13TH EDITION

HUMAN COMMUNICATION

The Basic Course

Joseph A. DeVito

Hunter College of the City University of New York

Boston Columbus Indianapolis New York San Francisco Upper Saddle River
Amsterdam Cape Town Dubai London Madrid Milan Munich Paris Montréal Toronto
Delhi Mexico City São Paulo Sydney Hong Kong Seoul Singapore Taipei Tokyo

Brief Contents

PART ONE Foundations of Human Communication 1

1 Preliminaries to Human Communication 1
2 Culture and Communication 27
3 The Self and Perception 50
4 Listening in Human Communication 78
5 Verbal Messages 100
6 Nonverbal Messages 121

PART TWO Interpersonal, Small Group, and Organizational Communication 150

7 Interpersonal Communication: Conversation 150
8 Interpersonal Relationship Stages and Theories 171
9 Friends, Lovers, and Families 192
10 Small Group Communication 210
11 Members and Leaders 227
12 Human Communication in the Workplace: Organizational Communication 245
13 Interpersonal, Group, and Workplace Conflict 263

PART THREE Public Speaking 281

14 Public Speaking Topics, Audiences, and Research 281
15 Supporting and Organizing Your Speech 311
16 Style and Delivery in Public Speaking 343
17 The Informative Speech 366
18 The Persuasive Speech 381

Appendix of Speeches: Public Speaking Sample Assistants 404
Glossary 419
References 435
Index 449
Credits 461

Detailed Contents

Welcome to *Human Communication: The Basic Course* xii

PART ONE Foundations of Human Communication 1

1 PRELIMINARIES TO HUMAN COMMUNICATION 1

FORMS, BENEFITS, AND MYTHS OF HUMAN COMMUNICATION 2
The Forms of Human Communication 2 ■ The Benefits of Human Communication 4 ■ The Myths of Human Communication 6

ELEMENTS OF HUMAN COMMUNICATION 7
Communication Context 7 ■ Source–Receiver 8 ■ Messages 8 ■ Channels 9 ■ Noise 9 ■ Effects 10

PRINCIPLES OF HUMAN COMMUNICATION 10
Communication Is Purposeful 10 ■ Communication Is Transactional 11 ■ Communication Is a Package of Signals 12 ■ Communication Is a Process of Adjustment 12 ■ Communication Involves Content and Relationship Dimensions 13 ■ Communication Is Ambiguous 14 ■ Communication Is Punctuated 15 ■ Communication Is Inevitable, Irreversible, and Unrepeatable 16

THE COMPETENT COMMUNICATOR 17
The Competent Communicator Makes Reasoned Choices 19 ■ The Competent Communicator Thinks Critically and Mindfully 19 ■ The Competent Communicator Is Culturally Sensitive 20 ■ The Competent Communicator Is Ethical 20 ■ The Competent Communicator Is an Effective Listener 21 ■ The Competent Communicator Is Media Literate 22

SUMMARY : PRELIMINARIES TO HUMAN COMMUNICATION 23
KEY TERMS 24
WORKING WITH THE PRELIMINARIES TO HUMAN COMMUNICATION 25
LOGON! MyCommunicationLab 26

2 CULTURE AND COMMUNICATION 27

WHAT IS CULTURE? 28
Sex and Gender 28 ■ The Transmission of Culture 29 ■ The Importance of Culture in Communication 30 ■ The Aim of a Cultural Perspective 31

CULTURAL DIFFERENCES 33
Individual and Collective Orientation 34 ■ High- and Low-Context Cultures 34 ■ Power Distances 35 ■ Masculine and Feminine Cultures 36 ■ High- and Low-Ambiguity-Tolerant Cultures 36 ■ Long- and Short-Term Orientation 37 ■ Indulgence and Restraint 37

INTERCULTURAL COMMUNICATION 38
The Nature and Forms of Intercultural Communication 38 ■ Improving Intercultural Communication 39

SUMMARY: CULTURE AND COMMUNICATION 47
KEY TERMS 47
WORKING WITH CULTURE AND COMMUNICATION 48
LOGON! MyCommunicationLab 49

3 THE SELF AND PERCEPTION 50

THE SELF IN HUMAN COMMUNICATION 51
Self-Concept 51 ■ Self-Awareness 52 ■ Self-Esteem 54

SELF-DISCLOSURE 56
Factors Influencing Self-Disclosure 56 ■ The Rewards and Dangers of Self-Disclosure 58 ■ Guidelines for Self-Disclosure 58

PERCEPTION 61
Stage 1: Stimulation 61 ■ Stage 2: Organization 61 ■ Stage 3: Interpretation–Evaluation 62 ■ Stage 4: Memory 63 ■ Stage 5: Recall 63

IMPRESSION FORMATION 64
Impression Formation Processes 64 ■ Increasing Accuracy in Impression Formation 68

IMPRESSION MANAGEMENT 70
To Be Liked: Affinity-Seeking Strategies and Politeness Strategies 70 ■ To Be Believed: Credibility Strategies 71 ■ To Excuse Failure: Self-Handicapping Strategies 71 ■ To Secure Help: Self-Deprecating Strategies 71 ■ To Hide Faults: Self-Monitoring Strategies 72 ■ To Be Followed: Influencing Strategies 73 ■ To Confirm Self-Image: Image-Confirming Strategies 73

SUMMARY: THE SELF AND PERCEPTION 74
KEY TERMS 75
WORKING WITH THE SELF AND PERCEPTION 75
LOGON! MyCommunicationLab 77

4 LISTENING IN HUMAN COMMUNICATION 78

THE IMPORTANCE OF LISTENING: TASK AND RELATIONSHIP BENEFITS 79

THE LISTENING PROCESS 79
Stage 1: Receiving 80 ■ Stage 2: Understanding 81 ■ Stage 3: Remembering 81 ■ Stage 4: Evaluating 84 ■ Stage 5: Responding 84

LISTENING BARRIERS 85
Distractions: Physical and Mental 85 ■ Biases and Prejudices 87 ■ Lack of Appropriate Focus 87 ■ Premature Judgment 87

STYLES OF EFFECTIVE LISTENING 87
Empathic and Objective Listening 88 ■ Nonjudgmental and Critical Listening 89 ■ Surface and Depth Listening 90 ■ Polite and Impolite Listening 91 ■ Active and Inactive Listening 92

LISTENING, CULTURE, AND GENDER 94
Culture and Listening 94 ■ Gender and Listening 95

SUMMARY: LISTENING IN HUMAN COMMUNICATION 97
KEY TERMS 98
WORKING WITH LISTENING 98
LOGON! MyCommunicationLab 99

5 VERBAL MESSAGES 100

PRINCIPLES OF VERBAL MESSAGES 101
Meanings Are in People 101 ■ Language Is Denotative and Connotative 102 ■ Meanings Depend on Context 102 ■ Messages Vary in Politeness 104 ■ Messages Can Be Onymous or Anonymous 105 ■ Messages Vary in Assertiveness 105 ■ Messages Can Deceive 106

DISCONFIRMATION AND CONFIRMATION 108
Racism 110 ■ Heterosexism 110 ■ Ageism 111 ■ Sexism 112 ■ Cultural Identifiers 112

USING VERBAL MESSAGES EFFECTIVELY 114
Language Symbolizes Reality (Partially) 115 ■ Language Expresses Both Facts and Inferences 116 ■ Language Is Relatively Static 117 ■ Language Can Obscure Distinctions 117

SUMMARY: VERBAL MESSAGES 118
KEY TERMS 119
WORKING WITH VERBAL MESSAGES 119
LOGON! MyCommunicationLab 120

6 NONVERBAL MESSAGES 121

THE PRINCIPLES OF NONVERBAL COMMUNICATION 122
Nonverbal Messages Interact with Verbal Messages 122 ■ Nonverbal Messages Help Manage Impressions 123 ■ Nonverbal Messages Help Form Relationships 124 ■ Nonverbal Messages Structure Conversation 125 ■ Nonverbal Messages Can Influence and Deceive 125 ■ Nonverbal Messages Are Crucial for Expressing Emotions 126

THE CHANNELS OF NONVERBAL COMMUNICATION 126
Body Communication 126 ■ Facial Communication 127 ■ Eye Communication 128 ■ Space Communication 131 ■ Artifactual Communication 133 ■ Touch Communication 134 ■ Paralanguage: The Vocal Channel 136 ■ Silence 136 ■ Time Communication 137 ■ Smell Communication 139

CULTURE AND NONVERBAL COMMUNICATION 140
Culture and Gesture 140 ■ Culture and Facial Expression 141 ■ Culture and Eye Communication 141 ■ Culture and Colors 141 ■ Culture and Touch 142 ■ Culture, Paralanguage, and Silence 142 ■ Culture and Time 142

SOME NONVERBAL COMMUNICATION SKILLS 144
Decoding Skills 144 ■ Encoding Skills 145

SUMMARY: NONVERBAL MESSAGES 146
KEY TERMS 147
WORKING WITH NONVERBAL COMMUNICATION 147
LOGON! MyCommunicationLab 149

PART TWO Interpersonal, Small Group, and Organizational Communication 150

7 INTERPERSONAL COMMUNICATION: CONVERSATION 150

PRINCIPLES OF CONVERSATION 152
The Principle of Process: Conversation Is a Developmental Process 152 ■ The Principle of Turn-Taking 153 ■ The Principle of Dialogue 155 ■ The Principle of Immediacy 156 ■ The Principle of Flexibility 156 ■ The Principle of Politeness: Conversation Is (Usually) Polite 157

EVERYDAY CONVERSATIONS 158
Making Small Talk 158 ■ Introducing People 162 ■ Making Excuses 163 ■ Apologizing 164 ■ Giving and Receiving Compliments 166 ■ Giving and Receiving Advice 167

SUMMARY: INTERPERSONAL COMMUNICATION: CONVERSATION 169
KEY TERMS 169
WORKING WITH CONVERSATION 169
LOGON! MyCommunicationLab 170

8 INTERPERSONAL RELATIONSHIP STAGES AND THEORIES 171

RELATIONSHIP STAGES 173
Contact 175 ■ Involvement 175 ■ Intimacy 176 ■ Deterioration 177 ■ Repair 178 ■ Dissolution 178

RELATIONSHIP THEORIES 179
Attraction Theory 179 ■ Relationship Rules Theory 180 ■ Relationship Dialectics Theory 182 ■ Social Penetration Theory 182 ■ Social Exchange Theory 183 ■ Equity Theory 184

THE DARK SIDE OF INTERPERSONAL RELATIONSHIPS 186
Jealousy 186 ■ Relationship Violence 188

SUMMARY: INTERPERSONAL RELATIONSHIP STAGES AND THEORIES 189
KEY TERMS 190
WORKING WITH INTERPERSONAL RELATIONSHIP STAGES AND THEORIES 190
LOGON! MyCommunicationLab 191

9 FRIENDS, LOVERS, AND FAMILIES 192

FRIENDSHIPS 193
Friendship Types 193 ■ Friendship and Communication 194 ■ Friendships, Culture, Gender, and Technology 195

ROMANTIC RELATIONSHIPS 197
Love Types 197 ■ Love and Communication 199 ■ Love, Culture, Gender, and Technology 200

FAMILIES 202
Types of Couples and Families 202 ■ Family Characteristics 204 ■ Families and Communication 204 ■ Families, Culture, Gender, and Technology 205

SUMMARY: FRIENDS, LOVERS, AND FAMILIES 207
KEY TERMS 207
WORKING WITH FRIENDS, LOVERS, AND FAMILIES 208
LOGON! MyCommunicationLab 209

10 SMALL GROUP COMMUNICATION 210

SMALL GROUPS AND TEAMS 211
The Small Group 211 ■ The Team 211 ■ Virtual Groups and Teams 212 ■ Small Group Stages 212 ■ Small Group Formats 213 ■ Small Group Culture 214 ■ Power in the Small Group 215

IDEA-GENERATION GROUPS 216

PERSONAL GROWTH GROUPS 217
The Encounter Group 218 ■ The Assertiveness Training Group 218 ■ The Consciousness-Raising Group 218 ■ The Intervention Group 218

INFORMATION-SHARING GROUPS 218
Educational or Learning Groups 219 ■ Focus Groups 219

PROBLEM-SOLVING GROUPS 219
The Problem-Solving Sequence 220 ■ Problem-Solving Groups at Work 222

SUMMARY: SMALL GROUP COMMUNICATION 225
KEY TERMS 225
WORKING WITH SMALL GROUP COMMUNICATION 226
LOGON! MyCommunicationLab 226

11 MEMBERS AND LEADERS 227

MEMBERS IN SMALL GROUP COMMUNICATION 228
Member Roles 228 ■ Interaction Process Analysis 230 ■ Member Functions and Skills 230

LEADERS IN SMALL GROUP COMMUNICATION 233
Myths about Leadership 234 ■ Approaches to Leadership 235 ■ Functions and Skills of Leadership 237

MEMBERSHIP, LEADERSHIP, AND CULTURE 239
Individualism and Collectivism 239 ■ Member Roles 241 ■ Belief Systems 241 ■ Leadership Style 241

SUMMARY: MEMBERS AND LEADERS 242
KEY TERMS 242
WORKING WITH MEMBERS AND LEADERS 243
LOGON! MyCommunicationLab 244

Specialized Table of Contents

MAKING ETHICAL CHOICES

Culture and Ethics (Chapter 2, p. 44)
The Ethics of Impression Management (Chapter 3, p. 72)
Listening Ethically (Chapter 4, p. 96)
Lying (Chapter 5, p. 108)
Silence (Chapter 6, p. 143)
Gossip (Chapter 7, p. 165)
Relationship Ethics (Chapter 8, p. 183)
Your Obligation to Reveal Yourself (Chapter 9, p. 198)
Telling Secrets (Chapter 10, p. 214)
The Leader's Ethical Responsibilities (Chapter 11, p. 240)
The Five Cs of Organizational Ethics (Chapter 12, p. 259)
Ethical Fighting (Chapter 13, p. 276)
Plagiarism (Chapter 14, p. 300)
Communicating in Cyberspace (Chapter 15, p. 313)
Criticizing Ethically (Chapter 16, p. 360)
Speaking Ethically (Chapter 17, p. 369)
The Ethics of Emotional Appeals (Chapter 18, p. 387)

UNDERSTANDING THEORY AND RESEARCH

Communication Theories (Chapter 1, p. 11)
Communication Research (Chapter 1, p. 16)
Cultural Theories (Chapter 2, p. 29)
Language and Thought (Chapter 2, p. 42)
The Pygmalion Effect (Chapter 3, p. 65)
The Just World Hypothesis (Chapter 3, p. 67)
Reconstructing Memory (Chapter 4, p. 83)
Cues to Lying (Chapter 4, p. 85)
Theories of Gender Differences (Chapter 5, p. 103)
The Verb *To Be* (Chapter 5, p. 115)
The Facial Feedback Hypothesis (Chapter 6, p. 129)
Space Violations (Chapter 6, p. 133)
The Development of Interpersonal Communication (Chapter 7, p. 151)
Opening Lines (Chapter 7, p. 163)
Relationship Commitment (Chapter 8, p. 176)
Online Relationship Theories (Chapter 8, p. 181)
Intimacy and Risk (Chapter 9, p. 199)
Love Styles and Personality (Chapter 9, p. 202)
Group Power (Chapter 10, p. 217)
Group Polarization (Chapter 10, p. 223)
Styles of Leadership (Chapter 11, p. 236)
Attila's Theory of Leadership (Chapter 11, p. 237)
Approaches to Organizations (Chapter 12, p. 248)
Peter and Dilbert (Chapter 12, p. 253)
Conflict Issues (Chapter 13, p. 267)
Conflict and Gender (Chapter 13, p. 268)
Performance Visualization (Chapter 14, p. 285)
Systematic Desensitization (Chapter 14, p. 288)
Primacy and Recency (Chapter 15, p. 315)
Culture and Speech Organization (Chapter 15, p. 325)
One-Sided versus Two-Sided Messages (Chapter 16, p. 345)
Speech Rate (Chapter 16, p. 355)
Information Theory (Chapter 17, p. 373)
Signal-to-Noise Ratio (Chapter 17, p. 375)
Balance Theories (Chapter 18, p. 383)
Foot-in-the-Door and Door-in-the-Face (Chapter 18, p. 392)

SELF-TESTS

The self-tests in this edition were reconfigured and are now integrated into the text narrative.

Myths of human communication (Chapter 1, p. 6)
Beliefs about ethics (Chapter 1, p. 21)
Cultural differences (Chapter 2, pp. 33–34)
Ethnic identity (Chapter 2, p. 41)
Willingness to self-disclose (Chapter 3, p. 56)
Listening styles (Chapter 4, pp. 87–88)
Assertiveness (Chapter 5, pp. 105–106)
Facts and inferences (Chapter 5, p. 116)
Nonverbal Communication myths (Chapter 6, p. 112)
Time orientation (Chapter 6, p. 137)
Conversational politeness (Chapter 7, p. 157)
Small talk (Chapter 7, pp. 160–161)
Relationship advantages and disadvantages (Chapter 8, pp. 172–173)
Intimacy and risk (Chapter 9, p. 199)
Power in the small group (Chapter 10, p. 215)
Group membership roles (Chapter 11, p. 228)
Group leadership (Chapter 11, p. 235)
Management style (Chapter 12, p. 250)
Conflict myths (Chapter 13, p. 266)
Conflict management strategies (Chapter 13, pp. 272–273)

Apprehension in public speaking (Chapter 14, p. 285)
Critical evaluations (Chapter 16, p. 360)
Credibility (Chapter 18, p. 388)

EXPANDING MEDIA LITERACY

Media Imperialism (Chapter 2, p. 32)
Media Messages "Construct" Reality (Chapter 3, p. 63)
Media Users Construct Meaning (Chapter 4, p. 91)
Media Messages Are Value-Laden (Chapter 5, p. 113)
Product Placement (Chapter 6, p. 125)
Conversation and Social Media (Chapter 7, p. 159)
Parasocial Relationships (Chapter 8, p. 173)
Interpersonal Relationships and the Media (Chapter 9, p. 196)
The Third-Person Effect (Chapter 10, p. 216)
The Knowledge Gap (Chapter 11, p. 234)
Advertising (Chapter 12, p. 250)
Public Relations (Chapter 13, p. 275)
Media Messages Are Often Stereotypes (Chapter 14, p. 295)
Agenda Setting (Chapter 15, p. 317)
Reversing Media's Influence (Chapter 16, p. 347)
Gatekeeping (Chapter 17, p. 372)
The Spiral of Silence (Chapter 18, p. 393)

PUBLIC SPEAKING SAMPLE ASSISTANTS

Speeches:
A Speech of Introduction (Appendix, p. 404)
A Poorly Constructed Informative Speech: "Biases" (Appendix, p. 406)
An Excellent Informative Speech, "Communication in an Ever-Changing World" by Marty Wiebe (Appendix, p. 408)
A Poorly Constructed Persuasive Speech: "Prenups" (Appendix, p. 411)
An Excellent Persuasive Speech, "It's Not the Addict, It's the Drug: Redefining America's War on Drugs" by Tunette Powell (Appendix, p. 412)
A Slide Show Speech: "Self-Disclosure" (Appendix, p. 417)

Outlines:
A Preparation Outline (Topical Organization) (Chapter 15, p. 335)
A Preparation Outline (Motivated Sequence Organization) (Chapter 15, p. 337)
A Template Outline (Chapter 15, p. 338)
A Phrase/Key-Word Presentation Outline (Chapter 15, p. 339)

Welcome to

Human Communication:

THE BASIC COURSE

THIRTEENTH EDITION

It's really an honor to present this new edition that has helped teach so many students about the amazing and fascinating subject of human communication. With this edition, as with all others, I hope to continue to serve that important function.

Human Communication: The Basic Course is designed for the introductory college course that offers comprehensive coverage of the fundamentals of human communication. The text covers classic approaches and new developments; it covers research and theory, but gives coordinated attention to communication skills.

This book is addressed to students who have little or no prior background in studying communication. If this will be your only communication course, *Human Communication* will provide you with a thorough foundation in the theory, research, and skills of this essential liberal art. For those of you who will take additional and advanced courses or who are beginning a major in communication, it will provide the significant foundation for more advanced and more specialized study.

NEW TO THIS EDITION: IN BRIEF

This thirteenth edition of *Human Communication: The Basic Course* contains a variety of structural and content changes. All of these changes were made to make the text narrative flow more freely and should make the book easier to read and more easily adaptable to different teaching and learning styles.

Structural Changes

Among the major structural changes are these:

- The chapter-opening objectives have been restructured into behavioral terms and highlight knowledge, application, and problem solving. The chapter-opening grid identifies these alongside the chapter's major headings/topics (which are repeated in the summary headings at the end of the chapter). This change helps coordinate the learning objectives and the chapter material and phrases the objectives in behavioral, measurable terms.
- The sample speeches in the public speaking chapters, formerly in boxes in the chapters, have been moved to a Public Speaking Sample Assistant Appendix. This change makes the text flow more smoothly and makes the speeches available whenever most appropriate. The outlines remain in the text chapter.
- The self-tests, formerly in boxes, have been integrated into the text narrative. This change was made to make these self-reflections a more integrated and integral part of the text.
- The Building Communication Skills boxes, from the previous edition, have been moved to the end of the chapters and now preface a variety of exercises and discussion starters. This change increases flexibility, making these features available at any point in the chapter coverage.
- The videos, formerly presented as chapter openers, now appear as the last item in the chapter. This change was made to emphasize the value of using these videos after the chapter material has been covered. This change also enabled us to brighten up the chapter openers with new photos that illustrate principles of communication from very different perspectives.

Content Changes

In addition to an updating of research, new examples, greater emphasis on social media, new exercises, and improved graphics, among the major content changes are these:

- **Part One (Foundations of Human Communication, Chapters 1–6).** New materials in these six introductory chapters include the addition of media literacy and choice making as characteristics of communication competence, a media literacy box on media imperialism, a table on the metaphors of culture, discussions of dialects and accents, online social comparisons, self-disclosure in the workplace, the impostor phenomenon, onymous and anonymous messages, and interpersonal time. In addition, new "In a Nutshell" tables summarize the principles of human communication, the competent communicator, improving intercultural communication, guidelines for self-disclosure, impression formation processes and strategies, listening styles, principles of verbal messages, and proxemic distances.
- **Part Two (Interpersonal, Small Group, and Organizational Communication, Chapters 7–13).** New materials include a self-test on small talk, politeness as a principle of conversation, an exercise on introductions, and discussions of types of families, the intervention group, social loafing, and the transition from membership to leadership. New "In a Nutshell" tables summarize the principles of conversation, relationship theories, small group types, membership, and leadership.
- **Part Three (Public Speaking, Chapters 14–18).** New materials include three new speeches with annotations and new excerpts to illustrate the various principles. Extensively revised sections include those on finding topics, research, voice, and bodily action. New "In a Nutshell" tables summarize the principles of informative speaking, the principles of persuasive speaking, and the types of persuasive speeches.

MAJOR FEATURES OF *HUMAN COMMUNICATION*

The thirteenth edition builds on the successful features of previous editions, in addition to incorporating much that is new.

Coverage of the Fundamentals of Communication

- **Part One (Foundations of Human Communication)** covers the fundamental concepts and principles of human communication, the self and perception, listening, and verbal and nonverbal messages (Chapters 1–6).
- **Part Two (Interpersonal, Small Group, and Organizational Communication)** covers interpersonal interaction and relationships, small group membership and leadership, organizational communication, and conflict (Chapters 7–13).
- **Part Three (Public Speaking)** covers the preparation and presentation of public speeches (Chapters 14–18).
- Because some courses cover interviewing but others do not, the interviewing material, included in earlier editions, is now a separate book, *The Interviewing Guidebook*, Second Edition, which is available for purchase, as a packaging option with new copies of this book, or on MyCommunicationLab (access code required).

The Concept of Choice

The concept of choice as central to all communication has been given greater prominence in this edition; it is now identified as a major characteristic of communication competence. This text aims to identify some of the available choices for a wide variety of communication situations and present the evidence and argument bearing on these various choices. This focus on choice is discussed throughout the text and is also highlighted in the online Analyzing Video Choices and in the photo program. In both of these features, at the point at which a communication decision needs to be made, the reader is asked to consider the available choices and the likely advantages and disadvantages of each.

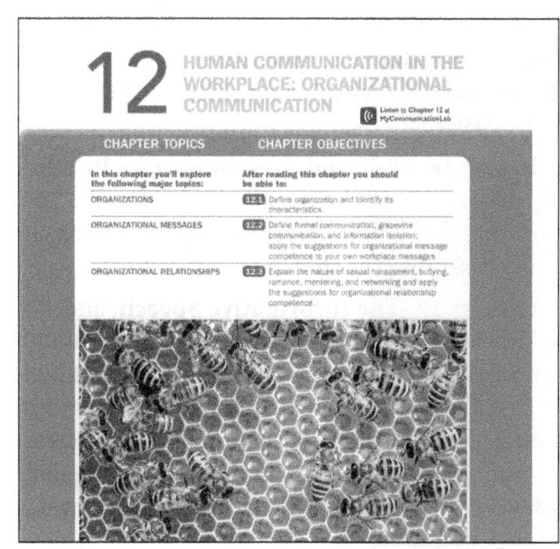

- **Exercises and Discussion Questions.** At the end of each chapter are exercises and discussion questions to stimulate you to expand on, evaluate, and apply the concepts, theories, and research findings discussed in the text to your own communications and to stimulate class discussion.
- **Key Terms and Glossaries.** A list of key terms at the end of each chapter will help you review the major terms discussed in the chapter. These terms are accompanied by references to the pages of the text on which they're introduced and defined. In addition, a combined glossary of concepts and skills provides brief definitions of the significant concepts in the study of human communication and of communication skills (skills appear in italics).
- **Choice Points.** The photo captions and the ***Analyzing Video Choices*** at the end of the chapter invite participation in working actively with the concepts discussed in the chapter. You can log on to MyCommunicationLab (www.mycommunicationlab.com; access code required) to view this end-of-the-chapter video. Click through to see how the characters make various communication choices and how these choices affect their effectiveness as communicators, and then answer the discussion questions to help you analyze each situation.

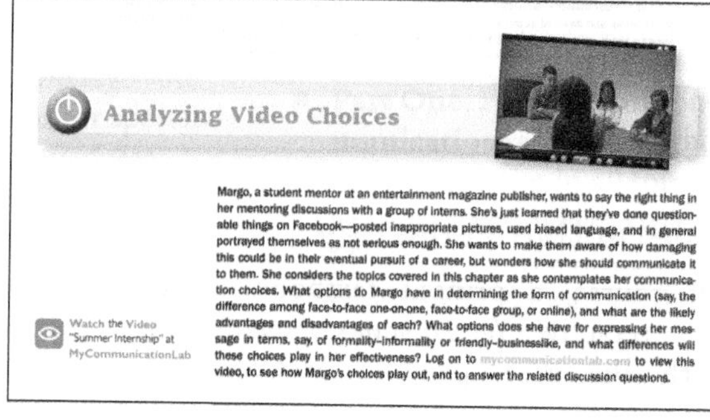

- **In a Nutshell Tables.** The few summary tables in the previous edition, praised by users, have been increased to 19 and are called "In a Nutshell." These tables summarize significant portions of the text and appear throughout the text as appropriate.
- **Summary Statements.** At the end of each chapter, a summary reviews the essential concepts and principles covered in the chapter. The summary is organized with the headings used in the chapter-opening grid and in the chapter itself.

RESOURCES IN PRINT AND ONLINE

Key instructor resources include an Instructor's Manual (ISBN 0-205-98105-4), Test Bank (ISBN 0-13-374647-X), and PowerPoint Presentation Package (ISBN 0-205-98094-5). These supplements are available at www.pearsonhighered.com/irc (access code required). MyTest online test generating software (ISBN 0-205-98106-2) is available at www.pearsonmytest.com (access code required).

For a complete listing of the instructor and student resources available with this text, please visit the *Human Communication* e-Catalog page at www.pearsonhighered.com/communication.

The student print version of this title is a three-hole punched, loose-leaf text packaged with a MyCommunicationLab access card (ISBN 0-205-99592-6). A MyCommunicationLab standalone access card is also available (ISBN 0-205-99595-0).

MyCommunicationLab

www.mycommunicationlab.com

MyCommunicationLab is an online homework, tutorial, and assessment program that truly engages students in learning. It helps students better prepare for class, quizzes, and exams—resulting in better performance in the course. It provides educators a dynamic set of tools for gauging individual and class performance. And MyCommunicationLab comes from Pearson, your partner in providing the best digital learning experiences.

- **Assessment** tied to videos, applications, and chapter content enables both instructors and students to track progress and get immediate feedback—and helps instructors find the best resources with which to help students.
- The **Pearson eText** lets students access their textbook anytime, anywhere, and any way they want—including listening online or accessing on a smartphone or tablet device.
- **Videos and Video Quizzes:** Sample student and professional speeches offer students models of the types of speeches they are learning to design and deliver. Many interactive videos include short, assignable quizzes that report to the instructor's gradebook.
- **PersonalityProfile:** Pearson's online library for self-assessment and analysis provides students with opportunities to evaluate their own and others' communication styles. Instructors can use these tools to show learning and growth over the duration of the course.
- **MediaShare:** A comprehensive file upload tool that allows students to post speeches, outlines, visual aids, video assignments, role plays, group projects, and more in a variety of formats, including video, Word, PowerPoint, and Excel. Structured much like a social networking site, MediaShare helps promote a sense of community among students. Uploaded files are available for viewing, commenting, and grading by instructors and class members in face-to-face and online course settings. Integrated video capture functionality allows students to record video directly from a webcam to their assignments, and allows instructors to record videos via webcam, in class or in a lab, and attach them directly to a specific student and/or assignment. In addition, instructors can upload files as assignments for students to view and respond to directly in MediaShare. Grades can be imported into most learning management systems, and robust privacy settings ensure a secure learning environment for instructors and students. Upload videos, comment on submissions, and grade directly from our new MediaShare app, available free from the iTunes store; search for Pearson MediaShare.
- **Class Preparation Tool:** Finding, organizing, and presenting your instructor resources is fast and easy with Pearson's class preparation tool. This fully searchable database contains hundreds of resources such as lecture launchers, discussion topics, activities, assignments, and video clips. Instructors can search or browse by topic and sort the results by type. You can create personalized folders to organize and store what you like or download resources, as well as upload your own content.
- **Pearson's Writing Space** is the best way to develop and assess concept mastery and critical thinking through writing. Writing Space provides a single place within MyCommunicationLab to create, track, and grade writing assignments, access writing resources, and exchange meaningful, personalized feedback quickly and easily. Plus, Writing Space will have integrated access to Turnitin, the global leader in plagiarism prevention.

ACKNOWLEDGMENTS

It's a pleasure to thank three groups of people who contributed greatly to this new edition. I want to thank the reviewers who shared insights and classroom experiences with me. Your suggestions have helped me improve this text significantly. Thank you,

Frannie Allan, Community College of Baltimore County

Marie Baker-Ohler, Northern Arizona University

David Bastien, St. Cloud State University

Ellen Bland, Central Carolina Community College

Laura Carr, Eastfield College

Michelle Christian, College of Southern Maryland

Preston Coleman, Gainesville State College

Shannon DeBord, Austin Community College

Jesse Jackson, Austin Community College

Dorman Picklesimer, Boston College

Sherry Rhodes, Collin College

I also want to again thank reviewers of previous editions whose comments I continue to turn to with each revision. Thank you,

Karen Anderson, University of North Texas

Michelle Bacino Thiessen, Rock Valley College

Kimberly Berry, Ozarka Technical Community College

Ellen B. Bremen, Highline Community College

David M. Butts, Harrisburg Area Community College

Judy Cannady, Ozarka Technical Community College

Tasha Davis, Austin Community College

Cynthia Graham, University of Wisconsin, Superior

Gwen A. Hullman, University of Nevada

Lori Norin, University of Arkansas, Fort Smith

Aleshia Panbamrung, Indiana University-Purdue University

Daniel M. Paulnock, Saint Paul College

Rachel C. Prioleau, University of South Carolina, Spartanburg

Charles V. Roberts, East Tennessee State University

Jill Tyler, University of South Dakota

Arnold Wood, Jr., Florida State College at Jacksonville

Alan Zaremba, Northeastern University

A special thank you goes to the members of the speech team at the University of Texas at Austin, especially Video Project Director Brendan Chan, for their work to create the Communication Choice Point videos: Taylor Adams, Kyle Akerman, Ryan Castillo, Brendan Chan, Kevin Chiu, Brianna Collins, Angelica Davis, Michelle Davis, Jaime Garcia, Brian Gaston, Caleb Graves, Natalie Groves, Chris Hiller, William Igbokwe, Anna Nicole Kreisberg, Melissa Lamb, Leah LeFebvre, Christy Liu, Colin Malinak, Joseph Muller, Rachael Phipps, Aviva Pinchas, Nathan Rarick, Rahul Sangal, Jeremy Vandermause, David Wang; to the University of Nebraska's David Tuck for his role in the videos; to Student Photographer Lara Grant; and to Freelance Writer Ziki Dekel who prepared the script.

I'm also greatly indebted to the many people at Pearson Inc. who worked to turn my manuscript into the book you now hold. Thank you Karon Bowers, Publisher, Communication; Carol Alper, Development Editor; Jen Nolan, Editorial Assistant; Blair Tuckman, Senior Marketing Manager; Sean Silver, Media Production Editor; Raegan Heerema, Project Manager; and Anne Ricigliano, Program Manager. All helped a great deal more than their job titles might indicate; their contributions were vital to all stages in the development and production of this book. I am in their collective debt.

Joseph A. DeVito
jadevito@earthlink.net
http://tcbdevito.blogspot.com
www.pearsonhighered.com/devito

1 PRELIMINARIES TO HUMAN COMMUNICATION

Listen to Chapter 1 at MyCommunicationLab

CHAPTER TOPICS	CHAPTER OBJECTIVES
In this chapter you'll explore the following major topics:	**After reading this chapter you should be able to:**
FORMS, BENEFITS, AND MYTHS OF HUMAN COMMUNICATION	1.1 Identify the major forms of human communication, its benefits, and its myths.
ELEMENTS OF HUMAN COMMUNICATION	1.2 Define the major elements of human communication: *context*, *source–receiver*, *messages*, *channels*, *noise*, *effects*, and *ethics*.
PRINCIPLES OF HUMAN COMMUNICATION	1.3 Paraphrase the principles of human communication.
THE COMPETENT COMMUNICATOR	1.4 Explain the characteristics of the competent communicator.

Human communication is a vast subject area and one that is likely new to you. In this chapter we look at some of the many benefits you'll derive from your exposure to the study of the forms of human communication, the elements involved in the communication process, some of the principles governing the way communication operates, and the nature of the effective or competent communicator.

1.1 FORMS, BENEFITS, AND MYTHS OF HUMAN COMMUNICATION

Of all the knowledge and skills you have, those concerning **communication** will prove among the most useful. Your ability to communicate will always play a crucial part in how effectively you live your personal and professional lives. It's vital to your success to learn how communication works and to master its most essential skills. Let's begin this introductory chapter with a clear explanation of the forms of communication that will be discussed and the benefits that you'll derive from your study of these forms of communication.

The Forms of Human Communication

You'll derive the benefits just mentioned through your exposure and mastery of the major forms of human communication, which can vary from one-person communication (in which you talk to yourself) to communication with millions (as in public speaking, mass communication, and computer-mediated communication). Here we look briefly at each of these forms (see the preview summary in Table 1.1).

Intrapersonal Communication

Intrapersonal communication is communication you have with yourself. Through intrapersonal communication you talk with, learn about, and judge yourself. You persuade yourself of this or that, reason about possible decisions to make, and rehearse messages that you plan to send to others. In intrapersonal communication you might, for example, wonder how you did in an interview and what you could have done differently.

You might conclude you did a pretty good job but that you need to be more assertive when discussing salary. Increasing your self-awareness, your mindfulness, and your ability to think critically about all types of messages will aid you greatly in improving your own intrapersonal communication. And this information—on the self, perception, listening, and verbal and nonverbal messages—will provide a foundation for learning about the various forms of human communication.

Interpersonal Communication

Interpersonal communication is communication between two persons or among a small group of persons. Most often, the communication emphasized in the study of interpersonal communication is communication of a continuing personal (rather than temporary and impersonal) nature; it's communication between or among intimates or those involved in close relationships—friends, romantic partners, family, and coworkers, for example. These relationships are interdependent, meaning that the actions of one person have some impact on the other person; whatever one person does influences the other person. Sometimes interpersonal communication is pleasant, but sometimes it erupts into conflict—making each person's communication especially significant for the other.

Interviewing

Interviewing is communication that proceeds by question and answer. Through interviewing you learn about others and what they know; you counsel or get counseling from others; or you get or don't get the job you want and ultimately the career you're preparing for in college. Today much interviewing (especially initial interviews) takes place through e-mail and (video) phone conferencing. Many of the skills for interviewing are the same skills noted for interpersonal and small group communication. The skills more specific to interviewing are covered in the companion text, *The Interviewing Guidebook*, second edition.

Small Group Communication

Small group communication is communication among members of groups of about five to ten people. Small group communication serves relationship needs such as those for companionship, affection, or support as well as task needs such as balancing the family budget, electing a new chairperson, or designing a new ad campaign. Through small group communication you interact with others, solve problems, develop new ideas, and share knowledge and experiences. You live your work and social life largely in groups, from school orientation meetings to executive board meetings; from informal social groups to formal meetings discussing issues of local or international concern. You also may live a good part of your life in online chat rooms,

TABLE 1.1 FORMS OF COMMUNICATION

This table identifies and arranges the forms of communication in terms of the number of persons involved, from one (in intrapersonal communication) to thousands and millions (in mass communication). It also offers a general preview of topics in this text. With the exception of intrapersonal communication, all other forms can be and are likely to be intercultural, a topic considered in depth in the next chapter.

Forms of Communication	Some Theory-Related Concerns	Some Skills-Related Concerns
Intrapersonal: communication with oneself	How do self-concept and self-esteem develop? How do they effect communication? How can problem-solving abilities be improved? What is the relationship between personality and communication?	Enhancing self-esteem, increasing self-awareness, improving problem solving and analyzing abilities, increasing self-control, managing communication apprehension, reducing stress, managing intrapersonal conflict
Interpersonal: communication between two or a few persons	What is interpersonal effectiveness? Why do people develop relationships? What holds relationships together? What tears them apart? How can relationships be repaired?	Increasing effectiveness in one-to-one communication, developing and maintaining productive relationships, improving conflict management abilities
Interviewing: communication that proceeds through questions and answers	What are the legal issues in interviewing? How can interviewing responses be analyzed? What is the role of nonverbal communication?	Phrasing questions to get the information you want, presenting your best self, writing résumés and cover letters
Small group: communication within a small group (say, 5 to 10) of people	What roles do people play in groups? What do groups do well and what do they fail to do well? What makes a leader? What types of leadership works best?	Increasing effectiveness as a group member, improving leadership abilities, using groups to achieve specific purposes (brainstorming, problem solving)
Organizational: communication within an organization	How and why do organizations grow and deteriorate? What role does culture play in the organization? What leadership styles prove most productive?	Transmitting information; motivating workers; dealing with feedback, the grapevine, and gossip; increasing worker satisfaction, productivity, and retention
Public: communication of speaker with audience	How can audiences be analyzed and adapted to? How can ideas be developed and supported for presentation to an audience? What kinds of organizational structures work best in informative and persuasive speeches?	Communicating information more effectively; increasing persuasive abilities; developing, organizing styling, and delivering messages effectively; becoming a more critical listener
Computer-mediated: communication between people via computers	Are there gender and age differences? In what ways is CMC more efficient? How can the various channels be incorporated into CMC?	Increasing security in e-communications, combining CMC with face-to-face communication; networking for social and professional purposes; beginning and maintaining relationships through social media
Mass: communication addressed to an extremely large audience, mediated by audio and/or visual means	What functions do media serve? How do media influence us? How can we influence the media? In what ways do the media filter the information we receive?	Improving abilities to use the media to greater effectiveness, increasing ability to control the media, avoiding being taken in by the media, becoming a more media-literate consumer and creator

where you may interact with people from different cultures living thousands of miles away, and in social networking (for example, Facebook, Google+, and LinkedIn) where you learn about and communicate with others.

Organizational Communication

Organizational communication is communication that takes place within an organization among members of the organization. Conferencing with colleagues, working in teams, talking with a supervisor, or giving employees directions are just a few examples of organizational communication. The study of organizational communication offers guidelines for improving your own formal and informal communication in an organizational setting.

Public Speaking

Public speaking, also termed public communication or presentational speaking, is communication between a speaker and an audience. Audiences range in size from several people to hundreds, thousands, and even millions. Through public communication, others inform and persuade you. And you, in turn, inform and persuade others—to act, to buy, or to think in a particular way.

Much as you can address large audiences face to face, you also can address such audiences electronically and through the mass media. Through newsgroups, blogs, or social networks, for example, you can post a "speech" for anyone to read and then read their reactions to your message. And with the help of the more traditional mass media of radio and television, you can address audiences in the hundreds of millions as they sit alone or in small groups scattered throughout the world.

Computer-Mediated Communication

Computer-mediated communication (CMC) is a general term that includes all forms of communication between people that take place through some computer, electronic, or Internet connection, for example, e-mail, texting, blogging, instant messaging, tweeting, or chatting on social network sites such as Facebook or MySpace or on your phone. All of these computer-mediated forms, like their face-to-face counterparts, are used both socially and in the world of business.

Some CMC (such as e-mail or blogging) is **asynchronous**, meaning that it does *not* take place in real time. You may send your message today, but the receiver may not read it for a week and may take another week to respond. Consequently, much of the spontaneity created by face-to-face real-time communication is lost in asynchronous communication. You may, for example, be very enthusiastic about a topic when you send your e-mail or post on your blog, but practically forget it by the time someone responds. Other forms of CMC (such as tweeting, chatting on social network sites, interactive websites, and instant messaging) are often **synchronous**—they occur at the same time and are similar to phone communication except that CMC is largely text-based rather than voice-based.

Table 1.2 presents some of the similarities and differences between face-to-face and computer-mediated communication. As you review the table, you may wish to add other similarities and differences or take issue with the ones identified here.

Mass Communication

Mass communication is communication from one source to many receivers, who may be scattered throughout the world. Mass communication takes place via at least the following media outlets: newspapers, magazines, television, radio, film, and video. The coverage of mass communication in this book focuses on media literacy and aims to help you to become a wiser, more critical user of the media. Beginning with the next chapter and in each subsequent chapter, Expanding Media Literacy boxes will help you achieve this crucial skill.

As you can see if you glance through your college catalogue, each of these forms of communication is likely to be covered in separate and more detailed courses in public speaking, small group communication, interpersonal communication, mass communication, and so on. In this course and in this text, the essentials of these communication forms are introduced, giving you the knowledge and skills to become a more effective communicator, and at the same time giving you the background to move on to more detailed study, whether in more in-depth courses or in your own reading.

The Benefits of Human Communication

A perfectly legitimate question to ask before beginning your study of any subject is "why?" Why should I learn about human communication? What will it do for me? What will I be able to do after taking this course that I wasn't able to do before? In short, how will I benefit from the study of human communication presented in this course and in this text? Actually, you'll benefit in lots of ways. Your knowledge of human communication and your mastery of many of its skills will enable you to improve

TABLE 1.2 FACE-TO-FACE AND COMPUTER-MEDIATED COMMUNICATION

Throughout this text face-to-face and computer-mediated communication are discussed, compared, and contrasted. Here is a brief summary of just some communication concepts and some of the ways in which these two forms of communication are similar and different.

Human Communication Element	Face-to-Face Communication	Computer-Mediated Communication
Sender ▪ Presentation of self and impression management ▪ Speaking turn	▪ Personal characteristics (sex, approximate age, race, etc.) are open to visual inspection; receiver controls the order of what is attended to; disguise is difficult. ▪ You compete for the speaker's turn and time with the other person(s); you can be interrupted.	▪ Personal characteristics are hidden and are revealed when you want to reveal them; anonymity is easy. ▪ It's always your turn; speaker time is unlimited; you can't be interrupted.
Receiver ▪ Number ▪ Opportunity for interaction ▪ Third parties ▪ Impression formation	▪ One or a few who are in your visual field. ▪ Limited to those who have the opportunity to meet; often difficult to find people who share your interests. ▪ Messages can be overheard by or repeated to third parties but not with complete accuracy. ▪ Impressions are based on the verbal and nonverbal cues the receiver perceives.	▪ Virtually unlimited. ▪ Unlimited. ▪ Messages can be retrieved by others or forwarded verbatim to a third party or to thousands. ▪ Impressions are based on text messages and posted photos and videos.
Context ▪ Physical ▪ Temporal	▪ Essentially the same physical space. ▪ Communication is synchronous; messages are exchanged at the same (real) time.	▪ Can be in the next cubicle or separated by miles. ▪ Communication may be synchronous (as in chat rooms) or asynchronous (where messages are exchanged at different times, as in e-mail).
Channel	▪ All senses participate in sending and receiving messages.	▪ Visual (for text, photos, and videos) and auditory.
Message ▪ Verbal and nonverbal ▪ Permanence	▪ Words, gestures, eye contact, accent, vocal cues, spatial relationships, touching, clothing, hair, etc. ▪ Temporary unless recorded; speech signals fade rapidly.	▪ Words, photos, videos, and audio messages. ▪ Messages are relatively permanent.

a variety of skills that will prove vital to your success and that are covered throughout this text. Here are some of the skills you'll acquire or improve as you study human communication to give you some idea of how important this study of human communication is: critical and creative thinking skills, interaction skills, relationship skills, leadership skills, presentation skills, and media literacy skills.

- **Critical and creative thinking skills,** emphasized throughout this book, help you approach new situations mindfully—with full conscious awareness, increase your ability to distinguish between a sound and valid argument and one that is filled with logical fallacies, and improve your ability to use language to reflect reality more accurately.
- **Interaction skills** help you improve your communication in a wide range of forms, from the seemingly simple small talk to the employment interview for the job of a lifetime. Interaction skills will enable you to communicate with greater ease, comfort, and effectiveness whether you're proposing a life-long relationship or apologizing for some transgression.

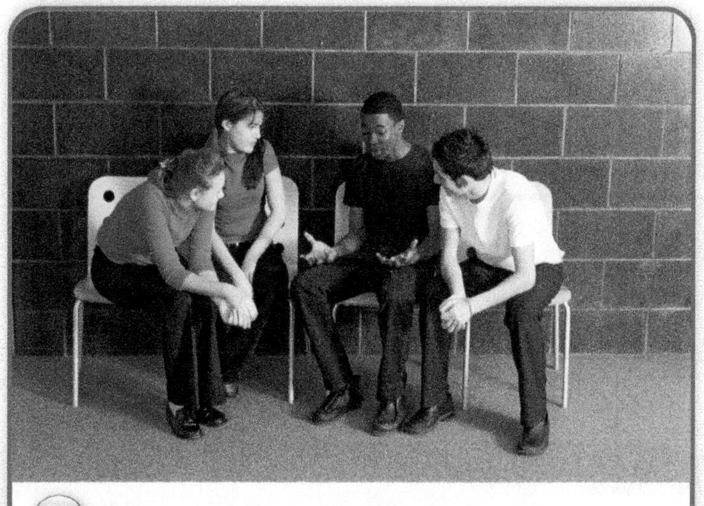

COMMUNICATION CHOICE POINT

HUMAN COMMUNICATION CHOICES *Paired with each photo is a Communication Choice Point, a point at which you need to examine your communication options and then make a decision and say something (or, of course, decide to remain silent). These choice points are designed to encourage you to apply the material discussed in the text to a wide variety of communication situations.*

- **Relationship skills** enable you to build friendships, enter into love relationships, work with colleagues, and interact with family members. These are the interpersonal and relationship skills for initiating, maintaining, repairing, and sometimes dissolving relationships of all kinds. And unless you're going to be living totally alone, these are skills you'll use every day, in every encounter. These are the skills that businesses of all kinds have on their lists of most important competencies for organizational success; they are an essential part of business competence (Bassellier & Benbasat, 2004).
- **Leadership skills** enable you to communicate information effectively in small groups or with large audiences, and your ability to influence others in these same situations are among your most important leadership skills. In a workplace world that operates largely on group interaction, these skills are increasingly essential if you are to be an effective organizational member and will help you rise in the organization. After all, people in power will often come to know you best through your communications. As you rise in the hierarchy, you'll need leadership skills to enable you to lead groups and teams in informative, problem-solving, and brainstorming sessions.
- **Presentation skills** enable you to present yourself as a confident, likable, approachable, and credible person. Your effectiveness in just about any endeavor depends heavily on your self-presentation—your ability to present yourself in a positive light, through your verbal and nonverbal messages. Incidentally, it is also largely through your skills of self-presentation (or lack of them) that you display negative qualities as well.
- **Media literacy skills** will help you interact with both mass and social media more effectively. These skills will help you understand how the media operate, how you can interact more effectively with the media, and how you can be a more effective media creator.

The Myths of Human Communication

One last point needs to be made to clarify what communication is before identifying its major elements and that is the myths about human communication, the things many people believe that simply aren't true. Which of the following statements do you believe are true, and which do you believe are false?

_____ **1.** Good communicators are born, not made.
_____ **2.** The more a couple communicates, the better their relationship will be.
_____ **3.** When two people are in a close relationship for a long period of time, one person should not have to communicate his or her needs and wants; the other person should know what these are.
_____ **4.** Complete openness should be the goal of any meaningful interpersonal relationship.
_____ **5.** Interpersonal or group conflict is a reliable sign that the relationship or group is in trouble.
_____ **6.** Like good communicators, leaders are born, not made.
_____ **7.** Fear of speaking in public is detrimental and must be eliminated.

As you may have figured out, all seven statements are generally false. As you read this text, you'll discover not only why these beliefs are false but also the trouble you can get into when you assume they're true. Briefly, here are some of the reasons why each of the statements is generally false:

1. Effective communication is a learned skill; although some people are born brighter or more extroverted than others, all can improve

their abilities and become more effective communicators.

2. If you practice bad communication habits, you're more likely to grow less effective than to become more effective; consequently, it's important to learn and follow the principles of effectiveness.
3. This assumption is at the heart of many interpersonal difficulties: People aren't mind readers, and to assume that they are merely sets up barriers to open and honest communication (see Chapters 8 and 9).
4. Although you may feel ethically obligated to be totally honest, this is generally not an effective strategy. In fact, "complete" anything is probably a bad idea.
5. Interpersonal conflict does not have to involve a winner and a loser; both people can win, as demonstrated in Chapter 12.
6. Leadership, like communication and listening, is a learned skill that you'll develop as you learn the principles of human communication in general and of group leadership in particular (Chapter 11).
7. Most speakers are nervous; managing, not eliminating, the fear will enable you to become effective regardless of your current level of fear (Chapter 14).

Consider how these beliefs about communication influence the way you communicate. Then, as you read this book and participate in class discussions and activities, reexamine your beliefs about communication and consider how new beliefs would influence the way you communicate. The theories and research discussed in this text will help you reconsider your own beliefs about communication, and the skill activities and experiences will help you practice new ways of communicating.

1.2 ELEMENTS OF HUMAN COMMUNICATION

Communication occurs when one person (or more) sends and receives messages that are distorted by noise, occur within a context, have some effect, and provide some opportunity for feedback. Figure 1.1 illustrates the elements present in all communication acts, whether intrapersonal, interpersonal, small group, public speaking, or mass communication—or whether face to face, by telephone, or over the Internet: (1) context, (2) sources-receivers, (3) messages, (4) channels, (5) noise, and (6) effects.

Communication Context

All communication takes place in a **context** that has at least four dimensions: physical, social-psychological, temporal, and cultural.

- **The physical context** is the tangible or concrete environment in which communication takes place—the room or hallway or park, for example.

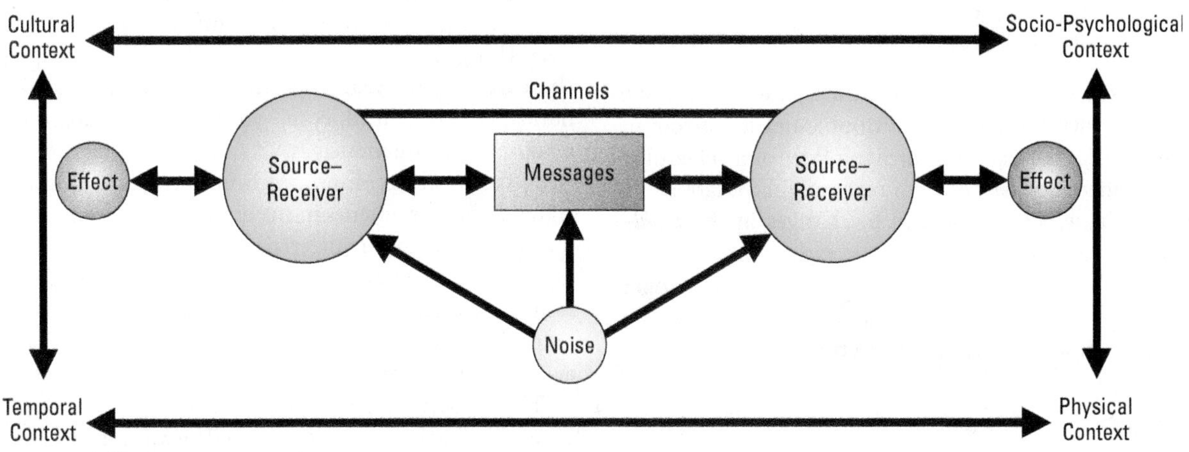

FIGURE 1.1 The Elements of Human Communication

This is a simplified view of the elements of human communication and their relationship to one another. Messages (including feedforward and feedback) are sent simultaneously through a variety of channels from one source-receiver to another. The communication process takes place in a context (physical, cultural, social-psychological, and temporal) and is subjected to interference by noise (physical, psychological, and semantic). The interaction of messages with each source-receiver leads to some effect.

This physical context exerts some influence on the content of your messages (what you say) as well as on the form (how you say it).

- **The social–psychological context** includes, for example, the status relationships among the participants, the roles and the games that people play, and the cultural rules of the society in which people are communicating. It also includes the friendliness or unfriendliness, formality or informality, and seriousness or humorousness of the situation. For example, communication that would be permitted at a graduation party might not be considered appropriate at a funeral.
- **The temporal (or time) context** includes (1) the time of day (for example, for some the morning is not a time for communication; for others, it's ideal), (2) the time in history in which the communication takes place (for example, messages on racial, sexual, or religious attitudes cannot be fully understood outside of their time in history), and (3) how a message fits into the sequence of communication events (for example, the meaning of a compliment would be greatly different depending on whether you said it immediately after your friend paid you a compliment, immediately before you asked your friend for a favor, or during an argument).
- **The cultural context** has to do with your (and others') culture: the beliefs, values, and ways of behaving that are shared by a group of people and passed down from one generation to the next. Cultural factors affect every interaction and influence what you say, how you say it, and how you respond to what others say.

These four dimensions of context interact with one another (symbolized by the double-headed arrow in Figure 1.1). For example, arriving late for a scheduled lunch meeting (*temporal* context) might violate a *cultural* rule, which might lead to changes in the *social–psychological* context, perhaps creating tension and unfriendliness, which in turn might lead to changes in the *physical* context—for example, choosing a less intimate restaurant for your meeting.

Source–Receiver

The compound term *source–receiver* emphasizes that each person involved in communication is both a **source** (or speaker) and a **receiver** (or listener). You send messages when you speak, write, gesture, or smile. You receive messages in listening, reading, smelling, and so on. As you send messages, however, you're also receiving messages. You're receiving your own messages (you hear yourself, you feel your own movements, you see many of your own gestures), and you're receiving the messages of the other person—visually, aurally, or even through touch or smell.

The act of producing messages—for example, speaking or writing—is called **encoding.** By putting your ideas into sound waves or into a computer program you're putting these ideas into a **code**, hence encoding. The act of receiving messages—for example, listening or reading—is called **decoding.** By translating sound waves or words on a screen into ideas you take them out of code, which is decoding. Thus, speakers or writers are called **encoders**, and listeners or readers, **decoders.**

As with sources–receivers, the compound term *encoding–decoding* emphasizes that you perform these functions simultaneously, at least in face-to-face communication. As you speak (encode), you also decipher the **responses** of the listener (decode). In computer communication this simultaneous exchange of messages occurs only sometimes. In e-mail (as well as snail mail) and social network sites, for example, the sending and receiving may be separated by several days or much longer. In chat groups and instant messaging, on the other hand, communication takes place in real time; the sending and receiving take place (almost) simultaneously.

Messages

Communication **messages** take many forms. You send and receive messages through any one or any combination of sensory organs. Although you may customarily think of messages as being verbal (oral or written), you also communicate nonverbally. Everything about you communicates. For example, the clothes you wear and the way you walk, shake hands, tilt your head, comb your hair, sit, and smile all communicate messages.

In face-to-face communication, the actual message signals (the movements in the air) are evanescent; they fade almost as they're uttered. Some written messages, especially computer-mediated messages such as those sent via e-mail, are unerasable. E-mails that are sent among employees in a large corporation, for example, are often stored on disk or tape.

Three special types of messages include metamessages, feedback messages, and feedforward messages.

Metamessages

A **metamessage** is a message that refers to another message; it is communication about communication. For example, remarks such as "This statement is false" or "Do you understand what I am trying to tell you?" refer to communication and are therefore

metacommunication. Nonverbal behavior may also be metacommunicational. Obvious examples include crossing your fingers behind your back or winking when telling a lie. On a less obvious level, consider the blind date. As you say, "I had a really nice time," your nonverbal messages—the lack of a smile, the failure to maintain eye contact, the extra long pauses—metacommunicate and contradict the verbal "really nice time," suggesting that you did not enjoy the evening.

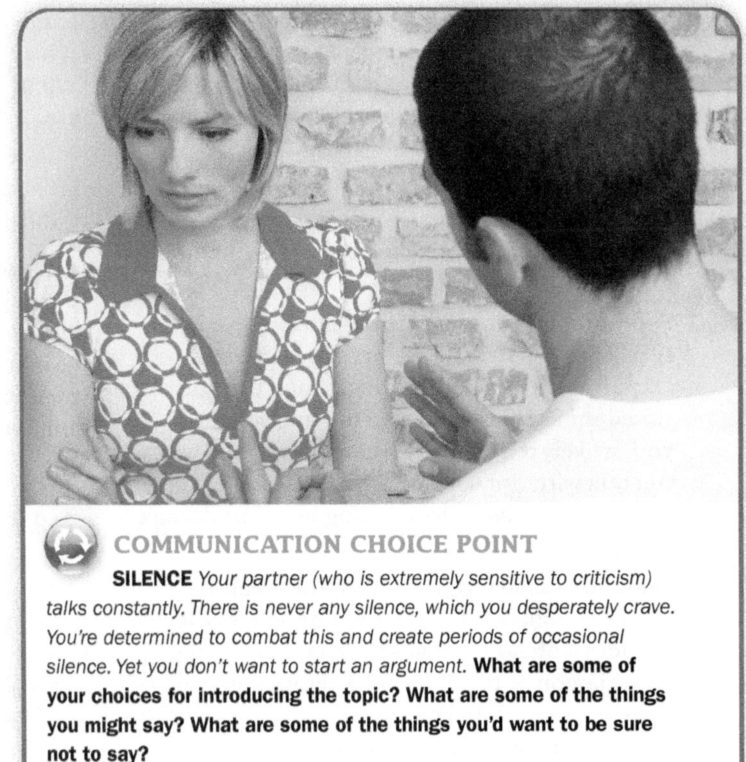

COMMUNICATION CHOICE POINT

SILENCE *Your partner (who is extremely sensitive to criticism) talks constantly. There is never any silence, which you desperately crave. You're determined to combat this and create periods of occasional silence. Yet you don't want to start an argument.* **What are some of your choices for introducing the topic? What are some of the things you might say? What are some of the things you'd want to be sure not to say?**

Feedback Messages

Throughout the listening process, a listener gives a speaker **feedback**—messages sent back to the speaker reacting to what is said. Feedback tells the speaker what effect he or she is having on the listener(s). This can take many forms: A frown or a smile, a yea or a nay, a pat on the back or a punch in the mouth are all types of feedback. Another type of feedback is the feedback you get from listening to yourself: You hear what you say, you feel the way you move, you see what you write. On the basis of this self-feedback you adjust your messages; for example, you may correct a mispronunciation, shorten your story, or increase your volume.

Feedforward Messages

Feedforward is information you provide before sending your primary messages; it reveals something about the messages to come (Richards, 1968). Feedforward includes such diverse examples as the preface or the table of contents in a book, the opening paragraph of a chapter, movie previews, magazine covers, and introductions in public speeches. Before you open your e-mail you get feedforward that tells you the sender's name and the subject matter. In communicating bad news you might give feedforward that aims to prepare the person to receive this news with something like, "I'm sorry I have to tell you this, but…"

Explore the Exercise "How to Give Feedforward" at MyCommunicationLab

Channels

The communication **channel** is the medium through which the message passes. Communication rarely takes place over only one channel; you may use two, three, or four different channels simultaneously. For example, in face-to-face interactions you speak and listen (vocal channel), but you also gesture and receive signals visually (visual channel). In chat groups you type and read words and use various symbols and abbreviations to communicate the emotional tone of the message and, in many cases, audio and video means as well. In addition, in face-to-face communication you emit and detect odors (olfactory channel). Often you touch another person, and this too communicates (tactile channel).

Explore the Exercise "Comparing Communication Channels" at MyCommunicationLab

Noise

Noise is anything that interferes with your receiving a message. At one extreme, noise may prevent a message from getting from source to receiver. A roaring noise or line static can easily prevent entire messages from getting through to your receiver. At the other extreme, with virtually no noise interference, the message of the source and the message received are almost identical. Most often, however, noise distorts some portion of the message as it travels from source to receiver. Four types of noise are especially relevant:

- **Physical noise** is interference that is external to both speaker and listener; it interferes with the physical transmission of the signal or message.

Examples include the screeching of passing cars, the hum of a computer, sunglasses, illegible handwriting, blurred type or fonts that are too small or difficult to read, misspellings and poor grammar, and popup ads.

- **Physiological noise** is created by barriers within the sender or receiver such as visual impairments, hearing loss, articulation problems, and memory loss.
- **Psychological noise** is mental interference in speaker or listener and includes preconceived ideas, wandering thoughts, biases and prejudices, closed-mindedness, and extreme emotionalism. You're likely to run into psychological noise when you talk with someone who is closed-minded and who refuses to listen to anything he or she doesn't already believe.
- **Semantic noise** is created when the speaker and listener have different meaning systems; it includes language or dialectical differences, the use of jargon or overly complex terms, and ambiguous or overly abstract terms whose meanings can be easily misinterpreted. You see this type of noise regularly, for example, in the medical doctor who uses "medicalese" without explanation or in the insurance salesperson who speaks in the jargon of the insurance industry.

As you can see from these examples, noise is anything that distorts your receiving the messages of others or their receiving your messages.

All communications contain noise. Noise can't be totally eliminated, but its effects can be reduced. Making your language more precise, sharpening your skills for sending and receiving nonverbal messages, adjusting your camera for greater clarity, and improving your listening and feedback skills are some ways to combat the influence of noise.

Effects

Communication always has some **effect** on one or more persons involved in the communication act. For every communication act, there is some consequence. Generally three types of effects are distinguished.

- **Intellectual (or cognitive) effects** are changes in your thinking. When you acquire information from a class lecture, for example, the effect is largely intellectual.
- **Affective effects** are changes in your attitudes, values, beliefs, and emotions. Thus, when you become frightened when watching the latest horror movie, its effect is largely affective. Similarly, after a great experience with, say, a person of another culture, your feelings about that culture may change. Again, the effect is largely affective (but perhaps also intellectual).
- **Psychomotor effects** are changes in behaviors such as, for example, learning new dance movements, to throw a curve ball, to paint a room, or to use different verbal and nonverbal behaviors.

These effects are not separate; rather, they interact. In many cases, a single message—say, a public speech on homelessness—may inform you (intellectual effect), move you to feel differently (affective effect), and lead you to be more generous when you come upon a homeless person (psychomotor effect).

1.3 PRINCIPLES OF HUMAN COMMUNICATION

Several principles are essential to an understanding of human communication in all its forms. These principles, as you'll see throughout the text, have numerous practical implications for your own communication effectiveness.

Watch the Video "Going Up" at **MyCommunicationLab**

Communication Is Purposeful

You communicate for a purpose; some motivation leads you to communicate. When you speak or write, you're trying to send some message and trying to accomplish some goal. Although different cultures emphasize different purposes and motives (Rubin, Fernandez-Collado, & Hernandez-Sampieri, 1992), five general purposes seem relatively common to most if not all forms of communication:

- **to learn:** to acquire knowledge of others, the world, and yourself
- **to relate:** to form relationships with others, to interact with others as individuals
- **to help:** to assist others by listening, offering solutions
- **to influence:** to strengthen or change the attitudes or behaviors of others
- **to play:** to enjoy the experience of the moment

Popular belief and research findings both agree that men and women use communication for different purposes. Generally, men seem to communicate more for information and women more for relationship purposes (Dindia & Canary, 2006; Helgeson, 2009). Gender differences also occur in computer communication. For example, women chat more for relationship reasons; men chat more to play and to relax (Leung, 2001).

the•o•ry *noun* statement of explanation, formulation of relationships, reasoned generalization

UNDERSTANDING THEORY AND RESEARCH
Communication Theories

In addition to the theory and research discussed throughout the text, two Understanding Theory and Research boxes appear in each chapter to highlight a particular theory or hypothesis about communication and to focus attention on the nature and function of theory and research in the study of human communication.

A **theory** is a generalization that explains how something works—for example, gravity, blood clotting, interpersonal attraction, or communication. In academic writing, the term *theory* is usually reserved for a well-established system of knowledge about how things work or how things are related. A theory is still fundamentally a generalization, but it's often supported by research findings and other well-accepted theories.

The theories you'll encounter in this book try to explain how communication works—for example, how you accommodate your speaking style to your listeners, how communication works when relationships deteriorate, how friends self-disclose, how problem-solving groups communicate, how speakers influence audiences, and how the media affect people. As you can see from even these few examples, theories provide general principles that help you understand an enormous number of specific events.

One great value of communication theories is that they help you predict future events. Because theories summarize what's been found, they can offer reasonable predictions for events that you've never encountered. For example, theories of persuasion will help you predict what kinds of emotional appeals will be most effective in persuading a specific audience. Or theories of conflict resolution will enable you to predict what strategies would be effective or ineffective in resolving differences. Despite their many values, theories don't reveal truth in any absolute sense. Rather, theories reveal some degree of accuracy, some degree of truth. In the natural sciences (such as physics and chemistry), theories are extremely high in accuracy. The same chemicals mixed the same way will produce the same effect, with little variation from one time to another. In social and behavioral sciences such as communication, sociology, and psychology, the theories are far less accurate in describing the way things work and in predicting how things will work in the future.

This failure to reveal truth, however, does not mean that theories are useless. In increasing your understanding and your ability to predict, theories are extremely helpful. Theories often have practical implications as you work on developing your own communication skills. For example, theories of interpersonal attraction offer practical insights into how to make yourself more attractive to others; theories of leadership offer practical advice on how you can more effectively exert your own leadership. This interrelationship between theories and skills is a theme you'll find throughout this book. The more you know about how communication works (that is, the theories and research), the more likely you'll be able to use it effectively (that is, build your communication skills).

Working with Theories and Research

Log on to one of the academic databases to which you have access and browse through issues of Quarterly Journal of Speech, Communication Monographs, *or* Communication Theory *(or scan similar journals in your own field of study); you'll be amazed at the breadth and depth of academic research and theory.*

Communication Is Transactional

Communication is **transactional**, which means that the elements in communication (1) are always changing, (2) are interdependent (each influences the other), (3) depend on the individual for their meaning and effect, and (4) each person in the communication act is both speaker and listener (Watzlawick, 1977, 1978; Watzlawick, Beavin, & Jackson, 1967). See Figure 1.2 on the following page.

1. **Communication is an ever-changing process.** It's an ongoing activity; all the elements of communication are in a state of constant change. You're constantly changing, the people with whom you're communicating are changing, and your environment is changing. Nothing in communication ever remains static.
2. **Each element relates integrally to every other element.** Each element exists in relation to the others. For example, there can be no source without a receiver. There can be no message without a source. Because of this interdependency, a change in any one element of the process produces changes in the other elements. For example, consider the change that might occur if you're talking with a group of your friends and your mother enters the group. This change in "audience" will lead to other changes. Perhaps you or your friends will adjust what you're saying or how you say it. Regardless of what change is introduced, other changes will be produced as a result.

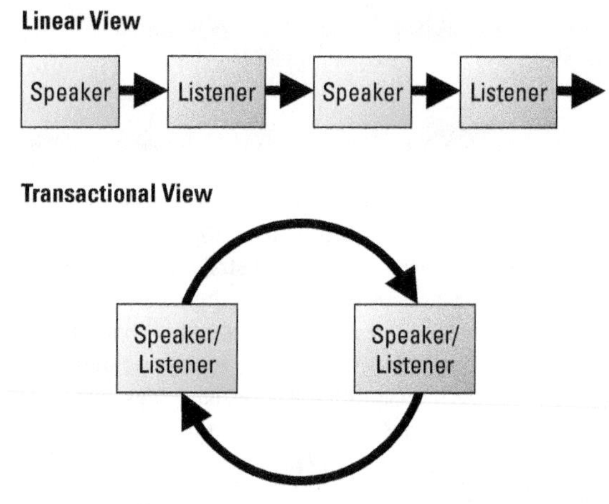

FIGURE 1.2 **Two Views of Communication**
The top diagram represents a linear view of communication, in which the speaker speaks and the listener listens. The bottom diagram represents a transactional view, the view that most communication theorists hold. In the transactional view, each person serves simultaneously as speaker and listener; at the same time that you send messages, you're also receiving messages from your own communications and also from the messages of the other person(s).

3. **Communication is influenced by a multitude of factors.** For example, the way you act in a communication situation will naturally depend on the immediate context, which in turn is influenced by your history, past experiences, attitudes, cultural beliefs, self-image, future expectations, emotions, and a host of related issues. One implication of this is that actions and reactions in communication are determined not only by what is said, but also by the way each person interprets what is said. Two people listening to the same message will often derive two very different meanings; although the words and symbols are the same, each person interprets them differently because each is influenced differently by their history, present emotions, and so on.
4. **Each person in an interaction is both sender and receiver.** Speaker and listener send each other messages at the same time. You send messages when you speak but also when you listen. Even your "refusal to communicate" is itself a communication.

Communication Is a Package of Signals

Communication behaviors, whether they involve verbal messages, gestures, or some combination thereof, usually occur in "packages," an important principle originally articulated some fifty years ago (Pittenger, Hockett, & Danehy, 1960). Usually, verbal and nonverbal behaviors reinforce or support each other. All parts of a message system normally work together to communicate a particular meaning. You don't express fear with words while the rest of your body is relaxed. You don't express anger through your posture while your face smiles. Your entire body works together—verbally and nonverbally—to express your thoughts and feelings.

In any form of communication, whether interpersonal, small group, public speaking, or mass media, you probably pay little attention to this "packaging." It goes unnoticed. But when there's an incongruity—when the weak handshake belies the confident verbal greeting or when the constant preening belies the verbal expressions of being comfortable and at ease—you take notice and begin to question the person's honesty.

Contradictory messages may be the result of the desire to communicate two different emotions or feelings. For example, you may like a person and want to communicate a positive feeling, but you may also feel resentment toward this person and want to communicate a negative feeling as well. The result is that you communicate both feelings; for example, you say that you're happy to see the person but your facial expression and body posture communicate your negative feelings (Beier, 1974). In this example, and in many similar cases, the socially acceptable message is usually communicated verbally while the less socially acceptable message is communicated nonverbally.

Communication Is a Process of Adjustment

Communication can take place only to the extent that the communicators use the same system of signals. You will only be able to communicate with another person to the extent that your language systems overlap. In reality, however, no two persons use identical signal systems, so a process of **adjustment** is relevant to all forms of communication. Parents and children, for example, not only have different vocabularies but also have different meanings for the terms they share. Different cultures, even when they use a common language, often have different nonverbal communication systems. To the extent that these systems differ, meaningful and effective communication will be difficult.

Part of the art of communication is identifying the other person's signals, learning how they're used, and understanding what they mean. If you want to understand what another person means (by smiling, by saying "I love you," by making self-deprecating comments), you have to learn that person's system of signals.

This principle of adjustment is especially important in **intercultural communication**, largely because people from different cultures use different signals—and sometimes also use the same signals to signify quite different things. Focused eye contact means honesty and openness in much of the United States. But in Japan and in many Hispanic cultures, it may signify arrogance or disrespect if, say, engaged in by a youngster with someone significantly older.

An interesting theory revolving largely around adjustment is **communication accommodation theory.** This theory holds that speakers adjust to, or accommodate to, the speaking style of their listeners in order to gain, for example, social approval and greater communication efficiency (Giles, 2008). For example, when two people have a similar speech rate, they seem to be attracted more to each other than to those with dissimilar rates (Buller, LePoire, Aune, & Eloy, 1992). In interethnic interactions, people who saw themselves as similar in communication styles were attracted to each other more than to those they perceived as having different communication styles (Lee & Gudykunst, 2001).

Communication Involves Content and Relationship Dimensions

Communications, to a certain extent at least, refer to the real world—to something external to both speaker and listener. At the same time, however, communications also refer to the relationships between the parties (Watzlawick, Beavin, & Jackson, 1967). In other words, communication has both **content and relationship dimensions.**

For example, an employer may say to a worker, "See me after the meeting." This simple message has a content aspect and a relational aspect. The **content message** refers to the behavioral response expected—namely, that the worker see the employer after the meeting. The **relationship message** tells how the communication is to be dealt with. For example, the use of the simple command says that there's a status difference between the two parties: The employer can command the worker. This aspect is perhaps seen most clearly if you imagine the worker giving this command to the employer; to do so would be awkward and out of place because it would violate the expected relationship between employer and worker.

In any communication situation, the content dimension may stay the same but the relationship aspect may vary. For example, the employer could say to the worker either "You had better see me after the meeting" or "May I please see you after the meeting?" In each case, the content is essentially the same; that is, the message being communicated about the behaviors expected is the same. But the relationship dimension is very different. The first example signifies a definite superior–inferior relationship and even a put-down of the worker. In the second, the employer signals a more equal relationship and shows respect for the worker.

Similarly, at times the content may be different but the relationship essentially the same. For example, a teenager might say to his or her parents, "May I go away this weekend?" or "May I use the car tonight?" The content of the two messages is clearly very different. The relationship dimension, however, is essentially the same. It clearly denotes a superior–inferior relationship in which permission to do certain things must be secured.

Ignoring Relationship Dimensions

Problems may arise when the distinction between the content and relationship levels of communication is ignored. Consider a couple arguing over the fact that Pat made plans to study with friends during the weekend without first asking Chris if that would be all right. Probably both would have agreed that to study over the weekend was the right choice to make. Thus, the argument is not at all related to the content level. The argument centers on the relationship level. Chris expected to be consulted about plans for the weekend. Pat, in not doing so, rejected this definition of the relationship.

Consider the following interchange:

Thom: I'm going bowling tomorrow. The guys at the plant are starting a team. [He focuses on the content and ignores any relational implications of the message.]

Sofia: Why can't we ever do anything together? [She responds primarily on a relational level, ignoring the content implications of the message and expressing her displeasure at being ignored in his decision.]

Thom: We can do something together anytime; tomorrow's the day they're organizing the team. [Again, he focuses almost exclusively on the content.]

Recognizing Relationship Dimensions

Here's essentially the same situation but with added sensitivity to relationship messages:

Thom: The guys at the plant are organizing a bowling team. I'd sure like to be on the team. Do you mind if I go to the organizational meeting tomorrow? [Although he focuses on content, he shows awareness of the relational dimensions by asking if this would be a problem. He also shows this in expressing his desire rather than his decision to attend this meeting.]

Sofia: That sounds great, but I'd really like to do something together tomorrow. [She focuses on the relational dimension but also acknowledges his content message. Note too that she does not respond as if she has to defend herself or her emphasis on relational aspects.]

Thom: How about you meet me at Luigi's for dinner after the organizational meeting? [He responds to the relational aspect without abandoning his desire to join the bowling team—and seeks to incorporate it into his communications. He attempts to negotiate a solution that will meet both Sofia's and his needs and desires.]

Sofia: Perfect. I'm dying for spaghetti and meatballs. [She responds to both messages, approving of both his joining the team and their dinner date.]

COMMUNICATION CHOICE POINT

RELATIONSHIP AMBIGUITY *You've been dating someone on and off for a year or so, and you'd like to invite your date to meet your parents as a friendly gesture but aren't sure how your date will perceive this invitation. You don't want your partner to think that meeting your parents means that you want a closer romantic bond; you're comfortable with the way things are.* **What are some of your choices for reducing the ambiguity? What would you say? In what context? Through what channel?**

Arguments over content are relatively easy to resolve. You can look something up in a book or ask someone what actually took place. Arguments on the relationship level, however, are much more difficult to resolve, in part because you may not recognize that the argument is in fact about your relationship.

Communication Is Ambiguous

Ambiguous messages are messages with more than one potential meaning. Sometimes this **ambiguity** occurs because we use words that can be interpreted differently. Informal time terms offer good examples; *soon, right away, in a minute, early, late,* and similar terms often mean different things to different people. The terms are ambiguous. A more interesting type of ambiguity is grammatical ambiguity. You can get a feel for this type of ambiguity by trying to develop two paraphrases (each with different meanings) for each of these sentences:

1. What has the cat in its paws?
2. Visiting relatives can be boring.
3. They are flying planes.

One set of possible paraphrases is this:

1. What monster has the cat in its paws? What does the cat have in its paws?
2. To visit relatives can be boring. Relatives who visit can be boring.
3. Those people are flying planes. Those planes are for flying.

Although these examples are particularly striking—and are the work of linguists who analyze language—some degree of ambiguity exists in all communication; all messages are ambiguous to some degree. When you express an idea, you never communicate your meaning exactly and totally; rather, you communicate your meaning with some reasonable accuracy—enough to give the other person a reasonably clear sense of what you mean. Sometimes, of course, you're less accurate than you anticipated: Your listener "gets the wrong idea," or "gets offended" when you only meant to be humorous, or "misunderstands your emotional meaning." Because of this inevitable uncertainty, you may qualify what you're saying, give an example, or ask, "Do you know what I mean?" These tactics help the other person understand your meaning and reduce uncertainty (to some degree).

Any communication situation can be ambiguous. In small group or organizational situations, you may be unsure of how you or your ideas are being evaluated. You may be unsure of the hierarchy in the organization. You may be unsure of what style of leadership will prove effective and what style will cause resentment. In public speaking you probably face the greatest ambiguity; namely, how your audience will respond to your speech. Will they be in favor of what you're advocating or against it? Will they understand certain technical terms, or will you have to define them? Will they be willing to pay attention?

Similarly, all relationships contain uncertainty. Consider a close relationship of your own and ask yourself, for example, if you know what topics will likely create problems or how your partner sees your relationship 10 years from now or what your partner's worst fears are or what fantasies your partner has. Very likely you have some ambiguity about these things. As a relationship progresses, it becomes less ambiguous but probably never totally unambiguous. You can look at the skills of communication presented in this course as ways of reducing ambiguity in communicating meaning and in relationships.

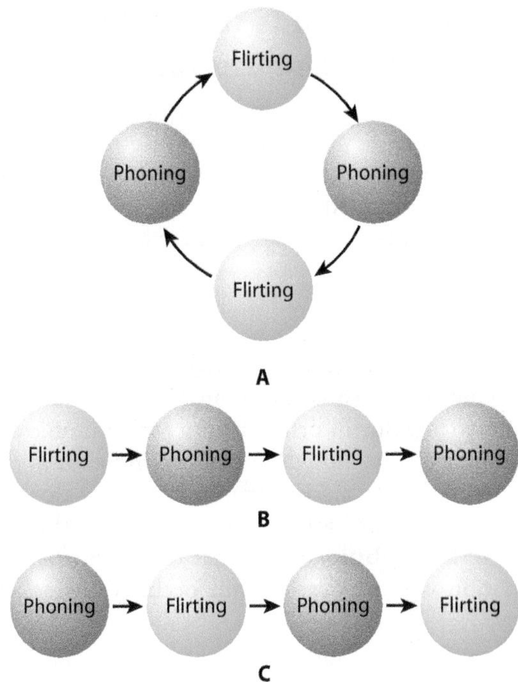

FIGURE 1.3 **Punctuation and the Sequence of Events**

(A) Shows the actual sequence of events as a continuous series of actions with no specific beginning or end. Each action (phoning and flirting) stimulates another action, but no initial cause is identified.

(B) Shows the same sequence of events as seen by the wife. She sees the sequence as beginning with the husband's flirting and her phoning behavior as a response to that stimulus.

(C) Shows the same sequence of events from the husband's point of view. He sees the sequence as beginning with the wife's phoning and his flirting as a response to that stimulus.

Try using this three-part figure, discussed in the text, to explain what might go on when a supervisor complains that workers are poorly trained for their jobs and when the workers complain that the supervisor doesn't know how to supervise.

Communication Is Punctuated

Communication events are continuous transactions. There is no clear-cut beginning and no clear-cut end. As participants in or observers of the communication act, you segment this continuous stream of communication into smaller pieces. You label some of these pieces causes or stimuli and others effects or responses.

Consider an example. A married couple is in a restaurant. The husband is flirting with another woman, and the wife is talking to her sister on her cell phone. Both are scowling at each other and are obviously in a deep nonverbal argument. Recalling the situation later, the husband might observe that the wife talked on the phone, so he innocently flirted with the other woman. The only reason for his behavior (he says) was his anger over her talking on the phone when they were supposed to be having dinner together. Notice that he sees his behavior as a response to her behavior. In recalling the same incident, the wife might say that she phoned her sister when he started flirting. The more he flirted, the longer she talked. She had no intention of calling anyone until he started flirting. To her, his behavior was the stimulus and hers was the response; he caused her behavior. Thus, the husband sees the sequence as going from phoning to flirting, and the wife sees it as going from flirting to phoning. This example is depicted visually in Figure 1.3 and is supported by research showing that, among marrieds at least, the individuals regularly see their partner's behavior as the cause of conflict (Schutz, 1999).

This tendency to divide communication transactions into sequences of stimuli and responses is referred to as **punctuation** (Watzlawick, Beavin, & Jackson, 1967). Everyone punctuates the continuous sequences of events into stimuli and responses for convenience. Moreover, as the example of the husband and wife illustrates, punctuation usually is done in ways that benefit the self and are consistent with a person's self-image.

Understanding how another person interprets a situation, how he or she punctuates, is a crucial step in interpersonal understanding. It is also essential in achieving empathy (feeling what the other person is feeling). In all communication encounters, but especially in conflicts, try to see how others punctuate the situation.

Communication Is Inevitable, Irreversible, and Unrepeatable

Communication is a process that is inevitable, irreversible, and unrepeatable. Communication messages are always being sent (or almost always), can't be reversed or uncommunicated, and are always unique and one-time occurrences. Let's look at these qualities in more detail.

Inevitability

Often communication is thought of as intentional, purposeful, and consciously motivated. In many instances it is. But in other instances communication takes place even though one of the individuals does not think he or she is communicating or does not want to communicate. Put more formally, the principle of **inevitability** means that in any interactional situation communication will occur. Consider, for example, the student sitting in the back of the classroom with an expressionless face, perhaps staring out the window. Although the student might claim not to be communicating with the teacher, the teacher may derive any of a variety of messages from this behavior; for example, that the student lacks interest, is bored, or is worried about something. In any event, the teacher is receiving messages even though the student may not intend to communicate. In an interactional situation you can't avoid communicating (Watzlawick, Beavin, & Jackson, 1967).

Further, when you're in an interactional situation you can't avoid responding to the messages of others. For example, if you notice someone winking at you, you must respond in some way. Even if you don't respond actively or openly, that lack of response is itself a response, and it communicates. Again, if you don't notice the winking, then obviously communication has not occurred.

the•o•ry *noun* statement of explanation, formulation of relationships, reasoned generalization

UNDERSTANDING THEORY AND RESEARCH
Communication Research

Research is usually conducted on the basis of some theory and its predictions—although sometimes the motivation to conduct research comes from a simple desire to answer a question. Communication research is a systematic search for information about communication, the very information that is discussed throughout this text; for example, information about perception and listening, verbal and nonverbal messages, interpersonal interactions, small group encounters, and public speaking situations.

Some research is designed to explore what exists; for example, what do people say after getting caught in a lie? Other research is designed to describe the properties of some communication behavior; for example, what are the various types of excuses? Still other research aims to predict what will happen in different situations; for example, what types of excuses will work best in a business relationship? Research findings bearing on these questions help explain how communication works and suggest ways to use communication more effectively.

In evaluating communication research (or any kind of research), ask yourself three questions:

- **Are the results reliable?** In establishing reliability, a measure of the extent to which research findings are consistent, you ask if another researcher, using the same essential tools, would find the same results. Would the same people respond in the same way at other times? If the answer to such questions is yes, then the results are reliable. If the answer is no, then the results may be unreliable.
- **Are the results valid?** Validity is a measure of the extent to which a measuring instrument measures what it claims to measure. For example, does your score on an intelligence test really measure what we think of as intelligence? Does your score on a test of communication apprehension measure what most people think of as constituting apprehension?
- **Do the results justify the conclusion?** Results and conclusions are two different things. Results are objective findings such as "men scored higher than women on this test of romanticism." Conclusions are the researcher's (or reader's) interpretation of the results and might include, for example, "Men are more romantic than women."

Working with Theories and Research

What question about communication would you like answered? Research the question and find out if the question has already been answered. If not, how might you go about conducting your own research to secure the answer?

Irreversibility

Notice that you can reverse the processes of only some systems. For example, you can turn water into ice and then the ice back into water. And you can repeat this reversal process as many times as you wish. Other systems, however, are irreversible. You can turn grapes into wine, but you can't turn the wine back into grapes—the process can go in only one direction. Communication is such an irreversible process. Once you say something, once you press the send key on your e-mail, you can't uncommunicate it. You can of course try to reduce the effects of your message by saying, for example, "I really didn't mean what I said" or "I was so angry I couldn't think straight." But regardless of how you try to negate or reduce the effects of a message, the message itself, once it has been sent and received, can't be reversed.

Because of **irreversibility** (and unerasability in the case of much electronic communication), be careful not to say things you may be sorry for later. Especially in conflict situations, when tempers run high, avoid saying things you may later wish to withdraw. Commitment messages—"I love you" messages and their variants—also need to be monitored. And in group and public communication situations, when messages are received by many people, it's crucial to recognize their irreversibility. Similarly, online messages (whether e-mail, blog posts, or Facebook photos) that could be interpreted as sexist, racist, homophobic, or ageist, which you thought were private or erased from your computer, may later be recalled and retrieved by others, creating all sorts of problems for you and your organization. Interestingly enough, only 55 percent of online teens say they do not post content that might reflect negatively on them in the future (Lenhart et al., 2011).

Unrepeatability

The reason for the **unrepeatability** of communication is simple: Everyone and everything is constantly changing. As a result, you can never recapture the exact same situation, frame of mind, or relationship dynamics that defined a previous communication act. For example, you can never repeat meeting someone for the first time, making a first impression in an interview, or resolving a specific group problem. You can, of course, try again, as when you say, "I'm sorry I came off so forward, can we try again?" But even after you say this, you have not erased the initial impression. Instead you try to counteract this initial and perhaps negative impression by going through the motions again.

COMMUNICATION CHOICE POINT

IRREVERSIBILITY *You post a really negative remark on your friend's Facebook wall which many of your mutual friends and work colleagues have seen. The next day you realize you shouldn't have been so negative. You really want to remain friends. You need to say something.* **What are your options for communicating your feelings? What communication channels could you use?**

Table 1.3, on page 18, summarizes these principles, basic ideas, and implications.

1.4 THE COMPETENT COMMUNICATOR

Communication competence refers both to your knowledge and understanding of how communication works and to your ability to use communication effectively (Spitzberg & Cupach, 1989, 2002, 2011).

Your understanding of communication would include a knowledge of the elements involved in communication, how these elements interact, and how each communication situation is both different from and similar to other situations. Your knowledge would also include an understanding of the choices you have for communicating in any given situation.

Explore at MyCommunicationLab Profile: "Self-Perceived Communication Competence"

Using communication effectively would involve your ability to select and implement the best choices for communicating and to read and adjust to the ongoing feedback that you receive from your own messages and that guide the choices you make in selecting future messages.

The more you know about communication, the more choices you'll have available for your day-to-day interactions. It's like learning vocabulary. The

TABLE 1.3

In A Nutshell A Summary of Some Principles of Human Communication

Here, in brief, are the major principles of human communication, their basic ideas, and some skill implications.

Principles	Basic Ideas	Some Skill Implications
Communication Is Purposeful	Communication may serve a variety of purposes, for example, to learn, to relate, to help, to influence, to play.	■ Use your purposes to guide your verbal and nonverbal messages. ■ Identify the purposes in the messages of others.
Communication Is Transactional	The elements in communication are (1) always changing, (2) interdependent (each influences the other), and (3) dependent on the individual for their meaning and effect. In addition (4) each person is both speaker and listener.	■ See messages as influenced by a variety of factors. ■ Base your message understanding on the words used and the person.
Communication Is a Package of Signals	Verbal and nonverbal messages work together in "packages," usually to communicate the same meaning but at other times different or even opposite meanings.	■ See messages as a combination of signals. ■ Look to both verbal and nonverbal messages for a clearer understanding of another's meaning.
Communication Is a Process of Adjustment	Communication can take place only to the extent that the communicators use the same system of signals.	■ Learn the other person's system of signaling. ■ Adjust your verbal and nonverbal messages to the situation and the other individuals.
Communication Involves Content and Relationship Dimensions	Messages may refer to the real world, to something external to both speaker and listener (the content), *and* to the relationships between the parties.	■ Distinguish between content and relationship messages. ■ Deal with relationship issues as relationship (not content) issues.
Communication Is Ambiguous	All messages and all relationships are potentially ambiguous.	■ Use clear and specific terms. ■ Ask if you're being understood. ■ Paraphrase complex ideas.
Communication Is Punctuated	Communication events are continuous transactions, punctuated into causes and effects for convenience.	■ See communication as an ongoing process rather than breaking it into causes and effects. ■ See alternative punctuations when trying to understand another's point of view.
Communication Is Inevitable, Irreversible, and Unrepeatable	Messages are (almost) always being sent, can't be uncommunicated, and are always unique, one-time occurrences.	■ Recognize that you're invariably communicating. ■ Remember that you can't reverse communication. ■ Realize that each communication situation is unique and cannot be repeated.

more vocabulary you know, the more choices you have to express yourself. In a similar way, the aim of this book is to give you a broad range of options to use in your own communications and thus increase your communicative competence. Let's spell out the nature of communication competence in more detail by discussing the major themes of competence that contemporary research and theory identify and that are highlighted in this text. Table 1.4, on page 22, provides a summary of the characteristics of competence.

The Competent Communicator Makes Reasoned Choices

Throughout your communication life and in each communication interaction you're presented with choice points—moments when you have to make a choice as to with whom you communicate, what you say, what you don't say, how you phrase what you want to say, and so on. Competence in communication choice-making can be viewed as a series of four interrelated characteristics.

1. The competent communication choice maker realizes that each communication situation can be approached in different ways. For example, there are lots of ways to offer an apology; there are lots of ways to lead a group; there are lots of ways to introduce a speech.
2. The competent communication choice maker has a large arsenal of available choices. For example, the competent communicator would know the characteristics of an effective apology, the varied leadership styles, and the numerous ways in which a speech can be introduced.
3. Because each communication situation is different from every other communication situation, the competent choice maker can effectively evaluate the available choices based on knowledge of the research and theory in human communication and can make reasonable predictions as to what choices will work and what choices won't. For example, the competent communicator would have the knowledge of human communication that would enable him or her to evaluate the type of apology, the style of leadership, or the specific introduction that would work best for this unique communication situation.
4. The competent communication choice maker has the interpersonal, small group, and public speaking skills for executing these choices effectively.

This course and this text aim to enlarge your communication options; regardless of your present level of competence, you should emerge from this course with a greater number of communication options under your control. In addition, this course and text provide you with the background—the theory and research bearing on these choices—to help you make more effective communication predictions and decisions. And this course and text will provide you with the skills enabling you to communicate your choices effectively.

The Competent Communicator Thinks Critically and Mindfully

An essential communication skill is the ability to think critically about the communication situations you face and the options for communicating that you have available; this is crucial to your success and effectiveness.

Without critical thinking there can be no competent exchange of ideas. **Critical thinking** is logical thinking; it's thinking that is well reasoned, unbiased, and clear. It involves thinking intelligently, carefully, and with as much clarity as possible. It's the opposite of what you'd call sloppy, illogical, or careless thinking.

A special kind of critical thinking is mindfulness. **Mindfulness** is a state of awareness in which you're conscious of your reasons for thinking or behaving. In its opposite, mindlessness, you lack conscious awareness of what or how you're thinking (Langer, 1989). To apply interpersonal skills effectively in conversation, you need to be mindful of the unique communication situation you're in, of your available communication options, and of the reasons why one option is likely to be better than the others (Burgoon, Berger, & Waldron, 2000; Elmes & Gemmill, 1990).

As you progress through your study of human communication, actively increase your own mindfulness (Langer, 1989):

- **Create and re-create categories.** Group things in different ways; remember that people are constantly changing, so the categories into which you may group them also should change. Learn to see objects, events, and people as belonging to a wide variety of categories. Try to see, for example, your prospective romantic partner in a variety of roles—child, parent, employee, neighbor, friend, financial contributor, and so on.
- **Be open to new information and points of view.** This is perhaps especially important when these contradict your most firmly held beliefs. New information forces you to reconsider what might be outmoded ways of thinking and can help you challenge long-held but now inappropriate beliefs and attitudes.

- **Beware of relying too heavily on first impressions.** Treat first impressions as tentative, as hypotheses that need further investigation. Be prepared to revise, reject, or accept these initial impressions.
- **Think before you act.** Especially in delicate situations such as anger or commitment messages, it's wise to pause and think over the situation mindfully. In this way you'll stand a better chance of acting and reacting appropriately.

You'll find frequent opportunities to apply mindful, critical thinking throughout your reading of the text but perhaps especially in the "Working With" experiences at the end of the chapters, in the Communication Choice Points that accompany the photos, and in the integrated self-tests.

The Competent Communicator Is Culturally Sensitive

Communication competence is **culture** specific; that is, the principles of effective communication vary from one culture to another, and what proves effective in one culture may prove ineffective in another. For example, in American culture you would call a person you wished to date three or four days in advance. In certain Asian cultures, you might call the person's parents weeks or even months in advance.

Cultures also differ in politeness; in the roles assigned to men and women; in the meanings of different nonverbal messages from facial expressions, colors, touch, silence, and time; in approaches to small group communication and leadership; and in their evaluation of different approaches in public speaking (for example, some cultures appreciate directness and a fully confident speaker, while others may prefer one who is indirect and modest).Because culture is so important in all forms of communication, the next chapter is devoted to culture in human communication and intercultural communication.

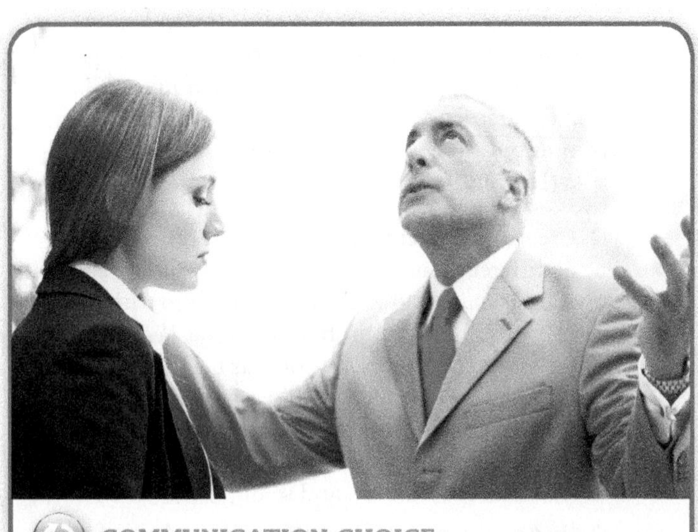

COMMUNICATION CHOICE

CONTENT AND RELATIONSHIP MESSAGES *An older relative frequently belittles you, though always in a playful way. But it's uncomfortable and probably not very good for your self-esteem. You're determined to stop the behavior but not lose the relationship.* **What are some of the things you might say? Through what channel?**

The Competent Communicator Is Ethical

Human communication also involves questions of **ethics**, the study of good and bad, of right and wrong, of moral and immoral. Ethics is concerned with actions, with behaviors; it's concerned with distinguishing between behaviors that are moral (ethical, good, right) and those that are immoral (unethical, bad, and wrong). Not surprisingly, there's an ethical dimension to any interpersonal communication act (Bok, 1978; Neher & Sandin, 2007).

Objective and Subjective Views of Ethics

Woven through these discussions of ethics are two interrelated questions that will influence all your ethical decisions: (1) Are ethical principles objective or subjective? and (2) Does the end justify the means?

In an **objective view** of ethics, you'd argue that the rightness or wrongness of an act is absolute and exists apart from the values or beliefs of any individual or culture. With this view, you'd hold that there are standards that apply to all people in all situations at all times. If lying, false advertising, using illegally obtained evidence, or revealing secrets you've promised to keep were considered unethical, then they would be unethical regardless of circumstances or of cultural values and beliefs. In an objective view the end can never justify the means; an unethical act is never justified regardless of how good or beneficial its results (or ends) might be.

In a **subjective view** of ethics, you'd argue that absolute statements about right and wrong are too rigid and that the ethics of a message depends on the culture's values and beliefs as well as on the particular circumstances. Thus, a subjective position would claim that lying might be wrong to win votes or sell cigarettes, but that it might be quite ethical if good would result from it—as when we try to make friends feel better by telling them that they look great or that they'll get well soon. In a subjective view a good end would often justify the use of means that would in other situations be considered unethical.

Beliefs about Ethics

As a preface to these future discussions, consider some of the popular beliefs about ethics—perhaps one or more of which you hold personally. For each of the following statements place a *T* (for True) if you feel the statement accurately explains what ethical behavior is and an *F* (for False) if you feel the statement does not accurately explain what ethical behavior is.

1. _____ My behavior is ethical when I feel (in my heart) that I'm doing the right thing.
2. _____ My behavior is ethical when it is consistent with my religious beliefs.
3. _____ My behavior is ethical when it is legal.
4. _____ My behavior is ethical when the majority of reasonable people would consider it ethical.
5. _____ My behavior is ethical when the effect of the behavior benefits more people than it harms.

These statements are based on responses given to the question "What does ethics mean to you?" on the Santa Clara University website on Ethical Decision Making and are presented here to stimulate thinking and discussion about what is and what is not a useful ethical theory. All five of these statements are false; none of them states a useful explanation of what is and what is not ethical.

1. Statement 1 is false simply because people often do unethical things they feel are morally justified. Jack the Ripper killing prostitutes is a good historical example, but there are many current ones such as stalking (*I'm so in love I need to be with this person*) or insurance scams (*My family needs the money more than the insurance company*). Even though Jack, the stalker, and the scam artist may feel justified in their own minds, it doesn't make their behavior moral or ethical.
2. Statement 2 must be false when you realize that different religions advocate very different kinds of behavior, often behaviors that contradict one another. Examples abound in almost every issue of a daily newspaper.
3. Statement 3 must be false when you realize so much discrimination against certain people is perfectly legal in many parts of the world, and, in many countries, war (even preemptive war) is legal.
4. Statement 4 is false because the thinking of the majority changes with the times and has often proven to be extremely immoral. The burning of people supposed to be witches or of those who spoke out against majority opinion (as in the Inquisition) are good examples.
5. Statement 5 is false because immoral acts frequently benefit the majority and harm the minority. The burning of witches, for example, was in the interest of the majority as were slavery and discrimination against gay men and lesbians, certain religions, or different races. But, despite this majority interest, we'd readily recognize these actions as immoral.

In addition to this introductory discussion, ethical dimensions of human communication are presented in each of the remaining chapters in the Making Ethical Choices boxes. As a kind of preview, here are just a few of the ethical issues raised in these boxes. As you read these questions, think about your own ethical beliefs and how these beliefs influence the way you'd answer the questions.

- What are your ethical obligations as a listener? See Ethics box, Chapter 4.
- When is it unethical to remain silent? See Ethics box, Chapter 6.
- When is gossiping ethical, and when is it unethical? See Ethics box, Chapter 8.
- At what point in a relationship do you have an obligation to reveal intimate details of your life? See Ethics box, Chapter 9.
- Are there ethical and unethical ways to engage in conflict and conflict resolution? See Ethics box, Chapter 11.

The Competent Communicator Is an Effective Listener

Often we tend to think of competence in interpersonal communication as "speaking effectiveness," paying little attention to listening. But listening is an integral part of interpersonal communication; you cannot be a competent communicator if you're a poor listener.

If you measured importance by the time you spend on an activity, then—according to the research studies available—listening would be your most important communication activity. Studies conducted from 1929 to 1980 show that listening was the most often used form of communication. For example, in a study of college students conducted in 1980 (Barker, Edwards, Gaines, Gladney, & Holley, 1980), listening also occupied the most time: 53 percent compared to reading (17 percent), speaking (16 percent), and writing (14 percent). In a more recent survey (Watkins, 2010), the figures for the four communication activities were: listening (40 percent), talking (35 percent), reading (16 percent), and writing (9 percent). Again, listening is the most often used of all communication activities.

Because of the importance of listening, Chapter 4 is devoted exclusively to listening and covers the nature and importance of listening, the steps you go through in listening, the role of culture and gender in listening, and ways to increase your listening effectiveness.

The Competent Communicator Is Media Literate

Media literacy, of both mass media and social media, covers a range of skills that are vital to dealing with media. Because these skills are so important, Expanding Media Literacy boxes are presented throughout the text, reminding you that the media are influencing you in ways you need to be aware of. Supplement these brief discussions by searching the Web for related and more detailed discussions. Citizens for Media Literacy and the Media Education Foundation maintain especially useful websites.

Because the media influence you in numerous ways (only some of which you may be conscious of), it's crucial that you learn how this influence is exerted so that you, rather than the media, can determine what influences you and what doesn't. Looked at in this way, media literacy is a form of empowerment. It can help you to use the media more intelligently: (1) to understand, analyze, and evaluate media messages more effectively; (2) to influence the messages that the media send out; and (3) to create your own mediated messages. Let's look at these three interrelated skills a bit more.

- Media literacy aims to enable you **to understand, analyze, and evaluate** the messages from the various media (television, film, music, radio, billboards, advertising, public relations, newspapers and magazines, books, websites and blogs, Facebook, Twitter, newsgroups, and chat rooms). Instead of just accepting what the media tell you, media literacy requires that you understand the purposes of the media message (from the media's point of view) and be able to analyze it for truth and fairness. Media literacy requires that you understand the difference between news and advocacy—something that gets blurred in most television and newspaper reporting. Most of the Media Literacy boxes in this text address this function.

TABLE 1.4

In A Nutshell The Competent Communicator

Here are six major characteristics of the competent communicator.

The Competent Communicator	Competent Behaviors
Makes reasoned choices	Understands that communication involves choices, has lots of available choices, can evaluate the choices from a knowledge of how communication works, and has the skills for executing the choices effectively.
Thinks critically and mindfully	Is aware of the uniqueness of each communication situation and thinks logically before acting.
Is culturally sensitive	Understands, acknowledges, and adapts to cultural differences.
Is ethical	Uses communication honestly and truthfully.
Is an effective listener	Listens for understanding and communicates this back to the speaker.
Is media literate	Understands, analyzes, and evaluates media messages and can use the available media resources effectively.

- Media literacy aims **to empower you to interact with the media,** to talk back to the media, and to provide the skills for your influencing the media rather than only the other way around. This function is addressed throughout the book; the skills of human communication are the skills you need to influence –whether it's your friend, a small group, a public speaking audience, or the media.
- Media literacy aims **to educate you to use the available resources to create your own media messages.** Blogs, Twitter, websites, and social network sites are making this function relatively easy. At the same time, many media are inviting readers and reviewers to comment on their articles and in most cases posting your comments along with the original articles.

Media literacy, then, may be defined as the ability to understand, analyze, and evaluate media messages, to interact with the media, and to use the available resources to create your own media messages.

Analyzing Video Choices

Margo, a student mentor at an entertainment magazine publisher, wants to say the right thing in her mentoring discussions with a group of interns. She's just learned that they've done questionable things on Facebook—posted inappropriate pictures, used biased language, and in general portrayed themselves as not serious enough. She wants to make them aware of how damaging this could be in their eventual pursuit of a career, but wonders how she should communicate it to them. She considers the topics covered in this chapter as she contemplates her communication choices. What options do Margo have in determining the form of communication (say, the difference among face-to-face one-on-one, face-to-face group, or online), and what are the likely advantages and disadvantages of each? What options does she have for expressing her message in terms, say, of formality–informality or friendly–businesslike, and what differences will these choices play in her effectiveness? Log on to mycommunicationlab.com to view this video, to see how Margo's choices play out, and to answer the related discussion questions.

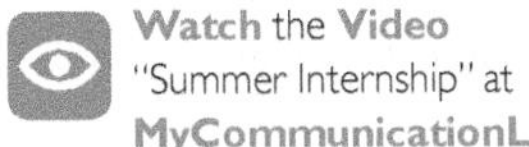

Study and **Review** materials for this chapter are at **MyCommunicationLab**

SUMMARY: PRELIMINARIES TO HUMAN COMMUNICATION

This chapter explained the forms, benefits, and purposes of human communication; the major elements of the human communication process, and several functional principles that explain how human communication works.

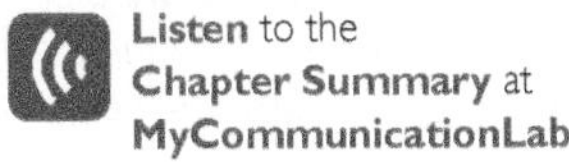

1.1 FORMS, BENEFITS, AND MYTHS OF HUMAN COMMUNICATION

1. Communication is the act, by one or more persons, of sending and receiving messages that occur within a context, are distorted by noise, have some effect (and some ethical dimension), and provide some opportunity for feedback.
2. The major types of human communication are intrapersonal, interpersonal, small group, organizational, public, computer-mediated, and mass communication.
3. Communication study will enable you to improve your presentation skills, relationship skills, interaction skills, thinking skills, and leadership skills.
4. Among the major myths about communication are that more communication is necessarily better communication and that fear of public speaking is necessarily detrimental.

1.2 ELEMENTS OF HUMAN COMMUNICATION

5. The communication context has at least four dimensions: physical, social–psychological, temporal, and cultural.

6. Sources–receivers are the individuals communicating, sending, and receiving messages.

7. Messages may be of varied forms and may be sent and received through any combination of sensory organs. The communication channel is the medium through which the messages are sent.

8. Metamessages are messages about messages; feedback messages are those messages that are sent back to the source and may come from the source itself or from the receiver; and feedforward messages are those that preface other messages and may be used to open the channels of communication.

9. The communication channel is the medium through which the messages are sent.

10. Noise is anything that distorts a message; it's present to some degree in every communication transaction and may be physical, physiological, psychological, or semantic in origin.

11. Communication always has an effect that may be cognitive, affective, or psychomotor or a combination.

1.3 PRINCIPLES OF HUMAN COMMUNICATION

12. Communication is multi-purposeful; we use communication to discover, to relate, to help, to persuade, and to play.

13. Communication is a transactional process in which each person simultaneously sends and receives messages.

14. Communication is normally a package of signals, each reinforcing the other. Opposing communication signals from the same source result in contradictory messages.

15. Communication is a process of adjustment and takes place only to the extent that the communicators use the same system of signals.

16. Communication involves both content dimensions and relationship dimensions.

17. Communication is ambiguous; messages can often be interpreted in different ways.

18. Communication is punctuated; different people divide up the communication sequence into stimuli and responses differently.

19. Communication is inevitable, irreversible, and unrepeatable: (1) In any interaction situation, communication is inevitable; you can't avoid communication, nor can you not respond to communication; (2) You can't uncommunicate; and (3) You can't duplicate a previous communication act.

1.4 THE COMPETENT COMMUNICATOR

20. Communication competence is knowledge of the elements and rules of communication, which vary from one culture to another.

21. The competent communicator is defined as one who makes effective choices, thinks critically and mindfully, understands the role of power, is culturally sensitive, is ethical, is an effective listener, and is media literate.

KEY TERMS

Here are the essential terms used in this chapter and the pages on which they are introduced. Many of these terms are also defined in the glossary at the end of the text. In addition, flash cards are available online at MyCommunicationLab (www.mycommunicationlab.com) to help you further master the vocabulary of human communication.

Study and **Review** the **Flashcards** at **MyCommunicationLab**

adjustment *12*
ambiguity *14*
asynchronous *4*
channel *9*
code *8*
communication *2*
communication accommodation theory *13*
communication competence *17*
computer-mediated communication *4*
content and relationship dimensions *13*
content message *13*
context *7*
critical thinking *19*
culture *20*
decoder *8*
decoding *8*
effect *10*
encoder *8*
encoding *8*
ethics *20*
feedback *9*
feedforward *9*
inevitability *16*
intercultural communication *13*
interpersonal communication *2*
interviewing *2*
intrapersonal communication *2*
irreversibility *17*
mass communication *4*
media literacy *23*
messages *8*
metacommunication *9*
metamessages *8*
mindfulness *19*
noise *9*
objective view *20*
organizational communication *4*
public speaking *4*
punctuation *15*
receiver *8*
relationship message *13*
responses *8*
small group communication *2*
source *8*
subjective view *20*
synchronous *4*
theory *11*
transactional *11*
unrepeatability *17*

WORKING WITH THE PRELIMINARIES TO HUMAN COMMUNICATION

1.1 Distinguishing Content from Relationship Messages. Content and relationship messages serve different communication functions. Being able to distinguish between these functions is a prerequisite for using and responding to messages effectively. In *You're Wearing That?* (2006), Deborah Tannen gives examples of content and relationship communication and the problems that can result from different interpretations. For example, the mother who says, "Are you going to wear those earrings?" may think she's communicating solely a content message. To the daughter, however, the message is largely relational and is a criticism of the way she intends to dress. (Of course, the mother may have intended criticism.) Often, questions that may appear to be objective and focused on content are perceived as attacks, as in the title of Tannen's book. Identify the possible content and relational messages that a receiver might get in being asked the following questions:

- You're calling me?
- Did you say you're applying to medical school?
- You're in love?
- You paid a hundred dollars for that?
- And that's all you did?

1.2 Resolving Ambiguity. Messages and relationships are often ambiguous; instead of assuming one interpretation is right and another wrong, it may be useful to try to disambiguate the message and find out more clearly what the speaker means.

Here are a few ambiguous situations; for each, indicate what you would say to resolve the ambiguity. If possible, try to share your responses with others in a small group and perhaps combine responses to come up with the ideal way to reduce the ambiguity. Or responses from a larger group can be written on index cards (anonymously), collected, and read aloud for the entire group to evaluate.

a. You've been dating Pat on and off for the past six months. Today, Pat asks you to come to dinner and meet the parents. You're not sure if this means that Pat wants to get more serious (which you do not want) or if it's a simple dinner invitation with no additional motives. How might you disambiguate this dinner invitation message?

b. At an appraisal interview, your supervisor says that your work over the last six months has improved considerably—then smiles and says, "But there's always more that we need to do" and then nonverbally indicates that the interview is over and you can return to work. Since you're considering other job offers, you want to know in more detail how your current employer sees you and your prospects for advancement. How might you disambiguate this job appraisal?

c. You receive an e-mail invitation to address the eighth-grade class of your local middle school on careers in communication. The invitation said little more than that a conference on careers is planned and that they'd like to schedule you as one of the speakers. This is too ambiguous for you; you need to know in more detail what will be expected of you. How might you disambiguate this invitation to speak?

1.3 Reading Feedback. Based on your own experiences, do you find that people who accurately read and respond to feedback are better liked than those who don't read feedback as accurately? Is there a relationship between the ability to read feedback and the ability to communicate information or to motivate or persuade an audience? In what ways might the ability to give effective feedback influence the growth or deterioration of a relationship?

1.4 To Communicate. Women often report that an essential quality—perhaps the most important quality—in a partner is one who can communicate. Compared to all the other factors you might take into consideration in choosing a partner, how important to you is the ability to communicate? What specific interpersonal communication skills would you consider "extremely important" in a life partner?

1.5 Feedback. The "feedback theory of relationships" holds that satisfying friendships, romantic relationships, or workplace relationships may be characterized by feedback that is positive, person focused, immediate, low in monitoring, and supportive—and that unsatisfying relationships are characterized by the opposites. How effective is this theory in explaining your social networking relationships?

1.6 Feedforward. In this book there are lots of examples of feedforward, for example: (1) the cover, (2) the "welcome" section, (3) the tables of contents, (4) each chapter's opening page, (5) each chapter's opening paragraph, and (6) the section headings within chapters. What kinds of feedforward can you identify on, for example, websites, newspapers, and television?

1.7 Online and Offline Activities. A Pew Internet and American Life Project report (Fallows, 2005) noted that people are more likely to "get news, play games, pay bills, send cards, look up phone numbers and addresses, buy tickets, check sports scores, listen to music, schedule appointments, and communicate with friends" offline than online. Do you think the items on this list have changed since 2005? How will they change over the next 5 years? Over the next 20 years?

1.8 Synchronous and Asynchronous Messaging. In face-to-face and chat room communication, messages are exchanged with virtually no delay; communication is synchronous. In other forms of communication—for example, snail or e-mail and blog posts—the messages may be exchanged with considerable delay; communication here is asynchronous. What differences does this lead to in the way you communicate in these various forms?

1.9 Inevitability, Irreversibility, and Unrepeatability. Identify one or two guidelines that the concepts of inevitability, irreversibility, and unrepeatability would suggest for any two or three of the following situations: (a) the first day at a new job, (b) asking for a date, (c) a face-to-face job interview, (d) chatting in an online group, (e) posting party photos on some social network site, (f) introducing yourself in class, (g) arguing with your romantic partner, (h) seeing an old friend after many years, (i) leading a group of colleagues in a brainstorming session, and (j) giving a speech to regain the goodwill of the people.

LogOn! MyCommunicationLab www.mycommunicationlab.com

Throughout this chapter, there are icons that highlight media content for selected topics. Go to **MyCommunicationLab** for additional materials on the forms of human communication, the elements involved in the communication process, some of the principles governing the way communication operates, and the nature of the effective or competent communicator. Here you'll find flashcards to help you learn key communication terms, videos that illustrate a variety of concepts, additional exercises, and discussions to help you continue your study of the preliminaries to human communication.

2 CULTURE AND COMMUNICATION

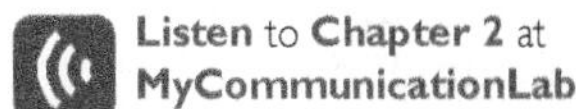

CHAPTER TOPICS	CHAPTER OBJECTIVES
In this chapter you'll explore the following major topics:	**After reading this chapter you should be able to:**
WHAT IS CULTURE?	**2.1** Explain the nature of and role of culture in human communication and define *culture, enculturation,* and *acculturation*.
CULTURAL DIFFERENCES	**2.2** Explain the seven cultural differences and how they affect human communication.
INTERCULTURAL COMMUNICATION	**2.3** Explain the nature of intercultural communication and apply the principles for improving intercultural communication.

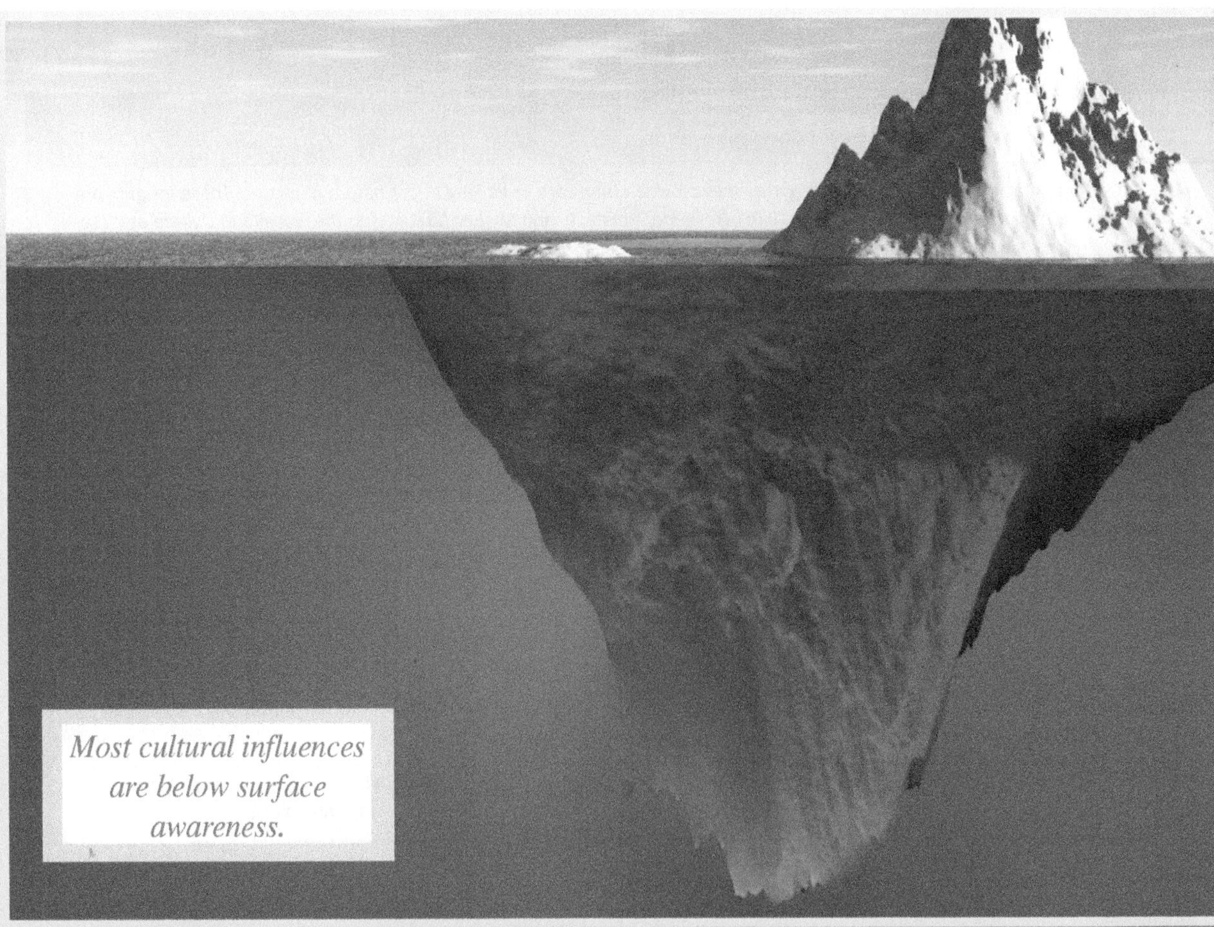

Most cultural influences are below surface awareness.

When you speak or listen, you're doing so as a member of a particular and unique culture—you're greatly influenced by the teachings of your religion, your racial and national history, the social expectations for your gender, and a host of other factors. This chapter explores this topic of culture and its relationship to human communication. As mentioned in the previous chapter, culture permeates all of communication. Here we look at the nature of culture (and answer the question, "What is culture?"), explain some major cultural differences, and look at intercultural communication and how we might improve it.

2.1 WHAT IS CULTURE?

Culture consists of (1) relatively specialized elements of the lifestyle of a group of people (2) that are passed on from one generation to the next through communication, not through genes.

1. Included in a social group's "culture" is everything that members of that group have produced and developed—their values, beliefs, artifacts, and language; their ways of behaving and ways of thinking; their art, laws, religion, and, of course, communication theories, styles, and attitudes.
2. Culture is passed on from one generation to the next through communication, not through genes. Thus, the term *culture* does not refer to color of skin or shape of eyes, as these are passed on through genes, not communication. But because members of a particular race or country are often taught similar beliefs, attitudes, and values, it's possible to speak of "Hispanic culture" or "African American culture." It's important to realize, however, that within any large group—especially a group based on race or nationality—there will be enormous differences. The Kansas farmer and the Wall Street executive may both be, say, German American, but may differ widely in their attitudes, beliefs, and lifestyles. In some ways the Kansas farmer may be closer in attitudes and values to a Chinese farmer than to the New York financier.

An interesting perspective on culture can be gained by looking at some of the popular metaphors for culture; seven of these are identified in Table 2.1.

Sex and Gender

In ordinary conversation *sex* and *gender* are often used synonymously. In academic discussions of culture, they're more often distinguished. **Sex** refers to the

TABLE 2.1 SEVEN METAPHORS OF CULTURE

Here are seven metaphors of culture; taken together they provide other ways of looking at the nature of culture. These insights are taken from a variety of sources, including Hall (1976), Hofstede, Hofstede, and Minkov (2010), and the website of Culture at Work and Culturally Teaching: Education across Cultures.

Metaphor	**Metaphor's Claim/Assumption**
Salad/jelly beans	Like items in a salad or bag of jelly beans, cultures are individual; yet, they work together with other cultures to produce an even better combination.
Iceberg	Like the iceberg, only a small part of culture is visible; most of culture and its influences are hidden from easy inspection.
Tree	Like the tree, you only see the trunk, branches, and leaves but the root system, which gives the tree its structure and function, is hidden from view.
Melting pot	Cultures blend into one amalgam and lose their individuality. But the blend is better than any one of the ingredients.
Software	Culture dictates what we do and don't do much as does a software program. Out of awareness, people are programmed, to some extent, to think and behave by their culture.
Organism	Culture, like an organism, uses the environment (other cultures) to grow but maintains boundaries so its uniqueness is not destroyed.
Mosaic	Like a mosaic is made up of pieces of different shapes, sizes, and colors, so is culture; the whole, the combination, is more beautiful than any individual piece.

biological and physiological qualities that characterize men and women; sex is determined by genes, by biology. **Gender,** on the other hand, refers to the socially constructed roles and behaviors that society deems appropriate for males and females. Gender is learned from society; it's the attitudes, beliefs, values, and ways of communicating that boys and girls learn as they grow up.

Thus, gender—although partly transmitted genetically and not by communication—may be considered a cultural variable, largely because cultures teach boys and girls different attitudes, beliefs, values, and ways of behaving. Thus, you act like a man or a woman in part because of what your culture has taught you about how men and women should act. This is not, of course, to deny that biological differences also play a role in the differences between male and female behavior. In fact, research continues to uncover biological roots of male/female differences we once thought were entirely learned (Helgeson, 2009; McCroskey, 1998).

Explore the Exercise "From Culture to Gender" at MyCommunicationLab

The Transmission of Culture

Culture is transmitted from one generation to another through **enculturation,** the process by which you learn the culture into which you're born (your native culture). Parents, peer groups, schools, religious institutions, and government agencies are the main teachers of culture.

A somewhat different process of learning culture is **acculturation,** the process by which you learn the rules and norms of a culture different from your native culture. In acculturation, your original or native culture is modified through direct contact with or exposure to a new and different "host" culture. For example, when immigrants settle in the United States (the host culture), their own culture becomes influenced by U.S. culture. Gradually, the values, ways of behaving, and beliefs of the host culture become more and more a part of the immigrants' culture, a process known as **assimilation**; the immigrant assimilates into the dominant culture's values, beliefs, and language, for example.

At the same time, of course, the host culture changes, too, as it interacts with the immigrants' culture. Generally, however, the culture of the immigrant changes more. The reasons for this are that the host country's members far outnumber the immigrant group and that the media are largely dominated by and reflect the values and customs of the host culture (Kim, 1988).

New citizens' acceptance of the new culture depends on many factors. Immigrants who come from cultures similar to the host culture will become acculturated more easily. Similarly, those who are younger and better educated become acculturated more quickly than do older and less well-educated people. Personality factors also play a part. Persons who are risk takers and open-minded, for example,

the•o•ry *noun* statement of explanation, formulation of relationships, reasoned generalization

UNDERSTANDING THEORY AND RESEARCH

Cultural Theories

Consider two very different theories of culture: cultural evolution and cultural relativism. The theory of *cultural evolution* (often called *social Darwinism*) holds that much as the human species evolved from lower life forms to Homo sapiens, cultures also evolve. Consequently, some cultures may be considered advanced and others primitive. Most contemporary scholars reject this view because the judgments that distinguish one culture from another have no basis in science and are instead based on individual values and preferences as to what constitutes "advanced" and what constitutes "primitive."

The *cultural relativism* approach, on the other hand, holds that all cultures are different but that no culture is either superior or inferior to any other (Berry, Poortinga, Segall, & Dasen, 1992). This view is generally accepted today and guides the infusion of cultural materials into contemporary textbooks on all academic levels (Jandt, 2004). But this position does not imply that all cultural practices are therefore equal or that you have to accept all cultural practices equally. As noted in the text, there are many cultural practices popular throughout the world that you may find, quite logically and reasonably, unacceptable.

Working with Theories and Research

Explore these two positions more fully by consulting one or more of the references cited in this chapter or by logging on to your favorite search engine or database and searching for such concepts as "cultural relativism," "cultural evolution," and "social Darwinism." What might you add to the brief discussion presented here?

have greater acculturation potential. Also, persons who are familiar with the host culture before immigration—through interpersonal contact or through media exposure—will be acculturated more readily than those who lack this familiarity.

The Importance of Culture in Communication

There are many reasons for the current cultural emphasis in the field of communication: (1) demographic changes, (2) increased sensitivity to cultural differences, (3) economic interdependency, (4) advances in communication technology, (5) the renewed concern for politeness, and (6) the fact that communication competence is specific to a culture (what works in one culture will not necessarily work in another). It's impossible to communicate effectively without being aware of how culture influences human communication.

Demographic Changes

Most obvious, perhaps, are the vast demographic changes taking place throughout the United States. Whereas at one time the United States was largely a country populated by northern Europeans, it's now a country greatly influenced by the enormous number of new citizens from Central and South America, Africa, and Asia. And the same is true to an even greater extent on college and university campuses throughout the United States. With these changes have come different customs and the need to understand and adapt to new ways of looking at communication.

Cultural Sensitivity

As a people, we've become increasingly sensitive to cultural differences. American society has moved from an *assimilationist perspective* (which holds that people should leave their native culture behind and adapt to their new culture) to a perspective that values *cultural diversity* (which holds that people should retain their native cultural ways). And, with some notable exceptions—hate speech, racism, sexism, homophobia, and classism come quickly to mind—we're more concerned with communicating respectfully and, ultimately, with developing a society where all cultures can coexist and enrich one another. At the same time, the ability to interact effectively with members of other cultures often translates into financial gain and increased employment opportunities and advancement prospects.

Economic Interdependency

Today most countries are economically dependent on one another. Consequently, our economic lives depend on our ability to communicate effectively across cultures. Similarly, our political well-being depends in great part on that of other cultures. Political unrest in any part of the world—the Far East, eastern Europe, or the Middle East, to take a few examples—affects our security in the United States. As a result of this interrelatedness among nations and peoples, often referred to as a "spaghetti bowl," business opportunities have an increasingly intercultural dimension. All this makes cultural awareness and intercultural communication competence essential skills for professional survival and success.

Communication Technology

The rapid spread of communication technology has brought foreign and sometimes very different cultures right into our living rooms. News from foreign countries is commonplace. You see nightly—in high definition—what is going on in remote countries. Technology has made intercultural communication easy, practical, and inevitable. Daily the media bombard you with evidence of racial tensions, religious disagreements, sexual bias, and all the other problems caused when intercultural communication fails. And, of course, the Internet has made intercultural communication as easy as writing a note on your computer. You now communicate by e-mail just as easily with someone in Europe or Asia as with someone down the street, and you make friends with people on Facebook from countries you never even knew existed.

Politeness

There can be little doubt that part of the emphasis on culture is because of the renewed emphasis on politeness. **Politeness** is probably universal across all cultures (Brown & Levinson, 1987), so we don't really have polite cultures on the one hand and impolite cultures on the other. Nevertheless, cultures differ widely in how they define politeness and in how important politeness is in comparison with, say, openness or honesty. For example, not interrupting, saying "please" and "thank you," maintaining focused eye contact, and asking permission to do something are all examples of politeness messages, but their importance differs from one culture to another.

Cultures also differ in their rules for expressing politeness or impoliteness. Some cultures, for example, may require you to give extended praise when meeting, say, an important scientist or educator; other cultures expect you to assume a more equal position regardless of the stature of the other person.

The varied forms of polite greetings provide excellent examples of the different ways cultures signal politeness, cleverly captured in the title of one guide to intercultural communication, *Kiss, Bow, or Shake Hands: How to do Business in Sixty Countries* (Morrison & Conaway, 2006). Chinese and Japanese will greet you with bows. In Chile, Honduras, and many other Latin countries women may pat each other on the arm or shoulder. In the Czech Republic men may kiss a woman's hand. In many Latin and Mediterranean cultures the polite greeting is to hug—a type of greeting that is gaining in popularity throughout the United States. And in many cultures the proper greeting is the handshake, but even this varies. For example, in the United States and Canada, the handshake is firm and short (lasting about 3 to 4 seconds), but it's soft (resembling a handclasp) and long (lasting about 10 to 12 seconds) in Indonesia. For more on the handshake, see Table 7.3, on page 162.

COMMUNICATION CHOICE POINT

CULTURE VERSUS CULTURE *You've been invited to dinner, along with several other students, at a faculty member's house. You follow strict religious dietary laws, and so you would likely not eat anything and perhaps embarrass your host.* **If you do attend, what are some of the things you might say about your eating rules? If you decide to refuse, how might you do so politely?**

There also are large gender differences (as well as similarities) in the expression of politeness (Helgeson, 2009; Holmes, 1995). Generally, studies from several different cultures show that women use more polite expressions than men (Brown, 1980; Holmes, 1995; Wetzel, 1988). Both in informal conversation and in conflict situations, women tend to seek areas of agreement more than do men (Holmes, 1995). There are also similarities. For example, both men and women in the United States and New Zealand seem to pay compliments in similar ways (Holmes, 1986, 1995; Manes & Wolfson, 1981), and both men and women use politeness strategies when communicating bad news in an organization (Lee, 1993).

Watch the Video "That's So Rude" at MyCommunicationLab

Communication Competence

Communication competence is specific to a given culture; what proves effective in one culture may be ineffective in another. For example, in the United States corporate executives get down to business during the first several minutes of a meeting. In Japan, however, business executives interact socially for an extended period and try to find out something about one another. Thus, the communication principle influenced by U.S. culture would advise participants to get down to the meeting's agenda during the first five minutes. The principle influenced by Japanese culture would advise participants to avoid dealing with business until everyone has socialized sufficiently and feels well acquainted enough to begin negotiations. Each principle seems effective within its own culture and ineffective outside its own culture. For example, Asians often find that the values they have learned—values that discourage competitiveness and assertiveness—work against them in Western cultures that endorse competition and outspokenness (Cho, 2000).

The Aim of a Cultural Perspective

Because culture permeates all forms of communication, it's necessary to understand its influences if you're to understand how communication works and master its skills. As illustrated throughout this text, culture influences communications of all types. It influences what you say to yourself and how you talk with friends, lovers, and family in everyday conversation. It influences how you interact in groups and how much importance you place on the group versus the individual. It influences the topics you talk about and the strategies you use in the workplace and in communicating information or in persuasion. And it influences how you use the media and the credibility you attribute to them. Success in communication—on your job and in your social life—will depend on your ability to communicate effectively with persons who are culturally different from yourself.

As demonstrated throughout this text, cultural differences exist across the communication spectrum—from the way you use eye contact to the way you develop or dissolve a relationship (Chang & Holt, 1996). But these should not blind you to the great number of similarities that also exist among even the most widely separated cultures. Close interpersonal relationships, for example, are common in all cultures, though they may be entered into for very different reasons by members of different cultures. Further, when reading about cultural differences, remember that these are usually matters of degree. Thus, most cultures value honesty, but not all value it to the same degree.

An emphasis on cultural awareness does not imply that you should accept all cultural practices or that all cultural practices are equal (Hatfield & Rapson, 1996). For example, cockfighting, foxhunting, and bullfighting are parts of the culture of some Latin American countries, England, and Spain, but you need not find these activities acceptable or equal to cultural practices in which animals are treated kindly. Further, a cultural emphasis does not imply that you have to accept or follow even the practices of your own culture. For example, even if the majority in your culture finds cockfighting acceptable, you need not agree with or follow the practice. Similarly, you can reject your culture's values and beliefs; its religion or political system; or its attitudes toward people who are homeless, handicapped, or culturally different. Of course, going against your culture's traditions and values is often very difficult. But it's important to realize that although culture influences you, it does not determine your values or behavior. Often, for example, personality factors (such as your degree of assertiveness, extroversion, or optimism) will prove more influential than culture.

me•di•a lit•er•a•cy *noun* ability to understand, interact with, and create media messages

EXPANDING MEDIA LITERACY

Media Imperialism

Political imperialism is a policy of expanding the dominion of one country over that of another. Cultural imperialism refers to a similar process; the expansion of dominion by one culture over another. Media imperialism is a subdivision of political and cultural imperialism and refers to the domination of one culture's media over those of other cultures. Generally, the media from developed countries such as the United States dominate the media from developing countries. This media dominance is also seen in online communication, in which the United States and the English language dominate.

Media products from the Unites States are likely to emphasize its dominant attitudes and values: for example, the preference for competition, the importance of individuality, the advantages of capitalism and democracy, safe sex, and health consciousness, and the importance of money. Through this media dominance, the attitudes and values of the dominant U.S. media will become the attitudes and values of the rest of the world.

Television programs, films, and music from the United States and Western Europe are so popular and so in demand in developing countries that they may actually inhibit the growth of native cultures' own talent. So, for example, instead of expressing their own vision in an original television drama or film, native writers in developing countries may find it easier and more secure to work as translators for products from more developed countries. And native promoters may find it easier and more lucrative to sell, say, U.S. music than to cultivate and promote native talent. The fact that it is cheaper to import and translate than it is to create original works gives the developed country's products an added advantage and the native culture's productions a decided disadvantage.

The popularity of U.S. and Western European media may also lead artists in developing countries to imitate. For example, media artists and producers may imitate films and television programs from the Untied States rather than develop their own styles, styles more consistent with their native culture.

Although the term *imperialism* is a negative one, the actual process of media influence may be viewed as negative or positive, depending on your cultural perspectives. Some people might argue that the media products from the U.S. are generally superior to those produced elsewhere and so serve as a kind of benchmark and standard for quality work throughout the world.

Also, it might be argued that such products introduce new trends and perspectives and hence enrich the native culture. Much as people in the United States profit from the influence of new cultural strains, the developing cultures profit when U.S. media introduce, for example, new perspectives on government and politics, foods, educational technologies, and health.

2.2 CULTURAL DIFFERENCES

For effective communication to take place in a global world, goodwill and good intentions are helpful—but they are not enough. If you're going to be effective, you need to know how cultures differ and how these differences influence communication. Research supports several major cultural distinctions that have an impact on communication: (1) individualist or collectivist orientation, (2) emphasis on context (whether high or low), (3) power structure, (4) masculinity–femininity, (5) tolerance for ambiguity, (6) long- and short-term orientation, and (7) indulgence and restraint. Each of these dimensions of difference has significant impact on all forms of communication (Gudykunst, 1994; Hall & Hall, 1987; Hofstede, Hofstede, & Minkov, 2010). Following the major researchers in this area, these differences are discussed in terms of countries, even though in many cases different nations have very similar cultures (and so we often speak of *Hispanic culture,* which would include a variety of countries). In other cases, the same country includes varied cultures (for example, Hong Kong, although a part of China, is considered separately because it has a somewhat different culture) (Hofstede, Hofstede, & Minkov, 2010).

Before reading about these dimensions, consider the statements below; they will help personalize the text discussion and make it more meaningful. For each of the items below, select either *a* or *b*. In some cases, you may feel that neither *a* nor *b* describes yourself accurately; in these cases simply select the one that is closer to your feeling. As you'll see when you read this next section, these are not *either/or* preferences, but *more-or-less* preferences.

1. Success, to my way of thinking, is better measured by
   a. the extent to which I surpass others.
   b. my contribution to the group effort.
2. My heroes are generally
   a. people who stand out from the crowd.
   b. team players.
3. If I were a manager, I would likely
   a. reprimand a worker in public if the occasion warranted.
   b. always reprimand in private regardless of the situation.
4. In communicating, it's generally more important to be
   a. polite rather than accurate or direct.
   b. accurate and direct rather than polite.
5. As a student (and if I feel well informed), I feel
   a. comfortable challenging a professor.
   b. uncomfortable challenging a professor.
6. In choosing a life partner or even close friends, I feel more comfortable
   a. with just about anyone, not necessarily one from my own culture and class.
   b. with those from my own culture and class.
7. In a conflict situation, I'd be more likely to
   a. confront conflicts directly and seek to win.
   b. confront conflicts with the aim of compromise.
8. If I were a manager of an organization I would stress
   a. competition and aggressiveness.
   b. worker satisfaction.
9. As a student, I'm more comfortable with assignments in which
   a. there is freedom for interpretation.
   b. there are clearly defined instructions.
10. Generally, when approaching an undertaking with which I've had no experience, I feel
    a. comfortable.
    b. uncomfortable.
11. Generally,
    a. I save money for the future.
    b. I spend what I have.
12. My general belief about child-rearing is that
    a. children should be cared for by their mothers.
    b. children can be cared for by others.
13. For the most part,
    a. I believe I'm in control of my own life.
    b. I believe my life is largely determined by forces out of my control.
14. In general,
    a. I have leisure time to do what I find fun.
    b. I have little leisure time.

- Items 1–2 refer to the **individualist–collectivist orientation;** *a* responses indicate an individualist orientation, and *b* responses indicate a collectivist orientation.
- Items 3–4 refer to the **high- and low-context** characteristics; *a* responses indicate a high-context focus, and *b* responses indicate a low-context focus.
- Items 5–6 refer to the **power distance** dimension; *a* responses indicate greater comfort with a low power distance, and *b* responses indicate comfort with a high power distance.
- Items 7–8 refer to the **masculine–feminine** dimension; *a* responses indicate a masculine orientation; *b* responses, a feminine orientation.
- Items 9–10 refer to the **tolerance for ambiguity** or uncertainty; *a* responses indicate high tolerance, and *b* responses indicate a low tolerance.

- Items 11–12 refers to the **long- or short-term orientation;** *a* responses indicate long-term orientation, and *b* responses indicate short-term orientation.
- Items 13–14 refer to **indulgent and restraint orientation;** *a* responses indicate indulgent, and *b* responses indicate restraint cultures.

Understanding your preferences in a wide variety of situations as culturally influenced (at least in part) is a first step to controlling them and to changing them should you wish to do so. This understanding also helps you modify your behavior as appropriate for greater effectiveness in certain situations. The remaining discussion in this section further explains these orientations and their implications.

Individual and Collective Orientation

Cultures differ in the way in which they promote individualist and collectivist thinking and behaving (Hofstede, Hofstede, & Minkov, 2010; Singh & Pereira, 2005). An **individualist culture** teaches members the importance of individual values such as power, achievement, hedonism, and stimulation. Examples include the cultures of the United States, Australia, United Kingdom, Netherlands, Canada, New Zealand, Italy, Belgium, Denmark, and Sweden. A **collectivist culture,** on the other hand, teaches members the importance of group values such as benevolence, tradition, and conformity. Examples of such cultures include Guatemala, Ecuador, Panama, Venezuela, Colombia, Indonesia, Pakistan, China, Costa Rica, and Peru.

One of the major differences between these two orientations is the extent to which an individual's goals or the group's goals are given greater importance. Of course, these goals are not mutually exclusive—you probably have both individualist and collectivist tendencies. For example, you may compete with other members of your basketball team for the most baskets or most valuable player award (and thus emphasize individual goals). At the same time, however, you will—in a game—act in a way that will benefit the entire team (and thus emphasize group goals). In actual practice, both individual and collective tendencies will help you and your team each achieve your goals. Yet most people and most cultures have a dominant orientation. In an individualist culture members are responsible for themselves and perhaps their immediate family. In a collectivist culture members are responsible for the entire group.

In some instances these tendencies may come into conflict. For example, do you shoot for the basket and try to raise your own individual score, or do you pass the ball to another player who is better positioned to score and thus benefit your team? You make this distinction in popular talk when you call someone a team player (collectivist orientation) or an individual player (individualist orientation).

Success, in an individualist culture, is measured by the extent to which you surpass other members of your group; you take pride in standing out from the crowd. And your heroes—in the media, for example—are likely to be those who are unique and who stand apart. In a collectivist culture success is measured by your contribution to the achievements of the group as a whole; you take pride in your similarity to other members of your group. Your heroes are more likely to be team players who don't stand out from the rest of the group's members.

Distinctions between in-group members and out-group members are extremely important in collectivist cultures. In individualistic cultures, which prize each person's individuality, the distinction is likely to be less important. In fact, closely related to individualism and collectivism is **universalism** and **exclusionism** (Hofstede, Hofstede, & Minkov, 2010). A universalist culture (highly correlated with individualism) is one in which people are treated as individuals, rather than in terms of the groups (racial, sexual, national, for example) to which they belong. A universalist orientation teaches a respect for other cultures, other beliefs, and other ways of doing things. An exclusionist orientation (highly correlated with collectivism) fosters a strong in-group affiliation with much less respect for out-group members. Special privileges are reserved for in-group members while indifference, impoliteness, and, in some cases, even hostility are directed at members of other cultures.

High- and Low-Context Cultures

Cultures also differ in the extent to which information is made explicit, on the one hand, or is assumed to be in the context or in the persons communicating, on the other. In a **high-context culture** much of the information in communication is in the context or in the person—for example, information that was shared through previous communications, through assumptions about each other, and through shared experiences. The information is thus known by all participants, but it is not explicitly stated in the verbal message. In a **low-context culture** most of the information is explicitly stated in the verbal message. In formal transactions it will be stated in written (or contract) form.

High-context cultures are also collectivist cultures (Gudykunst & Kim, 1992; Gudykunst, Ting-Toomey, &

Chua, 1988). These cultures (Japanese, Arabic, Latin American, Thai, Korean, Apache, and Mexican are examples) place great emphasis on personal relationships and oral agreements (Victor, 1992). Low-context cultures are also individualist cultures. These cultures (German, Swedish, Norwegian, and American are examples) place less emphasis on personal relationships and more emphasis on verbalized, explicit explanation—for example, on written contracts in business transactions.

A frequent source of intercultural misunderstanding that can be traced to the distinction between and low-context cultures is seen in **face-saving** (Hall & Hall, 1987). People in high-context cultures place a great deal more emphasis on face-saving, on avoiding one's own or another's possible embarrassment. For example, they're more likely to avoid argument for fear of causing others to lose face, whereas people in low-context cultures (with their individualist orientation) will use argument to win a point. Similarly, in high-context cultures criticism should take place only in private. Low-context cultures may not make this public–private distinction. Low-context managers who criticize high-context workers in public will find that their criticism causes interpersonal problems—and does little to resolve the difficulty that led to the criticism in the first place (Victor, 1992).

Members of high-context cultures are reluctant to say *no* for fear of offending and causing the person to lose face. So, for example, it's necessary to understand when the Japanese executive's *yes* means *yes* and when it means *no*. The difference is not in the words used but in the way in which they're used. It's easy to see how the low-context individual may interpret this reluctance to be direct—to say *no* when you mean *no*—as a weakness or as an unwillingness to confront reality.

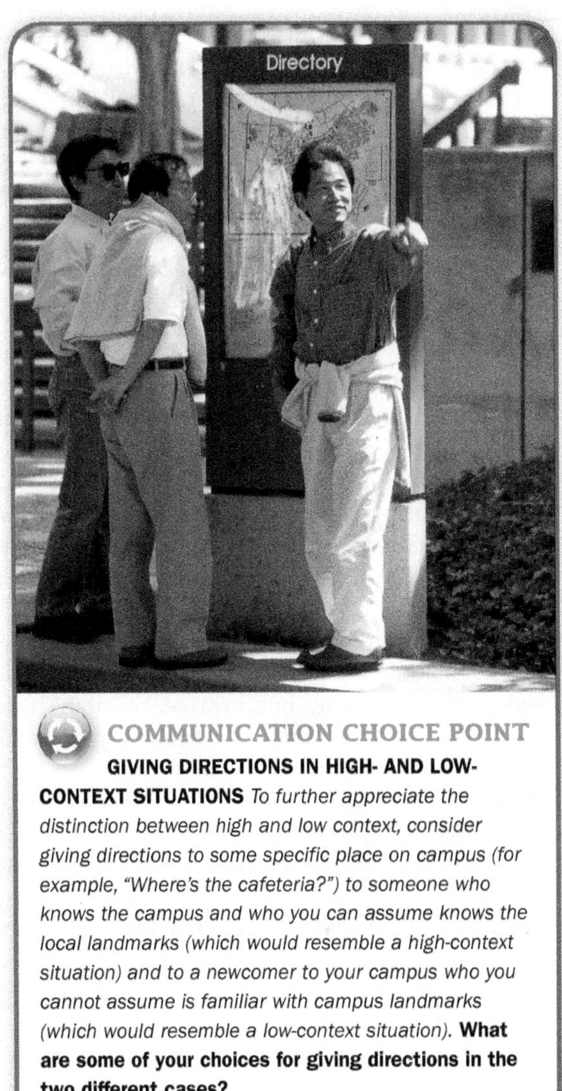

COMMUNICATION CHOICE POINT

GIVING DIRECTIONS IN HIGH- AND LOW-CONTEXT SITUATIONS *To further appreciate the distinction between high and low context, consider giving directions to some specific place on campus (for example, "Where's the cafeteria?") to someone who knows the campus and who you can assume knows the local landmarks (which would resemble a high-context situation) and to a newcomer to your campus who you cannot assume is familiar with campus landmarks (which would resemble a low-context situation).* **What are some of your choices for giving directions in the two different cases?**

Power Distances

In some cultures power is concentrated in the hands of a few, and there's a great difference between the power held by these people and the power of the ordinary citizen. These are called **high-power-distance cultures** (Malaysia, Slovakia, Guatemala, Panama, the Philippines, Russia, Romania, Serbia, Suriname, and Mexico are the top 10) (Hofstede, Hofstede, & Minkov, 2010; Singh & Pereira, 2005. In **low-power-distance cultures** power is more evenly distributed throughout the citizenry (Austria, Israel, Denmark, New Zealand, Switzerland, Ireland, Sweden, Norway, Finland, and Great Britain are the top ten) (Hofstede, Hofstede, & Minkov, 2010; Singh & Pereira, 2005). In a list of 76 countries, the United States ranks 59th (58 nations are higher in power distance). These differences affect communication in numerous ways. For example, in high-power-distance cultures there's a great power distance between students and teachers; students are expected to be modest, polite, and totally respectful. In low-power-distance cultures (and you can see this clearly in U.S. college classrooms) students are expected to demonstrate their knowledge and command of the subject matter, participate in discussions with the teacher, and even challenge the teacher—something many high-power-distance culture members wouldn't even think of doing.

Friendship and dating relationships also will be influenced by the power distance between groups (Andersen, 1991). In India, for example, such relationships are expected to take place within your cultural class. In Sweden a person is expected to select friends and romantic partners not on the basis of class or culture but on the basis of such individual factors as personality, appearance, and the like.

In low-power-distance cultures you're expected to confront a friend, partner, or supervisor assertively; there is in these cultures a general feeling of equality that is consistent with assertive behavior (Borden, 1991). In high-power-distance cultures, direct confrontation and assertiveness may be viewed negatively, especially if directed at a superior.

Masculine and Feminine Cultures

Especially important for self-concept is the culture's attitude about gender roles; that is, about how a man or woman should act. In fact, a popular classification of cultures is in terms of their masculinity and femininity (Hofstede, Hofstede, & Minkov, 2010). When denoting cultural orientations, the terms *masculine* and *feminine* should not be interpreted as perpetuating stereotypes but as reflecting some of the commonly held assumptions of a sizable number of people throughout the world. Some intercultural theorists note that equivalent terms would be *achievement* and *nurturance,* but because research is conducted under the terms *masculine* and *feminine* and because these are the terms you'd use to search the electronic databases, we use these terms here (Lustig & Koester, 2013).

A highly **masculine culture** values aggressiveness, material success, and strength. A highly **feminine culture** values modesty, concern for relationships and the quality of life, and tenderness. The 10 countries with the highest masculinity score are (beginning with the highest) Japan, Austria, Venezuela, Italy, Switzerland, Mexico, Ireland, Jamaica, Great Britain, and Germany. The 10 countries with the highest femininity score are (beginning with the highest) Sweden, Norway, the Netherlands, Denmark, Costa Rica, Yugoslavia, Finland, Chile, Portugal, and Thailand. Of the 53 countries ranked, the United States ranks 15th most masculine (Hofstede, Hofstede, & Minkov, 2010).

Masculine cultures emphasize success and so socialize their members to be assertive, ambitious, and competitive. For example, members of masculine cultures are more likely to confront conflicts directly and to fight out any differences competitively; they're more likely to emphasize conflict strategies that enable them to win and ensure that the other side loses (win–lose strategies). Feminine cultures emphasize the quality of life and so socialize their members to be modest and to highlight close interpersonal relationships. Feminine cultures, for example, are more likely to utilize compromise and negotiation in resolving conflicts; they're more likely to seek solutions in which both sides win (win–win strategies).

Similarly, organizations can be viewed as masculine or feminine. Masculine organizations emphasize competitiveness and aggressiveness. They stress the bottom line and reward their workers on the basis of their contributions to the organization. Feminine organizations are less competitive and less aggressive. They emphasize worker satisfaction and reward their workers on the basis of the needs of workers.

High- and Low-Ambiguity-Tolerant Cultures

Levels of **ambiguity tolerance** vary widely among cultures. In some cultures people do little to avoid uncertainty, and they have little anxiety about not knowing what will happen next. In some other cultures, however, uncertainty is strongly avoided and there is much anxiety about uncertainty.

High-Ambiguity-Tolerant Cultures

Members of high-ambiguity-tolerant cultures don't feel threatened by unknown situations; uncertainty is a normal part of life, and people accept it as it comes. The 10 countries with highest tolerance for ambiguity are Singapore, Jamaica, Denmark, Sweden, Hong Kong, Ireland, Great Britain, Malaysia, India, and the Philippines; the United States ranks 11th.

Because high-ambiguity-tolerant cultures are comfortable with ambiguity and uncertainty, they minimize the importance of rules governing communication and relationships (Hofstede, Hofstede, & Minkov, 2010; Lustig & Koester, 2013). People in these cultures readily tolerate individuals who don't follow the same rules as the cultural majority and may even encourage different approaches and perspectives.

Students from high-ambiguity-tolerant cultures appreciate freedom in education and prefer vague assignments without specific timetables. These students want to be rewarded for creativity and readily accept an instructor's lack of knowledge.

Low-Ambiguity-Tolerant Cultures

Members of low-ambiguity-tolerant cultures do much to avoid uncertainty and have a great deal of anxiety about not knowing what will happen next; they see uncertainty as threatening and as something that must be counteracted. The 10 countries with the lowest tolerance for ambiguity are Greece, Portugal, Guatemala, Uruguay, Belgium, Malta, Russia, El Salvador, Poland, and Japan (Hofstede, Hofstede, & Minkov, 2010).

Low-ambiguity-tolerant cultures create very clear-cut rules for communication that must not be broken. For example, students from strong-uncertainty-avoidance cultures prefer highly structured experiences with little ambiguity; they prefer specific objectives, detailed instructions, and definite timetables. An assignment to write a term paper on "anything" would be cause for alarm; it would not be clear or specific enough. These students expect to be judged on the basis of the right answers and expect the instructor to have all the answers all the time (Hofstede, Hofstede, & Minkov, 2010).

Long- and Short-Term Orientation

Another interesting distinction is that between long- and short-term orientation. Some cultures teach a **long-term orientation**, an orientation that promotes the importance of future rewards, and so, for example, members of these cultures are more apt to save for the future and to prepare for the future academically (Hofstede, Hofstede, & Minkov, 2010). The most long-term-oriented countries are South Korea, Taiwan, Japan, China, Ukraine, Germany, Estonia, Belgium, Lithuania, and Russia. The United States ranks 69th out of 93 countries, making it less long-term than most countries. In long-term cultures, marriage is a practical arrangement rather than one based on sexual or emotional arousal, and living with extended family (for example, in-laws) is common and considered quite normal. Members of these cultures believe that mothers should be home with their children, that humility is a virtue for both men and women, and that old age should be a happy time of life.

Cultures fostering a **short-term orientation** (Puerto Rico, Ghana, Egypt, Trinidad, Nigeria, Dominican Republic, Colombia, Iran, Morocco, and Zimbabwe are the top 10) look more to the past and the present. Instead of saving for the future, members of this culture spend their resources for the present and, not surprisingly, want quick results from their efforts. These cultures believe and teach that marriage is a moral arrangement, living with in-laws causes problems, children do not have to be cared for by their mothers (others can do that), humility is a virtue only for women (not men), and old age is an unpleasant time of life.

These cultures also differ in their view of the workplace. Organizations in long-term-oriented cultures look to profits in the future. Managers or owners and workers in such cultures share the same values and work together to achieve a common good. Organizations in short-term-oriented cultures, on the other hand, look to more immediate rewards. Managers and workers are very different in their thinking and in their attitudes about work.

Even in educational outlook there are significant differences. Students in long-term cultures will attribute their success or failure in school to their own efforts while students in short-term cultures will attribute their success or failure to luck or chance.

Another perspective on this difference is offered by a study that asked Asian (long-term cultures) and American (short-term culture) executives to rank order those values they considered most important in the workplace. The top six responses are presented in Table 2.2 and show a dramatic difference between the two cultural groups.

Indulgence and Restraint

Cultures also differ in their emphasis on indulgence or restraint (Hofstede, Hofstede, & Minkov, 2010). Cultures high in **indulgence** are those that

TABLE 2.2 VALUES OF THE WORKPLACE

This table presents the six highest-ranked values (beginning with the highest-ranked value) by Asian and American executives (Hofstede, Hofstede, & Minkov, 2010). Notice that "hard work" makes both lists but in very different positions.

Values Selected by Asian (Long-Term Orientation) Executives	Values Selected by American (Short-Term Orientation) Executives
Hard work	Freedom of expression
Respect for learning	Personal freedom
Honesty	Self-reliance
Openness to new ideas	Individual rights
Accountability	Hard work
Self-reliance	Personal achievement

emphasize the gratification of desires; they focus on having fun and enjoying life. Venezuela, Mexico, Puerto Rico, El Salvador, Nigeria, Colombia, Trinidad, Sweden, New Zealand, and Ghana are the top 10 in indulgence; the United States ranks 15th out of 93 countries, making it considerably more indulgent than most countries. These cultures have more people who are happy, which depends on two major factors:

- **Life control.** This is the feeling that you may do as you please (at least to a significant degree), that you have freedom of choice to do or not do what you want.
- **Leisure.** This is the feeling that you have leisure time to do what you find fun.

In addition, members of indulgent cultures have more positive attitudes and greater optimism and are more likely to remember positive emotions. They also have a more satisfying family life and loose gender roles (for example, household tasks are shared by both partners).

Cultures high in **restraint** (Pakistan, Egypt, Latvia, Ukraine, Albania, Belarus, Lithuania, Bulgaria, Estonia, and Iraq are the top 10), on the other hand, are those that foster the curbing of such gratification and its regulation by social norms. Restraint cultures have more people who are unhappy: people who see themselves as lacking control of their own lives and with little or no leisure time to engage in fun activities. In contrast to indulgent cultures, members of cultures high in restraint are more cynical, pessimistic, and less likely to remember positive emotions. They have less satisfying family lives, rigid gender roles, and an unequal distribution of household tasks.

As you might expect, indulgent cultures do not place great value on thrift; instead the value is on spending to gratify one's needs. Restrained cultures place a great value on thrift. Also predictable is the finding that indulgent cultures place great importance on friendship and having lots of friends whereas restrained cultures place less importance on friendships. Although there are no studies offering evidence, it's likely that the Facebook pages of indulgent culture members will have a lot more friends than will those of members of restrained cultures. And, not so predictably perhaps, is the finding that death rates from cardiovascular diseases are significantly higher in restrained than in indulgent cultures and significantly more indulgent culture members describe their health as "very good" (Hofstede, Hofstede, & Minkov, 2010).

2.3 INTERCULTURAL COMMUNICATION

Regardless of your own cultural background, you will surely come into close contact with people from a variety of other cultures—people who speak different languages, eat different foods, practice different religions, and approach work and relationships in very different ways. It doesn't matter whether you're a longtime resident of a country or a newly arrived immigrant: You are or you soon will be living, going to school, working, and forming relationships with people who are from very different cultures. Here we look first at the nature and forms of intercultural communication and second at guidelines for improving your own intercultural interactions.

The Nature and Forms of Intercultural Communication

As discussed in Chapter 1, the term **intercultural communication** refers to communication between persons who have different cultural beliefs, values, or ways of behaving. The model in Figure 2.1 illustrates this concept. The larger circles represent the culture of the individual communicators. The inner circles symbolize the communicators (the sources-receivers). In this model each communicator is a member of a different culture. In some instances the cultural differences are relatively slight—say, between persons from Toronto and New York. In other instances the cultural differences are great—say, between a farmer in Borneo and a surgeon in Germany.

All messages originate from within a specific and unique cultural context, and that context influences the messages' content and form. You communicate as you do largely as a result of your culture. Culture (along with the

Explore the Exercise "Cultural Beliefs" at MyCommunicationLab

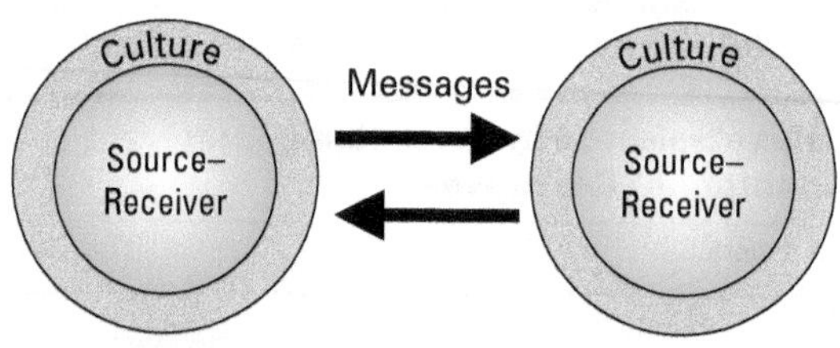

FIGURE 2.1 A Model of Intercultural Communication

This basic model of intercultural communication is designed to illustrate that culture is a part of every communication transaction. What other ways can you think of to illustrate the process of intercultural communication?

processes of enculturation and acculturation) influences every aspect of your communication experience.

The following types of communication may all be considered "intercultural" and, more important, subject to the varied barriers and gateways to effective communication identified in this chapter:

- Communication between people of different national cultures—for example, between Chinese and Portuguese individuals or between French and Norwegian individuals.
- Communication between people of different races (sometimes called *interracial communication*)—for example, between African Americans and Asian Americans.
- Communication between people of different ethnic groups (sometimes called *interethnic communication*)—for example, between Italian Americans and German Americans.
- Communication between people of different religions—for example, between Roman Catholics and Episcopalians or between Muslims and Jews.
- Communication between nations (sometimes called *international communication*)—for example, between the United States and Argentina or between China and Rwanda.
- Communication between genders—between men and women.
- Communication between smaller cultures existing within the larger culture—for example, between homosexuals and heterosexuals, doctors and patients, research scientists and the general public, or between those with and those without disabilities, a topic covered in Table 2.3, on page 40.

COMMUNICATION CHOICE POINT

Getting Your Foot Out of Your Mouth *At work you tell a homophobic joke only to discover that it was resented and clearly violated the organizational norms for polite and unbiased talk.* **What are some of your options for making this situation a little less awkward and potentially damaging to your work experience? What would you say? To whom? Through what channel?**

Improving Intercultural Communication

Murphy's law ("If anything can go wrong, it will") is especially applicable to intercultural communication. Intercultural communication is, of course, subject to all the same barriers and problems as are the other forms of communication discussed throughout this text. In this section, however, we'll consider some suggestions designed to counteract the barriers that are unique to intercultural communication (Barna, 1997; Ruben, 1985; Spitzberg, 1991).

Above all, intercultural communication depends on the cultural sensitivity of both individuals. **Cultural sensitivity** is an attitude and way of behaving in which you're aware of and acknowledge cultural differences. Cultural sensitivity is crucial on a global scale, as in efforts toward world peace and economic growth; it's also essential for effective interpersonal communication and for general success in life (Franklin & Mizell, 1995). Without cultural sensitivity there can be no effective interpersonal communication between people who are different in gender or race or nationality or affectional orientation. So be mindful of the cultural differences between yourself and the other person. For example, the close physical distance that is normal in Arab cultures may prove too familiar or too intrusive in much of the United States and northern Europe. The empathy that most Americans welcome may be uncomfortable for most Koreans (Yun, 1976).

The following guidelines can help you improve your intercultural communication: (1) prepare yourself; (2) reduce your ethnocentrism; (3) confront your stereotypes; (4) be mindful; (5) avoid overattribution; (6) recognize differences; and (7) adjust your communication. We'll take a look at each guideline in turn.

TABLE 2.3 COMMUNICATION TIPS **Between People with and without Disabilities**

Here we look at communication between those with general disabilities—for example, people in wheelchairs or with cerebral palsy—and those who have no such disability. The suggestions offered here are considered appropriate in the United States, although not necessarily in other cultures. For example, most people in the United States accept the phrase "person with mental retardation," but the term is considered offensive to many in the United Kingdom (Fernald, 1995).

TIPS

If you're the person without a general disability:

Generally	**Specifically**
Use person-first language where the person, rather than the disability, is emphasized.	Avoid terms that define the person as disabled. Avoid such expressions as "the disabled man" or "the handicapped child." Instead, using "person-first" language, say "person with a disability."
Respect assistive devices such as wheelchairs, canes, walkers, or crutches.	Don't move these out of your way; they're for the convenience of the person with the disability. Avoid leaning on a person's wheelchair; it's similar to leaning on a person.
Shake hands with the person with the disability if you shake hands with others in a group.	Don't avoid shaking hands because the individual's hand has lost some normal function, for example.
Avoid talking about the person with a disability in the third person.	For example, avoid saying, "Doesn't he get around beautifully with the new crutches." Direct your comments directly to the individual. Even if the person has an interpreter, direct your comments to the person with the disability, not the interpreter.
Don't assume that people who have a disability are intellectually impaired.	Slurred speech—such as may occur with people who have cerebral palsy or cleft palate—should not be taken as indicating a low-level intellect. Be careful not to talk down to such individuals as, research shows, many people do (Unger, 2001).
When you're not sure of how to act, ask.	For example, if you're not sure if you should offer walking assistance, say, "Would you like me to help you into the dining room?" And, more important, accept the person's response. If he or she says no, then that means no; don't insist.
Maintain similar eye level.	If the person is in a wheelchair, for example, it might be helpful for you to sit down or kneel down to get onto the same eye level.

If you're the person with a general disability:

Communicate your feelings.	For example, if you want someone to speak in a louder voice, ask. If you want to relax and have someone push your wheelchair, say so.
Be patient and understanding.	Many people mean well but may simply not know how to act or what to say. Put them at ease as best you can.
Demonstrate your own comfort.	If you detect discomfort in the other person, you might talk a bit about your disability to show that you're not uncomfortable about it—and that you understand that others may not know how you feel. But you're under no obligation to educate the public, so don't feel this is something you should or have to do.

Sources: These suggestions are based on a wide variety of sources, including www.empowermentzone.com/etiquet.txt (the website for the National Center for Access Unlimited), www.disabilityinfo.gov, www.drc.uga.edu, www.ndmig.com, and www.ucpa.org/.

Prepare Yourself

There's no better preparation for intercultural communication than learning about the other culture. Fortunately, there are numerous sources to draw on. View a video or film that presents a realistic view of the culture. Read what members of the culture as well as "outsiders" write about the culture. Scan magazines and websites from the culture. Talk with members of the culture. Chat in international chat rooms. Read blogs from members of the culture. Read materials addressed to people who need to communicate with those from other cultures. The easiest way to do this is to search the Internet for such keywords as *culture, international,* and *foreign travel.*

Another part of this preparation is to recognize and face fears that may stand in the way of effective intercultural communication (Gudykunst, 1994; Stephan & Stephan, 1985). For example, you may fear for your self-esteem. You may be anxious about your ability to control the intercultural situation, or you may worry about your own level of discomfort. You may fear saying something that will be considered politically incorrect or culturally insensitive.

You may fear that you'll be taken advantage of by a member of the other culture. Depending on your own stereotypes, you may fear being lied to, financially duped, or made fun of. You may fear that members of this other group will react to you negatively. You may fear, for example, that they will not like you or will disapprove of your attitudes or beliefs or perhaps even reject you as a person. Conversely, you may fear negative reactions from members of your own group. They might, for example, disapprove of your socializing with culturally different people.

Some fears, of course, are reasonable. In many cases, however, fears are groundless. Either way, you need to assess your concerns logically and weigh their consequences carefully. Then you'll be able to make informed choices about your communications.

Reduce Your Ethnocentrism

As you learn your culture's ways, you develop an **ethnic identity**—that is, a commitment to the beliefs and philosophy of your culture (Chung & Ting-Toomey, 1999). The degree to which you identify with your cultural group can be measured by your responses to such questions as the following (from Ting-Toomey, 1981). Using a scale ranging from 1 (strongly disagree) to 5 (strongly agree), indicate how true the following statements are for you:

- I am increasing my involvement in activities with my ethnic group.
- I involve myself in causes that will help members of my ethnic group.
- It feels natural being part of my ethnic group.
- I have spent time trying to find out more about my own ethnic group.
- I am happy to be a member of my ethnic group.
- I have a strong sense of belonging to my ethnic group.
- I often talk to other members of my group to learn more about my ethnic culture.

High scores (5s and 4s) indicate a strong commitment to your culture's values and beliefs; low numbers (1s and 2s) indicate a relatively weak commitment. **Ethnocentrism** is the tendency to see others and their behaviors through your own cultural filters, often as distortions of your own behaviors. It's the tendency to evaluate the values, beliefs, and behaviors of your own culture as more positive, superior, logical, and natural than those of other cultures. So although ethnocentrism may give you pride in your own culture and its achievements and may encourage you to sacrifice for that culture, it also may lead you to see other cultures as inferior and may foster an unwillingness to profit from the contributions of other cultures. For example, recent research shows a "substantial relationship" between ethnocentrism and homophobia (Wrench & McCroskey, 2003).

Ethnocentrism exists on a continuum. People are not either ethnocentric or not ethnocentric; rather, most are somewhere between these polar opposites. And, of course, your degree of ethnocentrism varies depending on the group on which you focus. For example, if you're Greek American, you may have a low degree of ethnocentrism when dealing with Italian Americans, but a high degree when dealing with Turkish Americans or Japanese Americans. Your degree of ethnocentrism (and we're all ethnocentric to at least some degree) will influence your communication in all its forms, an influence illustrated throughout this text.

Confront Your Stereotypes

Stereotypes, especially when they operate below the level of conscious awareness, can create serious communication problems. Originally, *stereotype* was a printing term that referred to the plate that printed the same image over and over. A sociological or psychological **stereotype** is a fixed impression of a group of people. Everyone has attitudinal stereotypes—of national groups, religious groups, or racial groups or perhaps of criminals, prostitutes, teachers, or plumbers. Ask yourself, for example, if you have any stereotypes of, say, bodybuilders, the opposite sex, a racial group different from your own, members of a religion very different from your

the•o•ry *noun* statement of explanation, formulation of relationships, reasoned generalization

UNDERSTANDING THEORY AND RESEARCH
Language and Thought

The linguistic relativity hypothesis claims (1) that the language you speak influences the thoughts you have and (2) that, therefore, people speaking widely differing languages will see the world differently and will think differently.

Theory and research, however, have not been able to find much support for this claim. A more modified hypothesis currently seems supported: The language you speak helps you to talk about what you see and perhaps to highlight what you see. For example, if you speak a language that is rich in color terms (English is a good example), you will find it easier to talk about nuances of color than will someone from a culture that has fewer color terms (some cultures, for example, distinguish only two, three, or four parts of the color spectrum). But this doesn't mean that people see the world differently, only that their language helps (or doesn't help) them to talk about certain variations in the world and may make it easier (or more difficult) to focus their thinking on such variations.

Nor does it mean that people speaking widely differing languages are doomed to misunderstand one another. Translation enables you to understand a great deal of the meaning in any foreign language message. And, of course, you have your communication skills; you can ask for clarification, for additional examples, for restatement. You can listen actively, give feedforward and feedback, use perception checking, and employ a host of other skills you'll encounter throughout this course.

Language differences don't make for very important differences in perception or thought. Difficulties in intercultural understanding are due more often to ineffective communication than to differences in languages.

Working with Theories and Research

Based on your own experience, how influential do you find language differences to be in perception and thought? Can you recall any misunderstandings that might be attributed to a particular language's leading its speakers to see or interpret things differently?

own, hard drug users, or college professors. It is very likely that you have stereotypes of several or perhaps all of these groups.

Although we often think of stereotypes as negative ("They're lazy, dirty, and only interested in getting high"), they may also be positive ("They're smart, hardworking, and extremely loyal"). But, even positive stereotypes have negative consequences; they reinforce the idea that members are fundamentally different and can be easily grouped together (thereby denying individual differences). Not surprisingly, even positive stereotypes generate negative feelings in those stereotyped (Kay, Day, & Zanna, in press).

If you have these fixed impressions, you might, upon meeting a member of a particular group, see that person primarily as a member of that group. Initially, a stereotype may provide you with some helpful orientation. However, it creates problems when you apply to a person all the characteristics you assign to members of that person's group without examining the unique individual. If you meet a politician, for example, you may apply to the person a series of stereotypical "politician" images. To complicate matters further, you may see in the person's behavior the manifestation of various characteristics that you would not see if you did not know that this person was a politician. In online communication, because there are few visual and auditory cues, it's not surprising to find that people form impressions of their online communication partner with a heavy reliance on stereotypes (Jacobson, 1999).

Consider another kind of stereotype: You're driving along a dark road and are stopped at a stop sign. A car pulls up beside you and three teenagers jump out and rap on your window. There may be a variety of reasons for this: They may need help, they may want to ask directions, or they may be planning a carjacking. Your self-protective stereotype may help you decide on "carjacking" and may lead you to pull away and into the safety of a busy service station. In doing that, of course, you may have escaped being carjacked, or you may have failed to assist innocent people who needed your help.

Stereotyping can lead to two major thinking and communication barriers. First, you will fail to appreciate the multifaceted nature of all people and all groups. The tendency to group a person into a class and to respond to that person primarily as a member of that class can lead you to perceive that a person possesses those qualities (usually negative) that you believe characterize the group to which he or she belongs. For example, consider your stereotype of an avid computer user. Very likely it's quite different from the research findings—which show that such users are as often female as male and are as sociable, popular, and self-assured as their peers who are not into heavy computer use (Schott & Selwyn, 2000).

Second, stereotyping also can lead you to ignore the unique characteristics of an individual; you therefore fail to benefit from the special contributions each person can bring to an encounter.

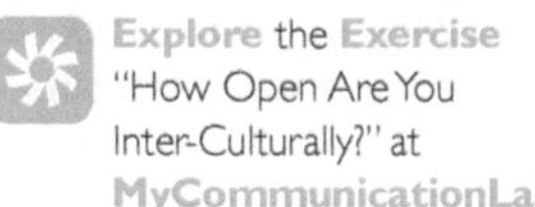
Explore the Exercise "How Open Are You Inter-Culturally?" at MyCommunicationLab

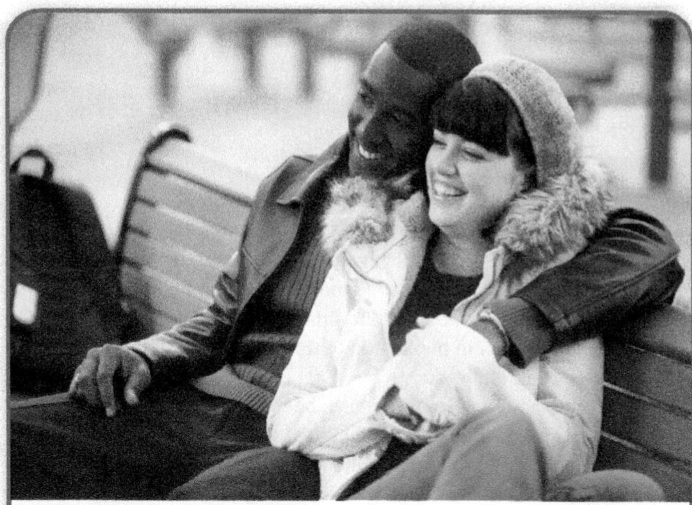

COMMUNICATION CHOICE POINT

CONFLICTING CULTURAL BELIEFS *You're dating a person from a culture very different from your own, and your views on important matters (for example, relationship responsibilities, finances, children, and religion) differ widely. You're now wondering if there's any future for this relationship.* **What are some of your options for exploring this question by yourself and with your dating partner? What are some of the things you might say to your partner?**

Increase Mindfulness

Being mindful rather than mindless (a distinction considered in more detail in Chapter 7) is generally helpful in intercultural communication situations (Burgoon, Berger, & Waldron, 2000). When you're in a mindless state, you behave on the basis of assumptions that would not normally pass intellectual scrutiny. For example, you know that cancer is not contagious, and yet you may still avoid touching cancer patients. You know that people who are blind generally don't have hearing problems, yet you may use a louder voice when talking to persons who are visually impaired. When the discrepancies between behaviors and available evidence are pointed out and your mindful state is awakened, you quickly realize that these behaviors are not logical or realistic.

You can look at this textbook and your course in human communication as means of awakening your mindful state about the way you engage in interpersonal, group, and public communication. After completing this course, you should be much more mindful and much less mindless about all your communication behavior.

Avoid Overattribution

Overattribution is the tendency to attribute too much of a person's behavior or attitudes to one of that person's characteristics (she thinks that way because she's a woman; he believes that because he was raised as a Catholic). In intercultural communication situations, overattribution appears in two ways. First, it's the tendency to see too much of what a person believes or does as caused by the person's cultural identification. Second, it's the tendency to see a person as a spokesperson for his or her particular culture—to assume that because a person is, say, African American, he or she is therefore knowledgeable about the entire African American experience or that the person's thoughts are always focused on African American issues. People's ways of thinking and ways of behaving are influenced by a wide variety of factors; culture is just one of them.

Recognize Differences

To communicate interculturally it's necessary to recognize (1) the differences between yourself and people from other cultures, (2) the differences within the other cultural group, (3) the numerous differences in meaning, and (4) differences in dialect and accent.

Differences between Yourself and the Culturally Different. A common barrier to intercultural communication occurs when you assume similarities and ignore differences. When you do, you'll fail to notice important distinctions and be more apt to miscommunicate. Consider this example: An American invites a Filipino coworker to dinner. The Filipino politely refuses. The American is hurt and feels that the Filipino does not want to be friendly. The Filipino is hurt and concludes that the invitation was not extended sincerely. Here, it seems, both the American and the Filipino assume that their customs for inviting people to dinner are the same when, in fact, they aren't. A Filipino expects to be invited several times before accepting a dinner invitation. When an invitation is given only once, it's viewed as insincere.

eth•ics *noun* morality, standards of conduct, moral judgment

MAKING ETHICAL CHOICES
Culture and Ethics

One of the most shocking revelations to come to world attention after the events of September 11, 2001, was the way in which women were treated under Taliban rule in Afghanistan: Females could not be educated or even go out in public without a male relative escort and when in public had to wear garments that covered their entire body.

Throughout history there have been cultural practices that today would be judged unethical. Sacrificing virgins to the gods, burning people who held different religious beliefs, and sending children to fight religious wars are obvious examples. But even today there are practices woven deep into the fabric of different cultures that you might find unethical. As you read these few examples of cultural practices with special relevance to interpersonal communication, consider what U.S. cultural practices people in other cultures might judge as unethical.

- only men can initiate divorce, and only men are permitted to drive
- female genital mutilation whereby part or all of a young girl's genitals are surgically altered so she can never experience sexual intercourse without extreme pain, a practice designed to keep her a virgin until marriage
- the belief and practice that a woman must be subservient to her husband's will
- women should not report spousal abuse because it will reflect negatively on the family
- sexual behavior between members of the same sex is punishable by imprisonment and even death

Ethical Choice Point

What ethical obligations do you have for communicating your beliefs about cultural practices you think are unethical when such topics come up in conversation or in class discussions? What are your ethical choices?

Here's another example: An American college student hears the news that her favorite uncle has died. She bites her lip, pulls herself up, and politely excuses herself from the group of foreign students with whom she is having dinner. The Russian thinks: "How unfriendly." The Italian thinks: "How insincere." The Brazilian thinks: "How unconcerned." To many Americans, it's a sign of bravery to endure pain (physical or emotional) in silence and without any outward show of emotion. To members of other groups, such silence is often interpreted negatively to mean that the individual does not consider them friends who can share such sorrow because, in their cultures, people are expected to reveal to friends how they feel.

Differences within the Culturally Different Group. Recognize that within every cultural group there are vast and important differences. As all Americans are not alike, neither are all Indonesians, Greeks, Mexicans, and so on. When you ignore these differences—when you assume that all persons covered by the same label (in this case a national or ethnic label) are the same—you're guilty of stereotyping. A good example of this is seen in the use of the term *African American*. The term stresses the unity of Africa and of those who are of African descent and is analogous to *Asian American* or *European American*. At the same time, it ignores the great diversity within the African continent when, for example, it's used as analogous to *German American* or *Japanese American*. More analogous terms would be *Nigerian American* or *Ethiopian American*. Within each culture there are smaller cultures that differ greatly from each other and from the larger culture.

Differences in Meaning. See the meaning of a message not only in the words used but also in the people using them (a principle we'll return to in Chapter 5). Consider, for example, the differences in meaning that exist for words such as *religion* to a born-again Christian and an atheist and *lunch* to a Haitian farmer and a Madison Avenue advertising executive. Even though the same word is used, its meanings will vary greatly depending on the listeners' cultural definitions.

The same is true of nonverbal messages. For example, a left-handed American who eats with the left hand may be seen by a Muslim as obscene. To the Muslim, the left hand isn't used for eating or for shaking hands but to clean oneself after excretory functions. So using the left hand to eat or to shake hands would generally be considered inappropriate.

Differences in Dialect and Accent. Dialects are variations in a language, mainly in the grammar and the semantics. The difference between language and dialect—at least as viewed by most linguists—is that different languages are mutually *un*intelligible; different dialects are mutually intelligent. So, for example, a person who grew up with only the English language would not be able to understand Russian and vice versa. But, people speaking different dialects of English (say, Southern and Northern) would be able to understand each other.

It's interesting to note that the Southerner, for example, will perceive the New Englander to speak with an accent but will not perceive another Southerner to have an accent. Similarly, the New Englander will perceive the Southerner to have an accent but not a fellow New Englander. Actually, linguists would argue that everyone speaks a dialect; it's just that we don't perceive speech like ours to be a dialect. We only think of speech different from ours as being a dialect.

Some dialects are popularly (but not scientifically) labeled "standard" and some are labeled "nonstandard." Standard dialect would be the language that is recommended by dictionaries and that is covered in the English handbooks you've likely already experienced. Nonstandard dialect would be any variation from this. This concept of dialect can easily and logically be extended to texting and social media language. Today, the abbreviated texting style would be considered nonstandard; tomorrow, things may be different.

Linguistically, all dialects are equal. But, although no one dialect is linguistically superior to any other dialect, it is equally true that judgments are made on the basis of dialect and the type of judgment made would depend on the person making the judgment. So, for example, you'd be advised to use standard dialect in applying to the traditional conservative law firm and to write your e-mails to them in Standard English, the kind recommended by the English handbooks. On the other hand, when you're out with friends or texting, you may feel more comfortable using nonstandard forms.

When differences in speech are differences in pronunciation we refer to them as **accents**, the emphasis or stress you place on various syllables. Just as everyone speaks with a particular dialect, everyone also speaks with a particular accent. Again, we notice accents that are different from our own and, in fact, don't refer to speech that sounds like ours as having any accent at all. But, all speakers speak with an accent. The "accents" that we probably notice most often are those that occur in speakers who learned the language in their teens or later. The second language is spoken through a kind of filter created by the original language. But, if you grew up in an English-speaking country with English-speaking parents, you also speak with an accent. It's just that you don't perceive it as such.

Linguistically, everyone speaks with an accent; it's simply a fact of life. In terms of communication, however, we need to recognize that accents are often used by people to pigeon-hole and stereotype others; for example, in some people's minds, certain accents are associated with lower class and others with upper class. Some accents are perceived as more credible, more knowledgeable, and more educated than others.

Adjust Your Communication

Intercultural communication (in fact, all communication) takes place only to the extent that you and the person you're trying to communicate with share the same system of symbols. As Chapter 1 discussed, your interaction will be hindered to the extent that your language and nonverbal systems differ (the principle of adjustment). Therefore, it's important to adjust your communication to compensate for cultural differences.

Furthermore, it helps if you share your own system of signals with others so they can better understand you. Although some people may know what you mean by your silence or by your avoidance of eye contact, others may not. Generally, avoid expecting others to decode your behaviors accurately without help.

Communication accommodation theory, as explained in Chapter 1, holds that speakers will adjust or accommodate to the communication style of their listeners in order to interact more pleasantly and efficiently. As you adjust your messages, recognize that each culture has its own rules and customs for communication (Barna, 1997). These rules identify what is appropriate and what is inappropriate. Thus, for example, in U.S. culture you would call a person you wished to date three or four days in advance. In certain Asian cultures you might call the person's parents weeks or even months in advance. In U.S. culture you say, as a general friendly gesture and not as a specific invitation, "come over and pay us a visit sometime." To members of other cultures, this comment is sufficient to prompt the listeners actually to visit at their convenience.

Table 2.4, on the following page, summarizes these guidelines for more effective intercultural communication.

TABLE 2.4

In A Nutshell Improving Intercultural Communication

Here are some guidelines for improving intercultural communication along with some specific strategies.

General Guidelines	Specific Strategies
Prepare Yourself	Read about, view images and videos of, and interact with culturally different individuals.
Reduce Your Ethnocentrism	Becoming aware of your own ethnocentrism can help you see its illogic.
Confront Your Stereotypes	Recognize that stereotypes are generalizations that prevent you from seeing the individual except through this stereotype.
Increase Mindfulness	Become aware of why you do or think what you do; act with awareness, and develop and question beliefs and attitudes mindfully.
Avoid Overattribution	Avoid attributing another's behavior to one or even a few factors; most often behavior is a combination of interrelated factors.
Recognize Differences	Recognize that differences exist between yourself and the culturally different, within the culturally different group, in meaning, and in dialect and accent. At the same time, don't fail to note the similarities.
Adjust Your Communication	Understanding the meanings that others have for gestures or for interpersonal interactions will help you adjust your own messages.

Analyzing Video Choices

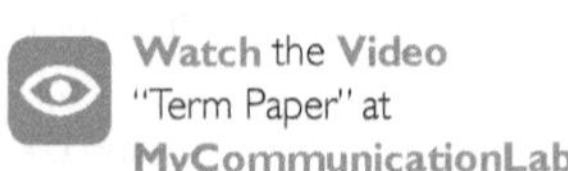

Watch the Video "Term Paper" at MyCommunicationLab

Jamie and Tim are in the same world history class. It is Friday afternoon, and their midterm papers are due Monday morning. Jamie has already turned in his paper, but Tim is just getting started. Tim's laptop is acting up, so he asks Jamie to borrow his for the weekend. Jamie wants to be polite and wants to help his friend, but isn't comfortable loaning out his laptop and wonders if their different cultures are affecting how they see the situation. Jamie considers the topics covered in this chapter as he contemplates his communication choices for dealing with these differences and the likely advantages and disadvantages of each choice. Log on to www.mycommunicationlab.com to view this video, to see how Jamie's choices played out, and to respond to a few discussion questions.

SUMMARY: CULTURE AND COMMUNICATION

This chapter introduced the study of culture and its relationship to communication and considered how cultures differ and some of the theories developed to explain how culture and communication affect each other. In addition, the chapter introduced the study of intercultural communication and its nature and principles.

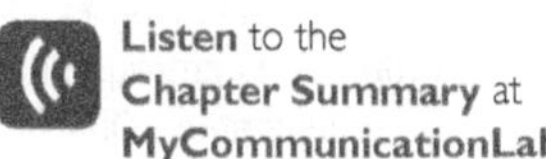

2.1 WHAT IS CULTURE?

1. Culture consists of the relatively specialized lifestyle of a group of people—their values, beliefs, artifacts, ways of behaving, and ways of communicating—that is passed on from one generation to the next through communication rather than through genes.
2. Enculturation is the process by which culture is transmitted from one generation to the next.
3. Acculturation involves the processes by which one culture is modified through contact with or exposure to another culture.

2.2 CULTURAL DIFFERENCES

4. Cultures differ in terms of individualist or collectivist orientations, high and low context, high and low power distance, masculinity and femininity, tolerance of ambiguity, long- and short-term orientation, and indulgence and restraint.
5. Individualist cultures emphasize individual values such as power and achievement, whereas collectivist cultures emphasize group values such as cooperation and responsibility to the group.
6. In high-context cultures much information is in the context or the person; in low-context cultures information is expected to be made explicit.
7. In high-power-distance cultures there are large differences in power between people; in low-power-distance cultures power is more evenly distributed throughout the population.
8. Masculine cultures emphasize assertiveness, ambition, and competition; feminine cultures emphasize compromise and negotiation.
9. High-ambiguity tolerant cultures feel little threatened by uncertainty; it's accepted as it comes. Low-ambiguity tolerant cultures feel uncomfortable with uncertainty and seek to avoid it.
10. Long-term-oriented cultures promote the importance of future rewards whereas short-term-oriented cultures look more to the past and the present.
11. Cultures high in indulgence emphasize the gratification of desires and having fun; cultures high in restraint emphasize the curbing and regulation of pleasures and fun.

2.3 INTERCULTURAL COMMUNICATION

12. Intercultural communication is communication among people who have different cultural beliefs, values, or ways of behaving.
13. Ethnocentrism, which exists on a continuum, is our tendency to evaluate the beliefs, attitudes, and values of our own culture positively and those of other cultures negatively.
14. Stereotyping is the tendency to develop and maintain fixed, unchanging impressions of groups of people and to use these impressions to evaluate individual members of these groups, ignoring unique individual characteristics.
15. Among the guidelines for more effective intercultural communication are: prepare yourself, recognize and reduce your ethnocentrism, confront your stereotypes, be mindful, avoid overattribution, recognize differences, and adjust your communication.

Study and **Review** the **Flashcards** at **MyCommunicationLab**

KEY TERMS

accent *45*
acculturation *29*
ambiguity tolerance *36*
assimilation *36*
collectivist culture *34*
cultural sensitivity *39*
dialect *45*
enculturation *29*
ethnic identity *41*
ethnocentrism *41*
exclusionism *34*
face-saving *35*
feminine culture *36*
gender *29*
high-context culture *34*
high-power-distance cultures *35*
individualist culture *34*
indulgence *37*
intercultural communication *38*
long-term orientation *37*
low-context culture *34*
low-power-distance cultures *35*
masculine culture *36*
politeness *30*
restraint *38*
sex *28*
short-term orientation *37*
stereotype *41*
universalism *34*

WORKING WITH CULTURE AND COMMUNICATION

2.1 Exploring Cultural Attitudes. Attitudes strongly influence communication. Understanding your cultural attitudes is prerequisite to effective intercultural communication. One of the best ways to appreciate the influence of culture on communication is to consider the attitudes people have about central aspects of culture. In a group of five or six—try for as culturally diverse a group as you can find—discuss how you think most of the students at your school feel (not how *you* feel) about each of the following. Use a five-point scale: 5 = most students strongly agree; 4 = most students agree; 3 = students are relatively neutral; 2 = most students disagree; 1 = most students strongly disagree.

1. _____ Most feminists are just too sensitive about sexism.
2. _____ Both females and males are victims of sexism.
3. _____ Gay rights means gay men and lesbians demanding special privileges.
4. _____ All men and women have a choice to be homosexual or not.
5. _____ Racism isn't going to end overnight, so minorities need to be patient.
6. _____ Minorities have the same opportunity as whites to succeed in our society.

Source: Koppelman, Kent L; Goodhart, R, Lee, *Understanding Human Differences: Multicultural Education for a Diverse America,* 3rd ed., ©2011. Adapted and Electronically reproduced by permission of Pearson Education, Inc., Upper Saddle River, New Jersey.

2.2 Confronting Intercultural Difficulties. How might you deal with any one or two of the following obstacles to intercultural communication? If you have the opportunity, share your responses with others in the class. You'll gain a wealth of practical insights.

a. You're in an interracial, interreligious relationship. Your partner's family ignores your "couplehood." For example, you and your partner are never invited to dinner as a couple or included in any family affairs. You decide to confront your partner's family.

b. Your parents persist in holding stereotypes about other religious, racial, and ethnic groups. These stereotypes come up in all sorts of conversations. You're really embarrassed by these attitudes and feel you must tell your parents how incorrect you think these stereotypes are.

c. George, a colleague at work, recently underwent a religious conversion. He now persists in trying to get everyone else—you included—to undergo this same religious conversion. You decide to tell him that you find this behavior offensive.

Confronting cultural insensitivity is not an easy task; most people do not see their own insensitivity. So approach these situations carefully; rely on all the communication skills presented throughout this text and in your course.

2.3 Cultural Differences. How do you feel about the following issues? As you respond, consider the ways in which culture has influenced your responses.

- refusing life-saving medical procedures for children on religious grounds
- same-sex marriage
- cockfighting, bullfighting, and foxhunting
- single-parent adoption
- physician-assisted suicide

2.4 Hofstede's Cultural Differences. The identification of the cultural differences is largely the work of Geert Hofstede and his associates. How important do you think these cultural differences are to your own personal and professional interactions? A good way to keep up with research in culture is to consult Hofstede's excellent website.

2.5 Choosing a Mate. In what ways do your cultural beliefs and values influence the kind of life partner you're looking for? Has your culture taught you to value certain qualities in a relationship partner and to devalue others?

2.6 Sexual Relations. Some cultures frown on sexual relationships outside of marriage; others consider sex a normal part of intimacy. Intercultural researchers (Hatfield & Rapson, 1996) recall a discussion between colleagues from Sweden and the United States on ways of preventing AIDS. When researchers from the United States suggested promoting abstinence, their Swedish counterparts asked, "How will teenagers ever learn to become loving, considerate sexual partners if they don't practice?" "The silence that greeted the question," note Hatfield and Rapson (1996, p. 36), "was the sound of two cultures clashing." How have your cultural beliefs influenced what you consider appropriate?

2.7 Men, Women, and Culture. It's been argued that in the United States women are more likely to view themselves as interdependents, having a more collectivist orientation, whereas men are more likely to view themselves as independents, having a more individualist orientation (Cross & Madson, 1997). Does your experience support this? What implications do you see for the workplace?

2.8 What's in a Name? Some researchers prefer to use the term *subculture* to refer to smaller cultures within larger cultures; other researchers do not use the term, feeling that it implies that some cultures are less important than others. Some researchers prefer to use the term *co-culture* to refer to a variety of cultures coexisting side by side, whereas others think this term is imprecise because all cultures coexist (Lustig & Koester, 2013); these theorists prefer simply to refer to all cultures as *cultures*. How do you feel about the terms *subculture, co-culture,* and just plain *culture*?

2.9 Cultural Defense. Assume you're a judge and the following case is presented to you: A Chinese immigrant killed his wife in New York because he suspected her of cheating. A "cultural defense" was offered, essentially claiming that infidelity so shames a man that he is uncontrollable in his anger. Would this cultural defense have influenced your judgment? In the actual case (reported in *Time,* December 2, 1993), influenced by an anthropologist's testimony that infidelity is so serious in Chinese culture that it pushed the defendant to commit the crime, the judge sentenced the defendant to five years' probation. How do you think a jury would decide on this issue today? How do you feel about "cultural defenses" in general? Are there some cultural defenses you'd accept and others you would not?

2.10 Cell Phone Etiquette. Cell phone users vary widely in how they use their phones in public places, and rules of cell phone etiquette abound. What rules of cell phone etiquette do you follow? Where are you most likely to turn off your cell phone? In what public situations are you likely to leave it on? What rules do you follow in the classroom?

LogOn! MyCommunicationLab www.mycommunicationlab.com

Throughout this chapter, there are icons that highlight media content for selected topics. Go to **MyCommunicationLab** for additional materials on culture and its relationship to human communication. Here you'll find flashcards to help you learn key communication terms, videos that illustrate a variety of concepts, additional exercises, and discussions to help you continue your study of culture and communication.

3 THE SELF AND PERCEPTION

Listen to Chapter 3 at MyCommunicationLab

CHAPTER TOPICS	CHAPTER OBJECTIVES
In this chapter you'll explore the following major topics:	**After reading this chapter you should be able to:**
THE SELF IN HUMAN COMMUNICATION	3.1 Define *self-concept*, *self-awareness*, and *self-esteem*.
SELF-DISCLOSURE	3.2 Define *self-disclosure* and identify its rewards and dangers; apply the guidelines for giving, receiving, and resisting self-disclosures.
PERCEPTION	3.3 Define *perception* and identify its five steps.
IMPRESSION FORMATION	3.4 Define *impression formation,* explain its major processes, and apply the guidelines for increasing your own accuracy in impression formation.
IMPRESSION MANAGEMENT	3.5 Use the suggestions for managing the impressions you communicate to others and to detect the impression management strategies of others.

Effective self-presentation seems a universal ambition.

In this chapter we look at the self and perception, particularly the processes that we use to make judgments of others and that they use to make judgments of us. First, let's look at the self.

3.1 THE SELF IN HUMAN COMMUNICATION

Who you are and how you see yourself influence not only the way you communicate, but also how you respond to the communications of others. First we'll explore the self: the self-concept and how it develops; self-awareness and ways to increase it; self-esteem and ways to enhance it; and self-disclosure, or communication that reveals who you are.

Self-Concept

Your **self-concept** is your image of who you are. It's how you perceive yourself: your feelings and thoughts about your strengths and weaknesses, your abilities and limitations. Self-concept develops from the images that others have of you, comparisons between yourself and others, your cultural experiences, and your evaluation of your own thoughts and behaviors (Figure 3.1). Let's explore each of these components of the self-concept.

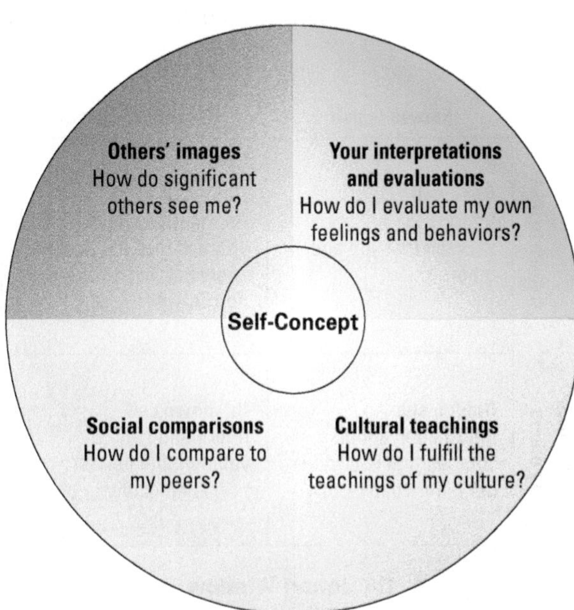

FIGURE 3.1 **The Sources of Self-Concept**

This diagram depicts the four sources of self-concept, the four contributors to how you see yourself. As you read about self-concept, consider the influence of each factor throughout your life. Which factor influenced you most as a preteen? Which influences you most now? Which will influence you most 25 or 30 years from now?

Others' Images of You

If you want to see how your hair looks, you probably look in a mirror. But what would you do if you wanted to see how friendly or how assertive you are? According to the concept of the **looking-glass self** (Cooley, 1922), you'd look at the image of yourself that others reveal to you through the way they communicate with you. Of course, you would not look to just anyone. Rather, you would look to those who are most significant in your life—to your *significant others,* such as your friends, family members, and romantic partners. If these significant others think highly of you, you will see a positive self-image reflected in their behaviors; if they think little of you, you will see a more negative image.

Comparisons with Others

Another way you develop self-concept is by comparing yourself with others, most often with your peers (Festinger, 1954). For example, after an exam, you probably want to know how you performed relative to the other students in your class. This gives you a clearer idea of how effectively you performed. If you play on a baseball team, it's important to know your batting average in comparison with the batting average of others on the team. You gain a different perspective when you see yourself in comparison to your peers.

Watch the Video "Sarah's Blog" at **MyCommunicationLab**

For good or ill, social media have provided us with the tools (all very easy to use) to compare ourselves to others to perhaps estimate our individual worth or perhaps make us feel superior. Here are just a half-dozen ways social media enable us to find out how we stand.

- **Search engine reports.** Type in your name on Google, Bing, or Yahoo!, for example, and you'll see the number of websites on which your name (and similarly named others) appears. Type in a colleague's name, and you get his or her score, which, you're hoping, is lower than yours.
- **Network spread.** Your number of friends on Facebook or your contacts on LinkedIn or Plaxo is in some ways a measure of your potential influence. Look at a friend's profile, and you have your comparison. Not surprisingly, there are programs and apps that will surf the Web to help you contact more social network friends.
- **Online influence.** Network sites such as Klout and Peer Index provide you with a score (from 0–100) of your online influence. Your Klout score, for example, is a combination of your "true reach" (the number of people you influence), "amplification" (the degree to which you influence them), and "network" (the influence of your network).

Postrank Analytics, on the other hand, provides you with a measure of engagement—the degree to which people interact with, pay attention to, read, or comment on what you write.

- **Twitter activities**. The number of times you tweet might be one point of comparison but more important is the number of times you are tweeted about or your tweets are repeated (retweets). Twitalyzer will provide you with a three-part score: an impact score, a Klout score, and a Peer Index score and will also enable you to search the "twitter elite" for the world as well as for any specific area (you can search by ZIP code). Assuming your Twitter score is what you'd like it to be, a single click will enable you to post this score on your own Twitter page.
- **Blog presence.** Your blog presence is readily available from your "stats" tab where you can see how many people visited your blog since inception or over the past year, month, week, or day. And you'll also see a map of the world indicating where people who are visiting your blog come from.
- **References to written works.** Google Scholar, for example, will enable you to see how many other writers have cited your works (and how many cited the works of the person you're comparing) and the works in which you were cited. And, of course, Amazon and other online book dealers provide rankings of your books along with a star system based on reviewers' comments.

Cultural Teachings

Your culture instills in you a variety of beliefs, values, and attitudes about such things as success (how you define it and how you should achieve it); the relevance of religion, race, or nationality; and the ethical principles you should follow in business and in your personal life. These teachings provide benchmarks against which you can measure yourself. Your ability to achieve what your culture defines as success, for example, contributes to a positive self-concept; in the same way, your failure to achieve what your culture encourages contributes to a negative self-concept.

Self-Interpretations and Self-Evaluations

Your **self-interpretations** (your reconstruction of the incident and your understanding of it) and **self-evaluations** (the value—good or bad—that you place on the behavior) also contribute to your self-concept. For example, let's say you believe that lying is wrong. If you then lie and you view it as a lie (rather than as, say, a polite way of avoiding an issue), you will probably evaluate this behavior in terms of your internalized beliefs about lying (*lying is wrong*) and you'll react negatively to your own behavior. You may, for example, experience guilt about violating your own beliefs. On the other hand, let's say that you pull someone out of a burning building at great personal risk. You will probably evaluate this behavior positively; you'll feel good about this behavior and, as a result, about yourself.

Self-Awareness

Self-awareness—your knowledge of who you are; of your traits, your strengths and limitations, your emotions and behaviors, your individuality—is basic to all communication. You can achieve self-awareness by examining the several aspects of yourself as they might appear to others as well as to yourself. One tool that is commonly used for this examination is called the **Johari window**, a metaphoric division of the self into four areas (Figure 3.2).

Your Four Selves

Divided into four areas or "panes," the Johari window shows different aspects or versions of the self. The four aspects are the open self, blind self, hidden self, and unknown self. These areas are not separate from one another, but interdependent. As one dominates, the others recede to a greater or lesser degree; or, to stay with our metaphor, as one windowpane becomes larger, one or another becomes smaller.

	Known to self	Not known to self
Known to others	**Open self** Information about yourself that you and others know	**Blind self** Information about yourself that you don't know but that others do know
Not known to others	**Hidden self** Information about yourself that you know but others don't know	**Unknown self** Information about yourself that neither you nor others know

FIGURE 3.2 **The Johari Window**

This diagram is a commonly used tool for examining what we know and don't know about ourselves. It can also help explain the nature of self-disclosure, covered later in this chapter. The window gets its name from its originators, Joseph Luft and Harry Ingham.

Source: Adapted from Joseph Luft, *Group Process: An Introduction to Group Dynamics* (3rd ed.). Copyright © 1984. New York: McGraw-Hill Companies. Reprinted by permission.

- **Open self.** This self represents all the information, behaviors, attitudes, and feelings about yourself that you know and that others also know. Such knowledge could include everything from your name, skin color, sex, and age to your religion and political beliefs. The size of the **open self** varies according to your personality and the people to whom you're relating. You may be more open with some people than you are with others. So, you may have a large open self about your romantic life with your friends (you tell them everything), but a very small open self about the same issues with, say, your parents.
- **Blind self.** This self represents knowledge about you that others have but you don't. **Blind self** might include your habit of finishing other people's sentences or your way of rubbing your nose when you become anxious. A large blind self indicates low self-awareness and interferes with accurate communication. So, it's important to reduce your blind self and learn what others know about you. You can do this by following the suggestions offered below, under "Growing in Self-Awareness."
- **Unknown self.** The **unknown self** represents those parts of yourself that neither you nor others know. This is information that is buried in your subconscious. You may, for example, learn of your obsession with money, your fear of criticism, or the kind of lover you are through hypnosis, dreams, psychological tests, or psychotherapy.
- **Hidden self.** This self represents all the knowledge you have of yourself but keep secret from others. The **hidden self** windowpane includes all your successfully kept secrets; for example, your fantasies, embarrassing experiences, and any attitudes or beliefs of which you may be ashamed. You probably keep secrets from some people and not from others; for example, you might not tell your parents you're dating someone of another race or religion, but you might tell a close friend.

Explore the Exercise "Disclosing Your Hidden Self" at MyCommunicationLab

Each person's Johari window will be different, and each individual's window will vary from one time to another and from one communication situation to another. By way of example, Figure 3.3 illustrates two possible configurations.

Growing in Self-Awareness

Because self-awareness is so important in communication, try to increase awareness of your own needs, desires, habits, beliefs, and attitudes. You can do this in various ways.

- **Listen to others.** Conveniently, others are constantly giving you the very feedback you need to increase self-awareness. In every interaction people comment on you in some way—on what you do, what you say, how you look. Sometimes these comments are explicit: "Loosen up" or "Don't take things so hard." Often they're "hidden" in the way others look at you—in the expressionless face that indicates disagreement or disappointment or the broad smile that says, "I think you're wonderful."
- **Increase your open self.** Revealing yourself to others will help increase your self-awareness. As you talk about yourself, you may see connections that you had previously missed. With feedback

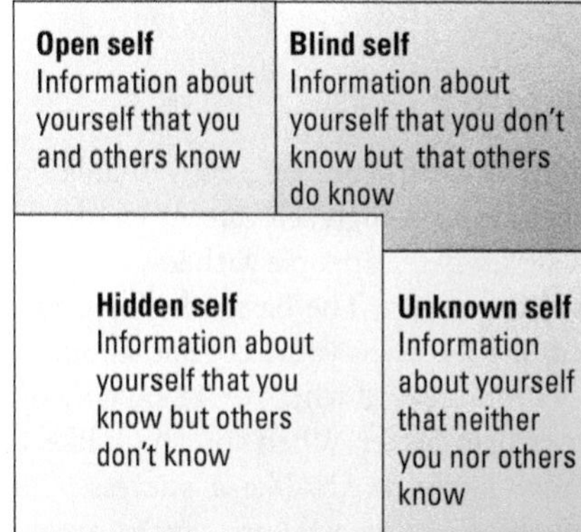

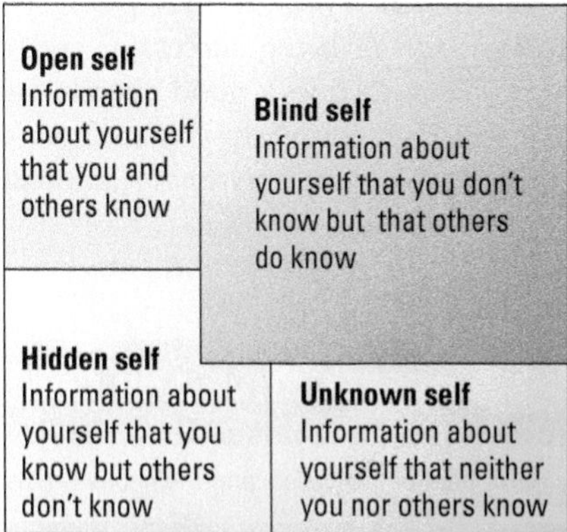

FIGURE 3.3 **Johari Windows of Different Structures**

Notice that as one self grows, one or more of the other selves shrink. Assume that these models depict the self-awareness and self-disclosure of two different people. How would you describe the type of communication (especially self-disclosure) that might characterize each of these two people?

Source: Adapted from Joseph Luft, *Group Process: An Introduction to Group Dynamics* (3rd ed.). Copyright © 1984. New York: McGraw-Hill Companies. Reprinted by permission.

from others, you may gain still more insight. By increasing your open self, you also increase the chances that others will reveal what they know about you.

- **Seek information about yourself.** Encourage people to reveal what they know about you. Use situations that arise every day to gain self-information: "Do you think I came down too hard on the kids today?" "Do you think I was assertive enough when asking for the raise?" But seek this self-awareness in moderation. If you do it too often, your friends will soon look for someone else with whom to talk.
- **Dialogue with yourself.** No one knows you better than you know yourself. Ask yourself self-awareness questions: What motivates me to act as I do? What are my short-term and long-term goals? How do I plan to achieve them? What are my strengths and weaknesses?

Self-Esteem

Self-esteem is a measure of how valuable you think you are; people with high self-esteem think very highly of themselves, whereas people with low self-esteem view themselves negatively. The basic idea behind building self-esteem is that when you feel good about yourself—about who you are and what you're capable of doing—you will perform better. When you think like a success, you're more likely to act like a success. Conversely, when you think you're a failure, you're more likely to act like a failure. When you get up to give a speech and you visualize yourself being successful and effective, you're more likely to give a good speech. Increasing self-esteem will, therefore, help you to function more effectively in school, in interpersonal relationships, and in careers. Here are six suggestions for increasing self-esteem.

Attack Self-Destructive Beliefs

Challenge those beliefs you have about yourself that are unproductive or that make it more difficult for you to achieve your goals (Einhorn, 2006). Here, for example, are some popular **self-destructive beliefs** (Butler, 1981):

- The belief that *you have to be perfect*; this causes you to try to perform at unrealistically high levels at work, school, and home; anything short of perfection is unacceptable.
- The belief that *you have to be strong* tells you that weakness and any of the more vulnerable emotions like sadness, compassion, or loneliness are wrong.
- The belief that *you have to please others* and that your worthiness depends on what others think of you.
- The belief that *you have to hurry up*; this compels you to do things quickly, to try to do more than can be reasonably expected in any given amount of time.
- The belief that *you have to take on more responsibilities* than any one person can be expected to handle.

These beliefs set unrealistically high standards and therefore almost always end in failure. As a result, you may develop a negative self-image, seeing yourself as someone who constantly fails. So, replace these self-destructive beliefs with more productive ones, such as "I succeed in many things, but I don't have to succeed in everything" and "It would be nice to be loved by everyone, but it isn't necessary to my happiness." See Table 3.1 for a summary and comparison of these destructive beliefs and constructive counterparts.

TABLE 3.1 DESTRUCTIVE AND CONSTRUCTIVE BELIEFS

Here are five destructive beliefs and their constructive counterparts.

Destructive Beliefs	Constructive Beliefs
I need to **be perfect**.	I'm not perfect, no one is; and I don't need to be perfect, but I'm not bad.
I need to **be strong**.	It's nice to be strong sometimes but also nice to be able to show weakness.
I need **to please** everyone.	It would be nice if I pleased everyone but that's really impossible; besides, there's no need to please everyone.
I need **to hurry**; I can't waste time.	I can stop and pause and not always be in a hurry.
I need to **do more**.	There is a limit on what one person can do; I do what I can do and don't do the rest.

Beware the Impostor Phenomenon

The impostor phenomenon refers to the tendency to disregard outward signs of success and to consider yourself an "impostor," a fake, a fraud, one who doesn't really deserve to be considered successful (Clance, 1985; Harvey & Katz, 1985). Even though others may believe you are a success, you "know" that they are wrong. One of the dangers of this belief is that it may prevent you from seeking advancement in your profession, believing you won't be up to the task. Becoming aware that such beliefs are not uncommon and that they are not necessarily permanent should help relieve some of these misperceptions. Another useful aid is to develop a relationship with an honest and knowledgeable mentor who not only will teach you the ropes but will let you know that you are successful.

Seek Out Nourishing People

Psychologist Carl Rogers (1970) drew a distinction between *noxious* and *nourishing* people. Noxious people criticize and find fault with just about everything. Nourishing people, on the other hand, are positive and optimistic. Most important, nourishing people reward us, they stroke us, they make us feel good about ourselves. To enhance your self-esteem, seek out these people—and avoid noxious people, those who make you feel negatively about yourself. At the same time, seek to become more nourishing yourself so you each build up the other's self-esteem.

Identification with people similar to yourself also seems to increase self-esteem. For example, in one study deaf people who identified with the larger deaf community had greater self-esteem than those who didn't so identify (Jambor & Elliott, 2005). Similarly, identification with your cultural group also seems helpful in developing positive self-esteem (McDonald et al., 2005).

Work on Projects That Will Result in Success

Some people want to fail (or so it seems). Often, they select projects that will result in failure simply because these projects are impossible to complete. Avoid this trap; select projects that will result in success. Each success will help build self-esteem, and each success will make the next success a little easier. If a project does fail, recognize that this does not mean that *you're* a failure. Everyone fails somewhere along the line. Failure is something that happens; it's not necessarily something you've created. It's not something inside you. Further, your failing once does not mean that you will fail the next time. So, learn to put failure in perspective.

Remind Yourself of Your Successes

Some people have a tendency to focus, sometimes too much, on their failures, their missed opportunities, their social mistakes. If your objective is to correct what you did wrong or to identify the skills that you need to correct these failures, then focusing on failures can have some positive value. But if you focus on failure without thinking about plans for correction, then you're probably just making life more difficult for yourself and limiting your self-esteem. To counteract the tendency to recall failures, remind yourself of your successes. Recall these successes both intellectually and emotionally. Realize why they were successes, and relive the emotional experience—the feelings you had when you sank that winning basketball or aced that test or helped that friend overcome a personal problem.

Secure Affirmation

An **affirmation** is simply a statement asserting that something is true. In discussions of self-concept and self-awareness, as noted in this chapter, the word *affirmation* is used to refer to positive statements about you, statements asserting that something good or positive is true of you. It's frequently recommended that you remind yourself of your successes with self-affirmations—that you focus on your good deeds; on your positive qualities, strengths, and virtues; and on your productive and meaningful relationships with friends, loved ones, and relatives (Aronson, Cohen, & Nail, 1998; Aronson, Wilson, & Akert, 2010).

Self-affirmations include statements such as "I'm a worthy person," "I'm responsible and can be depended upon," and "I'm capable of loving and being loved." The idea behind this advice is that the way you talk to yourself will influence what you think of yourself. If you *affirm* yourself—if you tell yourself that you're a success, that others like you, that you will succeed on the next test, and that you will be welcomed when asking for a date—you will soon come to feel more positive about yourself.

Some researchers, however, argue that self-affirmations—although extremely popular in self-help books—may not be very helpful. These critics contend that if you have low self-esteem, you're not going to believe your self-affirmations because you don't have a high opinion of yourself to begin with (Paul, 2001). They propose that the alternative to self-affirmation is to secure affirmation from others. You'd do this by, for example, becoming more competent in communication and interacting with more positive people. In this way, you'd get more positive feedback from others—which, these researchers argue, is more helpful than self-talk in raising self-esteem.

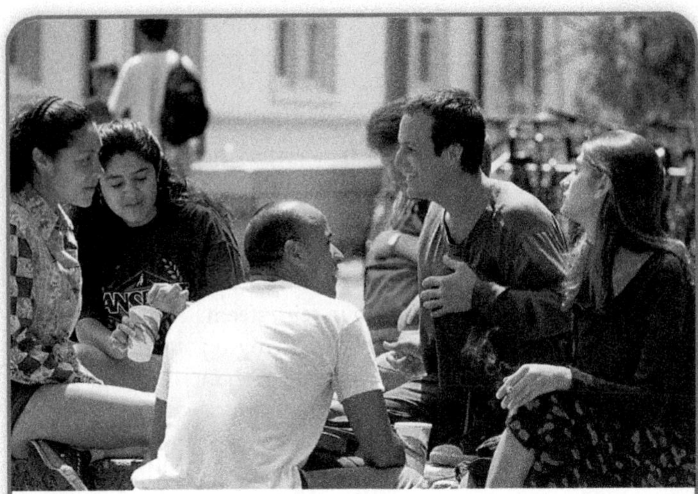

COMMUNICATION CHOICE POINT

SELF-ESTEEM *Your best friend at work has hit a new low in self-esteem—a long-term relationship failed, an expected promotion never materialized, a large investment went sour.* **What are some of your choices for helping your friend to regain some self-esteem? What are some of the things you might say? What channel would you use?**

3.2 SELF-DISCLOSURE

Self-disclosure is (1) a type of communication in which (2) you reveal information about yourself that (3) you normally keep hidden (Jourard, 1968, 1971a, 1971b; Tardy & Dindia, 2006).

1. Self-disclosure is a type of communication in which you take information from your hidden self and move it to the open self. Overt statements about the self (for example, "I'm getting fat"), as well as slips of the tongue (for example, using the name of an ex instead of your present lover), unconscious nonverbal movements (for example, self-touching movements or eye avoidance), and public confessions (for example, "Well, Jerry, it's like this…") can all be considered forms of self-disclosure. Usually, however, the term *self-disclosure* is used to refer to the conscious revealing of information, as in the statements "I'm afraid to compete" or "I love you."
2. In self-disclosure you reveal *information* about yourself; it is *information* in that it involves something that the receiver did not know about you. This information may vary from the relatively commonplace ("I'm really scared about that French exam") to the extremely significant ("I'm so depressed, I feel like committing suicide"). For self-disclosure to occur, you must reveal the information to someone else; the information must be received and understood by at least one other individual.
3. Generally, self-disclosure—at least the kind that's researched in communication and related fields—involves information that you normally keep hidden. To tell a listener something about yourself that you'd tell anyone is not self-disclosure but rather simply talking about yourself.

Factors Influencing Self-Disclosure

Before reading further about self-disclosure, consider your own willingness to self-disclose by responding to each of the following statements; indicate the likelihood that you would disclose such items of information to, say, other members of this class in three types of situations: (1) a one-on-one interpersonal situation, (2) a public speaking situation, and (3) online communication (say, blogs and social networking sites).

1. My attitudes toward other religions, nationalities, and races
2. My financial status, how much money I earn, how much I owe, how much I have saved
3. My feelings about my parents
4. My sexual fantasies
5. My physical and mental health
6. My ideal romantic partner
7. My drinking and/or drug behavior
8. My most embarrassing moment
9. My unfulfilled desires
10. My self-concept

Responding to these phrases, and ideally discussing your responses with others who also completed this experience, should get you started thinking about your own self-disclosing behavior and especially the factors that influence it, which we explain here in a bit more detail.

Who You Are

Highly sociable and extroverted people self-disclose more than those who are less sociable and more introverted. People who are comfortable communicating also self-disclose more than those who are apprehensive about talking in general. And competent people engage in self-disclosure more than less-competent people. Perhaps competent people have greater self-confidence and more positive things to reveal. Similarly, their self-confidence may make them more willing to risk possible negative reactions (McCroskey & Wheeless, 1976).

Your Culture

Different cultures view self-disclosure in different ways. Some cultures (especially those high in masculinity) view disclosing inner feelings as weakness. Among some groups, for example, it would be considered "out of place" for a man to cry at a happy occasion such as a wedding, whereas in some Latin cultures that same display of emotion would go unnoticed. Similarly, it's considered undesirable in Japan for colleagues to reveal personal information, whereas in much of the United States it's expected (Barnlund, 1989; Hall & Hall, 1987).

Your Gender

The popular stereotype of gender differences in self-disclosure emphasizes males' reluctance to speak about themselves. For the most part, research supports this view; women disclose more than men about their previous romantic relationships, their feelings about their closest same-sex friends, their greatest fears, and what they don't like about their partners (Sprecher, 1987). Women also increase the depth of their disclosures as the relationship becomes more intimate, whereas men seem not to change their self-disclosure levels. Women have fewer taboo topics—information that they will not disclose to their friends—than men do (Goodwin & Lee, 1994). Women also self-disclose more to members of their extended families than men (Argyle & Henderson, 1984, 1985; Komarovsky, 1964; Moghaddam, Taylor, & Wright, 1993).

There are exceptions, however. For example, in initial encounters men will disclose more intimately than women, perhaps "in order to control the relationship's development" (Derlega, Winstead, Wong, & Hunter, 1985). Still another exception is found in a study of Americans and Argentineans; here males in both cultures indicated a significantly greater willingness to self-disclose than females (Horenstein & Downey, 2003).

Your Listeners

Self-disclosure occurs more readily in small groups than in large groups. Dyads, or groups of two people, are the most hospitable setting for self-disclosure. With one listener, you can monitor your disclosures, continuing if there's support from your listener and stopping if there's not. With more than one listener, such monitoring becomes difficult, as the listeners' responses are sure to vary.

Not surprisingly, you disclose most to people you like (Derlega, Winstead, Wong, & Greenspan, 1987) and to people you trust (Wheeless & Grotz, 1977). You also come to like those to whom you disclose (Berg & Archer, 1983). At times self-disclosure is more likely to occur in temporary than in permanent relationships—for example, between strangers on a train or plane, in a kind of "in-flight intimacy" (McGill, 1985). In this situation two people set up an intimate, self-disclosing relationship during a brief travel period, but they don't pursue it beyond that point. In a similar way, you might set up a relationship with one or several people on the Internet and engage in significant disclosure. Perhaps knowing that you'll never see these other people, and that they will never know where you live or work, makes it easier to disclose.

You are more likely to disclose when the person you're with also discloses. This **dyadic effect** (what one person does, the other person also does) probably leads you to feel more secure and reinforces your own self-disclosing behavior. In fact, research shows that disclosures made in response to the disclosures of others are generally more intimate than those that are not the result of the dyadic effect (Berg & Archer, 1983). This dyadic effect, however, is not universal across all cultures. For example, Americans are likely to follow the dyadic effect and reciprocate with explicit self-disclosure; Koreans aren't (Won-Doornink, 1985). As you can appreciate, this difference can easily cause intercultural difficulties; the American may feel insulted if his or her Korean counterpart doesn't reciprocate with self-disclosures that are similar in depth.

Your Topic and Channel

You're more likely to disclose information about your job or hobbies than about your sex life or financial situation (Jourard, 1968, 1971a). Further, you're more likely to disclose favorable information than unfavorable information. Generally, the more personal and negative the topic, the less likely you are to self-disclose.

A **disinhibition effect** seems to occur in online communication; people seem less inhibited in communicating in e-mail or in social network sites, for example, than in face-to-face situations. Among the reasons for this seem to be that in online communication there is a certain degree of anonymity and invisibility (Suler, 2004). Research also finds that reciprocal self-disclosure occurs more quickly and at higher levels of intimacy online than it does in face-to-face interactions (Levine, 2000; Joinson, 2001).

The Rewards and Dangers of Self-Disclosure

Self-disclosure often brings rewards, but it can also create problems. Whether or not you self-disclose will depend on your assessment of the possible rewards and dangers.

Self-Disclosure Rewards

Among the rewards of self-disclosure are:

- **Self-knowledge.** Self-disclosure helps you gain a new perspective on yourself and a deeper understanding of your own behavior.
- **Improved coping abilities.** Self-disclosure helps you deal with problems, especially guilt. Because you feel that problems are a basis for rejection, you may develop guilt. By self-disclosing negative feelings and receiving support rather than rejection, you may be better able to deal with guilt, perhaps reducing or even eliminating it.
- **Communication enhancement.** Self-disclosure often improves communication. You understand the messages of others largely to the extent that you understand the individuals. You can tell what certain nuances mean, when a person is serious or joking, and when a person is being sarcastic out of fear or out of resentment.
- **More meaningful relationships.** By self-disclosing you tell others that you trust, respect, and care enough about them and your relationship to reveal yourself. This, in turn, leads the other individual to self-disclose and forms a good start to a relationship that is honest and open.

COMMUNICATION CHOICE POINT

CORRECTIVE SELF-DISCLOSURE *When you met your current partner—with whom you want to spend the rest of your life—you minimized the extent of your romantic past. You now want to come clean and disclose your "sordid" past.* **What are some of your options for introducing this topic? In what context would you want to do this? What channel would you use? What would you say?**

Self-Disclosure Dangers

Among the dangers of self-disclosure are:

- **Personal risks.** The more you reveal about yourself to others, the more areas of your life you expose to possible attack. Especially in the competitive context of work (or even romance), the more that others know about you, the more they'll be able to use against you.
- **Relationship risks.** Even in close and long-lasting relationships, self-disclosure can cause problems. Parents, normally the most supportive people in most individuals' lives, frequently reject children who disclose their homosexuality, their plans to marry someone of a different race, or their belief in another faith. Your best friends—your closest intimates—may reject you for similar self-disclosures.
- **Professional risks.** Sometimes self-disclosure may result in professional or material losses. Politicians who disclose that they have been in therapy may lose the support of their own political party and find that voters are unwilling to vote for them. Teachers who disclose disagreement with school administrators may find themselves being denied tenure, teaching undesirable schedules, and becoming victims of "budget cuts." In the business world self-disclosures of alcoholism or drug addiction often result in dismissal, demotion, or social exclusion.

Remember that self-disclosure, like any other communication, is irreversible (see Chapter 1). You cannot self-disclose and then take it back. Nor can you erase the conclusions and inferences listeners make on the basis of your disclosures. Remember, too, to examine the rewards and dangers of self-disclosure in terms of particular cultural rules. As with all cultural rules, following the rules about self-disclosure brings approval and violating them brings disapproval.

Guidelines for Self-Disclosure

Because self-disclosure is so important and so delicate a matter, here are some guidelines for (1) deciding whether and how to self-disclose, (2) responding to the disclosures of others, and (3) resisting the pressure to self-disclose.

Guidelines for Self-Disclosing

In addition to weighing the potential rewards and dangers of self-disclosure, consider the following factors as well. These hints will help you raise the right questions before you make what must be your decision. Additional suggestions that apply especially to the workplace are identified in Table 3.2.

- **Consider the motivation for the self-disclosure.** Self-disclosure should be motivated by a concern for the relationship, for the others involved, and for yourself.
- **Consider the appropriateness of the self-disclosure.** Self-disclosure should be appropriate to the context and to the relationship between you and your listener. Before making any significant self-disclosure, ask whether this is the right time (Do you both have the time to discuss this in the length it requires?) and place (Is the place private enough?). Ask, too, whether this self-disclosure is appropriate to the relationship. Generally, the more intimate the disclosure, the closer the relationship should be.

Explore the Exercise "The Timing of Self Disclosures" at MyCommunicationLab

- **Consider the disclosures of the other person.** During your disclosures, give the other person a chance to reciprocate with his or her own disclosures. If the other person does not reciprocate, reassess your own self-disclosures. It may be that, for this person at this time and in this context, your disclosures are not welcome or appropriate.
- **Consider the possible burdens self-disclosure might entail.** Carefully weigh the potential problems that you may incur as a result of your disclosure. Can you afford to lose your job if you disclose a disability? Are you willing to risk relational difficulties if you disclose your infidelities (on the *Jerry Springer Show,* for example)?

Also, ask yourself whether you're placing burdens on the listener. For example, consider the person who swears his or her mother-in-law to secrecy and then discloses having an affair with a neighbor. This disclosure clearly places an unfair burden on the mother-in-law.

Guidelines for Facilitating and Responding to Self-Disclosures

When someone discloses to you, it's usually a sign of trust and affection. In carrying out this most important receiver function, keep the following guidelines in mind.

Explore at MyCommunicationLab Profile: "Self-Disclosure Skills"

- **Practice the skills of effective and active listening.** Listen actively, listen politely, listen for different levels of meaning, listen with empathy, and listen with an open mind. Express an understanding of the speaker's feelings in order to give the speaker the opportunity to see his or her feelings more objectively and through the eyes of another. Ask questions to ensure your own understanding and to signal your interest and attention.
- **Support and reinforce the discloser.** Try to refrain from evaluation, concentrating on understanding

TABLE 3.2 SELF-DISCLOSURE IN THE WORKPLACE

Self-disclosure in the workplace involves somewhat different considerations from face-to-face disclosure with a friend, for example. Here are a few suggested cautions and comments.

Cautions for Workplace Disclosure	Comments
Assume that your disclosure will be repeated.	Although it may not be, assuming it will be will give you a useful "what if" perspective.
Realize that your disclosure may be used against you.	This seems especially true if you're in a highly competitive organization—from the relatively innocent office joking to the more serious issues of promotion and bonuses.
Disclosure very often leads to a loss of power.	Assess whether you're willing to give up some of the power you have when people are not quite sure about you.
Disclosure of a disability is your decision.	Whether or not you disclose a disability is entirely your decision, according to the U.S. Department of Labor's Office of Disability Employment Policy.
Realize that one colleague's disclosure does not obligate you to disclose.	Although reciprocating is a natural tendency, you are not required to also self-disclose. But you may be missing a great opportunity to connect with a colleague.

and empathizing. Make your supportiveness clear to the discloser through your verbal and nonverbal responses; for example, maintain eye contact, lean toward the speaker, ask relevant questions, and echo the speaker's thoughts and feelings.

- **Be willing to reciprocate.** Your own disclosures (made in response to the other person's disclosures) demonstrate your understanding of the other's meanings and your willingness to communicate on a meaningful level.
- **Keep the disclosures confidential.** If you reveal disclosures to others, negative effects are inevitable. It's interesting to note that one of the netiquette rules of e-mail is that you shouldn't forward mail to third parties without the writer's permission. This rule is useful for self-disclosure generally: Maintain confidentiality; don't pass on disclosures made to you to others without the person's permission.
- **Don't use the disclosures against the person.** Many self-disclosures expose vulnerability or weakness. If you later turn around and use a disclosure against the person, you betray the confidence and trust invested in you. Regardless of how angry you may get, resist the temptation to use the disclosures of others as weapons.

Guidelines for Resisting Pressure to Self-Disclose

You may, on occasion, find yourself in a position in which a friend, colleague, or romantic partner pressures you to self-disclose. In such situations, you may wish to weigh the pros and cons of self-disclosure and make your own decision as to whether and what you'll disclose. If your decision is to not disclose and you're still being pressured, then you need to say something. Here are a few suggestions.

- **Don't be pushed.** Although there may be certain legal or ethical reasons for disclosing, generally you don't have to disclose if you don't want to. Realize that you're in control of what you reveal and of when and to whom you reveal it. Remember that self-disclosure has significant consequence, so if you're not sure you want to reveal something, at least not until you've had additional time to think about it, then don't.
- **Be indirect and move to another topic.** Avoid the question that asks you to disclose, and change the subject. If someone presses you to disclose your past financial problems, move the conversation to financial problems in general or change the topic to a movie or to your new job. This is often a polite way of saying, "I'm not talking about it" and may be the preferred choice in certain situations and with certain people. Most often people will get the hint.
- **Be assertive in your refusal to disclose.** If necessary, say, very directly, "I'd rather not talk about that now" or "Now is not the time for this type of discussion."

A summary of these guidelines is presented in Table 3.3.

TABLE 3.3

In A Nutshell Guidelines and Strategies for Self-Disclosure

Here is a summary of the guidelines for self-disclosing, facilitating self-disclosure, and resisting self-disclosure.

General Guidelines	Specific Strategies
Self-disclosing	▪ Consider the motivation, the appropriateness, and the specific disclosures of the other person. ▪ Consider the possible burdens self-disclosure might entail.
Facilitating and responding to self-disclosures	▪ Practice the skills of effective and active listening. ▪ Support and reinforce the discloser. ▪ Be willing to reciprocate. ▪ Keep the disclosures confidential. ▪ Don't use the disclosures against the person.
Resisting pressure to self-disclose	▪ Don't be pushed. ▪ Be indirect and move to another topic. ▪ Be assertive in your refusal to disclose.

With an understanding of the self in human communication, we can explore perception, the processes by which you come to understand yourself and others (as well as the processes by which others come to understand you) and the way you manage the impressions you give to others.

3.3 PERCEPTION

Perception is your way of understanding the world; it is the process by which you make sense out of what psychologist William James called the "booming buzzing confusion" all around you. More technically, **perception** is the process by which you become aware of objects, events, and especially people through your senses: sight, smell, taste, touch, and sound. Perception is an active, not a passive, process. Your perceptions result from what exists in the outside world and from your own experiences, desires, needs and wants, loves and hatreds. Among the reasons why perception is so important in communication is that it influences your communication choices. The messages you send and listen to, the photos and messages you post and view and comment on, will depend on how you see the world, on how you size up specific situations, on what you think of the people with whom you interact.

Perception is a continuous series of processes that blend into one another. For convenience of discussion we can separate perception into five stages: (1) You sense, you pick up some kind of stimulation; (2) you organize the stimuli in some way; (3) you interpret and evaluate what you perceive; (4) you store your perception in memory; and (5) you retrieve it when needed (Figure 3.4).

Stage 1: Stimulation

At the first stage of perception, your sense organs are *stimulated*—you hear a new album, you read someone's tweet, you see a friend, you smell someone's perfume, you taste an orange, you feel another's sweaty palm. Naturally, you don't perceive everything; rather, you engage in selective perception, which includes selective attention and selective exposure.

In **selective attention** you attend to those things that you anticipate will fulfill your needs or will prove enjoyable. For instance, when daydreaming in class, you don't hear what the instructor is saying until he or she calls your name. Your selective attention mechanism focuses your senses on your name being called.

In **selective exposure** you tend to expose yourself to information that will confirm your existing beliefs, that will contribute to your objectives, or that will prove satisfying in some way. For example, after you buy a car, you're more apt to read and listen to advertisements for the car you just bought because these messages tell you that you made the right decision. At the same time, you will tend to avoid advertisements for the cars that you considered but eventually rejected because these messages would tell you that you made the wrong decision.

Stage 2: Organization

At the second stage of perception, you organize the information your senses pick up. Three interesting ways in which you organize your perceptions are (1) by rules, (2) by schemata, and (3) by scripts.

Organization by Rules

One frequently used rule of perception is that of **proximity**, or physical closeness. The rule says that things that are physically close together constitute a unit. Thus, using this rule, you would perceive people who are often together, or messages spoken one right after the other, as units, as belonging together. You also assume that the verbal and nonverbal signals sent at about the same time are related and constitute a unified whole.

Another rule is **similarity**, a principle stating that things that look alike or are similar in other ways belong together and form a unit. This principle leads you to see people who dress alike as belonging together. Similarly, you might assume that people who work at the same jobs, who are of the same religion, who live in the same building, or who talk with the same accent belong together.

You use the principle of **contrast** when you conclude that some items (people or messages, for

FIGURE 3.4 The Stages of Perception

Perception occurs in five stages: stimulation, organization, interpretation-evaluation, memory, and recall. Understanding how perception works will help make your own perceptions (of yourself and of others) more accurate.

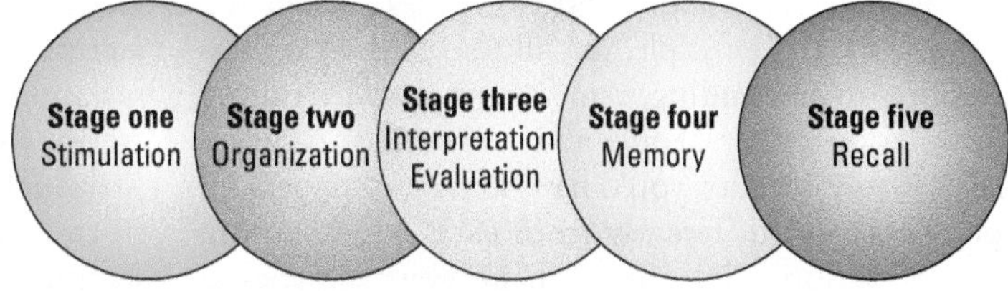

example) don't belong together because they're too different from each other to be part of the same unit. So, for example, in a conversation or a public speech, you'll focus your attention on changes in intensity or rate because these contrast with the rest of the message.

Organization by Schemata

Another way you organize material is by creating **schemata (or schemas)**, mental templates or structures that help you organize the millions of items of information you come into contact with every day as well as those you already have in memory. Schemata may thus be viewed as general ideas about people (Pat and Chris, Japanese, Baptists, New Yorkers); about yourself (your qualities, abilities, and even liabilities); or about social roles (the attributes of police officers, professors, or multimillionaires).

You develop schemata from your own experience—actual experiences as well as vicarious experiences from television, reading, and hearsay. Thus, for example, you may have a schema that portrays college athletes as strong, ambitious, academically weak, and egocentric. And, of course, you've probably developed schemata for different religious, racial, and national groups; for men and women; and for people of different affectional orientations. Each group that you have some familiarity with will be represented in your mind in some kind of schema. Schemata help you organize your perceptions by allowing you to classify millions of people into a manageable number of categories or classes. As you'll soon see, however, schemata can also create problems—they can influence you to see what is not there or to miss seeing what is there.

Organization by Scripts

A **script** is a type of schema. Like a schema, a script is an organized body of information; but a script focuses on an action, event, or procedure. It's a general idea of how some event should unfold; it's the rules governing events and their sequence. For example, you probably have a script for eating in a restaurant with the actions organized into a pattern something like this: Enter, take a seat, review the menu, order from the menu, eat your food, ask for the bill, leave a tip, pay the bill, and exit the restaurant. Similarly, you probably have scripts for how you do laundry, how you behave in an interview, the stages you go through in introducing someone to someone else, and the way you ask for a date.

Everyone relies on shortcuts—rules, schemata, and scripts, for example, are all useful shortcuts to simplify understanding, remembering, and recalling information about people and events. If you didn't have these shortcuts, you'd have to treat each person, role, or action differently from each other person, role, or action. This would make every experience totally new, totally unrelated to anything you already know. If you didn't use these shortcuts, you'd be unable to generalize, draw connections, or otherwise profit from previously acquired knowledge.

Shortcuts, however, may mislead you; they may contribute to your remembering things that are consistent with your schemata (even if they didn't occur) and distorting or forgetting information that is inconsistent. Judgments about members of other cultures are often ethnocentric. Because you form schemata and scripts on the basis of your own cultural beliefs and experiences, you can easily (but inappropriately) apply these to members of other cultures. It's easy to infer that when members of other cultures do things that conform to your scripts, they're right, and when they do things that contradict your scripts, they're wrong—a classic example of ethnocentric thinking. As you can appreciate, this tendency can easily contribute to intercultural misunderstandings.

A similar problem arises when you base your schemata for different cultural groups on stereotypes that you may have derived from television or movies. So, for example, you may have schemata for religious Muslims that you derived from stereotypes presented in the media. If you then apply these schemata to all Muslims, you risk seeing only what conforms to your script and failing to see or distorting what does not conform to your script.

Stage 3: Interpretation–Evaluation

The **interpretation–evaluation** step (a linked term because the two processes cannot be separated) is inevitably subjective and is greatly influenced by your experiences, needs, wants, values, expectations, physical and emotional state, gender, and beliefs about the way things are or should be, as well as by your rules, schemata, and scripts.

For example, when you meet a new person who is introduced to you as a college football player, you will tend to apply your schema to this person and may view him (perhaps) as strong, ambitious, academically weak, and egocentric. You will, in other words, see this person through the filter of your schema and evaluate him according to your schema for college athletes. Similarly, when viewing someone asking for a date, you will apply your script to this event and view the event through the script. You will interpret the actions of the suitor as appropriate or inappropriate depending on your script for date-requesting behavior and on the ways in which the suitor performs the sequence of actions.

Watch the Video "Art Appreciation" at MyCommunicationLab

Stage 4: Memory

You store in memory both your perceptions and their interpretations-evaluations. So, for example, you have in memory your schema for college athletes, and you know that Ben Williams is a football player. Ben Williams is then stored in memory with "cognitive tags" that tell you that he's strong, ambitious, academically weak, and egocentric. That is, despite the fact that you've not witnessed Ben's strength or ambitions and have no idea of his academic record or his psychological profile, you still may store your memory of Ben along with the qualities that make up your script for "college athletes."

Now, let's say that at different times you hear that Ben failed Spanish I (normally an A or B course at your school), that Ben got an A in chemistry (normally a tough course), and that Ben is transferring to Harvard as a theoretical physics major. Schemata act as filters or gatekeepers; they allow certain information to be stored in relatively objective form, much as you heard or read it, but may distort or prevent other information from being stored. As a result, these three items of information about Ben may get stored very differently in your memory along with your schema for college athletes.

For example, you may readily store the information that Ben failed Spanish because it's consistent with your schema; it fits neatly into the template that you have of college athletes. Information that's consistent with your schema—as in this example—will strengthen your schema and make it more resistant to change (Aronson, Wilson, & Akert, 2010). Depending on the strength of your schema, you may also store in memory (even though you didn't hear it) the "information" that Ben did poorly in other courses as well. The information that Ben got an A in chemistry, because it contradicts your schema (it just doesn't seem right), may easily be distorted or lost. The information that Ben is transferring to Harvard, however, is a bit different. This information also is inconsistent with your schema; but it is so drastically inconsistent that you may begin to look at this mindfully. Perhaps you'll begin to question your schema for athletes, or perhaps you'll view Ben as an exception to the general rule. In either case, you're going to etch Ben's transferring to Harvard very clearly in your mind.

What you remember about a person or an event isn't an objective recollection; it's more likely heavily influenced by your preconceptions or your schemata about what belongs and what doesn't belong. Your reconstruction of an event or person contains a lot of information that was not in your original experience and may omit a lot that was in this experience.

Stage 5: Recall

At some later date, you may want to recall or access information you have stored in memory. Let's say you want to retrieve your information about Ben because he's the topic of discussion among you and a few friends. As you'll see in the discussion of listening in

me•di•a lit•er•a•cy *noun* ability to understand, interact with, and create media messages

EXPANDING MEDIA LITERACY
Media Messages "Construct" Reality

Media messages do not reflect reality so much as construct it. The image of the world, of a specific country or city, that the media present is not so much simply what exists in reality but rather that portion of reality that the media want you to see. But, because it is largely through the media that we come to know the world, we really come to know the world as the media present it.

One theory built around this notion is **cultivation theory**, which holds, basically, that the media cultivate a view of the world in the mind of the viewer. For example, people who are heavy media viewers see the world existing as it is portrayed in the media more than those who are light viewers; heavy viewers, for example, think there is more violence in the world than there really is.

Some media messages are accurate, and some are not; some messages are slanted, and most of them are overly simplified. Listen to the ways in which the media influence how you see the world and to the ways they present distorted pictures of what is supposed to be reality.

Viewing the same event in a variety of different media is often a useful way of detecting possible biases. Another useful method is to ask yourself why this particular message was constructed as it was. Could the "same" event have been presented differently and given a totally different meaning or slant?

the next chapter, memory isn't reproductive; you don't simply reproduce what you've heard or seen. Rather, you *reconstruct* what you've heard or seen into a whole that is meaningful to you—depending in great part on your schemata and scripts—and it's this reconstruction that you store in memory. Now, when you want to retrieve this information from memory, you may recall it with a variety of inaccuracies. You're likely to:

- **Recall information that is consistent with your schema.** In fact, you may not even recall the specific information you're looking for (about Ben, for example) but actually just your schema (which contains the information about college athletes and therefore contains information about Ben).
- **Fail to recall information that is inconsistent with your schema.** You have no place to put that information, so you easily lose it or forget it.
- **Recall information that drastically contradicts your schema.** Because it forces you to think (and perhaps rethink) about your schema and its accuracy, it may even force you to revise your schema.

3.4 IMPRESSION FORMATION

With an understanding of the self and how perception works, we can look at the ways they are intimately connected first in impression formation and then in impression management—academic terms for what you do every day.

Impression formation (sometimes referred to as **person perception**) refers to the processes you go through in forming an impression of another person. Here you would make use of a variety of perception processes, each of which has pitfalls and potential dangers.

Certain characteristics are obvious and are open to ordinary inspection—sex, approximate age, height, and weight, not surprisingly, are all perceived with great accuracy. What is surprising is that we can judge with above-chance accuracy (we're accurate approximately 64.5 percent of the time) such characteristics as religion, sexuality, and even political leanings (Tskhay & Rule, 2013).

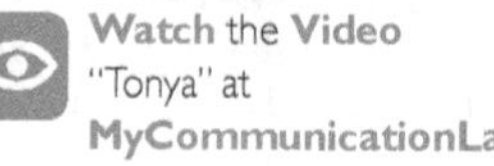
Watch the Video "Tonya" at MyCommunicationLab

Impression Formation Processes

How you perceive another person and ultimately come to some kind of evaluation or interpretation of him or her is influenced by a variety of processes. Here we consider some of the more significant: the self-fulfilling prophecy, personality theory, primacy-recency, consistency, and attribution. In addition to these five processes, recall from the previous chapter the discussion of stereotyping. This is another process many people use to help them form impressions of others.

Self-Fulfilling Prophecy

A **self-fulfilling prophecy** is a prediction that comes true because you act on it as if it were true. Put differently, a self-fulfilling prophecy occurs when you act on your schema as if it were true and in doing so make it true. Self-fulfilling prophecies occur in such widely different situations as parent–child relationships, educational settings, and business (Madon, Guyll, & Spoth, 2004; Merton, 1957; Rosenthal, 2002; Tierney & Farmer, 2004). There are four basic steps in the self-fulfilling prophecy:

1. You make a prediction or formulate a belief about a person or a situation. For example, you predict that Pat is friendly in social situations.
2. You act toward that person or situation as if that prediction or belief were true. For example, you act as if Pat is a friendly person.
3. Because you act as if the belief were true, it becomes true. For example, because of the way you act toward Pat, Pat becomes comfortable and friendly.
4. You observe your effect on the person or the resulting situation, and what you see strengthens your beliefs. For example, you observe Pat's friendliness, and this reinforces your belief that Pat is in fact friendly.

The self-fulfilling prophecy also can be seen when you make predictions about yourself and fulfill them. For example, suppose you enter a group situation convinced that the other members will dislike you. Almost invariably you'll be proved right; the other members will appear to you to dislike you. What you may be doing is acting in a way that encourages the group to respond to you negatively. In this way, you fulfill your prophecies about yourself.

Personality Theory

Everyone has a theory of personality (usually subconscious or implicit) that determines which characteristics of an individual go with other characteristics. Consider, for example, the following brief statements. Note the word in parentheses that you think best completes each sentence.

Carlo is energetic, eager, and (intelligent, stupid).

Kim is bold, defiant, and (extroverted, introverted).

Joe is bright, lively, and (thin, heavy).

the•o•ry *noun* statement of explanation, formulation of relationships, reasoned generalization

UNDERSTANDING THEORY AND RESEARCH
The Pygmalion Effect

A widely known example of the self-fulfilling prophecy is the **Pygmalion effect** (Rosenthal & Jacobson, 1992). The effect is named after Pygmalion, a sculptor in Greek mythology who created a statue of a beautiful woman and then fell in love with it. Venus, the goddess of love, rewarded Pygmalion for his artistry and love by making the statue come to life as a real woman, Galatea. George Bernard Shaw used this idea for his play *Pygmalion,* the story of a poor, uneducated London flower vendor who is taught "proper speech" and enters society's upper class. The musical *My Fair Lady* was in turn based on Shaw's play.

In a classic research study, experimenters told teachers that certain pupils were expected to do exceptionally well—that they were late bloomers (Rosenthal & Jacobson, 1968, 1992). And although the experimenters selected the "late bloomers" at random, the students who were labeled "late bloomers" did perform at higher levels than their classmates. Like the beautiful statue, these students became what their teachers thought they were. The expectations of the teachers may have caused them to pay extra attention to the students, and this may have positively affected the students' performance. The Pygmalion effect has also been studied in such varied contexts as the courtroom, the clinic, the work cubicle, management and leadership practices, athletic coaching, and stepfamilies (Eden, 1992; Einstein, 1995; McNatt, 2001; Rosenthal, 2002; Solomon et al., 1996).

Working with Theories and Research

Findings such as those cited above have led one researcher to suggest that companies apply the Pygmalion effect as a way to improve worker productivity—by creating in supervisors positive attitudes about employees and by helping employees to feel that their supervisors and the organization as a whole value them highly (McNatt, 2001). In what ways might this Pygmalion effect be applied at your own workplace?

Eve is attractive, intelligent, and (likable, unlikable).

Susan is cheerful, positive, and (outgoing, shy).

Angel is handsome, tall, and (friendly, unfriendly).

What makes some of these choices seem right and others wrong is your **implicit personality theory**, the system of rules that tells you which characteristics go with which other characteristics. Your theory may, for example, have told you that a person who is energetic and eager is also intelligent, not stupid—although there is no logical reason why a stupid person could not be energetic and eager.

The widely documented **halo effect** is a good example of how this personality theory works. If you believe a person has some positive qualities, you're likely to infer that she or he also possesses other positive qualities. There is also a reverse halo (or "horns") effect: If you know a person possesses several negative qualities, you're more likely to infer that the person also has other negative qualities. For example, you're more likely to perceive physically attractive people as more generous, sensitive, trustworthy, and interesting than

COMMUNICATION CHOICE POINT

IMPRESSION CORRECTION *You made a bad impression at work—you drank too much at an office party and played the clown. This is not the impression you want to give, and you need to change it fast. Although you know you can't erase that impression, you need to counteract it in some way.* **What are some of your choices? What might you say and do to help lessen the negative effects of that impression?**

those who are less attractive. And the **horns effect** or **reverse halo effect** will lead you to perceive those who are unattractive as mean, dishonest, antisocial, and sneaky (Katz, 2003).

In using personality theories, apply them carefully and critically so as to avoid perceiving qualities in an individual that your theory tells you should be present but aren't or seeing qualities that are not there (Plaks, Grant, & Dweck, 2005).

Primacy–Recency

Assume for a moment that you're enrolled in a course in which half the classes are extremely dull and half extremely exciting. At the end of the semester, you evaluate the course and the instructor. Would your evaluation be more favorable if the dull classes occurred in the first half of the semester and the exciting classes in the second? Or would it be more favorable if the order were reversed? If what comes first exerts the most influence, you have a **primacy effect.** If what comes last (or most recently) exerts the most influence, you have a **recency effect.**

In the classic study on the effects of **primacy–recency** in perception, college students perceived a person who was described as "intelligent, industrious, impulsive, critical, stubborn, and envious" more positively than a person described as "envious, stubborn, critical, impulsive, industrious, and intelligent" (Asch, 1946). Notice that the descriptions are identical; only the order was changed. Clearly, there's a tendency to use early information to get a general idea about a person and to use later information to make this impression more specific. The initial information helps you form a schema for the person. Once that schema is formed, you're likely to resist information that contradicts it.

One interesting practical implication of primacy–recency is that the first impression you make is likely to be the most important—and is likely to be made very quickly (Sunnafrank & Ramirez, 2004; Willis & Todorov, 2006). The reason for this is that the schema that others form of you functions as a filter to admit or block additional information about you. If the initial impression or schema is positive, others are likely (1) to readily remember additional positive information because it confirms this original positive image or schema; (2) to easily forget or distort negative information because it contradicts this original positive schema; and (3) to interpret ambiguous information as positive. You win in all three ways—if the initial impression is positive.

Consistency

The tendency to maintain balance among perceptions or attitudes is called **consistency.** You expect certain things to go together and other things not to go together. On a purely intuitive basis, for example, respond to the following sentences by noting your expected response.

1. I expect a person I like to (like, dislike) me.
2. I expect a person I dislike to (like, dislike) me.
3. I expect my friend to (like, dislike) my friend.
4. I expect my friend to (like, dislike) my enemy.
5. I expect my enemy to (like, dislike) my friend.
6. I expect my enemy to (like, dislike) my enemy.

According to most consistency theories, your expectations would be as follows: You would expect a person you liked to like you (1) and a person you disliked to dislike you (2). You would expect a friend to like a friend (3) and to dislike an enemy (4). You would expect your enemy to dislike your friend (5) and to like your other enemy (6). All these expectations are intuitively satisfying.

Further, you would expect someone you liked to possess characteristics you like or admire and would expect your enemies not to possess characteristics you like or admire. Conversely, you would expect people you liked to lack unpleasant characteristics and those you disliked to possess unpleasant characteristics. The downside here is that you might be wrong; your friend may possess negative qualities (which your friendship may lead you to miss) and your enemy may possess positive qualities (which your enmity may lead you to miss).

Attribution of Control

Another way in which you form impressions is through the **attribution of control**, a process by which you focus on explaining why someone behaved as he or she did on the basis of whether the person had control over his or her behavior. For example, suppose you invite your friend Desmond to dinner for 7 p.m. and he arrives at 9 p.m. Consider how you would respond to each of these reasons:

- **Reason 1:** I just couldn't tear myself away from the beach. I really wanted to get a great tan.
- **Reason 2:** I was driving here when I saw some guys mugging an old couple. I broke it up and took the couple home. They were so frightened that I had to stay with them until their children arrived. The storm knocked out all the cell towers and electricity, so I had no way of calling to tell you I'd be late.
- **Reason 3:** I got in a car accident and was taken to the hospital.

Depending on the reason, you would probably attribute very different motives to Desmond's

the•o•ry *noun* statement of explanation, formulation of relationships, reasoned generalization

UNDERSTANDING THEORY AND RESEARCH
The Just World Hypothesis

Many people believe that the world is just: Good things happen to good people and bad things to bad people (Aronson, Wilson, & Akert, 2010; Hunt, 2000). Put differently, the **just world hypothesis** suggests that you'll get what you deserve. Even if you mindfully dismiss this assumption, you may use it mindlessly when perceiving and evaluating other people. Consider a particularly vivid example: In certain cultures (for example, in Bangladesh, Iran, or Yemen), a woman who is raped is considered by many (though certainly not all) to have disgraced her family and to be deserving of severe punishment—in many cases, even death. Although most people reading this book will claim that this is unjust and unfair, it's quite common even in Western cultures to blame the victim. Much research, for example, shows that people often blame the victim for being raped (Bell, Kuriloff, & Lottes, 1994). In fact, accused rapists' defense attorneys routinely attack rape victims in court for dressing provocatively. And it's relevant to note that only two states—New York and Florida—currently forbid questions about the victim's clothing.

The belief that the world is just creates perceptual distortions by leading us to deemphasize the influence of situational factors and to overemphasize the influence of internal factors in our attempts to explain the behaviors of other people or even our own behaviors.

Working with Theories and Research

Take a look at your own behaviors. Do you act as you do because of your belief in a just world? For example, do you act fairly because you think you'll be rewarded for it? Do you know people who do act on the basis of this hypothesis—for example, doing good in anticipation of good things happening to them?

behavior. With reasons 1 and 2, you'd conclude that Desmond was in control of his behavior; with reason 3, that he was not. Further, you would probably respond negatively to reason 1 (Desmond was selfish and inconsiderate) and positively to reason 2 (Desmond was a Good Samaritan). Because Desmond was not in control of his behavior in reason 3, you would probably not attribute either positive or negative motivation to his behavior. Instead, you would probably feel sorry that he got into an accident.

In perceiving and especially in evaluating other people's behavior, you frequently ask if they were in control of the behavior. Generally, research shows that if you feel a person was in control of negative behaviors, you'll come to dislike him or her. If you believe the person was not in control of negative behaviors, you'll come to feel sorry for and not blame the person.

In your attribution of controllability—or in attributing motives on the basis of any other reasons (for example, hearsay or observations of the person's behavior) beware of several potential errors: (1) the self-serving bias, (2) overattribution, and (3) the fundamental attribution error.

- **Self-serving bias.** You commit the **self-serving bias** when you take credit for the positive and deny responsibility for the negative. For example, you're more likely to attribute your positive outcomes (say, you get an A on an exam) to internal and controllable factors—to your personality, intelligence, or hard work. And you're more likely to attribute your negative outcomes (say, you get a D) to external and uncontrollable factors—to the exam's being exceptionally difficult or to your roommate's party the night before (Bernstein, Stephan, & Davis, 1979; Duval & Silva, 2002).
- **Overattribution.** As noted in Chapter 2, **overattribution**—the tendency to single out one or two obvious characteristics of a person and attribute everything that person does to this one or these two characteristics—distorts perception. To prevent overattribution, recognize that most behaviors and personality characteristics result from lots of factors. You almost always make a mistake when you select one factor and attribute everything to it.
- **Fundamental attribution error.** The error occurs when you overvalue the contribution of internal factors (for example, a person's personality) and undervalue the influence of external factors (for example, the context or situation the person is in). The **fundamental attribution error** leads you to conclude that people do what they do because that's the kind of people they are, not because of the situation they're in. When Pat is late for an appointment, you're more likely to conclude that Pat is inconsiderate or irresponsible than to attribute the lateness to a possible bus breakdown or traffic accident.

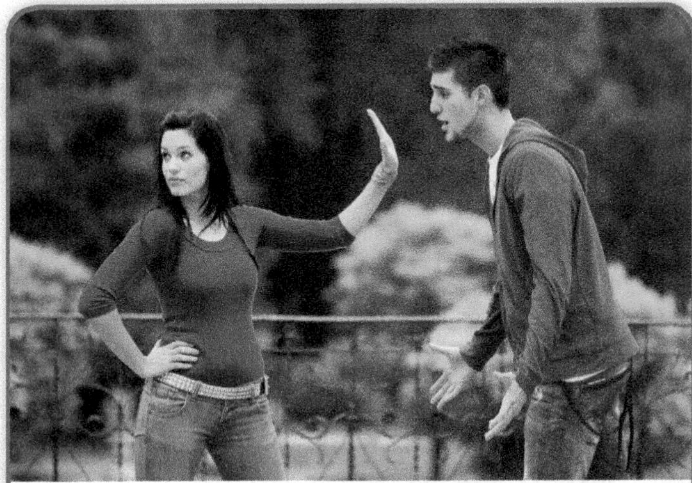

COMMUNICATION CHOICE POINT

OVERATTRIBUTION *Your partner overattributes your behavior, attitudes, values, and just about everything you do to your ethnic origins.* **What communication choices do you have for explaining the illogical nature of this overattribution but, at the same time, not insulting your partner? What would you say?**

Increasing Accuracy in Impression Formation

Successful communication depends largely on the accuracy of the impressions you form of others. We've already identified the potential barriers that can arise with each of the perceptual processes, for example, the self-serving bias or overattribution. In addition to avoiding these barriers, here are additional ways to increase your accuracy in impression formation.

Analyze Impressions

Subject your perceptions to logical analysis, to critical thinking. Here are two suggestions.

- **Recognize your own role in perception.** Your emotional and physiological state will influence the meaning you give to your perceptions. A movie may seem hysterically funny when you're in a good mood, but just plain stupid when you're in a bad mood.
- **Avoid early conclusions.** Formulate hypotheses to test against additional information and evidence (rather than conclusions). Look for a variety of cues pointing in the same direction. The more cues that point to the same conclusion, the more likely your conclusion will be correct. Be especially alert to contradictory cues that seem to refute your initial hypotheses. At the same time, seek validation from others. Do others see things in the same way you do? If not, ask yourself if your perceptions may be distorted in some way.

Check Perceptions

Perception checking will help you lessen your chances of misinterpreting another's feelings and will also give the other person an opportunity to elaborate on his or her thoughts and feelings. In its most basic form, perception checking consists of two steps.

- **Describe what you see or hear.** Try to do this as descriptively (not evaluatively) as you can. Sometimes you may wish to offer several possibilities, for example, "You've called me from work a lot this week. You seem concerned that everything is all right at home" or "You've not wanted to talk with me all week. You say that my work is fine, but you don't seem to want to give me the same responsibilities that other editorial assistants have."
- **Seek confirmation.** Ask the other person if your description is accurate. Avoid mind reading. Don't try to read the thoughts and feelings of another person just from observing their behaviors. Avoid phrasing your questions defensively, as in "You really don't want to go out, do you? I knew you didn't when you turned on the television." Instead, ask supportively, for example, "Would you rather watch TV?" or "Are you worried about the kids?" or "Are you displeased with my work? Is there anything I can do to improve my job performance?"

Reduce Uncertainty

In every communication situation, there is some degree of ambiguity. A variety of **uncertainty reduction strategies** you can use to help you reduce your own uncertainty about another person (Berger & Bradac, 1982; Brashers, 2007; Gudykunst, 1993).

- **Observe**. Observing another person while he or she is engaged in an active task, preferably interacting with others in an informal social situation, will often reveal a great deal about the person, as people are less apt to monitor their behaviors and more likely to reveal their true selves in informal situations.
- **Construct situations.** You can sometimes manipulate situations so as to observe the person in more specific and revealing contexts. Employment interviews, theatrical auditions, and student teaching are good examples of situations arranged to give you an accurate view of the person in action.
- **Lurk**. When you log on to an Internet group and lurk, reading the exchanges between the other group members before saying anything yourself,

you're learning about the people in the group and about the group itself, thus reducing uncertainty. When uncertainty is reduced, you're more likely to make contributions that will be appropriate to the group and less likely to violate the group's norms.

- **Ask.** Learn about a person through asking others. You might inquire of a colleague if a third person finds you interesting and might like to have dinner with you.
- **Interact.** Interacting with the individual will of course give you considerable information. For example, you can ask questions: "Do you enjoy sports?" "What would you do if you got fired?" You also gain knowledge of another by disclosing information about yourself. These disclosures help to create an environment that encourages disclosures from the person about whom you wish to learn more.

Increase Cultural Sensitivity

Recognizing and being sensitive to cultural differences will help increase your accuracy in perception. For example, Russian or Chinese artists such as ballet dancers will often applaud their audience by clapping. Americans seeing this may easily interpret this as egotistical. Similarly, a German man will enter a restaurant before the woman in order to see if the place is respectable enough for the woman to enter. This simple custom can easily be interpreted as rude when viewed by people from cultures in which it's considered courteous for the woman to enter first (Axtell, 2007).

Cultural sensitivity will help counteract the difficulty most people have in understanding the nonverbal messages of people from other cultures. For example, it's easier to interpret the facial expressions of members of your own culture than those of members of other cultures (Weathers, Frank, & Spell, 2002). This "in-group advantage" will assist your perceptual accuracy for members of your own culture but may hinder your accuracy for members of other cultures (Elfenbein & Ambady, 2002).

Within every cultural group there are wide and important differences. As all Americans are not alike, neither are all Indonesians, Greeks, or Mexicans. When you make assumptions that all people of a certain culture are alike, you're thinking in stereotypes. Recognizing differences between another culture and your own, and among members of the same culture, will help you perceive people and situations more accurately.

A summary of impression formation processes and the cautions to be observed is presented in Table 3.4.

Watch the Video "She Can Stay" at **MyCommunicationLab**

TABLE 3.4

In A Nutshell Impression Formation

Here is a brief summary of the impression formation processes and some cautions to observe.

Impression Formation Processes	Cautions to Observe
Self-Fulfilling Prophecy: you act on your prediction as if it were true, and it becomes true.	Beware of your predictions that come true; you may be influencing them in that direction.
Personality Theory: you expect certain qualities to go with other qualities.	Personalities are much too complex to easily predict one quality on the basis of others; beware of always finding fault with those you dislike or good with those you like.
Primacy–Recency: you are most influenced by what occurs first and by what occurs last.	Basing your impressions on the basis of early or late information may bias your perceptions.
Consistency: you assume that people are consistent; if you see them as "good people" then the things they do are likely to be seen as good.	People are not always consistent; don't expect them to be.
Attribution of Control: you evaluate what a person did on the basis of the control you perceive this person to have had on his or her behavior.	Beware of the self-serving bias, overattribution, and the fundamental attribution error.
Stereotyping: you form an impression of someone based on your racial, religious, or other stereotype.	Beware of stereotypes; often they were learned without conscious awareness and are often misleading.

3.5 IMPRESSION MANAGEMENT

Impression management (some writers use the terms *self-presentation* or *identity management*) refers to the processes you go through to communicate the impression you want other people to have of you.

Impression management is largely the result of the messages communicated. In the same way that you form impressions of others largely on the basis of how they communicate, verbally and nonverbally, they also form impressions of you based on what you say (your verbal messages) and how you act and dress (your nonverbal messages). Communication messages, however, are not the only means for impression formation and management. For example, you also communicate your self-image and judge others by the people with whom they associate; if you associate with VIPs, then surely you must be a VIP yourself, the conventional wisdom goes. Or you might form an impression of someone on the basis of that person's age or gender or ethnic origin. Or you might rely on what others have said about the person and from that form impressions. And, of course, they might well do the same in forming impressions of you.

Part of the art and skill of communication is to understand and be able to manage the impressions you give to others. Mastering the art of impression management will enable you to present yourself as you want others to see you—at least to some extent. The strategies you use to achieve this desired impression will depend on your specific goal. Here is a classification based on seven major communication goals and strategies. In addition to helping you communicate the impression you want to communicate, each of these strategies may backfire and communicate the opposite of your intended purpose.

To Be Liked: Affinity-Seeking and Politeness Strategies

If you're new at school or on the job and you want to be well liked, included in the activities of others, and thought of highly, you'd likely use affinity-seeking strategies and politeness strategies. Another set of strategies often used to increase likeability is immediacy strategies (these are discussed on page 156).

Affinity-Seeking Strategies

Using the **affinity-seeking strategies** that follow is likely to increase your chances of being liked (Bell & Daly, 1984). Such strategies are especially important in initial interactions, and their use has even been found to increase student motivation when used by teachers (Martin & Rubin, 1998; Myers & Zhong, 2004; Wrench, McCroskey, & Richmond, 2008).

- Present yourself as comfortable and relaxed.
- Follow the cultural rules for polite, cooperative, respectful conversation.
- Appear active, enthusiastic, and dynamic.
- Stimulate and encourage the other person to talk about himself or herself.
- Communicate interest in the other person.
- Appear optimistic and positive.
- Appear honest, reliable, and interesting.
- Communicate warmth, support, and empathy.
- Demonstrate shared attitudes and values.

Although this research was conducted before much of social media you can easily see how the same strategies could be used in online communication. For example, you can post photos to show that you're active and enthusiastic; you can follow the rules for polite interaction by giving "likes" and "+1s" to others; and you can communicate interest in the other person by inviting him or her to hang out, to join a group, by commenting on post, or by retweeting. Not surprisingly, plain old flattery also goes a long way toward making you liked. Flattery can increase your chances for success in a job interview, the tip a customer is likely to leave, and even the credibility you're likely to be seen as having (Seiter, 2007; Varma, Toh, & Pichler, 2006; Vonk, 2002).

There is also, however, a potential negative effect that can result from the use of affinity-seeking strategies. Using affinity-seeking strategies too often or in ways that may appear insincere may lead people to see you as attempting to ingratiate yourself for your own advantage and not really meaning "to be nice."

Politeness Strategies

Politeness strategies are another set of strategies often used to appear likeable. We can look at them in terms of negative and positive types (Brown & Levinson, 1987; Goffman, 1967; Goldsmith, 2007; Holmes, 1995). Both of these types of politeness are responsive to two needs that we each have:

1. **positive face needs**—the desire to be viewed positively by others, to be thought of favorably, and
2. **negative face needs**—the desire to be autonomous, to have the right to do as we wish.

Politeness in interpersonal communication, then, refers to behavior that allows others to maintain both positive and negative face, and impoliteness refers to behaviors that attack either positive face (for example, you criticize someone) or negative face (for example, you make demands on someone).

To help another person maintain positive face, you speak respectfully to and about the person, you give the person your full attention, you say "excuse me" when appropriate. In short you treat the person as you would want to be treated. In this way you allow the person to maintain positive face through what is called positive politeness. You attack the person's positive face when you speak disrespectfully about the person, ignore the person or the person's comments, and fail to use the appropriate expressions of politeness such as "thank you" and "please."

To help another person maintain negative face, you respect the person's right to be autonomous and so you request rather than demand that they do something; you say, "Would you mind opening a window" rather than "Open that window, damn it!" You might also give the person an "out" when making a request, allowing the person to reject your request if that is what the person wants. And so you say, "If this is a bad time, please tell me, but I'm really strapped and could use a loan of $100" rather than "Loan me a $100" or "You have to lend me $100." If you want a recommendation, you might say, "Would it be possible for you to write me a recommendation for graduate school" rather than "You have to write me a recommendation for graduate school." In this way you enable the person to maintain negative face through what is called negative politeness.

Of course, we do this almost automatically and asking for a favor without any consideration for the person's negative face needs would seems totally insensitive. In most situations, however, this type of attack on negative face often appears in more subtle forms. For example, your mother saying "Are you going to wear that?"—to use Deborah Tannen's (2006) example—attacks negative face by criticizing or challenging your autonomy. This comment also attacks positive face by questioning your ability to dress properly.

Politeness too may have negative consequences. Over-politeness, for example, is likely to be seen as phony and is likely to be resented, especially if it's seen as a persuasive strategy.

To Be Believed: Credibility Strategies

If you were a politician and wanted people to vote for you, at least part of your strategy would involve attempts to establish your **credibility** (which consists of your competence, your character, and your charisma). For example, to establish your competence, you might mention your great educational background or the courses you took that qualify you as an expert. To establish that you're of good character, you might mention how fair and honest you are, your commitment to enduring values, or your concern for those less fortunate. And to establish your charisma—your take-charge, positive personality—you might demonstrate enthusiasm, be emphatic, or focus on the positive while minimizing the negative.

If you stress your competence, character, and charisma too much, however, you risk being seen as someone who lacks the very qualities that you seem too eager to present to others. Generally, people who are truly competent need say little directly about their own competence; their actions and their success will reveal their competence.

To Excuse Failure: Self-Handicapping Strategies

If you were about to tackle a difficult task and were concerned that you might fail, you might use what are called **self-handicapping strategies.** In the more extreme form of this strategy, you actually set up barriers or obstacles to make the task impossible. That way, when you fail, you won't be blamed or thought ineffective—after all, the task was impossible. Let's say you aren't prepared for your human communication exam and you feel you're going to fail. Using this self-handicapping strategy, you might stay out late at a party the night before so that when you do poorly in the exam, you can blame it on the party rather than on your intelligence or knowledge. In a less extreme form, you might manufacture excuses for failure and have them ready if you do fail. For example, you might prepare to blame a poorly cooked dinner on your defective stove.

On the negative side, using self-handicapping strategies too often may lead people to see you as generally incompetent or foolish. After all, a person who parties the night before an exam for which he or she is already unprepared is clearly demonstrating poor judgment.

To Secure Help: Self-Deprecating Strategies

If you want to be taken care of and protected, or if you simply want someone to come to your aid, you might use **self-deprecating strategies.** Confessions of incompetence and inability often bring assistance from others. And so you might say, "I just can't fix that drain and it drives me crazy; I just don't know anything about plumbing" with the hope that the other person will offer help.

eth•ics *noun* morality, standards of conduct, moral judgment

MAKING ETHICAL CHOICES
The Ethics of Impression Management

Impression management strategies may also be used unethically and for less-than-noble purposes. For example, people may use affinity-seeking strategies to get you to like them so they can extract favors from you. Politicians frequently portray themselves as credible when they are not in order to win votes. The same could be said of the stereotypical used-car salesperson or insurance agent trying to make a sale. Some people use self-handicapping strategies or self-deprecating strategies to get you to see their behavior from a perspective that benefits them rather than you. Self-monitoring strategies are often deceptive and are designed to present a more polished image than one that might come out without this self-monitoring. And, of course, influence strategies have been used throughout history in deception as well as in truth. Even image-confirming strategies can be used to deceive, as when people exaggerate their positive qualities (or make them up) and hide their negative ones.

Ethical Choice Point

You're ready to join one (perhaps several) of the online dating services. You need to write your profile and are wondering if everyone (or nearly everyone) exaggerates, you shouldn't also. Specifically, you're considering saying that you earn a very good salary (actually, it's not so great but you're hoping for a promotion), 20 pounds lighter (actually, you intend to lose weight), and that you own a condo (actually, that's a goal once you get the promotion and save a down payment). If you don't exaggerate, you reason, you'll disadvantage yourself and not meet the people you want to meet. Also, you figure that people expect you to exaggerate and assume that you're probably a lot less ideal than your profile would indicate. Would this be ethical? Just how honest do you have to be?

But be careful: Your self-deprecating strategies may convince people that you are in fact just as incompetent as you say you are. Or people may see you as someone who doesn't want to do something and so pretends to be incompetent to get others to do it for you. This is not likely to benefit you in the long run.

COMMUNICATION CHOICE POINT

MAKING THE RIGHT IMPRESSION *You've just joined a social networking site that your future employers might look at.* **How might you write your profile and use the many features of the site to make yourself appear credible and a perfect future employee? What would you be sure not to do?**

To Hide Faults: Self-Monitoring Strategies

Much impression management is devoted not merely to presenting a positive image, but to suppressing the negative, to **self-monitoring strategies.** Here you carefully monitor (self-censor) what you say or do. You avoid your normal slang to make your colleagues think more highly of you; you avoid chewing gum so you don't look juvenile or unprofessional; you avoid posting the photos from the last party. While you readily disclose favorable parts of your experience, you actively hide the unfavorable parts.

But, if you self-monitor too often or too obviously, you risk being seen as someone unwilling to reveal himself or herself and perhaps as not trusting enough of others to feel comfortable disclosing. In more extreme cases, you may be seen as dishonest, as hiding your true self or trying to fool other people.

Explore at MyCommunicationLab Profile: "Self Monitoring Scale"

To Be Followed: Influencing Strategies

In many instances you'll want to get people to see you as a leader. Here you can use a variety of **influencing strategies.** One set of such strategies are those normally grouped under power—your knowledge (information power), your expertise (expert power), your right to lead by virtue of your position as, say, a doctor or judge or accountant (legitimate power). Or, using leadership strategies, you might stress your prior experience, your broad knowledge, or your previous successes.

Influencing strategies can also backfire. If you try to influence someone and fail, you'll be perceived to have less power than before your unsuccessful influence attempt. And, of course, if you're seen as someone who is influencing others for self-gain, your influence attempts might be resented or rejected.

To Confirm Self-Image: Image-Confirming Strategies

You may sometimes use **image-confirming strategies** to reinforce your positive perceptions about yourself. If you see yourself as the life of the party, you'll tell jokes, post photos in which you are in fact the life of the party, and try to amuse people. This behavior confirms your own self-image and also lets others know that this is who you are and how you want to be seen. At the same time that you reveal aspects of yourself that confirm your desired image, you actively suppress revealing aspects of yourself that would disconfirm this image. You'd quickly remove unfavorable wall postings, for example.

If you use image-confirming strategies too frequently, you risk being seen as too perfect to be genuine. If you try to project an exclusively positive image, it's likely to turn people off—people want to see their friends and associates as real people with some faults and imperfections. Also recognize that image-confirming strategies invariably involve your focusing on yourself, and with that comes the risk of seeming self-absorbed.

A knowledge of these impression management strategies and the ways in which they are effective and ineffective will give you a greater number of choices for achieving such widely diverse goals as being liked, being believed, excusing failure, securing help, hiding faults, being followed, and confirming your self image.

A summary of these strategies appears in Table 3.5.

TABLE 3.5

In A Nutshell Impression Management Strategies

Here is a summary of the impression management strategies discussed here along with the general goals of each.

Impression Management Strategies	Goals to Achieve
Affinity-seeking and politeness strategies	To be liked, to be thought of highly, to be seen in the right light.
Credibility strategies	To be seen as competent, of good character, and dynamic.
Self-handicapping strategies	To excuse actual or possible future failure.
Self-deprecating strategies	To secure help by making yourself seem unable to do the task.
To hide faults: self-monitoring strategies	To hide faults, to emphasize the positive and minimize the negative.
Influencing strategies	To be persuasive, to be in control, to be followed, to be the leader.
Image-confirming strategies	To seek reassurance of one's self-image; to be recognized for who you are.

Analyzing Video Choices

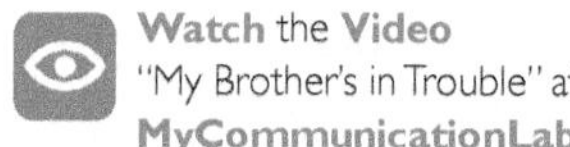

Watch the Video "My Brother's in Trouble" at MyCommunicationLab

Marisol and her older brother Jose have always been close, choosing to spend time together and confiding in each other. Lately, Jose's self-esteem has hit a new low and he and Marisol have drifted apart. Jose's long-term relationship ended, an expected A turned into a C, and a hoped-for job interview never materialized. "My Brother's in Trouble" looks at some of the ways of dealing with self-esteem, especially the choices you have available for helping to raise someone's self-esteem and the relative effectiveness of each of your choices. Log on to www.mycommunicationlab.com to view this video, see how the various choices play out, and then respond to a few discussion questions.

Study and **Review** materials for this chapter are at **MyCommunicationLab**

SUMMARY: THE SELF AND PERCEPTION

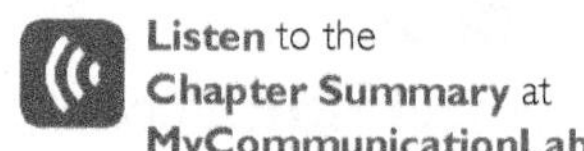

Listen to the **Chapter Summary** at **MyCommunicationLab**

This chapter explored the self, the ways you perceive yourself, and perception, the way you perceive others and others perceive you.

3.1 THE SELF IN HUMAN COMMUNICATION

1. Self-concept, the image that you have of yourself, is composed of feelings and thoughts about both your abilities and your limitations. Self-concept develops from the image that others have of you, the comparisons you make between yourself and others, the teachings of your culture, and your own interpretations and evaluations.

2. The Johari window model of the self is one way to view self-awareness. In this model there are four major areas or selves: open, blind, hidden, and unknown. To increase self-awareness, analyze yourself, listen to others to see yourself as they do, actively seek information from others about yourself, see yourself from different perspectives, and increase your open self.

3. Self-esteem is the value you place on yourself. To enhance self-esteem, attack self-destructive beliefs, seek out nourishing others, work on projects that will result in success, and secure affirmation.

3.2 SELF-DISCLOSURE

4. Self-disclosure is a form of communication in which information about the self that is normally kept hidden is communicated to one or more others.

5. Self-disclosure is more likely to occur when the potential discloser (1) feels competent and is sociable; (2) comes from a culture that encourages self-disclosure; (3) is a woman; (4) is talking to supportive listeners who also disclose; and (5) talks about impersonal topics and reveals positive information.

6. The rewards of self-disclosure include increased self-knowledge, the ability to cope with difficult situations and guilt, communication efficiency, and chances for more meaningful relationships. The dangers of self-disclosure include personal and social rejection and professional or material losses.

7. Before self-disclosing, consider the cultural rules operating, the motivation for the self-disclosure, the possible burdens you might impose on your listener or on yourself, the appropriateness of the self-disclosure, and the disclosures of the other person.

8. When listening to disclosures, take into consideration the cultural rules governing the communication situation, try to understand what the discloser is feeling, support the discloser, refrain from criticism and evaluation, and keep the disclosures confidential.

9. When you don't want to disclose, be firm, be indirect and change the topic, or assertively state your unwillingness to disclose.

3.3 PERCEPTION

10. Perception is the process by which you become aware of the many stimuli impinging on your senses. It occurs in five stages: Sensory stimulation occurs, sensory stimulation is organized, sensory stimulation

is interpreted–evaluated, sensory stimulation is held in memory, and sensory stimulation is recalled.

3.4 IMPRESSION FORMATION

11. Five important processes influence the way you form impressions: (1) self-fulfilling prophecies, which may influence the behaviors of others; (2) personality theory, which allows you to conclude that certain characteristics go with certain other characteristics; (3) primacy–recency, which influences you to give extra importance to what occurs first (a primacy effect) or to what occurs most recently (a recency effect); (4) consistency, which influences you to see what is consistent and to not see what is inconsistent; and (5) attributions of controllability, which may lead to the wrong conclusion through a self-serving bias, overattribution, or committing the fundamental attribution error.

12. To increase your accuracy in impression formation: Analyze your impressions and recognize your role in perception; check your impressions; reduce uncertainty; and become culturally sensitive.

3.5 IMPRESSION MANAGEMENT

13. Among the goals and strategies of impression management are: to be liked (affinity seeking and politeness strategies); to be believed (credibility strategies that establish your competence, character, and charisma); to excuse failure (self-handicapping strategies); to secure help (self-deprecating strategies); to hide faults (self-monitoring strategies); to be followed (influencing strategies); and to confirm one's self-image (image-confirming strategies).

14. Each of these impression management strategies can backfire and give others negative impressions. And each of these strategies may be used to reveal your true self or to present a false self and deceive others in the process.

Study and **Review** the **Flashcards** at **MyCommunicationLab**

KEY TERMS

affinity-seeking strategies *70*
affirmation *55*
attribution of control *66*
blind self *53*
consistency *66*
contrast *61*
credibility *71*
cultivation theory *63*
disinhibition effect *57*
dyadic effect *57*
fundamental attribution error *67*
halo effect *65*
hidden self *53*
horns effect *66*
image-confirming strategies *73*
implicit personality theory *65*
impression formation *64*
impression management *70*
influencing strategies *73*
interpretation–evaluation *62*
Johari window *52*
just world hypothesis *67*
looking-glass self *51*
open self *53*
overattribution *67*
perception *61*
perception checking *68*
person perception *64*
politeness strategies *70*
primacy effect *66*
primacy–recency *66*
proximity *61*
Pygmalion effect *65*
recency effect *66*
reverse halo effect *66*
schemata *62*
script *62*
selective attention *61*
selective exposure *61*
self-awareness *52*
self-concept *51*
self-deprecating strategies *71*
self-destructive beliefs *54*
self-disclosure *56*
self-esteem *54*
self-evaluations *52*
self-fulfilling prophecy *64*
self-handicapping strategies *71*
self-interpretations *52*
self-monitoring strategies *72*
self-serving bias *67*
similarity *61*
uncertainty reduction strategies *68*
unknown self *53*

WORKING WITH THE SELF AND PERCEPTION

3.1 Checking Your Perceptions. Perception checking is best thought of as a state of mind to seek clarification before forming conclusions. Practice your own perception checking; complete the following table by providing a description of how you perceive the incident and how you'd go about seeking confirmation. If you have several possible explanations for the incident, describe each of these in Column 2. In the third column indicate the ways you might go about seeking clarification of your initial impressions—what are your choices for seeking clarification?

Incident	Describe what you perceive and the possible interpretations or meanings	Seek clarification
You've extended an invitation to a classmate to be a Facebook friend but have heard nothing back.		
Your manager at work seems to spend a lot of time with your peers but very little time with you. You're concerned about the impression you're making.		
The person you've been dating for the last several months has stopped calling for a date. The messages have become fewer and less personal.		

3.2 Deciding about Self-Disclosure. Self-disclosure is a complex communication process and is especially important because its potential consequences, both positive and negative, are so significant. Disclose significant information only after mindfully considering the consequences. For any one or two of the following instances of impending self-disclosure, indicate whether you think the person should self-disclose and why. In making your decisions, consider each of the guidelines identified in this chapter.

a. Cathy has fallen in love with another man and wants to end her relationship with Tom, a coworker. She wants to call Tom on the phone, break the engagement, and disclose her new relationship.

b. Gregory plagiarized a term paper in anthropology. He's sorry, especially since the plagiarized paper only earned a grade of C+. He wants to disclose to his instructor and redo the paper.

c. Roberto, a college sophomore, has just discovered he is HIV positive. He wants to tell his parents and his best friends, but fears their rejection. In his Mexican American culture, information like this is rarely disclosed, especially by men. He wants the support of his friends and family and yet doesn't want them to reject him or treat him differently.

3.3 Using Impression Management Strategies. Try formulating impression management strategies for each of the following situations. In your responses, focus on one or two things you would say or do to achieve the stated goals.

- **To be liked.** You're new at work and want your colleagues to like you.
- **To be believed.** You're giving a speech on something you feel deeply about; you want others to believe you.
- **To excuse failure.** You know you're going to fail that midterm and you need a good excuse.
- **To secure help.** You need some computer help on something that would take you hours to do; you can't bear doing it alone.
- **To hide faults.** You don't have as many computer skills as your résumé might indicate and you need to appear to know a great deal.
- **To be followed.** You want members of the group to see you as the leader and, in fact, to elect you group leader.
- **To confirm self-image.** You want your colleagues to see you as a fun (but dedicated) worker.

All communication abounds with such strategies (not all of which are ethical); practicing with these strategies will help you understand the ways in which people (including yourself) manage the impressions they give to others.

3.4 Self-Esteem. Popular wisdom emphasizes the importance of self-esteem. The self-esteem camp, however, has come under attack from critics (for example, Baumeister, Bushman, & Campbell, 2000; Bower, 2001; Bushman & Baumeister, 1998; Coover & Murphy, 2000; Hewitt, 1998). These critics argue that high self-esteem is not necessarily desirable: It does nothing to improve academic performance, it does not predict success, and it may even lead to antisocial (especially aggressive) behavior. On the other hand, it's difficult to imagine how a person would function successfully without positive self-feelings. What do you think about the benefits or liabilities of self-esteem?

3.5 Predictability and Uncertainty. As you and another person develop a closer and more intimate relationship, you generally reduce your uncertainty about each other; you become more predictable to each other. Do you think this higher predictability makes a relationship more stable or less stable? More enjoyable or less enjoyable? Are there certain things about your partner (best friend, lover, or family member) that you are uncertain about, and do you want to reduce this uncertainty? What kinds of messages might you use to accomplish this uncertainty reduction?

3.6 Self-Disclosure. Some research indicates that self-disclosure occurs more quickly and at higher levels of intimacy online than in face-to-face situations (Joinson, 2001; Levine, 2000). In contrast, other research finds that people experience greater closeness and self-disclosure in face-to-face groups than in Internet chat groups (Mallen, Day, & Green, 2003). What has been your experience with self-disclosure in online and face-to-face situations?

3.7 Self-Disclosure and Relationship Maintenance. Research shows that self-disclosure is a significant part of relational maintenance (Craig & Wright, 2012). In what ways have you used (or witnessed being used) self-disclosure to maintain friendship or romantic relationships?

3.8 Your Public Messages. Will knowing that some undergraduate and graduate admissions offices and potential employers may examine your postings on sites such as MySpace or Facebook influence what you write? For example, do you avoid posting opinions that might be viewed negatively by schools or employers? Do you deliberately post items that you want schools or employers to find?

3.9 Online Dating. Online dating seems to be losing its stigma as an activity for introverts and the socially anxious. Why do you think perceptions are changing in the direction of greater acceptance of online relationships? What is your current implicit personality theory of the "online dater"?

3.10 The Gift Economy. In one experiment, three types of "invitations" to use a flower delivery service were offered: Group 1 users were offered $10 to invite friends to use the service; Group 2 users were offered the chance to give a $10 discount to someone they invited, but they received no money themselves; and Group 3 users and invitees were each offered $5. Which group of users do you think sent their friends more invitations? The answer from recent research (Aral, 2013) is that Groups 2 and 3 generated more "sends" than did Group 1. The researcher notes that this conforms to the notion of a "gift economy," where being generous increases ones status. Have you seen examples of this "gift economy" in your own social media experiences?

LogOn! MyCommunicationLab www.mycommunicationlab.com

Throughout this chapter, there are icons that highlight media content for selected topics. Go to **MyCommunicationLab** for additional materials on self and perception, particularly the processes that we use to make judgments of others and that they use to make judgments of us. Here you'll find flashcards to help you learn key communication terms, videos that illustrate a variety of concepts, additional exercises, and discussions to help you continue your study of the self and perception.

4 LISTENING IN HUMAN COMMUNICATION

Listen to **Chapter 4** at **MyCommunicationLab**

CHAPTER TOPICS	CHAPTER OBJECTIVES
In this chapter you'll explore the following major topics:	**After reading this chapter you should be able to:**
THE IMPORTANCE OF LISTENING: TASK AND RELATIONSHIP BENEFITS	4.1 Define *listening* and identify its major benefits
THE LISTENING PROCESS	4.2 Explain the five stages of listening and apply the suggestions for increasing accuracy at each of these stages.
LISTENING BARRIERS	4.3 Describe the four major barriers to effective listening and apply the suggestions for effectiveness in your own listening behavior.
STYLES OF EFFECTIVE LISTENING	4.4 Identify the five styles of listening and listen in the appropriate style for the specific situation.
LISTENING, CULTURE, AND GENDER	4.5 Explain the major cultural and gender differences found in listening and assess their influence on your own communication/listening.

Listening is a survival skill.

There can be little doubt that you listen a great deal. On waking, you listen to the radio or television. On the way to school, you listen to friends, people around you, screeching cars, singing birds, or falling rain. In school, you listen to the instructors, to other students, and to yourself. You listen to friends at lunch and return to class to listen to more instructors. You arrive home and again listen to family and friends. Perhaps you listen to music on your phone, news on the radio or your computer, or dramas and sitcoms on television. All in all, you listen for a good part of your waking day.

Traditionally, listening is concerned with spoken messages (Emmert, 1994; Brownell, 2010; Worthington & Fitch-Hauser, 2012). However, in light of Facebook, Twitter, wikis, and blogs, we need to expand this traditional definition of listening as the receiving and processing of only auditory signals. If posting messages on social media sites is part of human communication (which it surely is), then the reading of these messages must also be part of human communication and most logically a part of listening. **Listening**, then, may be defined as *the process of receiving, understanding, remembering, evaluating, and responding to verbal and/or nonverbal messages.*

In this chapter we will look at the importance of listening, the nature of the listening process, the varied styles of listening you might use in different situations, and some cultural and gender differences in listening. Throughout this chapter, we'll identify ways to avoid the major barriers to listening and provide guidelines for more effective listening.

4.1 THE IMPORTANCE OF LISTENING: TASK AND RELATIONSHIP BENEFITS

Regardless of what you do, listening will prove a crucial communication component and will serve both task and relationship functions. For example, one study concluded that in this era of technological transformation, employees' interpersonal skills are especially significant; workers' advancement will depend on their ability to speak and write effectively, to display proper etiquette, and *to listen attentively*. And in a revealing survey of 40 CEOs of Asian and Western multinational companies, respondents cited a lack of listening skills as *the major shortcoming* of top executives (Witcher, 1999).

It's also interesting to note that the effective listener—to take just a few examples of both task and relationship benefits—is more likely to emerge as group leader, a more effective salesperson, a more attentive and effective health-care worker, and a more effective manager (Castleberry & Shepherd, 1993; Johnson & Bechler, 1998; Kramer, 1997; Lauer, 2003; Levine, 2004; Stein & Bowen, 2003). And medical educators, claiming that doctors are not trained to listen to their patients, have introduced what they call "narrative medicine" to teach doctors how to listen to their patients and to help doctors recognize how their perceptions of their patients are influenced by their own emotions (Smith, 2003; Ubel, 2013).

Another way to appreciate the importance of listening is to consider its many benefits. Here are some, built around the purposes of human communication identified in Chapter 1.

- **Learning.** Listening enables you to acquire knowledge of others, the world, and yourself, so as to avoid problems and make better-informed decisions. For example, hearing Peter tell about his travels to Cuba will help you learn more about Peter and about life in another country. Listening to the difficulties of your sales staff may help you offer more pertinent sales training.
- **Relating.** Through attentive and supportive listening you can gain social acceptance and popularity. Others will increase their liking of you once they see your genuine concern for them.
- **Playing.** Listening can be enjoyable, letting you share pleasurable thoughts and feelings. Really listening to the anecdotes of coworkers will allow you to balance the world of work and the world of play.
- **Helping.** Listening often is vital in efforts to assist others. For example, listening to your child's complaints about her teacher will increase your ability to help your child cope with school and her teacher.
- **Influencing.** Listening can help you change the attitudes and behaviors of others. For example, workers are more likely to follow your advice once they feel you've really listened to their insights and concerns. You're also likely to be more influential when you listen with power, a topic addressed in Table 4.1, on page 80.

4.2 THE LISTENING PROCESS

The process of listening can be described as a series of five overlapping stages: (1) receiving (hearing and attending to the message), (2) understanding (deciphering meaning from the message you hear), (3) remembering (retaining what you hear in memory), (4) evaluating (thinking critically about and judging

TABLE 4.1 LISTENING POWER

In much the same way that you communicate power verbally and nonverbally—topics we'll consider in the next two chapters—you also can communicate your power through listening. Here are a few suggestions on how to listen with power.

Listening Behavior	Powerless	Powerful
Responding	Too little response says you aren't listening; too much response says you aren't listening critically.	Backchanneling cues—head nods and brief oral responses that say you're listening—are especially helpful in communicating power.
Adaptors	**Adaptors**—for example, playing with your hair or clicking a pen—may signal discomfort and hence a lack of power.	The absence of adaptors makes you appear in control of the situation and comfortable in the role of listener.
Posture	Covering your face, chest, or stomach with your hands may be interpreted as signaling defensiveness or vulnerability and hence powerlessness.	Maintaining a posture that is comfortable, that demonstrates attention and a willingness to listen will help to communicate power.
Note Taking	Taking too many or too few notes may communicate a lack of ability to identify what is really important.	Taking a modest amount of notes on information you'll need to refer to later demonstrates competence and power.
Eye Focus	Maintaining a low level of eye contact while talking and a higher level while listening will reduce power.	Maintaining a high level of eye contact while talking but a lower level while listening will increase power.

the message), and (5) responding (answering or giving feedback to the speaker). The process is visualized in Figure 4.1.

Note that the listening process is circular. The responses of person A serve as the stimuli for person B, whose responses in turn serve as the stimuli for person A, and so on. As will become clear in the following discussion of the five stages, listening is not a process of transferring an idea from the mind of a speaker to the mind of a listener. Rather, it is a process in which speaker and listener work together to achieve a common understanding.

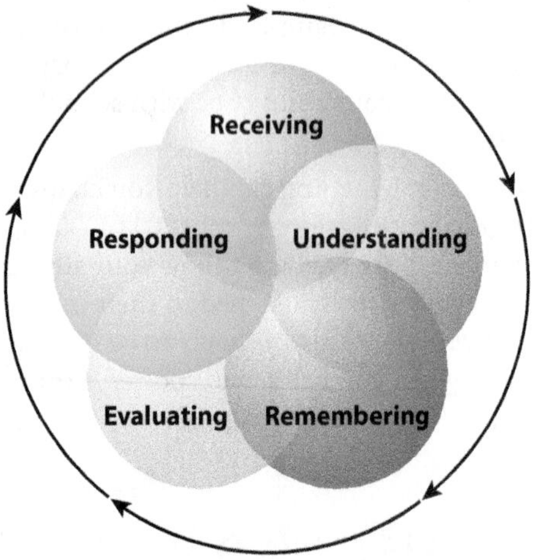

FIGURE 4.1 A Five-Stage Model of the Listening Process

This model, which depicts the various stages involved in listening, draws on a variety of previous models that listening researchers have developed (e.g., Alessandra, 1986; Barker, 1990; Brownell, 2010; Steil, Barker, and Watson, 1983). In what other ways might you visualize the listening process?

As you read this discussion of the five stages of listening, realize that listening can go wrong at any of the five stages. At the same time, you can enhance your listening ability by strengthening the skills needed at each listening stage.

Stage 1: Receiving

Unlike listening, hearing begins and ends with this first stage–receiving. Hearing is something that just happens when you open your ears or when you get within earshot of auditory stimuli.

Listening is quite different. Listening begins, but does not end, with receiving messages the speaker sends. In listening you receive both the verbal and the nonverbal messages–not only the words but also the gestures, facial expressions, variations in volume and rate, and lots more, as you'll discover when we discuss messages in more detail in Chapters 5 and 6. For improved reception:

- **Focus attention** on the speaker's verbal and nonverbal messages, on both what is said and what is not said.

- **Look for feedback** in response to previous messages as well as feedforward (Chapter 1), which can reveal how the speaker would like his or her message viewed.
- **Avoid distractions** in the environment and focus attention on the speaker rather than on what you'll say next.
- **Maintain your role as listener** and avoid interrupting the speaker until he or she is finished.

In this brief discussion of receiving (and in this entire chapter on listening), the unstated assumption is that both individuals can receive auditory signals without difficulty. But for the many people who have hearing impairments, listening presents a variety of problems. Table 4.2, on page 82, provides tips for communication between those with and those without hearing problems.

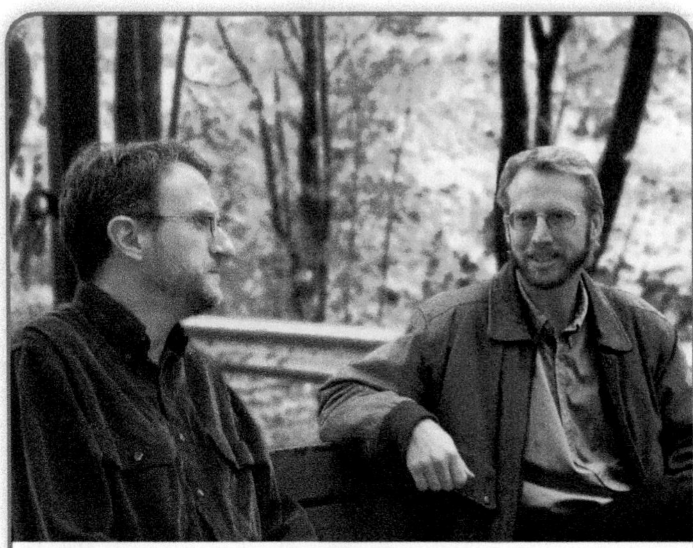

COMMUNICATION CHOICE POINT

LISTENING AVOIDANCE *Your best friend's latest relationship has just broken up, and your friend comes to you in the hope that you'll listen to all the details. This seems to happen about once a week. You're fed up; you're determined not to spend the next three hours listening to this tale of woe.* **What are some of the things you can say to get you out of listening to this boring recital but at the same time not alienate your friend?**

Stage 2: Understanding

Understanding is the stage at which you learn what the speaker means. This understanding must take into consideration both the thoughts that are expressed and the emotional tone that accompanies them—the urgency or the joy or sorrow expressed in the message. For improved understanding:

- **Relate new information** to what you already know.
- **See the speaker's messages** from the speaker's point of view. Avoid judging the message until you've fully understood it—as the speaker intended it.
- **Ask questions** to clarify or to secure additional details or examples if necessary.
- **Rephrase (paraphrase)** the speaker's ideas in your own words.

In addition to these few suggestions, consider the specific situation of listening in the classroom. Table 4.3, on page 83, provides a few suggestions unique to listening for understanding in the classroom.

Stage 3: Remembering

Effective listening depends on remembering. When Joe says his mother is ill, the effective listener remembers this and inquires about her health later in the week.

Perhaps the most important point to understand about memory is that what you remember is not what was said but what you remember was said. Memory for speech is not reproductive; you don't simply reproduce in your memory what the speaker said. Rather, memory is reconstructive; you actually reconstruct the messages you hear into a system that makes sense to you.

If you want to remember what someone says or the names of various people, this information needs to pass from your short-term memory (the memory you use, say, to remember a phone number just long enough to dial it) into long-term memory. Short-term memory is very limited in capacity—you can hold only a small amount of information there. Long-term memory is unlimited. To facilitate the passage of information from short- to long-term memory, here are FOUR suggestions:

- **Focus** your attention on the central ideas. Even in the most casual of conversations, there are central ideas. Fix these in your mind. Repeat these ideas to yourself as you continue to listen. Avoid focusing on minor details that often lead to detours in listening and in conversation.

TABLE 4.2

Between People with and without Hearing Difficulties

TIPS

People with hearing loss differ greatly in their hearing ability: Some are totally deaf and can hear nothing, others have some hearing loss and can hear some sounds, and still others have impaired hearing but can hear most speech. Although people with profound hearing loss can speak, their speech may appear labored and may be less clear than the speech of those with unimpaired hearing. Here are some suggestions for more effective communication between people who hear well and those who have hearing problems.

If you have unimpaired hearing:

Generally	**Specifically**
Set up a comfortable context.	Reduce the distance between yourself and the person with a hearing impairment. Reduce background noise. Make sure the lighting is adequate.
Avoid interference.	Make sure the visual cues from your speech are clearly observable; face the person squarely and avoid smoking, chewing gum, or holding your hand over your mouth.
Speak at an adequate volume.	But avoid shouting, which can distort your speech and may insult the person. Be careful to avoid reducing volume at the ends of your sentences.
Phrase ideas in different ways.	Because some words are easier to lip-read than others, it often helps if you can rephrase your ideas in different words.
Avoid overlapping speech.	In group situations only one person should speak at a time. Similarly, direct your comments to the person with hearing loss himself or herself; don't talk to the person through a third party.
Ask for additional information.	Ask the person if there is anything you can do to make it easier for him or her to understand you.
Don't avoid common terms.	Use terms like *hear*, *listen*, *music*, or *deaf* when they're relevant to the conversation. Trying to avoid these common terms will make your speech sound artificial.
Use nonverbal cues.	Nonverbals can help communicate your meaning; gestures indicating size or location and facial expressions indicating feelings are often helpful.

If you have impaired hearing:

Do your best to eliminate background noise.	Reduce the distance between yourself and the person with a hearing impairment. Reduce background noise. Make sure the lighting is adequate.
Move closer to the speaker if this helps you hear better.	Alert the speaker that this closer distance will help you hear better.
Ask for adjustments.	If you feel the speaker can make adjustments, ask the speaker to repeat a message, to speak more slowly, or to increase volume.
Position yourself for best reception.	If you hear better in one ear than another, position yourself accordingly and, if necessary, clue the speaker in to this fact.
Ask for additional cues.	If necessary, ask the speaker to write down certain information, such as phone numbers or website addresses. Carrying a pad and pencil will prove helpful for this and in the event that you wish to write something down for others.

Sources: These suggestions were drawn from a variety of sources including the Rochester Institute of Technology, the National Technical Institute for the Deaf, the Division of Public Affairs, and Department of Labor websites.

TABLE 4.3 LISTENING IN THE CLASSROOM

In addition to following the general guidelines for listening, here are a few additional suggestions for making your classroom listening more effective. After all, if you're going to spend the time, you might as well spend it efficiently.

General Principle	Specific Strategies
Prepare yourself to listen.	You listen with your eyes as well as your ears, so sit up front where you can see your instructor and any visual aids clearly and comfortably.
Avoid distractions.	Distractions are all around us; try to avoid distractions caused by mental daydreaming as well as physical distractions like your laptop, cell phone, or newspaper.
Pay special attention to the introduction.	The introduction will often contain a preview and will help you outline the lecture. Listen for key words and phrases such as "another reason," "three major causes," and "first." Use these cues to help you outline the lecture.
Take notes in outline form.	Listen for headings and use these as major headings in your outline. When the instructor says, for example, "there are four kinds of noise," you have your heading and you will have a numbered list of four items.
Assume relevance.	Assume what is said is relevant. It may eventually prove irrelevant (unfortunately), but if you listen with the assumption of irrelevancy, you'll never hear anything relevant.
Listen for understanding.	Avoid rehearsing in your own mind your arguments against what the instructor is saying. When you do this, you run the risk of missing additional explanation or qualification.

the•o•ry *noun* statement of explanation, formulation of relationships, reasoned generalization

UNDERSTANDING THEORY AND RESEARCH
Reconstructing Memory

When you remember a message, do you remember it as it was spoken, or do you remember what you think you heard? The common-sense response, of course, would be that you remember what was said. But before accepting this simple explanation, try to memorize the list of 12 words presented below, modeled on an idea from a research study (Glucksberg & Danks, 1975). Don't worry about the order of the words; only the number of words remembered counts. Take about 20 seconds to memorize as many words as possible. Then close the book and write down as many words as you can remember.

dining room	table	milk
cafeteria	shopping	hungry
green beans	steak	saucer
satisfied	knife	menu

Don't read any further until you've tried to memorize and reproduce the list of words.

If you're like most people, you not only remembered a good number of the words on the list, but also "remembered" at least one word that was not on the list: perhaps, *eat, dine, fork,* or some such word relating to the theme of the list. Most people would recall the extra words as being on the list (whether they read the list as you've done here or hear it spoken)—but, as you can see, they're not. What happens is that in remembering you don't simply reproduce the list; you reconstruct it. In this case you gave the list meaning, and part of that meaning included the word *eat* or some related word. Memory for speech, then, is not reproductive—you don't simply reproduce in your memory what the speaker said. Rather, memory is reconstructive: You reconstruct the messages you hear into a system that makes sense to you but, in the process, often remember distorted versions of what was said.

Working with Theories and Research

Log on to your favorite database or search engine and search for articles dealing with false memory. In what types of situations is false memory found? What are some of its implications for communication?

- **Organize** what you hear; summarize the message in a more easily retained form, but take care not to ignore crucial details or qualifications. If you chunk the material into categories, you'll be able to remember more information. For example, if you want to remember 15 or 20 items to buy in the supermarket, you'll remember more if you group them into chunks—say, produce, canned goods, and meats.
- **Unite** the new with the old; relate new information to what you already know. Avoid treating new information as totally apart from all else you know. There's probably some relationship, and if you identify it, you're more like to remember the new material.
- **Repeat** names and key concepts to yourself or, if appropriate, aloud. By repeating the names or key concepts, you in effect rehearse these names and concepts, and as a result they'll be easier to learn and remember. If you're introduced to Alice, you'll stand a better chance of remembering her name if you say, "Hi, Alice" than if you say just "Hi."

Stage 4: Evaluating

Evaluating consists of judging messages in some way. At times, you may try to evaluate the speaker's underlying intent. Often this evaluation process goes on without much conscious thought. For example, Elaine tells you that she is up for a promotion and is really excited about it. You may then try to judge her intention. Does she want you to use your influence with the company president? Is she preoccupied with her accomplishment and thus telling everyone about it? Is she looking for a pat on the back? Generally, if you know the person well, you'll be able to identify the intention and therefore be able to respond appropriately.

In other situations, evaluation is more in the nature of critical analysis. For example, in listening to proposals advanced in a business meeting, you will at this stage evaluate them. Is there evidence to show that these proposals are practical and will increase productivity? Is there contradictory evidence? Are there alternative proposals that would be more practical and more productive?

In evaluating, try to:

- **Resist evaluation** until you fully understand the speaker's point of view.
- **Assume that the speaker is a person of goodwill,** and give the speaker the benefit of any doubt by asking for clarification on issues that you feel you must object to (are there any other reasons for accepting this new proposal?).
- **Distinguish facts from inferences** (see Chapter 5), opinions, and personal interpretations by the speaker.
- **Identify any biases, self-interests, or prejudices** that may lead the speaker to slant unfairly what is presented.

Stage 5: Responding

Responding occurs in two phases: (1) responses you make while the speaker is talking and (2) responses you make after the speaker has stopped talking. These responses are feedback—information that you send back to the speaker and that tells the speaker how you feel and think about his or her messages. Responses made while the speaker is talking should be supportive and should acknowledge that you're listening. These include what researchers on nonverbal communication call **backchanneling cues:** "I see," "yes," "uh-huh," and similar signals that let the speaker know you're attending to the message.

Responses made after the speaker has stopped talking are generally more elaborate and might include expressing empathy ("I know how you must feel"), asking for clarification ("Do you mean that this new health plan is to replace the old one, or will it just be a supplement?"), challenging ("I think your evidence is weak here"), and agreeing ("You're absolutely right on this, and I'll support your proposal when it comes up for a vote"). For effective responding:

- **Be supportive** of the speaker throughout the speaker's talk by using and varying backchanneling cues; using only one backchanneling cue—for example, saying "uh-huh" throughout—may make it appear that you're not really listening.
- **Express support** for the speaker in your final responses.
- **Be honest;** the speaker has a right to expect honest responses, even if these express anger or disagreement.
- **State your thoughts and feelings** as your own, using I-messages. For example, say "I think the new proposal will entail greater expense than you outlined" rather than "Everyone will object to the plan for costing too much."

the•o•ry *noun* statement of explanation, formulation of relationships, reasoned generalization

UNDERSTANDING THEORY AND RESEARCH
Cues to Lying

In listening, you normally assume that the speaker is telling the truth and seldom even ask yourself if the speaker is lying. When you do wonder about a speaker's truthfulness, research shows, it may be because the speaker exhibits behaviors that often accompany lying. As you review these behaviors, ask yourself if you use these cues in making assumptions about whether or not people are telling the truth. Be careful that you don't fall into the trap of thinking that just because someone emits these cues, he or she is therefore lying; these cues are often used by truth-tellers as well and are not 100 percent reliable in indicating lying. In fact, in one study participants who held stereotypical views of how liars behave (for example, liars don't look at you or liars fidget) were less effective in detecting lying than were those who did not hold such beliefs (Vrij & Mann, 2001).

From a combination of research studies, the following behaviors were found to most often accompany lying (Al-Simadi, 2000; Andersen, 2004; Burgoon, 2005; Burgoon & Bacue, 2003; O'Hair, Cody, Goss, & Krayer, 1988; DePaulo et al., 2003; Knapp, 2008; Knapp & Hall, 2010; Leathers & Eaves, 2008; Bond & Atoum, 2000).

- **Liars hold back.** They speak more slowly (perhaps to monitor what they're saying), take longer to respond to questions (again, perhaps monitoring their messages), and generally give less information and elaboration.
- **Liars leak.** Very slight facial and eye movements (what we referred to earlier as micromomentary movements) may reveal the person's real feelings, a process referred to as leakage. Often this is the result of what has come to be called "duping delight"—the pleasure you get when you feel you're putting over a lie. Here you may leak your lying through slight movements in your lips or eyes.
- **Liars make less sense.** Liars' messages contain more discrepancies, more inconsistencies.
- **Liars give a more negative impression.** Generally, liars are seen as less willing to be cooperative, smile less than truth-tellers, and are more defensive.
- **Liars are tense.** The tension may be revealed by their higher-pitched voices and their excessive body movements.
- **Liars exhibit greater pupil dilation, more eyeblinks, and more gaze aversion.**
- **Liars speak with a higher vocal pitch**. Their voices often sound as if they are under stress.
- **Liars make more errors and use more hesitations in their speech**. They pause more and for longer periods of time;
- **Liars make more hand, leg, and foot movements.**
- **Liars engage in more self-touching movements.** For example, liars touch their face or hair more and engage in more object touching, for example, playing with a coffee cup or pen.

In detecting lying be especially careful that you formulate any conclusions with a clear understanding that you can be wrong and that accusations of lying (especially when untrue but even when true) can often damage a relationship to the point where it's beyond repair.

Working with Theories and Research

Can you recall a situation in which you made the assumption that someone was lying on the basis of such cues (or others)? What happened? Should you want to learn more about lying, search for such terms as "lying," "deception," "poker tells," and "falsehood." It's a fascinating subject of study.

Table 4.4, on page 86, identifies some types of difficult listeners—listeners who don't follow the suggestions for each of the five listening stages—and their problem-causing ways of responding, and some suggestions for dealing with them as both listener and speaker, as both speaker and listener are responsible for effective listening.

4.3 LISTENING BARRIERS

In addition to practicing the various skills for each stage of listening, consider some of the common barriers to listening. Here are just four such barriers

Distractions: Physical and Mental

Physical barriers might include, for example, hearing impairment, a noisy environment, or loud music. Multi-tasking (watching TV and listening to

TABLE 4.4 SOME PROBLEM-CAUSING WAYS OF RESPONDING IN LISTENING

Review this table and try to see if it includes some of your own listening behaviors.

Problem-Causing Responses	Corrective Strategies
The **static listener** gives no feedback, remains relatively motionless, and reveals no expression.	Give feedback as appropriate, smile, nod, and otherwise appropriately respond to the content and feeling of the message.
The **monotonous feedback giver** seems responsive, but the responses never vary, regardless of what is said.	Give varied feedback that is relevant to the conversation.
The **overly expressive listener** reacts to just about everything with extreme responses.	React in a tone consistent with the speaker's message.
The **eye avoider** looks all around the room and at others but never at you.	Look at the speaker; don't stare but make the speaker your eyes' main focus.
The **preoccupied listener** listens to other things at the same time, often with headphones turned up so loud that it interferes with the speaker's thinking.	Show the speaker that he or she is your primary focus; shut down the smartphone and the television; turn away from the computer screen.
The **waiting listener** listens for a cue to take over the speaking turn.	Hear the speaker out; refrain from giving cues that you want to speak while the speaker is in the middle of saying something.
The **thought-completing listener** listens a little and then finishes the speaker's thought.	Allow the speaker to complete his or her thoughts. Completing someone's thoughts often communicates that you find the speaker too predictable.
The **critical listener** evaluates everything you say, often negatively.	Avoid criticism, unless the situation calls for it, and always stress the positive.
The **advising listener** gives advice at the first mention of a problem or decision.	Avoid giving advice unless specifically asked and resist what is supposedly the male tendency to solve problems.
The **never-ending listener** just wants the speaker to keep talking, often long after the speaker has said what he or she wants to say.	Exchange speaking and listening roles frequently; they are each best when relatively short. Avoid unnecessarily prolonging conversations.

COMMUNICATION CHOICE POINT

LISTENING CUES *Friends have told you that people don't address comments directly to you because you don't give listening cues to let the other person know that you're listening and interested.* **What are some of the things you can do to help change this perception?**

someone) with the aim of being supportive, say, simply doesn't work. As both listener and speaker, try to remove whatever physical barriers can be removed; for those that you can't remove, adjust your listening and speaking to lessen the effects as much as possible. As a listener, focus on the speaker; you can attend to the room and the other people later.

Mental distractions are in many ways similar to physical distractions; they get in the way of focused listening. These barriers are often seen when you're thinking about your upcoming Saturday night date or becoming too emotional to think (and listen) clearly. In listening, recognize that you can think about your date later. In speaking, make what you say compelling and relevant to the listener.

Explore the Exercise "Sequential Listening" at MyCommunicationLab

Biases and Prejudices

Biases and prejudices against groups or individuals who are members of such groups will invariably distort listening. For example, a gender bias that assumes that only one sex has anything useful to say about certain topics will likely distort incoming messages that contradict this bias. Be willing to subject your biases and prejudices to contradictory information; after all if they're worth having, they should stand up to differences of opinion. When as a speaker you feel your listener may have certain prejudices, ask for a suspension of bias: "I know you don't think women are knowledgeable about sports, but just hear me out about why I think the team's offense isn't working..."

Another type of bias is closed mindedness, which is seen, for example, in the person who refuses to hear any feminist argument or anything about gay marriage. As a listener, assume that what the speaker is saying will be useful in some way. As a speaker, anticipate that many people are closed minded on a variety of issues and it often helps to simply ask for openness: "I know this is contrary to what many people think, but let's look at it logically..."

Lack of Appropriate Focus

Focusing on what a person is saying is obviously necessary for effective listening. And yet, there are many influences that can lead you astray. For example, listeners often get lost because they focus on irrelevancies, say, on an especially vivid example that conjures up old memories. Try not to get detoured from the main idea; don't get hung up on unimportant details. Try to repeat the idea to yourself and see the details in relation to this main concept. As a speaker, try to avoid language or examples that may divert attention from your main idea.

At times you might listen only for information with an obvious relevance to you. This type of listening prevents you from expanding your horizons; it's quite possible that information that you originally thought irrelevant will eventually prove helpful. As a speaker, be sure to make what you say relevant to your specific listener.

Another misplaced focus is often on the responses a listener is going to make while the speaker is still speaking. Anticipating how you're going to respond or what you're going to say (and even interrupting the speaker) prevents you from hearing the message in full. Instead, make a mental note of something and then get back to listening. As a speaker, when you feel someone is preparing to argue with you, ask them to hear you out: "I know you disagree with this, but let me finish and we'll get back to that."

Premature Judgment

Perhaps the most obvious form of premature judgment is assuming you know what the speaker is going to say and that there's no need to really listen. Let the speaker say what he or she is going to say before you decide that you already know it. As a speaker, it's often wise to assume that listeners will do exactly this, so it may be helpful to make clear that what you're saying will be unexpected.

A common listener reaction is to draw conclusions or judgments on incomplete evidence. Sometimes, listeners will stop listening after hearing, for example, an attitude they disagree with or some sexist or culturally insensitive remark. Instead, this is a situation that calls for especially concentrated listening so that you don't rush to judgment. Instead, wait for the evidence or argument; avoid making judgments before you gather all the information. Listen first; judge second. As a speaker, be aware of this tendency, and when you feel this is happening, ask for a suspension of judgment. A simple "Hear me out" is often sufficient.

Explore the Exercise "Your Listening Barriers" at MyCommunicationLab

4.4 STYLES OF EFFECTIVE LISTENING

Before reading about the styles of listening, examine your own listening habits and tendencies by responding to the following statements with the following scale: 1 = always, 2 = frequently, 3 = sometimes, 4 = seldom, and 5 = never.

_____ **1.** I listen actively, communicate acceptance of the speaker, and prompt the speaker to further explore his or her thoughts.

_____ **2.** I listen to what the speaker is saying and feeling; I try to feel what the speaker feels.

_____ **3.** I listen without judging the speaker.

_____ **4.** I listen to the literal meanings that a speaker communicates; I don't look too deeply into hidden meanings.

_____ **5.** I listen without active involvement; I generally remain silent and take in what the other person is saying.

_____ **6.** I never interrupt the speaker.

_____ **7.** I listen objectively; I focus on the logic of the ideas rather than on the emotional meaning of the message.

_____ **8.** I listen critically, evaluating the speaker and what the speaker is saying.

_____ **9.** I look for the hidden meanings: the meanings that are revealed by subtle verbal or nonverbal cues.

_____ **10.** I listen politely no matter who is speaking.

These statements focus on the ways of listening discussed in this chapter. All of these ways are appropriate at some times, but not at other times. It depends. So the only responses that are really inappropriate are "always" and "never." Effective listening is listening that is tailored to the specific communication situation. Listening is situational; the type of listening that is appropriate will vary with the situation, and each situation will call for a somewhat different combination of listening styles. A case in point is in listening to the emotions of others (see Table 4.5).

The art of effective listening is in making appropriate choices along the following five dimensions: (1) empathic and objective listening, (2) nonjudgmental and critical listening, (3) surface and depth listening, (4) polite and impolite listening, and (5) active and inactive listening. These dimensions exist on a continuum with, say, extremely empathic at one end and extremely objective at the other end. Most, if not all, listening exists somewhere between these extremes. Yet, they'll be an emphasis toward one side or the other depending on the specifics of the communication situation. Let's take a look at each of these dimensions.

Explore the Concept "Listening" at MyCommunicationLab

Empathic and Objective Listening

To understand what a person means and feels, listen with **empathy** (Rogers, 1970; Rogers & Farson, 1981). To empathize with others is to feel with them, to see

TABLE 4.5 LISTENING TO EMOTIONS (10 WAYS)

Situational listening is well illustrated in listening to emotions; your listening style will surely differ depending on the nature of the emotions being expressed. Here are a few general guidelines that you'll need to adapt to the uniqueness of each situation.

General Principles	Specific Strategies
Confirm the other person and his or her emotions.	A simple "You must be worried about finding another position" confirms the feelings of a person who has just lost a job.
Show interest by encouraging the person to explore his or her feelings.	Use simple encouragers like "I see" or "I understand." Or ask questions to let the speaker know that you're listening/interested.
Give the person permission to express feelings.	Let the person know that it's acceptable and okay with you if she or he expresses feelings in the ways that feel most comfortable—for example, by crying or talking about old times.
Don't try to force the person to talk about experiences or feelings she or he may not be willing to share.	A simple "Would you like to talk about it?" will cue the person that you're listening but not forcing him or her to talk.
Be especially sensitive to leave-taking cues. Don't overstay your welcome.	Notice especially comments like "It's getting late," a glance at the clock, or a polite yawn.
Empathize.	See the situation from the point of view of the speaker. Avoid comments such as "Don't cry; it wasn't worth it," which can be interpreted as a rejection of the person's feelings.
Focus on the other person; don't refocus the conversation on yourself.	Instead, provide a supportive atmosphere that encourages the person to express her or his feelings.
Don't try to solve the other person's problems.	Listening to another's emotions comes first; offer solutions only when asked.
Avoid trying to focus on the bright side.	Avoid expressions such as "You're lucky you have some vision left" or "It is better this way; Pat was suffering so much."
Avoid interrupting.	Emotional expression frequently involves extra-long pauses so wait before jumping in.

the world as they see it, to feel what they feel. Empathy will enable you to understand other people's meanings, and it will also enhance your relationships (Barrett & Godfrey, 1988; Snyder, 1992).

Empathy is best understood as having two distinct parts: thinking empathy and feeling empathy (Bellafiore, 2005). In *thinking empathy* you express an understanding of what the person means. For example, when you paraphrase someone's comment, showing that you understand the meaning the person is trying to communicate, you're communicating thinking empathy. The second part is *feeling empathy;* here you express your feeling of what the other person is feeling. You demonstrate a similarity between what you're feeling and what the other person is feeling. Often you'll respond with both thinking and feeling empathy in the same brief response; for example, when a friend tells you of problems at home, you may respond by saying, for example, "Your problems at home do seem to be getting worse. I can imagine how you feel so angry at times."

Empathic listening is the preferred mode of responding in most communication situations, but there are times when you need to go beyond it to measure meanings and feelings against some objective reality. It's important to listen to Peter tell you how the entire world hates him and to understand how Peter feels and why he feels this way. But then you need to look more objectively at Peter and perhaps see the paranoia or the self-hatred behind his complaints. Sometimes, in other words, you have to put your empathic responses aside and listen with objectivity and detachment.

In adjusting your empathic and objective listening focus, keep the following recommendations in mind:

- **Punctuate from the speaker's point of view** (Chapter 1). If you want to understand the speaker's perspective, see the sequence of events as the speaker does, and try to figure out how this can influence what the speaker says and does. Keep your focus (your thoughts and your messages) on the speaker.
- **Seek to understand both thoughts and feelings.** Don't consider your listening task finished until you've understood what the speaker is feeling as well as what he or she is thinking.
- **Avoid "offensive listening,"** the tendency to listen to bits and pieces of information that will enable you to attack the speaker or find fault with something the speaker has said.
- **Strive especially to be objective in listening to friends and foes alike.** Be aware that your attitudes may lead you to distort messages—for example, to block out positive messages about a foe or negative messages about a friend.
- **Avoid trying to solve the problem** or even giving advice when trying to achieve empathy. Being empathic is hard enough, and at this point it's better to communicate your support and understanding rather than your evaluation of the situation.
- **Encourage the speaker to explore his or her feelings further** by demonstrating a willingness to listen and an interest in what the speaker is saying.

Explore at MyCommunicationLab Activity: "Listening with Empathy"

Nonjudgmental and Critical Listening

Effective listening includes both nonjudgmental and critical responses. Listen nonjudgmentally (with an open mind and with a view toward understanding) and listen critically (with a view toward making some kind of evaluation or judgment). Listen first for understanding; only when you understand should you be willing to evaluate or judge the messages.

Listening with an open mind will help you understand messages better; listening with a critical mind will help you analyze and evaluate the messages. In adjusting your nonjudgmental and critical listening, focus on the following guidelines:

- **Keep an open mind.** Avoid prejudging. Delay your judgments until you fully understand the intention and the content the speaker is communicating. Avoid both positive and negative evaluation until you have a reasonably complete understanding.
- **Avoid filtering out or oversimplifying difficult or complex messages.** Similarly, avoid filtering out undesirable messages. Clearly, you don't want to hear that something you believe in is untrue, that people you care for are unkind, or that ideals you hold are self-destructive. Yet it's important that you reexamine your beliefs by listening to such messages.
- **Recognize your own biases.** These may interfere with accurate listening and cause you to distort message reception through the process of **assimilation**—the tendency to integrate and interpret what you hear or think you hear to conform to your own biases, prejudices, and expectations. For example, are your ethnic, national, or religious biases preventing you from appreciating a speaker's point of view?
- **Avoid uncritical listening when you need to make evaluations and judgments.** Recognize

and resist the normal tendency to sharpen—a process in which one or two aspects of a message become highlighted, emphasized, and perhaps embellished. Often the concepts that are sharpened are incidental remarks that somehow stand out from the rest of the message.

- **Recognize fallacies**—ways of using language to subvert instead of clarify truth and accuracy—and don't be persuaded by their pseudo-logic. Here are just a few types of words to which you'd want to give special critical listening:
    - **Weasel words.** These are terms whose meanings are slippery and difficult to pin down (Hayakawa & Hayakawa, 1989). Good examples can be easily found in commercials such as those claiming Medicine A works "better" than Medicine B but failing to specify how much or in what respect Medicine A performs better. It's quite possible that Medicine A performs better in one respect but less effectively according to nine other measures. Other weasel words are *help*, *virtually*, *as much as*, *like* (as in "it will make you feel like new"), and *more economical*. Ask yourself, "Exactly what is being claimed?" For example, "What does 'may reduce cholesterol' mean? What exactly is being asserted?"
    - **Euphemisms.** These terms make the negative and unpleasant appear positive and appealing as in an executive's reference to the firing of 200 workers as "downsizing" or "reallocation of resources." Often euphemisms take the form of inflated language designed to make the mundane seem extraordinary, the common seem exotic ("the vacation of a lifetime," "unsurpassed vistas"). Don't let words get in the way of accurate firsthand perception.
    - **Jargon.** This is the specialized language of a professional class, the language of the computer hacker, the psychologist, or the advertiser. When used to intimidate or impress, as when used with people who aren't members of the profession, jargon prevents meaningful communication. Don't be intimidated by jargon; ask questions when you don't understand.
    - **Gobbledygook.** This is overly complex language that overwhelms the listener instead of communicating meaning and usually consists of extra-long sentences, complex grammatical constructions, and rare or unfamiliar words. Some people just normally speak in complex language. But others use complexity to confuse and mislead. Ask for simplification when appropriate.

COMMUNICATION CHOICE POINT

EMPATHIC LISTENING *Your neighbors, who've avoided work all their lives and lived off unfairly obtained government disability payments, have just won the lottery for $236 million. They want you to share their joy and invite you over to help them celebrate.* **What are some of the things you can do to strengthen your ability to empathize with these people? What might you say to show empathic listening?**

Surface and Depth Listening

In Shakespeare's *Julius Caesar,* Marc Antony, in giving the funeral oration for Caesar, says: "I come to bury Caesar, not to praise him. / The evil that men do lives after them; / The good is oft interred with their bones." And later: "For Brutus is an honourable man; / So are they all, all honourable men." But if we listen beyond the surface of Marc Anthony's words, we can see that he does indeed come to praise Caesar and to convince the crowd that Brutus was dishonorable—despite the fact that at first glance his words seem to say quite the opposite.

In most messages there's an obvious meaning that you can derive from a literal reading of the words and sentences. But there's often another level of meaning. Sometimes, as in these famous lines from *Julius Caesar,* the deeper level is the opposite of the literal meaning. At other times it seems totally unrelated. In reality, most messages have more than one level of meaning. For example, suppose Carol asks you how you like her new haircut. On one level, the meaning is clear: Do you like the haircut? But there's also another, perhaps a more important level: Carol is asking you to say something positive about her appearance. In the same way, the parent who complains about working hard at the office or in the home may, on a deeper level, be asking for an expression of appreciation.

To appreciate these other meanings, engage in depth listening. If you respond only to the surface-level communication (the literal meaning), you miss the opportunity to make meaningful contact with the other person's feelings and needs. If you say to the parent, "You're always complaining. I bet you really love working so hard," you fail to respond to the call for understanding and appreciation. In regulating your surface and depth listening, consider the following guidelines:

- **Focus on both verbal and nonverbal messages.** Recognize both consistent and inconsistent "packages" of messages, and use these as guides for drawing inferences about the speaker's meaning. Ask questions when in doubt. Listen also to what is omitted. Remember that speakers communicate by what they leave out as well as by what they include.
- **Listen for both content and relational messages.** The student who constantly challenges the instructor is, on one level, communicating disagreement over content. However, on another level—the relationship level—the student may be voicing objections to the instructor's authority or authoritarianism. The instructor needs to listen and respond to both types of messages.
- **Make special note of statements that refer back to the speaker.** Remember that people inevitably talk about themselves. Whatever a person says is, in part, a function of who that person is. Attend carefully to those personal, self-reference messages.
- **Don't disregard the literal meaning of messages.** Balance your listening between surface and the underlying meanings. Respond to the different levels of meaning in the messages of others, as you would like others to respond to yours—sensitively but not obsessively, readily but not over-ambitiously.

Polite and Impolite Listening

Politeness is often thought of as the exclusive function of the speaker, as solely an encoding or sending function. But politeness (or impoliteness) may also be signaled through listening (Fukushima, 2000).

me•di•a lit•er•a•cy *noun* ability to understand, interact with, and create media messages

EXPANDING MEDIA LITERACY

Media Users Construct Meaning

Much as you reconstruct in your memory messages that you hear, you naturally reconstruct media messages—messages from a well-liked media personality will be given more weight and more credibility than will messages from a personality you don't like and don't respect.

The meaning that you get from the media messages will be somewhat different from the meaning that any other person gets. For example, the meaning that you derive from a television sitcom will depend on your values, beliefs, experiences, cultural training, and media literacy. The importance you place on a news story may be influenced by your culture, your interests, or your personal acquaintance with the news makers. As pointed out in the previous Media Literacy box (page 63) the media construct messages to give us the meanings they want us to have—that Brand X is better than Brand Y, for example. Often, they do exactly that; they're generally successful in constructing messages from which the viewer will construct the very meanings the media want.

Recall the previous discussion of selective attention and selective exposure in Chapter 3 (page 61). You attend to certain media and to certain media stories and not to others; you expose yourself to certain media and not to others. We each filter the media messages we receive; we filter out the messages that contradict our religious or political beliefs and we open the gate to all the messages that support our beliefs. We are our own gatekeepers. Not surprisingly, the media are also gatekeepers, a process examined in Media Literacy, Chapter 17.

Becoming conscious of the way you use the media is crucial to your gaining control over media messages. Become aware of the types of information you seek out and the types that you filter out. Consider if there is information that you internalize without any real analysis. Most important, ask yourself if your filtering process is productive for you. That is, does it help you achieve your goals?

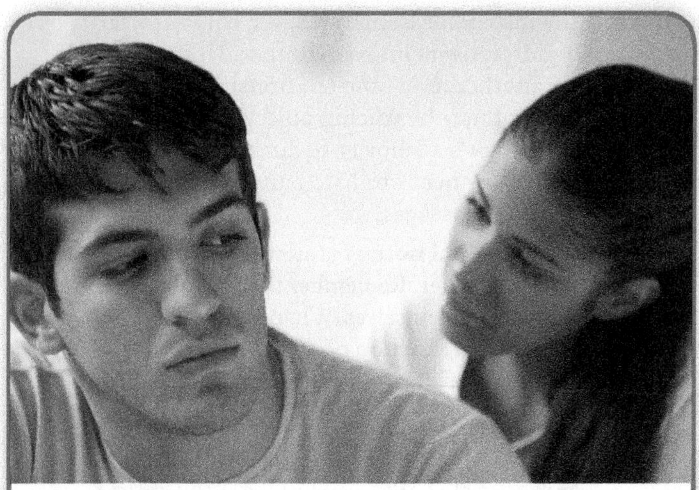

COMMUNICATION CHOICE POINT

DEALING WITH SADNESS AND JOY *The parents of your romantic partner (and best friend) were recently killed in a car accident. And now your partner, who has had many difficult financial times, will inherit a large estate.* **What are some of the things you can say to your partner at this time? What would you say?**

Of course, there are times when you would not want to listen politely (for example, if someone is being verbally abusive or condescending or using racist or sexist language). In these cases you might want to show your disapproval by showing that you're not even listening. But most often you'll want to listen politely and you'll want to express this politeness through your listening behavior. Here are a few suggestions for demonstrating that you are in fact listening politely. As you read these you'll notice that these are strategies designed to be supportive of the speaker's positive and negative face needs:

- **Avoid interrupting the speaker.** Avoid trying to take over the speaker's turn. Avoid changing the topic. If you must say something in response to something the speaker said and can't wait until he or she finishes, then say it as briefly as possible and pass the speaker's turn back to the speaker.
- **Give supportive listening cues.** These might include nodding your head, giving minimal verbal responses such as "I see" or "yes, it's true," or moving closer to the speaker. Listen in a way that demonstrates that what the speaker is saying is important. In some cultures, polite listening cues must be cues of agreement (Japanese culture is often used as an example); in other cultures, polite listening cues are attentiveness and support rather than cues of agreement (much of U.S. culture is an example).
- **Show empathy with the speaker.** Demonstrate that you understand and feel the speaker's thoughts and feelings by giving responses that show this level of understanding—smiling or cringing or otherwise echoing the feelings of the speaker. If you echo the speaker's nonverbal expressions, your behavior is likely to be seen as empathic.
- **Maintain eye contact.** In much of the United States this is perhaps the single most important rule. If you don't maintain eye contact when someone is talking to you, then you'll appear to be not listening and definitely not listening politely. This rule, however, does not hold in all cultures. In some Latin and Asian cultures, polite listening would consist of looking down and avoiding direct eye contact when, for example, listening to a superior or much older person.
- **Give positive feedback.** Throughout the listening encounter positive feedback will be seen as polite and negative feedback as impolite. If you must give negative feedback, then do so in a way that does not attack the person; for example, first mention areas of agreement or what you liked about what the person said and stress your good intentions. And, most important, do it in private. Public criticism is especially threatening and will surely be seen as a personal attack.

A somewhat different slant on politeness and listening can be seen in "forcing" people to listen when they don't want to. Generally, the polite advice is to be sensitive to when the other person wants to leave and to stop asking the person to continue listening. Closely related to this is the "forced" listening that many cell phone users impose on others, a topic addressed in Table 4.6.

Explore at MyCommunicationLab **Profile:** "Listening Preference Profile"

Active and Inactive Listening

One of the most important communication skills you can learn is active listening. Consider the following interaction. You say: "I can't believe I have to redo this entire budget report. I really worked hard on this project, and now I have to do it all over again." To this, you get three different responses.

Andy: That's not so bad; most people find they have to redo their first reports. That's the norm here.

TABLE 4.6 POLITENESS AND THE SMARTPHONE

The ubiquity of the smartphone has led to enormous increases in telephone communication and texting, but it has also created problems, many of which are problems of politeness. Because much smartphone use occurs in public spaces, people often are forced to listen to conversations that don't involve them.

General Rule	Specifics	Adjustments
Avoid using cell phones where inappropriate.	Especially avoid calling in restaurants, hospitals, theaters, museums, commuter buses or trains, and the classroom.	If you must make or take a call when in these various situations, try to move to a less public area.
Silence your cell phone.	Put your phone on vibrate mode, or let your voicemail answer and take a message when your call might interfere with others.	When you can't avoid taking a call, speak as quietly as possible and as briefly as possible.
Avoid unwanted photo-taking.	Don't take pictures of people who aren't posing for you, and erase photos if the person you photographed requests it.	Of course, if there's an accident or a robbery, you may want to photograph the events.
Avoid extended talking when your reception is weak.	Talking on your cell on a crowded street will probably result in poor reception, which is annoying to the other person.	In an emergency, caution trumps politeness.
Consider the other person.	It's easy to assume that when you have nothing better to do, the person you're calling also has nothing better to do.	As with any phone call, it's wise to ask if this is a good time to call—a strategy that helps maintain the autonomy (negative face) of the person you're calling.

Connie: You should be pleased that all you have to do is a simple rewrite. Peggy and Michael both had to completely redo their entire projects.

Greg: You have to rewrite that report you've worked on for the last three weeks? You sound really angry and frustrated.

All three listeners are probably trying to make you feel better. But they go about it in very different ways—and surely with very different results. Andy tries to lessen the significance of the rewrite. This well-intended and extremely common response does little to promote meaningful communication and understanding. Connie tries to give the situation a positive spin. In their responses, however, both Andy and Connie are also suggesting that you should not be feeling the way you do; they're saying that your feelings are not legitimate and should be replaced with more logical feelings.

Greg's response, however, is different from the others. Greg uses active listening. Active listening owes its development to Thomas Gordon (1975), who made it a cornerstone of his P.E.T. (parent effectiveness training) technique. **Active listening** is a process of sending back to the speaker what you as a listener think the speaker meant—both in content and in feelings. Active listening, then, is not merely repeating the speaker's exact words, but rather putting together into some meaningful whole your understanding of the speaker's total message. And, incidentally, when combined with empathic listening, it proves the most effective mode for success as a salesperson (Comer & Drollinger, 1999).

Active listening helps you check your understanding of what the speaker said and, more importantly, of what he or she meant. Reflecting back perceived meanings to the speaker gives the speaker an opportunity to offer clarification and to correct any misunderstandings. Active listening also lets the speaker know that you acknowledge and accept his or her feelings. In the sample responses given above, Greg listened actively and reflected back what he thought you meant while accepting what you were feeling. Note too that he also explicitly identified the feelings ("You sound angry and frustrated"), allowing you the opportunity to correct his interpretation. Still another function of active listening is that it stimulates the speaker to explore feelings and thoughts. Greg's response encourages you to elaborate on your feelings and perhaps to understand them better as you talk through them.

Three simple techniques may help you master the process of active listening: paraphrasing the speaker's meaning, expressing understanding, and asking questions.

- **Paraphrase the speaker's meaning.** Stating in your own words what you think the speaker means and feels helps ensure understanding and demonstrates your interest. Paraphrasing gives the speaker a chance to extend what was originally said. In paraphrasing, be objective; be especially careful not to lead the speaker in the direction you think he or she should go. Also, don't overdo paraphrasing. Paraphrase when you feel there's a chance for misunderstanding or when you want to express support for the other person and keep the conversation going.

Explore the Exercise "Paraphrasing to Ensure Understanding" at MyCommunicationLab

- **Express understanding of the speaker's feelings.** In addition to paraphrasing the content, echo the feelings the speaker expressed or implied ("You must have felt horrible"). This expression of feelings will help you further check your perception of the speaker's feelings and will allow the speaker to see his or her feelings more objectively (especially helpful when they're feelings of anger, hurt, or depression) and the opportunity to elaborate on these feelings.
- **Ask questions.** Asking questions ensures your own understanding of the speaker's thoughts and feelings and secures additional information ("How did you feel when you read your job appraisal report?"). Ask questions to provide just enough stimulation and support so that the speaker feels he or she can elaborate on these thoughts and feelings.

A summary of these listening choices appears in Table 4.7.

Watch the Video "Adapting to Serve a Client" at MyCommunicationLab

4.5 LISTENING, CULTURE, AND GENDER

Listening is difficult, in part, because of the inevitable differences in the communication systems between speaker and listener. Because each person has had a unique set of experiences, each person's communication and meaning system is going to be different from every other person's. When speaker and listener come from different cultures or are of different genders, the differences and their effects are naturally so much greater. Let's look first at culture.

Culture and Listening

In a global environment in which people from very different cultures work together, it's especially important to understand the ways in which cultural differences can influence listening. Four of these listening influences include: (1) language and speech, (2) nonverbal behaviors, (3) feedback, and (4) credibility.

TABLE 4.7

In A Nutshell Summary of Listening Style Choices

Here is a summary of the listening choices you normally have available; the appropriate mode will vary with the situation, the context, the participants, the goal of the interaction, and a host of factors considered throughout this text.

Choice A	Choice B
Empathic—generally the preferred mode for people in close relationships	Objective—to listen dispassionately and more as a scientist than a friend
Nonjudgmental—useful in expressing supportiveness	Critical—essential when decisions need to be made or when alternative courses of action need to be evaluated
Surface—useful for initially surveying your various options	Depth—when you really want to know what the person is thinking and feeling
Polite listening-makes the individual feel important and in control of his or her own behavior	Impolite listening—when you want to turn people off and offend them
Active listening—useful for checking your perceptions and expressive support	Inactive listening—rarely worth even the little effort expended

Language and Speech

Even when speaker and listener speak the same language, they speak it with different meanings and different accents. No two speakers speak exactly the same language. Speakers of the same language will, at the very least, have different meanings for the same terms because they have had different experiences.

Speakers and listeners who have different native languages and who may have learned English as a second language will have even greater differences in meaning. Translations are never precise and never fully capture the meaning in the other language. If your meaning for the word *house* was learned in a culture in which everyone lived in their own house with lots of land around it, then talking about houses with someone whose meaning was learned in a neighborhood of high-rise tenements is going to be difficult. Although you'll each hear the same word, the meanings you'll each develop will be drastically different. In adjusting your listening—especially in an intercultural setting—understand that the speaker's meanings may be very different from yours even though you're speaking the same language.

Watch the **Video** "American Spoken Here" at **MyCommunicationLab**

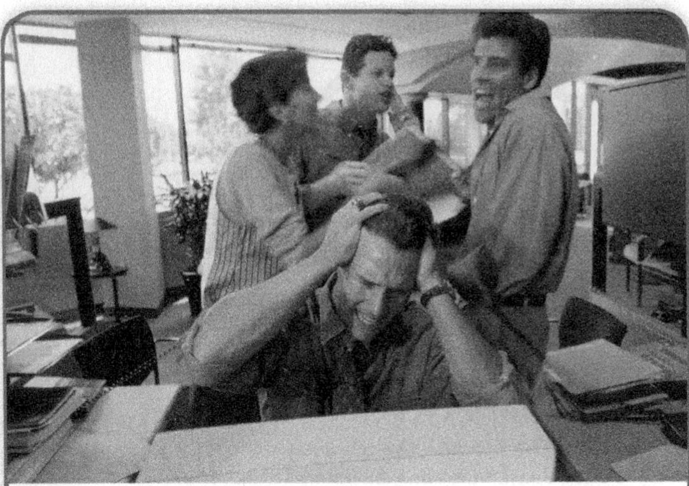

COMMUNICATION CHOICE POINT

HATE SPEECH *Your work colleagues in neighboring cubicles regularly use derogatory racial terms. You really don't want to listen to this and want to protest this kind of talk. At the same time, however, you don't want to alienate people you're going to have to work with for some time.* **What are some of the things you can say to register your protest (cooperatively)?**

Nonverbal Behaviors

Speakers from different cultures have different display rules—cultural rules that govern which nonverbal behaviors are appropriate and which are inappropriate in a public setting. As you listen to other people, you also "listen" to their nonverbal cues. If these are drastically different from what you expect on the basis of the verbal message, you may see them as a kind of noise or interference or even as contradictory messages. Also, of course, different cultures may give very different meanings to the same nonverbal gesture; for example, the thumb and forefinger forming a circle means "OK" in most of the United States, but it means "money" in Japan, "zero" in some Mediterranean countries, and "I'll kill you" in Tunisia.

Feedback

Members of some cultures give very direct and honest feedback. Speakers from these cultures—the United States is a good example—expect the feedback to be a forthright reflection of what their listeners are feeling. In other cultures—Japan and Korea are good examples—it's more important to be positive than to be truthful, so people may respond with positive feedback (say, in commenting on a business colleague's proposal) even though they don't actually feel positive. Listen to feedback, as you would all messages, with a full recognition that various cultures view feedback very differently.

Credibility

What makes a speaker credible, or believable, also will vary from one culture to another. In some cultures people would claim that competence is the most important factor in, say, the choice of a teacher for their preschool children. In other cultures the most important factor might be the goodness or morality of the teacher. Similarly, members of different cultures may perceive the credibility of various media very differently. For example, members of a repressive society in which the government controls television news may come to attribute little credibility to such broadcasts. After all, these listeners might reason, television news is simply what the government wants you to know. This reaction may be hard to understand or even recognize for someone raised in the United States, for example, where traditionally the media have been largely free of such political control.

Gender and Listening

Men and women learn different styles of listening, just as they learn different styles for using

Explore the **Exercise** "Typical Man, Typical Woman" at **MyCommunicationLab**

eth•ics *noun* morality, standards of conduct, moral judgment

MAKING ETHICAL CHOICES
Listening Ethically

Most often discussions of ethics in communication focus on the speaker. But listeners, too, have ethical obligations.

- **Give the speaker an honest hearing.** Avoid prejudging the speaker before hearing her or him. Try to put aside prejudices and preconceptions so you can understand and then evaluate the speaker's message fairly.
- **Empathize with the speaker.** You don't have to agree with the speaker, but try to understand emotionally as well as intellectually what the speaker means. In this way, you'll come to understand the speaker more fully.
- **Reflect honestly on the speaker's message.** Much as the listener has a right to expect an active speaker, the speaker has the right to expect a listener who will actively deal with, rather than just passively hear, the message.
- **Give the speaker honest feedback.** In a learning environment such as a communication class, this means giving honest and constructive criticism to help the speaker improve.

Ethical Choice Point

You're teaching a class in communication. In the public speaking segment, one of your students, a sincere and devout Iranian Muslim, gives a speech on "why women should be subservient to men." After the first two minutes of the speech, half the class walks out. During the next class you plan to give a lecture on the ethics of listening. What is your ethical obligation in this situation? What would you say?

verbal and nonverbal messages. Not surprisingly, these different styles can create difficulties in opposite-sex interpersonal communication.

Rapport and Report Talk

According to Deborah Tannen (1990) in her best-selling *You Just Don't Understand: Women and Men in Conversation*, women seek to share feelings, build rapport, and establish closer relationships, and they use listening to achieve these ends. Men, on the other hand, play up their expertise, emphasize it, and use it to dominate the interaction. Their focus is on reporting information. Tannen argues that in conversation a woman seeks to be liked, so she expresses agreement. The goal of a man, on the other hand, is to be given respect, so he seeks to show his knowledge and expertise.

Listening Cues

Men and women give different types of listening cues and consequently show that they're listening in different ways. In conversation, a woman is more apt to give lots of listening cues—interjecting "Yeah" or "Uh-huh," nodding in agreement, and smiling. A man is more likely to listen quietly, without giving lots of listening cues as feedback. Women also make more eye contact when listening than do men, who are more apt to look around and often away from the speaker (Brownell, 2010). As a result of these differences women seem to be more engaged in listening than do men.

Amount and Purposes of Listening

Tannen argues that men listen less to women than women listen to men. The reason, says Tannen (and on this not all researchers agree, see Goldsmith and Fulfs, 1999), is that listening places the person in an inferior position, whereas speaking places the person in a superior position. Men may seem to assume a more confrontational posture while listening and to ask questions that are argumentative or seek to puncture holes in the speaker's position as a way to play up their own expertise. Women are more likely than men to ask supportive questions and offer constructive criticism. Men and women act this way to both members of the same and of the opposite sex; their usual ways of speaking and listening don't seem to change depending on whether the person they're communicating with is male or female.

Gender differences are changing drastically and quickly; it's best to take generalizations about gender as starting points for investigation and not as airtight conclusions (Gamble & Gamble, 2003). Further, as you no doubt have observed from your own experiences, the gender differences—although significant—are far outnumbered by the similarities. It's important to be mindful of both similarities and differences.

Analyzing Video Choices

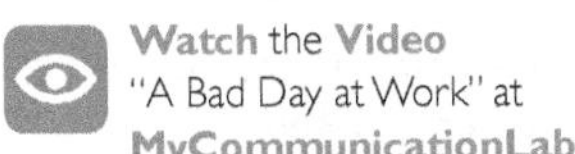

Watch the Video "A Bad Day at Work" at MyCommunicationLab

Sue is at home watching television when her partner Harry comes home from work. He is visibly upset about something, but Sue doesn't know what or why. She wants to communicate her concern for Harry, but is not sure of what she should say. This video, "A Bad Day at Work," focuses on the importance of listening in an interpersonal relationship and particularly the various styles of listening (empathic and objective listening, nonjudgmental and critical listening, surface and depth listening, polite and impolite listening, and active and inactive listening) and the effects these styles have on the individuals and on the relationship. Log on to www.mycommunicationlab.com to view the video for this chapter, to see how the choices played out, and then to consider some related discussion questions.

SUMMARY: LISTENING IN HUMAN COMMUNICATION

Study and **Review** materials for this chapter are at **MyCommunicationLab**

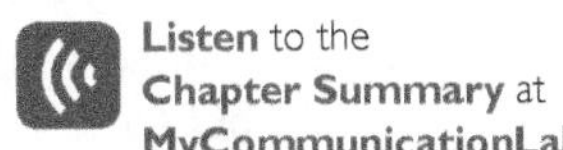

Listen to the **Chapter Summary** at **MyCommunicationLab**

This chapter discussed the importance of listening, the process of listening, the influence of culture and gender on the way people listen, and the principles for listening more effectively.

4.1 THE IMPORTANCE OF LISTENING: TASK AND RELATIONSHIP BENEFITS

1. Effective listening yields a wide variety of benefits, including more effective learning, relating, influencing, playing, and helping.

4.2 THE LISTENING PROCESS

2. Listening is a five-part process that begins with receiving and continues through understanding, remembering, evaluating, and responding.
3. Receiving consists of hearing the verbal signals and perceiving the nonverbal signals.
4. Understanding involves learning what the speaker means, not merely what the words mean.
5. Remembering involves retaining the received message, a process that involves considerable reconstruction.
6. Evaluating consists of judging the messages you receive.
7. Responding involves giving feedback while the speaker is speaking and taking your turn at speaking after the speaker has finished.

4.3 LISTENING BARRIERS

8. Among the barriers to listening are physical and mental distractions, biases and prejudices, lack of appropriate focus, and premature judgments.

4.4 STYLES OF EFFECTIVE LISTENING

9. Effective listening involves adjusting our behaviors on the basis of at least four dimensions: empathic and objective listening, nonjudgmental and critical listening, surface and depth listening, and active and inactive listening.
10. The empathic–objective dimension involves the degree to which the listener focuses on feeling what the speaker is feeling versus grasping the objective message.
11. The nonjudgmental–critical dimension involves the degree to which the listener evaluates what is said.
12. The surface–depth dimension has to do with the extent to which the listener focuses on literal or obvious meanings versus hidden or less obvious meanings.
13. The polite–impolite dimension refers to the presence or absence of civility and courtesy.
14. The active–inactive dimension involves the extent to which the listener reflects back and expresses support for the speaker.

4.5 LISTENING, CULTURE, AND GENDER

15. Listening is influenced by a wide range of cultural factors, such as differences in language and speech, nonverbal behaviors, credibility criteria, and feedback approaches.
16. Listening is influenced by gender: Men and women seem to view listening as serving different purposes.

Study and Review the Flashcards at MyCommunicationLab

KEY TERMS

active listening *93*
assimilation *89*
backchanneling cues *84*
empathy *88*
listening *79*

WORKING WITH LISTENING

4.1 Expressing Empathy. Expressing empathy is crucial to meaningful communication, but it is not an easily acquired skill; it takes practice. Here are a few practice examples. For any one or two of the following situations, indicate in one sentence (or more) how you'd respond to the speaker with *thinking empathy* and in one sentence (or more) how you'd respond with feeling empathy. Assume that all three people are your peers.

a. "I've never felt so alone in my life. Chris left last night and said it was all over. We were together for three years and now—after a 10-minute argument—everything is lost."

b. "I just got $20,000 from my aunt's estate. She left it to me! Twenty thousand! Now I can get that car and buy some new clothes!"

c. "A Camry! My parents bought me a Camry for graduation. What a bummer. They promised me a Lexus."

4.2 Empathy: The Negative Side. There is some evidence to show that empathy also has a negative side. For example, the more empathy you feel toward people who are similar to you racially and ethnically, the less empathy you feel toward those who are different. The same empathy that increases your understanding of your own group decreases your understanding of other groups. So although empathy may encourage understanding, it also can create dividing lines between your group and "them" (Angier, 1995). Have you ever witnessed these negative effects of empathy?

4.3 Regulating Your Listening Style. This exercise will help you see the importance of regulate your listening on the basis of the specific situation in which you find yourself. With specific reference to the five dimensions of effective listening discussed here, what styles would you use in each of the following situations? What types of listening would be obviously inappropriate in each situation?

a. Your steady dating partner for the last five years tells you that spells of depression are becoming more frequent and more long lasting.

b. Your history instructor lectures on the contributions of the ancient Greeks to modern civilization.

c. Your brother tells you he's been accepted into Harvard's MBA program.

d. Your supervisor explains the new e-mail system.

e. A newscaster reports on a recent Supreme Court decision.

4.4 Politeness in Social Media. Much of the thinking and research on listening and politeness has focused on them as face-to-face communication skills. How would you describe listening politeness on the phone or on social network sites? Are the same principles applicable or do we need an entirely different set to describe social networking listening politeness?

4.5 Using Active Listening Strategies. Active listening allows you to connect with another person by demonstrating your understanding and support. Here are three situations that might require active listening. For each situation compose an active listening response in which you (a) paraphrase the speaker's meaning, (b) express understanding of the speaker's meaning, and (c) ask questions to clarify any potential misunderstandings.

a. Your friend has just broken up a love affair and is telling you about it: *I can't seem to get Chris out of my head. All I do is think about what we used to do and all the fun we used to have.*

b. A young nephew tells you that he cannot talk with his parents. No matter how hard he tries, they just don't listen. *I tried to tell them that I can't play baseball and I don't want to play baseball. But they ignore me and tell me that all I need is practice.*

c. Your mother has been having a difficult time at work. She was recently passed up for a promotion and received one of the lowest merit raises given in the company. *I'm not sure what I did wrong. I do my work, mind my own business, don't take my sick days like everyone else. How could they give that promotion to Helen who's only been with the company for two years? Maybe I should just quit.*

4.6 Your Listening Self. Using the four dimensions of listening effectiveness discussed here (empathic–objective, nonjudgmental–critical, surface–depth, and active–inactive), how would you describe yourself as a listener when listening in class? When listening to your best friend? When listening to a romantic partner? When listening to your parents? When listening to your superiors at work?

4.7 Listening to Complaints. Would you find it difficult to listen to friends who were complaining that the insurance premium on their Bentley was going up? Would you find it difficult to listen to unemployed friends complain that their rent was going up and that they feared becoming homeless? If you do find a difference, to what do you attribute it?

4.8 Selling by Listening. Researchers have argued that effective listening skills are positively associated with salespeople's effectiveness in selling (Castleberrry & Shepherd, 1993). Can you think of examples from your own experience that would support this positive association between effective listening and effective selling?

4.9 Men and Women Listening. The popular belief, as noted in this chapter, is that men listen the way they do to prove themselves superior and that women listen as they do to ingratiate themselves. Although there is no evidence to support this belief, it persists in the assumptions people make about the opposite sex. What do you believe accounts for the differences in the way men and women listen?

4.10 Cell Phone Annoyances. Some researchers have argued that listening to the cell phone conversations of others is particularly annoying because you can hear only one side of the conversation; cell phone conversations were rated as significantly more intrusive than two people talking face to face (Monk, Fellas, & Ley, 2004). Do you find the cell phone conversations of people near you on a bus or in a store annoying, perhaps for the reason given here? For other reasons?

LogOn! MyCommunicationLab www.mycommunicationlab.com

Throughout this chapter, there are icons that highlight media content for selected topics. Go to **MyCommunicationLab** for additional materials on the importance of listening, the nature of the listening process, the varied styles of listening you might use in different situations, and some cultural and gender differences in listening. Here you'll find flashcards to help you learn key communication terms, videos that illustrate a variety of concepts, additional exercises, and discussions to help you continue your study of listening in human communication.

5 VERBAL MESSAGES

CHAPTER TOPICS	CHAPTER OBJECTIVES
In this chapter you'll explore the following major topics:	**After reading this chapter you should be able to:**
PRINCIPLES OF VERBAL MESSAGES	5.1 Paraphrase the seven principles of verbal messages.
DISCONFIRMATION AND CONFIRMATION	5.2 Define *disconfirmation, confirmation, racism, heterosexism, ageism,* and *sexism* and use appropriate cultural identifiers.
USING VERBAL MESSAGES EFFECTIVELY	5.3 Paraphrase the principles of intensional orientation, allness, fact-inference confusion, static evaluation, indiscrimination, and polarization and use these principles in your own verbal messaging.

Not all verbal messages are meaningful.

As you communicate, you use two major signal systems—the verbal and the nonverbal. Verbal messages are messages sent with words. It's important to remember that the word *verbal* refers to words, not to orality; verbal messages consist of both oral and written words. In contrast, verbal messages do not include laughter; vocalized pauses you make when you speak (such as *er, hmm,* and *ah*); and responses you make to others that are oral but don't involve words (such as *ha ha, aha,* and *ugh!*). These vocalizations are considered nonverbal—as are, of course, facial expressions, eye movements, gestures, and so on.

As explained in Chapter 1, your messages normally occur in "packages" consisting of both verbal and nonverbal signals that occur simultaneously. Usually, verbal and nonverbal behaviors reinforce or support each other. For example, you don't usually express fear with words while the rest of your body relaxes. You don't normally express anger with your body posture while your face smiles. Your entire being works as a whole—verbally and nonverbally—to express your thoughts and feelings.

This chapter focuses on the verbal system (the next will examine the nonverbal system) and discusses the principles of verbal messages, the concepts of confirmation and disconfirmation, and the ways you can use verbal messages most effectively.

5.1 PRINCIPLES OF VERBAL MESSAGES

As you grew up, you learned the language spoken by the people around you. You learned its phonological, or sound, system; its semantic system, or system of word meanings; and its syntactic system, which enabled you to put words into meaningful sentence patterns. Our concern in this chapter is not with the grammatical structure of language (that's the linguist's job), but with the verbal messages you speak and hear. These verbal messages, of course, rely on the rules of grammar; you can't just make up sounds or words or string words together at random and expect to be understood. But, as we'll see, following the rules of grammar is not enough to achieve effective communication. For this we need to understand several key principles of verbal messages: (1) meanings are in people, (2) language is denotative and connotative, (3) meanings depend on context, (4) messages vary in politeness, (5) messages can be onymous or anonymous, (6) messages vary in assertiveness, and (7) messages can deceive.

Watch the Video "Interpersonal Communication" at MyCommunicationLab

Meanings Are in People

If you wanted to know the meaning of the word *love,* you'd probably turn to a dictionary. There you'd find a definition such as Webster's: "the attraction, desire, or affection felt for a person who arouses delight or admiration or elicits tenderness, sympathetic interest, or benevolence." But where would you turn if you wanted to know what Pedro means when he says, "I'm in love"? Of course, you'd ask Pedro to discover his meaning. It's in this sense that meanings are not in words, but in people. Consequently, to uncover meaning, you need to look into people and not merely into words.

Also recognize that as you change, you also change the meanings you created out of past messages. Thus, although the message sent may not have changed, the meanings you created from it yesterday and the meanings you create today may be quite different. Yesterday, when a special someone said, "I love you," you created certain meanings. But today, when you learn that the same "I love you" was said to three other people, or when you fall in love with someone else, you drastically change the meanings you perceive from those three words.

As already noted in Chapter 2, this principle is especially important in intercultural communication, as meanings for the same words are often drastically different between members of different cultures. This became especially obvious after the tragedy of the World Trade Center attack: Terms like *justice, suicide,* and *terrorism* were given totally different meanings by those from different cultures.

A failure to recognize this important principle is at the heart of a common pattern of miscommunication called bypassing. **Bypassing** is a type of miscommunication that occurs when the sender's and the receiver's meanings are not the same (Haney, 1973). Bypassing can take either of two forms: two people in conversation using different words that have the same meaning or two people in conversation using the same words that have different meanings.

Bypassing: Different Words, Same Meaning

One type of bypassing occurs when two people use different words but give them the same meaning; on the surface there's disagreement, but at the level of meaning there's agreement. The two people actually agree but assume, because they use different words (some of which may actually never be verbalized), that they disagree. Here's an example:

Pat: I'm not interested in one-night stands. I want a permanent relationship. [Meaning: I want an exclusive dating relationship but not marriage]

Chris: I'm not ready for that. [Meaning: I'm not ready for marriage.]

Bypassing: Same Words, Different Meaning

The second type of bypassing is more common and occurs when two people use the same words but give the words different meanings. On the surface it looks like the two people agree (simply because they're using the same words). But if you look more closely, you see that the apparent agreement masks real disagreement, as in this example:

Pat: I don't really believe in religion. [Meaning: I don't really believe in God.]

Chris: Neither do I. [Meaning: I don't really believe in organized religions.]

Here Pat and Chris assume that they agree, but actually they disagree. At some later date the implications of these differences may well become crucial.

Language Is Denotative and Connotative

Denotation refers to the meaning you'd find in a dictionary; it's the meaning that members of the culture assign to a word. **Connotation** refers to the emotional meaning that specific speakers–listeners give to a word. Words have both kinds of meaning. Take as an example the word *death.* To a doctor this word might mean (or denote) the time when brain activity ceases. This is an objective description of a particular event. In contrast, when a mother is informed of her child's death, the word means (or connotes) much more. It recalls her child's youth, ambition, family, illness, and so on. To her it's a highly emotional, subjective, and personal word. These emotional, subjective, or personal reactions are the word's connotative meaning.

Take another example: Compare the term *migrants* (used to designate Mexicans coming into the United States to better their economic condition) with the term *settlers* (used to designate Europeans who came to the United States for the same reason) (Koppelman, 2005). Though both terms describe essentially the same activity (and are essentially the same denotatively), *migrants* is often negatively evaluated and *settlers* is often positively evaluated (they differ widely in their connotations).

Semanticist S. I. Hayakawa (Hayakawa & Hayakawa, 1989) coined the terms "snarl words" and "purr words" to clarify further the distinction between denotative and connotative meaning. **Snarl words** are highly negative ("She's an idiot," "He's a pig," "They're a bunch of losers"). Sexist, racist, and heterosexist language and hate speech provide lots of other examples. **Purr words** are highly positive ("She's a real sweetheart," "He's a dream," "They're the greatest"). Although they may sometimes seem to have denotative meaning and to refer to the "real world," snarl and purr words are purely connotative in meaning. They don't describe people or events; rather, they reveal the speaker's feelings about these people or events.

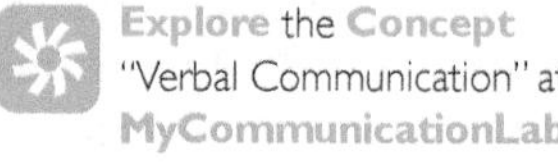
Explore the Concept "Verbal Communication" at MyCommunicationLab

Meanings Depend on Context

Verbal and nonverbal communications exist in a context, and that context to a large extent determines the meaning of any verbal or nonverbal behavior. The same words or behaviors may have totally different meanings when they occur in different contexts. For example, the greeting "How are you?" means "Hello" to someone you pass regularly on the street, but means "Is your health improving?" when said to a friend in the hospital. A wink to an attractive person on a bus means something completely different from a wink that says, "I'm kidding."

Similarly, the meaning of a given signal depends on the other behavior it accompanies or is close to in time. Pounding a fist on the table during a speech in support of a politician means something quite different from that same gesture in response to news of a friend's death. Focused eye contact may signify openness and honesty in one culture and defiance in another. In isolation from the context, it's impossible to tell what meaning was intended by merely examining the signals. Of course, even if you know the context in detail, you still may not be able to decipher the meaning of the message.

Perhaps the most important contexts to consider are the cultural and the gender contexts.

The Cultural Context

Your culture teaches you that certain ways of using verbal messages are acceptable and certain ways are not. For example, you may have learned to address older people by Title + Last Name (Ms. Winter), as with professors and doctors, but to address peers or people much younger than you by their first names. When you follow such cultural principles in communicating, you're seen as a properly functioning member of the culture. When you violate the principles, you risk being seen as deviant or perhaps as insulting. Here are a variety of such principles.

The Principle of Cooperation. The **principle of cooperation** holds that in any communication interaction, both parties will make an effort to help each other understand each other. That is, we assume cooperation. The ways in which we assume cooperation are identified in the principle's four corollaries or maxims. As you read down the list, ask yourself how you follow these maxims in your everyday conversation.

- ***The maxim of quality.*** Say what you know or assume to be true, and do not say what you know to be false.
- ***The maxim of relation.*** Talk about what is relevant to the conversation.
- ***The maxim of manner.*** Be clear, avoid ambiguities (as much as possible), be relatively brief, and organize your thoughts into a meaningful pattern. In e-mail and texting brevity is especially important, and as a result acronyms have become popular, especially in online communication: BTW for "by the way," BFF for "best friend forever," IMHO for "in my humble opinion," and TTYL for "talk to you later." For an ever-increasing list of acronyms see Net Lingua's website.
- ***The maxim of quantity.*** Be as informative as necessary to communicate the information.

The Principle of Peaceful Relations. This principle holds that when you communicate your primary goal is to maintain peaceful relationships. This means that you would never insult anyone and you may even express agreement with someone when you really disagree, a principle that violates the principle of cooperation and the maxim of quality (Midooka, 1990).

The Principle of Face-Saving. Face-saving messages are polite; they are messages that preserve the image of the other person and do nothing to insult the person or make him or her appear in a negative light. The principle holds that you should never embarrass anyone, especially in public. Always allow people to save face, even if this means avoiding the truth—as when you tell someone he or she did good work although the job was actually poorly executed. Many Asian and Latin American cultures stress the value of indirectness because it helps people avoid overt criticism and the loss of face.

The Principle of Self-Denigration. The principle of self-denigration advises you to avoid taking credit for accomplishments and to minimize your abilities or talents in conversation (Gu, 1997). At the same time, you would raise the image of the people with whom you're talking.

The Gender Context

Gender also influences our verbal communication. For example, studies from different cultures show that women's speech is generally more polite than men's speech, even on the telephone (Brown, 1980; Dindia & Canary, 2006; Holmes, 1995; Kapoor, Hughes, Baldwin, & Blue, 2003; Smoreda & Licoppe, 2000; Tannen, 1994b; Wetzel, 1988). Women seek areas of agreement in conversation and in conflict situations more often than men do. Similarly, young girls are more apt to try to modify disagreements, whereas young boys are more apt to express more

the•o•ry *noun* statement of explanation, formulation of relationships, reasoned generalization

UNDERSTANDING THEORY AND RESEARCH
Theories of Gender Differences

Throughout this text, gender differences are discussed in a wide variety of contexts. One researcher distinguishes three perspectives on gender differences in communication (Holmes, 1995):

- Gender differences are due to **innate biological differences**. Thus, gender differences in communication, such as differences in politeness or in listening behavior, are the result of these biological differences.
- Gender differences are due to **different patterns of socialization**, which lead to different forms of communication. Thus, the gender differences that you observe are due to the different ways boys and girls are raised and taught when growing up and throughout life—by being rewarded for "appropriate" gender communication and being punished for "inappropriate" gender communication.
- Gender differences are due to the **inequalities in social power.** For example, because of women's lesser social power, they're more apt to communicate with greater deference and politeness than are men.

Working with Theories and Research

What arguments could you offer in support of or in opposition to any of these positions? How might you go about conducting research to test any one of these hypotheses?

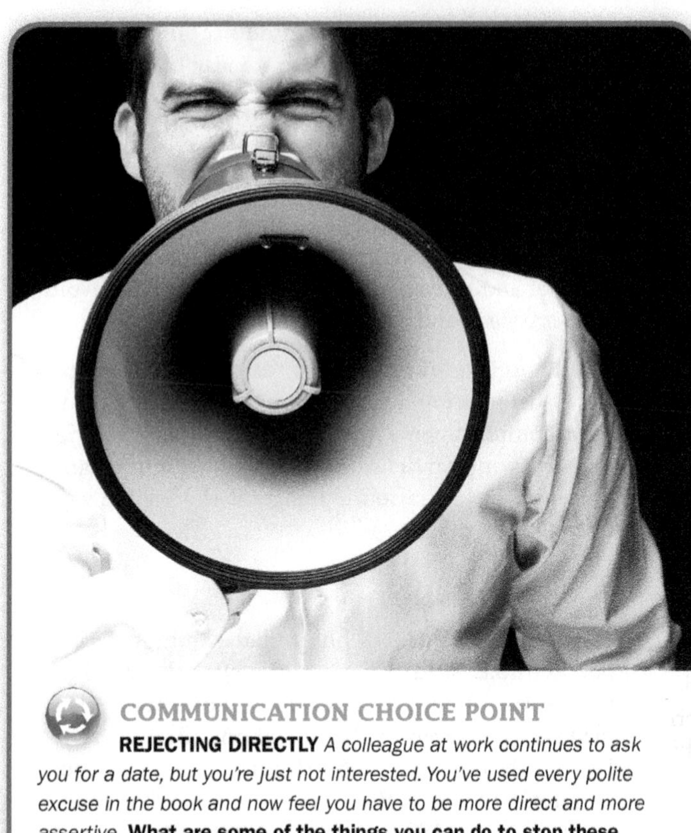

COMMUNICATION CHOICE POINT

REJECTING DIRECTLY *A colleague at work continues to ask you for a date, but you're just not interested. You've used every polite excuse in the book and now feel you have to be more direct and more assertive.* **What are some of the things you can do to stop these requests but not insult your colleague? What would you say?**

"bald disagreements" (Holmes, 1995). Women also use more polite speech when seeking to gain another person's compliance than men do (Baxter, 1984).

The popular stereotype in much of the United States holds that women tend to be indirect in making requests and in giving orders and that this indirectness communicates a powerlessness and discomfort with their own authority. Men, the stereotype continues, tend to be direct, sometimes to the point of being blunt or rude. This directness communicates men's power and comfort with their authority. Deborah Tannen (1994a) provides an interesting perspective on these stereotypes. Women are, it seems, more indirect in giving orders; they are more likely to say, for example, "It would be great if these letters could go out today" than "Have these letters out by three." But, Tannen (1994a, p. 84) argues, "issuing orders indirectly can be the prerogative of those in power" and does not necessarily show powerlessness. Power, to Tannen, is the ability to choose your own style of communication.

Men also can be indirect, and they are more likely to use indirectness when they express weakness, reveal a problem, or admit an error (Rundquist, 1992; Tannen, 1994a, 1994b). Men are more likely to speak indirectly when expressing emotions (other than anger). They are also more indirect when they refuse expressions of increased romantic intimacy. Men are thus indirect, the theory goes, when they are saying something that goes against the masculine stereotype. A few theories of gender differences are highlighted in the accompanying Understanding Theory and Research box.

There are also gender similarities. One of the best pieces of evidence comes from studies showing that when messages spoken by men and women are transcribed, native speakers of English cannot identify which were spoken by men and which by women (Mulac, 2006). There are also studies identifying specific similarities. For example, in both the United States and New Zealand, men and women seem to pay compliments in similar ways (Holmes, 1995; Manes & Wolfson, 1981), and both men and women use politeness strategies when communicating bad news in an organization (Lee, 1993).

Explore the Exercise "Recognizing Gender Differences" at MyCommunicationLab

Messages Vary in Politeness

It will come as no surprise that messages vary greatly in **politeness** Polite messages reflect positively on the other person (for example, compliments or pats on the back); that is, they help the other person maintain positive face (as explained more fully in Chapter 3). Politeness messages also respect the other person's right to be independent and autonomous (for example, asking permission or acknowledging the person's right to refuse); that is, they help the other person maintain autonomy. Impolite messages attack our needs to be seen positively (for example, criticism or negative facial expressions) and to be autonomous (making demands or forcing another to do something).

Direct messages ("Write me a recommendation," "Lend me $100") are usually less polite that indirect messages ("Do you think you could write a recommendation for me?" "Would it be possible to lend me $100?"). The reason that indirect messages are usually more polite is because they allow the person to maintain autonomy and provide an acceptable way for the person to refuse your request (thus helping to maintain the person's negative face needs). Direct messages may infringe on a person's need to maintain negative face.

Explore the Exercise "How Direct Are You?" at MyCommunicationLab

Indirect messages allow you to express a desire without insulting or offending anyone; they allow you to observe the rules of polite interaction. So instead of saying, "I'm bored with this group," you say, "It's getting late and I have to get up early tomorrow," or you look at your watch and pretend to be surprised by the time. Instead of saying, "This food tastes like cardboard," you say, "I just started my diet." In each instance you're stating a preference but are saying it indirectly so as to avoid offending someone.

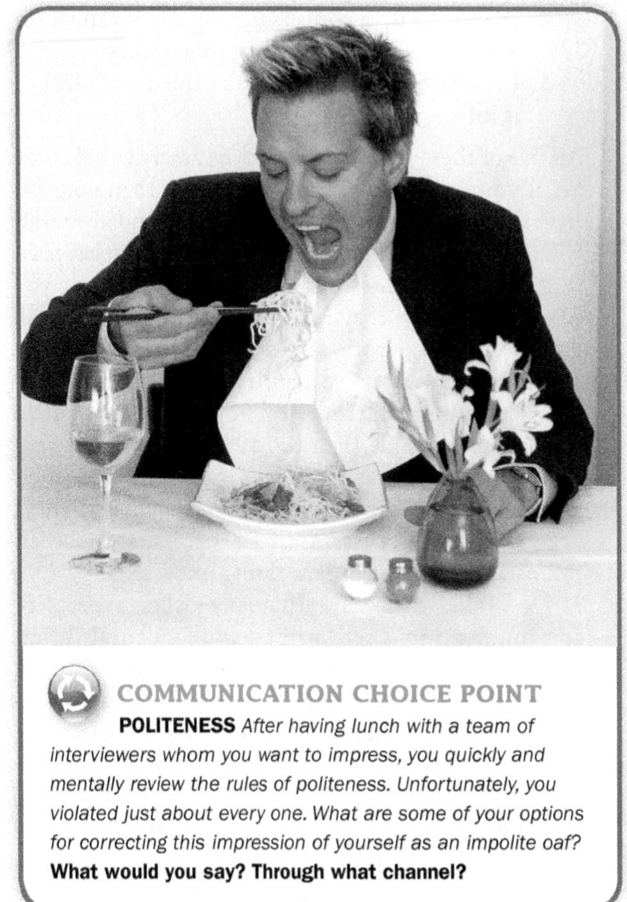

COMMUNICATION CHOICE POINT

POLITENESS *After having lunch with a team of interviewers whom you want to impress, you quickly and mentally review the rules of politeness. Unfortunately, you violated just about every one. What are some of your options for correcting this impression of yourself as an impolite oaf?* **What would you say? Through what channel?**

Messages Can Be Onymous or Anonymous

Some messages are onymous or "signed"; that is, the author of the message is clearly identified, as it is in your textbooks, news-related editorials, and feature articles and of course when you communicate face to face and, usually, by phone or chat. In many cases, you have the opportunity to respond directly to the speaker/writer and voice your opinions, your agreement or disagreement, for example. Other messages are anonymous: the author is not identified. For example, on faculty evaluation questionnaires and on RateMyProfessor.com, the ratings and the comments are published anonymously.

The Internet has made anonymity extremely easy, and there are currently a variety of websites that offer to send your e-mails to your boss, your ex-partner, your secret crush, your noisy neighbors, or your inadequate lawyer—all anonymously. Thus, your message gets sent but you are not identified with it. For good or ill, you don't have to deal with the consequences of your message.

One obvious advantage of anonymity is that it allows people to voice opinions that may be unpopular and may thus encourage greater honesty. In the case of RateMyProfessor.com, for example, anonymity ensures that the student writing negative comments about an instructor will not be penalized. An anonymous e-mail to a sexual partner informing him or her about your having an STD and suggesting testing and treatment might pass along a message that would never be shared in a face-to-face or phone conversation. The presumption is that anonymity encourages honesty and openness.

Anonymity also enables people to disclose their inner feelings, fears, hopes, and dreams with a depth of feeling that they may be otherwise reluctant to do. A variety of websites that enable you to maintain anonymity are available for these purposes. And, in these cases, not only are you anonymous but the people who read your messages are also anonymous, a situation that is likely to encourage a greater willingness to disclosure and to make disclosures at a deeper level than otherwise.

An obvious disadvantage is that anonymity might encourage people to go to extremes—as there are no consequences to the message—to voice opinions that are outrageous. This in turn can easily spark conflict that is likely to prove largely unproductive. With anonymous messages, you can't evaluate the credibility of the source. Advice on depression, for example, may come from someone who knows nothing about depression and may make useless recommendations.

Messages Vary in Assertiveness

Consider how true (or false) each of the following is of your own everyday behavior:

1. I would express my opinion in a group even if it contradicted the opinions of others.
2. When asked to do something that I really don't want to do, I can say no without feeling guilty.
3. I can express my opinion to my superiors on the job.

4. I can start up a conversation with a stranger on a bus or at a business gathering without fear.
5. I voice objection to people's behavior if I feel it infringes on my rights.

All five of these statements describe assertive behavior. So, if you responded mainly with True then your behavior is generally assertive; if you responded mainly with False then your behavior is generally nonassertive.

Assertive people operate with an "I win, you win" philosophy; they assume that both parties can gain something from an interaction, even from a confrontation. Assertive people are more positive and score lower on measures of hopelessness than do nonassertive people (Velting, 1999). Assertive people are willing to assert their own rights. Unlike their aggressive counterparts, however, they don't hurt others in the process. Assertive people speak their minds and welcome others' doing likewise.

Do realize that as with many other aspects of communication, there will be wide cultural differences when it comes to assertiveness. For example, the values of assertiveness are more likely to be extolled in individualist cultures than in collectivist cultures. Assertiveness will be valued more by those cultures that stress competition, individual success, and independence. It will be valued much less by those cultures that stress cooperation, group success, and interdependence of all members on one another. American students, for example, are found to be significantly more assertive than Japanese or Korean students (Thompson & Klopf, 1991; Thompson, Klopf, & Ishii, 1991). Most people are nonassertive in certain situations. If you're one of these people and if you wish to modify your behavior, here are some suggestions for communicating assertiveness (Bower & Bower, 2005; Dryden & Constantinou, 2005). (If you are always nonassertive and are unhappy about this, then you may need to work with a therapist to change your behavior.)

- ***Describe the problem.*** Don't evaluate or judge it. Be sure to use I-messages and to avoid messages that accuse or blame the other person: "We're all working on this advertising project together. And I need you to participate more actively."
- ***State how this problem affects you.*** Tell the person how you feel: "My job depends on the success of this project, and I don't think it's fair that I have to do extra work to make up for what you're not doing."
- ***Propose solutions.*** Suggest solutions that are workable and that allow the person to save face. Describe or visualize the situation if your solution were put into effect: "If you can get your report to the group by Tuesday, we'll still be able to meet our deadline. I could give you a call on Monday to remind you."
- ***Confirm understanding.*** Make sure your message is understood: "It's clear that we can't produce this project if you're not going to pull your own weight. Will you have the report to us by Tuesday?"

Keep in mind that assertiveness is not always the most desirable response. Assertive people are assertive when they want to be, but they can be nonassertive if the situation calls for it. For example, you might wish to be nonassertive in a situation in which assertiveness might emotionally hurt the other person. Let's say that an older relative wishes you to do something for her or him. You could assert your rights and say no, but in doing so you would probably hurt this person; it might be better simply to do as asked.

A note of caution should be added to this discussion. It's easy to visualize a situation in which, for example, people are talking behind you in a movie, and with your newfound enthusiasm for assertiveness, you tell them to be quiet. It's also easy to see yourself getting smashed in the teeth as a result. In applying the principles of assertive communication, be careful that you don't go beyond what you can handle effectively.

Messages Can Deceive

It comes as no surprise that some messages are truthful and some are deceptive. Although we operate in interpersonal communication on the assumption that people tell the truth, some people do lie. In fact, many view lying as quite common whether in politics, business, or interpersonal relationships (Amble, 2005; Knapp, 2008). Lying also begets lying; when one person lies, the likelihood of the other person lying increases (Tyler, Feldman, & Reichert, 2006). Furthermore, people like people who tell the truth more than they like people who lie. So lying needs to be given some attention in any consideration of interpersonal communication.

Lying refers to the act of (1) sending messages (2) with the intention of giving another person information you believe to be false.

1. Lying involves some kind of verbal and/or nonverbal message sending (and remember even the absence of facial expression or the absence of any verbal comment also communicates); it also requires reception by another person.
2. The message must be sent to intentionally deceive. If you give false information to

someone but you believe it to be true, then you haven't lied. You lie when you send information that you believe to be untrue and you intend to mislead the other person.

Types of Lies

Lies vary greatly in type; each lie seems a bit different from every other lie. Here is one useful system that classifies lies into four types (McGinley, 2000).

Explore the Exercise "Is Lying Unethical?" at MyCommunicationLab

- ***Pro-Social Deception: To Achieve Some Good.*** For example, praising a person's effort to give him or her more confidence or telling others they look great to simply make them feel good would be examples of pro-social lies. Some pro-social lies are expected and to not lie would be considered impolite. For example, it would be impolite to tell parents that their child is ugly (even if you firmly believe that the child is in fact ugly). The only polite course is to lie.
- ***Self-Enhancement Deception: To Make Yourself Look Good.*** Not all self-enhancement involves deception. For example, the impression management strategies discussed earlier (pages 70–73) may be used to simply highlight what is already true about you but that others may not see at first glance. In some cases, however, impression management strategies involve deception. For example, you might mention your good grades but omit the poor ones or present yourself as a lot more successful than you really are.
- ***Selfish Deception: To Protect Yourself.*** Sometimes it's something as simple as not answering the phone because you want to do something else. In this case, no one really gets hurt (usually). But some selfish deception strategies may involve hurting others; for example, you might imply that you did most of the work for a report—protecting yourself, but also hurting the reputation of your colleague. Or you might conceal previous failed relationships, an unsavory family history, or certain facts to protect yourself. Hiding an extra-relational affair is perhaps the classic example of selfish deception.
- ***Anti-Social Deception: To Harm Someone.*** Such lies might include spreading false rumors about someone you dislike or falsely accusing an opposing candidate of some wrongdoing (something you see regularly in political debates). Fighting parents may falsely accuse each other of a variety of wrongdoings to gain the affection of the child. Falsely accusing another person of a wrong you did yourself would be perhaps the clearest example of anti-social deception.

The Behavior of Liars

One of the more interesting questions about lying is how do liars act. Do they act differently from those telling the truth? And, if they do act differently, how can we tell when someone is lying to us? These questions are not easy to answer, and we are far from having complete answers to such questions. But we have learned a great deal; some of the behaviors of liars were identified in the Understanding Theory and Research box on page 85).

Despite the identification of "lying behaviors," it is still very difficult to detect when a person is lying and when telling the truth. The hundreds of research studies conducted on this topic find that in most instances people judge lying accurately in less than 60 percent of the cases, only slightly better than chance (Knapp, 2008). And there is some evidence to show that lie detection is even more difficult (that is, less accurate) in long-standing romantic relationships—the very relationships in which some of the most significant lying occurs (Guerrero, Andersen, & Afifi, 2007). One of the most important reasons for this is the **truth bias**. In most situations we assume that the person is telling the truth; as noted earlier in this chapter, we normally operate under the quality principle, which assumes that what a person says is true. This truth bias is especially strong in long-term relationships where it's taken for granted that each person tells the truth. There are also situations, however, where there is a **deception bias**. For example, in prison where lying is so prevalent and where lie detection is a crucial survival skill, prisoners often operate with a lie bias and assume that what the speaker is saying is a lie (Knapp, 2008).

In any attempt to detect lying be especially careful that you formulate any conclusions with a clear understanding that you may be wrong and that accusations of lying (especially when untrue but even when true) can often damage a relationship to the point where you may not be able to repair it. In addition, keep in mind all the cautions and potential errors in perception discussed earlier; after all, lie detection is a part of person perception.

eth•ics *noun* morality, standards of conduct, moral judgment

MAKING ETHICAL CHOICES
Lying

Not surprisingly, lies have ethical implications. In fact, one of the earliest cultural rules children are taught is that lying is wrong. At the same time, children also learn that in some cases lying is effective—in gaining some reward or in avoiding some punishment.

Some pro-social, self-enhancement, and selfish deception lies are considered ethical (for example, publicly agreeing with someone you really disagree with to enable the person to save face, saying that someone will get well despite medical evidence to the contrary, or simply bragging about your accomplishments). Some lies, as noted in the text, are considered not only ethical but required (for example, lying to protect someone from harm or telling the proud parents that their child is beautiful). Other lies (largely those in the anti-social category) are considered unethical (for example, lying to defraud investors or to falsely accuse someone).

However, a large group of lies are not that easy to classify as ethical or unethical. Here are a few such ethical dilemmas that present you with ethical choice points.

Ethical Choice Points

- Is it ethical to lie to get what you deserved but couldn't get any other way? For example, would you lie to get a well-earned promotion or raise? Would it matter if you hurt a colleague's chances of advancement in the process?
- Is it ethical to lie to your relationship partner to avoid a conflict and perhaps splitting up? In this situation, would it be ethical to lie if the issue was a minor one (you were late for an appointment because you wanted to see the end of the football game) or a major one (say, continued infidelity)?
- Is it ethical to lie to get yourself out of an unpleasant situation? For example, would you lie to get out of an unwanted date, an extra office chore, or a boring conversation?
- Is it ethical to exaggerate the consequences of an act in order to discourage it? For example, would you lie about the bad effects of marijuana in order to prevent your children or your students from using it?
- Is it ethical to lie about yourself in order to appear more appealing—for example, saying you were younger or richer or more honest than you really are? For example, would you lie in your profile on Facebook or MySpace or on a dating website to increase your chances of meeting someone really special?

5.2 DISCONFIRMATION AND CONFIRMATION

Consider this situation: You've been living with someone for the past six months, and you arrive home late one night. Your partner, let's say Pat, is angry and complains about your being so late. Which of the following is most likely to be your response?

1. Stop screaming. I'm not interested in what you're babbling about. I'll do what I want, when I want. I'm going to bed.
2. What are you so angry about? Didn't you get in three hours late last Thursday when you went to that office party? So knock it off.
3. You have a right to be angry. I should have called to tell you I was going to be late, but I got involved in a serious debate at work, and I couldn't leave until it was resolved.

In Response 1, you dismiss Pat's anger and even indicate dismissal of Pat as a person. In Response 2, you reject the validity of Pat's reasons for being angry but do not dismiss either Pat's feelings of anger or Pat as a person. In Response 3, you acknowledge Pat's anger and the reasons for it. In addition, you provide some kind of explanation and in doing so show that both Pat's feelings and Pat as a person are important and that Pat has the right to know what happened. The first response is an example of disconfirmation, the second of rejection, and the third of confirmation (Watzlawick, Beavin, & Jackson, 1967).

Disconfirmation is a communication pattern in which we ignore someone's presence as well as that

TABLE 5.1

In A Nutshell Summary of the Principles of Verbal Messages

Here is a brief summary of the principles of verbal messages and some implications for speaking and listening more effectively.

Principle	Verbal Message Strategies
Meanings are in people, not in things.	Look not only to the words used but to the person using the words.
Language is both denotative and connotative.	Look at both the objective meaning and the subjective meaning expressed.
Meanings are context based.	See messages within the context in which they occur; look especially at the cultural and gender context.
Messages (in all forms of communication) vary in politeness.	Use messages that reflect positively on others and allow them to be autonomous.
Meanings vary in assertiveness.	Acting assertively is most often the preferred mode of communication, but attitudes toward assertiveness vary greatly with the culture.
Message meanings can deceive.	Acting with a truth bias is usually appropriate, but realize that, in some situations, messages may be false and may be purposely designed to mislead you.

person's messages (Response 1). We say, in effect, that this person and what this person has to say are not worth serious attention or effort—that this person and this person's contributions are unimportant or insignificant and that there is no reason to concern ourselves with her or him. The Amish community practices an extreme form of disconfirmation called "shunning," in which the community members totally ignore a person who has violated one or more of their rules. The specific aim of shunning is to get the person to repent and to reenter the community of the faithful. It's likely that all cultures practice some form of exclusion for those who violate important cultural rules.

Note that disconfirmation is not the same as rejection. In **rejection,** you disagree with the person; you indicate your unwillingness to accept something the other person says or does (Response 2). In disconfirming someone, however, you deny that person's significance; you claim that what this person says or does simply does not count.

Confirmation, the opposite of disconfirmation, involves your acknowledging the presence of the other person, the person's importance, and your acceptance of this person (Response 3).

You can gain insight into a wide variety of offensive language practices by viewing them as types of disconfirmation—as language that alienates and separates. Four obvious practices, which we'll consider here, are racism, heterosexism, ageism, and sexism.

Another-ism is ableism—discrimination against people with disabilities. This particular practice is handled throughout the text in a series of tables offering tips for communicating between people with and without a variety of disabilities:

- between people with and without disabilities (Chapter 2).
- between people with and without hearing impairments (Chapter 4).
- between people with and without visual impairment (Chapter 6).
- between people with and without speech and language disorders (Chapter 7).

COMMUNICATION CHOICE POINT

CONFRONTING A LIE *You ask about the previous night's whereabouts of your romantic partner of two years and are told something you're almost certain is false. You don't want to break up the relationship over this, but you do want the truth and an opportunity to resolve the problems that contributed to this situation.* **What are some of the things you might say? What are some things you'd definitely want to avoid saying?**

Racism

According to Andrea Rich (1974), "any language that, through a conscious or unconscious attempt by the user, places a particular racial or ethnic group in an inferior position is racist." **Racist language** expresses racist attitudes. It also, however, contributes to the development of racist attitudes in those who use or hear the language. Even when racism is subtle, unintentional, or even unconscious, its effects are systematically damaging (Dovidio, Gaertner, Kawakami, & Hodson, 2002).

Racism exists on both individual and institutional levels, a distinction made by educational researchers and used throughout this discussion (Koppelman, 2005). The term *individual racism* refers to the negative attitudes and beliefs that people hold about specific races. Assumptions such as the idea that certain races are intellectually inferior to others or that certain races are incapable of certain achievements are clear examples of individual racism. Prejudice against American Indians, African Americans, Hispanics, and Arabs have been with us throughout history and are still a part of many people's lives today. Such racism is seen in the negative terms people use to refer to members of other races and to disparage their customs and accomplishments.

Institutionalized racism is seen in de facto school segregation, in companies' reluctance to hire members of minority groups, in banks' unwillingness to extend mortgages and business loans to members of some races, or in lenders' charging higher interest rates to members of certain groups.

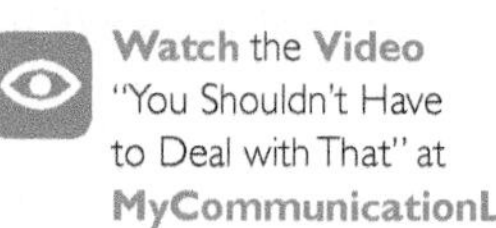

Watch the Video "You Shouldn't Have to Deal with That" at **MyCommunicationLab**

Here are a few guidelines on racist messages.

- Avoid using derogatory terms for members of a particular race.
- Avoid interacting with members of other races through stereotypes perpetuated by the media.
- Make sure not to refer to race when it's irrelevant, as in "an African American surgeon" or "an Asian athlete."
- Avoid attributing economic or social problems to the race of the individuals rather than to institutionalized racism or to general economic problems that affect everyone.

Heterosexism

Heterosexism also exists on both an individual and an institutional level. Individual heterosexism involves attitudes, behaviors, and language that disparage gay men and lesbians as well as a belief that all sexual behavior that is not heterosexual is unnatural and deserving of criticism and condemnation. These beliefs are at the heart of antigay violence and "gay bashing." Individual heterosexism also includes such beliefs as the notions that homosexuals are more likely than heterosexuals to commit crimes (there's actually no difference) or to molest children (actually, heterosexual, married men are overwhelmingly the child molesters) (Abel & Harlow, 2001; Koppelman, 2005). It also includes the belief that homosexuals cannot maintain stable relationships or effectively raise children, a belief that contradicts research evidence (Fitzpatrick, Jandt, Myrick, & Edgar, 1994; Johnson & O'Connor, 2002).

Although great strides have been made in the United States against institutionalized heterosexism, as of this writing 38 states still prevent same-sex marriage, the Boy Scouts of America will not allow gay men to serve as Scoutmasters, and many religions ban gay men and lesbians from the ministry. In some cultures, homosexual relations are illegal (for example, in India, Malaysia, Pakistan, and Singapore); penalties range from a "misdemeanor" conviction in Liberia, to life in jail in Singapore, to death in Pakistan.

Heterosexist language includes the obvious derogatory terms used for lesbians and gay men but also the more subtle forms of language usage: for example, when you qualify a reference to a professional—as in "gay athlete" or "lesbian doctor"—and, in effect, say that athletes and doctors are not normally gay or lesbian.

Still another instance of heterosexism is the presumption of heterosexuality. Usually, people assume the person they're talking to or about is heterosexual. And usually they're correct because the majority of people are heterosexual. At the same time, however, this presumption denies the lesbian or gay identity a certain legitimacy. The practice is very similar to the presumptions of whiteness and maleness that we have made significant inroads in eliminating. Here are a few additional suggestions for avoiding heterosexist (or what some call homophobic) language.

- Avoid offensive nonverbal mannerisms that parody stereotypes when talking about gay men and lesbians. Avoid the "startled eye blink" with which some people react to gay couples (Mahaffey, Bryan, & Hutchison, 2005).
- Avoid "complimenting" gay men and lesbians by saying that they "don't look it." To gay men and lesbians, this is not a compliment. Similarly, expressing disappointment that a person is gay—often thought to be a compliment, as in comments such as "What a waste!"—is not really a compliment.
- Avoid making the assumption that every gay or lesbian knows what every other gay or lesbian is thinking. It's very similar to asking a Japanese person why Sony is investing heavily in the United States or, as one comic put it, asking an African American, "What do you think Jesse Jackson meant by that last speech?"
- Avoid denying individual differences. Comments like "Lesbians are so loyal" or "Gay men are so open with their feelings," which ignore the reality of wide differences within any group, are potentially insulting to all members of the group.

Ageism

Although used mainly to refer to prejudice against older people, the term **ageism** can also refer to prejudice against other age groups. For example, if you describe all teenagers as selfish and undependable, you're discriminating against group members purely because of their age and thus are using ageist language. In some cultures—some Asian and some African cultures, for example—the old are revered and respected. Younger people seek them out for advice on economic, ethical, and relationship issues.

Individual ageism is seen in negative stereotypes and in the general disrespect many have for older people. Institutional ageism is seen in mandatory retirement laws and age restrictions in certain occupations (as opposed to requirements based on demonstrated competence). In less obvious forms, ageism is seen in the media's portrayal of old people as incompetent, complaining, and, perhaps most clearly evidenced in both television and films, without romantic feelings. Rarely, for example, does television or film show older people working productively, being cooperative and pleasant, and engaging in romantic and sexual relationships.

Popular language is replete with examples of linguistic ageism; terms like *little old lady, old hag, old-timer, over the hill, old coot,* and *old fogy* are a few examples. As with sexism, qualifying a description of someone in terms of his or her age demonstrates ageism. For example, if you refer to "a quick-witted 75-year-old" or "an agile 65-year-old" or "a responsible teenager," you're implying that these qualities are unusual in people of these ages and thus need special mention. You're saying that "quick-wittedness" and "being 75" do not normally go together. The problem with this kind of stereotyping is that it's simply wrong. There are many 75-year-olds who are extremely quick-witted (and many 30-year-olds who aren't).

You also communicate ageism when you speak to older people in overly simple words or explain things that don't need explaining. Nonverbally, you demonstrate ageist communication when, for example, you avoid touching an older person but touch others, or when you avoid making direct eye contact with the older person but readily do so with others, or when you speak at an overly high volume (suggesting that all older people have hearing difficulties).

One useful way to avoid ageism is to recognize and avoid the illogical stereotypes that ageist language is based on. Here are a few suggestions.

- Avoid talking down to or refreshing an older person's memory. Older people are not mentally slow, and most have good memories.
- Avoid implying that relationships (particularly romantic and sexual) are no longer important. Older people continue to be interested in relationships.
- Speak at a normal volume and maintain a normal physical distance. Being older does not mean being hard of hearing or being unable to see; most older people hear and see quite well, sometimes with hearing aids or glasses.
- Engage older people in conversation as you would wish to be engaged. Older people are interested in the world around them.

Even though you want to avoid ageist communication, there are times when you may wish to make adjustments when talking with someone who does have language or communication difficulties. The American Speech and Hearing Association's website offers several useful suggestions:

- Reduce as much background noise as you can.
- Speak in relatively short sentences and questions.
- Give the person added time to respond. Some older people react more slowly and need extra time.
- Listen actively. Practice the skills of active listening discussed in Chapter 4.

Sexism

Sexism—like all the -isms discussed here—exists on both an individual and institutional level. Individual sexism consists of prejudicial attitudes and beliefs about men or women based on rigid beliefs about gender roles. These might include beliefs such as the ideas that women should be caretakers, should be sensitive at all times, and should acquiesce to a man's decisions concerning political or financial matters. Sexist attitudes would also include beliefs that men are insensitive, interested only in sex, and incapable of communicating feelings.

Institutional sexism, on the other hand, involves customs and practices that discriminate against people because of their gender. Two very clear examples are the widespread practice of paying women less than men for the same job and the discrimination against women in the upper levels of management. Another clear example of institutionalized sexism is seen in the divorce courts' practice of automatically or near-automatically granting child custody to the mother rather than the father.

Of particular interest here is **sexist language:** language that puts down someone because of his or her gender (a term usually used to refer to language derogatory toward women). The National Council of Teachers of English has proposed guidelines for nonsexist (gender-free, gender-neutral, or sex-fair) language. These guidelines concern the use of the generic word *man*, the use of generic *he* and *his*, and sex-role stereotyping (Penfield, 1987). Consider a few suggestions for avoiding sexist language:

- Avoid using *man* generically. Gender-neutral terms can easily be substituted. Instead of *mankind*, say *humanity*, *people*, or *human beings*. Similarly, the use of terms such as *policeman* or *fireman* and other terms that presume maleness as the norm—and femaleness as a deviation from this norm—are clear and common examples of sexist language.
- Refrain from using *he* and *his* as generic. Instead, you can alternate pronouns, restructure your sentences to eliminate any reference to gender, use *he and she* or *her and him*, or rephrase into the plural form.
- Stay away from sex-role stereotyping. When you make the hypothetical elementary school teacher female and the college professor male or refer to doctors as male and nurses as female, you're sex-role stereotyping; the same is true when you identify the sex of a professional in phrases such as *woman doctor* or *male nurse*.

Explore the Concept "Sexist Language" at MyCommunicationLab

Cultural Identifiers

Perhaps the best way to develop nonsexist, nonheterosexist, nonracist, and nonageist language is to examine the preferred cultural identifiers to use in talking to and about members of different groups. Remember, however, that preferred terms frequently change over time, so keep in touch with the most current preferences.

Race and Nationality

Generally, most African Americans prefer *African American* to *black* (Hecht, Collier, & Ribeau, 1993), although *black* is often used with *white*, as well as in a variety of other contexts (for example, Department of Black and Puerto Rican Studies, the Journal of Black History, and Black History Month). The terms *Negro* and *colored*, although used in the names of some organizations (for example, the United Negro College Fund and the National Association for the Advancement of Colored People), are not used outside these contexts.

White is generally used to refer to those whose roots are in European cultures and usually does not include Hispanics. Analogous to *African American* (which itself is based on a long tradition of terms such as Irish American and Italian American) is the phrase *European American*. Few European Americans, however, call themselves that; most prefer their national origins emphasized, as in German American or Greek American. This preference may well change as Europe moves toward becoming a more cohesive and united entity. *People of color*—a more literary-sounding term appropriate perhaps to public speaking but awkward in most conversations—is preferred to *non-white*, which implies that whiteness is the norm and non-whiteness is a deviation from that norm. The same is true of the term *non-Christian:* It implies that people who have other beliefs deviate from the norm.

Generally, the term *Hispanic* refers to anyone who identifies himself or herself as belonging to a

me•di•a lit•er•a•cy *noun* ability to understand, interact with, and create media messages

EXPANDING MEDIA LITERACY

Media Messages Are Value-Laden

Media messages are value-laden. This means that the media promote the values of the producer and often of the primary audience. These values may range widely: capitalism is good, God is just, good deeds get rewarded, crime gets punished, drugs are bad, and so on. And these media messages ethicize and socialize you; they give you an ethical standard and teach you the social rules you should follow. Because many mass media messages (feature films and television shows, for example) are expensive to produce, they are likely to reflect the values of the rich and powerful. In contrast, electronic media—blogs, websites, and social networks such as LinkedIn or Facebook—are free or relatively inexpensive, and through these media people normally without influence can voice their opinions and send out persuasive messages. So listen to television programs, for example, with a consciousness of the values that are embedded in the production—the sitcom as well as the news broadcast—and how these might influence your thoughts and behaviors.

More specifically, ask yourself: What values are being expressed? What values do the media personalities embody? How are these values presented? What values are they trying to teach me? And, most important, ask if these values are productive ***for you***.

Spanish-speaking culture. *Latina* (female) and *Latino* (male) refer to persons whose roots are in one of the Latin American countries, such as Haiti, the Dominican Republic, Nicaragua, or Guatemala. *Hispanic American* refers to U.S. residents whose ancestry is in a Spanish culture; the term includes people from Mexico, the Caribbean, and Central and South America. In emphasizing a Spanish heritage, however, the term is really inaccurate because it leaves out the large numbers of people in the Caribbean and in South America whose origins are African, Native American, French, or Portuguese. The words *Chicana* (female) and *Chicano* (male) refer to persons with roots in Mexico, although these terms often connote a nationalist attitude (Jandt, 2004) and are considered offensive by many Mexican Americans. *Mexican American* is generally preferred.

Inuk (plural *Inuit*), also spelled with two n's (*Innuk* and *Innuit*), is preferred to *Eskimo* (a term the U.S. Census Bureau uses), which was applied to the indigenous peoples of Alaska and Canada by Europeans and literally means "raw meat eaters."

The word *Indian* technically refers only to someone from India, not to citizens of other Asian countries or to the indigenous peoples of North America. *American Indian* or *Native American* is preferred, even though many Native Americans do refer to themselves as Indians and Indian people. The word *squaw*, used to refer to a Native American woman and still used in the names of some places in the United States and in some textbooks, is clearly a term to be avoided; its usage is almost always negative and insulting (Koppelman, 2005).

In Canada indigenous people are called *first people* or *first nations*. The term *native American* (with a lowercase *n*) is most often used to refer to persons born in the United States. Although technically the term could refer to anyone born in North or South America, people outside the United States generally prefer more specific designations such as Argentinean, Cuban, or Canadian. The term *native* describes an indigenous inhabitant; it is not used to indicate "someone having a less developed culture."

Muslim (rather than the older *Moslem*) is the preferred form to refer to a person who adheres to the religious teachings of Islam. *Quran* (rather than *Koran*) is the preferred term for the scriptures of Islam. *Jewish people* is often preferred to *Jews*, and *Jewess* (a Jewish female) is considered derogatory. *Jew* is never used as an adjective.

When history was being written from a European perspective, Europe was taken as the focal point and the rest of the world was defined in terms of its location relative to that continent. Thus, Asia became the East or the Orient, and Asians became *Orientals*—a term that is today considered inappropriate or Eurocentric. Thus, people from Asia are Asians, just as people from Africa are Africans and people from Europe are Europeans.

Affectional Orientation

Generally, *gay* is the preferred term to refer to a man who has an affectional orientation toward other men, and *lesbian* is the preferred term for a woman who has an affectional orientation toward other women (Lever, 1995). (*Lesbian* means "homosexual woman," so the term *lesbian woman* is redundant.) *Homosexual* refers to both gay men and lesbians, but more often to a sexual orientation to members of one's own sex. *Gay* and *lesbian* refer to a lifestyle and not merely to sexual orientation. *Gay* as a noun, although widely used, may prove offensive in some contexts, as in "We have two gays on the team." Because much scientific thinking holds that sexuality is not a matter of choice, the terms *sexual orientation* and *affectional orientation* are preferred to *sexual preference* or *sexual status.* In the case of same-sex marriages, there are two husbands or two wives. In a male-male marriage, each person is referred to as *husband* and in the case of female-female marriage, each person is referred to as *wife*. Some same-sex couples—especially those who are not married—prefer the term *partner* or *lover*.

Age and Sex

Older person is preferred to *elder, elderly, senior,* or *senior citizen* (the last term technically refers to someone older than 65). Usually, however, language designating age is unnecessary. There are times, of course, when you'll need to refer to a person's age group, but most of the time age is beside the point—in much the same way that racial or affectional orientation terms are usually irrelevant.

Generally, the term *girl* should be used only to refer to very young females and is equivalent to *boy*. Neither term should be used for people older than age 17 or 18. *Girl* is never used to refer to a grown woman, nor is *boy* used to refer to people in blue-collar positions, as it once was. *Lady* is negatively evaluated by many because it connotes the stereotype of the prim and proper woman. *Woman* or *young woman* is preferred.

The term *ma'am*, originally an honorific used to show respect, is probably best avoided because today it's often used as a verbal tag to comment (indirectly) on the woman's age or marital status (Angier, 2010).

Transgendered people (people who identify themselves as members of the sex opposite to the one they were assigned at birth and who may be gay or straight, male or female) are addressed according to their self-identified sex. Thus, if the person identifies herself as a woman, then the feminine name and pronouns are used—regardless of the person's biological sex. If the person identifies himself as a man, then the masculine name and pronouns are used.

Transvestites (people who prefer at times to dress in the clothing of the sex other than the one they were assigned at birth and who may be gay or straight, male or female) are addressed on the basis of their clothing. If the person is dressed as a woman—regardless of the birth-assigned sex—she is referred to and addressed with feminine pronouns and feminine name. If the person is dressed as a man—regardless of the birth-assigned sex—he is referred to and addressed with masculine pronouns and masculine name.

COMMUNICATION CHOICE POINT

HOMOPHOBIA *You're bringing your college roommate home for the holidays. She's an outspoken lesbian and your parents are homophobic. You want to prepare them for their holiday get-together.* **What are some things you might say to prepare your roommate and your family for what will probably be a bumpy weekend?**

Let's turn now from issues of confirmation to some guidelines for using language effectively by avoiding common mistakes and applying some simple principles.

5.3 USING VERBAL MESSAGES EFFECTIVELY

A chief concern in using verbal messages is to recognize what critical thinking theorists call "conceptual distortions"; that is, mental mistakes, misinterpretations, or reasoning fallacies. Avoiding these distortions and substituting a more critical, more realistic analysis is probably the best way to improve your own use of verbal messages (DeVito, 1974). Let's look at several principles of language that are often ignored or misunderstood, along with the conceptual distortions that result from such misunderstandings (Korzybski, 1933).

Language Symbolizes Reality (Partially)

Language symbolizes reality; it's not the reality itself. Of course, this is obvious. But consider: Have you ever reacted to the way something was labeled or described rather than to the actual item? Have you ever bought something because of its name rather than because of the actual object? If so, you were probably responding as if language were the reality, a distortion called intensional orientation.

Intensional Orientation

Intensional orientation (the *s* in *intensional* is intentional) is the tendency to view people, objects, and events according to the way they're talked about—the way they're labeled. For example, if Sally were labeled "uninteresting," you would, responding intensionally, evaluate her as uninteresting even before listening to what she had to say. You'd see Sally through a filter imposed by the label "uninteresting." **Extensional orientation**, on the other hand, is the tendency to look first at the actual people, objects, and events and only afterward at their labels. In this case, it would mean looking at Sally without any preconceived labels, guided by what she says and does, not by the words used to label her.

To avoid intensional orientation, **extensionalize**. Never give labels greater attention than the actual thing. Give your main attention to the people, things, and events in the world as you see them and not as they're presented in words. For example, when you meet Jack and Jill, observe and interact with them. Then form your impressions. Don't respond to them as "greedy, money-grubbing landlords" because Harry labeled them this way. Don't respond to George as "lazy" just because Elaine told you he was.

The accompanying Understanding Theory and Research box explores the concept of intensional orientation and its connection with the verb *to be*.

Allness

A related distortion is **allness:** forgetting that language symbolizes only a portion of reality, never the whole. When you assume that you can know all or say all about anything, you're into allness. In reality, you never can see all of anything. You never can experience anything fully. You see a part, then conclude what the whole is like. You have to draw conclusions on the basis of insufficient evidence (because you always have insufficient evidence). A useful extensional device to help combat the tendency to think that all can or has been said about

the•o•ry *noun* statement of explanation, formulation of relationships, reasoned generalization

UNDERSTANDING THEORY AND RESEARCH
The Verb *To Be*

The theory of **E-prime** (or E9) argues that if you wrote and spoke English without the verb *to be*, you'd describe events more accurately (Bourland, 1965–1966; Bourland & Johnston, 1998; Klein, 1992; Wilson, 1989). For example, when you say, "Johnny is a failure," the verb is implies that "failure" is in Johnny rather than in your observation or evaluation of Johnny. The verb *to be* (in forms such as *is, are,* and *am*) also implies permanence; the implication is that because failure is in Johnny, it will always be there; Johnny will always be a failure. A more accurate and descriptive statement might be "Johnny failed his last two math exams."

Consider this theory as applied to your thinking about yourself. When you say, for example, "I'm not good at public speaking" or "I'm unpopular" or "I'm lazy," you imply that these qualities are in you. But these are simply evaluations that may be incorrect or, if at least partly accurate, may change over time (Joyner, 1993).

Working with Theories and Research

How might you apply the E-prime principle to gain greater understanding of the ways in which you view yourself? To answer this question you might try first to identify yourself (who you are, what you are) in a few sentences using forms of the verb to be and then to rephrase these same sentences in E-prime. What different perspectives do these two versions give you?

anything is to end each statement mentally with **et cetera**—a reminder that there's more to learn, more to know, and more to say and that every statement is inevitably incomplete. Instead of saying, for example, "I wouldn't like her; I saw the way she treated her father," you'd say, "I don't think I'd like her; I saw the way she treated her father, but I haven't seen her with other people, and I really don't know her father, et cetera." Of course, some people overuse the "et cetera." They use it not as a mental reminder, but as a substitute for being specific. This obviously is to be avoided and merely adds to conversational confusion.

To avoid allness, recognize that language symbolizes only a part of reality, never the whole. Whatever someone says—regardless of what it is or how extensive it is—represents only a part of the story.

Language Expresses Both Facts and Inferences

Language enables you to form statements of both facts and inferences without making any linguistic distinction between the two. Similarly, in speaking and listening you often don't make a clear distinction between statements of fact and statements of inference. Yet there are great differences between the two. Barriers to clear thinking can be created when inferences are treated as facts, a tendency called **fact-inference confusion.**

For example, you can say, "She's wearing a blue jacket," and you can say, "He's harboring an illogical hatred." Although the sentences have similar structures, they're different. You can observe the jacket and its color, but how do you observe "illogical hatred"? Obviously, this is not a factual statement but an **inferential statement**. It's a statement you make on the basis not only of what you observe, but of what you infer. For a statement to be considered a **factual statement**, it must be made by the observer after observation and must be limited to what is observed (Weinberg, 1958). You can test your ability to distinguish facts from inferences by taking the fact-inference self-test below (based on the tests constructed in Haney, 1973). Carefully read the following report and the observations based on it. Indicate whether you think the observations are true, false, or doubtful on the basis of the information presented in the report. Write ***T*** if the observation is definitely true, ***F*** if the observation is definitely false, and ***?*** if the observation may be either true or false. Judge each observation in order. Don't reread the observations after you've indicated your judgment, and don't change any of your answers.

A well-liked college teacher had just completed making up the final examinations and had turned off the lights in the office. Just then a tall, broad figure with dark glasses appeared and demanded the examination. The professor opened the drawer. Everything in the drawer was picked up and the individual ran down the corridor. The dean was notified immediately.

_____ **1.** The thief was tall and broad and wore dark glasses.
_____ **2.** The professor turned off the lights.
_____ **3.** A tall figure demanded the examination.
_____ **4.** The examination was picked up by someone.
_____ **5.** The examination was picked up by the professor.
_____ **6.** A tall, broad figure appeared after the professor turned off the lights in the office.
_____ **7.** The man who opened the drawer was the professor.
_____ **8.** The professor ran down the corridor.
_____ **9.** The drawer was never actually opened.
_____ **10.** Three persons are referred to in this report.

Statement 3 is true, statement 9 is false, and all the rest are ?. Review your answers by referring back to the story. To get you started, consider: Is there necessarily a thief? Might the dean have demanded to see the instructor's examination (statement 1)? Did the examination have to be in the drawer (statements 4 and 5)? How do you know it was the professor who turned off the lights (statement 6)? Need the professor have been a man (statement 7)? Do the instructor and the professor have to be the same person (statement 10)?

There is nothing wrong with making inferential statements. You must make them in order to talk about much that is meaningful to you. The problem arises when you act as if those inferential statements were factual. To avoid fact-inference confusion, phrase inferential statements in such a way as to show that they are tentative. Inferential statements should leave open the possibility of alternatives. If, for example, you treat the statement "Our biology teacher was fired for poor teaching" as factual, you eliminate any alternatives. But if you preface your statement with, say, "Pat told me ..." or "I'm wondering if ..." the inferential nature of your statement will be clear. Be especially sensitive to this distinction when you're listening. Most talk is inferential. Beware of the speaker who presents everything as fact. Analyze closely and you'll uncover a world of inferences.

Language Is Relatively Static

Language changes only very slowly, especially when compared to the rapid change in people and things. **Static evaluation** is the tendency to retain evaluations without change while the reality to which they refer is changing. Often a verbal statement you make about an event or person remains static ("That's the way he is; he's always been that way") while the event or person may change enormously.

The mental **date** is an extensional device that helps you keep your language (and your thinking) up to date and helps you guard against static evaluation. The procedure is simple: date your statements and especially your evaluations. Remember that Pat Smith_{2012} is not Pat Smith_{2015}; academic abilities_{2012} are not academic abilities_{2015}. T. S. Eliot, in *The Cocktail Party*, said, "What we know of other people is only our memory of the moments during which we knew them. And they have changed since then ... at every meeting we are meeting a stranger." In listening, look carefully at messages that claim that what was true still is. It may or may not be. Look for change.

Language Can Obscure Distinctions

Language can obscure distinctions among people or events that are covered by the same label but are really quite different (indiscrimination); it can also make it easy to focus on extremes rather than on the vast middle ground between opposites (polarization).

Indiscrimination

Indiscrimination is the failure to distinguish between similar but different people, objects, or events. This error occurs when you focus on categories or classes and fail to see that each phenomenon is unique and needs to be looked at individually.

Everything is unlike everything else. Our language, however, provides you with common nouns, such as teacher, student, friend, enemy, war, politician, and liberal. These lead you to focus on similarities—to group together all teachers, all students, and all politicians. At the same time, the terms divert attention away from the uniqueness of each person, each object, and each event.

This misevaluation is at the heart of stereotyping on the basis of nationality, race, religion, sex, and affectional orientation. A stereotype, as you know, is a fixed mental picture of a group that is applied to each individual in the group without regard to his or her unique qualities. Whether stereotypes are positive or negative, they create the same problem: They provide you with shortcuts that are often inappropriate.

A useful antidote to indiscrimination (and stereotyping) is another extensional device called the **index**. This mental subscript identifies each individual as an individual—even though both may be covered by the same label. Thus, politician_1 is not politician_2, teacher_1 is not teacher_2. The index helps you to discriminate among without discriminating against. Although the label (*politician*, for example) covers all politicians, the index makes sure that each is thought about as an individual. The index would, for example, prevent you from grouping all Muslims or all Christians or all Jews in the same category. Each Muslim, each Christian, and each Jew is unique and needs a unique index number. So at the same time that you have to generalize and appreciate similarities, the index reminds you also to look at differences.

Polarization

Another way in which language can obscure differences is in its preponderance of extreme terms and its relative lack of middle terms, a characteristic that often leads to polarization. **Polarization** is the tendency to look at the world in terms of opposites and to describe it in extremes—good or bad, positive or negative, healthy or sick, intelligent or stupid. Polarization is often referred to as the fallacy of "either/or" or "black or white." Most people exist somewhere between the extremes. Yet there's a strong tendency to view only the extremes and to categorize people, objects, and events in terms of polar opposites.

Problems are created when opposites are used in inappropriate situations. For example, "So-and-so is either for us or against us." These options don't include all possibilities. The person may be for us in some things and against us in other things or may be neutral.

To correct this polarizing tendency, beware of implying (and believing) that two extreme classes include all possible classes—that an individual must be one or the other, with no alternatives ("Are you pro-choice or pro-life?"). Most people, most events, most qualities exist between polar extremes. When others imply that there are only two sides or alternatives, look for the middle ground.

Explore the Exercise "How Do You Talk about the Middle?" at MyCommunicationLab

Analyzing Video Choices

Margo is a sophomore at a college that is about to throw its annual homecoming party. She has her eye on a dorm mate named Kevin who she'd like to take as a date to the party, but Kevin is DJing the event. While Margo is talking to a friend in the dorm lounge, her good friend Luis walks up to her and asks her if she'd like to go to the party with him. Margo isn't interested in dating Luis, but she'd like to go to the party, and she doesn't want to show up alone. She also doesn't know if Luis is asking her out on a date or if he just doesn't want show up alone, as well. She wants to know Luis's intentions and wants to find out without jeopardizing their friendship. She considers the topics covered in this chapter as she contemplates her communication choices in an effort to make her messages clear and unambiguous, confirming rather than disconfirming, and say what she means. Log on to www.mycommunicationlab.com to view this video, "Homecoming Party," see how the choices played out, and then answer the related discussion questions.

Watch the Video "Homecoming Party" at MyCommunicationLab

Study and Review materials for this chapter are at MyCommunicationLab

SUMMARY: VERBAL MESSAGES

This chapter focused on verbal messages and specifically on the nature of language and the ways language works; the concept of disconfirmation and how it relates to racism, heterosexism, ageism, and sexism; and the ways in which language can be used more effectively.

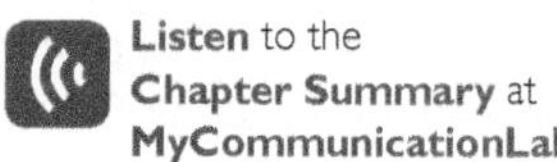

Listen to the Chapter Summary at MyCommunicationLab

5.1 PRINCIPLES OF VERBAL MESSAGES

1. Meanings are in people, not in things.
2. Language is both denotative (objective and generally easily agreed upon) and connotative (subjective and generally highly individual in meaning).
3. Meanings are context based; the same message in a different context will likely mean something different. Among the most important contexts are the cultural and the gender contexts.
4. Messages (in all forms of communication) vary in politeness.
5. Meanings vary in assertiveness.
6. Message meanings can deceive.
7. Messages are influenced by culture and gender.

5.2 DISCONFIRMATION AND CONFIRMATION

8. Disconfirmation is the process of ignoring the presence and the communications of others. Confirmation is accepting, supporting, and acknowledging the importance of the other person.
9. Racist, heterosexist, ageist, and sexist language puts down and negatively evaluates members of various groups.

5.3 USING VERBAL MESSAGES EFFECTIVELY

10. Using language effectively involves eliminating conceptual distortions and substituting more accurate assumptions about language.
11. Language symbolizes reality; it's not the reality itself, so avoid intensional orientation and allness.
12. Language can express both facts and inferences, so learn to make distinctions between them.
13. Language is relatively static, but reality changes rapidly; try to constantly revise the way you talk about people and things.
14. Language can obscure distinctions in its use of general terms and in its emphasis on extreme rather than middle terms, so be careful to avoid indiscrimination and polarization.

 **Study** and **Review** the **Flashcards** at **MyCommunicationLab**

KEY TERMS

ageism *111*
allness *115*
bypassing *101*
confirmation *109*
connotation *102*
date *117*
deception bias *107*
denotation *102*
direct messages *104*
disconfirmation *108*
E-prime *115*
et cetera *116*
extensionalize *115*
extensional orientation *115*
fact–inference confusion *116*
factual statement *116*
heterosexism *110*
heterosexist language *110*
index *117*
indirect messages *105*
indiscrimination *117*
inferential statement *116*
intensional orientation *115*
lying *106*
polarization *117*
politeness *104*
principle of cooperation *102*
purr words *102*
racism *110*
racist language *110*
rejection *109*
sexism *112*
sexist language *112*
snarl words *102*
static evaluation *117*
truth bias *107*

WORKING WITH VERBAL MESSAGES

5.1 Confirming, Rejecting, or Disconfirming. Here are three practice situations. For each situation, (a) write the three potential responses as indicated; then, (b) after completing all three situations, indicate what effects each type of response is likely to generate. As you'll see each type of response communicates a different message; generally, however, confirming messages are likely to increase relationship satisfaction and disconfirming messages are likely to decrease relationship satisfaction.

a. Enrique receives this semester's grades in the mail; they're a lot better than previous semesters' grades but are still not great. After opening the letter, Enrique says, "I really tried hard to get my grades up this semester." Enrique's parents respond:

With disconfirmation:

With rejection:

With confirmation:

b. Elizabeth, who has been out of work for the past several weeks, says, "I feel like such a failure; I just can't seem to find a job. I've been pounding the pavement for the last five weeks and still nothing." Elizabeth's friend responds:

With disconfirmation:

With rejection:

With confirmation:

c. Candi's colleague at work comes to her overjoyed and tells her that she was just promoted to vice president of marketing, skipping three steps in the hierarchy and tripling her salary. Candi responds:

With disconfirmation:

With rejection:

With confirmation:

5.2 Talking about the Middle. Although most things, people, and events fall between extremes, the common but illogical tendency is to concentrate on the extremes and ignore the middle. This exercise should illustrate one reason why we may focus on extremes. Fill in the word that would logically be the term's opposite in the column marked "opposite."

		Opposite
hot	____:____:_?_:____:____	____
high	____:____:_?_:____:____	____
good	____:____:_?_:____:____	____
popular	____:____:_?_:____:____	____
sad	____:____:_?_:____:____	____

Filling in these opposites was probably easy—the words you supplied were probably short, and, if various different people supplied opposites, you'd probably find a high level of agreement among them.

Now fill in the middle positions with words meaning, for example, "midway between hot and cold," "midway between high and low." Do this before reading further.

You probably had greater difficulty here. You probably took more time to think of these middle terms, and you also probably used multiword phrases. Further, you would probably find less agreement among different people completing this same task. From this brief experience what implications can you draw about polarization?

5.3 Changing Communication Styles. When researchers asked men and women what they would like to change about the communication style of the opposite sex, most men said they wanted women to be more direct, and most women said they wanted men to stop interrupting and offering advice (Noble, 1994). What one change would you like to see in the communication style of the opposite sex? Of your own sex?

5.4 Importance of a Concept. A widely held assumption in anthropology, linguistics, and communication is that the importance of a concept to a culture can be measured by the number of words the language has for talking about the concept. So, for example, in English there are lots of words for money, transportation, and communication, as all these concepts are important in English-speaking cultures. With this principle in mind, consider the findings of Julia Stanley, for example, who researched terms indicating sexual promiscuity. Stanley found 220 English-language terms referring to a sexually promiscuous woman but only 22 terms for a sexually promiscuous man (Thorne, Kramarae, & Henley, 1983). What does this suggest about cultural attitudes and beliefs about promiscuity in men and women?

5.5 Directness. How would you describe the level of directness you use when talking face to face versus the level you use in texting or in e-mail or chat rooms? If you do notice differences, to what do you attribute them?

5.6 Using Assertiveness Strategies. For any one of the following situations, compose (a) an aggressive, (b) a nonassertive, and (c) an assertive response. Then, in one sentence, explain why your message of assertiveness will be more effective than the aggressive or nonassertive message.

a. You've just redecorated your apartment, making it exactly as you want it. A good friend of yours brings you a house gift—the ugliest poster you've ever seen—and insists that you hang it over your fireplace, the focal point of your living room.

b. Your friend borrows $30 and promises to pay you back tomorrow. But tomorrow passes, as do 20 subsequent tomorrows. You know that your friend has not forgotten about the debt, and you also know that your friend has more than enough money to pay you back.

c. Your next-door neighbor repeatedly asks you to take care of her 4-year-old while she runs some errand or another. You don't mind helping out in an emergency, but this occurs almost every day.

5.7 Negative Terms. Many people feel that it's permissible for members of a particular culture to refer to themselves in terms that if said by outsiders would be considered racist, sexist, or heterosexist. Some researchers suggest a possible problem with this—the idea that these terms may actually reinforce negative stereotypes that the larger society has already assigned to the group (Guerin, 2003). Others would argue that by using such labels groups weaken the terms' negative impact. Do you refer to yourself using terms that would be considered offensive or politically incorrect if said by "outsiders"? What effects, if any, do you think such self-talk has?

LogOn! MyCommunicationLab www.mycommunicationlab.com

Throughout this chapter, there are icons that highlight media content for selected topics. Go to **MyCommunicationLab** for additional materials on verbal messages. Here you'll find flashcards to help you learn key communication terms, videos that illustrate a variety of concepts, additional exercises, and discussions to help you continue your study of the verbal system.

6 NONVERBAL MESSAGES

CHAPTER TOPICS	CHAPTER OBJECTIVES
In this chapter you'll explore the following major topics:	**After reading this chapter you should be able to:**
THE PRINCIPLES OF NONVERBAL COMMUNICATION	6.1 Define *nonverbal communication* and paraphrase the principles of nonverbal communication
THE CHANNELS OF NONVERBAL COMMUNICATION	6.2 Identify the major channels of nonverbal communication and give examples of the messages sent and received through these channels.
CULTURE AND NONVERBAL COMMUNICATION	6.3 Explain the role of culture in nonverbal communication.
SOME NONVERBAL COMMUNICATION SKILLS	6.4 Apply the skills for effective encoding and decoding of nonverbal messages.

Meaning is often communicated without words.

When you smile, nod your head in agreement, or wave your hand to someone, you're communicating nonverbally. In fact, some researchers argue that you actually communicate more information nonverbally than you do with words.

Watch at MyCommunicationLab Video: "Judee Burgoon Discusses Nonverbal Communication"

Nonverbal communication is communication without words. You communicate nonverbally when you gesture, smile or frown, widen your eyes, move your chair closer to someone, wear jewelry, touch someone, raise your vocal volume, or even say nothing. The crucial aspect of nonverbal communication is that the message you send is in some way received by one or more other people. If you gesture while alone in your room and no one is there to see you, then, most theorists would argue, communication has not taken place. The same, of course, is true of verbal messages; if you recite a speech and no one hears it, then communication has not taken place.

Using nonverbal communication effectively can yield two major benefits (Burgoon, Guerrero, & Floyd, 2010). First, the greater your ability to send and receive nonverbal signals, the higher your attractiveness, popularity, and psychosocial well-being are likely to be. Second, the greater your nonverbal skills, the more successful you're likely to be at communicating information and in influencing others.

Perhaps the best way to begin the study of nonverbal communication is to look at your own beliefs. Which of the following statements do you think are true?

1. Nonverbal communication conveys more meaning than verbal communication.
2. Liars avoid eye contact.
3. Studying nonverbal communication will enable you to read a person like a book.
4. Unlike verbal communication, nonverbal communication is universal throughout the world.
5. When verbal and nonverbal messages contradict each other, it's wise to believe the nonverbal.

Actually, all of these statements are popular myths about nonverbal communication. Briefly:

1. In some instances nonverbal messages may communicate more meaning than verbal messages, but in most cases it depends on the situation. You won't get very far discussing science and mathematics nonverbally, for example.
2. Some liars do avoid eye contact but others don't. And some truth-tellers avoid eye contact.
3. Studying nonverbal communication will yield lots of benefits, but not the ability to read a person's inner thoughts.
4. Actually, the same nonverbal signals may communicate very different meanings in different cultures.
5. People can be deceptive verbally as well as nonverbally; it's best to look at the entire group of signals before making a judgment but even then it won't be an easy or sure thing.

6.1 THE PRINCIPLES OF NONVERBAL COMMUNICATION

Let's begin the study of nonverbal communication by examining several principles that, as you'll see, also identify the different functions that nonverbal messages serve (Afifi, 2007; Burgoon & Bacue, 2003; Burgoon & Hoobler, 2002).

Explore at MyCommunicationLab Exercise: "Recognizing Verbal and Nonverbal Message Functions"

Nonverbal Messages Interact with Verbal Messages

Verbal and nonverbal messages interact with each other in six major ways: to accent, to complement, to contradict, to control, to repeat, and to substitute for each other.

- **Accent.** Nonverbal communication is often used to accent or emphasize some part of the verbal message. You might, for example, raise your voice to underscore a particular word or phrase, bang your fist on the desk to stress your commitment, or look longingly into someone's eyes when saying "I love you."
- **Complement.** Nonverbal communication may be used to complement, to add nuances of meaning not communicated by your verbal message. Thus, you might smile when telling a story (to suggest that you find it humorous) or frown and shake your head when recounting someone's deceit (to suggest your disapproval).
- **Contradict.** You may deliberately contradict your verbal messages with nonverbal movements; for example, by crossing your fingers or winking to indicate that you're lying.
- **Control.** Nonverbal movements may be used to control, or to indicate your desire to control, the flow of verbal messages, as when you purse your lips, lean forward, or make hand movements to

indicate that you want to speak. You might also put up your hand or vocalize your pauses (for example, with "um") to indicate that you have not finished and aren't ready to relinquish the floor to the next speaker.

- **Repeat.** You can repeat or restate the verbal message nonverbally. You can, for example, follow your verbal "Is that all right?" with raised eyebrows and a questioning look, or you can motion with your head or hand to repeat your verbal "Let's go."
- **Substitute.** You may also use nonverbal communication to substitute for verbal messages. You can, for example, signal "OK" with a hand gesture. You can nod your head to indicate yes or shake your head to indicate no.

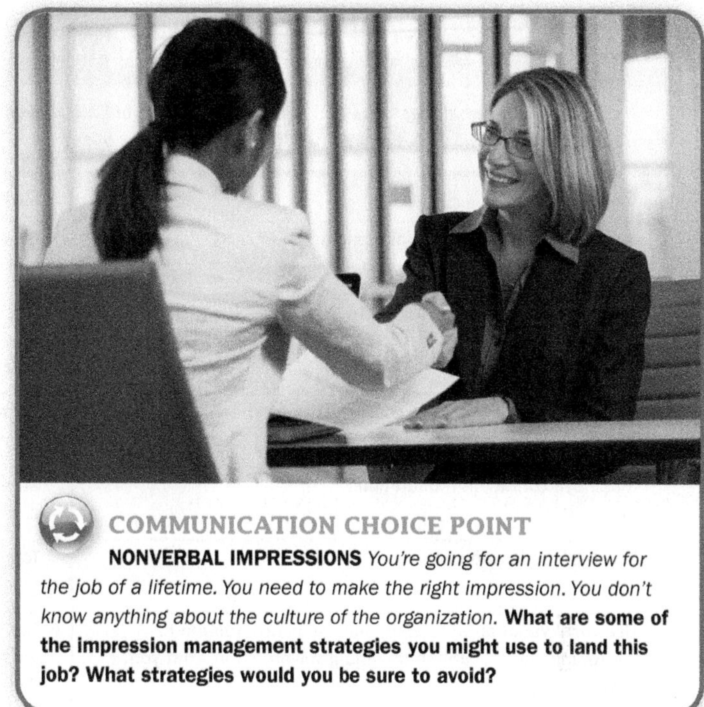

COMMUNICATION CHOICE POINT

NONVERBAL IMPRESSIONS *You're going for an interview for the job of a lifetime. You need to make the right impression. You don't know anything about the culture of the organization.* **What are some of the impression management strategies you might use to land this job? What strategies would you be sure to avoid?**

When you communicate electronically, of course, your message is communicated by means of typed letters without facial expressions or gestures that normally accompany face-to-face communication and without the changes in rate and volume that are a part of normal telephone communication. To compensate for this lack of nonverbal behavior, the emoticon was created (see Table 6.3 on page 128). Sometimes called a "smiley," the emoticon is a typed symbol that communicates through a keyboard the nuances of the message normally conveyed by nonverbal expression. The absence of the nonverbal channel through which you can clarify your message—for example, smiling or winking to communicate sarcasm or humor—make such typed symbols extremely helpful. And of course you can post photos and book and music album covers, for example, to further communicate your emotional meaning.

Nonverbal Messages Help Manage Impressions

It is largely through the nonverbal communications of others that you form impressions of them. Based on a person's body size, skin color, style of dress, eye contact, and facial expressions, you form an impression—you judge who the person is and what the person is like. Perhaps the most important nonverbal expression related to impressions is the smile.

Some smiles are real and are genuine expressions of our feelings; these are called Duchene smiles. Some smiles, however, are fake and are expressions of what we want others to think we're feeling. According to much facial research, we're not very good at distinguishing the real from the fake but it doesn't seem to matter; the real smile and the fake smile both seem to be appreciated (Ekman, 2009; Ekman & Friesen, 1975/2003; Skenazy, 2013).

It's also interesting to note that women perceive men who are smiled at by other women as being more attractive than men who are not smiled at. But, men—perhaps being more competitive—perceive men who women smile at as being less attractive than men who are not smiled at (Jones, DeBruine, Little, Burriss, & Feinberg, 2007). Smiles, however, also signal a lack of dominance; people who smile are generally perceived as having less power than those who don't smile (Skenazy, 2013).

At the same time that you form impressions of others, you are also managing the impressions they form of you. As explained in the discussion of impression management in Chapter 3 (pages 70–73), use different strategies to achieve different impressions. And of course many of these strategies involve nonverbal messages. Also, as noted earlier, each of these strategies may be used to present a false self and to deceive others. For example:

Watch at MyCommunicationLab **Video:** "Louder Than Words"

- **To be liked** you might smile, pat someone on the back, and shake hands warmly. See Table 6.1 on page 124 for some additional ways in which nonverbal communication may make you seem more attractive and more likeable.
- **To be believed** you might use focused eye contact, a firm stance, and open gestures.

TABLE 6.1 TEN NONVERBAL MESSAGES AND ATTRACTIVENESS

Here are 10 nonverbal messages that help communicate your attractiveness and 10 that will likely create the opposite effect (Andersen, 2004; Riggio & Feldman, 2005).

Dos	Don'ts
Gesture to show liveliness and animation in ways that are appropriate to the situation and to the message.	Gesture for the sake of gesturing or gesture in ways that may prove offensive to members of other cultures.
Nod and lean forward to signal that you're listening and are interested.	Go on automatic pilot, nodding without any coordination with what is being said, or lean so forward that you intrude on the other's space.
Smile and otherwise show your interest, attention, and positivity in your facial expressions.	Overdo it; inappropriate smiling is likely to be perceived negatively.
Make eye contact in moderation.	Stare, ogle, glare, or otherwise make the person feel that he or she is under scrutiny.
Touch in moderation when appropriate.	Touch excessively or too intimately. When in doubt, avoid touching another.
Use vocal variation in rate, rhythm, pitch, and volume to communicate your animation and involvement in what you're saying.	Falling into the pattern where, for example, your voice goes up and down, up and down, up and down without any relationship to what you're saying.
Use silence to listen. Show that you're listening with facial reactions, posture, and backchanneling cues.	Listen motionlessly or in ways that suggest you're only listening half-heartedly.
Stand reasonably close to show a connectedness.	Exceed the other person's comfort zone.
Present a pleasant smell and be careful to camouflage the onions, garlic, or smoke that you don't notice.	Overdo the cologne or perfume.
Dress appropriately to the situation.	Wear clothing that is uncomfortable or that calls attention to itself and hence away from your message.

- **To excuse failure** you might look sad, cover your face with your hands, and shake your head.
- **To secure help** while indicating helplessness you might use open hand gestures, a puzzled look, and inept movements.
- **To hide faults** you might avoid self-adaptors.
- **To be followed** you might dress the part of a leader or put your diploma or awards where others can see them.
- **To confirm self-image and to communicate it to others** you might dress in certain ways or decorate your apartment with things that reflect your personality.

Nonverbal Messages Help Form Relationships

Much of your relationship life is lived nonverbally. You communicate affection, support, and love, in part at least, nonverbally (Floyd & Mikkelson, 2005). At the same time, you also communicate your displeasure, anger, and animosity throughout nonverbal signals.

You also use nonverbal signals to communicate the nature of your relationship to another person; and you and that person communicate nonverbally with each other. These signals that communicate your relationship status are known as "tie signs" because they indicate the ways in which your relationship is tied together (Afifi & Johnson, 2005; Goffman, 1967; Knapp & Hall, 2010). Tie signs vary in intimacy and may extend from the relatively informal handshake through the more intimate forms such as hand holding and arm linking to very intimate forms like full mouth kissing (Andersen, 2004). Tie signs are also used to confirm the level of the relationship. For instance, you might hold hands to see if your partner responds positively. And of course tie signs are often used to communicate your relationship status to others.

You also use nonverbal signals to communicate your relationship dominance and status (Dunbar & Burgoon, 2005; Knapp & Hall, 2010). The large corner office with the huge desk communicates high status just as the basement cubicle communicates low status.

Nonverbal Messages Structure Conversation

When you're in conversation, you give and receive cues that you're ready to speak, listen, or comment on what the speaker just said. These cues regulate and structure the interaction. These turn-taking cues may be verbal (as when you say, "What do you think?"), but most often they're nonverbal: A nod of the head in the direction of someone else, for example, signals that you're ready to give up your speaking turn and want this other person to say something. You also show that you're listening and that you want the conversation to continue (or that you're not listening and want the conversation to end) largely through nonverbal signals.

Nonverbal Messages Can Influence and Deceive

You can influence others not only through what you say, but you also exert influence through your nonverbal signals. A focused glance that says you're committed; gestures that further explain what you're saying; appropriate dress that says, "I'll easily fit in with this organization" are a few examples of ways in which you can exert nonverbal influence.

And with the ability to influence, of course, comes the ability to deceive–to lie, to mislead another person into thinking something is true when it's false or that something is false when it's true (see Chapter 5, pages 106–108). One common example of nonverbal deception is using your eyes and facial

me•di•a lit•er•a•cy *noun* ability to understand, interact with, and create media messages

EXPANDING MEDIA LITERACY
Product Placement

In much the same way that you make judgments about people on the basis of the products they use (jewelry, furs, and name brands from Prada to Old Navy), you also make judgments about products on the basis of the people who use them, a tendency that has spawned huge product placement efforts by major corporations. Product placement refers simply to the placement of a product—for a fee but without any explicit advertising statements—within a scene of a movie or television show to give the product a certain image. The advertiser's hope is that you'll identify with the actor using the product (i.e., you want to be like the character in some way) and that you too will then also buy the product. The actor and the movie give the product an image that the advertiser assumes will help sell the product.

In the 2012 James Bond movie *Skyfall*, for example, Heineken paid $45 million to have Bond drink its beer (*New York Daily News*, November 9, 2012). In addition, Bond wears a Tom Ford suit and an Omega watch, while Q uses a Sony Vaio—all very clear to the viewer. The more recent Superman *Man of Steel* 2013 movie currently holds the record for product placement, according to MSNBC. The film earned $160 million just from the placement of products in the film—for example, the Caspi Sun that Superman drinks and the Gillette razors he uses. The same is true on television; the Cheesecake Factory on *The Big Bang Theory* and McDonald's on *30 Rock* are good examples. Product placement is, of course, nothing new; recall James Bond's Aston Martin in the 1964 movie *Goldfinger* and E.T. eating Reese's Pieces in the 1982 movie *E. T. The Extra-Terrestrial*.

As you no doubt already know, product placement is occurring in television sitcoms and dramas and in feature films with ever increasing frequency. The fact that this type of advertising aims to influence you below the level of conscious awareness raises all sorts of serious ethical issues. Those who favor or defend product placement, such as the American Advertising Federation, argue:

> Product placement is a legitimate source of advertising revenue and is not deceptive. It benefits both content producers and consumers and adds verisimilitude to fictional programming. We oppose proposals that would require simultaneous "pop up" notices of every instance of product placement, believing this would make television unwatchable. We instead believe the current practice of disclosures at the end of the program works well.

Those who oppose product placement argue that it's deceptive because viewers are not aware that it's a paid advertisement. It is subliminal advertising—messages that somehow get communicated without mindfulness or awareness. And, despite the AAF's statement, no one can really read the disclosures at the end of a television program, nor would anyone want to. Furthermore, the enormous profits to be made from product placement will likely lead to its spread to news shows, which will further erode fairness and objectivity. Regardless of the possible ethical violations, product placement is likely to remain a part of movies and television; it is too lucrative a market for it to disappear anytime soon. Media literacy is here a survival skill.

expressions to communicate a liking for other people when you're really interested only in gaining their support in some endeavor. Not surprisingly, you also interpret nonverbal signals to try to detect deception in others. For example, you may well suspect a person of lying if he or she avoids eye contact, fidgets, and conveys inconsistent verbal and nonverbal messages. Relying on nonverbal cues to detect lying is likely to get you into trouble by leading you to formulate incorrect conclusions (Burgoon, Guerrero, & Floyd, 2010; Knapp, 2008).

A particularly clear example of the use of nonverbal messages to influence (and perhaps deceive) is seen in the media's use of what has come to be called product placement, a topic addressed in the accompanying Expanding Media Literacy box.

Nonverbal Messages Are Crucial for Expressing Emotions

Although people often explain and reveal emotions verbally, nonverbal expressions communicate a great part of your emotional experience. For example, you reveal your level of happiness, sadness, or confusion largely through facial expressions. You also reveal your feelings by posture (for example, whether tense or relaxed), gestures, eye movements, and even the dilation of your pupils.

Nonverbal messages often help people communicate unpleasant messages—messages they might feel uncomfortable putting into words (Infante, Rancer, & Avtgis, 2010). For example, you might avoid eye contact and maintain large distances between yourself and someone with whom you didn't want to interact or with whom you wanted to decrease the intensity of your relationship.

At the same time, you also use nonverbal messages to hide your emotions. You might, for example, smile even though you feel sad so as not to dampen the party spirit. Or you might laugh at someone's joke even though you think it silly.

Explore at MyCommunicationLab Exercise: "Communicating Emotions Nonverbally"

6.2 THE CHANNELS OF NONVERBAL COMMUNICATION

Nonverbal communication is probably most easily explained in terms of the various channels through which messages pass. Here we'll survey 10 channels: (1) body, (2) face, (3) eye, (4) space, (5) artifactual, (6) touch, (7) paralanguage, (8) silence, (9) time, and (10) smell.

Explore at MyCommunicationLab Activity: "Nonverbal Communication"

Body Communication

Two areas of the body are especially important in communicating messages. First, the movements you make with your body communicate; second, the general appearance of your body communicates.

Body Gestures

Researchers in **kinesics,** or the study of nonverbal communication through face and body movements, identify five major types of movements: emblems, illustrators, affect displays, regulators, and adaptors (Ekman & Friesen, 1969; Knapp & Hall, 2010).

Emblems are body gestures that directly translate into words or phrases; for example, the OK sign, the thumbs-up for "good job," and the V for victory. You use these consciously and purposely to communicate the same meaning as the words. But emblems are culture specific, so be careful when using your culture's emblems in other cultures. Here are a few cultural differences in the emblems you may commonly use (Axtell, 1993, 2007):

- In the United States, to say "hello" you wave with your whole hand moving from side to side, but in a large part of Europe that same signal means "no." In Greece such a gesture would be considered insulting.
- In Texas the raised fist with little finger and index finger held upright is a positive expression of support, because it represents the Texas longhorn steer. But in Italy it's an insult that means "Your spouse is having an affair with someone else." In parts of South America it's a gesture to ward off evil, and in parts of Africa it's a curse: "May you experience bad times."
- In the United States and in much of Asia, hugs are rarely exchanged among acquaintances; but among Latins and southern Europeans, hugging is a common greeting gesture, and failing to hug someone may communicate unfriendliness.

Illustrators enhance (literally "illustrate") the verbal messages they accompany. Most often you illustrate with your hands, but you can also illustrate with head and general body movements. You might, for example, turn your head or your entire body toward the left when referring to something on the left. You might also use illustrators to communicate the shape or size of objects you're talking about. Interestingly enough, illustrators increase your ability to remember. In one study, for example, people who illustrated their verbal messages with gestures remembered some 20 percent more than those who didn't gesture (Goldin-Meadow, Nusbaum, Kelly, & Wagner, 2001).

Affect displays are movements of the face (smiling or frowning, for example) but also of the hands and general body (body tension or relaxation, for example) that communicate emotional meaning. Often affect displays are unconscious; you often smile or frown without awareness. At other times, however, you may smile consciously, trying to convey your pleasure or satisfaction. Not surprisingly, people who smile spontaneously are judged to be more likable and more approachable than people who don't smile or people who pretend to smile (Gladstone & Parker, 2002.

Regulators are behaviors that monitor, control, coordinate, or maintain the speaking of another individual. When you nod your head, for example, you tell the speaker to keep on speaking; when you lean forward and open your mouth, you tell the speaker that you would like to say something.

Adaptors are gestures that satisfy some personal need, such as scratching to relieve an itch or moving your hair out of your eyes. **Self-adaptors** are self-touching movements (for example, rubbing your nose). **Alter-adaptors** are movements directed at the person with whom you're speaking, such as removing lint from someone's jacket or straightening a person's tie or folding your arms in front of you to keep others a comfortable distance from you. **Object-adaptors** are gestures focused on objects, such as doodling on or shredding a Styrofoam coffee cup. Table 6.2 summarizes these five types of body movements.

Body Appearance

Your general body appearance also communicates. Height, for example, has been shown to be significant in a wide variety of situations. Tall presidential candidates have a much better record of winning the election than do their shorter opponents. Tall people seem to be paid more and are favored by interviewers over shorter job applicants (Guerrero & Hecht, 2008; Keyes, 1980; Knapp & Hall, 2010). Taller people also have higher self-esteem and greater career success than do shorter people (Judge & Cable, 2004).

Your body also reveals your ethnicity (through skin color and tone) and may also give clues as to your more specific nationality. Your weight in proportion to your height will also communicate messages to others, as will the length, color, and style of your hair.

Your general **attractiveness** is also a part of body communication. Attractive people have the advantage in just about every activity you can name. They get better grades in school, are more valued as friends and lovers, and are preferred as coworkers (Burgoon, Guerrero, & Floyd, 2010).

Facial Communication

Your face communicates various messages, especially your emotions. Facial movements alone seem to communicate the degree of pleasantness, agreement, and sympathy felt; the rest of the body doesn't provide any additional information. But for other emotional messages—for example, the intensity with which an emotion is felt—both facial and bodily cues send messages (Graham & Argyle, 1975; Graham, Bitti, & Argyle, 1975). The importance of these cues seems to have led to the creation of the ubiquitous smiley face and emoticons generally used in e-mail and text messaging (see Table 6.3 on page 128).

Some researchers in nonverbal communication claim that facial movements may express at least the following eight emotions: happiness, surprise, fear, anger, sadness, disgust, contempt, and interest (Ekman, Friesen, & Ellsworth, 1972). Facial expressions of these emotions are generally called primary affect displays: They indicate relatively pure, single emotions. Other

TABLE 6.2 FIVE BODY MOVEMENTS

What other examples can you think of for these five movements?

Name and Function	Examples
EMBLEMS directly translate words or phrases; they are especially culture specific.	"OK" sign, "come here" wave, hitchhiker's sign
ILLUSTRATORS accompany and literally "illustrate" verbal messages.	Circular hand movements when talking of a circle; hands far apart when talking of something large
AFFECT DISPLAYS communicate emotional meaning.	Expressions of happiness, surprise, fear, anger, sadness, disgust/contempt
REGULATORS monitor, maintain, or control the speech of another.	Facial expressions and hand gestures indicating "keep going," "slow down," or "what else happened?"
ADAPTORS satisfy some need.	Scratching your head

TABLE 6.3 SOME POPULAR EMOTICONS

Here are a few of the many popular emoticons used in computer communication. The first nine are popular in the United States; the last three are popular in Japan and illustrate how culture influences such symbols. That is, because Japanese culture considers it impolite for women to show their teeth when smiling, the emoticon for a woman's smile shows a dot signifying a closed mouth. An excellent website that contains extensive examples of smileys, emoticons, acronyms, and shorthand abbreviations is the website of Net Lingo. Also look up "emoji," the Japanese smileys that are much more elaborate and diversified.

Emoticon	Meaning	Emoticon	Meaning
:-)	Smile; I'm kidding	*This is important*	Substitutes for underlining or italics
:-(	Frown; I'm feeling down	<G>	Grin; I'm kidding
*	Kiss	<grin>	Grin; I'm kidding
{}	Hug	^.^	Woman's smile
{*****}	Hugs and kisses	^_^	Man's smile
This is important	Gives emphasis, calls special attention to	^o^	Happy

emotional states and other facial displays are combinations of these various primary emotions and are called affect blends. You communicate these blended feelings with different parts of your face. For example, you may experience both fear and disgust at the same time. Your eyes and eyelids may signal fear, and movements of your nose, cheek, and mouth area may signal disgust.

Facial Management

As you learned your culture's nonverbal system of communication, you also learned certain **facial management techniques** that enable you to communicate your feelings to achieve the effect you want—for example, ways to hide certain emotions and to emphasize others. Here are several purposes such techniques may serve (Malandro, Barker, & Barker, 1989; Metts & Planalp, 2002).

- ***To intensify:*** to exaggerate your astonishment at a surprise party to make your friends feel better.
- ***To deintensify:*** to cover up your own joy about good news in the presence of a friend who didn't receive any such news.
- ***To neutralize:*** to cover up your sadness so as not to depress others.
- ***To mask:*** to express happiness in order to cover up your disappointment at not receiving a gift you expected.
- ***To simulate:*** to express an emotion you didn't feel.

These tactics of facial management help you display emotions in socially acceptable ways. For example, when someone gets bad news in which you may secretly take pleasure, the cultural display rule dictates that you frown and otherwise nonverbally signal your displeasure. If you place first in a race and your best friend barely finishes, the display rule requires that you minimize your expression of pleasure in winning and avoid any signs of gloating. If you violate these display rules, you'll seem insensitive. So, although facial management techniques may be deceptive, they're also expected—in fact required—by the rules of polite interaction.

Explore at MyCommunicationLab Exercise: "Facial Expressions"

Encoding–Decoding Accuracy

Research in 11 different countries shows that women are better than men at both encoding and decoding nonverbal cues (Rosenthal & DePaulo, 1979). It may be argued that because men and women play different roles in society, they've learned different adaptive techniques and skills to help them perform these roles. Thus, in most societies women are expected to be more friendly, nurturing, and supportive and so learn these skills (Eagly & Crowley, 1986)..

Accuracy also varies with the emotions themselves. Some emotions are easier to encode and decode than others. In one study, for example, people judged facial expressions of happiness with an accuracy ranging from 55 to 100 percent, surprise from 38 to 86 percent, and sadness from 19 to 88 percent (Ekman, Friesen, & Ellsworth, 1972).

Eye Communication

Research on the messages communicated by the eyes (a study known technically as oculesis) shows

the•o•ry *noun* statement of explanation, formulation of relationships, reasoned generalization

UNDERSTANDING THEORY AND RESEARCH
The Facial Feedback Hypothesis

The **facial feedback hypothesis** claims that your facial expressions influence physiological arousal (Cappella, 1993). In one study, for example, participants held a pen in their teeth to simulate a sad expression and then rated a series of photographs. Results showed that mimicking sad expressions actually increased the degree of sadness the subjects reported feeling when viewing the photographs (Larsen, Kasimatis, & Frey, 1992). Further support for this hypothesis comes from a study that compared (1) participants who felt emotions such as happiness and anger with (2) participants who both felt and expressed these emotions. In support of the facial feedback hypothesis, people who felt and expressed the emotions became emotionally aroused faster than did those who only felt the emotion (Burgoon, Guerrero, & Floyd, 2010; Hess et al., 1992).

Generally, research finds that facial expressions can produce or heighten feelings of sadness, fear, disgust, and anger. But this effect does not occur with all emotions; smiling, for example, doesn't seem to make us feel happier. Further, it has not been demonstrated that facial expressions can eliminate one feeling and replace it with another. So if you're feeling sad, smiling will not eliminate the sadness and replace it with gladness. A reasonable conclusion seems to be that your facial expressions can influence some feelings, but not all (Burgoon, Guerrero, & Floyd, 2010).

Working with Theories and Research

What effect do you observe when you express your emotions? Do your feelings get stronger? Weaker?

that these messages vary depending on the duration, direction, and quality of the eye behavior. For example, in every culture there are strict, though unstated, rules for the proper duration for eye contact. In U.S. culture the average length of gaze is 2.95 seconds. The average length of mutual gaze (two persons gazing at each other) is 1.18 seconds (Argyle, 1988; Argyle & Ingham, 1972). When eye contact falls short of this amount, you may think the person is uninterested, shy, or preoccupied. When the appropriate amount of time is exceeded, you may perceive the person as showing unusually high interest.

The direction of the eye also communicates. In much of the United States, you're expected to glance alternately at the other person's face, then away, then again at the face, and so on. The rule for the public speaker is to scan the entire audience, not focusing for too long on or ignoring any one area of the audience. When you break these directional rules, you communicate different meanings—abnormally high or low interest, self-consciousness, nervousness over the interaction, and so on. The quality of eye behavior—how wide or how narrow your eyes get during interaction—also communicates meaning, especially interest level and such emotions as surprise, fear, and disgust. Some researchers note that eye contact serves to enable gay men and lesbians to signal their homosexuality and perhaps their interest in the other person—an ability referred to as "gaydar" (Nicholas, 2004).

Eye Contact

Eye contact can serve a variety of functions. One such function is to seek feedback. In talking with someone, we look at her or him intently, as if to say, "Well, what do you think?" As you might predict, listeners gaze at speakers more than speakers gaze at listeners. In public speaking, you may scan hundreds of people to secure this feedback.

A second function is to inform the other person that the channel of communication is open and that he or she should now speak. You see this regularly in conversation, when one person asks a question or finishes a thought and then looks to you for a response. And one study found that eye contact was the most frequently noted nonverbal behavior used to tell library users that the librarian was approachable (Radford, 1998).

Eye movements may also signal the nature of a relationship, whether positive (an attentive glance) or negative (eye avoidance). You can also signal your power through **visual dominance** behavior (Exline, Ellyson, & Long, 1975). The average person, for example, maintains a high level of eye contact while listening and a lower level while speaking. When people want to signal dominance, they may reverse this pattern—maintaining a high level of eye contact while talking but a much lower level while listening.

By making eye contact you psychologically lessen the physical distance between yourself and another person. When you catch someone's eye at a party, for example, you become psychologically close though physically far apart.

Explore at MyCommunicationLab Exercise: "Eye Contact"

Eye Avoidance

Eye avoidance, too, can serve several different functions. When you avoid eye contact or avert your glance, you may help others maintain their privacy. For example, you may do this when you see a couple arguing in public. You turn your eyes away (though your eyes may be wide open) as if to say, "I don't mean to intrude; I respect your privacy," a behavior referred to as **civil inattention** (Goffman, 1971).

Eye avoidance can also signal lack of interest—in a person, a conversation, or some visual stimulus. At times, too, you may hide your eyes to block out unpleasant stimuli (a particularly gory or violent scene in a movie, for example) or close your eyes to block out visual stimuli and thus heighten other senses. For example, you may listen to music with your eyes closed. Lovers often close their eyes while kissing, and many prefer to make love in a dark or dimly lit room.

In some cases, the visual channel may be damaged and adjustments have to be made. Table 6.4 gives you an idea of how such adjustment between people with visual impairments and those without such impairments can make communication more effective.

TABLE 6.4 COMMUNICATION TIPS

Between People with and People without Visual Impairments

TIPS

People vary greatly in their visual abilities; some are totally blind, some are partially sighted, and some have unimpaired vision. Ninety percent of people who are "legally blind" have some vision. All people, however, have the same need for communication and information. Here are some tips for making communication better between those who have visual impairments and those without such difficulties.

If you're the person without visual impairment and are talking with a person with visual impairment:

Generally	**Specifically**
Identify yourself.	Don't assume the visually impaired person will recognize your voice.
Face your listener; you'll be easier to hear.	Don't shout. Most people who are visually impaired are not hearing impaired. Speak at your normal volume.
Encode into speech all the meanings you wish to communicate.	Remember that your gestures, eye movements, and facial expressions cannot be seen by the visually impaired.
Use audible turn-taking cues.	When you pass the role of speaker to a person who is visually impaired, don't rely on nonverbal cues; instead, say something like "Do you agree with that, Joe?"
Use normal vocabulary and discuss topics that you would discuss with sighted people.	Don't avoid terms like *see* or *look* or even *blind*. Don't avoid discussing a television show or the way your new car looks; these are normal topics for all people.

If you are a person with visual impairment and are talking with a person without visual impairment:

Help the sighted person meet your special communication needs.	If you want your surroundings described, ask. If you want the person to read the road signs, ask.
Be patient with the sighted person.	Many people are nervous talking with people who are visually impaired for fear of offending. Put them at ease in a way that also makes you more comfortable.
Demonstrate your comfort.	When appropriate, let the other person know that you're comfortable with the interaction, verbally or nonverbally.

Source: These suggestions were drawn from a variety of sources, including the websites of the Cincinnati Association for the Blind and Visual Impaired, the Association for the Blind of WA, the National Federation of the Blind, and the American Foundation for the Blind, all accessed October 25, 2013.

Space Communication

Space is an especially important factor in interpersonal communication, although we seldom think about it. Edward T. Hall (1959, 1963, 1976) pioneered the study of spatial communication and called this research area **proxemics.** We can examine this broad area by looking at (1) proxemic distances and (2) territoriality.

Proxemic Distances

Hall (1959, 1963, 1976) distinguishes four **proxemic distances,** or **spatial distances:** the physical distances that define the types of relationships between people and the types of communication in which they are likely to engage (see Table 6.5).

- ***Intimate Distance.*** Ranging from actual touching to 18 inches, in **intimate distance** the presence of the other individual is unmistakable. Each person experiences the sound, smell, and feel of the other's breath. You use intimate distance for lovemaking, comforting, and protecting. This distance is so short that most people don't consider it proper in public.
- ***Personal Distance.*** The protective "bubble" that defines your personal space, ranging from 18 inches to 4 feet is **personal distance.** This imaginary bubble keeps you protected and untouched by others. At the outer limit of personal distance, you can touch another person only if both of you extend your arms. This is the distance at which you conduct most of your interpersonal interactions; for example, talking with friends and family.
- ***Social Distance.*** Ranging from 4 to 12 feet, at **social distance** you lose the visual detail you have at personal distance. You conduct impersonal business and interact at a social gathering at this social distance. The more distance you maintain in your interactions, the more formal they appear. In offices of high officials, the desks are positioned so the official is assured of at least this distance from clients.
- ***Public Distance.*** The space around you that protects you from others, referred to as **public distance,** ranges from 12 to more than 25 feet.

TABLE 6.5

In A Nutshell Relationships and Proxemic Distances

Note that these four distances can be further divided into close and far phases and that the far phase of one level (say, personal) blends into the close phase of the next level (social). Do your relationships also blend into one another? Or are, say, your personal relationships totally separate from your social relationships?

Relationship	Distance
Intimate relationship	Intimate distance 0 inches ______ 18 inches close phase — far phase
Personal relationship	Personal distance 1 foot ______ 4 feet close phase — far phase
Social relationship	Social distance 4 feet ______ 12 feet close phase — far phase
Public relationship	Public distance 12 feet ______ 25+ feet close phase — far phase

At this distance you could take defensive action if threatened. On a public bus or train, for example, you might keep at least this distance from a drunken passenger. Although at this distance you lose fine details of the face and eyes, you're still close enough to see what is happening.

The specific distances that we maintain between ourselves and other people depend on a wide variety of factors (Burgoon & Bacue, 2003; Burgoon, Guerrero, & Floyd, 2010). Among the most significant are *gender* (in same-sex dyads women sit and stand closer to each other than do men, and people approach women more closely than they approach men); *age* (people maintain closer distances with similarly aged others than they do with those much older or much younger); and *personality* (introverts and highly anxious people maintain greater distances than do extroverts). Not surprisingly, we maintain shorter distances with people with whom we're familiar and with people we like. One theoretical explanation of the dynamics of spatial distances is discussed in the accompanying Understanding Theory and Research box.

Watch at **MyCommunicationLab** **Video:** "Personal Space"

COMMUNICATION CHOICE POINT

PROXEMICS *Like the close-talker in a classic episode of* Seinfeld, *one of your team members at work maintains an extremely close distance when talking. Coupled with the fact that this person is a heavy smoker and reeks of smoke, you need to say something.* **In what ways might you deal with this issue? What would you say (if anything)? Through what channel?**

Territoriality

One of the most interesting concepts in ethology (the study of animals in their natural surroundings) is **territoriality,** a possessive or ownership reaction to an area of space or to particular objects. Two interesting dimensions of territoriality are territory types and territorial markers.

Territory Types. Three types of territory are often distinguished: primary, secondary, and public (Altman, 1975). **Primary territories** are your exclusive preserve: your desk, room, house, or backyard, for example. In these areas you're in control. The effect is similar to the **home field advantage** that a sports team has when playing in its own ballpark. When you're in these home territories, you generally have greater influence over others than you would in someone else's territory. For example, in their own home or office, people generally take on a kind of leadership role; they initiate conversations, fill in silences, assume relaxed and comfortable postures, and maintain their positions with greater conviction. Because the territorial owner is dominant, you stand a better chance of getting your raise approved, your point accepted, or a contract resolved in your favor if you're in your own primary territory (home, office) rather than in someone else's (Marsh, 1988).

Secondary territories, although they don't belong to you, are associated with you—perhaps because you've occupied them for a long time or they were assigned to you. For example, your desk in a classroom may become a secondary territory if it is assigned to you or if you regularly occupy it and others treat it as yours. Your neighborhood turf, a cafeteria table where you usually sit, or a favorite corner of a local coffee shop may be secondary territories. You feel a certain "ownership-like" attachment to the place, even though it's really not yours in any legal sense.

Public territories are areas that are open to all people, such as a park, movie house, restaurant, or beach. European cafés, food courts in suburban malls, and the open areas in large city office buildings are public spaces that bring people together and stimulate communication.

Territory is closely linked to status, power, and dominance. Generally, the size and location of a person's territory communicates a person's status and power (Burgoon, Guerrero, & Floyd, 2010). A large apartment or office in midtown Manhattan or downtown Tokyo, for example, is extremely high-status territory; the cost of the territory restricts it to those who have lots of money (and are likely to be of high status and powerful).

the•o•ry *noun* statement of explanation, formulation of relationships, reasoned generalization

UNDERSTANDING THEORY AND RESEARCH
Space Violations

Expectancy violations theory, developed by Judee Burgoon, explains what happens when you increase or decrease the distance between yourself and another person in an interpersonal interaction (Burgoon, Guerrero, & Floyd, 2010). Each culture has certain expectancies for the distance that people are expected to maintain in their conversations. And, of course, each person has certain idiosyncrasies. Together, these determine expected distance. If you violate the expected distance to a great extent (small violations most often go unnoticed), the relationship itself comes into focus; the other person begins to turn attention away from the topic of conversation to you and to your relationship with him or her.

If this other person perceives you positively—for example, if you're a high-status person or you're particularly attractive—then you'll be perceived even more positively if you violate the expected distance. If, on the other hand, you're perceived negatively and you violate the norm, you'll be perceived even more negatively.

Working with Theories and Research

Do your own experiences support this theory of space expectancy violations? What do you see happening when space expectations are violated?

Territory Markers. Much as animals mark their territory, humans mark theirs with three types of **markers:** central markers, boundary markers, and earmarkers (Moore, Hickson, & Stacks, 2010).

- *Central markers.* **Central markers** are items you place in a territory to reserve it. For example, you place your coffee on a table, books on your desk, or a sweater over the chair to let others know that these territories belong to you.
- *Boundary markers.* These markers set boundaries that divide your territory from "theirs." In the supermarket checkout line, the bar placed between your groceries and those of the person behind you is a **boundary marker.** Similarly, the armrests separating your seat from those of the people on either side at a movie theater and the molded plastic seats on a bus or train are boundary markers.
- *Earmarkers.* A term taken from the practice of branding animals on their ears, **earmarkers** are those marks that indicate your ownership of a territory or object. Trademarks, nameplates, initials on an attaché case, and markings of gang boundaries are all examples of earmarkers.

Watch at MyCommunicationLab Video: "Hey Roomie"

Artifactual Communication

Artifactual communication is communication via objects made by human hands. Thus, color, clothing, jewelry, and the decoration of space would be considered artifactual. Let's look at each of these briefly.

Color Communication

There is some evidence that colors affect us physiologically. For example, respiratory movements increase with red light and decrease with blue light. Similarly, eye blinks increase in frequency when eyes are exposed to red light and decrease when exposed to blue. These responses seem consistent with our intuitive feelings about blue being more soothing and red more arousing. When a school changed the color of its walls from orange and white to blue, the blood pressure of the students decreased and their academic performance increased (Ketcham, 1958; Malandro, Barker, & Barker, 1989).

Color also influences perceptions and behaviors (Kanner, 1989). People's acceptance of a product, for example, is largely determined by its packaging—especially its color. In one study the very same coffee taken from a yellow can was described as weak, from a dark brown can as too strong, from a red can as rich, and from a blue can as mild. Even your acceptance of a person may depend on the colors he or she wears. Consider, for example, the comments of one color expert (Kanner, 1989): "If you have to pick the wardrobe for your defense lawyer heading into court and choose anything but blue, you deserve to lose the case." Black is so powerful it could work against the lawyer with the jury. Brown lacks sufficient authority. Green would probably elicit a negative response.

Explore at MyCommunicationLab Exercise: "Color Meaning"

Clothing and Body Adornment

People make inferences about who you are, at least in part, from the way you dress. Your socioeconomic class, your seriousness, your attitudes (for example, whether you're conservative or liberal), your concern for convention, your sense of style, and perhaps even your creativity will all be judged in part by the way you dress (Burgoon, Guerrero, & Floyd, 2010; Knapp & Hall, 2010; Molloy, 1981). In the business world, your clothing may communicate your position within the hierarchy and your willingness and desire to conform to the norms of the organization. It also may communicate your professionalism, which seems to be the reason why some organizations favor dress codes (Smith, M. H., 2003).

The way you wear your hair says something about your attitudes—from a concern about being up to date, to a desire to shock, to perhaps a lack of interest in appearances. Men with long hair will generally be judged as less conservative than those with shorter hair. Your jewelry also communicates about you. Wedding and engagement rings are obvious examples that communicate specific messages. College rings and political buttons likewise communicate specific messages. If you wear a Rolex watch or large precious stones, others are likely to infer that you're rich.

Body piercings are now common, especially among the young. Nose, nipple, tongue, and belly button jewelry (among other piercings) send a variety of messages. Although people wearing such jewelry may wish to communicate positive meanings, research indicates that those interpreting these messages seem to infer that the wearer is communicating an unwillingness to conform to social norms and a willingness to take greater risks than people without such piercings (Forbes, 2001). And, in a study of employers' perceptions, applicants with eyebrow piercings were rated and ranked significantly lower than those without such piercings (Acor, 2001). In another study, nose-pierced job candidates were scored lower on measures of credibility such as character and trust as well as sociability and the likelihood of being hired (Seiter & Sandry, 2003). And in health-care situations, tattoos and piercings may communicate such undesirable traits as impulsiveness, unpredictability, and a tendency toward being reckless or violent (Rapsa & Cusack, 1990; Smith, M. H., 2003). This situation and these impressions may well change as body jewelry becomes more and more common.

Tattoos, whether temporary or permanent, likewise communicate a variety of messages—often the name of a loved one or some symbol of allegiance or affiliation. Tattoos also communicate to the wearers themselves. For example, tattooed students see themselves (and perhaps others do as well) as more adventurous, creative, individualistic, and risk-prone than those without tattoos (Drews, Allison, & Probst, 2000). Attitudes toward tattoos are also likely to change as they become more popular with both men and women.

Space Decoration

The way you decorate your private spaces also communicates about you. The office with a mahogany desk and bookcases and oriental rugs communicates your importance and status within an organization, just as a metal desk and bare floor indicate a worker much further down in the hierarchy.

Similarly, people will make inferences about you based on the way you decorate your home. The expensiveness of the furnishings may communicate your status and wealth; their coordination may convey your sense of style. The magazines may reflect your interests, and the arrangement of chairs around a television set may reveal how important watching television is to you. The contents of bookcases lining the walls reveal the importance of reading in your life. In fact, there's probably little in your home that will not send messages from which others will draw inferences about you. Similarly, the absence of certain items will communicate something about you. Consider what messages you'd get from a home where no television, phone, or books can be seen.

People will also make judgments as to your personality on the basis of room decorations. They will evaluate your openness to new experiences (distinctive decorating usually communicates this, as would different types of books and magazines and travel souvenirs) and even about your conscientiousness, emotional stability, degree of extroversion, and agreeableness. Not surprisingly, bedrooms prove more revealing of personality than offices (Gosling, Ko, Mannarelli, & Morris, 2002).

Touch Communication

The study of **touch communication,** technically referred to as **haptics,** suggests that touch is perhaps the most primitive form of communication (Montagu, 1971). Developmentally, touch is probably the first sense to be used. Even in the womb the child is stimulated by touch. Soon after birth the child is fondled, caressed, patted, and stroked. In turn, the child explores its world through touch. In a short time the child learns to communicate many different meanings through touch.

The Meanings of Touch

Researchers in the field of haptics have identified the major meanings of touch (Burgoon, Guerrero, & Floyd, 2010; Jones & Yarbrough, 1985). Here are five of the most important:

- **Emotional communication.** Touch may communicate positive emotions such as support, appreciation, inclusion, sexual interest or intent, and affection (Matsumoto & Hwang, 2013). When you hug someone in greeting or when you put your arm around someone's shoulder, you're likely touching to express positive emotions, to say you like them, to express warmth and supportiveness. Touch, however, can also communicate such emotions as anger, fear, sadness, and disgust (Hertenstein, Holmes, McCullough, & Keltner, 2009).

- **Playfulness**. Touch often communicates playfulness. Sometimes this playful touching is affectionate, when, for example, you'd "punch" someone in the arm as if to say "good job." Playful touching may also be more aggressive, as when you push someone as if to say "you've got to be kidding."
- **Task-related touching**. Task touching occurs while you are performing some function—for example, removing a speck of dust from another person's face or helping someone out of a car. You'd engage in task-related touching if, for example, you were showing someone how to grasp a football or how to swing a golf club.
- **Ritual touching.** Ritual touching centers on greetings and departures as in hugging, kissing, putting your arm around another's shoulder when greeting or saying farewell, or shaking hands to say hello or good-bye.
- **Control**. Touch may also control or direct the behaviors, attitudes, or feelings of another person. To get attention, for example, you may touch a person as if to say "look at me" or "look over here." Or you may control an elderly person's movements to help him or her get on a bus or out of a car. A great deal of research has been directed at the connection between touch and compliance, influence, or persuasion (Guéguen & Fischer-Lokou, 2003). For example, in one study 53 men and 67 women were asked to look after a large and excited dog for 10 minutes while the owner went into a store that didn't allow dogs. Half the subjects were touched during the request while half were not touched. Fifty-five percent of those who were touched complied with this request but only 35 percent of those who weren't touched complied (Guéguen & Fischer-Lokou, 2002). And, in a study with more practical implications, patients were either touched or not touched as the health-care worker asked them to promise that they would take their medication as prescribed. Not surprisingly, those who were touched complied more closely with the prescription than those who were not touched (Guéguen & Vion, 2009). And, in a widely cited study, servers in a restaurant who touched the customers on the hand received larger tips than those who didn't touch (Crusco & Wetzel, 1984).

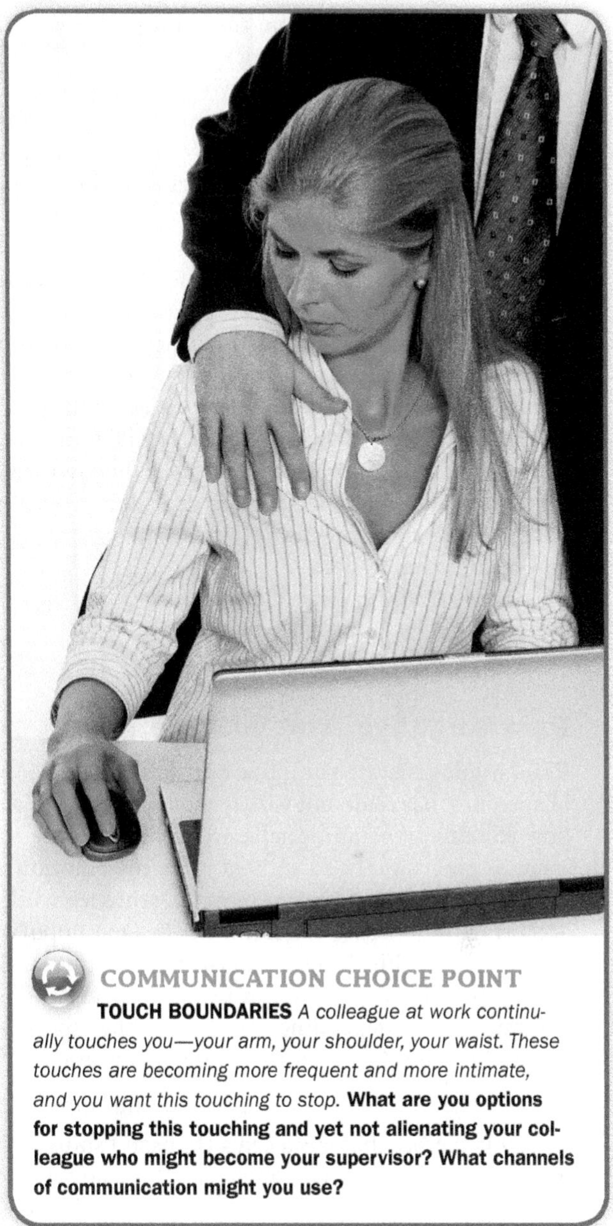

COMMUNICATION CHOICE POINT

TOUCH BOUNDARIES *A colleague at work continually touches you—your arm, your shoulder, your waist. These touches are becoming more frequent and more intimate, and you want this touching to stop.* **What are you options for stopping this touching and yet not alienating your colleague who might become your supervisor? What channels of communication might you use?**

Explore at MyCommunicationLab **Profile:** "Touch Apprehension Scale"

Touch Avoidance

Much as you have a need and desire to touch and be touched, you also have a tendency to avoid touch from certain people or in certain circumstances (Andersen, 2005; Andersen & Leibowitz, 1978).

Researchers have found several interesting connections between touch avoidance and other factors. For example, **touch avoidance** is positively related to communication apprehension. If you have a strong fear of oral communication, then you probably also have strong touch avoidance tendencies. Touch avoidance is also high in those who self-disclose less.

Both touch and self-disclosure are intimate forms of communication. People who are reluctant to get close to another person by self-disclosing also seem reluctant to get close by touching.

Older people avoid touch with opposite-sex persons more than younger people do. As people get older they're touched less by members of the opposite sex; this decreased frequency of touching may lead them to avoid touching.

Not surprisingly, touch also varies with your relationship stage. In the early stages of a relationship, you touch little; in intermediate stages (involvement and intimacy), you touch a great deal; and at stable or deteriorating stages, you again touch little (Guerrero & Andersen, 1991, 1994).

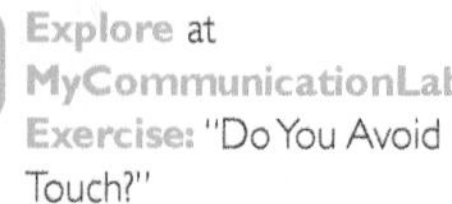

Explore at MyCommunicationLab Exercise: "Do You Avoid Touch?"

Paralanguage: The Vocal Channel

Paralanguage is the vocal but nonverbal dimension of speech. It has to do not with what you say, but with how you say it. A traditional exercise students use to increase their ability to express different emotions, feelings, and attitudes is to repeat a sentence while accenting or stressing different words. One popular sentence is, "Is this the face that launched a thousand ships?" Significant differences in meaning are easily communicated depending on where the speaker places the stress. Consider the following variations:

- Is *this* the face that launched a thousand ships?
- Is this the *face* that launched a thousand ships?
- Is this the face that *launched* a thousand ships?
- Is this the face that launched a *thousand ships*?

Each sentence communicates something different; in fact, each asks a different question, even though the words are exactly the same. All that distinguishes the sentences is stress, one aspect of paralanguage. In addition to stress and **pitch** (highness or lowness), paralanguage includes such **voice qualities** as **rate** (speed), **volume** (loudness), rhythm, and pauses or hesitations as well as the vocalizations you make in crying, whispering, moaning, belching, yawning, and yelling (Argyle, 1988; Trager, 1958, 1961). A variation in any of these features communicates. When you speak quickly, for example, you communicate something different than when you speak slowly. Even though the words may be the same, if the speed (or volume, rhythm, or pitch) differs, the meanings people receive will also differ.

Judgments about People

Paralanguage cues are often used as a basis for judgments about people; for example, evaluations of their emotional state or even their personality. A listener can accurately judge the emotional state of a speaker from vocal expression alone if both speaker and listener speak the same language. Paralanguage cues are not so accurate when used to communicate emotions to those who speak a different language (Albas, McCluskey, & Albas, 1976). Also, some emotions are easier to identify than others; it's easy to distinguish between hate and sympathy but more difficult to distinguish between fear and anxiety. And, of course, listeners vary in their ability to decode and speakers in their ability to encode emotions (Scherer, 1986).

Judgments about Communication Effectiveness

In one-way communication (when one person is doing all or most of the speaking and the other person is doing all or most of the listening), those who talk fast (about 50 percent faster than normal) are more persuasive (MacLachlan, 1979). People agree more with a fast speaker than with a slow speaker and find the fast speaker more intelligent and objective.

When we look at comprehension, rapid speech shows an interesting effect. When the speaking rate is increased by 50 percent, the comprehension level drops by only 5 percent. When the rate is doubled, the comprehension level drops only 10 percent. These 5 and 10 percent losses are more than offset by the increased speed; thus, the faster rates are much more efficient in communicating information. If speeds are more than twice the rate of normal speech, however, comprehension begins to fall dramatically.

Do exercise caution in applying this research to all forms of communication (MacLachlan, 1979). For example, if you increase your rate to increase efficiency, you may create an impression so unnatural that others will focus on your speed instead of your meaning.

Silence

Like words and gestures, **silence,** too, communicates important meanings and serves important functions (Ehrenhaus, 1988; Jaworski, 1993; Johannesen, 1974). Here are a few functions silence might serve.

- ***To give time to think.*** Silence allows the speaker time to think; time to formulate and organize his or her verbal communications. Before messages of intense conflict, as well as before those confessing undying love, there's often silence. Again, silence seems to prepare the receiver for the importance of these future messages.

- ***To hurt.*** Some people use silence as a weapon to hurt others and give them "the silent treatment." After a conflict, for example, one or both individuals may remain silent as a kind of punishment. Silence used to hurt others may also take the form of refusing to acknowledge the presence of another person, as in disconfirmation (see Chapter 5); here silence is a dramatic demonstration of the indifference one person feels toward the other.
- ***To lessen anxiety.*** Sometimes silence is used to lessen the anxiety you might experience if you said something. For example, you may feel anxious or shy among new people and prefer to remain silent. By remaining silent you preclude the chance of rejection. Only when you break your silence and make an attempt to communicate with another person do you risk rejection.
- ***To prevent communication.*** In conflict situations, for example, silence is sometimes used to prevent certain topics from surfacing and to prevent one or both parties from saying things they may later regret. In such situations silence often allows us time to cool off before expressing strong emotions or criticism, which, as we know, are irreversible. Silence may also be used when you simply have nothing to say.
- ***To communicate emotions.*** Like the eyes, face, and hands, silence can also be used to communicate emotions. Sometimes silence communicates defiance and an unwillingness to cooperate; by refusing to engage in verbal communication, you defy the authority or the legitimacy of the other person's position. Silence is also often used to communicate annoyance, particularly when accompanied by a pouting expression, arms crossed in front of the chest, and nostrils flared. Silence may also express affection or love, especially when coupled with long and longing gazes into each other's eyes.

Time Communication

The study of **temporal communication,** known technically as **chronemics,** concerns the use of time—how you organize it, react to it, and communicate messages through it (Bruneau, 1985, 2010). Here we'll look at psychological and interpersonal time and, in the section on culture, some cultural dimensions of time.

Psychological Time

Before reading about psychological time, consider your own time orientation. For each of the following statements, indicate whether it is true or false in terms of your general attitude and behavior.

_____ **1.** I often turn to the past for guidance in the present.
_____ **2.** Old people have wisdom that I can learn from.
_____ **3.** I enjoy learning about and from the past.
_____ **4.** Knowing about the past helps me in the present.
_____ **5.** I enjoy life as it comes.
_____ **6.** I avoid looking too far ahead.
_____ **7.** I frequently put off work to enjoy the moment.
_____ **8.** I look for immediate payoffs/rewards.
_____ **9.** I work hard today basically because of tomorrow's expected rewards.
_____ **10.** I enjoy planning for tomorrow and the future generally.
_____ **11.** I'm willing to endure difficulties if there's a payoff/reward at the end.
_____ **12.** I prepare "to do" lists fairly regularly.

These questions were designed to raise the issue of time orientation, whether you focus more on the past, the present, or the future. The idea for this test and the insights on psychological time owe their formulation to Gonzales and Zimbardo (1985). Past-oriented individuals would (as you can tell from the questions) respond with *true* to questions 1–4 and with either *true* or *false* for the remaining statements. Present-oriented individuals would response with *true* to questions 5–8, *false* to questions 9–12, and either *true* or *false* for questions 1–4. Future-oriented individuals would respond with *true* to questions 9–12, *false* for questions 5-8, and either *true* or *false* for questions 1–4. As you'll see, your time orientation has important implications for both your college and your professional career.

Consider the emphasis you place on the past, present, and future. In a past orientation, you have special reverence for the past. You relive old times and regard old methods as the best. You see events as circular and recurring, so the wisdom of yesterday is applicable also to today and tomorrow. In a present orientation, however, you live in the present: for now, not tomorrow. In a future orientation, you look toward and live for the future. You save today, work hard in college, and deny yourself luxuries because you're preparing for the future.

The time orientation you develop depends largely on your socioeconomic class and your personal experiences (Gonzales & Zimbardo, 1985). For example, parents with unskilled and semiskilled occupations are likely to teach their children a present-orientated fatalism and a belief that enjoying yourself is more important than planning for the future. Parents who are teachers or managers, for instance, teach their children the importance of planning and preparing for the future, along with strategies for success.

Interpersonal Time

Interpersonal time refers to a wide variety of time-related elements that figure into interpersonal interaction. Here are several of the more important (Andersen, 2004; Burgoon, Guerrero, & Floyd, 2010; DeVito, 2013).

- **Punctuality** refers to being on time for a variety of occasions—for company meetings, for class, for teacher-student appointments, for a ball game, for a movie or television show, and for completing assignments, to take just a few examples. Some people are always on time or early and others are consistently late, likely a personality difference. But much of it is learned by observing examples or by explicit instruction. Generally, those of higher status have greater leeway when it comes to punctuality; the boss may be late but the workers need to be on time. As a patient you're expected to be on time though the doctor rarely is.
- **Wait time** refers to the amount of time it's considered appropriate to wait for something or someone. Generally, the rule is that you'd wait longer for higher-status people than for lower-status people. You'd wait long if your supervisor is late but may wait only a few minutes for a colleague. There are of course factors other than status that figure into this equation. For example, if this was the first time you were meeting face to face with someone you've communicated with for two years via a social network and the person was late, you'd probably wait a lot longer than if this were someone you didn't care about or if you were not looking forward to the meeting.
- **Duration** refers to the length of time that a particular interaction will take. When you go to the doctor or dentist you're likely given a specific amount of time. If you use a consultant, lawyer, or accountant you may be charged for the length of time you interact and the length of time he or she works on your project. Appropriately enough, the practice is referred to as being "on the clock." The more important the topic is, generally, the longer the duration. And, not surprisingly, higher-status people will ration their time more rigidly than will a lower-status person. For example, you'd normally talk for a longer duration with your immediate supervisor than with the president of the company.
- **Talk time** refers to, for example, who initiates and who terminates a conversation, who talks more, who selects and directs the topics for discussion. As with so many such factors, status plays an important role here. It's the higher-status person who makes the decisions. But, perhaps the best example of high status and talk time is the privilege to interrupt. The person higher up in the hierarchy interrupts lower-hierarchical members and not the other way around. It's a way of saying and meaning: "What I have to say is more important than what you have to say. And since I'm the boss, that's the way it's going to be."
- **Work time** refers to the time schedule of your working life. If you're a low-level employee, you may have to punch a clock. And you're probably paid per unit of time, per hour or per day. You need to arrive on time and not leave before the workday is finished. And you need to wait for your lunch break to eat even if you were hungry for the last two hours. If you're a high-level employee or the boss, you may actually spend more time at work but it will be of your own choosing; you won't have to punch a time clock or get permission to arrive late or leave early, and of course you don't have to wait for your lunch break to eat.
- **Relationship time** is similar to work time but refers to the time one gives or should give to the various people with whom one has a relationship. In our culture, committed romantic couples normally spend a considerable amount of time together, and when that time is abbreviated (and considered too little by one of the partners), the relationship may be headed for trouble. Even long-distance relationships normally have relationship time—whether on the phone, through periodic visits, or via Skype. Even at social gatherings you're expected to devote your time on the basis of the relationships you have with the other members. So you're expected to spend more time with close friends (especially if you've not seen them for a long time) than with acquaintances. Parents are expected to devote a great deal of time to their children (especially when the children are young), and those who don't are often criticized by those who do. And adult children are expected to spend less and less time with their parents and more and more time with their romantic partner or friends.
- **Response time** refers to the time it takes a person to respond. Response time is observed in both synchronous and asynchronous communication. For example, in face-to-face communication, the response time to some statements and questions

must be immediate. There should be very little response lag between one's person's "Will you marry me?" and the other's "Yes." When the response time is inappropriately long, you may sense some kind of disagreement or lack of certainty. A recent article in *The Week* (June 1, 2012, p. 12) gives a perfect example of inappropriate response time. An Indian woman filed a motion for divorce from her husband of two months because he took too long to change his relationship status on Facebook to "married." Her reasoning was that this was an indication that he was probably cheating; the judge didn't agree and ordered them to undergo counseling.

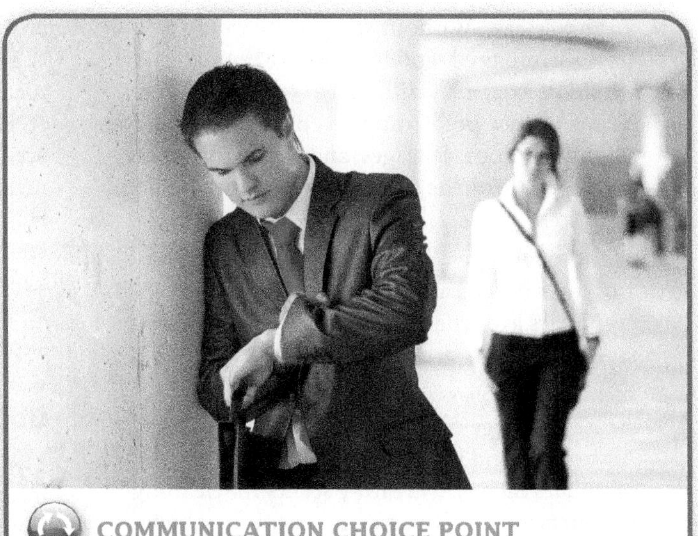

COMMUNICATION CHOICE POINT

TIME DIFFERENCES *You've just started dating a wonderful person who, unfortunately, has no sense of time and is constantly late for appointments and rarely responds to social media messages without a long delay. You, on the other hand, are always punctual and respond immediately or with very little delay. You need to get on the same page.* **What are some of the things you can say that might help this relationship?**

You also expect people to respond immediately when you're in need of support or comfort; if not, you may perceive any eventual support as forced or not genuine. But response time is also extremely important in asynchronous communication—for example, the time it takes someone to respond to your e-mail or poke or invitation to connect on some social media site will communicate some message. With different response times, you send different messages—messages of interest and concern and immediacy and messages of indicating the opposite. Sometimes our impressions are correct and sometimes not.

All of these types of interpersonal time will be influenced by a variety of factors involved in the interpersonal communication process. Status differences, as already illustrated, will influence significantly the way in which interpersonal time is treated. But other factors also come into play. For example, your personality will likely influence your punctuality, how long you wait for someone, whether or not you interrupt others, and your response time to invitations. Similarly, the context and purpose of the communication will influence how you'll treat interpersonal time. For example, if you're interviewing for the job of a lifetime and the interviewer is late, you'll no doubt wait. But if you're simply meeting someone to walk to classes with and the person is late, you'd be more likely to move on. Also, the relationship between you and the other person or persons will influence your interpersonal time. For example, if the relationship is an important one to you personally you'll likely excuse the lack of punctuality. But if the relationship is only a casual one or perhaps one of hostility, you might become annoyed, increase your dislike for this person who has no consideration for your time, and resolve not to wait any longer.

Smell Communication

Smell communication, or **olfactory communication,** is extremely important in a wide variety of situations and is now big business. For example, there's some evidence (though clearly not very conclusive evidence) that the smell of lemon contributes to a perception of health, the smells of lavender and eucalyptus increase alertness, and the smell of rose oil reduces blood pressure. Findings such as these have contributed to the growth of aromatherapy and to a new profession of aromatherapists (Furlow, 1996). Because humans possess "denser skin concentrations of scent glands than almost any other mammal," it has been argued that it only remains for us to discover how we use scent to communicate a wide variety of messages (Furlow, 1996, p. 41). Research also finds that smells can influence your body's chemistry, which in turn influences your emotional state. For example, the smell of chocolate results in the reduction of theta brain waves, which produces a sense of relaxation and a reduced level of attention (Martin, 1998).

Here are some of the most important messages scent seems to communicate.

- ***Attraction messages.*** Humans use perfumes, colognes, after-shave lotions, powders, and the like to enhance their attractiveness to others and to themselves. After all, you also smell yourself. When the smells are pleasant, you feel better about yourself.

- ***Taste messages.*** Without smell, taste would be severely impaired. For example, without smell it would be extremely difficult to taste the difference between a raw potato and an apple. Street vendors selling hot dogs, sausages, and similar foods are aided greatly by the smells, which stimulate the appetites of passersby.
- ***Memory messages.*** Smell is a powerful memory aid; you often recall situations from months and even years ago when you encounter a similar smell.
- ***Identification messages.*** Smell is often used to create an image or an identity for a product. Advertisers and manufacturers spend millions of dollars each year creating scents for cleaning products and toothpastes, for example, which have nothing to do with their cleaning power. And in some cases, we may be able to identify other people by their smell.

6.3 CULTURE AND NONVERBAL COMMUNICATION

This chapter has already noted a few cultural and gender differences in nonverbal communication. The importance of culture in certain areas of nonverbal communication, however, has become the focus of sustained research. Here we consider just a sampling of research on gesture, facial expression, eye communication, colors, touch, silence, and time.

Research shows that of the two genders, women are the better senders and receivers of nonverbal messages in most contexts (Burgoon & Hoobler, 2002; Hall, 2006). For example, in a review of 21 research studies, 71 percent of the findings showed women to be superior nonverbal senders. And in a review of 61 studies on decoding, 84 percent showed women to be superior receivers (Hall, 2006).

Culture and Gesture

There is much variation in gestures and their meanings among different cultures (Axtell, 2007). Consider a few common gestures that you might use even without thinking, but that could easily get you into trouble if you used them in another culture (also, take a look at Figure 6.1).

- Folding your arms over your chest would be considered defiant and disrespectful in Fiji.
- Waving your hand would be insulting in Nigeria and Greece.
- Gesturing with the thumb up would be rude in Australia.
- Tapping your two index fingers together would be considered an invitation to sleep together in Egypt.

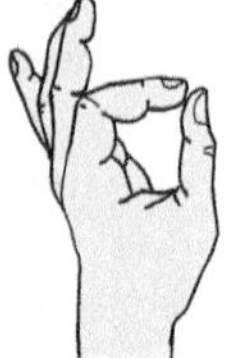

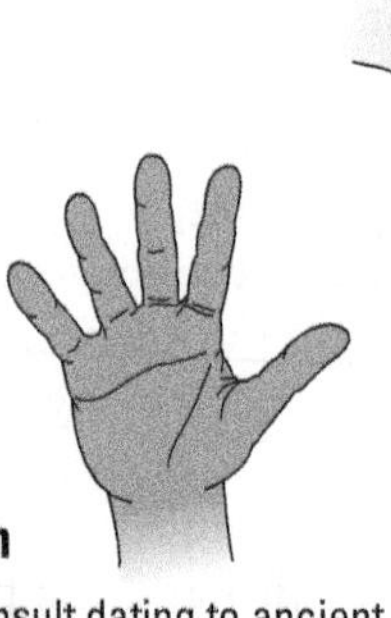

FIGURE 6.1 Some Cultural Meanings of Gestures

Cultural differences in the meanings of nonverbal gestures are often significant. The over-the-head clasped hands that signify victory to an American may signify friendship to a Russian. To an American, holding up two fingers to make a V signifies victory or peace. To certain South Americans, however, it is an obscene gesture that corresponds to the American's extended middle finger. This figure highlights some additional nonverbal differences. Can you identify others?

- Pointing with your index finger would be impolite in many Middle Eastern countries.
- Bowing to a lesser degree than your host would be considered a statement of your superiority in Japan.
- Inserting your thumb between your index and middle finger in a clenched fist would be viewed as a wish that evil fall on the person in some African countries.
- Resting your feet on a table or chair would be insulting and disrespectful in some Middle Eastern cultures.

Culture and Facial Expression

The wide variations in facial communication that we observe in different cultures seem to reflect different attitudes about what reactions are permissible in public rather than differences in the way humans show emotions. For example, Japanese and American students watched a film of a surgical operation (Ekman, 1985). The students were videotaped both in an interview situation about the film and alone while watching the film. When alone the students showed very similar reactions; in the interview, however, the American students displayed facial expressions indicating displeasure, whereas the Japanese students did not show any great emotion. Similarly, it's considered "forward" or inappropriate for Japanese women to reveal broad smiles, and so many Japanese women will hide their smile, sometimes with their hands (Ma, 1996). Women in the United States, on the other hand, have no such restrictions and so are more likely to smile openly. Thus, the difference may not be in the way people in different cultures express emotions, but rather in the cultural rules for displaying emotions in public (Matsumoto, 1991).

Similarly, people in different cultures may decode the meanings of facial expression differently (Matsumoto & Juang, 2008). For example, American and Japanese students judged the meaning of a smiling and a neutral facial expression. The Americans rated the smiling face as more attractive, more intelligent, and more sociable than the neutral face. In contrast, the Japanese rated the smiling face as more sociable but not as more attractive—and they rated the neutral face as more intelligent (Matsumoto & Kudoh, 1993).

Culture and Eye Communication

Not surprisingly, eye messages vary with both culture and gender (Helgeson, 2009). Americans, for example, consider direct eye contact an expression of honesty and forthrightness, but the Japanese often view this as a lack of respect. A Japanese person will glance at the other person's face rarely, and then only for very short periods (Axtell, 1990). Interpreting another's eye contact messages with your own cultural rules is a risky undertaking; eye movements that you may interpret as insulting may have been intended to show respect.

Women make eye contact more and maintain it longer (both in speaking and in listening) than men. This holds true whether women are interacting with other women or with men. This difference in eye behavior may result from women's greater tendency to display their emotions (Wood, 1994). When women interact with other women, they display affiliative and supportive eye contact, whereas when men interact with other men, they avert their gaze (Gamble & Gamble, 2003).

Culture and Colors

Colors vary greatly in their meanings from one culture to another. To illustrate this cultural variation here are just some of the many meanings that popular colors communicate in a variety of different cultures (Dresser, 1996; Dreyfuss, 1971; Hoft, 1995; Singh & Pereira, 2005). As you read this section, you may want to consider your own meanings for these colors and where your meanings came from.

- ***Red.*** In China red signifies prosperity and rebirth and is used for festive and joyous occasions; in France and the United Kingdom it indicates masculinity, in many African countries blasphemy or death, and in Japan anger and danger. Red ink, especially among Korean Buddhists, is used only to write a person's name at the time of death or on the anniversary of the person's death; this can create problems when American teachers use red ink to mark homework.
- ***Green.*** In the United States green signifies capitalism, go ahead, and envy; in Ireland patriotism; among some Native Americans femininity; to the Egyptians fertility and strength; and to the Japanese youth and energy.
- ***Black.*** In Thailand black signifies old age, in parts of Malaysia courage, and in much of Europe death.
- ***White.*** In Thailand white signifies purity, in many Muslim and Hindu cultures purity and peace, and in Japan and other Asian countries death and mourning.

- ***Blue.*** In Iran blue signifies something negative, in Ghana joy; among the Cherokee it signifies defeat, for the Egyptian virtue and truth, and for the Greek national pride.
- ***Yellow.*** In China yellow signifies wealth and authority, in the United States caution and cowardice, in Egypt happiness and prosperity, and in many countries throughout the world femininity.
- ***Purple.*** In Latin America purple signifies death, in Europe royalty, in Egypt virtue and faith, in Japan grace and nobility, in China barbarism, and in the United States nobility and bravery.

Culture and Touch

The several functions and examples of touching discussed so far have been based on studies in North America; in other cultures these functions are not served in the same way (Burgoon, Guerrero, & Floyd, 2010). In some cultures, for example, some task-related touching is viewed negatively and is to be avoided. Among Koreans, it is considered disrespectful for a store owner to touch a customer in, say, handing back change; it is considered too intimate a gesture. Members of other cultures that are used to such touching may consider the Korean's behavior cold and aloof. Muslim children are socialized not to touch members of the opposite sex—a practice that can easily be interpreted as unfriendly by American children who are used to touching each other (Dresser, 1996).

Some cultures—including many in southern Europe and the Middle East—are contact cultures; others are noncontact cultures, such as those of northern Europe and Japan. Members of contact cultures maintain close distances, touch one another in conversation, face one another more directly, and maintain longer and more focused eye contact. Members of noncontact cultures maintain greater distance in their interactions, touch one another rarely (if at all), avoid facing one another directly, and maintain much less direct eye contact. As a result, southern Europeans may perceive northern Europeans and Japanese as cold, distant, and uninvolved. Southern Europeans may in turn be perceived as pushy, aggressive, and inappropriately intimate.

Culture, Paralanguage, and Silence

Cultural differences also need to be taken into consideration when evaluating the results of the studies on speech rate, as different cultures view speech rate differently. For example, in one study Korean male speakers who spoke rapidly were given unfavorable credibility ratings, as opposed to the results obtained by Americans who spoke rapidly (Lee & Boster, 1992). Researchers have suggested that in individualistic societies a rapid-rate speaker is seen as more competent than a slow-rate speaker, whereas in collectivist cultures a speaker who uses a slower rate is judged as more competent.

Similarly, all cultures do not view silence as functioning in the same way (Vainiomaki, 2004). In the United States, for example, silence is often interpreted negatively. At a business meeting or even in an informal social group, the silent member may be seen as not listening, having nothing interesting to add, not understanding the issues, being insensitive, or being too self-absorbed to focus on the messages of others. Other cultures, however, view silence more positively. In many situations in Japan, for example, silence is a response that is considered more appropriate than speech (Haga, 1988; Matsumoto & Juang, 2008).

The traditional Apache, to take another example, regard silence very differently than do European Americans (Basso, 1972). Among the Apache, mutual friends do not feel the need to introduce strangers who may be working in the same area or on the same project. The strangers may remain silent for several days. This period enables them to observe and to form judgments about each other. Once this assessment is made, the individuals talk. When courting, especially during the initial stages, the Apache remain silent for hours; if they do talk, they generally talk very little. Only after a couple has been dating for several months will they have lengthy conversations. These periods of silence are generally attributed to shyness or self-consciousness; but the use of silence is explicitly taught to Apache women, who are especially discouraged from engaging in long discussions with their dates. Silence during courtship is a sign of modesty to many Apache.

Culture and Time

People in different cultures view time very differently. Here are three aspects of time that illustrate important cultural differences: the social clock, formal and informal time, and monochronism versus polychronism.

The Social Clock

Your culture maintains an implicit "schedule" for the right time to do a variety of important things; for example, the right time to start dating, to finish college, to buy your own home, or to have a child. This unspoken timetable provides you with a **social clock,** a schedule that tells you if you're keeping pace with your peers, are ahead of them, or are falling behind (Neugarten, 1979). On the basis of this social clock, which you learned as you grew up, you evaluate your own social and professional development. If you're in synch with the rest of your peers—for example, if you started dating at the "appropriate" age or if you're finishing college at the "appropriate" age—then you'll feel well adjusted, competent, and a part of the group. If you're late, you'll probably experience feelings of dissatisfaction. And although in some cultures the social clock is becoming more flexible and more tolerant of deviations from the conventional timetable, it still exerts pressure to keep pace with your peers (Peterson, 1996).

Formal and Informal Time

Days are astronomically determined by the earth's rotation on its axis, months by the moon's movement around the earth, and years by the earth's rotation around the sun. But the rest of our time divisions are cultural (largely religious) in origin.

In the United States and in most of the world, formal time divisions include seconds, minutes, hours, days, weeks, months, and years. Some cultures, however, may use phases of the moon or the seasons to delineate their most important time periods. Other formal time units exist, too. For example, in the United States, if your college is on the semester system, your courses are divided into 50- or 75-minute periods that meet two or three times a week for 14-week periods. Eight semesters of 15 or 16 periods per week equal a college education. As these examples illustrate, formal time units are arbitrary. The culture establishes them for convenience.

Informal time terms are more hazy and subject to interpretation—terms such as *forever, immediately, soon, right away,* or *as soon as possible.* This type of time creates the most communication problems because the terms have different meanings for different people.

Attitudes toward both formal and informal time vary from one culture to another. One study, for example, measured the accuracy of clocks in six cultures—those of Japan, Indonesia, Italy, England, Taiwan, and the United States. Japan had the most accurate and Indonesia had the least accurate clocks. The researchers also measured the speed at which

eth•ics *noun* morality, standards of conduct, moral judgment

MAKING ETHICAL CHOICES
Silence

Remaining silent is at times your right. For example, you have the right to remain silent so as not to incriminate yourself. You have a right to protect your privacy—to withhold information that has no bearing on the matter at hand. And thus, your previous relationship history, affectional orientation, or religion is usually irrelevant to your ability to function in a job and may be kept private in most job-related situations. On the other hand, these issues may be relevant when, for example, you're about to enter a more intimate phase of a relationship. At this point there may be an obligation to reveal information about yourself that could have been kept hidden at earlier relationship stages.

At other times, however, you have an obligation not to remain silent; and in fact in some cases it may be unlawful to say nothing. For example, you do not have the right to remain silent and to refuse to reveal information about crimes you've seen others commit. You have a legal obligation to report such crimes and in some cases even suspicions of crime. Psychiatrists, clergy, and lawyers—fortunately or unfortunately—are often exempt from this requirement to reveal information about criminal activities when the information had been gained through privileged communication with clients.

Ethical Choice Point

Your college roommate is selling term papers and uses your jointly owned computer to store them. You're becoming increasingly uncomfortable about the situation and want to distance yourself from this unethical behavior. What are some of your options for distancing yourself or severing yourself entirely from this operation, without creating too much trouble in the same dorm room you'll have to continue sharing for the rest of the year? What are some of the things you might say?

people in these six cultures walked, and results showed that the Japanese walked the fastest, the Indonesians the slowest (LeVine & Bartlett, 1984).

Monochronism and Polychronism

Another important distinction is that between **monochronic** and **polychronic time orientations** (Hall, 1959, 1976; Hall & Hall, 1987). Monochronic people or cultures—such as those of the United States, Germany, Scandinavia, and Switzerland—generally schedule one thing at a time. In these cultures time is compartmentalized and there is a time for everything. Polychronic people or cultures, on the other hand—groups such as Latin Americans, Mediterranean people, and Arabs—tend to schedule more than one thing at the same time. Eating, conducting business with several different people, and taking care of family matters may all be conducted simultaneously. No culture is entirely monochronic or polychronic; rather, these are general tendencies that are found across a large part of the culture. Some cultures combine both time orientations; in Japan and in some American groups, for example, both orientations are found. Table 6.6 identifies some of the distinctions between these two time orientations.

Understanding these culturally different perspectives on time should make intercultural communication a bit easier, especially if these time differences are discussed in a culturally sensitive atmosphere. After all, one view of time is not any more correct than any other. However, like all cultural differences, these different time orientations have consequences. Automobile accidents occur regularly because of drivers' obsession with time. And members of future-oriented cultures are more likely to succeed in competitive markets like the United States, but may be viewed negatively by members of cultures that stress living in and enjoying the present.

6.4 SOME NONVERBAL COMMUNICATION SKILLS

Throughout the discussion of nonverbal communication, you've probably deduced a number of suggestions for improving your own nonverbal communication. Here we bring together some suggestions for both receiving and sending nonverbal messages.

Perhaps the most general skill that applies to both receiving and sending is to become mindful of nonverbal messages—those of others as well as your own. Observe those whose nonverbal behavior you find particularly effective and those you find ineffective and try to identify exactly what makes one effective and one ineffective. Consider this chapter a brief introduction to a lifelong study.

In addition to mindfulness, general suggestions can be offered under two headings: decoding (or interpreting) nonverbal messages and encoding (or sending) nonverbal messages.

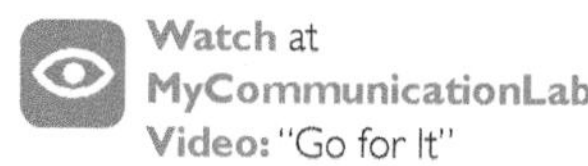

Decoding Skills

When you make judgments or draw conclusions about another person on the basis of her or his nonverbal messages, consider these suggestions:

- Be tentative. Resist the temptation to draw conclusions from nonverbal behaviors. Instead, develop hypotheses (educated guesses) about what is going on, and test the validity of your hypotheses on the basis of other evidence.
- When making judgments, mindfully seek alternative judgments. Your first judgment may be in error, and one good way to test it is to consider alternative judgments. When your

TABLE 6.6 MONOCHRONIC AND POLYCHRONIC TIME

As you read down this table, based on Hall and Hall (1987), note the potential for miscommunication that these differences might create when M-time and P-time people interact. Have any of these differences created interpersonal misunderstandings for you?

The Monochronic-Time Person	The Polychronic-Time Person
Does one thing at a time.	Does several things at once.
Treats time schedules and plans very seriously; feels they may be broken only for the most serious of reasons.	Treats time schedules and plans as useful (not sacred); feels they may be broken for a variety of causes.
Considers the job the most important part of life, ahead of even family.	Considers the family and interpersonal relationships more important than the job.
Considers privacy extremely important; seldom borrows or lends to others; works independently.	Is actively involved with others; works in the presence of and with lots of people at the same time.

romantic partner creates a greater than normal distance between you, it may signal an annoyance with you, but it can also signal that your partner needs some space to think something out.

- Notice that messages come from lots of different channels and that reasonably accurate judgments can only be made when multiple channels are taken into consideration. Although textbooks (like this one) must present the areas of nonverbal communication separately, the various elements all work together in actual communication situations.
- Even after you've explored the different channels, consider the possibility that you are incorrect. This is especially true when you make a judgment that another person is lying based on, say, eye avoidance or long pauses. These nonverbal signals may mean lots of things (as well as the possibility of lying).
- Interpret your judgments and conclusions against a cultural context. Consider, for example, if you interpret another's nonverbal behavior through its meaning in your own culture. So, for example, if you interpret someone's "overly close" talking distance as intrusive or pushy because that's your culture's interpretation, you may miss the possibility that this distance is simply standard in the other person's culture or it's a way of signaling closeness and friendliness.
- Consider the multitude of factors that can influence the way a person behaves nonverbally; for example, a person's physical condition, personality, or particular situation may all influence a person's nonverbal communication. A sour stomach may be more influential in unpleasant expressions than any communication factor. A low grade on an exam may make your normally pleasant roommate scowl and grumble. Without knowing these factors, it's difficult to make an accurate judgment.

Encoding Skills

In using nonverbal messages to express your meanings, consider these suggestions:

- Consider your choices for your nonverbal communication just as you do for your verbal messages. Identify and think mindfully about the choices you have available for communicating what you want to communicate.
- Keep your nonverbal messages consistent with your verbal messages; avoid sending verbal messages that say one thing and nonverbal messages that say something else—at least not when you want to be believed.
- Monitor your own nonverbal messages with the same care that you monitor your verbal messages. If it's not appropriate to say "this meal is terrible," then it's not appropriate to have a negative expression when you're asked if you want seconds.
- Avoid extremes and monotony. Too little nonverbal communication or too much is likely to be responded to negatively. Similarly, always giving the same nonverbal message—say, continually smiling and nodding your head when listening to a friend's long story—is likely to be seen as insincere.
- Take the situation into consideration. Effective nonverbal communication is situational; to be effective adapt your nonverbal messages to the specific situation. Nonverbal behavior appropriate to one situation may be totally inappropriate in another.
- Maintain eye contact with the speaker—whether at a meeting, in the hallway, or on an elevator; it communicates politeness and says that you are giving the person the consideration of your full attention. Eye contact that is too focused and too prolonged is likely to be seen as invasive and impolite.
- Avoid using certain adaptors in public—for example, combing your hair, picking your teeth, or putting your pinky in your ear; these will be seen as impolite. And, not surprisingly, the greater the formality of the situation, the greater the perception of impoliteness is likely to be. So, for example, combing your hair while sitting with two or three friends would probably not be considered impolite (or perhaps only mildly so), but in a classroom or at a company meeting, it would be considered inappropriate.
- Avoid strong cologne or perfume. While you may enjoy the scent, those around you may find it unpleasant and intrusive. Much like others do not want to hear your cell messages, they probably don't want to have their sense of smell invaded, either.
- Be careful with touching; it may or may not be considered appropriate or polite depending on the relationship you have with the other person and on the context in which you find yourselves. The best advice to give here is to avoid touching unless it's part of the culture of the group or organization.

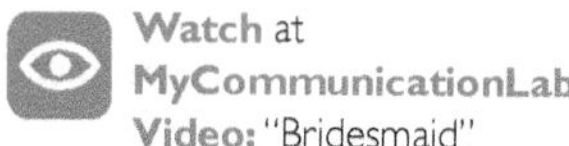

Vicki is getting married in a few months and she has asked her best friend Marisol to be in the wedding party. Vicki is clearly tense about her wedding, and Marisol doesn't want to make things worse, but Marisol can't afford the designer dress that Vicki has selected for the wedding party. She also feels that the dress is unflattering on her. Marisol is from Brazil and this is the first American wedding she has been asked to participate in. She doesn't know what expectations Vicki has of her. Log on to mycommunicationlab.com to view this video, called "Bridesmaid," see how the choices play out, and respond to a few related discussion questions.

SUMMARY: NONVERBAL MESSAGES

In this chapter we explored nonverbal communication—communication without words. We considered body movements, facial and eye movements, spatial and territorial communication, artifactual communication, touch communication, paralanguage, silence, time communication, and smell communication. Finally, we looked at cultural variations in many types of nonverbal communication.

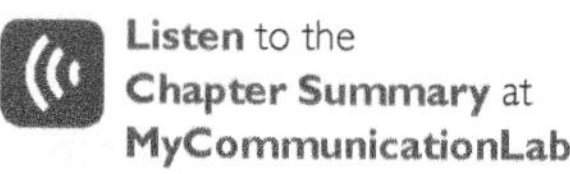

6.1 THE PRINCIPLES OF NONVERBAL COMMUNICATION

1. Nonverbal messages are governed by a variety of principles: nonverbal messages integrate with verbal messages, and they help form and manage impressions, define relationships, structure conversation, influence and deceive, and express emotions.

6.2 THE CHANNELS OF NONVERBAL COMMUNICATION

2. The five types of body gestures are emblems (nonverbal behaviors that directly translate words or phrases); illustrators (nonverbal behaviors that accompany and literally "illustrate" verbal messages); affect displays (nonverbal movements that communicate emotional meaning); regulators (nonverbal movements that coordinate, monitor, maintain, or control the speaking of another individual); and adaptors (nonverbal behaviors that are emitted without conscious awareness and that usually serve some kind of need, as in scratching an itch).
3. Facial movements may communicate a variety of emotions. The most frequently studied are happiness, surprise, fear, anger, sadness, disgust, and contempt. Facial management techniques enable you to control the extent to which you reveal the emotions you feel.
4. The facial feedback hypothesis claims that facial display of an emotion can lead to physiological and psychological changes.
5. Through eye contact you may seek feedback, signal others to speak, indicate the nature of a relationship, or compensate for increased physical distance. Eye avoidance may help you avoid prying or may signal a lack of interest.
6. Proxemics is the study of the communicative functions of space and spatial relationships. Four major proxemic distances are (1) intimate distance, ranging from actual touching to 18 inches; (2) personal distance, ranging from 18 inches to 4 feet; (3) social distance, ranging from 4 to 12 feet; and (4) public distance, ranging from 12 to more than 25 feet.
7. Your treatment of space is influenced by such factors as status, culture, context, subject matter, gender, age, and positive or negative evaluation of the other person.
8. Territoriality focuses on your possessive reaction to an area of space or to particular objects.
9. Artifactual communication consists of messages conveyed through human-made articles; for example, communication through color, clothing and body adornment, and space decoration.
10. The study of haptics indicates that touch may convey a variety of meanings, the most important being positive affect, playfulness, ritual, task-relatedness, and control. Touch avoidance is the desire to avoid touching and being touched by others.

11. Paralanguage involves the vocal but nonverbal dimensions of speech. It includes rate, pitch, volume, rhythm, and vocal quality as well as pauses and hesitations. Paralanguage helps us make judgments about people, their emotions, and their believability.

12. Silence may communicate a variety of meanings, from messages aimed at hurting another (the silent treatment) to deep emotional responses.

13. The study of time communication (chronemics) explores the messages communicated by our treatment of time.

14. Smell can communicate messages of attraction, taste, memory, and identification.

6.3 CULTURE AND NONVERBAL COMMUNICATION

15. Among the cultural differences that researchers have focused on are facial expressions and displays, eye communication, the meanings of color, the appropriateness and uses of touch, the uses of silence, and the ways in which different cultures treat time.

6.4 SOME NONVERBAL COMMUNICATION SKILLS

16. The skills of nonverbal encoding and decoding will help you communicate your meanings more effectively in a wide variety of communication situations.

KEY TERMS

Study and **Review** the **Flashcards** at **MyCommunicationLab**

adaptors ***127***
affect displays ***126***
alter-adaptors ***127***
artifactual communication ***133***
attractiveness ***127***
boundary marker ***133***
central marker ***133***
chronemics ***137***
civil inattention ***130***
earmarker ***133***
emblems ***126***
expectancy violations theory ***133***
facial feedback hypothesis ***129***
facial management techniques ***128***
haptics ***134***
home field advantage ***132***
illustrators ***126***
informal time ***143***
interpersonal time ***138***
intimate distance ***131***
kinesics ***126***
markers ***133***
monochronic time orientation ***144***
nonverbal communication ***122***
object-adaptors ***127***
olfactory communication ***139***
paralanguage ***136***
personal distance ***131***
pitch ***136***
polychronic time orientation ***144***
primary territories ***132***
proxemic distances ***131***
proxemics ***131***
public distance ***131***
public territories ***132***
rate ***136***
regulators ***127***
secondary territories ***132***
self-adaptors ***127***
silence ***136***
social clock ***143***
social distance ***131***
spatial distance ***131***
temporal communication ***137***
territoriality ***132***
touch avoidance ***135***
touch communication ***134***
visual dominance ***129***
voice qualities ***136***
volume ***136***

WORKING WITH NONVERBAL COMMUNICATION

6.1 Choosing a Seat. Every nonverbal (and verbal) message that you send has an impact, even the seat you select at a meeting. Your messages always reveal (to some extent) who you are and what others will think of you. Look at the diagram here, which represents a table with 12 chairs, one of which is already occupied by the "boss." Below are listed five messages you might want to communicate. For each of these messages, indicate (a) where you would sit to communicate the desired message and (b) any other messages that your seating position will make it easier for you to communicate.

a. You want to polish the apple and ingratiate yourself with your boss.

b. You aren't prepared and want to be ignored.

c. You want to challenge your boss on a certain policy that will come up for a vote.

d. You want to be accepted as a new (but important) member of the company.

e. You want to get to know the person already seated at position number 5.

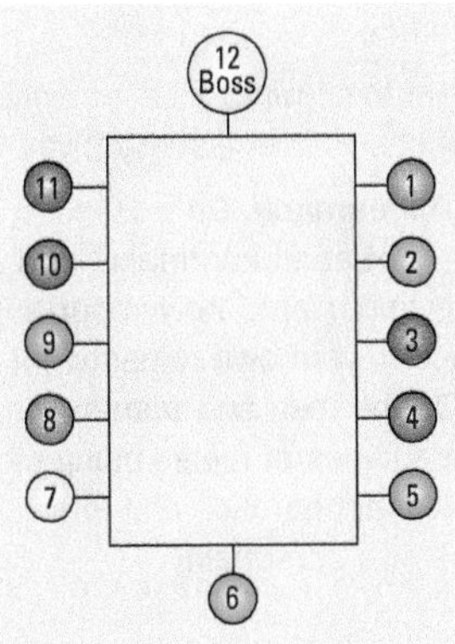

6.2 Expressing Praise and Criticism. You cannot speak a sentence without using nonverbal signals, and these signals influence the meaning the receiver gets. Acquiring the skills of nonverbal communication will help you communicate your meanings more effectively whether in interpersonal, small group, or public speaking. Consider here how nonverbal messages can communicate praise and criticism by reading each of the following statements, first to communicate praise and second to communicate criticism. In the second and third columns, record the nonverbal signals you used to help you communicate these differences in meaning between praise and criticism.

Message	Nonverbal cues to communicate praise	Nonverbal cues to communicate criticism
You lost weight.	____	____
You look happy.	____	____
You're an expert.	____	____
Your parents are something else.	____	____

6.3 Using Nonverbal Impression Management Strategies. Now that you've read about how nonverbal messages may help you manage impressions, consider how you would manage yourself nonverbally in the following situations. For each of these situations, indicate (1) the impressions you'd want to create (e.g., an image of a hardworking self-starter); (2) the nonverbal cues you'd use to create these impressions; and (3) the nonverbal cues you'd be especially careful to avoid.

a. You want a job at a conservative, prestigious law firm and are meeting for your first face-to-face interview.

b. You want a part in a movie in which you'd play a homeless drug addict.

c. You're single and you're applying to adopt a child.

d. You want to ask another student to go out with you.

e. You want to convince your romantic partner that you did not see your ex last night; you were working.

6.4 Physical Appearance. On a 10-point scale, with 1 indicating "not at all important" and 10 indicating "extremely important," how important is body appearance to your own romantic interest in another person? Do the men and women you know conform to the stereotypes of males being more concerned with physical appearance and females more concerned with personality?

6.5 Status and Invasion. One signal of status is an unwritten "law" granting the right of invasion. Higher-status individuals have more of a right to invade the territory of others than vice versa. The boss, for example, can invade the territory of junior executives by barging into their offices, but the reverse would be unacceptable. In what ways do you notice this "right" of territorial invasion in your workplace (or your dorm room)?

6.6 Signature Size. In a study of the size of over 600 CEOs' signatures, research found that those CEOs who had large signatures overspent, had lower returns on the company's assets, and earned larger salaries than their peers who wrote with smaller signatures (Seybert, 2013). Do you make inferences about people on the basis of the size of their signature?

6.7 Blaming the Victim. A popular defense tactic in criminal trials for sex crimes against women, gay men, and lesbians is to blame the victim by implying that the way the victim was dressed provoked the attack. (Some states prohibit this type of defense while others allow it.) What do you think of this tactic? Is this a legitimate and ethical defense tactic?

6.8 Gender and Nonverbal Communication. Here is a brief summary of findings from research on gender differences in nonverbal expression (Burgoon, Guerrero, & Floyd, 2010; Guerrero & Hecht, 2008; Pearson, West, & Turner, 1995): (1) Women smile more than men; (2) women stand closer to one another than do men and are generally approached more closely than men; (3) both men and women, when speaking, look at men more than at women; (4) women both touch and are touched more than men; (5) men extend their bodies, taking up greater areas of space, more than women. What problems might these differences create when men and women communicate with each other?

6.9 Liking Cues. What nonverbal cues should you look for in judging whether someone likes you? List cues in the order of their importance, beginning with 1 for the cue that is of most value in making your judgment. Do you really need two lists? One for judging a woman's liking and one for a man's?

6.10 Office Set Up. Culture will also influence the way in which offices are set up (Congdon & Gall, 2013). For example:

- In an individualist culture (where self-reliance and autonomy are stressed), the cubicle is eliminated in favor of allowing workers to choose their own spaces; in a collectivist culture (where group cohesion and group cooperation are stressed), workers are grouped closely together, which encourages interaction.
- In a masculine culture, outward symbols of one's importance (for example, private offices) are in

clear evidence; in a feminine culture, the spaces are more fluid and attempt to encourage equality.

- In a short-term culture, where the emphasis is on fast returns, work spaces are flexible and encourage movement from individual to group work; long-term cultures (where the emphasis is on long term growth) emphasize their history and longevity with private executive offices, for example.

How do the workplaces with which you're familiar reflect their culture?

LogOn! MyCommunicationLab www.mycommunicationlab.com

Throughout this chapter, there are icons that highlight media content for selected topics. Go to **MyCommunicationLab** for additional materials on nonverbal communication. Here you'll find flashcards to help you learn key communication terms, videos that illustrate a variety of concepts, additional exercises, and discussions to help you continue your study of nonverbal messages.

7 INTERPERSONAL COMMUNICATION: CONVERSATION

Listen to **Chapter 7** at **MyCommunicationLab**

CHAPTER TOPICS	CHAPTER OBJECTIVES
In this chapter you'll explore the following major topics:	**After reading this chapter you should be able to:**
PRINCIPLES OF CONVERSATION	**7.1** Define *conversation* and paraphrase the principles of *process, turn-taking, dialogue, immediacy, flexibility,* and *politeness.*
EVERYDAY CONVERSATIONS	**7.2** Engage in small talk, formulate credible excuses and apologies, give and receive compliments comfortably, and give and receive advice appropriately.

Compliments come in many forms.

Talking with another person seems so simple and so natural that most people are surprised to learn that the conversational process actually follows a complex set of rules and customs. In this chapter we dissect this process and explain how it operates and the kinds of problems that can be created when these rules and customs are broken. In addition, we look at a variety of everyday conversations and especially at ways in which these can be made more effective.

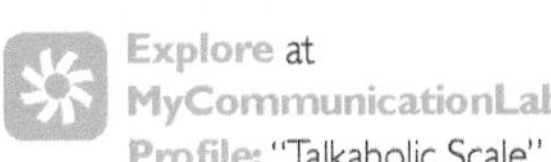

Conversation is the essence of interpersonal communication. These two concepts are so closely

the•o•ry *noun* statement of explanation, formulation of relationships, reasoned generalization

UNDERSTANDING THEORY AND RESEARCH

The Development of Interpersonal Communication

You can view communication as a continuum that has impersonal messages at one end and personal or intimate communication at the other (somewhat like that presented here). Interpersonal communication occupies a part of the continuum toward the more personal and intimate end and is distinguished from impersonal communication by three factors: (1) psychologically based predictions, (2) explanatory knowledge, and (3) personally established rules (Miller, 1978).

PREDICTIONS ARE BASED ON PSYCHOLOGICAL DATA

In impersonal encounters, you respond to another person on the basis of sociological data—the classes or groups to which the person belongs. For example, a student responds to a particular college professor the way students respond to college professors generally. Similarly, the professor responds to the student the way professors respond to students generally. As the relationship becomes more personal, however, both professor and student begin to respond to each other not just as members of their groups, but as individuals. They respond (to some degree) on the basis of psychological data, that is, on the basis of the ways the individual differs from the members of his or her group.

KNOWLEDGE OF EACH OTHER IS EXPLANATORY

In interpersonal interactions, you base your communications on explanatory knowledge of each other. When you know a particular person, you can predict how that person will act in a variety of situations. But as you get to know the person better, you can predict not only how the person will act, but also why the person behaves as he or she does; you can explain the behavior. For example, in an impersonal relationship the professor may be able to predict Pat's behavior and know that Pat will be late to class each Friday. But in an interpersonal situation, the professor can also offer explanations for the behavior, giving reasons for Pat's lateness.

RULES OF INTERACTION ARE PERSONALLY ESTABLISHED

Society sets up rules for interaction in impersonal situations. As noted in the example of the student and professor, however, the social rules of interaction set up by the culture lose importance as the relationship becomes more personal. In the place of these social rules, the individuals set up personal rules. When individuals establish their own rules for interacting with each other rather than using the rules set down by the society, the situation becomes increasingly interpersonal.

Working with Theories and Research

Try applying these three factors to your own experiences in interpersonal relationships. Do you experience the kind of progression identified here?

Impersonal
Taxi driver and passenger
Real estate agent and client
Doctor and patient
Neighbors
Work colleagues
Casual friends
Nieces/nephews and aunts/uncles
Close and best friends
Parents and children
Longtime lovers
Interpersonal

An Interpersonal Continuum *Here is one possible interpersonal continuum; others might position the relationships differently. Try constructing an interpersonal continuum of your own relationships.*

related that we often think of them as the same. Conversation is probably best thought of as the more general term for almost any two- (or a few) person interaction. Interpersonal communication, then, would be a more personal type of conversation. If you view conversation on a continuum (such as the one depicted in the figure in the accompanying Understanding Theory and Research box), interpersonal communication would occupy some significant portion of the right side of this continuum. Exactly where impersonal ends and interpersonal begins is a matter of disagreement.

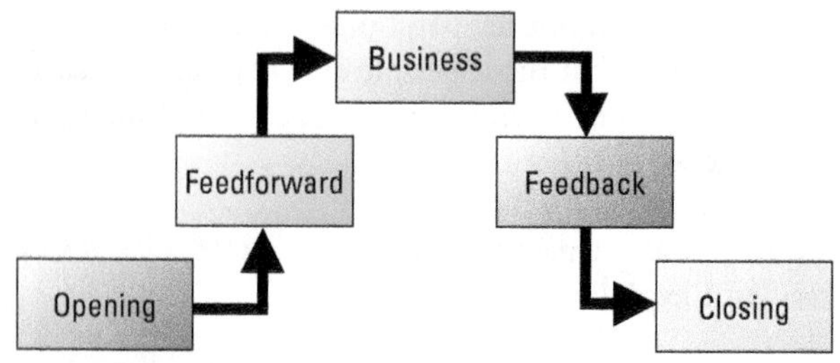

FIGURE 7.1 The Process of Conversation

This model of the stages of conversation is best seen as a way of looking at conversation and not as defining unvarying stages that all conversations follow. As you read about conversation, consider how accurately you think this model reflects the progression of your last conversation.

7.1 PRINCIPLES OF CONVERSATION

Although conversation is an everyday process and one we seldom think about, it is, like most forms of communication, governed by several principles.

The Principle of Process: Conversation Is a Developmental Process

Conversation is best viewed as a process rather than as an act. It's convenient to divide up this process into chunks or stages and to view each stage as requiring a choice as to what you'll say and how you'll say it. Here we divide the sequence into five steps: opening, feedforward, business, feedback, and closing (Figure 7.1). These stages and the way people follow them will vary depending on the personalities of the communicators, their culture, the context in which the conversation occurs, the purpose of the conversation, and the entire host of factors considered throughout this text.

- **Opening.** The first step is to open the conversation, usually with some kind of greeting: "Hi. How are you?" "Hello, this is Joe." The greeting is a good example of phatic communion. It's a message that establishes a connection between two people and opens up the channels for more meaningful interaction. Openings, of course, may be nonverbal as well as verbal. A smile, kiss, or handshake may be as clear an opening as "Hello." Greetings are so common that they often go unnoticed. But when they're omitted—as when the doctor begins the conversation by saying, "What's wrong?"—you may feel uncomfortable and thrown off guard.
- **Feedforward.** At the second step, you (usually) provide some kind of feedforward, which gives the other person a general idea of the conversation's focus: "I've got to tell you about Jack," "Did you hear what happened in class yesterday?" or "We need to talk about our vacation plans." Feedforward also may identify the tone of the conversation ("I'm really depressed and need to talk with you") or the time required ("This will just take a minute") (Frentz, 1976; Reardon, 1987). Conversational awkwardness often occurs when feedforwards are used inappropriately, for example, using overly long feedforwards or omitting feedforward before a truly shocking message.
- **Business.** The third step is the "business," the substance or focus of the conversation. The term *business* is used to emphasize that most conversations are goal directed. That is, you converse to fulfill one or several of the general purposes of interpersonal communication: to learn, relate, influence, play, or help (see Chapter 1). The term is also sufficiently general to incorporate all kinds of interactions. In general, the business is conducted through an exchange of speaker and listener roles. Brief, rather than long, speaking turns characterize most satisfying conversations. In the business stage, you talk about Jack, what happened in class, or your vacation plans. This is obviously the longest part of the conversation and the reason for the opening and the feedforward.
- **Feedback.** The fourth step is feedback, the reverse of the second step. Here you (usually) reflect back on the conversation to signal that, as far as you're concerned, the business is completed: "So you want to send Jack a get-well card," "Wasn't that the craziest class you ever heard of?" or "I'll call for reservations, and you'll shop for what we need."
- **Closing.** The fifth and last step, the opposite of the first step, is the closing, the goodbye, which often reveals how satisfied the persons were with the conversation: "I hope you'll call soon" or "Don't call us, we'll call you." The closing also may be used to schedule future conversations: "Give me

a call tomorrow night" or "Let's meet for lunch at 12." When closings are indefinite or vague, conversation often becomes awkward; you're not quite sure if you should say goodbye or if you should wait for something else to be said.

The Principle of Turn-Taking

Throughout the speaking-listening process, both speaker and listener exchange cues for what are called **conversational turns** (Burgoon, Guerrero, & Floyd, 2010). These cues enable the speaker and listener to communicate about the communication in which they're currently engaged; that is, a form of **metacommunication** takes place through the exchange of these often very subtle cues. The use of turn-taking cues—like just about every other aspect of human communication—will naturally vary from one culture to another. The description that follows here is largely valid for the United States and many Western cultures (Grossin, 1987; Iizuka, 1993; Lee, 1984; Ng, Loong, He, Liu, & Weatherall, 2000. As you read the following discussion, take a look at Figure 7.2; it provides a visual guide to the various turn signals.

Speaker Cues

Speakers regulate the conversation through two major types of cues: turn-maintaining cues and turn-yielding cues. Using these cues effectively not only ensures communication efficiency but also increases likability (Heap, 1992; Place & Becker, 1991).

Turn-Maintaining Cues. Through **turn-maintaining cues** you can communicate your wish to maintain the role of speaker in a variety of ways:

- Audibly inhaling breath to show that you have more to say.
- Continuing a gesture or series of gestures to show that you've not yet completed your thought.
- Avoiding eye contact with the listener so as not to indicate that you are passing along your speaking turn.
- Sustaining the intonation pattern to indicate that you're going to say more.
- Vocalizing pauses ("er," "umm") to prevent the listener from speaking and to show that you're still talking.

COMMUNICATION CHOICE POINT

FEEDFORWARD *You want to break up your relationship with someone you've been dating rather steadily over the past eight months. You want to remain friends but end the romance, something your partner has no idea about. The reason is simply that you realize you're not in love and want to move on and find great love.* **What are some of the things you might say as a preface (as feedforward) to your breakup speech? What would you say in your breakup speech?**

Conversational Wants

	To speak	To listen
Speaker	1 Turn-maintaining cues	2 Turn-yielding cues
Listener	3 Turn-requesting cues	4 Turn-denying cues

FIGURE 7.2 **Turn-Taking and Conversational Wants**

Quadrant 1 represents the speaker who wants to speak (continue to speak) and uses turn-maintaining cues; quadrant 2, the speaker who wants to listen and uses turn-yielding cues; quadrant 3, the listener who wants to speak and uses turn-requesting cues; and quadrant 4, the listener who wants to listen (continue listening) and uses turn-denying cues. Backchanneling cues would appear in quadrant 4 because they are cues that listeners use while they continue to listen.

In most conversations we expect the speaker to maintain relatively brief speaking turns and to turn over the speaking role to the listener willingly (when so signaled by the listener). People who don't follow those unwritten rules are likely to be evaluated negatively.

Turn-Yielding Cues. **Turn-yielding cues** tell the listener that the speaker is finished and wishes to exchange the role of speaker for the role of listener. They tell the listener (and, if in a group, such cues may be addressed to a specific listener or to just any listener) to take over the role of speaker. For example, at the end of a statement you may add some cue such as "okay?" or "right?" to ask one of the listeners to assume the role of speaker. You also can indicate that you've finished speaking by dropping your intonation or by pausing at length (Wennerstrom & Siegel, 2003), by making direct eye contact with a listener, by asking a question, or by nodding in the direction of a particular listener.

In much the same way that you expect a speaker to yield the role of speaker, you also expect the listener to assume the speaking role willingly. Those who don't may be regarded as reticent or as unwilling to involve themselves and take equal responsibility for the conversation.

Listener Cues

As a listener you can regulate the conversation by using three types of cues: turn-requesting cues, turn-denying cues, and backchanneling cues and interruptions.

Turn-Requesting Cues. **Turn-requesting cues** let the speaker know that you would like to say something and take a turn as speaker. Sometimes you can do this simply by saying, "I'd like to say something," but often it's done more subtly through some vocalized "er" or "um" that tells the speaker that you would now like to speak. The request to speak is also often made with facial and mouth gestures. Frequently a listener will indicate a desire to speak by opening his or her eyes and mouth wide as if to say something, by beginning to gesture with a hand, or by leaning forward.

Turn-Denying Cues. You can use **turn-denying cues** to indicate your reluctance to assume the role of speaker; for example, by intoning a slurred "I don't know" or by giving some brief grunt that signals you have nothing to say. Often people accomplish turn denying by avoiding eye contact with the speaker (who wishes them now to take on the role of speaker) or by engaging in some behavior that is incompatible with speaking—for example, coughing or blowing their nose.

Backchanneling Cues. **Backchanneling cues** are used to communicate various types of information back to the speaker without assuming the role of speaker. Some researchers call these "acknowledgment tokens"—brief utterances such as "mm-hm," "uh-huh," and "yeah,"—that tell the speaker you're listening (Drummond & Hopper, 1993; Schegloff, 1982). Other researchers call them "overlaps" to distinguish them from those interruptions that are aimed at taking over the speaker's turn (Tannen, 1994a, b). Backchanneling cues are generally supportive and confirming and show that you're listening and are involved in the interaction (Kennedy & Camden, 1988).

You can communicate a variety of messages with these backchanneling cues (Burgoon, Buller, & Woodall, 1996; Pearson & Spitzberg, 1990):

- **To indicate agreement or disagreement.** Smiles, nods of approval, brief comments such as "Right" and "Of course," or a vocalization like "uh-huh" signal agreement. Frowning, shaking your head, and making comments such as "No" or "Never" signal disagreement.
- **To indicate degree of involvement.** An attentive posture, forward leaning, and focused eye contact tell the speaker that you're involved in the conversation. An inattentive posture, backward leaning, and avoidance of eye contact communicate a lack of involvement.
- **To pace the speaker.** Ask the speaker to slow down by raising your hand near your ear and leaning forward or to speed up by continued nodding of your head. Cue the speaker verbally by asking the speaker to slow down or to speed up.
- **To ask for clarification.** Puzzled facial expressions, perhaps coupled with a forward lean, or direct interjection of "Who?," "When?," or "Where?" signal your need for clarification.

Interruptions. **Interruptions,** in contrast to backchanneling cues, *are* attempts to take over the role of the speaker. These are not supportive and are often disconfirming. Interruptions are often interpreted as attempts to change the topic to one that the person knows more about or to emphasize one's authority. Interruptions are seen as attempts to assert power and to maintain control. Not surprisingly, research finds that superiors (bosses and supervisors) and those in positions of authority (police officers and interviewers) interrupt those in inferior positions more than the other way around (Ashcraft, 1998; Carroll, 1994). In fact, it would probably strike you as strange to see a worker repeatedly interrupting a supervisor or a student repeatedly interrupting a professor.

Numerous studies have focused on gender differences in interruption. The popular belief is that men interrupt more than women. This belief, research finds, is basically accurate. Men interrupt other men and women more than women interrupt. For example, one analysis of 43 published studies on interruptions and gender differences showed that men interrupted significantly more than women (Anderson, 1998). In addition, the more male-like the person's gender identity—regardless of the person's biological sex—the more likely it is that the person will interrupt (Drass, 1986). Fathers interrupt their children more than mothers do (Greif, 1980). Some research, however, finds no differences (Crown & Cummins, 1998; Donaldson, 1992; Smith-Lovin & Brody, 1989; Stratford, 1998).

Whatever gender differences do exist, however, seem small. More important than gender in determining who interrupts whom is the specific type of situation; some situations (for example, task-oriented situations) may call for more interruptions while relationship discussions may call for more backchanneling cues (Anderson, 1998).

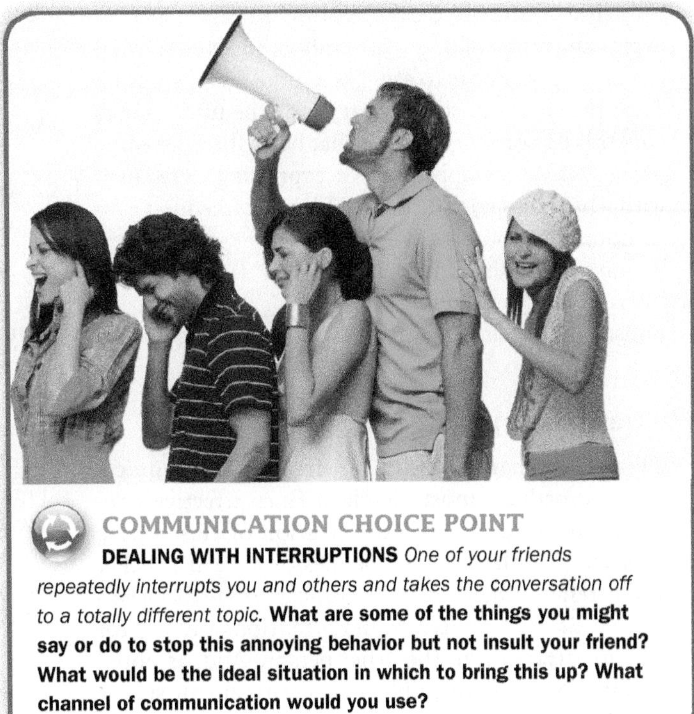

COMMUNICATION CHOICE POINT

DEALING WITH INTERRUPTIONS *One of your friends repeatedly interrupts you and others and takes the conversation off to a totally different topic.* **What are some of the things you might say or do to stop this annoying behavior but not insult your friend? What would be the ideal situation in which to bring this up? What channel of communication would you use?**

The Principle of Dialogue

Often the term *dialogue* is used as a synonym for *conversation*. But dialogue is more than simple conversation; it's conversation in which there is genuine two-way interaction (Buber, 1958; McNamee & Gergen, 1999; Yau-fair Ho, Chan, Peng, & Ng, 2001). It's useful to distinguish the ideal dialogic communicator from his or her opposite, the totally monologic communicator. Of course, no one totally and always engages in dialogue, and no one is totally monologic. These types are extremes and are intended to clarify the differences between these two types of communicators.

In **dialogue** each person is both speaker and listener; sender and receiver. It's conversation in which there is deep concern for the other person and for the relationship between the two. The objective of dialogue is mutual understanding and empathy. There is respect for the other person—not because of what this person can do or give but simply because this person is a human being and therefore deserves to be treated honestly and sincerely.

In a dialogic interaction you respect the other person enough to allow that person the right to make his or her own choices without coercion, without the threat of punishment, without fear or social pressure. A dialogic communicator believes that other people can make decisions that are right for them and implicitly or explicitly lets them know that whatever choices they make, they will still be respected as people.

The dialogic communicator avoids negative criticism and negative personal judgments and instead practices using positive criticism ("I liked those first two explanations best; they were really well reasoned"). This person avoids dysfunctional communication patterns and keeps the channels of communication open by displaying a willingness to listen. While listening, this person lets you know it by giving you cues (nonverbal nods, brief verbal expressions of agreement, paraphrasing) that tell you he or she is paying attention. When in doubt the dialogic communicator asks for clarification—asks for your point of view, your perspective—and thus signals a real interest in you and in what you have to say.

Monologic communication is the opposite side: In **monologue** one person speaks and the other listens—there's no real interaction between participants. The monologic communicator is focused only on his or her own goals and has no real concern for the listener's feelings or attitudes; this speaker is interested in the other person only insofar as that person can serve his or her purposes.

The monologic communicator frequently uses negative criticism ("I didn't like that explanation") and negative judgments ("You're not a very good listener, are you?"). This communicator also often uses dysfunctional communication patterns such as expressing an unwillingness to talk or to listen to what the other person has to say. The monologic communicator rarely demonstrates that he or she understands you; this person gives no cues that he or she is listening (cues such as paraphrasing or expressing agreement with what you say). Nor would this person request clarification of your ideas because he or she is less interested in you than in himself or herself.

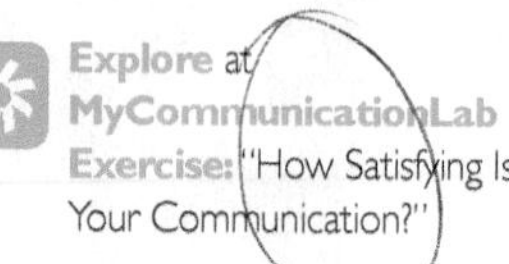

The Principle of Immediacy

Of all the characteristics of effective communication, immediacy most clearly defines effective conversation. **Immediacy** is the creation of closeness, a sense of togetherness, of oneness, between speaker and listener. When you communicate immediacy you convey a sense of interest and attention, a liking for and an attraction to the other person. And, as noted in our discussion of impression management strategies (pages 70–73), immediacy strategies are often used to make someone like us.

Not surprisingly, people respond to communication that is immediate more favorably than to communication that is not. You can increase your interpersonal attractiveness (the degree to which others like you and respond positively toward you) by using immediacy behaviors. In addition there is considerable evidence to show that immediacy behaviors are effective in teaching and in health care (Richmond, McCroskey, & Hickson, 2008; Richmond, Smith, Heisel, & McCroskey, 2001).

You can communicate immediacy with both verbal and nonverbal messages (Richmond, McCroskey, & Hickson, 2008).

- **Self-disclose;** reveal something significant about yourself.
- **Refer to the other person's good qualities** of, say, dependability, intelligence, character; for example, "You're always so reliable."
- **Express your positive view of the other person and of your relationship;** for example, "I'm sure glad you're my roommate; you know everyone."
- **Talk about commonalities,** things you and the other person have done together or share.
- **Demonstrate your responsiveness** by giving feedback cues that indicate you want to listen more and that you're interested; for example, "And what else happened?"
- **Express psychological closeness and openness** by, for example, maintaining physical closeness and arranging your body to exclude third parties.
- **Maintain appropriate eye contact** and limit looking around at others.
- **Smile** and express your interest in the other person.
- **Focus on the other person's remarks.** Make the speaker know that you heard and understood what was said, and give the speaker appropriate verbal and nonverbal feedback.

At the same time that you'll want to demonstrate these immediacy messages, try also to avoid nonimmediacy messages such as interrupting the other person, avoiding small talk, making potentially offensive or condescending comments, closing off the channels of communication ("I don't have the time to chat"), or talking about things for which the other person has no reference or no experience. Nonverbally, avoid speaking in a monotone, looking away from the person you're talking to, frowning while talking, having a tense body posture, or avoiding gestures (Richmond, McCroskey, & Hickson, 2008).

Not all cultures or all people respond in the same way to immediacy messages. For example, in the United States (and in individualist and low-power-distance cultures generally) immediacy behaviors are seen as friendly and appropriate. In other cultures (many of the collectivist and high-power-distance cultures), however, the same immediacy behaviors may be viewed as overly familiar—as presuming that a relationship is close when only acquaintanceship exists (Axtell, 2007).

Also, recognize that some people may take your immediacy behaviors as indicating a desire for increased intimacy in the relationship. So, while you're trying to signal a friendly closeness, the other person may perceive a romantic invitation. Recognize too that because immediacy behaviors prolong and encourage in-depth communication, they may not be responded to favorably by persons who are fearful about communication and who want to get the interaction over with as soon as possible (Richmond, McCroskey, & Hickson, 2008).

The Principle of Flexibility

Because conversations vary depending on the people involved, the topic being talked about, the context in which it takes place, and a host of other factors discussed throughout this text, the effective conversationalist needs to be flexible. To get a clearer idea of **flexibility** in conversation, take the following self-test, which asks you (1) to imagine that you're in a specific situation, (2) to consider the course of action identified, and (3) to estimate how much this choice would be similar to the choice you'd make in the same or similar situation.

You can increase your flexibility by following a few simple steps.

- **Analyze the specific conversational situation** asking yourself what is unique or different about this specific situation and using the concepts and principles discussed throughout the text.
- **Mindfully consider your available choices** for any given conversational situation, a suggestion offered throughout this text.
- **Estimate the potential advantages and disadvantages** of each potential choice, using the theories and research evidence discussed throughout the text.
- **Competently communicate your choice,** using the skills learned throughout this course.

The Principle of Politeness: Conversation Is (Usually) Polite

Not surprisingly, conversation is expected (at least in many cases) to follow the principle of politeness. Six maxims/fundamental principles/general rules/ accepted truths of politeness have been identified by linguist Geoffrey Leech (1983) and seem to encompass a great deal of what we commonly think of as conversational politeness. Before reading about these maxims, take the following self-test to help you personalize the material that follows. Try estimating your own level of politeness. For each of the statements below, indicate how closely they describe your typical communication. Avoid giving responses that you feel might be considered "socially acceptable"; instead, give responses that accurately represent your typical communication behavior. Use a 10-point scale with 10 being "very accurate description of my typical conversation" and 1 being "very inaccurate description of my typical conversation."

_____ **1.** I tend not to ask others to do something or to otherwise impose on others.

_____ **2.** I tend to put others first, before myself.

_____ **3.** I maximize the expression of approval of others and minimize any disapproval.

_____ **4.** I seldom praise myself but often praise others.

_____ **5.** I maximize the expression of agreement and minimize disagreement.

_____ **6.** I maximize my sympathy for another and minimize any feelings of antipathy.

All six statements would characterize politeness, so high numbers, say 8–10, would indicate politeness whereas low numbers, say 1–4, would indicate impoliteness. As you read this material, personalize it with examples from your own interpersonal interactions, and try to identify specific examples and situations in which increased politeness might have been more effective. Each of these six statements refers to a specific maxim or rule of politeness:

- The **maxim of tact** (statement 1 in the self-test) helps to maintain the other's autonomy (what we referred to earlier as negative face, page 70). Tact in your conversation would mean that you do not impose on others or challenge their right to do as they wish. For example, if you wanted to ask someone a favor, using the maxim of tact, you might say something like, "I know you're very busy but..." or "I don't mean to impose, but..." Not using the maxim of tact, you might say something like, "You have to lend me your car this weekend" or "I'm going to use your ATM card."
- The **maxim of generosity** (statement 2) helps to confirm the other person's importance, for example, the importance of the person's time, insight, or talent. Using the maxim of generosity, you might say, "I'll walk the dog; I see you're busy," and violating the maxim, you might say, "I'm really busy, why don't you walk the dog; you're not doing anything important."
- The **maxim of approbation** (statement 3) refers to praising someone or complimenting the person in some way (for example, "I was really moved by your poem") and minimizing any expression of criticism or disapproval (for example, "For a first effort, that poem wasn't half bad").
- The **maxim of modesty** (statement 4) minimizes any praise or compliments *you* might receive. At the same time, you might praise and compliment the other person. For example, using this maxim you might say something like, "Well, thank you, but I couldn't have done this without your input; that was the crucial element." Violating this maxim, you might say, "Yes, thank you, it was one of my best efforts, I have to admit."
- The **maxim of agreement** (statement 5) refers to your seeking out areas of agreement and expressing them ("That color you selected was just right; it makes the room exciting") and at the same time avoiding and not expressing (or at least minimizing) disagreements ("It's an interesting choice, very different"). In violation of this maxim, you might say, "That color—how can you stand it?"
- The **maxim of sympathy** (statement 6) refers to the expression of understanding, sympathy, empathy, supportiveness, and the like for the other person. Using this maxim, you might say, "I understand your feelings; I'm so sorry."

If you violated this maxim, you might say, "You're making a fuss over nothing" or "You get upset over the least little thing; what is it this time?"

A summary of these principles of conversation appears in Table 7.1.

Explore at MyCommunicationLab Exercise: "How Polite Is Your Conversation?"

7.2 EVERYDAY CONVERSATIONS

Now that we have covered the basic principles of conversation, we can explore a variety of everyday conversation situations: making small talk, introducing other people or ourselves, excusing, apologizing, complimenting, and offering advice. When reading about and thinking about conversation, keep in mind that not everyone speaks with the fluency and ease that many textbooks often assume. Speech and language disorders, for example, can seriously disrupt the conversation process when some elementary guidelines aren't followed. Table 7.2 on page 160 offers suggestions for making such conversations run more smoothly.

Making Small Talk

Small talk is pervasive; all of us engage in small talk. Sometimes, we use small talk as a preface to big talk. For example, before a conference with your boss or even an employment interview, you're likely to engage in some preliminary small talk. "How are you doing?" "I'm pleased this weather has finally cleared up." "That's a great-looking jacket." The purpose here is to ease into the major topic or the big talk.

Sometimes, small talk is a politeness strategy and a bit more extensive way of saying hello as you pass someone in the hallway or meet a neighbor at the post office. You might say, "Good seeing you, Jack. You're looking ready for the big meeting" or "See you in Geology at 1."

Sometimes your relationship with another person revolves totally around small talk—perhaps with your barber or hair dresser, a colleague at work, your next door neighbor, or a fellow student you sit next to in class. In these relationships, neither person makes an effort to deepen the relationship and it remains on a small talk level.

Despite its name, small talk serves important purposes. One obvious purpose is simply to pass the time more pleasantly than you might in silence. Small talk also demonstrates that the normal rules of politeness are operating. In the United States, for example, you would be expected to smile and at least say hello to people on an elevator in your apartment building and perhaps at your place of work. Furthermore, small talk confirms to others that all is well with you. Should you scowl and avoid eye contact with someone in your apartment house elevator, you'd signal that something is wrong.

Watch at MyCommunicationLab Video: "Talk, Talk, Talk"

TABLE 7.1

In A Nutshell A Summary of the Principles of Conversation

General Principle	Principle in Conversation
The Principle of Process	Conversation is a developmental process and can be viewed as a five-stage process: opening, feedforward, business, feedback, and closing.
The Principle of Turn-Taking	Conversation works best when speaking turns are relatively short and easily exchanged.
The Principle of Dialogue	Conversation relies on each person listening and responding as well as speaking.
The Principle of Immediacy	Effective conversation is immediate; there is a sense of togetherness.
The Principle of Flexibility	Being flexible and responsive to the moment will contribute to conversational effectiveness.
The Principle of Politeness	Polite conversations generally follow the maxims of tact, generosity, approbation, modesty, agreement, and sympathy.

me•di•a lit•er•a•cy *noun* ability to understand, interact with, and create media messages

EXPANDING MEDIA LITERACY
Conversation and Social Media

Of course a great deal of your conversation takes place over social media, and part of media literacy is using these channels to communicate more effectively and to build more effective relationships. In all of these lists of suggestions, the recommendations are generally applicable to all social networks and yet some seem more logically placed with one medium rather than another.

Tweeting. Unlike other social network sites, people can follow you on Twitter whether you like it or not. But, assuming that you want some kind of relationship between yourself and those who follow you, consider these suggestions.

- Leave room for retweets (if you want retweets). Keep your tweet to 120 characters.
- Avoid "fast following" tools. These will likely create problems for you.
- Tweet items of interest to yourself but also keep in mind your readers.
- Treat criticism as the start of a dialogue rather than a personal attack.
- Tweet in moderation. Not everything that happens deserves a tweet.
- Tweet positively; avoid angry tweets.
- Create a complete profile, revealing what you want and keeping hidden what you don't want revealed.
- Limit promotional materials; Twitter is personal.
- Retweet if you wish to be retweeted.
- Use direct messaging when the entire group.

Blogging. Although many people view blogs are monologic, they are best viewed as dialogic. Their great value is in creating dialogue, and so a blog post, at least for the traditional blog, is ideally one that provides information with a personal slant for a specific audience that creates some measure of discussion. Assuming that this is your aim or close to it, here are a few suggestions for making this a more effective interaction.

- Offer syndication. RSS feeds will greatly help in spreading the word.
- Be both informational and personal; blog posts are more personal in nature than are articles or websites, which are more purely informational.
- Be consistent in style and format. It will help brand your blog as unique—not unlike McDonald's; readers will know what to expect.
- Build your blog and your posts around a theme. Posts unrelated to the theme are generally perceived as noise and are likely to lose your readers.
- Reply to comments. Dialogue.
- Track statistics so you can get insight into the posts that are read often and those that aren't.
- Create attractive titles and relevant identifying labels. Make it as easy as possible for others to retrieve your materials.

Social/Workplace Networking. Perhaps the social medium that comes first to mind is Facebook, by far the largest of the social networking sites. But, Google+ and MySpace serve similar purposes as do numerous others. LinkedIn and Plaxo, on the other hand, serve mainly business purposes, for example, getting a job or promotion, finding likely candidates for a job, networking, or mentoring. Despite these differences, some similar suggestions govern effective conversation and relationships in these types of sites.

- Be careful of uploading photos that will reflect on you negatively, especially with alcohol or drugs. Interestingly enough, one research student found that 85 percent of 225 profiles examined (average age 19.9 years) make alcohol references (Egan & Moreno, 2011).
- Be positive about your current position. Complaining about your job online for all to see is likely to make management less positive toward you and also to lead prospective employers to see you as a complainer and someone who would be critical of the new organization as well.
- Avoid revealing any negative work habits or discussing inappropriate workplace behavior—even if (especially if) you think it's funny.
- Use the Friends List or the Google+ Circles to distinguish the people you want to see certain information and those you wouldn't. But, remember, again, that anyone who receives your message can post it to anyone, even those you'd rather not see it.
- Give your social network profile even more attention than you give to dressing up for a long-anticipated face-to-face date. After all, a lot more people are going to see your online profile than the way you dressed for a date.
- Keep your posts (at least on Facebook and Google+) personal and informative. Avoid promoting any commercial enterprise.
- Poke and tag in moderation. Learn first the norms of the group with which you're communicating.
- Avoid asking to be friends with anyone you think may have difficulty with your seeing their more personal side.

TABLE 7.2

Between People with and without Speech and Language Disorders

TIPS

Speech and language disorders vary widely—from fluency problems such as stuttering, to indistinct articulation, to difficulty in finding the right word (aphasia). Following a few simple guidelines can facilitate communication between people with and without speech and language disorders.

If you're the person without a speech or language disorder:

Generally	**Specifically**
Avoid finishing another's sentences.	Finishing the person's sentences may communicate the idea that you're impatient and don't want to spend the extra time necessary to interact effectively.
Avoid giving directions to the person with a speech disorder.	Saying "slow down" or "relax" will often seem insulting and will make further communication more difficult.
Maintain eye contact.	Show interest and at the same time avoid showing any signs of impatience or embarrassment.
Ask for clarification as needed.	If you don't understand what the person said, ask him or her to repeat it. Don't pretend that you understand when you don't.
Don't treat people who have language problems like children.	A person with aphasia, say, who has difficulty with names or nouns generally, is in no way childlike. Similarly, a person who stutters is not a slow thinker; in fact, stutterers differ from non-stutterers only in their oral fluency.

If you're the person with a speech or language disorder:

Let the other person know what your special needs are.	If you stutter, you might tell others that you have difficulty with certain sounds and so they need to be patient.
Demonstrate your own comfort.	Show that you have a positive attitude toward the interpersonal situation. If you appear comfortable and positive, others will also.
Be patient	For example, have patience with those who try to finish your sentences; they're likely just trying to be helpful.

***Sources:** These suggestions were drawn from a variety of sources, including the websites of the National Stuttering Association, the National Aphasia Association, the U.S. Department of Labor, and the American Speech and Hearing Association, all accessed May 9, 2012.*

Before reading about the guidelines for effective small talk, respond to the following situations:

1. On an elevator with three or four strangers, I'd be most likely to:
   a. seek to avoid interacting
   b. respond to another but not initiate interaction
   c. be the first to talk
2. When I'm talking with someone and I meet a friend who doesn't know the person I'm with, I'd be most apt to:
   a. avoid introducing them
   b. wait until they introduce each other
   c. introduce them to each other
3. At a party with people I've never met before, I'd be most likely to:
   a. wait for someone to talk to me
   b. nonverbally indicate that you're receptive to someone interacting with you
   c. initiate interaction with others nonverbally and verbally

4. When confronted with someone who doesn't want to end the conversation I'd be most apt to:
   a. just stick it out and listen
   b. tune out the person and hope time goes by quickly
   c. end it firmly myself
5. When the other person monologues, I'd be most apt to:
   a. listen politely
   b. try to change the focus
   c. exit as quickly as possible

COMMUNICATION CHOICE POINT

MAKING SMALL TALK *At the company cafeteria, you regularly sit next to someone from another department who you would like to get to know better.* **How might you use small talk to see if this other person is receptive to your overtures?**

The *a* responses are unassertive, the *b* responses are indirect (not totally unassertive but not assertive, either), and the *c* responses are direct and assertive. Very likely, if you answered with 4 or 5 *c* responses, you're comfortable and satisfied with your small talk experiences. Lots of *a* responses would indicate some level of dissatisfaction and discomfort with the experience of small talk. If you had lots of *b* responses then you probably experience both satisfaction and dissatisfaction with small talk. If your small talk experiences are not satisfying to you, read on. The entire body of interpersonal skills will prove relevant here as will a number of suggestions unique to small talk.

The Topics and Contexts of Small Talk

Small talk topics must be non-controversial in the sense that they must not be something about which you and the other person are likely to disagree. If a topic is likely to arouse deep emotions or different points of view, then it is probably not a suitable topic for small talk.

Most often the topics are relatively innocuous. The weather is perhaps the most popular small talk topic. "Trivial" news, for example, news about sports (although criticizing the other person's favorite team would not be considered non-controversial by many), athletes, and movie or television stars are also popular small talk topics. Current affairs—as long as there is agreement—might also be used in small talk: "Did you see the headline in the news?" Sometimes small talk grows out of the context; waiting on line for tickets may prompt a comment to the person next to you about your feet hurting or if they know how long it will be until the tickets go on sale.

Small talk is also relatively short in duration. The context in which small talk occurs allows for only a brief interaction. Waiting in line to get into a movie, riding in an elevator, and stopping briefly in the hallway of a school on the way to class are the kinds of occasions that create small talk opportunities. A party, at which guests are meant to mingle and exchange pleasantries, is perhaps the classic example.

Guidelines for Effective Small Talk

Although "small," this talk still requires the application of the communication skills for "big" talk. As already noted, remember that the best topics are non-controversial and that most small talk is relatively brief. Here are a few additional guidelines for more effective small talk.

- **Be positive.** No one likes a negative doom-sayer. So comment on the weather when it's nice; move to another topic when it isn't.
- **Be sensitive to leave-taking cues.** Small talk is necessarily brief, but at times one person may want it to be a preliminary to the big talk and another person may see it as the sum of the interaction.
- **Stress similarities rather than differences.** This is a good way to ensure that the small talk stays non-controversial.
- **Answer questions with sufficient elaboration.** This will give the other person information that can then be used to interact with you. Let's say someone sees a book you're carrying and says, "I see you're taking Accounting." If you say, simply "yes," you've not given the other person anything

to talk with you about. Instead, if you say, "Yes, it's a great course; I think I'm going to major in it" then you have given the other person information that can be used to further the conversation. The more elaborate answer also signals your willingness to engage in small talk. Of course, if you do not want to interact, then the simple one-word response will help you achieve your goal.

- **Avoid monologuing.** Listen and be responsive to the other person. Even small talk is two-way and requires each person to talk and each person to listen. Remember the principles of turn-taking and dialogue.
- **Choose topics carefully.** In selecting the topics of your small talk, remember that you will be associated with the topics you frequently talk about. If all your small talk concerns Britney Spears, Justin Bieber, Lindsay Lohan, and Paris Hilton then you might become defined as someone who is only interested in shallow celebrity gossip.

Introducing People

One of the interpersonal communication situations that often creates difficulties is the introduction of one person to another. Let's say you're with Jack and bump into Jill who stops to talk. Because they don't know each other, it's your job to introduce them. Generally, it's best to do this simply but with enough detail to provide a context for further interaction. It might go something like this:

> Jill Williams, this is Jack Smith, who works with me at XYZ as marketing manager. I went to college with Jill and, if I'm not mistaken, she has just returned from Hawaii.

With this introduction Jack and Jill can say something to each other based on the information provided in this brief (32-word) introduction. They can talk about working at XYZ, what it's like being a marketing manager, what Jill majored in, what Hawaii is like, what Jill did in Hawaii, and so on. If you simply said, "Jill, this is Jack" there would be virtually nothing for Jack and Jill to talk about.

Also, if you know that the two people have something in common, you might mention this—for example, Jack is also a native New Yorker or Jill is also a marathon runner. This will help to ease the communication between Jack and Jill and is likely to make the interaction more meaningful and satisfying. If you're unsure about what to reveal in your introduction, it's best to leave it out. The safest policy is to include only obviously public information. Avoid repeating things either of the individuals might have disclosed to you in confidence or that might be kept hidden from outsiders. Introducing Jack as "soon to be single" may reveal more than Jack would like.

In the United States the handshake is the most essential gesture of the introduction and generally follows rather specific rules (see Table 7.3). In other cultures, different rules operate. For example, in Muslim cultures people of the same sex will hug, but not people of the opposite sex. In Latin America, South America, and the Mediterranean, people are more likely to hug (and perhaps kiss on the cheek) than are Northern Europeans, Asians, and many from the United States. Given the great Hispanic influence on the United States today, it's probable that the hug-kiss will grow in general popularity. Asians are more reluctant to extend their hands and more often bow, with lower bows required when people of lower status meet someone of higher status.

TABLE 7.3 SIX STEPS TO AN EFFECTIVE HANDSHAKE

Dos	Don'ts
Make eye contact at the beginning and maintain it throughout the handshake.	Look away from the person or down at the floor or at your shaking hand.
Smile and otherwise signal positiveness.	Appear static or negative. You shake hands not just with your hands but with your whole body.
Extend your entire right hand.	Extend just your fingers or your left hand.
Grasp the other person's hand firmly but without discomforting pressure.	Grasp the other person's fingers as if you really don't want to shake hands but you're making a gesture to be polite.
Pump three times for about 3 to 4 seconds.	Give the person a "dead fish." Be careful that the other person's pumping doesn't lead you to withdraw your own pumping.
Release grasp while still maintaining eye contact.	Hold grasp for an overly long time or releasing too early.

When one of the people being introduced has a right hand that is disabled in some way, the general rule is that if one person shakes hands with other people in the group, he or she should also shake hands with the person who has a disability. The person with a disabled right hand is free to use the left hand in most cultures, although in Muslim countries the left hand is considered unclean.

As you can imagine, cultural differences may create intercultural difficulties and misunderstandings. For example, if you shake hands in a culture that hugs and kisses, you may appear standoffish. If you hug and kiss in a culture that is used to shaking hands, you may seem presumptuous and overly friendly. The best advice is to watch what the people of the culture you're in do and try to do likewise. At the same time, don't get upset if members of other cultures unknowingly "violate" your own culture's rituals. After all, one ritual is no more inherently logical or correct than any other.

Making Excuses

Excuses are explanations that are designed to reduce any negative reactions to what you've said or done; the objective is to maintain your positive image (Snyder, 1984; Snyder, Higgins, & Stucky, 1983). Excuses are especially appropriate when you say or are accused of saying something that runs counter to what is expected, sanctioned, or considered "right" by the people with whom you're in conversation. Ideally, you hope, the excuse will lessen the negative impact of your message.

The major motives for excuse making seem to be to maintain your self-esteem and to project a positive image of yourself to others. Excuses also represent an effort to reduce stress: You may feel that if you can offer an excuse—especially a good one that is accepted by those around you—it will reduce the negative reaction and the subsequent stress that accompanies a poor performance.

Excuses also may enable you to maintain effective interpersonal relationships after some negative behavior. For example, after criticizing a friend's behavior and observing his or her negative reaction to your criticism, you might offer an excuse such as, "I'm really exhausted. I'm just not thinking straight." Excuses enable you to place your messages—even your possible failures—in a more favorable light.

Types of Excuses

Different researchers have classified excuses into varied categories (Cody & Dunn, 2007; Scott & Lyman, 1968). One of the best typologies classifies excuses into three main types (Snyder, Higgins, & Stucky, 1983).

- **Denial.** Here you deny that you have done what you're being accused of. You may then bring up an alibi to prove you couldn't have done it, or perhaps you may accuse another person of doing what you're being blamed for ("I never said that" or "I wasn't even near the place when it happened").

the•o•ry *noun* statement of explanation, formulation of relationships, reasoned generalization

UNDERSTANDING THEORY AND RESEARCH
Opening Lines

How do you strike up a conversation with someone you're meeting for the first time? How have people tried to open conversations with you? Researchers investigating this question found three basic types of opening lines (Kleinke, 1986).

- **Cute–flippant openers** are humorous, indirect, and ambiguous as to whether or not the person opening the conversation really wants an extended encounter. Examples: "Is that really your hair?" "Bet I can outdrink you."
- **Innocuous openers** are highly ambiguous as to whether these are simple comments that might be made to just anyone or whether they're in fact openers designed to initiate an extended encounter. Examples: "What do you think of the band?" "Could you show me how to work this machine?"
- **Direct openers** demonstrate clearly the speaker's interest in meeting the other person. Examples: "I feel a little embarrassed about this, but I'd like to meet you." "Would you like to have a drink after dinner?"

Studies indicate that the opening lines most preferred by both men and women are generally those that are direct or innocuous. Least preferred by both men and women are opening lines that are cute–flippant; women, however, dislike these openers more than men (Kleinke & Dean, 1990).

Working with Theories and Research

Do you find support for these conclusions from your own experience? For example, do you find significant gender differences in preferences? What openers do you yourself find most effective? What types do you dislike?

- **Minimize.** Here you admit to doing it but claim the offense was not really so bad or perhaps that there was justification for the behavior ("I only padded the expense account, and even then only modestly" or "Sure, I hit him, but he was asking for it").
- **Qualify.** Here you claim that extenuating circumstances accounted for the behavior; for example, that you weren't in control of yourself at the time or that you didn't intend to do what you did ("I was too upset to think" or "I never intended to hurt him; I was actually trying to help").

Good and Bad Excuses

The most important question for most people is what makes a good excuse and what makes a bad excuse (Slade, 1995; Snyder, 1984). Good excuse makers use excuses in moderation; bad excuse makers rely on excuses too often. Good excuse makers accept responsibility for their failures and avoid blaming others, while bad excuse makers won't acknowledge their mistakes and are quick to pass the blame. Not surprisingly, excuse makers who accept responsibility will be perceived as more credible, competent, and likable than those who deny responsibility (Dunn & Cody, 2000).

What makes one excuse effective and another ineffective will vary from one culture to another and will depend on factors already discussed such as the culture's individualism-collectivism, its power distance, the values it places on assertiveness, and various other cultural tendencies (Tata, 2000). But, at least in the United States, researchers seem to agree that the best excuses in interpersonal communication contain four or five elements (Coleman, 2002; Slade, 1995).

1. You demonstrate that you understand the problem and that your partner's feelings are legitimate and justified. Avoid minimizing the issue or your partner's feelings ("It was only $100; you're overreacting," "I was only two hours late," or "It was only one time").
2. You acknowledge your responsibility. If you did something wrong, avoid qualifying your responsibility ("I'm sorry *if* I did anything wrong") or expressing a lack of sincerity ("Okay, I'm sorry; it's obviously my fault—*again*"). On the other hand, if you can demonstrate that you had no control over what happened and therefore cannot be held responsible, your excuse is likely to be highly persuasive (Heath, Stone, Darley, & Grannemann, 2003).
3. You acknowledge your own displeasure at what you did; you make it clear that you're not happy with yourself for your actions.
4. You make it clear that your misdeed will never happen again.
5. Some researchers include a fifth step, which is actually an apology. Here you would express your sorrow or regret and perhaps ask forgiveness for what you did.

Watch at **MyCommunicationLab** **Video:** "Getting Even"

Apologizing

Apologies are expressions of regret or sorrow for having said or done something that you most likely shouldn't have. Often the apology is blended with the excuse—"I didn't realize how fast I was driving" (the excuse); "I'm really sorry" (the apology). The most basic of all apologies is simply, "I'm sorry." In popular usage, the apology includes some admission of wrongdoing on the part of the person making the apology. Sometimes the wrongdoing is acknowledged explicitly ("I'm sorry I lied") and sometimes only by implication ("I'm sorry you're so upset").

In many cases the apology also includes a request for forgiveness and some assurance that the behavior won't be repeated ("Please forgive my lateness; it won't happen again").

According to the Harvard Business School Working Knowledge website, apologies are useful for two main reasons: (1) to help repair relationships and (2) to repair the reputation of the wrongdoer. If you do something wrong in your relationship, for example, an apology will help you repair the relationship with your partner and perhaps reduce the level of conflict. At the same time, however, realize that other people know about your behavior and an apology will help improve their image of you.

An effective apology, like an effective excuse, must be crafted for the specific situation. Effective apologies to a long-time lover, to a parent, or to a new supervisor are likely to be very different because the individuals and your relationships are different. Therefore, the first rule of an effective apology is to take into consideration the uniqueness of the situation—the people, context, cultural rules, relationship, specific wrongdoing—for which you might want to apologize. Here are some general guidelines that would have to be adjusted to the uniqueness of each situation.

Watch at **MyCommunicationLab** **Video:** "I Didn't Do It"

Some Dos for Effective Apologies

- Admit wrongdoing if indeed wrongdoing occurred. Accept responsibility. Own your own actions; don't try to pass them off as the work of someone else. Instead of "Smith drives so slow, it's a wonder I'm only 30 minutes late," say "I should have taken traffic into consideration."

eth•ics *noun* morality, standards of conduct, moral judgment

MAKING ETHICAL CHOICES
Gossip

There can be no doubt that we spend a great deal of time gossiping. In fact, gossip seems universal among all cultures (Laing, 1993), and among some groups gossip is a commonly accepted ritual (Hall, 1993).

Gossip involves making social evaluations about a person who is not present during the conversation; it generally occurs when two people talk about a third party (Eder & Enke, 1991).

In the organization, gossip has particularly important consequences and in many instances has been shown to lead to firings, lawsuits, and damaged careers. And because of the speed and ease with which members of an organization can communicate with each other (instant messaging, e-mail, and blogs, for example) gossip can spread quickly and broadly (Armour, 2007).

People often gossip in order to get some kind of reward; for example, to hear more gossip, gain social status or control, have fun, cement social bonds, or make social comparisons (Leaper & Holliday, 1995; Miller & Wilcox, 1986; Rosnow, 1977). Gossiping, however, often leads others to see you more negatively—regardless of whether your gossip is positive or negative or whether you're sharing this gossip with strangers or with friends (Turner, Mazur, Wendel, & Winslow, 2003).

In addition to its negative impact on the gossiper, gossiping often has ethical implications. In many instances gossiping would be considered unethical; for example, when you use it to unfairly hurt another person, when you know it's not true, when no one has the right to such personal information, or when you are breaking a promise of secrecy.

Ethical Choice Point

You and your longtime friend Pat are now working in the same company and are competing for the position of sales manager. You know that Pat's résumé contains many lies—claiming, for example, a long history of experience. And it is this claimed experience that is likely to land Pat the position over you. Pat's lying hasn't bothered you before, but now it's likely to work against your own promotion. You wonder if it would be ethical to let it be known, through informal gossip channels, that Pat doesn't really have all the experience claimed. What are your ethical obligations to yourself, to your family, to your company? What would you do?

- Be apologetic. Say (and mean) "I'm sorry" or "What I did was wrong."
- State in specific rather than general terms what you've done. Instead of "I'm sorry for what I did," say "I'm sorry for getting drunk at the party and flirting with everyone."
- Express understanding of how the other person feels and acknowledge the legitimacy of these feelings. For example, "You have every right to be angry; I should have called."
- Express your regret that this has created a problem for the other person: "I'm sorry I made you miss your appointment."
- Offer to correct the problem (whenever this is possible): "I'm sorry I didn't clean up the mess I made; I'll do it now."
- Give assurance that this will not happen again. Say, quite simply, "It won't happen again" or better and more specifically, "I won't be late again."

Some Don'ts for Effective Apologies

At the same time that you follow the suggestions for crafting an effective apology, try to avoid these common "don'ts."

- Apologize when it isn't necessary.
- Justify your behavior by mentioning that everyone does it, for example, "Everyone leaves work early on Friday."
- Minimize your wrongdoing by saying that the other person has done something equally wrong. "So I play poker; you play the lottery."
- Accuse the other person of contributing to the problem. "I should have known you're overly anxious about receiving the figures exactly at 9 a.m."
- Minimize the hurt that this may have caused. Avoid such comments as, "So the figures arrived a little late. What's the big deal?"
- Include excuses with the apology. Avoid such combinations as "I'm sorry the figures are late, but I had so much other work to do." An excuse often negates the apology by saying, in effect, "I'm really not sorry because there was good reason for what I did, but I'm saying 'I'm sorry' to cover all my bases and to make this uncomfortable situation go away."

COMMUNICATION CHOICE POINT

APOLOGIZING *You totally forget that you were scheduled to give your speech in class and instead cut class to study for a chemistry test. One norm of your particular class is that if you miss a speech, you're required to give a 1-minute speech of apology to both the instructor and the class members.* **What are some of your options for expressing this apology? What would you say?**

- Take the easy way out and apologize through e-mail (unless the wrongdoing was committed in e-mail or if e-mail is your only or main form of communication). Generally, it's preferable to use a more personal mode of communication—face-to-face or phone, for example. It's more difficult, but it's more effective.

Giving and Receiving Compliments

A **compliment** is a message of praise, flattery, or congratulations. The compliment functions like a kind of interpersonal glue; it's a way of relating to another person with positiveness and immediacy. It's also a conversation starter, "I like your watch; may I ask where you got it?" Another purpose the compliment serves is to encourage the other person to compliment you—even if not immediately (which often seems inappropriate).

Compliments can be unqualified or qualified. The unqualified compliment is a message that is purely positive. "Your paper was just great, an A." The qualified message is not entirely positive: "Your paper was great, an A; if not for a few problems, it would have been an A+." You might also give a qualified compliment by qualifying your own competence; for example, "That song you wrote sounded great, but I really don't know anything about music."

A "backhanded compliment" is really not a compliment at all; it's usually an insult masquerading as a compliment. For example, you might give a backhanded compliment if you say "That sweater takes away from your pale complexion; it makes you look less washed out" (it compliments the color of the sweater but criticizes the person's complexion) or "Looks like you've finally lost a few pounds, am I right?" (It compliments a slimmer appearance but points out the person's being overweight). Compliments are sometimes difficult to give and even more difficult to respond to without discomfort or embarrassment. Fortunately, there are easy-to-follow guidelines.

Explore at MyCommunicationLab Exercise: "Giving and Receiving Compliments"

Giving a Compliment

Here are a few suggestions for giving a compliment.

- Be real and honest. Say what you mean and refrain from giving compliments you don't believe in. They'll likely sound insincere.
- Compliment in moderation. A compliment that is too extreme (say, for example, "That's the best decorated apartment I've ever seen in my life") may be viewed as dishonest. Similarly, don't compliment at every possible occasion; if you do, your compliments will seem too easy to win and not really meaningful.
- Be totally complimentary; avoid qualifying your compliments. If you hear yourself giving a compliment and then adding a "but" or a "however," stop and rethink what you are going to say. Many people will remember the qualification rather than the compliment and the qualified compliment will instead feel like a criticism.
- Be specific. Direct your compliment at something specific rather than something general. Instead of saying "I liked your speech," you might say "I liked your speech—the introduction gained my attention immediately and you held it throughout."

- Be personal in your own feelings—"Your song really moved me; it made me recall so many good times"—but not personal about the other person—"Your hair looks so natural; is that a weave or a toupee?" At the same time, avoid any compliment that can be misinterpreted as overly sexual. Depending on your relationship with the person, you might use his or her name; people like to hear their name spoken and doubly so when it's associated with a compliment.
- Some interpersonal watchers recommend that you compliment people for their accomplishments rather than for who they are or for things over which they have no control. So, for example, you would compliment people for their clear reports, their poetry, their problem solving, their tact, and so on, and you would not compliment someone for being attractive or having beautiful green eyes.

Receiving a Compliment

In receiving a compliment, people generally take either one of two options: denial or acceptance.

Many people deny the compliment ("It's nice of you to say, but I know I was terrible"), minimize it ("It isn't like I wrote the great American novel; it was just an article that no one will read"), change the subject ("So, where should we go for dinner?"), or say nothing. Each of these responses denies the legitimacy of the compliment. Accepting the compliment seems the much better alternative. An acceptance might consist simply of (1) a smile with eye contact—avoid looking at the floor; (2) a simple "thank you," and, if appropriate, (3) a personal reflection in which you explain (very briefly) the meaning of the compliment and why it's important to you (for example, "I really appreciate your comments; I worked really hard on the project and it's great to hear it was effective").

Giving and Receiving Advice

Most people like to give advice. Advising someone else about what they should do might make you feel competent and authoritative. In some cases giving advice may be part of your job description. For example, if you're a teacher, lawyer, health-care provider, religious leader, or psychiatrist, you are in the advice-giving business. Advice is often solicited from relatives and friends as well as professionals.

Advice is best viewed as a process of giving another person a suggestion for thinking or behaving, usually to effect a change. In many cases it will take the form of a suggestion to solve a problem. For example, you might advise a friend to change his or her way of looking at a broken love affair, a financial situation, or a career path. Or you might advise someone to do something such as to start dating again, to invest in certain stocks, or to go back to school to complete a degree. Sometimes, the advice serves to encourage the person to stick with what they are currently thinking or doing—for example, to stay with Pat despite the difficulties, to hold the stocks the person already has, or to continue on his or her current career path.

One of the most important types of advice is what we might call **meta-advice,** advice about advice. At least three types of meta-advice can be identified.

- **To explore options and choices.** This type of meta-advice would focus on helping the person explore the available options. For example, if a friend asks what he or she should do about never having a date, you might help your friend explore the available options (such as dating websites, speed dating, or singles groups) and the advantages and disadvantages of each.
- **To seek expert advice.** If confronted with a request for advice about a subject you know little about, the best advice is often to seek advice from someone who is an expert in the field. When a friend asks what to do about a persistent cough, the best advice seems to be the meta-advice to "talk to your doctor."
- **To delay decision.** If asked for advice about a decision that doesn't have to be made immediately, one form of meta-advice would be to delay the decision while additional information is collected. So, for example, if your advice-seeker has two weeks to decide on whether to take a job with XYZ Company, meta-advice would suggest that the decision be delayed while the company is researched more thoroughly.

Meta-advice is one of the safest types of advice to give. When you meta-advise to explore options more thoroughly, you're not so much giving advice as you are helping the advice-seeker to collect the information needed to make his or her own decision.

Giving Advice

The following are some suggestions for giving advice effectively:

- **Listen.** This is the first rule for advice giving. Listen to the person's thoughts and feelings to discern what he or she really wants. The person who says, for example, "I just don't know what to do" may be requesting support and active listening rather than advice. The person may simply want to ventilate in the presence of a friend. The person who says, "What do you think I can do to make the room look better?" might be looking for praise. Rather than advice about what to change, this person may want the response to be, "It's perfect as it is. I wouldn't touch a thing." If you're in doubt as to what the person is seeking, ask.

- **Empathize.** Try to feel what the other person is feeling. Perhaps you might recall similar situations you were in or similar emotions you experienced. Think about the importance of the issue to the person and, in general, try to put yourself in his or her position.
- **Be tentative.** If you give advice, give it with the qualifications it requires. The advice seeker has a right to know how sure (or unsure) you are of the advice or what evidence (or lack of evidence) you have that the advice will work.
- **Offer options.** When appropriate, offer several options and give the pros and cons of each: "If you do X, then A and B are likely to follow." Even better, allow the advice seeker to identify the possible consequences of each option.
- **Ensure understanding.** Often people seeking advice are emotionally upset and may not remember everything in the conversation. Seek feedback after giving advice by saying, for example, "Does that make sense?" or "Is my suggestion workable?"
- **Keep the interaction confidential.** People often seek advice about very personal matters. It's best to keep such conversations confidential, even if you're not explicitly asked to do so.
- **Avoid should statements.** People seeking advice still ultimately have to make their own decisions. It's better to say, "You *might* do X" or "You *could* do Y" rather than "You *should* do Z." Avoid demanding—or even implying—that the person has to follow your advice. This attacks the person's negative face, his or her need for autonomy.

Receiving Advice

Here are just a few suggestions for receiving advice.

- If you asked for advice, then accept what the person says. You owe it to the advice giver to listen to and consider the advice, even if you decide not to follow it.
- Resist the temptation to retaliate or criticize the advice giver, even if you didn't ask for advice. Instead of responding with "Well, your hair doesn't look that great, either," consider if the advice has any merit. If you decide to reject the advice, ask yourself why someone would think you were in need of such advice in the first place.
- Interact with the advice. Talk about it with the advice giver. A process of asking and answering questions is likely to produce added insight into the problem.
- Express your appreciation for the advice. It's often difficult to give advice. Showing the advice giver some gratitude in return is a good idea.

Watch at MyCommunicationLab Video: "First Day of Class"

It's the first day of Intro to Biology, and Tim and Emad are both early for class. The classroom is rather large, but the two students both choose to sit at opposite ends of the room. Tim feels awkward, but wants to approach Emad to start a conversation. Log on to mycommunicationlab.com to view this "First Day of Class" video, see how the choices play out, and then answer the related discussion questions.

SUMMARY: INTERPERSONAL COMMUNICATION: CONVERSATION

Study and **Review** at **MyCommunicationLab**

This chapter explored interpersonal communication and conversation in a variety of forms including small talk, making excuses and apologies, complimenting, and advising.

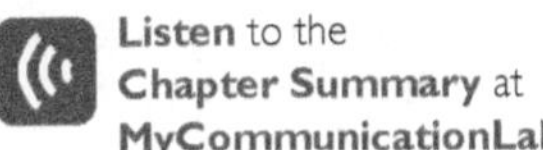

Listen to the **Chapter Summary** at **MyCommunicationLab**

7.1 PRINCIPLES OF CONVERSATION

1. Conversation is a developmental process that can be viewed as consisting of five general stages: opening, feedforward, business, feedback, and closing.
2. Throughout the speaking–listening process, both speaker and listener exchange cues for what are called conversational turns that enable the speaker and listener to communicate about the communication in which they're currently engaged.
3. Speakers regulate the conversation through two major types of cues: turn-maintaining cues and turn-yielding cues. Listeners regulate the conversation by using three types of cues: turn-requesting cues, turn-denying cues, and backchanneling cues and interruptions.
4. Dialogue is conversation in which there is genuine two-way interaction and each person is both speaker and listener, sender and receiver. Monologue communication is the opposite side; here one person speaks and the other listens—there's no real interaction between participants.
5. Immediacy is the creation of closeness, a sense of togetherness, of oneness, between speaker and listener.
6. Flexibility refers to the ability to adapt to different circumstances.
7. Politeness refers to conversation that follows the maxims of generosity, approbation, modesty, agreement, and sympathy.

7.2 EVERYDAY CONVERSATIONS

8. Small talk is pervasive and non-controversial and often serves as a polite way of introducing one's self or a topic.
9. Introducing one person to another or yourself to others will vary with the culture.
10. Excuses are explanations designed to lessen any negative implications of a message.
11. Apologies are expressions of regret or sorrow for having done what you did or for what happened.
12. A compliment is a message of praise, flattery, or congratulations and often enables you to interact with positiveness and immediacy.
13. Advice can be specific or advice about advice (meta-advice).

Study and **Review** the **Flashcards** at **MyCommunicationLab**

KEY TERMS

apology *164*
backchanneling cues *154*
compliment *166*
conversation *151*
conversational turns *153*
dialogue *155*
excuses *163*
flexibility *156*
gossip *165*
immediacy *156*
interruptions *154*
leave-taking cues *161*
meta-advice *167*
metacommunication *153*
monologue *155*
turn-denying cues *154*
turn-maintaining cues *153*
turn-requesting cues *154*
turn-yielding cues *154*

WORKING WITH CONVERSATION

7.1 Formulating Excuses and Apologies. Excuses and apologies are often helpful in lessening the possible negative effects of a mishap. Here are several situations in which you might want to offer an excuse and/or an apology. Excuses and apologies will not reverse your errors or eliminate their negative impacts, but they may help repair—at least to some extent—conversational or relationship damage. For each of the following situations, formulate one excuse or apology that you think will prove effective.

1. Your boss confronts you with your office telephone log. The log shows that you've been making lots of long-distance personal phone calls, a practice that is explicitly forbidden.
2. In talking with your supervisor, you tell a joke that puts down lesbians and gay men. Your supervisor tells you she finds the joke homophobic and offensive; she adds that she has a gay son and is proud of him. This supervisor's approval is essential to your retention.
3. You're caught in a lie. You told your romantic partner that you were going to visit your parents, but were discovered to have visited a former lover. You don't want to break up your relationship over this.

7.2 Giving and Receiving Compliments. Complimenting another and receiving compliments gracefully are acquired communication skills. This exercise is in two parts. First, formulate a compliment in which you say something favorable and positive about another person's reliability, intelligence, sense of style, fair mindedness, independence, perceptiveness, warmth, or sense of humor. Second, assume that the compliment you just formulated was addressed to you. What would you say in response?

7.3 Introductions: Special Handling. Of course, not all introductions are easy; some are actually quite difficult. Indicate what you would do in each of the following situations:

a. You're walking along the street with your romantic partner and you meet a colleague from work. You work closely with this colleague and yet you just can't think of her name. Yet you have to introduce her to your partner. What are some of your choices? What do you say?

b. You're walking along the street with someone with whom you have a clandestine romantic relationship. You meet a neighbor from your apartment building who stops to chat. You have to introduce these two people, but you really don't want to reveal anything about your relationship. What are your choices? What would you say?

c. You're walking along the street with a friend who is, like you, an entry-level employee of a huge corporation. You meet one of the vice presidents who stops to chat. What are some of your choices for introducing these people? Who would you introduce to whom? What would you say?

7.4 The Negatives of Empathy. Although empathy is almost universally considered positive, there is some evidence to show that it has a negative side. For example, people are most empathic with those who are similar—racially and ethnically as well as in appearance and social status. The more empathy we feel toward our own group, the less empathy—possibly even the more hostility—we feel toward other groups. The same empathy that increases our understanding of our own group decreases our understanding of other groups. So while empathy may encourage group cohesiveness and identification, it can also create dividing lines between "us" and "them" (Angier, 1995). Have you ever witnessed these negative effects of empathy?

7.5 Conversational Etiquette. Another way of looking at conversational rule violations is as breaches of etiquette. When you fail to follow the rules of etiquette, you're often breaking a conversational rule. A variety of websites focus on etiquette in different communication situations. Use your favorite search engine and search for such terms as "etiquette + conversation," "cell phone etiquette," or "communication etiquette." Visit one or more websites and record any rules you find particularly applicable to interpersonal communication and conversation.

7.6 Conversational Taboos. Not surprisingly, each culture has its own conversational taboos—topics that should be avoided, especially by visitors from other cultures. A few examples: In Norway avoid talk of salaries and social status; in Spain avoid discussing family, religion, or jobs, and don't make negative comments on bullfighting; in Egypt avoid talk of Middle Eastern politics; in Japan avoid talking about World War II; in the Philippines avoid talk of politics, religion, corruption, and foreign aid; in Mexico avoid talking about the Mexican-American war and illegal aliens; in the Caribbean avoid discussing race, local politics, and religion (Axtell, 1993). Do you consider some topics taboo? In particular, are there topics that you do not want members of other cultures to talk about? Why?

7.7 Interruptions. In an analysis of 43 published studies on interruptions and gender differences, men interrupted significantly more than women (Anderson, 1998). Among the reasons offered to explain why men interrupt more is men's desire to shift the focus to their areas of competence (and away from their areas of incompetence) and to maintain power and control. Do you find that your own experience supports these findings on gender differences in interrupting? Based on your experiences, how would you explain the reasons for interrupting? Do you notice gender differences in interrupting or in responding to another's interruptions?

LogOn! MyCommunicationLab www.mycommunicationlab.com

Throughout this chapter, there are icons that highlight media content for selected topics. Go to **MyCommunicationLab** for additional materials on the principles of conversation and everyday conversation. Here you'll find flashcards to help you learn key communication terms, videos that illustrate a variety of concepts, additional exercises, and discussions to help you continue your study of conversation.

8 INTERPERSONAL RELATIONSHIP STAGES AND THEORIES

CHAPTER TOPICS	CHAPTER OBJECTIVES
In this chapter you'll explore the following major topics:	**After reading this chapter you should be able to:**
RELATIONSHIP STAGES	8.1 Explain the stages relationships go through.
RELATIONSHIP THEORIES	8.2 Paraphrase the main assumptions of the theories of interpersonal relationships.
THE DARK SIDE OF INTERPERSONAL RELATIONSHIPS	8.3 Define *jealousy* and *relationship violence* and explain apply the suggestions for dealing with these dark sides of relationships.

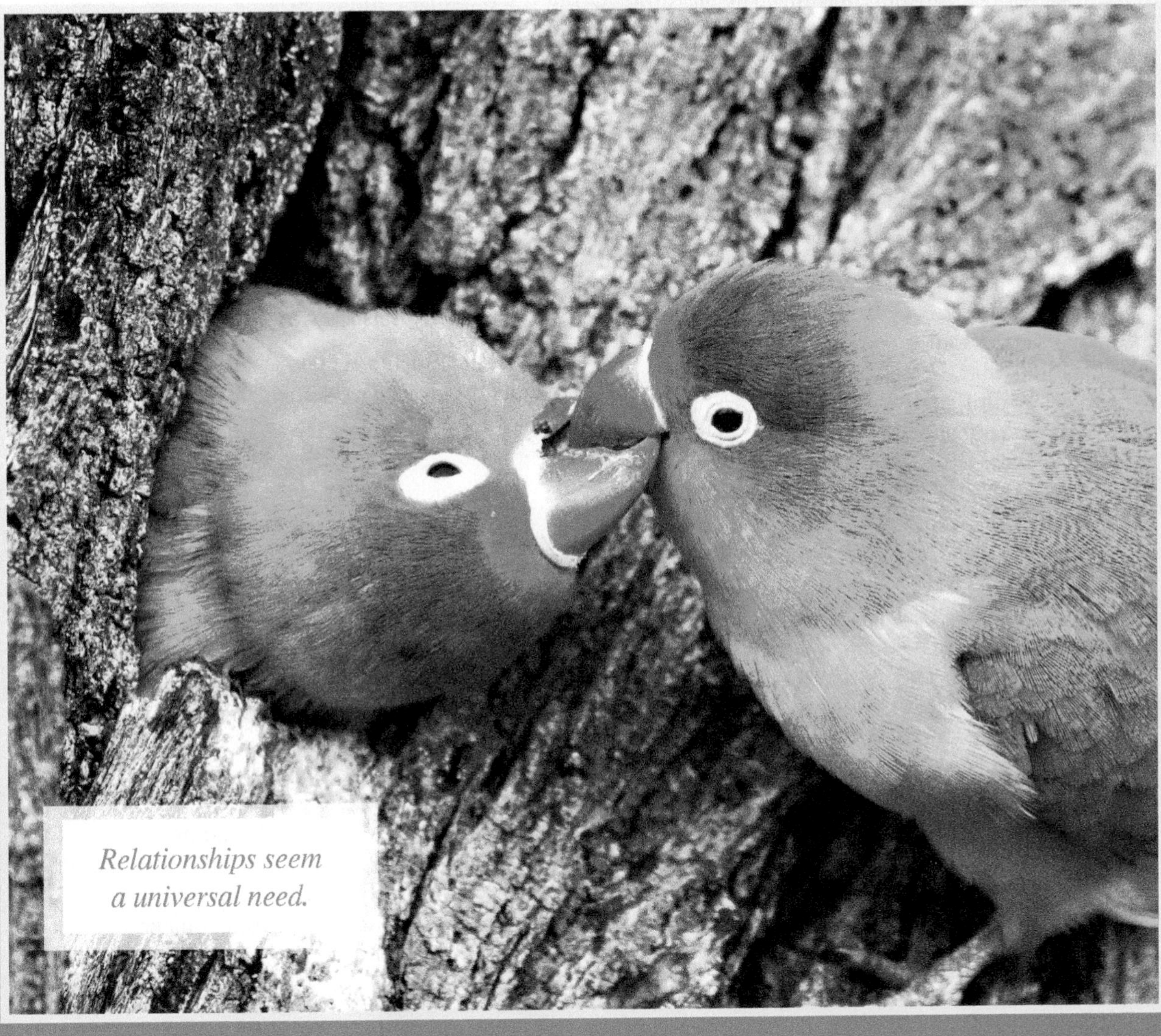

Relationships seem a universal need.

A good way to begin the study of interpersonal relationships is to examine your own relationships (past, present, or those you look forward to) by asking yourself what your relationships do for you. What are the advantages and the disadvantages? Focus on your own relationships in general (friendship, romantic, family, and work); focus on one particular relationship (say, your life partner or your child or your best friend); or focus on one type of relationship (say, friendships), and respond to the following statements by indicating the extent to which your relationship(s) serve each of these functions. Visualize a 10-point scale on which 1 indicates that your relationship(s) never serves this function, 10 indicates that your relationship(s) always serves this function, and the numbers in between indicate levels between these extremes.

_____ **1.** My relationships help to lessen my loneliness.
_____ **2.** My relationships help me gain in self-knowledge and in self-esteem.
_____ **3.** My relationships help enhance my physical and emotional health.
_____ **4.** My relationships maximize my pleasures and minimize my pains.
_____ **5.** My relationships help me to secure stimulation (intellectual, physical, and emotional).

Let's elaborate just a bit on each of these commonly accepted advantages of interpersonal communication.

1. One of the major benefits of relationships is that they help to lessen loneliness (Rokach, 1998; Rokach & Brock, 1995). They make you feel that someone cares, that someone likes you, that someone will protect you, that someone ultimately will love you.
2. Through contact with others you learn about yourself and see yourself from different perspectives and in different roles, as a child or parent, as a coworker, as a manager, as a best friend. Healthy interpersonal relationships help enhance self-esteem and self-worth. Simply having a friend or romantic partner (at least most of the time) makes you feel desirable and worthy.
3. Research consistently shows that interpersonal relationships contribute significantly to physical and emotional health (Goleman, 1995a, b; Pennebaker, 1991; Rosen, 1998; Rosengren et al., 1993) and to personal happiness (Berscheid & Reis, 1998). Without close interpersonal relationships you're more likely to become depressed—and this depression, in turn, contributes significantly to physical illness. Isolation, in fact, contributes as much to mortality as high blood pressure, high cholesterol, obesity, smoking, or lack of physical exercise (Goleman, 1995a, b).
4. The most general function served by interpersonal relationships, and the function that encompasses all the others, is that of maximizing pleasure and minimizing pain. Your good friends, for example, will make you feel even better about your good fortune and less hurt when you're confronted with hardships.
5. As plants are heliotropic and orient themselves to light, humans are stimulotropic and orient themselves to sources of stimulation (Davis, 1973). Human contact is one of the best ways to secure this stimulation—intellectual, physical, and emotional. Even an imagined relationship seems better than none, one type of which is covered in the accompanying Expanding Media Literacy box.

Now, respond to these sentences as you did to the above.

_____ **6.** My relationships put uncomfortable pressure on me to expose my vulnerabilities.
_____ **7.** My relationships increase my obligations.
_____ **8.** My relationships prevent me from developing other relationships.
_____ **9.** My relationships scare me because they may be difficult to dissolve.
_____ **10.** My relationships hurt me.

These statements express what most people would consider disadvantages of interpersonal relationships.

6. Close relationships put pressure on you to reveal yourself and to expose your vulnerabilities. While this is generally worthwhile in the context of a supporting and caring relationship, it may backfire if the relationship deteriorates and these weaknesses are used against you.
7. Close relationships increase your obligations to other people, sometimes to a great extent. Your time is no longer entirely your own. And although you enter relationships to spend more time with these special people, you also incur time (and perhaps financial) obligations with which you may not be happy.
8. Close relationships can lead you to abandon other relationships. Sometimes the other relationship involves someone you like, but

me•di•a lit•er•a•cy *noun* ability to understand, interact with, and create media messages

EXPANDING MEDIA LITERACY
Parasocial Relationships

Parasocial relationships are relationships that viewers perceive themselves to have with media personalities (Giles, 2001; Rubin & McHugh, 1987). Some viewers develop these relationships with real media personalities—Ellen DeGeneris, Jerry Springer, or Oprah Winfrey, for example. As a result they may watch these people faithfully and communicate with them in their own imaginations. In other cases these relationships are with fictional characters—Sherlock Holmes or Joan Watson on *Elementary,* a firefighter on *Chicago Fire,* or a forensic pathologist on *Bones, Body of Proof,* or *Rizzoli and Isles.* In fact, actors who portray doctors frequently get mail asking for medical advice. And soap opera stars who are about to be "killed" frequently get warning letters from their parasocial relationship fans.

Parasocial relationships develop in a three-stage process (Rubin & McHugh, 1987):

- **Initial attraction.** Parasocial relationships start from an initial attraction based on the character's social and task roles.
- **Perceived relationship.** With this initial attraction established, the relationship progresses to a perceived relationship. We begin to see the relationship as real.
- **Importance.** The third stage is the recognition that this relationship is important and significant.

As might be expected, research indicates that these parasocial relationships are most important to those who spend a great deal of time with the media, who have few interpersonal relationships, and who are generally anxious (Cole & Leets, 1999; Rubin, Perse, & Powell, 1985).

In many ways the media encourage the development of parasocial relationships. Television shows like *Extra, Access Hollywood, and Omg!Insider* and their corresponding websites present the kinds of information about celebrities that enable you to feel you know them and like them. In fact, the more you know about the person or character, the more likely you are to develop a parasocial relationship with that character (Perse & Rubin, 1989). Similarly, the chat sessions that celebrities hold on the Internet foster the illusion of a real interpersonal relationship. And in reality shows you have people very much like yourself who, simply by virtue of their appearance in the media, become celebrities, making it even easier to develop parasocial relationships.

As you interact with the media, ask yourself in what other ways the media encourage parasocial relationships between viewers on the one hand and television and film characters on the other. In what ways does the culture encourage such relationships? All things considered, what do you think about parasocial relationships?

your partner can't stand. More often, however, it's simply a matter of time and energy; relationships take a lot of both and you have less to give to these other and less intimate relationships.

9. The closer your relationships, the more emotionally difficult they are to dissolve, a feeling which may be uncomfortable for some people. If a relationship is deteriorating, you may feel distress or depression. In some cultures, for example, religious pressures may prevent married couples from separating. And if lots of money is involved, dissolving a relationship can often mean giving up the fortune you've spent your life accumulating.
10. And, of course, your partner may break your heart. Your partner may leave you—against all your pleading and promises. Your hurt will be in proportion to how much you care and need your partner. If you care a great deal, you're likely to experience great hurt; if you care less, the hurt will be less—it's one of life's little ironies.

To complement this discussion of the disadvantages of interpersonal relationships, we'll look also at what has come to be called the "dark side of interpersonal relationships" later in this chapter.

8.1 RELATIONSHIP STAGES

It's useful to look at interpersonal relationships as created and constructed by the individuals involved. That is, in any interpersonal relationship—say between Pat and Chris—there are actually several relationships: (1) the relationship as Pat sees it, (2) the relationship as Chris sees it, (3) the relationship that Pat wants and is striving for, (4) the relationship that Chris wants and is striving for. And then, of course, there are the many relationships that friends and relatives see and that they reflect back in their communications. For example, the relationship that Pat's mother (who dislikes Chris) sees and reflects in her communication with Pat and Chris is very likely to influence Pat and Chris in some ways. And then there's the relationship that a dispassionate researcher/observer would see. Looked at in this way, there are an infinite number of interpersonal relationships in any interpersonal relationship.

This is not to say that there is no *real* relationship; it's just to say that there are many real relationships. And because there are these differently constructed relationships, people often disagree about a wide variety of issues and evaluate the relationship very differently. Regularly on *The Jerry Springer Show* and *Maury*, you see couples where each individual sees the relationship very differently. The first guest thinks all is going well until the second guest comes on and explodes—often identifying long-held dissatisfactions and behaviors that shock the partner.

The quality that makes a relationship interpersonal is **interdependency**; that is, the actions of one person have an impact on the other; one person's actions have consequences for the other person. The actions of a stranger (for example, actions such as working overtime or flirting with a coworker) will have no impact on you; you and the proverbial stranger are *in*dependent—your actions have no effect on each other. If, however, you were in an interpersonal relationship and your partner worked overtime or flirted with a coworker, it would affect you and the relationship in some way.

The six-stage model shown in Figure 8.1 describes the significant stages a relationship may go through. As a general description of relationship development (and sometimes dissolution), the stages seem standard: They apply to all relationships, whether friendship or love, whether face-to-face or computer-mediated. The six stages are contact, involvement, intimacy, deterioration, repair, and dissolution. Each stage can be divided into an initial and a final phase.

Explore at MyCommunicationLab Activity: "Relationships"

As important as the stages themselves is the movement from stage to stage, depicted in Figure 8.1 by the different types of arrows. The exit arrows show that each stage offers the opportunity to exit the relationship: After saying hello, you can say goodbye and exit. The vertical or movement arrows going to the next stage and back again represent the fact that you can move either to a more intense stage (say, from involvement to intimacy) or to a less intense stage (say, from intimacy to deterioration). The self-reflexive arrows—the arrows that return to the beginning of the same level or stage—signify that any relationship may become stabilized at any point. You may, for example, remain at the contact stage without getting any further involved—a situation that exists among residents of many large apartment complexes.

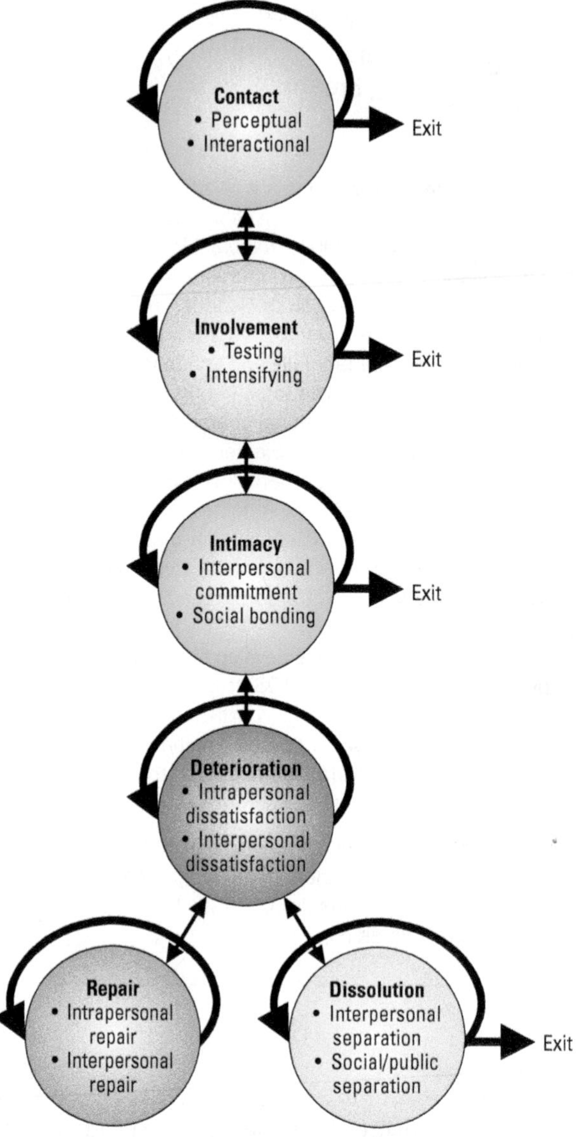

FIGURE 8.1 A Six-Stage Relationship Model

Because relationships differ so widely, it's best to think of this or any relationship model as a tool for talking about relationships rather than as a specific map that indicates how you move from one relationship position to another. Can you identify other steps or stages that would further explain what goes on in relationship development? What happens when the two people in a relationship experience the stages differently? Can you provide an example from literature or from your own experience?

Movement from one stage to another depends largely on your relationship communication skills—the skills you deploy to initiate and open a relationship, present yourself as likable, express affection, and self-disclose appropriately—and, in fact, all the interpersonal skills you've been acquiring throughout this course (Dindia & Timmerman, 2003). Recognize that these skills will prove relevant in both face-to-face and in computer-mediated relationships, though the specific ways in which you express empathy, for example, will vary depending on your expressing it with only written cues or with facial, vocal, and body as well as verbal cues.

Explore at MyCommunicationLab Exercise: "Analyzing Stage Talk"

COMMUNICATION CHOICE POINT

RELATIONSHIP RÉSUMé *Although you've been mostly honest is your Internet relationship, now that you're living together, you want to come clean about past relationships and your poor financial situation.* **What might you say in preface to this revelation? What might you say? What are some of the things you would want to avoid saying?**

Contact

At the **contact** stage, there is first *perceptual contact*—you see what the person looks like, you hear what the person sounds like, you may even smell the person. From this, you get a physical picture: gender, approximate age, height, and so on. Or you might browse a group of photos and profiles from an online dating site. If this is an online relationship, this initial perception relies on cues from the messages, photos, and perhaps video and audio.

After this perception, there is usually *interactional contact*. Here the interaction is superficial and impersonal. This is the stage of "Hello, my name is Joe"—the stage at which you exchange basic information that needs to come before any more intense involvement. This interactional contact may also be nonverbal, as in exchanging smiles, concentrating your focus on one person, or decreasing the physical distance between the two of you.

This is the stage at which you initiate interaction ("May I join you?") and engage in invitational communication ("May I buy you a cup of coffee?" or, if on Facebook, say, an invitation to friendship). With online relationships, each of you will have read the other's profile and so will know quite a lot about each other before you even begin to talk. According to some researchers, it's at this contact stage—within the first 4 minutes of initial interaction—that you decide whether you want to pursue the relationship (Zunin & Zunin, 1972).

Physical appearance (whether revealed face to face or in online photos) is especially important in the initial development of attraction because it's the characteristic most readily available to sensory inspection. Yet through both verbal and nonverbal behaviors, qualities such as friendliness, warmth, openness, and dynamism are also revealed at the contact stage. With online relations people may profile themselves as warm or open or dynamic and, as a result, you may actually see the person's messages confirming this labeling.

Involvement

At the **involvement** stage a sense of mutuality, of being connected, develops. During this stage you experiment and try to learn more about the other person. At the initial phase of involvement, a kind of preliminary testing goes on. You want to see if your initial judgment—made perhaps at the contact stage—proves reasonable. So you may ask questions: "Where do you work?" "What are you majoring in?" If you're doing this online, you probably can find most of this type of information in the person's profile. If you're committed to getting to know the person even better, you continue your involvement by intensifying your interaction. In this process you not only try to get to know the other person better, but also begin to reveal yourself. It's at this stage that you begin to share your feelings and your emotions. If this is to be a romantic relationship, you might date. If it's to be a friendship, you might share in activities related to mutual interests—go to the movies or to some sports event together.

And throughout the relationship process—but especially during the involvement and early stages of intimacy—partners continue testing each other. Each person tries to find out how the other feels about the relationship. For example, you might ask your partner directly how he or she feels; or you might disclose your own feelings on the assumption that your partner will also self-disclose; or you might joke about a shared future together, touch more intimately, or hint that you're serious about the relationship; or you might question mutual friends as to your partner's feelings (Baxter & Wilmot, 1984; Bell & Buerkel-Rothfuss, 1990).

Intimacy

One way to define **intimacy** is as a feeling that you can be honest and open when talking about yourself, that you can express thoughts and feelings you wouldn't reveal in other relationships (Mackey, Diemer, & O'Brien, 2000). At the intimacy stage, you commit yourself still further to the other person and, in fact, establish a kind of relationship in which this individual becomes your best or closest friend, lover, or companion. Because intimacy is essentially an emotional/communication connection, it can occur in face-to-face and in online relationships equally. You also come to share each other's social networks, a practice followed by members of widely different cultures (Gao & Gudykunst, 1995). This is seen most clearly on social network sites where the site itself identifies people with whom you might want to become "friends" based on mutual friends or interests.

Your communication becomes more personalized, more synchronized, and easier (Gudykunst, Nishida, & Chua, 1987). Usually the intimacy stage divides itself quite neatly into two phases: an *interpersonal commitment* phase, in which you commit yourselves to each other in a kind of private way, and a *social bonding* phase, in which the commitment is made public—revealed perhaps to family and friends, perhaps to the public at large through a formal ceremony, or with a simple "married to" on Facebook. Here the two of you become a unit, a pair.

In addition, in the intimacy stage you increase your display of **affiliative cues** (signs that show you love the other person), including head nods, gestures, and forward leaning. You give **Duchenne smiles**, smiles that are beyond voluntary control and that signal genuine joy (Gonzaga, Keltner, Londahi, & Smith, 2001). These Duchenne smiles give you crow's-feet around the eyes, raise up your cheeks, and puff up the lower eyelids (Lemonick, 2005). In online relationships and on social networking sites, you exchange a variety of messages, bumper stickers, icons, and the like to demonstrate your closeness.

Commitment may take many forms; it may be an engagement or a marriage, a commitment to help the person or to be with the person, or a commitment to reveal your deepest secrets. It may consist of living together or agreeing to become lovers. Or it may consist of becoming a romantic pair either in face-to-face or in online relationships. The type of commitment varies with the relationship and with the individuals. The important characteristic is that the commitment made is a special one; it's a commitment that you do not make lightly or to everyone. Each of us reserves this level of intimacy for very few people at any given time—sometimes just one person; sometimes two, three, or perhaps more. In computer-mediated communication, there is the potential for a much greater number of intimates.

the•o•ry *noun* statement of explanation, formulation of relationships, reasoned generalization

UNDERSTANDING THEORY AND RESEARCH
Relationship Commitment

An important factor influencing the course of relationship deterioration (as well as relationship maintenance) is the degree of commitment the individuals have toward each other and toward the relationship. Three types of commitment are often distinguished and can be identified from your answers to the following questions (Johnson, 1973, 1982, 1991; Knapp & Taylor, 1995; Kurdek, 1995):

- Do I want to stay in this relationship? Do I have a desire to stay?
- Do I have a moral obligation to stay in this relationship?
- Do I have to stay in this relationship? Is it a necessity for me to stay?

All relationships are held together, in part, by desire, obligation, or necessity or by some combination of these elements. The strength of the relationship, including its resistance to possible deterioration, is related to the degree of commitment. When a relationship shows signs of deterioration and yet there's a strong commitment to preserving it, the individuals may well surmount the obstacles and reverse the process. In contrast, when commitment is weak and the individuals doubt that there are good reasons for staying together, the relationship deteriorates faster and more intensely.

Working with Theories and Research

Has commitment or the lack of it (from either or both of you) ever influenced the progression of one of your relationships? What happened?

One important characteristic of intimacy is that we talk more affectionately, more lovingly, more deeply. Exercise 8.1 explores a particular type of intimacy talk, cherishing.

Deterioration

Although many relationships remain at the intimacy stage, some enter the stage of **relationship deterioration**—the stage that sees the weakening of bonds between the parties and represents the downside of the relationship progression. Relationships deteriorate for many reasons. When the reasons for coming together are no longer present or change drastically, relationships may deteriorate. Thus, for example, when your relationship no longer lessens your loneliness or provides stimulation or self-knowledge, or when it fails to increase your self-esteem or maximize pleasures and minimize pains, it may be in the process of deteriorating. Table 8.1 presents some of the causes of relationship deterioration and some preventives.

Watch at **MyCommunicationLab**
Video: "Give Me a Break"

TABLE 8.1 SOME CAUSES OF RELATIONSHIP DETERIORATION

In addition to the problems caused by relationships not meeting the reasons the relationship was developed to serve in the first place, here are some additional reasons for relationship deterioration. The preventives noted should not be taken to mean that all relationship partners should stay together; there are many good reasons for breaking up. The accompanying Understanding Theory and Research box examines relationship commitment, which greatly influences the course of relationship deterioration.

Problems	**Reasons**	**Preventive Strategies**
Poor Communication	Communication that is excessively critical or unsupportive or disconfirming will create dissatisfaction that can easily lead to a breakdown in friendship, love, or family relationships.	Talk about your communication; voice your expectations.
Third-Party Relationships	When a person's goals cease to be met within the relationship, a new relationship may be pursued, and if this new relationship serves the goals better, then the original relationship is likely to deteriorate.	Talk about needs openly, explaining what you want from the relationship and listening to what the other person wants.
Relationship Changes	The development of incompatible attitudes, vastly different intellectual interests and abilities, or major goal changes may contribute to relationship deterioration.	Discuss the changes as you develop them and listen openly to the changes of your partner. If appropriate and possible, participate in the changes of the other.
Sex- and Work-Related Problems	Problems within the relationship (for example, sex) or outside the relationship (for example, work) can put a strain on a relationship with the frequent result that other, more supportive relationships may be sought.	Discussing these problems with each other or with a therapist can help prevent them from escalating.
Financial Difficulties	Money (in part because of its close association with power and control) often proves to be a cause of major problems as people settle into their relationship.	Discuss your attitudes and beliefs about money before entering a relationship.
Beliefs about Relationships	If you and your partner hold widely different beliefs about, say, gender or financial expectations then your relationship is more likely to experience instability and interpersonal distancing (Goodwin & Gaines, 2004).	Try to be more open minded and flexible; differences do not have to lead to deterioration.

Repair

The first phase of the **relationship repair** stage is *intrapersonal repair*, in which you analyze what went wrong and consider ways of solving your relational difficulties. At this stage, you may consider changing your behaviors or perhaps changing your expectations of your partner. You may also weigh the rewards of your relationship as it is now against the rewards you could anticipate if your relationship ended.

If you decide that you want to repair your relationship, you may discuss this with your partner at the *interpersonal repair* level. Here you may talk about the problems in the relationship, the corrections you would want to see, and perhaps what you would be willing to do and what you would want the other person to do.

This is the stage of negotiating new agreements, new behaviors. You and your partner may try to solve your problems yourselves, seek the advice of friends or family, or perhaps enter professional counseling.

Fortunately, social media sites offer considerable help in making relationship repair by providing ready access to cards and virtual gifts, for example, to help you express your desire to repair the relationship.

You can look at the strategies for repairing a relationship in terms of the following six suggestions—which conveniently spell out the word *REPAIR*, a useful reminder that repair is not a one-step but a multistep process: Recognize the problem, Engage in productive conflict resolution, Pose possible solutions, Affirm each other, Integrate solutions into normal behavior, and Risk giving.

- **Recognize the problem.** What, in concrete terms, is wrong with your present relationship? What changes would be needed to make it better—again, in specific terms? Create a picture of your relationship as you would want it to be and compare that picture to the way the relationship looks now.
- **Engage in productive conflict resolution.** Interpersonal conflict is an inevitable part of relationship life. It's not so much the conflict that causes relationship difficulties, as the way in which the conflict is approached (as we'll see in Chapter 12). If it's confronted through productive strategies, the conflict may be resolved and the relationship may actually emerge stronger and healthier. If, however, unproductive and destructive strategies are used, the relationship may well deteriorate further.
- **Pose possible solutions.** Ideally, each person will ask, "What can we do to resolve the difficulty that will allow both of us to get what we want?"
- **Affirm each other.** For example, happily married couples engage in greater positive behavior exchange; that is, they communicate more agreement, approval, and positive affect than do unhappily married couples (Dindia & Fitzpatrick, 1985).
- **Integrate solutions.** Put the solutions to work in your daily life—make the solutions a part of your normal behavior.
- **Risk giving.** Risk giving favors without certainty of reciprocity. Risk rejection by making the first move to make up or say you're sorry. Be willing to change, adapt, and take on new tasks and responsibilities.

Explore at MyCommunicationLab Exercise: "Giving Repair Advice"

Dissolution

The **dissolution** stage, in both friendship and romance, is the cutting of the bonds tying you together. At first it usually takes the form of *interpersonal separation*, in which you may not see each other anymore or may not return messages or even de-friend or uncircle the person. If you live together, you may move into separate apartments and begin to lead lives apart from each other. If this relationship is a marriage, you may seek a legal separation. If this separation period proves workable and if the original relationship is not repaired, you may enter the phase of *social or public separation*. In marriage, this phase corresponds to divorce. Avoidance of each other and a return to being "single" are among the primary identifiable features of dissolution. In some cases, however, the former partners change the definition of their relationship; for example, ex-lovers become friends or ex-friends become "just" business partners.

The final, "good-bye" phase of dissolution is the point at which you become an ex-lover or ex-friend. In some cases this is a stage of relief and relaxation; finally, it's over. In other cases this is a stage of anxiety and frustration, of guilt and regret, of resentment over time ill spent and now lost. In more materialistic terms, the good-bye phase is the stage when property is divided and when legal battles may ensue over who should get what.

No matter how friendly the breakup, dissolution is likely to bring some emotional difficulty. Here are some suggestions for dealing with this.

- **Break the loneliness–depression cycle.** Avoid sad passivity, a state in which you feel sorry for yourself, sit alone, and perhaps cry. Instead, try to engage in active solitude (exercise, write, study, play computer games) and seek distraction (do things to put loneliness out of your mind; for example, take a long drive or shop). The most effective way to deal with loneliness is through social action, especially through helping people in need.
- **Take time out.** Take some time for yourself. Renew your relationship with yourself. Get to know

yourself as a unique individual—standing alone now but fully capable of entering a meaningful relationship in the future.

- **Bolster self-esteem.** Positive and successful experiences are most helpful in building self-esteem. As in dealing with loneliness, helping others is one of the best ways to raise your own self-esteem.
- **Seek the support of others.** Avail yourself of your friends and family for support; it's an effective antidote to the discomfort and unhappiness that occurs when a relationship ends.
- **Avoid repeating negative patterns.** Ask, at the start of a new relationship, if you're entering a relationship modeled on the previous one. If the answer is yes, be especially careful that you do not repeat the problems. At the same time, avoid becoming a prophet of doom. Do not see in every new relationship vestiges of the old. Use past relationships and experiences as guides, not filters.

Explore at MyCommunicationLab Exercise: "Learning to Hear Stage Talk"

COMMUNICATION CHOICE POINT

RELATIONSHIP DISSOLUTION *You realize that your 6-month relationship is going nowhere, and you want to break it off. It's just not exciting and not taking you where you want to go. You want to avoid making a scene.* **What would you say? Where would you say it? What kinds of feedforward would you use before breaking the news?**

8.2 RELATIONSHIP THEORIES

Many theories offer insight into why and how we develop and dissolve our relationships. Here we'll examine six relationship theories: theories focusing on attraction, relationship rules, relationship dialectics, social penetration, social exchange, and equity. Two theories that address online relationships are highlighted in the accompanying Understanding Theory and Research box.

Explore at MyCommunicationLab Exercise: "Mate Preferences: I Prefer Someone Who…"

Attraction Theory

Attraction theory holds that people form relationships on the basis of **attraction**. You are no doubt drawn or attracted to some people and not to others. In a similar way, some people are attracted to you and some are not. If you're like most people, then you're attracted to others on the basis of four major factors.

Similarity

If you could construct your mate, according to the **similarity** principle, it's likely that your mate would look, act, and think very much like you (Burleson, Kunkel, & Birch, 1994; Burleson, Samter, & Luccetti, 1992). Generally, people like those who are similar to them in nationality, race, abilities, physical characteristics, intelligence, and attitudes (Pornpitakpan, 2003).

Research also finds that you're more likely to help someone who is similar in race, attitude, and general appearance. Even the same first name or coming from the same state or city is significant (Wyer, 2012). Even the same first name is significant. For example, when an e-mail (asking receivers to fill out surveys of their food habits) identified the sender as having the same name as the receiver, there was a greater willingness to comply with the request (Gueguen, 2003). Sometimes people are attracted to their opposites, in a pattern called **complementarity**; for example, a dominant person might be attracted to someone who is more submissive. Generally, however, people prefer those who are similar.

Proximity

If you look around at people you find attractive, you will probably find that they are the people who live or work close to you. People who become friends are the people who have the greatest opportunity to interact with each other. **Proximity**, or physical closeness, is most important in the early stages of interaction—for example, during the first days of school (in class or in dormitories). It decreases in importance, though always remaining significant, as the opportunity to interact with more distant others increases.

Reinforcement

Not surprisingly, you're attracted to people who give rewards or **reinforcements**, which can range from a simple compliment to an expensive cruise. You're also attracted to people you reward (Aronson, Wilson, & Akert, 2010; Jecker & Landy, 1969). That is, you come to like people for whom you do favors; for example, you've probably increased your liking for persons after buying them an expensive present or going out of your way to do them a special favor. In these situations you justify your behavior by believing that the person was worth your efforts; otherwise, you'd have to admit to spending effort on people who might not deserve it.

Physical Attractiveness and Personality

It's easily appreciated that people like physically attractive people more than they like physically unattractive people. What isn't so obvious is that we also feel a greater sense of familiarity with more attractive people than with less attractive people; that is, we're more likely to think we've met a person before if that person is attractive (Monin, 2003). Also, although culture influences what people think is physical attractiveness and what isn't, some research indicates that there are certain facial features that seem to be thought attractive in all cultures—a kind of universal attractiveness (Brody, 1994). Additionally, you probably tend to like people who have a pleasant rather than an unpleasant personality (although people will differ on what is and what is not an agreeable personality).

Relationship Rules Theory

You can gain an interesting perspective on interpersonal relationships by looking at them in terms of the rules that govern them (Shimanoff, 1980). The general assumption of **rules theory** is that relationships—friendship and love in particular—are held together by adherence to certain rules. When those rules are broken, relationships may deteriorate and even dissolve.

Relationship rules theory helps us clarify several aspects of relationships. First, these rules help identify successful versus destructive relationship behavior. In addition, these rules help pinpoint more specifically why relationships break up and how they may be repaired. Further, if we know what the rules are, we will be better able to master the social skills involved in relationship development and maintenance. And because these rules vary from one culture to another, it is important to identify those unique to each culture so that intercultural relationships may be more effectively developed and maintained.

Friendship Rules

One approach to friendship argues that friendships are maintained by rules (Argyle, 1986; Argyle & Henderson, 1984). When these rules are followed, the friendship is strong and mutually satisfying. When these rules are broken, the friendship suffers and may die. For example, the rules for keeping a friendship include such behaviors as standing up for your friend in his or her absence, sharing information and feelings about successes, demonstrating emotional support for a friend, trusting and offering to help a friend in need, and trying to make a friend happy when you're together. On the other hand, a friendship is likely to be in trouble when one or both friends are intolerant of the other's friends, discuss confidences with third parties, fail to demonstrate positive support, nag, and/or fail to trust or confide in the other. The strategy for maintaining a friendship, then, depends on your knowing the rules and having the ability to apply the appropriate interpersonal skills (Blieszner & Adams, 1992; Trower, 1981).

Romantic Rules

Other research has identified the rules that romantic relationships establish and follow. These rules, of course, will vary considerably from one culture to another. For example, the different attitudes toward permissiveness and sexual relations with which Chinese and American college students view dating influence the romantic rules each group will establish and live by (Tang & Zuo, 2000). Leslie Baxter (1986) has identified eight major romantic rules. Baxter argues that these rules keep the relationship together—or, when broken, lead to deterioration and eventually dissolution. The general form for each rule is that if people are in a close relationship, then they should:

1. Acknowledge each other's identities and recognize that each has a life beyond the relationship.
2. Express similarities in attitudes, beliefs, values, and interests.
3. Enhance the value and self-esteem of the other person
4. Be open and honest with each other.
5. Be faithful.
6. Spend a significant amount of shared time together.
7. Obtain rewards that are proportional to the effort expended.
8. Experience a "magic" in each other.

Family Rules

Family communication research points to the importance of rules in defining and maintaining the family (Galvin, Bylund, & Brommel, 2007). Family rules concern three main interpersonal communication issues (Satir, 1983).

- **What can you talk about?** Can you talk about the family finances? Grandpa's drinking? Your sister's lifestyle?

the•o•ry *noun* statement of explanation, formulation of relationships, reasoned generalization

UNDERSTANDING THEORY AND RESEARCH

Online Relationship Theories

Here are two theories of online relationships that raise issues that are unique to online communication and that the other theories do not address.

Social presence theory argues that the "bandwidth" (the number of message cues exchanged) of communication influences the degree to which the communication is personal or impersonal (Walther & Parks, 2002; Wood & Smith, 2005). When lots of cues are exchanged (especially nonverbal cues), as in face-to-face communication, you feel great social presence—the whole person is there for you to communicate with and exchange messages with. When the bandwidth is smaller (as in e-mail or chat communication), then the communication is largely impersonal. So, for example, personal communication is easier to achieve in face-to-face situations (where tone of voice, facial expressions, eye contact, and similar nonverbal cues come into play) than in computer-mediated communication, which essentially contains only written cues. It's more difficult, the theory goes, to communicate supportiveness, warmth, and friendliness in text-based chat or e-mail exchanges because of the smaller bandwidth. Of course, as noted elsewhere, as video and audio components become more widely used this bandwidth will increase.

Social information processing (SIP) theory argues, contrary to social presence theory, that whether you're communicating face to face or online, you can communicate the same degree of personal involvement and develop similar close relationships (Walther, 1992; Walther & Parks, 2002). The idea behind this theory is that communicators are clever people: Given whatever channel they have available to send and receive messages, they will make adjustments to communicate what they want and to develop the relationships they want. It is true that when the time span studied is limited—as it is in much of the research—it is probably easier to communicate and develop relationships in face-to-face interaction than in online situations. But SIP theory argues that when the interaction occurs over an extended time period, as it often does in ongoing chat groups and in repeated e-mail exchanges, then the communication and the relationships can be as personal as those you develop in face-to-face situations.

Working with Theories and Research

How would you compare the level of closeness that you can communicate in face-to-face and in online situations? Do you feel it's more difficult (even impossible) to communicate, say, support, warmth, and friendship in online communication than in face-to-face communication?

- **How can you talk about something?** Can you joke about your brother's disability? Can you address directly questions of family history or family skeletons?
- **To whom can you talk?** Can you talk openly to extended family members such as cousins and aunts and uncles? Can you talk to close neighbors about family health issues?

Like the rules governing relationships between friends and lovers, family rules tell you which behaviors will be rewarded (and therefore what you should do) and which will be punished (and therefore what you should not do). Family rules also provide a kind of structure that defines the family as a cohesive unit and that distinguishes it from other similar families.

Not surprisingly, the rules a family develops are greatly influenced by the culture. Although there are many similarities among families throughout the world, there are also differences (Georgas et al., 2001). For example, members of collectivist cultures are more likely to shield family information from outsiders as a way of protecting the family than are members of individualist cultures. As already noted, this tendency to protect the family can create serious problems in cases of wife abuse. Many women will not report spousal abuse because they feel they must protect the family image and must not let others know that things aren't perfect at home (Dresser, 1996, 2005).

Family communication theorists argue that rules should be flexible so that special circumstances can be accommodated; there are situations that necessitate changing the family dinner-time, vacation plans, or savings goals (Noller & Fitzpatrick, 1993). Rules should also be negotiable so that all members can participate in their modification and feel a part of family government.

Workplace Rules

Rules also govern your workplace relationships. These rules are usually a part of the corporate culture that an employee would learn from observing other employees (especially those who move up the hierarchy) as well as from official memos on dress, sexual harassment, and the like. Of course, each organization will have different rules, so it's important to see what rules are operating in any given situation. Among the rules that you might find are:

- Work very hard.
- Be cooperative in teams; the good of the company comes first.
- Don't reveal company policies and plans to workers at competing firms.
- Don't form romantic relationships with other workers.
- Avoid even the hint of sexual harassment.

Watch at MyCommunicationLab Video: "Power Moment"

Relationship Dialectics Theory

Relationship dialectics theory argues that people in a relationship experience dynamic tensions between pairs of opposing motives or desires. Research generally finds three such pairs of opposites (Baxter, 1988, 1990; Baxter & Simon, 1993; Rawlins, 1989, 1992):

- **The tension between *closedness and openness*** has to do with the conflict between the desire to be in a closed, exclusive relationship and the wish to be in a relationship that is open to different people. You like the exclusiveness of your pairing, and yet you want also to relate to a larger group.
- **The tension between *autonomy and connection*** involves the desire to remain an autonomous, independent individual and the wish to connect intimately to another person and to a relationship. This tension, by the way, is a popular theme in women's magazines, which teach readers to want both autonomy and connection (Prusank, Duran, & DeLillo, 1993).
- **The tension between *novelty and predictability*** centers on the competing desires for newness, different experiences, and adventure on the one hand and for sameness, stability, and predictability on the other. You're comfortable with being able to predict what will happen, and yet you also want newness, difference, and novelty.

The closedness-openness tension occurs most during the early stages of relationship development. The autonomy-connection and novelty-predictability tensions occur more often as the relationship progresses. Each individual in a relationship may experience a somewhat different set of desires. For example, one person may want exclusivity above all, whereas that person's partner may want greater openness. Sometimes a happy combination can be negotiated; at other times these differences are irreconcilable, with the result that the couple becomes dissatisfied with their relationship or dissolves it.

Perhaps the major implication of relationship dialectics theory is that these tensions will influence a wide variety of behaviors. For example, the person who finds the primary relationship excessively predictable may seek novelty elsewhere, perhaps with a vacation to exotic places, perhaps with a different partner. The person who finds the primary relationship too connected (even suffocating) may need physical and psychological space to meet his or her autonomy needs. As you can appreciate, meeting your partner's needs—while also meeting your own needs—is one of the major relationship challenges you'll face.

Social Penetration Theory

Social penetration theory is a theory not of why relationships develop, but of what happens when they do develop; it describes relationships in terms of the number of topics that people talk about and their degree of "personalness" (Altman & Taylor, 1973). The **breadth** of a relationship has to do with the number of topics you and your partner talk about. The **depth** of the relationship involves the degree to which you penetrate the inner personality—the core—of the other individual. We can represent an individual as a circle and divide that circle into various parts, as in Figure 8.2. This figure illustrates different models of social penetration. Each circle in the figure contains eight topic areas to depict breadth (identified as A through H) and five levels of intimacy to depict depth (represented by the concentric circles).

Note that in Circle 1, only three topic areas are penetrated. Of these, one is penetrated only to the first level and two to the second. In this type of interaction, three topic areas are discussed, and only at rather superficial levels. This is the type of relationship you might have with an acquaintance. Circle 2 represents a more intense relationship, one that has greater breadth and depth; more topics are discussed and to deeper levels of penetration. This is the type of relationship you might have with a friend. Circle 3 represents a still more intense relationship. Here there is considerable breadth (seven of the eight areas are penetrated) and depth (most of the areas are penetrated to the deepest levels). This is the type of relationship you might have with a lover or a parent.

When a relationship begins to deteriorate, the breadth and depth will, in many ways, reverse themselves, in a process called **depenetration**. For example, while ending a relationship, you might cut out certain topics from your interpersonal communications. At the same time, you might discuss the remaining topics in less depth. In some instances of relational deterioration, however, both the breadth and the depth of interaction increase. For example, when a couple breaks up and each is finally free from an oppressive

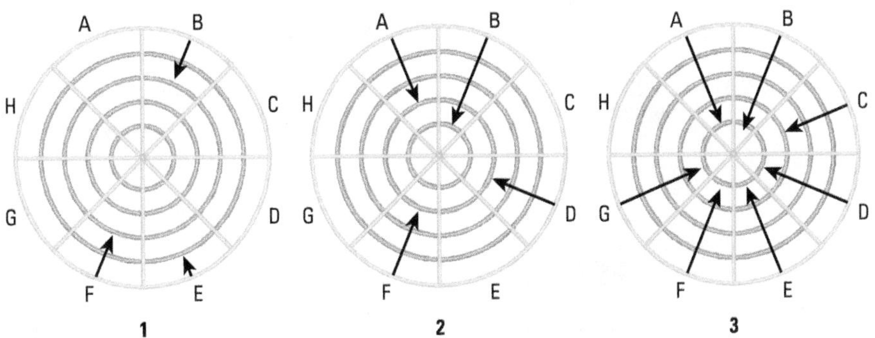

FIGURE 8.2 Models of Social Penetration
Can you visualize your own relationships in terms of these varying levels of depth and breadth? What can you do to increase both depth and breadth? What can you do to decrease both depth and breadth?

relationship, the partners may—after some time—begin to discuss problems and feelings they would never have discussed when they were together. In fact, they may become extremely close friends and come to like each other more than when they were together. In these cases the breadth and depth of their relationship may increase rather than decrease (Baxter, 1983).

Watch at MyCommunicationLab Video: "Friends"

Social Exchange Theory

Social exchange theory claims that you develop relationships that will enable you to maximize your profits (Chadwick-Jones, 1976; Gergen, Greenberg, & Willis, 1980; Thibaut & Kelley, 1986)—a theory based on an economic model of profits and losses. The theory begins with the following equation:

Profits = Rewards – Costs

eth·ics *noun* morality, standards of conduct, moral judgment

MAKING ETHICAL CHOICES
Relationship Ethics

Ethics is a significant part of meaningful relationship communication. Relationships built and maintained on lies are not likely to survive in the long run. But there is more to relationship ethics than the injunction not to lie. For a beginning perspective, the ethical issues and guidelines that operate within a friendship, romantic, family, or workplace relationship can be reviewed with the acronym ETHICS—Empathy (Cheney & Tompkins, 1987), Talk rather than force, Honesty (Krebs, 1990), Interaction management, Confidentiality, and Supportiveness (Johannesen, 2001). As you read these guidelines, think about whether you and your relationship partners follow them.

- **Empathy:** People in a relationship have an ethical obligation to try to understand what others are feeling and thinking from their point of view. This is especially important when relationship members from different cultures communicate.
- **Talk:** Decisions in a relationship should be arrived at by talk, not by force—by persuasion rather than coercion.
- **Honesty:** Relationship communication should be honest and truthful.
- **Interaction management:** Relationship communication should be satisfying and comfortable and is the responsibility of all individuals.
- **Confidentiality:** People in a relationship have a right to expect that what they say in confidence will not be made public or even whispered about.
- **Supportiveness:** A supportive and cooperative climate should characterize interpersonal interactions in a relationship.

Ethical Choice Point

You're managing a work team of four colleagues charged with redesigning the company website. The problem is that Jack doesn't do any work and misses most of the meetings. You spoke with him about it, and he confided that he's going through a divorce and can't concentrate. You've been carrying him for the past few months, but you now realize that you'll never be able to bring the project in on time if you don't replace Jack. In addition, you really don't want to get a negative appraisal because of Jack; in fact, you were counting on the raise that this project was going to get you. What are your ethical obligations in this situation—to yourself? to the other team members? to your employer? What are your options for dealing with this problem?

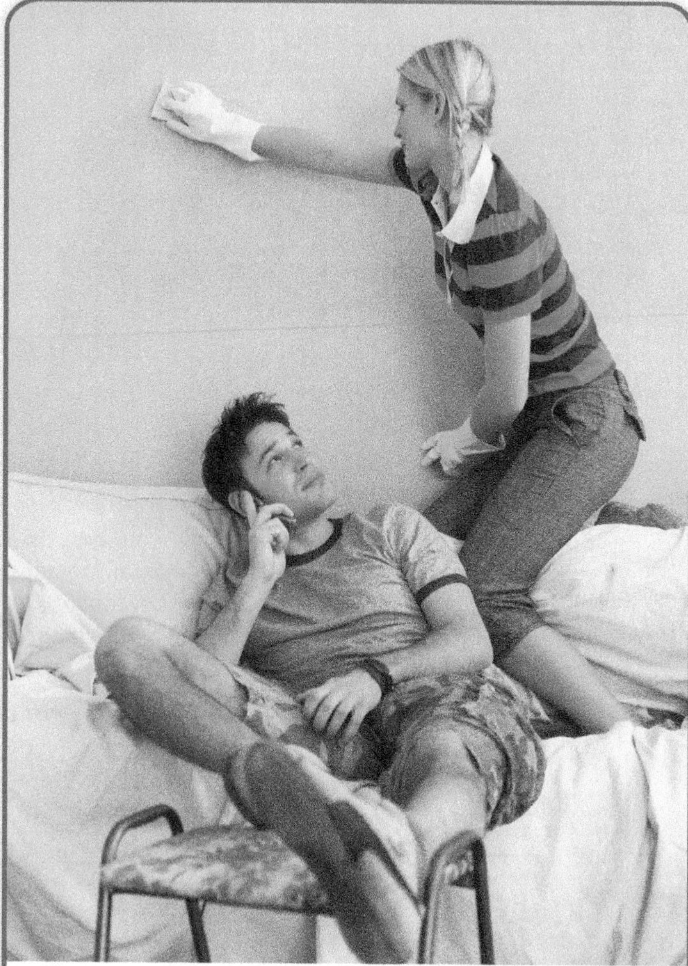

COMMUNICATION CHOICE POINT

NEGOTIATING EQUITY *You feel your romantic relationship of the last three months has become inequitable—you seem to do more of the work but get few benefits, while your partner does less work but gets more benefits. You want to correct this imbalance before the relationship goes any further.* **What are some options you have for negotiating greater equity? What are some of the things you might say?**

- **Rewards** are anything that you would incur costs to obtain. Research has identified six types of rewards in a love relationship: money, status, love, information, goods, and services (Baron & Byrne, 1984). For example, to get the reward of money, you might have to work rather than play. To earn the status of an A in an interpersonal communication course, you might have to write a term paper or study more than you want to.
- **Costs** are things that you normally try to avoid, that you consider unpleasant or difficult. Examples might include working overtime; washing dishes and ironing clothes; watching your partner's favorite television show, which you find boring; or doing favors for those you dislike.
- **Profit** is what results when the rewards exceed the costs.

Using this basic economic model, social exchange theory claims that you seek to develop the friendships and romantic relationships that will give you the greatest profits, that is, relationships in which the rewards are greater than the costs. When you enter a relationship, you have in mind a **comparison level**—a general idea of the kinds of rewards and profits that you feel you ought to get out of such a relationship. This comparison level consists of your realistic expectations concerning what you feel you deserve from this relationship. For example, a study of married couples found that most people expect high levels of trust, mutual respect, love, and commitment. Couples' expectations are significantly lower for time spent together, privacy, sexual activity, and communication (Sabatelli & Pearce, 1986). When the rewards that you get equal or surpass your comparison level, you feel satisfied with your relationship.

However, you also have a comparison level for alternatives. That is, you compare the profits that you get from your current relationship with the profits you think you could get from alternative relationships. Thus, if you see that the profits from your present relationship are below the profits that you could get from an alternative relationship, you may decide to leave your current relationship and enter a new, more profitable relationship.

Equity Theory

Equity theory uses the ideas of social exchange, but goes a step further and claims that you develop and maintain relationships in which the ratio of your rewards relative to your costs is approximately equal to your partner's (Messick & Cook, 1983; Walster, Walster, & Berscheid, 1978). For example, if you and a friend start a business—you put up two-thirds of the money and your friend puts up one-third—equity would demand that you get two-thirds of the profits and your friend gets one-third. An *equitable relationship*, then, is simply one in which each party derives rewards that are proportional to their costs. If you contribute more toward the relationship than your partner, then equity requires that you should get greater rewards. If you both work equally hard, then equity demands that you should both get approximately equal rewards. Conversely, inequity will exist in a relationship if you pay more of the costs (for example, if you do more of the unpleasant tasks) but your partner enjoys more of the rewards. Inequity will also exist if you and your partner work equally hard, but one of you gets more of the rewards.

Much research supports this idea that people want equity in their interpersonal relationships (Ueleke et al., 1983). The general idea behind the theory is that if you are underbenefited (you get less than you put in), you'll be angry and dissatisfied. If, on the other hand, you are overbenefited (you get more than you put in), you'll feel guilty. Some research, however, has questioned this rather neat but intuitively unsatisfying assumption and finds that the overbenefited person is often quite happy and contented; guilt from getting more than you deserve seems easily forgotten (Noller & Fitzpatrick, 1993).

Equity theory puts into clear focus the sources of the relational dissatisfaction we all hear about every day. For example, in a relationship both partners may have full-time jobs, but one partner may also be expected to do the major share of the household chores. Thus, although both may be deriving equal rewards—they have equally good cars, they live in the same three-bedroom house, and so on—one partner is paying more of the costs. According to equity theory, this partner will be dissatisfied because of this lack of equity.

Equity theory claims that you will develop, be satisfied with, and maintain relationships that are equitable. You will not develop, will be dissatisfied with, and will terminate relationships that are inequitable. The greater the inequity, the greater the dissatisfaction, and the greater the likelihood that the relationship will end. Though each relationship is unique, relationships for many people possess similar characteristics, and it is these general patterns that these theories tried to explain.

Taken together, the theories actually explain a great deal about why you develop relationships, the way relationships work, the ways you seek to maintain relationships, and the reasons why some relationships are satisfying and others are not. Table 8.2 presents a summary of the major theories and their basic assumptions. Figure 8.3 on page 186 illustrates the predictions of the theories and maps them onto the model of relationships presented earlier in the chapter.

TABLE 8.2

In A Nutshell A Summary of Relationship Theories

Theory	Basic Assumptions
Attraction	You are attracted to those who are similar and nearby, who reinforce you, and who you think are physically attractive and have a pleasant personality.
Relationship Rules	Relationships are bound together by rules; when the rules are followed relationships are maintained, and when the rules are broken the relationship is in trouble
Relationship Dialectics	Relationships experience conflicts over, for example, the desire to be free and the desire to be connected.
Social Penetration	Describes relationships in terms of the number of topics that people talk about (breadth) and their degree of "personalness" (depth).
Social Exchange	Relationships develop and are maintained when the rewards exceed the costs.
Equity	Relationships are satisfying when there is equity; when one person's rewards are proportional to their costs.

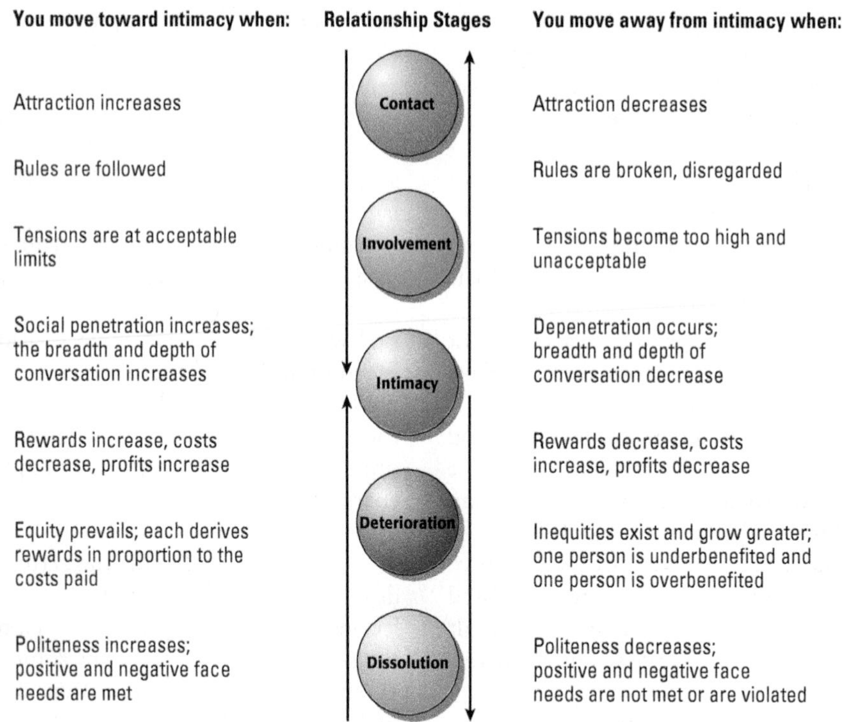

FIGURE 8.3 **Movement among the Stages as Predicted by Relationship Theories**

As you examine this figure, try to identify specific behaviors that would increase or decrease as the relationship becomes more or less intimate.

8.3 THE DARK SIDE OF INTERPERSONAL RELATIONSHIPS

Although relationships serve a variety of vital functions and provide enormous advantages (as already noted) not all relationships are equally satisfying and productive. Consequently, it's necessary to explore this "dark" side. Here we consider two such sides: jealousy and violence.

Jealousy

Jealousy is similar to envy in that, in both cases, we experience a negative emotion about our relationship and we often use the terms interchangeably. But they are actually very different. Envy is an emotional feeling that we experience when we desire what someone else has or has more of than we do. And so we might feel envious of a friend who has lots of friends or romantic partners or money when we have significantly less. When we feel *envy* we may feel that we are inferior to or of lesser importance than someone else. **Jealousy,** on the other hand, is a feeling (most researchers would view it as a type or form of anger) we have when we feel our relationship is in danger due to some rival. Jealousy is a reaction to relationship threat: If you feel that someone is moving in on your relationship partner, you may experience jealousy—especially if you feel that this interloper is succeeding. Usually, the rival is a potential romantic partner but it could also be a close friend or a job that occupies all our partner's time and thoughts. When we feel jealousy we may feel angry and anxious.

Jealousy has at least three components (Erber & Erber, 2011): a cognitive, an emotional, and a behavioral.

- **Cognitive jealousy.** Cognitive jealousy would involve your suspicious thinking, worrying, or imagining the different scenarios in which your partner may be interested in another person.
- **Emotional jealousy.** Emotional jealousy would involve the feelings you have when you see your partner, say, laughing or talking intimately with or kissing a rival.
- **Behavioral jealousy.** Behavioral jealousy refers to what you actually do in response to the jealous feelings and emotions, for example, reading your partner's e-mail, looking on Facebook for incriminating photos, or going through the back seat of the car with the proverbial fine-tooth comb.

Sometimes we feel jealousy because of some suspicion that a rival is looking to steal our relationship partner. In this case, we may do a variety of things to guard our relationship and our relationship partner, a process called *mate guarding* (Buss, 1988; Erber & Erber, 2011). One popular strategy is concealment. We don't introduce our partner to any potential rival and avoid interaction with any potential rivals. Another strategy is vigilance; we constantly look out for occasions when we might lose our partner to a rival. The least suspicious glance becomes a major problem. Still another strategy is to monopolize the partner; to always be together and to avoid leaving the partner without anything to do for too long a time. Of course, we also would experience jealousy if our rival actually succeeded.

Much research has reported that heterosexual men and women experience jealousy for different reasons, which are rooted in our evolutionary development (Buller, 2005; Buss, 2000; Buunk & Dijkstra, 2004). Basically, research finds that men experience jealousy from their partner being *physically* intimate with another man whereas women experience jealousy from their partner being *emotionally* intimate with another woman. The evolutionary reason given is that a man provided food and shelter for the family and would resent his partner's physical intimacy with another because he would then be providing food and shelter for another man's child. Women, because they depended on men for food and shelter, became especially jealous when their partner was emotionally intimate with another because this might mean he might leave her and she'd thus lose the food and shelter protection.

COMMUNICATION CHOICE POINT

JEALOUSY *Your partner is excessively jealous—at least from your point of view. You can't meet other people or even communicate with them online without your partner questioning your fidelity. You're fed up.* **What might you do to reduce (or ideally stop) this jealousy without destroying the relationship?**

Not all research supports this finding and not all theory supports this evolutionary explanation (Harris, 2003). For example, among Chinese men only 25 percent reported physical infidelity was the more distressing, while 75 percent reported emotional infidelity to be more distressing.

Another commonly assumed gender difference is that jealous men are more prone to respond with violence. This assumption, however, does not seem to be the case; men and women apparently are equally likely to respond with violence (Harris, 2003).

So what do you do when you experience jealousy (short of violence)? Communication researchers find several popular but generally negative interactive responses (Dindia & Timmerman, 2003; Guerrero, Andersen, Jorgensen, Spitzberg, & Eloy, 1995). You may:

- nonverbally express your displeasure; for example, cry or express hurt.
- threaten to become violent or actually engage in violence.
- be verbally aggressive; for example, be sarcastic or accusatory.
- withdraw affection or be silent, sometimes denying that anything is wrong.

On the more positive side are responses known as "integrative communication": messages that attempt to work things out with your partner, such as self-disclosing your feelings, being honest, practicing effective conflict management, listening actively, and, in short, all the skills we talk about in this text.

Relationship Violence

Three types of **relationship violence** may be distinguished: physical abuse, verbal or emotional abuse, and sexual abuse (Rice, 2007).

- **Physical abuse** involves threats of violence as well as acts such as pushing, hitting, slapping, kicking, choking, throwing things, and breaking things. Often, relationship violence causes physical injuries, which can range from scratches and bruises to broken bones, knife wounds, and damage to the central nervous system.
- **Verbal or emotional abuse** might involve humiliating a partner, isolating the partner from significant others, constant criticizing, or stalking the partner. Even when physical injuries are relatively minor, the psychological injuries caused by relationship violence may be major. They may include, for example, depression, anxiety, fear of intimacy, and of course low self-esteem. A related emotional abuse would involve controlling the finances or preventing the partner from working or making any financial decisions.
- **Sexual abuse** involves touching that is unwanted, accusations of sexual infidelity without reason, forced sex, and referring to a partner with abusive sexual terms.

A great deal of research has centered on identifying the warning signs of relationship violence. Here, for example, are a few signs compiled by the State University of New York at Buffalo and posted on their website. Your partner:

- belittles, insults, or ignores you.
- controls pieces of your life; for example, the way you dress or who you can be friends with.
- gets jealous without reason.
- can't handle sexual frustration without anger.
- is so angry or threatening that you've changed your life so as not to provoke additional anger.

The Alternatives to Violence

Here are some ways in which a nonviolent relationship differs from a violent relationship, from the website of the University of Texas.

- Instead of emotional abuse, there is fairness; you look for resolutions to conflict that will be fair to both of you.
- Instead of control and isolation, there is communication that makes the partner feel safe and comfortable expressing himself or herself.
- Instead of intimidation, there is mutual respect, mutual affirmation, and valuing of each other's opinions.
- Instead of economic abuse, the partners make financial decisions together.
- Instead of threats, there is accountability—each person accepts responsibility for his or her own behavior.
- Instead of a power relationship in which one person is the boss and the other the servant, there is a fair distribution of responsibilities.
- Instead of sexual abuse, there is trust and respect for what each person wants and doesn't want.

Dealing with Violence

Whether you're a victim or a perpetrator of relationship violence, in addition to seeking professional help (and of course the help of friends and family where appropriate), please consider the following suggestions, compiled from the website of the University of Texas.

If your partner has been violent:

- Realize that you're not alone.
- Realize that you are not at fault. You did not deserve to be the victim of violence.
- Plan for your safety. Violence, if it occurred once, is likely to occur again.
- Know your resources—the phone numbers you need to contact help, the location of money and a spare set of keys.

If you are the violent partner:

- Realize that you too are not alone. Review the statistics.
- Know that you can change. It won't necessarily be easy or quick, but you can change.
- Own your own behaviors; take responsibility. This is an essential step if any change is to occur.

Relationship violence is not an inevitable part of interpersonal relationships; in fact, it occurs in a minority of relationships. Yet it's important to know that there is the potential for violence in all relationships, as there is the potential for friendship, love, support, and all the positive things we look for in relationships. Knowing the difference between productive and destructive relationships seems the best way to make sure that your own relationships are as you want them to be.

Analyzing Video Choices

Watch at MyCommunicationLab Video: "Taking the Next Step"

Tim and Marisol have been dating for several weeks, and things between them have been going well. Tim now realizes that he wants the relationship to be permanent and exclusive, and he wants to express his feelings to Marisol. He isn't sure how to bring this issue up in conversation because he's never felt this strongly about someone before. "Taking the Next Step" explores the stages in interpersonal relationships and the options you have for communicating at the various stages and to initiate movement from one stage to another. Log on to mycommunicationlab.com to view this video, see the choices made, and then answer the related discussion questions.

SUMMARY: INTERPERSONAL RELATIONSHIP STAGES AND THEORIES

Study and **Review** at **MyCommunicationLab**

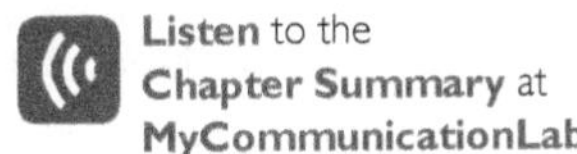

Listen to the **Chapter Summary** at **MyCommunicationLab**

In this chapter we looked at interpersonal relationships: some of the reasons we enter relationships, relationship stages, and the theories that try to explain what happens in an interpersonal relationship.

1. Interpersonal relationships have both advantages and disadvantages. Among the advantages are that these relationships stimulate you, help you learn about yourself, and generally enhance your self-esteem. Among the disadvantages are that they force you to expose your vulnerabilities, make great demands on your time, and often cause you to abandon other relationships.

8.1 RELATIONSHIP STAGES

2. Most relationships involve various stages. Recognize at least these: contact, involvement, intimacy, deterioration, repair, and dissolution.
3. In contact there is first perceptual contact and then interaction.
4. Involvement includes a testing phase (will this be a suitable relationship?) and an intensifying of the interaction; often a sense of mutuality, of connectedness, begins.
5. In intimacy there is an interpersonal commitment, and perhaps a social bonding, in which the commitment is made public.
6. Some relationships deteriorate, proceeding through a period of intrapersonal dissatisfaction to interpersonal deterioration.
7. Along the process, repair may be initiated. Intrapersonal repair generally comes first (should I change my behavior?); it may be followed by interpersonal repair, in which you and your partner discuss your problems and seek remedies.
8. If repair fails, the relationship may dissolve—moving first to interpersonal separation and later, perhaps, to public or social separation.

8.2 RELATIONSHIP THEORIES

9. Theories that focus on attraction, relationship rules, social penetration, social exchange, and relationship equity offer five explanations for what happens when you develop, maintain, and dissolve interpersonal relationships.
10. Attraction depends on four factors: similarity (especially attitudinal), proximity (physical closeness), reinforcement, and attractiveness (physical attractiveness and personality).
11. The relationship rules approach views relationships as held together by adherence to an agreed-on set of rules.
12. Social penetration theory describes relationships in terms of breadth and depth: respectively, the number of topics partners talk about and the degree of personalness with which the partners pursue topics.
13. Social exchange theory holds that we develop relationships that yield the greatest profits. We seek relationships in which our rewards exceed our costs, and we are more likely to dissolve relationships when costs exceed rewards.
14. Equity theory claims that we develop and maintain relationships in which each partner's rewards are distributed in proportion to his or her costs. When our share of the rewards is less than would be demanded by equity, we are likely to experience dissatisfaction and to exit the relationship.

8.3 THE DARK SIDE OF INTERPERSONAL RELATIONSHIPS

15. Jealousy is a reaction to relationship threat and often leads to relationship problems, especially if carried to extremes.

16. Verbal or emotional abuse, physical abuse, and sexual abuse are the major types of relationship violence. Relationship violence may result in psychological, physical, and economic injuries.

Study and **Review** the **Flashcards** at **MyCommunicationLab**

KEY TERMS

affiliative cues *176*
attraction *179*
attraction theory *179*
breadth *182*
cherishing behaviors *190*
comparison level *184*
complementarity *179*
contact *175*
depenetration *182*
depth *182*
dissolution *178*
Duchenne smiles *176*
equity theory *184*
interdependency *174*
intimacy *176*
involvement *175*
jealousy *186*
parasocial relationships *173*
proximity *179*
reinforcements *179*
relationship deterioration *177*
relationship dialectics theory *182*
relationship repair *178*
relationship violence *188*
rules theory *180*
similarity *179*
social exchange theory *183*
social penetration theory *182*

WORKING WITH INTERPERSONAL RELATIONSHIP STAGES AND THEORIES

8.1 Talking Cherishing. Cherishing behaviors are an especially insightful way to affirm another person and to increase favor exchange, a concept that comes from the work of William Lederer (1984). **Cherishing behaviors** are those small gestures you enjoy receiving from your partner (a smile, a wink, a squeeze, a kiss, a phone call, a text message). Prepare a list of 10 cherishing behaviors that you would like to receive from your real or imagined relationship partner. Identify cherishing behaviors that are:

- specific and positive—nothing overly general or negative.
- focused on the present and future rather than on issues about which the partners have argued in the past.
- capable of being performed daily.
- easily executed—nothing you really have to go out of your way to accomplish.

In an actual relationship each partner would prepare a list; then the partners would exchange lists. Ideally, each partner would then perform the cherishing behaviors the other had chosen during their normal activities. In time, these behaviors should become a normal part of your interaction, which is exactly what you'd hope to achieve. Lists of cherishing behaviors will also give you insight into your own relationship needs and the kind of communicating partner you want.

8.2 Repairing Relationships. Whether expert or novice, each of us tries to repair relationships—not only our own, but also those of others. Here are three situations that call for repair. Can you use what you've read about here (as well as your own experiences, readings, observations, and so on) to come up with some reasonable repair advice? What specific suggestions would you offer to each of the people in these situations?

1. **Friends and colleagues.** Mike and Jim, friends for 20 years, have had a falling out over the fact that Mike supported another person for promotion over Jim. Jim is resentful and feels that Mike should have helped him; Mike feels that his first obligation was to the company and that he chose the person he believed would do the best job. Mike feels that if Jim resents him and can't understand or appreciate his motives, then he no longer cares to be friends. Assuming that both Mike and Jim want the friendship to continue or will do so at some later time, what do you suggest that Mike and Jim do?
2. **Coming out.** Tom, a junior in college, recently came out as gay to his family. Contrary to his every expectation, they went ballistic. His parents want him out of the house, and his two brothers refuse to talk with him. Assuming that all parties will be sorry at some later time if the relationship is not repaired, what would you suggest that each of the individuals do?
3. **Betraying a confidence.** Pat and Chris have been best friends since elementary school. Even now, in their twenties, they speak every day and rely on each other for emotional support. Recently Pat betrayed a confidence and told several mutual friends that Chris had been having emotional problems and had been considering suicide. Chris found out and no longer wants to maintain the friendship. Assuming that the friendship is more good than bad and that both parties will regret it if they don't patch up the friendship, what do you suggest that Pat and Chris do?

8.3 **Positive Behaviors.** One way to improve communication during difficult times is to ask your partner for positive behaviors rather than to try to stop negative behaviors. How might you use this suggestion to replace the following statements? (1) "I hate it when you ignore me at business functions." (2) "I can't stand going to these cheap restaurants; when are you going to start spending a few bucks?" (3) "Stop being so negative; you criticize everything and everyone."

8.4 **Sexual Relationships.** As noted earlier, different cultures look at relationships very differently. How do your own cultural beliefs and values influence what you consider an appropriate and an inappropriate relationship? Do your cultural beliefs and values influence what you consider appropriate relationship behavior? In what ways do your cultural beliefs and values influence what you actually do as a relationship partner (as friend, lover, or family member)?

8.5 **Turning Points.** Throughout the life of a relationship, there exist "turning points"—jumps or leaps that project you from one relationship level to another. Do men and women see turning points in the same way? For example, what turning points are most important to women? Which are most important to men?

8.6 **Flirting Online.** One research study found that women flirt online by stressing their physical attributes, whereas men flirt by focusing on their socioeconomic status (Whitty, 2003). Do you observe flirting on the Internet? If so, how would you describe the way men and women flirt?

8.7 **Internet Courage.** Anonymity often leads people to feel more courageous, enabling them to say or do things they would not say or do if their identity was known (Barrett, 2006). It may be argued that when communicating in chat rooms, where you can conceal your true identity, you're likely to be more assertive, take more chances, and risk possible failure than you would in face-to-face situations. Do you display "Internet courage"? Do others you know display "Internet courage"?

LogOn! MyCommunicationLab www.mycommunicationlab.com

Throughout this chapter, there are icons that highlight media content for selected topics. Go to **MyCommunicationLab** for additional materials on interpersonal relationship stages and theories. Here you'll find flashcards to help you learn key communication terms, videos that illustrate a variety of concepts, additional exercises, and discussions to help you continue your study of interpersonal relationship stages and theories.

9 FRIENDS, LOVERS, AND FAMILIES

Listen to **Chapter 9** at **MyCommunicationLab**

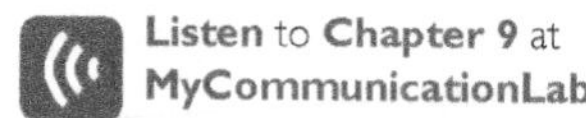

CHAPTER TOPICS	CHAPTER OBJECTIVES
In this chapter you'll explore the following major topics:	**After reading this chapter you should be able to:**
FRIENDSHIPS	**9.1** Define *friendship* and identify its major types.
ROMANTIC RELATIONSHIPS	**9.2** Define *love* and explain its six major types.
FAMILIES	**9.3** Explain the three types of couples and the three types of families and their respective communication patterns.

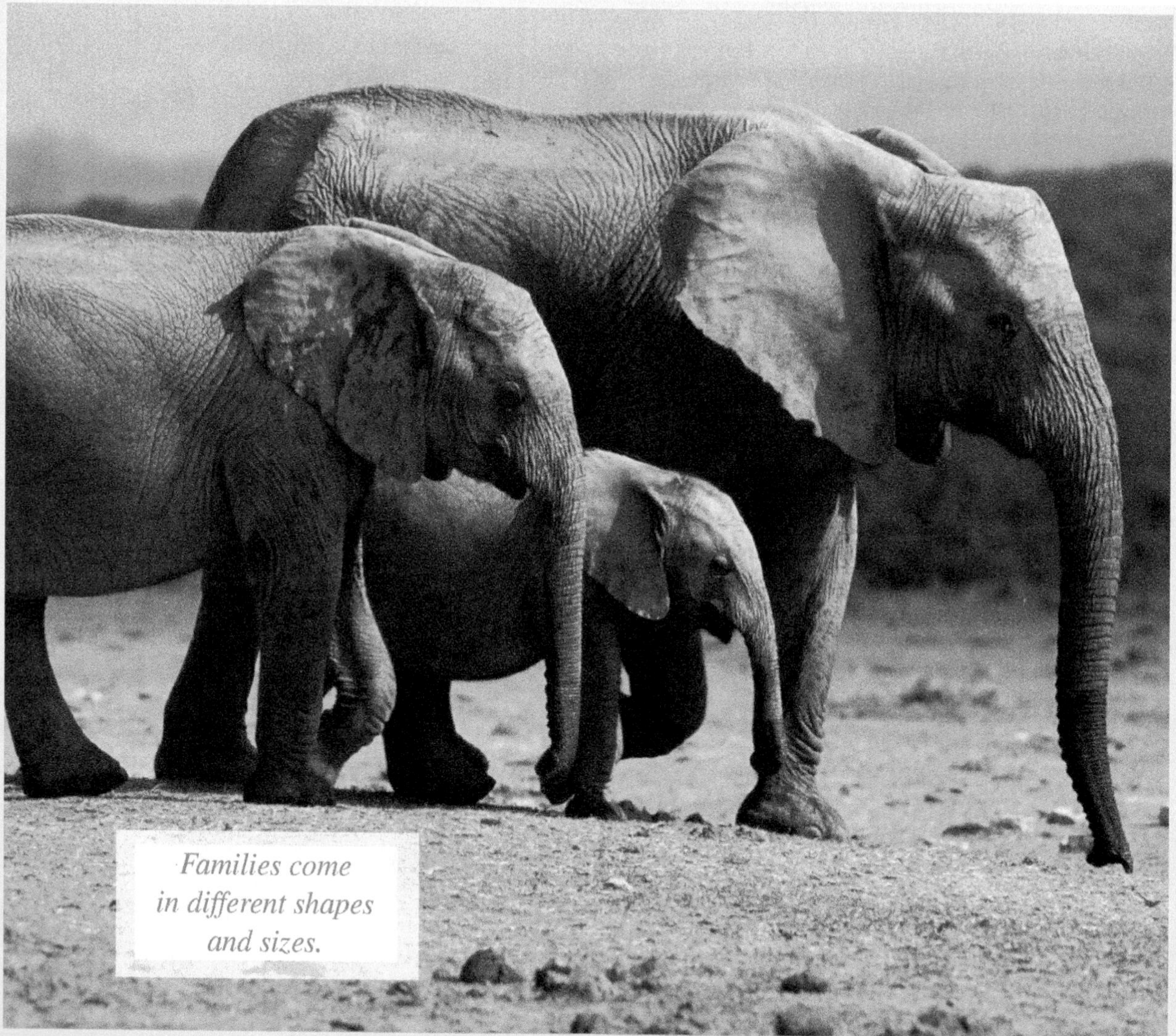

Families come in different shapes and sizes.

Interpersonal relationships come in a variety of forms: between friends, between lovers, between mentors and protégés, between family members, and between work colleagues, for example. Building on the discussion of the stages and theories of relationships in Chapter 8, this chapter considers three major types of relationships: friendships, romantic relationships, and family.

9.1 FRIENDSHIPS

Throughout your life you'll meet many people, but out of this wide array you'll develop relatively few relationships you would call friendships. Yet despite the low number of friendships you may form, their importance is great.

Friendship is an interpersonal relationship between two persons that is mutually productive and characterized by mutual positive regard. Let's take a closer look at the components of this definition.

- **Friendship is an interpersonal relationship.** This means that communication interactions must have taken place between the people. Further, the interpersonal relationship involves a "personalistic focus" (Wright 1978, 1984). Friends react to each other as complete persons; as unique, genuine, and irreplaceable individuals.
- **Friendships must be mutually productive.** This qualifier emphasizes that, by definition, they cannot be destructive to either of the involved parties. Once destructiveness enters into a relationship, it can no longer be characterized as a friendship. Unlike almost all other types of relationships, friendship must enhance the potential of each person and can only be productive.
- **Friendships are characterized by mutual positive regard.** You like your friend and your friend likes you. Liking people is essential if we are to call them friends. Three major characteristics of friends—trust, emotional support, and sharing of interests (Blieszner & Adams 1992)—testify to this positive regard.

The closer friends are, the more interdependent they become; that is, when friends are especially close, the actions of one will more significantly affect the other than they would if the friends were just casual acquaintances. At the same time, however, the closer friends are, the more independent they are of, for example, the attitudes and behaviors of others. Also, they're less influenced by the societal rules that govern more casual relationships (as explained in the Understanding Theory and Research box, "The Development of Interpersonal Communication," page 151). Close friends are likely to make up their own rules for interacting with each other; they decide what they will talk about and when, what they can say to each other without offending and what they can't, when and for what reasons they can call each other, and so on.

In North America, friendships clearly are a matter of choice; you choose—within limits—who your friends will be. The density of the cities and the ease of communication and relocation make friendships voluntary, a matter of choice. But in many parts of the world—in small villages miles away from urban centers, for example, where people are born, live, and die without venturing much beyond their home community—relationships aren't voluntary. In these cases, you simply form relationships with those in your village. In fact, you must interact with and form relationships with the people in your village simply because these people are the only ones you come into contact with on a regular basis (Moghaddam, Taylor, and Wright 1993).

Friendship Types

Not all friendships are the same. But how do they differ? One way of answering this question is by distinguishing among the three major types of friendship: friendships of reciprocity, receptivity, and association (Reisman, 1979, 1981).

- The **friendship of reciprocity** is the ideal type, characterized by loyalty, self-sacrifice, mutual affection, and generosity. A friendship of reciprocity is based on equality: Each individual shares equally in giving and receiving the benefits and rewards of the relationship.
- In the **friendship of receptivity,** in contrast, there is an imbalance in giving and receiving; one person is the primary giver and one the primary receiver. This imbalance, however, is a positive factor because each person gains something from the relationship. The different needs of both the person who receives and the person who gives affection are satisfied. This is the friendship that may develop between a teacher and a student or between a doctor and a patient. In fact, a difference in status is essential for the friendship of receptivity to develop.

- The **friendship of association** is a transitory one. It might be described as a friendly relationship rather than a true friendship. Associative friendships are the kind we often have with classmates, neighbors, or coworkers. There is no great loyalty, no great trust, no great giving or receiving. The association is cordial, but not intense.

COMMUNICATION CHOICE POINT

FRIENDSHIP FUNCTIONS *When thinking about your own friendships and the needs they serve, you notice that your friendships all seem to be built around just one of the needs.* **What are some of your options for expanding the needs that friendships serve in your life?**

Another answer to the question of how friendships differ can be based on the needs that friends serve. On the basis of our experiences or our predictions, we select as friends those who will help to satisfy our basic growth needs. Selecting friends on the basis of need satisfaction is similar to choosing a life partner, an employee, or any person who may be in a position to satisfy our needs. Thus, for example, if you need to be the center of attention or to be popular, you might select friends who allow and even encourage you to be the center of attention or who tell you, verbally and nonverbally, that you're popular.

As your needs change, the qualities you look for in friendships also change. In many instances, old friends are dropped from your close circle to be replaced by new friends who better serve these new needs. Here are some popular needs that friendships may serve (Wright 1978, 1984).

1. **Utility:** Someone who may have special talents, skills, or resources that will help you achieve your specific goals and needs. For example, you might become friends with someone who is particularly bright because such a person might assist you in getting better grades, in solving problems, or in getting a better job.
2. **Affirmation:** Someone who will affirm your personal value and help you to recognize your attributes. For example, you might develop a friendship with someone who would help you see more clearly your leadership abilities, your athletic prowess, or your sense of humor.
3. **Ego support:** Someone who behaves in a supportive, encouraging, and helpful manner. For example, you might seek friendships with people who would help you view yourself as worthy and competent.
4. **Stimulation:** Someone who introduces you to new ideas and new ways of seeing the world and helps you to expand your worldview. For example, you might form friendships with those who could provide you with new and exciting experiences.
5. **Security:** Someone who does nothing to hurt you or to emphasize or call attention to your inadequacies or weaknesses. For example, you might select a friend because you'd not have to worry about him or her betraying you or making negative comments about you.

Friendship and Communication

Friendships develop over time in stages. At one end of the friendship continuum are strangers, or two persons who have just met, and at the other end are intimate friends. What happens between these two extremes?

As you progress from the initial contact stage to intimate friendship, the depth and breadth of communications increase (see Chapter 8). You talk about issues that are closer and closer to your inner core. Similarly, the number of communication topics increases as your friendship becomes closer. As depth and breadth increase, so does the satisfaction you derive from the friendship. This increase in depth and breadth can and does occur in all forms of communication—face-to-face as well as online. Even some 10 years ago, research was finding that friendship was the primary goal for Internet communication among college students (Knox, Daniels, Sturdivant, & Zusman, 2001; Nice & Katzev, 1998).

We can distinguish three main stages of friendship development. The assumption made here is that as the friendship progresses from initial contact and acquaintanceship through casual friendship to close and intimate friendship, the level of effective interpersonal communication increases.

Initial Contact and Acquaintanceship

The first stage of friendship development is obviously an initial meeting of some kind. This does not mean that what has happened prior to the encounter is unimportant—quite the contrary. In fact, your prior history of friendships, your personal needs, and your readiness for friendship development are extremely important in determining whether the relationship will develop.

At the initial stage, you're guarded rather than open or expressive, lest you reveal aspects of yourself that might be viewed negatively. Because you don't yet know the other person, your ability to empathize with or to orient yourself significantly to the other is limited, and the relationship—at this stage, at least—is probably viewed as too temporary to be worth the effort. At this stage there is little genuine immediacy; the two individuals see themselves as separate and distinct, rather than as a unit. The confidence that is demonstrated is probably more a function of the individual personalities than of the relationship. Because the relationship is so new and because the people don't know each other very well, the interaction is often characterized by awkwardness—for example, by overlong pauses, uncertainty over topics to be discussed, and ineffective exchanges of speaker and listener roles.

Casual Friendship

In this second stage, there is a **dyadic consciousness**, a clear sense of "we-ness," of togetherness; communication demonstrates a sense of immediacy. At this stage you participate in activities as a unit rather than as separate individuals. A casual friend is one we would go with to the movies, sit with in the cafeteria or in class, or ride home with from school.

At this casual-friendship stage, you start to express yourself openly and become interested in the other person's disclosures. You begin to own your feelings and thoughts and respond in an open and honest way to the person's communications. There is an ease at this stage, a coordination in the interaction between you and the other person. You communicate with confidence, maintain appropriate eye contact and flexibility in body posture and gesturing, and use few adaptors signaling discomfort.

Close and Intimate Friendship

At the stage of close and intimate friendship, there is an intensification of the casual friendship; you and your friend see yourselves more as an exclusive unit, and each of you derives greater benefits (for example, emotional support) from intimate friendship than from casual friendship (Hays, 1989).

Because you know each other well (for example, you know one another's values, opinions, attitudes), your uncertainty about each other has been significantly reduced—you're able to predict each other's behaviors with considerable accuracy. This knowledge makes possible significant interaction management. Similarly, you can read your friend's nonverbal signals more accurately and can use these signals as guides to your interactions—avoiding certain topics at certain times or offering consolation on the basis of facial expressions. At this stage, you exchange significant messages of affection, messages that express fondness, liking, loving, and caring for the other person.

You view this friend as one who is important in your life; as a result, conflicts—inevitable in all close relationships—become important to work out and resolve through compromise and empathic understanding rather than through, for example, refusal to negotiate or a show of force.

Explore at MyCommunicationLab Profile: "Friendship Inventory"

Friendships, Culture, Gender, and Technology

Your friendships and the way you look at friendships will be influenced by your culture and your gender. Let's look first at culture.

Culture and Friendships

In the United States, you can be friends with someone, yet never really be expected to go much out of your way for this person. Many Middle Easterners, Asians, and Latin Americans would consider going significantly out of their way an essential ingredient in friendship; if you're not willing to sacrifice for your friend, then this person is really not your friend (Dresser, 1996).

Generally, friendships are closer in collectivist cultures than in individualist cultures (see Chapter 2). In their emphasis on the group and on cooperation, collectivist cultures foster the development of close friendship bonds. Members of a collectivist culture are expected to help others in the group. When you help or do things for someone else, you increase your own attraction to this person (recall the discussion in Chapter 8 on attraction and reinforcement), and this is certainly a good start for a friendship. And, of course, the collectivist culture continues to reward these close associations.

Members of individualist cultures, on the other hand, are expected to look out for Number One—themselves. Consequently, they're more likely to compete and to try to do better than each other—conditions that don't support (generally at least) the development of friendships.

As noted in Chapter 2, these characterizations are extremes; most people have both collectivist and individualist values but have them to different degrees, and that is what we are talking about here—differences in degree of collectivist and individualist orientation.

me•di•a lit•er•a•cy *noun* ability to understand, interact with, and create media messages

EXPANDING MEDIA LITERACY
Interpersonal Relationships and the Media

Far from merely reflecting society, the media put forth their own beliefs and values about relationships (friendship, romantic, and family) and influence your thinking about what makes for appropriate and inappropriate relationship behavior. Consider your own beliefs about what constitutes a good friend, what an ideal romantic partner would be like, and what makes for a happy and productive family. Very likely, your ideas about these relationships came from the media; you were taught by television, film, and other media about friendship, love, and family.

To increase your media literacy try this: Select a television sitcom or drama or film that deals with interpersonal relationships, and analyze it for at least the following: (1) What does the show say about relationships generally? Does it make some relationships seem better than others? Are some relationships denigrated? (2) What does it say about men and women? (3) What relationship characteristics are valued? Which are devaluated? (4) What role does communication play in the relationships depicted? Are specific principles of communication advocated or discouraged? (5) If an alien who knew nothing about relationships among Earthlings were to view just this television show, for example, what would this alien conclude about interpersonal relationships?

Gender and Friendships

Gender influences who becomes your friend and the way you look at friendships. Perhaps the best-documented finding—already noted in Chapter 3's discussion of self-disclosure—is that women self-disclose more than men do. This difference holds throughout male and female friendships. Male friends self-disclose less often and with fewer intimate details than female friends do. Some research has argued that men generally don't view intimacy as a necessary quality of their friendships (Hart, 1990).

Women engage in significantly more affectional behaviors with their friends than do males; this difference may account for the greater difficulty men experience in beginning and maintaining close friendships (Hays, 1989). Women engage in more casual communication; they also share greater intimacy and more confidences with their friends than do men. Communication, in all its forms and functions, seems a much more important dimension of women's friendships.

Men's friendships are often built around shared activities—attending a ball game, playing cards, working on a project at the office. Women's friendships, on the other hand, are built more around a sharing of feelings, support, and "personalism." Similarity in status, in willingness to protect one's friend in uncomfortable situations, in academic major, and even in proficiency in playing the game *Password* were significantly related to the relationship closeness of male–male friends, but not of female–female or female–male friends (Griffin & Sparks, 1990).

Given the present state of research in gender differences, we need to be careful not to exaggerate and to treat small differences as if they are highly significant. We need to avoid stereotypes and the stress on opposites to the neglect of the huge number of similarities between men and women (Deaux & LaFrance, 1998; Wright, 1988).

Technology and Friendships

Perhaps even more obvious than culture is the influence of technology on friendships. In 2011, for example, the average number of Facebook friends was 319 for adults between the ages of 18 and 34; 198 for ages 35 to 46, and 124 for ages 47 to 65 (Hampton, 2011). Clearly, online interpersonal friendships are on the increase. The number of Internet users is rapidly increasing throughout the world, and commercial websites devoted to helping people meet other people are proliferating, making it especially easy to meet people online. Daytime television talk shows frequently focus on computer-mediated relationships, especially bringing together individuals who have established a relationship online but who have never met. As mentioned earlier, many people are turning to the Internet to find a friend or romantic partner. And college students as well as others are making the most of sites such as Facebook and Google+ to meet other students on their own or other campuses.

As relationships develop on the Internet, **network convergence** occurs; that is, as a relationship between two people develops, they begin to share their network of other communicators with each other (Parks, 1995; Parks & Floyd, 1996). And, as you've no doubt noticed, Facebook and similar social networking sites encourage this by reminding you of people you know who know people you might want to know. This, of course, is similar to relationships formed through face-to-face contact.

Many would argue that the friendships on social networking sites are not the same as those established and maintained face to face. After all, they would argue, can you really be friends with more than 300 people? Surely, there are differences between these kinds of friendships but exactly what these differences are seem to vary with the individual.

9.2 ROMANTIC RELATIONSHIPS

Of all the qualities of interpersonal relationships, none seems as important as love. "We are all born for love," noted famed British Prime Minister Benjamin Disraeli; "It is the principle of existence and its only end." It's also an interpersonal relationship developed, maintained, and sometimes destroyed through communication.

Love Types

Like friendships, romantic partnerships come in different styles as well.

- **Eros: Beauty and sexuality. Eros love** or the erotic lover focuses on beauty and physical attractiveness, sometimes to the exclusion of qualities you might consider more important and more lasting. The erotic lover has an idealized image of beauty that is unattainable in reality. Consequently, the erotic lover often feels unfulfilled. Not surprisingly, erotic lovers are particularly sensitive to physical imperfections in the ones they love.
- **Ludus: Entertainment and excitement. Ludus love** is experienced as a game, as fun. The better the lover can play the game, the greater the enjoyment. Love is not to be taken too seriously; emotions are to be held in check lest they get out of hand and make trouble; passions never rise to the point where they get out of control. The ludic lover retains a partner only as long as the partner is interesting and amusing. When interest fades, it's time to change partners. Perhaps because love is a game, sexual fidelity is of little importance. In fact, research shows that people who score high on ludic love are more likely to engage in "extradyadic" dating and sex than those who score low on ludus (Wiederman & Hurd, 1999).
- **Storge: Peaceful and slow. Storge love** lacks passion and intensity. Storgic lovers don't set out to find lovers but to establish a companionable relationship with someone they know and with whom they can share interests and activities. Storgic love is a gradual process of unfolding thoughts and feelings; the changes seem to come so slowly and so gradually that it's often difficult to define exactly where the relationship is at any point in time. Sex in storgic relationships comes late, and when it comes, it assumes no great importance.
- **Pragma:** Practical and traditional. Someone looking for **pragma love** is practical and seeks a relationship that will work. Pragma lovers want compatibility and a relationship in which their important needs and desires will be satisfied. They're concerned with the social qualifications of a potential mate even more than with personal qualities; family and background are extremely important to the pragma lover, who relies not so much on feelings as on logic. The pragma lover views love as a useful relationship—one that makes the rest of life easier. So the pragma lover asks such questions as "Will this person be of financial help? "Will this person help me advance in my career?" Pragma lovers' relationships rarely deteriorate. This is partly because pragma lovers choose their mates carefully and emphasize similarities. Another reason is that they have realistic romantic expectations.
- **Mania: Elation and depression. Mania love** is characterized by extreme highs and extreme lows. The manic lover loves intensely and at the same time intensely worries about the loss of the love.

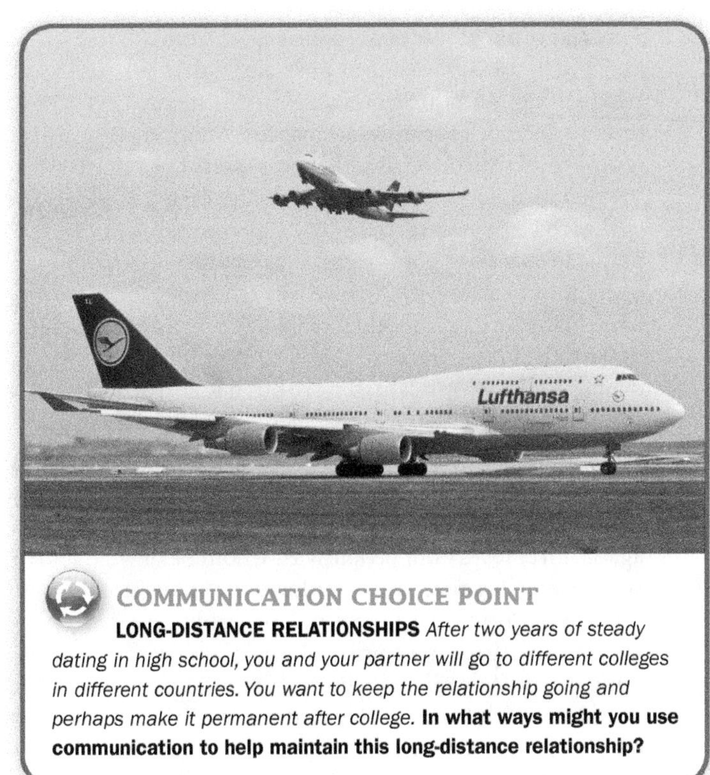

COMMUNICATION CHOICE POINT

LONG-DISTANCE RELATIONSHIPS *After two years of steady dating in high school, you and your partner will go to different colleges in different countries. You want to keep the relationship going and perhaps make it permanent after college.* **In what ways might you use communication to help maintain this long-distance relationship?**

eth•ics *noun* morality, standards of conduct, moral judgment

MAKING ETHICAL CHOICES
Your Obligation to Reveal Yourself

At some point in any close relationship, an ethical issue arises as to your obligation to reveal information about yourself. After all, people in a close relationship have considerable impact on each other (recall, as we noted earlier, that people in an interpersonal relationship are *inter*dependent), so you *may* have an obligation to reveal certain things about yourself. Conversely, you may feel that the other person—because he or she is so close to you—has an ethical obligation to reveal certain information to you.

Ethical Choice Point

At what point—*if any*—do you feel you have an ethical obligation to reveal each of the 10 items of information listed here? Record your answers for romantic relationships in the first column and for close friendship relationships in the second column. Use numbers from 1 to 10 to indicate at what point you would feel your partner or friend has a right to know this information about you by visualizing a relationship as existing on a continuum on which 1 = initial contact and 10 = extreme intimacy. If you feel you would never have the obligation to reveal this information, use 0.

At what point do you feel you have an ethical obligation to reveal:

Romantic Partner	Close Friend	
______	______	**1.** Age
______	______	**2.** Family genetic history
______	______	**3.** HIV status
______	______	**4.** Sexual experiences
______	______	**5.** Salary/net financial worth
______	______	**6.** Affectional orientation
______	______	**7.** Race and nationality
______	______	**8.** Religious beliefs
______	______	**9.** Past criminal activities
______	______	**10.** Political attitudes and beliefs

This fear often prevents the manic lover from deriving as much pleasure as possible from the relationship. With little provocation, the manic lover may experience extreme jealousy. Manic love is obsessive; the manic lover has to possess the beloved completely. In return, the manic lover wishes to be possessed; to be loved intensely. The manic lover's poor self-image seems capable of being improved only by love; self-worth comes from being loved rather than from any sense of inner satisfaction. Because love is so important, danger signs in a relationship are often ignored; the manic lover believes that if there is love, then nothing else matters.

- **Agape: Compassionate and selfless. Agape love** is a compassionate, egoless, self-giving love. The agapic lover loves even people with whom he or she has no close ties. This lover loves the stranger on the road even though they will probably never meet again. Agape is a spiritual love, offered without concern for personal reward or gain. This lover loves without expecting that the love will be reciprocated. Jesus, Buddha, and Gandhi preached this unqualified love, agape (Lee, 1976). In one sense, agape is more a philosophical kind of love than a love that most people have the strength to achieve. People who believe in *yuan*, a Chinese concept that comes from the Buddhist belief in predestiny, are more likely to favor agapic (and pragmatic) love and less likely to favor erotic love (Goodwin & Findlay, 1997).

Each of these varieties of love can combine with others to form new and different patterns (for example, manic and ludic or storge and pragma). These six, however, identify the major types of love and illustrate the complexity of any love relationship. The six styles should also make it clear that different people want different things, that each person seeks satisfaction in a unique way. The love that may seem lifeless or crazy or boring to you may be ideal for someone else.

Also keep in mind that love changes. A relationship that began as pragma may develop into ludus or eros. A relationship that began as erotic may develop into manic or storge.

Explore at MyCommunicationLab Profile: "Love Style Preference"

Love and Communication

How do you communicate when you're in love? What do you say? What do you do nonverbally? According to research, you exaggerate your beloved's virtues and minimize his or her faults. You share emotions and experiences and speak tenderly, with an extra degree of courtesy, to each other; "please," "thank you," and similar polite expressions abound. You frequently use "personalized communication." This type of communication includes secrets you keep from other people and messages that have meaning only within your specific relationship (Knapp, Ellis, & Williams, 1980). You also create and use personal idioms (and pet names)—words, phrases, and gestures that carry meaning only for the particular relationship and that say you have a special language that signifies your special bond (Hopper, Knapp, & Scott 1981). When outsiders try to use personal idioms—as they sometimes do—the expressions seem inappropriate, at times even an invasion of privacy.

You engage in significant self-disclosure. There is more confirmation and less disconfirmation among lovers than among either nonlovers or those who are going through romantic breakups. You're also highly aware of what is and is not appropriate to the one you love. You know how to reward, but also how to punish, each other. In short, you know what to do to obtain the reaction you want.

Among your most often used means for communicating love are telling the person face to face or by telephone (in one survey 79 percent indicated they did it this way), expressing supportiveness, and talking things out and cooperating (Marston, Hecht, & Robers, 1987).

Nonverbally, you also communicate your love. Prolonged and focused eye contact is perhaps the clearest nonverbal indicator of love. So important is eye contact that its avoidance almost always triggers a "what's wrong?" response. You also have longer periods of silence than you do with friends (Guerrero, 1997).

You grow more aware not only of your loved one but also of your own physical self. Your muscle tone is heightened, for example. When you're in love, you engage in preening gestures, especially immediately prior to meeting your lover, and you position your body attractively—stomach pulled in, shoulders square, legs arranged in appropriate masculine or feminine positions. Your speech may even have a somewhat different vocal quality. There is some evidence to show that sexual excitement enlarges the nasal membranes, which introduces a certain nasal quality into the voice (Davis, 1973).

You eliminate socially taboo adaptors, at least in the presence of the loved one. You would curtail, for example, scratching your head, picking your teeth, cleaning your ears, and passing gas. Interestingly enough, these adaptors often return after the lovers have achieved a permanent relationship.

You touch more frequently and more intimately (Guerrero, 1997). You also use more "tie signs," nonverbal gestures that show that you're together, such as holding hands, walking with arms entwined, kissing, and the like (Knapp & Vangelisti, 2009). You may even dress alike. The styles of clothes and even the colors

the•o•ry *noun* statement of explanation, formulation of relationships, reasoned generalization

UNDERSTANDING THEORY AND RESEARCH
Intimacy and Risk

To some people, relational intimacy, whether in face-to-face or in computer mediated communication, seems extremely risky. To others, intimacy involves only low risk. Consider your own view of relationship risk by responding to the following questions.

- Is it dangerous to get really close to people?
- Are you afraid to get really close to someone because you might get hurt?
- Do you find it difficult to trust other people?
- Do you believe that the most important thing to consider in a relationship is whether you might get hurt?

People who answer yes to these and similar questions see intimacy as involving considerable risk (Pilkington & Richardson, 1988). Such people have fewer close friends, are less likely to have romantic relationships, have less trust in others, have lower levels of dating assertiveness, have lower self-esteem, are more possessive and jealous, and are generally less sociable and extroverted than those who see intimacy as involving little risk (Pilkington & Woods, 1999).

Working with Theories and Research

How would you describe your willingness to take relationship risks? What exactly are you willing to risk in establishing a relationship? What exactly are you unwilling to risk? Do you perceive different levels of risk in online versus face-to-face interaction?

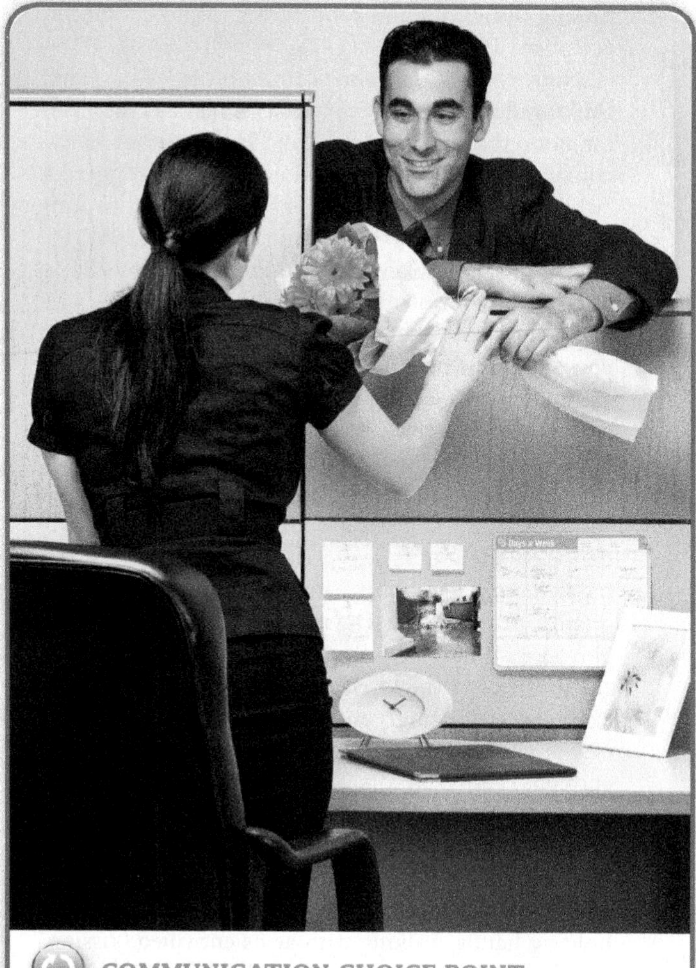

COMMUNICATION CHOICE POINT

FROM FRIENDSHIP TO LOVE *You have a great friendship with a colleague at work, but recently these feelings of friendship are turning to feelings of love.* **What are some of the things you can do or say to move this friendship to love or at least discover if the other person would be receptive to this change?**

selected by lovers are more similar than those worn by nonlovers.

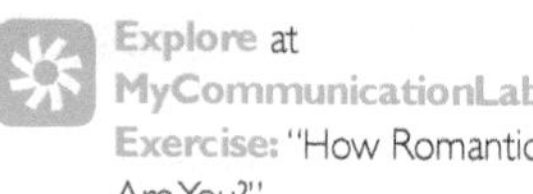

Explore at MyCommunicationLab Exercise: "How Romantic Are You?"

Love, Culture, Gender, and Technology

Like friendship, love is heavily influenced by culture and by gender (Dion & Dion, 1996). Let's consider first some of the cultural influences on the way you look at love and perhaps on the love you're seeking or maintaining.

Culture and Love

Although most of the research on love styles has been done in the United States, some research has been conducted in other cultures (Bierhoff & Klein, 1991). Here is a small sampling of the research findings—just enough to illustrate that culture is an important factor in love. Asians have been found to be more friendship oriented in their love style than are Europeans (Dion & Dion, 1993b). Members of individualist cultures (for example, Europeans) are likely to place greater emphasis on romantic love and on individual fulfillment. Members of collectivist cultures are likely to spread their love over a large network of relatives (Dion & Dion, 1993a).

One study finds a love style among Mexicans characterized as calm, compassionate, and deliberate (Leon et al., 1994). In comparisons between loves styles in the United States and France, it was found that subjects from the United States scored higher on storge and mania than the French; in contrast, the French scored higher on agape (Murstein, Merighi, & Vyse, 1991). Caucasian women, when compared to African American women, scored higher on mania, whereas African American women scored higher on agape. Caucasian and African American men, however, scored very similarly; no statistically significant differences have been found (Morrow, Clark, & Brock, 1995).

At least one research study shows that romanticism seems to increase on the basis of the amount of choice you have in selecting a partner. In countries where there is much choice, as in the United States and Europe, romanticism is high; in countries where there is less choice, as in India and parts of Africa, romanticism is lower (Medora, Larson, Hortacsu, & Dave, 2002). Internet dating provides greater choice than do face-to-face interactions, so it may be argued that romanticism will be higher in Internet than in face-to-face interactions.

Gender and Love

Gender also influences love (Knapp & Vangelisti, 2009). In the United States, the differences between men and women in love are considered great. In poetry, novels, and the mass media, women and men are depicted as acting very differently when falling in love, being in love, and ending a love relationship. As Lord Byron put it in *Don Juan,* "Man's love is of man's life a thing apart, / 'Tis woman's whole existence." Women are portrayed as emotional, men as logical. Women are supposed to love intensely; men are supposed to love with detachment.

Women indicate greater love than men do for their same-sex friends. This may reflect a real difference between the sexes, or it may be a function of the greater social restrictions on men. A man is not supposed to admit his love for another man, but women are permitted greater freedom to communicate their love for other women.

Men and women also differ in the types of love they prefer (Hendrick, Hendrick, Foote, & Slapion-Foote, 1984). For example, on one version of the love self-test presented earlier, men have been found to score higher on erotic and ludic love, whereas women score higher on manic, pragmatic, and storgic love. No difference has been found for agapic love.

In much research, men are found to place more emphasis on romance than women. For example, when college students were asked the question "If a man (woman) had all the other qualities you desired, would you marry this person if you were not in love with him (her)?" approximately two-thirds of the men responded no, which seems to indicate that a high percentage were concerned with love and romance. However, less than one-third of the women responded no (LeVine, Sato, Hashimoto, & Verma, 1994).

Despite such differences, women and men seem to experience love to a similar degree, and research continues to find great similarities between men's and women's conceptions of love (Fehr & Broughton, 2001; Rubin, 1973).

Technology and Love

A 2006 report from the Pew Internet Research Center notes that 11 percent of all Internet users (and 37 percent of single Internet users) have visited internet dating sites. And 17 percent report that they've begun long-term relationships with people they met online (Madden & Lenhart, 2006). According to another report, between 2007 and 2009, 21 percent of heterosexual couples and 61 percent of same-sex couples met online (Rosenbloom, 2011). And *Time* magazine reports that 23 million Americans log on to one of the 4,000 online dating sites each month (Steinmetz, 2013). Match.com, in its 2013 advertisements, reports that one out of five relationships begin online. Clearly, the Internet is growing in importance in the development, maintenance, and even the deterioration of romantic relationships. And, according to the 2013 FBI website, dating and romantic relationship scams are likewise becoming more common (and more sophisticated).

In face-to-face relationships, you perceive the other person through nonverbal cues—you see the person's eyes, face, body—and you form these perceptions immediately. In online relationships of just a few years ago, physical attractiveness was signaled exclusively through words and self-descriptions (Levine, 2000). Under such circumstances, as you can appreciate, the face-to-face encounter strongly favored those who were physically attractive, whereas the online encounter favored those who were verbally adept at self-presentation and did not disadvantage less-attractive individuals. Today, with photos, videos, and voice a part of online dating and social networking sites, this distinction is fading—though probably not entirely erased.

There are many advantages to establishing romantic relationships online. For example, online relationships are safe in terms of avoiding the potential for physical violence or sexually transmitted diseases. Unlike relationships established in face-to-face encounters, in which physical appearance tends to outweigh personality, Internet communication reveals your inner qualities first. Rapport and mutual self-disclosure become more important than physical attractiveness in promoting intimacy (Cooper & Sportolari, 1997). And, contrary to some popular opinions, online relationships rely just as heavily on the ideals of trust, honesty, and commitment as do face-to-face relationships (Whitty & Gavin, 2001). Friendship and romantic interaction on the Internet are a natural boon to shut-ins and extremely shy people, for whom traditional ways of meeting someone are often difficult. Computer talk is empowering for those who have been disfigured or have certain disabilities. For them, face-to-face interactions often are superficial and end with withdrawal (Bull & Rumsey, 1988; Lea & Spears, 1995). By eliminating the physical cues, computer talk equalizes the interaction and doesn't put the person with a disfigurement, for example, at an immediate disadvantage in a society in which physical attractiveness is so highly valued.

Another obvious advantage is that the number of people you can reach is so vast that it's relatively easy to find someone who matches what you're looking for. The situation is like finding a book that covers just what you need from a library of millions of volumes, rather than from a collection holding only several thousand.

Of course, there are also disadvantages. For one thing, you may not be able to see the person. And even if photos are exchanged, how certain can you be that the photos are of the person or that they were taken recently? In addition, you may not be able to hear the person's voice, and this too hinders you as you seek to develop a total picture of the other person.

Online, people can present a false self with little chance of detection; minors may present themselves as adults, and adults may present themselves as children in order to conduct illicit and illegal sexual

the•o•ry *noun* statement of explanation, formulation of relationships, reasoned generalization

UNDERSTANDING THEORY AND RESEARCH
Love Styles and Personality

In reading about the six love styles, you may have felt that certain personality types would be likely to favor one type of love over another. Consider your own assumptions about which of the following personality characteristics would go with which love style—eros, ludus, storge, pragma, mania, and agape (Taraban & Hendrick, 1995):

1. inconsiderate, secretive, dishonest, selfish, and dangerous
2. honest, loyal, mature, caring, loving, and understanding
3. jealous, possessive, obsessed, emotional, and dependent
4. sexual, exciting, loving, happy, and optimistic
5. committed, giving, caring, self-sacrificing, and loving
6. family-oriented, planning, careful, hard-working, and concerned

Very likely you perceived these personality factors in the same way as did the participants in research from which this list was drawn: 1 = ludus, 2 = storge, 3 = mania, 4 = eros, 5 = agape, and 6 = pragma. Do note, of course, that these results do not imply that ludus lovers *are* necessarily inconsiderate, secretive, and dishonest. They merely mean that people in general (and perhaps you in particular) *think* of ludus lovers as inconsiderate, secretive, and dishonest.

Working with Theories and Research

Consider your own love style preferences. Do you possess the personality characteristics identified with your particular love style? Do others you know possess the personality characteristics associated with their preferred love style?

communications and, perhaps, meetings. Although people can also misrepresent themselves in face-to-face relationships, the fact that it's easier to do online probably accounts for greater frequency of misrepresentation in computer relationships (Cornwell & Lundgren, 2001).

9.3 FAMILIES

Families are central to contemporary life. It will come as no surprise to note that families come in various configurations and are undergoing major changes.

Here are several findings on the American family from the United States census. As you read these findings, consider the reasons for the changes and what the possible trends might be.

- The percentage of one-person households increased from 25% in 1990 to 27% in 2010.
- The percentage of multigenerational households increased from 14% in 1990 to 16% in 2010.
- The percentage of births by unmarried women increased from 26% in 1990 to 41% in 2010.
- Fifty percent of women who marry did so at 24 in 1990; in 2010 fifty percent married at 26.
- In 2000 (the first year the census bureau allowed people to indicate more than one race) 1.6 percent indicated mixed race; in 2010 it was 2 percent.
- In 2005, 53 percent of men and 46 percent of women between the ages of 18 and 24 lived with their parents; in 2011 the percentage was 59 percent for men and 50 percent for women.
- In 2000, 57 percent of all adults were married; in 2010, 51 percent were married.
- In 2000 the average size of the family was 2.62; in 2010 it was 2.59.

The communication principles that apply to the traditional nuclear family (i.e., the mother-father-child family) also apply to all family configurations. In the following discussion, the term **primary relationship** denotes the relationship between two principal parties–husband and wife, husband-husband, wife-wife, lovers, or domestic partners, for example–and the term **family** may denote a broader constellation that includes children, relatives, and assorted significant others.

Types of Couples and Families

A primary relationship is a relationship between two people that the partners see as their most important interpersonal relationship. An interesting typology of primary relationships (based on more than 1,000 couples' responses to questions concerning their degree of sharing, their space needs, their conflicts, and the time they spend together) identifies three basic types: traditionals, independents, and separates (Fitzpatrick, 1983, 1988, 1991; Noller & Fitzpatrick, 1993).

- **Traditionals** share a basic belief system and philosophy of life. They see themselves as a blending of two persons into a single couple rather than as two separate individuals. They're interdependent and believe that each individual's independence must be sacrificed for the good of the relationship. In their communication traditionals are highly responsive to each other. They lean toward each other, smile, talk a lot, interrupt each other, and finish each other's sentences.
- **Independents** stress their individuality. The relationship is important, but never more important than each person's individual identity. Although independents spend a great deal of time together, they don't ritualize it, for example, with schedules. Each individual spends time with outside friends. The communication between independents is responsive. They engage in conflict openly and without fear. Their disclosures are quite extensive and include high-risk and negative disclosures that are typically absent among traditionals.
- **Separates** live together, but they view their relationship more as a matter of convenience than a result of their mutual love or closeness. They seem to have little desire to be together and, in fact, usually are together only at ritual occasions such as mealtime or holiday get-togethers. It's important to these separates that each has his or her own physical as well as psychological space. The most significant characteristic of this type is that each person sees himself or herself as a separate individual and not as a part of a "we."

Explore at MyCommunicationLab Exercise: "What Type of Relationship Do You Prefer?"

Like couples, families can also be classified in any number of ways, for example, according to the number of people in the family, their affectional orientation, the presence or absence of children or of extended family members. Here is a communication-oriented typology (Anderson & Sabatelli, 2011; Arnold, 2008; Galvin, Byland, & Brommel, 2012; Koerner & Fitzpatrick, 1997, 2002). In this system families are looked at in terms of conformity and conversation.

Conformity-orientation refers to the degree to which family members express similar or dissimilar attitudes, values, and beliefs. So, we can speak of high-conformity families as those who express highly similar attitudes, beliefs, and values and try to avoid conflict and low-conformity families as those whose members express highly divergent attitudes, beliefs, and values and may frequently engage in conflict interactions. As you can appreciate, families high in conformity are likely to be harmonious with children who are expected to obey their parents, largely without question. Families low in conformity are likely to be less harmonious with children who are given greater freedom to say or do as they wish.

Conversation-orientation refers to the degree to which family members can speak their mind. A family high on conversation orientation encourages members to discuss a variety of issues and the voicing of members' opinions. A family low on conversation orientation discourages discussion and the voicing of opinions.

With these two dimensions in mind, we can identify four types of families:

- **Consensual families**: high in conversation and high in conformity. These families encourage open communication and agreement.
- **Protective families**: high in conformity and low in conversation. These families stress agreement and strive to avoid conflict but with little communication.
- **Pluralistic families**: low in conformity and high in conversation. These family members are encouraged to express different attitudes and points of view and to engage in open communication while being supportive of each other.

COMMUNICATION CHOICE POINT

FAMILIES *You and your dating partner (for about a year) want to move your relationship to a more exclusive and public one. And you both think it's time for your families to meet (who are different in culture, politics, religion, and just about everything else).* **What are some of your options for making this meeting a pleasant and productive one? Where would you hold this get-together? How would you invite family members? How might you prepare them?**

- **Laissez-faire families**: low in conformity and low in conversation. These families avoid interaction and communication and encourage privacy and a "do what you want" attitude.

These family types are simply descriptions and are not meant to be evaluations; no assumption is made that one family type is better or more productive than another. What works for some people will not work for others.

Family Characteristics

Despite this diversity, all families have some characteristics in common; for example, defined roles, recognition of responsibilities, shared history and future, and shared living space.

Defined Roles

Family members have relatively defined roles that each person is expected to play in relation to the other and to the relationship as a whole. Each has acquired the rules of the culture and social group; each knows approximately what his or her obligations, duties, privileges, and responsibilities are. The partners' roles might include those of wage earner, cook, housecleaner, child caregiver, social secretary, home decorator, plumber, carpenter, food shopper, money manager, nurturer, philosopher, comedian, organizer, and so on. At times the roles may be shared, but even then it's often assumed that one person has *primary* responsibility for certain tasks and the other person for others.

Recognition of Responsibilities

Family members recognize their responsibilities to one another; for example, responsibilities to help others financially; to offer comfort when family members are distressed; to take pleasure in family members' pleasures, to feel their pain, to raise their spirits. Each person in a couple also has a temporal obligation to reserve some large block of time for the other. Time-sharing seems important to all relationships, although each family may define it a bit differently.

Shared History and Future

Family members have a history that is at least partly shared by other members, and the prospect is that they will share the future together as well. This history has enabled the members to get to know one another, to understand one another a little better, and ideally to like and even love one another. And, in most cases, family members view the relationship as persisting into the future.

Shared Living Space

Most families in the United States share their living space, although an increasing number of couples retain their original apartments or houses and may spend substantial time apart. These relationships, it should be stressed, are not necessarily less satisfying. In some cultures, in fact, men and women don't share the same living space; the women may live with the children while the men live together in a communal arrangement (Harris & Johnson, 2007).

COMMUNICATION CHOICE POINT

FAMILY CHARACTERISTICS AND COMMUNICATION *You always had a pleasant family life but never really thought much about its characteristics or its communication patterns.* **What characteristics of your family stand out most in your mind? How would you describe the communication pattern? Would you like to change anything?**

Families and Communication

One helpful way to understand families and primary relationships is to look at the communication patterns that dominate the relationship. Four general communication patterns are identified here; each interpersonal relationship may then be viewed as a variation on one of these basic patterns.

Equality

The *equality* pattern exists more in theory than in practice, but it's a good starting point for looking at communication in primary relationships and families In the equality pattern, each person shares equally in the communication transactions and each person is accorded a similar degree of credibility. Each is equally open to the ideas, opinions, and beliefs of the other; each engages in self-disclosure on a more or less equal basis. The communication is open, honest, direct, and free of the power plays that characterize so many other interpersonal relationships. There is no leader or follower, no opinion giver or opinion seeker; rather, both parties play these roles equally.

Both parties share equally in decision-making processes—in the insignificant choices, such as which movie to attend, as well as in the significant decisions, such as where to send the child to school, whether to attend religious services, and what house to buy. Conflicts in equality relationships may occur with some frequency, but they're not seen as threatening to the individuals or to the relationship. They're viewed, rather, as exchanges of ideas, opinions, and values.

Balanced Split

In the *balanced split* pattern, an equality relationship is maintained, but each person has authority over different domains. Each person is seen as an expert or a decision maker in different areas. For example, in the traditional nuclear family, the husband maintains high credibility in business matters and perhaps in politics. The wife maintains high credibility in such matters as child care and cooking. These gender roles are breaking down in many cultures, although they still define lots of families throughout the world (Hatfield & Rapson, 1996).

Conflict is generally viewed as nonthreatening by these individuals because each has specified areas of expertise. Consequently, the outcome of the conflict is almost predetermined.

Unbalanced Split

In the *unbalanced split* relationship, one person dominates; one person is seen as an expert in more than half the areas of mutual communication. In many unions this expertise takes the form of control. Thus, in the unbalanced split, one person is more or less regularly in control of the relationship. In some cases this person is the more intelligent or more knowledgeable, but in many cases he or she is the more physically attractive or the higher wage earner. The less attractive or lower-income partner compensates by giving in to the other person, allowing the other to win the arguments or to have his or her way in decision making.

The person in control makes more assertions, tells the other person what should or will be done, gives opinions freely, plays power games to maintain control, and seldom asks for opinions in return. The noncontrolling person, conversely, asks questions, seeks opinions, and looks to the other for decision-making leadership.

Monopoly

In a *monopoly* relationship, one person is seen as the authority. This person lectures rather than communicates. Rarely does this person ask questions to seek advice, and he or she always reserves the right to have the final say. In this type of couple, the arguments are few because both individuals already know who is boss and who will win the argument should one arise. When the authority is challenged, there are arguments and bitter conflicts.

The controlling person tells the partner what is and what is not to be. The controlling person talks more frequently and goes off the topic of conversation more than does the noncontrolling partner (Palmer, 1989). The noncontrolling person looks to the other to give permission, to voice opinion leadership, and to make decisions, almost as a child looks to an all-knowing, all-powerful parent.

Families, Culture, Gender, and Technology

As with friendship and love, families too vary from one culture to another, are viewed differently by men and women, and are influenced by technology.

Culture, Gender, and Families

In U.S. society it is assumed, in discussions of relationship development such as the model presented in this text, that you voluntarily choose your relationship partners. You consciously choose to pursue certain relationships and not others. In some cultures, however, your romantic partner is chosen for you by your parents. In some cases your husband or wife is chosen to unite two families or to bring some financial advantage to your family or village. An arrangement such as this may have been entered into by your parents when you were an infant or even before you were born. In most cultures, of course, there's pressure to marry the "right" person and to be friends with certain people and not others.

Similarly, U.S. researchers study and textbook authors write about dissolving relationships and how to survive relationship breakups. It's assumed that you have the right to exit an undesirable relationship. But in some cultures you cannot simply dissolve a relationship once it's formed or once there are children. In the practice of Roman Catholicism, once people are validly married, they're always married and cannot dissolve that relationship. More important in such cultures may be such issues as "How do you maintain a relationship that has problems?," "What can you do to survive in this unpleasant relationship?," or "How can you repair a troubled relationship?" (Moghaddam, Taylor, & Wright, 1993).

Culture also seems to influence the kind of love people want. For example, when compared to their Chinese counterparts, American men scored higher on ludic and agapic love and lower on erotic and pragma love. American men are also less likely to view emotional satisfaction as crucial to relationship maintenance (Sprecher & Toro-Morn, 2002).

Culture influences heterosexual relationships by assigning different roles to men and women. In the United States men and women are supposed to be equal—at least that is the stated ideal. As a result, both men and women can initiate relationships, and both can dissolve them. Both men and women are expected to derive satisfaction from their interpersonal relationships; and when that satisfaction isn't present, either person may seek to exit the relationship. In Iran, on the other hand, only the man has the right to dissolve a marriage without giving reasons.

Gay and lesbian relationships are accepted in some cultures and condemned in others. In some areas of the United States, "domestic partnerships" may be registered and in some states same-sex marriages are legal; in these cases gay men, lesbians, and (in some cases) unmarried heterosexuals have rights that were formerly reserved only for married couples, such as health insurance benefits and the right to make decisions when one member is incapacitated. In Belgium, the Netherlands, Spain, South Africa, and Canada, same-sex couples can marry; and in Norway, Sweden, and Denmark, same-sex relationship partners have the same rights as married partners. And, as mentioned in the discussion of heterosexism in Chapter 5, in many countries same-sex couples would be considered criminals and could face severe punishment; in some cultures they could even face death.

Technology and Families

You know from your own family interactions that technology has greatly changed the communication among family members. Cell phones enable parents and children to keep in close touch in case of emergencies or just to chat or text. College students today stay in closer touch with their parents than did earlier generations, in part because of the cell phone but also through e-mail and texting. On the other hand, some people—in some cases parents, in most cases children—become so absorbed with their online community that they have little time for their biological family members. In some cases (in South Korea, for example), Internet use seems to be contributing further to the already significant generational conflict between children and parents (Rhee & Kim, 2004).

Research on young people (ages 10–17) finds that for both girls and boys, those who form close online relationships are more likely to have low levels of communication with their parents and to be more "highly troubled" than those who don't form such close online relationships (Wolak, Mitchell, & Finkelhor, 2003). More recent research offers contradictory conclusions. Some research indicates that both parents and children are reaching a comfortable stage and are using technology to communicate more often and more effectively (Barna Group, 2013). Other research indicates that technology has created a division between parents and children (Taylor, 2013).

Charles and Mei Li have been dating for several months. Mei Li has met Charles's family several times and Mei Li is now ready to introduce Charles to her family. Charles has been invited to celebrate the Chinese New Year with Mei Li's brother and her cousins, a prospect that makes both of them nervous. "Meet the Family" explores the options you have for communicating in a cultural setting different from the one you grew up in. Illustrated here are choices that are both effective and ineffective communication among friends, romantic partners, and families. Log on to mycommunicationlab.com to view this video, to explore the choices, and to then answer a few related discussion questions.

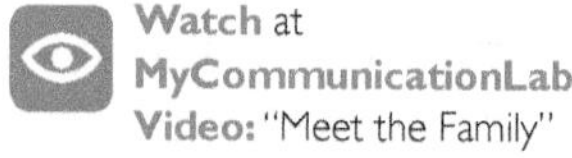

SUMMARY: FRIENDS, LOVERS, AND FAMILIES

Study and Review at MyCommunicationLab

This chapter looked at three of our most important relationships—friendship, romantic, and family—and examined their types and the role of communication in these relationships.

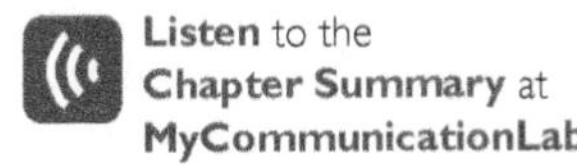

Listen to the Chapter Summary at MyCommunicationLab

9.1 FRIENDSHIPS

1. Friendship is an interpersonal relationship between two persons that is mutually productive and characterized by mutual positive regard.
2. The types of friendships are: (1) reciprocity, characterized by loyalty, self-sacrifice, mutual affection, and generosity; (2) receptivity, characterized by a comfortable and positive imbalance in the giving and receiving of rewards, in which each person's needs are satisfied by the exchange; and (3) association, a transitory relationship, more like a friendly relationship than a true friendship.
3. Friendships serve a variety of needs and give us a variety of rewards, among which are utility, affirmation, ego support, stimulation, and security.
4. Friendships, their development, and the expectations you have for them are greatly influenced by culture and gender as well as by technology.

9.2 ROMANTIC RELATIONSHIPS

5. Love is a feeling that may be characterized by passion and caring and by intimacy, passion, and commitment.
6. Six types of love have been distinguished by research: (1) Eros love focuses on beauty and sexuality, sometimes to the exclusion of other qualities. (2) Ludus love is seen as a game and focuses on entertainment and excitement. (3) Storge love is a kind of companionship, peaceful and slow. (4) Pragma love is practical and traditional. (5) Mania love is obsessive and possessive, characterized by elation and depression. (6) Agape love is compassionate, selfless, and altruistic.
7. Verbal and nonverbal messages echo the intimacy of a love relationship. With increased intimacy, you share more, speak in a more personalized style, engage in prolonged eye contact, and touch each other more often.
8. The kind of love you look for and the place it occupies in your life will be influenced by your culture and your gender and by the opportunities afforded by computer-mediated communication.

9.3 FAMILIES

9. Among the characteristics of families are (1) defined roles—members understand the roles each of them serves; (2) recognition of responsibilities—members realize that each person has certain responsibilities to the relationship; (3) shared history and future—members have an interactional past and an anticipated future together; and (4) shared living space—generally, members live together.
10. Among the family types, (1) traditionals see themselves as a blending of two people into a single couple; (2) independents see themselves as primarily separate individuals, an individuality that is more important than the relationship or the connection between the individuals; and (3) separates see their relationship as a matter of convenience rather than of mutual love or connection.
11. Communication patterns in families include (1) equality—in which each person shares equally in the communication transactions and decision making; (2) balanced split—each person has authority over different but relatively equal domains; (3) unbalanced split—one person maintains authority and decision-making power over a wider range of issues than the other; and (4) monopoly—one person dominates and controls the relationship and the decisions made.
12. Families and the attitudes toward them vary from one culture to another and are being heavily influenced by the new computer-mediated communication.

Study and Review the Flashcards at MyCommunicationLab

KEY TERMS

agape love *198*
dyadic consciousness *195*
eros love *197*
family *202*
friendship *193*
friendship of association *193*
friendship of receptivity *193*
friendship of reciprocity *193*
independents *203*
ludus love *197*
mania love *197*
network convergence *196*
pragma love *197*
primary relationship *202*
separates *203*
storge love *197*
traditionals *203*

WORKING WITH FRIENDS, LOVERS, AND FAMILIES

9.1 Using Affinity-Seeking Strategies. In Chapter 3 we introduced the concept of affinity-seeking strategies, ways in which you communicate so another person comes to like you (Bell & Daly, 1984). From the list of affinity-seeking strategies presented below, compose at least one message that would help you communicate the desired qualities to a friend. Be sure to include both verbal and nonverbal messages.

AFFINITY-SEEKING STRATEGIES

Altruism: Be of help to the other person.
Assumption of equality: Present yourself as socially equal to the other.
Comfortable self: Present yourself as comfortable and relaxed with the other.
Conversational rule-keeping: Follow the cultural rules for polite, cooperative conversation.
Dynamism: Appear active, enthusiastic, and dynamic.
Self-concept confirmation: Show respect for the other person and help the person feel positive about himself or herself.

All communication involves such strategies. Practicing with these strategies will help increase your arsenal of ways to best achieve one of your most important interpersonal purposes.

9.2 Until This Do Us Part. This exercise is designed to stimulate you to examine the factors that might lead you to dissolve a romantic relationship. Here are listed a number of factors that might lead someone to end a romantic relationship. For each factor identify the likelihood that you would dissolve romantic relationships of various types, using a 10-point scale on which 10 = "would definitely dissolve the relationship" and 1 = "would definitely not dissolve the relationship," with the numbers 2 through 9 representing intermediate levels. Use 5 for "don't know what I'd do."

Factor	Budding romantic relationship of 1 or 2 weeks	Steady dating for the last few months	Romantic relationship of about a year	Committed romantic relationship of 5 or more years
1. Person lies frequently about insignificant and significant issues				
2. Person abuses you emotionally or physically				
3. Person is sexually unfaithful				
4. Person has an addiction to gambling, alcohol, or drugs				
5. Person is close to relatives and friends you dislike				
6. Person has a serious illness that will require lots of your time, energy, and financial resources				
7. Person lacks ambition and doesn't want to do anything of significance				
8. Person has a commitment phobia and seems unwilling to increase the intimacy of the relationship				
9. Person has very different religious beliefs from you				

Factor	Budding romantic relationship of 1 or 2 weeks	Steady dating for the last few months	Romantic relationship of about a year	Committed romantic relationship of 5 or more years
10. Person embarrasses you because of bad manners, poor grammar, and inappropriate dress				
11. Person has really poor hygiene habits				
12. Person spends 4 to 5 hours a day talking in chat rooms				

A significant part of relationship competence is to recognize behaviors that are likely to cause problems and to work on eliminating these from your own communication patterns or at least to deal effectively with their consequences.

9.3 Matching Hypothesis. The *matching hypothesis* claims that people date and mate those who are similar to themselves in physical attractiveness (Walster & Walster, 1978). When this does not happen—when a very attractive person dates someone of average or low attractiveness—there are likely to be "compensating factors," factors that the less attractive person possesses that compensate or make up for being less physically attractive. What evidence can you find to support or contradict this theory? How would you go about testing this theory?

9.4 Romantic Love. When researchers asked college students to identify the features that characterize romantic love, the five qualities most frequently noted were trust, sexual attraction, acceptance and tolerance, spending time together, and sharing thoughts and secrets (Regan, Kocan, & Whitlock, 1998). How would you characterize love? Do you notice any differences in the way people talk about love based on gender or cultural differences?

9.5 Family Characteristics. How would you describe your own family in terms of (1) the defined roles, recognition of responsibilities, shared history and future, and shared living space and (2) the most often used communication pattern (equality, balanced split, unbalanced split, or monopoly)?

9.6 Virtual Infidelity. Generally online infidelity is seen as a consequence of a failure in communication between the couple (Young, Griffin-Shelley, Cooper, O'Mara, & Buchanan, 2000). How would you describe online infidelity? What are some potential consequences (positive as well as negative) of online infidelity?

9.7 Safety Precautions. One study suggests that people who make friends online take safety precautions such as protecting anonymity and talking on the phone before meeting face to face (McCown, Fischer, Page, & Homant, 2001). What safety precautions do you think are reasonable to take in online relationships?

LogOn! MyCommunicationLab www.mycommunicationlab.com

Throughout this chapter, there are icons that highlight media content for selected topics. Go to **MyCommunicationLab** for additional materials on the three major types of relationships: friendships, romantic, and family. Here you'll find flashcards to help you learn key communication terms, videos that illustrate a variety of concepts, additional exercises, and discussions to help you continue your study of friendships, romantic, and family relationships.

10 SMALL GROUP COMMUNICATION

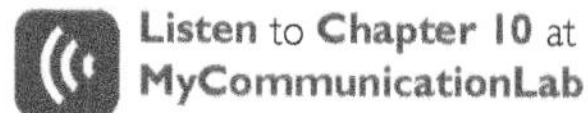

CHAPTER TOPICS	CHAPTER OBJECTIVES
In this chapter you'll explore the following major topics:	**After reading this chapter you should be able to:**
SMALL GROUPS AND TEAMS	10.1 Define *small group* and *team.*
IDEA-GENERATION GROUPS	10.2 Define *brainstorming* and explain its four rules.
PERSONAL GROWTH GROUPS	10.3 Define *personal growth groups* and give examples of several types.
INFORMATION-SHARING GROUPS	10.4 Define the *educational* or *learning group* and the *focus group.*
PROBLEM-SOLVING GROUPS	10.5 Explain the steps involved in the problem-solving sequence and define the *nominal group*, the *Delphi method*, and *quality circles.*

All groups are unique.

This chapter (and the next) focuses on small group communication. Here we explore the nature and types of groups, and in the next we focus on effective group membership and leadership.

10.1 SMALL GROUPS AND TEAMS

Let's begin with some basic definitions of the small group and the team, both face-to-face and virtual. We'll then look at small group stages, formats, culture, and power.

The Small Group

A **small group** is (1) a collection of individuals who (2) are connected to one another by some common purpose, (3) are interdependent, (4) have some degree of organization among them, and (5) see themselves as a group. Each of these characteristics needs to be explained a bit further.

1. **Collection of Individuals.** Generally, a small group consists of approximately 3 to 12 people. A small group is a collection of individuals few enough in number so that all members may communicate with relative ease as both senders and receivers. In face-to-face situations, there are also limits that the available space imposes; in online groups, no such spatial barrier exists. If the group gets much larger than 12, however, even online group communication becomes difficult. On Facebook and similar social networking sites, the number of individuals in a group may number in the hundreds of friends. These would not be small groups—communicating via these sites is more akin to public speaking—but the subgroups that form would likely fall into the small group category.
2. **Common Purpose.** The members of a group must be connected to one another through some common purpose. People on a bus normally do not constitute a group because they're not working at some common purpose. But if the bus gets stuck in a ditch, the riders may quickly become a group and work together to get the bus back on the road. Generally there must be some similarity in the individuals' reasons for interacting. Social media sites provide easy ways of connecting with others who have similar purposes. Social media groups—whether professional as on LinkedIn or more purely social (although there are now apps to establish more professional groups) such as Facebook or a mixture as on Google+)—enable you to form groups on just about any topic you'd like. If you're interested in something, there are probably others out there who are interested in the same thing and who would like to get together in virtual space. By joining a social media site group you can, depending on which one you join, receive e-mails from group members about group activities, network for a variety of reasons, discuss topics of mutual interest, plan events or hangouts, or solve problems—the very same purposes that face-to-face groups serve.
3. **Interdependence.** In a small group, members are interdependent; the behavior of one member is significant for and has an impact on all other members. When one member attacks or supports the ideas of another member, that behavior influences the other members and the group as a whole.
4. **Organizing Rules.** Members of small groups must be connected by some organizing rules or structure. At times the structure is rigid—as in groups operating under parliamentary procedure, in which each comment must follow prescribed rules. At other times, as in a social gathering, the structure is very loose.
5. **Self-Perception as a Group.** Members of small groups feel they are, in fact, members of this larger whole. This doesn't mean that individuality is ignored or that members do not see themselves as individuals; it simply means that each member thinks, feels, and acts as a part of the group. The more members see themselves as part of the group, the greater the group cohesion (or sense of "groupness"), satisfaction, and productivity.

Watch at MyCommunicationLab Video: "The Interns"

The Team

A **team** is a particular kind of small group. As such it possesses all of the characteristics of the small group, as well as some additional qualities. Drawing on a number of small group researchers in communication and organizational theory, we can define the team as a small group (1) constructed for a specific task, (2) whose members have clearly defined roles, (3) whose members are committed to achieving the same goal, and (4) that is content focused (Beebe & Masterson, 2012; Hofstrand, 2006; Kelly, 2006):

1. **Specific Purpose.** A team is often constructed for a specific task. After the task is completed the members may be assigned to other teams or go their separate ways. Players on a baseball team,

COMMUNICATION CHOICE POINT

IMPRESSION MANAGEMENT *You've been assigned to join a team of four others to work on new accounting procedures. As the new member you want to be perceived as both likeable and competent.* **Thinking back to the discussion of impression management strategies (Chapter 3, pages 70–73), what are some of your communication choices for achieving the impression you want? What would you say? What behaviors would you want to avoid?**

for example, come together for practice and for the actual game, but after the game, they each go their separate ways. After the book is published, members of the book team may go on to work on different books with different team members.

2. **Clearly Defined Roles.** In a team, member's roles are rather clearly defined. A sports team is a good example. Each player has a unique function; the shortstop's functions are very different from the pitcher's or the catcher's, for example. In business, the team that is responsible for publishing a book, say, would also consist of people with clearly defined roles and might include the editor, the designer, the marketing manager, the sales manager, the photo researcher, the author, and so on. Each brings a unique perspective to the task, and each is an authority in a specific area.
3. **Goal Directed.** In a team all members are committed to achieving the same, clearly identified goal. Again, a sports team is a good example; all members are committed to winning the game. In the book business example, all members of the team are committed to producing a successful book.
4. **Content Focused.** Teams are generally more content focused. In terms of the distinction between content and relationship messages introduced in Chapter 1, teams are generally more focused on content and their communication proceeds largely through the exchange of content messages—on winning the game or creating the book—than they are on exchanging messages about the interpersonal relationships of its members.

Virtual Groups and Teams

Small groups and teams use a wide variety of channels. Often, interactions take place face to face; this is the channel that probably comes to mind when you think of groups. Nowadays much small group and team interaction also takes place online, among geographically separated members who communicate as a group via computer or phone connections. These *virtual groups and teams* serve both relationship and social purposes on the one hand (these are best thought of as small groups) and business and professional purposes on the other (these are best thought of as teams).

Watch at MyCommunicationLab Video: "Listening in Virtual Meetings"

Perhaps the best example of **virtual groups** serving relationship purposes are the social networking sites like Twitter and Facebook, where friends interact in groups but may be separated by classrooms or by oceans. And, increasingly, these social networking sites are also serving business task purposes as well. They are used for finding jobs, conducting business, solving organizational problems, and conducting just about any kind of function that a face-to-face group would serve.

The business and professional purposes of virtual groups are usually served by virtual teams. Some of these team members may be working at home, but increasingly virtual teams consist of people who are in different work spaces, perhaps in different parts of an office building, perhaps in different countries.

The same principles of effective group communication apply to all kinds of groups and teams, whether social or business, face-to-face or virtual (we'll use the most inclusive term *small group* to refer to all types of groups). Whether you're working on a team project with colleagues in different countries, communicating with new friends on Facebook, or interacting face to face with your extended family, the principles we discuss here will prove useful.

Watch at MyCommunicationLab Video: "Virtual Miscommunication"

Small Group Stages

The small group develops in much the same way that a conversation develops. As in conversation, there are five **small group stages:** (1) opening, (2) feedforward, (3) business, (4) feedback, and (5) closing.

- **Opening.** A small group's *opening stage* is usually a getting-acquainted time in which members introduce themselves and engage in social small talk.
- **Feedforward.** After this preliminary get-together, there's usually *a feedforward stage* in which members attempt to identify what needs to be done, who will do it, and so on. In formal business groups, the meeting agenda (which is a perfect example of feedforward) may be reviewed and the tasks of the group identified. In informal social groups, the feedforward may consist simply of introducing a topic of conversation or talking about what the group's members should do.
- **Business.** The *business stage* is the actual work on the tasks—the problem solving, the sharing of information, or whatever else the group needs to do.
- **Feedback.** At the *feedback stage*, the group may reflect on what it has done and perhaps on what remains to be done. Some groups may even evaluate their performance at this stage.
- **Closing.** At the *closing stage*, the group members again return to their focus on individuals and will perhaps exchange closing comments—"Good seeing you again," and the like.

These stages are rarely distinct from one another. Rather, they blend into one another. For example, the opening stage is not completely finished before the feedforward begins. Rather, as the opening comments are completed, the group begins to introduce feedforward; as the feedforward begins to end, the business starts.

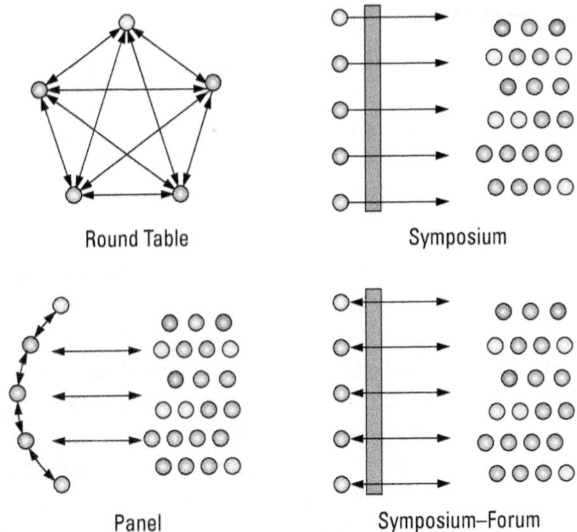

FIGURE 10.1 **Small Group Formats**

These four formats are general patterns that may describe a wide variety of groups. Within each type there will naturally be considerable variation. For example, in the symposium-forum there's no set pattern for how much time will be spent on the symposium part and how much time will be spent on the forum part. Similarly, combinations may be used. Thus, for example, group members may each present a position paper (basically a symposium) and then participate in a round table discussion.

Small Group Formats

Small groups serve their functions in a variety of formats. Among the most popular small group formats for relatively formal functions are the round table, the panel, the symposium, and the symposium-forum (Figure 10.1).

The Round Table

In the **round table format,** group members arrange themselves in a circular or semicircular pattern. They share the information or solve the problem without any set pattern of who speaks when. Group interaction is informal, and members contribute as they see fit. A leader or moderator may be present; he or she may, for example, try to keep the discussion on the topic or encourage more reticent members to speak up.

The Panel

In the **panel,** group members are "experts" but participate informally and without any set pattern of who speaks when, as in a round table. The difference is that there's an audience whose members may interject comments or ask questions. A variation is the two-panel format, with an expert panel and a lay panel. The lay panel discusses the topic but may turn to the expert panel members when in need of technical information, additional data, or direction.

The Symposium

In the **symposium,** each member delivers a prepared presentation much like a public speech. All speeches are addressed to different aspects of a single topic. A symposium leader introduces the speakers, provides transitions from one speaker to another, and may provide periodic summaries.

The Symposium–Forum

The symposium-forum consists of two parts: a symposium, with prepared speeches, and a **forum,** with questions from the audience and responses by the speakers. The leader introduces the speakers and moderates the question-and-answer session.

Small Group Culture

Small groups, especially those of long standing, develop their own culture. Especially relevant to understanding this cultural dimension of small groups are the group norms and the high or low context with which the group operates. Let's look at each in turn.

Small Group Norms

Group norms are rules or standards of behavior identifying which behaviors are considered appropriate (for example, being willing to take on added tasks or directing conflict toward issues rather than toward people) and which are considered inappropriate (for example, coming in late or not contributing actively). Sometimes these rules for appropriate behavior are *explicit*; they're clearly stated in a company contract or policy, such as "All members must attend department meetings." Sometimes the rules are *implicit*; it is understood that members will be polite or well groomed.

Small group norms apply to individual members as well as to the group as a whole and, of course, will differ from one society to another (Axtell, 1993). For example, in the United States men and women in business are expected to interact when making business decisions as well as when socializing. In Muslim and Buddhist societies, however, religious restrictions prevent mixed-gender groups. In groups in some societies, including those of the United States, Bangladesh, Australia, Germany, Finland, and Hong Kong, punctuality for business meetings is very important. But in Morocco, Italy, Brazil, Zambia, Ireland, and Panama, time is less highly regarded; being late is no great insult and is even expected. In many Persian Gulf states the business executive is likely to conduct meetings with several different people—sometimes dealing with totally different issues—at the same time. In this situation you have to expect to share what in the United States would be "your time" with these other parties.

Norms that regulate a particular group member's behavior, called **role expectations,** identify what each person in an organization is expected to do; for example, Pat is great at formatting and editing and so should play the role of secretary.

You're more likely to accept the norms of your group's culture when you feel your group membership is important and want to continue your membership in the group. You're also more likely to accept these norms when your group is cohesive. **Cohesiveness** means that you and the other members are closely connected, are attracted to one another, and depend on one another to meet your needs. Lastly, you're more apt to accept these norms if you'd be punished by negative reactions or exclusion from the group for violating them (Napier & Gershenfeld, 1992).

eth•ics *noun* morality, standards of conduct, moral judgment

MAKING ETHICAL CHOICES
Telling Secrets

In groups of close friends, family members, or workplace committees, people often exchange secrets with the explicit or implied assumption that these secrets will not be revealed to outsiders. Revealing or not revealing such secrets often has ethical implications.

In *Secrets* (1983) ethicist Sissela Bok identifies three types of situations in which she argues it would be *unethical* to reveal the secrets of another person. These conditions aren't always easy to identify in any given instance, but they do provide excellent starting points for asking whether it's ethical to reveal what we know about another person. And, of course, for any situation, there may be legitimate exceptions.

It's unethical *to reveal information that you have promised to keep secret.*

It's unethical *to say things about another person when you know the information to be false.*

It's unethical *to invade the privacy to which everyone has a right*—to reveal information that no one else has a right to know.

In other situations, however, you may actually have an obligation to reveal a secret. For example, Bok (1983) argues that you have an obligation to reveal a secret when keeping the information hidden will do more harm than good. For example, if a teenager confided in you that he or she intended to commit suicide, you'd have an ethical obligation to say something.

Ethical Choice Point

How would you handle the following situations? (1) An instructor who supervises your study group confides that she is a confirmed racist and proud of it. (2) A 16-year-old member of the wilderness group you're leading confides that she's having unprotected sex with her supervisor at work, a married man. (3) A community religious leader confides that he's skimming a portion of the members' contributions to fund his retirement.

High- and Low-Context Cultures

The distinction between high- and low-context cultures, introduced in Chapter 2, has special relevance to small group communication (and to public speaking, which is considered in Chapters 14–18). A high-context culture, you'll recall, is a culture in which much of the information in communication is in the context or in the person rather than explicitly coded in the verbal messages. In a high-context culture people have lots of information in common, so it does not have to be made explicit. A low-context culture, on the other hand, is a culture in which most of the information in communication is explicitly stated in the verbal messages. In a low-context culture people do not assume they share certain information and so make all crucial details explicit.

As you might expect, group members in high-context cultures spend a lot of time getting to know one another before engaging in any important transactions. Because of this prior personal knowledge, a great deal of information is shared and therefore does not have to be explicitly stated in the group's deliberations. Members of low-context cultures, on the other hand, spend less time getting to know one another and therefore do not have that shared knowledge. As a result, everything has to be stated explicitly during the group's discussions. When this simple difference is not taken into account, misunderstandings can easily result. For example, the directness and explicitness characteristic of the low-context culture may prove insulting, insensitive, or unnecessary to members of a high-context culture.

Conversely, to members of a low-context culture, someone from a high-context culture may appear vague, underhanded, even dishonest in his or her reluctance to be explicit or to engage in communication that a low-context culture would consider open and direct.

Power in the Small Group

Power permeates all small groups and all relationships. It influences what you do, when, and with whom. It influences the employment you seek and the employment you get. It influences the friends you choose and don't choose and those who choose you and those who don't. It influences your romantic and family relationships—their success, failure, and level of satisfaction or dissatisfaction.

Power is what enables one person (the one with power) to control the behaviors of others. Thus, if A has power over B and C, then A, by virtue of this power and through the exercise of this power (or the threat of exercising it), can control the behaviors of B and C. Differences in individuals' amounts and types of power influence who makes important decisions, who will prevail in an argument, and who will control the finances.

Although all relationships involve power, they differ in the types of power that the people use and to which they respond. Examine your own power by responding to the following statements. For each statement, indicate which of the following descriptions is generally an accurate description of your power and which is a generally inaccurate description.

_____ **1.** My position is such that I often have to tell others what to do. For example, a mother's position demands that she tell her children what to do, a manager's position demands that he or she tell employees what to do, and so on.

_____ **2.** People wish to be like me or identified with me. For example, high school football players may admire the former professional football player who is now their coach and want to be like him.

_____ **3.** People see me as having the ability to give them what they want. For example, employers have the ability to give their employees increased pay, longer vacations, or improved working conditions.

_____ **4.** People see me as having the ability to administer punishment or to withhold things they want. For example, employers have the ability to reduce voluntary overtime, shorten vacation time, or fail to improve working conditions.

_____ **5.** Other people realize that I have expertise in certain areas of knowledge. For example, a doctor has expertise in medicine and so others turn to the doctor to tell them what to do. Someone knowledgeable about computers similarly possesses expertise.

_____ **6.** Other people realize that I possess the communication ability to present an argument logically and persuasively.

These statements refer to the six major types of power to be described. As you read these descriptions, consider your own satisfaction-dissatisfaction with your level of power and possible ways of increasing it. The six types of power covered in the above statements are (1) legitimate, (2) referent, (3) reward, (4) coercive, (5) expert, and (6) information or persuasion power (French & Raven, 1968; Raven, Centers, & Rodrigues, 1975).

You have **legitimate power** (statement 1) over another person when this person believes you have a right by virtue of your position (for example, you're the appointed group leader) to influence or control his or her behavior. Legitimate power usually comes from the leadership roles people occupy. Teachers are often seen to have legitimate power, and this is doubly true for religious teachers. Parents are seen as having legitimate power over their children. Employers, judges, managers, doctors, and police officers are others who may hold legitimate power.

You have **referent power** (statement 2) over another person when that person wishes to be like you or identified with you. Your referent power over another person increases when you're well liked and well respected, when you're seen as attractive and prestigious, when you're of the same gender, and when you have attitudes and experiences similar to those of the other person.

You have **reward power** (statement 3) over a person if you have the ability to give that person rewards—either material (money, promotions, jewelry) or social (love, friendship, respect). Reward power increases attractiveness; we like those who have the power to reward us and who do in fact give us rewards.

Conversely, you have **coercive power** (statement 4) if you have the ability to remove rewards or to administer punishments. Usually, the two kinds of power go hand in hand; if you have reward power, you also have coercive power. For example, parents may grant as well as deny privileges to their children.

You possess **expert power** (statement 5) if group members regard you as having expertise or knowledge—whether or not you truly possess such expertise. Expert power increases when you are seen as being unbiased and having nothing to gain personally from influencing others. It decreases if you are seen as biased and as having something to gain from securing the compliance of others.

You have **information power,** or persuasion power (statement 6), if you're seen as someone who can communicate logically and persuasively. Generally, persuasion power is attributed to people who are seen as having significant information and the ability to use that information in presenting a well-reasoned argument.

Now that the general nature of the small group is clear, let's look at several of the more important types of small groups you'll encounter: idea-generation groups, personal growth groups, information-sharing groups, and problem-solving groups.

10.2 IDEA-GENERATION GROUPS

Idea-generation groups are small groups that exist solely to generate ideas and often follow a pattern called brainstorming (Beebe & Masterson, 2012; DeVito, 1996; Osborn, 1957). **Brainstorming** is a technique for bombarding a problem and generating as many ideas as possible. This technique involves two stages. The first is the brainstorming period proper; the second is the evaluation period.

The procedures are simple. A problem is selected that is amenable to many possible solutions or ideas. Group members are informed of the problem to be brainstormed before the actual session so they can think about the topic. When the group meets, each person contributes as many ideas as he or she can think of. All ideas are recorded either in writing or on tape.

me•di•a lit•er•a•cy *noun* ability to understand, interact with, and create media messages

EXPANDING MEDIA LITERACY
The Third-Person Effect

The *third-person effect* is a theory of media influence claiming that people routinely believe they are influenced less by the media than their peers are. According to this theory, you believe that your friends, neighbors, and coworkers are influenced more by the media than you are. You mistakenly believe yourself to be more resistant to media influence than others. A variety of studies conducted on college students have supported this theory (Davison, 1983). Whether the topic was political advertising, rap music, or pornography, students felt they were less susceptible to media influence than were their peers (Hoffner et al., 2001). This belief, research finds, is especially strong when the media message is a negative or socially unacceptable one; for example, people think that messages of violence, racism, or sexism influence them much less than their peers. The effect is weakened but still present when the message is a more acceptable one (for example, public service announcements).

Try testing out this theory. For example, survey 10 to 20 people and ask them how influenced they feel they are by, say, media violence or racism. Then ask them if their friends and relatives are influenced by such media messages more than they are. Then conduct the same type of two-step survey with a more socially acceptable message, such as a media campaign on the value of education or the importance of proper diet. On the basis of your research, what can you add to this discussion?

A variation on this idea is known as *electronic brainstorming* (EBS). Often aided by special software, members of this virtual group gather at their individual computers, which may be spread out throughout the world, and respond to a question with ideas. The ideas are immediately submitted to the screens of other members anonymously. This anonymity of contributions makes it easier for members to disagree with ideas (when that time comes), but also prevents the eventual solution or grand idea from being identified with any one person; instead, the result is the property of the group.

During this idea-generating session, four general rules are followed.

- **Brainstorm Rule 1: Don't criticize.** In a brainstorming session all ideas are recorded. They're not evaluated, nor are they even discussed. Any negative criticism—whether verbal or nonverbal—is itself criticized by the leader or the members. This is a good general rule to follow in all creative thinking: Allow your idea time to develop before you look for problems with it. At the same time, don't praise the ideas, either. All evaluations should be suspended during the brainstorming session.
- **Brainstorm Rule 2: Strive for quantity.** If you need an idea, you're more likely to find it in a group of many than in a group of few. Thus, in brainstorming, the more ideas, the better.
- **Brainstorm Rule 3: Combine and extend ideas.** Although you may not criticize a particular idea, you're encouraged to extend it or combine it in some way. The value of a particular idea may be the way it stimulates someone to combine or extend it. Even if your modification seems minor or obvious, say it. Don't censor yourself.
- **Brainstorm Rule 4: Develop the wildest ideas possible.** The wilder the idea, the better. It's easier to tone an idea down than to build it up. A wild idea can easily be tempered, but it's not so easy to elaborate on a simple or conservative idea.

After all the ideas are generated—a period lasting no longer than 15 to 20 minutes—the group evaluates the entire list of ideas, using the critical thinking skills developed throughout this text. The ideas that are unworkable are thrown out; those that show promise are retained and evaluated. During this stage, negative criticism is allowed.

10.3 PERSONAL GROWTH GROUPS

Some **personal growth groups,** sometimes referred to as support groups, aim to help members cope with particular difficulties—such as drug addiction, not being assertive enough, having an alcoholic parent, being an ex-convict, or having a hyperactive child or a promiscuous spouse. Other groups are more clearly therapeutic and are designed to change significant

the•o•ry *noun* statement of explanation, formulation of relationships, reasoned generalization

UNDERSTANDING THEORY AND RESEARCH
Group Power

Recall (from Chapter 2) that high-power-distance cultures are those in which power is concentrated in the hands of a few and there's a great difference between the power held by these people and the power held by the ordinary citizen. In contrast, in low-power-distance cultures power is more evenly distributed throughout the citizenry (Hofstede, Hofstede, & Minkov, 2010). Groups also may be viewed in terms of high and low power distance. In high-power-distance groups, the leader is far more powerful than the members. In low-power-distance groups, leaders and members differ much less in their power.

Of the groups in which you'll participate—as a member or as a leader—some will be high in power distance and others will be low. The skill is to recognize which is which, to follow the rules generally, and to break the rules only after you've thought through the consequences. For example, in low-power-distance groups, you're expected to confront a group leader (or friend or supervisor) assertively; acting assertively denotes a general feeling of equality (Borden, 1991). In high-power-distance groups, direct confrontation and assertiveness toward the leader (or toward any person in authority, such as a teacher or doctor) may be viewed negatively (Bochner & Hesketh, 1994; Westwood, Tang, & Kirkbride, 1992).

Working with Theories and Research

Visit one of the online databases to which you have access and search the communication and sociology databases for "group power." What types of questions engage the attention of researchers?

aspects of an individual's personality or behavior. Still other groups are devoted to making healthy individuals function even more effectively.

Personal growth groups vary widely in their procedures, so it's not possible to provide a standard pattern that all such groups follow (as is the case with brainstorming groups, discussed above, or with problem-solving groups, discussed later in this chapter). But let's look briefly at three well-known types of personal growth groups: the encounter group, the assertiveness training group, the consciousness-raising group, and the intervention group.

A word of caution should be injected here: These groups are highly personal and ego-involving, and although they will all seem easy and reasonable to set up and participate in, they are actually very complex and difficult. They are discussed here (briefly) to give you an idea of the types of personal growth groups available rather than to provide a set of guidelines for using these groups.

The Encounter Group

Encounter groups, also known as "sensitivity groups" or "T [Training]-groups," for example, constitute a form of psychotherapy; these groups try to facilitate members' personal growth and foster their ability to deal effectively with other people (Hirsch, Kett, & Trefil, 2002; Rogers, 1970). One of the encounter group's assumptions is that the members will be more effective, both psychologically and interpersonally, if they get to know and like themselves better. Consequently, members are encouraged to look at themselves and their relationships honestly and in depth and to react to others in the group openly and honestly. Members are encouraged to express their inner thoughts, fears, and doubts in the encounter group, in which interactions are always characterized by total acceptance and support.

The Assertiveness Training Group

The **assertiveness training group** aims to increase the willingness of its members to stand up for their rights and to act more assertively in a wide variety of situations (Adler, 1977; Bishop, 2006). Distinctions are made between being assertive (which is good and effective); being nonassertive (which is ineffective because your own wants and needs are unlikely to be met); and being aggressive (which also is ineffective because it contributes to escalating the conflict and causing resentment). The group aims to increase the assertiveness skills of its members, who are likely to be people who feel they are not assertive enough. The skill of assertiveness is covered in more detail in the discussion of conflict in Chapter 13.

The Consciousness-Raising Group

The **consciousness-raising group** aims to help people cope with the problems society confronts them with. The members of a consciousness-raising group all have one characteristic in common (for example, they may all be women, unwed mothers, gay fathers, or recently unemployed executives). It's this commonality that leads the members to join together and help one another. In the consciousness-raising group the assumption is that similar people are best equipped to assist one another's personal growth. The procedures generally followed are simple: A topic is selected, and each member speaks on the topic as it relates to the general group topic. For example, if the group consists of unwed mothers, then whatever the topic (taxes, children, school, prejudice), the members address it in the context of the group's focus on unwed motherhood. No interruptions are allowed. After each member has finished, the other group members may ask questions of clarification. The feedback from other members is to be totally supportive. After the last member has spoken, a general discussion follows. This procedure is designed to help raise members' consciousness by giving them an opportunity to formulate and verbalize their thoughts on a particular topic, hear how others feel and think about the same topic, and formulate and answer questions of clarification.

The Intervention Group

In the **intervention group** people gather to help one of their members overcome some problem. For example, family members may gather to confront an alcoholic member. Other commonly confronted issues are drug, gambling, and sex addiction and eating disorders. Usually a leader is designated (sometimes a professional intervention leader and sometimes a group member). Under the leader's guidance the group expresses its support and love for the person, explains the impact of this member's behavior on all connected others, and offers to help the person with the problem behavior. As you can imagine the skills of empathy, supportiveness, and immediacy are especially important in the intervention.

10.4 INFORMATION-SHARING GROUPS

The purpose of **information-sharing groups** is to enable members to acquire new information or skills through a sharing of knowledge. In most information-sharing groups, all members have something to teach and something to learn. In some, however, the interaction takes place because some members have information and some don't.

Educational or Learning Groups

In **educational or learning groups**, the members pool their knowledge to the benefit of all, as in the popular law and medical student learning groups. Members may follow a variety of discussion patterns. For example, a historical topic might be developed chronologically, with the discussion progressing from the past into the present and perhaps predicting the future. Issues in developmental psychology, such as physical maturity or language development in the child, also might be discussed chronologically. Other suitable patterns, depending on the nature of the topic and the needs of the participants, might be developed in terms of causes and effects, problems and solutions, or structures and functions.

Perhaps the most popular is the topical pattern. A group might discuss the challenges of raising a hyperactive child by itemizing and discussing each of the major problems. The structure of a corporation might also be considered in terms of its major divisions. As can be appreciated, topical approaches may be further systematized; for instance, a learning group might rank the problems of hyperactivity in terms of their importance or complexity or might order the major structures of the corporation in terms of decision-making power.

COMMUNICATION CHOICE POINT

STIMULATING CONTRIBUTIONS *You're in charge of a focus group discussing what members like and dislike about the websites they visit. The problem you anticipate, based on past experience, is that a few members will do all the talking and the rest will hardly talk at all. You want to encourage all members to participate fully.* **What are some of the ways you can confront this problem? What might you say?**

Focus Groups

A different type of learning group is the **focus group,** a small group assembled for a kind of in-depth interview. The aim here is to discover what people think about an issue or product; for example, what do men between 18 and 25 think of the new aftershave lotion and its packaging? What do young executives earning more than $100,000 think about buying a foreign luxury car?

In the focus group, a leader tries to discover the beliefs, attitudes, thoughts, and feelings that members have so as to help an organization make decisions on changing the scent or redesigning the packaging of aftershave lotion or constructing advertisements for luxury cars. It is the leader's task to prod members to analyze their thoughts and feelings on a deeper level and to use the thoughts of one member to stimulate the thoughts of others.

Generally, approximately 12 people are assembled. The leader explains the process, the time limits, and the general goal of the group—let's say, to discover why these 12 individuals requested information on the XYZ health plan but purchased a plan from another company. The idea, of course, is that these 12 people are representing a wider population. The leader, who is usually a professional focus group facilitator rather than a member of the client organization itself, asks a variety of questions such as: How did you hear about the XYZ health plan? What other health plans did you consider before making your actual purchase? What influenced you to buy the plan you eventually bought? Were any other people influential in helping you make your decision? Through the exploration of these and similar questions, the facilitator and the relevant members of the client organization (who may be seated behind a one-way mirror, watching the discussion) may put together a more effective health plan or more effective advertising strategies.

10.5 PROBLEM-SOLVING GROUPS

A **problem-solving group** is a collection of individuals who meet to solve a problem or to reach a decision. In one sense this is the most exacting kind of group to participate in. It requires not only a knowledge of small group communication techniques, but also a thorough knowledge of the particular problem. And it usually demands faithful adherence to a somewhat rigid set of rules. We'll look at this group first in terms of the classic and still popular problem-solving approach, whereby we identify the steps to go through in solving a problem. In the context of this sequence, we'll consider the major decision-making methods. Finally, we'll survey some types of groups that are popular in organizations today: the nominal group, the Delphi method, and quality circles.

The Problem-Solving Sequence

The approach developed by philosopher John Dewey (1910), the **problem-solving sequence,** is probably the technique used most often. The six steps of the sequence (see Figure 10.2) are designed to make problem solving more efficient and effective: (1) Define and analyze the problem, (2) establish criteria, (3) identify possible solutions, (4) evaluate solutions, (5) select the best solution(s), and (6) test the selected solution(s).

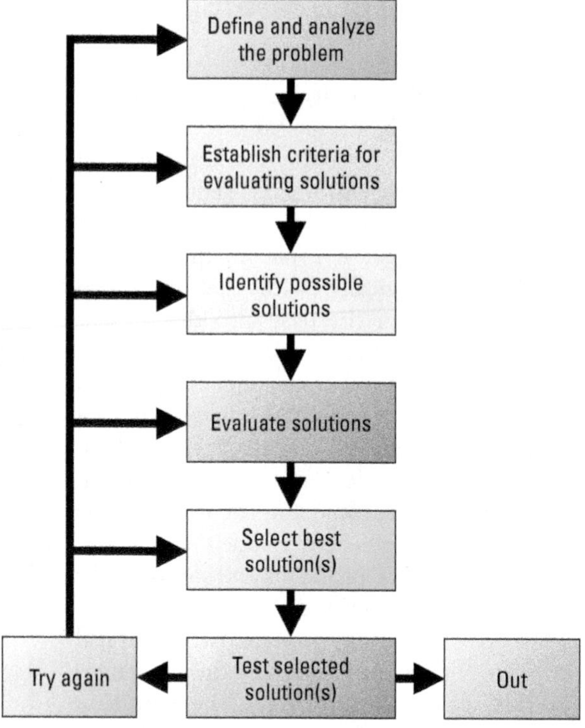

FIGURE 10.2 **Steps in Problem-Solving Discussion**

Although most small group theorists would advise you to follow the problem-solving pattern as presented here, others would alter it somewhat. For example, the pattern here advises you first to define the problem and then to establish criteria for identifying possible solutions. You would then keep these criteria in mind as you generated possible solutions (step 3). Another school of thought, however, would advise you to generate solutions first and to consider how they will be evaluated only after these solutions are proposed (Brilhart & Galanes, 1992). The advantage of this second approach is that you may generate more creative solutions if you're not restricted by standards of evaluation. The disadvantage is that you may spend a great deal of time generating impractical solutions that would never meet the standards you'll eventually propose.

Step 1: Define and Analyze the Problem

In many instances the nature of the problem is clearly specified. For example, a group of designers might discuss how to package a new soap product. In other instances, however, the problem may be vague, and it may remain for the group to define it in concrete terms. Thus, the general problem may be that your company wants to increase profits, and the solution that needs to be found is a way to make the company more profitable. But such a broad and general topic is difficult to tackle in a single problem-solving discussion, so it may be helpful to specify the problem in more specific and limited terms. Perhaps this hypothetical problem will need to be dealt with in a series of problem-solving discussions on "How to reduce waste," "How to increase market visibility," and/or "How to improve the company website."

Define the problem as an open-ended question ("How can we improve the company website?") rather than as a statement ("The company website needs to be improved") or a yes/no question ("Does the website need improvement?"). The open-ended question allows greater freedom of exploration. Some appropriate questions for most problems revolve around the following issues:

- **Duration.** How long has the problem existed? Is it likely to continue in the future? What is the predicted course of the problem? For example, will it grow or lessen in impact?
- **Causes.** What are the major causes of the problem? How certain can we be that these are the actual causes?
- **Effects.** What are the effects of the problem? How significant are they? Who is affected by this problem? How significantly are they affected? Is this problem causing other problems? How important are these other problems?

Step 2: Establish Criteria for Evaluating Solutions

Before any solutions are proposed, the group should decide on the criteria or standards for evaluating the solution. This step will enable you to rule out unacceptable solutions and to devote your time to solutions that seem possible and workable. At this stage you identify the standards or criteria that you'll use in evaluating solutions or in selecting one solution over another. Generally, two types of criteria need to be considered:

- **Practical criteria.** For example, you might decide that solutions to the website problem must not increase the budget, must lead to a higher volume of business, must be constructed in-house, must load almost immediately, and so on.
- **Value criteria.** These are usually more difficult to identify. These might include, for example, requirements that the website reflect the culture of the company, that it represent the company's commitment to multiculturalism, or that it serve to benefit the community.

Step 3: Identify Possible Solutions

At this stage identify as many solutions as possible. Focus on quantity rather than quality. Brainstorming may be particularly useful at this point (see the earlier discussion of idea-generation groups). Solutions to the website problem might include incorporating reviews of publications by company members, reviews of restaurants in the area, recruitment guidelines, and new employment opportunities within the company.

Step 4: Evaluate Solutions

After all the solutions have been proposed, go back and evaluate each according to the criteria you have established. For example, to what extent does incorporating reviews of area restaurants meet the evaluation criteria? Will it increase the budget? Each potential solution should be matched against the criteria.

An especially insightful technique for evaluating solutions is presented in Table 10.1.

Step 5: Select the Best Solution(s)

At this stage the best solution or solutions are selected and put into operation. For instance, in the company website example, if "reviews of area restaurants" and "listings of new positions" best met the evaluation criteria, the group might then incorporate these two new items in the redesign of the website.

Groups may use different decision-making methods in deciding, for example, which criteria to use or which solutions to accept. Generally, groups use one of three methods: decision by authority, majority rule, or consensus.

Watch at **MyCommunicationLab** **Video:** "Helping Annie"

Decision by authority. In decision by authority, members voice their feelings and opinions, but the leader, boss, or CEO makes the final decision. Sometimes, the authority is an expert who is called in to make the ultimate decision–as might be the case in, say, deciding what surgical procedure to use in a specific case. This is surely an efficient method; it gets things done quickly, and the amount of discussion can be limited as desired. Another advantage is that experienced and informed members (for example, those who have the most experience with these types of operations) will

TABLE 10.1 THE SIX CRITICAL THINKING HATS

This technique involves thinking with six different "hats" and, in doing so, subjecting an issue to a six-part analysis (deBono, 1987).

Hat	Focus	Possible Questions to Ask
The Fact Hat	Focuses on the data—the facts and figures that bear on the problem.	■ What are the relevant data on the website? ■ How much does it cost to establish and maintain a website?
The Feeling Hat	Focuses on your feelings, emotions, and intuitions concerning the problem.	■ How do we feel about the current website? ■ How do we feel about making changes?
The Negative Argument Hat	Focuses on the possible negative aspects of a proposed solution.	■ Why might this proposed solution fail? ■ What is the worst-case scenario?
The Positive Benefits Hat	Focuses on the possible positive aspects of a proposed solution.	■ What benefits will this website provide for employees? ■ What is the best case scenario?
The Creative New Idea Hat	Focuses on new ways of looking at a problem and can be easily combined with the techniques of brainstorming.	■ In what other ways can we look at this problem? ■ How can the website provide a service to the community?
The Control of Thinking Hat	Focuses on the thinking processes that are going into finding a solution.	■ Have we adequately defined the problem? ■ Are we focusing too much on insignificant issues?

probably exert a greater influence on the final decision. The great disadvantage is that group members may not feel the need to contribute their insights and may become distanced from the power within the group or organization. Another disadvantage is that this method may lead members to tell the decision maker what they feel she or he wants to hear, a condition that can easily lead to groupthink (Chapter 11).

Decision by majority rule. With this method the group members agree to abide by the majority decision and may vote on various issues as the group works toward solving its problem. Majority rule is efficient, as there's usually the option of calling for a vote when the majority is in agreement. One disadvantage of this method is that it can lead to fractioning, in which various minorities align against the majority. The method may also lead to limiting discussion once a majority has agreed and a vote is called.

Decision by consensus. In small group decision making, consensus means reaching agreement. The agreement does not have to be unanimous; it is, rather, something that the group members can live with. The members agree that they can and will do whatever the group's solution requires (Kelly, 1994).

Consensus also implies that all members of the group had their say and that their opinions were carefully considered. The best of these opinions (in the group's estimation) are then combined and synthesized into a solution that the group as a whole gives agreement and permission to follow. It does not imply that you—as an individual group member—agree with the solution but only that you agree that (at this time, for this situation, for this group) this solution should be adopted and followed.

Here are a few hints to working in a group designed to achieve its solution by consensus; members and leader should:

- understand the nature of consensus, what it is and what it isn't.
- be willing to abide by the group's decisions.
- feel free to express their opinions, openly and honestly, while listeners must be open-minded, with a willingness to change their own initial opinions.
- make an honest attempt to incorporate as many of the members' needs, thoughts, and proposals into the final solution as reasonable and possible.
- be willing to put the group's needs ahead of their individual needs.

Consensus is the most time-consuming of the decision-making methods. However, it is also the method that best secures the cooperation and participation of all members in implementing the group's decisions. If you want members of the group to be satisfied and committed to the decision, consensus seems the best way to select a solution (Beebe & Masterson, 2012).

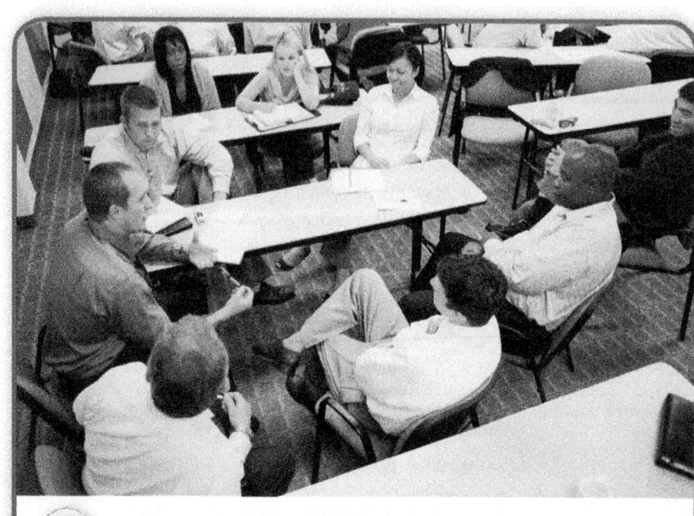

COMMUNICATION CHOICE POINT

CRITICAL THINKING *You're on a team (all equal in your organizational position) charged with designing the packaging for a new cell phone, and you need to establish how a decision will be made.* **What are some of your decision-making options? What are the advantages and disadvantages of each decision-making option?**

Step 6: Test Selected Solution(s)

After solutions are put into operation, test their effectiveness. The group might, for example, poll employees about the website changes, examine the number of hits, or analyze the advertising revenue.

If the solutions you have adopted prove ineffective, you will need to go back to one of the previous stages and repeat part of the process. Often this takes the form of selecting other solutions to test. But it may also involve going further back—for example, to a reanalysis of the problem, an identification of other solutions, or a restatement of evaluation criteria.

Problem-Solving Groups at Work

The problem-solving sequence discussed here is used widely in business in a variety of different types of groups. Let's examine three group approaches popular in business that rely largely on the problem-solving techniques just discussed: the nominal group technique, the Delphi method, and quality circles.

As you read these discussions, realize that the available technology will dictate some of the ways in which these groups operate. If all the members have is a whiteboard, then much will be recorded on the board. If all members have laptops or tablets connected to the company website, then much of the record keeping will go onto each laptop or tablet.

The Nominal Group Technique

The **nominal group** technique is a method of problem solving that uses limited discussion and confidential voting to obtain a group decision. It's especially helpful when some members may be reluctant to voice their opinions in a regular problem-solving group or when the issue is controversial or sensitive. The nominal group approach can be divided into eight steps (Kelly, 1994):

1. The problem is defined and clarified for all members.
2. Each member writes down (without discussion or consultation with others) his or her ideas on or possible solutions to the problem.
3. Each member–in sequence–states one idea from his or her list, which is recorded on a board or flip chart so everyone can see it. This process is repeated until all suggestions are stated and recorded.
4. Each suggestion is clarified (without debate). Ideally, each suggestion is given equal time.
5. Each member rank-orders the suggestions in writing.
6. The rankings of the members are combined to get a group ranking, which is then written on the board.
7. Clarification, discussion, and possible reordering may follow.
8. The highest-ranking or several high-ranking solutions may then be put into operation and tested.

The Delphi Method

In the **Delphi method** a group of "experts" is established, but there's no interaction among them; instead, they communicate by repeatedly responding to questionnaires (Kelly, 1994; Tersine & Riggs, 1980). The Delphi method is especially useful when you want to involve people who are geographically distant from one another, when you want all members to become part of the solution and to uphold it, or when you want to minimize the effects of dominant members or even of peer pressure. The method is best explained as a series of steps (Kelly, 1994).

1. The problem is defined (for example, "We need to improve intradepartmental communication"). What each member is expected to do is specified (for example, each member should contribute five ideas on this specific question).
2. Each member then anonymously contributes five ideas in writing.
3. The ideas of all members are combined, written up, and distributed to all members.
4. Members then select the three or four best ideas from this composite list and submit these.
5. From these responses another list is produced and distributed to all members.
6. Members then select the one or two best ideas from the new list and submit these.
7. From these responses another list is produced and distributed to all members. The process

the•o•ry *noun* statement of explanation, formulation of relationships, reasoned generalization

UNDERSTANDING THEORY AND RESEARCH
Group Polarization

Groups frequently make more extreme decisions than individuals—a tendency known as *group polarization* (Brauer, Judd, & Gliner, 1995; Bullock, et al., 2002; Friedkin, 1999). For example, a group will take greater risks if the individual members are already willing to take risks (a condition known as the "risky shift phenomenon") or will become more cautious if the members are already cautious. What seems to happen is that as a group member you estimate how others in the group feel about risk taking. If you judge the group as one of high-risk takers, you're likely to become more willing to take risks than you were before the group interaction. Similarly, if you judge the group members as cautious and as low-risk takers, you'll become even more cautious than you were before the interaction. In other words—and not surprisingly—your own attitudes toward risk will be heavily influenced by the attitudes you think the group possesses. Further, you're likely to change your attitudes to more closely match those of the group.

Working with Theories and Research

Have you ever observed group polarization? What happened? What implications does this theory have for, say, gang members, professors joining a new faculty, or investment analysts?

TABLE 10.2

In A Nutshell Small Group Types

Here is a brief summary of four types of groups and their basic uses.

Group	Basic Uses
Idea Generation [brainstorming groups]	▪ to generate ideas ▪ to gain new perspectives
Personal Growth [encounter, assertiveness, consciousness-raising, and intervention groups]	▪ to achieve greater self-understanding ▪ to help others
Information Sharing [educational and focus groups]	▪ to learn ▪ to teach
Problem Solving [nominal, Delphi, quality circle groups]	▪ to solve problems ▪ to manage conflict ▪ to realign/resolve differences

may be repeated any number of times, but usually three rounds are sufficient for achieving a fair degree of agreement.

8. The "final" solutions are identified and are communicated to all members.

Quality Circles

A **quality circle** is a group of workers (usually about 6 to 12) whose task it is to investigate and make recommendations for improving the quality of some organizational function. The members are drawn from the workers whose area is being studied; for example, if the problem were how to improve advertising on the Internet, then the quality circle membership would be drawn from the advertising and technology departments. The basic assumption is that people who work on similar tasks will be best able to improve their departments or jobs by pooling their insights and working through problems they share.

Quality circle members investigate problems using any method they feel might be helpful; for example, they may form face-to-face problem-solving groups or use nominal groups or Delphi methods. The group then reports its findings and its suggestions to those who can implement the proposals.

As you can see from just this one chapter, small groups exist in a variety of forms or types—each with their own rules and goals. Knowing how these groups can be used most effectively will prove a great asset in personal life and perhaps especially in the workplace. Another essential part of small group competence is knowing how to function as both a group member and a group leader, topics we cover in the next chapter.

Table 10.2 provides a brief summary of the groups just discussed.

Angie is an accounting major who has just landed her first job out of college with a large accounting firm. She has been assigned to join a team of four others to work on new accounting procedures for a major client. As the newest member, she wants to be perceived as both likeable and competent. "First Impressions," as the title implies, explores the importance of first impressions and how the choices you make in your verbal and nonverbal messages influence your effectiveness. As you'll see, some choices result in effective communication and other choices in ineffective communication. Log on to mycommunicationlab.com to view this video, the choices, and some discussion questions.

SUMMARY: SMALL GROUP COMMUNICATION

Study and **Review** at **MyCommunicationLab**

This chapter introduced the nature of the small group and team and discussed four major types of groups (idea-generation, personal growth, information-sharing, and problem-solving) along with their functions and procedures.

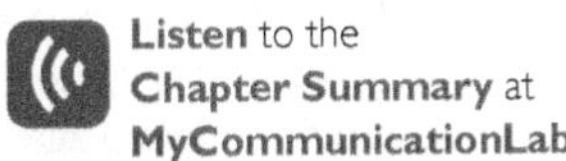

10.1 SMALL GROUPS AND TEAMS

1. A small group is a collection of individuals who are connected to one another by some common purpose, are interdependent, have some degree of organization among them, and see themselves as a group.
2. Small groups make use of four major formats: the round table, the panel, the symposium, and the symposium–forum.
3. Most small groups develop norms or rules that operate much like cultural norms, identifying what is considered appropriate behavior for the group members.
4. Power operates in all groups. Six types of power may be identified: legitimate, referent, reward, coercive, expert, and information or persuasion.

10.2 IDEA-GENERATION GROUPS

5. The idea-generation or brainstorming group attempts to generate as many ideas as possible.

10.3 PERSONAL GROWTH GROUPS

6. The personal growth group helps members to deal with personal problems and to function more effectively. Popular types of personal growth groups are the encounter group, the assertiveness training group, the consciousness-raising group, and the intervention group.

10.4 INFORMATION-SHARING GROUPS

7. Information-sharing groups attempt to enable members to acquire new information or skill through a mutual sharing of knowledge or insight. In educational or learning groups, the members pool their knowledge to the benefit of all. The focus group aims to discover what people think about an issue or product through a kind of in-depth group interview.

10.5 PROBLEM-SOLVING GROUPS

8. The problem-solving group attempts to solve a particular problem or at least to reach a decision that may cause the problem to solve itself.
9. The six steps in the problem-solving sequence are: Define and analyze the problem; establish criteria for evaluating solutions; identify possible solutions; evaluate solutions; select best solution(s); and test solution(s).
10. Decision-making methods include decision by authority, decision by majority rule, and decision by consensus.
11. Small group approaches that are widely used in business today include the nominal group, the Delphi method, and quality circles.

Study and **Review** the **Flashcards** at **MyCommunicationLab**

KEY TERMS

assertiveness training group *218*
brainstorming *216*
coercive power *216*
cohesiveness *214*
consciousness-raising group *218*
Delphi method *223*
educational or learning groups *219*
encounter groups *218*
expert power *216*
focus group *219*
forum *213*
group norms *214*
idea-generation groups *216*
information power *216*
information-sharing groups *218*
intervention group *218*
legitimate power *215*
nominal group *223*
panel *213*
personal growth groups *217*
power *215*
problem-solving group *219*
problem-solving sequence *220*
quality circle *224*
referent power *216*
reward power *216*
role expectations *214*
round table format *213*
small group *211*
small group stages *213*
symposium *213*
team *211*
virtual groups *212*

WORKING WITH SMALL GROUP COMMUNICATION

10.1 Combating Idea Killers. Creativity needs a great deal of freedom to develop, and this is one of the advantages of brainstorming. Think about how you can be on guard against negative criticism and how you can respond to "idea killers" or "killer messages." Some expressions aim to stop an idea from being developed—to stop it in its tracks before it can even get going. As you read down the list of these commonly heard killer messages, formulate at least one response you might give if someone used one of these on you or if you yourself used it to censor your own creative thinking.

a. It'll never work.

b. No one would vote for it.

c. It's too complex.

d. It's too simple.

e. It would take too long.

f. It's too expensive.

g. It's not logical.

h. What we have is good enough.

i. It just doesn't fit us.

j. It's impossible.

10.2 Listening to New Ideas. A useful skill for listening to new ideas is PIP'N, a technique that derives from Carl Rogers's (1970) emphasis on paraphrasing as a means for ensuring understanding and Edward deBono's (1976) PMI (*plus, minus,* and *interesting*) technique. PIP'N involves four steps:

P = Paraphrase. State in your own words what you think the other person is saying. This will ensure that you and the person proposing the idea are talking about the same thing. Your paraphrase also will provide the other person with the opportunity to elaborate or clarify his or her ideas.
I = Interesting. State something interesting that you find in the idea. Say why you think this idea might be interesting to you, to others, to the organization.
P = Positive. Say something positive about the idea. What is good about it? How might it solve a problem or make a situation better?
N = Negative. State any negatives that you think the idea might entail. Might it prove expensive? Difficult to implement? Is it directed at insignificant issues?

It's often easier to analyze an idea when you follow specific steps; in this way there's less likelihood that you'll omit some crucial element in the process. Try using PIP'N the next time you hear about a new idea; say, in conversation or in a small group. For practice, try PIP'N on the PIP'N technique itself: (1) Paraphrase the PIP'N technique; (2) say why the technique is interesting; (3) say something positive about it; and (4) say something negative about it.

10.3 Small Group Creativity. Studies find that persons high in communication apprehension are generally less effective in idea-generation groups than those who are low in apprehension (Comadena, 1984; Cragan & Wright, 1990; Jablin, 1981). Why do you think this is so?

10.4 Group Norms. What norms govern your class in human communication? What norms govern your family? What norms govern your place of work? Do you have any difficulty with these norms?

10.5 Chat Groups. In research on chat groups, it was found that people were more likely to comment on a participant's message when that message was negative than when it was positive (Rollman, Krug, & Parente, 2000). Do you find this to be true? If so, why do you think this occurs?

10.6 Developing Criteria. What type of criteria would an advertising agency use in evaluating a campaign to sell soap? A university, in evaluating a new multicultural curriculum? Parents, in evaluating a preschool for their children?

10.7 Uses and Gratifications. One study identified seven gratifications you derive from online communication: being in a virtual community, seeking information, aesthetic experience, financial compensation, diversion, personal status, and maintaining relationships (Song, LaRose, Eastin, & Lin, 2004). How would you describe the gratifications you receive from online groups?

LogOn! MyCommunicationLab www.mycommunicationlab.com

Throughout this chapter, there are icons in the margin that highlight media content for selected topics. Go to **MyCommunicationLab** for additional materials on the nature and types of small group communication. Here you'll find flashcards to help you learn key communication terms, videos that illustrate a variety of concepts, additional exercises, and discussions to help you continue your study of small group communication.

11 MEMBERS AND LEADERS

CHAPTER TOPICS	CHAPTER OBJECTIVES
In this chapter you'll explore the following major topics:	**After reading this chapter you should be able to:**
MEMBERS IN SMALL GROUP COMMUNICATION	11.1 Define *group task roles, group building and maintenance roles,* and *individual roles* and give examples of each; and apply the suggestions for member participation.
LEADERS IN SMALL GROUP COMMUNICATION	11.2 Define *leadership* and distinguish among the traits, functional, transformation, and situation approaches; and apply the suggestions for effective group leadership.
MEMBERSHIP, LEADERSHIP, AND CULTURE	11.3 Explain the impact of culture on small group membership and leadership behavior.

Groups without leaders are rare.

Throughout your life, you'll participate in a wide variety of groups—as a member of a work group, as a part of a social or neighborhood group, or as a player on a team. Probably you'll also lead some of these social or work groups, and your leadership responsibilities are likely to increase as you rise in the group hierarchy. In this chapter we continue our coverage of small group communication with a focus on members and leaders. Let's look at small group membership first.

11.1 MEMBERS IN SMALL GROUP COMMUNICATION

You can view membership in small group communication situations from a variety of perspectives—in terms of the roles that members serve, the types of contributions they make, and the principles for more effective participation.

Member Roles

Each of us serves many **roles,** patterns of behaviors that we customarily perform and that we're expected by others to perform. Javier, for example, is a part-time college student, father, bookkeeper, bowling team captain, and sometime poet. That is, he acts as a student—attends class, reads textbooks, takes exams, and does the things we expect of college students. He also performs those behaviors associated with fathers, bookkeepers, and so on. In a similar way, you develop ways of behaving when participating in small groups. Before reading about the roles of members in small groups, respond to each of the following statements by noting True (if the statement is often or generally true of your small group behavior and False (if the statement is often or generally untrue of your membership behavior.

_____ **1.** I present new ideas and suggest new strategies.
_____ **2.** I ask for facts and opinions.
_____ **3.** I stimulate the group.
_____ **4.** I give examples and try to look for positive solutions.
_____ **5.** I positively reinforce group members.
_____ **6.** I try to reconcile differences.
_____ **7.** I go along with the other members.
_____ **8.** I offer compromises as ways of resolving conflict.
_____ **9.** I express negative evaluation of the actions and feelings of the group members.
_____ **10.** I try to run the group.
_____ **11.** I express personal perspectives and feelings.
_____ **12.** I express confusion or deprecate myself.

As you'll see as you read further, these behaviors are characteristic of the three general types of group member roles—a classification introduced in early research (Benne & Sheats, 1948) and still widely used today (Beebe & Masterson, 2012). Statements 1–4 refer to your taking on group task roles, and statements 5–8 refer to your taking on group building and maintenance roles. Both of these types of roles are productive. Statements 9–12, however, refer to your taking an individual rather than a group focus; these are the behaviors that often work against the group's achieving its goals. As you read the following sections on member roles, try to relate these roles to your own behavior or to group behavior you've witnessed. Then ask yourself what worked and what didn't work. What roles were productive, and what roles were unproductive?

Group Task Roles

Group task roles are those that help the group focus more specifically on achieving its goals. In serving any of these roles, you act not as an isolated individual, but rather as a part of the larger whole. The needs and goals of the group dictate the task roles you serve. As an effective group member you would serve several of these functions.

Some people, however, lock into a few specific roles. For example, one person may almost always seek the opinions of others, another may concentrate on elaborating details, still another on evaluating suggestions. Usually this kind of single focus is counterproductive. It's usually better for group task roles to be spread more evenly so each member may serve many roles. The 12 specific group task roles are the following.

- **Initiator–contributor.** Presents new ideas or new perspectives on old ideas, suggests new goals, or proposes new procedures or organizational strategies.
- **Information seeker.** Asks for facts and opinions and seeks clarification of the issues being discussed.
- **Opinion seeker.** Tries to discover the values underlying the group's task.
- **Information giver.** Presents facts and opinions to the group members.
- **Opinion giver.** Presents values and opinions and tries to spell out what the values of the group should be.

- **Elaborator.** Gives examples and tries to work out possible solutions, trying to build on what others have said.
- **Coordinator.** Spells out relationships among ideas and suggested solutions and coordinates the activities of the different members.
- **Orienter.** Summarizes what has been said and addresses the direction the group is taking.
- **Evaluator–critic.** Evaluates the group's decisions, questions the logic or practicality of the suggestions, and thus provides the group with both positive and negative feedback.
- **Energizer.** Stimulates the group to greater activity.
- **Procedural technician.** Takes care of various mechanical duties such as distributing group materials and arranging seating.
- **Recorder.** Writes down the group's activities, suggestions, and decisions; he or she serves as the memory of the group.

Group Building and Maintenance Roles

Most groups focus not only on the task to be performed but also on interpersonal relationships among members. If the group is to function effectively and if members are to be both satisfied and productive, these relationships must be nourished. When these needs are not met, group members may become irritable when the group process gets bogged down, may engage in frequent conflicts, or may find the small group process as a whole unsatisfying. The group and its members need the same kind of support that individuals need. The **group building and maintenance roles** serve this general function. Group building and maintenance functions are broken down into seven specific roles.

- **Encourager.** Supplies members with positive reinforcement in the form of social approval or praise for their ideas.
- **Harmonizer.** Mediates differences among group members.
- **Compromiser.** Offers compromises as a way to resolve conflicts between his or her ideas and those of others.
- **Gatekeeper–expediter.** Keeps the channels of communication open by reinforcing the efforts of others.
- **Standard setter.** Proposes standards for the functioning of the group or for its solutions.
- **Group observer and commentator.** Keeps a record of the proceedings and uses this in the group's evaluation of itself.
- **Follower.** Goes along with the members of the group, passively accepts the ideas of others, and functions more as an audience than as an active member.

Individual Roles

The group task and group building and maintenance roles just considered are productive roles; they aid the group in achieving its goals. **Individual roles,** on the other hand, are counterproductive; they hinder the group's productivity and member satisfaction, largely because they focus on serving individual rather than group needs. As you read about these eight specific types, consider what you'd say to each of them if you were a member or a leader of the group and wanted to deal with this dysfunctional role-playing but, at the same time, didn't want to alienate the individual or the group.

- **Aggressor.** Expresses negative evaluation of the actions or feelings of the group members; he or she attacks the group or the problem being considered.
- **Blocker.** Provides negative feedback, is disagreeable, and opposes other members or suggestions regardless of their merit.
- **Recognition seeker.** Tries to focus attention on himself or herself rather than on the task at hand, boasting about his or her own accomplishments.
- **Self-confessor.** Expresses his or her own feelings and personal perspectives rather than focusing on the group.
- **Playboy/playgirl.** Jokes around without any regard for the group process.
- **Dominator.** Tries to run the group or the group members by pulling rank, flattering members of the group, or acting the role of the boss.
- **Help seeker.** Expresses insecurity or confusion or deprecates himself or herself and thus tries to gain sympathy from the other members.
- **Special interest pleader.** Disregards the goals of the group and pleads the case of some special group.

As you might expect, your tendency to play group versus individual roles will be influenced by your culture—and especially by your individualist or collectivist orientation, as discussed in Chapter 2, and your power orientation, as discussed in Chapter 10.

Watch at **MyCommunicationLab**
Video: "Politics of Sociology"

Interaction Process Analysis

Another way of looking at the contributions group members make is through **interaction process analysis** (IPA), developed by Robert Bales (1950). In this system you analyze the contributions of members under four general categories: (1) social-emotional positive contributions, (2) social-emotional negative contributions, (3) attempted answers, and (4) questions. Each of these four areas contains three sub-divisions, yielding a total of 12 categories into which you can classify group members' contributions (Table 11.1). Note that the categories under social-emotional positive are the natural opposites of those under social-emotional negative, and those under attempted answers are the natural opposites of those under questions. You may want to try out Bales's IPA system by listening to a small group discussion or a televised situation comedy or drama and recording the interactions using Bales's IPA.

Both the member role classification and the IPA categories are useful for analyzing the contributions members make in small group situations. When you look at member contributions through these systems, you can see, for example, if one member is locked into a particular role or if the group process is breaking down because too many people are serving individual rather than group goals or because social-emotional negative comments dominate the discussion. You should also be in a better position to offer improvement suggestions for individual members based on this analysis.

Member Functions and Skills

For another perspective on group membership, let's consider some of the functions and skills for effective participation in small group communication.

Be Group or Team Oriented

In the small group you're a member of a team, a larger whole. As a group your task is to pool your talents, knowledge, and insights so as to arrive at a better solution than any one person could have developed. This call for group orientation is not to be taken as a suggestion that members abandon their individuality or give up their personal values or beliefs for the sake of the group, however. Individuality with a group orientation is what is advocated here.

Center Conflict on Issues

It's particularly important in the small group to center conflict on issues rather than on personalities. When you disagree, make it clear that your disagreement is with the solution suggested or with the ideas expressed, not with the person who expressed them. Similarly, when someone disagrees with what you say, don't take it as a personal attack. Instead, view this as an opportunity to discuss issues from an alternative point of view.

TABLE 11.1 INTERACTION PROCESS ANALYSIS FORM

The names of participants appear in the top spaces, as shown by the examples here. In the column under each participant's name, you place a slash mark for each contribution in each of the 12 categories. (Based on Robert Bales, 1950.)

		Joe	Judy	Liz	Mike	Peg
Social-Emotional Positive Contributions	Shows solidarity					
	Shows tension release					
	Shows agreement					
Social-Emotional Negative Contributions	Shows disagreement					
	Shows tension					
	Shows antagonism					
Attempted Answers	Gives suggestions					
	Gives opinions					
	Gives information					
Questions	Asks for suggestions					
	Asks for opinions					
	Asks for information					

Be Critically Open-Minded

Because the most effective and creative solutions often emerge from a combination of ideas, approach small group situations with flexibility; come to the group with ideas and information but without firmly formulated conclusions. Advance any solutions or conclusions tentatively rather than with certainty. Be willing to alter your suggestions and revise them in light of the discussion.

Beware of Social Loafing

Visualize yourself in a rope-pulling contest—you need to successfully pull the members of the other side into the pond or they will pull you. With this vision in mind, consider whether you would exert more effort if you were alone or if you were part of a group of five or six. The concept of **social loafing** resulted from experiments like this that measured the amount of effort people actually exerted alone versus in groups; it holds that you exert less effort when you're a part of the group than when alone (Latané, Williams, & Harkins, 2006). Being aware of this tendency is a useful first step in combating it. It's often an unproductive group tendency that leads to less productive group interactions and decisions. And it is probably noticed by others and so hurts you professionally. Some of the factors that influence social loafing and corresponding correctives are identified in Table 11.2.

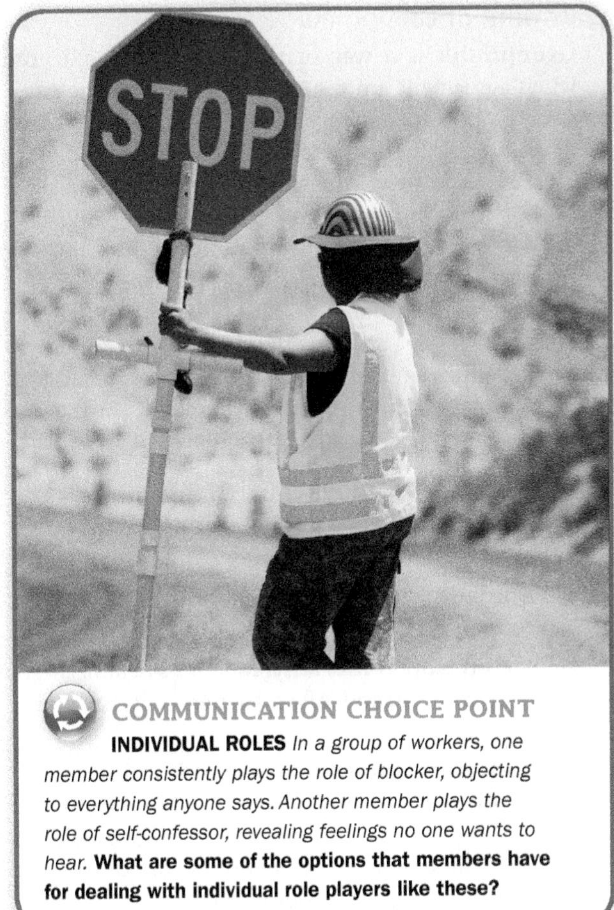

COMMUNICATION CHOICE POINT
INDIVIDUAL ROLES *In a group of workers, one member consistently plays the role of blocker, objecting to everything anyone says. Another member plays the role of self-confessor, revealing feelings no one wants to hear.* **What are some of the options that members have for dealing with individual role players like these?**

Ensure Understanding

Make sure that your ideas are understood by all participants. If something is worth saying, it's worth saying clearly. When in doubt, ask: "Is that clear?" "Did I explain that clearly?" Make sure, too, that you understand fully the contributions of other members, especially before you take issue with them. In fact, as explained in Chapter 10, it's often wise to preface any extended disagreement with some kind of paraphrase to give the other person the opportunity to clarify, deny, or otherwise alter what was said. For example, you might say, "As I understand it, you want to exclude freshmen from playing on the football team. Is that correct? I disagree with that idea, and I'd like to explain why I think that would be a mistake."

TABLE 11.2 SOCIAL LOAFING

Here are a few factors that influence the likelihood of social loafing to occur and some correctives (Kenrick, Neuberg, & Cialdini, 2010).

Social loafing is more likely to occur when:	Corrective Strategies
An individual group member's contributions cannot be easily identified.	Make contributions easily identifiable and make members aware of this.
The punishment for poor performance is insignificant.	Reward excellent performance and/or punish poor performance.
The group lacks cohesion.	Stress the importance of being part of a group or team; follow the suggestions for membership and leadership.
The task has little personal importance.	Stress the personal connection between the members of the group and the task.

Beware of Groupthink

Groupthink is a way of thinking that people use when agreement among members has become excessively important. Groupthink is most likely to occur when there is high stress, when like-minded individuals are isolated from others, and when there is an especially strong and opinionated leader. Overemphasis on agreement among members tends to shut out realistic and logical analysis of a problem or of possible alternatives (Janis, 1983; Mullen, Tara, Salas, & Driskell, 1994). The following symptoms should help you recognize groupthink in groups you observe or participate in (Janis, 1983; Richmond, McCroskey, & McCroskey, 2005; Schafer & Crichlow, 1996).

- **Illusion of invulnerability.** Group members think the group and its members are invulnerable, that they are virtually beyond being harmed.
- **Avoidance.** Members create rationalizations to avoid dealing with warnings or threats.
- **Assumption of morality.** Members believe their group is moral and, often, that any opposition is immoral.
- **Intolerance of differences of opinion.** Those opposed to the group are perceived in simplistic, stereotyped ways, and group pressure is applied to any member who expresses doubts or questions the group's arguments or proposals.
- **Self-censorship.** Members censor their own doubts.
- **Assumption of unanimity.** Group members believe that all members are in unanimous agreement, whether this is stated or not. This belief is encouraged, of course, by members censoring their own doubts and not allowing differences of opinion to be discussed.
- **Gatekeeping.** Group members emerge whose function it is to guard the information that gets to other members, especially when it may create diversity of opinion.
- **Peer pressure.** Groupthinkers pressure others to go along with the group and not to express any disagreement.

Here are three suggestions for combating groupthink.

1. When too-simple solutions are offered to problems, try to illustrate (with specific examples, if possible) for the group members how the complexity of the problem is not going to yield to the solutions offered.
2. When you feel that members are not expressing their doubts about the group or its decisions, encourage members to voice disagreement. Ask members to play devil's advocate, to test the adequacy of the solution. Or, if members resist, do it yourself. Similarly, if you feel there is unexpressed disagreement, ask specifically if anyone disagrees. If you still get no response, it may be helpful to ask everyone to write his or her comments anonymously, then read them aloud to the group.
3. To combat the group pressure toward agreement, reward members who do voice disagreement or doubt. Say, for example, "That's a good argument; we need to hear more about the potential problems of this proposal. Does anyone else see any problems?"

Explore at **MyCommunicationLab** **Activity:** "Enhancing Groups"

A summary of these membership functions and skills appears in Table 11.3.

COMMUNICATION CHOICE POINT
ASSERTING YOURSELF IN A GROUP *In your casual conversations with groups of friends as well as at work meetings, people consistently ignore your cues that you want to say something. And when you do manage to say something, no one reacts. You're determined to change this situation.* **Thinking back to the discussion of assertiveness (pages 105–106) and power (pages 215–216), what are some of the things you can do to speak more assertively and more powerfully? What are some of the things you'd be sure to avoid doing or saying?**

From Member to Leader

Throughout your small group experiences, you'll serve the role of member most often. In many cases, groups have no appointed leader. In these situations, one member often emerges as leader and becomes the de facto leader. Here are a few behaviors that seem to contribute to a member emerging as leader.

- The member/leader listens to all members equally and in the process gives positive listening cues, for example, head nods and minimal verbal responses like "I see" or "yes" (without taking over the role of speaker).
- The member/leader gives positive affiliative cues; the behaviors demonstrate a liking for the members and would include smiling, making eye contact when the person is talking, and maintaining an open posture.
- The member/leader is prepared and demonstrates this with an in-depth knowledge of the issues and also a knowledge of the members—who they are and what they do, for example.
- The member/leader positively reinforces other members by acknowledging their contributions with both verbal and nonverbal responses as appropriate.
- The member/leader shows flexible strength. This person has opinions and doesn't hesitate to voice them but is also flexible; this person is neither a Gumby nor a stone wall.
- The member/leader is responsive to conversational signals from other members.
- The member/leader is culturally sensitive and avoids all sorts of stereotypes and -isms. If the group is of even moderate size, such remarks are sure to offend someone.
- The member/leader displays the traits associated with leadership, for example, honesty, dominance, and cooperativeness.
- The member/leader focuses criticisms and conflict on issues rather than on people.
- The member/leader is fair and treats others and their positions as important to the group.

11.2 LEADERS IN SMALL GROUP COMMUNICATION

Leadership is defined in two very different ways in research and theory.

- Leadership is the process of influencing the thoughts, feelings, and behaviors of group members and establishing the direction that others follow; leadership and influence are parts of the same skill.
- Leadership is the process of empowering others; the leader is the person who helps others to maximize their potential and to take control of their lives.

These two definitions are not mutually exclusive; in fact, most effective leaders do both; they influence and they empower. As you read the remaining discussion of leadership, keep these two definitions in mind and see leadership as embodying both power and empowerment.

In many small groups one person serves as leader. In other groups, leadership may be shared by several persons. In some cases a person may be appointed

TABLE 11.3

In A Nutshell A summary of some membership functions and skills

Membership Functions and Skills	Specifically
Be Group or Team Oriented	Avoid trying to dominate the group or its decisions.
Center Conflict on Issues	Focus on the content issues but don't ignore the personality conflicts.
Be Critically Open-Minded	Be open, especially to ideas you may disagree with, and be critical even of ideas that you do agree with.
Beware of Social Loafing	Groups work best when members pull their own weight.
Ensure Understanding	Ask periodically if what you're saying is clear.
Beware of Groupthink	It's easy to fall into this so be careful; when there is too much agreeing, there is probably too little thinking.

the leader or may serve as leader because of her or his position within the company or hierarchy. In other cases the leader may emerge as the group proceeds in fulfilling its functions or may be elected leader by the group members. Two significant factors exert considerable influence on who emerges as group leader. One is the extent of active participation: The person who talks the most is more likely to emerge as leader (Mullen, Salas, & Driskell, 1989; Shaw & Gouran, 1990). The second factor is effective listening: Members who listen effectively will emerge as leaders more often than those who don't (Bechler & Johnson, 1995; Johnson & Bechler, 1998).

The **emergent leader** performs the duties of leadership, though not asked or expected to, and gradually becomes recognized by the members as the group's leader. And because this person has now proved herself or himself an effective leader, it's not surprising that this emergent leader often becomes the designated leader for future groups.

The role of the leader or leaders is vital to the well-being and effectiveness of the group. Even in leaderless groups in which all members are equal, leadership functions must still be served.

Myths about Leadership

As with many important concepts, beliefs about leadership have grown. Some of these beliefs are erroneous and need to be recognized as such. Here are just three myths about leadership offered by—and here paraphrased from—small group theorists (Bennis & Nanus, 2003).

- Myth: The skills of leadership are rare. Actually, all of us have the potential for leadership; and, of course, there are millions of leaders throughout the world who are serving a variety of functions in government, business, education, and countless other fields.
- Myth: Leaders are born. Actually, the major leadership skills can be learned by just about everyone. No specific genetic endowment is necessary. We all can improve our leadership abilities.
- Myth: All leaders are charismatic. Actually, only some leaders are. According to one survey of leaders (Bennis & Nanus, 2003), some were short and some were tall, some were articulate and some inarticulate, and some dressed well and some poorly. They were of all types and personalities.

me•di•a lit•er•a•cy *noun* ability to understand, interact with, and create media messages

EXPANDING MEDIA LITERACY
The Knowledge Gap

The *knowledge gap* refers to the difference in knowledge between one group and another; it's the difference between those who have a great deal of knowledge about some subject and those who have significantly less. Much of the research in this area has focused on the influence of the media in widening this knowledge gap though it is perhaps even more applicable to computer-mediated communication (Severin, 1988; Tichenor, Donohue, & Olien, 1970; Viswanath & Finnegan, 1995).

Information is valuable; it brings wealth and power. It gives you the means you need to get a high-paying job, to live a healthy life, to plan for retirement, or to accomplish just about any task you set for yourself (Mastin, 1998).

But information is expensive, and not everyone has equal access to it. This is especially true as we live more of our lives in cyberspace. The new communication technologies—computers, cell phone, e-book readers, high-speed Internet connections, satellite and cable television, for example—are major ways for gaining information. Better-educated people have the money to own and the skills to master the new technologies and thus acquire more information. Less-educated people don't have the money to own or the skills to master the new technologies and thus cannot acquire more information. Thus, the educated have the means for becoming even better educated, and the gap widens.

You also see the knowledge gap when you compare different cultures. Developed countries, for example, have the new technologies in schools and offices, and people in these countries can afford to buy their own computers and satellite systems. Access to the new technologies helps these countries develop even further. Developing countries, with significantly less financial resources, have less access to such technologies and, therefore, cannot experience the same gain in knowledge and information as those with significantly greater access.

Become more mindful of the knowledge gap as it operates around you—in your community or school or nationally and internationally. Consider next what you might do—as an individual—to address the inequities caused by the knowledge gap.

Approaches to Leadership

Not surprisingly, leadership has been the focus of considerable attention from theorists and researchers, who have used numerous approaches to understand this particular communication behavior. Before reading about these approaches, respond to the following statements about how you see yourself as a leader.

I generally see myself as one who is:

1. generally popular with group members.
2. knowledgeable about the topics and subjects discussed.
3. dependable.
4. effective in establishing group goals.
5. competent in giving directions.
6. capable of energizing group members.
7. charismatic (dynamic, engaging, powerful).
8. empowering of group members.
9. moral and honest.
10. skilled in balancing the concerns of getting the task done and satisfying group members' personal needs.
11. flexible in adjusting leadership style on the basis of the unique situation.
12. able to delegate responsibility.

These statements were presented to encourage you to look at yourself in terms of the four approaches to leadership that will be discussed. Statements 1–3 refer to the traits approach to leadership, which defines a leader as a person who possesses certain qualities. Statements 4–6 refer to the functional approach, which defines a leader as a person who performs certain functions. Statements 7–9 refer to the transformational approach, which defines a leader as a person who inspires the group members to become the best they can be. Statements 10–12 refer to the situational approach, which defines a leader as someone who can adjust his or her style to balance the needs of the specific situation. As you read the remainder of this chapter and the rest of the book, try to identify specific skills and competencies you might learn that would enable you to increase your scores on all four approaches to leadership. Also, try searching the Web for information on "leadership" as well as, say, "business leadership" and "political leaders."

Traits Approach

The **traits approach to leadership** argues that leaders must possess certain qualities if they're to function effectively. Some of the traits found to be associated with leadership are intelligence, dominance, honesty, foresight, altruism, popularity, sociability, cooperativeness, knowledge, and dependability (Hackman & Johnson, 1991). The problem with the traits approach is that the specific qualities called for will vary with the situation, with the members, and with the culture in which the leader functions. Thus, for example, the leader's knowledge and personality are generally significant factors; but for some groups a knowledge of financial issues and a serious personality might be effective, whereas for other groups a knowledge of design and a more humorous personality might be effective.

Functional Approach

The **functional approach to leadership** focuses on what the leader should do in a given situation. We have already considered some of these functions in the discussion of group membership, which identified group roles. Other functions found to be associated with leadership are setting group goals, giving direction to group members, and summarizing the group's progress (Schultz, 1996). Still other functions are identified in the section titled "Functions and Skills of Leadership," later in this chapter.

Transformational Approach

In the **transformational approach to leadership,** the leader elevates the group's members, enabling them not only to accomplish the group task but also to emerge as more empowered individuals (Li & Shi, 2003). At the center of the transformational approach is the concept of charisma—that quality of an individual that makes us believe in or want to follow him or her. Gandhi, Martin Luther King Jr., and John F. Kennedy may be cited as examples of transformational leaders. These leaders were seen as role models of what they asked of their members, were perceived as extremely competent and able leaders, and articulated moral goals (Northouse, 1997). We'll return to this concept of charisma in the discussion of credibility in Chapter 18.

Situational Approach

The **situational approach to leadership** focuses on the two major responsibilities of the leader—accomplishing the task at hand and ensuring the satisfaction of the members—and recognizes that the leader's style must vary on the basis of the specific situation. Just as you adjust your interpersonal style in conversation or your motivational appeals in public speaking on the basis of the particular situation, so you must adjust your leadership style. Leadership effectiveness, then, depends on combining the concerns for task and people according to the specifics of the situation. Some situations will call for

the•o•ry *noun* statement of explanation, formulation of relationships, reasoned generalization

UNDERSTANDING THEORY AND RESEARCH
Styles of Leadership

Small group communication researchers distinguish three basic types of group leaders: laissez-faire, democratic, and authoritarian (Bennis & Nanus, 2003; Hackman & Johnson, 1991).

The **laissez-faire leader** takes no initiative in directing or suggesting alternative courses of action. Rather, this leader allows the group to develop and progress on its own—even allowing it to make its own mistakes. The laissez-faire leader answers questions and provides information only when specifically asked. During the group interaction, this leader neither compliments nor criticizes the group's members or their progress. Generally, this type of leadership results in a satisfied but inefficient group.

The **democratic leader** provides direction but allows the group to develop and progress the way its members wish. This leader encourages group members to determine their own goals and procedures and works to stimulate the self-direction and self-actualization of group members. Unlike the laissez-faire leader, the democratic leader does contribute suggestions and does comment on member and group performance. Generally, this form of leadership results in both satisfaction and efficiency.

The **authoritarian leader,** the opposite of the laissez-faire leader, determines group policies and makes decisions without consulting or securing agreement from the members. This leader discourages member-to-member communication but encourages communication from member to leader. The authoritarian leader is concerned with getting the group to accept his or her decisions rather than making its own. If the authoritarian leader is competent, the group may be highly efficient, but its members are likely to be less personally satisfied.

Working with Theories and Research

Which leadership style—say, in a classroom exercise with other students—are you likely to feel most comfortable using? What leadership style would you have difficulty working with as a group member?

high concentration on task issues, but will need little in the way of people encouragement. For example, a group of scientists working on AIDS research would probably need a leader primarily to provide them with the needed information to accomplish their task. They would be self-motivating and would probably need little in the way of social and emotional encouragement. On the other hand, a group of recovering alcoholics might require leadership that stressed the social and emotional needs of the members.

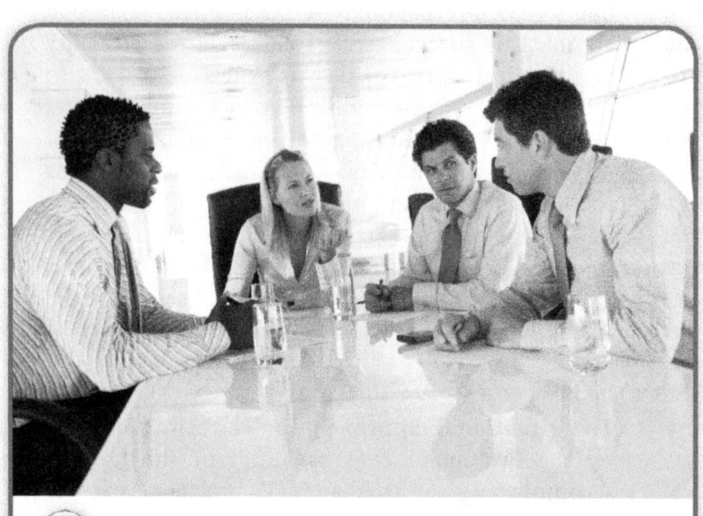

COMMUNICATION CHOICE POINT

SITUATIONAL LEADERSHIP *You're a member of an introductory Internet design team whose leader uses a delegating style that isn't working. Group members are all new to this business and need more direction and guidance. The group members have elected you to clue the leader into appropriate and inappropriate styles.* **What are some options for dealing with this problem? What preliminary information might you want to collect before saying anything? What might you say? Where would you say it?**

An interesting extension of the situational approach portrays four basic leadership styles (Hersey, Blanchard, & Johnson, 2001). This theory claims that groups differ in their degree of readiness. A group that contains members who are knowledgeable and experienced and can demonstrate their skill at a sustained and acceptable level have a high degree of readiness. Because of that readiness, group members are able to set realistic and attainable goals. Continued success and supportive behavior from others tend to build confidence that leads to higher levels of readiness where group members are willing to appropriately take responsibility for their decisions. A group this high in readiness is characterized by members who are both willing and able to perform the task in question. This is a critical point. A group or individual's readiness varies with the task; an individual may be skilled at—and more than happy to engage

the•o•ry *noun* statement of explanation, formulation of relationships, reasoned generalization

UNDERSTANDING THEORY AND RESEARCH
Attila's Theory of Leadership

From a totally different perspective, consider these leadership qualities, paraphrased from Wes Roberts's *Leadership Secrets of Attila the Hun* (1987), a study of the warrior who united many of the nomadic tribes in first-century Asia.

- **Empathy.** Leaders must develop an appreciation for and an understanding of other cultures and the values of their group members.
- **Courage.** Leaders should be fearless and should have the courage to complete their assignments; they must not complain about obstacles or be discouraged by adversity.
- **Dependability.** Leaders must be dependable in carrying out their responsibilities; leaders must also be willing to depend on their group members to accomplish matters they themselves can't oversee.
- **Credibility.** Leaders must be seen as believable by both friends and enemies; they must possess the integrity and intelligence needed to secure and communicate accurate information.
- **Stewardship.** Leaders must be caretakers of their group members' interests and well-being; they must guide and reward subordinates.

Working with Theories and Research

Of these five qualities, which do you see as being the most important to you in your personal and social life? What about in your business and professional life?

in—discussions about food and exercise, but less than amenable when it comes to talking about finances.

Effective leadership, then, depends on the leader's assessment of the group's ability and willingness to do the task. To complicate matters even more, the readiness of the group will also change as the group develops or regresses over time—so the style of leadership will have to change in response to the changes in the group. The different styles of leadership, their focuses, and their uses are presented in Table 11.4 on page 238.

Explore at MyCommunicationLab Activity: "Leadership Style"

Functions and Skills of Leadership

In relatively formal small group situations, as when politicians plan a strategy, advertisers discuss a campaign, or teachers consider educational methods, the leader has several specific functions. These functions—a mixture of task and people functions—are not the exclusive property of the leader. Nevertheless, when there's a specific leader, he or she is expected to perform them.

As you read these functions, keep in mind that an effective leader needs not only knowledge of the topic of the discussion but also communication competence—the ability to effectively use the group process as well as to use the varied communication skills that are discussed throughout this text. One of the most important of these skills is the ability to manage conflict, a topic we discuss in detail in Chapter 13.

Get Ready

It often falls to the leader to provide members with necessary materials prior to the meeting. Prediscussion functions may include, for example, arranging a convenient meeting time and place; informing members of the purposes and goals of the meeting; providing them with materials they should read or view; and recommending that they come to the meeting with, for example, general ideas or specific proposals.

Similarly, groups form gradually and need to be eased into meaningful discussion. Diverse members should not be expected to sit down and discuss a problem without becoming familiar with one another. Put more generally, the leader is responsible for any preparations and preliminaries necessary to ensure an orderly and productive group experience.

Ensure Member Satisfaction

Group members have different psychological needs and wants; in fact, many people enter groups primarily to satisfy these personal concerns. Even though a group may, for example, deal with economic problems, the members may have come together for reasons that are more psychological than economic. If a group is to be effective, it must meet not only the surface purposes of the group but also the underlying or interpersonal purposes that motivated many of the members to come together in the first place.

Depending on the specific people involved, special adjustments may have to be made to accommodate group members with disabilities. You can easily adapt

TABLE 11.4 **LEADERSHIP STYLES**

This table presents four different leadership styles that provide the highest probability of successfully and effectively influencing the behaviors of others based on their level of readiness for a specific task. As you can tell from these descriptions, the leader exerts more control with groups that are new or that lack knowledge (telling and selling) and less control with more established, more knowledgeable groups (participating and delegating).

Style	Leadership Focus	Uses
Telling Style	This leader focuses almost exclusively on the task and offers little, if any, relationship support.	Appropriate for a group that lacks knowledge of the issues involved and needs the direct guidance of a leader who tells the members what they should do.
Selling Style	This leader is a persuasive one, giving specific guidance on the task and also relationship support. The aim is to get the group members to "buy into" the ideas and to do as directed.	Appropriate for a group that is trying hard but still lacks the needed skills or information to accomplish their task.
Participating Style	This leader relies heavily on communicating, facilitating, and encouraging group members. This leader participates in the group's problem solving but provides little direction.	Appropriate for groups that know what to do but may not be so willing to do it.
Delegating Style	This leader monitors and observes, rather than provides direction or relationship support.	Appropriate for groups that know what to do and are eager to do it.

to group situations the principles identified in the special TIPS tables in Chapters 2, 4, 6, and 7 that deal with communication between people with and without disabilities.

Activate the Group Agenda

Most groups have an agenda. An **agenda** is simply a list of the tasks the group wishes to complete. It's an itemized listing of what the group should devote its attention to. In some cases the supervisor or consultant or CEO prepares the agenda and simply presents it to the group; the group is then expected to follow the agenda item by item. In other cases the group will develop its own agenda, usually as its first or second order of business. Generally, the more formal the group, the more important the agenda becomes. In informal groups the agenda may simply consist of general ideas in the minds of the members (for example, "We'll review the class assignment and then make plans for the weekend"). In formal business groups the agenda will be much more detailed and explicit. Some agendas specify not only the items that must be covered but also the order in which they should be covered and even the amount of time that should be devoted to each item.

Promote Group Interaction

Many groups need some prodding to interact. Perhaps the group is newly formed and the members feel a bit uneasy with one another. One of the leader's functions is to stimulate the members to interact. A leader also serves this function when members act as individuals rather than as a group. In this instance the leader needs to focus the members on their *group* task.

Suppose that you are leading a group and have successfully stimulated group interaction, but now the discussion begins to drag. Your job is to prod the group to maintain effective interaction: "Do we have any additional comments on the proposal to eliminate required courses?" "What do those of you who are members of the college curriculum committee think about the English Department's proposal to restructure required courses?" "Does anyone want to make any additional comments on eliminating the minor area of concentration?" As the leader, you'll want to ensure that all members have an opportunity to express themselves.

Many individuals are egocentric and will pursue only their own interests and concerns, even in a group setting. In promoting effective group interaction, you'll need to keep all members reasonably on track. Here are a few ways you might accomplish this.

- **Ask questions.** Ask questions that focus on the specific topic at hand, especially of those who seem to be wandering off in other directions.
- **Summarize.** Interject internal summaries in which you briefly identify what has been accomplished and what the group needs to move on to next.
- **Set an agenda.** Consider setting a formal agenda (if you don't already have one) and sticking to it.
- **Focus your attention.** Focus your own attention on the topics at hand; your example will influence the behavior of the other members.

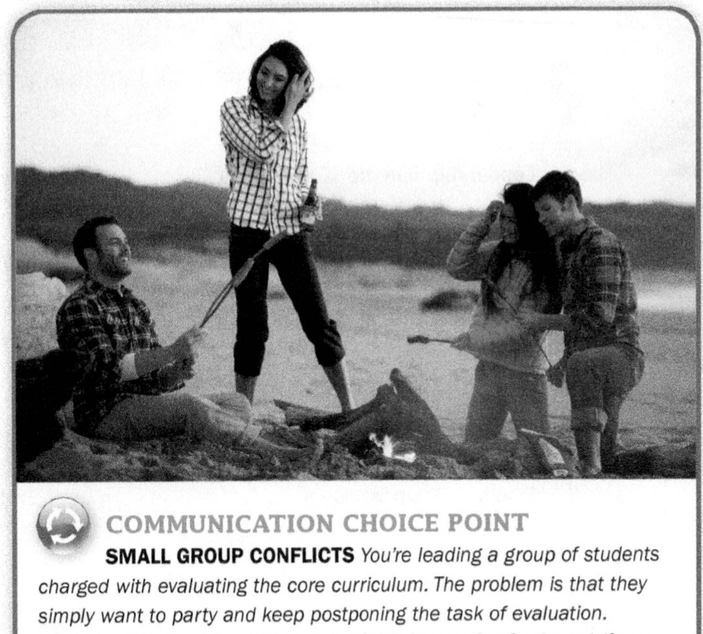

COMMUNICATION CHOICE POINT

SMALL GROUP CONFLICTS *You're leading a group of students charged with evaluating the core curriculum. The problem is that they simply want to party and keep postponing the task of evaluation.* **What are some of the things you might do as a leader to get them to focus on the task at hand?**

Empower Group Members

An important function in at least some leadership styles (though not limited to leadership) is to empower others—to help other group members (but also your relational partner, coworkers, employees, other students, or siblings) to gain increased power over themselves and their environment. Some ways to empower others include the following.

- **Raise the person's self-esteem.** Compliment, reinforce, and resist faultfinding; it doesn't benefit anyone (and in fact disempowers).
- **Share skills.** Be willing to share your skills as well as decision-making power and authority.
- **Be constructively critical.** Be willing to offer your perspective, to lend an ear to an intern's first proposal, for example. Be willing to react honestly to suggestions from all group members and not just those in high positions.
- **Encourage growth.** Encourage growth and development in all forms: academic, relational, and professional, among others. The growth and empowerment of the other person enhances your own growth and power.

Follow Up

Just as the leader is responsible for getting ready, the leader is also responsible for following up the discussion. Such follow-up functions might include summarizing the group's discussion, organizing future meetings, or presenting the group's decisions to some other group. All in all, the leader is responsible for doing whatever needs to be done to ensure that the group's experience is productive.

A brief summary of these leadership functions appears in Table 11.5 on page 240.

Watch at MyCommunicationLab Video: "Director's Cut"

11.3 MEMBERSHIP, LEADERSHIP, AND CULTURE

Not surprisingly, culture influences the ways in which group members and leaders act and are expected to act.

Individualism and Collectivism

Most research on and theories about small group communication, membership, and leadership have emerged from universities in the United States and reflect U.S. culture. For example, in the United States—and in individualist cultures generally—each group member is important. But in collectivist cultures the individual is less important; it's the *group* that is the significant entity. Individuals become fulfilled and satisfied as members of the group (Cathcart & Cathcart, 1985). In the United States, in contrast, individual fulfillment and satisfaction is attained by the individual and through his or her own efforts, not by the group.

TABLE 11.5

In A Nutshell — A summary of some leadership functions and skills

Leadership Functions and Skills	Specifically
Get Ready	Be prepared yourself and do whatever is needed to prepare members.
Ensure Member Satisfaction	Don't forget that groups consist of individuals who have needs the group is often expected to satisfy.
Activate the Group Agenda	Get the group started on its task.
Promote Group Interaction	Ask questions; reward member contributions.
Empower Group Members	Empowered members are likely to be more effective group contributors.
Follow Up	Most group deliberations or decisions need to be communicated in some way to someone.

It's often thought that because group membership and group identity are so important in collectivist cultures, it's the group that makes important decisions. Actually, this does not seem to be the case. In fact, a study of 48 (highly collectivist) Japanese organizations found that participating in decision-making groups did not give the members decision-making power. Group members were encouraged to contribute ideas, but the decision-making power was reserved for the CEO or for managers higher up the organizational ladder (Brennan, 1991).

Explore at MyCommunicationLab **Exercise:** "How Individualistic Are You?

eth·ics *noun* morality, standards of conduct, moral judgment

MAKING ETHICAL CHOICES
The Leader's Ethical Responsibilities

In addition to mastering the skills of effective and efficient leadership, the leader needs also to consider the ethical issues involved in leading a group or an organization. Because the leader is often a chairperson, CHAIR seems an appropriate acronym to help identify at least some of the characteristics of the ethical leader:

- **Concern for the welfare of their members.** Leaders who are more concerned with their own personal interests, rather than with the group task or the interpersonal needs of the members, would clearly be acting unethically.
- **Honesty.** Leaders should be honest with the group members by, for example, revealing any hidden agendas and presenting information fairly.
- **Accountability.** Leaders should take responsibility for their actions and decisions, admit making mistakes, and take corrective action when necessary.
- **Integrity.** Leaders have integrity; they take the high road. They don't lie or deceive. And they avoid any actions that might violate the basic rights of others.
- **Responsiveness.** The leader must be responsive to all members of the group or the organization.

Ethical Choice Point

You're leading a discussion among a group of high school freshmen whom you're mentoring. The topic turns to marijuana, and the students ask you directly if you smoke pot. The truth is that on occasion you do—but it's a very controlled use, and you feel that it would only destroy your credibility and lead the students to experiment with or continue smoking pot if they knew you did (something you do not want to do). At the same time, you wonder if you can ethically lie to them and tell them that you do not smoke. What is your ethical obligation in this situation? What would you do?

Member Roles

The discussion of member roles earlier in this chapter devoted an entire category to individual roles—roles adopted by individuals to satisfy individual rather than group goals. In other cultures (notably collectivist cultures) these roles probably would not even be mentioned—simply because they wouldn't be acted out often enough to deserve such extended discussion. For example, in many collectivist cultures the group orientation is too pervasive for individuals to violate it by acting as the blocker, the recognition seeker, or the dominator.

Belief Systems

In a similar way, each culture's belief system influences group members' behavior. For example, members of many Asian cultures, influenced by Confucian principles, believe that "the protruding nail gets pounded down" and are therefore not likely to voice disagreement with the majority of the group. Americans, on the other hand, influenced by the belief that "the squeaky wheel gets the grease," are more likely to voice disagreement or to act differently from other group members in order to get what they want.

Leadership Style

Each culture has its own rules of preferred and expected leadership style. In the United States the general and expected style for a group leader is democratic. Our political leaders are elected by a democratic process; similarly, boards of directors are elected by the shareholders of a corporation. In other situations, of course, leaders are chosen by those in authority. The directors choose the president of a company, and the president will normally decide who will supervise and who will be supervised within the organization. Even in this situation, however, we expect the supervisor to behave democratically—to listen to the ideas of employees, to take their views into consideration when decisions are to be made, to keep them informed of corporate developments, and generally to respect their interests. Also, we expect that leaders will be changed fairly regularly, much as we elect a president every four years and company directors each year.

The most important implication of these differences in the ways in which group leaders and members interact is to be mindful that your membership and leadership styles (and the ways you respond to the membership and leadership styles of others) are influenced by the culture in which you were raised. Consequently, when in a group with members of different cultures, be sensitive to the inevitable differences in their small group behavior. For example, a member who plays individual roles may be tolerated in many groups in the United States and in some cases may even be thought amusing and different. That same member playing the same roles in a group with a more collectivist orientation is likely to be evaluated much more negatively. Multicultural groups may find it helpful to discuss members' views of group membership and leadership and what constitutes comfortable interaction for them.

Charles has been assigned to work with a group of three other students for the service learning component of his communication class. The other members of the group have already been working together for a week when Charles joins them. He is finding that the other members consistently ignore his cues when he wants to say something. And when he does manage to say something, no one reacts. He's determined to change this situation. "Leading in Service Learning" focuses on the small group experience and especially on the varied roles that members and leaders choose to serve—some, as you'll see, are productive (and get the task done) while others are unproductive; some are likely to lead to satisfaction with the group experience while others are likely to create dissatisfaction. Log on to mycommunicationlab.com to view this video and the choices, and then answer the related discussion questions.

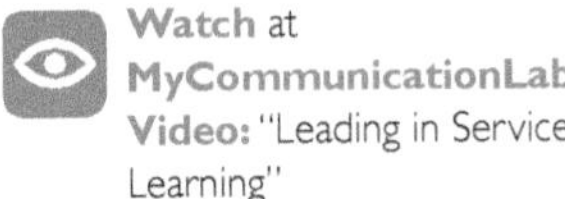

SUMMARY: MEMBERS AND LEADERS

Study and **Review** at **MyCommunicationLab**

This chapter examined the roles of members and leaders of small groups and the principles that govern effective small group interaction.

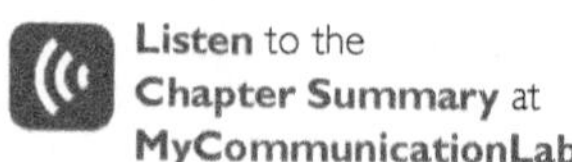

11.1 MEMBERS IN SMALL GROUP COMMUNICATION

1. A popular classification of small group member roles divides them into group task roles, group building and maintenance roles, and individual roles.
2. Twelve group task roles are: initiator–contributor, information seeker, opinion seeker, information giver, opinion giver, elaborator, coordinator, orienter, evaluator–critic, energizer, procedural technician, and recorder.
3. Seven group building and maintenance roles are: encourager, harmonizer, compromiser, gatekeeper–expediter, standard setter, group observer and commentator, and follower.
4. Eight individual roles are: aggressor, blocker, recognition seeker, self-confessor, playboy/playgirl, dominator, help seeker, and special interest pleader.
5. Interaction process analysis categorizes group members' contributions into four areas: social–emotional positive contributions, social–emotional negative contributions, attempted answers, and questions.
6. Membership functions and skills include being group oriented, centering conflict on issues, being critically open-minded, avoiding social loafing, ensuring understanding, and being careful not to fall into the groupthink trap.
7. Groupthink is a way of thinking that develops when concurrence seeking in a cohesive group overrides realistic appraisal of alternative courses of action.

11.2 LEADERS IN SMALL GROUP COMMUNICATION

8. Among the major myths about leadership are that leaders are rare, that leaders are born, and that all leaders are charismatic.
9. The traits approach to leadership focuses on personal characteristics that contribute to leadership; the functional approach centers on what the leader does (the functions the leader serves); and the transformational approach focuses on the leader's empowerment of the group members.
10. In the situational theory of leadership, leadership is seen as concerned with both accomplishing the task and serving the interpersonal needs of the members. The degree to which either concern is emphasized should depend on the specific group and the unique situation.
11. An extension of this situational approach to leadership identifies four leadership styles: the telling style, the selling style, the participating style, and the delegating style. The appropriate style to use depends on the group's level of task and relationship maturity.
12. Among the leader's functions are getting ready for the group interaction, ensuring member satisfaction, activating the group agenda, promoting group interaction, empowering group members, and following up.

11.3 MEMBERSHIP, LEADERSHIP, AND CULTURE

13. The culture in which people are raised will greatly influence the ways in which members and leaders interact in small groups.

KEY TERMS

Study and **Review** the **Flashcards** at **MyCommunicationLab**

agenda *238*
authoritarian leader *236*
delegating style *238*
democratic leader *236*
emergent leader *234*
functional approach to leadership *235*
group building and maintenance roles *229*
group task roles *228*
groupthink *232*
individual roles *229*
interaction process analysis *230*
laissez-faire leader *236*
leadership *233*
participating style *238*
roles *228*
selling style *238*
situational approach to leadership *235*
social loafing *231*
telling style *238*
traits approach to leadership *235*
transformational approach to leadership *235*

WORKING WITH MEMBERS AND LEADERS

11.1 Combating Groupthink. Groupthink prevents creativity and logical analysis; watch out for it and try to reduce its influence whenever you can. Practice this by developing specific messages you might use as a member or a leader of a group in which you see the signs of groupthink noted on the left and you wish to use the combat tactic noted in the center column.

Suspected Problem	Combat Tactic	Messages to Accomplish Your Combat Goal
Group members assume there's unanimous agreement.	Ask for a poll of opinion; survey the group members.	
Members are not expressing their doubts about the group or its decisions.	Encourage members to voice disagreement, or ask if anyone disagrees.	
There's lots of group pressure toward agreement.	Reward members who voice disagreement, or voice it yourself.	

11.2 Empowering Others. For each situation below, indicate what you might say to help empower the other person(s), using such strategies as (a) raising the other person's self-esteem; (b) listening actively and supportively; (c) being open, positive, and empathic; and (d) avoiding verbal aggressiveness or any unfair conflict strategies. As you'll experience, empowering others, far from reducing your own power, will actually increase it.

a. Your partner is having lots of difficulties—recently he lost his job, received poor grades in a night class, and started gaining a lot of weight. At the same time, you're doing extremely well. What are some of the things you can do or say that might help bring back your partner's confidence?

b. You're managing four college interns who are redesigning your company's website—three men and one woman. The men are extremely supportive of one another and regularly contribute ideas. Although equally competent, the woman doesn't contribute; she seems to lack confidence. But the objective of this redesign is to increase the number of female visitors, so you really need her input and want to empower her. What are some of your options for empowering her and thereby getting her to contribute more actively? What might you say?

c. You're a third-grade teacher. Most of the students are from the same ethnic–religious group; three, however, are from a very different group. The problem is that these three have not been included in the social groupings of the students; they're considered outsiders. As a result, these children stumble when they have to read in front of the class and make a lot of mistakes at the whiteboard (though they consistently do well in private). You want to empower these students. What do you say?

11.3 Responding to Individual Roles. One major value of small group interaction is that everyone profits from the insights of everyone else; individual roles can get in the way. For each of the five individual roles, compose a response or two that you as a leader might make in order to deal with this dysfunctional role playing. Be careful that your responses don't alienate the individual or the group.

Individual, Dysfunctional Roles	Responding to Individual Roles
The aggressor:	
The recognition seeker or self-confessor:	
The blocker:	
The special interest pleader:	
The dominator:	

11.4 Group Roles in Interpersonal Relationships. Can you identify roles that you habitually or frequently serve in certain groups? Do you serve these roles in your friendship, love, and family relationships as well?

11.5 Groupthink. Have you ever been in a group when groupthink was operating? If so, what were its symptoms? What effect did groupthink have on the process and conclusions of the group?

11.6 Leadership Style. How would you characterize the leadership style of one of your local politicians, religious leaders, college instructors, or talk show hosts? How would you characterize your own leadership style? For example, are you usually more concerned with people or with tasks? Are you more likely to be a laissez-faire, democratic, or authoritarian leader? Most important, why?

11.7 The Emergent Leader. The member with the highest rate of participation is the one most likely to be chosen group leader (Mullen, Salas, & Driskell, 1989). Do you find this to be true of the groups in which you've participated? Why do you suppose this relationship exists?

11.8 Gender Differences. Do you find that women and men respond similarly to the different leadership styles? Do women and men exercise the different leadership styles with equal facility, or are women more comfortable and more competent in certain leadership styles and men more comfortable and competent in other styles?

LogOn! MyCommunicationLab www.mycommunicationlab.com

Throughout this chapter, there are icons in the margin that highlight media content for selected topics. Go to **MyCommunicationLab** for additional materials on members and leaders of small group communication. Here you'll find flashcards to help you learn key communication terms, videos that illustrate a variety of concepts, additional exercises, and discussions to help you continue your study of members and leaders.

12 HUMAN COMMUNICATION IN THE WORKPLACE: ORGANIZATIONAL COMMUNICATION

Listen to Chapter 12 at MyCommunicationLab

CHAPTER TOPICS	CHAPTER OBJECTIVES
In this chapter you'll explore the following major topics:	**After reading this chapter you should be able to:**
ORGANIZATIONS	12.1 Define *organization* and identify its characteristics.
ORGANIZATIONAL MESSAGES	12.2 Define *formal communication*, *grapevine communication*, and *information isolation*; apply the suggestions for organizational message competence to your own workplace messages
ORGANIZATIONAL RELATIONSHIPS	12.3 Explain the nature of sexual harassment, bullying, romance, mentoring, and networking and apply the suggestions for organizational relationship competence.

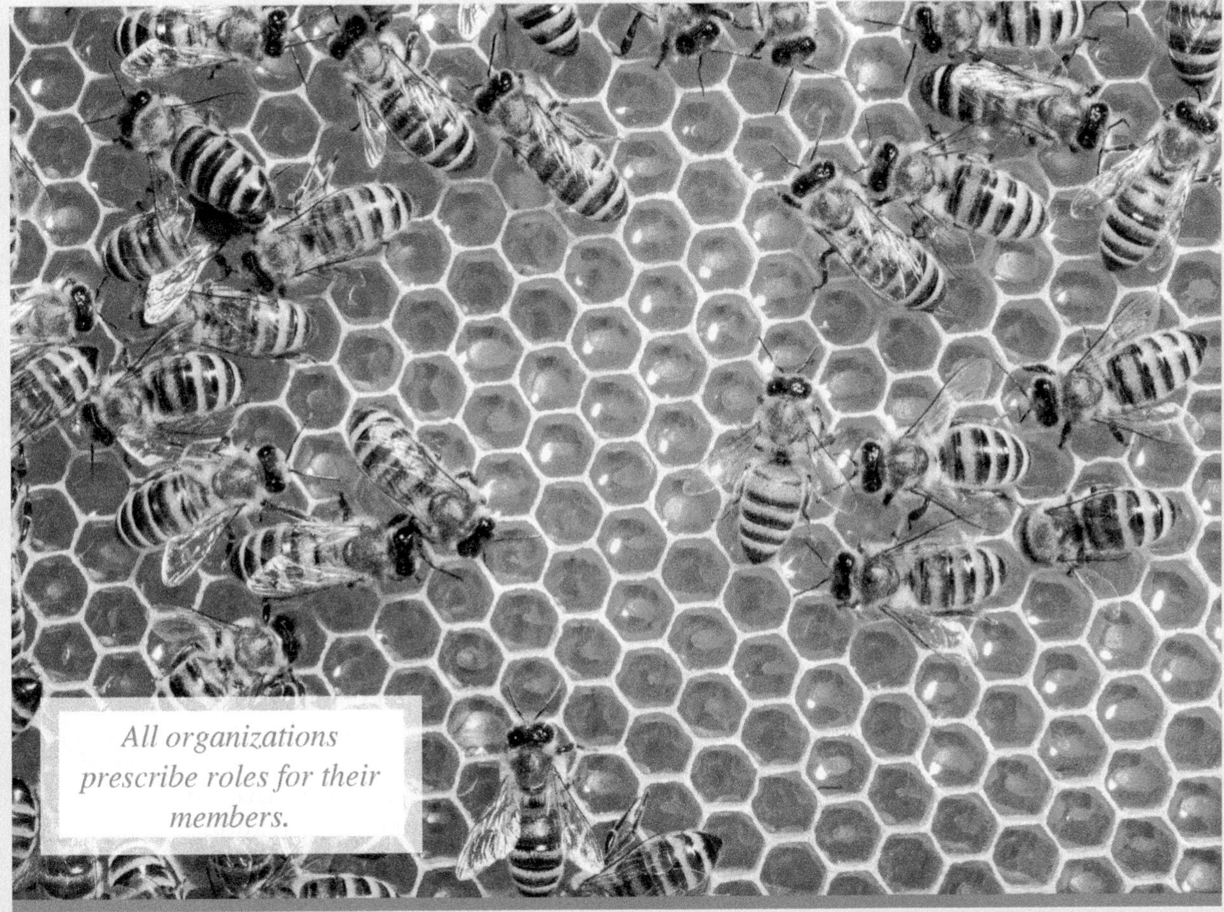

All organizations prescribe roles for their members.

Success at your job, regardless of what that job is, will depend heavily on your mastery of the theories and skills of communication discussed throughout this text and course. This chapter looks specifically at communication in the workplace, a popular area of communication called organizational communication.

12.1 ORGANIZATIONS

Here we look at the importance of the organization, the nature of the organization, and the major characteristics of organizations.

The Importance of Organizational Communication

Studying organizations and organizational communication is important for a variety of reasons.

- **Employment.** Perhaps the most obvious reason is that the vast majority of jobs are in organizations. A significant part of your work life is likely to be spent within an organization regardless of what profession you enter. In addition to employing people, organizations provide health and pension benefits, work space, continuing education, and so on.
- **Complexity.** A second reason is that organizations are becoming larger and more complex; mergers and acquisitions are frequent events in the corporate world. And with this increase in size comes an increase in complexity. If you are to function effectively within an organization, it's crucial that you understand how organizations work.
- **Influence.** A third reason is that organizations exert major influence over public policy—they are, for example, among the largest contributors to political candidates—and thus over just about everyone. Because of this, they exert significant influence on our lives—our health care, our international reputation, our financial system, and much more.

When you visualize an organization, the one activity that comes to mind most quickly is communication. Communication is what keeps an organization running, and it's through communication that most of the work of an organization gets done. We have moved from a society of organizations concerned with manufacturing to a society of organizations specializing in information transfer, in communicating.

Watch at **MyCommunicationLab** **Video:** "James McCroskey: Organizational Communication"

What Is an Organization?

An **organization** may be defined as (1) an organized (2) group of people (3) who work together (4) to achieve compatible goals.

1. **Organized.** The word *organized* in this definition refers to the fact that all organizations are structured in some way. Some are rigidly structured where each person's role and position within the hierarchy is clearly defined. You know exactly where you stand. Other organizations are more loosely structured; roles may be interchanged, and a person's status and function within the organization may be less clear. Figure 12.1 depicts a representative organizational chart of a publishing company, which shows the hierarchical structure of an organization and how the varied functions of the organization are related and coordinated.

   Within any organization there are both formal and informal structures that are much like channels of communication. For example, in a college there is a formal academic structure, with the president at the top, the provost at the next level, deans at the next, department chairs at the next, and faculty next. These structures identify

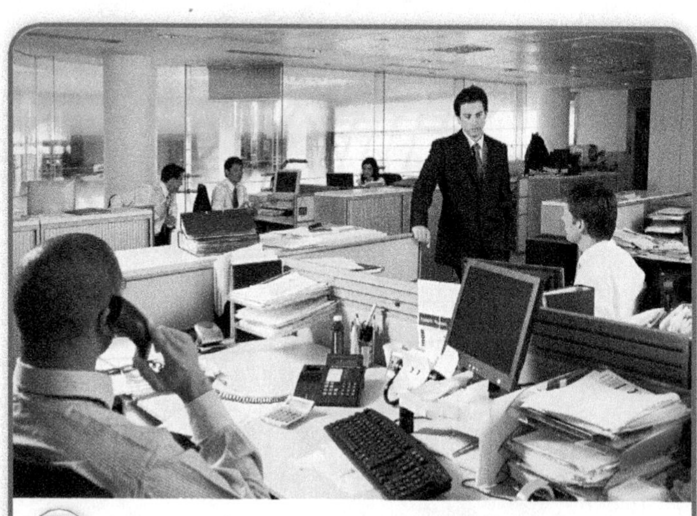

COMMUNICATION CHOICE POINT

NETWORKING *You're new on a job that you think you want to remain in for the foreseeable future; the commute is good, the salary is fine, and the workplace environment is ideal. You want to be accepted, and you want to advance in the company.* **What are some of your options for accomplishing these two goals?**

the formal channels of communication—the president communicates to the provost, who communicates to the deans, and so on down the line. There are also informal structures throughout the university, and in many cases these cross hierarchical lines. They might include, for example, the three computer science professors who play *Dungeons and Dragons* together or the public relations professor and the dean of arts who attend AA meetings together.

2. **Group of people.** The number of individuals varies greatly from one organization to another—from three or four members working in close contact to thousands of members working in a variety of different cultures throughout the world.
3. **Working together.** Each person's job is related and connected to the jobs of others within the organization. Even when members are separated geographically—as is true in many of today's organizations—the job of one person is connected in some way with the job of the other persons in the organization.
4. **Compatible goals.** The goals that each person works for are not necessarily the same, but they are compatible. For example, one person may work to earn money (the objective we think of most readily when we think of why someone works), but another may work to learn the business (as in the case of interns or apprentices), to be close to someone he or she loves, or even to satisfy conditions of parole. Yet these varied goals do not contradict each other. Regardless of the specific motivation, each person's job contributes to the goal of the organization.

Characteristics of Organizations

To understand organizations on a somewhat deeper level, we need to look at some of the major characteristics of all organizations: Organizations have rules and regulations, rely on a division of labor, use systems of rewards and consequences, and have their own cultures.

Rules and Regulations

Like all large groups, organizations have rules and regulations. Some of these are written down in company policy—what is required for promotion, salary schedules, vacation leave, health benefits, the use of office equipment, using the office e-mail system, and so on. Written rules, as you can imagine, help to reduce uncertainty and ambiguity. Some of the rules are unwritten but are known by the workers nevertheless. These are the "rules" against, say,

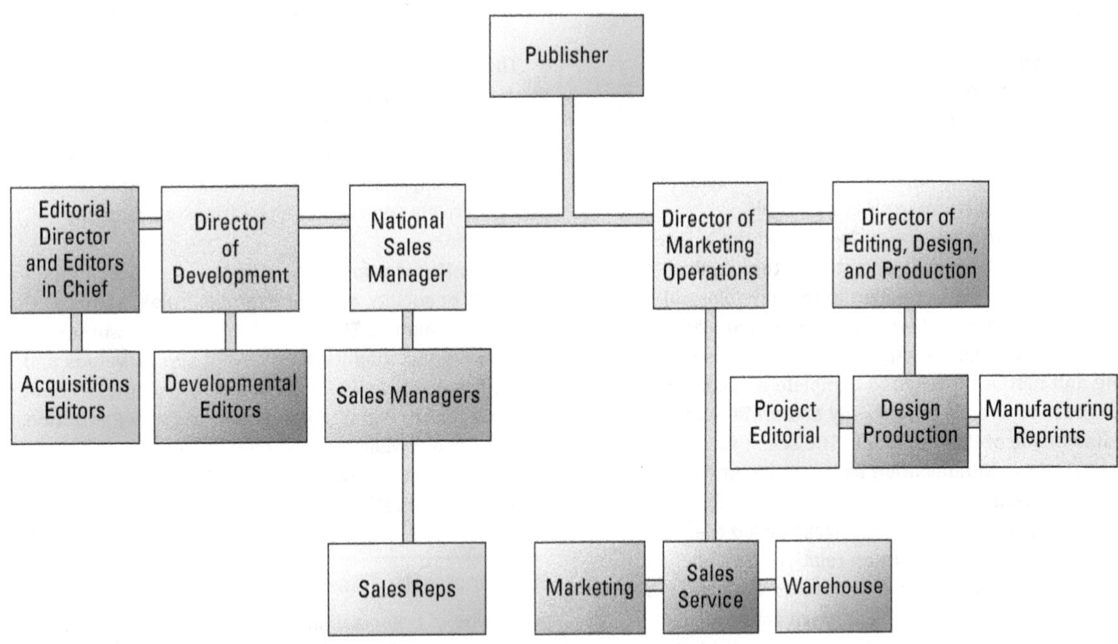

FIGURE 12.1 **Hierarchy of an Organization**

Organizations differ widely in the number of hierarchical levels they maintain. Tall organizations are those with many levels between the CEO and the trainee; flat organizations are those with few hierarchical levels. How would you describe the organization of your college? The U.S. government? The organization you work for?

sexual harassment or romantic relationships among coworkers and "rules" promoting punctuality and appropriate dress. Increasingly, organizations are, in fact, writing these formerly unwritten rules into policy statements in an attempt to avoid lawsuits. Still, unwritten rules are generally less certain and more ambiguous than are the written rules.

Division of Labor

Organizations, especially large ones, have a clear division of labor; workers are increasingly specialized. When you call for computer assistance, for example, the response system asks you a series of questions—what platform you use, what edition of the operating system you are using, the nature of your problem (whether it's Internet related or has to do with accessing software programs), and so on—in order to direct your question to a specialist in your specific problem. Workers are responsible for limited areas within a company; the accountant is not responsible for the cafeteria menu, and the cooks are not responsible for getting paychecks to members.

Systems of Rewards and Consequences

Organizations rely largely on a system of rewards and punishments. If you do the job expected of you and do it well, you'll be rewarded with bonuses, pay raises, a corner office, a better parking space, or a promotion, for example. If you don't do your job, you're likely to be punished; you'll be denied the bonus or promotion and may even be fired. The power to reward and punish is always controlled by those above you. Ideally, whether you're rewarded or punished will depend on your performance, though in reality it often depends on how much those above you like you (see Table 12.1).

Organizational Culture

Each organization has its own culture and, like any cultural group, it has its own rituals, norms, and rules for communicating. These **cultural rules**—whether in an interview situation or in a friendly conversation—delineate appropriate and inappropriate verbal and nonverbal behavior, specify rewards (or punishments

the•o•ry *noun* statement of explanation, formulation of relationships, reasoned generalization

UNDERSTANDING THEORY AND RESEARCH
Approaches to Organizations

Organizations may be viewed from several different theoretical perspectives, each of which will give you different insights into what an organization is and how organizational communication may be understood. Four approaches are particularly significant: the scientific, the behavioral, the systems, and the cultural.

The **scientific approach** focuses on the science of increasing productivity and studies the physical demands of the job in relation to the physiological capabilities of the workers. Time and motion studies—designed to enable the organization to reduce the time and motions it takes to complete a specific task and thus to increase productivity and profit—are most characteristic of this approach. The scientific approach emphasizes communication as the giving of orders, from management down to the workers.

The **behavioral approach**—also called the humanistic, organic, or human relations approach—holds that increased worker satisfaction will result in increased productivity. This approach acknowledges the importance of informal social groups within the organization and gives special consideration to the interpersonal communication within the subgroups of these organizations.

The **systems approach** combines the scientific and the behavioral approaches and views an organization as a system in which all parts interact and in which each part influences every other part. Communication, in this approach, is what holds the organization together and effectively coordinates the various parts of the organization.

The **cultural approach** views the organization as a culture or society with, for example, rules, norms, values, and heroes. This approach views the workers and the organization itself as having similar values and goals. Teamwork, pride in work and in accomplishment, commitment to high standards and to the organization, honesty, and a willingness to change in order to grow despite difficulties from competition characterize the effective organization in this view.

Working with Theories and Research

What type of organizational approach characterized the work environments you've experienced? What do you see as the advantages and disadvantages of each approach to organizations? If you owned a large company, which management approach would you adopt?

TABLE 12.1 HOW TO BE LIKED AT WORK

Whether in a job interview, in the early days on a new job, or in meeting new colleagues, first impressions are especially important—because they're so long lasting and so powerful in influencing future impressions and interactions (Flocker, 2006; Grobart, 2007; Parsons, Liden, & Bauer, 2001). Here are a few guidelines that will help you make a good first impression and should increase your likability on the job.

General Guideline	Specific Strategies
Look the Part	■ Dress appropriately; even "casual Fridays" have dress codes. ■ Any drastic deviation from the standard dress for your position may communicate that you don't fit in.
Be Positive	■ Express positive attitudes toward the organization, the job, and your colleagues. ■ Avoid negative talk and sarcasm (even in humor).
Be Culturally Sensitive	■ Avoid stereotyping and talk that might be considered racist, heterosexist, ageist, or sexist; you're sure to offend someone with any of these -isms. ■ Demonstrate respect for and an openness toward different cultural practices and beliefs.
Be Respectful and Friendly	■ Be respectful of other people's time or personal quirks. ■ At the same time, be available, helpful, and cooperative as appropriate.
Be Interested	■ Focus attention on the other person. ■ Express interest in who the person is and what he or she says and does. ■ Maintain eye contact, a pleasant facial expression, an open posture, and relatively close proximity. ■ Be a good listener.

for breaking the rules), and tell you what will help you get the job and what won't. For example, the general advice given throughout this text is to emphasize your positive qualities, to highlight your abilities, and to minimize any negative characteristics or failings. But in some organizations—especially in collectivist cultures such as those of China, Korea, and Japan—workers are expected to show modesty (Copeland & Griggs, 1985). If you stress your own competencies too much, you may be seen as arrogant, brash, and unfit to work in an organization where teamwork and cooperation are emphasized.

In collectivist organizational cultures, great deference is to be shown to managers, who represent the company. If you don't treat managers with respect, you may appear to be disrespecting the entire company. In contrast, in the individualist cultures that prevail in many U.S. companies, too much deference may make you appear unassertive, unsure of yourself, and unqualified to assume a position of authority.

When you join an organization, you learn the rules and norms of a culture different from, say, the college culture from which you came or the culture of another organization for which you worked previously. Put differently, and in terms of the concepts discussed in Chapter 2, you become acculturated—much as you would if you moved to a foreign country.

When the new organizational culture is similar to the culture from which you come, acculturation is simple and easy. For workers who move from one division of GM to another division, the process is likely to be smooth; both divisions are likely to be governed by an overall General Motors culture. Moving from Google to IBM, however, might be more difficult because the corporate cultures are very different.

As you can appreciate, it's essential to learn the organization's culture to know what the rules of the game are—and especially to learn the rules of organizational communication and to understand what kinds of messages will get you rewarded and what will get you punished.

12.2 ORGANIZATIONAL MESSAGES

Organizational communication refers to the process of sending and receiving verbal and nonverbal messages that convey meaning and that occur within an organizational context. Organizational communication is thus limited to messages occurring within the organization's formal and informal groups. Communication from the organization to the public would be part of advertising and public relations. These forms of communication are covered briefly in the Media Literacy boxes in this chapter and the next.

As an organization becomes larger and more complex, so do the members' communications. In a three-person organization, communication is relatively simple; but in a multinational organization of thousands, communication becomes highly complex.

Your organizational communication—as sender and as receiver—will be greatly influenced by the way in which you view the organization and the workers within that organization. To help you explore some of your own attitudes and beliefs, respond to each of the following statements with T if you believe the statement is generally or usually true or with F for false if you believe the statement is generally or usually false:

The average worker:

_____ **1.** must be persuaded, even motivated by fear, to do work.
_____ **2.** has little real ambition and will avoid work if possible.
_____ **3.** wants to be directed as a way of avoiding responsibility.
_____ **4.** will accept and even seek responsibility.
_____ **5.** will direct himself or herself to achieve organizational objectives.
_____ **6.** is capable and willing to learn new tasks.
_____ **7.** focuses on the entire organization rather than just his or her own department.
_____ **8.** favors group decision making and responsibility.
_____ **9.** seeks to expand career opportunities within the organization.

These statements refer to theories of management that have been labeled X, Y, and Z (McGregor, 1980; 2005). Statements 1, 2, and 3 would be believed by a Theory X manager, who holds that the worker is unmotivated and really does not want to work. Statements 4, 5, and 6 would be believed by a Theory Y manager, who holds that the worker is in fact motivated, responsible, and eager to work. Statements 7, 8, and 9 would be believed by a Theory Z manager, who holds that the worker focuses on the entire organization rather than on just his or her own area and wants to advance within the organization (Ouchi, 1981).

The important principle to derive from this brief excursion into management beliefs is that your

me•di•a lit•er•a•cy *noun* ability to understand, interact with, and create media messages

EXPANDING MEDIA LITERACY
Advertising

Organizations use advertising to communicate with their customers and other publics. Advertising is a communication strategy designed to persuade listeners, readers, or viewers to do something—usually to buy a product. Advertising both informs and persuades. It informs you by:

- making you aware of a particular product or service, a function that's especially important with new products. Advertising also informs you about the product and its ingredients, features, or uses.
- telling you where to buy the product, its cost, and other details.
- correcting erroneous claims made in previous ads. For example, Listerine was required to advertise that it doesn't kill germs that cause colds—as had been previously advertised.

Of course, the real business of advertising is persuasion, ultimately to get you to buy something. An advertiser seeks to persuade you by:

- establishing a favorable image of its product—making you think a certain way about the product, or associate a positive feeling with it, so you will want to buy the product. Advertising also may try to associate a product with negative feelings. The American Cancer Society's advertisements against smoking regularly attack the glamorous image of smoking by showing pictures of wrinkled and sick smokers.
- convincing you of the superiority of the advertiser's product and the inferiority of the competition. This comparative advertising pits one product against another.
- getting you to buy the product. Whether it's a product or a service, the advertiser wants to get you to the point where you'll go to the store, make the phone call, or type in your credit card number and complete the sale.

Try keeping a log for one day of all the advertising with which you come into contact. Be prepared—it's going to be a very extensive log. In what ways did these advertisements influence you? Which two or three techniques can you identify that these advertisers use to achieve their purposes?

beliefs about other workers will influence the way you communicate and interact with other workers. If, for example, you believe that the average worker doesn't really want to work, you may respond to workers as if this belief were true—and, in an example of the self-fulfilling prophecy, may actually influence workers to act as if they do not want to work. If you believe that the worker is motivated and wants to assume responsibility, you'll communicate with workers in ways that assume this is true and, in turn, may influence workers to motivate themselves and assume responsibility.

Formal Communication

Organizational communication may be both formal and informal. Let's look at formal communication first. **Formal communication** consists of messages that are sanctioned by the organization itself and are organizationally focused. They deal with the workings of the organization, with productivity, and with the various jobs done by the employees. Most often they follow the organizational chart and may be looked at in terms of their direction, whether upward, downward, or lateral.

Upward Communication

Upward communication consists of messages sent from the lower levels of a hierarchy to the upper levels—for example, line worker to manager or faculty member to dean. This type of communication usually is concerned with job-related activities and problems; ideas for change and suggestions for improvement; and feelings about the organization, work, other workers, or similar issues.

Upward communication is vital to the growth of any organization. It provides management with feedback on worker morale and possible sources of dissatisfaction and offers leaders the opportunity to acquire new ideas from workers. At the same time, it gives subordinates a sense of belonging to and being a part of the organization. Among the guidelines for improving upward communication are, for managers:

- Set up a nonthreatening system for upward communication that is acceptable to the cultural norms of the workforce; for example, a suggestion box or periodic meetings. Realize that from a worker's point of view, upward communication involves risk.
- Be open to hearing worker comments (even when critical), and eliminate unnecessary gatekeepers that prevent important messages from traveling up the organizational hierarchy (Callan, 1993).

And for employees:

- Be especially careful to avoid messages that may be perceived as disconfirming fellow workers.
- Avoid sending too many messages and contributing to information overload. Too many messages may also make it difficult for managers to distinguish the really important from the routine.
- Beware of sending messages that may be ambiguous or that may contradict previous messages. Usually, it's better to err on the side of excess explanation.

Downward Communication

Watch at MyCommunicationLab Video: "What Was That?"

Downward communication consists of messages sent from the higher levels to the lower levels of the hierarchy; for example, messages sent by managers to workers or by deans to faculty members. Common forms of downward communication include orders; explanations of procedures, goals, and changes; and appraisals of workers. Among the guidelines for effective downward communication are:

- Use a vocabulary known to the workers. Keep technical jargon to a minimum, especially with workers who are not native speakers of the managers' language.
- Provide workers with sufficient information for them to function effectively, but avoid information overload.
- When criticizing, be especially careful not to damage the image or face of those singled out.

Lateral Communication

Lateral communication refers to messages between equals—manager-to-manager, worker-to-worker. Such messages may move within the same subdivision or department of the organization or across divisions. Lateral communication, for example, is the kind of communication that takes place between two history professors at Illinois State University, between a psychologist at Ohio State and a communicologist at Kent State, or between a bond trader and an equities trader at a brokerage house.

Lateral communication facilitates the sharing of insights, methods, and problems. It helps the organization to avoid some problems and to solve others. Lateral communication also builds morale and worker satisfaction. Good relationships and meaningful communication between workers are among the main sources of worker satisfaction. More generally, lateral communication serves the purpose of coordinating the various activities of the organization and enabling the various divisions to pool insights and expertise.

Among the guidelines for improving lateral communication are the following.

- Recognize that your own specialty has a technical jargon that others outside your specialty might not know. Clarify when and as needed.
- See the entire organizational picture, and recognize the importance of all areas. Seeing one's own area as important and all others as unimportant does little to foster meaningful communication.
- Balance the needs of an organization that relies on cooperation and yet rewards competition. In most cases it seems that cooperation can be increased without doing any individual damage.

Informal Organizational Communication: The Grapevine

As noted earlier, the **informal communication** of organizational messages may concern just about any topic germane to workers and the organization. These messages are called grapevine messages because they follow twisting routes reminiscent of grapevines.

Explore at MyCommunicationLab Exercise: "How Machiavellian Are You?"

Grapevine messages don't follow any of the formal, hierarchical lines of communication established in an organization; rather, they seem to have a life of their own. Grapevine messages, like the formal organizational messages, concern job-related issues that you want to discuss in a more interpersonal setting; for example, organizational issues that have not yet been made public, the real relationship among the regional managers, or possible changes that are being considered but not yet finalized. Not surprisingly, the grapevine also grows as the size of the organization increases. In fact, large organizations often have several grapevines: The grapevine among interns is not the same as the grapevine used by upper management, and the student grapevine is not the same as the faculty grapevine. Sometimes, of course, they overlap; interns and management or students and faculty may exchange grapevine messages with each other.

The grapevine is most likely to be used when (Crampton, Hodge, & Mishra, 1998):

- the issues are considered important to the workers (the more important the topic, the more likely the grapevine will focus on it).
- there is ambiguity or uncertainty about what an organization is going to do (a lack of clarity encourages grapevine communication).
- the situation is perceived as threatening or insecure and anxiety may be running high (in such circumstances grapevine messages will be rampant).

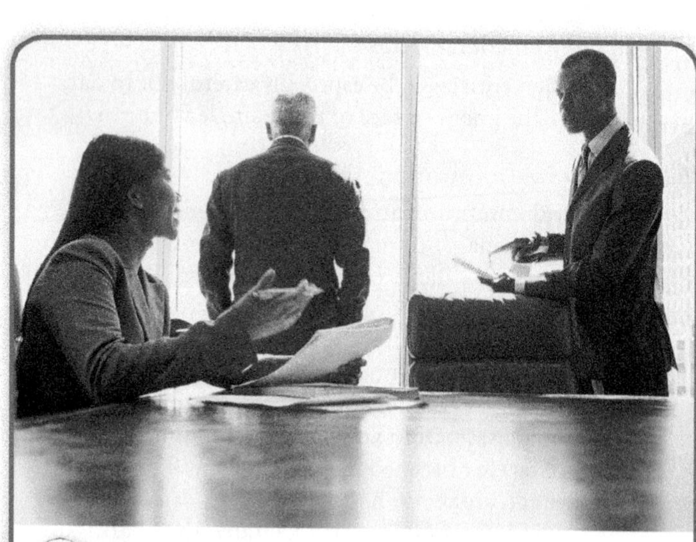

COMMUNICATION CHOICE POINT

VIOLATING ORGANIZATIONAL NORMS *In an animated discussion with an influential colleague you criticize one of the managers who, you discover a day later, is one of the most loved workers in the organization—no one talks negatively about this person (except you, as it turns out).* ***What are some of your options for smoothing over this? What specifically might you say?***

One research study notes that workers spend between 65 and 70 percent of their time on the grapevine during a crisis. And even in non-crisis times, workers spend 10 to 15 percent of their time on the grapevine (Smith, 1996). As you can imagine, listening to grapevine messages will therefore give you insight into what workers consider important, what needs added clarification, and what issues make workers anxious.

The grapevine is surprisingly accurate, with estimates of accuracy ranging from 75 to 95 percent. Workers hear about organizational matters first through the grapevine about 75 percent of the time. And, perhaps equally important, workers believe the grapevine to be accurate—at times, even more accurate than management's formal messages (Davis, 1980; Hellweg, 1992; Smith, 1996).

Here are a few useful suggestions for dealing with the inevitable office grapevine:

- **Understand grapevine purposes.** Its speed and general accuracy make it an ideal medium to carry many of the social communications that so effectively bind workers together. So listen carefully; it will give you an insider's view of the organization and will help you understand those with whom you work.

- **Treat grapevine information as tentative.** Although grapevine information is generally accurate, it's often incomplete and ambiguous; it may also contain crucial distortions.
- **Repeat with discretion.** Repeat only what you know or strongly believe to be true, and indicate your own level of belief in your grapevine messages; for example, "I heard we're all getting a nice bonus, but it may be just wishful thinking from the mailroom staff."
- **Tap into the grapevine.** Whether you're a worker or a member of management, it's important to hear grapevine information. It may clue you into events that will affect your future with the organization, and it will help you network with others in the organization.
- **Assume your messages will be repeated.** In this way, you'll be more mindful of your message sending, realizing, for example, that the potentially offensive joke that you e-mail a colleague can easily be forwarded to the very people who may take offense (Hilton, 2000; Smith, 1996).

Communication Channels in Organizations

Organizations use the same communication channels that everyone else uses. The major difference—depending on an organization's finances—is that usually the organization's methods are at the cutting edge of technology and make use of the most sophisticated equipment available. The organization makes use of all the forms of communication discussed in this text. Face-to-face interpersonal communication, small group meetings, and public presentations are all used in today's organizations. But organizations also make use of instant messaging, blogs, interactive websites, and video conferencing, for example.

All communication channels are potentially useful; the channels used in any given situation are chosen on the basis of what's best for the specific task being addressed. If editors want to solicit the opinions of authors who are widely scattered

the•o•ry *noun* statement of explanation, formulation of relationships, reasoned generalization

UNDERSTANDING THEORY AND RESEARCH
Peter and Dilbert

Two interesting "principles" will give you an idea of how some critics of the organization view organizational practices.

The **Peter Principle,** developed by college professor Lawrence J. Peter, states that in any organization, people will rise to their level of incompetence (Peter & Hull, 1969). The principle applies to all levels of the organization. For example, a publishing house may reward a great salesperson (for being a great salesperson) by promoting him or her to, say, editor. If the person proves a good editor, he or she will again be removed from a job he or she does extremely well and will be promoted to another job. The person will keep moving up in the hierarchy until he or she no longer performs well and so no longer deserves to be rewarded with another promotion. You see this regularly in education; the great teacher becomes dean (a position that requires a totally different set of skills). The great teacher may make a lousy dean and so will not advance further to, say, president. Put in terms of the Peter Principle, this person has now risen to his or her level of incompetence. This principle is clearly stated in an exaggerated form, but there seems enough truth to it to keep it a very lively organizational topic.

A somewhat similar principle is the **Dilbert Principle,** articulated by satirist Scott Adams (1997) who also writes the popular Dilbert comic strip: Organizations promote the most incompetent workers to managerial positions where they'll be able to do the least damage. All organizations have these people—workers who have served the company for many years but are now incompetent. Rather than have these people go to other organizations (and reveal trade secrets perhaps), the organization holds on to them, pays them a salary, but doesn't expect them to do much.

Working with Theories and Research

What evidence can you find that would support or refute either of these principles? Can you identify **Peters** *and* **Dilberts** *from the organizations you know or from those portrayed in film and television?*

throughout the world on an issue, then e-mail will probably work most efficiently. Face-to-face meetings would be prohibitively expensive and would probably not be any more effective than e-mail. When short messages need to be sent and quick responses are needed, instant messaging seems the logical option. When a CEO wants to present a reorganization plan to top-level management, a face-to-face public presentation may serve best.

Communication Networks

Organizations use a variety of different **communication networks**—configurations of channels through which messages pass from one person to another. The five types of networks shown in Figure 12.2 are among the most commonly used organizational communication patterns. These networks are defined by the exchange of messages, which may be transmitted face to face or via telephone, e-mail, intranet, teleconferencing, informal memos, or formal reports.

- **Circle.** In the circle, members may communicate with the two members on either side. The circle has no leader; all members have exactly the same authority or power to influence the group.
- **Wheel.** In the wheel, all messages must go through the central position or leader. Members may not communicate directly with each other.
- **Y.** In the Y, the messages pass mainly to the third person from the bottom and to a lesser extent to the person second from the bottom.
- **Chain.** In the chain, messages may be sent only to the person next to you. In this pattern there are some power differences; the middle positions receive more messages than the end positions.
- **All-channel.** In the all-channel or star pattern, each member may communicate with any other member, allowing for the greatest member participation. All members, as in the circle, have the same power to influence others.

Information Overload

Information overload is a condition in which a worker has to deal with an excessive amount of information. Information overload is created not only by the vast number of messages that a worker receives, but also by the ambiguity and complexity that often characterize such messages. Together, these factors make it extremely difficult for workers to process and respond to the messages that come across their desk. As you can easily appreciate, advances in information technology have made it easier to send more and more information in less and less time, increasing the likelihood of greater and greater overload.

Information is now generated at such a rapid rate that it's impossible to keep up with all that's relevant to your job. Invariably, you must select only certain information to attend to. The junk mail and spam are a perfect example. Today the American worker is exposed to more information in one year than a person living in 1900 was exposed to in his or her entire life. Technology has made it easy (perhaps too easy) to create and disseminate information on the Web, on blogs, and through mailing lists; and there seems every reason to expect this trend to increase.

One of the problems with information overload is that it absorbs an enormous amount of time for workers at all levels of an organization. The more messages you have to deal with, the less time you have for those messages or tasks that are central to your functions. Research finds, for example, that when you're overloaded, you're more likely to respond to simpler messages and to generate simpler messages, which may not always be appropriate (Jones, Ravid, & Rafaeli, 2004). Similarly, errors become more likely under conditions of information overload simply because you cannot devote the needed time to any one item.

Other communication problems include the risk that you will lower your normally high standards of precision or assign responsibility for responding to messages to subordinates or interns who may not have the knowledge and background to respond as

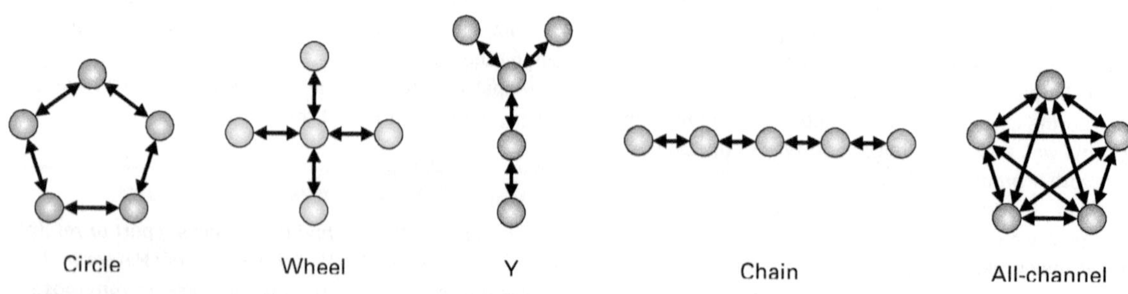

FIGURE 12.2 Five Network Structures
These figures represent some of the more common patterns that organizational messages follow.

appropriately as you might. Or you may seek to escape the overload by not accessing information—for example, by not reading your e-mails, ignoring memos, or not responding to phone messages (Timm & DeTienne, 1995).

Information overload has even been linked to health problems in more than one-third of managers (Lee, 2000). *Technostress* is a new term that denotes the anxiety and stress resulting from a feeling of being controlled by the overwhelming amount of information and from the inability to manage the information in the time available.

Several suggestions should help you deal with information overload (Timm & DeTienne, 1995; Uris, 1986).

- **Think before passing on messages.** Not all messages must be passed on; not everyone needs to know everything.
- **Use the messages as they come to you.** Record the relevant information and then throw them out or delete them. Similarly, throw out or delete materials that contain information that you can easily find elsewhere.
- **Organize your messages.** Create folders to help you store and retrieve the information you need quickly.
- **Get rid of extra copies.** When you receive multiple copies of an item, get rid of all but the one (if any) that you need. And back it up on your computer.
- **Take inventory.** Periodically take inventory of the messages you receive regularly and, where appropriate, eliminate one or more sources of unnecessary messages.

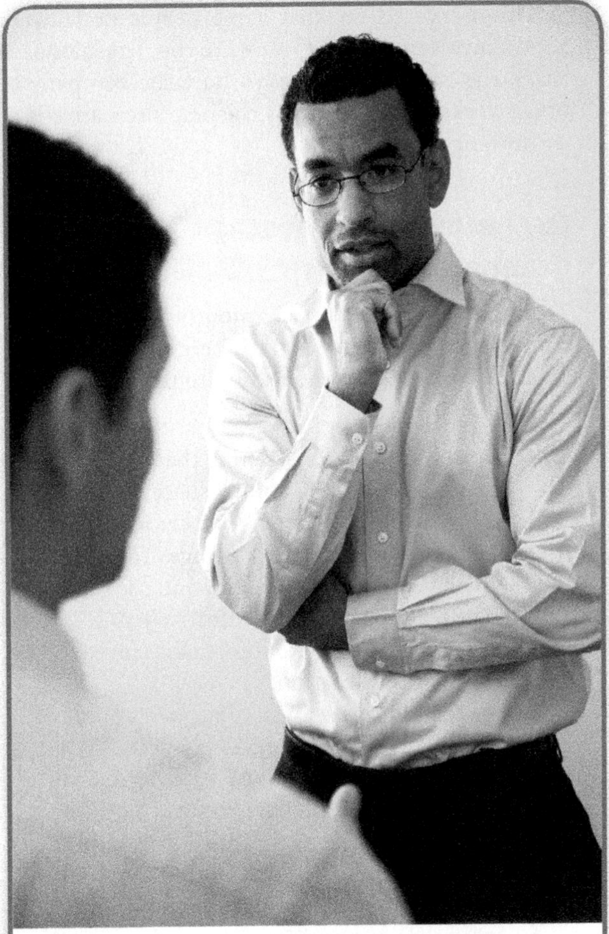

COMMUNICATION CHOICE POINT

DEALING WITH INFORMATION ISOLATION *One of the workers you're supervising has been isolated, largely because the individual has been extremely negative and doesn't socialize with others in the organization.* **What are some of your options for getting this person to participate more actively in day-to-day operations? What are some of the things you might say?**

Information Isolation

At the other extreme is **information isolation,** the situation that exists when a worker is given little or no information. Such isolation may occur when formal messages are not sent to certain people or when some people are excluded from informal gossip and grapevine messages.

Information isolation also may occur when workers are at remote locations or work at home; when a worker has an unpleasant personality or is difficult to work with; or when someone is isolated because of prejudice toward his or her race, gender, or affectional orientation.

Information isolation makes it difficult for the individual to do the job assigned, deprives the organization of potentially useful input from the individual, and generally creates an unhappy and unmotivated worker.

Several suggestions can be offered to combat information isolation. If you're the isolated person, consider if you may be contributing to this isolation by, for example, not answering your e-mails promptly, avoiding meetings, replying to the contributions of others negatively, or expressing negative attitudes toward the company or to other workers. If any of these are true, then consider changing your behavior.

If another worker is isolated, consider attempting to involve the person, for example, by making sure the worker is copied on relevant matters, is brought up to date regularly, and is positively reinforced for involvement (even if only minor).

This is not to say that some people don't want active involvement and want to be left alone. If that's the case, and it doesn't hurt the company or other workers, then perhaps the best alternative is to do nothing.

Organizational Message Competence

Throughout this text the importance of message competence has been stressed; here is a brief list of 10 skills with specific application to the workplace.

1. Listen actively, empathically, critically, and in depth. It's through listening that you'll learn the rules for organizational success.
2. Apologize when you make an error, following the suggestions offered on pages 164–166. No one is expected to be right all the time, so be ready to apologize effectively.
3. Avoid contributing to information overload or information isolation.
4. Use the grapevine appropriately. It contains important information.
5. Demonstrate the communication skills of leadership. Be prepared to lead a group successfully and to give an effective public presentation. And be able to do this with the latest and most appropriate technology.
6. Avoid the various -isms discussed on pages 110–112. Speech that is racist, heterosexist, ageist, or sexist will invariably offend someone, and you don't need that kind of hostility.
7. Help manage conflict; don't aggravate it, as some do, to stir up excitement. To the organization, conflict is not excitement—it's a headache.
8. Use power effectively. Learn the power structure of the organization. Use verbal and nonverbal messages that communicate power, and avoid those that signal a lack of power.
9. Understand the communication flow. Understand the channels that various messages are expected to go through and how you can make the available patterns work best for you.
10. Prepare all messages as if they are going to be graded by your instructor.

12.3 ORGANIZATIONAL RELATIONSHIPS

Within any organization there are interpersonal relationships. Understanding these relationships will further your understanding of organizations and organizational competence. Here we look at sexual harassment, bullying, romance in the workplace, mentoring, and networking.

Sexual Harassment

No discussion of communication in the workplace can omit a discussion of **sexual harassment,** one of organizations' major problems today. In conjunction with this section, take a look at some of the many websites devoted to this topic. Perhaps the first visit should be to the many state and federal websites dealing with sexual harassment. There you'll find the laws and the statistics on sexual harassment. Many universities also maintain websites devoted to this topic.

There are two general categories of workplace sexual harassment: quid pro quo (a Latin term that literally means "something for something") harassment and the creation of a hostile environment.

In **quid pro quo harassment,** employment opportunities (as in hiring and promotion) may be made dependent on the granting of sexual favors. Quid pro quo harassment also can include threats of reprisals or of various negative consequences that would result from a person's failure to grant such sexual favors.

Hostile environment harassment is a much broader category and includes all sexual behaviors (verbal and nonverbal) that make a worker uncomfortable. For example, putting sexually explicit pictures on the office bulletin board, using sexually explicit screen savers, telling sexual jokes and stories, and using sexual and demeaning language or gestures all constitute hostile environment harassment.

How can you avoid sexual harassment behaviors? You can avoid conveying messages that might be considered sexual harassment by following these suggestions (Bravo & Cassedy, 1992; Geffner, Braverman, Galasso, & Marsh, 2004). First, begin with the assumption that others at work are not interested in your sexual advances, sexual stories and jokes, or sexual gestures. Second, listen and watch for negative reactions to any sex-related discussion. Use the suggestions and techniques discussed throughout this book (such as perception checking and critical listening) to become aware of such reactions. When in doubt, find out; ask questions, for example. Third, avoid saying or doing anything you think your parent, partner, or child would find offensive in the behavior of someone with whom she or he worked.

What can you do about sexual harassment? If you think you're being sexually harassed, consider these suggestions (Bravo & Cassedy, 1992; Marshall, 2005; Petrocelli & Repa, 1992; Rubenstein, 1993):

1. Talk to the harasser. Tell this person, assertively, that you do not welcome the behavior and that you find it offensive. If this doesn't solve the problem, then consider the next suggestion.
2. Collect evidence—perhaps get corroboration from others who have experienced similar harassment and/or keep a log of the offensive behaviors.
3. Use the channels established by the organization to deal with such grievances. If this doesn't stop the harassment, consider going further, for example, to your human resources officer.
4. File a complaint with an organization or governmental agency, or perhaps take legal action.
5. Don't blame yourself. Like many who are abused, you may tend to blame yourself, feeling that you are responsible for being harassed. You aren't; however, you may need to secure emotional support from friends or perhaps from trained professionals.

Bullying

Workplace bullying is much like bullying in the playground—it's abusive acts repeatedly committed by one person (or a group) against another. Bullying is behavior that has become a pattern; it's repeated frequently rather than being an isolated instance. On the playground bullying often involves physical abuse; in the workplace (at least in most civilized countries) bullying is generally verbal and might involve, for example:

- gossiping about someone, making others the butt of jokes.
- treating others as inferior, for example, frequently interrupting them or otherwise not giving their ideas due attention.
- excluding members from social functions.
- verbal insults, name calling.
- negative facial expressions, sneering, avoiding eye contact.
- excessive blaming.
- being supervised (watched, monitored) more closely than others.
- being unnecessarily criticized, often with shouting and in public.

Sometimes, bullying is a part of the organization's culture, where, for example, first-year interns in a law office are treated unfairly and often abused by their superiors (demonstrated on a variety of lawyer TV shows such as *The Good Wife*). Sometimes it's perpetrated by a group who perhaps bully the newcomers or those who do less creative jobs.

The problem with bullying from the employer's point of view is that it reduces productivity and hurts the bottom line. If one or even a few workers are bullied they're probably not going to be as productive as they would be if they weren't bullied. It also is likely to lead to workers leaving the company—after the company has trained them but before they have become productive team members—with the added cost of hiring and training new people (and perhaps attendant lawsuits). According to a Washington State Department of Labor & Industries website report victims of bullying may suffer significant mental and physical problems including high stress, financial problems, reduced self-esteem, and sleep and digestion disturbances. From the point of view of the worker being bullied, it obviously creates an uncomfortable atmosphere, perhaps a desire to avoid going to work, perhaps a preoccupation with the bullying rather than the job. And this is likely to spill over into the person's private life; after all, it would be strange if bullying at work did not create problems with other aspects of life. And although the bullies probably derive some personal satisfaction from their wielding power over someone else, they too are likely to fail to be as productive as they might be and may well be personally troubled. From an ethical point of view, bullying destroys a person's right to personal dignity and a workplace free from intimidation and is therefore unethical. And yet bullying is not illegal in the United States, unless it involves harassment based on a person's gender or race, for example.

Among the actions recommended for combating bullying are the following.

1. Workers and organizations need to be clear about their opposition to bullying and that it doesn't profit anyone and will not be tolerated. Accusations of bullying will be investigated promptly and fairly.
2. If possible and there is no danger (physical or institutional) sometimes confronting the bully assertively (not aggressively) will be enough—"I don't like it when you make fun of the way I dress and I want you to stop—it's not funny and it just makes me feel bad."
3. Taking action when you or someone else is bullied. This suggestion is not always easy to implement, especially if the bullying is part of the corporate culture or if the bully is your boss, unfortunately, a not uncommon situation. But well-kept records of such incidents will often convince even the most reluctant.

Romance in the Workplace

Opinions vary widely concerning workplace romances. On the positive side, the work environment seems a perfect place to meet a potential partner. By virtue of the fact that you're working in the same office, you're probably both interested in the same field, have similar training and ambitions, and spend considerable time together—all factors that foster the development of a successful interpersonal relationship. In one survey, 59 percent of the participants felt that office romances were nothing to worry about; 23 percent said they had had affairs within office walls; and 19 percent said they had dated a subordinate (Flocker, 2006).

If you're romantically attracted to another worker, it can make going to work, working together, and even working added hours more enjoyable. If the relationship is mutually satisfying, you're likely to develop empathy for each other and to act in ways that are supportive, cooperative, friendly, and beneficial to the organization.

On the negative side, even if a workplace relationship is good for the lovers themselves, it may not necessarily be good for other workers. They may see the lovers as a team that has to be confronted as a pair and may feel that they can't criticize one partner without incurring the wrath of the other. Such relationships may also cause problems for management—for example, when a promotion is to be made or when relocation decisions are necessary.

Of course, if an office romance goes bad or if it's one-sided, it can be stressful for the individuals involved to see each other regularly and perhaps to work together. In addition, other workers may feel they have to take sides, being supportive of one partner and critical of the other. This can easily cause friction throughout the organization and damage the team ethic.

Management is reasonably concerned with the potential that office romances gone bad could lead to charges of sexual harassment. This concern has prompted a large number of organizations to consider "love contracts"—agreements between management and workers as to what constitutes appropriate and inappropriate romantic behavior in the workplace.

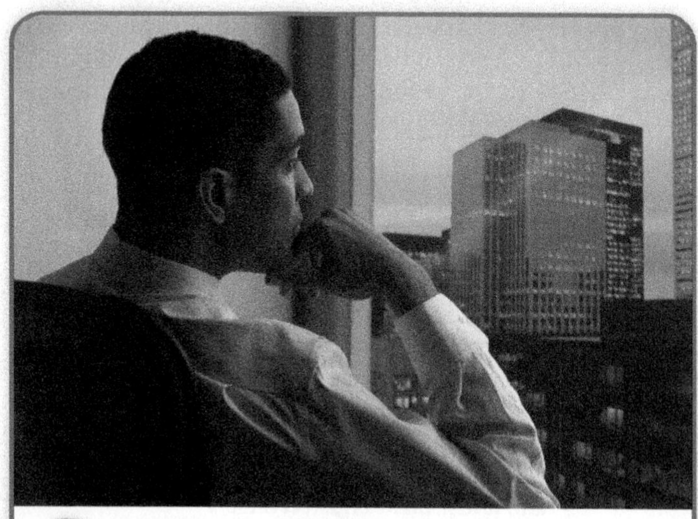

COMMUNICATION CHOICE POINT

ROMANCE IN THE WORKPLACE *After working together with a coworker you think you're falling in love. At the same time, you want to be cautious about pursuing an office romance.* **What are some of your communication choices for dealing with this touchy issue? To whom would you speak about this first? What would you say? What channel would you use (at least initially)?**

Mentoring

In a **mentoring** relationship, an experienced individual (mentor) helps to train a less-experienced person who is sometimes referred to as a mentee or, more often, a protégé (Ragins & Kram, 2007). An accomplished teacher, for example, might mentor a newly arrived or novice teacher. The mentor guides the new person through the "ropes," teaches the strategies and techniques for success, and otherwise communicates his or her knowledge and experience to the newcomer.

Mentoring usually involves a one-on-one relationship between an expert and a novice—a relationship that is supportive and trusting. There's a mutual and open sharing of information and thoughts about the job. The relationship enables the novice to try out new skills under the guidance of an expert, to ask questions, and to obtain the feedback so necessary in learning complex skills.

In a study of middle-level managers, those who had mentors and participated in mentoring relationships were found to earn more frequent promotions and higher salaries than those who didn't (Scandura, 1992). And the mentoring relationship is one of the three primary paths to career achievement among African American men and women (Bridges, 1996). It's also interesting to note that similarity in race or gender between mentor and protégé doesn't seem to influence the mentoring experience (Barr, 2000).

At the same time that a mentor helps a novice, the mentor benefits from clarifying his or her thoughts, from seeing the job from the perspective of a newcomer, and from considering and formulating answers to a variety of questions. Much the way a teacher learns from teaching and from his or her students, a mentor learns from mentoring and from his or her protégés.

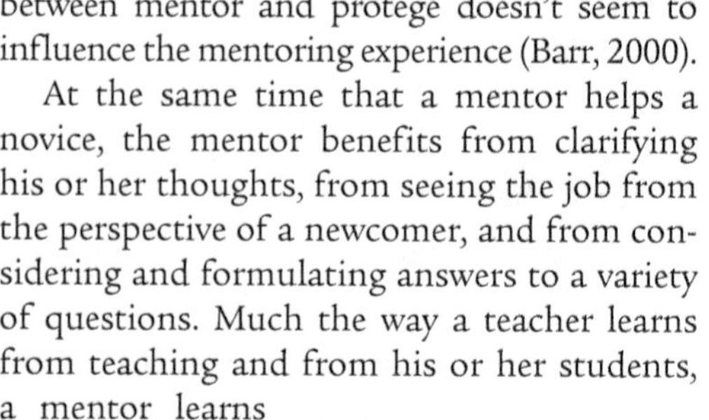

eth•ics *noun* morality, standards of conduct, moral judgment

MAKING ETHICAL CHOICES
The Five Cs of Organizational Ethics

Considering the importance of ethics in organizations and the frequent ethics violations that appear in the news, there is surprisingly little of substance written on the ethical guides an organization and workers should follow. Here, then, is an attempt to identify at least some of the principles an ethical organization should follow.

- **Clear policies and expectations.** Management has an obligation to set forth clear and unambiguous policies concerning organizational matters; people have a right to know what is expected of them.
- **Comfortable work environment.** The work environment should be free of harassment and bullying. No one should have to endure harassment or intimidation.
- **Channels for communication.** Communication channels need to be open and listened to. Everyone has a right to hear what is relevant to their position and to be listened to.
- **Cooperation.** Each person has a right to expect that cooperation will yield benefits to the organization and to the workers.
- **Commitment.** Contracts, verbal agreements, and job descriptions need to be accurate and followed through. People have a right to expect promises to be kept.

Ethical Choice Point

At your workplace, management seems to condone sexual harassment; at least managers do nothing to stop it. You've witnessed both quid pro quo and hostile environment sexual harassment toward women and gay men and lesbians. What are your ethical obligations in this situation? What would you do?

Networking

Networking is more than a technique for securing a job. It is a broad process of enlisting the aid of other people to help you solve a problem or to offer insights that bear on your problem—for example, on how to publish your manuscript, where to go for low-cost auto insurance, how to find an apartment, or how to empty your e-mail cache (Heenehan, 1997). Here are a few principles for effective networking, which have special application to the workplace but which you'll find useful generally.

- **Start with people you already know.** You can also network with people who know the people you know. Thus, you may contact a friend's friend to find out if the firm where he or she works is hiring. Or you may contact people with whom you have no connection from, say, a blog post or website reference. Newsgroups and social andprofessional networking sites such as Facebook and LinkedIn are other obvious networking avenues.
- **Seek mutually beneficial relationships.** If you can provide others with helpful information, it's more likely that they'll provide helpful information for you. In this way you establish a mutually satisfying and productive network.
- **Create folders, files, and directories.** For example, if you're a freelance artist, you might develop a list of persons in positions to offer you work or who might lead you to others who could offer work, such as authors, editors, art directors, or people in advertising.
- **Be proactive.** Initiate contacts rather than waiting for them to come to you. If you're also willing to help others, there's nothing wrong in asking these same people to help you. If you're respectful of your contacts' time and expertise, it's likely that they will respond favorably to your networking attempts.

Organizational Relationship Competence

The importance of relationship competence has been a keynote of this text. Here is a list of 10 relationship competence skills that are particularly applicable to the workplace.

1. Be a mentor and a network giver as well as a protégé and network seeker. From a purely practical point of view, those you mentor or help are likely to reward you in various ways.
2. Be supportive of your coworkers; avoid being either overly critical or unconcerned with their specific jobs.
3. Exercise caution in the development of office romances, and understand your company's policies regarding such relationships. At the same time, be careful of getting in the middle of the office romances of others.

4. Self-disclose selectively. Be especially careful with disclosures that may be negative or may be too intimate for the relationship you have with your colleagues.
5. Although there are exceptions, it's generally best to avoid bringing your relationship problems to work with you. Unless you have a very close friend at work or a company counselor you can go to with problems, it's best not to mix at-home and at-work relationship issues.
6. Learn the cultural rules of the organization, and unless there's an outstanding reason, don't break them. And don't denigrate them; many consider these rules and norms valuable and personally meaningful and will be offended by any negative attitudes. Further, when appropriate, display **value congruence,** your own agreement with the values of the organization (Shockley-Zalabak, 2012).
7. Stress the positive. Be friendly, helpful, and generally positive. At the same time, act as politely toward subordinates as you do toward superiors.
8. Remember that your colleagues may one day be your superiors or you may be theirs. Visualize yourselves in these roles, and regulate your communications accordingly.
9. Relate to others at your appropriate relationship stage. Trying to be overly friendly with your superior may appear pushy.
10. Watch out for any ethnocentrism on your part. In an organization all people are treated according to rank, not gender or race.

Angie was hired last year as a marketing assistant in a small but successful computer microchip company. She realizes that she still has a lot to learn before she can move up the career ladder; nonetheless, she has established a personal goal of achieving success and a promotion to the sales team in the next year. Now she just has to come up with a plan and put it into action. "Succeeding at Work" provides an inside view of life in the organization and explores some of the effective and ineffective strategic choices for getting ahead in the organization, messages that are effective and messages that are ineffective. Log on to www.mycommunicationlab.com to view this video and the choices made, and then answer the related discussion questions.

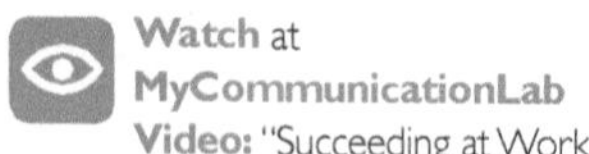

SUMMARY: HUMAN COMMUNICATION IN THE WORKPLACE

This chapter looked at organization communication and defined the nature of the organization, described some of the major organizational messages, and looked at some of the important relationships in organizations.

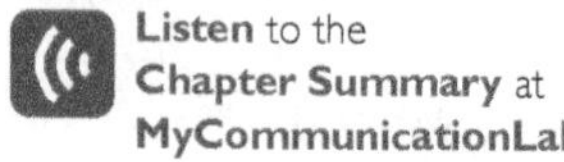

12.1 ORGANIZATIONS

1. An organization may be defined as (1) an organized (2) group of people (3) who work together (4) to achieve compatible goals.
2. Within any organization, there are both formal and informal structures that are much like channels of communication. These structures define the communication patterns of the organization.
3. All organizations have rules and regulations, rely on a division of labor, use systems of rewards and punishments to motivate workers, and have their own cultures.

12.2 ORGANIZATIONAL MESSAGES

4. Organizational communication is the process of sending and receiving verbal and nonverbal messages that convey meaning and that occur within an organizational context.

5. Formal communications are those that are sanctioned by the organization itself and deal with the workings of the organization, with productivity, and with the various jobs served by the employees.

6. Informal messages are socially sanctioned. They are oriented more to the individual members and their relationship to the organization.

7. Organizational networks are the configurations of channels through which messages pass from one person to another.

8. In any hierarchical organization, communication flows upward, downward, and across, or laterally.

9. Upward communication consists of messages sent from the lower levels of a hierarchy to the upper levels—for example, from line worker to manager or from faculty member to dean.

10. Downward communication consists of messages sent from the higher levels to the lower levels of the hierarchy; for example, messages sent by managers to workers or by deans to faculty members.

11. Lateral communication refers to messages between equals—manager-to-manager, worker-to-worker. Such messages may move within the same subdivision or department of the organization or across divisions.

12. Grapevine messages, unlike formal messages, don't follow any of the formal lines of communication established in an organization; rather, they seem to have a life of their own.

13. Information overload refers to the excessive amount of information that workers have to deal with, the lack of clarity in many messages, and the increasing complexity of messages. Information isolation is the opposite and refers to the situation in which certain workers receive little or no information or when some people are excluded from the informal gossip and grapevine messages.

14. Organizational message competence involves, for example, active listening, using power effectively, using the grapevine appropriately, and avoiding contributing to information overload or isolation.

12.3 ORGANIZATIONAL RELATIONSHIPS

15. Sexual harassment is the sending of unwanted sexual messages. Two general categories of workplace sexual harassment are quid pro quo (Latin term for "something for something") harassment and the creation of a hostile environment.

16. Avoid bullying or expressing positive attitudes toward such behavior. Take action when appropriate.

17. Opinions vary widely concerning workplace romances. On the positive side, the work environment seems a perfect place to meet a potential partner. On the negative side, even if a workplace relationship is good for the lovers themselves, it may not necessarily be good for other workers or the organization as a whole.

18. In a mentoring relationship, an experienced individual (mentor) helps to train a less-experienced person (mentee or protégé).

19. Networking is a broad process of enlisting the aid of other people to help you solve a problem or offer insights that bear on your problem.

20. Organizational competence involves, for example, supportiveness toward others, a general positiveness, a lack of ethnocentrism, selective self-disclosure, and adherence to organizational culture and norms.

Study and **Review** the **Flashcards** at **MyCommunicationLab**

KEY TERMS

communication networks *254*
cultural rules *248*
Dilbert Principle *253*
downward communication *251*
formal communication *251*
grapevine *252*
hostile environment harassment *256*
informal communication *252*
information isolation *255*
information overload *254*
lateral communication *251*
mentoring *258*
networking *259*
organization *246*
organizational communication *249*
Peter Principle *253*
quid pro quo harassment *256*
sexual harassment *256*
upward communication *251*
value congruence *260*

WORKING WITH HUMAN COMMUNICATION IN THE WORKPLACE

12.1 Workplace Analysis. Much as you would analyze an audience so as to tailor your messages to its members (as will be detailed in Chapter 14), you can analyze a workplace to reduce your uncertainty. In this way you'll be better able to fit your messages to the organization, the hierarchy, and your coworkers. Here are five kinds of information you might focus on in your workplace analysis; for each, create an example of how this specific knowledge might help a worker new to the organization.

- **Cultural norms.** All organizations have rules for interacting, beliefs about their mission, and values that they seek to cultivate. Discover what these are.
- **Communication pathways.** Organizations have specific pathways that they expect communication to follow; for example, interns do not send messages directly to the CEO of a large corporation but may address them to other interns or to those who are supervising the internship program.
- **Grapevine.** In most organizations, grapevines flourish; tap into the grapevine to learn about your workplace. The grapevine often will clue you in to what is going on in the organization and will provide the very information that you need to interact effectively with a wide variety of individuals.
- **Power.** All members of organizations exercise power over those who work for them. Seek to understand who has power and what types of power are used. Ultimately, you'll want to learn how to acquire such power yourself and to empower others.
- **Reward system.** All organizations exercise control through a system of rewards (promotions, raises, bonuses, choice offices, and the like) and punishments (termination, no bonuses, undesirable offices, and the like). Seek to discover the behaviors that are rewarded and those that are punished as well as who controls the reward system.

12.2 Dealing with Organizational Complaints. Assume that you're the leader of a work team consisting of members from each of the major departments in your company. For any one of the complaints listed below, explain what you would say and the objectives you'd hope to achieve. In framing your responses, follow these guidelines: (a) Let the other person know that you're open to complaints and that you do view complaints as essential sources of information; (b) show that you're following the suggestions for effective listening discussed in Chapter 4, such as listening supportively and with empathy; (c) show that you understand both the thoughts and the feelings that go with the complaint; and (d) ask the other person what he or she would like you to do about the complaint.

a. You're calling these meetings much too often and much too early to suit us. We'd like fewer meetings scheduled for later in the day.

b. That's not fair. Why do I always have to take the minutes of these meetings? Can't we have a real secretary here?

c. There's a good reason why I don't contribute to the discussion. I don't contribute because no one listens to what I say.

12.3 Facilitating Upward and Downward Communication. If you ran a company of, say, 40 or 50 employees, how would you go about facilitating both upward and downward communication?

12.4 Organizational Behaviors. How would you describe the communication behaviors of the following organizational members:

a. The person who is determined to rise to the top in the shortest time possible

b. The person who just wants to have fun

c. The person who wants to meet relationship partners

12.5 Networking. Develop a network list of people who might help you get a job in your chosen profession.

12.6 Romance on the Job. You've just taken a position at a new firm, and you find that your manager is romantically interested in you. You decide to do a cost-benefit analysis. List all the costs (potential problems and disadvantages) and the benefits (potential advantages) of pursuing this relationship.

12.7 Organizational Hierarchies. Some theorists believe that computer-mediated communication will eventually eliminate the hierarchical structure of organizations, largely because CMC encourages participation from all members of the organization and greater honesty. It is encourages an organizational culture in which merit is more important than status (Kollock & Smith, 1996). What evidence can you find to support or refute this claim?

LogOn! MyCommunicationLab

www.mycommunicationlab.com

Throughout this chapter, there are icons in the margin that highlight media content for selected topics. Go to **MyCommunicationLab** for additional materials on organizational communication. Here you'll find flashcards to help you learn key communication terms, videos that illustrate a variety of concepts, additional exercises, and discussions to help you continue your study of human communication in the workplace.

13 INTERPERSONAL, GROUP, AND WORKPLACE CONFLICT

Listen to Chapter 13 at MyCommunicationLab

CHAPTER TOPICS	CHAPTER OBJECTIVES
In this chapter you'll explore the following major topics:	**After reading this chapter you should be able to:**
INTERPERSONAL, GROUP, AND WORKPLACE CONFLICT	13.1 Define *conflict* and its various types.
PRINCIPLES OF CONFLICT	13.2 Explain the four principles of conflict.
PRELIMINARIES TO CONFLICT MANAGEMENT	13.3 Identify and apply the suggestions for approaching and dealing with conflict management.
CONFLICT MANAGEMENT STRATEGIES	13.4 Explain the various conflict strategies and use them as appropriate.

Interpersonal conflict does not have to have a loser; both can win.

No matter how effective a communicator you are, you'll still experience conflict and disagreements in interpersonal relationships and in the social and work groups of which you are a part. At some point you are bound to find yourself in conflict with another person or even with an entire group. Because conflict is an inevitable part of interpersonal and group life, it's essential to learn how it works, how it can go wrong, and what you can do to resolve conflicts effectively. Let's begin our discussion of conflict with some basic definitions and dispel some myths about conflict.

13.1 INTERPERSONAL, GROUP, AND WORKPLACE CONFLICT

Pat wants to go to the movies with Chris; Chris wants to stay home. Pat's insisting on going to the movies interferes with Chris's staying home, and Chris's determination to stay home interferes with Pat's going to the movies. Carl is a member of a work team and wants to convince the group to change advertising agencies; other members don't want any change. Each person in these scenarios has goals that interfere with someone else's desired goals.

Interpersonal, small group, and workplace conflicts may concern goals to be pursued (for example, parents get upset that their child wants to become an actor instead of a doctor); the allocation of resources such as money or time (for example, group members differ on how to spend the advertising dollar); decisions to be made (for example, some people want a holiday party and others want a cash bonus); or behaviors that are considered appropriate or desirable by one person but inappropriate or undesirable by the other (for example, two people disagree over whether one of them was flirting or drinking or not working at full speed).

A Definition of Interpersonal Conflict

As these examples illustrate, **interpersonal conflict** (we'll use the shorthand "interpersonal conflict" to refer to interpersonal, group, and workplace conflicts) occurs (Cahn & Abigail, 2014; Folger, Poole, & Stutman, 2013) when people:

- are interdependent (they're connected in some significant way); what one person does has an impact or an effect on the other person.
- are mutually aware that their goals are incompatible; if one person's goal is achieved, then the other person's goal cannot be achieved. For example, if one person wants to buy a new car and the other person wants to pay down the mortgage (and there is not enough money to do both) there is conflict.
- perceive each other as interfering with the attainment of their own goals. For example, you may want to study but your roommate may want to party; the attainment of either goal would interfere with the attainment of the other goal.

One of the implications of this concept of interdependency is that the greater the interdependency (1) the greater the number of issues around which conflict can center and (2) the greater the impact of the conflict and the conflict management interaction on the individuals and on the relationship (see Figure 13.1). Looked at in this way, it's easy to appreciate the importance of understanding interpersonal conflict and the learning strategies for effective conflict management.

Another implication of interdependency is the inevitability of conflict. It is a part of every interpersonal relationship—between parents and children, brothers and sisters, friends, lovers, and coworkers. One study found that the average person has approximately seven conflicts per week (Benoit & Benoit, 1990). A more recent poll, from 2007, claims that married couples, for example, have 182 conflicts each year (approximately 3.5 conflicts per week), each lasting on average 25 minutes, with another 30 minutes for sulking (www.24dash.com, 2007).

Online and Workplace Conflicts

When we think of interpersonal conflict, we most likely think of conflict between lovers or friends. Two special conflict situations should be noted. The first is online conflict. Just as you can experience disagreement in face-to-face communication, you can experience conflict online; but there are a few conflict situations that are unique to online communication, and we'll look at them here. The second is conflict in the workplace or formal group—in any group that consists of a leader and various members of the organization.

Online Conflict

Sending commercial messages to those who didn't request them often creates conflict. Junk mail is junk mail; but on the Internet, junk mail slows down the entire Internet system, as well as the individual who has to sit through the downloading of unwanted messages. In many cases (when you access your e-mail from an Internet café, for example), you have to pay for the time it takes to download junk mail.

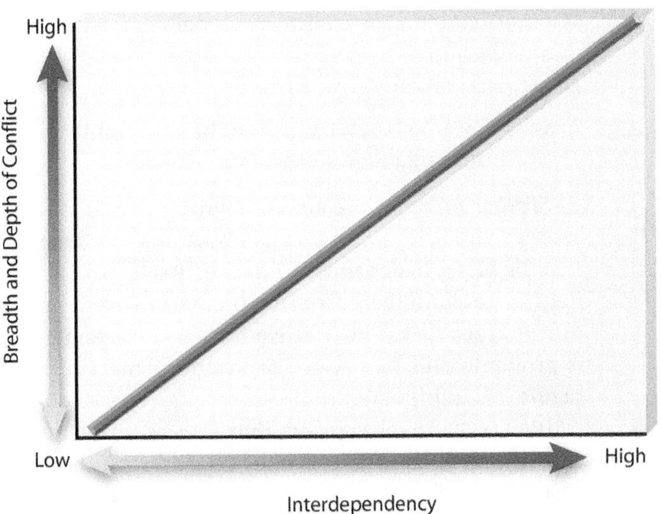

FIGURE 13.1 Conflict and Interdependency

This figure illustrates that, as interdependency increases, so do the potential for and the importance of conflict. Does this diagram effectively depict the likelihood and the significance of your own interpersonal conflicts?

Spamming often causes conflict. Spamming is sending someone unsolicited mail, repeatedly sending the same mail, or posting the same message on lots of bulletin boards, even when the message is irrelevant to the focus of the group.

Flaming, especially common in newsgroups, is sending messages that personally attack another user. Flaming frequently leads to flame wars, in which everyone in the group gets into the act and attacks other users. Generally, flaming and flame wars prevent us from achieving our goals and so are counterproductive.

Workplace and Formal Group Conflicts

Unlike conflicts that might occur in an informal group of friends or in a family (which are more similar to interpersonal encounters), disagreements in the workplace group present a specific set of issues.

In formal groups it's often the leader's responsibility to manage conflict. Small group communication researchers distinguish between procedural and people conflicts and offer a wide variety of conflict management strategies (Cahn & Abigail, 2014; Folger, Poole, & Stutman, 2013).

Procedural conflicts involve disagreements over who is in charge (who is the leader or who should be the leader), what the agenda or task of the group should be, and how the group should conduct its business. The best way to deal with procedural problems is to prevent them from occurring in the first place by establishing early in the group's interaction who is to serve as leader and what the agenda should be.

People conflicts can occur when one member dominates the group, when several members battle for control, or when some members refuse to participate. The leader should try to secure the commitment of all members and to convince them that the progress of the group depends on everyone's contributions. At times, it may be necessary to concentrate on people needs—on the importance of satisfying members' needs for group approval, for periodic rewards, or for encouragement. The conflict management strategies presented later in this chapter are applicable to the workplace or formal group situation. In addition, here are four principles that have special relevance to conflict in this type of group (Kindler, 1996).

- **Preserve the dignity and respect of all members.** Assume, for example, that each person's disagreement is legitimate and stems from a genuine concern for the good of the group. Therefore, treat disagreements kindly; even if someone attacks you personally, it's generally wise not to respond in kind, but to redirect the criticism to the issue at hand.
- **Listen empathically.** See the perspectives of the other members; try to feel what they're feeling without making any critical judgments. Try to ask yourself why others see the situation differently from the way you see it.
- **Seek out and emphasize common ground.** Even in the midst of disagreement, there are areas of common interest, common beliefs, and common aims. Find these and build on them.
- **Value diversity and differences.** Creative solutions often emerge from conflicting perspectives. So don't gloss over differences; instead, explore them for the valuable information they can give you.

Myths about Conflict

One of the problems many people have in dealing with conflict is that they may be operating on the basis of false assumptions about what conflict is and what it means. Think about your own assumptions about interpersonal and small group conflict, which were probably derived from the communications you witnessed in your family and in your social interactions. For example, do you think the following are true or false?

- Conflict is best avoided.
- If two people are in a relationship conflict, it means they have a bad relationship.
- Conflict damages an interpersonal relationship or small group.
- Conflict is bad because it reveals our negative selves—our pettiness, our need to be in control, our unreasonable expectations.

COMMUNICATION CHOICE POINT

CONFRONTING A PROBLEM *Your neighbor never puts out the garbage in time for pickup, and so the garbage—often broken into by stray animals—remains until the next pickup. You're fed up with the rodents the garbage draws, the smell, and the horrible appearance. You're determined to stop this problem and yet not have your next-door neighbor hate you.* **What communication choices do you have for dealing with this problem? What might you say? To whom? Through what channel?**

Simple answers are usually wrong. In this case, each of the four assumptions above may be true or may be false. It depends. In and of itself, conflict is neither good nor bad. Conflict is a part of every interpersonal relationship—if it isn't, then the interaction is probably dull, irrelevant, or insignificant. Conflict seems inevitable.

It's not so much conflict that creates problems as the way in which you approach and deal with the conflict. Some ways of approaching conflict can resolve difficulties and actually improve a relationship. Other ways can hurt the relationship; it can destroy self-esteem, create bitterness, and foster suspicion. Your task, therefore, is not to try to create relationships or groups that will be free of conflict but rather to learn appropriate and productive ways of managing conflict.

Similarly, it's not the conflict (the disagreement itself) that will reveal your negative side but the fight strategies you use. Thus, if you attack other people, use force, or use personal rejection or manipulation, you will reveal your negative side. But in fighting you can also reveal your positive self—your willingness to listen to opposing points of view, your readiness to change unpleasant behaviors, your willingness to accept imperfection in others.

Explore at MyCommunicationLab Activity: "Conflict"

13.2 PRINCIPLES OF CONFLICT

We can further our understanding of interpersonal conflict by looking at some general principles: (1) conflict can center on content or relationship issues, (2) conflict can be negative or positive, (3) conflict takes place in a context, and (4) conflict styles have consequences.

Conflict Can Center on Content and Relationship Issues

Using concepts developed in Chapter 1, you can distinguish between content conflict and relationship conflict. **Content conflict** centers on objects, events, and persons that are usually, though not always, external to the parties involved in the conflict. Content conflicts have to do with the millions of issues that we argue and fight about every day—the merit of a particular movie, what to watch on television, the fairness of the last examination or job promotion, the way to spend our savings.

the•o•ry *noun* statement of explanation, formulation of relationships, reasoned generalization

UNDERSTANDING THEORY AND RESEARCH
Conflict Issues

Think about your own interpersonal conflicts, and particularly about the issues you fight over. What exactly do you fight about? Here are the results of a few studies that investigated what couples fight about.

One study focused on heterosexual couples and identified the four conditions that most often led up to a couple's "first big fight" (Siegert & Stamp, 1994): uncertainty over commitment, jealousy, violation of expectations, and personality differences.

Another study asked what heterosexual, gay, and lesbian couples argued about most and found that all three types of couples were amazingly similar in their conflict issues. All three types argued primarily about these six issues (Kurdek, 1994): intimacy issues such as affection and sex; power issues such as excessive demands or possessiveness, lack of equality in the relationship, friends, and leisure time; personal flaws issues such as drinking or smoking, personal grooming, and driving style; personal distance issues such as frequently being absent and school or job commitments; social issues such as politics, friendships, parents, and personal values; and distrust issues such as previous lovers and lying.

According to the eHarmony website (accessed July 20, 2013) nine issues are at the heart of couple conflicts: free time, money, household responsibilities, politics, sex, children and pets, religion, jealousy, and stress.

In the workplace, conflicts are especially important because of their potential negative effects such as personnel leaving the job (necessitating new recruitment and retraining), low morale, and a lessening desire to perform at top efficiency. Workplace conflicts, according to one study, center on such issues as these (Psychometrics, 2010):

- Personality differences and resulting clashes, 86 percent.
- Ineffective leadership, 73 percent.
- Lack of openness, 67 percent.
- Physical and emotional stress, 64 percent.
- Differences in values and resulting clashes, 59 percent.

Working with Theories and Research

For at least 3 consecutive days, maintain a log of all the interpersonal, group, and workplace conflicts that you witness and/or participate in. What issues do these conflicts revolve around? What might you or others do to lessen these conflicts or at least make them less harmful?

Relationship conflicts are equally numerous. Examples include clashes that arise when a younger brother refuses to obey his older brother, two partners each want an equal say in making vacation plans, or a mother and daughter each want to have the final word concerning the daughter's lifestyle. Here the conflicts are concerned not so much with external objects as with the relationships between the individuals—issues like who is in charge, how equal the members in a primary relationship are, or who has the right to set down rules of behavior.

Of course, content and relationship dimensions are always easier to separate in a textbook than they are in real life. Many conflicts contain elements of both content and relationship conflicts. For example, you can probably imagine both content and relationship dimensions in each of the "content" issues mentioned. Yet certain issues seem oriented more toward one dimension than the other. For example, differences on political and social issues are largely content focuses, whereas intimacy and power issues are largely relational.

Conflict Can Be Negative or Positive

Although interpersonal conflict is always stressful, it's important to recognize that it has both negative and positive aspects.

Negative Aspects

Conflict often leads to increased negative regard for the opponent. One reason for this is that many conflicts involve unfair fighting methods (which we'll examine shortly) and are focused largely on hurting the other person. When one person hurts the other, increased negative feelings are inevitable; even the strongest relationship has limits.

At times, conflict may lead you to close yourself off from the other person. When you hide your true self from an intimate, you prevent meaningful communication from taking place. Because the need for intimacy is so strong, one or both parties may then seek intimacy elsewhere. This often leads to further conflict, mutual hurt, and resentment—qualities that add heavily to the costs carried by the relationship. Meanwhile, rewards may become difficult to

the•o•ry *noun* statement of explanation, formulation of relationships, reasoned generalization

UNDERSTANDING THEORY AND RESEARCH
Conflict and Gender

Not surprisingly, there are significant gender differences in interpersonal conflict. For example, men are more apt to withdraw from a conflict situation than are women. It's been argued that this may be due to the fact that men become more psychologically and physiologically aroused during conflict (and retain this heightened level of arousal much longer) than do women and so may try to distance themselves and withdraw from the conflict to prevent further arousal (Canary, Cupach, & Messman, 1995; Goleman, 1995a, b; Gottman & Carrere, 1994). Women, on the other hand, want to get closer to the conflict; they want to talk about it and resolve it. Another study showed that young girls used more pro-social strategies (behaviors designed to help others rather than oneself) than boys (Rose & Asher, 1999).

Other research finds that women are more emotional and men are more logical when they argue (Canary, Cupach, & Messman, 1995; Schaap, Buunk, & Kerkstra, 1988). Women have been defined as conflict "feelers" and men as conflict "thinkers" (Sorenson, Hawkins, & Sorenson, 1995).

It should be noted, however, that much research fails to support the gender "differences" in conflict style that cartoons, situation comedies, and films portray so readily and so clearly. For example, numerous studies of both college students and men and women in business found no significant differences in the ways men and women engage in conflict (Canary & Hause, 1993; Gottman & Levenson, 1999; Wilkins & Andersen, 1991).

Working with Theories and Research

Log on to and search the communication, psychology, and sociology databases for research on gender and conflict. What can you add to the discussion presented here?

exchange. In this situation, the costs increase and the rewards decrease, a condition that often results in relationship deterioration and eventual dissolution.

Positive Aspects

The major value of interpersonal conflict is that it forces you to examine a problem and work toward a potential solution. If both you and your opponent use productive conflict strategies (which will be described below), the relationship may well emerge from the encounter stronger, healthier, and more satisfying than before. And you may emerge stronger, more confident, and better able to stand up for yourself (Bedford, 1996).

Through conflict and its resolution, you also can stop resentment from increasing and let your needs be known. For example, suppose I need lots of attention when I come home from work, but you need to review and get closure on the day's work. If we both can appreciate the legitimacy of these needs, then we can find solutions. Perhaps you can make your important phone call after my attention needs are met, or perhaps I can delay my need for attention until you get closure about work. In this way both of us get what we want—a situation we refer to later as win–win.

Consider, too, that when you try to resolve conflict within an interpersonal relationship, you're saying in effect that the relationship is worth the effort. Usually, confronting a conflict indicates commitment and a desire to preserve the relationship.

Conflict Takes Place in a Context

Conflict, like any form of communication, takes place in a context that influences the way conflict and conflict resolution are carried out. Here we look at the physical, socio-psychological, and temporal contexts and—perhaps the most important—the cultural context.

The Physical, Socio-psychological, and Temporal Contexts

The *physical context*—for example, whether you engage in conflict privately or publicly, alone or in front of children or relatives—will influence the way the conflict is conducted as well as the effects that this conflict will have.

The *socio-psychological context* also will influence the conflict. If the atmosphere is one of equality, for example, the conflict is likely to progress very differently than it would in an atmosphere of inequality. A friendly or a hostile context will exert different influences on the conflict.

The *temporal context* will likewise prove important to understand. A conflict that follows a series of similar conflicts will be seen differently than a conflict that follows a series of enjoyable experiences and an absence of conflict. A conflict immediately after a hard day of work will engender feelings different from a conflict after an enjoyable dinner.

The Cultural Context

Culture influences not only the issues that people fight about, but also what is considered appropriate and inappropriate in terms of dealing with conflict. For example, cohabiting 18-year-olds are more likely to experience conflict with their parents about their living style if they live in the United States than if they live in Sweden, where cohabitation is much more accepted. Similarly, male infidelity is more likely to cause conflict between American spouses than in southern European couples. Students from the United States are more likely to engage in conflict with another U.S. student than with someone from another culture. Chinese students, on the other hand, are more likely to engage in a conflict with a non-Chinese student than with another Chinese (Leung, 1988).

The types of conflicts that arise depend on the cultural orientation of the individuals involved. For example, in collectivist cultures, such as those of Ecuador, Indonesia, and Korea, conflicts are more likely to center on violations of collective or group norms and values. Disagreeing in public or proving a colleague wrong in front of others and causing this person to lose face (and violate important cultural norms) is likely to create conflict. Conversely, in individualist cultures, such as those of the United States, Canada, and western Europe, conflicts are more likely to occur when people violate individual norms; for example, if bonuses are not distributed according to merit (Ting-Toomey, 1985).

The cultural norms of organizations also influence the types of conflicts that occur and the ways people may deal with them. Some work environments, for example, would not tolerate the expression of disagreement with high-level management; others might welcome it. In individualist cultures there is greater tolerance for conflict, even when it involves different levels of an organizational hierarchy. In collectivist cultures, there's less tolerance. And, not surprisingly, the culture influences how the conflict will be resolved. For example, managers in the United States (an individualist culture) deal with workplace conflict by seeking to integrate the demands of the different sides; managers in China (a collectivist culture) are more likely to call on higher management to make decisions—or not to resolve the conflict at all (Tinsley & Brett, 2001).

Conflict Styles Have Consequences

The way in which you approach and engage in conflict has consequences for the resolution of the conflict and for the relationship between the conflicting parties. Consider five basic ways in which people approach interpersonal, group, or organizational conflict (Blake & Mouton, 1984).

Watch at MyCommunicationLab Video: "Time Troubles"

Competing: I Win, You Lose

The competitive style involves great concern for your own needs and desires and little for those of others. As long as your needs are met, the conflict has been dealt with successfully (for you). In conflict motivated by competitiveness, you'd be likely to be verbally aggressive and to blame the other person.

This style represents an "I win, you lose" philosophy. This is the conflict style of a person who simply imposes his or her will on the other: "I make the money, and we'll vacation at the beach or not at all." But this philosophy often leads to resentment on the part of the person who loses, which can cause additional conflicts. Further, the fact that you win and the other person loses probably means that the conflict hasn't really been resolved but has only concluded (for now).

Avoiding: I Lose, You Lose

Conflict avoiders are relatively unconcerned with their own or with their opponents' needs or desires. They avoid any real communication about the problem, change topics when the problem is brought up, and generally withdraw both psychologically and physically.

As you can appreciate, the avoiding style does little to resolve any conflicts and may be viewed as an "I lose, you lose" philosophy. If a couple can't agree about where to spend their vacation, but each person refuses to negotiate a resolution to the disagreement, the pair may not take any vacation at all, and both sides lose. Interpersonal problems rarely go away of their own accord; rather, if they exist, they need to be faced and dealt with effectively. Avoidance merely allows the conflict to fester and probably grow—only to resurface in another guise.

Accommodating: I Lose, You Win

When you accommodate, you sacrifice your own needs for the needs of the other person(s). Your primary goal is to maintain harmony and peace in the relationship or group. This style may help maintain peace and may satisfy the opposition; but it does little to meet your own needs, which are unlikely to go away.

Accommodation represents an "I lose, you win" philosophy. If your partner wants to vacation in the mountains and you want to vacation at the beach, and you, instead of negotiating an agreement acceptable to both, give in and accommodate, then you lose and your partner wins. And although this style may make your partner happy (at least on this occasion), it's not likely to prove a lasting resolution to an interpersonal conflict. You'll eventually sense unfairness and inequality and may easily come to resent your partner and perhaps even yourself.

COMMUNICATION CHOICE POINT

WIN–WIN SOLUTIONS *Let's say that you and your partner have just received an unexpected $5,000. You want a new car (your old one is unreliable), and your partner wants to spend it on a vacation (your partner is exhausted and feels the need for a rest).* **What are some of your communication choices for achieving win–win solutions in this conflict?**

Collaborating: I Win, You Win

In collaborating you address both your own and the other person's needs. This style, often considered the ideal, takes time and a willingness to communicate—especially to listen to the perspectives and needs of the other person.

Collaboration enables each person's needs to be met, an "I win, you win" situation. For example, you might both agree to split the vacation—one week in the mountains and one week at the beach. Or you might agree to spend this year's vacation at one resort and next year's at the other. This is obviously the style that, in an ideal world, most people would choose for interpersonal conflict.

Compromising: I Win and Lose, You Win and Lose

Compromise is the kind of strategy you might refer to as "meeting each other halfway," "horse trading," or "give and take." There's some concern for your own needs and some concern for the other's needs. This strategy is likely to result in maintaining peace, but there will be a residue of dissatisfaction over the inevitable losses that each side has to endure.

Compromise represents an "I win and lose, you win and lose" philosophy. So, if you and your partner can't vacation at both the beach and the mountains, then you might settle for weekend trips or use the money to have a hot tub installed instead. These may not be your first choices, but they're not bad and may satisfy (to some degree at least) each of your vacation wants.

Table 13.1 summarizes these five conflict styles and their possible consequences.

13.3 PRELIMINARIES TO CONFLICT MANAGEMENT

In managing conflict, you can choose from a variety of strategies, which the next section will describe. Before getting to the specific conflict management strategies, however, we need to consider some preliminaries. You're more likely to select appropriate strategies if you prepare for and follow up the conflict appropriately, understand the influences on your choice of conflict strategies, and apply the stages of conflict management.

Before the Conflict

Try to fight in private—within the relationship or within the group. When you air your conflicts in front of others, you create a wide variety of other problems. You may not be willing to be totally honest when third parties are present; you may feel you have to save face and therefore must win the fight at all costs. This may lead you to use strategies aimed at winning the argument rather than strategies aimed at resolving the conflict. Also, of course, you run the risk of embarrassing or upsetting others, which will cause resentment and hostility.

Be sure everyone is ready to fight. Although conflicts arise at the most inopportune times, you can choose the time when you will try to resolve them. The moment when your partner comes home after a hard day of work may not be the right time for a confrontation. When a group is completing the company's most important project on a deadline, it may not be the wisest time to raise minor conflict issues. In general, make sure that all individuals are relatively free of other problems and ready to deal with the conflict at hand.

Fight about problems that can be solved. Fighting about past behaviors or about family members or situations over which you have no control solves nothing; instead, it creates additional difficulties. Any attempt at resolution is doomed because, by their nature, such problems can't be solved. Often such conflicts are concealed attempts at expressing frustration or dissatisfaction.

Consider what beliefs you hold that may need to be reexamined. Unrealistic beliefs are often at the heart of interpersonal and group conflicts. Such

TABLE 13.1

In A Nutshell A Summary of Conflict Styles

Here is a brief summary of the five conflict styles, their basic ideas, and some possible, but not inevitable, consequences.

Conflict Style	Basic Idea	Possible Consequences
Competing: I Win, You Lose	You have great concern for your own needs and desires and little for those of the other person.	■ Doesn't resolve the conflict. ■ Can lead to resentment on the part of the person who loses.
Avoiding: I Lose, You Lose	You both avoid the conflict and withdraw from it.	■ The problem causing the conflict doesn't go away and is likely to grow. ■ No one benefits here.
Accommodating: I Lose, You Win	You sacrifice your own needs for the needs of the other person(s) in order to keep the peace.	■ Unlikely to provide a long-lasting resolution. ■ You may come to resent your partner and the relationship.
Collaborating: I Win, You Win	You focus on both your needs and the other person's.	■ Enables each person's needs to be met, an "I win, you win" situation.
Compromising: I Win and Lose, You Win and Lose	You have some concern for your needs and some concern for the other's.	■ May lead to dissatisfaction by both parties over the losses.

beliefs include ideas like "If my partner really cared, he or she would do what I ask," "If people really cared about the success of the group, they'd devote 100 percent of their time to the project," or "People don't listen to what I have to say."

After the Conflict

After the conflict is resolved, there's still work to be done. Often, after one conflict is supposedly settled, another conflict will emerge—because, for example, one person may feel harmed and may feel the need to retaliate and take revenge in order to restore self-worth (Kim & Smith, 1993). So it's especially important that the conflict be resolved in such a way that it does not generate other, perhaps more significant, conflicts.

Learn from the conflict and from the process you went through in trying to resolve it. For example, can you identify the fight strategies that aggravated the situation? Do some people need a cooling-off period? Do you need extra space when upset? Can you identify when minor issues are going to escalate into major arguments? Does avoidance make matters worse? What issues are particularly disturbing and likely to cause difficulties? Can these be avoided?

Negative feelings frequently arise after a conflict, most often because unfair fight strategies were used—strategies such as personal rejection, manipulation, or force. Resolve to avoid such unfair tactics in the future, but at the same time let go of guilt and blame for yourself and others. If you think it would help, discuss these feelings with your partner, your group members, or even a therapist.

Increase the exchange of rewards and cherishing behaviors to demonstrate your positive feelings and to show that you're over the conflict. It's a good way of saying you want the relationship or the group to survive and to flourish.

Influences on Your Choice of Conflict Strategies

A variety of factors will influence the strategies you choose to manage your interpersonal conflicts (Koerner & Fitzpatrick, 2002). Understanding these factors may help you select more appropriate and more effective strategies to manage conflict with success (Neff & Harter, 2002; Weitzman, 2001; Weitzman & Weitzman, 2000).

- **Goals.** The goals (short-term and long-term) you wish to achieve will influence what strategies seem appropriate to you. If you just want to enjoy the moment, you might want to simply "give in" and ignore the difficulty. On the other hand, if you want to build a long-term relationship, you might want to fully analyze the cause of the problem and look for strategies that will enable both parties to win.
- **Emotional state.** Your emotional state will influence your strategies; you're not likely to select the same strategies when you're sorry as when you're angry. When sorry, you're likely to use conciliatory strategies designed to make peace; but when you're angry, you're more likely to use strategies that attack the other person.
- **Cognitive assessment.** Your cognitive assessment of the situation will exert powerful influence on your selection of strategies. For example, your attitudes and beliefs about what is fair and equitable will influence your readiness to acknowledge the fairness in the other person's position. Your own assessment of who (if anyone) is the cause of the problem also will influence your conflict style. You may also assess the likely effects of your various strategies. For example, what do you risk if you fight with your boss by using blame or personal rejection? As a parent, do you risk alienating your teenager if you use force?
- **Personality and communication competence.** Your personality and communication competence will influence the way you engage in conflict. For example, if you're shy and unassertive, you may want to avoid conflict rather than fight actively. If you're extroverted and have a strong desire to state your position, you may be more likely to fight actively and forcefully.
- **Family history.** Your family history influences the strategies you use, the topics you choose to fight about, and perhaps your tendencies to obsess or forget about interpersonal conflicts. People often imitate their parents.

The Stages of Conflict Management

Earlier, in Chapter 10 (pages 220–222), we looked at the stages of problem solving in small group communication. If you make the assumption that a conflict is a problem to be resolved, then the steps you go through in managing interpersonal and small group conflict will (generally, at least) follow the problem-solving stages. In brief review, you'll recall these steps:

- **Define and analyze the problem**—just what is causing the conflict?
- **Establish criteria for evaluating solutions**—what will a productive resolution look like?
- **Identify possible solutions**—what changes will help resolve or manage the conflict?
- **Evaluate solutions**—which solutions seem to best meet the criteria already identified and thus go furthest in managing the conflict?
- **Select the best solution**—what solution seems to satisfy all sides the most?
- **Test the selected solution**—how does the relationship do under this new solution?

13.4 CONFLICT MANAGEMENT STRATEGIES

Before reading about the various conflict management strategies, examine your own conflict management tendencies by responding to the following statements with True if the statement is a generally accurate description of your interpersonal conflict behavior and False if the statement is a generally inaccurate description of your behavior.

_____ **1.** I strive to seek solutions that will benefit both of us.

_____ **2.** I look for solutions that will give me what I want.

_____ **3.** I confront conflict situations as they arrive.

_____ **4.** I avoid conflict situations as best I can.

_____ **5.** My messages are basically descriptive of the events leading up to the conflict.

_____ **6.** My messages are often judgmental.

_____ **7.** I take into consideration the face needs of the other person.

_____ **8.** I advance the strongest arguments I can find even if these attack the other person.

_____ **9.** I center my arguments on issues rather than on personalities.

_____ **10.** I use messages that may attack a person's self-image if this will help me win the argument.

These statements were designed to sensitize you to some of the conflict strategies to be discussed in this section of the chapter. They are not intended to give you a specific score. Generally, however, you'd be following the principles of effective interpersonal conflict management if you answered True to the odd-numbered statements (1, 3, 5, 7, and 9) and False to the even-numbered statements (2, 4, 6, 8, and 10). As you think about your responses and read the text discussion ask yourself what you can do to improve your own conflict management skills.

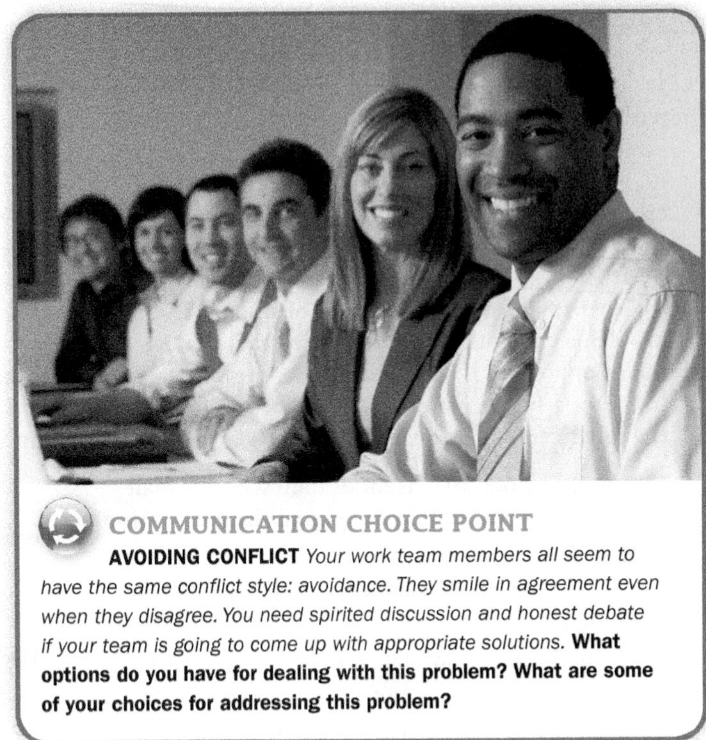

COMMUNICATION CHOICE POINT

AVOIDING CONFLICT *Your work team members all seem to have the same conflict style: avoidance. They smile in agreement even when they disagree. You need spirited discussion and honest debate if your team is going to come up with appropriate solutions.* **What options do you have for dealing with this problem? What are some of your choices for addressing this problem?**

Win–Lose and Win–Win Strategies

If you look at interpersonal and small group conflict in terms of winning and losing, you'll see that there are four potential outcomes: (1) A wins, B loses; (2) A loses, B wins; (3) A loses, B loses; and (4) A wins, B wins.

In managing conflict you have a choice and can seek to achieve any one of those combinations of winning and losing. You can look for solutions in which one person or one side wins (usually you or your side) and the other person or other side loses: **win–lose solutions.** Or you can look for solutions in which both you and the other person or side win: **win–win solutions.**

Obviously, win–win solutions are the most desirable. Perhaps the most important reason is that win–win solutions lead to mutual satisfaction and prevent the resentment that win–lose solutions often engender. Looking for and developing win–win solutions makes the next conflict less unpleasant; the participants can more easily view conflict as "solving a problem" rather than as "fighting." Still another advantage is that win–win solutions promote mutual face-saving: Both parties can feel good about themselves.

Avoidance and Active Fighting

One nonproductive conflict strategy is **avoidance.** Avoidance may involve actual physical flight: You may leave the scene (walk out of the apartment or meeting room). Or you may simply psychologically tune out all incoming arguments or problems. In the United States men are more likely to use avoidance than women (Markman, Silvern, Clements, & Kraft-Hanak, 1993; Oggins, Veroff, & Leber, 1993), often additionally denying that anything is wrong (Haferkamp, 1991–92).

Nonnegotiation is a special type of avoidance. Here you refuse to discuss the conflict or to listen to the other person's argument. At times, nonnegotiation takes the form of hammering away at your point of view until the other person gives in, a method referred to as "steamrolling."

Instead of avoiding the issues, take an active role in your conflicts. Don't close your ears (or mind) or walk out during an argument. This does not mean that taking time out to cool off is not a useful first strategy. Sometimes it is. In an e-mail conflict, for example, a cooling-off period is an easy-to-use and often effective strategy. By delaying your response until you've had time to think things out more logically and calmly, you'll be better able to respond constructively and to address possible ways to resolve the conflict and get the relationship back to a less hostile stage.

Another part of active fighting involves taking responsibility for your thoughts and feelings. For example, when you disagree with your partner or with other group members, say, "I disagree with..." or "I don't like it when you..." Avoid statements that deny your responsibility, as in, "Everybody thinks you're wrong about..." or "Even the photography department thinks we shouldn't..."

Force and Talk

When confronted with conflict, many people prefer not to deal with the issues but rather to force their position on the other person. **Force** may be emotional or physical. In either case, it is an unproductive strategy: The issues are avoided, and the person who "wins" is merely the combatant who exerts the most force. This is the technique used by warring nations, children, and even some normally sensible and mature adults. It seems also to be the technique of some persons who are dissatisfied with the power they perceive themselves to have in a relationship, as research shows that perpetrators of violence against both men and women often are motivated to gain control or to defend their own image (Felson, 2002; Ronfeldt, Kimerling, & Arias, 1998).

The use of force is surely one of the most serious problems confronting relationships today, although many approach it as if it were a minor—or even humorous—issue. Here are some sobering facts from the American Bar Association (2006):

- Approximately 20 percent of high school female students report physical or sexual abuse by dating partners.
- Teen dating violence occurs among all races and socioeconomic groups.
- About 50 percent of date rapes are of teenagers.
- More than 80 percent of parents surveyed believe teen dating violence is not a problem.
- More than 50 percent of parents admit to not having spoken about dating violence with their teenagers.

The only real alternative to force is talk. Instead of using force, you need to talk and listen. The qualities of empathy, openness, and positiveness (see Chapter 7), for example, are suitable starting points.

Blame and Empathy

Conflict is rarely caused by a single, clearly identifiable problem or by only one of the parties. Usually, conflict occurs because of a wide variety of factors, and all concerned play a role. Any attempt to single out one person for **blame** is sure to be unproductive. Even so, a frequently used fight strategy is to blame another person. Consider, for example, the couple who fight over their child's getting into trouble with the police. Instead of dealing with the conflict itself, the parents may blame each other for the child's troubles. Such blaming, of course, does nothing to resolve the problem or to help the child.

Often, when you blame someone, you attribute motives to the person, a process often referred to as "mind reading." Thus, if the person forgot your birthday and this disturbs you, tackle the actual behavior—the forgetting of the birthday. Try not to presuppose motives: "Well, it's obvious you just don't care about me. If you really cared, you could never have forgotten my birthday!"

Empathy is an excellent alternative to blame. Try to feel what the other person is feeling and to see the situation as the other person does. Try to see the situation as punctuated by the other person and think about how this differs from your own punctuation.

Demonstrate empathic understanding. Once you have empathically understood the feelings of the other person or group members, validate those feelings as appropriate. If your partner is hurt or angry and you feel that such feelings are legitimate and justified (from the other person's point of view), say so; say, "You have a right to be angry; I shouldn't have said what I did. I'm sorry. But I still don't want to go on vacation with your college roommate." In expressing validation you're not necessarily expressing agreement on the point at issue; you're merely stating that your partner's feelings are legitimate and that you recognize them as such.

Gunnysacking and Present Focus

A gunnysack is a large bag, usually made of burlap. The unproductive conflict strategy known as **gunnysacking** is the practice of storing up grievances so as to unload them at another time (Bach & Wyden, 1968). The occasion for unloading may be relatively minor (or so it might seem at first); for example, you come home late without calling, or you fail to fulfill your assigned task before a meeting at work. Instead of addressing the immediate problem, the gunnysacker unloads all past grievances. The birthday you forgot, the times you were absent from meetings, the hotel reservations you forgot to make. As you probably know from experience, gunnysacking begets gunnysacking. When one person gunnysacks, the other person gunnysacks. The result is that both sides dump their stored-up grievances on each other. Frequently, the trigger problem never gets addressed. Instead, resentment and hostility escalate.

Focus your conflict on the here and now rather than on issues that occurred 2 months ago. Similarly, focus your conflict on the person with whom you're fighting, not on the person's mother, child, or friends.

Manipulation and Spontaneity

Manipulation involves an avoidance of open conflict. The manipulative individual tries to divert conflict by being especially charming (disarming, actually). The manipulator gets the other individual into a receptive and non-combative frame of mind, then presents his or her demands to a weakened opponent. The manipulator relies on our tendency to give in to people who are especially nice to us.

me•di•a lit•er•a•cy *noun* ability to understand, interact with, and create media messages

EXPANDING MEDIA LITERACY
Public Relations

Public relations (PR) is a communication strategy designed to convey information so as to establish positive relationships between a corporation, agency, or other group and the public (Folkerts, Lacy, & Larabee, 2008; Rodman, 2001; Vivian, 2011).

Public relations practitioners engage in a wide variety of activities to accomplish their purposes:

- **Lobbying.** Lobbying to influence government officials or agencies to fund a proposal, support a nominee, or vote for or against an upcoming bill.
- **Raising money.** Raising funds for colleges, political candidates, charities, or public broadcasting stations.
- **Controlling crises.** The work of PR practitioners often involves efforts to repair potentially damaged images, whether in regard to defective or problematic products—cars, dietary supplements, or drugs—or in regard to an organization's financial problems.
- **Influencing public opinion.** PR professionals try to persuade you, for example, to support a political candidate or initiative or to change your attitudes on a variety of issues—abortion, campaign financing, gay rights, and a host of other issues you read about daily.
- **Establishing and repairing images.** PR practitioners might try, for example, to establish good relationships between a community and a company that wants to erect a mall in the neighborhood, improve the image of the police department in a community, or repair a company's image after some wrongdoing.

Public relations persuasion is all around us, but its strategies are well hidden. For one day become especially mindful of the influence of public relation professionals. In what ways are they exerting persuasion on you?

Instead of manipulating, try expressing your feelings with **spontaneity** and honesty. Remember that in conflict situations there's no need to plan a strategy to win a war. The objective is not to win but to increase mutual understanding and to reach a decision that both parties can accept.

Personal Rejection and Acceptance

A person practicing **personal rejection** withholds approval and affection from his or her opponent in conflict, seeking to win the argument by getting the other person to break down in the face of this withdrawal. The individual acts cold and uncaring in an effort to demoralize the other person. In a group situation a person might practice rejection by not listening, not giving any positive feedback, or perhaps even giving negative feedback, making you think everything you're saying is gibberish. In withdrawing positive messages, the rejecting individual hopes to make the other person question his or her own self-worth. Once the other is demoralized and feels less than worthy, it's relatively easy for "rejecters" to get their way. They hold out the renewal of approval and affection as a reward for a resolution in their own favor.

Instead of rejection, express positive feelings for the other person and for the relationship or group. Throughout any conflict, harsh words will probably be exchanged, later to be regretted. The words cannot be unsaid or uncommunicated, but they can be partially offset by the expression of positive statements.

Fighting below and above the Belt

Much like boxers in a ring, each of us has a "belt line." When you hit someone below the emotional belt line, a tactic called **beltlining,** you can inflict serious injury. When you hit above the belt, however, the person is able to absorb the blow. With most interpersonal relationships, especially those of long standing, we know where the belt line is. You know, for example, that to hit Pat with the inability to have children is to hit below the belt. You know that to hit Chris with the failure to get a permanent job is to hit below the belt. You know that to stress the number of years your colleague has been in the same position without a promotion is to hit below the belt. Hitting below the belt line causes everyone involved added problems. Keep blows to areas your opponent can absorb and handle.

eth•ics *noun* morality, standards of conduct, moral judgment

MAKING ETHICAL CHOICES
Ethical Fighting

This chapter emphasizes the differences between effective and ineffective conflict strategies. But every conflict strategy also has an ethical dimension. Consider just a few examples.

- Does conflict avoidance have an ethical dimension? For example, is it unethical for one romantic partner to refuse to discuss issues of disagreement with the other?
- Is it ever ethical to force someone to accept your position? Can you identify a situation in which it would be appropriate for someone with greater physical strength to overpower another person to enforce his or her point of view?
- Is it ever ethical to use face-detracting strategies? Are face-detracting strategies inherently unethical, or might it be appropriate to use them in certain situations? Can you identify such situations?
- What are the ethical implications of verbal aggressiveness? Why might it be argued that argumentativeness is more ethical than verbal aggressiveness?

Ethical Choice Point

At your high-powered and highly stressful job you sometimes use cocaine with your colleagues. This happens several times a month. You don't use drugs of any kind at any other times. Your partner—who you know hates drugs and despises people who use any recreational drug—asks you if you take drugs. Because your use is so limited, but mostly because you know that admitting it will cause a huge conflict in a relationship that's already having difficulties, you wonder if you can ethically lie about this. What ethical choices do you have in this situation? What is your ethical obligation? What would you say?

Remember that the aim of interpersonal and small group conflict is not to win and have your opponent lose. Rather, it's to resolve a problem and strengthen the relationship or group. Keep this ultimate goal always in clear focus, especially when you're angry or hurt.

Face-Detracting and Face-Enhancing Strategies

Another dimension of conflict strategies is that of *face orientation*. Face-detracting or face-attacking strategies involve treating the other person as incompetent or untrustworthy, as unable or bad (Donohue, 1992). These attack a person's need for positive face. Such attacks can vary from mildly embarrassing to severely damaging to the other person's ego or reputation (Imahori & Cupach, 1994). When such attacks become extreme, they may be similar to verbal aggressiveness—another unproductive tactic that we'll consider shortly. Protecting our image (or face), especially in the midst of conflict, is important to everyone, but especially important to members of the collectivist cultures of Asia (Zane & Yeh, 2002). Another type of face-detracting strategy is to demand that someone do something or force them to do it; this attacks their need for autonomy, their need for negative face.

Face-enhancing techniques, in contrast, help the other person maintain a positive image—an image as competent and trustworthy, able and good. There's some evidence to show that even when, say, you get what you want in a bargaining situation, it is wise to help the other person retain positive face. This makes it less likely that future conflicts will arise (Donohue, 1992).

Not surprisingly, people are more likely to make a greater effort to support their opponent's "face" if they like the opponent than if they don't (Meyer, 1994). So be especially careful to avoid "fighting words"—words that are sure to escalate the conflict rather than to help resolve it. Words like *stupid, liar,* and *bitch,* as well as words like *always* and *never* (as in "you always" or "you never"), invariably create additional problems. In contrast, confirming the other person's definition of self, avoiding attack and blame, and using excuses and apologies as appropriate are some generally useful face-enhancing strategies.

Aggressiveness and Argumentativeness

An especially interesting perspective on conflict has emerged from researchers' work on verbal aggressiveness and argumentativeness (Avtgis & Rancer, 2010; Infante, 1988; Rancer, 1998; Wigley, 1998). Understanding these two concepts will help you understand some of the reasons why things go wrong and some of the ways in which you can use conflict to actually improve your relationships.

Verbal aggressiveness is an unproductive conflict strategy in which one person tries to win an argument by inflicting psychological pain, by attacking the other person's self-concept. The technique relies on many of the other unproductive conflict strategies we've already considered. It's a type of disconfirmation in that it seeks to discredit the individual's view of self (see Chapter 5).

Contrary to popular usage, **argumentativeness** is a quality to be cultivated rather than avoided. The term *argumentativeness* in this context refers to your willingness to argue for a point of view, your tendency to speak your mind on significant issues. It's the mode of dealing with disagreements that is the preferred alternative to verbal aggressiveness (Infante & Rancer, 1996). Assess your own degree of argumentativeness by taking the accompanying self-test.

Watch at MyCommunicationLab Video: "Jim and Jack Joust"

As you can appreciate, there are numerous differences between argumentativeness and verbal aggressiveness. A few of these differences are presented in Table 13.2, on page 278.

Most relevant here are the suggestions for developing argumentativeness—and for preventing it from degenerating into aggressiveness (Atvgis & Rancer, 2010; Infante, 1988; Infante & Rancer, 1996).

COMMUNICATION CHOICE POINT

VERBAL AGGRESSIVENESS *Your work colleague persists in being verbally aggressive whenever you have an argument. Regardless of what the conflict is about, your self-concept is attacked.* **What are some of the things you might say or do to stop these attacks? What channel(s) would you use?**

- Treat disagreements as objectively as possible; avoid assuming that because someone takes issue with your position or your interpretation, they're attacking you as a person.
- Center your arguments on issues rather than personalities. Avoid attacking a person (rather than the person's arguments), even if this would give you a tactical advantage—it will probably backfire at some later time and make your relationship or group participation more difficult.
- Reaffirm the other person's sense of competence; compliment the other person as appropriate.
- Allow the other person to state her or his position fully before you respond; avoid interrupting.
- Stress equality, and stress the similarities that you have with the other person or persons; stress your areas of agreement before attacking the disagreements.
- Express interest in the other person's position, attitude, and point of view.
- Avoid getting overemotional; using an overly loud voice or interjecting vulgar expressions will prove offensive and eventually ineffective.
- Allow people to save face; never humiliate another person.

Explore at MyCommunicationLab Exercise: "Analyzing a Conflict Episode"

TABLE 13.2 DIFFERENCES BETWEEN ARGUMENTATIVENESS AND VERBAL AGGRESSIVENESS

Here are just a few differences between arguing and being verbally aggressive (Atvgis & Rancer, 2010; Infante & Rancer, 1996; Rancer & Atvgis, 2006). As you read this table consider your own conflict tendencies.

Argumentativeness	Verbal Aggressiveness
Is **constructive**; the outcomes are positive in a variety of communication situations.	Is **destructive**; the outcomes are negative in a variety of communication situations.
Leads to **relationship satisfaction**.	Leads to **relationship dissatisfaction**, not surprising for a strategy that aims to attack another's self-concept.
May **prevent relationship violence**, especially in domestic relationships.	May lead to **relationship violence**.
Enhances organizational life; for example, subordinates prefer supervisors who encourage argumentativeness.	**Damages organizational life** and demoralizes workers on varied levels.
Enhances parent–child communication and enables parents to gain greater compliance.	**Prevents meaningful parent–child communication** and makes corporal punishment more likely.
Increases the user's credibility; argumentatives are seen as trustworthy, committed, and dynamic.	**Decreases the user's credibility**, in part because it's seen as a tactic to discredit the person rather than address the argument.
Increases the user's power of persuasion; argumentatives are more likely to be seen as leaders.	**Decreases the user's power** of persuasion.

Tim's dorm mate Luis is very popular and has an open-door policy. Day and night, friends drop by to chat, borrow books, check their e-mail, and socialize—all of which prevents Tim from studying. Normally Tim puts up with the heavy traffic, but midterms are coming up and he needs to focus. "Dorm Room Conflict" looks at the process of interpersonal conflict and some of the choices you might make to resolve the conflict and some of the choices that aggravate the conflict and that you'd want to avoid. Log on to www.mycommunicationlab.com to view this video and the varied choices, and then answer the related discussion questions.

SUMMARY: INTERPERSONAL, GROUP, AND WORKPLACE CONFLICT

Study and **Review** at MyCommunicationLab

Listen to the **Chapter Summary** at MyCommunicationLab

This chapter explored interpersonal, small group, and workplace conflict, the principles of conflict, and the effective and ineffective conflict management strategies.

13.1 INTERPERSONAL, GROUP, AND WORKPLACE CONFLICT

1. Relationship and small group conflict occurs among people who are connected but who have opposing goals that interfere with others' desired goals. Conflicts may occur face to face or on the Internet, through e-mail, in newsgroups, and in other contexts.
2. Interpersonal conflicts may yield both positive and/or negative results.

13.2 PRINCIPLES OF CONFLICT

3. Content conflicts center on objects, events, and persons in the world that are usually (though not always) external to the parties involved.

4. Relationship conflicts are concerned not so much with some external object as with relationships between individuals—with such issues as who is in charge, how equal the partners are in a primary relationship, or who has the right to set down rules of behavior.

13.3 PRELIMINARIES TO CONFLICT MANAGEMENT

5. In preparation for conflict, try to fight in private and when all are ready to fight. Have a clear idea of what you want to fight about, and be specific; fight about things that can be solved; and reexamine beliefs that may be unrealistic. Consider, too, the value of following a standard sequence of steps in dealing with the conflict.

6. After the conflict, assess what you've learned, keep the conflict in perspective, let go of negative feelings, and increase positiveness.

7. Among the conflict styles are competing, avoiding, accommodating, collaborating, and compromising.

13.4 CONFLICT MANAGEMENT STRATEGIES

8. Unproductive and productive conflict strategies include: win–lose and win–win approaches, avoidance and fighting actively, force and talk, blame and empathy, gunnysacking and present focus, manipulation and spontaneity, personal rejection and acceptance, fighting below and above the belt, face-detracting and face-enhancing tactics, nonassertive and assertive approaches, and fighting aggressively and argumentatively.

9. To cultivate constructive argumentativeness, treat disagreements objectively and avoid attacking the other person, reaffirm the other's sense of competence, avoid interrupting, stress equality and similarities, express interest in the other's position, avoid presenting your arguments too emotionally, and allow the other to save face.

Study and **Review** the **Flashcards** at **MyCommunicationLab**

KEY TERMS

argumentativeness 277
avoidance 273
beltlining 275
blame 274
content conflict 266
empathy 274
force 273
gunnysacking 274
interpersonal conflict 264
manipulation 274
nonnegotiation 273
personal rejection 275
public relations 275
relationship conflict 267
spontaneity 275
verbal aggressiveness 277
win–lose solution 273
win–win solution 273

WORKING WITH INTERPERSONAL, GROUP, AND WORKPLACE CONFLICT

13.1 Managing Conflicts Early. This exercise helps you look at your own way of dealing with conflict starters—something someone says that signals to you that this is the start of an interpersonal conflict. Recognizing conflict starters may enable you to deal with them at an early stage when they are more easily resolved. For each situation, (a) write an unproductive response (a response that is likely to cause the conflict to escalate); (b) write a productive response (a response that will likely lessen the potential conflict); and (c) in one sentence explain the major difference that you see between the productive and the unproductive responses.

a. You're late again. You're always late. Your lateness is so inconsiderate!

b. I just can't bear another weekend of sitting home watching cartoon shows with the kids.

c. Well, there goes another anniversary that you forgot.

d. You think I'm fat, don't you?

e. You never want to do what I want. We always have to do what you want.

13.2 Finding Win–Win Solutions. As this section explains, win–win conflict strategies are preferable to win–lose approaches, at least when the conflict is interpersonal. Often, however, people fail even to consider what possible win–win solutions might exist. To get into the habit of looking for these types of solutions, try generating as many win–win solutions as possible (that you feel the individuals could reasonably accept) for the following scenarios. Give yourself 2 minutes for each case. If possible, share your win–win solutions with other individuals or groups; also, consider ways in which you might incorporate win–win strategies into your own conflict management behavior.

a. Pat and Chris plan to take a 2-week vacation in August. Pat wants to go to the shore and relax by the water. Chris wants to go the mountains and go hiking and camping.

b. Pat recently got a totally unexpected $3,000 bonus. Pat wants to buy a new computer and printer for the home office; Chris wants to take a much-needed vacation.

c. Philip has recently come out as gay to his parents. He wants them to accept him and his life (which include a committed relationship with a man). His parents want him to seek religious counseling for help in changing his orientation.

13.3 **Gender Differences.** Why do you think men are more likely to withdraw from conflict than women? For example, what arguments can you present for or against any of these reasons (Noller, 1993): (a) Because men have difficulty dealing with conflict? (b) Because the culture has taught men to avoid it? (c) Because withdrawal is an expression of power?

13.4 **Culture and Conflict.** What does your own culture teach about conflict and its management? For example: What strategies does it prohibit? Are some strategies prohibited in conflicts with certain people (say, your parents) but not in conflicts with others (say, your friends)? Does your culture prescribe certain ways of dealing with conflict? Does it have different expectations for men and for women? To what degree do these teachings have on your actual conflict behaviors?

13.5 **Conflict Style.** How would you describe your conflict style in your own close relationships in terms of competing-avoiding-accommodating-collaborating-compromising? Is it the same at work?

13.6 **Online Communication and Interpersonal Conflict.** In what ways do you find that online communication can escalate interpersonal conflict? In what ways might texting, e-mailing, or posting on Facebook, for example, help resolve interpersonal conflict?

13.7 **Positiveness.** One study found that, at least in general, people are more positive in dealing with conflict in face-to-face situations than in computer-mediated communication (Zornoza, Ripoll, & Peiró, 2002). Do you find this to be true? If so, why do you think it's true?

LogOn! MyCommunicationLab www.mycommunicationlab.com

Throughout this chapter, there are icons in the margin that highlight media content for selected topics. Go to **MyCommunicationLab** for additional materials on conflict and disagreements in interpersonal relationships and in the social and work groups of which you are a part. Here you'll find flashcards to help you learn key communication terms, videos that illustrate a variety of concepts, additional exercises, and discussions to help you continue your study of interpersonal, group, and workplace conflict.

14 PUBLIC SPEAKING TOPICS, AUDIENCES, AND RESEARCH

CHAPTER TOPICS	CHAPTER OBJECTIVES
In this chapter you'll explore the following major topics:	**After reading this chapter you should be able to:**
INTRODUCING PUBLIC SPEAKING	14.1 Define *public speaking* and identify some of its historical roots and its benefits.
MANAGING YOUR APPREHENSION	14.2 Explain and apply the suggestions for managing public speaking apprehension.
STEP 1: SELECT YOUR TOPIC, PURPOSES, AND THESIS	14.3 Explain the characteristics of good public speaking topics, purposes, and theses.
STEP 2: ANALYZE YOUR AUDIENCE	14.4 Analyze an audience's sociology and psychology.
STEP 3: RESEARCH YOUR TOPIC	14.5 Identify the major research sources, the criteria for evaluating research, and the ways to integrate and cite the research.

What's understandable to one audience, may not be to another.

Public speaking is one of the essential skills people need to function effectively in today's society. The higher you move in any chain of command—say, from intern, to junior analyst, to manager, to CEO—the more important public speaking becomes. This section of *Human Communication* explains these essential skills—the skills you'll need to prepare and present effective public speeches. As you'll see throughout this and the next five chapters, these skills will also prove useful to you in a variety of other situations as well. As you read these chapters, refer to the speeches in the appendix; these speeches and the accompanying annotations will help illustrate the principles discussed here.

14.1 INTRODUCING PUBLIC SPEAKING

In **public speaking** a speaker presents a relatively continuous message to a relatively large audience in a unique context (see Figure 14.1). Like all forms of communication, public speaking is transactional (Watzlawick 1978; Watzlawick, Beavin, & Jackson 1967): Each element in the public speaking process depends on and interacts with all other elements. For example, the way in which you organize a speech will depend on such factors as the speech topic, the specific audience, the purpose you hope to achieve, and a host of other variables—all of which are explained in the remainder of this chapter and in the chapters to follow.

Especially important is the mutual interaction and influence between speaker and listeners. True, when you give a speech, you do most of the speaking and the listeners do most of the listening. However, the listeners also send messages in the form of feedback—for example, applause, bored looks, nods of agreement or disagreement, and attentive glances. The audience also influences how you'll prepare and present your speech. It influences your arguments, your language, your method of organization, and, in fact, every choice you make. You would not, for example, present the same speech on saving money to high school students as you would to senior citizens.

A Brief History

Although public speaking principles were probably developed soon after our species began to talk, it was in ancient Greece and Rome that our Western tradition of public speaking got its start. This Greco-Roman tradition has been enriched by the experiments, surveys, field studies, and historical studies that have been done since classical times and that continue to be done today.

Aristotle's *Rhetoric*, written some 2,300 years ago in ancient Greece, was one of the earliest systematic studies of public speaking. It was in this work that the three kinds of persuasive appeals—*logos* (or logical proof), *pathos* (emotional appeals), and *ethos* (appeals based on the character of the speaker)—were introduced. This three-part division is still followed today; Chapter 18 discusses the three kinds of persuasive appeals in more detail.

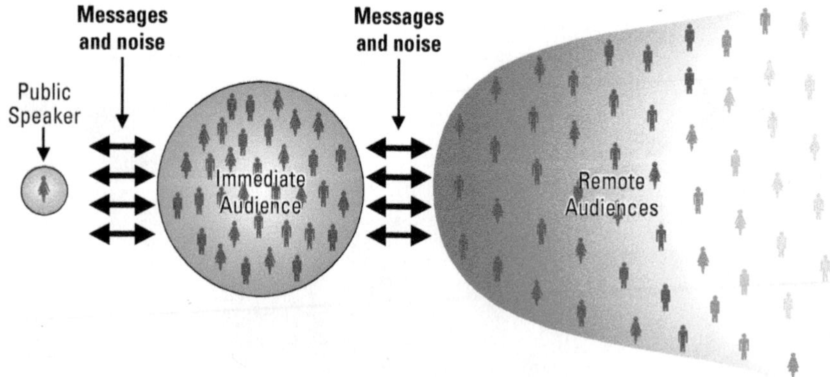

FIGURE 14.1 **Process and Elements of Public Speaking**

This diagram is designed to illustrate the interplay of elements in the public speaking process and to emphasize that there are a variety of audiences of public speaking: (1) the immediate audience that hears the speaker as it is spoken, whether in person, on television, over the Internet, or even via cell phone, and (2) the remote audiences that get the material secondhand; for example, they read the speech, read about the speech, or hear from those who heard the speech or from those who heard about the speech from immediate audience members or from those who heard about the speech from those who heard about the speech. As you can appreciate, the immediate audience is finite (limited to the number of people who heard the speech first hand) but the remote audience is potentially infinite (and hence is indicated with a parabola).

Roman rhetoricians added to the work of the Greeks. Quintilian, who taught in Rome during the first century, built an entire educational system—from childhood through adulthood—based on the development of the effective and responsible orator. Over the following 2,000 years, the study of public speaking continued to grow and develop.

Contemporary public speaking—the kind discussed in this text—builds on this classical heritage but also incorporates insights from the humanities, the social and behavioral sciences, and computer science and information technology. Likewise, perspectives from different cultures are being integrated into our present study of public speaking. Table 14.1 shows some of the contributors to contemporary public speaking and illustrates the wide research and theory base from which the principles of this discipline are drawn.

The Benefits of Public Speaking

Here are just a few of the benefits you'll derive from this section of the text and from your course work in public speaking.

Improve Your Public Speaking Abilities

Speakers aren't born; they're made. Through instruction, exposure to different speeches, experience with diverse audiences, feedback on your own speeches, and individual learning experiences, you can become an effective speaker. Regardless of your present level of competence, you can improve through proper training.

At the end of your public speaking training, you'll be a more competent, confident, and effective public speaker. You'll also be a more effective listener—more open yet more critical, more empathic yet more discriminating. And you'll emerge a more competent and discerning critic of public communication. You'll learn to organize and explain complex concepts and processes clearly and effectively to a wide variety of listeners. You'll learn to support an argument with all the available means of persuasion and to present a persuasive appeal to audiences of varied types.

Improve Your Personal and Social Abilities

In your study of public speaking you'll also learn a variety of personal and social competencies. Perhaps one of the most important is to manage your fear of

TABLE 14.1 GROWTH AND DEVELOPMENT OF PUBLIC SPEAKING

Academic Roots	Contributions to Public Speaking
Rhetoric and Public Address	■ Emphasis on substance ■ Ethical responsibilities of the speaker ■ Use of a combination of logical, ethical, and emotional appeals ■ Strategies of organization ■ Insights into how famous speakers dealt with varied purposes and audiences to achieve desired effects
Philosophy	■ Emphasis on the logical validity of arguments ■ Continuing contribution to ethics
Psychology	■ How language is made easier to understand and remember ■ Principles of attitude and behavior change ■ Emphasis on behavioral effects of communication
Communication Theory and Interpersonal Communication	■ Insights on information transmission ■ The importance of viewing the whole of the communication act ■ The understanding of such concepts as feedback, noise, channel, and message ■ The emphasis on mutual influence of speaker and audience
Sociology and Anthropology	■ Data on audiences' attitudes, values, opinions, and beliefs and how these influence exposure to and responses to messages ■ Insights into the attitudes, beliefs, and values of different cultures and how these influence communication in general and public speaking in particular
Language, Linguistics, Semantics, General Semantics	■ Insights into style ■ Emphasis on using language to describe reality accurately ■ Techniques for avoiding common thinking errors that faulty language usage creates
Computer Science and Information Technology	■ The virtual audience ■ Design, outlining, and presentation software ■ Search tools for research and easily accessed databases

communication situations in general and of public speaking in particular. You may not eliminate your fear entirely, but you'll be able to manage it so that it works for you rather than against you.

You'll also develop greater self-confidence in presenting yourself and your ideas to others—competencies that are consistently ranked high in lists of what employers look for in hiring and promoting (Morreale & Pearson, 2008).

As you master the skills of public speaking, you'll grow in power; you'll become more effective in influencing the thinking and behavior of others. At the same time, power enables you to empower others, whether as organizational manager, political leader, older sibling, or member of any of hundreds of groups.

Improve Your Academic and Career Skills

As you learn public speaking, you'll also learn a wide variety of academic and career skills, many of which are largely communication skills (as you can tell from reading the employment ads, especially for middle-management positions in just about every field you can name). For example, you will learn to:

- conduct research efficiently and effectively, using the latest and the best techniques available.
- critically analyze and evaluate arguments and evidence from any and all sources.
- understand human motivation and make effective use of your insights in persuasive encounters.
- develop an effective communication style (whether for conversation or for that important job interview) that you feel comfortable with.
- give and respond appropriately to criticism so as to increase your insight into your own strengths and weaknesses.
- communicate your competence, character, and charisma to make yourself believable.

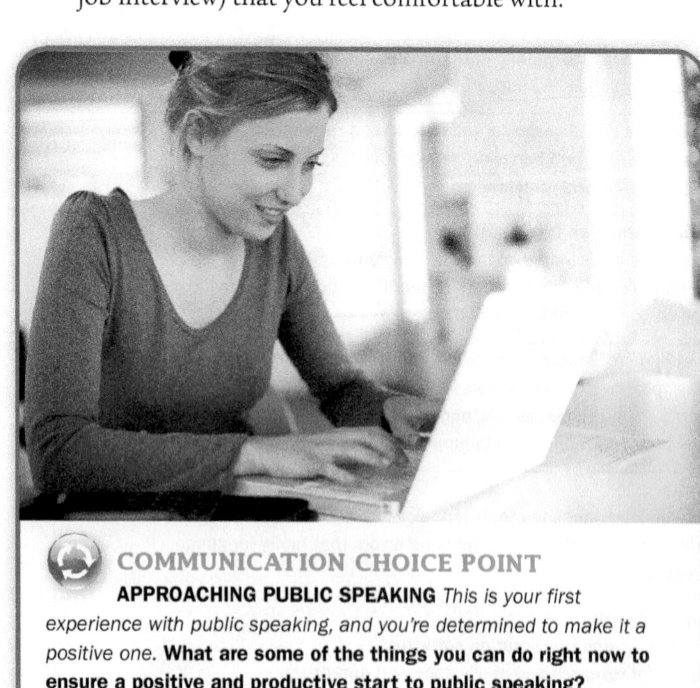

COMMUNICATION CHOICE POINT

APPROACHING PUBLIC SPEAKING *This is your first experience with public speaking, and you're determined to make it a positive one.* **What are some of the things you can do right now to ensure a positive and productive start to public speaking?**

14.2 MANAGING YOUR APPREHENSION

Apprehension in public speaking is normal; everyone experiences some degree of fear in the relatively formal public speaking situation. After all, in public speaking you're the sole focus of attention and are usually being evaluated for your performance. Experiencing nervousness or anxiety is a natural reaction. You are definitely not alone in these feelings.

Some people have a general **communication apprehension** that shows itself in all communication situations. These people suffer from *trait apprehension*—a general fear of communication, regardless of the specific situation. Their fear appears in conversations, small group settings, and public speaking situations. Not surprisingly, if you have high trait apprehension, you're also more likely to experience embarrassment in a variety of social situations (Withers & Vernon, 2006). Similarly, high apprehensives are likely to have problems in the work environment; for example, they may perform badly in employment interviews and may contribute few ideas on the job (Butler, 2005).

Other people experience communication apprehension in only certain communication situations. These people suffer from *state apprehension*—a fear that is specific to a given communication situation. For example, a speaker may fear public speaking but have no difficulty in talking with two or three other people. Or a speaker may fear job interviews but have no fear of public speaking. State apprehension is extremely common. Most people experience it for some situations; not surprisingly, it is public speaking that most people fear.

Communication apprehension exists on a continuum. Some people are so apprehensive that they're unable to function effectively in any communication situation and will try to avoid communication as much as possible. Other people are so mildly apprehensive that they appear to experience no fear at all; they're the ones who actively seek out communication opportunities. Most of us are between these extremes.

Watch at **MyCommunicationLab** **Video:** "Fear of Public Speaking"

Although you may at first view communication apprehension as harmful, it's not necessarily so. In fact, apprehension can work for you. Fear can energize you. It may motivate you to work a little harder—to produce a speech that will be better than it might have been had you not been fearful. And fear may encourage you to avoid procrastinating and even to start earlier than you might have were it not for your apprehension.

You may wish to pause here and examine your own apprehension in public speaking by responding to these six statements, which come from James McCroskey's (1997) widely used measure of public speaking apprehension, using the following scale: 1 = strongly agree; 2 = agree; 3 = are undecided; 4 = disagree; 5 = strongly disagree. There are no right or wrong answers. Don't be concerned that some of the statements are similar to others. Work quickly; just record your immediate response.

_____ **1.** I have no fear of giving a speech.

_____ **2.** Certain parts of my body feel very tense and rigid while giving a speech.

_____ **3.** I feel relaxed while giving a speech.

_____ **4.** My thoughts become confused and jumbled when I am giving a speech.

_____ **5.** I face the prospect of giving a speech with confidence.

_____ **6.** While giving a speech, I get so nervous that I forget facts I really know.

To obtain your public speaking apprehension score, begin with the number 18 (selected so that you won't wind up with negative numbers) and add to it the scores for items 1, 3, and 5. Then, from this total, subtract the scores from items 2, 4, and 6. A score above 18 shows some degree of apprehension. Most people score above 18, so if you scored relatively high, you're among the vast majority of people. As you read the suggestions for managing apprehension, consider what you can do to incorporate these into your own public speaking experiences. Consider too how these suggestions might be useful in reducing apprehension more generally; for example, in social situations and in small groups and meetings.

Explore at **MyCommunicationLab** **Profile:** "Personal Report of Speaking Anxiety"

Here are several ways you can deal with and manage your own public speaking apprehension by reversing the factors that cause apprehension (Beatty, 1988; Bodie, 2010; Richmond & McCroskey, 1998). Additional methods are considered in the two Understanding Theory and Research boxes (here and page 288). These same techniques will also prove useful in managing apprehensiveness in social and work situations.

- **Reduce the newness of public speaking by gaining experience.** New and different situations such as public speaking are likely to make anyone anxious, so try to reduce their newness and differentness. One way to do this is to get as much public speaking experience as you can.
- **Reduce your self-focus by visualizing public speaking as conversation.** When you're the center of attention, as you are in public speaking, you feel especially conspicuous, and this often increases anxiety. It may help, therefore, to think of public speaking as another type of

the•o•ry *noun* statement of explanation, formulation of relationships, reasoned generalization

UNDERSTANDING THEORY AND RESEARCH
Performance Visualization

The theory of **performance visualization** argues that you can reduce the outward signs of apprehension and the negative thinking that often creates anxiety through a few simple techniques (Ayres & Hopf, 1992, 1993; Ayres, Hopf, & Ayres, 1994).

First, develop a positive attitude and a positive self-perception. Visualize yourself in the role of the effective public speaker. Visualize yourself walking to the front of the room—fully and totally confident, fully in control of the situation. The audience pays rapt attention to your talk and bursts into wild applause as you finish. Throughout this visualization, avoid all negative thoughts. As you visualize yourself as this effective speaker, take note of how you walk, look at your listeners, handle your notes, and respond to questions; especially, think about how you feel about the public speaking experience.

Second, model your performance on that of an especially effective speaker. View a particularly competent public speaker on video, for example, and make a mental "movie" of it. As you review the actual video and mental movie, shift yourself into the role of speaker; become this speaker.

Working with Theories and Research

Try performance visualization as you rehearse for your next speech. Did it help reduce your apprehension?

conversation (some theorists call it "enlarged conversation").

- **Reduce your perceived differentness from the audience.** When you feel similar to your audience, your anxiety is likely to lessen. Therefore, try to emphasize the similarities between yourself and your audience. This is especially important when your audience consists of people from cultures different from your own.
- **Reduce your fear of failure by thoroughly preparing and practicing.** Much of the fear you experience is a fear of failure. Adequate and even extra preparation will lessen the possibility of failure and the accompanying apprehension (Smith & Frymier, 2006).
- **Reduce your anxiety by moving about and breathing deeply.** Physical activity—including movements of the whole body as well as small movements of the hands, face, and head—lessens apprehension. Also try breathing deeply a few times before getting up to speak. You'll feel your body relax, and this will help you overcome your initial fear of walking to the front of the room.
- **Avoid chemicals as tension relievers.** Unless prescribed by a physician, avoid any chemical means for reducing apprehension. Tranquilizers, marijuana, or artificial stimulants are likely to create problems rather than reduce them. These chemicals can impair your ability to remember the parts of your speech, to accurately read audience feedback, and to regulate the timing of your speech.

Explore at MyCommunicationLab Activity: "Overcoming Nervousness"

With the nature of public speaking and its benefits in mind and with an understanding of communication apprehension and some ways for managing it, we can look at the essential steps for preparing an effective public speech (Figure 14.2): (1) Select your topic, purposes, and thesis; (2) analyze your audience; (3) research your topic; (4) collect supporting materials; (5) develop your main points; (6) organize your speech materials; (7) construct your introduction, conclusion, and transitions and outline your speech; (8) word your speech; (9) rehearse your speech; and (10) present your speech. The first three of these steps are discussed in the remainder of this chapter; the remaining seven are discussed over the next two chapters.

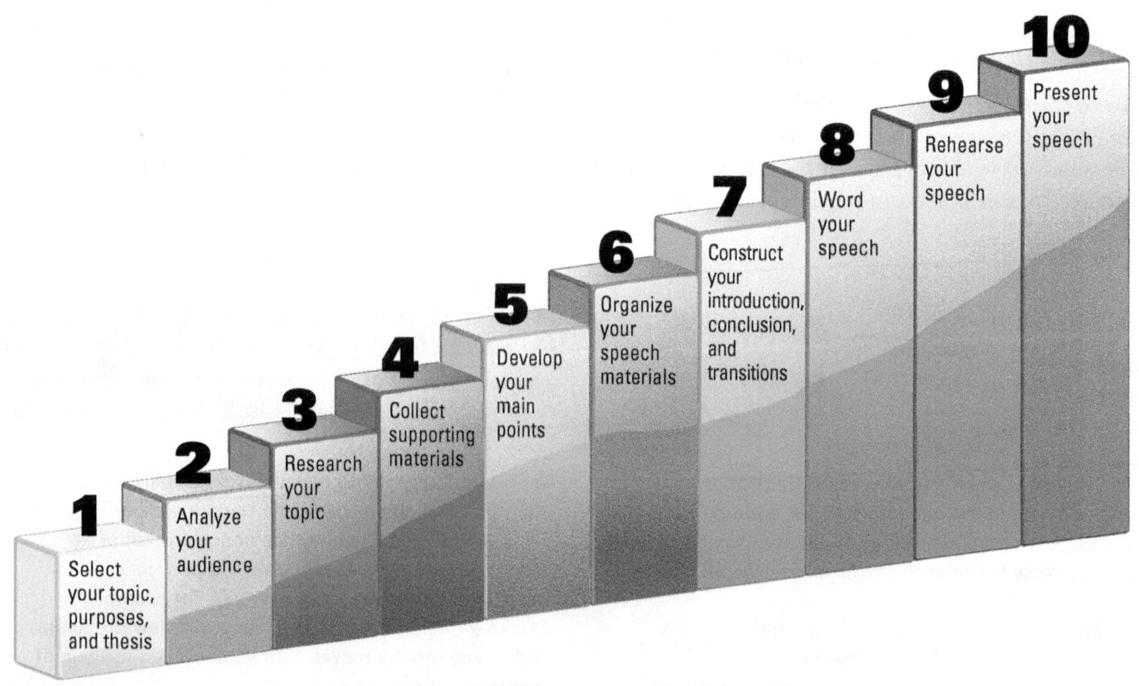

FIGURE 14.2 **The Steps in Public Speaking Preparation and Delivery**

Speakers differ in the order in which they follow these steps. Some speakers, for example, prefer to begin with audience analysis; they ask themselves what the audience is interested in and then select the topic and purpose. Some speakers prefer to identify their main points before conducting extensive research, whereas others prefer to allow the points to emerge from the research. The order presented here will prove useful to most speakers for most situations, but you can vary the order to serve your purposes. As long as you cover all steps, you should be in good shape.

14.3 STEP 1: SELECT YOUR TOPIC, PURPOSES, AND THESIS

Your first step in preparing to give a speech is to select your topic, purposes, and thesis.

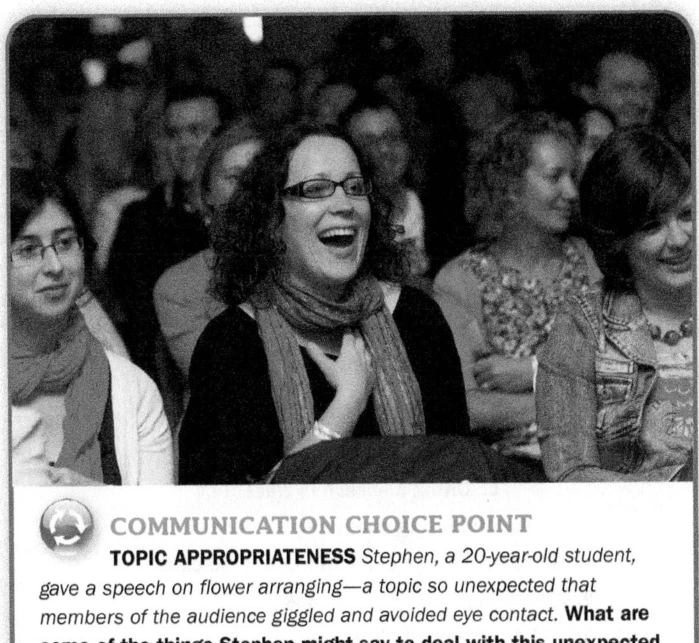

COMMUNICATION CHOICE POINT

TOPIC APPROPRIATENESS *Stephen, a 20-year-old student, gave a speech on flower arranging—a topic so unexpected that members of the audience giggled and avoided eye contact.* **What are some of the things Stephen might say to deal with this unexpected reaction? What would you say?**

Your Topic

As you begin to think about public speaking, (and especially about your own speech) perhaps the first questions you have are "What do I speak about?" "What **topic** would be appropriate?" The answer to these questions will change as your life situation changes; in the years ahead you'll most likely speak on topics that grow out of your job or your social or political activities.

In the classroom, however, where your objective is to learn the skills of public speaking, there are literally thousands of subjects to talk about. Nevertheless, the question remains: "What do I speak about?" To answer this question, focus on three related questions: "What makes a good topic?" "How do I find such a topic?" and "How do I focus or limit my topic?"

Watch at **MyCommunicationLab** **Video:** "Martin Cox Discusses Tips on Developing a Topic for a Speech"

A good public speaking topic is one that deals with matters of substance, is appropriate to you and the audience, and is culturally sensitive. These three characteristics suggest some guidelines for selecting a good topic.

- **Substantive.** The most important criterion of a good topic is that it be *substantive*—that it deal with matters of substance. Select a topic that is important enough to merit the time and attention of a group of intelligent people. Ask yourself: Would this topic engage the attention of my classmates? Would a reputable newspaper cover such a topic? Would students find this topic relevant to their social or professional lives?
- **Appropriate.** Select a topic that is *appropriate to you as the speaker.* For example, if you're male, it probably isn't a good idea to give a speech on the stages of childbirth. On the other hand, if you're female and have just given birth, this might be a good topic. If you've never been incarcerated, then a speech on what life is like in prison is probably not going to ring true to your audience. The best way to look at this criterion is to ask if—given what audience members already know about you and what you'll tell them during your speech—your listeners will see you as a knowledgeable and believable spokesperson on this topic. If the answer is yes, then you have a topic appropriate to you as a speaker. Also, select a topic that is *appropriate to your audience.* Giving a speech to students in your class on the need to have a computer would be inappropriate, simply because they already know the importance of the computer. But that same topic might be quite appropriate if given at a senior center where most of the members did not own computers. Giving a speech advocating a specific religious belief might well prove insulting to members of the audience who don't share your religious beliefs. Yet that same speech might be very well received by members of a particular religious congregation. Always look to audience members when thinking about a topic and try to gauge their reaction to it.
- **Culturally sensitive.** A good topic is *culturally sensitive.* Select a topic that will not offend members of other cultures (who may even be in your audience). At the same time, recognize that we live in a time when a person's level of cultural sensitivity is taken as a sign of education and sophistication—qualities that can only help a speaker. For example, in many Arab, Asian, and African cultures, discussing sex in an audience of both men and women would be considered obscene and offensive. In Scandinavian cultures, on the other hand, sex is discussed openly and without embarrassment or discomfort.

the•o•ry *noun* statement of explanation, formulation of relationships, reasoned generalization

UNDERSTANDING THEORY AND RESEARCH
Systematic Desensitization

The theory of **systematic desensitization** holds that you can reduce fear through a process of gradually adapting to lesser and then successively greater versions of the thing you fear. This technique has been used to deal with many kinds of fear, including public speaking fears (Richmond & McCroskey, 1998; Wolpe 1957). In the case of public speaking, the general idea of systematic desensitization is to create a hierarchy of behaviors leading up to the desired but feared behavior. One specific hierarchy might look like this:

5. Giving a speech in class
4. Introducing another speaker to the class
3. Speaking in a group in front of the class
2. Answering a question in class
1. Asking a question in class

The main objective of desensitization is to learn to relax, beginning with relatively easy tasks and progressing to the behavior you're apprehensive about—in this case giving a speech in class. You begin at the bottom of this hierarchy and rehearse behavior number 1 mentally over a period of days until you can clearly visualize asking a question in class without any uncomfortable anxiety. Once you can accomplish this, move to the second level. Here you visualize a somewhat more threatening behavior: answering a question. Once you can do this, move to the third level, and so on until you get to the desired behavior.

Working with Theories and Research

Create a hierarchy for dealing with communication apprehension. Use small steps to help you get from one step to the next more easily.

Finding Topics

Public speaking topics are all around you. Select a topic that you're interested in and know something about. And, of course, select a topic that your audience will find interesting and worthwhile. Here are a few ways you can find topics:

- **Yourself.** What are you interested in? What news articles or blogs do you read, what feeds do you subscribe to? What titles of articles would interest you enough so that you would open them and read them? If you plan a speech on a topic that you're interested in your enthusiasm for your topic is likely to make your delivery more exciting, less anxiety-provoking, and more engaging to the audience.

Watch at **MyCommunicationLab** **Video:** "Tall Girls"

- **Brainstorming.** The small group technique of brainstorming can also be used by yourself to generate speech topics. Begin with your "problem"—what will I talk about?—and follow the four rules of brainstorming discussed earlier (page 217). In just a few minutes, you should have a sizable list of potential topics.

Explore at **MyCommunicationLab** **Activity:** "Visual Brainstorming"

- **Surveys.** To see what your audience finds important, take a look at some of the national and regional polls concerned with the issues people feel are most significant. Search for polling sites with your favorite search engine or start with some of the more widely known such as the Gallup Poll, the Marist Poll, or Pew Research Center, for example. Or, take a look at what people are talking about on social media sites. What are people tweeting about? What are they posting about? Or you can conduct a survey yourself through a variety of social media sites or classroom management systems.
- **News items.** Still another useful starting point is your online news page. Here you'll find the important international, domestic, financial, and social issues all conveniently accessible from one screen. But, of course, news items also appear on Twitter and on blogs and a variety of social media sites.
- **Topic lists.** For example, the interactive topic selector on MyCommunicationLab (available at **www.mycommuniationlab.com**) lists hundreds of appropriate topics for informative and persuasive speeches (see Figure 14.3). A variety of educational and commercial websites contain topic generators, similar to that on MyCommunicationLab, where you can view a wide variety of topics, for example, those provided by WritingFix and McMaster eBusiness Research Center. Just search for "public speaking topics + .edu."

Limiting Topics

To be suitable for a public speech, a topic must be limited in scope; it must be narrowed down so as to fit the time restrictions and yet permit some depth of coverage.

Limiting your topic will help you focus your collection of research materials. With a relatively narrow topic, you can search for research materials more efficiently. Here are three methods for narrowing and limiting your topic: topoi, tree diagrams, and search directories.

Topoi, the System of Topics

Topoi, the system of topics, is a technique that comes from the classical rhetorics of ancient Greece and Rome but today is used more widely as a stimulus to creative thinking (DeVito, 1996). When using the method of topoi, you ask yourself a series of questions about your general subject. The process will help you see divisions of your general topic on which you might want to focus. Table 14.2 provides an example.

Tree Diagrams

Tree diagrams help you to divide your topic repeatedly into its constituent parts. Starting with the general topic, you divide it into its parts. Then you

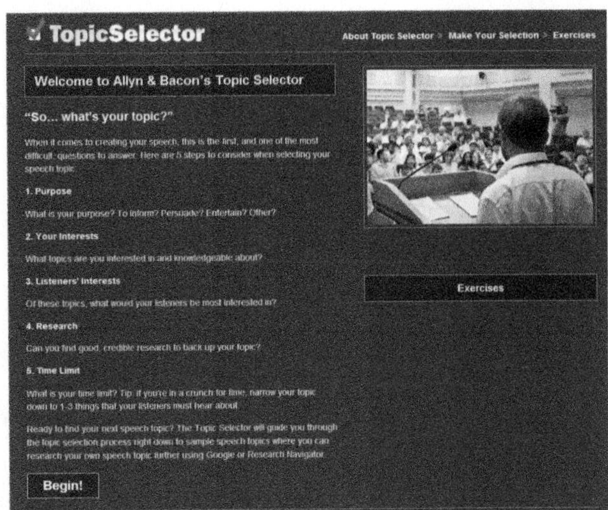

FIGURE 14.3 Interactive Topic Selector on MyCommunicationLab (www.mycommunicationlab.com)

TABLE 14.2 TOPOI: THE SYSTEM OF TOPICS

These questions should enable you to use general topics to generate more specific ideas for your speeches. You'll be amazed at how many topics you'll be able to find. Your problem will quickly change from "What can I speak on?" to "Which one of these should I speak on?" Here's an example on the topic of homelessness.

General Questions	Subject-Specific Questions
Who? Who is he or she? Who is responsible? To whom was it done?	■ Who are the homeless? ■ Who is the typical homeless person? ■ Who is responsible for the increase in homelessness? ■ Who cares for the homeless?
What? What is it? What effects does it have? What is it like? What is it different from? What are some examples?	■ What does it mean to be homeless? ■ What does homelessness do to the people themselves? ■ What does homelessness do to the society in general? ■ What does homelessness mean to you and me?
Why? Why is there homelessness? Why does it happen? Why does it not happen?	■ Why are there so many homeless people? ■ Why did this happen? ■ Why does it happen in the larger cities more than in smaller towns? ■ Why is it more prevalent in some countries than in others?
When? When did it happen? When will it occur? When will it end?	■ When did homelessness become so prevalent? ■ When does it occur in the life of a person?
Where? Where did it come from? Where is it going? Where is it now?	■ Where is homelessness most prevalent? ■ Where is there an absence of homelessness?
How? How does it work? How is it used? How do you do it? How do you operate it? How is it organized?	■ How does someone become homeless? ■ How can we help the homeless? ■ How can we prevent others from becoming homeless?
So? What does it mean? What is important about it? Why should I be concerned with this? Who cares?	■ Why is homelessness such an important social problem? ■ Why must we be concerned with homelessness? ■ How does all this affect me?

take one of these parts and divide it into its subparts. You continue with this dividing process until the topic seems manageable—until you believe you can reasonably cover it in some depth in the time allotted. Figure 14.4 illustrates the process.

Search Directories

A more technologically sophisticated way of both selecting and limiting your topic is to let a **search directory** do some of the work for you. A search directory is a nested list of topics. You go from the general to the specific by selecting a topic, then a subdivision of that topic, then a subdivision of that subdivision. Eventually you'll be directed to relatively specific areas and websites that will suggest topics that may be suitable for a classroom speech.

Explore at MyCommunicationLab Activity: "Topic"

Your Purposes

The *purpose* of your speech is the goal you want to achieve; it identifies the effect that you want your speech to have on your audience. In constructing your speech you'll first identify your general purpose and then your specific purpose.

Watch at MyCommunicationLab Video: "Martin Cox Discusses Tips on Developing the Purpose of a Speech"

General Purpose

Because you're now in a learning environment, your general purpose will likely be chosen for you. In this way, the classroom is like the real world. The situation, the audience you'll address, the nature of your job will dictate your **general purpose**—whether informative or persuasive. If you're a lawyer giving a closing at a trial, your speech must be persuasive. If you're an engineer explaining blueprints to clients, your speech must be informative. If you're a college professor, your speeches will be largely informative; if you're a politician, they will be mostly persuasive.

To inform and to persuade are the two general purposes of most public speeches. Another purpose is to serve some special occasion function—to toast, to bid farewell, to present an award. **Special occasion speeches** are in many ways combinations of informative and persuasive purposes (see the Special Occasion boxes in Chapters 17 and 18).

In **informative speeches** (for example, a speech to inform your audience about a career seminar), you seek to create understanding: to clarify, to enlighten, to correct misunderstandings, to demonstrate how something works, to define what something means. In this type of speech, you'll rely most heavily on materials that amplify—examples, illustrations, definitions, testimony, visual aids, and the like.

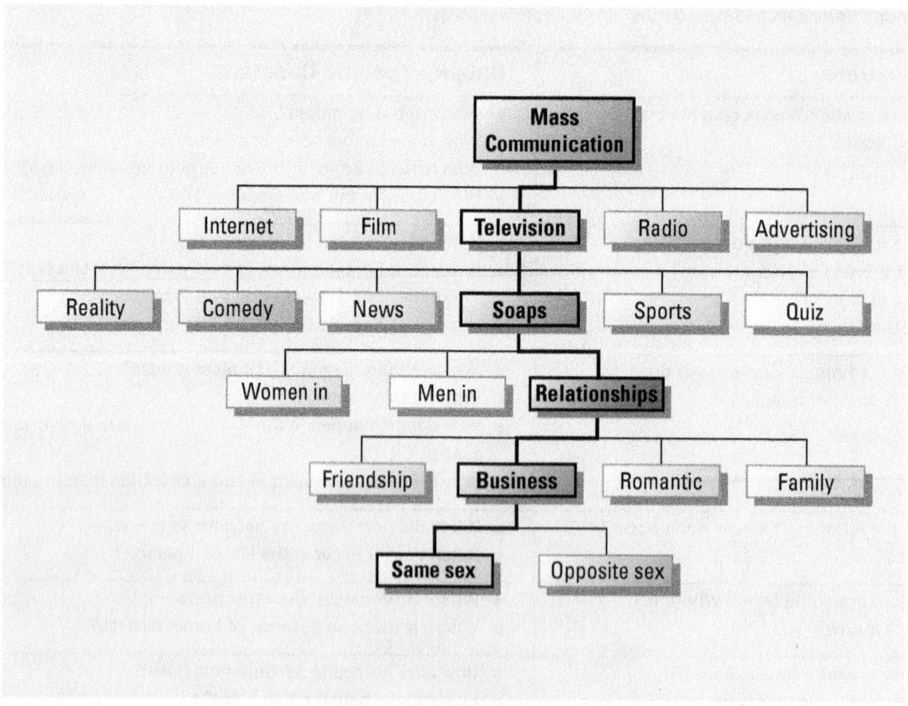

FIGURE 14.4 A Tree Diagram for Limiting Speech Topics

Here is a tree diagram illustrating how a topic can be divided until it becomes manageable for a short speech: "Same-Sex Business Relationships in Television Soaps." Construct a different tree diagram by selecting Internet, film, radio, Television, or advertising as a topic and subdividing it until you reach a level that would be appropriate for a 5- to 10-minute informative or persuasive speech.

In **persuasive speeches** (for example, a speech aimed at persuading your audience to vote in the next election), you try to influence **attitudes** or behaviors; you seek to strengthen or change existing attitudes or to get the audience to take some action. In this type of speech, you'll rely heavily on materials that offer proof—on evidence, argument, and psychological appeals, for example.

Specific Purpose

Once you have chosen your general purpose, develop your **specific purpose** by identifying more precisely what you aim to accomplish. For example, in an informative speech your specific purpose will identify the information you want to convey to your audience:

General purpose:	To inform.
Specific purposes:	To inform my audience of the differences between embryonic and adult stem cell research.
	To inform my audience about two areas of stem cell research progress.
	To inform my audience of the current federal regulations for funding stem cell research.

You may find it helpful to view your specific informative purposes in behavioral terms: identifying how you want the audience to demonstrate what they've learned from your speech:

- After listening to my speech, listeners should be able to describe the procedures for systematic desensitization.
- After listening to my speech, listeners should be able to define the three major differences between communism and capitalism.
- After listening to my speech, listeners should be able to demonstrate the five steps of active listening.

In a persuasive speech, your specific purpose identifies what you want your audience to believe, to think, or perhaps to do:

General purpose:	To persuade.
Specific purposes:	To persuade listeners to use systematic desensitization to reduce their apprehension.
	To persuade listeners to believe that capitalism is superior to communism.
	To persuade listeners to use active listening more often.

As you formulate your specific purposes, follow these five guidelines: Use an infinitive phrase; focus your purpose on your audience; limit it to one idea; limit it to what you can reasonably expect to achieve; and use specific terms.

Use an Infinitive Phrase. Begin the statement of each specific purpose with your general purpose (to inform, to persuade) and then elaborate on your general purpose. For example:

- To inform my audience of the new registration procedures.
- To persuade my audience to contribute a book for the library fund-raiser.
- To introduce the main speaker of the day to my audience.

Focus on the Audience. Right now, your audience is your public speaking class. It may at first seem unnecessary to include reference to the audience in each specific purpose statement. Actually, including the words "my audience" is crucial because it keeps you focused on the people you want to inform or persuade; it's a reminder that everything you do in your speech needs to be directed by the purpose you want to achieve with this specific audience. Your speech purpose must be relevant to your audience. And in your career in years to come, you'll probably address a variety of different audiences; you need to keep each unique and distinct audience clearly in focus.

Limit Your Specific Purpose to One Idea. Don't try to accomplish too much in too short a time. For example, consider the following statement of a specific purpose:

> To persuade audience members of the prevalence of date rape in our community and that they should attend the dating seminars offered on campus.

This statement contains two specific purposes: (1) informing my audience of the prevalence of date rape in our community and (2) persuading my audience to attend the dating seminars offered on campus. This speaker needs to limit the specific purpose statement by selecting one specific purpose or the other. As you construct your specific purpose statement, beware of the word *and*—it's often a sign that your statement contains more than one specific purpose.

Limit Your Specific Purpose to What Is Reasonable. Limit your specific purpose to what you can reasonably develop and achieve in the allotted time. Specific purposes that are too broad are useless. Note how broad and overly general are such purposes as "To inform my audience about clothing design" or "To persuade audience members to improve their health." You couldn't hope to cover such topics in one speech. It would be much more reasonable to have such purposes as "To inform my audience of the importance of color in clothing design" or "To persuade audience members to exercise three times a week."

Use Specific Terms. Phrase your specific purposes with specific terms. The more precise your specific purpose statement, the more effectively it will guide you in the remaining steps of preparing your speech. Notice that the purposes used as examples of covering too much are also overly general and very unspecific ("clothing design" can mean hundreds of things, as can "improve your health"). Instead of the overly general "To persuade my audience to help the homeless," consider the more specific "To persuade my audience to donate a few hours a month to make phone calls for the Homeless Coalition."

Your Thesis

Like your specific purpose, your **thesis** needs to be given special attention. This section defines the thesis and explains how you should word and use it in your preparation and in your actual speech.

What Is a Thesis?

Your thesis is your central idea; it's the theme, the essence of your speech. It's your point of view; it's what you want the audience to get out of your speech. The thesis of Lincoln's Second Inaugural Address was that Northerners and Southerners should work together for the entire nation's welfare; the thesis of Martin Luther King Jr.'s "I have a dream" speech was that true equality is a right of African Americans and all people; and the thesis of political campaign speeches is generally something like: "Vote for me," or "I'm the better candidate," or "My opponent is the wrong choice."

In an informative speech your thesis states what you want your audience to learn. For example, a suitable thesis for an informative speech on jealousy might be "There are two main theories of jealousy." Notice that here, as in all informative speeches, the thesis is relatively neutral and objective.

In a persuasive speech your thesis states what you want your audience to believe or accept; it summarizes the claim you're making, the position you're taking. For example, let's say that you're planning to present a speech against using animals for experimentation. Your thesis statement might be something like "Animal experimentation should be banned." Here are a few additional examples of persuasive speech theses:

- We should all contribute to the Homeless Shelter Project.
- Everyone over 50 should get tested for colon cancer.
- Condoms should be distributed free of charge.

As you can see, these thesis statements identify what you want audience members to believe or do as a result of your speech—you want them to contribute to the homeless shelter, to believe that everyone over 50 should be tested for colon cancer, and to be convinced that condoms should be distributed without charge. Notice that in persuasive speeches the thesis statement puts forth a point of view, an opinion. The thesis is arguable; it's debatable.

How Do Thesis and Specific Purpose Differ?

The thesis and the specific purpose are similar in that they are both guides to help you select and organize your speech materials. Because they both serve these similar goals, they are often confused—so let's consider some of the ways in which they are different.

First, the thesis and purpose differ in their form of expression. The specific purpose is worded as an infinitive phrase; for example, "To inform my audience of the provisions of the new education budget" or "To persuade my audience to vote in favor of the new education budget." The thesis, on the other hand, is phrased as a complete declarative sentence; for example, "The education budget must be increased."

Second, they differ in their focus. The specific purpose is audience-focused; it identifies the change you hope to achieve in your audience. For example, your specific purpose may be for the audience to gain information, to believe something, or to act in a certain way. The thesis, on the other hand, is message-focused. It identifies the main idea of your speech; it summarizes—it epitomizes—the content of your speech. It's the one idea that you want audience members to remember even if they forget everything else.

Third, the specific purpose and thesis differ in their concern for practical limitations. No matter how sweeping or ambitious the thesis, the specific purpose must take into consideration the time you have to speak and the attitudes of the audience toward you and your topic. The specific purpose, therefore, needs to be phrased with these practical limitations in mind. For example, the thesis might be that "Colleges are not educating students for today's world." The speech, however, might have any one of several different specific purposes. For example, (1) To persuade my audience that colleges must change to keep pace with today's world, (2) To persuade my audience to adapt the Illinois Educational Proposal, or (3) To persuade my audience to quit college. The thesis epitomizes the speech without regard to practical limitations of, say, time or current audience attitudes.

The following examples may clarify further the difference between purpose and thesis:

General purpose:	To inform.
Specific purpose:	To inform audience members of three ways to save on their phone bills.
Thesis:	You can reduce your phone bills.

General purpose:	To persuade.
Specific purpose:	To persuade my audience to take a computer science course.
Thesis:	Computer science knowledge is essential.

Wording and Using Your Thesis

Here are a few suggestions on how to word and use your thesis.

Limit Your Thesis to One Central Idea. Be sure to limit your thesis statement to one and only one central idea. A statement such as "Animal experimentation should be banned and companies engaging in it should be prosecuted" contains not one but two basic ideas. Whenever you see an *and* or a semicolon (;) in a thesis statement it probably contains more than one idea.

State Your Thesis as a Complete Declarative Sentence. In phrasing your thesis, word it as a complete declarative sentence; for example:

Hate speech corrupts.
Speak out against hate speech.
Support the college's new hate speech code.

This will help you focus your thinking, your collecting of materials, and your organizational pattern. Avoid stating your thesis as a question or a sentence fragment; these will not provide the clear and specific focus you need to use the thesis effectively.

Use Your Thesis to Focus Audience Attention. Because the thesis sentence focuses the audience's attention on your central idea and reveals what you hope to achieve in your speech, you'll want to consider the options you have for stating your thesis. Here are a few guidelines that will help you make a strategically effective decision about how and when to present your thesis to your audience.

- In an informative speech, state your thesis early, clearly, and directly:

  Immigration patterns are predicted to change drastically over the next 50 years.
  Carpal tunnel syndrome can be corrected with surgery.
  A smart phone can organize your life.

- In a persuasive speech addressed to an audience already in agreement with you, state your thesis explicitly and early in your speech:

  Immigration laws should be changed.
  You can avoid carpal tunnel syndrome with rest and exercise.
  Medical marijuana should be legal in all states.

- In a persuasive speech addressed to an audience opposed to your position, give your evidence and arguments first and gradually move the audience into a more positive frame of mind before stating your thesis explicitly.
- When you are speaking to a relatively uneducated or uninformed audience, it is probably best to state your thesis explicitly. If the thesis is not explicit, the listeners may fail to grasp what your thesis is and therefore may be less likely to change their attitudes or behaviors.
- Recognize, too, that there are cultural differences in the way a thesis should be stated. In some Asian cultures, for example, making a point too directly or asking directly for audience compliance may be considered rude or insulting.

Table 14.3 provides a summary of some of the differences between informative and persuasive speeches, the two main types you'll focus on in this course.

TABLE 14.3 DIFFERENCES BETWEEN INFORMATIVE AND PERSUASIVE SPEECHES

Here are some of the major differences between speeches that aim primarily to inform and speeches that aim primarily to persuade.

Element of speech	**Informative speeches**, e.g., classroom lectures, demonstrations of how things work	**Persuasive speeches**, e.g., political speeches, religious sermons
Topic/subject	Significant but generally noncontroversial	Significant and controversial or debatable
Purpose	To communicate new information to listeners	To change the attitudes, beliefs, or behaviors of listeners
Thesis	States the central idea of the speech	States the debatable position to be argued

14.4 STEP 2: ANALYZE YOUR AUDIENCE

The characteristic that seems best to define an audience is common purpose: A public speaking **audience** is a group of individuals gathered together to hear a speech. If you're to be a successful speaker, then you must know your audience. This knowledge will help you in selecting your topic; phrasing your purpose; establishing a relationship between yourself and your audience; and choosing examples, illustrations, and logical and emotional appeals.

Your first step in **audience analysis** is to construct an audience profile in which you analyze audience members' sociological or demographic characteristics. These characteristics help you estimate the attitudes, beliefs, and values of your audience. If you want to effect changes in these attitudes, beliefs, and values, you have to know what they are.

Explore at MyCommunicationLab Activity: "Audience Analysis"

Analyzing the Sociology of the Audience

In analyzing an audience, be careful not to assume that people covered by the same label are necessarily all alike. As soon as you begin to think about a sociological characteristic in terms of an expressed or implied "all," consider the possibility that you may be stereotyping. Don't assume that all women or all older people or all highly educated people think or believe the same things. They don't.

Nevertheless, there are characteristics that seem to be more common among one group than another, and it is these characteristics that you want to explore in your sociological analysis of your audience. Let's look at four major sociological or demographic variables: (1) cultural factors, (2) age, (3) gender, (4) affectional orientation, and (5) religion and religiousness. Additional factors are considered in Table 14.4.

TABLE 14.4 OTHER AUDIENCE FACTORS

No list of audience characteristics can possibly be complete, and the list presented in the text is no exception. Here are some additional audience factors you may want to consider and some questions you may want to ask, depending on your specific thesis and audience.

Audience Factor	Questions to Ask
Educational Levels	■ Does the educational level of the audience suggest any stylistic adjustment? ■ Will technical terms have to be defined? ■ Will the educational level suggest different persuasive strategies or supporting materials?
Occupation and Income	■ Is your audience's level of job security and occupational pride related to your topic, purpose, or examples? ■ Will people from different economic levels have different preferences for immediate or long-range goals?
Relational Status	■ Will singles be interested in hearing about the problems of selecting preschools? ■ Will those in long-term relationships be interested in the depression many people who are not in close relationships experience during the holidays?
Special Interests	■ What special interests do the audience members have? What occupies their leisure time? ■ How can you integrate these interests into your examples and illustrations or use them as you select quotations?
Political Beliefs	■ Will audience members' political affiliations influence how they view your topic or purpose? ■ Are they politically liberal? Conservative? Might this influence how you develop your speech?
Organizational Memberships	■ Might audience members' affiliations give you cues as to their other beliefs and values? ■ Might you use references to these organizations in your speech, perhaps as examples or illustrations?

Cultural Factors

Cultural factors such as nationality, race, and cultural identity are crucial in audience analysis. Largely because of different training and experiences, the interests, values, and goals of various cultural groups will differ. Further, cultural factors will influence each of the remaining sociological factors; for example, attitudes toward age and gender will differ greatly from one culture to another. Perhaps the primary question to ask is "Are the cultural beliefs and **values** of the audience relevant to your topic and purpose?" That is, might the cultural background(s) of your audience members influence the way they see your topic? If so, find out what these **beliefs** and values are and take these into consideration as you build your speech.

Age

Different age groups have different attitudes and beliefs, largely because they have had different experiences in different contexts. Take these differences into consideration in preparing your speeches. For example, let's say that you're an investment counselor and you want to persuade your listeners to invest their money to increase their earnings. Your speech to an audience of retired people (say in their 60s) would be very different from an address to an audience of young executives (say in their 30s). In considering the age of your audience, ask yourself if the age groups differ in goals, interests, and day-to-day concerns that may be related to your topic and purpose. Graduating from college, achieving corporate success, raising a family, and saving for retirement are concerns that differ greatly from one age group to another.

Gender

In recent decades rapid social changes have made it difficult to pin down the effects of gender. As you analyze your audience in terms of gender, ask yourself if men and women are both interested in your topic or if it might appeal to just one gender. Men and women prefer different television programs, movies, and speech topics. For example, traditionally, men have been found to place greater importance on theoretical, economic, and political values. Traditionally, women have been found to place greater importance on aesthetic, social, and religious values. In framing appeals and in selecting examples, take into account the values your audience members consider most important. Ask too if men and women might have different attitudes toward the topic. Men and women do not, generally, at least, respond in the same way to such topics as abortion, rape, and equal pay for equal work. Select your topics and supporting materials in light of the gender of your audience members.

Affectional Orientation

Yet you can be reasonably sure that in all your public speaking experiences, you will never address an audience that is totally heterosexual. Consequently, consider if the affectional orientation of your audience will influence how they view a topic. If your topic is politics, the military's current policies on gay men and lesbians, taxes, marriage, or any of a host of other topics, the answer is probably yes. Polls and frequent news items consistently report on attitudes among gay men and lesbians that differ from those of heterosexuals in significant ways. But

me•di•a lit•er•a•cy *noun* ability to understand, interact with, and create media messages

EXPANDING MEDIA LITERACY

Media Messages Are Often Stereotypes

In all forms of communication, be especially careful not to rely on media stereotypes. The media are responsible for propagating many discriminatory stereotypes, and a media-literate individual needs to be able to recognize these and to see that such stereotypes are not reality but extreme examples, often created for comic effect or to maintain a viewer's attention. Men and women on comedy shows are often seen in an unpleasant light; most men on television are portrayed as incompetent, relationally inept, absorbed with sports, and ignorant of the important things in life. Men will never learn how to relate to women and are doomed to be insensitive clods. And women are portrayed as complaining, never satisfied, and abnormally thin. Old folks are portrayed as inept, complaining, loud, and offensive. And of course old people have lost and will never again find romance; for older people the kisses, for example, have to be nonsexual.

Racism is rampant in the media's portrayal of Muslims; almost all the Muslims on television are negatively constructed and are much more likely to be terrorists than they are to be teachers or lawyers or store owners or carpenters. Also, consider the negative stereotypes of gay men and lesbians; they're extremes that you rarely see in real life.

An excellent exercise in media literacy is to try to identify examples that support or contradict the idea that media engage in stereotyping.

don't assume that heterosexuals and homosexuals necessarily see things differently on every topic. There are differences, but there are also many similarities.

Religion and Religiousness

Religion permeates all topics and all issues. On a most obvious level, such issues as attitudes toward birth control, abortion, censorship, and divorce are often connected to religion. Similarly, people's views on premarital sex, marriage, child rearing, money, cohabitation, responsibilities toward parents, and thousands of other issues are frequently influenced by religion. Religion also influences many people's ideas concerning such topics as obedience to authority; responsibility to government; and the usefulness of such qualities as honesty, guilt, and happiness. Take these differences into consideration as you prepare your supporting materials.

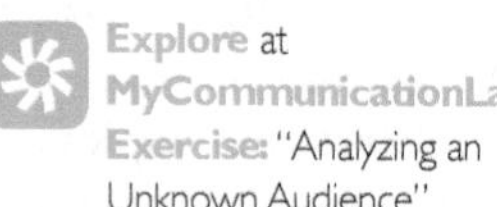
Explore at MyCommunicationLab Exercise: "Analyzing an Unknown Audience"

Analyzing the Psychology of the Audience

In addition to looking at the sociological characteristics of audience members, it's often useful to consider their psychological characteristics—particularly their willingness to listen to you, their favorableness to your purpose, and their background knowledge.

COMMUNICATION CHOICE POINT
UNFAVORABLE AUDIENCE *In presenting her persuasive speech, Marie sees from the audience's initial reactions that they are totally against her thesis and are tuning her out.* **What are some options Marie has for regaining the attention, interest, and goodwill of her audience?**

How Willing Is Your Audience?

Do your listeners come to hear your speech because they have to, or do they come because they're interested in what you'll say? If they're a willing group, then you have few problems. And even if they're an unwilling group, all is not lost; you just have to work a little harder in preparing your speech. Here are a few suggestions to help change your listeners from unwilling to willing:

- Secure their interest and attention as early in your speech as possible, and reinforce their interest throughout the speech by using little-known facts, quotations, startling statistics, examples, narratives, audiovisual aids, and the like.
- Reward audience members for their attendance and attention. Let them know you're aware they're making a sacrifice in coming to hear you speak. Tell them you appreciate it.
- Relate your topic and supporting materials directly to your audience's needs and wants. Show audience members how they can—for example—save time, make money, solve important problems, or become more popular.

How Favorable Is Your Audience?

Audiences vary in the degree to which their ideas and attitudes will be favorable or unfavorable toward you, your topic, or your point of view. If you conclude that your audience will be unfavorable to your chosen topic or viewpoint, the following suggestions should help.

- **Build on commonalities;** stress what you and the audience share as people, as interested citizens, or as fellow students. When audience members see similarity or common ground between themselves and you, they become more favorable to both you and your speech.
- **Organize your speech inductively.** Try to build your speech from areas of agreement, through areas of slight disagreement, up to the major differences between the audience's attitudes and your position. Once areas of agreement are established, it's easier to bring up differences.
- **Strive for small gains.** Don't try, in a 5-minute speech, to convince a pro-life group to contribute money for a new abortion clinic. Be content to get the audience to listen fairly and to see some validity in your position.

- **Acknowledge differences.** If it's clear to audience members that they and you are at opposite ends of an issue, you might want to acknowledge this fact and use it as a takeoff point to stress what you both agree on. You might say, for example, "I know that our differences on this issue are great, but what I also know is that we have the same ultimate goals."

How Knowledgeable Is Your Audience?

Listeners differ greatly in the knowledge they have. Some listeners will be quite knowledgeable about a given topic; others will be almost totally ignorant. Mixed audiences are the most difficult to address. Treat audiences that lack knowledge of your topic very carefully. Never confuse a lack of audience knowledge with a lack of ability to understand.

- **Don't talk down to your audience.** No one wants to listen to a speaker putting them down.
- **Don't confuse a lack of knowledge with a lack of intelligence.** An audience may have no knowledge of your topic but be quite capable of following a clearly presented, logically developed argument. Fill in background details as required. Avoid jargon and other specialized terminology that may not be clear to someone new to the subject.
- **Let audience members know that you're aware of their knowledge and expertise.** Emphasize that what you have to say will be relevant and valuable. Tell them that you'll be presenting recent developments or new approaches. Let them know that they will not be wasting their time listening to your speech.
- **Emphasize your credibility,** especially your competence in this general subject area.

Analyzing and Adapting during the Speech

In addition to analyzing your audience and making adaptations in your speech *before* delivering it, devote attention to analysis and adaptation *during* the speech. Although this during-the-speech analysis is especially important when you know little of your audience or find yourself facing a very different audience than you expected, it is always crucial to public speaking success. Here are a few suggestions.

Focus on Listeners as Message Senders

As you're speaking, look at your audience. Remember that just as you're sending messages to your listeners, they're also sending messages to you. Pay attention to these messages; on the basis of what they tell you, make the necessary adjustments.

Remember that members of different cultures operate with different display rules, cultural rules that state what types of expressions are appropriate to reveal—and what expressions are inappropriate to reveal and should be kept hidden. Some display rules call for open and free expression of feelings and responses; these listeners will be easy to read. Other display rules call for little expression, and these listeners will be difficult to read.

Address Audience Responses Directly

Another way of dealing with audience responses is to confront them directly. To those who are giving disagreement feedback, for example, you could say something like:

> **You may disagree with this position, but all I ask is that you hear me out and see if this new way of doing things will not simplify your accounting procedures.**

Or, to those who seem puzzled, you might say:

> **I know this plan may seem confusing, but bear with me; it will become clear in a moment.**

Or, to those who seem impatient, you might respond:

> **I know this has been a long day, but give me just a few more minutes and you'll be able to save hours recording your accounts.**

By responding to your listeners' reactions and feedback, you acknowledge your audience's priorities. You let them know that you hear them, that you're with them, and that you're responding to their very real needs.

Use Answers to Your "What If" Questions

The more preparation you put into your speech, the better prepared you'll be to make on-the-spot adjustments and adaptations. For example, let's say you have been told that you're to explain the opportunities available to the nontraditional student at your college. You've been told that your audience will consist mainly of working women in their 30s and 40s who are just beginning college. As you prepare your speech with this audience in mind, ask yourself "what if" questions. For example:

- What if the audience has a large number of men?
- What if the audience consists of women much older than 40?
- What if the audience members also come with their spouses or their children?

Keeping such questions in mind will force you to consider possible answers as you prepare your speech. Use these answers to make on-the-spot adjustments.

14.5 STEP 3: RESEARCH YOUR TOPIC

Throughout the process of preparing your public speeches, you'll need to find information to use as source material in your speech. This means doing research. Through research you'll find examples, illustrations, and definitions to help you inform your listeners; testimony, statistics, and arguments to support your major ideas; and personal anecdotes, quotations, and stories to help you bring your topics to life.

Research, however, also serves another important function: It helps you persuade your listeners because it makes you appear more believable. For example, if your listeners feel you've examined lots of research, they'll be more apt to see you as competent and knowledgeable and therefore more apt to believe what you say. And, of course, presenting the research is itself convincing. When you present research to your listeners, you give them the very reasons they need to draw conclusions or decide on a course of action.

Research is a systematic search for information; it's an investigation of the relevant information on a topic; it's an inquiry into what is known or thought about a subject. The University of Idaho's research website notes that research is undertaken, almost always, to discover an answer to one of several types of questions.

- **Research for specifics.** Research as a search for specific facts, examples, illustrations, statistics, definitions. Here your question is simple: How is socialism defined? What is the population of Japan? What is the average salary for accountants? You'll make use of this type of research in all your speeches as you search for supporting materials.
- **Research to discover what is known.** Here your question is how?—how might you describe some person or object or how you can describe an event or process? Or you might want to discover how a term or theory is defined and the differences and similarities among terms and systems. Or you might want to discover how to do something or how something operates. These types of research are at the heart of informative speech making.
- **Research to support a position.** Here your questions can revolve around a variety of issues. For example, you might conduct research to discover which explanation or position is the closest to being true (Questions of Fact)—Are the parents guilty of child negligence? Do "stand your ground" laws reduce crime? Another type of question focuses on what is just or moral (Questions of Value)—Can bullfighting ever be morally justified? What procedures will be most humane? Still another type of question focuses on the policies that should or should not be adopted (Questions of Policy)—Should medical marijuana be made legal nationally? What should the government's policy be on immigration? These three types of research questions are at the heart of persuasive speech making and are considered in more detail in Chapter 18.

Of course, your time is limited and you cannot research all that has been written and said about a topic. But you can learn to use your research time more effectively and more efficiently. Table 14.5 identifies some principles of time management.

Research Notes

The more accurate your research notes are, the less time you'll waste going back to sources to check on a date or a spelling. Accurate records also will prevent you from going to sources you've already consulted but may have forgotten about. The following suggestions may prove helpful to you as you take notes during the research process.

Create Folders

If you want to collect your material on paper, looseleaf notebooks or simple manila folders work well to keep everything relating to a speech or article in the same place. If you want to file your material electronically, create a general folder and subfolders as you need them. This will work especially well if you can scan into your folder material you find in print. In this notebook or folder, you can consolidate the sources consulted, quotations, ideas, arguments, suggested references, preliminary outlines, and material you've printed or downloaded.

Key Your Notes

Notes are most effective when they're keyed to specific topics. For example, let's say that your speech is to be on animal experimentation. Your notebook or major folder might be titled "Animal Experimentation." The notebook divisions or subfolders might then be labeled "Basic Information" (statistics on animal experimentation, people to contact, organizations involved in this issue), "Arguments for Animal Experimentation," and "Arguments against Animal Experimentation." Taking notes with reference to your preliminary outline will help focus your research and will remind you of those topics for which you need more information. It will also help you keep the information logically organized.

TABLE 14.5 PRINCIPLES OF TIME MANAGEMENT

Generally	Specifically
Understand your use of time.	Take a look at what takes up most of your time. Once you know how you spend your time, you'll be able to see what can be and should be cut back.
Attack your time wasters.	Identify your time wasters and get rid of the one time waster that you can most easily do without. Then tackle the next.
Avoid procrastination.	Avoid the tendency to delay things to the last minute, another strategy that college students often use in the mistaken belief that they work better under pressure.
Use tools.	Whether you use the low-tech schedule book or the Google Calendar or Rescue Time's app on your smartphone, use a tool.
Prioritize.	Make lists of items you need to accomplish and classify them in terms of importance. Lists help you put order into your work life.
Break up large tasks.	Divide large tasks into units or steps (as we do here in preparing and presenting a public speech); the steps will seem more manageable and not as daunting.
Set realistic time limits.	When the task is large, it often helps to set time limits; in this way the task will not seem oppressive or overly difficult.
Reward yourself.	Reward yourself after completing a unit of work, but keep the reward in proportion. Don't reward yourself with unhealthy food or overly long "breaks."
Do things once rather than twice.	Try to look only once at a piece of paper or electronic message, act on it, and then file or get rid of it.

Take Complete Notes

Make sure your notes are complete (and legible). If you have to err, then err on the side of too much detail. You can always cut the quotation or select one example out of the three at a later time. As you take notes, be sure to identify the source of the material—so you can find that reference again should you need it, and so you can reference it in your speech outline. When you use material from a Web source, be sure to print out or save to the folder the Web page, noting the URL and the date you accessed this site. This way you'll be able to cite a source even if the Web page disappears, a not unlikely possibility.

Libraries and Bookstores

Libraries, the major depositories of stored information, have evolved from a concentration on print sources to their current focus on computerized databases. Starting your research at the library (and with the librarian's assistance) is probably a wise move.

Here are a few online libraries that you'll find especially helpful.

- Quick Study, the University of Minnesota's Library Research Guide, will help you learn how to find the materials you need and will answer lots of questions you probably have about research.
- The largest library in the United States is the Library of Congress which houses millions of books, maps, multimedia, and manuscripts.
- Maintained by the National Archives and Records Administration, the presidential libraries will prove useful for a variety of purposes.
- The Virtual Library is a collection of links to 14 subject areas; for example, agriculture, business and economics, computing, communication and media, and education.
- If you're not satisfied with your own college library, visit the libraries of some of the large state universities, such as the University of Pennsylvania or the University of Illinois.
- The Internet Public Library is a collection of links to a wide variety of materials and will function much like the reference desk at any of the world's best libraries.

Of course, you'll also need to go to a brick-and-mortar library because it houses materials that are not on the Web and/or that you want to access in print. Because each library functions somewhat differently, your best bet in learning about a specific library—such as your own college library—is to talk with your librarian about what the library has available, what kinds of training or tours it offers, and how materials are most easily accessed.

eth•ics *noun* morality, standards of conduct, moral judgment

MAKING ETHICAL CHOICES
Plagiarism

One of the most complex issues in a public speaking course—and, actually, in every course—is that of **plagiarism**. Very often plagiarism is committed because of a lack of understanding of proper citation, and so this ethics box aims to clarify what plagiarism is, why it's unacceptable, and how you can avoid even the suggestion of plagiarism.

What Is Plagiarism?

The word *plagiarism* refers to the process of passing off the work (ideas, words, illustrations) of others as your own. Understand that plagiarism is not the act of using another's ideas—we all do that. It is using another's ideas without acknowledging that they are the ideas of this other person; it is passing off the ideas as if they were yours.

Plagiarism exists on a continuum, ranging from representing as your own an entire term paper or speech written by someone else (this is often called "direct plagiarism") to using a quotation or research finding without properly citing the author (this is often called "misattribution plagiarism"). Plagiarism also can include getting help from a friend without acknowledging this assistance.

In some cultures—especially collectivist cultures (cultures that emphasize the group and mutual cooperation, such as Korea, Japan, and China)—teamwork is strongly encouraged. Students are encouraged to help other students with their work. In the United States and in many other individualist cultures (cultures that emphasize individuality and competitiveness), teamwork without acknowledgment is considered plagiarism.

Why Is Plagiarism Unacceptable?

In U.S. colleges and universities, plagiarism is a serious violation of the rules of academic honesty and can bring serious penalties, sometimes even expulsion. And it's interesting to note that instructors are mobilizing and are educating themselves in techniques for detecting plagiarism. Further, as with all crimes, ignorance of the law is not an acceptable defense against charges of plagiarism. This last point is especially important because many people plagiarize through a lack of information as to what does and what does not constitute plagiarism.

Here are just a few reasons why plagiarism is wrong.

- Plagiarism is a violation of another's intellectual property rights. Much as it would be unfair to take another person's watch without permission, it's unfair to take another person's ideas without acknowledging that you did it.
- You're in college to develop your own ideas and your own ways of expressing them; plagiarism defeats this fundamental purpose.
- Evaluations (everything from grades in school to promotions in the workplace) assume that what you present as your work is in fact your work.

How Can You Avoid Plagiarism?

Here are a few guidelines to help you avoid plagiarism.

Let's start with the easy part. You do not have to, and should not, cite sources for common knowledge—information that is readily available in numerous sources and is not likely to be disputed. For example, the population of Thailand, the amendments to the U.S. Constitution, the actions of the United Nations, or the way the heart pumps blood all are widely available knowledge, and you would not cite the almanac or the political science text from which you got this information. On the other hand, if you were talking about the attitudes of people from Thailand or the reasons the constitutional amendments were adopted, then you would need to cite your sources because this information is not common knowledge and may well be disputed.

For information that is not common knowledge, you need to acknowledge your source. Three simple rules will help you avoid even the suggestion of plagiarism:

1. Acknowledge the source of any ideas you present that are not your own. If you learned of an idea in your history course, then cite the history instructor or the textbook. If you read an idea in an article, then cite the article.
2. Acknowledge the words as well as the ideas of another. If you're in doubt as to whether to cite another person, see, for example, Purdue University's writing center.
3. Acknowledge help from others. If your roommate gave you examples or ideas or helped you style your speech, acknowledge the help. But you don't need to acknowledge the assistance of, say, a librarian who helped you find a book or website.
4. When in doubt as to whether you should cite a source or how you might best do it, ask your instructor.

Ethical Choice Point

While listening to an impressive speech in your class, you recognize that you've read this exact same material in an obscure online publication. You're annoyed that this student has not done the work that everyone else has done and yet will probably earn a high grade. However, you wonder if you want to or should take on being the ethical conscience of your class. What is your ethical obligation in this case? What would you do?

Interviewing for Information

One research activity that you may find helpful is to interview people who have special information that you might use in your speech. For example, you might want to interview a veterinarian for information on proper nutrition for household pets; an eyewitness for information on living through a hurricane; or average people for their opinions on politics, religion, or any of a wide variety of topics. In these interviews, a great part of your effectiveness will hinge on your ability to listen actively, for total meaning, with empathy, with an open mind, and ethically, all of the interpersonal communication skills already covered. Here are six steps you might follow:

- **Select the person you wish to interview.** You might, for example, look through your college catalog for an instructor teaching a course that involves your topic. Or visit blogs and look for people who have posted articles on your topic. If you want to contact a book author, you can always write to the author in care of the publisher or editor (listed on the copyright page), though many authors are now including their e-mail address.
- **Secure an appointment.** Phone the person or send an e-mail requesting an interview. State the purpose of your request and say that you hope to conduct a brief interview by phone or that you'd like to send this person a series of questions by e-mail.
- **Create a cheat sheet.** A cheat sheet is a list of what you want to say during the interview. If this is a phone or chat interview, you can keep the cheat sheet in front of you; if a face-to-face interview, review the cheat sheet immediately before the interview.
- **Ask open-ended questions.** Generally, ask questions that provide the interviewee with room to discuss the issues you want to raise. Avoid questions that can be answered with *yes* or *no*.
- **Ask for permission to record or print the interview.** It's a good idea to keep an accurate record of the interview, so ask permission to record the interview if it's in person or by telephone.
- **Close and follow up with an expression of appreciation.** Even though you thank the person at the end of the interview, it's polite to follow up with a thank-you note later that day or the next day. Or perhaps you might send the person you interviewed a copy of your speech (e-mail would work well here) with a note of thanks.

Primary, Secondary, and Tertiary Source Material

As you research your speeches distinguish between primary, secondary, and tertiary source material whether your materials come from print or online.

Primary sources are firsthand, contemporary accounts written or spoken by someone who has had direct experience with or witnessed a particular event. Also considered primary sources are reports of original research by the researcher himself or herself. Primary sources include, for example, an original research study reported in an academic journal, a corporation's annual report, and an eyewitness report of an accident. With primary sources there is nothing (or very little) standing between the event (say, an accident) and the reporting of it (the eyewitness testimony).

Secondary sources are those that interpret, comment on, analyze, or summarize primary source material. Secondary source material includes, for example, a summary of research appearing in a popular magazine, a television news report on a corporation's earnings, and a report by someone who talked to someone who witnessed an accident. With secondary sources someone stands between the actual event and the report; for example, a science reporter reads the scientist's monograph (primary source), then writes up a summary for the popular press (secondary source).

Tertiary sources are a combination of primary and secondary sources and would include, for example, articles in encyclopedias, almanacs, handbooks, and guidebooks. Also considered tertiary are statistical compilations such as movie attendance figures or Nielsen figures. Your textbooks are in part secondary source material (they interpret and summarize the primary source material that appears in scholarly journals) and in part tertiary source material (they also make use of summaries of research and theories, i.e., secondary source material).

As a listener and speaker you'll hear and use all three types of source material. Yet there are important differences that you should keep in mind. Secondary source material is usually less reliable than primary source material because it's a step removed from the actual facts or events. The writer of secondary material may have forgotten important parts, may be biased, or may have misunderstood the data. On the other hand, the writer may have been able to express complicated data in simple language—often making it easier for a non-expert to understand than the original report. Tertiary material (say, an encyclopedia article) is usually an excellent starting place, but your research needs to go beyond that and include secondary and perhaps primary source materials.

COMMUNICATION CHOICE POINT

ASKING A FAVOR *Cary is preparing a speech on sustainable energy and wants to ask some of the famous environmentalists a few questions so he can integrate their most recent thoughts (and interject a more personalized note) into his speech.* **What are some specific things Cary can do to help secure these interviews?**

Scholarly and Popular Journals

Throughout your research, you'll use both scholarly journals and popular magazines, each for different purposes. If you want scientifically reliable information then the scholarly journals are what you need to look at, though they'll prove difficult to read—especially if they're outside your area of expertise. If you want more popular material in easy-to-understand language, then you should consult popular magazines. The type of information you seek will determine which types of publications you'll need to consult. If you want to read the original research studies on, say, emotional contagion, then you'll consult scholarly journals; if you want to get a broad and general overview of the nature of emotional contagion, then an article written in a popular magazine might prove more useful. If you want information on Madonna's latest concert, then a popular magazine would likely have what you need. If you want information on Madonna and feminist theory, then a scholarly journal might be more helpful.

Some publications are not so easy to classify. For example, *Psychology Today* would normally be considered a popular magazine, and yet it often contains scholarly articles by academic researchers. *National Geographic* is both a scholarly publication and a popular magazine. With this caveat in mind, Table 14.6 presents a chart comparing these two types of publications on a variety of criteria.

General Reference Works

General reference works are tertiary sources and are excellent starting points for researching your topic.

Encyclopedias

One of the best general reference works is the standard encyclopedia. Any good encyclopedia will give you a general overview of your subject and suggestions for additional reading. One way to search for these is to visit Freeality and search through the available general and specific encyclopedias. Perhaps the most widely known online encyclopedia, and one that you'll find extremely useful, is Wikipedia. The articles in Wikipedia—some brief and some extremely long and detailed—are written by people who are not necessarily experts. Many of the articles are reviewed, updated, and corrected periodically. But because this work doesn't have the authority of the more traditional encyclopedias, you'll need to check the facts and statistics—most of which you'll find easy to do because of the extensive hot links written into each article and the list of additional sources provided for most articles.

Almanacs

Another excellent general reference work is the almanac, in print or online. Start with InfoPlease, which contains a wide variety of hot links to almanacs and similar works covering such categories as the world, U.S. history and government, biography, sports, business, society and culture, health and science, and arts and entertainment. Another useful source is the Internet Public Library's list of almanac resources.

Biographical Materials

As a speaker you'll often need information about particular individuals. For example, in using expert testimony, it's helpful to stress your experts' qualifications, which you can easily learn about from even brief biographies. Knowing something about your sources enables you to more effectively evaluate their competence, convey their credibility to the audience, and answer audience questions about them. Just searching for the person's name will enable you to find information that you'll find useful in establishing the person's credibility for yourself and for your audience.

Statistical Information

A variety of organizations collect statistics but none as thoroughly as the government and its various agencies. Each government department

TABLE 14.6 A COMPARISON OF SCHOLARLY JOURNALS AND POPULAR MAGAZINES

	Scholarly Journals	**Popular Magazines**
Purpose	To report research studies; to advance and stimulate research and theory building; to communicate specialized knowledge and research findings	To entertain and inform people about general issues and concerns; to communicate general interest knowledge, to summarize and popularize more specialized knowledge
Types of Articles	Original scientific research studies; critical analyses; usually written in the jargon of the particular field, making it difficult for outsiders to understand	Personality profiles; news summaries; usually written in easy-to-understand, fast-paced prose
Article Authors	Professors, researchers, scientists, graduate students	Professional writers, journalists, and some academics
Hardcopy and Online Accessibility	Available by subscription, usually fairly expensive; online access available for a fee that libraries, publishers, or individuals pay for	Available by subscription, usually fairly inexpensive and at newsstands and book-stores; online copies are often free
Review Process	Often blind review by peers (ideally the reviewers do not know the author when they review the article)	Varies greatly from a review board to a general editor
Reliability	Probably the most reliable types of articles available	Varies greatly depending on the magazine
Readers/Audience	Academics, scientists, researchers, undergraduate and graduate students	The general reading public or those interested in specific areas, for example, photography, finance, movies, or sports
Design and Appearance	Scholarly looking, one color, little variation in typeface, seldom containing photos (with obvious exceptions as in art and architecture journals); few advertisements, perhaps of other scholarly journals or books	Glossy, colorful, varied fonts, lots of photos, advertisements for all sorts of products
Examples of Journals and Magazines	*Communication Monographs, Journal of Personality and Social Psychology, New England Journal of Medicine*	*People, Wired, Time, Fast Company, Reader's Digest, Forbes, Everyday with Rachael Ray*
Examples of Articles	■ Attachment and relational satisfaction: the mediating effect of emotional communication ■ Managing self-uncertainty through group identification ■ The interface between academic education and the professional training of accountants	■ "How to Ace Your Interview" ■ "What Exactly Is the Fight over Health Care?" ■ "Procrastination: 5 Strategies to Get Started" ■ "Create a Comfy Cottage-Style Living Room"
Publication Schedule	Usually quarterly; articles are often published 9–12 months after they are accepted (a process that itself can take 6 months or more) for publication. As a result most articles do not address immediate concerns or very recent issues.	Usually, weekly or monthly; articles are likely to be published within days of the happenings they report.

publishes statistics, and you can go to the specific department (for example, the Department of the Treasury) to get relevant statistics. An even easier way is to log on to the federal government's statistical website. Here you'll find statistics from more than 100 U.S. federal agencies, including statistical profiles of each state, country, and city as well as statistics on crime, population, economics, mortality, and energy, along with comparisons with other countries.

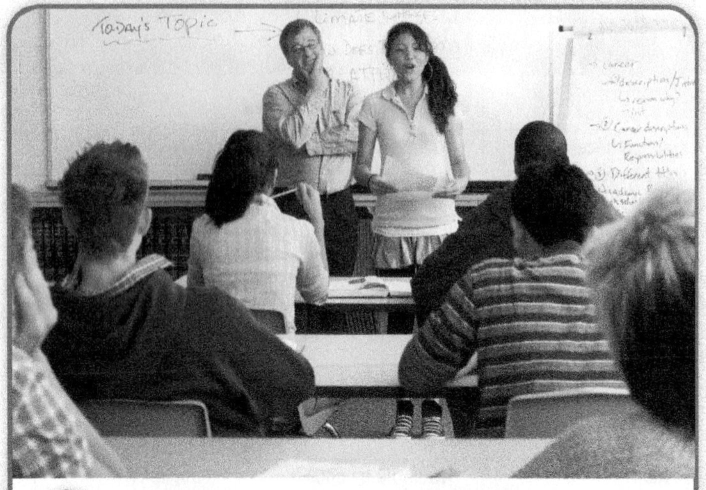

COMMUNICATION CHOICE POINT

CORRECTING ERRORS *In her speech Lena says that more than 70 percent of the students favored banning alcohol. Toward the end of the speech, she realizes that she mixed up the figures (only 30 percent favored banning alcohol). During the question-and-answer period no one asks about the figures.* **What are some of Lena's options for dealing with this error?**

The Government

Governmental bodies and agencies throughout the United States (at the federal, state, and municipal levels) publish an enormous amount of information that you're sure to find useful in speeches on almost any topic. One excellent starting point is Google's government search (www.google.com/unclesam). This engine covers all websites in the *.gov* domain. Another way is to visit one or more of the 13 relevant departments of the federal government (these are the Departments of Agriculture, Commerce, Defense, Education, Energy, Health and Human Services, Housing and Urban Development, Interior, Justice, Labor, State, Treasury, and Transportation). All departments issue reports, pamphlets, books, and assorted documents dealing with their various concerns. Here are a few of the topics on which some of the departments have information that you'll find useful for your speeches.

- Department of the Treasury: taxes, property auctions, savings, economy, financial markets, international business, and money management.
- Department of Justice: drugs and drug enforcement; Patriot Act information; trafficking in persons; inmate locator; Americans with Disabilities Act; sentencing statistics; and information from the Bureau of Alcohol, Tobacco, Firearms, and Explosives.
- Department of Health and Human Services: aging, AIDS, disease, safety issues, food and drug information, disaster and emergency protection, families and children, disabilities, homelessness, and immigration.
- Department of Education: teaching resources in science, math, history, and language arts; innovations in education; reports on performance and accountability, "no child left behind," at-risk and gifted students, the Pell grant program, and religious expression in the schools.
- Department of Labor: pensions, unemployment, wages, insurance, and just about any other topic even remotely related to labor.

News Sources

Often you'll want to read reports on scientific breakthroughs, political speeches, congressional actions, obituaries, financial news, international developments, UN actions, or any of a host of other topics. Or you may wish to locate the date of a particular event and learn something about what else was going on in the world at that particular time. For this type of information, you may want to consult one or more of the many news sources available. Especially relevant are newspaper and newsmagazine websites, news wire services, and broadcast news networks.

- **Newspaper and newsmagazine websites.** Most newspapers and magazines maintain their own websites from which you can access current and past issues. Among the best are these: *Los Angeles Times*, *USA Today*, *The Wall Street Journal*, *The New York Times*, and *The Washington Post*.
- **News wire services.** Four wire services should prove helpful. Check out the Associated Press, Reuters, United Press International, and PR Newswire.
- **News networks online.** All of the television news stations maintain extremely useful websites. Some of the most useful are CNN, ESPN, ABC News, CBS News, and MSNBC News.

The Web

It's convenient to think of the Web as a three-part system consisting of the open, the deep, and the social Web.

The **open Web** (or visible or surface) consists of those materials that you'd be able to access with a simple search from most of your favorite search engines or directories. When you do a simple Google search, for example, you'd be accessing the open Web.

The **deep Web** (or invisible or hidden or deepnet)—estimated to be perhaps 50 times the size of the open Web—contains that collection of documents that are not accessible through simple searches on general search engines or directions. These include databases of scholarly articles and academic research journals that are available only for a fee that is paid for by your college library and your textbook publishers. It also includes all those websites you need a password to enter. Images and video files would also be considered as residing on the deep Web.

The **social Web** (actually a part of the deep web but because it deals with a unique type of material, it's helpful to consider it as a separate category) consists of the millions of blogs, Facebook pages, tweets, newsgroups, and listservs. Blogs are now extremely popular and often contain information that may be useful in public speaking. But don't assume that anything on a blog is necessarily reliable and accurate; check first.

In most cases, searching the Web efficiently requires the use of search engines and subject directories, plus some knowledge of how these tools operate. A *search engine* is a program that searches a database or index of Internet sites for the specific words you submit. Search engines search an enormous number of websites but do not distinguish between reliable and unreliable information. A high school student's term paper may well be listed next to that of a world-famous scientist with no distinction between them.

In using search engines (and in searching many CD-ROM databases), you'll find it helpful to limit your search with *operators*—words and symbols that define relationships among the terms for which you're searching. Perhaps the most common are AND (or +), OR, NOT (or -), and quotation marks. Searching for *drugs AND violence* will limit your search to only those documents that contain both words—in any order. Searching for *drugs OR violence* will expand your search to all documents containing either word. And searching for *violence AND schools NOT elementary* will yield documents containing both *violence* and *schools* except those that contain the word *elementary*. Quotation marks around the phrase will yield only those sources that use the exact phrase.

A *directory* is a list of subjects or categories of Web links. You select the category you're most interested in, then a subcategory of that, then a subcategory of that until you reach your specific topic. A directory doesn't cover everything; rather, the documents that it groups under its various categories are selected by the directory's staff members from those they deem to be especially worthwhile. Many search engines also provide directories, so you can use the method you prefer.

You can also search the net by setting up alerts on Google, Bing, or Yahoo! Here you enter your speech topic, the kind of search you want (whether news, Web, news and Web, or groups), and how often you want to receive alerts (daily, weekly, or as-it-happens). You'll then receive in your e-mail alerts with hot links to sites that include your speech topic.

Evaluating Internet Resources

As you research your topic, keep in mind that anyone can "publish" on the Internet, making it essential that you subject everything you find on the Web to critical analysis. An article on the Internet can be written by world-renowned scientists or by elementary school students; by fair and objective reporters or by people who would spin the issues to serve their own purposes. It's not always easy to tell which is which. Here are five questions—built around the acronym FACQS to help you remember—to ask concerning the **f**airness, **a**ccuracy, **c**urrency, **q**ualifications, and **suf**ficiency of Internet resources (as well as information from print media, from interpersonal interaction, or from film and electronic media).

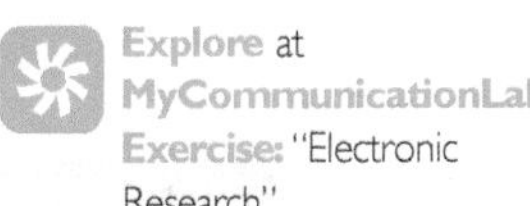

- **Fairness.** Does the author present the information fairly and objectively, or is there a bias favoring one position? Some websites, although objective on the surface, are actually organs of political, religious, or social organizations; so it's often useful to go to the home page and look for information on the nature of the organization sponsoring the website. Reviewing a range of research in the area will help you see how other experts view the issue and if this author's view of the situation is fair.
- **Accuracy.** Is the information presented accurate? Determining accuracy is not easy, but the more you learn about your topic, the more able you'll be to judge the accuracy of information. Is the information primary, secondary, or tertiary? Is it worthwhile to check the primary source when using secondary or tertiary information? Check to see if the information is consistent with information found in other sources and if the recognized authorities in the field accept this information.
- **Currency.** When was the information published? When were the sources cited in the article written? Generally, the more recent the material, the more

useful it will be. With some topics—for example, unemployment statistics, developments in AIDS research, tuition costs, stem cell research, or attitudes toward the war, same-sex marriage, or organized religion—the currency of the information is crucial to its usefulness, simply because these things change so rapidly. Other topics, such as historical or literary subjects, may well rely on information that was written even hundreds of years ago. Even here, however, new information frequently sheds light on events that happened in the far distant past.

- **Qualifications.** Does the author have the necessary credentials? For example, does the author have a background in science or medicine to write authoritatively on health issues? Do an Internet search using one of the biography sites or simply enter the author's name in your favorite search engine.
- **Sufficiency.** Is the information presented sufficient to establish the claim or conclusion? The opinion of one dietitian is insufficient to support the usefulness of a particular diet; statistics on tuition increases at five elite private colleges are insufficient to illustrate national trends in tuition costs. Generally, the broader your conclusion, the greater the information you'll need to meet the requirements for sufficiency. If you want to claim the usefulness of a diet for all people, then you're going to need a great deal of information from different populations—men and women, old and young, healthy and sick, and so on.

Integrating and Citing Research

Even the best and most extensive research would count for little if you didn't integrate it into your speech. By integrating and acknowledging your sources of information in your speech, you'll give fair credit to those whose ideas and research findings you're using, and you'll lessen the risk that anything you say can be interpreted as plagiarism (see page 300). At the same time, you'll help establish your own reputation as a responsible researcher and thus increase your own credibility. Suggestions for citing sources in your speech as well as in your written outline are provided in Table 14.7.

Explore at MyCommunicationLab Activity: "Avoiding Plagiarism"

TABLE 14.7 THE ORAL CITATION

Here are a few examples and notes on citing your sources in your speech. The written citations would be included at the end of your speech in a list of references. The American Psychological Association (APA) style is used here. Numerous websites are available that will convert your sources into the desired style.

Source and Written Citation	Oral Citation	Research and Presentation Notes
Book Knapp, M. (2008). *Lying and deception in human interaction.* Boston, MA: Penguin.	Mark Knapp, an authority on nonverbal communication, and the author of *Lying and Deception in Human Interaction,* notes some of the cues to look for when judging lying.	Try to establish the importance of the author to add weight to your argument.
Magazine Article Kashdan, T., & Biswas-Diener, R. (2013, July/August). What happy people do differently. *Psychology Today, 46,* 50–59.	A recent article in *Psychology Today* magazine identifies some of the factors making for happiness.	If the magazine is well known, as is *Psychology Today,* it's sufficient to name the magazine. If it were less well known, then you might establish its credibility for your listeners by noting, for example, its reputation for fairness, its longevity, or its well-known authors.

TABLE 14.7 (CONTINUED)

Source and Written Citation	Oral Citation	Research and Presentation Notes
Newspaper Article Hauslohner, A., & al-Hourani, S. (2013, July 3). Morsi aide: Coup is underway. *Washington Post* Retrieved from http://www.Washingtonpost.com. If a letter to the editor or an editorial, then insert [Letter to the Editor] or [Editorial] after the article title.	An article in the online *Washington Post,* one of the world's great newspapers, dated July 3, 2013 reports that…	It sometimes helps to establish the credibility of the newspaper—some are more reputable than others. And always include reference to the date of the article. You should also indicate whether it was a regular news item or a letter to the editor or editorial.
Encyclopedia article *Encyclopaedia Britannica* (2013, September 12). USDA Rule Takes a Bite Out of Online Puppy Mills. Retrieved from www.britannica.com.	The *Encyclopaedia Britannica,* which I accessed on September 13, 2013) reports on recent legislation concerning animal rights.	It isn't necessary to say "www.britiannica.com." Your audience members will know how to access the encyclopedia—especially if they're in this course.
Research Study Hefner, V., & Wilson, B. J. (2013, June). From love at first sight to soul mate. *Communication Monographs, 80,* 150–175.	In the June 2013 issue of *Communication Monographs,* one of the official journals of the National Communication Association, the influence of movies on relationships…	In citing a research study, make it clear that what you're reporting is from the primary source and not a secondary sources such as a magazine's summary of the research.
Blog Murphy, B. (2013, July 3). Aaron Hernandez's past brushes with violence. *The Huffington Post.* Retrieved from www.huffingtonpost.com.	Just this week, the Huffington Post, perhaps the most widely read of all blogs, posted an article on Aaron Hernandez.	Anyone can maintain a blog. If the blog is used for more than examples or illustrations, you need to establish the authority of the blog or blogger and the currency of the post.
Television Show National Geographic. (2013, July 3). The realities of war [Television broadcast].	*National Geographic* covered this issue in detail earlier this week.	It's helpful to name the network as well as the specific show. If the program is an interview, then identify the person being interviewed and perhaps the interviewer.
Personal Interview Because this is not retrievable, this is not included in the reference list.	In an e-mail interview I conducted with Margaret Wilder, the sheriff of Forest County, in September of this year, Wilder wrote that…	State how the interview was conducted—in person, by telephone, or through e-mail—and establish the currency of the interview.
Classroom Lecture Brommel, B. (2013, April 7) Communication at Hunter College in New York City.	In a lecture last week in "Communication in the Family," Professor Bernard Brommel noted that…	Citations of classroom lectures should include the professor's name, the course, and the approximate time the comment was made.
Statistics Centers for Disease Control and Prevention. (2013, June 27). Autism spectrum disorders. Retrieved from http://www.cdc.gov, July 3, 2013.	The Centers for Disease Control and Prevention website, which I accessed earlier this week, provides sobering statistics on the numbers of people with autism It notes…	It's important with most statistics to stress the authority of the source that collected the statistics (.gov sites are more reliable than .com sites) and the recency of the statistics. Providing information on the date of the page and when you accessed the website will further establish the currency of the statistics.

Watch at MyCommunicationLab Video: "Preparing for a Speech"

Margo is planning to give a speech on baseball for her communication course. She feels confident about her knowledge of the topic, but she's concerned about her ability to apply that in the speaking arena and is especially concerned that her audience may not find her a credible speaker. She has asked her friend Vicki for help. "Preparing for a Speech" looks at the initial steps involved in public speaking, the preparation of the speech itself, the form of its presentation, and the attitudinal approach important for public speaking effectiveness. All of these individual steps involve choices between doing one thing and doing another. Log on to www.mycommunicationlab.com to view this video and the various choices, and then respond to a few related discussion questions.

SUMMARY: PUBLIC SPEAKING TOPICS, AUDIENCES, AND RESEARCH

Study and Review at MyCommunicationLab

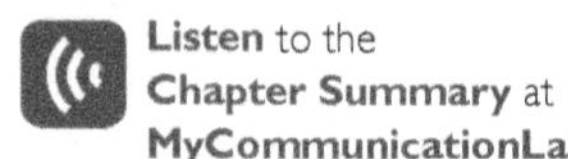

Listen to the Chapter Summary at MyCommunicationLab

This chapter introduced the nature of public speaking and covered selecting and limiting the topic and purpose, analyzing and adapting to your audience, and researching your speech.

14.1 INTRODUCING PUBLIC SPEAKING

1. Public speaking provides training to improve your personal and social competencies, academic and career skills, and general communication abilities.

14.2 MANAGING YOUR APPREHENSION

2. Apprehension in public speaking is normal and can be managed by reversing the factors that cause anxiety, practicing performance visualization, and systematically desensitizing yourself.
3. The preparation of a public speech involves 10 steps: (1) select the topic, purposes, and thesis; (2) analyze the audience; (3) research the topic; (4) formulate the thesis and identify the main points; (5) support the main points; (6) organize the speech materials; (7) construct the conclusion, introduction, and transitions; (8) outline the speech; (9) word the speech; and (10) rehearse and deliver the speech. The first three of these steps were discussed in this chapter; the remaining seven are discussed over the next two chapters.

14.3 STEP 1: SELECT YOUR TOPIC, PURPOSES, AND THESIS

4. Speech topics should deal with significant issues that interest the audience. Subjects and purposes should be limited in scope.
5. The thesis is your central idea; it is the one thing you want your audience to remember.

14.4 STEP 2: ANALYZE YOUR AUDIENCE

6. In analyzing an audience, consider the audience members' attitudes, beliefs, and values.
7. In analyzing the audience, also consider age, gender, cultural factors, religion and religiousness, the occasion, and the specific context.
8. Also analyze and adapt to your audience's willingness to hear your speech, how favorable the audience is to your point of view, and the knowledge that your audience has of your topic.

14.5 STEP 3: RESEARCH YOUR TOPIC

9. Research the topic, beginning with general sources and gradually exploring more specific and specialized sources.
10. Useful sources of information include libraries, interviews, scholarly articles, popular publications, reference works, news media, biographical material, government publications, electronic databases, and more.
11. Integrate research into your speech by mentioning the sources and any additional relevant information.
12. Avoid plagiarism by clearly acknowledging the source of any words or ideas you use that are not your own.
13. Critically evaluate your research by asking if the research is current, if it is fair and unbiased, and if the evidence is sufficient and accurate.

Study and **Review** the **Flashcards** at **MyCommunicationLab**

KEY TERMS

attitudes *290*
audience *294*
audience analysis *294*
belief *295*
communication apprehension *284*
deep Web *305*
general purpose *290*
informative speeches *290*
open Web *305*
performance visualization *285*
persuasive speech *290*
plagiarism *300*
primary sources *301*
public speaking *282*
search directory *290*
secondary sources *301*
social Web *305*
special occasion speech *290*
specific purpose *291*
systematic desensitization *288*
tertiary sources *301*
thesis *292*
topic *287*
topoi *289*
tree diagrams *289*
value *295*

WORKING WITH TOPICS, AUDIENCES, AND RESEARCH

14.1 Brainstorming for Topics. With a small group of students or with the entire class sitting in a circle, brainstorm for suitable speech topics. Be sure to appoint someone to write down all the contributions or use a recorder.

After this brainstorming session, consider:

a. Did any members give negative criticism (even nonverbally)?
b. Did any members hesitate to contribute really wild ideas? Why?
c. Was it necessary to re-stimulate the group members at any point? Did this help?
d. Did some useful speech topics emerge in the brainstorming session?

14.2 Limiting a Topic. As a general rule, focus on depth rather than breadth; avoid trying to cover too much in short speeches. Here are some overly general speech topics. Limit each of these topics to a subtopic that would be reasonable for a 5- to 10-minute speech.

a. Dangerous sports
b. Race relations
c. Parole
d. Censorship on the Internet
e. Ecological problems
f. Problems faced by college students
g. Morality
h. Health and fitness
i. Ethical issues in politics
j. Urban violence

14.3 Using Cultural Beliefs as Assumptions. There are probably few topics that the audience has not been culturally influenced about. So don't neglect cultural analysis regardless of your specific topic or audience. Evaluate each of the cultural beliefs listed below in terms of how effective each would be if used as a basic assumption by a speaker addressing your public speaking class. Use the following scale:

A = The audience would accept this assumption and would welcome a speaker with this point of view.
B = Some audience members would listen receptively and others wouldn't.
C = The audience would reject this assumption and would not welcome a speaker with this point of view.

a. A return to religious values is the best hope for the world.
b. The welfare of our country must come first, even before our own individual interests.
c. Sex outside of marriage is wrong and sinful.
d. Winning is all-important; it's not how you play the game, it's whether you win that matters.

14.4 Winning Over the Unwilling. Jack is scheduled to give a speech on careers in computer technology to a group of high school students who have been forced to go to a Saturday "career day" and to attend at least three of the speeches. The audience is definitely an unwilling group. What advice can you give Jack to help him deal with this type of audience?

14.5 Biographical Information. Jill wants to give a speech on television talk shows and wants to include biographical information on some of the talk show hosts. What sources might Jill go to in order to get authoritative and current information on these hosts? What sources might she go to in order to get "fan"-type information? What advice would you give Jill for distinguishing the two types of sources and their information?

14.6 2-Minute Speeches. Prepare and deliver a 2-minute speech in which you do one of the following:

- Evaluate the topics of recent talk shows against the criteria for a worthwhile and appropriate topic.
- Explain the cultural factors operating in this class that need to be taken into consideration by the speaker selecting a topic and purpose.
- Explain a particularly strong belief that you hold.
- Describe members of your class in terms of how willing, favorable, and knowledgeable you believe them to be about any specific topic or speaker.
- Describe the audience of a popular magazine, television show, or movie.
- Explain the value of one reference book, website, database, listserv, or newsgroup for research in public speaking.

14.7 Libraries. Visit one of the online libraries, using one of the suggestions presented in this chapter or one from your own search. How might this library help you in researching your speeches?

LogOn! MyCommunicationLab www.mycommunicationlab.com

Throughout this chapter, there are icons in the margin that highlight media content for selected topics. Go to **MyCommunicationLab** for additional materials on public speaking—one of the essential skills people need to function effectively in today's society. Here you'll find flashcards to help you learn key communication terms, videos that illustrate a variety of concepts, additional exercises, and discussions to help you continue your study of public speaking topics, audiences, and research.

15 SUPPORTING AND ORGANIZING YOUR SPEECH

Listen to Chapter 15 at MyCommunicationLab

CHAPTER TOPICS	CHAPTER OBJECTIVES
In this chapter you'll explore the following major topics:	**After reading this chapter you should be able to:**
STEP 4: COLLECT SUPPORTING MATERIALS	15.1 Identify the major types of supporting material and provide examples of each.
STEP 5: DEVELOP YOUR MAIN POINTS	15.2 Develop main points for a speech.
STEP 6: ORGANIZE YOUR SPEECH MATERIALS	15.3 Explain the major patterns of organization and organize your speech with the appropriate pattern.
STEP 7: CONSTRUCT YOUR INTRODUCTION, CONCLUSION, AND TRANSITIONS	15.4 Construct effective introductions, conclusions, and transitions.
OUTLINING YOUR SPEECH	15.5 Create preparation and presentation outlines for your speeches.

An organized pattern is almost always helpful.

Now that you've selected your topic, purpose, and thesis, analyzed your audience, and researched your topic, you're ready to develop and organize your main points and develop your introduction, conclusion, and transitions—the topics of this chapter.

15.1 STEP 4: COLLECT SUPPORTING MATERIALS

Now that you've identified your main points, you can devote attention to your next step: collecting supporting materials for your main points. Supporting materials (such as examples, statistics, and presentation aids) are essential to the public speaker: They give life to the main points; they help maintain attention; and they contribute to your purpose, whether that is to inform or to persuade. Presenting examples of homelessness, for instance, helps you show your listeners what homelessness is, how it happens, and how it affects people. Presenting statistics on the new health insurance plans helps your listeners understand why they should make certain decisions and not others.

In this section we cover examples, illustrations, and narratives; analogies; definitions; testimony; numerical data; and presentation aids. For each, we'll examine the varied types and offer some guidelines for using these materials effectively.

Explore at MyCommunicationLab Activity: "Testing for Relevance of Supporting Ideas"

Examples, Illustrations, and Narratives

Examples, illustrations, and narratives are specific instances that are explained in varying degrees of detail and will help greatly in helping the audience remember your speech.

Types of Examples, Illustrations, and Narratives

Examples (and we'll use the shorthand "examples" to refer to these forms of support) may be distinguished on the basis of their being real or hypothetical. Examples may also be distinguished on the basis of length. Generally, a relatively brief specific instance is referred to as an **example**; a longer and more detailed example is referred to as an **illustration**; and an example told in story-like form is referred to as a **narrative**.

The main value of examples is that they allow you to bring an abstract concept down to specifics. For example, to clarify what you mean by determination, you might give a specific instance or illustration from history or tell the story of any of the numerous great people who rose to prominence against the odds. Here is a good example of a specific instance used to illustrate the violation of human rights from a speech by Kyle Akerman from 2010:

> Initially, a Human Rights Watch report on March 19, 2009, substantiates that there are reports of detainees being shackled, and denied basic medical procedures. The January 9, 2010, *New York Times* tells the story of Nery Romero, a 22-year-old detainee who repeatedly begged for treatment of unbearable pain, and was repeatedly denied. The Office of Professional Responsibility discovered falsified documents saying that Romero received medication. Falsification was easy to detect... because [he] died days before he supposedly received his last treatment. This article notes that there have been 107 deaths of this type since October of 2003.

Guides for Using Examples, Illustrations, and Narratives

Keep in mind that the function of examples is to make your ideas vivid and easily understood; they are not ends in themselves. Make your examples only as long as necessary to ensure that your purpose is achieved.

Stress relevancy. Make sure your example is directly relevant to the proposition you want it to support, and make its relationship with your assertion explicit. Remember that although this relationship is clear to you (because you've constructed the speech), the audience is going to hear your speech only once. Show the audience exactly how your example relates to the assertion or concept you're explaining.

Distinguish between real and hypothetical examples. Don't try to foist a hypothetical example on the audience as a real one. If audience members recognize the deception, they'll resent your attempt to fool them. Let the audience know when you're using a real example and when you're using a hypothetical example.

Real examples	Hypothetical examples
▪ A situation such as this occurred recently; it involved...	▪ We could easily imagine a situation such as...
▪ I have a friend who...	▪ I think an ideal friend would be someone who...
▪ An actual example of this was reported in the...	▪ A hypothetical example of this type of friendship would be like...

Use examples to emphasize the widespread nature or significance of an issue or problem. Here, for example, New York Governor Andrew Cuomo (Associated Press, 2013) uses two recent examples to make the point that we need greater gun control:

> The tragic events of just the last few weeks in Newtown, Conn., and West Webster, N.Y., have

indelibly taught us guns can cut down small children, firefighters and policemen in a moment.

Analogies

Analogies are comparisons that are often extremely useful in making your ideas clear and vivid to your audience.

Types of Analogies

Analogies may be of two types: figurative and literal. **Figurative analogies** compare items from different classes—for example, the flexibility afforded by a car with the freedom of a bird, a college degree with a passport to success, playing baseball with running a corporation. Figurative analogies are useful for illustrating possible similarities and provide vivid examples that are easily remembered.

Literal analogies compare items from the same class, such as two cars or two cities. For example, in a literal analogy you might argue (1) that two companies are similar—both are multinational, multibillion-dollar pharmaceutical companies, both have advertising budgets in the hundreds of millions of dollars, and so on; and (2) that therefore the advertising techniques that worked for one company will work for the other.

Guides in Using Analogies

Analogies do not constitute evidence of the truth or falsity of an assertion. Avoid presenting analogies as proof and beware of speakers who do this; they may be doing this because there is no real evidence.

Select figurative analogies that are not overly fanciful; you want the audience to see that the comparison is a reasonable one. In using literal analogies stress that the cases compared (say, two corporations) are alike in essential respects. Let the audience see that it's the similarities that are important and any differences of only minor consequence.

Definitions

A **definition** is a statement explaining the meaning of a term or concept; it explains what something is.

Types of Definitions

Some of the most important ways in which you can define a term are by etymology, authority, negation, and specific examples.

Definition by Etymology. One way to define a term is to trace its historical or linguistic development. In defining the word *communication,* for example, you might note that it comes from the Latin *communis,* meaning "common"; in "communicating" you seek to establish a commonness, a sharing, a similarity with another individual. And *woman* comes from the Anglo-Saxon *wifman,* which meant literally a "wife man," where the word *man* was applied to

eth•ics *noun* morality, standards of conduct, moral judgment

MAKING ETHICAL CHOICES
Communicating in Cyberspace

Because of the explosion in computer communication, the ethics of Internet communication (sometimes referred to as *nethics*) has become an important part of ethical communication. Of course, the same principles that govern ethical public speaking should also prevail when you communicate on the Internet. Here, however, are a few ethical principles with special relevance to computer communication. It is unethical to:

Invade the privacy of others. Reading the files of another person or breaking into files that you're not authorized to read is unethical.

Harm others or their property. Creating computer viruses; publishing instructions for making bombs; and creating websites that promote racism, heterosexism, ageism, or sexism are some examples of unethical computer use.

Spread falsehoods. Lying on the Internet—about other people, the powers of medical or herbal treatment, or yourself—is just as unethical as it is in other forms of communication.

Plagiarize. Appropriating the work of another as your own—whether the original work appeared on the Internet or in a book or journal—is unethical.

Steal passwords, PINs, or authorization codes that belong to others.

Copy software programs that you haven't paid for.

Ethical Choice Point

As an experiment, you develop a computer virus that can destroy websites. Recently, you've come across a variety of websites that market child pornography. You wonder if you can ethically destroy these websites. Indeed, you wonder if not destroying them is actually more unethical than using your newly developed virus. What is your ethical obligation in this situation? What would you do?

both sexes. Through phonetic change *wifman* became woman. Most larger dictionaries and, of course, etymological dictionaries will help you find useful etymological definitions.

Definition by Authority. You can often clarify a term by explaining how a particular authority views it. You might, for example, define lateral thinking by authority and say that Edward deBono, who developed lateral thinking in 1966, has noted that "lateral thinking involves moving sideways to look at things in a different way. Instead of fixing on one particular approach and then working forward from that, the lateral thinker tries to find other approaches." Or you might use the authority of cynic and satirist Ambrose Bierce and define love as nothing but "a temporary insanity curable by marriage" and friendship as "a ship big enough to carry two in fair weather, but only one in foul."

Definition by Negation. You also might define a term by noting what the term is not; that is, define it by negation. "A wife," you might say, "isn't a cook, a cleaning person, a babysitter, a seamstress, a sex partner. A wife is..." or "A teacher isn't someone who tells you what you should know but rather one who...."

Definition by Specific Examples. An example is not a definition, but it can serve defining functions; it can help clarify terms or phrases. Here, for example, Ohio Congressman Dennis Kucinich (2007) uses a series of specific examples to clarify what he means by "human rights" in a speech presented to the Wall Street Project Conference on January 8, 2007:

> We have a right to a job.
>
> We have a right to a living wage.
>
> We have a right to an education.
>
> We have a right to health care.
>
> We have a right to decent and affordable housing.
>
> We have a right to a secure pension.
>
> We have a right to air fit to breathe.
>
> We have a right to water fit to drink.
>
> We have a right to be free of the paralyzing fear of crime.

Guides in Using Definitions

Use definitions when you wish to explain difficult or unfamiliar concepts or when you wish to make a concept more vivid or forceful. If the purpose of the definition is to clarify, then it must do just that. Avoid defining terms that don't need defining.

Make sure your definitions don't sound like you're talking down to your audience. Integrate the definitions into your speech, rather than announce that you'll define a term. Definitions in a speech often sound best when they are inserted parenthetically, for example: "Rhetoric, the art of persuasive communication, was one of the original liberal arts in the academies of Ancient Greece and Rome."

Take a look at some of the numerous websites devoted to defining terms; they offer a variety of definitions, often along with great quotations, the correct pronunciation, and lots more.

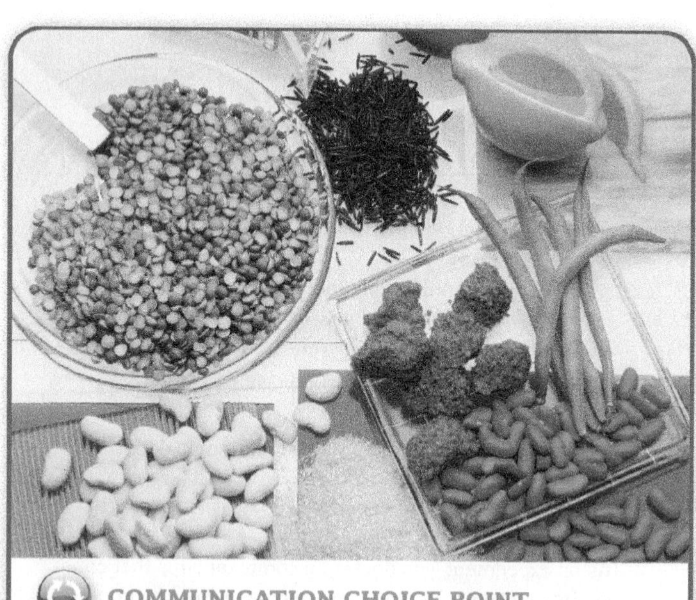

COMMUNICATION CHOICE POINT

USING DEFINITIONS *Marilyn wants to define vegan and vegetarian and distinguish between them using a variety of types of definitions.* **What are some of Marilyn's options for clarifying these two similar but different terms?**

Testimony

Testimony is often a useful form of support and involves using the opinions of others to clarify or support your assertions.

Types of Testimony

Testimony is of two basic types: expert and eyewitness. In using **expert witness testimony** the speaker cites the opinions, beliefs, predictions, or values of some authority or expert. For example, you might want to state an economist's predictions concerning inflation and depression, or you might want to support your analysis by citing an art critic's evaluation of a painting or art movement. The faculty of your college or university is one of the best, if rarely used, sources of expert information for almost any speech topic. Regardless of what your topic is, a faculty member of some department likely knows a great deal about the subject. At the very least, faculty members will be able to direct you to appropriate sources. Experts in the community can serve similar functions. Local politicians, religious leaders, doctors, lawyers, museum directors, and the like often are suitable sources of information.

Of course, if 500 public speaking students all descend on the faculty or on the community, chaos can easily result. So going to these experts is often discouraged as a class assignment. But it's often a useful practice for speeches you'll give later in life.

The second type is that of **eyewitness testimony** to some event or situation. For example, you might cite the testimony of someone who saw an accident, of a person who spent time in a maximum-security prison, or of a person who had a particular kind of operation.

Guides in Using Testimony

Whether you use the testimony of a world-famous authority or draw on an eyewitness account, you need to establish your source's credibility—to demonstrate to the audience that your expert is in fact an authority or that your eyewitness is believable.

Stress the competence of the person. Whether the person is an expert or a witness, make sure the audience sees this person as competent. To cite the predictions of a world-famous economist of whom your audience has never heard will mean little, so first explain the person's competence. To prepare the audience to accept what this person says, you might introduce the testimony by saying, for example:

> This prediction comes from the world's leading economist, who has successfully predicted all major financial trends over the past 20 years.

Stress the unbiased nature of the testimony. If listeners perceive the testimony to be biased—whether or not it really is—it will have little effect. You want to check out the biases of a witness so that you may present accurate information. But you also want to make the audience see that the testimony is in fact unbiased. You might say something like this:

> Researchers and testers at *Consumer Reports*, none of whom have any vested interest in the products examined, found wide differences in car safety. Let's look at some of these findings. In the October 2011 issue, for example,...

Stress the recency of the testimony. When you say, for example,

> General Bailey, who was interviewed last week in *The Washington Post*, spoke on U.S. military power and said....

you show your audience that your information is recent and up to date.

the•o•ry *noun* statement of explanation, formulation of relationships, reasoned generalization

UNDERSTANDING THEORY AND RESEARCH
Primacy and Recency

Let's say that you have three points that you intend to arrange in topical order. How will you determine which to put first? The theory and research on primacy and recency offer help. As explained in Chapter 3, the rule of primacy tells you that what an audience hears first will be remembered best and will have the greatest effect. The rule of recency tells you that what the audience hears last (or most recently) will be remembered best and will have the greatest effect. Research findings on these seemingly incompatible "rules" offer a few useful general suggestions.

- The middle is remembered least and has the least general effect. Thus, if you have a speech with three points, put the weakest one in the middle.
- If your listeners are favorable or neutral, lead with your strongest point. In this way you'll strengthen the conviction of those who are already favorable and you'll get the neutrals on your side early.
- If your audience is hostile or holds very different views than you, put your most powerful argument last and work up to it gradually—assuming, that is, that you can count on the listeners' staying with you until the end.

Research on memory tells us that the audience will remember very little of what you say in a speech. Therefore, repeat your main assertions—whether you put them first or last in your speech—in your conclusion.

Working with Theories and Research

Examine your previous speech or the speech you're currently working on in terms of the order of the main points. What insights does primacy-recency theory give you for ordering your main points?

Numerical Data

Numerical data are often essential and will help to support what you mean by, say, high tuition, reasonable wage, or appropriate executive compensation.

Types of Numerical Data

Numerical data is of two basic types: raw numbers and statistics. **Raw numbers** are simply figures unmodified by any mathematical operation. For example, if you want to show that significant numbers of people now get their news from the Internet, you could give the total number of online users for each of the past 10 years and compare that with the numbers of newspaper readers and television news viewers in those same years. These data would then allow you to show that the number of people who get their news from the Internet is increasing while the number of those getting the news from papers and television is declining.

Statistics, on the other hand, are summary figures that help you communicate the important characteristic of a complex set of numbers such as the mean (the average—the average grade on the test was 86), the mode (the most frequent score in an array—more students scored 85 than any other grade), percentages (the portion of a total, expressed as a portion of 100—96 percent of the students passed). For example, you might compare the percentage of a tuition increase at your school to the national average or to the rate of inflation. To illustrate the growth of instant messaging or Twitter as a means of communication, you might note the percentage that usage has grown over the past few years.

In a speech on auto safety, Meagan Hagensick of Wartburg College used numbers effectively to drive home the importance of seat belts (Schnoor, 2008):

> One fatality every 13 minutes. One injury every 10 seconds. One accident every 5 seconds. Six million crashes. 2.8 million injuries. 43,000 people killed each year. These numbers are not spawned from a deadly virus or new strain of bacteria; they are the result of avoidable human error.

Guides for Using Numerical Data

In using numerical data of any kind, make sure the numbers are clear, remembering that your audience will hear the figures only once. Round off figures so they're easy to comprehend and retain. If your numbers are difficult to remember, reinforce your oral presentation with some type of presentation aid—perhaps a slide or a chart. Numbers presented without some kind of visual reinforcement are often difficult to grasp and remember.

Make explicit the meaning of the numbers you're using. For example, if you state that the average home health aide makes less than $30,000 a year, you need to compare this figure to the salaries of other workers and to your proposition that salaries need to be increased.

Use numbers in moderation. Most listeners' capacity for numerical data presented in a speech is limited, so use figures sparingly.

Use only reliable and current numerical data and make sure that your audience is aware of their reliability and currency.

Presentation Aids

As you plan your speech, consider using some kind of **presentation aid**—a visual or auditory means for clarifying ideas. Ask yourself how you can visually present what you want your audience to remember. For example, if you want your audience to see the growing impact of the sales tax, consider showing them a chart of rising sales tax over the past 10 years. If you want them to see that Brand A is superior to Brand X, consider showing them a comparison chart identifying the superiority of Brand A. Presentation aids are not added frills—they are integral parts of your speech. They will help you gain your listeners' attention and maintain their interest; they can add clarity, reinforce your message, and contribute to your credibility and confidence (Sojourner & Wogalter, 1998).

Explore at MyCommunicationLab Exercise: "Analyzing Presentation Aids"

- **Presentation aids help you gain attention and maintain interest.** We perk up when the speaker says, "I want you to look at this chart showing the employment picture for the next 5 years" or "Listen to the vocal range in this voice." Presentation aids provide variety in what we see and hear—something audiences will appreciate and respond to favorably.
- **Presentation aids add clarity.** If you want to illustrate the growth in Facebook since it started in 2003, you might recite the number of members on Facebook for each year. But that would be almost impossible for an audience to appreciate. However, if you couple this verbal explanation with a graph, they'll more easily understand (and see) the growth you're trying to illustrate.
- **Presentation aids reinforce your message.** Presentation aids help ensure that your listeners understand and remember what you've said. They help you present the same information in two different ways: verbally, as audience members hear you explain the aid, and visually, as they see the chart, map, or model.

- **Presentation aids contribute to credibility and confidence.** If you use appropriate and professional-looking presentation aids—a topic that will be covered later in this chapter—your listeners are likely to see you as a highly credible speaker, as someone who cares enough about both them and the topic to do this "extra" work.
- **Presentation aids help reduce apprehension.** When you concentrate on coordinating your speech with your presentation aids, you're less likely to focus on yourself—and self-focus often increases apprehension. In addition, the movement involved in using presentation aids relaxes many speakers.

Types of Presentation Aids

Among the presentation aids you have available are the object itself, models of the object, graphs, word charts, maps, people, photographs, and illustrations.

- **The object itself.** As a general rule (to which there are many exceptions), the best presentation aid is the object itself. Bring it to your speech if you can. Notice that infomercials sell their products not only by talking about them but by showing them to potential buyers. You see what George Foreman's Lean Mean Grilling Machine looks like and how it works. You see the jewelry, the clothing, the new mop from a wide variety of angles and in varied settings.
- **Models. Models**—replicas of the actual object—are useful for a variety of purposes. For example, if you want to explain complex structures such as the human auditory or vocal mechanism, the brain, or the structure of DNA, a model will prove useful. Models help to clarify the relative sizes and positions of parts and how each part interacts with each other part.
- **Graphs.** Graphs are useful for showing differences over time, clarifying how a whole is divided into parts, and comparing different amounts or sizes. Figure 15.1 on the next page shows a variety of graphs that can be drawn freehand or generated with the graphics capabilities of any word-processing or presentation software. Keep your graphs as simple as possible. In a **pie graph,** for example, don't have more than five segments. Similarly, in a bar graph limit the number of items to five or fewer. As in the graphs shown in Figure 15.1, be sure you add the legend, the labels, and the numerical values you wish to emphasize.
- **Word charts.** Word charts (which also can contain numbers and even graphics) are useful for identifying the key points in one of your propositions or in your entire speech—in the order in which you cover them, of course. Or you could use a word chart to identify the steps in a process—for example, the steps in programming TiVo, in dealing with sexual harassment, or in downloading the latest version of Adobe Photoshop. Another use of charts is to show information you want your audience to write down, for example, emergency phone numbers, addresses, or titles of recommended books or websites.
- **Maps.** If you want to illustrate the locations of geographic features such as cities, lakes, rivers, or mountain ranges, maps will obviously prove useful

me•di•a lit•er•a•cy *noun* ability to understand, interact with, and create media messages

EXPANDING MEDIA LITERACY
Agenda Setting

The media are agenda-setting organizations; the media tell you what is and what is not important and they do this by focusing attention on certain topics and certain people (the "important" issues and personalities) and giving no or little attention to others (the "unimportant" issues and personalities). Because the media are so important and so pervasive in our lives, we believe them. We believe that the topics the media cover a great deal are, in fact, the important topics of the day. But, on more sober reflection and with our media literacy hat on, we can see that the personalities the media focuses on are not the really important people. For example, on Google News of July 19, 2013, there were 622,000 news items on Kim Kardashian and 65,300 news items about *Dancing with the Stars,* but only 13,400 on New York Governor Andrew Cuomo and 35,000 on New Jersey Governor Chris Christie.

"The media tell you what is and what is not important."

A good way to see agenda setting is to compare the coverage of two very different media outlets; you'll quickly see agenda setting in action. In viewing or reading any of the media's presentation of "important issues" keep in mind that they have each made selections and their selections are telling you what you should be concerned with and what you can dismiss.

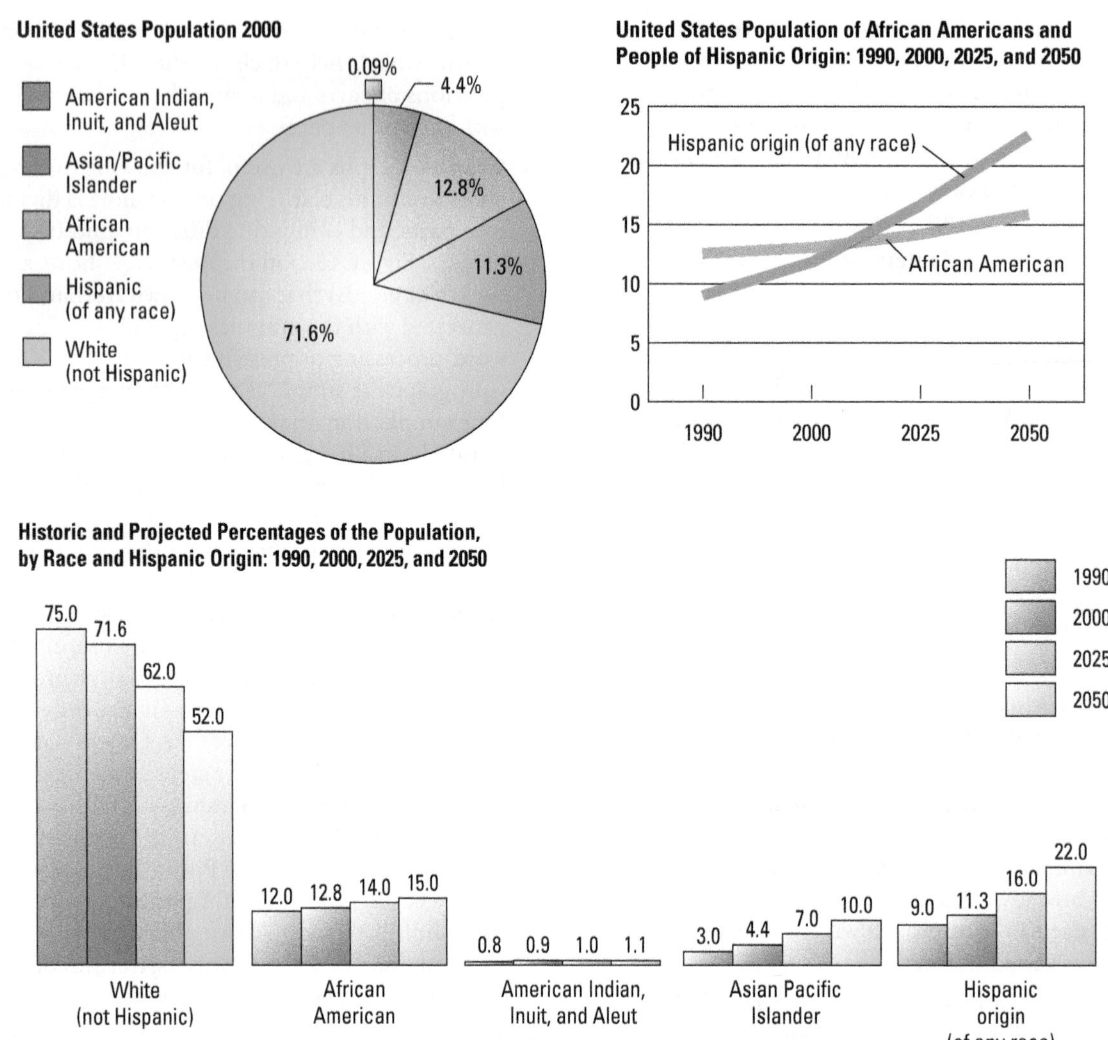

FIGURE 15.1 Assorted Graphs

Notice that each of the graphs serves a somewhat different purpose. The pie graph is especially useful if you want to show how some whole is divided into its parts and the relative sizes of the parts. From the pie graph you can easily see the relative percentages of the different groups in the U.S. population. Pie graphs are especially helpful when you have three to five values to illustrate. The line graph shows how comparisons can be visualized with a very simple illustration. Notice that the graph is especially clear because it focuses on only two groups. The bar graph presents the same information as the pie graph but for four different time periods.

as presentation aids. But maps also can be used for illustrating population densities, immigration patterns, world literacy rates, varied economic conditions, the spread of diseases, and hundreds of other issues you may wish to examine in your speeches. A wide variety of maps may be downloaded from the Internet and then shown as slides or transparencies. Chances are you'll find a map on the Internet for exactly the purpose you need.

- **People.** If you want to demonstrate the muscles of the body, different voice patterns, skin complexions, or hairstyles, consider using people as your aids. Aside from the obvious assistance they provide in demonstrating their muscles or vocal qualities, people help to secure and maintain the attention and interest of the audience.
- **Photographs and illustrations.** Types of trees, styles of art, kinds of exercise machines, or the horrors of war—all can be made more meaningful with photographs and illustrations. The best way to use these is to convert these to images so that they can be projected on a wall or screen and can be seen clearly by everyone in the audience. You can also convert the images to transparencies to use with a transparency projector. Passing pictures around the room is generally a bad idea.

Listeners will wait for the pictures to circulate to them, wonder what the pictures contain, and miss a great deal of your speech in the interim.

Once you've decided on the type of presentation aid you'll use, you need to decide on the medium you'll use to present it. Acquire skill in using both low-tech (the whiteboard or flip chart) and high-tech (the computerized slide show) resources. A variety of media, with their major uses, and some suggestions for using them effectively are presented in Table 15.1.

Using Presentation Aids

Your presentation aids will be more effective if you follow a few simple guidelines.

- **Know your aids intimately.** Be sure you know in what order your aids are to be presented and how you plan to introduce them. Know exactly what goes where and when. Do all your rehearsal with your presentation aids so that you'll be able to introduce and use them smoothly and effectively.

TABLE 15.1 THE MEDIA OF PRESENTATION AIDS

Here, in brief, are some of the media you might use along with some suggestions for using them effectively.

Media	Uses	Suggestions
Whiteboards	Use to record key terms or names, important numerical data, or even the main points of your speech (in very abbreviated form).	■ Keep what you write brief. ■ Don't turn your back to the audience; maintain eye contact even when writing ■ Erase material you no longer want the audience to focus on.
Chartboards Large semi-rigid boards come in a variety of colors and sizes.	Useful when you have one or two relatively simple graphs, a few word charts, or diagrams that you want to display during your speech.	■ Be sure you have a way of holding them up. ■ Black lettering on a white board generally works best. ■ Remove the chart after you're finished with it.
Flip Charts Large pads of paper (usually about 24 × 24 inches) mounted on a stand or easel.	Use to record a variety of information, for example, key concepts or main points. Writing these out before the speech saves you the time of writing them during the speech (as you're forced to do with a chalkboard).	■ Be sure the print is legible to the back of the audience. ■ Keep the charts simple. ■ Make sure the pages are in the correct order and that you can navigate the flip chart with ease.
Slides and Transparencies Projected on a screen.	Useful in showing a series of visuals that may be of very different types; for example, photographs, illustrations, charts, or tables.	■ Follow the general suggestions for using computer-assisted presentations. ■ Low-tech transparencies are often still of value.
Audios and Videos You can play a scene from a film or television show at the appropriate time in your speech or you can create your own video.	Add variety to your presentation and help to maintain audience attention. A speech on advertising jingles or music styles would be greatly helped by having actual samples for the audience to hear.	■ Videos are best used in small doses; in many instances just 20- or 30-second excerpts will prove sufficient. ■ Do not pass your smartphone around for audience members to view.
Handouts Printed materials that you distribute to the audience. A variety of handouts can be easily prepared with many of the computer presentation packages that we'll consider in the last section of this chapter.	Helpful in explaining complex material and also in providing listeners with a permanent record of some aspect of your speech. Also useful for presenting complex information that you want your audience to refer to throughout the speech. Handouts encourage listeners to take notes—especially if you leave enough white space or even provide a specific place for notes—which keeps them actively involved in your presentation.	■ Be careful: If you distribute your handouts during your speech, encourage your audience to listen to you when you want them to and to look at the handout when you want them to by simply telling them "Look at the graph on the top of page 2" or "We'll get back to the handout in a minute; now, I want to direct your attention to the second argument"). ■ If you distribute your handouts at the end of the speech, they may never get read. Encourage your audience to read them by including additional material.

- **Rehearse your speech with the presentation aids.** Practice your actual movements with the aids you'll use. If you're going to use a chart, how will you use it? Will it stand by itself? Will you ask another student to hold it for you? Can it be seen from all parts of the room?
- **Integrate presentation aids into your speech seamlessly.** Just as a verbal example should flow naturally into the text and seem an integral part of the speech, so should the presentation aid. It should appear not as an afterthought.
- **Avoid talking to your aid.** Talk to your audience at all times. Know your aids so well that you can point to what you want without breaking eye contact with your audience.
- **Use your aid only when it's relevant.** Show each aid when you want the audience to concentrate on it and then remove it. If you don't remove it, the audience's attention may remain focused on the visual when you want it to focus on what you're saying.

Computer-Assisted Presentations

A variety of **presentation software** packages are available. The speech presented in the Appendix on pages 417–418 illustrates what a set of slides might look like; the slides are built around the speech outline discussed later in this chapter (pages 335–336) and were constructed in Microsoft's PowerPoint. As you review this figure, try to visualize how you'd use a slide show to present your next speech.

Computer-assisted presentations possess all of the advantages of aids already noted (for example, maintaining interest and adding clarity). In addition, however, they have advantages all their own. They give your speech a professional, up-to-date look and in the process add to your credibility. They show you're prepared and care about your topic and audience.

Ways of Using Presentation Software

Presentation software enables you to produce a variety of aids. If you're speaking to a very small group, it may be possible to have your listeners gather around your computer as you speak. With larger audiences, however, you'll need a computer projector or LCD projection panel. Assuming you have a properly equipped computer in the classroom, you can copy your entire presentation to a CD-ROM or external drive, for example, and bring it with you the day of the speech.

Computer presentation software also enables you to print out a variety of materials: slides, slides with speaker's notes, slides with room for listener notes, and outlines of your speech. You can print out your complete set of slides to distribute to your listeners. Or you can print out a select portion of the slides, or even slides that you didn't have time to cover in your speech but that you'd like your audience to look at later. The most popular options are to print out two, three, or up to six slides per page. The two-slide option provides for easy readability and would be especially useful for slides of tables or graphs that you want to present to your listeners in an easy-to-read size. The three-slide option is probably the most widely used; it prints the three slides down the left side of the page with space for listeners to write notes on the right. This option is useful if you want to interact with audience members and you want them to take notes as you're speaking. Naturally, you'll distribute this handout before you begin your speech, during your introduction, or perhaps at that point when you want your listeners to begin taking notes. A sample three-slide printout with space for notes is provided in Figure 15.2. If you want to provide listeners with a complete set of slides, then the six-slide option may be the most appropriate. You can, of course, also print out any selection of slides you wish—perhaps only those slides that contain graphs or only those slides that summarize your talk.

Another useful option is to print out your slides with your speaker's notes. In that way you'll have your slides and any notes you may find useful—for example, statistics that would be difficult to memorize or quotations that you want to read to your audience. The audience will see the slides but not your speaker's notes. It's generally best to record these notes in outline form, with key words rather than complete sentences. This will prevent you from falling into the trap of reading your speech. A sample printout showing a slide plus speaker's notes is provided in Figure 15.3 on page 322.

Suggestions for Designing Slides

Your slides will be more effective and easier to produce if you follow these few simple suggestions.

- **Use the templates provided by your software.** Allow the design wizards to help you choose colors and typefaces. The templates are created by professional designers who are experts at blending colors, fonts, and designs into clear and appealing renderings.
- **Use consistent typeface, size, and color.** Give each item in your outline that has the same level head (for example, all your main points) the same typeface, size, and color throughout your presentation. This will help your listeners better follow the organization of your speech. If you're using

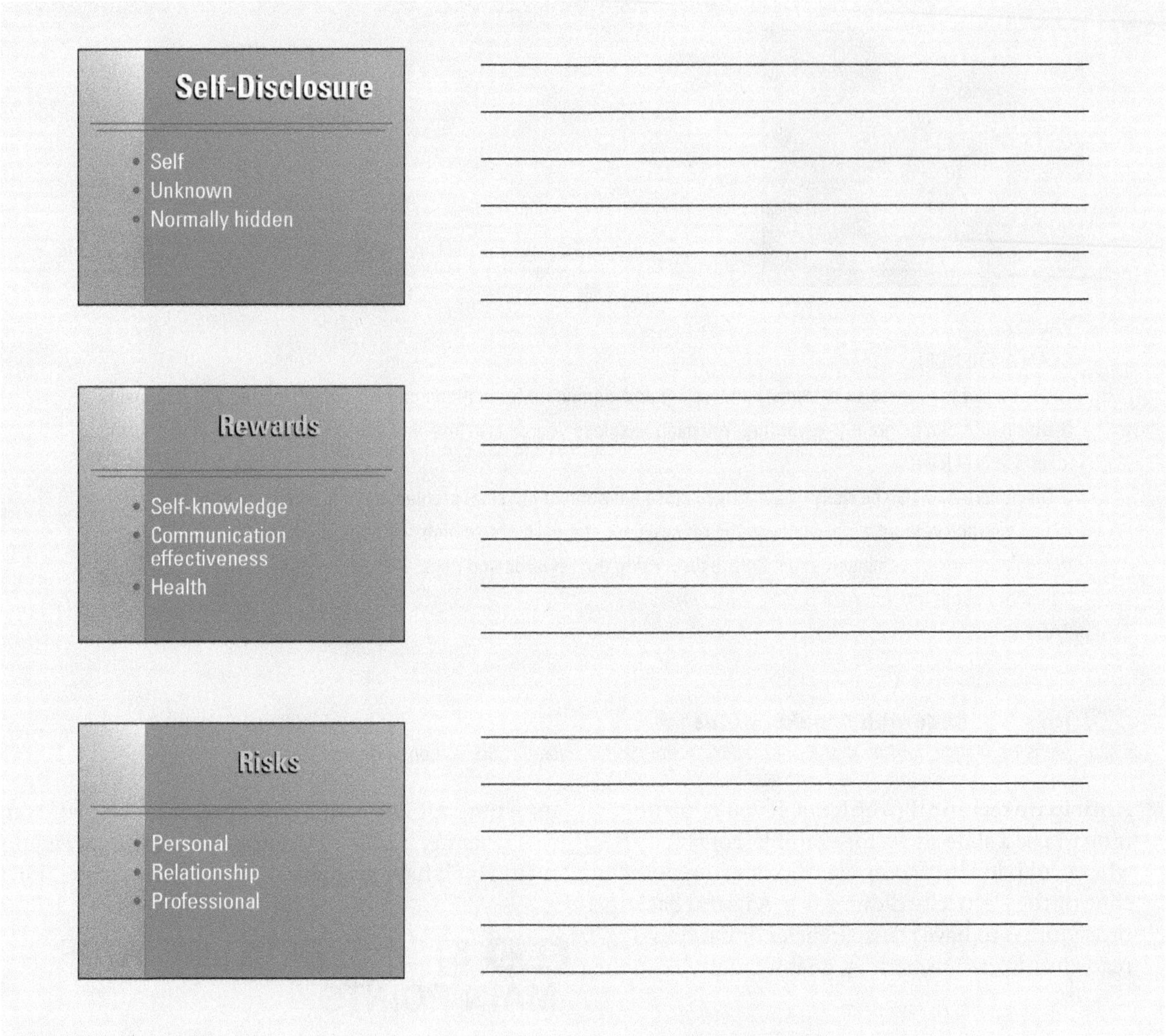

FIGURE 15.2 **Slides with Space for Listeners' Notes**

one of the predesigned templates, this will be done for you. Also, use the spell-check.

- **Be brief.** Your objective in designing these slides is to provide the audience with key words and ideas that will reinforce what you're saying in your speech; you don't want your audience to spend time reading rather than listening. Generally, put one complete thought on a slide, and don't try to put too many words on one slide.
- **Use colors wisely.** Generally, use colors for contrast. Many people have difficulty distinguishing red from green; so if you want to distinguish ideas, it is probably best to avoid this color pairing. Remember, too, the cultural attitudes toward different colors; for example, among some Asian cultures, writing a person's name in red means that the person has died.
- **Use only the visuals that you really need.** Use visuals only when you have room on the slide and when the visual is directly related to your speech thesis and purpose. If the inclusion of a visual will advance the purpose of your speech, use it; if it doesn't, don't.
- **Use charts and tables when appropriate.** Charts and tables are useful when you want to communicate complex information that would take too much text for one slide to explain. You have a tremendous variety of chart and graph types (for example, pie, bar, and cumulative charts) and tables to choose from.
- **Anticipate questions.** If there's a question-and-answer period following your speech, consider preparing a few extra slides for responses to questions you anticipate being asked.

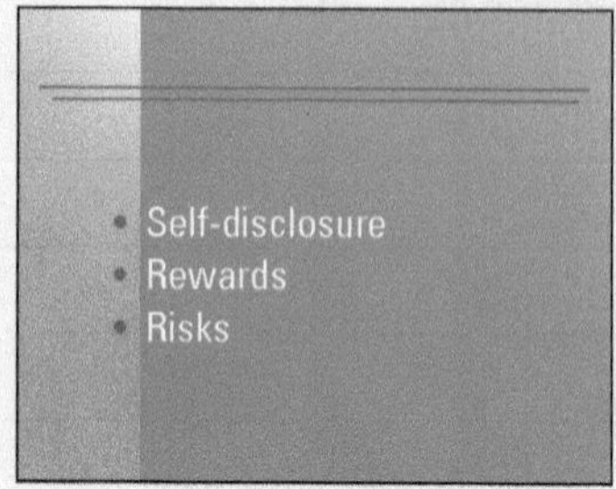

PAUSE!
SCAN AUDIENCE!
Today I'd like to discuss an extremely interesting and significant form of communication. It's called self-disclosure.
S-Disclosure can be greatly **rewarding**. You might disclose your secret love and find that you too are your secret lover's secret lover.
S-Disclosure can also be **risky**. You might disclose a mental or physical problem to your employer, only to find yourself without a job. Because the rewards and the risks are so high, we need to understand this unique form of communication. Before discussing the rewards and risks, we need to understand a little more about the nature of S-D.
PAUSE!

FIGURE 15.3 **Slide with Speaker Notes**
This example is from slide number 4, the orientation, in the "Self-Disclosure" speech on page 417.

- **Anticipate technical problems.** If you're planning to use a slide show, for example, consider what you'd do if the computer didn't arrive on time or the electricity didn't work. A useful backup procedure is to have transparencies or handouts ready just in case something goes wrong.

Rehearsing with Presentation Programs

Presentation packages are especially helpful for rehearsing your speech and timing it precisely. As you rehearse, the computer program records the time you spend on each slide and will display that time under each slide; it will also record the presentation's total time. You can use these times to program each slide so you can set it to run automatically. Or you can use the times to see if you're devoting the amount of time to each of your ideas that you want to. If you find in your rehearsal that your speech is too long, these times can help you see which parts may be taking up too much time and perhaps could be shortened.

Presentation software allows you to rehearse individually selected slides as many times as you want. But make sure that you go through the speech from beginning to end toward the end of your rehearsal period. Rehearse with this system as long as improvements result; when you find that rehearsal no longer serves any useful purpose, then stop.

Another type of rehearsal is to check out the equipment available in the room you'll speak in and its compatibility with the presentation software you're using. If possible, rehearse with the very equipment you'll have available on the day you're speaking.

15.2 STEP 5: DEVELOP YOUR MAIN POINTS

Your **thesis**, as already noted (pages 292–293), is your main assertion; it's what you want the audience to absorb from your speech. The thesis of the *Rocky* movies is that the underdog can win; the thesis of the Martin Luther King Jr. "I have a dream" speech is that true equality must be granted to African Americans and to all people. From your thesis you'll be able to derive your main points, the major ideas that you will explore in order to prove or support your thesis.

To see how this works in detail, imagine that you're giving a speech on the values of a college education to a group of high school students. Your thesis is: "A college education is valuable." You then ask, "Why is it valuable?" From this question you generate your main points. Your first step might be to brainstorm this question and generate as many answers as possible without evaluating them. You might come up with answers such as the following:

1. It helps you get a good job.
2. It increases your earning potential.
3. It gives you greater job mobility.

4. It helps you secure more creative work.
5. It helps you appreciate the arts more fully.
6. It helps you understand an extremely complex world.
7. It helps you understand different cultures.
8. It allows you to avoid taking a regular job for a few years.
9. It helps you meet lots of people and make new friends.
10. It helps you increase your personal effectiveness.

There are, of course, many other possibilities—but for purposes of illustration, these 10 possible main points will suffice. Even with only these 10 you can see that not all are equally valuable or relevant to your audience. So look over the list to see how to make it shorter and more meaningful. Try these suggestions.

- Eliminate those points that seem least important to your thesis. On this basis you might want to eliminate number 8, as this seems least consistent with your emphasis on the positive values of college.
- Combine those points that have a common focus. Notice, for example, that the first four points all center on the value of college in terms of jobs. You might, therefore, consider grouping these four items into one proposition: A college education helps you get a good job. This main point and its elaboration (all aspects of a "good job") might look like this in your speech outline:

  I. A college education helps you get a good job.
  A. College graduates earn higher salaries.
  B. College graduates enter more creative jobs.
  C. College graduates have greater job mobility.

- Select points that are most relevant or interesting to your audience. You might decide that high school students would be interested in increasing personal effectiveness, so you might select point 10 for inclusion as a second main point.
- For your class speeches, which will generally range from 5 to 15 minutes, use two, three, or four major ideas. Too many main points will result in a speech that is confusing, contains too much information and too little amplification, and proves difficult for listeners to remember.
- Word each of your main points in the same (parallel) style. When outlining, phrase points labeled with Roman numerals in a similar (parallel) style. Likewise, phrase points labeled with capital letters and subordinate to the same Roman numeral (for example, A, B, and C under point I) in a similar style. Parallel style was used in the example on college education and getting a good job, presented above. This parallel styling helps the audience follow and remember your speech.
- Develop your main points so they're separate and discrete; don't allow them to overlap one another. Each section labeled with a Roman numeral should be a separate entity.

Not This	This
I. Color and style are important in clothing selection.	I. Color is important in clothing selection. II. Style is important in clothing selection.

15.3 STEP 6: ORGANIZE YOUR SPEECH

When you organize your ideas, you derive a variety of benefits. Here are just four:

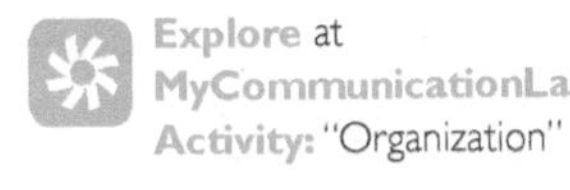

- **Organizing will help guide the speech preparation process.** As you develop your organization, you'll be able to see the speech more clearly and as a whole (even in a preliminary and unfinished form). This will help you to see what needs further development, what needs paring down, or what should be rearranged or repositioned.
- **Organizing will help your audience understand your speech.** Because audience members will hear your speech only once, it must be instantly clear to them. If they can visualize the pattern or outline you're following, it will be easier for them to understand your speech and to see, for example, how an example supports a main point or how two arguments are related to your thesis.
- **Organizing will help your audience remember your speech.** People simply remember organized material better than unorganized material. Help them by presenting them with information in an easily identifiable and memorable organizational pattern.
- **Organizing will help establish your credibility.** When you present an effectively organized speech, you say in effect that you put work into this and that you're concerned with the audience understanding and remembering your speech.

Once you've identified the main points you wish to include in your speech, you need to devote attention to how you'll arrange these points in the **body**, or main part, of your speech. Here are several options.

Temporal Pattern

When you use a **temporal pattern**, you organize your speech into two, three, or four major parts, beginning with the past and working up to the present or future—or beginning with the present and working back to the past.

The temporal (sometimes called "chronological") pattern is especially appropriate for informative speeches in which you wish to describe events or processes that occur in a time sequence. It's also useful when you wish to tell a story, demonstrate how something works, or examine the steps involved in some process. Directions for making lasagna, the steps toward a college education, or the history of writing would all be appropriate for temporal patterning. A speech on the development of language in the child might be organized in a temporal pattern and could be broken down something like this:

I. Babbling occurs around the 5th month.
II. Lallation occurs around the 6th month.
III. Echolalia occurs around the 9th month.
IV. "Communication" occurs around the 12th month.

Spatial Pattern

You can also organize your main points on the basis of space. The **spatial pattern** is especially useful when you wish to describe objects or places. Like the temporal pattern, it's an organizational pattern that listeners will find easy to follow as you progress—from top to bottom, from left to right, from inside to outside, or from east to west, for example. The structure of a place, an object, or even an animal is easily placed into a spatial pattern. You might describe the layout of a hospital, a school, a skyscraper, or a dinosaur with a spatial pattern. Here's an example of an outline describing the structure of the traditional textbook and using a spatial pattern:

I. The front matter contains the preface and the table of contents.
II. The text proper contains the chapters.
III. The back matter contains the glossary, bibliography, and index.

Topical Pattern

When your topic conveniently divides itself into subdivisions, each of which is clear and approximately equal in importance, the **topical pattern** is most useful. A speech on important cities of the world might be organized into a topical pattern, as might be speeches on problems facing the college graduate, great works of literature, the world's major religions, and the like. The topical pattern would be an obvious choice for organizing a speech on the powers of the government. The topic itself divides into three parts: legislative, executive, and judicial. A sample outline might look like this:

Watch at MyCommunicationLab Video: "Intercultural Communication in Italy"

I. The legislative branch is controlled by Congress.
II. The executive branch is controlled by the president.
III. The judicial branch is controlled by the courts.

Problem–Solution Pattern

The **problem–solution pattern** is especially useful in persuasive speeches in which you want to convince the audience that a problem exists and that your solution would solve or lessen the problem. Let's say that you want to persuade your audience that jury awards for damages should be limited. A problem–solution pattern might be appropriate here. In the first part of your speech, you'd identify the problem(s) created by these large awards; in the second part, you'd propose the solution. A sample outline for such a speech might look something like this:

I. Jury awards for damages are out of control. [the general problem]
  A. These awards increase insurance rates. [a specific problem]
  B. These awards increase medical costs. [a second specific problem]
  C. These awards place unfair burdens on business. [a third specific problem]
II. Jury awards need to be limited. [the general solution]
  A. Greater evidence should be required before a case can be brought to trial. [a specific solution]
  B. Part of the award should be turned over to the state. [a second specific solution]
  C. Realistic estimates of financial damage must be used. [a third specific solution]

Cause–Effect/Effect–Cause Pattern

Similar to the problem–solution pattern is the cause–effect or effect–cause pattern. This pattern is useful in persuasive speeches when you want to convince your audience of the causal connection existing between two events or elements. In the **cause–effect pattern** you divide the speech into two major sections: causes and effects. For example, a speech on the reasons for highway accidents or birth defects might lend itself to a cause–effect pattern. Here you might first consider, say, the causes of highway accidents or birth defects, then turn to some of the effects; for example, the number of deaths, the number of accidents, and so on.

Or suppose you wanted to demonstrate the causes for the increase in AIDS in your state. In this case you might use an **effect–cause pattern** that might look something like this:

- **I. AIDS is increasing.** [general effect]
  - **A. AIDS is increasing among teenagers.** [a specific effect]
  - **B. AIDS is increasing among IV drug users.** [a second specific effect]
  - **C. AIDS is increasing among women.** [a third specific effect]
- **II. Three factors contribute to this increase.** [general causal statement]
  - **A. Teenagers are ignorant about how HIV is transmitted.** [a specific cause]
  - **B. IV drug users exchange contaminated needles.** [a second specific cause]
  - **C. Women are not practicing safe sex.** [a third specific cause]

As you can see from this example, this type of speech is often combined with the problem–solution type. For example, after identifying the causes, the speaker might then treat the causes as problems and offer solutions for each problem/cause (for example: education for teens, free needle exchange programs, and education on safer sex for men and women).

The Motivated Sequence

The **motivated sequence** is an organizational pattern in which you arrange your information so as to motivate your audience to respond positively to your purpose (German, Gronbeck, Ehninger, & Monroe, 2010). In contrast to the previous organizational patterns, which provided ways of organizing the main ideas in the body of the speech, the motivated sequence is a pattern for organizing the entire speech. Here the speech (introduction, body, and conclusion) is divided into five parts or steps: (1) attention, (2) need, (3) satisfaction, (4) visualization, and (5) action.

1. The **attention step** makes audience members give you their undivided attention. You can gain audience attention through a variety of means, for example, asking a question (rhetorical or actual) or making reference to audience members. These methods are presented in the "Introduction" discussion in the Step 7 section of this chapter.
2. In the **need step**, you establish that a need exists for some kind of change. The audience should feel that something has to be learned or something has to be done because of this demonstrated need.
3. The **satisfaction step** presents the answer or the solution to the need you demonstrated in step 2 of the motivated sequence. On the basis of this satisfaction step, audience members should now believe that what you are informing them about or persuading them to do will satisfy the need.
4. In the **visualization step** you intensify the audience's feelings or beliefs. You enable your listeners to imagine the situation as it would

the•o•ry *noun* statement of explanation, formulation of relationships, reasoned generalization

UNDERSTANDING THEORY AND RESEARCH
Culture and Speech Organization

Members of low-context cultures (see Chapter 2) are usually direct in their messages and appreciate directness in others. But directness may be unnecessary or even insulting to the high-context cultural member. Conversely, the indirectness of the high-context member may appear vague or even dishonest to a member of a low-context culture.

High-context cultures prefer indirectness. Speakers in Japan, to take one well-researched example, need to be careful lest they make their point too obvious or too direct and insult the audience. Speakers in Japan are expected to lead their listeners to the conclusion through example, illustration, and various other indirect means (Lustig & Koester, 2010). In contrast, in the United States (a low-context culture) speakers are encouraged to be explicit and direct—to tell the listeners, for example, exactly what the speaker wants them to do.

Another cultural difference influences how focused the speech ought to be. For example, in the United States, each main point of a speech or written composition should be developed by itself. Only when one point is fully developed and finalized does the speaker or writer move on to the next. Hindu culture, however, is less rigid and allows for many ideas being considered in the same paragraph of an essay or in the same part of a speech (Lustig & Koester, 2010).

Working with Theories and Research

As a listener, what type of organization do you prefer? For example, do you prefer a speaker who is direct or indirect? Do you prefer speakers who clearly separate the main points or who consider several points together?

be if the need were satisfied as you suggested in step 3. You might, for example, demonstrate the benefits that people would receive if your ideas were put into operation or the negative effects they would suffer if your plan were not adopted.

5. The **action step** spells out what you want audience members to do, the action that you want them to take to ensure that the need (step 2) is satisfied (step 3) as visualized (step 4). Here you want to move the audience in a particular direction—for example, to contribute free time to read to the blind. You can accomplish this step by stating what audience members should do, using a variety of supporting materials and logical, emotional, and ethical appeals.

Chapter 18 discusses the use of the motivated sequence in persuasive speeches. Table 15.2 presents a variety of other organizational patterns.

TABLE 15.2 ADDITIONAL ORGANIZATIONAL PATTERNS

The six patterns just considered are the most common and the most useful for organizing most public speeches. But there are other patterns that might be appropriate for different topics.

Organizational Structure	Uses	Possible Outlines
In the **structure–function pattern** there are generally two main points, one for structure and one for function.	Useful in informative speeches in which you want to discuss how something is constructed (its structure) and what it does (its function). It might prove useful, for example, in a speech explaining what a business organization is and what it does, identifying the parts of a university and how they operate, or describing the nature of a living organism: its anatomy (its structures) and its physiology (its functions).	Thesis: To understand the brain you need to understand its structure and its function. I. The brain consists of two main parts [explanation of structures] A. The cerebrum consists of... B. The cerebellum consists of... II. The brain enables us to do a variety of things [explanations of functions] A. The cerebrum enables us to... B. The cerebellum enables us to...
In the **comparison-and-contrast pattern** your main points might be the main divisions of your topic.	This pattern is often useful in informative speeches in which you want to analyze two different theories, proposals, departments, or products in terms of their similarities and differences. In this type of speech you would be concerned not only with explaining each theory or proposal but also with clarifying how they're similar and how they're different.	Thesis: Liberal and conservative political philosophies differ in important ways. I. Government regulation... A. The liberal attitude is... B. The conservative attitude is... II. Redistribution of income... A. Liberals view this... B. Conservatives view this...
In the **pro-and-con pattern**, sometimes called the **advantages–disadvantages pattern**, the speech has two main points—the advantages of Plan A and the disadvantages of Plan A (or Plan B).	Useful in informative speeches in which you want to explain objectively the advantages (the pros) and the disadvantages (the cons) of a plan, method, or product. Or you can use this pattern in a persuasive speech in which you want to show the superiority of Plan A (identifying its advantages) over Plan B (identifying its disadvantages).	Thesis: The proposals of the two health plans differ in co-payments, hospital benefits, and sick leave. I. Co-payments... A. Plan A provides... B. Plan B provides... II. Hospital benefits.... A. Plan A provides... B. Plan B provides... III. Sick leave... A. Plan A provides... B. Plan B provides...

TABLE 15.2 ***(CONTINUED)***

Organizational Structure	Uses	Possible Outlines
In the **claim-and-proof pattern** your thesis would essentially be your claim and then each main point would be support for your claim.	Useful in a persuasive speech in which you want to prove the truth or usefulness of a particular proposition. It's the pattern that you see frequently in trials, where the claim made by the prosecution is that the defendant is guilty and the proof is the varied evidence designed to show that the defendant had a motive, opportunity, and no alibi.	Thesis/claim: The city must become proactive in dealing with the drug addicted. I. Drug usage is increasing. [Proof No. 1] A. A particularly vivid example... B. Recent statistics... II. Drug related crimes are increasing. [Proof No. 2] A. Street crimes have increased... B. Business break-ins...
In the **multiple-definition pattern** each of your main points would consist of a different type of definition.	Useful for informative speeches in which you want to explain the nature of a concept.	Thesis: The nature of creative thinking is often misunderstood. I. Creative thinking is not [definition by negation] II. According to Webster's dictionary...[dictionary definition] III. Edward deBono defines...[a creative thinking theorist's view] IV. A good example of creative thinking...[definition by example]
In the **5W pattern** (who? what? why? where? when?) your main points are explanations of who, what, why, where, and/or when.	Useful when you wish to report or explain an event; for example, a robbery, political coup, war, or trial; it's the journalist's pattern.	Thesis: Understanding the Constitution is a first step toward responsible citizenship. I. The Constitution is a document that sets forth...[answers the question What is the Constitution?] II. The Constitution was needed because...[answers the question Why was it written?] III. The Constitution was written at a time...[answers the question When was it written?] IV. The Constitution was written by...[answers the question Who wrote it?]
In the **fiction–fact pattern** your main points would be the fiction and under these would be the facts.	Useful in informative speeches when you wish to clarify misconceptions that people have about various things. In persuasive speeches this pattern might be used to defend or attack, whether a proposal, belief, or person.	Thesis: Three main misconceptions exist about the flu shot. I. The first misconception is that you can get the flu from the flu shot. A. Studies show... B. The flu shot contains... II. The second misconception is that antibiotics will help with the flu. A. Actually, antibiotics.... B. Viruses, such as the flu, however,... III. The third misconception is that older people spread the flu. A. Actually, children... B. In studies done....

15.4 STEP 7: CONSTRUCT YOUR INTRODUCTION, CONCLUSION, AND TRANSITIONS

Now that you have the body of your speech organized, devote your attention to the introduction, conclusion, and transitions that will hold the parts of your speech together.

Introduction

Together with your general appearance and your nonverbal messages, the introduction gives your audience its first impression of you and your speech. Your introduction sets the tone for the rest of the speech; it tells your listeners what kind of a speech they'll hear.

Your **introduction** may serve three functions: gain attention (an essential part of the speech), establish a speaker–audience–topic connection (almost always useful), and orient the audience as to what is to follow (always needed, in some form). Let's look at how you can accomplish each of these functions.

Watch at MyCommunicationLab Video: "Effective Introductions"

Gain Attention

In your introduction, gain the attention of your audience and focus it on your speech topic. (Then, of course, maintain that attention throughout your speech.) You can secure attention in numerous ways. Here are just a few of them.

- **Ask a question.** Questions are effective because they are a change from declarative statements and call for an active response from listeners.
- **Refer to audience members.** Talking about audience members makes them perk up and pay attention because you are involving them directly in your talk.
- **Refer to recent happenings.** Citing a previous speech, recent event, or prominent person currently making news helps you gain attention because the audience will want to see how you're going to connect it to your speech topic.
- **Use humor.** A clever (and appropriate) anecdote is often useful in holding attention.
- **Stress the importance of the topic.** People pay attention to what they feel is important to them and ignore what seems unimportant or irrelevant.
- **Use a presentation aid.** Presentation aids are valuable because they're new and different. They engage our senses and thus our attention.
- **Tell the audience to pay attention.** A simple, "I want you to listen to this frightening statistic," or "I want you to pay particularly close attention to...," used once or twice in a speech, will help gain audience attention.
- **Use a quotation.** Quotations are useful because audience members are likely to pay attention to the brief and clever remarks of someone they've heard of or read about.
- **Cite a little-known fact or statistic.** Little-known facts or statistics (on unemployment, crime in the schools, or political corruption, for example) will help perk up an audience's attention.
- **Use an illustration or dramatic story.** Much as we are drawn to soap operas, so are we drawn to illustrations and stories about people. Here's a good example from a speech by U.S. Senator (California) Dianne Feinstein (2006):

> On September 24 of this year, Los Angeles experienced a new low. Three-year-old Kaitlyn Avila was shot point-blank by a gang member who mistakenly thought her father was a member of a rival gang. The gang member shot and wounded her father, then intentionally fired into little Kaitlyn's chest. This is the first time law enforcement officials remember a young child being "targeted" in a gang shooting.

Establish a Speaker–Audience–Topic Relationship

In addition to gaining attention, you may also want to establish connections amongst yourself as the speaker, the audience members, and your topic. Try to answer your listeners' inevitable question: Why should we listen to you speak on this topic? You can establish an effective **speaker–audience–topic connection**, or S-A-T connection, in many different ways.

- **Refer to others present.** Not only will this help you to gain attention; it will also help you to establish a bond with the audience.
- **Refer to the occasion.** Often your speech will be connected directly with the occasion. By referring to the reason the audience has gathered, you can establish a connection between yourself, the audience, and the topic.
- **Express your pleasure or interest in speaking.**
- **Establish your competence in the subject.** Show the audience that you are really interested in and knowledgeable about the topic.
- **Express similarities with the audience.** By stressing your own similarities with members of the audience, you create a relationship with them and become an "insider" instead of an "outsider."

COMMUNICATION CHOICE POINT

AROUSING THE AUDIENCE *Paul notices that his audience doesn't seem to pay much attention to those who have spoken before him. And his speech topic, at least on first acquaintance, isn't one with a lot of audience appeal. He needs to gain their attention early in the speech.* **What are some of the things he might say to secure his listeners' attention?**

- **Compliment the audience.** Complimenting the audience is a commonly used technique to establish an S-A-T connection in much professional public speaking. In the classroom this technique may seem awkward and obvious, so it is probably best avoided here. But in other settings paying the audience an honest and sincere compliment (though never overdoing it) will not only encourage your listeners to give you their attention, but also help make them feel a part of your speech. In some cultures—Japan and Korea are good examples—the speaker is expected to compliment the audience, the beauty of the country, or its culture. It's one of the essential parts of the introduction. In this example, musician Billy Joel (1993) compliments his audience, the graduating class of the Berklee College of Music, directly and honestly:

  > I am truly pleased that the road has twisted and turned its way up the East Coast to Boston. The Berklee College of Music represents the finest contemporary music school there is, and I am honored to be here with you this morning to celebrate.

Orient the Audience

The introduction should orient the audience in some way as to what is to follow in the body of the speech. Preview for the audience what you're going to say. The **orientation** may be covered in a variety of ways.

- **Give a general idea of your subject.** You might say very simply, "Tonight I'm going to discuss atomic waste" or "I want to talk with you about the problems our society has created for the aged." In a speech at the groundbreaking ceremony for the Dr. Martin Luther King Jr. National Memorial, President Barack Obama (2006a), then Senator from Illinois, gave a general idea of what he'd say in the main part of his speech:

  > I have two daughters, ages five and eight. And when I see the plans for this memorial, I think about what it will [be] like when I first bring them here upon the memorial's completion.... And at some point, I know that one of my daughters will ask, perhaps my youngest, will ask, "Daddy, why is this monument here? What did this man do?" How might I answer them?

- **Identify the main points you'll cover.** In your orientation you may want to identify very briefly the main points you'll cover. Here's how one student, Christi Liu from the University of Texas did it:

> So to better understand WiTricity and its possibilities, we will first explore the phenomenon of wireless electricity, next plug in the uses of WiTricity, and finally take a look at the shocking implications.

Give a Detailed Preview. Or you may wish to give a detailed preview of the main points of your speech. After giving an introduction to the topic of devocalizing animals, Chelsea Anthony (2012), a student from Louisiana State University, Shreveport, oriented her audience in this way:

> [F]irst, we need to understand what convenience devocalization is, second, we need to investigate the reasons some people feel this barbaric act is necessary, and the, we will examine what must be done to help give a voice back to those who can't speak, or bark, for themselves.

- **Identify your goal.** Here California Governor Arnold Schwarzenegger (2007) orients the audience by giving a general idea of the goal he hopes to achieve.

> Hello everybody. Thank you for being here. I believe that in Sacramento this year, we are going to make history. Using a comprehensive approach built on shared responsibility where everyone does their part we will fix California's broken health care system and create a model that the rest of the nation can follow. I know everyone has been eager to hear exactly what we are proposing.

Conclusion

Your **conclusion** is especially important because it's often the part of the speech that the audience remembers most clearly. It's your conclusion that in many cases determines what image of you is left in the minds of the audience. Devote special attention to this brief but crucial part of your speech. Your conclusion may serve three major functions: to summarize, motivate, and provide closure. A summary of the speech is useful to both the speaker and the listener in nearly any circumstance. Motivation is appropriate in many persuasive speeches and in some informative speeches. Providing closure in any speech is essential.

Watch at MyCommunicationLab Video: "Effective Conclusions"

Summarize

The **summary** function is particularly important in an informative speech; it is less so in persuasive speeches or in speeches to entertain. You may summarize your speech in a variety of ways.

- **Restate your thesis or purpose.** In this type of brief summary, you restate the essential thrust of your speech, repeating your thesis or perhaps the goals you hoped to achieve.
- **Restate the importance of the topic.** Tell the audience again why your topic or thesis is so important.
- **Restate your main points.** That is, restate both your thesis and the major points you used to support it.

Motivate

A second function of the conclusion—most appropriate in persuasive speeches—is to motivate the people in the audience to do what you want them to do. In your conclusion you have the opportunity to give the audience one final push in the direction you wish them to take. Whether it's to buy stock, vote a particular way, or change an attitude, you can use the conclusion for a final **motivation**, a final appeal. Here are two excellent ways to motivate.

- **Ask for a specific response.** Specify what you want the audience to do after listening to your speech.
- **Provide directions for future action.** Another type of motivational conclusion is to spell out the action you wish the audience to take. Here's an example from a speech by Brett Martz (2012) from Ohio University:

> First, I want you to give the clothes off your back, literally. Hold your horses, not right now; you can leave that jacket on. But seriously, we as competitors and coaches are in ready supply of something that so many people need...our dress clothes. Do what I did. I pledged to donate one of my suits at the end of the season. And don't worry what condition it is in, the people at most food pantries will be able to find someone to mend anything. If you go to my Facebook page, "Just Do Something," you will find a link where you can donate your old suits.

Close

The third function of your conclusion is to provide **closure**. Often your summary will accomplish this, but in some instances it will prove insufficient. End your speech with a conclusion that is crisp and definite. Make the audience aware that you have definitely and clearly ended. Some kind of wrap-up, some sort of final statement, is helpful in providing this feeling of closure. You may achieve closure through a variety of methods.

- **Use a quotation.** A quotation is often an effective means of providing closure.
- **Refer to subsequent events.** You may also achieve closure by referring to future events—events taking place either that day or soon afterward.
- **Pose a challenge or question.** You may close your speech by leaving the audience with a provocative question to ponder or a challenge to consider. Or you can pose a question and answer it by recapping your thesis and perhaps some of your major arguments or propositions.
- **Thank the audience.** Speakers frequently conclude their speeches by thanking audience members for their attention or for their invitation to address them. In almost all cases, the "thank you" should be brief—A simple "thank you" or "I appreciate your attention" is all that's usually necessary.
- **Refer back to the introduction.** It's sometimes useful to connect your conclusion with your introduction. One student, David DePino (2012) from North Central College, Illinois, accomplished this neatly. After introducing his speech with a dramatic illustration of the savage beating of Chrissy Lee, a transgendered 22-year-old, he concludes his speech by referring back to this introductory story.

> **Unfortunately for Chrissy Lee, change came far too late. As she lay upon the McDonald's bathroom floor convulsing, the police were called but no one arrested and hers became one more story shrouded in silence. I hope that our community, the forensics community will WAKE UP. It is time to hear those stories that haven't been told, because it is those that must come through the loudest.**

COMMUNICATION CHOICE POINT

ORGANIZATIONAL PATTERNS What might be some of your patterns for organizing a speech of information on surveillance cameras in public places? What might be some appropriate patterns for a persuasive speech for (or against) surveillance cameras?

Transitions

Remember that audience members will hear your speech just once. They must understand it as you speak it, or your message will be lost. Transitions help listeners understand your speech more effectively and efficiently.

Transitions are words, phrases, or sentences that help your listeners follow the development of your thoughts and arguments and get an idea of where you are in your speech.

You can think of transitions as serving four functions: to connect, to preview, to review, and to signal where the speaker is in the speech. All of these functions work to provide coherence to your speech and to make it easier for the audience to follow your train of thought.

Explore at MyCommunicationLab Activity: "Better Transitions"

Connectives

Use connective transitions to connect the major parts of your speech. Use transitions in at least the following places:

- between the introduction and the body of the speech
- between the body and the conclusion
- between the main points in the body of the speech

You might say, for example, "Now that we have a general idea of...we can examine it in more detail." This helps the listener see that you've finished your introduction and are moving into the first main point. Or you might say, "Not only are prison sentences too long, they are often incorrect." This would help the listener see that you've concluded your argument about prison sentence length and are now going to illustrate that sentences are often incorrect. Other common phrases useful as connective transitions include: "In contrast to...," "consider also...," "Not only...but also...," "In addition to...we also need to look at...," and "Not only should we...but we should also...."

These transitions are generally indicated in your outline in square brackets.

Previews

Preview transitions help the audience get a general idea of where you're going. For example, you might want to signal the part of your speech you're approaching and say something like, "By way of introduction...," or "In conclusion...," or "Now, let's discuss why we are here today...," or "So, what's the solution? What should we do?"

At other times, you might want to announce the start of a major proposition or piece of evidence and say something like, "An even more compelling argument," or "A closely related problem," or "My next point," or "If you want further evidence, just look at..."

Reviews

It often helps to provide periodic reviews (sometimes called internal summaries), especially if your speech is long or complex. Incorporate internal summaries into your speech—perhaps working them into the transitions connecting your main points. Notice how the internal summary presented below reminds listeners of what they've just heard and previews what they'll hear next.

> **Inadequate recreational facilities, poor schooling, and a lack of adequate role models seem to be the major problems facing our youngsters. Each of these, however, can be remedied and even eliminated. Here's what we can do.**

Signposts

Signpost transitions are individual words that tell listeners where you are in your speech and would include such terms as these:

> **First,..., A second argument..., Next, consider..., Thus,...Therefore,..., So, as you can see..., It follows, then, that...**

Pitfalls in Introductions, Conclusions, and Transitions

In addition to understanding the principles of effective pubic speaking, it often helps to become aware of common mistakes. Here, then, are some of the common mistakes you'll want to avoid.

In your introduction:

- Don't apologize (generally). In the United States and western Europe, an apology may be seen as an excuse and so is to be avoided. In certain other cultures (those of Japan, China, and Korea are good examples), however, speakers are expected to begin with an apology. It's a way of complimenting the audience.
- Avoid promising something you won't deliver. The speaker who promises to tell you how to make a fortune in the stock market or how to be the most popular person on campus (and fails to deliver such insight) quickly loses credibility.
- Avoid gimmicks that gain attention but are irrelevant to the speech or inconsistent with your treatment of the topic. For example, slamming a book on the desk or telling a joke that bears no relation to your speech may accomplish the limited goal of gaining attention, but quickly audience members will see that they've been fooled and they'll resent it.
- Don't introduce your speech with ineffective statements such as "I'm really nervous, but here goes" or "Before I begin my talk, I want to say...." These statements will make audience members uncomfortable and will encourage them to focus on your delivery rather than on your message.

In your conclusion:

- Don't introduce new material. Instead, use your conclusion to reinforce what you've already said and to summarize.
- Don't dilute your position. Avoid being critical of your own material or your presentation. Saying, for example, "The information I presented is probably dated, but it was all I could find" or "I hope I wasn't too nervous" will detract from the credibility you've tried to establish.
- Don't drag out your conclusion. End crisply.

In your transitions:

- Avoid too many or too few transitions. Either extreme can cause problems. Use transitions to help your listeners, *who will hear the speech only once*, to understand the structure of your speech.
- Avoid transitions that are out of proportion to the speech parts they connect. If you want to connect the two main points of your speech, you need something more than just "and" or "the next point." In contrast, if you want to connect two brief examples, then a simple "another example occurs when..." will do.

15.5 OUTLINING YOUR SPEECH

As you collected supporting materials, developed and organized your main points, and constructed the introduction, conclusion, and transitions, you were, ideally, organizing your thoughts and materials into some kind of outline. The various types of outlines that you can use in public speaking, and presented here, can be looked at as ways of visualizing your entire speech, but should be especially helpful while working through Steps 5, 6, and 7, which focus on organization.

The **outline** is a blueprint for your speech; it lays out the elements of the speech and their relationship to one another. With this blueprint in front of you, you can see at a glance all the elements of organization—the functions of the introduction and conclusion, the transitions, the main points and their relationship to the thesis and purpose, and the adequacy of the supporting materials. And, like a blueprint for a building, the outline enables you to spot weaknesses that might otherwise go undetected.

Begin outlining when you start constructing your speech. In this way, you'll take the best advantage of one of the major functions of an outline—to tell you where change is needed. Change and alter the outline as necessary at every stage of the speech construction process.

Outlines may be extremely detailed or extremely general. But because you're now in a learning environment whose objective is to make you a more proficient public speaker, a detailed full-sentence outline will serve best. The more detail you put into the outline, the easier it will be for you to examine the parts of the speech for all the qualities and characteristics that make a speech effective.

Explore at MyCommunicationLab Activity: "Annotated Outline: Helen Keller International"

Constructing the Outline

After you've completed your research and mapped out an organizational plan for your speech, put this plan (this blueprint) on paper. Construct a "preparation outline" of your speech, using the following guidelines.

Preface the Outline with Identifying Data

Before you begin the outline proper, identify the general and specific purposes as well as your thesis. This prefatory material should look something like this:

Title:	**What Media Do**
General purpose:	**To inform.**
Specific purpose:	**To inform my audience of four major functions of the mass media.**
Thesis:	**The mass media serve four major functions.**

These identifying notes are not part of your speech proper. They're not, for example, mentioned in your oral presentation. Rather, they're guides to the preparation of the speech and the outline. They're like road signs to keep you going in the right direction and to signal when you've gone off course. One additional bit of identifying data should preface the statements of purposes and thesis: the title of your speech.

Outline the Introduction, Body, and Conclusion as Separate Units

The introduction, body, and conclusion of the speech, although intimately connected, should be labeled separately and should be kept distinct in your outline. Like the preliminary identifying data, these labels are not spoken to the audience but are further guides to your preparation.

By keeping the introduction, body, and conclusion separate, you'll be able to see at a glance if they do in fact serve the functions you want them to serve. You'll be able to see where further amplification and support are needed. In short, you'll be able to see where there are problems and where repair is necessary.

At the same time, make sure that you examine the speech as a whole and that you can see how the introduction leads to the body and how the conclusion summarizes your propositions and brings your speech to a close.

Insert Transitions

Insert [using square brackets, like these] transitions between the introduction and the body, the body and the conclusion, the main points of the body, and wherever else you think they might be useful.

Include a List of References

Some instructors require that you include a list of references in your preparation outline. If this is requested, then do so at the end of the outline or on a separate page. Some instructors require that only sources cited in the speech be included in the list of references, whereas others require that the full list of sources consulted be provided (those mentioned in the speech as well as those not mentioned).

Your research and references will prove most effective with your audience if you carefully integrate them into the speech. It will count for little if you consulted the latest works by the greatest authorities but never mention this to your audience. So, when appropriate, weave into your speech the source material you've consulted. In your outline, refer to the source material by the author's name, date, and page in parentheses and then provide the complete citation in your list of references.

In your actual speech, a source citation might be phrased something like this:

Sheena Iyenar, in her recent *The Art of Choosing*, argues that to be able to make effective choices, we need to first evaluate all our possible options.

Regardless of what specific sourcing system is required (find out before you prepare your outline), make certain to include all sources of information, not just written materials. Personal interviews, information derived from course lectures, and data learned from television should all be included in your list of references.

Use a Consistent Set of Symbols

The following is the standard, accepted sequence of symbols for outlining:

I.
  A.
    1.
      a.
        (1)
          (a)

Begin the introduction, the body, and the conclusion with Roman numeral I. Treat each of the three major parts as a complete unit.

Use Visual Aspects to Reflect the Organizational Pattern

Use proper and clear indentation. The outlining function of word-processing programs has many of these suggestions built into them.

Not this:

I. Television caters to the lowest possible intelligence.
II. Talk shows illustrate this.
III. *General Hospital*

This:

I. Television caters to the lowest possible intelligence.
  A. Talk shows illustrate this.
    1. *The Wendy Williams Show*
    2. *Maury*
    3. *The Jerry Springer Show*
  B. Soap operas illustrate this.
    1. *Days of Our Lives*
    2. *General Hospital*
    3. *The Young and the Restless*

Use One Discrete Idea per Symbol

If your outline is to reflect the organizational pattern structuring the various items of information, use just one discrete idea per symbol, and make sure each item does not overlap with any other item. Instead of the overlapping "Education might be improved if teachers were better trained and if students were better motivated," break this statement into two propositions: "I. Education would be improved if teachers were better trained" and "II. Education would be improved if students were better motivated."

Use Complete Declarative Sentences

Phrase your ideas in the outline in complete declarative sentences rather than as questions or as phrases. This will further assist you in examining the essential relationships. It's much easier, for example, to see if one item of information supports another if both are phrased in the declarative mode. If one is a question and one is a statement, this will be more difficult.

Explore at MyCommunicationLab Exercise: "Organizing a Scrambled Outline"

Sample Outlines

Now that the principles of outlining are clear, let's look at some specific examples to illustrate how those principles are put into operation in specific outlines. We'll look first at preparation outlines with two different organizational patterns; then at a template outline, a kind of skeletal pattern for a speech; and finally at a delivery outline, the type of outline you might take with you when you deliver your speech.

The Preparation Outline

Two **preparation outlines** are presented in the Public Speaking Sample Assistant boxes on pages 335–336 and 337. One uses a topical organizational pattern, perhaps the most common pattern among public speeches; the other uses the motivated sequence, an extremely popular pattern both for informative talks (see Chapter 17) and for persuasive speeches (see Chapter 18).

These full-sentence outlines are similar to the written materials you might prepare in constructing your own speeches. The side notes in the boxes are designed to clarify both the content and the format of full-sentence outlines.

Template Outline

Another useful type of outline is the **template outline.** Much as a template in PowerPoint guides you to fill in certain information in particular places, the template outline serves a similar function; it ensures that you include all the relevant material in reasonable order. At the same time, it also helps you see your speech as a whole—perhaps with gaps that need to be filled in or items that are discussed at too great a length. In some sense the template outline is mechanical (some might say too mechanical), but it's an extremely useful device for organizing a speech. As you become more familiar

PUBLIC SPEAKING SAMPLE ASSISTANT

A PREPARATION OUTLINE (TOPICAL ORGANIZATION)

Self-Disclosure

General purpose: To inform.
Specific purpose: To inform my audience of the advantages and disadvantages of self-disclosing.
Thesis: Self-disclosure has advantages and disadvantages.

Generally, the title, thesis, and general and specific purposes of the speech are prefaced to the outline. When the outline is an assignment that is to be handed in, additional information may be requested.

Introduction

Note the general format for the outline: the headings (introduction, body, and conclusion) are clearly labeled, and the sections are separated visually.

I. We've all heard them:

Notice that the introduction serves the three functions discussed in the text: it gains attention (by these extreme confessions); establishes an S-A-T connection (by noting that all of us, speaker and audience, have had this experience); and orients the audience (by identifying the three major ideas of the speech).

A. I'm in love with my nephew.

Note how the indenting helps you to see clearly the relationship that one item bears to another. For example, in Introduction I, the outline format helps you to see that A, B, and C are explanations (amplification and support) for I.

B. My husband is not my baby's father.
C. I'm really a woman.

These brief statements are designed to get attention, perhaps a laugh or two, but also to introduce the nature of the topic.

II. We've all disclosed.
A. Sometimes it was positive, sometimes negative, but always significant.
B. Knowing the potential consequences will help us make better decisions.

Here the speaker seeks to establish a speaker–audience–topic connection.

III. We look at this important form of communication in three parts:
A. First, we look at the nature of self-disclosure.
B. Second, we look at the potential rewards.
C. Third, we look at the potential risks.
[Let's look first at the nature of this type of communication.]

Here the speaker orients the audience and explains the three parts of the speech. The use of guide phrases (*first, second, third*) helps the audience fix clearly in mind the major divisions of the speech.

This transition cues the audience that the speaker will consider the first of the major parts of the speech. Notice that transitions are inserted between all major parts of the speech. Although they may seem too numerous in this abbreviated outline, transitions will be appreciated by your listeners because they will help them follow and understand your speech.

Body

I. Self-disclosure is a form of communication (Petronio, 2000).
A. S-D is about the self.
1. It can be about what you did.
2. It can be about what you think.
B. S-D is new, previously unknown information.
C. S-D is normally about information usually kept hidden.
1. It can be something about which you're ashamed.
2. It can be something for which you'd be punished in some way.
[Knowing what self-disclosure is, we can now look at its potential rewards.]

This transition helps the audience see that the speaker is finished discussing what self-disclosure is and will now consider the potential rewards.

II. Self-disclosure has three potential rewards.
A. It gives us self-knowledge.
B. It increases communication effectiveness (Schmidt & Cornelius, 1987).

Notice the parallel structure throughout the outline. For example, note that II and III in the body are phrased in similar style. Although this may seem unnecessarily redundant, it will help your audience follow your speech more closely and will also help you in logically structuring your thoughts.

C. It improves physiological health (Sheese, Brown, & Graziano, 2004).

[Although these benefits are substantial, there are also risks.]

III. Self-disclosure has three potential risks.

A. It can involve personal risks.

1. This happened to a close friend.

2. This also happened with well-known celebrities.

B. It can involve relationship risks (Petronio, 2000).

1. This happens on *Jerry Springer* five times a week.

2. It also happened to me.

C. It can involve professional risks (Korda, 1975; Fesko, 2001).

1. This occurred recently at work.

2. There are also lots of political examples.

[Let me summarize this brief excursion into self-disclosure.]

Note that the references are integrated throughout the preparation outline just as they would be in a term paper. In the actual speech, the speaker might say something like: "Communication theorist Sandra Petronio presents evidence to show that . . ."

These examples would naturally be recounted in greater detail in the actual speech. One of the values of outlining these examples is that you'll be able to see at a glance how many you have and how much time you have available to devote to each of these examples. Examples, especially personal ones, have a way of growing beyond their importance to the speech.

Note that each statement in the outline is a complete sentence. You can easily convert this outline into a phrase or key-word outline for use in presentation (see Public Speaking Sample Assistant box, page 339). The full sentences, however, will help you see more clearly the relationships among items.

Conclusion

I. Self-disclosure is a type of communication.

A. It's about the self, concerns something new, and concerns something that you usually keep hidden.

B. Self-disclosure can lead to increased self-knowledge, better communication, and improved health.

C. Self-disclosure can also create risks to your personal, relational, and professional lives.

This first part of the conclusion summarizes the major parts of the speech. The longer the speech, the more extensive the summary should be.

Notice that the Introduction's III A, B, and C correspond to the Body's I, II, and III, and to the Conclusion's I A, B, and C. This pattern will help you emphasize the major ideas in your speech—first in the orientation, second in the body of the speech, and third in the conclusion's summary.

II. Self-disclosure is not only an interesting type of communication; it's also vital.

A. You may want to explore this further by simply typing "self-disclosure" in your favorite search engine.

B. If you want a more scholarly presentation, take a look at Sandra Petronio's *Balancing the Secrets of Private Disclosures* in the library or online.

III. The bottom line, of course: Should you self-disclose?

A. Yes.

B. No.

C. Maybe.

This step, in which the speaker motivates the listeners to continue learning about self-disclosure, is optional in informative speeches. In persuasive speeches, you'd use this step to encourage listeners to act on your purpose—to vote, to donate time, to give blood, and so on.

This step provides closure; it makes it clear that the speech is finished. It also serves to encourage reflection on the part of the audience as to their own self-disclosing communication.

References

Korda, M. (1975). *Power! How to get it, how to use it.* New York, NY: Ballantine.

Fesko, S. L. (2001). Disclosure of HIV status in the workplace: Considerations and strategies. *Health and Social Work* 26 (November), 235–244.

Petronio, S. (Ed.). (2000). *Balancing the secrets of private disclosures*. Mahwah, NJ: Erlbaum.

Schmidt, T. O., & Cornelius, R. R. (1987). Self-disclosure in everyday life. *Journal of Social and Personal Relationships, 4,* 365–373.

Sheese, B. E., Brown, E. L, & Graziano, W. G. (2004). Emotional expression in cyberspace: Searching for moderators of the Pennebaker disclosure effect via e-mail. *Health Psychology, 23* (September), 457–464.

This reference list includes just those sources that appear in the completed speech.

PUBLIC SPEAKING SAMPLE ASSISTANT

A PREPARATION OUTLINE (MOTIVATED SEQUENCE ORGANIZATION)

This outline illustrates how you might construct an outline and a speech using the motivated sequence. The five steps of the motivated sequence (attention, need, satisfaction, visualization, and action) take the place of the introduction, body, and conclusion structure of many outlines discussed earlier.

The Youth Center

General purpose: To persuade.
Specific purpose: To persuade my listeners to vote in favor of Proposition 14, which would establish a community youth center.
Thesis: A youth center will reduce juvenile crime.

I. If you could reduce juvenile crime by some 20 percent by just flipping a lever, would you do it?
- **A.** Thom's drugstore was broken into by teenagers.
- **B.** Loraine's video store windows were broken by teenagers.

Step 1: Attention

The speaker asks a question to gain attention and follows it with specific examples of juvenile crime that audience members have experienced. The question and the specific examples focus on one single issue: the need to reduce juvenile crime. If the speech were a broader and longer one and included other reasons for the youth center, then it would have been appropriate to preview them here as well.

II. Juvenile crime is on the rise.
- **A.** The overall number of crimes has increased.
  - **1.** In 2008 there were 32 juvenile crimes.
  - **2.** In 2010 there were 47 such crimes.
  - **3.** In 2012 there were 63 such crimes.
- **B.** The number of serious crimes also has increased.
  - **1.** In 2008 there were 20 misdemeanors and 12 felonies.
  - **2.** In 2012 there were 38 misdemeanors and 25 felonies.

Step 2: Need

The speaker states directly and clearly the need and shows that a problem exists. The speaker then demonstrates that the rise in crime is significant both in absolute numbers and in the severity of the crimes. To help the listeners understand these figures, the speaker could display these figures on a chalkboard, on a prepared chart, or on PowerPoint slides. In a longer speech, other needs might also be identified in this step; for example, teenagers' needs for vocational and social skills.

III. A youth center will help reduce juvenile crime.
- **A.** Three of our neighboring towns reduced juvenile crime after establishing a youth center.
  - **1.** In Marlboro there was a 20 percent decline in overall juvenile crime.
  - **2.** In both Highland and Ellenville the number of serious crimes declined 25 percent.
- **B.** The youth center will not increase our tax burden.
  - **1.** New York State grants will pay for most of the expenses.
  - **2.** Local merchants have agreed to pay any remaining expenses.

Step 3: Satisfaction

In this step, the speaker shows the listeners that the proposal to establish a youth center offers great benefits and no significant drawbacks.

The speaker argues that the youth center will satisfy the need to reduce juvenile crime by showing statistics from neighboring towns. The speaker also preemptively answers any objections about increased taxes. If the speaker had reason to believe that listeners had other possible objections, these concerns too should be addressed in this step.

IV. Juvenile crime will decrease as a result of the youth center.
- **A.** If we follow the example of our neighbors, our juvenile crime rates are likely to decrease by 20 to 25 percent.
- **B.** Thom's store would not have been broken into.
- **C.** Loraine's windows would not have been broken.

Step 4: Visualization

Here the speaker visualizes what the town would be like if the youth center were established, using both the statistics developed earlier and the personal examples introduced in the beginning of the speech.

V. Vote yes on Proposition 14.
- **A.** In next week's election you'll be asked to vote on Proposition 14, establishing a youth center.
- **B.** Vote yes if you want to help reduce juvenile crime.
- **C.** Urge your family members, your friends, and your work colleagues also to vote yes.

Step 5: Action

In this step the speaker asks the audience for a specific action—to vote in favor of the youth center—and urges listeners to influence others to do the same. The speaker also reiterates the main theme of the speech; namely, that the youth center will help reduce juvenile crime.

PUBLIC SPEAKING SAMPLE ASSISTANT

A TEMPLATE OUTLINE

This template outline would be appropriate for a speech using a temporal, spatial, or topical organization pattern. Note that in this template outline there are three main points (I, II, and III in the body). These correspond to the III A, B, and C in the introduction (where you'd orient the audience) and to the A, B, and C in the conclusion (where you'd summarize your main points). The phrases printed in light ink will remind you of the functions of each outline item. Additional template outlines are available at MyCommunicationLab (www.mycommunicationlab.com).

Title: short, relevant, and attention-getting

General purpose: your general aim (to inform, to persuade, to entertain)

Specific purpose: what you hope to achieve from this speech

Thesis: your main assertion: the core of your speech

Introduction

I. gain attention

II. establish S-A-T connection

III. Orient audience

- **A.** first main point; same as I in body
- **B.** second main point; same as II in body
- **C.** third main point; same as III in body

[**Transition:** connect the introduction to the body]

Body

I. first main point

- **A.** support of I (the first main point)
- **B.** further support for I

[**Transition:** connect the first main point to the second]

II. second main point

- **A.** support for II (the second main point)
- **B.** further support for II

[**Transition:** connect the second main point to the third]

III. Third main point

- **A.** support for III (the third main point)
- **B.** further support for III

[**Transition:** connect the third main point (or all main points) to the conclusion]

Conclusion

I. summary

- **A.** first main point; same as I in body
- **B.** second main point; same as II in body
- **C.** third main point; same as III in body

II. motivation

III. closure

References

Alphabetical list of sources cited

PUBLIC SPEAKING SAMPLE ASSISTANT

A PHRASE/KEY-WORD PRESENTATION OUTLINE

Self-Disclosure

PAUSE!
LOOK OVER THE AUDIENCE!

Introduction

I. We've heard them:
- **A.** I'm in love with my nephew.
- **B.** My husband is not my baby's father.
- **C.** I'm really a woman.

II. We've all S-D.
- **A.** Sometimes 1, 2, significant
- **B.** consequences = better decisions.

III. 3 parts: (WRITE ON BOARD)
- **A.** 1. nature of S-D
- **B.** 2. rewards
- **C.** 3. risks

[1st = type of communication.]
PAUSE, STEP FORWARD

Body

I. S-D: communication
- **A.** about self
- **B.** new
- **C.** hidden information

[Knowing what self-disclosure is, now rewards.]

II. 3 rewards.
- **A.** self-knowledge
- **B.** communication effectiveness
- **C.** physiological health

[Benefits substantial, there are also risks.]
PAUSE!

III. 3 risks
- **A.** personal
- **B.** relationship
- **C.** professional

[Summarize: S-D]

Conclusion

I. S-D = communication.
- **A.** about self, new, and usually hidden
- **B.** rewards: increased self-knowledge, better communication, and improved health
- **C.** risks: personal, relational, and professional

II. S-D, not only interesting, it's vital
- **A.** Explore further "S-D" on www
- **B.** Scholarly: Sandra Petronio's *Boundaries*.

III. Should you S-D?
- **A.** Yes
- **B.** No
- **C.** Maybe

PAUSE!
ANY QUESTIONS?

with the public speaking process, as with PowerPoint, you'll develop your speech, and your slides, without any template or wizard. As you review the template outline in the Public Speaking Sample Assistant box on page 338, the phrases printed in light ink will remind you of the functions of each outline item.

The Phrase/Key-Word Presentation Outline

Now that you've constructed a preparation outline perhaps using a template outline for guidance, you need to construct a presentation outline (also called a delivery outline). Resist the temptation to use your preparation outline to deliver the speech. If you use your preparation outline, you'll tend to read from the outline instead of presenting a seemingly extemporaneous speech in which you attend to and respond to audience feedback. Instead, construct a brief **presentation outline:** an outline that will assist, rather than hinder, your delivery of the speech. Here are some guidelines to follow in preparing this delivery outline.

Explore at MyCommunicationLab Activity: "Creating a Speaking Outline"

- **Be brief.** Try to limit yourself to one side of one sheet of paper.
- **Be clear.** Be sure that you can see the outline while you're speaking. Use different colored inks, underlining, or whatever system will help you communicate your ideas.
- **Be delivery minded.** Include any guides to delivery that will help while you're speaking. Note in the outline when you'll use your presentation aid and when you'll remove it. A simple "show PA" or "remove PA" should suffice. You might also wish to note some speaking cues, such as "slow down" when reading a poetry excerpt, or perhaps a place where an extended pause might help.
- **Rehearse with the presentation outline.** In your rehearsals, use the delivery outline only. Remember, the objective is to make rehearsals as close to the real thing as possible.

The Public Speaking Sample Assistant box on page 339 shows a sample presentation outline constructed from the preparation outline on self-disclosure (on pages 335–336). Note that the outline is brief enough so that you'll be able to use it effectively without losing eye contact with the audience. It uses abbreviations (for example, S-D for self-disclosure) and phrases rather than complete sentences. Yet it's detailed enough to include all essential parts of your speech, including transitions. It contains delivery notes specifically tailored to your own needs, such as pause suggestions and guides to using visual aids. Note also that it's clearly divided into introduction, body, and conclusion and uses the same numbering system as the preparation outline.

Harry is a member of the university's computer science faculty and has been asked to give a speech on careers in computer technology to a group of students attending a career day event. It is Saturday morning, and the students are required to attend the speech. Harry is concerned his audience won't pay attention to his speech and has asked his partner Sue for her advice. "Career Day" looks at the steps involved in supporting and organizing your speech and the options you have for collecting and using supporting materials and for organizing speeches of information and persuasion. Log on to www.mycommunicationlab.com to view this video and the choices made, and then answer the related discussion questions.

Watch at MyCommunicationLab Video: "Career Day"

SUMMARY: SUPPORTING AND ORGANIZING YOUR SPEECH

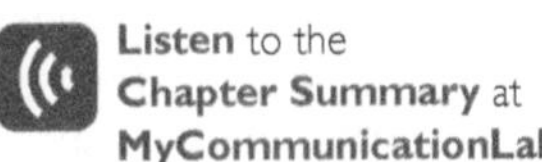

This chapter covered ways of collecting and using supporting materials; developing and organizing your main points; developing your introduction, conclusion, and transition; and outlining your speech.

15.1 STEP 4: COLLECT SUPPORTING MATERIALS

1. Collect a variety of materials that support your thesis and main points. Suitable supporting materials include examples, narratives, analogies, definitions, testimony, statistics, and presentation aids as well as such devices as quotations, comparisons, statements of facts, and repetition and restatement.
2. Among the presentation aids you might consider are the actual object, models of the object, graphs, word charts, maps, people, photographs and illustrations, and tapes and CDs. Presentation aids work best when they add clarity to your speech, are appealing to listeners, and are culturally sensitive.
3. Computer-assisted presentations such as PowerPoint allow you to communicate lots of information in an interesting format, to print handouts to coordinate with your speech, and to create an outline and speaker's notes for your speech.

15.2 STEP 5: DEVELOP YOUR MAIN POINTS

4. Use your thesis to develop your main points.

15.3 STEP 6: ORGANIZE YOUR SPEECH MATERIALS

5. Organize the speech materials into a clear, easily identifiable thought pattern. Suitable organizing principles include temporal, spatial, topical, problem–solution, cause–effect/effect–cause, and the motivated sequence (as well as the structure–function, comparison-and-contrast, pro-and-con, claim-and-proof, multiple-definition, and who? what? why? where? when? [5W] patterns).

15.4 STEP 7: CONSTRUCT YOUR INTRODUCTION, CONCLUSION, AND TRANSITIONS

6. Introductions should gain attention, establish a speaker–audience–topic (S-A-T) connection, and orient the audience as to what is to follow.
7. Conclusions should summarize the main ideas, provide a final motivation, and provide a crisp closing to the speech.
8. Transitions and internal summaries help connect and integrate the parts of the speech; they also help the listeners to better remember the speech.

15.5 OUTLINING YOUR SPEECH

9. An outline is a blueprint that helps you organize and evaluate your speech.
   - The preparation outline is detailed and includes all of your main points, supporting materials, introduction, conclusion, transition, and references.
   - The template outline can help you see where certain material can be placed.
   - The presentation outline is a brief version of your preparation outline that you use as a guide when presenting your speech.

KEY TERMS

Study and Review the Flashcards at MyCommunicationLab

5W pattern **327**
action step **326**
advantages–disadvantages pattern **326**
analogies **313**
attention step **325**
body **323**
cause–effect pattern **324**
claim-and-proof pattern **327**
closure **330**
comparison-and-contrast pattern **326**
conclusion **330**
definition **313**
effect–cause pattern **325**
example **312**
expert witness testimony **314**
eyewitness testimony **315**
fiction–fact pattern **327**
figurative analogies **313**
illustration **312**
introduction **328**
literal analogies **313**
models **317**
motivated sequence **325**
motivation **330**
multiple-definition pattern **327**
narrative **312**
need step **325**
orientation **329**
outline **333**
pie graph **317**
preparation outline **334**
presentation aid **316**
presentation outline **340**
presentation software **320**
pro-and-con pattern **326**
problem–solution pattern **324**
raw numbers **316**
satisfaction step **325**
spatial pattern **324**
speaker–audience–topic connection **328**
statistics **316**
structure–function pattern **326**
summary **330**
template outline **334**
temporal pattern **324**
testimony **314**
thesis **322**
topical pattern **324**
transitions **331**
visualization step **325**

WORKNG WITH SUPPORT AND ORGANIZATION

15.1 Generating Main Points. Try generating two or three main points (suitable for an informative or persuasive speech) from any one of the following thesis statements by asking strategic questions of each. The more main points you generate, the more likely you'll find ones that will be especially appropriate for your thesis and audience. Try following the general format illustrated in the text (pages 322–323) in the example of the values of a college education.

- **a.** Property owned by religious organizations should be taxed.
- **b.** Adoption agencies should be required to reveal the names of birth parents to all children when they reach 18 years of age.
- **c.** The growing of tobacco should be declared illegal.
- **d.** Medicinal marijuana should be legalized.
- **e.** Stand-your-ground laws should be repealed.

15.2 Constructing Conclusions and Introductions. Because the conclusion and introduction are often what listeners remember best, give these opening and closing remarks careful attention. Prepare a conclusion and an introduction to a hypothetical speech on one of the topics listed below.

- **a.** Proficiency in a foreign language should be required of all college graduates.
- **b.** All killing of wild animals should be declared illegal.
- **c.** Suicide and its assistance by qualified medical personnel should be legalized.
- **d.** Gambling should be legalized by all states.
- **e.** Maximum sentences should be imposed for hate crimes.

15.3 Strategies of Arrangement. What strategies of arrangement would you use if you were giving a pro-choice speech to a pro-life audience? What strategies would you use if you were giving a speech in favor of domestic partnership insurance to gay rights activists?

15.4 Vivid Support. Jamie, a student at a community college in Texas, wants to give a speech on the cruelty of cockfighting. Most people in the predominantly Hispanic audience come from Mexico, where cockfighting is a legal and popular sport. Among the visuals Jamie is considering are extremely vivid photographs of cocks literally torn to shreds by their opponents, which have razor blades strapped to their feet. Would you advise Jamie to use these photographs? Why? With which type of audience might these photos be effective?

15.5 Quotations. Visit one of the many websites for quotations. Select a quotation suitable for use with the slide show of the speech on self-disclosure in the Appendix on pages 417–418, and explain how you would use this on a slide.

15.6 Presentation Aids. Shana wants to illustrate the rise and fall in the prices of 12 stocks over the past 10 years to show that her investment club should sell 3 stocks and keep the other 9. This is the first time Shana will be using visual aids, and she needs advice on what aids best serve her purpose. What suggestions do you have for Shana?

15.7 Prepare and Deliver a 2-Minute Speech. Here are a few suggestions:

- Tell a personal story to illustrate a specific point.
- Explain a print ad that relies on statistics, and show how the advertiser uses statistics to make a point.
- Describe the events portrayed in a recently seen television program, using a temporal pattern.
- Discuss a recent newspaper editorial or op-ed letter, using a problem–solution or cause–effect pattern.
- Explain how television commercials get your attention.

LogOn! MyCommunicationLab

www.mycommunicationlab.com

Throughout this chapter, there are icons that highlight media content for selected topics. Go to **MyCommunicationLab** for additional materials on developing and organizing your main points and developing your introduction, conclusion, and transitions. Here you'll find flashcards to help you learn key communication terms, videos that illustrate a variety of concepts, additional exercises, and discussions to help you continue your study of supporting and organizing your speech.

16 STYLE AND DELIVERY IN PUBLIC SPEAKING

Listen to Chapter 16 at MyCommunicationLab

CHAPTER TOPICS	CHAPTER OBJECTIVES
In this chapter you'll explore the following major topics:	**After reading this chapter you should be able to:**
STEP 8: WORD YOUR SPEECH	16.1 Choose words to add clarity, vividness, appropriateness, personal style, and forcefulness to your speeches and phrase sentences effectively.
STEP 9: REHEARSE YOUR SPEECH	16.2 Rehearse your speech effectively and efficiently.
STEP 10: PRESENT YOUR SPEECH	16.3 Present your speech with effective voice and bodily action.
SPEECH CRITICISM	16.4 Give and receive criticism positively and with a view toward improvement.

Style and delivery are always important.

In this chapter we examine the final three steps in public speaking: wording your speech, rehearsing your speech, and presenting your speech.

16.1 STEP 8: WORD YOUR SPEECH

You're a successful public speaker when your listeners create in their minds the meanings you want them to create. You're successful when your listeners adopt the attitudes and behaviors you want them to adopt. The language choices you make—the words you select and the sentences you form—will greatly influence the meanings your listeners receive and, thus, how successful you are.

Generally, oral style is recommended for most public speeches. **Oral style** refers to the degree to which a communication style resembles that of informal conversation as opposed to the more formal style of writing. You don't speak as you write, nor should you. The main reason why spoken and written language should differ is that the listener hears a speech only once; therefore, speech must be *instantly intelligible.* The reader can reread an essay or look up an unfamiliar word; the reader can spend as much time as he or she wishes with the written page. The listener, however, must move at the pace set by the speaker. The reader may reread a sentence or paragraph if there's a temporary attention lapse; the listener doesn't have this option.

Generally, spoken language, or oral style, uses shorter, simpler, and more familiar words than does written language. Also, there's more qualification in speech than in writing. For example, when speaking you probably make greater use of such expressions as *although, however, perhaps,* and the like. When writing, you probably edit these out.

Choosing Words

Choose words to achieve clarity, vividness, appropriateness, a personal style, and forcefulness.

Clarity

Clarity in speaking style should be your primary goal. Here are some guidelines to help you make your speech clear.

Be Economical. Don't waste words. Notice the wasted words in such expressions as "at nine *a.m. in the morning,*" "we *first* began the discussion," "I *myself personally,*" and "blue *in color.*" By withholding the italicized terms you eliminate unnecessary words and move closer to a more economical and clearer style.

Use Specific Terms and Numbers. As we get more and more specific, we get a clearer and more detailed picture. Be specific. Don't say *dog* when you want your listeners to picture a St. Bernard. Don't say *car* when you want them to picture a limousine. The same is true of numbers. Don't say "earned a good salary" if you mean "earned $90,000 a year." Don't say "taxes will go up" when you mean "taxes will increase 7 percent."

Explore at **MyCommunicationLab** **Exercise:** "Making Concepts Specific"

Use Signposts. Use signpost phrases to help listeners see that you're moving from one idea to another—phrases such as "now that we have seen how . . . , let us consider how . . . ," and "my next argument. . . ." Terms such as *first, second, and also, although,* and *however* will help your audience follow your line of thinking.

Use Short, Familiar Terms. Generally, favor the short word over the long one, the familiar over the unfamiliar, and the more commonly used over the rarely used term. For example, use *harmless* instead of *innocuous, clarify* instead of *elucidate,* and *use* instead of *utilize.*

Carefully Assess Idioms. Idioms are expressions that are unique to a specific language and whose meaning cannot be deduced from the individual words used. Expressions such as "kick the bucket" and "doesn't have a leg to stand on" are idioms. Either you know the meaning of the expression or you don't; you can't figure it out from only a knowledge of the individual words.

The positive side of idioms is that they give your speech a casual and informal air; they make your speech sound like a speech and not like a written essay. The negative side of idioms is that they create problems for listeners who are not native speakers of your language. Many non-native speakers will simply not understand the meaning of your idioms. This problem is especially important because audiences are becoming increasingly intercultural and because the number of idioms we use is extremely high.

Vividness

Select words to make your ideas vivid and to help your arguments come alive in the minds of your listeners. To achieve **vividness**, use active verbs, strong verbs, figures of speech, and imagery.

Use Active Verbs. Favor verbs that communicate activity rather than passivity. The verb *to be,* in all its forms—*is, are, was, were, will be*—is relatively inactive. Try using verbs of action instead. Rather than saying "The teacher was in the middle of the crowd," say "The teacher stood in the middle of the crowd."

Instead of saying "The report was on the president's desk for three days," try "The report rested [or slept] on the president's desk for three days." Instead of saying "Management will be here tomorrow," consider "Management will descend on us tomorrow" or "Management jets in tomorrow."

Use Strong Verbs. The verb is the strongest part of your sentence. Choose verbs carefully, and choose them so they accomplish a lot. Instead of saying "He walked through the forest," consider such terms as *wandered, prowled, rambled,* or *roamed.* Consider whether one of these might not better suit your intended meaning. Consult a thesaurus for any verb you suspect might be weak.

Use Figures of Speech. Figures of speech help achieve vividness, in addition to making your speech more memorable and giving it a polished, well-crafted tone. **Figures of speech** are stylistic devices that have been a part of rhetoric since ancient times. Here are some of the major figures of speech; you may wish to incorporate a few of these into your next speech.

- **Alliteration** is the repetition of the same initial sound in two or more words, as in "fifty famous flavors" or the "cool, calculating leader."
- **Antithesis** is the presentation of contrary ideas in parallel form, as in "My loves are many, my enemies are few." Charles Dickens's opening words in *A Tale of Two Cities* are a famous antithesis: "It was the best of times; it was the worst of times."
- **Hyperbole** is the use of extreme exaggeration, as in "He cried like a faucet" or "I'm so hungry I could eat a whale."
- **Irony** is the use of a word or sentence whose literal meaning is the opposite of the message actually conveyed; for example, a teacher handing back failing examinations might say, "So pleased to see how many of you studied so hard."
- **Metaphor** compares two unlike things by stating that one thing "is" the other, as in "She's a lion when she wakes up" or "He's a real bulldozer."
- **Metonymy** is the substitution of a name for a title with which it's closely associated, as in "City Hall issued the following news release," in which

the•o•ry *noun* statement of explanation, formulation of relationships, reasoned generalization

UNDERSTANDING THEORY AND RESEARCH
One-Sided versus Two-Sided Messages

When you're presenting persuasive arguments, should you devote all your time to your side of the case, or should you also mention the other side and show why that side is not acceptable? Originally studied during the 1940s, this question continues to engage the attention of researchers. Early studies found that one-sided presentations were more effective with less-educated audiences, whereas two-sided presentations were more effective with more-educated listeners. One-sided presentations also were more effective with people who were already in favor of the speaker's point of view, whereas two-sided presentations were more persuasive with those who were initially opposed to the speaker's position.

Whether you choose to use a one-sided or a two-sided persuasive approach will depend on your topic (are there two competing positions?), the time you have available (limited time may prevent you from covering both sides), audience members' existing attitude (if they already reject the other position, there may not be a need to include it), and perhaps other factors as well.

If you do decide to present both sides, here are a few points to consider.

1. Using a two-sided presentation generally helps establish your credibility; by mentioning the other side, you demonstrate your knowledge of the entire area and by implication tell the audience that you understand both positions.
2. In a two-sided presentation, be sure to demonstrate the superiority of your position and the reasons why the other position is not as good as yours (O'Keefe, 1999). If you merely mention the other position without pointing out its flaws, then you risk creating doubt in the minds of your listeners about the superiority of your position.
3. If your audience is aware of an alternative position, then you need to demonstrate that you too are aware of it but that it's not as good as your position.
4. Demonstrate that you have analyzed the alternative position as carefully and thoroughly as the position you're supporting.

Working with Theories and Research

Take a look at print, television, or Internet ads and identify a few ads that use a two-sided approach (Brand A is better than Brand X). What makes a two-sided advertisement effective?

"City Hall" stands for "the mayor" or "the city council."

- **Personification** is the attribution of human characteristics to inanimate objects, as in "This room cries for activity" or "My car is tired and wants a drink."
- **Rhetorical questions** are questions used to make a statement or to produce a desired effect rather than to secure an answer, as in "Do you want to be popular?" or "Do you want to get well?"
- **Simile**, like metaphor, compares two unlike objects; but simile explicitly uses the words *like* or *as;* for example, "The manager is as gentle as an ox."
- **Synecdoche** is the use of a part of an object to stand for the whole object, as in "All hands were on deck" (where *hands* stands for "sailor" or "crew member") or "green thumb" for "expert gardener."
- **Oxymoron** is a term or phrase that combines two normally opposite qualities: *bittersweet, the silent roar, poverty-stricken millionaires, the ignorant genius, a war for peace* or *a peaceful war.*

Use Imagery. Appeal to the senses, especially your listeners' visual, auditory, and tactile senses. Make your audience see, hear, and feel what you're talking about.

- Use **visual imagery** to create word "pictures" of people or objects. When appropriate, describe such visual qualities as height, weight, color, size, shape, length, and contour. Let audience members see the sweat pouring down the faces of the coal miners; let them see the short, overweight, cigar-smoking executive in his pin-striped suit.
- Use **auditory imagery** to describe sounds; let your listeners hear the car's tires screeching, the wind whistling, the bells chiming, the angry professor roaring.
- Use **tactile imagery** to let the audience feel the temperature and texture of the object you're talking about. Let your listeners feel the cool water running over their bodies, the punch of the prize-fighter, the smooth skin of the newborn baby.

COMMUNICATION CHOICE POINT

UNEXPECTED FEEDBACK *Cathy introduces her speech with a story she found extremely humorous and laughed out loud after she finished it. Unfortunately, the audience just didn't get it—not one smile in the entire audience.* **What are some of the things Cathy might say to deal with this situation and turn it to her advantage?**

Appropriateness

Use language that is appropriate to you as the speaker—and that is appropriate to your audience, the occasion, and the speech topic. Here are some general guidelines to help you achieve **appropriateness**.

Speak on the Appropriate Level of Formality. The most effective public speaking style is less formal than the written essay, but more formal than conversation. One way to achieve an informal style is to use contractions. Say *don't* instead of *do not, I'll* instead of *I shall,* and *wouldn't* instead of *would not.* Contractions give a public speech the sound and rhythm of conversation—a quality that most listeners react to favorably. Also use personal pronouns rather than impersonal expressions. Say "I found" instead of "It has been found," or "I will present three arguments" instead of "Three arguments will be presented."

Avoid Unfamiliar Terms. Avoid using terms the audience doesn't know. Avoid foreign and technical terms unless you're certain the audience is familiar with them. Similarly, avoid **jargon** (the technical vocabulary of a specialized field) unless you're sure the meanings are clear to your listeners. Some acronyms (such as NATO, UN, NOW, and CORE) are probably familiar to most audiences; many, however, are not. When you wish to use any specialized terms or abbreviations, explain their meaning fully to the audience.

Avoid Slang. Slang is language that is used by special groups but is generally considered impolite or not quite proper. *Webster's New World College Dictionary* defines *slang* as "highly informal speech that is outside conventional or standard usage and consists both of coined words and phrases and of new or extended meanings attached to established terms." Generally, it's best to avoid slang, which may offend or embarrass your audience. If you're in doubt about whether a word is considered slang, consult a dictionary; usually, dictionaries identify slang terms as "informal."

Avoid Ethnic Expressions (Generally). Chapter 5 discussed the dangers of using racist, heterosexist, ageist, or sexist terms; these can only insult the audience members themselves or people they know and care about. So avoid these terms at all costs. In addition, avoid ethnic expressions, at least generally. Ethnic expressions are words and phrases that are used extensively by members of a particular ethnic group but not usually by others. At times these expressions are known only by members of the ethnic group; at other times they may be known more widely but still recognized as ethnic expressions.

Personal Style

Audiences favor speakers who speak in a personal rather than an impersonal style—speakers who speak with them rather than at them. You can achieve a more **personal style** by using personal pronouns, asking questions, and creating immediacy.

Use Personal Pronouns. Say *I, me, he, she,* and *you.* Avoid impersonal expressions such as *one* (as in "One is led to believe ..."), *this speaker,* or *you, the listeners.* These expressions distance the audience and create barriers rather than bridges.

Use Questions. Ask audience members questions to involve them. In a small audience, you might even briefly entertain responses. In larger audiences, you might ask the question, pause to allow the audience time to consider their responses, and then move on. When you direct questions to your listeners they feel a part of the public speaking transaction.

Create Immediacy. Immediacy, as discussed in Chapter 7, is a connectedness, a relatedness with one's listeners. Immediacy is the opposite of disconnectedness and separation. Here are some suggestions for creating immediacy through language.

- Use personal examples.
- Use terms that include both you and the audience; for example, *we* and *our.*
- Address the audience directly; say *you* rather than *students;* say "You'll enjoy reading" instead of

me•di•a lit•er•a•cy *noun* ability to understand, interact with, and create media messages

EXPANDING MEDIA LITERACY
Reversing Media's Influence

Although you generally think of the media influencing you, you can also influence the media—on radio, television, newspapers and magazines, film, and the Internet (Jamieson & Campbell, 2006; Media Education Foundation, 2006a, b; Postman & Powers, 1992):

- **Register your complaints.** Write letters, send e-mails, call a television station or advertiser, tweet, post on your blog, or fill out the feedback forms available on many websites expressing your views. Write to a public forum, such as a newspaper or newsgroup, or to the Federal Communication Commission or other regulatory agencies. Use any of the variety of federal, state, or city websites that encourage users to voice their opinions and then forward these to the appropriate agencies.
- **Exert group pressure.** Join with others who think the same way you do. Bring group pressure to bear on television networks, newspapers, advertisers, Internet sites, and manufacturers.
- **Protest through an established organization.** There's probably an organization already established for the issue with which you're concerned. Search the Internet for relevant newsgroups, professional organizations, and chat rooms that focus on your topic.
- **Join a social protest movement.** This technique has been used throughout history to gain civil rights. Such movements have the potential advantage of securing media coverage that might enable you to communicate your message to a large audience.
- **Create legislative pressure.** Exert influence on the state or federal level by influencing your local political representatives (through voting and through calls, letters, and e-mails), who will in turn influence representatives on higher levels of the political hierarchy.

For example, if you think a national and local media (television and newspapers) organization unfairly treated a controversy you're interested in, consider the options you have for protesting and for correcting the unfairness you perceive.

"Everyone will enjoy reading"; say "I want you to see" instead of "I want people to see."

- Use specific names of audience members when appropriate.
- Refer directly to commonalities between you and the audience; for example, "We are all children of immigrants" or "We all want to see our team in the playoffs."
- Refer to shared experiences and goals; for example, "We all want, we all need, a more responsive PTA."

Forcefulness/Power

Forceful or powerful language will help you achieve your purpose, whether it be informative or persuasive. **Forcefulness** in language enables you to direct the audience's attention, thoughts, and feelings. To make your speech more forceful, eliminate weakeners, vary intensity, and avoid overused expressions.

Eliminate Weakeners. Delete **weakeners,** or phrases that weaken your sentences. Among the major weakeners are uncertainty expressions and weak modifiers. Uncertainty expressions such as "I'm not sure of this, but"; "Perhaps it might"; or "Maybe it works this way" communicate a lack of commitment and conviction and will make your audience wonder if you're worth listening to. Weak modifiers such as "It works pretty well," "It's kind of like," or "It may be the one we want" make you seem unsure and indefinite about what you're saying.

Here are a few types of words and phrases that you'll want to avoid.

- **Hesitations** ("I, er, want to say that, ah, this one is, er, the best, you know") make you sound unprepared and uncertain.
- **Too many intensifiers** ("Really, this was the greatest; it was truly phenomenal.") may lead the audience to doubt the speaker who uses too many superlatives.
- **Tag questions** ("I'll review the report now, okay?" "That is a great proposal, don't you think?") signal your need for approval and your own uncertainty and lack of conviction.
- **Self-critical statements** ("I'm not very good at this," "This is my first speech") signal a lack of confidence and make public your sense of inadequacy.
- **Slang and vulgar expressions** may signal low social class and hence little power.

Table 16.1 identifies a few suggestions for nonverbal action that will also help you to communicate forcefulness and power.

Vary Intensity as Appropriate. Just as you can vary your voice in intensity, you can also phrase your ideas with different degrees of stylistic intensity. You can, for example, refer to an action as "failing to support our position" or as "stabbing us in the back"; you can say that a new proposal will "endanger our goals" or will "destroy us completely"; you can refer to a child's behavior as "playful," "creative," or "destructive." Vary your language to express different degrees of intensity—from mild through neutral to extremely intense.

Avoid Bromides and Clichés. **Bromides** are trite sayings that are worn out because of constant usage. A few examples: "Honesty is the best policy;" "If I can't do it well, I won't do it at all;" and "It is what it is."

TABLE 16.1 POWERFUL BODILY ACTION

Here are some nonverbal behaviors that are likely to help you communicate power in public speaking (Burgoon, Guerrero, & Floyd, 2010; DeVito, 2014).

Suggestions for Communicating Power with Bodily Action	Reasons
Avoid self-manipulations (playing with your hair or touching your face, for example); avoid leaning backward.	These signals communicate a lack of comfort and an ill-at-ease feeling and are likely to damage your persuasiveness.
Walk slowly and deliberately to and from the podium.	To appear hurried is to appear powerless, as if you were rushing to meet the expectations of those who have power over you.
Use facial expressions and gestures as appropriate.	These help you express your concern for the audience and for the interaction and help you communicate your comfort and control of the situation.
Use consistent packaging; be careful that your verbal and nonverbal messages do not contradict each other.	Inconsistency between verbal and nonverbal messages may be seen as uncertainty and a lack of conviction.

When we hear these hackneyed statements, we recognize them as unoriginal and uninspired.

Clichés are phrases that have lost their novelty and part of their meaning through overuse. Clichés call attention to themselves because of their overuse. Here are some examples of clichés to avoid: "in this day and age," "tell it like it is," "free as a bird," "in the pink," "no sooner said than done," "it goes without saying," "few and far between," "over the hill," "no news is good news," "the life of the party," and "keep your shirt on."

A summary of these guidelines appears in Table 16.2.

Phrasing Sentences

Give the same careful consideration that you give to words to the sentences of your speech as well. Some guidelines follow.

Use Short Sentences

Short sentences are more forceful and economical. They are also easier for your audience to comprehend and remember. Listeners don't have the time or the inclination to unravel long and complex sentences. Help them to listen more efficiently. Use short rather than long sentences.

Use Direct Sentences

Direct sentences are easier to understand. They are also more forceful. Instead of saying "I want to tell you of the three main reasons why we should not adopt Program A," say "We should not adopt Program A. There are three main reasons."

Use Active Sentences

Active sentences—that is, sentences whose verbs are in the active voice—are easier to understand than passive ones. They also make your speech seem livelier and more vivid. Instead of saying "The lower court's decision was reversed by the Supreme Court," say "The Supreme Court reversed the lower court's decision." Instead of saying "The proposal was favored by management," say "Management favored the proposal."

Use Positive Sentences

Positive sentences are easier to comprehend and remember. Notice that the sentences under "This" are easier to understand that those under "Not This."

Not This	This
The committee did not accept the proposal.	The committee rejected the proposal.
This committee does not work within the normal company hierarchy.	This committee works outside the normal company hierarchy.

Vary the Types of Sentences

The preceding advice to use short, direct, active, positive sentences is valid most of the time. Yet too many sentences of the same type or length will make your speech sound boring. So follow (generally) the preceding advice, but add variations as well. Here are a few special types of sentences that should prove useful, especially for adding variety, vividness, and forcefulness to your speech.

Parallel Sentences. Parallel sentences convey ideas in parallel (similar, matching) style for ease of comprehension and memory. Note the parallelism in "This" and its absence in the "Not This" sentences.

TABLE 16.2

In A Nutshell A Summary of Guidelines for Wording Your Speech

Goal	Strategies
Clarify	Use specific terms, signposts, and short and familiar terms; watch out for idioms.
Vividness	Use active and strong words, add figures of speech, use imagery.
Appropriate	Vary formality as appropriate; avoid unfamiliar, slang, and ethnic expressions.
Personal	Use personal pronouns and questions; create immediacy.
Power	Eliminate weakeners, vary intensity, and avoid clichés.

Not This	This
The professor prepared the lecture, the examination was graded, and she read the notices.	The professor prepared the lecture, graded the examination, and read the notices.
Love needs two people. Just one can create jealousy.	Love needs two people to flourish. Jealousy needs but one.

Antithetical Sentences. **Antithetical sentences** juxtapose contrasting ideas in parallel fashion. In his inaugural speech, President John F. Kennedy phrased one of his most often quoted lines in antithetical structure:

> Ask not what your country can do for you; ask what you can do for your country.

Periodic Sentences. In **periodic sentences** you reserve the key word until the end of the sentence. In fact, the sentence is not grammatically complete until you say this last word. For example, in "Looking longingly into his eyes, the old woman fainted," the sentence doesn't make sense until the last word is spoken.

16.2 STEP 9: REHEARSE YOUR SPEECH

Use your rehearsal time effectively and efficiently for the following purposes:

- To develop a delivery that will help you achieve the objectives of your speech.
- To time your speech; if you time your rehearsals, you'll be able to see if you can add material or if you have to delete something.
- To see how the speech will flow as a whole and to make any changes and improvements you think necessary.
- To test the presentation aids and to detect and resolve any technical problems.
- To learn the speech thoroughly.
- To reduce any feelings of apprehension and gain confidence.
- The following procedures should assist you in achieving these goals.

Rehearse the Speech as a Whole

Rehearse the speech from beginning to end, not in parts. Rehearse it from getting out of your seat through the introduction, body, and conclusion to returning to your seat. Be sure to rehearse the speech with all the examples and illustrations (and any audiovisual aids) included. This will enable you to connect the parts of the speech and see how they interact.

Time the Speech

Time the speech during each rehearsal. Make the necessary adjustments on the basis of this timing. If you're using computer presentation software, you'll be able to time your speech very precisely. Also time the individual parts of your speech so you can achieve the balance you want—for example, you might want to spend twice as much time on the solutions as on the problems, or you might want to balance the introduction and conclusion so that each portion constitutes about 10 percent of your speech.

Approximate the Actual Speech Situation

Rehearse the speech under conditions as close as possible to those under which you'll deliver it. If possible, rehearse the speech in the same room where you'll present it. If this is impossible, try to simulate the actual conditions as closely as you can—even in your living room or bathroom. If possible, rehearse the speech in front of a few supportive listeners. It's always helpful (and especially for your beginning speeches) that your listeners be supportive rather than too critical. Merely having listeners present during your rehearsal will further simulate the conditions under which you'll eventually speak. Get together with two or three other students in an empty classroom where you can take turns as speakers and listeners.

See Yourself as a Speaker

Rehearse the speech in front of a full-length mirror. This will enable you to see yourself and see how you'll appear to the audience. This may be extremely difficult at first, and you may have to force yourself to watch. After a few attempts, however, you'll begin to see the value of this experience. Practice your eye contact, your movements, and your gestures in front of the mirror.

Incorporate Changes and Make Delivery Notes

Make any needed changes in the speech between rehearsals. Do not interrupt your rehearsal to make notes or changes; if you do, you may never experience the entire speech from beginning to end. While making these changes note any words whose pronunciation you wish to check. Also, insert pause notations, "slow down" warnings, and other delivery suggestions into your outline.

If possible, record your speech (ideally, on video) so you can hear exactly what your listeners will hear: your volume, rate, pronunciation, and pauses. You'll thus be in a better position to improve these qualities.

COMMUNICATION CHOICE POINT

TIME PROBLEM *Jack's speech has run overtime, and he's been given the 30-second stop signal. He still has about 5 more minutes remaining in his speech.* **What are some of the options Jack has for dealing with this problem (caused by a lack of effective rehearsal)?**

Rehearse Often

Rehearse the speech as often as seems necessary. Two useful guides are: (1) Rehearse the speech at least three or four times; less rehearsal than this is sure to be too little. (2) Rehearse the speech as long as your rehearsals continue to result in improvements in the speech or in your delivery.

Undertake a Long-Term Delivery Improvement Program

To become a truly effective speaker, you may need to undertake a long-term delivery improvement program. Approach this project with a positive attitude: Tell yourself that you can do it and that you will do it.

1. First, seek feedback from someone whose opinion and insight you respect. Your public speaking instructor may be a logical choice, but someone majoring in communication or working in a communication field might also be appropriate. Get an honest and thorough appraisal of both your voice and your bodily action.
2. Learn to hear, see, and feel the differences between effective and ineffective patterns. For example, is your volume too loud? A recorder will be very helpful. Learn to feel your rigid posture or your lack of arm and hand gestures. Once you've perceived these voice and/or body patterns, concentrate on learning more effective habits. Practice a few minutes each day. Avoid becoming too conscious of any source of ineffectiveness. Just try to increase your awareness and work on one problem at a time. Do not try to change all your patterns at once.
3. Seek additional feedback on the changes. Make certain that listeners agree that the new patterns you're practicing really are more effective. Remember that you hear yourself through bone conduction as well as through air transmission. Others hear you only through air transmission. So what you hear and what others hear will be different.
4. For voice improvement, consult a book on voice and diction for practice exercises and for additional information on the nature of volume and rate.
5. If difficulties persist, see a professional. For voice problems, see a speech clinician. Most campuses have a speech clinic, and you can easily avail yourself of its services. For bodily action difficulties, talk with your public speaking instructor.
6. Seek professional help if you're psychologically uncomfortable with any aspect of your voice or bodily action. It may be that all you have to do is to hear yourself or see yourself on a videotape—as others hear and see you—to convince yourself that you sound and look just fine. Regardless of what is causing this discomfort, however, if you're uncomfortable, do something about it. In a college community there's more assistance available to you at no cost than you'll ever be offered again. Make use of it.

16.3 STEP 10: PRESENT YOUR SPEECH

Perhaps the most important characteristic of effective public speaking presentation is that it depends. What makes for effectiveness in one situation and with one speaker will not necessarily prove effective in another situation with a different speaker. And to complicate matters just a bit, audiences differ in what they consider effective delivery—some audiences expect and enjoy a lively entertaining style while others will prefer a more subtle, intellectualized presentation.

You'll want to develop a presentation style that works for you while remaining flexible in adjusting that presentation style to the uniqueness of the specific public speaking situation. Nevertheless, amid these qualifications we can offer a few suggestions as to what constitutes effective presentation.

- **Comfortable.** Your presentation style should be comfortable to you. It should feel natural to you and it should look natural to the audience. It should not appear phony or in any way unnatural.
- **Consistent.** Your presentation style should be consistent with all the other public speaking factors you've considered throughout your preparation. If your speech is on a humorous topic, then your presentation style is likely to be lighthearted. If your speech were on a more somber topic such as the death penalty, then your presentation style would likely be fairly serious.
- **Interesting.** Your presentation should add interest and some variety into your speech. Much like how your language contributes to the interest of your speech, so does your delivery. If you stand motionless, it's not likely to prove terribly interesting. At the same time, you don't want to run around the room just to add interest—which, in this case, would draw attention away from your speech.
- **Contributes to the content of the speech.** Your presentation style should contribute to your speech; it should add some degree of clarity to what you're saying. For example, moving a half step forward or to the side when introducing a main point might help reinforce your verbal transition. In addition, your presentation style—whatever that is—should not call attention to itself and away from the message of your speech. Your presentation style should reinforce your verbal message.

Methods of Presentation

Speakers vary widely in their methods of presentation. Some speak off-the-cuff, with no apparent preparation; others read their speeches from manuscript. Some memorize their speeches word for word; others construct a detailed outline, rehearse often, then speak extemporaneously.

Explore at MyCommunicationLab Activity: "Methods of Delivery"

Speaking Impromptu

When you give an **impromptu speech,** you talk without any specific preparation. You and the topic meet for the first time and immediately the speech begins. On some occasions you will not be able to avoid speaking impromptu. For example, in a classroom, after someone has spoken, you might give a brief impromptu speech of evaluation. In asking or answering questions in an interview situation, you're giving impromptu speeches, albeit extremely short ones. At a meeting, you may find yourself explaining a proposal or defending a plan of action; these too are impromptu speeches. Of course, impromptu speeches don't permit attention to the details of public speaking such as audience adaptation, research, and style.

Speaking from Manuscript

When you give a **manuscript speech,** you read aloud the entire speech, which you've written out word for word. The manuscript speech allows you to control the timing precisely—a particularly important benefit when you are delivering a speech that will be recorded (on television, for example). Also, there's no risk of forgetting, no danger of being unable to find the right word. Another feature of the manuscript method is that it allows you to use the exact wording that you (or a team of speechwriters) want. In the political arena, this is often crucial. And, of course, because the speech is already written out, you can distribute copies and are therefore less likely to be misquoted.

Many audiences, however, don't like speakers to read their speeches, except perhaps with teleprompters on television. In face-to-face situations, audiences generally prefer speakers who interact with them. Reading a manuscript makes it difficult to respond to listener feedback. You cannot easily make adjustments on the basis of feedback. And with the manuscript on a stationary lectern, as it most often is, it's impossible for you to move around.

Speaking from Memory

When presenting a **memorized speech,** you write out the speech word for word (as in the manuscript method); but instead of reading it, you memorize it and recite it or "act it out." Speaking from memory allows you freedom to move about and otherwise concentrate on delivery. It doesn't, however, allow easy adjusting to feedback, and you thus lose one of the main advantages of face-to-face contact.

One potential problem with this method is the risk of forgetting your speech. In a memorized speech, each sentence cues the recall of the following sentence. Thus, when you forget one sentence, you may forget the rest of the speech. This danger, along with the natural nervousness that speakers feel, makes the memorizing method a poor choice in most situations.

Speaking Extemporaneously

An **extemporaneous speech** involves thorough preparation, but no commitment to the exact wording to be used during the speech. Speaking extemporaneously is the recommended method for your classroom speeches and most of the speeches you'll deliver outside this class. It often involves memorizing your opening lines (perhaps the first few sentences), your closing lines (perhaps the last few sentences), and your main points and the order in which you'll present them. You can also, if you wish, memorize selected phrases, sentences, or quotations. Memorizing the opening and closing lines will help you to focus your complete attention on the audience and will also put you more at ease. Once you know exactly what you'll say in opening and closing the speech, you'll feel more in control.

The extemporaneous method is useful in most speaking situations. Good college lecturers use the extemporaneous method. They prepare thoroughly and know what they want to say and in what order they want to say it, but they've made no commitment to exact wording. This method allows you to respond easily to feedback. Should a point need clarification, you can elaborate on it at the moment when it will be most effective. This method makes it easy to be natural, too, because you're being yourself. It's the method that comes closest to conversation. With the extemporaneous method, you can move about and interact with the audience.

Making Your Presentation More Effective

Here are a few guidelines for making your presentation an effective one.

Watch at **MyCommunicationLab** **Video:** "Tips for Speech Delivery"

Be Natural

Listeners will enjoy and believe you more if you speak naturally, as if you were conversing with a small group of people. Don't allow your delivery to call attention to yourself. Your ultimate aim should be to deliver the speech so naturally that the audience won't even notice your presentation. This will take some practice, but you can do it. When voice or bodily action is so prominent that it's distracting, the audience concentrates on the delivery and will fail to attend to your speech.

Use Presentation Style to Reinforce Your Message

Effective presentation style should aid instant intelligibility. Your main objective is to make your ideas understandable to an audience. A voice that listeners have to strain to hear, a decrease in volume at the ends of sentences, or slurred diction will obviously hinder comprehension.

Vary Your Presentation

Listening to a speech is hard work for the audience. Flexible and varied presentation eases the listeners' task. Be especially careful to avoid **monotonous patterns** and **predictable patterns.**

Speakers who are monotonous keep their voices at the same volume and rate throughout the speech. Like the drone of a motor, this easily puts the audience to sleep. Vary your volume and your rate of speaking. In a similar way, avoid monotony in bodily action. Use your body to express your ideas, to communicate to the audience what is going on in your head.

A predictable vocal pattern is a pattern in which, for example, the volume levels vary but they are always in the same sequence. Through repetition, the sequence soon becomes predictable. For example, each sentence may begin loud and then decline to a barely audible volume. In bodily action, the predictable speaker repeatedly uses the same movements or gestures. For example, a speaker may scan the audience from left to right to left to right throughout the entire speech. A patterned and predictable delivery will draw the audience's attention away from what you're saying.

Dress Appropriately

When you give a public speech, everything about you communicates. You cannot prevent yourself from sending messages to others. The way in which you dress is no exception. In fact, your attire will figure significantly in the way audience members assess your credibility and even the extent to which they give you attention.

- **Avoid extremes.** Don't allow your clothes, hairstyle, and so on to detract attention from what you're saying.
- **Dress comfortably.** Be both physically and psychologically comfortable with your appearance so you can concentrate your energies on what you're saying.
- **Dress appropriately.** Your appearance should be consistent with the specific public speaking occasion.

Be Conversational

Although more formal than conversation, presentation in public speaking should have some of the most important features of conversation. These qualities include immediacy, eye contact, expressiveness, and responsiveness to feedback.

Make your listeners feel that you're talking directly and individually to each of them. For example:

- **Maintain appropriate eye contact.** Look directly into your listeners' eyes. Lock eyes with different audience members for short periods.
- **Maintain a physical closeness that reinforces a psychological closeness.** Don't stand behind a desk or lectern.
- **Smile.** Express yourself facially as appropriate to your message.
- **Stand with a direct and open body posture.**
- **Talk directly to your audience.** Avoid the appearance of talking to your notes or to your presentation aids.

Be Expressive

When you're expressive, you communicate genuine involvement in the public speaking situation. You can communicate this quality of expressiveness, of involvement, in several ways:

- **Personalize what you say.** Express responsibility for your own thoughts and feelings.
- **Communicate involvement nonverbally.** Allow your facial muscles and your entire body to reflect and echo this inner involvement.
- **Use gestures appropriately.** Too few gestures may signal lack of interest, but too many can communicate uneasiness, awkwardness, or anxiety.

Read carefully the feedback signals sent by your audience. Then respond to these signals with verbal, vocal, and bodily adjustments. For example, respond to audience feedback signals communicating lack of comprehension or inability to hear with added explanation or increased volume.

Avoid Common Mistakes

Be sure to avoid the frequently made mistakes that detract from the power of your speech. Here are a few.

- **Don't start your speech immediately.** Instead, survey your audience; make eye contact and engage listeners' attention. Stand in front of the audience with a sense of control. Pause briefly, then begin speaking.
- **Don't display any discomfort or displeasure.** When you walk to the speaker's stand, display enthusiasm and your desire to speak. People much prefer listening to a speaker who seems to enjoy speaking to them.
- **Don't race away from the speaker's stand.** Once you've finished your presentation (after your last statement), pause, maintain audience eye contact, and then walk (don't run) to your seat. Show no signs of relief; focus your attention on whatever activity is taking place, glance over the audience, and sit down.

Use Notes Appropriately

For some speeches it may be helpful for you to use notes. As one public speaking consultant put it, "By using notes you are demonstrating that you 'plan your work and work your plan.' You are a well-organized speaker. You have more sense than to spend valuable time memorizing an entire presentation" (Fensholt, 2003).

In Chapter 15, PowerPoint (pages 320–322) and the delivery outline (pages 339–340) were discussed as types of notes that will help you remember your speech and contain certain quotations or figures you want to recall exactly. Some speakers, however, prefer to use an abbreviated outline put on one piece of paper or one or a few index cards. To make the most effective use of such notes, keep in mind the following guidelines.

- **Keep your notes to a minimum.** The fewer notes you take with you, the better off you'll be. One reason so many speakers bring notes with them is that they want to avoid the face-to-face interaction required. With experience, however, you should find this face-to-face interaction the best part of the public speaking experience.
- **Resist the normal temptation to use your entire speech outline as your notes.** You may rely on it too heavily and lose direct contact with the audience. Bring with you only as much information as you absolutely need, but never so much that it will interfere with your direct contact with the audience.
- **Use your notes with "open subtlety."** Don't make your notes more obvious than necessary. Don't gesture with your notes and thus make them more obvious than they need be. At the same time, don't try to hide them. Use them openly and honestly but gracefully, with "open subtlety." Rehearse at least twice with the same notes that you'll take with you to the speaker's stand.
- **Don't allow your notes to prevent directness.** When using your notes, pause to look at them. Then regain eye contact with the audience and continue your speech. Don't read from your notes; just take cues from them. The one exception to this is an extensive quotation or complex set of statistics that you have to read; read it and then, almost immediately, resume direct eye contact with the audience.

Watch at MyCommunicationLab **Video:** "Untreated Depression"

the•o•ry *noun* statement of explanation, formulation of relationships, reasoned generalization

UNDERSTANDING THEORY AND RESEARCH

Speech Rate

You've probably noticed that advertisers and salespeople generally talk at a rate faster than normal speech. But is this effective? Are people who speak faster more persuasive? The answer is: It depends (Smith & Shaffer, 1991, 1995). The rapid speaker who speaks *against* your existing attitudes is generally more effective than the speaker who speaks at a normal rate. But the rapid speaker who speaks *in favor of* your existing attitudes (say, in an attempt to strengthen them) is actually less effective than the speaker who speaks at a normal rate. The reason for this is quite logical. In the case of the speaker speaking against your existing attitudes, rapid speech doesn't give you the time you need to think of counterarguments to rebut the speaker's position. So you're more likely to be persuaded because you don't have time to consider why the speaker may be incorrect. In the case of the speaker speaking in favor of your existing attitudes, rapid speech doesn't give you time to mentally elaborate on the speaker's arguments; consequently, they don't carry as much persuasive force as they would if you had the time to add the speaker's arguments to those you already have.

Working with Theories and Research

With specific reference to your next speech, how might you apply this research to increase your own persuasiveness?

Voice

Chapter 6 discussed paralanguage as one of the major nonverbal communication channels (page 136). In public speaking it's especially important to give attention to such paralanguage dimensions as volume, rate, articulation and pronunciation, and pauses. Using these features appropriately will help you use your voice to complement and reinforce your message.

Volume

Volume refers to the relative loudness or softness of your voice. When your voice is adequately controlled, you adjust its volume according to factors such as the distance between you and your listeners, the competing noise, and the emphasis you want to give an idea. Vary your volume to best reflect your ideas—perhaps increasing volume for key words or phrases, lowering volume when talking about something extremely serious. Be especially careful not to fade away at the ends of sentences.

Rate

Rate refers to the speed at which you speak. About 140 words per minute is average for speaking as well as for reading aloud. If you talk too fast, you deprive your listeners of the time they need to digest what you're saying. If your rate is too slow, your listeners' thoughts will wander. So speak at a pace that engages but doesn't bore and that allows listeners time for reflection.

Articulation and Pronunciation

Articulation results from movements of the speech organs as they modify and interrupt the air stream from the lungs. Different movements of the tongue, lips, teeth, palate, and vocal cords produce different sounds. **Pronunciation** is the production of syllables or words according to some accepted standard, such as that of a dictionary. The most common problems associated with faulty articulation and pronunciation are these:

- **Errors of omission** (articulation). Omitting sounds or even syllables is a common articulation problem that you can easily overcome with concentration and practice. Some examples include saying "gov-a-ment," "studyin," or "comp-ny" instead of the correct "gov-ern-ment," "studying," and "comp-a-ny."
- **Errors of substitution** (articulation). Substituting an incorrect sound for the correct one is also easy to fix. Among the most common substitutions are [d] for [t] and [d] for [th]; for example, "wader," "dese," "bedder," and "ax" for the correct "waiter," "these," "better," and "ask." Other common substitution errors include "ek cetera," "congradulations," and "lenth" for the correct "et cetera," "congratulations," and "length."
- **Errors of addition** (articulation). These errors involve adding sounds where they don't belong, as in saying "acrost," "athalete," and "Americar" instead of the correct "across," "athlete," and "America."
- **Errors of accent** (pronunciation). Each word has its own accepted accent, or stress pattern. Examples of words that are often accented

incorrectly include "New Orleáns," "ínsurance," "compárable," and "orator" for the correct "New Órleans," "insúrance," "cómparable," and "órator."

- **Errors of adding sounds** (pronunciation). For some words, many people add sounds that are not part of the standard pronunciation, in many cases because they are part of the written word. Such errors would include saying "Illinois" or "evening" instead of the correct "Illinoi" and "evning."

Pauses

Pauses are interruptions in the flow of speech. Filled pauses are gaps that you fill with vocalizations such as *er*, *um*, and *ah*. Even expressions such as *well* and *you know*, when used merely to fill up silence, are filled pauses. These pauses are ineffective and detract from the strength of your message. They will make you appear hesitant, unprepared, and unsure.

Unfilled pauses, silences interjected into the stream of speech, can be especially effective if used correctly. Here are a few examples of places where unfilled pauses—silences of a second or two—can enhance your speech.

- Pause at transitional points. This will signal that you're moving from one part of the speech or from one idea to another. It will help listeners separate the main issues you're discussing.
- Pause at the end of an important assertion. This allows the audience to think about its significance.
- Pause after asking a rhetorical question. This will give audience members time to think about how they would answer.
- Pause before an important idea. This will help signal that what comes next is especially significant.
- Pause before you begin your speech (to scan and assess the audience and gather your thoughts) and after you finish it (to allow your ideas to sink in and to dispel any idea that you're anxious to escape).

Explore at MyCommunicationLab Activity: "Speech Delivery"

Body Action

You speak with your body as well as with your mouth, a point made clear in Chapter 6's discussion of the various nonverbal channels. The four aspects of body action that are especially important in public speaking are eye contact, facial expression, gestures and posture, and movement. As you read about these four channels, be sure to follow the most important and general rule: use consistent packaging. Be careful that your verbal and your nonverbal messages do not contradict each other. So, if you say you're happy to be speaking today, your nonverbals (facial expression, general enthusiasm, posture and eye contact, for example) should echo that sentiment. You don't want to give your audience conflicting cues. Consistency among verbal and nonverbal messages will also communicate your self-confidence and conviction.

Eye Contact

The most important single aspect of bodily communication is eye contact. The two major problems with eye contact are not enough eye contact and eye contact that does not cover the audience fairly. Speakers who do not maintain enough eye contact appear distant, unconcerned, and less trustworthy than speakers who look directly at their audience. And, of course, without eye contact, you will not be able to secure that all-important audience feedback. Maintain eye contact with the entire audience. Communicate equally with the audience members on the left and on the right, in both the back and the front of the room. Keep in mind, however, that cultures differ widely on the amount and intensity of eye contact they consider appropriate. In some cultures, eye contact that is too intense may be considered offensive.

Facial Expression

Appropriate facial expressions help you express your concern for the public speaking interaction and will help you communicate your comfort and control of the public speaking situation. Nervousness and anxiety, however, can prevent you from relaxing enough for your positive emotions to come through. Time and practice will allow you to relax, and your feelings will reveal themselves appropriately and automatically.

Gestures and Posture

Spontaneous and natural gestures will help illustrate your verbal messages. If you feel relaxed and comfortable with yourself and your audience, you'll generate natural body action without conscious or studied attention. When delivering your speech, stand straight but not stiffly. Try to communicate your command of the situation rather than any nervousness you may feel. Avoid putting your hands in your pockets or leaning on the desk or chalkboard. Avoid self-manipulation (e.g., playing with your hair or touching your face) and backward leaning, which can signal an ill-at-ease feeling.

Movement

Use movement to emphasize transitions and to introduce important assertions. For example, when making a transition, you might step forward to signal that something new is coming. Similarly, use movement to signal an important assumption, bit of evidence, or closely reasoned argument. Walk slowly and deliberately (but not too slowly, of course) to and from the podium. Avoid appearing hurried, as if you want to get your speech over with as soon as possible. Walking more slowly will help you convey an air of control.

Explore at MyCommunicationLab Activity: "Physical Delivery"

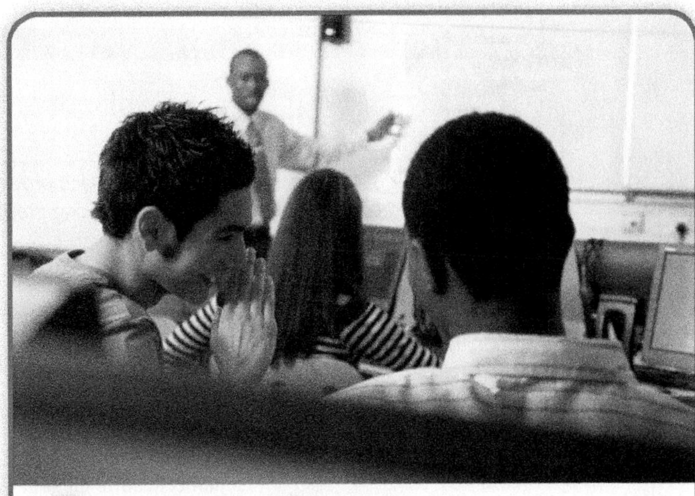

COMMUNICATION CHOICE POINT

AUDIENCE INATTENTION *Kenneth is giving a speech on the problems of teenage drug abuse and notices that the entire back rows of his audience have totally tuned him out; they're reading, chatting, working on their laptops, tweeting.* **What are some of Kenneth's options for gaining the attention of his entire audience and to put an end to this back-row inattention?**

Handling Audience Questions

In many public speaking situations, a question-and-answer period will follow the speech, so be prepared to answer questions. Generally a question-and-answer session is helpful because the ensuing dialogue gives the speaker an opportunity to talk more about something he or she is interested in. In some cases, too, there seems an ethical obligation for the speaker to entertain questions; after all, if audience members sat through what the speaker wanted to say, the speaker should listen to what they want to say.

In most public speaking situations, the question-and-answer session focuses on the message of the speech. In the public speaking classroom, however, the question-and-answer session may focus, in whole or in part, on the speech preparation, the effectiveness of organization, the style of language and delivery, the sufficiency of the evidence, and so on. In either case, here are 10 suggestions for making this Q&A session more effective.

1. Anticipate questions you're likely to be asked and prepare answers to them as you're preparing your speech.
2. If you wish to encourage questions, preface the question period with some kind of encouraging statement, for example, "I'll be happy to respond to your questions—especially on how the new health program will work and how we'll finance it. Anyone?"
3. Maintain eye contact with the audience. Let audience members know that you're still speaking with them.
4. After you hear a question, pause to think about the question and about your answer. If you're not sure of what the question is asking you, seek clarification. If you suspect that some members of the audience didn't hear the question, repeat it; then begin your answer.
5. If a question is too personal or you just don't want to get into that area, avoid responding by saying something like, "I'd like to stick to the matter at hand" or "That's a great question, but I really don't think this is the place to discuss that."
6. Don't assume that a question is a personal attack. Assume, instead, that the question is an attempt to secure more information or perhaps to challenge a position you've taken.
7. If appropriate, thank the questioner or note that it's a good question. This will encourage others also to ask questions.
8. Don't bluff. If you're asked a question and you don't know the answer, say so. If appropriate, note that you'll try to find the answer and get back to the questioner.
9. Question-and-answer sessions often give you opportunities to further advance your purpose by connecting the question and its answer with one or more of your major points: "I'm glad you asked about child care because that's exactly the difference between the two proposals we're here to vote on. The plan I'm proposing . . ."
10. Don't allow one person to dominate the Q&A session. Often there is an unstated rule that each questioner may also ask one follow-up question. If that is in effect, you'll want to follow it. Just be careful that this doesn't become a private dialogue.

Table 16.3 on the next page provides a checklist of the 10 steps for preparing and presenting a speech. Use this to make sure you've covered all the essential steps.

TABLE 16.3

In A Nutshell Public Speaking Checklist

Here is a checklist that summarizes the 10 steps and provides a convenient means to ensure that you've covered each of them in your public speaking preparation.

The 10 Steps	Questions to Ask
Step 1. Select your topic, general and specific purposes, and your thesis.	■ Is the topic substantive, appropriate, and culturally sensitive? ■ Is the topic limited so that you cover a small topic in some depth? ■ Is your purpose worded as an infinitive, focused on the audience, limited to one idea, limited to what you can reasonably accomplish, and phrased with precise terms? ■ Is the thesis limited to one central idea, stated as a complete declarative sentence, useful for generating main points and suggesting organizational patterns, and able to focus the audience's attention?
Step 2. Analyze your audience: Seek to discover what is unique about your listeners and how you might adapt your speech to them.	■ Have you taken into consideration the age, gender, affectional orientation, educational levels, religion, and culture of the audience, and have you adapted your speech in light of these characteristics? ■ Have you taken into consideration additional audience and context characteristics? ■ Have you taken into consideration the audience's willingness, favorableness, and knowledge of your subject and adapted to these factors?
Step 3. Research your topic so that you know as much as you possibly can.	■ Is your speech adequately researched (is the research current, reliable, and appropriate to the topic)? ■ Have you incorporated research citations into your speech?
Step 4. Collect your supporting materials.	■ Are the supporting materials varied, interesting, and relevant to the topic? ■ Are your presentation aids clear, well organized, and tested?
Step 5. Develop your main points.	■ Do the main points support your thesis? ■ Are the main points few in number, focused on your audience, and worded as separate and discrete?
Step 6. Organize your main points into an easily comprehended pattern.	■ Is your speech organized into a logical pattern? ■ Will the audience be able to understand the organizational pattern you use?
Step 7. Construct your introduction, conclusion, and transitions.	■ Does the introduction gain attention, establish a speaker–audience–topic connection, and orient the audience? ■ Does the conclusion summarize, motivate, and close? ■ Do the transitions hold the parts together and make going from one part to another clear to your audience?
Step 8. Word your speech, focusing on being as clear as possible.	■ Is the language clear, vivid, appropriate, and personal? ■ Are the sentences powerful, short, direct, active, positive, and varied in type?
Step 9. Rehearse your speech until you feel confident and comfortable with the material and with your audience interaction.	■ Have you rehearsed the speech from beginning to end sufficiently? ■ Have you rehearsed the speech a sufficient number of times?
Step 10. Present your speech to your intended audience.	■ Does your voice use appropriate volume, rate, pausing, articulation, and pronunciation? ■ Do your general appearance, eye contact, facial expressions, posture, dress, gestures, and movements contribute to your speech purpose?

16.4 SPEECH CRITICISM

In learning the art of public speaking, you can gain much insight from the criticism offered by others as well as from your own efforts to critique others' speeches. This section considers the nature of criticism in a learning environment, the influence of culture on criticism, and the standards and principles for evaluating a speech and for making criticism easier and more effective.

COMMUNICATION CHOICE POINT

CRITICIZING A SPEECH *A student has just given a speech on the glory of bullfighting, something Liz views as animal cruelty. To the speaker, however, bullfighting is an important part of the culture. As Liz bristles inside, the instructor asks her to critique the speech.* **What are some of the things Liz might say in this awkward situation?**

What Is Criticism?

Critics and criticism are essential parts of any art. The word *criticism* comes into English from the Latin *criticus*, which means "able to discern," "able to judge." In the context of public speaking, therefore, **criticism** is the process of evaluating a speech; of rendering a judgment of its value. Note that there is nothing inherently negative about criticism. Criticism may be negative, but it also may be positive.

Perhaps the major value of criticism in the classroom is that it helps you improve your public speaking skills. Through the constructive criticism of others, you'll learn the principles of public speaking more effectively. You'll be shown what you do well; what you could improve; and, ideally, how to improve. As a listener-critic, you'll also learn the principles of public speaking through assessing the speeches of others. Just as you learn when you teach, you also learn when you criticize.

When you give criticism—as you do in a public speaking class—you're telling the speaker that you've listened carefully and that you care enough about the speech and the speaker to offer suggestions for improvement.

Watch at MyCommunicationLab Video: "The After Dinner Speech: Critique"

Culture and Criticism

There are vast cultural differences in what is considered proper when it comes to criticism. For example, criticism will be viewed very differently depending on whether members come from an individualist culture (which emphasizes the individual, placing primary value on the individual's goals) or a collectivist culture (which emphasizes the group, placing primary value on the group's goals). Those who come from cultures that are highly individualist and competitive (the United States, Germany, and Sweden are examples) may find public criticism a normal part of the learning process. Those who come from cultures that are more collectivist and therefore emphasize the group rather than the individual (Japan, Mexico, and Korea are examples) are likely to find giving and receiving public criticism uncomfortable. Thus, people from individualist cultures may readily criticize speakers and are likely to expect the same "courtesy" from listeners. "After all," such a person might reason, "if I'm going to criticize your skills to help you improve, I expect you to help me in the same way." Persons from collectivist cultures, on the other hand, may feel that it's more important to be polite and courteous than to help someone learn a skill. Cultural rules that maintain peaceful relations among the Japanese (Midooka, 1990) and norms of politeness among many Asian cultures (Fraser, 1990) may conflict with the classroom cultural norm that promotes the expression of honest criticism. In some cultures, being kind to the person is more important than telling the truth, so members may say things that are complimentary, but that are untrue in a strict literal sense.

Collectivist cultures place a heavy emphasis on face-saving—on allowing people always to appear in a positive light (James, 1995). In these cultures people may prefer not to say anything negative in public. In fact, they may even be reluctant to say anything positive, lest any omission be construed as negative. In cultures in which face-saving is especially important, communication rules such as the following tend to prevail.

- Don't express negative evaluation in public; instead, compliment the person.
- Don't prove someone wrong, especially in public; express agreement even if you know the person is wrong.

eth•ics *noun* morality, standards of conduct, moral judgment

MAKING ETHICAL CHOICES
Criticizing Ethically

Just as speakers and listeners have ethical obligations, so do critics. To be an ethical critic, keep in mind these guidelines:

- Separate personal feelings about the speaker from your evaluations. Liking the speaker should not lead you to evaluate a speech positively, nor should disliking the speaker lead you to evaluate a speech negatively.
- Separate personal feelings about the issues from your evaluation of the validity of the arguments. Recognize the validity of an argument even if it contradicts a deeply held belief; by the same token, recognize the fallaciousness of an argument even if it supports a deeply held belief.
- Demonstrate cultural sensitivity and be conscious of your own ethnocentrism. Beware of evaluating customs and forms of speech negatively simply because they differ from your own. Conversely, be careful not to evaluate a speech positively just because it supports your own cultural beliefs and values. Avoid any inclination to discriminate for or against speakers simply because they're of a particular gender, race, nationality, religion, age group, or affectional orientation.

Ethical Choice Point

You and your best friend are taking this course together. Your friend just gave a pretty terrible speech, and unfortunately, the instructor has asked you to offer a critique. The wrinkle here is that the instructor's grades seem to be heavily influenced by what student critics say. So in effect your critique will largely determine your friend's grade. You'd like to give your friend a positive critique so he can earn a good grade—which he badly needs—and you figure you can always tell him the truth later and even help him to improve. What is your ethical obligation in this situation? What would you do?

- Don't correct someone's errors; don't even acknowledge them.
- Don't ask difficult questions, lest the person not know the answer and lose face or be embarrassed; generally, avoid asking questions.

The difficulties that these differences can cause may be lessened if they're discussed openly. Some people may become comfortable with public criticism once it's explained that the cultural norms of most public speaking classrooms include public criticism, just as they incorporate informative and persuasive speaking and written outlines. Others may feel more comfortable offering written criticism as a substitute for oral and public criticism. Or perhaps private consultations can be arranged.

Guidelines for Criticizing More Effectively

A useful standard to use in evaluating a classroom speech is the speech's degree of conformity to the principles of the art. Using this standard, you'll evaluate a speech positively when it follows the principles of public speaking established by the critics, theorists, and practitioners of public speaking (as described throughout this text) and evaluate it negatively if it deviates from these principles. These principles include, for example, speaking on a subject that is worthwhile, relevant, and interesting to listeners; designing a speech for a specific audience; and constructing a speech that is based on sound research.

Before reading the specific suggestions for making critical evaluations a more effective part of the total learning process and avoiding some of the potentially negative aspects of criticism, take a look at the following statements. What's wrong with each of them?

1. The speech didn't do anything for me.
2. I loved the speech. It was great. Really great.
3. The speech was weak.
4. Your position was unfair to those of us on athletic scholarships; we earned those scholarships.
5. I liked the speech; we need more police on campus.
6. The introduction didn't gain my attention.
7. I found four things wrong with your speech. First, ...
8. You needed better research.
9. Nobody was able to understand you.
10. We couldn't hear you clearly.

Let's look now at some principles for giving criticism and why the above statements are not appropriate.

Stress the Positive

Egos are fragile, and public speaking is extremely personal. Speakers understand what Noel Coward meant when he said, "I love criticism just as long as it's unqualified praise." Part of your function as a critic is to strengthen the already positive aspects of someone's public speaking performance. Positive criticism is particularly important in itself, but it's almost essential as a preface to negative comments. There are always positive characteristics about any speech, and it's more productive to concentrate on these first. Thus, instead of saying (as in the above 10 statements), "The speech didn't do anything for me," tell the speaker what you liked first, then bring up a weak point and suggest how it might be improved.

When criticizing a person's second or third speech, it's especially helpful if you can point out specific improvements ("You really held my attention in this speech," "I felt you were much more in control of the topic today than in your first speech").

Remember, too, that communication is irreversible. Once you say something, you can't take it back. Remember this when offering criticism, especially criticism that may be negative. If in doubt, err on the side of gentleness.

Be Specific

Criticism is most effective when it's specific. General statements such as "I thought your presentation was bad," "I thought your examples were good," or, as in the preceding list, "I loved the speech… . Really great" or "The speech was weak" are poorly expressed criticisms. These statements don't specify what the speaker might do to improve his or her presentation or to capitalize on the examples used. In commenting on presentation, refer to such specifics as eye contact, vocal volume, or whatever else is of consequence. In commenting on the examples, tell the speaker why they were good. Were they realistic? Were they especially interesting? Were they presented dramatically?

In giving negative criticism, specify and justify—to the extent that you can—positive alternatives. Here's an example.

> **I thought the way you introduced your statistics was vague. I wasn't sure where the statistics came from or how recent or reliable they were. It might have been better to say something like "The U.S. Census figures for 2010 show… ." That way we would know that the statistics were as recent as possible and the most reliable available.**

Be Objective

In criticizing a speech, transcend your own biases as best you can, unlike the preceding example ("Your position was unfair … we earned those scholarships"). See the speech as objectively as possible. Suppose, for example, that you're strongly for a woman's right to choose to have an abortion and you encounter a speech diametrically opposed to your position. In this situation, you'll need to take special care not to dismiss the speech because of your own biases. Examine the speech from the point of view of a detached critic; evaluate, for example, the validity of the arguments and their suitability to the audience, the language, and the supporting materials. Conversely, take special care not to evaluate a speech positively because it presents a position with which you agree, as in "I liked the speech; women should have the right to choose."

Be Constructive

Your primary goal should be to provide the speaker with insight that will prove useful in future public speaking transactions. For example, to say that "The introduction didn't gain my attention" doesn't tell the speaker how he or she might have gained your attention. Instead, you might say, "The example about the computer crash would have more effectively gained my attention in the introduction."

Another way you can be constructive is to limit your criticism. Cataloging a speaker's weak points, as in "I found four things wrong with your speech," will overwhelm, not help, the speaker. If you're the sole critic, your criticism naturally will need to be more extensive. But if you're one of many critics, limit your criticism to one or perhaps two points. In all cases, your guide should be the value your comments will have for the speaker.

Focus on Behavior

Focus criticism on what the speaker said and did during the actual speech. Try to avoid the very natural tendency to read the mind of the speaker—to assume that you know why the speaker did one thing rather than another. Compare the critical comments presented in Table 16.4 on page 362. Note that those in the first column, "Criticism as Attack," try to identify the reasons the speaker did as he or she did; they try to read the speaker's mind. At the same time, they blame the speaker for what happened. Those in the second column, "Criticism as Support," focus on the specific behavior. Note, too, that those in the first column are likely to encourage defensiveness; you can almost hear the speaker saying, "I was so interested in the topic." Those in the second column are less likely to create

TABLE 16.4 CRITICISM AS ATTACK AND AS SUPPORT

Can you develop additional examples to illustrate criticism as attack and as support?

Criticism as Attack	Criticism as Support
You weren't interested in your topic.	I would have liked to see greater variety in your presentation. It would have made me feel that you were more interested.
You should have put more time into the speech.	I think it would have been more effective if you had looked at your notes less.
You didn't care about your audience.	I would have liked it if you had looked more directly at me while speaking.
You didn't know your topic enough.	I would have liked you to tell us more about your research on the topic and your experiences with this issue.

defensiveness and are more likely to be appreciated as honest reflections of how the critic perceived the speech.

Own Your Criticism

In giving criticism, own your comments; take responsibility for them. The best way to express this ownership is to use "I-messages" rather than "you-messages." Instead of saying, "You needed better research," say, "I would have been more persuaded if you had used more recent research."

Avoid attributing what you found wrong to others. Instead of saying, "Nobody was able to understand you," say, "I had difficulty understanding you. It would have helped me if you had spoken more slowly." Remember that your criticism is important precisely because it's your perception of what the speaker did and what the speaker could have done more effectively.

Employing I-messages also will prevent you from using "should messages," a type of expression that almost invariably creates defensiveness and resentment. When you say "You should have done this" or "You shouldn't have done that," you assume a superior position and imply that what you're saying is correct and that what the speaker did was incorrect. On the other hand, when you own your evaluations and use I-messages ("I would have explained deflation by noting ..." or "I didn't see the connection between ...") you're giving your perceptions; it's then up to the speaker to accept or reject them.

Sue works in the public relations department of a large art museum. She has been asked to speak to a local women's group about special programs and classes the museum is offering this season. She wants to prepare and deliver a speech that will hold the attention of this group of highly educated women and give them a good feeling for the museum. She has shared her speech with her coworker, Stephanie, who has offered to help Sue refine her words. "Speaking on the Arts" focuses on selecting words and sentences to best express your meaning and the choices you have in presenting your speech to your audience. Also illustrated are some suggestions for rehearsing your speech. Log on to mycommunicationlab.com to view this video and the choices, and then answer the related discussion questions.

SUMMARY: STYLE AND DELIVERY IN PUBLIC SPEAKING

Study and **Review** at **MyCommunicationLab**

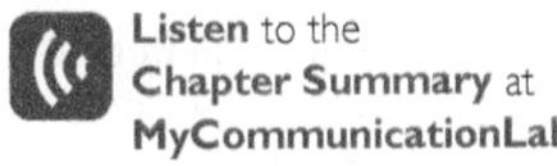

This chapter focused on style, rehearsal, and presentation and offered suggestions for choosing words and phrasing sentences; for rehearsing and presenting your speech; and for delivering impromptu, manuscript, memorized, or extemporaneous speeches. In addition, this chapter discussed guidelines for giving and receiving criticism.

16.1 STEP 8: WORD YOUR SPEECH

1. Compared with written style, oral style contains shorter, simpler, and more familiar words; greater qualification; and more self-referential terms.
2. Effective public speaking style should be clear (be economical and specific; use guide phrases; and stick to short, familiar, and commonly used terms), vivid (use active verbs, strong verbs, figures of speech, and imagery), appropriate to audience (speak on a suitable level of formality; avoid jargon and technical expressions; avoid slang, vulgarity, and offensive terms), personal (use personal pronouns, ask questions, and create immediacy), and forceful (eliminate weakeners, vary intensity, and avoid trite expressions).
3. In constructing sentences for public speeches, favor short, direct, active, and positively phrased sentences. Vary the type and length of sentences.

16.2 STEP 9: REHEARSE YOUR SPEECH

4. Use rehearsal to time your speech; perfect your volume and rate; incorporate pauses and other delivery notes; and perfect your bodily action.

16.3 STEP 10: PRESENT YOUR SPEECH

5. There are four basic methods of presenting a public speech. The impromptu method involves speaking without any specific preparation. The manuscript method involves writing out the entire speech and reading it to the audience. Memorized delivery involves writing out the speech, memorizing it, and reciting it. The extemporaneous method involves thorough preparation and memorizing of the main ideas and their order of appearance but no commitment to exact wording.
6. Effective presentation is natural, reinforces the message, is varied, and has a conversational quality. When you present your speech, regulate your voice for greatest effectiveness. Adjust your vocal volume and rate as appropriate. Check your articulation and pronunciation of key terms.
7. Use unfilled pauses to signal a transition between the major parts of the speech, to allow the audience time to think, to allow the audience to ponder a rhetorical question, or to signal the approach of a particularly important idea. Avoid filled pauses; they weaken your message.
8. Effective body action involves maintaining eye contact with your entire audience, allowing your facial expressions to convey your feelings, using your posture to communicate command of the public speaking interaction, gesturing naturally, and moving around a bit.
9. In Q&A sessions after the speech, encourage questions, maintain eye contact, repeat the question if necessary, avoid any signs of defensiveness, express thanks for the question (if appropriate), don't bluff, and consider the usefulness of a persuasive answer.

16.4 SPEECH CRITICISM

10. Criticism, a process of judging and evaluating a work, is crucial to mastering the principles of public speaking.
11. Criticism can (1) identify strengths and weaknesses and thereby help you improve as a public speaker, (2) identify standards for evaluating all sorts of public speeches, and (3) show that the audience is listening and is concerned about the speaker's progress.
12. Cultures differ in their views of criticism and in the rules they consider appropriate. For example, members of individualist cultures may find public criticism easier and more acceptable than people from collectivist cultures.
13. Among the guidelines for effective criticism are these: Stress the positive, be specific, be objective, be constructive, focus on behavior, and own your criticism.

Study and **Review** the **Flashcards** at **MyCommunicationLab**

KEY TERMS

accent *355*
antithetical sentences *350*
appropriateness *346*
articulation *355*
auditory imagery *346*
bromides *348*
clarity *344*
clichés *349*
criticism *359*
extemporaneous speech *353*
figures of speech *345*
forcefulness *348*
impromptu speech *352*
jargon *346*
manuscript speech *352*
memorized speech *352*
monotonous patterns *353*
oral style *344*
parallel sentences *349*
pauses *356*
periodic sentences *350*
personal style *347*
predictable patterns *353*
pronunciation *355*
rate *355*
slang *346*
tactile imagery *346*
visual imagery *346*
vividness *344*
volume *355*
weakeners *348*

WORKING WITH STYLE AND PRESENTATION IN PUBLIC SPEAKING

16.1 Distinguish between Commonly Confused Words. Using the wrong term is likely to divert audience attention from your main ideas and perhaps damage your credibility. When in doubt, check it out. Many words, because they sound alike or are used in similar situations, are commonly confused. Underline the word in parentheses that you would use in each sentence.

a. He (accepted, excepted) the award and thanked everyone (accept, except) the producer.

b. The professor (affected, effected) her students greatly and will now (affect, effect) a complete curriculum overhaul.

c. Are you deciding (between, among) red and green or (between, among) red, green, and blue?

d. I (can, may) scale the mountain but I (can, may) not reveal its hidden path.

e. The table was (cheap, inexpensive) but has great style whereas the chairs cost a fortune but look (cheap, inexpensive).

f. The explorer's dream was to (discover, invent) uncharted lands but also to (discover, invent) computer programs.

g. She was (explicit, implicit) in her detailed description of the crime but made only (explicit, implicit) observations concerning the perpetrator.

h. He was evasive and only (implied, inferred) that he'd seek a divorce. You can easily (imply, infer) his reasons.

i. The wedding was (tasteful, tasty) and the food really (tasteful, tasty).

j. The student seemed (disinterested, uninterested) in the test while, in assigning grades, the teacher was always (disinterested, uninterested).

Here are the principles that govern correct usage. (1) Use *accept* to mean "to receive" and *except* to mean "with the exclusion of." (2) Use to *affect* to mean "to have an effect or to influence" and to *effect* to mean "to produce a result." (3) Use *between* when referring to two items and *among* when referring to more than two items. (4) Use *can* to refer to ability and *may* to refer to permission. (5) Use *cheap* to refer to something that is inferior and *inexpensive* to describe something that costs little. (6) Use *discover* to refer to the act of finding something out or learning something previously unknown, and use *invent* to refer to the act of originating something new. (7) Use *explicit* to mean "specific" and *implicit* to describe something that's indicated but not openly stated. (8) Use to *imply* to mean "to state indirectly" and to *infer* to mean "to draw a conclusion." (9) Use *tasteful* to refer to good taste and *tasty* to refer to something that tastes good. (10) Use *uninterested* to refer to a lack of interest, and use *disinterested* to mean "objective or unbiased."

16.2 Checking Your Pronunciation. Mispronouncing words in public speaking may significantly damage your credibility. Feeling unsure about how to pronounce any word or words in your speech is also likely to contribute to your communication apprehension. Here are some words that are often mispronounced. Consult a print or online dictionary (ideally, one with audio capabilities) and record the correct pronunciations here.

Words Often Mispronounced	Correct Pronunciation
abdomen	________
accessory	________
arctic	________
ask	________
buffet	________
cavalry	________
clothes	________
costume	________
diagnosis	________
especially	________
espresso	________
et cetera	________
February	________
foliage	________
forte	________
herb	________
hierarchy	________
library	________
nausea	________
nuclear	________
probably	________
prostate	________
realtor	________
relevant	________
repeat	________
salmon	________
sandwich	________
similar	________
substantive	________
xenophobia	________

16.3 **Wording the Speech for Different Audiences.** Francisco is scheduled to give two speeches, one to a predominantly female audience of health professionals and one to a predominantly male audience of small business owners. His topic for both groups is the same: neighborhood violence. What advice—if any—would you give Francisco for tailoring his speech to the two different audiences?

16.4 **Using Humor.** John has this great joke that is only tangentially related to his speech topic. But the joke is so great that it will immediately get the audience actively involved in his speech; this, John thinks, outweighs the fact that the joke isn't integrally related to the speech. John asks your advice; what do you suggest?

16.5 **Projecting an Image.** Michael has a very formal type of personality; he's very restrained in everything he does. But he wants to try to project a different image—a much more personable, friendly, informal quality—in his speeches. What are some of the things Michael might do to project this new image? What advice would you give Michael?

16.6 **E-Talk and Public Speaking.** How would you describe your language—word and sentence choices—in online and in public speaking communication? What are the major differences between online and public communication?

16.7 **The 2-Minute Speech.** Prepare and deliver a 2-minute speech in which you do one of the following:

- Describe the language of a noted personality
- Introduce an excerpt from literature and read the excerpt as you might a manuscript speech
- Analyze an advertisement in terms of one or two of the characteristics of effective style: clarity, vividness, appropriateness, personal style, or forcefulness
- Describe an object in the room using visual, auditory, and tactile imagery

LogOn! MyCommunicationLab www.mycommunicationlab.com

Throughout this chapter, there are icons that highlight media content for selected topics. Go to **MyCommunicationLab** for additional materials on the final three steps in public speaking: wording your speech, rehearsing your speech, and presenting your speech. Here you'll find flash-cards to help you learn key communication terms, videos that illustrate a variety of concepts, additional exercises, and discussions to help you continue your study of style and delivery in public speaking.

17 THE INFORMATIVE SPEECH

CHAPTER TOPICS	CHAPTER OBJECTIVES
In this chapter you'll explore the following major topics:	**After reading this chapter you should be able to:**
PRINCIPLES OF INFORMATIVE SPEAKING	17.1 Paraphrase the principles of informative speaking and apply them in constructing informative speeches.
SPEECHES OF DESCRIPTION	17.2 Define the *speech of description* and construct and present speeches of description.
SPEECHES OF DEFINITION	17.3 Define the *speech of definition* and construct and present speeches of definition.
SPEECHES OF DEMONSTRATION	17.4 Define the *speech of demonstration* and construct and present speeches of demonstration.

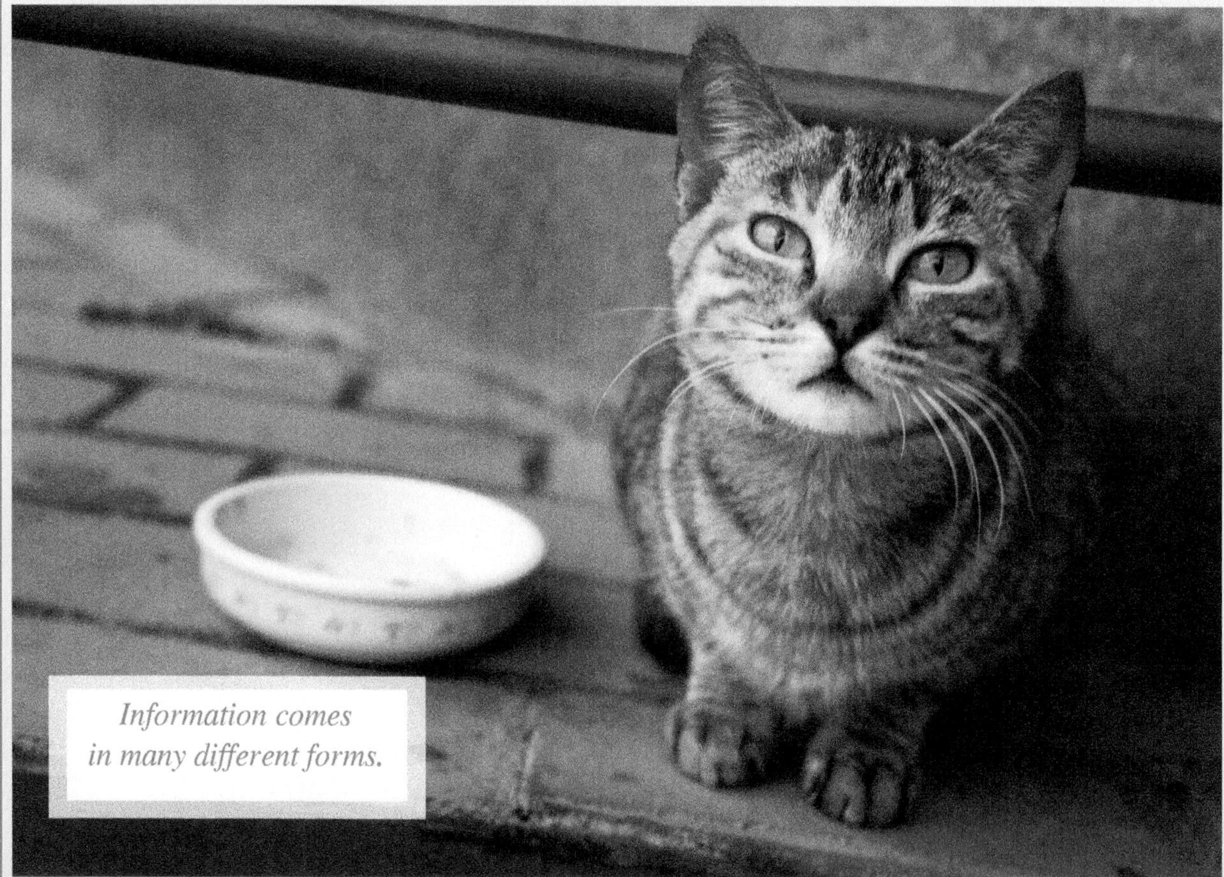

Information comes in many different forms.

This chapter and the next focus on types of public speeches. This chapter looks at informative speaking and Chapter 18 at persuasive speaking. More specifically, this chapter considers the general goals of informative speaking, the principles for communicating information, and the varied types of informative speeches and how you can develop these most effectively.

17.1 PRINCIPLES OF INFORMATIVE SPEAKING

When you communicate **information**, you tell your listeners something new—something they don't know. You may tell them about a new way of looking at old things or an old way of looking at new things. You may discuss a theory not previously heard of or a familiar theory not fully understood. You may discuss events that the audience may be unaware of or may have misconceptions about. Regardless of what type of informative speech you intend to give, the following guidelines should help.

Explore at MyCommunicationLab Activity: "Informative Speeches"

In addition, the Public Speaking Sample Assistant boxes in the Appendix illustrate some of the pitfalls you'll want to avoid in a poorly constructed informative speech (see pages 406–408) and some of the principles you'll want to follow in an excellent informative speech (see pages 408–410).

Focus on Your Audience

Your audience will—to some extent—influence the information you'll present and how you'll present it. Consequently, it's wise to look to your audience as a first principle. As I write this, Microsoft's Windows 8 operating system is making its debut and provides a good illustration of how the same topic can be pursued with different goals in mind. So let's say you want to give an informative speech on Windows 8.

Watch at MyCommunicationLab Video: "Eat Right"

- To an audience of dedicated Mac users, the information may be entirely new, so your goal will be to introduce a topic unknown to the audience.
- To an audience of dedicated Mac users who think there's little or no difference between the systems, you'll be clarifying misconceptions.
- To an audience of students using Windows 7 or Vista, you may wish to demonstrate how this new operating system is different. For example, you might explain the ways in which Windows 8 is superior to Windows 7.

As you can appreciate, each of these speeches would have to be somewhat different depending on the knowledge and experience of the audiences.

Stress Relevance and Usefulness

Listeners remember information best when they see it as relevant and useful to their own needs or goals. Notice that as a listener you yourself regularly demonstrate this principle of relevance and usefulness. For example, you may remember a given piece of information because it will help you make a better impression in your job interview, make you a better parent, or enable you to deal with relationship problems. If you want audience members to listen to your speech, relate your information to their needs, wants, or goals. Throughout your speech, but especially in the beginning, make sure audience members know that the information you're presenting is or will be relevant and useful to them now or in the immediate future. For example, you might say something like:

> We all want financial security. We all want to be able to buy those luxuries we read so much about in magazines and see every evening on television. Wouldn't it be nice to be able to buy a car without worrying about where you're going to get the down payment or how you'll be able to make the monthly payments? Actually, that is not an unrealistic goal, as I'll demonstrate in this speech. In fact, I'll show you several investment strategies that have enabled many people to increase their income by as much as 20 percent.

Limit the Information

There's a limit to the amount of information that a listener can take in at one time. Resist the temptation to overload your listeners with information. Instead of enlarging the breadth of information you communicate, expand its depth. It's better to present two new items of information and explain them in depth with examples, illustrations, and descriptions than to present five items without this needed amplification. The speaker who attempts to discuss the physiological, psychological, social, and linguistic differences between men and women, for example, is clearly trying to cover too much and is going to be forced to cover these areas only superficially, with the result that little new information will be communicated. Even covering one of these areas completely is likely to prove difficult. Instead, select one subdivision of one area—say, language development or differences in language problems—and develop that in depth.

Adjust the Level of Complexity

As you know from attending college classes, information can be presented in very simple or very complex form. Adjusting the level of complexity on which you communicate your information is crucial. This adjustment should depend on the wide variety of factors considered throughout this book: the level of knowledge your audience has, the time you have available, the purpose you hope to achieve, the topic on which you're speaking, and so on. If you simplify a topic too much, you risk boring or, even worse, insulting your audience. On the other hand, if your talk is too complex, you risk confusing your audience and failing to communicate your message.

Generally, beginning speakers err by being too complex and not realizing that a 5- or 10-minute speech isn't long enough to make an audience understand sophisticated concepts or complicated processes. At least in your beginning speeches, try to keep it simple. Make sure the words you use are familiar to your audience; alternatively, explain and define any unfamiliar terms as you use them. For example, remember that jargon and technical vocabulary familiar to the computer hacker may not be familiar to the person who still uses a typewriter. Always see your topic from the point of view of audience members; ask yourself how much they know about your topic and its particular terminology.

Watch at MyCommunicationLab Video: "Transcranial Magnetic Stimulation"

COMMUNICATION CHOICE POINT

UNEXPECTED EVENTS *Ronald is going to speak on the newest Microsoft operating system that he's been using the past few weeks. Unfortunately, the preceding speaker turns out to be a Microsoft program designer who gives a speech on exactly this topic.* **What are some of the things Ronald can say (or should he say nothing?) in his introduction to deal with this awkward situation?**

Relate New Information to Old

Listeners will learn information more easily and retain it longer when you relate it to what they already know. So relate the new to the old, the unfamiliar to the familiar, the unseen to the seen, the untasted to the tasted. Here, for example, Betsy Heffernan, a student from the University of Wisconsin (Reynolds & Schnoor, 1991), relates the problem of sewage to a familiar historical event:

> During our nation's struggle for independence, the citizens of Boston were hailed as heroes for dumping tea into Boston Harbor. But not to be outdone, many modern day Bostonians are also dumping things into the harbor: five-thousand gallons of human waste every second. The New England Aquarium of Boston states that since 1900, Bostonians have dumped enough human sewage into the harbor to cover the entire state of Massachusetts chest deep in sludge. Unfortunately, Boston isn't alone. All over the country, bays, rivers, and lakes are literally becoming cesspools.

Vary the Levels of Abstraction

You can talk about freedom of the press in the abstract by talking about the importance of getting information to the public, by referring to the Bill of Rights, and by relating a free press to the preservation of democracy. But you can also talk about freedom of the press on a low level of abstraction—a level that is specific and concrete; for example, you can describe how a local newspaper was prevented from running a story critical of the town council or how Lucy Rinaldo was fired from the *Accord Sentinel* after she wrote a story critical of the mayor.

Varying the **levels of abstraction**—combining high abstraction (the very general) and low abstraction (the very specific)—seems to work best. Too many generalizations without the specifics or too many specifics without the generalizations will prove less effective than the combination of abstract and specific.

Here, for example, is an excerpt from a speech on the homeless. Note that in the first paragraph we have a relatively abstract description of homelessness. In

eth•ics *noun* morality, standards of conduct, moral judgment

MAKING ETHICAL CHOICES
Speaking Ethically

One interesting approach to ethics that has particular relevance to public speaking identifies four key rules for speakers (Johannesen, 2001; Wallace, 1955). As an ethical speaker, you should be guided by the following principles:

Have a thorough knowledge of the topic, an ability to answer relevant questions, and an awareness of the significant facts and opinions bearing on the issues you discuss.

Present both facts and opinions fairly, without bending or spinning them to personal advantage. You must allow listeners to make the final judgment.

Reveal the sources of these facts and opinions, and help listeners evaluate any biases and prejudices in the sources.

Acknowledge and respect opposing arguments and evidence; advocate a tolerance for diversity.

Ethical Choice Point

You're giving an informative speech to explain how the new condom machines on campus will work. Among the important items that should logically be covered is their cost, which is going to come from an increase in student fees. Because you are in favor of these machines, you'd like to eliminate discussing cost largely because the students may vote against installing the machines if they knew their fees would be raised. You figure you don't have time to include all issues, that it's really the responsibility of the audience to ask where the money is coming from, and that the machines will help prevent sexually transmitted diseases. What is your ethical obligation in this situation? What would you do?

the second paragraph, we get into specifics. In the last paragraph the abstract and the concrete are connected.

Here the speaker begins with relatively general or abstract statements.

Homelessness is a serious problem for all metropolitan areas throughout the country. It's currently estimated that there are now more than 200,000 homeless in New York City alone. But what is this really about? Let me tell you what it's about.

Here the speaker gets to specifics, for example, the age, the cardboard box, the blanket.

It's about a young man. He must be about 25 or 30, although he looks a lot older. He lives in a cardboard box on the side of my apartment house. We call him Tom, although we really don't know his name. All his possessions are stored in this huge box. I think it was a box from a refrigerator. Actually, he doesn't have very much, and what he has easily fits in this box. There's a blanket my neighbor threw out, some plastic bottles Tom puts water in, and some Styrofoam containers he picked up from the garbage from Burger King. He uses these to store whatever food he finds.

The conclusion combines the general (homelessness) and the specific (the case of Tom).

What is homelessness about? It's about Tom and 200,000 other "Toms" in New York and thousands of others throughout the rest of the country. And not all of them even have boxes to live in.

Make Your Speech Easy to Remember

The principles of public speaking (principles governing use of language, delivery, and supporting materials, for example) will all help your listeners remember your speech. If, for example, you stress interest and relevance—as already noted—audience members are more likely to remember what you say because they will see it as important and relevant to their own lives. But here are a few extra suggestions.

Watch at MyCommunicationLab **Video:** "Communication in an Ever-Changing World"

- **Repeat the points you want the audience to remember.** Help audience members to remember what you want them to remember by repeating your most important points.
- **Use signposts.** Guide your audience's attention to your most memorable points by saying, for example, "the first point to remember is that . . . ," "the argument I want you to remember when you enter that voting booth is . . . ."
- **Use internal summary transitions.** Internal summary transitions will remind the audience of what you have said and how it relates to what is to follow. This kind of repetition will reinforce your message and help your listeners remember your main points.

- **Pattern your messages.** If audience members can see the logic of your speech, they'll be better able to organize what you say in their own minds. If they can see that you're following a temporal pattern or a spatial pattern, for example, it will be easier for them to retain more of what you say because they'll have a framework into which they can fit what you say.
- **Focus audience attention.** The best way to focus the listeners' attention is to tell them to focus their attention. Simply say, "I want you to focus on three points that I will make in this speech. First,..." or "What I want you to remember is this:..."

A summary of these principles for communicating information appears in Table 17.1.

Now that the principles of information speaking have been identified, let's consider the main types of informative speeches and some suggestions for developing your thesis and main points, support, and organization.

- **Speeches of description** are speeches in which you describe an object (the human heart), person (a genius, artist, or inventor), event (a hurricane), or process (adopting a child).
- **Speeches of definition** are speeches in which you define a term (linguistics), a system or theory (evolution), or similar and dissimilar terms (nature/nurture, communism/socialism).
- **Speeches of demonstration** are speeches in which you show how to do something (protecting yourself against identity theft) or how something works (search spiders).

17.2 SPEECHES OF DESCRIPTION

In a **speech of description** you're concerned with explaining an object, person, event, or process. Here are a few examples:

Describing an Object or Place

- The structure of DNA
- The parts of a cell phone
- The geography of Africa
- The hierarchy of a corporation

Describing a Person, Real or Generalized

- The power of Nancy Pelosi, Bill Gates, Tiger Woods, or Meg Whitman
- The significance of Benjamin Franklin, Rosa Parks, or Martin Scorsese
- The contributions of a philanthropist
- The vegan and the vegetarian

Describing an Event or Process

- The events leading to war with Iraq
- Organizing a bodybuilding contest

TABLE 17.1

In A Nutshell Principles of Informative Speaking

Principle	The Logic of the Principle
Focus on Your Audience	Audience members are the reason for your speech; focus on them.
Stress Relevance and Usefulness	People get bored easily; they pay attention to what is meaningful and useful to them.
Limit the Information	Too much information will confuse rather than clarify.
Adjust the Level of Complexity	People will ignore what is too complex or too simple.
Relate New Information to Old	People want to make connections and will understand information better if it's connected to something familiar.
Vary the Levels of Abstraction	People want to see the big picture but also specifics.
Make Your Speech Easy to Remember	Remembering is key to achieving your goal.

- How a book is printed
- Purchasing stock online

Thesis and Main Points

The thesis of a speech, as explained in Chapter 15, is your single most important concept; it is what you most want your audience to remember. The thesis of a speech of description simply states what you'll describe in your speech; for example:

- A child acquires language in four stages.
- There are three steps to purchasing stock online.
- Four major events led to the Iraq war.

The main points of your speech of description are the major subdivisions of the thesis. You derive your main points from the thesis by asking strategic questions, for example:

- What are the four stages in child language acquisition?
- What are the three steps to purchasing stock online?
- What events led to the Iraq war?

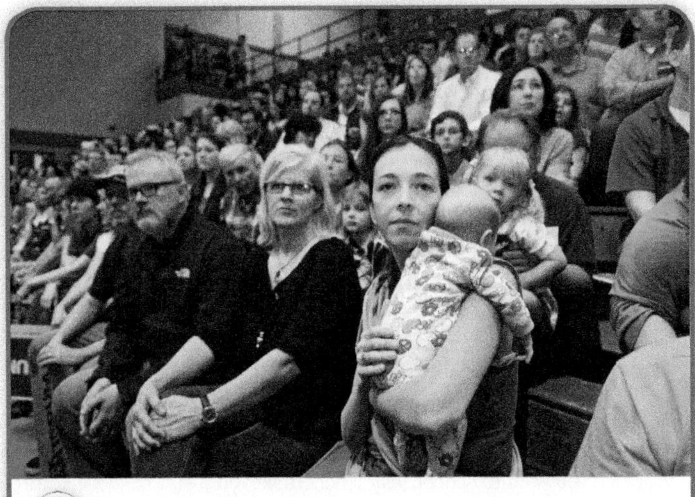

COMMUNICATION CHOICE POINT

SPEECH OF DESCRIPTION *Angela is giving a speech of description on how children acquire language and notices a woman with a child of the age she's talking about in the audience.* **What are some of Angela's options if she wanted to integrate this situation into her speech?**

Support

Obviously, you don't want simply to list your main points, but rather to flesh them out and to make them memorable, interesting, and most of all clear. You do this by using a variety of materials that amplify and support your main ideas—the examples, illustrations, testimony, statistics, and the like that have already been explained. So, for example, in describing the babbling stage of language learning, you might give examples of babbling, the age at which babbling first appears, the period of time that babbling lasts, or the differences between the babbling of girls and boys.

Because this is a speech of description, give extra consideration to the types of description you might use in your supporting materials. Try to describe the object or event with lots of different descriptive categories. With physical categories, for example, ask yourself questions such as these: What color is it? How big is it? What is it shaped like? How much does it weigh? What is its volume? How attractive/unattractive is it? Also consider social, psychological, and economic categories. In describing a person, for example, consider such categories as friendly/unfriendly, warm/cold, rich/poor, aggressive/meek, and pleasant/unpleasant.

Consider how you might use presentation aids. In describing an object or a person, show your listeners a picture; show them the inside of a telephone, pictures of the brain, the skeleton of the body. In describing an event or process, show them a diagram or flowchart to illustrate the stages or steps; for example, the steps involved in buying stock, in publishing a newspaper, in putting a parade together.

Organization

Consider using a spatial or a topical organization when describing objects and people. Consider using a temporal pattern when describing events and processes. For example, if you were to describe the layout of Philadelphia, you might start from the north and work down to the south (using a spatial pattern). If you were to describe the contributions of Thomas Edison, you might select the three or four major contributions and discuss each of these equally (using a topical pattern).

If you were describing the events leading up to World War II, you might use a temporal pattern, starting with the earliest and working up to the latest. A temporal pattern would also be appropriate for describing how a hurricane develops or how a parade is put together.

Consider the 5W (who? what? where? when? and why?) pattern of organization discussed in Chapter 15. These journalistic categories are especially useful when you want to describe an event or a process. For example, if you're going to describe how to purchase a house, you

me•di•a lit•er•a•cy *noun* ability to understand, interact with, and create media messages

EXPANDING MEDIA LITERACY

Gatekeeping

The concept of *gatekeeping*, introduced by Kurt Lewin in his *Human Relations* (1947), concerns both *the process* by which a message passes through various "gates" and *the people or groups*, or "gatekeepers," that allow the message to pass.

As you were growing up, your parents—your first gatekeepers—gave you certain information and withheld other information. For example, depending on the culture in which you were raised, you may have been told about Santa Claus and the tooth fairy but not about cancer or mutual funds. When you went to school, your teachers served a similar gatekeeping function. They taught you about certain historical events, for example, but not others. Textbook authors also serve as gatekeepers. Editors of newspapers and magazines; television producers, writers, and advertisers; and those who regulate and monitor Internet messages are all gatekeepers: They allow certain information to come through and other information to be filtered out (Bodon, Powell, & Hickson, 1999; Lewis, 1995).

Often the media gatekeeps to increase profits, as when they emphasize (open the gates for) stories of celebrities, violence, and sex—because these sell—and deemphasize (close the gates on) minority issues, classical drama, or antireligious statements. At times they may gatekeep because of legal restrictions.

So, when you hear a news broadcast, read an article, or listen to a commentator, ask yourself if you're seeing or hearing an incomplete or unrealistic picture. Ask yourself, what might not have passed through the gate?

As you interact with the media, consider how gatekeeping operates, who is doing the gatekeeping, and for what purpose. Consider too how the following people function as gatekeepers: the editor of your local or college newspaper, your romantic partner (past or present), the president of the United States, network news shows, or the advertising department of a large corporation.

might want to consider the people involved (who?), the steps you have to go through (what?), the places you'll have to go (where?), the time or sequence in which the steps have to take place (when?), and the advantages and disadvantages of buying the house (why?).

Here are two examples of the main components a descriptive speech might contain. In this first example, the speaker describes four suggestions for reducing energy bills. Notice that the speaker derives the main points from asking a question of the thesis.

General purpose: To inform.

Specific purpose: To describe how you can reduce energy bills.

Thesis: Energy bills can be reduced. (How can energy bills be reduced?)

I. Caulk window and door seams.
II. Apply weather stripping around windows and doors.
III. Insulate walls.
IV. Install storm windows and doors.

In this second example, the speaker describes the way in which fear works in intercultural communication.

General purpose: To inform.

Specific purpose: To describe the way fear works in intercultural communication.

Thesis: Fear influences intercultural communication. (How does fear influence intercultural communication?)

I. We fear disapproval.
II. We fear embarrassing ourselves.
III. We fear being harmed.

In delivering such a speech, a speaker might begin by saying:

Three major fears interfere with intercultural communication. First, we fear disapproval—from members of our own group as well as from members of the other person's group. Second, we fear embarrassing ourselves, even making fools of ourselves, by saying the wrong thing or appearing insensitive. And third, we may fear being harmed—our stereotypes of the other group may lead us to see its members as dangerous or potentially harmful to us.

Let's look at each of these fears in more detail. We'll be able to see clearly how they influence our own intercultural communication behavior. Consider, first, the fear of disapproval. [The speaker would then amplify and support this fear of disapproval, giving examples of disapproval seen in his or her own experience, the testimony of communication theorists on the importance of such fear, research findings on the effects that such fear might have on intercultural communication, and so on.]

the•o•ry *noun* statement of explanation, formulation of relationships, reasoned generalization

UNDERSTANDING THEORY AND RESEARCH
Information Theory

In the 1940s, engineers working at Bell Telephone Laboratories developed the mathematical theory of communication—which became known as information theory (Shannon & Weaver, 1949). This theory defined *information* as that which reduces uncertainty. For example, if I tell you my name and you already know it, then I haven't communicated information—because my message (my name) didn't reduce uncertainty; you already knew my name and so had no uncertainty in this connection. If, on the other hand, I tell you my salary or my educational background or my fears and dreams, that constitutes information because these are things you presumably didn't already know. Although this theory doesn't explain many of the complexities of human communication very well (see Chapter 1), it is helpful when you are thinking about the purpose of the informative speech: to communicate information, to tell the members of the audience something they didn't already know, or to send messages that reduce the uncertainty of your listeners about your speech topic. If you don't communicate enough information, audience members will be bored (they'll already know what you're saying). But if you communicate too much information, they'll be overwhelmed. The art of the effective speaker is to strike an appropriate balance.

Working with Theories and Research

Review the speech you're working on now. How much is information? How much does the audience already know? Is this the appropriate balance, or do you need to make adjustments?

17.3 SPEECHES OF DEFINITION

What is leadership? What is a born-again Christian? What is the difference between sociology and psychology? What is a cultural anthropologist? What is safe sex? These are all topics for informative **speeches of definition**.

Watch at MyCommunicationLab Video: "Sweat"

A definition is a statement of the meaning of a term. In giving a speech of definition (as opposed to using a definition as a form of supporting material, as explained in Chapter 15, pages 313–314), you may focus on defining a term, defining a system or theory, or pinpointing the similarities and/or differences among terms or systems. A speech of definition may be on a subject new to the audience or may present a familiar topic in a new and different way. Here are a few examples.

Defining a Term

- What is a smart house?
- What is cloud storage?
- What is perjury?
- What is restless leg syndrome?

Defining a System or Theory

- Buddhism: its major beliefs
- What is virtual reality?
- What is futurism?
- The "play theory" of mass communication

Defining Similar and Dissimilar Terms or Systems

- Football and soccer: What's the difference?
- What do Christians and Muslims have in common?
- Twitter and Facebook: How do they differ?
- Animal and human rights

Thesis and Main Points

The thesis in a speech of definition is a statement identifying the term or system and your intention to define it or to contrast it with other terms; for example:

- Christianity and Islam have much in common.
- You can search for definitions in print or in online dictionaries.

You derive the main points for your speech of definition by asking questions of your thesis; for example:

- What do Christianity and Islam have in common?
- How do print and online dictionaries differ?

Your main points will then consist of, say, the factors that Christianity and Islam have in common or the several ways in which print and online dictionaries differ.

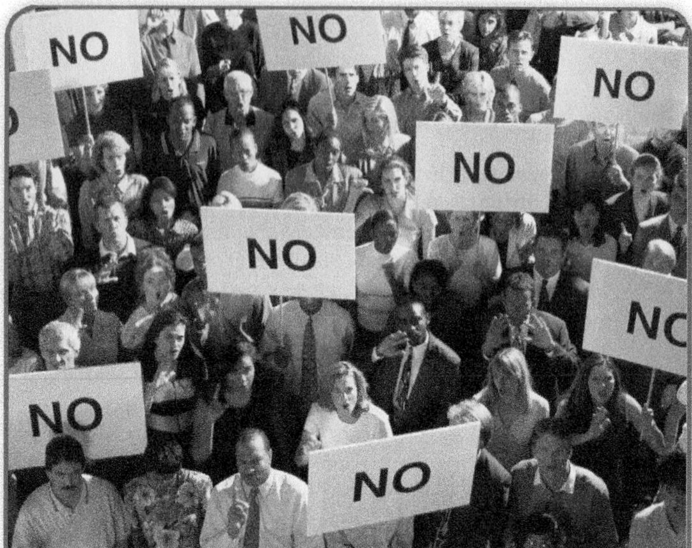

COMMUNICATION CHOICE POINT

DEFINING *In visualizing his next speech, in which he plans to define the basic tenets of his religion, Michael realizes that most members of his audience have a negative view of his religion.* **What are some of Michael's options for acknowledging his understanding of these negative attitudes? What specifically might he say?**

Support

Once you have each of your main points, you'll support them with examples, testimony, and the like. For example, one of your main points in the Christianity–Islam example might be that both religions believe in the value of good works. You might then quote from the New Testament and from the Quran to illustrate this belief, or you might give examples of noted Christians and Muslims who exemplified this characteristic, or you might cite the testimony of religious leaders who talked about the importance of good works.

Because this is a speech of definition, you'll want to give special attention to different types of definitions, as detailed in Chapter 15 (pages 313–314).

Organization

In addition to the obvious organizational pattern of multiple definitions (see Chapter 15, page 327), consider using a topical order, in which each main idea is treated equally. In either case, however, proceed from the known to the unknown. Start with what your audience knows and work up to what is new or unfamiliar. This will help the audience to bring to consciousness the material you want to build on. Let's say you want to explain the concept of phonemics (with which your audience is totally unfamiliar). The specific idea you wish to get across is that each phoneme stands for a unique sound. You might proceed from the known to the unknown and begin your definition with something like this:

> We all know that in the written language each letter of the alphabet stands for a unit of the written language. Each letter is different from every other letter. A *t* is different from a *g* and a *g* is different from a *b*, and so on. Each letter is called a *grapheme*. In English we have 26 such letters.
>
> We can look at the spoken language in much the same way. Each sound is different from every other sound. A *t* sound is different from a *d* and a *d* is different from a *k*, and so on. Each individual sound is called a *phoneme*.
>
> Now, let me explain in a little more detail what I mean by a *phoneme*.

Here are two examples of how you might go about constructing a speech of definition. In this first example, the speaker explains the parts of a résumé and follows a spatial order, going from the top to the bottom of the page.

General purpose: To inform.

Specific purpose: To define the essential parts of a résumé.

Thesis: There are four major parts to a résumé. (What are the four major parts of a résumé?)

I. Identify your career goals.
II. Identify your educational background.
III. Identify your work experience.
IV. Identify your special competencies.

In this second example, the speaker selects three major types of lying for discussion and arranges these in a topical pattern.

General purpose: To inform.

Specific purpose: To define lying by explaining the major types of lying.

Thesis: There are three major kinds of lying. (What are the three major kinds of lying?)

I. Concealment is the process of hiding the truth.
II. Falsification is the process of presenting false information as if it were true.
III. Misdirection is the process of acknowledging a feeling but misidentifying its cause.

the•o•ry *noun* statement of explanation, formulation of relationships, reasoned generalization

UNDERSTANDING THEORY AND RESEARCH
Signal-to-Noise Ratio

A useful way of looking at information is in terms of its **signal-to-noise ratio**. *Signal* in this context refers to information that is useful to you, information that you want. *Noise,* on the other hand, is what you find useless; it's what you do not want. So, for example, if a mailing list or newsgroup contained lots of useful information, it would be high on signal and low on noise; if it contained lots of useless information, it would be high on noise and low on signal. Spam is high on noise and low on signal, as is static that interferes with radio, television, or telephone transmission.

From the public speaker's point of view, noise is anything that diverts audience attention away from the speech (the signal)—pictures on the walls, writing on the whiteboard, people talking in the hallway, the rustle of newspapers, and so on. The speaker's task is to keep the audience's focus on the speech instead of the noise.

Working with Theories and Research

Look around the classroom in which you give your speeches. What sources of potential noise can you identify? What can you do to prevent the audience from focusing on the noise instead of your speech?

In delivering such a speech, a speaker might begin the speech by saying:

> A lie is a lie is a lie. True? Well, not exactly. Actually, there are a number of different ways we can lie. We can lie by concealing the truth. We can lie by falsification: by presenting false information as if it were true. And we can lie by misdirection: by acknowledging a feeling but misidentifying its cause.
>
> Let's look at the first type of lie—the lie of concealment. Most lies are lies of concealment. Most of the time when we lie we simply conceal the truth. We don't actually make any false statements. Rather we simply don't reveal the truth. Let me give you some examples I overheard recently.

17.4 SPEECHES OF DEMONSTRATION

Whether in using demonstration within a speech or in giving a speech devoted entirely to demonstration, you show the audience how to do something or how something operates. Here are some examples of topics of **speeches of demonstration**.

Watch at MyCommunicationLab **Video:** "How to Unlock Your Car if You Lock Your Keys Inside"

Demonstrating How to Do Something

- How to use Google Drive to share files and photos.
- How to drive defensively
- How to burglarproof your house
- How to give mouth-to-mouth resuscitation

Demonstrating How Something Operates

- How the body maintains homeostasis
- How an MRI works
- How LinkedIn connects people
- How a hurricane develops

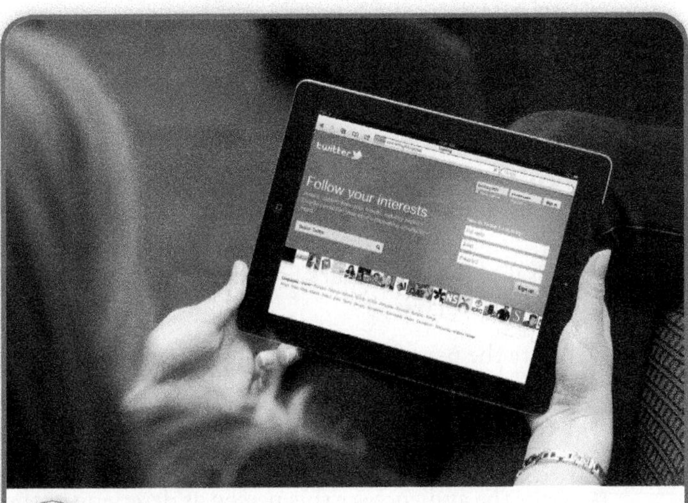

COMMUNICATION CHOICE POINT

DEMONSTRATING *Anne wants to demonstrate to her audience how Twitter works. Her audience is probably mixed in terms of members' knowledge of Twitter. She wants to make sure that all audience members will pay attention, and she'd like to accomplish that right at the start of her speech.* **What are some of Anne's options for convincing audience members that what she has to say will prove relevant regardless of their level of expertise?**

SPECIAL OCCASION SPEECHES

[Largely Informative]

In addition to the speeches of description, definition, and demonstration, there are what are called special occasion speeches. These are speeches that are dominated by the context and occasion for the speech. Here are a few such speeches that are largely (though not exclusively) informative.

THE SPEECH OF INTRODUCTION

The **speech of introduction** is usually designed to introduce a speaker or a topic area that a series of speakers will address. For example, before a speaker addresses an audience, another speaker often sets the stage by introducing both the speaker and the topic. At conventions, where a series of speakers address an audience, a speech of introduction might introduce the general topic on which the speakers will focus.

The speech of introduction is basically informative and follows the general patterns already discussed for the informative speech. The main difference is that instead of discussing a topic's issues, you discuss who the speaker is and what the speaker will talk about. In your speeches of introduction, follow these general principles:

- Establish the significance of the speech.
- Establish relevant connections among the speaker, the topic, and the audience.
- Stress the speaker's credibility (see Chapter 18).
- Speak in a style and manner that is consistent with the main speech.
- Be brief (relative to the length of the main speech).
- Don't cover the substance of the topic the speaker will discuss.

THE EULOGY

The **eulogy**, a speech of tribute to praise someone who has died, puts a person's life and contributions in a positive light. This type of speech is often given at a funeral or at the anniversary of the person's birth or death. This is not the time for a balanced appraisal of the individual's life. Rather, it's a time for praise. In developing the eulogy, consider the following:

- Relate the person whose life you're celebrating to yourself and to those in the audience.
- Be specific; show that you really knew the person or know a great deal about the person.
- Make the audience see this person as deserving of the praise you're bestowing.
- Show audience members what they can learn from this individual.

THE SPEECH OF PRESENTATION OR ACCEPTANCE

In a **presentation speech** you seek to (1) place an award or honor in some kind of context and (2) give the award an extra air of dignity or status. A speech of presentation may focus on rewarding a colleague for an important accomplishment (being named Teacher of the Year) or on recognizing a particularly impressive performance (winning an Academy Award). It may honor an employee's service to a company or a student's outstanding grades or athletic abilities.

The **acceptance speech** is the other side of this honoring ceremony. Here the recipient accepts the award and attempts to place the award in some kind of context.

In your speeches of presentation, follow these three principles:

- State the reason for the presentation. Make clear why this particular award is being given to this particular person.
- State the importance of the award.
- Be brief.

In preparing and presenting your speech of acceptance:

- Thank the people responsible for giving you the award.
- Acknowledge those who helped you achieve the award.
- Put the award into personal perspective.

THE TOAST

The **toast** is a brief speech designed to celebrate a person or an occasion. You might, for example, toast the next CEO of your company, a friend who just got admitted to a prestigious graduate program, or a colleague on the occasion of a promotion. Often toasts are given at weddings or at the start of a new venture. The toast is designed to say hello or good luck in a relatively formal sense. In developing your toast consider the following:

- Be brief; realize that people want to get on with the festivities.
- Focus attention on the person or persons you're toasting, not on yourself.
- Avoid inside jokes that only you and the person you're toasting understand.
- When you raise your glass in the toast—an almost obligatory part of toasting—make audience members realize that they should drink and that your speech is at an end.

MyCommunicationLab ***Visit mycommunicationlab.com to see additional examples of excellent special occasion speeches.***

Thesis and Main Points

The thesis for a speech of demonstration identifies what you will show the audience how to do or how something operates; for example:

- E-mail works through a series of electronic connections from one computer to a server to another computer.
- You can burglarproof your house in three different ways.
- Three guidelines will help you get that raise.

You can derive the main points for your speech of demonstration by asking a simple how or what question of your thesis, for example:

- How do these electronic connections work?
- What are the methods you can use to burglarproof your house?
- What are the guidelines for asking for a raise?

Support

Support each of your main ideas with a variety of materials. For example, you might show diagrams of houses that use different burglarproofing methods, demonstrate how various locks work, or show how different security systems work.

Presentation aids are especially helpful in speeches of demonstration. A good example of this is the signs in restaurants demonstrating the Heimlich maneuver. These signs demonstrate the sequence of steps with pictures as well as words. The combination of verbal and graphic information makes it easy for restaurant-goers to understand this important process. In a speech on this topic, however, it would be best to use only the pictures so that the written words would not distract your audience from your oral explanation.

Organization

In most cases a temporal pattern will work best in speeches of demonstration. Demonstrate each step in the sequence in which it's to be performed. In this way you'll avoid one of the major difficulties in demonstrating a process—backtracking. Don't skip steps even if you think they're familiar to the audience. They may not be. Connect each step to the next with appropriate transitions. For example, in explaining the Heimlich maneuver, you might say:

> **Now that you have your arms around the choking victim's chest, your next step is to...**

Assist your listeners by labeling the steps clearly; for example, "the first step," "the second step," and so on.

Begin with an overview. It's often helpful when demonstrating to give a broad general picture and then present each step in turn. For example, suppose you were talking about how to prepare a wall for painting. You might begin with a general overview to give your listeners a general idea of the process, saying something like this:

> **In preparing the wall for painting, you want to make sure that the wall is smoothly sanded, free of dust, and dry. Sanding a wall isn't like sanding a block of wood. So let's look at the proper way to sand a wall.**

Following are two examples of the speech of demonstration. In this first example, the speaker explains the proper way to paint a wall by rag rolling. As you can see, the speaker uses a temporal organizational pattern and covers three stages in the order in which they would be performed.

General purpose: To inform.
Specific purpose: To demonstrate how to rag roll.
Thesis: Rag rolling is performed in three steps. (What are the three steps of rag rolling?)

I. Apply the base coat of paint.
II. Apply the glaze coat.
III. Roll a rag through the wet glaze.

In the next example, the speaker identifies and demonstrates how to listen actively.

General purpose: To inform.
Specific purpose: To demonstrate three techniques of active listening.
Thesis: We can engage in active listening. (How can we engage in active listening?)

I. Paraphrase the speaker's meaning.
II. Express understanding of the speaker's feelings.
III. Ask questions.

In delivering the speech, the speaker might begin by saying:

> **Active listening is a special kind of listening. It's listening with total involvement, with a concern for the speaker. It's probably the most important type of listening you can engage in. Active listening consists of three steps: paraphrasing the speaker's meaning, expressing understanding of the speaker's feelings, and asking questions.**
>
> **Your first step in active listening is to paraphrase the speaker's meaning. What is a paraphrase? A paraphrase is a restatement in your own words of the speaker's meaning. That is, you express in your own words what you think the speaker meant. For example, let's say that the speaker said...**

Analyzing Video Choices

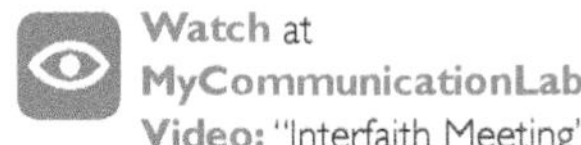

Watch at MyCommunicationLab Video: "Interfaith Meeting"

Chigoze is a Nigerian student at an American university. He is one of the few Africans and Muslims on campus. A friend of his who is active in the school's Interfaith Club has asked him to come to its next meeting and talk a little bit about his culture. "Interfaith Meeting" focuses on the principles for communicating information and the choices you have available for most effectively communicating information to an audience and illustrates how an effective information speech is constructed and delivered. Log on to www.mycommunicationlab.com to view this video and the choices, and then answer the related discussion questions.

Study and **Review** at **MyCommunicationLab**

SUMMARY: THE INFORMATIVE SPEECH

Listen to the **Chapter Summary** at **MyCommunicationLab**

This chapter focused on the informative speech, examining the principles of informative speaking and the various types of informative speeches.

17.1 PRINCIPLES OF INFORMATIVE SPEAKING

1. Informative speeches are more likely to be effective when they adhere to the following principles of informative speaking:
   - Focus on your audience.
   - Stress relevance and usefulness.
   - Limit the information you communicate.
   - Adjust the level of complexity.
   - Relate new information to old.
   - Vary the levels of abstraction.
   - Make your speech easy to remember.

17.2 SPEECHES OF DESCRIPTION

2. Speeches of description describe a process or procedure, an event, an object, or a person.

17.3 SPEECHES OF DEFINITION

3. Speeches of definition define a term, system, or theory or explain similarities and/or differences among terms.

17.4 SPEECHES OF DEMONSTRATION

4. Speeches of demonstration show how to do something or how something operates.

Study and **Review** the **Flashcards** at **MyCommunicationLab**

KEY TERMS

acceptance speech *377*
eulogy *376*
information *367*
levels of abstraction *368*
presentation speech *377*
signal-to-noise ratio *375*
speeches of definition *373*
speeches of demonstration *375*
speeches of description *370*
speech of introduction *376*
toast *377*

WORKING WITH THE INFORMATIVE SPEECH

17.1 Climbing the Abstraction Ladder. Words exist at different levels of abstraction. As you get more specific, you more clearly communicate your own meanings and more easily direct the listeners' attention to what you wish. For each of the terms listed on page 380, indicate at least four possible terms that indicate increasing specificity. The first example is provided as an illustration.

Level 1	Level 2	Level 3	Level 4	Level 5
	more specific than 1	more specific than 2	more specific than 3	more specific than 4
Building	*Masonry building*	*Masonry office building*	*Office skyscraper*	*New York's Empire State Building*
Transportation	______	______	______	______
Communication	______	______	______	______
Toy	______	______	______	______
Sport	______	______	______	______

17.2 Preparing an Informative Speech. Working repeatedly with the process of preparing a speech will ultimately make the process easier, more efficient, and more effective. Select a topic suitable for an informative speech and develop a preparation outline by doing the following.

- Formulate a thesis and a specific purpose suitable for an informative speech of approximately 10 minutes.
- Analyze members of this class as your potential audience and identify ways that you can relate this topic to their interests and needs.
- Generate at least two main points from your thesis.
- Support these main points with examples, illustrations, definitions, testimony, and so on.
- Construct a conclusion that summarizes your main ideas and brings the speech to a definite close.
- Construct an introduction that gains attention and orients your audience.

Discuss these outlines in small groups or with the class as a whole. Try to secure feedback from other members on how you can improve these outlines.

17.3 Communicating Unknown Concepts. You want to give an informative speech on virtual reality simulation, but most of your audience members have never experienced it. How would you communicate this concept and this experience to your audience?

17.4 Informative Strategies. You're planning to give an informative speech on the history of doctor-assisted suicide and are considering the strategies that you might use. What organizational pattern would be appropriate? What types of presentation aids might you use? How would you define "doctor-assisted suicide"? How would you introduce your speech?

17.5 Same-Topic Speech. You're scheduled to be the third speaker in a series of six presentations today. Unfortunately, the first speaker presented a really excellent speech on the same topic you're speaking on—how the Internet works. What should you do?

17.6 Definitions. Take a look at the ways in which textbooks define terms. Examine one of your textbooks—this one if you want—and identify the kinds of definitions used. Which types do you find particularly helpful? Do you find some definitions that are unnecessary?

17.7 The 2-Minute Speech. Prepare and deliver a 2-minute informative speech in which you do one of the following:

- Explain a card game: Explain the way a card game such as solitaire, poker, gin rummy, bridge, canasta, or pinochle is played.
- Explain a board game: Explain the way a board game such as chess, backgammon, Chinese checkers, Go, Othello, Scrabble, Yahtzee, or Monopoly is played.
- Explain food preparation: Explain how to make a pie, a soup, a western omelet, a pizza, roast beef, a dip, or a casserole (any kind you'd like).
- Explain a sport: Explain the way a sport such as football, baseball, basketball, hockey, soccer, tennis, or golf is played.

LogOn! MyCommunicationLab www.mycommunicationlab.com

Throughout this chapter, there are icons that highlight media content for selected topics. Go to **MyCommunicationLab** for additional materials on the general goals of informative speaking, the principles for communicating information, and the varied types of informative speeches and how you can develop these most effectively. Here you'll find flashcards to help you learn key communication terms, videos that illustrate a variety of concepts, additional exercises, and discussions to help you continue your study of the informative speech.

18 THE PERSUASIVE SPEECH

CHAPTER TOPICS	CHAPTER OBJECTIVES
In this chapter you'll explore the following major topics:	**After reading this chapter you should be able to:**
GOALS OF PERSUASIVE SPEAKING	18.1 Paraphrase the goals of persuasive speaking.
THE THREE PERSUASIVE PROOFS	18.2 Define and distinguish among logical, emotional, and credibility appeals.
PRINCIPLES OF PERSUASIVE SPEAKING	18.3 Paraphrase the principles of persuasive speaking.
PERSUASIVE SPEECHES ON QUESTIONS OF FACT	18.4 Define the speech on questions of fact and construct and present speeches on questions of fact.
PERSUASIVE SPEECHES ON QUESTIONS OF VALUE	18.5 Define the speech on questions of value and construct and present speeches on questions of value.
PERSUASIVE SPEECHES ON QUESTIONS OF POLICY	18.6 Define the speech on questions of policy and construct and present speeches on questions of policy.

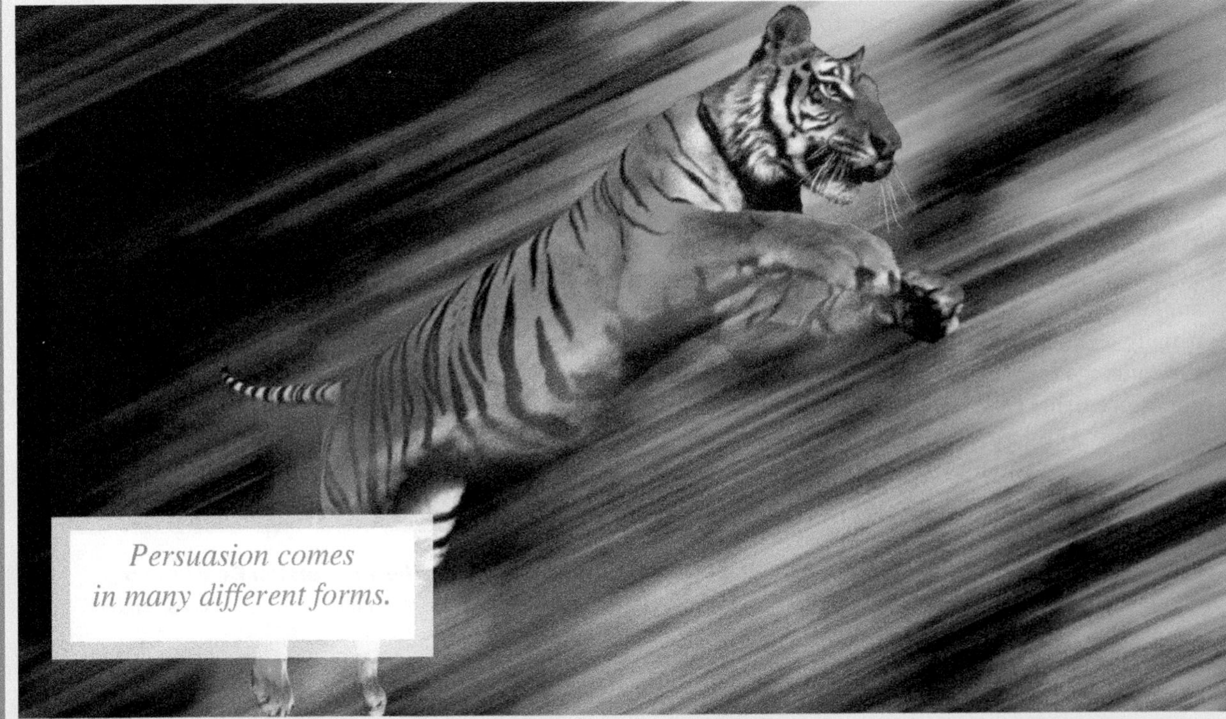

Persuasion comes in many different forms.

The previous chapter focused on informative speaking; it examined the goals of such speaking, essential principles for communicating information, and the varied types of informative speeches. This chapter looks at persuasive speaking and considers the goals of persuasive speaking, the three major proofs, the essential principles of persuasion, and the varied types of persuasive speeches you might give.

18.1 GOALS OF PERSUASIVE SPEAKING

Generally, the word **persuasion** refers to the process of influencing another person's attitudes, beliefs, values, and/or behaviors. Briefly, an *attitude* is a tendency to behave in a certain way. For example, if you have a positive attitude toward science fiction, then you're likely to watch science fiction movies or read science fiction books; if you have a negative attitude, you'll be likely to avoid such movies and books. A *belief* is a conviction in the existence or reality of something or in the truth of some assertion. For example, some believe that God exists, that democracy is the best form of government, or that soft drugs lead to hard drugs. A *value* is an indicator of what you feel is good or bad, ethical or unethical, just or unjust. Many people in your audience will positively value "college education" or "free speech" and negatively value "discrimination" or "war." In the context of persuasion, the word *behavior* refers to overt, observable actions such as voting for a particular person, contributing money to the Red Cross, or buying a hybrid automobile.

Your persuasive speeches may focus on influencing listeners' attitudes, beliefs, values, and/or behaviors. You may want to accomplish any one of the following three general goals of persuasive speaking.

Explore at MyCommunicationLab Activity: "Persuasion"

- **To strengthen or weaken attitudes, beliefs, or values.** Persuasion often aims to strengthen audience views. For example, religious sermons usually seek to strengthen the existing beliefs of the congregation. Similarly, many public service announcements try to strengthen existing beliefs about, say, recycling, smoking, or safe sex. At times, however, you may want to weaken the existing beliefs of audience members—to suggest that what they currently believe may not be entirely true. For example, you might want to weaken the favorable attitudes people might have toward a particular political party or policy.
- **To change attitudes, beliefs, or values.** Sometimes you'll want to change how audience members feel. You might want to change their attitudes regarding the college's no-smoking rules, to change their beliefs about television's influence on viewer violence, or to change their values about the efficacy of war.
- **To motivate to action.** Most often your goal is to get people to do something—for example, to vote for one person rather than another, to donate money to a fund for the homeless, or to take a course in personal finance.

It's useful to view the effects of persuasion as a continuum ranging from one extreme to another. Let's say, to take one issue currently in the news, that you want to give a persuasive speech on same-sex marriage. You might visualize your audience as existing on a continuum ranging from strongly in favor to strongly opposed, as shown in Figure 18.1. Your task is to move your audience in the direction of your persuasive purpose, which you can do in any of three ways (corresponding to the goals of persuasion identified above). You can design your persuasive speech to attempt to:

- Strengthen or weaken your listeners' attitudes, beliefs, or values about same-sex marriage.
- Change your listeners' attitudes, beliefs, or values about same-sex marriage.
- Move your listeners to act—to protest, write letters, or sign a petition.

If your purpose is to persuade the audience to *oppose* same-sex marriage, then in Figure 18.1 any movement toward the right will be successful persuasion; if your purpose is to persuade listeners to *support* same-sex marriage, then any movement toward the left will be successful persuasion. Notice, however, that it's quite possible to give a speech in which you hope to move your listeners in one direction but actually move them in the other direction. This "negative persuasion" effect can occur, for example, if the audience members perceive you as dishonest or self-promoting or if they feel you presented biased evidence or faulty reasoning.

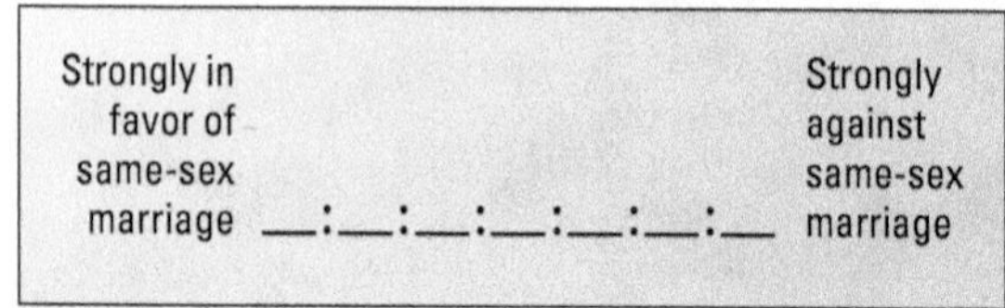

FIGURE 18.1 **The Persuasion Continuum**
Any movement along the continuum would be considered persuasion.

18.2 THE THREE PERSUASIVE PROOFS

As mentioned in the first chapter, classical rhetoric (as well as contemporary research) identifies three kinds of persuasive proofs: logical (or *logos*), emotional (or *pathos*), and credibility (or *ethos*).

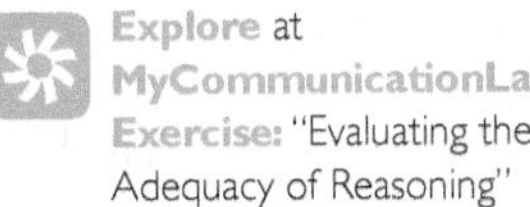

Explore at MyCommunicationLab Exercise: "Evaluating the Adequacy of Reasoning"

Logical Proof

When a speaker persuades listeners with **logical arguments**—focusing on facts and evidence rather than on emotions or credibility claims—the listeners are more likely to remain persuaded over time and are more likely to resist counterarguments that may come up in the future (Petty & Wegener, 1998). We'll look at the three main categories of logical appeals, then at some fallacies of reasoning.

Reasoning from Specific Instances and Generalizations

In **reasoning from specific instances** (or examples), you examine several specific instances and then conclude something about the whole. This form of reasoning, known as *induction,* is useful when you want to develop a general principle or conclusion but cannot examine the whole. For example, you sample a few communication courses and conclude something about communication courses in general; you visit several Scandinavian cities and conclude something about the whole of Scandinavia. Critically analyze reasoning from specific instances (your own or those of speakers you're listening to) by asking the following questions.

Watch at MyCommunicationLab Video: "Interstate Commerce Commission"

- **Were enough specific instances examined?** Two general guidelines will help you determine how much is enough. First, the larger the group you wish to cover with your conclusion, the greater the number of specific instances you should examine. If you wish to draw conclusions about members of an entire country or culture, you'll have to examine a considerable number of people before drawing even tentative conclusions. On the other hand, if you're attempting to draw a conclusion about a bushel of 100 apples, sampling a few is probably sufficient. Second, the greater the diversity of items in the class, the more specific instances you will have to examine. Some classes or groups of items are relatively homogeneous, whereas others are more heterogeneous; this will influence how many specific instances constitute a sufficient number. Pieces of spaghetti in boiling water are all about the same; thus, sampling one usually tells you something about all the others. On the other hand, communication courses are probably very different from one another, so valid conclusions about the entire range of communication courses will require a much larger sample.
- **Are there significant exceptions?** When you examine specific instances and attempt to draw

the•o•ry *noun* statement of explanation, formulation of relationships, reasoned generalization

UNDERSTANDING THEORY AND RESEARCH
Balance Theories

An especially interesting group of theories of persuasion go under the general term *balance theories.* The general assumption of balance theories is that people strive to maintain consistency between their beliefs and their behaviors. For example, if you believe that people should exercise regularly (because you believe it's the healthy thing to do) but you don't exercise (because you feel exercise is difficult and boring), then you'll be in a state of imbalance or dissonance. According to balance theory, you will then strive either to change your beliefs about exercise (to make them consistent with your behavior) or to change your behavior (to make it consistent with your beliefs).

Applied to persuasion, balance theories claim that people look for information that will maintain or restore balance or consonance. For example, if you as a speaker demonstrate that you offer an easy and enjoyable (not difficult and boring) exercise plan, you stand a good chance of influencing audience members—because they are looking for the very means to restore balance that you are now providing. Conversely, of course, you might assert that exercise is unhealthy; the belief that exercise is unhealthy would be consistent with their no-exercise behavior and also would restore balance.

Working with Theories and Research

How might you use the insights of balance theories in preparing a speech on why the audience should start investing, give up junk food, or quit smoking?

a conclusion about the whole, take into consideration the exceptions. Thus, if you examine the GPA of computer science majors and discover that 70 percent have GPAs above 3.5, you may be tempted to draw the conclusion that computer science majors are especially bright. But what about the 30 percent who have lower GPAs? How much lower are these scores? This may be a significant exception that must be taken into account when you draw your conclusion and would require you to qualify your conclusion in significant ways. Exactly what kind of or how many exceptions will constitute "significant exceptions" will depend on the unique situation.

Reasoning from Causes and Effects

In **reasoning from causes and effects,** you may go in either of two directions. You may reason from cause to effect (from observed cause to unobserved effect) or from effect to cause (from observed effect to unobserved cause). In testing your own reasoning from cause to effect or from effect to cause and in evaluating the causal reasoning of others, ask yourself the following questions.

- **Might other causes be producing the observed effect?** If you observe a particular effect (say, high crime or student apathy), you need to ask if causes other than the one you're postulating might be producing these effects. Thus, you might postulate that poverty leads to high crime, but there might be other factors actually causing the high crime rate. Or poverty might be one cause but not the most important cause. Therefore, explore the possibility of other causes producing the observed effects.
- **Is the causation in the direction postulated?** If two things occur together, it's often difficult to determine which is the cause and which is the effect. For example, a lack of interpersonal intimacy and a lack of self-confidence often occur in the same person. The person who lacks self-confidence seldom has intimate relationships with others. But which is the cause and which is the effect? It might be that the lack of intimacy "causes" low self-confidence; it might also be, however, that low self-confidence "causes" a lack of intimacy. Of course, it might also be that some other previously unexamined cause (a history of negative criticism, for example) might be producing both the lack of intimacy and the low self-confidence.

Reasoning from Sign

Reasoning from sign involves drawing a conclusion on the basis of the presence of clues or symptoms that frequently occur together. Medical diagnosis is a good example of reasoning by sign. The general procedure is simple. If a sign and an object, event, or condition are frequently paired, the presence of the sign is taken as proof of the presence of the object, event, or condition. For example, fatigue, extreme thirst, and overeating serve as signs of hyperthyroidism because they frequently accompany the condition. In using reasoning from sign and in evaluating the reasoning by sign of others, ask yourself the following questions.

- **Do the signs necessitate the conclusion drawn?** Given extreme thirst, overeating, and the like, how certain are you of the "hyperthyroid" conclusion? With most medical and legal matters we can never be absolutely certain, but we can be certain beyond a reasonable doubt.
- **Are there other signs that point to the same conclusion?** In the thyroid example, extreme thirst could be brought on by any number of factors. Similarly, the fatigue and the overeating could be attributed to other causes. Yet taken together, the three signs seem to point to only one reasonable diagnosis. Generally, the more signs that point toward the conclusion, the more confidence you can have that it's valid.
- **Are there contradictory signs?** Are there signs pointing toward contradictory conclusions? For example, if the butler had a motive and a history of violence (signs supporting the conclusion that the butler was the murderer) but also had an alibi (a sign pointing to the conclusion of innocence), then the conclusion of guilt would have to be reconsidered or discarded.

Listening to Logical Arguments and the Fallacies of Reasoning

When listening to logical or seemingly logical arguments, in addition to asking yourself the questions suggested for the various types of reasoning, also listen for what are called the *fallacies of reasoning:* arguments that appear to address issues but really don't. Here are 10 such fallacies (Herrick, 2004; Lee & Lee, 1972, 1995; Pratkanis & Aronson, 1991). Learn to spot fallacies in the speeches of others and be sure to avoid them in your own speeches.

- **Anecdotal evidence.** Often you'll hear people use **anecdotal evidence** to "prove" a point: "Women are like that; I know because I have three sisters." "That's the way Japanese managers are; I've seen plenty of them." One reason this type of "evidence" is inadequate is that it relies on too few observations. A second reason anecdotal evidence is inadequate is that one person's observations may be unduly clouded by his or her

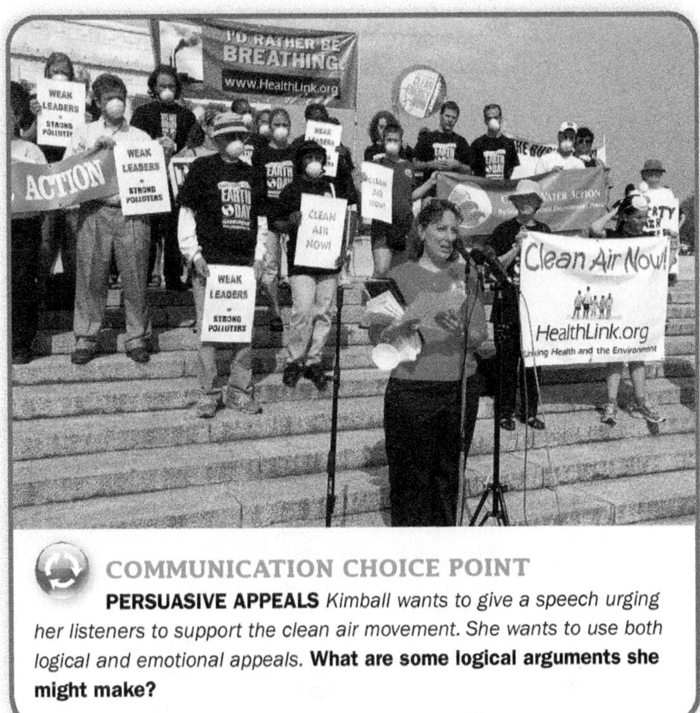

COMMUNICATION CHOICE POINT

PERSUASIVE APPEALS *Kimball wants to give a speech urging her listeners to support the clean air movement. She wants to use both logical and emotional appeals.* **What are some logical arguments she might make?**

own attitudes and beliefs; your personal attitudes toward women or Japanese-style management, for example, may influence your perception of their behaviors.

- **Straw man.** A **straw man** argument (like a man made of straw) is a contention that's easy to knock down. In this fallacy a speaker creates an easy-to-destroy simplification of an opposing position (that is, a straw man) and then proceeds to smash it. But, of course, if the opposing case were presented fairly and without bias, it wouldn't be so easy to demolish.
- **Appeal to tradition.** Often used as an argument against change by those who do not want change, the **appeal to tradition** claims that some proposed innovation is wrong or should not be adopted because it was never done before. But, of course, the fact that something has not been done before says nothing about its value or whether it should be done now.
- **Bandwagon.** In the **bandwagon** fallacy, often referred to as an argument *ad populum* (to the people), the speaker tries to persuade the audience to accept or reject an idea or proposal because "everybody's doing it" or because the "right" people are doing it. This is a popular technique in political elections; campaigns trumpet the results of polls in an effort to get undecided voters to jump on the bandwagon of the leading candidate. After all, you don't want to vote for a loser. When this technique is used ethically—when it's true—it's referred to a social proof (discussed later in this chapter, page 394).
- **Testimonial.** The **testimonial** technique involves using the image associated with some person to secure your approval (if you respect the person) or your rejection (if you don't respect the person). This is the technique of advertisers who use actors dressed up to look like doctors or plumbers or chefs to sell their products. Sometimes this technique takes the form of using only vague and general "authorities," as in "experts agree," "scientists say," "good cooks know," or "dentists advise."
- **Thin entering wedge.** In using the **thin entering wedge**, a speaker argues against a proposal or new development on the grounds that it will be a "thin entering wedge" that will open the floodgates to all sorts of catastrophes (Chase, 1956). Though often based on no evidence, this argument has been used throughout history to oppose change. Some examples are "wedge" claims that school integration and interracial marriage will bring the collapse of American education and society, same-sex unions will destroy the family, and banning smoking in public places will lead to the collapse of the restaurant industry.

Emotional Proof

Emotional appeals (or motivational appeals) are appeals to your listeners' feelings, needs, desires, and wants and can be powerful means of persuasion (Wood, 2000). Specifically, when you use emotional appeals, you appeal to those forces that energize, move, or motivate people to develop, change, or strengthen their attitudes or ways of behaving. For example, one motive might be the desire for status. This desire might motivate someone to enter a high-status occupation or to dress a certain way.

Developed in the late 1960s, one of the most useful analyses of human motives remains Abraham Maslow's fivefold **hierarchy of needs**, reproduced in Figure 18.2 on page 386 (Benson & Dundis, 2003; Maslow, 1970). One of the assumptions contained in this theory is that people seek to fulfill the needs at the lowest level first. When those needs are satisfied, the needs at the next level begin to influence behavior. For example, people would not concern themselves with the need for security or freedom from fear if they were starving (if their need for food had not been fulfilled). Similarly, they would not be concerned with friendship if their need for protection and security had not been fulfilled. The implication for you as a speaker is that you have to know what

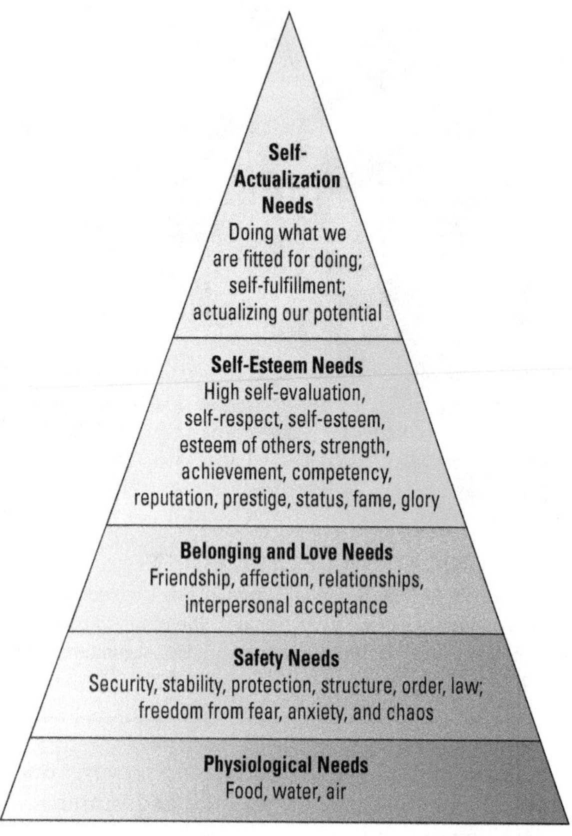

FIGURE 18.2 **Maslow's "Hierarchy of Needs"**

Abraham Maslow's model of lower-order and higher-order needs has long influenced theories of persuasion. As you read about these needs, consider which would work best with your specific class members. Are there some that would not work, at least generally?

Source: Adapted from A. Maslow. *Motivation and Personality,* 3rd ed. Copyright © 1954 by HarperCollins.

needs of your audience are unsatisfied. These are the needs you can appeal to most effectively in motivating audience members.

Here are several useful motivational appeals organized around Maslow's hierarchy. As you review these, try to visualize how you would use each one in your next speech.

Physiological Needs

In many parts of the world and even in parts of the United States, the basic physiological needs of people are not fully met and thus, as you can appreciate, are powerful motivating forces. In many of the poorest countries of the world, the speaker who promises to meet fundamental physiological needs is the one the people will follow. Most college students in the United States, however, have their physiological needs for food, water, and air well satisfied, so these issues will not prove helpful in motivating and persuading them.

Safety Needs

Those who do not have their basic safety and freedom-from-fear needs met will be motivated by appeals to security, protection, and freedom from physical harm and from psychological distress. You see appeals to this need in advertisements for burglar protection devices for home and car, in political speeches promising greater police protection on the streets and in schools, and in the speeches of motivational gurus who promise psychological safety and freedom from anxiety. Many people fear what is unknown, and order and structure seem to make things predictable and therefore safe.

Belonging and Love Needs

Belonging and love needs are extremely powerful; most people are motivated to love and be loved. If you can teach your audience how to be loved and how to love, your audience will be not only attentive but also grateful. We also want affiliation—friendship and companionship. We want to be a part of a group, despite our equally potent desire for independence and individuality. Notice how advertisements for singles clubs, cruises, and dating services appeal to this need for affiliation. On this basis alone they successfully gain the attention, interest, and participation of thousands.

Self-Esteem Needs

We have a need for positive **self-esteem:** a favorable self-image, a view of ourselves that casts us in the best possible light. We want to see ourselves as self-confident, worthy, and contributing human beings. Inspirational speeches, speeches of the "you're the greatest" type, never seem to lack receptive and suggestible audiences. People want to achieve in whatever they do. In using the achievement motive, be explicit in stating how your speech, ideas, and recommendations will contribute to the listeners' achievements. At the same time, recognize that different cultures will view achievement very differently. To some achievement may mean financial success, to others it may mean group popularity, to still others it may mean security. Show your listeners how what you have to say will help them achieve the goals they seek, and you'll likely have an active and receptive audience.

Self-Actualization Needs

At the top of Maslow's hierarchy is the self-actualization motive. According to Maslow (1970), this motive influences attitudes and behaviors only after all other needs are satisfied. Regardless of how satisfied or unsatisfied your other desires may be, you have a desire to self-actualize—to become what you

eth•ics *noun* morality, standards of conduct, moral judgment

MAKING ETHICAL CHOICES
The Ethics of Emotional Appeals

Emotional appeals are all around. Persons who want to restrict the media's portrayal of violence may appeal to your fear of increased violence in your community; the real estate broker may appeal to your desire for status; the friend who wants a favor may appeal to your desire for social approval; the salesperson may appeal to your desire for sexual rewards. But are such appeals ethical?

Most communication theorists would argue that emotional appeals are ethical when, for example, they are used in combination with logical appeals, used in moderation, and directed at our better selves. Emotional appeals are considered unethical when, for example, they're used instead of logical evidence, directed at our baser selves, or aimed at children. In actual practice, however, it's often difficult to distinguish between the ethical and unethical use of emotional appeals.

Ethical Choice Point

You want to dissuade your teenaged sons and daughters from engaging in sexual relationships. Would it be ethical to use emotional appeals to scare them so that they'll avoid sexual relationships? Would it be ethical to use the same appeals to get them to avoid associating with teens of other races? What ethical obligations do you have in using emotional appeals in these situations? What would you do?

feel you're fit for. If you see yourself as a poet, you must write poetry. If you see yourself as a teacher, you must teach. Appeals to self-actualization needs—to the yearning "to be the best you can be"—encourage listeners to strive for their highest ideals and are often welcomed by the audience.

Listening to Emotional Appeals

Emotional appeals are all around you, urging you to do all sorts of things—usually to buy a product or to support a position or cause. As you listen to these inevitable appeals, consider the following.

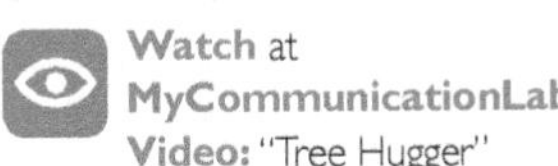
Watch at MyCommunicationLab Video: "Tree Hugger"

- **Emotional appeals do not constitute proof.** No matter how passionate the speaker's voice or bodily movement, no matter how compelling the language, passion does not prove the case a speaker is presenting.
- **Feelings are not open to public inspection.** You really can't tell with certainty what the speaker is feeling. The speaker may, in fact, be using facial management techniques or clever speechwriters to communicate emotions without actually feeling them.
- **Emotional appeals may be used to divert attention from the lack of real evidence.** If emotional appeals are being used to the exclusion of argument and evidence, or if you suspect that the speaker seeks to arouse your emotions so you forget that there's no evidence, ask yourself why.
- **Emotional appeals may be to high or low motives.** A speaker can arouse feelings of love and peace, but also feelings of hatred and war. In asking for charitable donations, an organization may appeal to high motives such as your desire to help those less fortunate than you or to lower motives such as guilt and fear.
- **Be especially on the lookout for the appeal to pity.** This is what logicians call *argumentum ad misericordiam,* as in "I really tried to do the work, but I've been having terrible depression and find it difficult to concentrate."

Credibility Proof

Your **credibility** is the degree to which your audience regards you as a believable spokesperson. If your listeners see you as competent and knowledgeable, of good character, and charismatic or dynamic, they will find you credible. As a result, you'll be more effective in changing their attitudes or in moving them to do something. Credibility is not something you have or don't have in any objective sense; rather, it's a function of what the audience thinks of you.

Explore at MyCommunicationLab Exercise: "Comparative Credibility Judgments"

You form an impression of a speaker as credible on the basis of two sources of information (Figure 18.3 on page 388). First, you assess the reputation of the speaker as you know it. This is initial—or what theorists call "extrinsic"—credibility. Second, you evaluate the degree to which that reputation is confirmed or refuted by what the speaker says and does during the speech. This is derived—or "intrinsic"—credibility. In

FIGURE 18.3 **Credibility Impressions**

The credibility impressions you form are a combination of the speaker's reputation and what the speaker does during the speech.

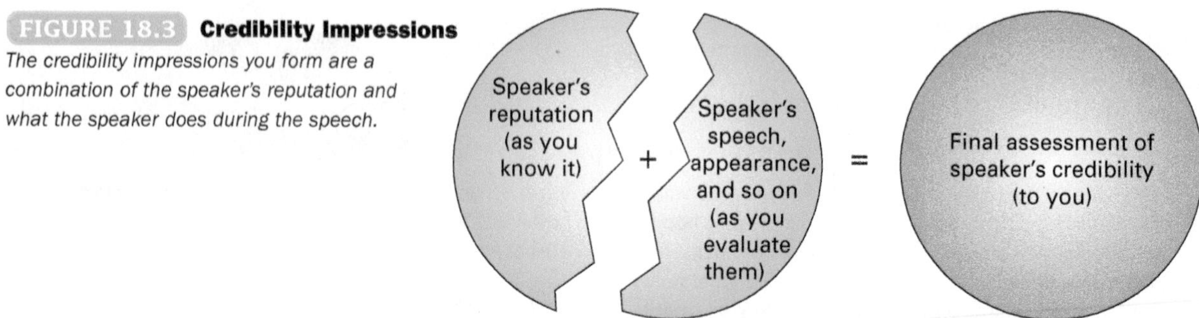

other words, you merge what you know about the speaker's reputation with the more immediate information you get from present interactions in order to form a combined final assessment of credibility.

What makes a speaker credible will vary from one culture to another. In some cultures people would see competence as the most important factor in, say, their choice of a teacher for their preschool children. In other cultures the most important factor might be the goodness or morality of the teacher or perhaps the reputation of the teacher's family.

At the same time, each culture may define each of the factors in credibility differently. For example, "character" may mean following the rules of a specific religion in some cultures and following the individual conscience in others. To take another example, the Quran, the Torah, and the New Testament will be ascribed very different levels of credibility depending on the religious beliefs of the audience. And this will be true even when all three religious books say essentially the same thing on a given point.

Before reading any more about the ways to establish your credibility, you may wish to respond to the following phrases, indicating how you think members of your class see you when you deliver a speech. Use the following scale: **5** = definitely true; **4** = probably true; **3** = neither true nor untrue; **2** = probably untrue; and **1** = definitely untrue.

The audience/class generally sees me as someone who is:

_____ **1.** knowledgeable
_____ **2.** a thorough researcher
_____ **3.** informed about the subject matter
_____ **4.** fair in the presentation of material (i.e., evidence and argument)
_____ **5.** concerned with the audience's needs
_____ **6.** honest; unlikely to bend the truth
_____ **7.** assertive in personal style
_____ **8.** enthusiastic about the topic and in general
_____ **9.** active rather than passive

These phrases focus on the three qualities of credibility—competence, character, and charisma—and is based on a large body of research (see McCroskey, 2006; Riggio, 1987). Items 1 to 3 refer to perceived competence: How capable do you seem to the audience? Items 4 to 6 refer to character: Does the audience see you as a good and moral person? Items 7 to 9 refer to charisma: Does the audience see you as dynamic and active? Total scores will range from a high of 45 to a low of 9. If you scored relatively high (around 32 or higher), then you feel your audience sees you as credible. If you scored relatively low (below 27), then you feel your audience sees you as lacking in credibility. As you read further about credibility consider how you might go about increasing your credibility. What specific steps can you take to change undesirable audience perceptions of your credibility? How might you strengthen the perception of your competence, character, and/or charisma?

Competence

Your perceived **competence** is the knowledge and expertise an audience thinks you have. The more knowledge and expertise the audience sees you as having, the more likely the audience will believe you. Similarly, you're likely to believe a teacher or doctor if you think he or she is knowledgeable on the subject at hand. You can demonstrate your competence to your audience in a variety of ways.

- **Tell listeners of your competence.** Let the audience know of any special experience or training that qualifies you to speak on this specific topic. If you're speaking on communal living and you've lived on a commune yourself, then say so in your speech. This recommendation to tell listeners of your competence generally applies to most audiences you'll encounter in the United States. But in some cultures—notably collectivist cultures such as those of Japan, China, and Korea, for example—to stress your own competence or that of your corporation may be taken as a suggestion that your audience members are inferior or that their corporations are not as good as yours. In other cultures—notably individualist cultures such as those of

Scandinavia, the United States, and western Europe, for example—if you don't stress your competence, your listeners may assume it's because you don't have any.

- **Cite a variety of research sources.** Make it clear to your audience that you've thoroughly researched your topic. Do this by mentioning some of the books you've read, the persons you've interviewed, the articles you've consulted. Weave these references throughout your speech. Don't bunch them together at one time.
- **Stress the competencies of your sources.** If your audience isn't aware of them, then emphasize the particular competencies of your sources. In this way it becomes clear to the audience that you've chosen your sources carefully so as to provide the most authoritative sources possible. For example, saying simply, "Senator Cardova thinks . . ." does nothing to establish the senator's credibility. Instead, consider saying something like "Senator Cardova, who headed the finance committee for three years and was formerly a professor of economics at MIT, thinks . . ."

Character

Audience members will see you as credible if they perceive you as being someone of high moral **character,** someone who is honest, and someone they can trust. When an audience perceives your intentions as good for them (rather than for your own personal gain), they'll think you credible and they'll believe you. You can establish your high moral character in a number of ways.

- **Stress fairness.** If delivering a persuasive speech, stress that you've examined both sides of the issue (if indeed you have). If you're presenting both sides, then make it clear that your presentation is accurate and fair. Be particularly careful not to omit any argument the audience may already have thought of—this is a sure sign that your presentation isn't fair or balanced.
- **Stress concern for audience.** Make it clear to audience members that you're interested in their welfare rather than seeking self-gain. Make it clear that the audience's interests are foremost in your mind. Tell audience members how the new legislation will reduce *their* taxes, how recycling will improve *their* community, how a knowledge of sexual harassment will make *their* workplace more comfortable and stress free.
- **Stress concern for enduring values.** We view speakers who are concerned with small and insignificant issues as less credible than speakers who demonstrate a concern for lasting truths and general principles. Thus, make it clear to audience members that your position—your thesis—is related to higher-order values; show them exactly how this is true.

Here, for example, Kofi Annan (2006), in giving his farewell speech as secretary general of the United Nations on September 19, 2006, stressed his concern for enduring values:

> **Yes, I remain convinced that the only answer to this divided world must be a truly United Nations. Climate change, HIV/AIDS, fair trade, migration, human rights—all these issues, and many more, bring us back to that point. Addressing each is indispensable for each of us in our village, in our neighborhood, and in our country. Yet each has acquired a global dimension that can only be reached by global action, agreed and coordinated through this most universal of institutions.**

Charisma

Charisma is a combination of your personality and dynamism as seen by the audience. Audience members will perceive you as credible (and believable) if they like you and if they see you as friendly and pleasant rather than aloof and reserved. They'll perceive you as less credible if they see you as shy, introverted, and soft-spoken rather than as an extroverted and forceful individual. As a speaker there's much that you can do to increase your charisma and hence your perceived credibility.

- **Demonstrate a positive outlook.** Show the audience that you have a positive orientation to the public speaking situation and to the entire speaker–audience encounter. We see positive and forward-looking people as more credible than negative and backward-looking people. Stress your pleasure at addressing the audience. Stress hope rather than despair; stress happiness rather than sadness.
- **Demonstrate enthusiasm.** The lethargic speaker, the speaker who somehow plods through the speech, is the very opposite of the charismatic speaker. Try viewing a film of Martin Luther King Jr. or Billy Graham speaking—they're totally absorbed with the speech and with the audience. They're excellent examples of the enthusiasm that makes a charismatic speaker.
- **Be emphatic.** Use language that's emphatic. Use gestures that are clear and decisive. Demonstrate a firm commitment to the position you're

advocating; the audience will be much more likely to agree with a speaker who believes firmly in the thesis of the speech.

Listening to Credibility Appeals and Character Attacks

When you listen to credibility appeals, evaluate them critically. Here are three questions you'll find helpful to ask in assessing credibility appeals.

- **Is the dimension of credibility used relevant to the issue at hand?** For example, are the politician's family members (nice though they may be) relevant to his or her position on gun control or social security or immigration? Is the politician's former military service (or the lack of it) relevant to the issue being discussed?
- **Are credibility appeals being used instead of argument and evidence?** In typical examples of invalid credibility appeals, speakers may emphasize their educational background (to establish "competence"), appear at religious rituals (to establish "moral character"), or endeavor to present themselves as take-charge, alpha-type individuals (to demonstrate "charisma"). When used to divert attention from the issues or to mask the absence of evidence, such appeals are meaningless.
- **Are the credibility appeals true?** The actor who advertises toothpaste dressed as a dentist is still an actor doing a modeling job, not a dentist. Too often people unconsciously attribute credibility to a performance because of a uniform. Even when the endorser is a real dentist, remember that this dentist is getting paid for the endorsement. Although this doesn't necessarily make the endorsement false, it does (or should) make you skeptical.

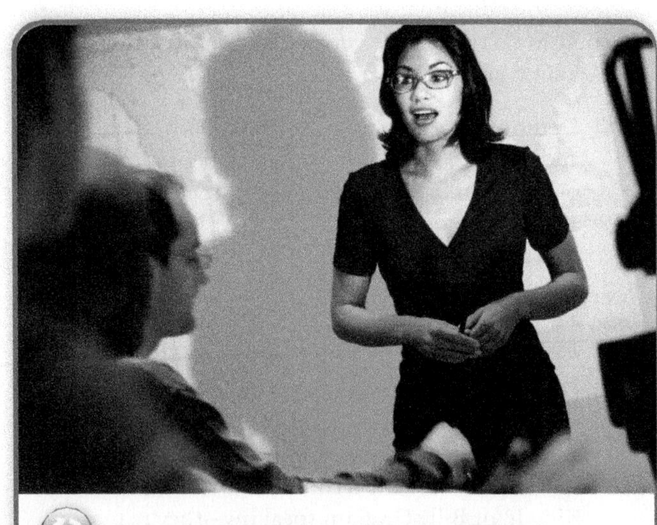

COMMUNICATION CHOICE POINT

INTRODUCING CREDIBILITY *Teresa has been assigned to compose a brief introduction (about 1 minute in length or about 150 words) about you that she will present before you speak.* **What are some of the things Teresa might say to establish your competence, character, and charisma?**

In addition to these general questions, become conscious of fallacious strategies that focus on attacking the person. Be alert for fallacies like the following in the speeches of others, and eliminate them from your own reasoning.

- **Personal interest. Personal interest** attacks may take either of two forms. In one form the speaker disqualifies someone from having a point of view because he or she isn't directly affected by an issue or proposal or doesn't have firsthand knowledge; for example, a speaker might dismiss an argument on abortion merely because it was made by a man. In another form the speaker disqualifies someone because he or she will benefit in some way from a proposal. For example, arguing that someone is rich, middle class, or poor and thus will benefit greatly from a proposed tax cut does not mean that the argument for the tax cut is invalid. The legitimacy of an argument can be judged only on the basis of the evidence and reasoning presented.
- **Character attacks.** Often referred to as *ad hominem* arguments, **character attacks** involve accusing another person (usually an opponent) of some wrongdoing or of some character flaw. The purpose is to discredit the person or to divert attention from the issue under discussion. Arguments such as "How can we support a candidate who has smoked pot [or avoided the military]?" or "Do you want to believe someone who has been unfaithful on more than one occasion?" are often heard in political discussions but probably have little to do with the logic of the argument.
- **Name-calling.** In **name-calling**, often referred to as "poisoning the well," the speaker gives an idea, a group of people, or a political philosophy a bad name ("bigoted," "soft on terrorism,") to try to get listeners to condemn an idea without analyzing the argument and evidence. The opposite of name-calling is the use of "**glittering generalities**," in which the speaker tries to make you accept some idea by associating it with things you value highly ("democracy," "free speech," "academic freedom"). By using these "virtue words," the speaker tries to get you to ignore the evidence and simply approve of the idea.

18.3 PRINCIPLES OF PERSUASIVE SPEAKING

To succeed in strengthening or changing attitudes or beliefs and in moving your listeners to action, follow these guidelines for persuasive speaking.

Motivate Your Listeners with Limited Choices

If you want to persuade your listeners, you have to motivate them to believe or to act in some way. One way to motivate, as explained in Chapter 15 (pages 325–326), is to use the motivated sequence—the organizational structure in which you gain your listeners' attention, demonstrate that a need exists, demonstrate how that need can be satisfied, show them what things will be like if the need is satisfied as you suggest, and urge them to do something to solve the problem.

In using this principle, it is more effective to offer listeners a limited number of choices for action. For example, if you want your listeners to participate more in community affairs, be specific and suggest a limited number of ways in which they can participate. If you suggest too many choices, your listeners are more likely to do nothing (Goldstein, Martin, & Cialdini, 2008; Iyengar, 2010; Schwartz, 2005).

Table 18.1 summarizes the motivated sequence as a persuasive strategy and will help you develop your speeches whether they deal with questions of fact, value, or policy—the topics to which we turn later in the chapter.

Focus on Your Audience

Just as the first principle of informative speaking was to focus on your audience, so it is with persuasion. Begin thinking about your persuasive strategies in terms of the audience's existing beliefs, attitudes, and values. The more you know about your audience, the more you'll be able to address their needs and tailor your persuasive appeals to them specifically. At this point you may want to review the discussion of audience analysis and adaptation presented in Chapter 14, pages 294–297.

Identify with Your Audience

A closely related principle is that of **identification**, a process of demonstrating a similarity with your audience. If you can show audience members that you and they share important attitudes, beliefs, and values, you'll advance your persuasive goal. Other similarities are also important. For example, in some

TABLE 18.1 THE MOTIVATED SEQUENCE AS A PERSUASIVE STRATEGY

This table summarizes the motivated sequence as used in persuasive speeches.

Step and Purpose	Audience Question Speaker Should Answer	Ideal Audience Response	Cautions to Observe
Attention: Focus listeners' attention on you and your message.	Why should I listen? Is this worth my time?	▪ This sounds interesting. ▪ Tell me more.	Make attention relevant to speech topic.
Need: Demonstrate that there is a problem that affects them.	Why do I need to know or do anything?	▪ Okay, I understand; there's a problem. ▪ Something needs to be done.	Don't overdramatize the need.
Satisfaction: Show listeners how they can satisfy the need.	How can I do anything about this?	▪ I know what I can do to change things. ▪ I'm empowered.	Answer any objections listeners might have to your plan.
Visualization: Show listeners what the situation will be like with the need satisfied.	How would anything be different or improved?	▪ *Wow!* Things look a lot better this way. ▪ That change was really needed.	Be realistic; don't visualize the situation as perfect.
Action: Urge listeners to act, to do something.	What can I do to effect this change?	▪ Let me sign up; I'll participate. ▪ Here's my contribution.	Be specific. Ask for small changes and behaviors.

cases similarity of cultural, educational, or social background may help you identify yourself with your audience. Be aware, however, that insincere or dishonest identification is likely to backfire and create problems. So avoid even implying similarities between yourself and your audience that don't exist.

Secure a Yes Response

Research evidence clearly supports the importance of securing a yes response in influencing further compliance (Goldstein, Martin, & Cialdini, 2008). If you can get your listeners to give a yes response to some related issue, they will be more likely to give another yes response (ideally to your thesis). Even if the yes response is to some small request (say, Can I look at your notes from yesterday's lecture?), it will still pave the way to a yes response for a larger request (say, Can I borrow your notes for the weekend?).

Anticipate Selective Exposure

As noted earlier (Chapter 3, page 61), listeners follow the law of selective exposure: (1) Listeners actively seek out information that supports their opinions, beliefs, values, decisions, and behaviors; and (2) listeners actively avoid information that contradicts their existing opinions, beliefs, attitudes, values, decisions, and behaviors.

If you want to persuade audience members who hold attitudes different from your own, anticipate selective exposure and proceed inductively; that is, hold back on your thesis until you've given them your evidence and argument. Only then relate this evidence and argument to your initially contrary thesis. If you were to present your listeners with your thesis first, they might tune you out without giving your position a fair hearing.

Let's say you're giving a speech on the need to reduce spending on college athletic programs. If your audience is composed of listeners who agree with you and want to cut athletic spending, you might lead with your thesis. Your introduction might go something like this:

Our college athletic program is absorbing money that we can more profitably use for the library, science labs, and language labs. Let me explain how the money now going to unnecessary athletic programs could be better spent in these other areas.

the•o•ry *noun* statement of explanation, formulation of relationships, reasoned generalization

UNDERSTANDING THEORY AND RESEARCH
Foot-in-the-Door and Door-in-the-Face

When you have the opportunity to persuade your audience on several occasions (rather than simply delivering one speech), two strategies will prove helpful: the foot-in-the-door and door-in-the-face techniques (Goldstein, Martin, & Cialdini, 2008).

As its name implies, the **foot-in-the-door technique** involves requesting something small, something that audience members will easily agree to. Once they agree to this small request, you then make your real request. People are more apt to comply with a large request after they have complied with a similar but much smaller request. For example, in one study the objective was to get people to put a "Drive Safely" sign on their lawn (a large request). When this (large) request was made first, only about 17 percent of the people were willing to agree. However, when this request was preceded by a much smaller request (to sign a petition), between 50 and 76 percent granted permission to install the sign. Agreement with the smaller request paves the way for the larger request and puts the audience into an agreeable mood.

With the **door-in-the-face technique**, the opposite of foot-in-the-door, you first make a large request that you know will be refused and then follow it with a more moderate request. For example, your large request might be "We're asking people to donate $100 for new school computers." When this is refused, you make a more moderate request, the one you really want your listeners to comply with (for example, "Might you be willing to contribute $10?"). In changing from the large to the more moderate request, you demonstrate your willingness to compromise and your sensitivity to your listeners. The general idea here is that your listeners will feel that because you've made concessions, they should also make concessions and at least contribute something. Listeners will probably also feel that $10 is actually quite a small amount considering the initial request and are more likely to donate the $10.

Working with Theories and Research

What kinds of opportunities might you have for using either of these techniques? Have they ever been used on you? With what effect?

On the other hand, suppose you're addressing alumni who strongly favor the existing athletic programs. In this case, you may want to lead with your evidence and hold off stating your thesis until the end of your speech.

Use Positive Labeling

People generally act in ways consistent with the way in which they are labeled, especially if the label is a favorable one that reflects positively on the individual. So if you describe your listeners as possessing a particular attitude or trait (and for ethical reasons, you need to truly believe that they actually do possess such attitudes or traits), they'll be more apt to act in accordance with the label (Goldstein, Martin, & Cialdini, 2008). For example, let's say that you want to motivate your audience to devote time to working with students who have disabilities. If you describe your audience as caring, compassionate, and helpful, for example, its members will be more apt to think of themselves in that way and be more apt to agree to requests that other caring, compassionate, and helpful people do.

Ask for Reasonable Amounts of Change

Generally, people change gradually, in small degrees over a long period of time. Persuasion, therefore, is most effective when it strives for small changes and works over a period of time. For example, a persuasive speech stands a better chance when it tries to get an alcoholic to attend just one AA meeting rather than asking the person to give up alcohol for life. If you try to convince audience members to change their attitudes radically or to engage in behaviors to which they're initially opposed, your attempts may backfire. In this type of situation, the audience may close its ears to even the best and most logical arguments.

When you're addressing audience members that is opposed to your position and you're trying to change their attitudes and beliefs, be especially careful to seek change in small increments. Let's say, for example, that your ultimate goal is to get an antiabortion group to favor abortion on demand. Obviously, this goal is too great to achieve in one speech. Therefore, strive for small changes. For example, in the following excerpt the speaker attempts to get an audience that opposes legalized abortion to agree that at least some abortions should be legalized. The speaker begins:

> **One of the great lessons I learned in college was that most extreme positions are wrong. Most of the important truths lie somewhere between the extreme opposites. And today I want to talk with you about one of these truths. I want to talk with you about rape and the problems faced by the mother carrying a child conceived in this most violent of all violent crimes.**

me•di•a lit•er•a•cy *noun* ability to understand, interact with, and create media messages

EXPANDING MEDIA LITERACY
The Spiral of Silence

The spiral of silence theory argues that you're more likely to voice agreement than disagreement (Noelle-Neumann, 1973, 1980, 1991; Windahl, Signitzer, & Olson, 1992). The theory claims that when a controversial issue arises, you try to estimate public opinion on the issue and figure out which views are popular and which are not, largely by attending to the media (Gonzenbach, King, & Jablonski, 1999; Jeffres, Neuendorf, & Atkin, 1999). At the same time, you also judge the likelihood and the severity of punishment for expressing minority opinions. You then use these estimates to regulate your expression of opinions.

The theory continues: When you agree with the majority, you're more likely to voice your opinions than when you disagree. You may avoid expressing minority opinions because you don't want to be isolated from the majority or confront the unpleasant possibility of being proven wrong. Or you may assume that the majority, because they're a majority, are right.

Not all people seem affected equally by this spiral (Noelle-Neumann, 1991). For example, younger people and men are more likely to express minority opinions than are older people and women. Educated people are more likely to express minority opinions than are those who are less educated. Similarly, the tendency to voice minority opinions will vary from one culture to another (Scheufele & Moy, 2000).

In any case, the "spiral" effect occurs when, as people with minority views remain silent, the media position gets stronger (because those who agree with it are the only ones speaking). As the media's position grows stronger, the voice of the opposition also gets weaker. Thus, the situation becomes an ever-widening spiral of silence.

As you think about the spiral of silence, consider the ways the process of silence operates in your own media life. For example, do you contribute to this spiral of silence? Under what conditions are you most likely to conform to the predictions of this theory? What are its effects on your self-image and on your popularity with peers?

Notice that the speaker does not state a totally pro-choice position, but instead focuses on one area of the abortion issue and attempts to get audience members to ask themselves, "What if my daughter was raped and abortion was unavailable?" and perhaps ultimately to agree that in some cases the possibility of abortion should be available.

Provide Social Proof

You provide social proof when you give your listeners examples of other people doing what you want them to do (Goldstein, Martin, & Cialdini, 2008; Surowiecki, 2005). So, for example, let's say you want your listeners to turn off their cell phones during classes. How might you achieve this? Consider these two alternatives.

1. So many people leave on their cell phones, which annoy others. This is just an example of gross inconsideration for the rights of others.
2. So many people are turning off their cell phones and acting with consideration for others.

Which strategy is likely to prove more effective? In (1) you offer what is called **negative social proof**—you're showing your listeners that many people do what they should not do. And, they may reason, if everyone is doing it, why shouldn't I? In (2) you offer **positive social proof**—you're showing your listeners that many people do what you want them to also do. And, again, they're more likely to do what others are doing, namely what you want them to do. This "herd instinct" is a powerful impulse.

Table 18.2 presents a summary of the principles of persuasive speaking.

18.4 PERSUASIVE SPEECHES ON QUESTIONS OF FACT

Questions of fact concern what is or is not true, what does or does not exist, what did or did not happen. Some questions of fact are easily answered. These include many academic questions you're familiar with: Who was Aristotle? How many people use the Internet to get news? When was the first satellite launched? Questions of fact also include more mundane questions like: What's on television? When is

Explore at MyCommunicationLab Activity: "Annotated Outline: Untreated Depression"

TABLE 18.2

In A Nutshell A Summary of the Principles of Persuasive Speaking

Principle	The Logic of the Principle
Motivate Your Listeners with Limited Choices	People prefer fewer choices; too many choices and there's a tendency to do nothing
Focus on Your Audience	The audience is the reason for the speech; without the audience, there would be no public speaking.
Identify with Your Audience	People tend to agree with those who they perceive are similar to them.
Secure a Yes Response	A yes response to a simple request will often pave the way to a yes response to a major request.
Anticipate Selective Exposure	Start with areas of agreement to hold your audience listening.
Use Positive Labeling	Labels are remembered because they're short and simple.
Ask for Reasonable Amounts of Change	People want to change gradually and are more apt to change in small ways than in major ways.
Provide Social Proof	People tend to do what others do and not do what others do not do.

the meeting? What's Jenny's e-mail address? You can easily find answers to these questions by looking at some reference book, finding the relevant website, or asking someone who knows the answer.

The questions of fact that we deal with in persuasive speeches are a bit different. Although these questions also have answers, the answers are not that easy to find and in fact may never be found. The questions concern controversial issues for which different people have different answers. Daily newspapers and Internet websites abound in questions of fact. For example, on July 13, 2013—from Google, Bing, and Yahoo! online news—there were such questions of fact as these: Is George Zimmerman guilty? What caused the French train crash? Is the U.S. economy healing? Did GlaxoSmithKline bribe doctors to prescribe their drugs? Is the IRS guilty of illegal activities?

Thesis and Main Points

For a persuasive speech on a question of fact, you'll formulate a thesis on the basis of a factual statement such as:

- **This company has a glass ceiling for women.**
- **The plaintiff was slandered (or libeled or defamed).**
- **The death was a case of physician-assisted suicide.**
- **Gay men and lesbians make competent parents.**
- **Television violence leads to violent behavior in viewers.**

If you were preparing a persuasive speech on the first example given above, you might phrase your thesis as "This company discriminates against women." Whether or not the company does discriminate is a question of fact; clearly the company either does or does not discriminate. Whether you can prove it does discriminate or it doesn't, however, is another issue.

Once you've formulated your thesis, you can generate your main points by asking the simple question "How do you know this?" or "Why would you believe this is true (factual)?" The answers to one of these questions will enable you to develop your main points. The essential components of your speech might then look something like this:

General purpose:	To persuade.
Specific purpose:	To persuade my listeners that this company discriminates against women.
Thesis:	This company discriminates against women. (How can we tell that this company discriminates against women?)

I. Women earn less than men.
II. Women are hired less often than men.
III. Women occupy fewer managerial positions than men.

Make sure that you clearly connect your main points to your thesis in your introduction, when introducing each of the points, and again in your summary. Don't allow the audience to forget that the lower salaries that women earn directly supports the thesis that this company discriminates against women.

Support

Having identified your main points, begin searching for information to support them. Taking the first point, you might develop it something like this:

I. Women earn less than men.
A. Over the past five years, the average salary for editorial assistants was $6,000 less for women than it was for men.
B. Over the past five years, the entry-level salaries for women averaged $4,500 less than the entry-level salaries for men.
C. Over the past five years, the bonuses earned by women were 20 percent below the bonuses earned by men.

The above speech focuses entirely on a question of fact; the thesis itself is a question of fact. In other speeches, however, you may want just one of your main points to center on a question of fact. So, for example, let's say you're giving a speech advocating that the military give gay men and lesbians full equality. In this case, one of your points might focus on a question of fact: You might seek to establish that gay men and lesbians make competent parents. Once you've established that, you'd then be in a better position to argue for equality in the right to adopt children.

In a speech on questions of fact, you want to emphasize logical proof. Facts are your best support. The more facts you have, the more persuasive you'll be in dealing with questions of fact. For example, the more evidence you can find that women earn less than men, the more convincing you will be in proving that women do in fact earn less and, ultimately, that women are discriminated against.

Use the most recent materials possible. The more recent your materials, the more relevant they will be to the present time and the more persuasive they're likely to be. Notice, in our example, that if you said that in 1980 women earned on average $13,000 less than men, that fact would be meaningless in relation to the question of whether the company discriminates against women *now*.

Organization

Speeches on questions of fact probably fit most readily into a topical organizational pattern, in which each reason for your thesis is given approximately equal weight. Notice, for example, that the outline of the speech under "Main Points" uses a topic order in which all of the reasons pointing to discrimination are treated as equal main points.

18.5 PERSUASIVE SPEECHES ON QUESTIONS OF VALUE

Questions of value concern what people consider good or bad, moral or immoral, just or unjust. Bing, Yahoo!, and Google news (July 13, 2013) reported on such questions of value as these: Is Edward Snowdon a hero? A terrorist? Is the immigration bill fair to all? What is the value of the IRS? Is Patrice Bergeron worth $52 million?

Speeches on questions of value will seek to strengthen audiences' existing attitudes, beliefs, or values. This is true of much religious and political speaking; for example, people who listen to religious speeches usually are already believers, so these speeches strive to strengthen the beliefs and values the people already hold. In a religious setting, the listeners already share the speaker's values and are willing to listen. Speeches that seek to change audience values are much more difficult to construct. Most people resist change. When you try to get people to change their values or beliefs, you're fighting an uphill (though not necessarily impossible) battle.

Be sure that you clearly define the specific value on which you're focusing. For example, let's say that you're developing a speech to persuade high school students to attend college. You want to stress that college is of value, but what type of value do you focus on? The financial value (college graduates earn more money than nongraduates)? The social value (college is a lot of fun and a great place to make friends)? The intellectual value (college will broaden your view of the world and make you a more critical and creative thinker)? Once you clarify the type of value on which you'll focus, you'll find it easier to develop the relevant points. You'll also find it easier to locate appropriate supporting materials.

Thesis and Main Points

Theses devoted to questions of value might look something like this:

- **The death penalty is unjustifiable.**
- **Bullfighting is inhumane.**
- **Discrimination on the basis of affectional orientation is wrong.**
- **Chemical weapons are immoral.**
- **Human cloning is morally justified.**
- **College athletics minimize the importance of academics.**

As with speeches on questions of fact, you can generate the main points for a speech on a question of value by asking a strategic question of your thesis, such as "Why is this good?" or "Why is this immoral?" For example, you can take the first thesis given above and ask, "Why is the death penalty unjustifiable?" The answers to this question will give you the speech's main points. The body of your speech might then look something like this:

General purpose:	**To persuade.**
Specific purpose:	**To persuade my listeners that the death penalty is unjustifiable.**
Thesis:	**The death penalty is unjustifiable. (Why is the death penalty unjustifiable?)**

I. The criminal justice system can make mistakes.

II. The death penalty constitutes cruel and unusual punishment.

III. No one has the moral right to take another's life.

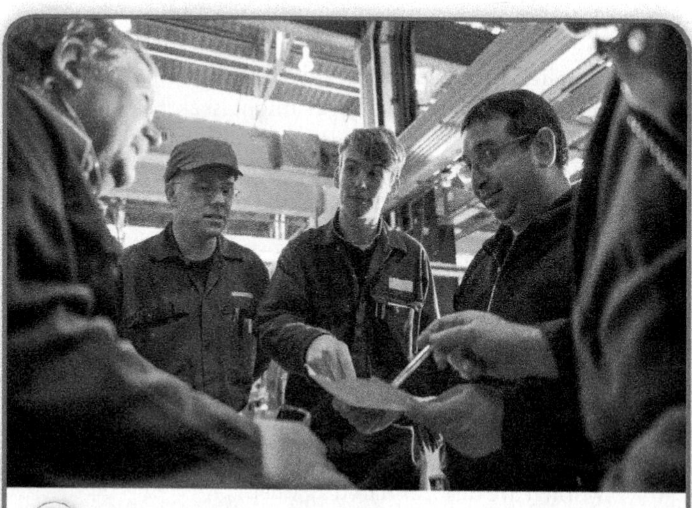

COMMUNICATION CHOICE POINT

CHANGING BEHAVIOR *Patrick is supervising a small work force. His problem is that some members are just not doing their job, and he's been assigned the task of making sure they start working.* **What are some of the techniques of persuasion that Patrick might use in getting his message across and getting the others to do their jobs?**

Support

To support your main points, search for relevant evidence. For example, to show that mistakes have been made, you might itemize three or four high-profile cases in which people were put to death and later, through DNA, found to have been innocent.

At times, and with certain topics, it may be useful to identify the standards you would use to judge something moral or justified or fair or good. For example, in the "bullfighting is inhumane" speech, you might devote your first main point to defining when an action can be considered inhumane. In this case, the body of your speech might look like this:

- **I. An inhumane act has two qualities.**
  - **A. It is cruel and painful.**
  - **B. It serves no human necessity.**
- **II. Bullfighting is inhumane.**
  - **A. It is cruel and painful.**
  - **B. It serves no necessary function.**

Notice that in the example of capital punishment, the speaker aims to strengthen or change the listeners' beliefs about the death penalty. The speaker is not asking the audience to do anything about capital punishment, but merely to believe that it's not justified. However, you might also use a question of value as a first step toward persuading your audience to take some action. For example, once you got your listeners to see the death penalty as unjustified, you might then ask them to take certain actions—perhaps in your next speech—to support an anti-death penalty politician, to vote for or against a particular proposition, or to join an organization fighting against the death penalty.

Organization

Like speeches on questions of fact, speeches on questions of value often lend themselves to topical organization. For example, the speech on capital punishment cited earlier uses topical order. But even within this topical order there is another level of organization, an organization that begins with those items on which there is least disagreement or opposition and moves on to the items on which your listeners are likely to have very different ideas. It's likely that even people in favor of the death penalty would agree that mistakes can be made; and they probably would be willing to accept evidence that mistakes have in fact been made—especially if you cite reliable statistical evidence and expert testimony. By starting with this issue, you secure initial agreement and can use that as a basis for approaching areas where you and the audience are more likely to disagree.

18.6 PERSUASIVE SPEECHES ON QUESTIONS OF POLICY

When you move beyond a focus on value to urging your audience to do something about an issue, you're then into a question of policy. For example, in a speech designed to convince your listeners that bullfighting is inhumane, you'd be focusing on a question of value. If you were to urge that bullfighting should therefore be declared illegal, you'd be urging the adoption of a particular policy. Items on Yahoo!, Bing, and Google news (July 13, 2013) that suggested questions of policy included these: What should be Russian policy toward Edward Snowdon? What should be U.S. policy toward Egypt's new government? What should be done about air pollution? Should the IRS be abolished?

Questions of policy concern what should be done, what procedures should be adopted, what laws should be changed; in short, what policy should be followed. In some speeches you may want to propose a new policy or to defend an existing policy; in others you may wish to argue that a current policy should be discontinued.

Explore at MyCommunicationLab **Exercise:** "The Persuasive Speech on Questions of Fact, Value, and Policy"

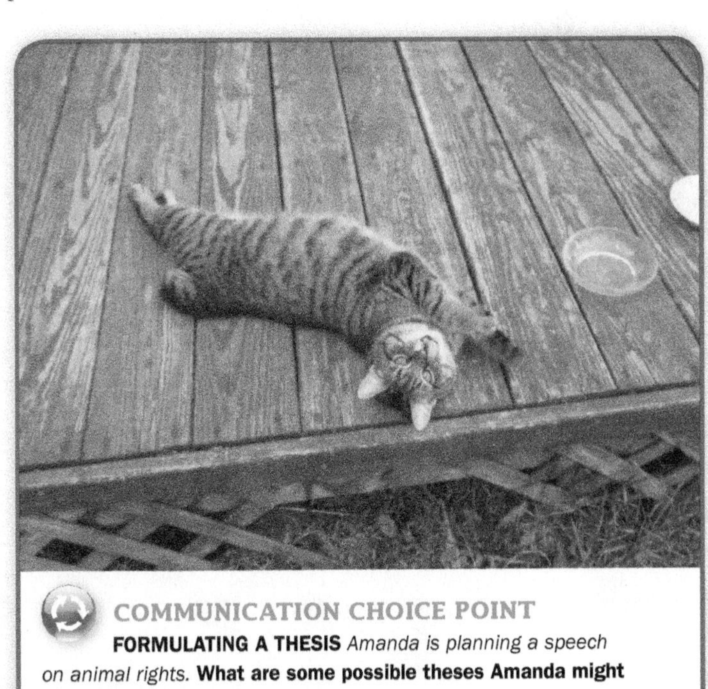

COMMUNICATION CHOICE POINT

FORMULATING A THESIS *Amanda is planning a speech on animal rights.* **What are some possible theses Amanda might develop for speeches of fact, value, and policy?**

SPECIAL OCCASION SPEECHES

[Largely Persuasive]

In addition to the speeches on fact, value, and policy there are also special occasion speeches that are largely (though not exclusively) persuasive. Here are several such special occasion speeches.

THE SPEECH TO SECURE GOODWILL

The **goodwill speech** is part information and part persuasion. On the surface, the speech informs the audience about a product, company, profession, institution, or person. Beneath this surface, however, lies a more persuasive purpose: to heighten the image of a person, product, or company—to create a more positive attitude toward this person or thing. Many speeches of goodwill have a further persuasive purpose: to get audience members ultimately to change their behavior toward the person, product, or company.

A special type of goodwill speech is the speech of self-justification, in which the speaker seeks to justify his or her actions to the audience. In securing goodwill, whether for another person or for yourself, consider the following suggestions:

- Demonstrate the contributions that deserve goodwill.
- Establish credibility.
- Don't be obvious. The effective goodwill speech looks, on the surface, very much like an objective informative speech. It will not appear to ask for goodwill, except on close analysis.

THE COMMENCEMENT SPEECH

The **commencement speech** is designed to congratulate and inspire the recent graduates and is often intended to mark the transition from school to the next stage in life. In giving a commencement speech, consider the following:

- Organize the speech in a temporal pattern, beginning with the past, commenting on the present, and projecting into the future.
- Do your research. Learn something about the school, the student body, and the goals and ambitions of the graduates, and integrate these into your speech.
- Be brief. Recognize that your audience has other things on their minds.
- Congratulate the graduates, parents, and instructors.
- Offer the graduates some kind of motivational message, some guidance.
- Offer your own good wishes to the graduates.

THE SPEECH OF INSPIRATION

A great many special occasion speeches are designed to inspire; the **speech of inspiration is designed** to raise the spirits of an audience. Many religious speeches are of this type. Similarly, speeches that corporate leaders give to stockholders when introducing a new product or a new CEO, for example, would be designed to inspire investors. In speaking to inspire:

- Demonstrate your oneness with the audience. Try to show in some way that you and your listeners have significant similarities.
- Demonstrate your own intense involvement, the kind of intensity you want your audience to show.
- Stress emotional appeals. Inspiring an audience has to do more with emotions than with logic.
- Stress the positive. Especially, end your speech on a positive note. Inspirational speeches are always positive.

MyCommunicationLab *Visit mycommunicationlab.com to see additional examples of excellent special occasion speeches.*

Table 18.3 presents a brief summary of these questions of fact, value, and policy.

Thesis and Main Points

Persuasive speeches frequently revolve around questions of policy and may use theses such as the following:

- **Hate speech should be banned in colleges.**
- **Our community should adopt a zero tolerance policy for guns in schools.**
- **Abortion should be available on demand.**
- **Music albums and singles should be rated for violence and profanity.**
- **Medical marijuana should be legalized.**
- **Smoking should be banned from all public buildings and parks.**

As you can tell from these examples, questions of policy almost invariably involve questions of values. For example, the argument that hate speech should be banned in colleges is based on the value judgment that hate speech is wrong. To argue for a zero tolerance policy on guns in schools implies that you think it's wrong for students or faculty to carry guns to school.

You can develop your speech on a question of policy by asking a strategic question of your thesis. With policy issues the question will be "Why should the policy be adopted?" or "Why should this policy be discontinued?" or "Why is this policy better than what we now have?" Taking our first example, we might ask, "Why should hate speech be banned on campus?" From the answers to this question, you would develop your main points, which might look something like this:

I. **Hate speech encourages violence against women and minorities.**
II. **Hate speech denigrates women and minorities.**
III. **Hate speech teaches hate instead of tolerance.**

Support

Having chosen your main points, you then support each point with a variety of supporting materials that will help convince your audience that hate speech should be banned from college campuses.

TABLE 18.3

In A Nutshell — A Summary of Questions of Fact, Value, and Policy

This table summarizes the three types of persuasive speeches in terms of their purposes, examples of the types of questions such speeches deal with, and the questions the audience is likely to ask and that you will likely want to have answers for somewhere in your speech.

Question Purposes	Examples	Question Audience May Want Answered
Questions of Fact To persuade listeners that something is true or false	▪ Higgins is guilty (not guilty). ▪ What he did was criminal (legal). ▪ The stock market will go much higher (much lower).	▪ Is this the most likely interpretation of the issue? ▪ Are other, more likely, explanations possible? ▪ How do we know that this is true or that this is false?
Questions of Value To persuade listeners in the value of something, that something is good, moral, or just	▪ Higgins deserves the chair (to go free). ▪ Universal health care is essential (not essential).	▪ Why is this good or just or the right thing to do? Are there alternatives that would be more just or fairer? ▪ The war is just (unjust)
Questions of Policy To persuade listeners that this is the policy to adopt or not adopt	▪ The verdict must be guilty (not guilty). ▪ Plan B needs to be enacted (discarded). ▪ The war needs to be continued (discontinued).	▪ Might there be better courses of action to follow? ▪ Are there downsides to this course of action?

For example, you might cite the websites put up by certain groups that advocate violence against women and minority members or quote from the lyrics of performers who came to campus. Or you might cite examples of actual violence that had been accompanied by hate speech or hate literature.

In some speeches on questions of policy, you may simply want your listeners to agree that the policy you're advocating is a good idea. In other cases you may want them to do something about the policy—to vote for a particular candidate, to write to their elected officials, to participate in the walkathon, to wear an AIDS awareness ribbon, and so on.

Watch at **MyCommunicationLab**
Video: "Same Sex Marriage"

Organization

Speeches on questions of policy may be organized in a variety of ways. For example, if you're comparing two policies, consider the comparison-and-contrast method. If the existing policy is doing harm, consider using a cause-to-effect pattern. If your policy is designed to solve a problem, consider the problem-solution pattern. For example, in a speech advocating zero tolerance for guns in school, the problem-solution pattern would seem appropriate; your speech would thus be divided into two basic parts:

I. **Guns are destroying our high schools. (problem)**
II. **We must adopt a zero tolerance policy. (solution)**

Margo has been volunteering as a Big Sister for the past year and has made excellent progress with her mentee. The organization is planning a service day for at-risk high school girls on the importance of planning for college, and Margo has been asked to give a speech to the entire group of volunteers and mentees. "Planning for Success" focuses on using the principles of persuasion to influence another's behavior and the choices you have for most effectively persuading others and illustrates how wise choices can result in an effective persuasive presentation. Log on to mycommunicationlab.com to view this video and the choices, and then answer the related discussion questions.

SUMMARY: THE PERSUASIVE SPEECH

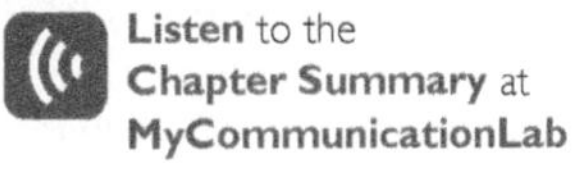

This chapter focused on persuasive speeches and examined the goals of persuasion, several principles of persuasion, and three types of persuasive speeches.

18.1 GOALS OF PERSUASIVE SPEAKING

1. Persuasive speeches may have one of three main goals: (1) to strengthen or weaken the attitudes, beliefs, or values of your listeners; (2) to change their attitudes, beliefs, or values; and (3) to motivate them to act in some way, to do something.

18.2 THE THREE PERSUASIVE PROOFS

2. The three persuasive proofs are:
   - logical proof, the evidence and arguments
   - emotional proof, the motivational appeals
   - ethical proof or credibility appeals

18.3 PRINCIPLES OF PERSUASIVE SPEAKING

3. Among the guidelines for preparing persuasive speeches are the following:
   - Focus on the audience.
   - Identify with your audience.
   - Secure a yes response.
   - Anticipate selective exposure.
   - Use positive labeling.
   - Ask for reasonable amounts of change.
   - Provide social proof.
   - Motivate your listeners.

18.4 PERSUASIVE SPEECHES ON QUESTIONS OF FACT

4. Persuasive speeches on **questions of fact** focus on what is or is not true. In a speech on a question of fact:
   - Emphasize logical proof.
   - Use the most recent materials possible.
   - Use highly competent sources.
   - Clearly connect your main points to your thesis.

18.5 PERSUASIVE SPEECHES ON QUESTIONS OF VALUE

5. Speeches on **questions of value** focus on issues of good and bad, justice or injustice. In designing speeches to strengthen or change attitudes, beliefs, or values:
   - Define clearly the specific value on which you're focusing.
   - Begin with shared assumptions and beliefs, then progress gradually to areas of disagreement.
   - Use sources that the audience values highly.

18.6 PERSUASIVE SPEECHES ON QUESTIONS OF POLICY

6. Speeches on **questions of policy** focus on what should or should not be done, what procedures should or should not be adopted. In designing speeches to move listeners to action:
   - Prove that the policy is needed.
   - Emphasize that the policy you're supporting is practical and reasonable.
   - Show your listeners how the policy will benefit them directly.
   - When asking for action, ask for small, easily performed, and very specific behaviors.
   - Use an organizational pattern that best fits your topic.

Study and **Review** the **Flashcards** at **MyCommunicationLab**

KEY TERMS

anecdotal evidence *384*
appeal to tradition *385*
bandwagon *385*
character *389*
character attacks *390*
charisma *389*
commencement speech *398*
competence *388*
credibility *387*
door-in-the-face technique *392*
emotional appeals *385*
foot-in-the-door technique *392*
glittering generality *390*
goodwill speech *398*
hierarchy of needs *385*
identification *391*
logical arguments *383*
name-calling *390*
negative social proof *394*
personal interest *390*
persuasion *382*
positive social proof *394*
questions of fact *394*
questions of policy *397*
questions of value *396*
reasoning from causes and effects *384*
reasoning from sign *384*
reasoning from specific instances *383*
self-esteem *386*
speech of inspiration *399*
straw man *385*
testimonial *385*
thin entering wedge *385*

WORKING WITH THE PERSUASIVE SPEECH

18.1 Constructing Logical, Motivational, and Credibility Appeals. Below are statements suitable as theses for a variety of persuasive speeches. Select any one statement (or its opposite) and construct (a) a logical appeal, (b) an emotional appeal, and (c) a credibility appeal that would prove effective in persuading your class.

a. Sports involving cruelty to animals—such as bullfighting, cockfighting, and foxhunting—should (not) be universally condemned and declared illegal.

b. Government surveillance must be curtailed.

c. Retirement should (not) be mandatory at age 65 for all government employees.

d. The death penalty is (not) morally wrong.

e. Too little (too much) government money is spent on accommodating people with disabilities.

18.2 Questions of Fact, Value, and Policy. Understanding how purposes and theses can be identified from a wide variety of questions of fact, value, and policy will help you construct more effective speeches. To develop this understanding, select a newspaper (Sunday's edition will work best), a weekly newsmagazine, or an Internet news site and identify the questions of fact, value, and policy covered in this one issue (as was done in this chapter). From these, select one question of fact, value, or policy and develop a general purpose, a specific purpose, a thesis that would be appropriate for a speech in this class, and two or three main ideas that you might want to develop based on this thesis.

18.3 Gender and Persuasion. You're planning to give a speech urging more conscientious recycling to two separate audiences. One audience will be composed solely of women and the other audience solely of men. Otherwise the audience members will be similar: college-educated professionals about 30 years old. In what ways would you make the two speeches differ? What general principles or assumptions about gender are you making as you differentiate these two speeches?

18.4 Foot-in-the-Door or Door-in-the-Face. You want to get your listeners to contribute 1 hour a week to your college's program of helping high school students prepare for college. You're considering using the foot-in-the-door or the door-in-the-face technique. How would you develop each of these strategies? Which would you eventually use?

18.5 Fact, Value, and Policy in the News. Examine one issue of a national newspaper. What are the questions of fact, value, and policy that this newspaper edition covers? Then read the editorials. What types of questions do the editorials address?

18.6 The Persuasiveness of Blogs. Visit a few blogs and analyze them in terms of the principles of persuasion discussed in this chapter. How are blogs like persuasive speeches? How are they different?

18.7 The 2-Minute Speech. Prepare and deliver a 2-minute speech in which you do one of the following:

- Explain an interesting attitude, belief, or value that you have come across.
- Explain how a speech strengthened or changed one of your attitudes or beliefs.
- Explain an advertisement in terms of the principles of persuasion.

LogOn! MyCommunicationLab www.mycommunicationlab.com

Throughout this chapter, there are icons that highlight media content for selected topics. Go to **MyCommunicationLab** for additional materials on persuasive speaking and consider the goals of persuasive speaking, the three major proofs, the essential principles of persuasion, and the varied types of persuasive speeches you might give. Here you'll find flashcards to help you learn key communication terms, videos that illustrate a variety of concepts, additional exercises, and discussions to help you continue your study of the persuasive speech.

APPENDIX OF SPEECHES

PUBLIC SPEAKING SAMPLE ASSISTANTS

1. A Speech of Introduction
2. A Poorly Constructed Informative Speech, "Biases"
3. An Excellent Informative Speech, "Communication in an Ever-Changing World" by Marty Wiebe
4. A Poorly Constructed Persuasive Speech, "Prenups"
5. An Excellent Persuasive Speech, "It's Not the Addict, It's the Drug: Redefining America's War on Drugs" by Tunette Powell
6. A Slide Show Speech, "Self-Disclosure"

The speeches in this appendix will help you to see the public speech as a whole and to ask critical questions about structure, support, language, and numerous other public speaking factors we consider in the public speaking chapters. The annotations will help you explore important principles that you're likely to find helpful in your own speeches.

Two of the speeches, one informative ("Biases") and one persuasive ("Prenups"), are purposely designed to illustrate ineffective speeches (no one really gives speeches this bad). Not surprisingly, research shows that we learn a great deal from negative examples (Goldstein, Martin, & Cialdini, 2008; Hesketh & Neal, 2006). All other speeches included here as well as the outlines integrated into the chapters are presented as models of effectiveness.

A SPEECH OF INTRODUCTION

One of the first speeches you may be called upon to make is the speech in which you introduce yourself or (as illustrated in this particular speech) some other person. This speech also will let you see a public speech as a whole and will give you reference points for examining each of the 10 steps for preparing and delivering a public speech.

THE SPEECH	COMMENTS/QUESTIONS
Introduction It's a real pleasure to introduce Joe Robinson to you. I want to tell you a little about Joe's background, his present situation, and his plans for the future.	In this introduction, the speaker accomplishes several interrelated purposes: to place the speech in a positive context, to explain the purpose of the speech and orient audience members, to tell them what the speech will cover and that it will follow a time pattern—beginning with the past, moving to the present, and then ending with the proposed future. **What other types of opening statements might be appropriate? In what other ways might you organize a speech of introduction?**
Transition Let's look first at Joe's past.	This transitional statement alerts listeners that the speaker is moving from the introduction to the first major part of what is called the "body" of the speech.
Body, first main point (*the past*) Joe comes to us from Arizona, where he lived and worked on a small ranch with his father and grandparents—mostly working with dairy cows. Working on a farm gave Joe a deep love and appreciation for animals that he carries with him today and into his future plans.	The speaker here gives us information about Joe's past that makes us see him as a unique individual. We also learn something pretty significant about Joe, namely that his mother died when he was very young. The speaker continues here to answer one of the questions that audience members probably have; namely, why this somewhat older person is in this class and in this college. **If this were a longer speech, what else might the speaker cover here? What else would you want to know about Joe's past?**
Joe's mother died when he was 3 years old, and so he lived with his father most of his life. When his father, an air force lieutenant, was transferred to Stewart Air Force Base here in the Hudson Valley, Joe thought it would be a great opportunity to join his father and continue his education.	Here the speaker shows that Joe has a sense of humor in his identifying why he wanted to stay with his father, the very same things that a father would say about a son. **Can you make this more humorous?**

Joe also wanted to stay with his father to make sure he eats right, doesn't get involved with the wrong crowd, and meets the right woman to settle down with.

Transition
So Joe and his father journeyed from the dairy farm in Arizona to the Hudson Valley.

Here's simple transition, alerting the audience that the speaker is moving from the first main point (the past) to the second (the present). **In what other ways might you state such a transition?**

Second main point (*the present*)
Right now, with the money he saved while working on the ranch and with the help of a part-time job, Joe's here with us at Hudson Valley Community College.

Like many of us, Joe is a little apprehensive about college and worries that it's going to be a difficult and very different experience, especially at 28. Although an avid reader—mysteries and biographies are his favorites—Joe hasn't really studied, taken an exam, or written a term paper since high school, some 10 years ago. So he's a bit anxious, but at the same time he's looking forward to the changes and the challenges of college life.

And, again, like many of us, Joe's a bit apprehensive about taking a public speaking course.

Joe is currently working for a local animal shelter. He was especially drawn to this particular shelter because of its no-kill policy; lots of shelters will kill the animals they can't find adopted homes for, but this one sticks by its firm no-kill policy.

Here the speaker shifts to the present and gives Joe a very human dimension by identifying his fears and concerns about being in college and taking this course and his concern for animals. The speaker also explains some commonalities between Joe and the rest of the audience (for example, being apprehensive in a public speaking class is something shared by nearly everyone). **Some textbook writers would suggest that telling an audience that a speaker has apprehension about speaking is a bad idea. What do you think of its disclosure here?**

Transition
But it's not the past or the present that Joe focuses on, it's the future.

This transition tells listeners that the speaker has finished talking about the past and present and is now moving on to the future.

Third main point (*the future*)
Joe is planning to complete his AB degree here at Hudson Valley Community and then to move on to the State University of New Paltz, where he intends to major in communication with a focus on public relations.

His ideal job would be to work for an animal rights organization. He wants to help make people aware of the ways in which they can advance animal rights and stop so much of the cruelty to animals common throughout the world.

From the present, the speaker moves to the future and identifies Joe's educational plans. This is the one thing that everyone has in common and something that most in the class would want to know. The speaker also covers Joe's career plans: again, something the audience is likely to be interested in. In this the speaker also reveals important aspects of Joe's interests and belief system—his concern for animals and his dedication to building his career around this abiding interest. **What kinds of information might this speech of introduction give you about the attitudes and beliefs of its listeners?**

Transition, internal summary
Joe's traveled an interesting road from a dairy farm in Arizona to the Hudson Valley, and the path to New Paltz and public relations should be just as interesting.

This transition (a kind of internal summary) tells you that the speaker has completed the three-part discussion (past, present, and future) and offers a basic summary of what has been discussed.

Conclusion
Having talked with him for the past few days, I'm sure he'll do well—he has lots of ideas, is determined to succeed, is open to new experiences, and

In this concluding comment the speaker appropriately expresses a positive attitude toward Joe and summarizes some of Joe's positive qualities. These qualities are then

enjoys interacting with people. I'd say that gives this interesting dairy farmer from Arizona a pretty good start as a student in this class, as a student at Hudson Valley Community, and as a soon-to-be public relations specialist.

tied to the past-present-future organization of the speech. Although the speaker doesn't say "thank you"—which can get trite when 20 speakers in succession say this—it's clear that this is the end of the speech from the last sentence, which brings Joe into his future profession. **How effective do you think this conclusion is? What other types of conclusions might the speaker have used?**

A POORLY CONSTRUCTED INFORMATIVE SPEECH: "BIASES"

You may find it useful to return to this speech at different points in the course; as the course progresses, your analysis will become more complete, more insightful, and more effective. After you have reviewed the speech and the comments on the right, offer a 1- or 2-minute critique of the speech.

THE SPEECH

Title: Biases

Thesis: What are confirmation, disconfirmation, in-group, and belief biases?

General purpose: To inform.

Specific purpose: To inform you about biases.

PROBLEMS/CORRECTIVES

The title is likely to lead listeners to think of racial or religious bias—which the speech is not about. **Select a title that is interesting, attention-getting, and relevant to the speech. After reading the speech, give the speech an interesting, attention-grabbing title.**

Stating the thesis as a question will prove confusing. **Instead, state the thesis as a declarative sentence, for example: Types of biases include confirmation, disconfirmation, in-group, and belief.**

The general purpose is fine, although when you read the speech, you'll see the speaker moves beyond informing.

The specific purpose is too general. **It needs to be more specific: To define confirmation, disconfirmation, in-group, and belief biases.**

Introduction

Whew! I'm here. This public speaking is all new to me. My major requires public speaking so I may be a bit nervous—I mean, a lot nervous.

These kinds of introductory comments are best avoided. They merely focus the listeners' attention on your weaknesses. **Instead, encourage listeners to focus on your strengths.**

Let's see [shuffles through notes, arranging them and mumbling,] page 1, page 2—OK, it's all here.

Things like this reveal a decided lack of preparation. **Instead, have your notes arranged and in order before getting up to speak.**

I want to talk with you about bias and biases—confirmation, disconfirmation, in-group, and belief. I read an interesting article on this on the Internet, and I thought, you know, since I have to give an informative speech this would be really good. It's interesting; really it is.

Getting right into the topic is not necessarily a bad idea. **But some more attention-grabbing way of gaining attention might have worked better. Perhaps a question or a dramatic illustration.**

I have a lot of biases, so I'm really concerned with this topic, and I know you all have lots of biases, so this might help you. So you should listen, like our textbook says.

Confessing to having biases—which are almost universally considered negative—is probably not a very good way to establish a connection with the audience. And saying the audience has biases will likely prove insulting to many listeners. **Again, stress strengths rather than weaknesses.**

The "So you should listen…" sentence was intended to get a laugh but is likely to fall on its face. **Pretest your humor; it may not be as funny to others as it is to you.**

So, like I said, I mean, that I'm going to talk about biases.

This statement functions as a transition—a sentence or phrase that guides the listeners from one part of the speech to another—but is too brief. A more elaborate transition here might have identified the four biases and the reason why these are being discussed.

Body

Confirmation bias—this means, like, you know, that you seek the kinds of information that will confirm your beliefs. And, not only this, but you also would give more importance to information that confirms your beliefs than to information that would not confirm your beliefs. I guess this could be about anything—religion or politics, maybe. I can give you a good example of this. My sister thinks that Chevrolet is the best car and only reads advertisements for Chevys.

The speaker begins here with the first bias but doesn't define bias. It needs to be defined first and then the other four biases could be introduced as types of bias. Further, you would want to answer the audience's inevitable question, Why these four biases? Some reason for selecting these biases or some unifying thread would be effective in answering the audience's question.

Another example is if you want to persuade an audience to believe X, then you're going to do your research to find information that makes you believe X. But that may be because you just want to get the speech prepared and don't want to waste time looking at information you won't use.

This X example doesn't work; it says that the speaker didn't think hard enough about this topic. It tells listeners that the speaker hasn't thought about this sufficiently to come up with a good specific example. Generally, specific examples work better than the unidentified "X."

Disconfirmation bias—this means that people will reject information that goes against their beliefs. So, my sister would reject advertisements that claim that BMW is a better car. It's crazy but she does that. BMW is definitely the better car. That's what I want to get when I get a permanent job and make the big bucks.

The sister example is trite. And the personal asides about BMW and the car the speaker wants to get just detract from the speech and, again, make you think the speaker didn't think this out clearly. Examples are extremely important; think them out and rehearse them carefully.

Let's say, for example, that you believe X and someone gives you the information in favor of X and against X. You would believe the information in favor of your belief about X and will also reject information that goes against what you believe about X. This was actually shown in a research study on capital punishment.

Again, the X adds little to clarity. But, the research study cited on capital punishment would have made an excellent example and could have easily explained how those who were for capital punishment believed the studies that supported capital published more than the studies that did not support capital punishment. Also, the study on capital punishment requires an oral citation, a more specific identification of the study cited.

In-group bias—this is also called intergroup bias—this means that people like people who are in the same groups as they are. So, if you're in the photography club and you hear that someone else is in the club, you'll probably have positive feelings for this person. I don't know about this, though; I'm in the photography club and I don't like a lot of the people. And I think some of them don't like me—actually a lot of them. This is supposed to work, but I'm not sure.

Notice that the speaker is evaluating the concept rather than simply explaining it. If the speech were on evaluating these bias theories, then this personal example would not have been so inappropriate. In a speech of definition, stick to defining.

Wikipedia says that there are two theories about in-group bias: realistic conflict theory and social identity theory. I'm not sure that helps, but that's what Wikipedia says.

Introducing these two theories without any explanation will confuse rather than clarify, unless audience members were very sophisticated in their knowledge of this topic. Further, some instructors may frown upon using Wikipedia as a source. So, know your audience.

Belief bias—this means that people will accept a conclusion if it fits in with the beliefs they have. And, at the same time, people will reject a conclusion if it doesn't fit in with the beliefs they have. So, what happens here is that people don't look at the

By this time, the sister example is likely to seem silly to the audience. Avoid examples that might be considered silly; one laugh at the wrong time is likely to prove upsetting even to a seasoned speaker.

evidence; they only look at the conclusion. Like my sister doesn't examine the research on BMW; she just goes with the conclusion that Chevys are the best.

This is really confusing and has to do with the validity of arguments. It seems if you have belief bias you don't care about the validity of the argument. That's because you just look at the conclusion.

The term *validity* might have been defined though it's a complex term and would likely take up too much time. **It may have been easier to not use the term and say something like "the strength or truthfulness of the arguments."**

Conclusion

There are four biases—confirmation bias (like my sister and her car), disconfirmation bias (my sister and her car again), in-group bias (the photography club), and belief bias (my sister again).

This summary does little to help listeners remember what was discussed; they're likely to remember the example of the speaker's sister and not the four types of biases. **It might also have helped to use a transitional sentence to guide the listener from the body of the speech to the conclusion, for example, "As we've seen there are four biases…."or even "In summary, we've seen there are four biases that …."**

BTW, I got most of my information from a website that I can't remember.

This type of source credit is woefully inadequate. **As shown in the discussion of the oral citation (pages 306–307), citing sources is an essential component of the speech. And, of course, one or two sources are hardly sufficient for such a complex topic.**

If you want to read more about these they are on the Internet.

This is much too general and more of a throw-away line. **Something more specific might have helped, for example, a handout on the terms and where listeners can get more information.**

Further, the speaker seems almost without concern about whether or not listeners will want to learn more about these biases. **Express enthusiasm about your topic, from the start of the speech to the very end. Listeners prefer speakers who are enthusiastic about their topic and really want to share their knowledge.**

AN EXCELLENT INFORMATIVE SPEECH: "COMMUNICATION IN AN EVER-CHANGING WORLD"

This speech was delivered by Marty Wiebe, a student at Centralia College in Washington, in an introductory communication course taught by Jeff McQuarrie that used the previous edition of this textbook. You can view this speech at MyCommunicationLab. Here is a transcript of that speech with annotations to help guide your reading/viewing and questions to help guide your analysis. Some of the key terms we used throughout the section on public speaking appear in the annotations in boldface. This particular speech assignment did not require the citation of references.

SPEECH

Good morning. Drumming [the sound of drumming on the desk]. That's one of the things we just did today. My name is Marty Wiebe, and drumming, we just did, is one form of communication. Talking to you like I am doing right now is another form of communication.

COMMENTS/QUESTIONS

This speech is appropriately titled Communication in a Changing World. It gives you a very clear idea of what the speech will be about. **What other titles might be appropriate if you were giving this speech to your class? [Read or view the speech before creating a title.]**

Notice that the speaker not only gained **attention** by drumming but she related this attention-getter to the topic of the speech. **In what other ways might she have introduced the speech?**

My speech is going to be about how communication is changing and how the media is changing and how we as communicators have got to become better and more acquainted with the new modes of communication and some of the new rules that we're going to have to learn.

Here the speaker gives a very direct **orientation**, telling her audience what her speech will be about. How would you define the **purpose** and **thesis** of this speech? How appropriate would this speech be if delivered in your class? Why?

There are two main forms of communication: verbal, which is what I'm doing right now, and nonverbal, like our drums. They're nonverbal. Music is nonverbal. When I smile at you, it's nonverbal. So verbal and nonverbal go hand in hand, and it's really, really important that we use both, verbal and nonverbal communication, when we are doing presentations.

You'll notice that the speaker effectively uses lots of specific **examples** as **supporting materials** throughout this speech. What other types of supporting materials would be useful in this speech? For example, if this were a longer speech, in what way might the speaker have used **illustrations, testimony, numerical data,** and **definitions?**

We live in a shrinking world. When I grew up back in the stone age, face-to-face was the normal type of communication that we did. We met somebody. We talked to them face to face. We sat down, and we wrote a letter, and we sent them, but which is now considered by snail mail. We had newspapers and televisions and probably in the 70's when I was just graduating from high school, we did phone conferencing, which was a really, really big deal.

Here the speaker describes communication as it was in the 70s. How effectively did the speaker describe communication in the "stone age"? What else might the speaker have said?

Because up to that point, our world was just what was around us. We weren't global at this point. Computers were just getting developed. My first computer was a Commodore 64, and we had little 5 and a half inch floppy disks that we used, but there was no Internet. Bill Gates was still in the baby stage of developing Microsoft.

Here the speaker describes the state of computing in the 70s. If this were a longer speech, what else might she have mentioned to emphasize this contrast between then and now?

But today we've got tons and tons of communication. Lots of us have Facebook accounts. We can now communicate with people around the world. We have a classmate in here, name is CJ, he lives in Africa, and we can actually communicate with him after he gets back to Africa. We can also use Skype.

Referring to specific audience members is often a useful technique to maintain interest and attention. If you were giving this speech in your class, what specific references might you make? If the speaker had chosen to use **visual aids**, what types would have been useful?

We have cell phones. When I was growing up, we were just still using landlines and long distance charges applied, which don't anymore. Now cell phones, we can talk internationally. We couldn't even talk internationally on our landlines many, many years ago. We now have something called teleconferencing. In other words, you can be sitting here in this classroom, studying, and someone from Australia could be in the same classroom with you, and you can be discussing things and learning together.

This particular speech assignment did not call for citing **research**. If it had, what types of research might the speaker have used?

Here the speaker introduces the element of cultural differences in a neat transition from the discussion of changing communication technology to culture.

Our communicating world is shrinking, but with new communications, we also have to realize that there are cultural differences.

We have to learn whether it is proper to speak or not to speak. In this culture, speaking is fine. In Asian cultures, you need to listen first. In our culture, we're more individualism. In other words, if you make a mistake, you're responsible for it. But on the other

The distinction between individualist and collectivist cultures is made clear with a simple example contrasting the cultures of the United States and Asia. If this were a longer speech what other examples might have been used to emphasize this distinction?

hand, if you live in a collective culture, such as our Asian counterparts, their thinking is different. They work as a group. If you make a mistake, the whole group makes a mistake. So it's really important that we learn that cultural differences can make the difference between communication skills that you're learning are going to be effective or not.

How would you describe the speaker's delivery style? Would this be effective in your class? What can you learn from this model? How would you describe the speaker's adherence to the suggestions for informative speaking: Focus on the audience? Limiting the amount of information? Adjustment of the level of complexity? Relating new information to old?

You have to realize that just because we're allowed to speak in our culture doesn't necessarily mean that you can speak in another. Remember, once the words are out there, you can't go stop, come back. They're out there for the whole world, and it isn't just our little world or the neighborhood that I grew up in. It's the world. We're talking Sweden, Australia, the Congo, South America. Those words that you spoke that you thought were just for you to hear are no longer your words. They're out there. You can't say come back. I made a mistake.

Before you press that send button on your Facebook page, or before you press any send button or even talk in teleconferencing, you have to make sure that what you're saying is not going to be offensive to someone else. Again, once it's said, there are no do overs. And what you can say may be very offensive to someone else. So, again, in our culture, in our communication, those are the things that we have to remember. There are no do overs. There are no stop, come back moments

The speaker uses **repetition** in making the point that communication is irreversible and unerasable in this technological world. In what other ways might this point have been made?

And in conclusion, we have different forms of communication. It isn't just me talking to you face to face. It's Facebook. It's Skype. It's mass media. There are different platforms. We've got Facebook. I've got a general account. I can Skype. I can talk to someone on a cell phone. I can e-mail them on my computer. Those weren't available several years ago, and I suspect as time progresses that our platforms are going to be changing.

Lots of speakers announce their **conclusion** with the word "conclusion." What other ways might be used to signal that you're going into your conclusion?

Technology's going to allow us to even further communicate with those people that we were unable to do so even ten years ago. We live in a shrinking world, and because the world is shrinking, it is important to realize that what we here in the United States may think is normal, someone in Asia may find very offensive. So the bottom line is communication is really important, but it's also an awareness.

Here the speaker provides a kind of **motivation**—to learn more about communication and especially the cultural implications. If this speech were given in your class, what would you say in motivating your classmates to learn more about communication and culture?

It's a challenge to each student every day that when we learn to communicate, we communicate on a level that is both effective and not offensive, and with that, I thank you.

Here it's clear that the speaker is providing crisp **closure** to her speech. What would you say in closing?

A POORLY CONSTRUCTED PERSUASIVE SPEECH: "PRENUPS"

This speech was written to illustrate some really broad as well as some more subtle errors that a beginning speaker might make in constructing a persuasive speech. First, read the entire speech without reading any of the "Problems/Correctives." As you read the speech, consider what errors are being demonstrated and how you might correct them. Then, after you've read the entire speech, reread each paragraph and combine your own analysis with the "Problems/Correctives" annotations.

SPEECH	PROBLEMS/CORRECTIVES
Title: Prenups Topic: Prenuptial agreements Purpose: Prenuptials are bad. Thesis: Why do we need prenuptial agreements?	This title sounds like an informative speech title and doesn't give the idea that a position will be argued. In addition, the topic, purpose, and thesis are not clearly focused or appropriately worded. **A more appropriate title might be something like "Prenups Have Got to Go" or "The Dangers of Prenups." The topic would need to be narrowed by some qualification such as "The negative aspects of prenuptial agreements." The purpose should be stated as an infinitive phrase: To persuade my audience that prenuptial agreements should be declared illegal. The thesis needs to be stated as a declarative sentence: Prenuptial agreements should be declared illegal.**
Introduction You're probably not worried about prenuptial agreements yet. But maybe you will be. At any rate, that's what my speech is on. I mean that prenuptial agreements should be made illegal.	This opening is weak and can easily turn off audience members. After all, if they're not worried about it now, why listen? The speaker could have made a case for the importance of this topic in the near future, however. It appears as if the speaker knows the topic's not important but will speak on it anyway. **A more effective introduction would have (1) captured the audience's attention—perhaps by citing some widely reported celebrity prenup; (2) provided a connection among the speaker-audience-topic, perhaps by noting the consequences one might suffer with or without a prenup; and (3) oriented the audience as to what is to follow.**
Body	Here a transition would help. In fact, transitions should be inserted between the introduction and the body and between the body and the conclusion. Using transitions between the main points and signposts when introducing each main point would help. **The speaker might have said something like: "There are three main reasons why prenups should be banned."**
Prenuptial agreements make marriage a temporary arrangement. If you have a prenuptial agreement, you can get out of a marriage real fast—and we know that's not a good thing. So if we didn't have prenups—that's short for prenuptial agreements—marriages would last longer.	This is the speaker's first argument but it isn't introduced in a way the audience will find easy to understand. Abbreviations should be introduced more smoothly. **A simple signpost like, "My first argument against prenups is. ..." would make the audience see where the speaker is and get a visual of the outline. To introduce the abbreviation that will be used throughout the speech, the speaker might have incorporated it into the first sentence—"Prenuptial agreements—for short, prenups—make a marriage. . . ."**
Right now, most people don't have prenups and yet somewhere around 50 percent of marriages last. That would be equivalent to a baseball player batting .500. If we had prenups that number would go up—I mean down—I mean the number of marriages that last will go up if we had prenups, I mean if we didn't.	The fact that 50 percent of the marriages fail seems to be the more telling statistic, yet the speaker treats a 50 percent success rate as good—something the audience is likely to see very differently. And the baseball analogy seems weak at best. The speaker also betrays a lack of preparation in confusing up with down.

Poor people are going to be discriminated against. Poor people won't be able to marry rich people because rich people will want a prenup and if a poor person doesn't want a prenup they wouldn't get married.

This argument just doesn't seem logical, and the speaker would have been better served by omitting this entirely. **For this argument to be useful in advancing the speaker's purpose, the speaker would have had to show that in fact poor people suffer in, say, divorce proceedings because of prenups.**

These agreements are difficult to discuss. I mean, how do you tell someone you've told you love that you now want a prenup just in case the marriage gets screwed up? I guess you can say something like, "By the way, how about signing a prenup?"

This argument too doesn't seem important or logical. The fact that something is difficult to discuss doesn't mean you shouldn't discuss it; it merely means it's difficult to discuss. The speaker seems to be implying that if something is difficult to discuss it should be abandoned—clearly a poor communication strategy.

And they're expensive. I mean you need a lawyer and all. I don't know what a lawyer charges but I'd guess it's a lot. So it's expensive and a young couple could use the money on other things.

This argument also seems weak simply because if there is enough money involved to warrant a prenup, there's probably enough money to hire a lawyer. **If the speaker wanted to make this argument, specific costs should have been cited.**

I had a prenup 2 years ago. And when we got divorced, I got nothing. If we didn't have a prenup I'd be rich and I'd be at some private college instead of here.

Here the audience is likely thinking that there was a personal and emotional reason for arguing against prenups and not any logical reasons. And yet the audience is probably asking itself, what were the specifics of the prenup, and how much money was involved? **The speaker probably should have disclosed this earlier in the speech and assured the audience that this personal experience led to a thorough study of the subject. And if a personal experience is going to be used—and there's no reason it shouldn't—then it needs to be discussed more fully and, at the least, answer the audience's obvious questions.**

Conclusion

My conclusions. So you can see that prenups are not a good thing. Like they're unfair to poor people. And it creates a lot of stress for the couple, especially for the one who didn't want the prenup in the first place, like myself.

Using the word "conclusion" is not a bad idea, but it stands out like a heading in a textbook. This speech also needed a more detailed conclusion, reiterating the main points in the speech. This speaker also commits one of the common faults of conclusions and that is to introduce new material—notice that we hadn't heard of the stress factor before. **The speaker might have said something like: "In conclusion, we can see there are three main arguments against prenups. First, ..."**

Any questions?

This seems too abrupt. **A good pause should preface this request for questions and perhaps a more inviting request could be offered, something like, "If anyone has any questions, I'd be happy to respond."**

AN EXCELLENT PERSUASIVE SPEECH: "IT'S NOT THE ADDICT, IT'S THE DRUG"

This speech was delivered by Tunette Powell of the University of Nebraska, Omaha (and coached by Abbie Syrek and Vanessa Hatfield-Reeker) and took first place in the 139th Annual Contest of the Interstate Oratorical Association (Emerson College, Boston, MA), April 27–28, 2012. The speech is taken from Tunette Powell, *Winning Orations*, 2012, pp. 100–102. Interstate Oratorical Association, Mankato, IL. Ed. Larry Schnoor etc.

Title:	It's Not the Addict, It's the Drug: Redefining America's War on Drugs
Thesis:	Drug addiction should be treated as a disease rather than a crime.
General Purpose:	To persuade.
Specific Purpose:	To persuade the audience to view drug addiction as a disease.

SPEECH	COMMENTS/QUESTIONS
	This speech had strict time limits and so the speaker could not possibly include the "extras" that are noted in these comments and questions; rather, these are opportunities to explore different choices that might be available if this was a 30- or 40-minute speech.
Bruce Callis grew up in one of the poorest projects in San Antonio, Texas. His mother was a housekeeper; his father, a full-time alcoholic. Bruce downed his first beer at age 13, smoked marijuana at 14, and at 21 he was addicted to crack cocaine. By the time he was 30 Bruce was convicted of possession of crack cocaine and sentenced to 15 years behind bars.	Here the speaker gains attention by relaying this dramatic incident; it's the kind of illustration that piques audience members' interest; it makes them want to hear what else has happened in Bruce's life.
Forty years ago, Richard Nixon launched the "War on Drugs" to eliminate drug use and the illegal drug trade in our country. Sadly, Nixon and presidents after him waged the wrong war. This 40-year fight has become less about preventing drug distribution and more about the criminalization of addiction.	Here the speaker gives a little necessary background, which often helps if your audience is not well informed on the topic.
According to the New York Times on March 7, 2012, the United States currently incarcerates 2.3 million people, of which 23 percent are non-violent drug offenders.	Notice the integration of research here and throughout. You get the feeling that the speaker really did her homework; it gives you confidence that what the speaker is saying is reliable and current. **Does 2.3 million sound like a lot to you? If so, how might you have expressed the enormity of this figure?**
Yes, drug distribution in our country is a serious concern, but according to the Law Office for the Southern Center for Human Rights, last updated October 6, 2011, our misguided attitudes and policies toward drugs have created a culture that is intolerant of addiction. Although many people recognize addiction as a disease, we are still more likely to punish people for it than to help them with recovery.	The use of "yes" is interesting; it signals speaker and audience agreement that, ideally, will be carried over to the acceptance of the speaker's thesis.
According to the Office of National Drug Control Policy, "The U.S. federal government spent over $15 billion dollars in 2010 on the War on Drugs, at a rate of about $500 per second."	This is an enormous amount of money and the speaker makes it all the more real by noting that this comes to $500 per second. **What else might the speaker have said to make this amount more real in the minds of the audience?**
But the cost of criminalizing addiction isn't just paid in dollars, it is paid in lives. According to the Summer 2011 issue of YES Magazine, only one-fifth of addicts behind bars have adequate access to rehabilitation programs, making it almost impossible for them to recover and become functioning members of society, which not only hurts them, but society as a whole.	Some references may be unknown to the audience. **How might you establish the magazine's credibility in this context?**
Today, let's set aside what we've previous been told about drug use in America and focus on the person behind the addiction by discussing the problems, impacts, and solutions of criminalizing addiction. Attitude is the paint that can change the color of any room. And the walls of America are in dire need of a touch up.	Here the speaker provides an orientation, a preview, of her speech. You know the speech is going to deal with the problems, the impacts, and the solutions to criminalizing addiction. The organization is basically problem-solution with a section on the impacts of criminalization.

According to *USA Today* on September 10, 2011, over 20 million Americans struggling with addictions never receive help with recovery. Let's ask ourselves not what the problem is, but who the problem is. We are the problem for two reasons, one: we demonize addiction as dirty and morally wrong, and two: our policies reinforce this by putting addicts behind bars without rehabilitation.

Here the speaker identifies two problems—the demonization of the addict and incarceration without rehabilitation—and begins to discuss the first problem.

First, we are guilty of branding addiction as morally wrong when it is really an issue of public health. Maia Szalavitz wrote in the *New York Times* on September 27, 2011: "Prejudice against people based on the substances they use is one of the few remaining acceptable biases." She explains that we are blinded by a cultural perception that addicts are expendable; that they "deserve to die because they have violated the law and aren't taking responsibility for the consequences of their actions." Just proving her point further, in response to the article one reader explained, "Is it really in the social interest to save the lives of junkies who overdoes?"

The speaker later identifies Maia Szalavitz as a neuroscience journalist. **How might the speaker have first introduced or qualified this authority?**

Unfortunately, this voice is only one in a chorus of intolerance toward addicts, which leads to our second problem: we incarcerate addicts instead of giving them treatment. As we discussed earlier, the United States currently incarcerates over 500,000 non-violent drug users, all despite this: *USA Today* explained on August 16, 2011, that two decades of neuroscience have uncovered how addiction hijacks different parts of the brain and changes the cognitive and behavioral functions of drug users. According to the National Institute on Drug Abuse in 2011, "Addiction is a chronic disease similar to other chronic diseases such as type II diabetes, cancer, and cardiovascular disease."

Here the speaker introduces the second problem: incarceration without rehabilitation.

If cancer were treated the same as addiction, we would refuse treatment to inmates suffering from lung cancer simply because they have a history of smoking cigarettes.

This is a particularly effective analogy that makes you see the similarity between addiction and lung cancer and at the same time the very different responses of society. **Does this section convince you that addicts are not given adequate treatment? If so, what specifically convinced you? If not, what might the speaker have said that would have convinced you?**

According to *News Weekly* on June 28, 2010, only one-fifth of prison inmates get any form of drug treatment and nowhere does our public health policy stipulate that such treatment has to be "effective." Bruce Callis was in and out of prison from his early 20s to his late 40s. Most prisons didn't offer him treatment, and the ones that did were ineffective. Criminalizing addictions results in two alarming impacts: on the addict and society. According to a 2011 Public Safety Performance Project conducted by the Pew Research Center, four out of 10 drug offenders returned to state prison within three years of their release. And with little treatment available this shouldn't surprise us. A cycle is created the first time an addict goes to prison. They go from a sick person to a criminal. The addict is then released back into society. The sickness is ignored and the cycle repeats itself all over again.

As previously cited neuroscience journalist Maia Szalavitz points out, “even when drug users are released, their criminal record makes it impossible for them to find meaningful employment.” Not only are many addicts fighting disease without medical assistance, but many do so as unemployed, sometimes homeless, members of our society.

Second, this leads to startling social impacts. According to Uniform Crime Reports published by the FBI in October of 2011, every 20 seconds someone in America is arrested for violating a drug law. However, many of theses arrests are for drug possession with no intent to distribute. For example, according to that same report approximately 900,000 people in 2009 were arrested for marijuana, of which 89 percent were charged with possession with non intent to distribute.

Note the transition to the second major part of the body of the speech—the impacts of this incarceration without rehabilitation. **Do you personally feel this impact? If so, what made you feel it? If not, what might the speaker have said that would have made you feel this impact?**

Our economy is in a state of emergency, yet our eagerness to criminalize drugs and put users behind bars is costing us billions of dollars a year. *The Fiscal Times* reported on February 9, 2011, that in California, alone, it costs about $45,000 per year to incarcerate a drug user; the same price as one year at Harvard University with room and board. By contrast, rehabilitation would costs less that $5,000 per year. Our tax collars continue to be wasted on room and board for inmates who will never benefit or recover as long as they're incarcerated.

This comparison with Harvard is particularly interesting because it makes listeners see how an amount as large as a year at Harvard is used but accomplishes nothing or very little. **How would you have emphasized that $45,000 is a lot of money? That is, what other comparisons might you have used?**

Bruce Callis was released from prison for the final time when he was 47 years old.

After one week his son found him slumped over at a bus station, high on crack and barely able to walk. Notice that nowhere in Callis' story have I mentioned drug treatment, only incarceration. What can we do to help people like him? Let's look at personal, organizational, and governmental solutions.

Here the speaker gives an orientation to the section of her speech dealing with the solutions; from this sentence we know that she will address personal, organizational, and governmental solutions in that order.

Our personal solution comes first, because it is the foundation for all other solutions: we must change our attitudes about addiction.

Dr. Ellen Friedman, a psychologist, told the Huffington Post on October 3, 2011: “The profile of the addict as an amoral thrill-seeker is . . . scientifically wrong.” We don't shame people for cancer diagnoses; we cannot continue to demonize drug users.

Second, we have to get involved to promote rehabilitation and fight incarceration for non-violent drug users. There are existing organizations that need our support, such as A New Path, an organization that is dedicated to reducing the stigma of addictive illness and advocates for therapeutic rather than punitive drug policies. Visit their website

Notice the transitional terms (*Second*) here and throughout. They help the listeners follow the speaker's train of thought. **Do you think you'll visit this website? If so, what in the speech lead to your decision? If not, what might the speaker have said to move you to access the website and to look into this organization?**

at **anewpathsite.org**. This organization publishes updates on national drug legislation; check it out to learn more about legislation in your area.

On a government level, the first step is for policy to reflect the differences between possession and distribution, which would greatly reduce the number of drug users behind bars. This would help law enforcement distinguish between the crime of distributing drugs and the person who is addicted to them.

Finally, perhaps our government can look to Portugal who has set a noble example. Ten years ago, Portugal decriminalized the use of drugs, according to *Matador Magazine* in July, 2011. People caught using illegal substances are sent before a panel of psychologists and social workers instead of a judge in a criminal court. *Matador Magazine* reported that since the 2001 law was enacted the number of addicts has been cut in half. Portugal is a real life example of what happens when a country treats drug addiction as a health issue and not a criminal one.

This example is especially well chosen because it demonstrates that the speaker's proposal has worked elsewhere. **How might you have expressed the credentials of *Matador Magazine*?**

Now is the time to separate the war on drugs from the war on addiction. Today, you've head the problems, impacts, and solutions of criminalizing addiction. Bruce Callis is 50 years old now. And he is still struggling with his addiction. While you all are sitting out there listening to this, I'm living it. Bruce Callis is my father and for my entire life, I have watched our misguided system destroy him. The irony here is that we live in a society where we are told to recycle. We recycle paper, aluminum, and old electronics. But why don't we ever consider recycling the most previous thing on earth—the human life.

This is a particularly dramatic conclusion where we discover that Bruce Callis is the speaker's father. It's a personal connection that could also have been used in the introduction to stress the speaker's personal involvement with the topic. But in the conclusion it leaves perhaps a more lasting impression. **Where in the speech do you think this revelation would have been most effective?**

A SLIDE SHOW SPEECH: "SELF-DISCLOSURE"

This PowerPoint speech is intended to illustrate the general structure of a slide show speech and is derived from the speech in the Public Speaking Sample Assistant box in Chapter 16 (pages 335–336); you may find it helpful to look back at that speech to consider how you might improve this purposely sparse slide show. This PowerPoint presentation is available online at MyCommunication-Lab. Copy it to your computer and try altering this basic outline as you learn more about PowerPoint or similar presentation software.

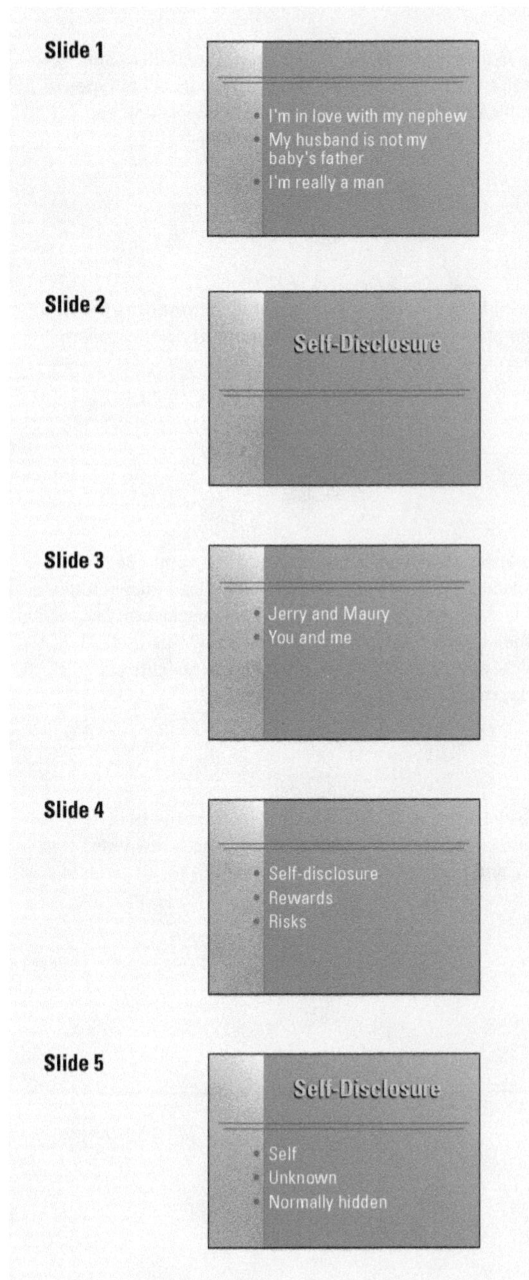

This first slide aims to gain attention with these provocative confessions. These three bullets would come up one at a time, with the speaker pausing for (with luck) some laughter. After you review the entire list of slides, try inserting graphics where you think they'd be appropriate.

This second slide introduces the topic of the speech, self-disclosure.

This slide recalls the popular confessions heard on the *Jerry Springer Show* and *Maury* but also relates the process of self-disclosure to the speaker and the audience, establishing an S-A-T connection.

This slide orients the audience by identifying the three main ideas to be discussed in the speech: the nature of self-disclosure, its rewards, and its risks. As with slide number 1, these three bullets should come up one at a time to give the speaker a chance to elaborate on each item and to give the audience a chance to digest the information. Note that this slide show does not contain transitions; if you think they might help, insert transitions.

This fifth slide focuses on the first major idea, the nature of self-disclosure as communication about the self, about something previously unknown, and about something that is normally kept hidden. Note here that very few words are used in the actual slide; the speaker will elaborate on each of these items in the actual speech. The words on the slide are best thought of as tags you want the audience to hang on to as you explain each point.

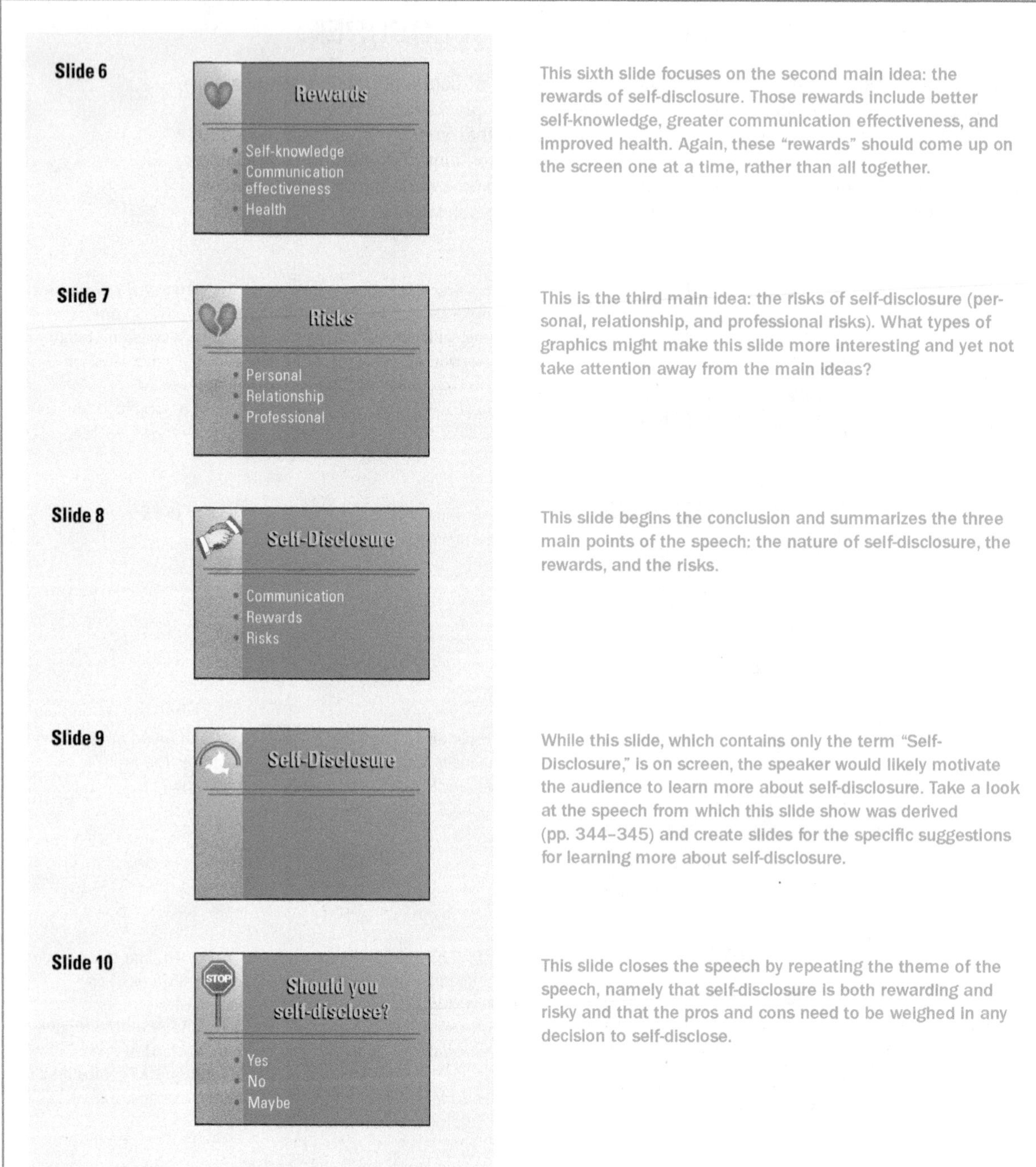

This sixth slide focuses on the second main idea: the rewards of self-disclosure. Those rewards include better self-knowledge, greater communication effectiveness, and improved health. Again, these "rewards" should come up on the screen one at a time, rather than all together.

This is the third main idea: the risks of self-disclosure (personal, relationship, and professional risks). What types of graphics might make this slide more interesting and yet not take attention away from the main ideas?

This slide begins the conclusion and summarizes the three main points of the speech: the nature of self-disclosure, the rewards, and the risks.

While this slide, which contains only the term "Self-Disclosure," is on screen, the speaker would likely motivate the audience to learn more about self-disclosure. Take a look at the speech from which this slide show was derived (pp. 344–345) and create slides for the specific suggestions for learning more about self-disclosure.

This slide closes the speech by repeating the theme of the speech, namely that self-disclosure is both rewarding and risky and that the pros and cons need to be weighed in any decision to self-disclose.

Glossary of Human Communication Concepts and Skills

Listed here are definitions of the technical terms of human communication—the words that are peculiar or unique to this discipline along with relevant skills where applicable. These definitions and skill statements should make new or difficult terms a bit easier to understand and should serve as reminders of the skills discussed throughout this text. All boldface terms within the definitions appear as separate entries in the glossary

5W pattern An organizational pattern for a speech that divides the speech into who? what? why? where? and when? *Consider this pattern for speeches in which you wish to report or explain an event.*

A

ableism Discrimination against people with disabilities. *Use person-first language; put the person first and the disability second, not "the blind boy" but "the boy who is blind ..."*

abstraction A general concept derived from a class of objects; a partial representation of some whole. *Use both abstract and specific terms when describing or explaining.*

abstraction process The process by which a general concept is derived from specifics; the process by which some (never all) characteristics of an object, person, or event are perceived by the senses or included in some term, phrase, or sentence. *Use both abstract and specific terms when describing or explaining.*

accent The stress or emphasis placed on a syllable when it is pronounced.

acceptance speech A speech in which the speaker accepts an award or honor of some kind and attempts to place the award in some kind of context.

accommodation The process of adjusting your communication patterns to those with whom you're interacting. *Accommodate to the speaking style of your listeners in moderation; too much mirroring of the other's style may appear manipulative.*

acculturation The processes by which a person's culture is modified or changed through contact with or exposure to another culture.

action step The fifth step in the **motivated sequence** which spells out what you want audience members to do, the action that you want them to take to ensure that the need is satisfied as visualized.

active listening A process of putting together into some meaningful whole the listener's understanding of the speaker's total message—the verbal and the nonverbal, the content and the feelings. *If you wish to listen actively, paraphrase the speaker's meaning, express understanding of the speaker's feelings, and ask questions when you need something clarified.*

adaptors Nonverbal behaviors that satisfy some personal need and usually occur without awareness; for example, scratching to relieve an itch or moistening your lips to relieve dryness. Three types of adaptors are often distinguished: **self-adaptors, alter-adaptors,** and **object-adaptors.**

adjustment The principle of verbal interaction that claims that communication takes place only to the extent that the parties communicating share the same system of signals.

advantages–disadvantages pattern In evaluating your own relationship choices, consider both the advantages and the disadvantages of your relationships in general and of your specific relationships.

affect displays Movements of the facial area that convey emotional meaning—for example, expressions showing anger, fear, or surprise.

affiliative cues Verbal or nonverbal signals that show love for another person.

affinity-seeking strategies Behaviors designed to increase our interpersonal attractiveness. *Use in moderation.*

affirmation The communication of support and approval.

agape love A type of love that is compassionate, egoless, and self-giving.

ageism Discrimination based on age, usually against the elderly. *Avoid it.*

agenda A list of the items that a small group must deal with in the order in which they should be covered. *As a leader or member, keep focused on the agenda.*

agenda-setting A persuasive technique in which the speaker states or implies that XYZ is the issue and that all others are unimportant.

aggressiveness See **verbal aggressiveness.**

allness A language distortion; the assumption that all can be known or is known about a given person, issue, object, or event. *Avoid allness statements (for example, statements containing such words as* all, never, *or* always*); they invariably misstate the reality and will often offend the other person.*

alter-adaptors Body movements you make in response to your current interactions; for example, crossing your arms over your chest when someone unpleasant approaches or moving closer to someone you like.

altercasting Placing the listener in a specific role for a specific purpose and asking that the listener approach a question or problem from the perspective of this specific role.

ambiguity Uncertainty of meaning; the possibility of interpreting a message in more than one way. *Recognize that all messages are potentially ambiguous so clarify as necessary.*

ambiguity tolerance A cultural orientation concerned with the degree of discomfort with uncertainty.

amount of change principle A principle of persuasion stating that the greater and more important the change desired by the speaker, the more difficult its achievement will be.

analogies Comparisons that are often extremely useful in making your ideas clear and vivid to your audience

analogy, reasoning from A type of reasoning in which you compare like things and conclude that since they are alike in so many respects that they are also alike in some previously unknown respect.

anecdotal evidence A fallacious persuasive tactic in which the speaker offers specific examples or illustrations as "proof."

anger management The methods and techniques by which anger is controlled and managed. *Calm down as best you can; then consider your communication options and the relevant communication skills for expressing your feelings.*

antithesis A figure of speech in which contrary ideas are presented in parallel form, as in Charles Dickens's opening lines in *A Tale of Two Cities:* "It was the best of times, it was the worst of times."

antithetical sentences A type of sentence patterning in which contrasting ideas are placed together in parallel style.

apology A type of excuse in which you acknowledge responsibility for your behavior, generally ask forgiveness, and claim that this behavior will not happen again.

apology, speech of A speech in which the speaker apologizes for some transgression and tries to restore his or her credibility.

appeal to authority A fallacy of reasoning in which someone is passed off as an authority when the person logically has little authority, expertise, or knowledge in the subject under discussion. *Ask for evidence.*

appeal to numbers Appeals to numbers in which the speaker argues that truth is determined by popularity.

appeal to tradition A fallacy often used as an argument against change, as when a speaker claims that a proposed plan should not be adopted because it was never done before.

apprehension See **communication apprehension.**

appropriateness A quality of public speaking language making it suitable for a particular audience.

arbitrariness The feature of human language that reflects the absence of a real or inherent relationship between the form of a word and its meaning. If we do not know anything of a particular language, we cannot examine the form of a word and thereby discover its meaning.

argument Evidence (for example, facts or statistics) and a conclusion drawn from the evidence.

argumentativeness Willingness to argue for a point of view, to speak your mind. *In conflict, avoid attacking the other person's* *self-concept. Instead, focus logically on the issues, emphasize finding solutions, and work to ensure that what is said will result in positive self-feelings for both individuals.* Distinguished from **verbal aggressiveness.**

articulation The physiological movements of the speech organs as they modify and interrupt the air stream emitted from the lungs.

artifactual communication Communication that takes place through the wearing and arrangement of various items made by human hands—for example, clothing, jewelry, buttons, or the furniture in your house and its arrangement. *Use artifacts (for example, color, clothing, body adornment, space decoration) to communicate your desired messages. But check to find out whether others are in fact receiving the messages you think you are communicating.*

assertiveness Willingness to stand up for your own rights while respecting the rights of others. *Increase your own assertiveness by analyzing the assertive messages of others, rehearsing assertive messages, and communicating assertively by describing the problem, saying how the problem affects you, proposing solutions, confirming your understanding, and reflecting on your own assertiveness.*

assertiveness training group A type of small group focusing on increasing assertive behavior of members.

assimilation A process of distortion in which messages are reconstructed to conform to our own attitudes, prejudices, needs, and values.

asynchronous Communication in which sending and receiving of a message takes place at different times. Opposed to **synchronous.**

attack A persuasive technique that involves accusing another person (usually an opponent) of some serious wrongdoing so that the issue under discussion never gets examined. *Avoid this as a speaker and recognize it for what it is as a listener.*

attention The process of responding to a stimulus or stimuli; usually involves some consciousness of responding.

attention step The first step in the **motivated sequence**; makes audience members give you their undivided attention.

attitude A predisposition to respond for or against an object, person, or position.

attraction The state or process by which one individual is drawn to another and forms a highly positive evaluation of that other person.

attraction theory A theory holding that we form relationships on the basis of our attraction to another person.

attractiveness The degree to which a person is perceived to be physically appealing and to possess a pleasing personality.

attribution A process through which we attempt to understand the behaviors of others (as well as our own), particularly the reasons or motivations for these behaviors.

attribution of control A process by which you focus on explaining why someone behaved as he or she did on the basis of whether the person had control over his or her behavior.

audience Those who hear the speech first-hand (the immediate audience) and those who hear it second-hand (the remote audience).

audience analysis The process of analyzing a speaker's intended listeners. *Analyze the audience in terms of its sociological and psychological characteristics and adapt your speech based on these findings.*

audience participation principle A principle of persuasion stating that persuasion is achieved more effectively when the audience participates actively.

auditory imagery Imagery that describes sounds and enable listeners to "hear" the car's tires screeching, for example.

authoritarian leader A group leader who determines group policies or makes decisions without consulting or securing agreement from group members.

avoidance An unproductive **conflict** strategy in which a person takes mental or physical flight from the actual conflict. *Avoid avoidance; engaging in conflict actively is generally the more effective management strategy.*

B

backchanneling cues Listener responses to a speaker that do not ask for the speaking role.

bandwagon A persuasive technique in which the speaker tries to gain compliance by saying that "everyone is doing it" and urging listeners to jump on the bandwagon.

barriers to communication Factors (physical or psychological) that prevent or hinder effective communication.

behavioral synchrony The similarity in the behavior, usually nonverbal, of two persons. Generally, it is taken as an index of mutual liking.

belief Confidence in the existence or truth of something; conviction.

beltlining An unproductive **conflict** strategy in which one person hits at the level at which the other person cannot withstand the blow. *Avoid it; beltlining is likely to cause resentment that may extend well beyond the argument itself.*

blame An unproductive **conflict** strategy in which we attribute the cause of the conflict to the other person or devote our energies to discovering who is the cause and avoid talking about the issues causing the conflict. *Focus on resolving the conflict rather than affixing blame.*

blind self The self that contains knowledge about you that others have but that you do not.

boundary marker An object that divides one person's territory from another's—for example, a fence.

brainstorming A technique for generating ideas either alone or, more usually, in a small group. *Follow these general rules: Avoid negative criticism, strive for quantity, combine and extend the contributions of others, and contribute as wild ideas as possible. Appropriately re-stimulate a brainstorming group that has lost its steam by asking for additional contributions or for further extensions of previously contributed ideas.*

breadth In the **social penetration theory** of interpersonal relationships, the number of topics about which individuals in a relationship communicate.

bromides Trite sayings that are worn out because of constant usage.

bypassing A pattern of miscommunication occurring when the speaker and the listener miss each other with their meanings.

C

card stacking A persuasive technique in which the speaker selects only the evidence and arguments that build his or her case and omits or distorts any contradictory evidence.

causes and effects, reasoning from A form of reasoning in which you conclude that certain effects are due to specific causes or that specific causes produce certain effects. *Be careful that you don't fall into the trap of assuming that because things occur in sequence, that one necessarily causes the other.*

cause–effect pattern An organizational pattern in which the speech is divided into two main parts: causes and effects.

censorship Restriction on people's rights to produce, distribute, and/or receive various communications.

central marker An item that is placed in a territory to reserve it for a specific person—for example, the sweater thrown over a library chair to signal that the chair is taken.

certainty An attitude of closed-mindedness that creates a defensiveness among communication participants; opposed to **provisionalism.**

channel The vehicle or medium through which signals are sent. *Assess your channel options (for example, speaking face to face, sending e-mail, or leaving a voicemail message when you know the person won't be home) before communicating important messages.*

character An individual's honesty and basic nature; moral qualities that contribute to **credibility.**

character attacks Attacks on a person's personal qualities, usually accusing the person (often an opponent) of some wrongdoing or of some character flaw.

charisma An individual's dynamism or forcefulness; one of the qualities that contribute to **credibility.**

cherishing behaviors Small behaviors we enjoy receiving from others, especially from our relational partner—for example, a kiss, a smile, or a gift of flowers. *Exchanging such behaviors is one way of increasing relationship satisfaction.*

chronemics The study of the communicative nature of time—of the way you treat time and use it to communicate. Two general areas of chronemics are **cultural time** and **psychological time.**

civil inattention Polite ignoring of others so as not to invade their privacy.

claim-and-proof pattern An organizational pattern in which the thesis is the claim and each main point offers proof in support of this claim.

clarity A quality of language that makes messages understandable to listeners.

cliché An overused expression that has lost its novelty and part of its meaning and that calls attention to itself because of its overuse, such as "tall, dark, and handsome" as a description of a man.

closed-mindedness An unwillingness to receive certain communication messages. *Listen openly even to messages that may contradict existing attitudes and beliefs.*

closure A recommended part of the conclusion of a public speech in which you wrap up everything and let the audience know that the speech is ending.

code A set of symbols used to translate a message from one form to another.

coercive power Power derived from an individual's ability to punish or to remove rewards from another person.

cognitive restructuring A theory for substituting logical and realistic beliefs for unrealistic ones; used in reducing communication apprehension and in raising self-esteem.

cohesiveness The property of togetherness. In group-communication situations, cohesiveness has to do with the mutual attraction among members; it's a measure of the extent to which individual group members work together as a group.

collective orientation A cultural orientation that stresses the group's, rather than the individual's, goals and preferences. Opposed to **individual orientation.**

collectivist culture A culture in which the group's goals are given greater importance than the individual's and in which, for example, benevolence, tradition, and conformity are given special emphasis. Opposed to **individualist culture.**

color communication The meanings that different colors communicate in various cultures. *Use color to reinforce your meanings and recognize the cultural differences in the way colors are given meaning.*

commencement speech A speech given to celebrate the end of some training period, often at school graduation ceremonies.

communication (1) The process or act of communicating; (2) the actual message or messages sent and received; (3) the study of the processes involved in the sending and receiving of messages.

communication accommodation theory Theory holding that speakers adjust their speaking style to their listeners to gain social approval and achieve greater communication effectiveness.

communication apprehension Fear or anxiety over communicating; may be "trait apprehension" (fear of communication generally, regardless of the specific situation) or "state apprehension" (fear that is specific to a given communication situation). *Acquire communication skills and experiences, focus on your prior successes, reduce unpredictability, and put apprehension in perspective.*

communication competence A knowledge of the rules and skills of communication; the term often refers to the qualities that make for effectiveness in communication.

communication network The pathways of messages; the organizational structure through which messages are sent and received.

communicology The study of communication, particularly the subsection concerned with human communication.

comparison and contrast pattern A pattern for organizing a speech in which you compare and contrast two different items.

comparison level A general idea of the profits you feel you should get from a relationship.

competence A person's ability and knowledge; one of the qualities that contribute to **credibility.**

complementarity A principle of **attraction** stating that we are attracted by qualities that we do not possess or that we wish to possess and to people who are opposite or different from ourselves; opposed to **similarity.**

complementary relationship A relationship in which the behavior of one person (e.g., energetic activity) serves as the stimulus for the complementary behavior of the other (e.g., laziness); in complementary relationships behavioral differences are maximized.

compliance-gaining strategies Behaviors that are directed toward gaining the agreement of others; behaviors designed to persuade others to do as we wish.

compliance-resisting strategies Behaviors directed at resisting the persuasive attempts of others.

compliment A message of praise, flattery, or congratulations.

computer-mediated communication A general term denoting all forms of communication between people that take place through some computer, electronic, or Internet connection.

conclusions Conclusions to speeches should summarize the main points and bring the speech to a crisp close.

confidence A quality of interpersonal effectiveness; a comfortable, at-ease feeling in interpersonal communication situations.

confirmation A communication pattern that acknowledges another person's presence and also indicates an acceptance of this person, this person's definition of self, and the relationship as defined or viewed by this other person. *When you wish to be confirming, acknowledge (verbally and/or nonverbally) others in your group and their contributions.* Opposed to **disconfirmation**.

conflict An extreme form of competition in which interdependent persons perceive their respective goals to be incompatible and see each other as interfering with their own attainment of desired goals.

conflict, culture, and gender Approach conflict with an understanding of cultural and gender differences in what constitutes conflict and in how it should be pursued.

conflict styles Adjust your conflict style to the specific conflict in which you find yourself.

congruence A condition in which both verbal and nonverbal behaviors reinforce each other.

connotation The feeling or emotional aspect of meaning, generally viewed as consisting of the evaluative (for example, good–bad), potency (strong–weak), and activity (fast–slow) dimensions; the associations of a term. *As a speaker, clarify your connotative meanings if you have any doubts that your listeners might misunderstand you; as a listener, ask questions if you have doubts about the speaker's connotations.* See also **denotation.**

consciousness-raising group A small group of people who help each other to cope with the problems society confronts them with.

consensus A principle of attribution through which we attempt to establish whether other people react or behave in the same way as the person on whom we are now focusing. If the person is acting in accordance with the general consensus, then we seek reasons for the behavior outside the individual; if the person is not acting in accordance with the general consensus, then we seek reasons that are internal to the individual.

consistency A perceptual process that influences us to maintain balance among our perceptions; a process that makes us tend to see what we expect to see and to be uncomfortable when our perceptions run contrary to our expectations.

contact The first stage of an interpersonal relationship, in which perceptual and interactional contact occurs.

contamination A form of territorial encroachment that renders another's territory impure.

content and relationship dimensions A principle of communication stating that messages refer both to content (the world external to both speaker and listener) and to the relationship existing between the individuals who are interacting. *Listen to both the content and the relationship aspects of messages, distinguish between them, and respond to both. In conflict, analyze messages in terms of content and relationship dimensions and respond to each accordingly.*

content conflict Interpersonal conflict that centers on objects, events, and persons that are usually, though not always, external to the parties involved in the conflict.

content message A message that refers to events or objects external to a relationship; opposed to **relationship message**.

context The physical, social-psychological, temporal, and cultural environment in which communication takes place.

context of communication The physical, psychological, social, and temporal environment in which communication takes place. *Adjust your messages to the unique communication context, taking into consideration its physical, cultural, social–psychological, and temporal aspects.*

contrast (principle of) Often-followed rule of perception: If messages or people are very different from each other, they probably don't belong together and do not constitute a set or group.

controllability One of the factors we consider in judging whether or not a person is responsible for his or her behavior. If the person was in control, then we judge that he or she was responsible. A principle in **attribution theory.**

conversation Communication engaged in by two or three people and usually including an opening, feedforward, a business stage, feedback, and a closing.

conversational management The conduct of a conversation by means of **conversational turns.**

conversational maxims Principles that are followed in conversation to ensure that the goal of the conversation is achieved. *Follow (generally) the basic maxims of conversation, such as the maxims of quantity, quality, relations, manner, and politeness.*

conversational turns The process of exchanging the speaker and listener roles during conversation. *Maintain relatively short conversational turns and then pass the speaker's turn to another person nonverbally or verbally.*

cooperation An interpersonal process by which individuals work together for a common end; the pooling of efforts to produce a mutually desired outcome. In communication, an implicit agreement that calls for speaker and listener to work together to achieve mutual comprehension.

credibility The degree to which a speaker is perceived to be believable; **competence**, **character**, and **charisma** (dynamism) are its major dimensions.

credibility appeals Seek to establish credibility by displaying **competence,** high moral character, and dynamism or **charisma.**

critical analysis Critically analyze reasoning from specific instances to generalizations, causes and effects, and sign.

critical thinking The process of logically evaluating reasons and evidence and reaching a judgment on the basis of this analysis.

critical thinking hats technique Technique developed by Edward deBono in which a problem or issue is viewed from six distinct perspectives: facts, feelings, negative arguments, positive benefits, creative new ideas, and control of thinking.

criticism The reasoned judgment of some work; although often equated with fault finding, criticism can involve both positive or negative evaluations.

cultivation theory A theory of media influence that claims that the media cultivate a view of the world in the mind of the viewer.

cultural display Signs that communicate a person's cultural identification, for example, clothing or religious jewelry.

cultural rules Rules that are specific to a given cultural group. *Increase your sensitivity to these rules by learning about different cultures, recognizing and facing your own fears of intercultural interaction, recognizing differences between yourself and others, and becoming conscious of the cultural rules and customs of other cultures.*

cultural sensitivity An attitude and way of behaving in which you're aware of and acknowledge cultural differences without negative evaluation.

cultural time The perspective on time shared by members of a particular culture.

culture The relatively specialized lifestyle of a group of people—consisting of their values, beliefs, artifacts, ways of behaving, and ways of communicating—that is passed on from one generation to the next.

culture shock The psychological reaction we experience at being placed in a culture very different from our own or from what we are used to.

D

date An **extensional device** used to emphasize the notion of constant change and symbolized by a mental subscript: for example, John Smith 1999 is not John Smith 2008. *Use the date (verbally or mentally) to guard against static evaluation.*

deception bias The assumption that the other person is lying; opposed to a truth bias.

deception cues Verbal or nonverbal cues that reveal the person is lying.

decoder Something that takes a message in one form (for example, sound waves) and translates it into another form (for example, nerve impulses) from which meaning can be formulated (for example, in vocal-auditory communication). In human communication the decoder is the auditory mechanism; in electronic communication the decoder is, for example, the telephone earpiece. See also **encoder.**

decoding The process of extracting a message from a code—for example, translating speech sounds into nerve impulses. See also **encoding.**

dedication speech A special occasion speech in which you commemorate the opening or start of a project.

deep web That part of the web that contains that collection of documents that are not accessible through simple searches on general search engines or directions.

definition A statement explaining the meaning of a term or concept.

defensiveness An attitude of an individual or an atmosphere in a group characterized by threats, fear, and domination; messages evidencing evaluation, control, strategy, neutrality, superiority, and certainty are assumed to lead to defensiveness; opposed to **supportiveness.**

delayed reactions Reactions that are consciously delayed while a situation is analyzed.

delegating style A style of leadership in which the leader observes but doesn't provide much direction or support.

delivery outline The outline the speaker brings to the public speaking situation and refers to during the speech.

Delphi method A type of problem-solving group in which questionnaires are used to poll members (who don't interact among themselves) on several occasions so as to arrive at a group decision on, for example, the most important problems a company faces or activities a group might undertake. *Use the Delphi method to solve problems when group members are separated geographically.*

democratic leader A group leader who stimulates self-direction and self-actualization on the part of the group members.

denial One of the obstacles to the expression of emotion; the process by which we deny our emotions to ourselves or to others. *Become mindful of the reasons for denial and the negative impact this generally has on communication.*

denotation Referential meaning; the objective or descriptive meaning of a word. See also **connotation.**

depenetration A reversal of penetration; a condition in which the **breadth** and **depth** of a relationship decrease. See **social penetration theory.**

depth In **social penetration theory** of interpersonal relationships, the degree to which the inner personality—the inner core—of an individual is penetrated in interpersonal interaction.

determinism The principle of verbal interaction that holds that all verbalizations are to some extent purposeful—that there is a reason for every verbalization.

dialogue A form of **communication** in which each person is both speaker and listener; communication characterized by involvement, concern, and respect for the other person. *Treat conversation as a dialogue rather than a monologue; show concern for the other person, and for the relationship between you, with other-orientation.* Opposed to **monologue.**

Dilbert Principle A principle of organizations that claims that organizations will promote incompetent workers to managerial positions where they'll be able to do the least damage.

direct message Speech in which the speaker states his or her intentions clearly and forthrightly.

disclaiming A form of feedforward in which you ask listeners to hear you favorably and without bias.

disconfirmation The process by which one person ignores or denies the right of another person even to define himself or herself. *Avoid sexist, heterosexist, racist, and ageist language; such language is disconfirming and insulting and invariably contributes to communication barriers.* Opposed to **confirmation.**

disinhibition effect A tendency to be more open, less inhibited, in some forms of communication, often social network communication.

display rules Cultural norms for what is and what is not appropriate to display in public.

dissolution The breaking of the bonds holding an interpersonal relationship together.

door-in-the-face technique A persuasive strategy in which the speaker first makes a large request that will be refused and then follows with the intended and much smaller request.

downward communication Messages sent from the higher levels to the lower levels of an organizational hierarchy; for example, messages sent by managers to workers or by deans to faculty members. See **upward communication, lateral communication.** *To improve downward communication, use a vocabulary known to the workers, keeping technical jargon to a minimum; provide workers with sufficient information; and be especially careful not to damage others' image or face.*

Duchenne smile Smiles that are beyond voluntary control and that signal genuine happiness.

dyadic communication Two-person communication.

dyadic consciousness An awareness of an interpersonal relationship or pairing of two individuals; distinguished from situations in which two individuals are together but do not perceive themselves as being a unit or twosome.

dyadic effect The process by which one person in a dyad imitates the behavior of the other person, usually used to refer to the tendency of one person's self-disclosures to prompt the other to also self-disclose. *Pay attention to the dyadic effect; it may indicate the other person's degree of involvement in the conversation.*

E

earmarker A physical sign that identifies an item as belonging to a specific person—for example, a nameplate on a desk or initials on an attaché case. *Use earmarkers with a consideration for the rights of others as well as your own.*

effect The outcome or consequence of an action or behavior; communication is assumed always to have some effect.

effect-cause pattern An organizational structure of a speech into both effects and causes.

emblems Nonverbal behaviors that directly translate words or phrases—for example, the signs for "OK" and "peace." *Use these with an awareness of the great cultural differences in the meanings given to various emblems.*

emergent leader A leader who is not appointed but rather "emerges" during the group process.

emotional appeals Persuasive strategies designed to influence the emotions of the audience. *In persuasive speaking use emotional appeals—for example, appeals to fear; power, control, and influence; safety; achievement; and financial gain—as appropriate to the speech and the audience.*

emotional communication To communicate emotions effectively, (1) describe feelings, (2) identify the reasons for the feelings, (3) anchor feelings to the present, and (4) own your feelings and messages.

emotional display Express your emotions and interpret the emotions of others in light of the cultural rules dictating what is and what isn't "appropriate" emotional expression.

emotional understanding Be able to identify and describe emotions (both positive and negative) clearly and specifically. Learn the vocabulary of emotional expression.

emotionality in interpersonal communication Include the inevitable emotionality of your thoughts and feelings in your interpersonal communication, verbally and nonverbally.

emotions The feelings we have—for example, our feelings of guilt, anger, or sorrow. *Express your emotions and interpret the emotions of others in light of the cultural rules dictating what is and what isn't appropriate emotional expression.*

empathy Feeling another person's feeling or perceiving something as does another person. *Communicate empathy when appropriate: resist evaluating the person's behaviors, focus concentration on the person, express active involvement through facial expressions and gestures, reflect back the feelings you think are being expressed, self-disclose, and address any mixed messages.*

encoder Something that takes a message in one form (for example, nerve impulses) and translates it into another form (for example, sound waves). In human communication the encoder is the speaking mechanism; in electronic communication the encoder is, for example, the telephone mouthpiece. See also **decoder.**

encoding The process of putting a message into a code—for example, translating nerve impulses into speech sounds. See also **decoding.**

encounter groups A type of small group in which members facilitate each other's personal growth.

enculturation The process by which culture is transmitted from one generation to another.

E-prime A form of the English language that omits the verb *to be* except when used as an auxiliary or in statements of existence; also called E'. Designed to eliminate the tendency toward **projection.** *When you feel that you may be over-generalizing or making assumptions about all from only a few instances, try thinking in E-prime by eliminating the verb "to be."*

equality An attitude that recognizes that each individual in a communication interaction is equal, that no one is superior to any other; encourages supportiveness; opposed to **superiority.**

equilibrium theory A theory of **proxemics** holding that intimacy and physical closeness are positively related; as relationship becomes more intimate, the individuals will use shorter distances between them.

equity theory A theory of interpersonal relationships claiming that we experience relational satisfaction when there is an equal distribution of rewards and costs between the two persons in the relationship.

eros A type of love characterized by a focus on physical qualities.

et cetera An **extensional device** used to emphasize the notion of infinite complexity; because we can never know all about anything, we should end any statement about the world or an event with an explicit or implicit "etc." *Think with the etc., being mindful that there is more to say, see, hear, etc.*

ethics The rightness or wrongness of actions; the branch of philosophy that studies moral values.

ethnic identity A commitment to the beliefs and philosophy of your culture.

ethnocentrism The tendency to see others and their behaviors through our own cultural filters, often as distortions of our own behaviors; the tendency to evaluate the values and beliefs of our own culture more positively than those of another culture. *Recognizing our own ethnocentrism may help to prevent evaluating different cultural practices negatively.*

etymology The historical or linguistic development of a word or phrase and often a useful way to help define a word.

eulogy A speech of tribute in which the speaker praises someone who died.

euphemism A polite word or phrase used to substitute for some taboo or otherwise offensive term; often used as a persuasive strategy to make the negative appear positive.

example A relatively brief specific instance.

excluding talk Talk about a subject or in a vocabulary that only certain people understand, often in the presence of someone who does not belong to this group and therefore does not understand; use of terms unique to a specific culture as if they were universal.

exclusionist orientation A cultural orientation that fosters a strong in-group affiliation with much less respect for out-group members; opposed to **universalism.**

excuse An explanation designed to lessen the negative consequences of something done or said. *When using excuses, for example, to repair a conversation problem (1) demonstrate that you understand the problem, (2) acknowledge your responsibility, (3) acknowledge your regret for what you did, (4) request forgiveness, and (5) make it clear that this will never happen again.*

expectancy violations theory A theory of **proxemics** holding that people have a certain expectancy for space relationships. When that expectancy is violated (for example, when a person stands too close to you or a romantic partner maintains abnormally large distances from you), the relationship comes into clearer focus and you wonder why this "normal distance" is being violated.

experiential limitation The limit of an individual's ability to communicate, as set by the nature and extent of that individual's experiences.

expert power Power that a person possesses because others believe the individual to have expertise or knowledge.

expert witness testimony Support for a public speech in which the speaker cites the opinions, beliefs, predictions, or values of some authority or expert.

extemporaneous speech A speech that is thoroughly prepared and organized in detail and in which certain aspects of style are predetermined.

extensional device Linguistic device to help make language a more accurate means for talking about the world. Proposed by Alfred Korzybski, the extensional devices include **et cetera, date,** and **index**, among others. *Thinking mindfully with these devices in mind.*

extensionalize The tendency to give more attention to the actual person or thing and less to the labels used.

extensional orientation A tendency to give primary consideration to the world of experience and only secondary consideration to labels. Opposed to **intensional orientation.**

eye movements Use eye movements to seek feedback, exchange conversational turns, signal the nature of your relationship with others, and compensate for increased physical distance. At the same time, look for such meanings in the eye movements of others.

F

face-attacking conflict strategies Strategies that attack a person's positive face or self-esteem or a person's negative face or need for autonomy and independence. *Avoid these.*

face-enhancing conflict strategies Strategies that support and confirm a person's positive face or self-esteem or a person's negative face or need for autonomy. *Use these when appropriate.*

face-saving Maintaining a positive public self-image in the minds of others. *In conflict use face-saving strategies to allow your opponent to save face; avoid beltlining, or hitting your opponent with attacks that he or she will have difficulty absorbing and will resent.*

facial feedback hypothesis The theory that your facial expressions can produce physiological and emotional effects.

facial management techniques Techniques used to mask certain emotions and to emphasize others; for example, intensifying your expression of happiness to make a friend feel good about a promotion. *Use these ethically as well as effectively. Use facial expressions to communicate that you're involved in the interaction. As a listener, look to the emotional facial expressions of others as additional cues to their meaning.*

facial messages Use facial expressions to communicate that you're involved in the interaction. As a listener, look to the emotional expressions of others as additional cues to their meaning.

fact, questions of Questions that concern what is or is not true, what does or does not exist, what did or did not happen; questions that potentially have answers.

fact-inference confusion A misevaluation in which a person makes an inference, regards it as a fact, and acts upon it as if it were a fact. *Distinguish facts (verifiably true past events) from inferences (guesses, hypotheses, hunches), and act on inferences with tentativeness and with mindfulness that they may turn out to be incorrect.*

factual statement A statement made after observation and limited to what is observed. Opposed to **inferential statement.**

fallacies of language Ways of using language that may appear logical on the surface but in fact have no logical foundation and are often (though not always) used to persuade (for example, weasel words, euphemisms, and jargon).

family A group of people who consider themselves related and connected to one another and among whom the actions of one have consequences for others.

farewell speech A speech designed to say goodbye to a position or to colleagues and to signal that you're moving on.

fear appeal The appeal to fear used to persuade an individual or group of individuals to believe or to act in a certain way.

feedback Information that is given back to the source. Feedback may come from the source's own messages (as when we hear what we are saying) or may come from the receiver(s) in the form of applause, yawning, puzzled looks, questions, letters to the editor of a newspaper, increased or decreased subscriptions to a magazine, and so forth. *Listen to both verbal and nonverbal feedback—from yourself and from others—and use these cues to help you adjust your messages for greatest effectiveness.* See also **negative feedback; positive feedback.**

feedforward Information that is sent prior to a regular message telling the listener something about what is to follow. *Preface your messages with some kind of feedforward when you feel your listener needs some background or when you want to ease into a particular topic, such as bad news.*

feminine culture A cultural orientation characterized by a concern for relationships and the quality of life. Opposed to **masculine culture.**

fiction-fact pattern An organizational pattern in which the speech is organized into two main parts, the fictions and then the facts of a particular issue.

field of experience The sum total of an individual's experiences, which influences his or her ability to communicate. In some views of communication, two people can communicate only to the extent that their fields of experience overlap.

figurative analogies Comparison of items from different classes; opposed to **literal analogies.**

figures of speech Stylistic devices that give added life and emphasis to your messages.

flexibility The ability to adjust communication strategies on the basis of the unique situation. *Because no two communication situations are identical, because everything is in a state of flux, and because everyone is different, cultivate flexibility and adjust your communication to the unique situation.*

flirting A type of communication in which you signal romantic interest.

focus group A group designed to explore the feelings and attitudes of its individual members; usually follows a question-and-answer format.

foot-in-the-door technique A persuasive strategy in which the speaker first asks for something small (to get a foot in the door) and then, once a pattern of agreement has been achieved, follows with the real and larger request.

force An unproductive **conflict** strategy in which a person attempts to win an argument by physical force or threats of force.

forcefulness A quality of language that makes messages more powerful, more intense.

formal communications In an organization, the communications that are sanctioned by the organization itself and deal with the workings of the organization, with productivity, and with the various jobs served by the employees.

forum A small group format in which members of the group answer questions from the audience; often follows a symposium.

free information Information that is revealed implicitly and that may be used as a basis for opening or pursuing conversations.

friendship An interpersonal relationship between two persons that is mutually productive, established and maintained through perceived mutual free choice, and characterized by mutual positive regard. *Establish friendships to help serve such needs as utility, ego support, stimulation, and security. At the same time, seek to serve similar needs that your friends have.*

functional approach to leadership An approach to leadership that focuses on what the leader should do in a given situation.

fundamental attribution error The tendency to attribute a person's behavior to the kind of person he or she is (to the person's personality, perhaps) and to give too little importance to the situation the person is in. *Avoid the fundamental attribution error by mindfully focusing on the possible influence of situational forces.*

G

game A simulation of some situation with rules governing the behaviors of the participants and with some payoff for winning; in transactional analysis, "game" refers to a series of ulterior transactions that lead to a payoff; the term also refers to a basically dishonest kind of transaction in which participants hide their true feelings.

gender The socially constructed roles and behaviors for males and females that society teaches as appropriate. Distinguished from sex, which refers to biological qualities of men and women.

general semantics The study of the relationships among language, thought, and behavior.

glittering generality Attempt by a speaker to gain listeners' acceptance of an idea by associating it with things they value highly; the opposite of **name calling.**

gobbledygook Overly complex language that overwhelms the listener instead of communicating meaning. *Simplify your own language and ask for clarification when in doubt.*

goodwill speech A special occasion speech in which the speaker seeks to make the image of a person, product, or company more positive.

gossip Communication about someone not present, some third party; usually concerns matters that are private to this third party.

grapevine The informal lines through which messages in an organization may travel; these informal routes resemble a physical grapevine, with its twists and turns and its unpredictable pattern of branches. *To deal with the office grapevine, understand the variety of purposes the grapevine serves and listen to it carefully, treat grapevine information as tentative, repeat only what you know or believe to be true, tap into the grapevine frequently, and always assume that what you say in grapevine communication will be repeated to others.*

group A collection of individuals connected to one another by some common purpose and with some structure among them.

group building and maintenance roles Group roles that focus not only on the task to be performed but also on interpersonal relationships among members.

group norms Rules or expectations of appropriate behavior for members of groups. *Actively seek to discover the norms of a group, and take these norms into consideration when interacting in the group.*

group self-esteem A person's positive (or negative) evaluation of himself or herself as a member of a particular cultural group.

group task roles Group roles that help the group focus more specifically on achieving its goals.

groupthink A tendency observed in some groups in which agreement among members becomes more important than the exploration of the issues at hand. *Recognize and actively counter any groupthink tendencies evidenced in a group.*

gunnysacking An unproductive **conflict** strategy of storing up grievances—as if in a gunnysack—and holding them in readiness to dump on the opponent in a disagreement.

H

halo effect The tendency to generalize an individual's positive or negative qualities from one area to another; opposed to the **horns effect.**

haptics The study of touch communication.

heterosexist language Language that assumes all people are heterosexual and thereby denigrates lesbians and gay men.

hidden self The self knowledge that you have but that is kept hidden from others.

hierarchy of needs A view of human needs that argues that certain basic needs (e.g., for food and shelter) have to be satisfied before higher-order needs (e.g., for self-esteem or love) can be effective in motivating listeners.

high-context culture A culture in which much of the information in communication is in the context or in the person rather than explicitly coded in the verbal messages. **Collectivist cultures** are generally high context. *Adjust your messages and your listening in light of the differences between high- and low-context cultures.* Opposed to **low-context** culture.

high-power-distance culture A culture in which there is a great difference in power between groups; for example, between teachers and students or managers and workers.

home field advantage The increased power that comes from being in your own territory.

home territories Territories about which individuals have a sense of intimacy and over which they exercise control—for example, a professor's office.

horns effect Assuming that because a person possesses some negative qualities that the person also possesses other negative qualities; a reverse **halo effect.**

hostile environment harassment A form of sexual harassment that includes all sexual behaviors (verbal and nonverbal) that make a worker uncomfortable.

hyperbole A figure of speech in which something is exaggerated for effect but is not intended to be taken literally.

hyphen An **extensional device** used to illustrate that what may be separated verbally may not be separable on the event level or on the nonverbal level; although we may talk about body and mind as if they were separable, in reality they are better referred to as body-mind.

I

idea-generation group A group whose purpose is to generate ideas. See also **brainstorming.**

identification A principle of persuasion in which a speaker demonstrates a similarity with the audience (identifying with who they are and what they believe).

idioms Expressions that are unique to a specific language and whose meaning cannot be deduced simply from an analysis of the individual words

illustration A relatively long and more detailed example.

illustrators Nonverbal behaviors that accompany and literally illustrate verbal messages—for example, an upward gesture accompanying the verbalization "It's up there."

image-confirming strategies Communication techniques to reinforce your positive perceptions about yourself.

I-messages Messages in which the speaker accepts responsibility for his or her own thoughts and behaviors; messages in which the speaker's point of view is acknowledged explicitly. *Use I-messages* *when communicating your feelings; take responsibility for your own feelings (as in "I get angry when you ...") rather than attributing them to others (as in "you make me angry").* Opposed to **you-messages.**

immediacy A quality of interpersonal effectiveness that creates a sense of contact and togetherness and conveys interest in and liking for the other person. *Maintain nonverbal immediacy through close physical distances, eye contact, and smiling; maintain verbal immediacy by using the other person's name and focusing on the other's remarks.*

implicit personality theory A theory of personality, complete with rules or systems, that each individual maintains and through which the individual perceives others. *Bring to your mindful state your implicit personality theory to subject your perceptions and conclusions to logical analysis.*

impression formation The processes involved in forming impressions of others.

impression management The processes you go through to communicate the impression you want others to have of you.

impromptu speech A speech given without any explicit prior preparation.

independents Couples who see themselves as primarily separate individuals; their individuality is more important than the relationship or the connection between the individuals.

index An **extensional device** used to emphasize the notion of nonidentity (no two things are the same) and symbolized by a mental subscript—for example, politician 1 is not politician 2.

indirect messages Use indirect messages when a more direct style might prove insulting or offensive; but be aware that indirectness can create communication problems because indirect statements are easier to misunderstand than direct ones.

indirect speech Speech that may hide the speaker's true intentions or that may be used to make requests and observations in a roundabout way. *Make judicious use of indirect messages when a more direct style might prove insulting or offensive. But be aware that indirect messages can create communication problems, because they are easier to misunderstand than direct messages.*

indiscrimination A misevaluation caused by categorizing people, events, or objects into a particular class and responding to them only as members of the class; a failure to recognize that each individual is unique; a failure to apply the **index.** *Avoid indiscrimination by treating each situation and each person as unique (when possible) even when they're covered by the same label or name. Index your key concepts.*

individual orientation A cultural orientation that stresses the individual's rather than the group's goals and preferences. *Adjust your messages and your listening on the basis of differences between individualistic and collectivist cultures.* Opposed to **collective orientation.**

individual roles (in groups) Behavior in groups that is usually dysfunctional and works against a sense of groupness. *In a group avoid playing the popular but dysfunctional individual roles—those of the aggressor, blocker, recognition seeker, self-confessor, or dominator.*

individualist culture A culture in which the individual's goals and preferences are given greater importance than the group's. Opposed to **collectivist culture.**

indulgence A cultural orientation that emphasizes the gratification of desires, a focus on having fun and enjoying life.

inevitability A principle of communication stating that communication cannot be avoided; all behavior in an interactional setting is communication.

inferential statement A statement that can be made by anyone, is not limited to what is observed, and can be made at any time. Opposed to **factual statement.**

informal messages In an organization, the communication that is socially sanctioned; messages that are oriented more to the individual members and their relationship to the organization than to the performing the specific jobs within the organization.

informal time Approximate rather than exact time, denoted in terms such as *soon, early,* and *in a while.*

information That which reduces uncertainty.

information isolation The situation in which certain workers receive little or no information or when some people are excluded from the informal gossip and grapevine messages.

information overload A condition in which the amount of information is too great to be dealt with effectively or the number or complexity of messages is so great that an individual or organization is not able to deal with them. *To prevent or manage information overload, pass on only messages that the other person needs to have, use messages as they come to you, organize your messages, rid yourself of extra copies, and periodically review and eliminate the sources of unnecessary messages.*

information power Power that a person possesses because others see that individual as having significant information and the ability to communicate logically and persuasively. Also called "persuasion power."

information-sharing groups Groups designed to share new information or skills.

informative interview A type of **interview** in which the interviewer asks the interviewee, usually a person of some reputation and accomplishment, questions designed to elicit his or her views, predictions, and perspectives on specific topics.

informative speech A public speech in which you describe, demonstrate, or define something. *Follow the principles of informative speaking: Stress the information's usefulness, relate new information to information the audience already knows, present information through several senses, adjust the level of complexity, vary the levels of abstraction, avoid information overload, and recognize cultural variations.*

inoculation principle A principle stating that persuasion will be more difficult to achieve when the would-be persuader attacks beliefs and attitudes that have already been challenged previously, because the listener has built up defenses (has been "inoculated") against such attacks.

insulation A reaction to territorial encroachment in which you erect some sort of barrier between yourself and the invaders.

intensional orientation A point of view in which primary consideration is given to the way things are labeled and only secondary consideration (if any) to the world of experience. *Avoid intensional orientation by responding to things first and to labels second; the way a person is talked about is not the best measure of who that person really is.* Opposed to **extensional orientation.**

interaction management A quality of interpersonal effectiveness; the control of interaction to the satisfaction of both parties. Includes managing conversational turns, fluency, and message consistency.

interaction process analysis A content analysis method that classifies messages into four general categories: social emotional positive, social emotional negative, attempted answers, and questions.

intercultural communication Communication that takes place between or among persons of different cultures or persons who have different cultural beliefs, values, or ways of behaving. *When communicating interculturally, become mindful of (1) the differences between yourself and culturally different individuals, (2) the differences within the other cultural group, (3) cultural differences in meanings for both verbal and nonverbal signals, and (4) different cultural rules and customs. Communicate interculturally with appropriate openness, empathy, positiveness, immediacy, interaction management, expressiveness, and other orientation.*

interdependency The quality of communication referring to the dependency of each element on each other element in the process.

interpersonal communication Communication between two persons or among a small group of persons and distinguished from public or mass communication; communication of a personal nature and distinguished from impersonal communication; communication between or among intimates or those involved in a close relationship; often, dyadic and small group communication in general.

interpersonal conflict Conflicts between and among individuals who are interdependent, mutually aware that their goals are incompatible, and perceive each other as interfering with the attainment of their own goals.

interpersonal time The ways in which we treat time in our interpersonal relationships and interactions.

interruptions In conversation, attempts to take over the role of the speaker.

interviewing A particular form of interpersonal communication in which two persons interact largely in a question-and-answer format for the purpose of achieving specific goals.

intimacy The closest interpersonal relationship; usually, a close **primary relationship.**

intimacy claims Obligations incurred by virtue of being in a close and intimate relationship.

intimate distance The closest **proxemic distance,** ranging from touching to 18 inches. See also **proxemics.**

intrapersonal communication Communication with yourself.

introduction, speech of A speech designed to introduce the speaker himself or herself to an audience, or a speech designed to introduce another speaker or group of speakers.

introductions Introductions to speeches should gain attention and preview what is to follow.

invasion The unwarranted entrance into another's territory that changes the meaning of the territory.

involvement The stage in an interpersonal relationship that normally follows **contact;** in this stage the individuals get to know each other better and explore the potential for greater intimacy.

irony A figure of speech employed for special emphasis, in which a speaker uses words whose literal meaning is the opposite of the speaker's actual message or intent.

irreversibility A principle of communication holding that communication cannot be reversed; once something has been communicated, it cannot be uncommunicated.

J

jargon The technical language of any specialized group, often a professional class, that is unintelligible to individuals not belonging to the group; "shop talk."

jealousy A reaction to relationship threats.

Johari window A diagram of the four selves (open, blind, hidden, and unknown) that details the different kinds of information in each self.

just world hypothesis The belief that good things happen to good people because they're good and that bad things happen to bad people because they're bad—because the world is just.

K

kinesics The study of the communicative dimensions of facial and bodily movements.

laissez-faire leader A group leader who allows the group to develop and progress (or make mistakes) on its own.

L

lateral communication Messages between equals in an organization—manager to manager, worker to worker. Such messages may move within the same subdivision or department of the organization or across divisions. *To improve lateral communication, reduce jargon and clarify terminology as needed, recognize the importance of all areas, and balance the needs of an organization that relies on cooperation and a system that rewards competition.* See **downward communication, upward communication.**

leadership The quality by which one individual directs or influences the thoughts and/or the behaviors of others. See also **laissez-faire leader, democratic leader,** and **authoritarian leader.**

leave-taking cues Verbal and nonverbal cues that indicate a desire to terminate a conversation.

legitimate power Power that a person possesses because others believe that the individual has a right, by virtue of position, to influence or control their behavior.

level of abstraction The relative distance of a term or statement from an actual perception. A low-order abstraction would be a description of the perception, whereas a high-order abstraction would consist of inferences about descriptions of the perception.

leveling A process of message distortion in which a message is repeated but the number of details is reduced, some details are omitted entirely, and some details lose their complexity.

listening An active process of receiving messages sent orally; this process consists of five stages: receiving, understanding, remembering, evaluating, and responding.

literal analogies Comparison of items from the same class, such as two cars or two cities; opposed to **figurative analogies**.

logic The science of reasoning; the study of the principles governing the analysis of inference making.

logical arguments Arguments based on facts and evidence rather than on emotions or credibility claims.

long-term-orientation A cultural orientation that promotes the importance of future rewards; opposed to **short-term orientation.**

looking-glass self The self-concept that results from the image of yourself that others reveal to you.

loving An interpersonal process in which one feels a closeness, a caring, a warmth, and an excitement in relation to another person.

low-context culture A culture in which most of the information in communication is explicitly stated in the verbal messages. **Individualist cultures** are usually low-context cultures. Opposed to **high-context culture.**

low-power-distance culture A culture in which there is little difference in power between groups; for example, between doctors and patients or men and women.

ludus love A type of love emphasizing fun and enjoyment.

lying The act of deliberately trying to mislead another person by communicating information you believe to be false.

M

magnitude of change principle A principle of persuasion stating that the greater and more important the change desired by the speaker, the more difficult its achievement will be.

maintenance strategies Specific behaviors designed to preserve an interpersonal relationship. Compare to **relationship repair.**

maintenance A stage of relationship stability at which the relationship does not progress or deteriorate significantly; a continuation as opposed to a dissolution of a relationship.

mania love A style of love characterized by extreme highs and extreme lows.

manipulation An unproductive **conflict** strategy in which a person avoids open conflict but instead attempts to divert the conflict by being especially charming and getting the opponent into a noncombative frame of mind.

manuscript speech A speech designed to be read verbatim from a script.

markers Devices that signify that a certain territory belongs to a particular person. *Become sensitive to the markers (central, boundary, and ear) of others, and learn to use these markers to define your own territories and to communicate the desired impression.* See also **boundary marker, central marker,** and **earmarker.**

masculine and feminine cultures A cultural distinction based on qualities traditionally thought of as masculine and feminine.

mass communication Communication addressed to an extremely large audience, mediated by audio and/or visual transmitters, and processed by gatekeepers before transmission.

matching hypothesis An assumption that we date and mate with people who are similar to ourselves—who match us—in degree of physical attractiveness.

meaningfulness A perception principle that refers to your assumption that people's behavior is sensible, stems from some logical antecedent, and is consequently meaningful rather than meaningless.

media literacy The skills needed to understand, influence, and create media messages.

mediated communication Messages sent by a source through some electronic device to a receiver; includes both mass media and computer communication.

mentoring The process by which an experienced individual (mentor) helps to train a less experienced person referred to as a mentee or, more often, a protégé.

mere exposure hypothesis The theory that repeated or prolonged exposure to a stimulus may result in a change in attitude toward the stimulus object, generally in the direction of increased positiveness.

message Any signal or combination of signals transmitted to a **receiver.**

message isolation The situation that exists when a worker is given little or no information; may occur when formal messages are not sent to certain people or when some people are excluded from the informal gossip and grapevine messages.

meta-advice Advice about advice, for example, suggesting that they seek more expert advice.

metacommunication Communication about communication. *Metacommunicate when you want to clarify the way you're talking or what you're talking about; for example, give clear feedforward and paraphrase your own complex messages.*

metalanguage Language used to talk about language.

metamessage A message that makes reference to another message. For example, comments like "Did I make myself clear?" or "That's a lie" refer to other messages and are therefore considered metamessages.

metaphor A figure of speech in which there is an implied comparison between two unlike things; for example, "That CEO is a jackal."

metonymy A figure of speech in which some particular thing is referred to by something with which it is closely associated, for example, *Rome* for the *Catholic Church* or *the White House* for the *U.S. government.*

mindfulness A state of awareness in which we are conscious of the logic and rationality of our behaviors and the logical connections existing among elements. In a mindless state we are unaware of this logic and rationality. *Increase your mindfulness by creating and recreating categories, being open to new information and points of view, and avoiding excessive reliance on first impressions.*

mixed messages Messages that contradict themselves; messages that ask for two different (often incompatible) responses. *Avoid encoding mixed messages by focusing clearly on your purposes when communicating and by increasing conscious control over your verbal and nonverbal behaviors.*

model A representation of an object or process.

monochronic time orientation A view of time in which things are done sequentially; one thing is scheduled at a time. Opposed to **polychronic time orientation.**

monologue A form of **communication** in which one person speaks and the other listens; there is no real interaction among participants. Opposed to **dialogue.**

motivated sequence An organizational pattern for arranging the information in a speech to motivate an audience to respond positively to the speaker's purpose. *In using the motivated sequence: gain attention, establish a need, satisfying the need, visualize the need satisfied, and move to action.*

multiple-definition pattern An organizational structure for a public speech in which each of your main points consists of a different type of definition.

N

name-calling A persuasive tactic in which the speaker gives an idea a derogatory name.

narrative A long example presented in the form of an anecdote or short story, for example, Aesop's fables.

need step The second step in the **motivated sequence** where you establish that a need exists for some kind of change.

negative face need The need and desire to be autonomous, to have the right to do as one wishes.

negative feedback Feedback that serves a corrective function by informing the source that his or her message is not being received in the way intended. Negative feedback serves to redirect the source's behavior. Looks of boredom, shouts of disagreement, letters critical of newspaper policy, and teachers' instructions on how better to approach a problem are examples of negative feedback. See also **positive feedback.**

negative social proof A generally ineffective persuasive technique in which examples of other people doing what the speaker does not want the audience to do are presented.

negatives and positives of conflict Approach conflict to minimize negative outcomes and to maximize the positive benefits of conflict and its resolution.

netiquette The rules for polite communication over the Internet. *Learn what these are and follow them.*

network convergence The process by which persons who are connected share their other connections.

networking A broad process of enlisting the aid of other people to help you solve a problem or offer insights that bear on your problem. *Establish a network of relationships to provide insights into issues relevant to your personal and professional life, and be willing to lend your expertise to the networks of others.*

noise Anything that interferes with a person's receiving a message as the source intended the message to be received. Noise is present in a communication system to the extent that the message received is not the message sent. *Reduce the influence of physical, physiological, psychological, and semantic noise to the extent that you can; use repetition and restatement and, when in doubt, ask if you're being clear.*

nominal group A collection of individuals who record their thoughts and opinions, which are then distributed to others. Without direct interaction, the thoughts and opinions are gradually pared down until a manageable list (of solutions or decisions) is produced. When this occurs, the nominal group (a group in name only) may restructure itself into a problem-solving group that analyzes the final list. *Use the nominal group technique to solve problems when anonymity in suggesting ideas may be desirable.*

nonallness An attitude or point of view in which it is recognized that one can never know all about anything and that what we know, say, or hear is only a part of what there is to know, say, or hear.

nonnegotiation An unproductive **conflict** strategy in which an individual refuses to discuss the conflict or to listen to the other person.

nonverbal communication Communication without words; communication by means of space, gestures, facial expressions, touching, vocal variation, and silence, for example.

nonverbal dominance Nonverbal behavior through which one person exercises psychological dominance over another.

norm See **group norms.**

O

object-adaptors Movements that involve manipulation of some object; for example, punching holes in or drawing on a Styrofoam coffee cup, clicking a ballpoint pen, or chewing on a pencil.

olfactory communication Communication by smell.

openness A quality of interpersonal effectiveness encompassing (1) willingness to interact openly with others, to self-disclose as appropriate; (2) willingness to react honestly to incoming stimuli; and (3) willingness to own our own feelings and thoughts.

open self That self that is known by others and by yourself.

open web That part of the web that consists of those materials that you'd be able to access with a simple search from most search engines or directories.

operational definition A type of definition in which the steps to construct the object are identified.

oral style The style of spoken discourse. When compared with written style, consists of shorter, simpler, and more familiar words; more qualification, self-reference terms, allness terms, verbs, and adverbs; and more concrete terms and terms indicative of consciousness of projection—for example, "as I see it."

organization An organized group of people who work together to achieve compatible goals; in public speaking, the pattern of the speech.

organizational communication The process of sending and receiving verbal and nonverbal messages that convey meaning and that occur within an organizational context.

organizational message competence The ability to send and receive organizational messages effectively. *For example, listen actively, empathically, critically, and in depth; apologize for errors; avoid contributing to information overload or information isolation; follow the rules of netiquette; use the grapevine; demonstrate the communication skills of group leadership and membership; avoid racist, heterosexist, ageist, or sexist language; help reduce conflict; use power effectively; use the expected channels of communication; treat all your messages as if they were being graded by your instructor.*

organizational relationship competence The ability to form effective relationships in a work environment. *For example, be a mentor and a network giver as well as a protégé and network seeker; be supportive of your coworkers, and avoid being either overly critical or unconcerned with their specific jobs; exercise caution in the development of office romances, and understand your company's policies regarding such relationships; self-disclose selectively; avoid bringing relationship problems into work with you; follow the cultural rules of the organization, and break them only for an outstanding reason; stress the positive.*

orientation In public speaking, a preview of what is to follow in the speech.

other-orientation A quality of interpersonal effectiveness involving attentiveness, interest, and concern for the other person. *Acknowledge the importance of the other person; use focused eye contact and appropriate facial expressions; smile, nod, and lean toward the other person; express agreement when appropriate.*

outing Disclosing information about another person that others do not know and that the person wishes to keep secret, most often referred to in connection with one's affectional orientation.

overattribution The process of attributing one's behavior to one or a few particular characteristics. *Avoid overattribution; rarely is any one factor an accurate explanation of complex human behavior.*

owning feelings The process by which you take responsibility for your own feelings instead of attributing them to others.

oxymoron A figure of speech in which two opposite qualities are combined, as in *bittersweet.*

P

packaging Make your verbal and nonverbal messages consistent; inconsistencies between, say, verbal and nonverbal messages often create uncertainty and misunderstanding.

panel A small group format in which "expert" participants speak without any set pattern and respond to questions from an audience.

paralanguage The vocal but nonverbal aspect of speech. Paralanguage consists of voice qualities (for example, pitch range, resonance, tempo); vocal characterizers (laughing or crying, yelling or whispering); vocal qualifiers (intensity, pitch height); and vocal segregates ("uh-uh" meaning "no," or "sh" meaning "silence"). *Vary paralinguistic features such as rate, pausing, pitch, and volume to communicate your meanings and to add interest and color to your messages.*

parallel sentences Sentences having the same grammatical structure.

parasocial relationship Relationship between a real person and an imagined or fictional character; also, relationship between a viewer and a real or fictional television personality.

participating style A style of leadership in which the leader facilitates and encourages group members.

pauses Silent periods in the normally fluent stream of speech. Pauses are of two major types: filled pauses (interruptions in speech that are filled with such vocalizations as "er" or "um") and unfilled pauses (silences of unusually long duration). *Use pauses to signal transitions, to allow listeners time to think, and to signal the approach of a significant idea.*

perception The process of becoming aware of objects and events from the senses. *Increase accuracy in interpersonal perception by (1) identifying the influence of your physical and emotional state; (2) making sure that you're not drawing conclusions from too little information; and (3) identifying any perceptions that may be the result of mind reading.* See also **interpersonal perception.**

perception checking The process of verifying your understanding of some message or situation or feeling to reduce uncertainty.

perceptual accentuation A process that leads you to see what you expect to see and what you want to see—for example, seeing people you like as better looking and smarter than people you do not like.

performance visualization A method for reducing communication apprehension in which you visualize yourself performing effectively and confidently.

periodic sentence A type of sentence in which the key word is placed at the end of the sentence.

personal attack A fallacy of argument in which the speaker attacks the person instead of the person's arguments. *Avoid this in your own reasoning and reject these when used by others.*

personal distance The second-closest **proxemic distance,** ranging from 18 inches to four feet. See also **proxemics.**

personal growth groups A type of small group which aims to help members cope with particular difficulties—such as drug addiction, not being assertive enough, having an alcoholic parent, being an ex-convict, or having a hyperactive child or a promiscuous spouse.

personal interest A persuasive fallacy that attempts to divert attention from the issues and arguments in one of two ways: (1) The speaker argues that the opponent should be disqualified because he or she isn't directly affected by the proposal or doesn't have firsthand knowledge, or (2) the speaker tries to disqualify someone because he or she will benefit in some way from the proposal.

personal rejection An unproductive **conflict** strategy in which one individual withholds love and affection and seeks to win the argument by getting the other person to break down under this withdrawal.

personality theory A theory or set of assumptions about personality, complete with rules or systems, that each individual maintains and through which the individual perceives others. *In order to subject your perceptions and conclusions about people to logical analysis, bring to your mindful state your personality theory.*

personification A figure of speech in which human characteristics are attributed to inanimate objects for special effect; for example, "After the painting, the room looked cheerful and energetic."

persuasion The process of influencing attitudes and behavior. *Apply (where relevant) the principles of persuasion: selective exposure, audience participation, identification, and amounts of change.*

persuasive speech A type of speech designed to influence the attitudes or behaviors or listeners.

Peter Principle A principle that claims that in any hierarchical organization, employees will rise to their level of incompetence.

phatic communication Communication that is primarily social; communication designed to open the channels of communication rather than to convey substantive information. "Hello" and "How are you?" in everyday interaction are examples.

pitch The highness or lowness of the vocal tone.

plagiarism The act of passing off the work of someone else as your own without acknowledging the source. *Avoid even the suggestion of plagiarism.*

plain folks A persuasive tactic in which the speaker seeks to identify himself or herself (and his or her proposal) with the audience.

polarization A form of fallacious reasoning in which only two extremes are considered; also referred to as "black-or-white" or "either/or" thinking or as a two-valued orientation. *Avoid thinking and talking in extremes by using middle terms and qualifiers. At the same time, remember that too many qualifiers may make you appear unsure of yourself.*

policy, questions of Questions that focus on what should be done (the policy that should be adopted).

politeness Civility, consideration, refinement, respect, and regard for others as expressed verbally and nonverbally; interaction that follows the socially accepted rules for interpersonal interaction.

politeness strategies Strategies that support another's face needs and may be used as a strategy to appear likeable.

polychronic time orientation A view of time in which several things may be scheduled or engaged in at the same time. Opposed to **monochronic time orientation.**

positive face need The need and desire to be viewed positively by others, to be thought of favorably.

positive feedback Feedback that supports or reinforces the continuation of behavior along the same lines in which it is already proceeding—for example, applause during a speech. See also **negative feedback.**

positive labeling A persuasive technique in which the audience is labeled in ways that are consistent with the way you want them to act.

positive social proof A persuasive strategy in which the speaker gives examples of people who do as you wish your listeners do.

positiveness A characteristic of effective communication involving positive attitudes toward the self and toward the interpersonal interaction. Also can mean complimenting another and expressing acceptance and approval. *Communicate positiveness by expressing your own satisfaction with the interaction, compliment others by expressing your positive thoughts and feelings about and to the other person, and express acceptance and approval.*

power The ability to control the behaviors of others. *Communicate power by avoiding such powerless message forms as hesitations, too many intensifiers, disqualifiers, tag questions, one-word answers, self-critical statements, overly polite statements, and vulgar and slang expressions.*

power distance A cultural dimension referring to the degree of distance between those with power and those without power. *Adjust your messages and listening based on the power distance orientation of the culture in which you find yourself.*

power play A consistent pattern of behavior in which one person tries to control the behavior of another. *Respond to power plays with cooperative strategies: (1) Express your feelings, (2) describe the behavior to which you object, and (3) state a cooperative response.*

pragma love A type of love that is practical.

pragmatic implication An assumption that seems logical but is not necessarily true.

premature self-disclosures Disclosures that are made before the relationship has developed sufficiently.

presentation speech During the presentation of a speech, maintain eye contact with the entire audience, allow facial expressions to convey feelings, gesture naturally, and incorporate purposeful body movements.

presentation method In general, use the extemporaneous method of delivery for speeches.

present-focus conflict Focus conflict resolution messages on the present; avoid dredging up old grievances and unloading them on the other person (gunnysacking).

primacy effect The condition in which what comes first exerts greater influence in our perceptions than what comes later. See also **recency effect.**

primacy–recency Processes of perception in which we give more credence to that which occurs first (primacy) or to that which occurs last or most recently (recency).

primary relationship The relationship between two people that they consider their most (or one of their most) important; for example, the relationship between spouses or domestic partners.

primary source Original information about a topic or event, for example, the original research study. See *secondary source.*

primary territories Areas that a person can consider his or her own exclusive preserve—for example, someone's room or office.

principle of cooperation A principle that holds that in any communication interaction, both parties will make an effort to help each other understand each other.

pro-and-con pattern A pattern for organizing a speech in which the arguments for the thesis are advanced and the arguments against the thesis are noted and attacked.

problem–solution pattern An organizational structure for a public speech divided into the problem and the solution, a structure that's especially useful in persuasive speeches in which you want to convince the audience that a problem exists and that your solution would solve or lessen the problem.

problem-solving group A group whose primary task is to solve a problem or, perhaps more often, to reach a decision.

problem-solving sequence A logical step-by-step process for solving a problem that is frequently used by groups; consists of defining and analyzing the problem, establishing criteria for evaluating solutions, identifying possible solutions, evaluating solutions, selecting the best solution(s), and testing the selected solution(s).

process Ongoing activity; by thinking of communication as a process, we emphasize that it is always changing, always in motion.

progressive differentiation A relational problem caused by the exaggeration or intensification of differences or similarities between individuals.

projection A psychological process whereby we attribute characteristics or feelings of our own to others; often, the process whereby we attribute our own faults to others.

pronunciation The production of syllables or words according to some accepted standard; for example, as presented in a dictionary.

protection theory A theory of **proxemics** referring to the fact that people establish a body-buffer zone to protect themselves from unwanted closeness, touching, or attack.

provisionalism An attitude of open-mindedness that leads to the creation of supportiveness; opposed to **certainty.**

proxemic distances The spatial distances that people maintain in communication and social interaction. *Use spatial distance to signal the type of relationship you are in: intimate, personal, social, or public. Let your spatial relationships reflect your interpersonal relationships. Maintain spatial distances that are comfortable (neither too close nor too far apart) and that are appropriate to the situation and to your relationship with the other person.*

proxemics The study of the communicative function of space; the study of how people unconsciously structure their space—the distances between people in their interactions, the organization of spaces in homes and offices, and even the design of cities.

proximity Physical closeness; one of the qualities influencing **attraction.** Also, as a principle of **perception,** the tendency to perceive people or events that are physically close as belonging together or representing some unit.

psychological time orientation The importance you place on past, present, or future time.

public distance The longest **proxemic distance,** ranging from 12 to more than 25 feet. See also **proxemics.**

public relations A communication strategy designed to convey information so as to establish positive relationships between a corporation, agency, or other group and the public.

public speaking Communication in which a speaker presents a relatively continuous message to a relatively large audience in a unique context.

public territories Areas that are open to all people—for example, restaurants or parks.

punctuation of communication The breaking up of continuous communication sequences into short sequences with identifiable beginnings and endings or stimuli and responses.

punishment Noxious or aversive stimulation.

pupillometrics The study of communication through changes in the size of the pupils of the eyes.

purr words Highly positive words that express the speaker's feelings rather than referring to any objective reality; opposite of **snarl words.**

Pygmalion effect Condition in which we make a prediction of success, act as if it were true, and thereby make it come true; a type of **self-fulfilling prophecy.**

Q

quality circle Group of workers whose task it is to investigate and make recommendations for improving the quality of some organizational function. *Use the quality circle technique to improve organizational functions.*

questions of fact Questions concerned with what is or is not true, what does or does not exist, what did or did not happen.

questions of policy Questions concerning what should be or should not be done (or what policy should be adopted).

questions of value Issues focused on what is good or bad, just or unjust.

quid pro quo harassment A form of workplace sexual harassment in which employment opportunities (as in hiring and promotion) are made dependent on the granting of sexual favors.

quotes An **extensional device** to emphasize that a word or phrase is being used in a special sense and should therefore be given special attention.

R

racism Bias or prejudice against a particular racial or ethnic group.

racist language Language that denigrates or is derogatory toward members of a particular racial or ethnic group.

rate The speed with which you speak, generally measured in words per minute.

reasoning from causes and effects See **causes and effects.**

reasoning from sign See **sign**.

reasoning from specific instances See **specific instances.**

receiver Any person or thing that takes in messages. Receivers may be individuals listening to or reading a message, a group of persons hearing a speech, a scattered television audience, or machines that store information.

receiving In receiving messages, focus your attention on both the verbal and the nonverbal messages, because both communicate meaning.

recency effect The condition in which what comes last (that is, most recently) exerts greater influence in our perceptions than what comes first. See also **primacy effect.**

reducing uncertainty To increase accuracy in perception, reduce your uncertainty, using passive, active, and interactive strategies.

redundancy The quality of a message that makes it totally predictable and therefore lacking in information. A message of zero redundancy would be completely unpredictable; a message of 100 percent redundancy would be completely predictable. All human languages contain some degree of built-in redundancy, generally estimated to be about 50 percent.

referent power Power that a person possesses because others desire to identify with or be like that individual.

regulators Nonverbal behaviors that regulate, monitor, or control the communications of another person, such as nods or changes in body posture.

rehearsal The process of fixing in mind the delivery of your public speech. *Rehearse your speech often, perfect your delivery, rehearse the speech as a whole, time the speech at each rehearsal, approximate the specific speech situation as much as possible, see and think of yourself as a public speaker, and incorporate any delivery notes that may be of value during the actual speech presentation.*

reinforcements In **attraction theory,** rewards or favors that tend to promote interpersonal relationships.

rejection A response to an individual that rejects or denies the validity of that individual's ideas or actions.

relational communication Communication between or among intimates or those in close relationships; used by some theorists as synonymous with **interpersonal communication.**

relationship conflicts Interpersonal conflicts, concerned not so much with some external object as with the relationship between the individuals.

relationship deterioration The stage of a relationship during which the connecting bonds between the partners weaken and the partners begin drifting apart; can lead to **dissolution.** *To cope with the ending of a relationship, break the loneliness–depression cycle, take time out, bolster your self-esteem, seek the support of nourishing others, and avoid repeating negative patterns.*

relationship development The stages of a relationship that lead up to **intimacy;** in the model of relationships presented here, relationship development includes the **contact** and **involvement** stages.

relationship dialectics theory A theory that describes relationships in terms of the tensions between a series of competing opposite desires or motivations, such as the desire for autonomy versus the desire to belong to someone, desires for novelty versus predictability, and desires for closedness versus openness.

relationship maintenance The processes by which individuals attempt to keep an interpersonal relationship stable and satisfying.

relationship message Message that comments on the relationship between the speakers rather than on matters external to them. *Formulate messages that are appropriate to the stage of the relationship. And listen to messages from relationship partners that may reveal differences in perception about your relationship stage.*

relationship message A message that refers to the relationship in some way; opposed to **content message**.

relationship repair Efforts to reverse the process of **relationship deterioration.** *Recognize the problem, engage in productive conflict resolution, pose possible solutions, affirm each other, integrate solutions into normal behavior, and take risks as appropriate.*

relationship rules Principles that relationship partners establish to help define their relationship. *Follow the rules for maintaining relationships when you do in fact wish to maintain and even strengthen them.*

relationship violence Physical abuse, verbal or emotional abuse, or sexual abuse that occurs within an interpersonal relationship.

reliability A quality of research or support that can be counted on as accurate and trustworthy.

remembering To enhance your ability to remember messages, identify the central ideas, summarize the message in an easy-to-retain form, and repeat (aloud or to yourself) key terms and names.

research A systematic search for information; an investigation of the relevant information on a topic; an inquiry into what is known or thought about a subject.

response Any overt or covert behavior.

restatement A message that repeats an idea in different words, often used to achieve emphasis or clarity.

restimulating brainstorming If appropriate, restimulate a brainstorming group that has lost its steam by asking for additional contributions or for further extensions of previously contributed ideas.

restraint A cultural orientation that fosters the curbing of gratification and its regulation by social norms.

reverse halo effect The tendency to assume that someone who possesses several negative qualities, also possesses other negative qualities; opposed to **halo effect.**

reward power Power derived from an individual's ability to reward another person.

rhetoric The study of the means of persuasion.

rhetorical question A figure of speech in which a question is asked to make a statement rather than to secure an answer.

rigid complementarity The inability to break away from a **complementary relationship** that once was appropriate but is no longer.

role The part an individual plays in a group; an individual's function or expected behavior.

romantic workplace relationships Approach any romantic relationship at work with a clear understanding of the potential problems.

round table format A small group format in which members arrange themselves in a circular or semicircular pattern and interact informally, with or without a moderator.

rules theory A theory that describes relationships as interactions governed by series of rules that couples agree to follow. When the rules are followed, a relationship is maintained; when they are broken, the relationship experiences difficulty.

S

satisfaction step The third step in the **motivated sequence** presents the answer or the solution to the need you demonstrated in establishing the need.

schemata Mental templates or structures that help us organize the millions of items of information we come into contact with every day (singular: schema).

script A general idea of how an event should unfold; a rule governing the sequence of occurrences in some activity. A type of **schema.**

secondary source A summary or interpretation of information, for example, a newspaper's summary of a research study. See *primary source.*

secondary territories Areas that do not belong to a particular person but that have been occupied by that person and are therefore associated with her or him—for example, the seat you normally take in class.

selective attention A principle of **perception** that states that listeners attend to those things that they anticipate will fulfill their needs or will prove enjoyable.

selective exposure A principle of **perception** and **persuasion** that states that listeners actively seek out information that supports their opinions and actively avoid information that contradicts their existing opinions, beliefs, attitudes, and values.

self-acceptance Being satisfied with ourselves, our virtues and vices, and our abilities and limitations.

self-actualization needs A basic need to become and do what you feel you must do; a need that is only satisfied, in Maslow's theory, after all other needs are satisfied.

self-adaptors Movements that usually satisfy a physical need, especially a need to be more comfortable; for example, scratching your head to relieve an itch, moistening your lips because they feel dry, or pushing your hair out of your eyes.

self-affirmation A positive statement about oneself.

self-attribution A process through which we seek to account for and understand the reasons and motivations for our own behaviors.

self-awareness The degree to which a person knows himself or herself. *Increase self-awareness by listening to others, increasing your open self as appropriate, and seeking out information (discreetly) to reduce any blind spots.*

self-concept An individual's self-evaluation; an individual's self-appraisal. *Learn who you are: See yourself through the eyes of others; compare yourself to similar (and admired) others; examine the influences of culture; and observe, interpret, and evaluate your own message behaviors.*

self-deprecating strategies Impression management strategies in which one confesses incompetence in order to have others help.

self-destructive beliefs Beliefs that are harmful to your growth and development.

self-disclosure The process of revealing something about ourselves to another; usually, revealing information that would normally be kept hidden. *In considering self-disclosure, consider the legitimacy of your motives for disclosing, the appropriateness of the disclosure, the listener's responses (is the dyadic effect operating?), and the potential burdens self-disclosures might impose.*

self-esteem The value you place on yourself; your self-evaluation; usually, the positive value you place on yourself. *Raise your self-esteem: Increase your communication effectiveness, challenge self-destructive beliefs, seek out nourishing people with whom to interact, work on projects that will result in success, and engage in self-affirmation.*

self-fulfilling prophecy The situation in which we make a prediction or prophecy and fulfill it ourselves—for example, expecting a class to be boring and then fulfilling this expectation by not listening and thus becoming bored. *Take a second look at your perceptions when they correspond very closely to your initial expectations; the self-fulfilling prophecy may be at work.*

self-handicapping strategies Impression management strategies in which the person sets up obstacles to make the task impossible and thus is given an excuse for failure.

self-monitoring strategies The manipulation of the image we present to others in interpersonal interactions so as to create the most favorable impression.

self-serving bias A bias that operates in the **self-attribution** process and leads us to take credit for the positive consequences and to deny responsibility for the negative consequences of our behaviors. *Become mindful of any self-serving bias; that is, of giving too much weight to internal factors (when explaining your positives) and too little weight to external factors (when explaining your negatives).*

self-talk Talk about oneself.

selling style A style of leadership in which the leader gives both task guidance and emotional support.

semantics The area of language study concerned with meaning.

separates Couples who see their relationship as a matter of convenience rather than of mutual love or connection.

sex The biological and physiological qualities that characterize men and women.

sexism Bias or prejudice against a particular sex.

sexist language Language derogatory to one sex, usually women; also, language that seems to prefer one gender over the other, as in the use of *man* for *humankind.*

sexual harassment Unsolicited and unwanted sexual messages. *In dealing with sexual harassment: First, talk to the harasser; if this doesn't stop the behavior, then consider collecting evidence, using appropriate channels within the organization, and filing a complaint. Do not blame yourself. At the same time: Avoid behaviors that could be interpreted as sexual harassment: behavior that's sexual in nature, that might be considered unreasonable, that is severe or pervasive, and that is unwelcome and offensive.*

short-term-orientation A cultural orientation that emphasizes the present rather than the future; opposed to **long-term orientation**.

shyness The condition of discomfort and uneasiness in interpersonal situations.

sign, reasoning from A form of reasoning in which the presence of certain signs (clues) are interpreted as leading to a particular conclusion.

signal reaction A conditioned response to a signal; a response to some signal that is immediate rather than delayed.

signal-to-noise ratio In verbal interaction, the relative amounts of signal (meaningful information) and noise (interference). Messages high in information and low in noise would have a high signal/noise ratio; messages low in information and high in noise would have a low signal/noise ratio.

silence The absence of vocal communication. Often mistakenly thought to be the absence of any and all communication, silence actually can communicate feelings or can serve to prevent communication about certain topics. *Because silence can communicate lots of different meanings (e.g., your anger or your need for time to think), examine your use of silence just as you would eye movements or body gestures.*

similarity A principle of **attraction** holding that we are attracted to qualities similar to those we possess and to people who are similar to ourselves; opposed to **complementarity.** Also, in **perception,** rule stating that things that look alike belong together and form a unit.

simile A figure of speech in which two unlike objects are compared using the words *like* or *as.*

situational approach to leadership An approach to leadership that emphasizes that the leader's style must vary on the basis of the specific situation.

situational leadership An approach to leadership stresses that leadership styles need to be adapted to the specific group situation.

situational listening A view of listening holding that effective listening needs to be adjusted to the specific situation; one style of listening does not fit all forms of communication.

slang Language used by particular groups that is highly informal, nonstandard, and often considered improper.

slippery slope A reasoning fallacy involving the assumption that one event (the one the person is arguing against) will inevitably or most likely lead to another event that everyone agrees would be undesirable. *Seek proof of causality.*

small group A collection of individuals who are connected to one another by some common purpose, are interdependent, have some degree of organization among them, and see themselves as a group.

small group communication Communication among a collection of individuals small enough in number that all members may interact with relative ease as both senders and receivers, the members being connected to one another by some common purpose and with some degree of organization or structure.

snarl words Highly negative words that express the feelings of the speaker rather than referring to any objective reality; opposite to **purr words.**

social clock An internalized schedule—based on cultural teachings—for the ages at which important events should be done; for example, the approximate ages for getting married or for buying a house.

social comparison processes The processes by which you compare yourself (for example, your abilities, opinions, and values) with others and then assess and evaluate yourself; one of the sources of **self-concept.**

social distance The third **proxemic distance,** ranging from 4 to 12 feet; the distance at which business is usually conducted. See also **proxemics.**

social exchange theory A theory hypothesizing that we develop relationships in which our rewards or profits will be greater than our costs and that we avoid or terminate relationships in which the costs exceed the rewards.

social loafing The tendency of people to exert less effort when in a group than they would if working individually.

social penetration theory A theory describing how relationships develop from the superficial to the intimate level and from few to many areas of interpersonal interaction.

social web A part of the deep web through which people exchange messages with each other.

source Any person or thing that creates messages. A source may be an individual speaking, writing, or gesturing or a computer sending an error message.

spatial distance Physical distance that signals the type of relationship you are in: intimate, personal, social, or public.

spatial pattern An organizational pattern for a public speech in which points are discussed in a spatial sequence—high to low, east to west.

special occasion speeches Speeches designed for special occasions, usually a combination of information and persuasion.

specific instances, reasoning from A form of reasoning in which several specific instances are examined and then a conclusion about the whole is formed.

specific purpose The information you want to communicate (in an informative speech) or the attitude or behavior you want to change (in a persuasive speech).

speech Messages utilizing a vocal-auditory channel.

speech of definition An informative speech in which a concept or theory is explained. *For a speech of definition, consider using a variety of definitions, choose credible sources, and proceed from the known to the unknown.*

speech of demonstration An informative speech in which you show how something works or how something is constructed. *For a speech of demonstration, consider using a temporal pattern, employ transitions to connect the steps, present a broad overview and then the specific steps, and incorporate visual aids.*

speech of description An informative speech devoted to describing an object or person. *For a speech of description, consider using a spatial, topical, or 5W organizational pattern, a variety of descriptive categories, and visual aids.*

speech of inspiration A type of speech designed to raise the spirits of an audience.

spontaneity Communication pattern in which a person verbalizes what he or she is thinking without attempting to develop strategies for control; encourages **supportiveness;** opposed to **manipulation.**

stability Principle of **perception** that refers to the fact that our perceptions of things and of people are relatively consistent with our previous perceptions.

state apprehension A fear that is specific to a given communication situation. Opposed to **trait apprehension.**

static evaluation An orientation that fails to recognize that the world is characterized by constant change; an attitude that sees people and events as fixed rather than as constantly changing. *Mentally date your statements to avoid thinking and communicating that the world is static and unchanging. In your messages, reflect the inevitability of change.*

statistics Summary numbers such as the mean (or average) or the median (or most common score).

status The relative level a person occupies in a hierarchy; because status always involves a comparison, one individual's status is only relative to the status of another.

stereotype In communication, a fixed impression of a group of people through which we then perceive specific individuals; stereotypes are most often negative but also may be positive. *Be careful of thinking and talking in stereotypes; recognize that members of all groups are different, and focus on the individual rather than on the individual's membership in one group or another.*

stimuli External or internal changes that impinge on or arouse an organism (singular: stimulus).

storge love A style of love characterized by its peacefulness and slowness in terms of developing.

straw man An argument (like a person made of straw) that is set up only to be knocked down. In this fallacy a speaker creates a "straw man"—an easy-to-destroy simplification of the opposing position—and then proceeds to demolish it.

structure–function pattern An organizational pattern for a public speech in which the speech is divided into two parts: its form or structure and what it does or its functions.

supporting materials Usually used in reference to public speaking, enlarging a concept or principle through the use of examples, illustrations, and narratives; testimony; definitions; statistics; and visual aids. *Use supporting materials that will prove interesting to your audience, that are consistent in style with the rest of the speech, and that clearly related to the concept and principle which they are designed to explain.*

supportiveness An attitude of an individual or an atmosphere in a group that is characterized by openness, absence of fear, and a genuine feeling of equality. *Try to respond supportively by expressing your empathy, being open to even opposing viewpoints, and acting as an equal in the interaction.*

symmetrical relationship Relationship between two or more persons in which one person's behavior prompts the same type of behavior in the other person(s). For example, anger in one person may encourage or serve as a stimulus for anger in another person, or a critical comment by one person may lead the other person to criticize in return.

symposium A small group format in which each member of the group delivers a relatively prepared talk on some aspect of the topic. Also see **symposium–forum.**

symposium–forum A moderated group presentation with prepared speeches on various aspects of a topic, followed by a question-and-answer session with the audience.

synchronous Communication in which the sending and receiving of a message takes place at the same time. Opposed to **asynchronous.**

synecdoche A figure of speech in which a part of an object is used to stand for the entire object as in *green thumb* for *gardener.*

systematic desensitization A theory and technique for dealing with fears (such as communication apprehension) in which you gradually expose yourself to and develop a comfort level with the fear-causing stimulus.

T

taboo Forbidden; culturally censored. Taboo language is language that is frowned on by "polite society." Topics and specific words may be considered taboo—for example, death, sex, certain forms of illness, and various words denoting sexual activities and excretory functions. *Generally, avoid violating any cultural taboo; the more formal the situation, the more important it is to avoid such taboos.*

tactile imagery Imagery that communicates feelings normally conveyed by touch.

tag questions Questions that ask for another's agreement and often signal weakness or uncertainty, for example, "That dinner was fine, don't you think?" *Avoid these when you want your speech to have power.*

team A particular kind of small group that is constructed for a specific task, whose members have clearly defined roles, are committed to achieving the same goal, and content focused.

telling style A style of leadership that focuses almost exclusively on the task.

template outline An outline in which the essential parts of the speech are identified with spaces for these essential parts to be filled in; a learning device for developing speeches.

temporal communication The messages communicated by a person's time orientation and treatment of time.

temporal pattern A public speech organizational pattern in which points are ordered in a time sequence, usually past-present-future.

territoriality A possessive or ownership reaction to an area of space or to particular objects.

tertiary sources A combination of primary and secondary sources, for example, articles in encyclopedias, almanacs, handbooks, and guidebooks.

testimonial A persuasive tactic in which the speaker tries to use the authority or image of some positively evaluated person to gain your approval—or the image of some negatively evaluated person to gain your rejection.

testimony A form of supporting material consisting of an experts' opinions or witnesses' accounts and may add an authoritative tone to your arguments.

theory A general statement or principle applicable to related phenomena.

thesis The main assertion of a message—for example, the theme of a public speech.

thin entering wedge A persuasive fallacy in which a speaker argues against a position on the grounds that it is a thin entering wedge that will open the floodgates to all sorts of catastrophes, though there is no evidence to support such results.

toast A brief speech designed to celebrate a person or an occasion.

topical pattern An organizational pattern for a public speech in which the topic is organized into its subtopics or component parts.

topoi A system for analyzing a topic according to a pre-established set of categories.

touch avoidance The tendency to avoid touching and being touched by others. *Respect the touch-avoidance tendencies of others; pay special attention to cultural and gender differences in touch preferences and in touch avoidance.*

touch communication Communication through tactile means.

traditionals Couples who see themselves as a blending of two people into a single couple.

trait apprehension A general fear of communication, regardless of the specific situation. Opposed to **state apprehension.**

traits approach to leadership An approach to leadership that argues that leaders must possess certain qualities if they're to function effectively.

transactional Characterizing the relationship among elements whereby each influences and is influenced by each other element; communication, in which no element is independent of any other element, is a transactional process.

transfer A persuasive tactic in which a speaker associates an idea with something you respect to gain your approval or with something you dislike to gain your rejection.

transformational approach to leadership An approach to leadership that views the leader as one who elevates the group's members, enabling them not only to accomplish the group task but also to emerge as more empowered individuals.

transitions Words or statements that connect what was said to what will be said. *Use transitions and internal summaries to connect the parts of a speech and to help listeners remember the speech.*

tree diagram A method for narrowing a topic in which each topic is branched off into subtopics and each of these subtopics is branched off into additional subtopics.

truth bias The assumption that the other person is telling the truth; opposed to a deception bias.

turn-denying cues Verbal or nonverbal cues indicating that the listener does not want to assume the role of speaker.

turn-maintaining cues Verbal or nonverbal cues that communicate your wish to maintain the role of speaker.

turn-requesting cues Verbal or nonverbal cues that indicate a desire to assume the speaker's turn.

turn-yielding cues Verbal or nonverbal cues indicating the speaker's desire to give up the speaker's role.

U

uncertainty reduction strategies Passive, active, and interactive ways of increasing accuracy in interpersonal perception.

uncertainty reduction theory The theory holding that as relationships develop, uncertainty is reduced; relationship development is seen as a process of reducing uncertainty about each other.

universalism A cultural orientation that emphasizes treating people as individuals, rather than in terms of the groups (racial, sexual, national, for example) to which they belong.

unknown self That self that contains information not known to either the person himself or herself or to others.

unrepeatability Principle of communication stating that no communication can ever be re-created in quite the same way because circumstances are never the same.

upward communication Messages sent from the lower levels of a hierarchy to the upper levels—for example, line worker to manager or faculty member to dean. See **downward communication, lateral communication.**

V

value Relative worth; a quality that makes something desirable or undesirable; an ideal or custom about which we have emotional responses, whether positive or negative.

value congruence In organizational communication, a merging of employees values with those of the organization.

verbal aggressiveness An unproductive **conflict** strategy that involves trying to win an argument by attacking the other person's **self-concept**. Often considered opposed to **argumentativeness.**

virtual group A group whose members communicate through some electronic means and who may be separate widely geographically.

visual dominance The use of the eyes to maintain a superior or controlling position; for example, when making an especially important point, you might look intently at the other person.

visual imagery Imagery that creates word "pictures" of people or objects.

visualization step The fourth step in the **motivated sequence** where you intensify the audience's feelings or beliefs.

vividness A quality of language that makes your messages stand out.

voice qualities Aspects of **paralanguage**—specifically, pitch range, vocal lip control, glottis control, pitch control, articulation control, rhythm control, resonance, and tempo.

volume The relative loudness of the voice. *Use volume to reinforce the meanings you want to communicate.*

W

weasel words Words whose meanings are difficult (slippery like a weasel) to pin down to specifics. *Ask for specifics when confronted with weasel words.*

win–lose solutions In interpersonal conflict, a solution in which one person wins and one person loses. Opposed to **win-win solutions.**

win–win solutions Solutions that benefit both parties in a conflict. *Consider the possibility of solutions in which both parties gain from the conflict. Focus on these rather than solutions in which one person wins and the other loses.*

withdrawal (1) A reaction to territorial encroachment in which we leave the territory. (2) A tendency to close oneself off from conflicts rather than confront the issues.

Y

you-messages Messages in which you deny responsibility for your own thoughts and behaviors; messages that attribute your perception to another person; messages of blame. Opposed to **I-messages.**

References

A

Abel, G. G., & Harlow, N. (2001). *The stop child molestation book.* Philadelphia: Xlibris.

Acor, A. A. (2001). Employers' perceptions of persons with body art and an experimental test regarding eyebrow piercing. (Doctoral dissertation, Marquette University, 2001). *Dissertation Abstracts International, 61,* 3885B.

Adams, S. (1997). *The Dilbert principle.* New York, NY: HarperCollins.

Adler, R. B. (1977). *Confidence in communication: A guide to assertive and social skills.* New York, NY: Holt, Rinehart & Winston.

Afifi, W. A., & Johnson, M. L. (2005). The nature and function of tie-signs. In V. Manusov (Ed.), *The sourcebook of nonverbal measures: Going beyond words* (pp. 189–198). Mahwah, NJ: Erlbaum.

Afifi, W. A. (2007). Nonverbal communication. In B. B. Whaley & W. Samter (Eds.), *Explaining communication: Contemporary theories and exemplars* (pp. 39–60). Mahwah, NJ: Erlbaum.

Albas, D. C., McCluskey, K. W., & Albas, C. A. (1976). Perception of the emotional content of speech: A comparison of two Canadian groups. *Journal of Cross-Cultural Psychology, 7* (December), 481–490.

Al-Simadi, F. A. (2000). Detection of deception behavior: A cross-cultural test. *Social Behavior & Personality, 28,* 455–461.

Altman, I. (1975). *The environment and social behavior.* Monterey, CA: Brooks/Cole.

Altman, I., & Taylor, D. (1973). *Social penetration: The development of interpersonal relationships.* New York, NY: Holt, Rinehart & Winston.

Amble, B. (2005). Corporate culture encourages lying. Retrieved from http://www.management-issues.com

American Advertising Federation. (2008). Product placement. Retrieved from http://aaf.org/default.asp?id=349

American Bar Association. (2006). Retrieved from http://www.americanbarassociation.org/unmet/teendating/facts.pdf

Andersen, P. A. (1991). Explaining intercultural differences in nonverbal communication. In L. A. Samovar & R. E. Porter (Eds.), *Intercultural communication: A reader* (6th ed., pp. 286–296). Belmont, CA: Wadsworth.

Andersen, P. A. (2004). *The complete idiot's guide to body language.* New York, NY: Penguin Group.

Andersen, P. A. (2005). The touch avoidance measure. In V. Manusov (Ed.), *The sourcebook of nonverbal measures* (pp. 57–66). Mahwah, NJ: Erlbaum.

Andersen, P. A. (2006). The evaluation of biological sex differences in communication. In Dindia, K., & Canary, D. J. (Eds.), *Sex differences and similarities in communication* (2nd ed., pp. 117–135). Mahwah, NJ: Lawrence Erlbaum.

Andersen, P. A., & Bowman, L. L. (1999). Postiions of power: Nonverbal influence in organizational communication. In L. K. Guerrero, J. A. DeVito, & M. L. Hecht (Eds.), *The nonverbal communication reader: Classic and contemporary readings* (2nd ed., pp. 317–334). Prospect Heights, IL: Waveland.

Andersen, P. A., & Leibowitz, K. (1978). The development and nature of the construct touch avoidance. *Environmental Psychology and Nonverbal Behavior, 3,* 89–106.

Anderson, K. J. (1998). Meta-analysis of gender effects on conversational interruption: Who, what, when, where, and how. *Sex Roles, 39* (August), 255–252.

Anderson, S. A. & Sabatelli, R. M. (2011). *Family interaction: A multigenerational developmental perspective* (5th ed.). Boston, MA: Pearson.

Angier, N. (1995, May 9). Scientists mull role of empathy in man and beast. *New York Times,* pp. C1, C6.

Angier, N. (2010). Just don't call me... *New York Times* (August 29), Weekend, p. 3.

Annan, K. (2007). *General Assembly Sixty-first Session 10th plenary meeting.* Retrieved from http://unbisnet.un.org

Anthony, C. (2012). Put an end to convenience devocalization. In L. G. Schnoor (Ed.), *Winning orations* (pp. 63–66). Mankato, MN: Interstate Oratorical Association.

Aral, S. (2013). What would Ashton do—and does it matter? *Harvard Business Review 91,* 25–27.

Argyle, M. (1986). Rules for social relationships in four cultures. *Australian Journal of Psychology, 38* (December), 309–318.

Argyle, M. (1988). *Bodily communication* (2nd ed.). New York, NY: Methuen.

Argyle, M., & Henderson, M. (1984). The rules of friendship. *Journal of Social and Personal Relationships, 1* (June), 211–237.

Argyle, M., & Henderson, M. (1985). *The anatomy of relationships: And the rules and skills needed to manage them successfully.* London, UK: Heinemann.

Argyle, M., & Ingham, R. (1972). Gaze, mutual gaze, and distance. *Semiotica, 1,* 32–49.

Armour, S. (2007). Office gossip has never traveled faster, "thanks" to tech. Retrieved from http://www.USAToday.com

Aronson, E., Wilson, T. D., & Akert, R. M. (2010). *Social psychology: The heart and the mind* (6th ed.). New York, NY: Longman.

Aronson, J., Cohen, J., & Nail, P. (1998). Self-affirmation theory: An update and appraisal. In E. Harmon-Jones & J. S. Mills (Eds.), *Cognitive dissonance theory: Revival with revisions and controversies* (pp. 127–147). Washington, DC: American Psychological Association.

Asch, S. (1946). Forming impressions of personality. *Journal of Abnormal and Social Psychology, 41,* 258–290.

Ashcraft, M. H. (1998). *Fundamentals of cognition.* New York, NY: Longman.

Avtgis, T., & Rancer, A. S. (2010). Eds. *Arguments, aggression, and conflict: New directions in theory and research.* Clifton, NJ: Routledge.

Axtell, R. E. (1990). *Do's and taboos of hosting international visitors.* New York, NY: Wiley.

Axtell, R. E. (1993). *Do's and taboos around the world* (3rd ed.). New York, NY: Wiley.

Axtell, R. E. (2007). *Essential do's and taboos: The complete guide to international business and leisure travel.* Hoboken, NJ: Wiley.

Ayres, J., & Hopf, T. S. (1992). Visualization: Reducing speech anxiety and enhancing performance. *Communication Reports, 5,* 1–10.

Ayres, J., & Hopf, T. S. (1993). *Coping with speech anxiety.* Norwood, NJ: Ablex.

Ayres, J., Hopf, T. S., & Ayres, D. M. (1994). An examination of whether imaging ability enhances the effectiveness of an intervention designed to reduce speech anxiety. *Communication Education, 43* (July), 252–258.

B

Bach, G. R., & Wyden, P. (1968). *The intimate enemy.* New York, NY: Avon.

Bales, R. F. (1950). *Interaction process analysis: A method for the study of small groups.* Cambridge, MA: Addison-Wesley.

Barker, L., Edwards, R., Gaines, C., Gladney, K., & Holley, F. (1980). An investigation of proportional time spent in various communication activities by college students. *Journal of Applied Communication Research, 8,* 101–109.

Barker, L. L., & Gaut, D. (2002). *Communication* (8th ed.). Boston, MA: Allyn & Bacon.

Barker, L., Edwards, R., Gaines, C., Gladney, K., & Holley, F. (1980). An investigation of proportional time spent in various communication activities by college students. *Journal of Applied Communication Research, 8,* 101–109.

Barna Group (2013). Barna research. Retrieved from www.barna.org/

Barna, L. M. (1997). Stumbling blocks in intercultural communication. In L. A. Samovar & R. E. Porter (Eds.), *Intercultural communication: A reader* (7th ed., pp. 337–346). Belmont, CA: Wadsworth.

Barnlund, D. C. (1989). *Communicative styles of Japanese and Americans: Images and realities.* Belmont, CA: Wadsworth.

Baron, R. A., & Byrne, D. (1984). *Social psychology: Understanding human interaction* (4th ed.). Boston, MA: Allyn & Bacon.

Barr, M. J. (2000). Mentoring relationships: A study of informal/formal mentoring, psychological type of mentors, and mentor/protégé type combinations. *Dissertation Abstracts International, 60,* 2568A.

Barrett, G. (2006, December 24). Glossary. *New York Times,* Wk 4.

Barrett, L., & Godfrey, T. (1988). Listening. *Person-Centered Review, 3* (November), 410–425.

Bassellier, G., & Benbasat, I. (2004). Business competence of information technology professionals: Conceptual development and influence on IT-business partnerships. *MIS Quarterly, 28* (December), 673–694.

Basso, K. H. (1972). To give up on words: Silence in Apache culture. In P. P. Giglioli (Ed.), *Language and social context.* New York, NY: Penguin.

Baumeister, R. F., Bushman, B. J., & Campbell, W. K. (2000). Self-esteem, narcissism, and aggression: Does violence result from low self-esteem or from threatened egotism? *Current Directions in Psychological Science, 9* (February), 26–29.

Baxter, L. A. (1983). Relationship disengagement: An examination of the reversal hypothesis. *Western Journal of Speech Communication, 47,* 85–98.

Baxter, L. A. (1984). An investigation of compliance-gaining as politeness. *Human Communication Research, 10,* 427–456.

Baxter, L. A. (1986). Gender differences in the heterosexual relationship rules embedded in break-up accounts. *Journal of Social and Personal Relationships, 3,* 289–306.

Baxter, L. A. (1988). A dialectical perspective on communication strategies in relationship development. In S. Duck (Ed.), *Handbook of Personal Relationships.* New York, NY: Wiley.

Baxter, L. A. (1990). Dialectical contradictions in relationship development. *Journal of Social and Personal Relationships, 7* (February), 69–88.

Baxter, L. A., & Simon, E. P. (1993). Relationship maintenance strategies and dialectical contradictions in personal relationships. *Journal of Social and Personal Relationships, 10* (May), 225–242.

Baxter, L. A., & Wilmot, W. W. (1984). "Secret tests": Social strategies for acquiring information about the state of the relationship. *Human Communication Research, 11,* 171–201.

Beatty, M. J. (1988). Situational and predispositional correlates of public speaking anxiety. *Communication Education, 37,* 28–39.

Beatty, M. J., Rudd, J. E., & Valencic, K. M. (1999). A re-evaluation of the verbal aggressiveness scale: One factor or two? *Communication Research Reports, 16,* 10–17.

Bechler, C., & Johnson, S. D. (1995). Leadership and listening: A study of member perceptions. *Small Group Research, 26,* 77–85.

Bedford, V. H. (1996). Relationships between adult siblings. In A. E. Auhagen & M. von Salisch (Eds.), *The diversity of human relationships* (pp. 120–140). New York, NY: Cambridge University Press.

Beebe, S. A., & Masterson, J. T. (2012). *Communicating in small groups: Principles and practices* (10th ed.). Boston, MA: Allyn & Bacon.

Beier, E. (1974). How we send emotional messages. *Psychology Today, 8* (October), 53–56.

Bell, R. A., & Buerkel-Rothfuss, N. L. (1990). S(he) loves me, s(he) loves me not: Predictors of relational information-seeking in courtship and beyond. *Communication Quarterly, 38,* 64–82.

Bell, R. A., & Daly, J. A. (1984). The affinity-seeking function of communication. *Communication Monographs, 51,* 91–115.

Bell, S. T., Kuriloff, P. J., & Lottes, I. (1994). Understanding attributions of blame in stranger rape and date rape situations: An examination of gender, race, identification, and students' social perceptions of rape victims. *Journal of Applied Social Psychology, 24* (October), 1719–1734.

Bellafiore, D. (2005). *Interpersonal conflict and effective communication.* Retrieved from http://www.drbalternatives.com/articles/cc2.html

Benne, K. D., & Sheats, P. (1948). Functional roles of group members. *Journal of Social Issues, 4,* 41–49.

Bennis, W., & Nanus, B. (2003). *Leaders: Strategies for taking charge.* New York: Harpercollins.

Benoit, W. L., & Benoit, P. J. (1990). Memory for conversational behavior, *Southern Communication Journal, 55,* 17–23.

Benson, S. G., & Dundis, S. P. (2003). Understanding and motivating health care employees: Integrating Maslow's hierarchy of needs, training and technology. *Journal of Nursing Management, 11,* 315–320.

Berg, J. H., & Archer, R. L. (1983). The disclosure-liking relationship. *Human Communication Research, 10,* 269–281.

Berger, C. R., & Bradac, J. J. (1982). *Language and social knowledge: Uncertainty in interpersonal relations.* London: Edward Arnold.

Bernstein, W. M., Stephan, W. G., & Davis, M. H. (1979). Explaining attributions for achievement: A path analytic approach. *Journal of Personality and Social Psychology, 37,* 1810–1821.

Berscheid, E., & Reis, H. T. (1998). Attraction and close relationships. In D. Gilbert, S. Fiske, & G. Lindzey (Eds.), *The Handbook of Social Psychology,* 4th ed. (Vol. 2, pp. 193–281).

Berry, J. N. III (2004). Can I quote you on that? *Library Journal, 129,* 10.

Berry, J. W., Poortinga, Y. H., Segall, M. H., & Dasen, P. R. (1992). *Cross-cultural psychology: Research and applications.* New York, NY: Cambridge University Press.

Bierhoff, H. W., & Klein, R. (1991). Dimensionen der Liebe: Entwicklung einer Deutschsprachigen Skala zur Erfassung von Liebesstilen. *Zeitschrift for Differentielle und Diagnostische Psychologie, 12,* 53–71.

Bishop, S. (2006). *Develop your assertiveness.* London, UK: Kogan Page.

Blake, R. R., & Mouton, J. S. (1984). *The managerial grid III* (3rd ed.). Houston, TX: Gulf Publishing.

Blieszner, R., & Adams, R. G. (1992). *Adult friendship.* Thousand Oaks, CA: Sage.

Blumstein, P., & Schwartz, P. (1983). *American couples: Money, work, sex.* New York, NY: Morrow.

Bochner, S., & Hesketh, B. (1994). Power, distance, individualism/collectivism, and job-related attitudes in a culturally diverse work group. *Journal of Cross-Cultural Psychology, 25* (June), 233–257.

Bodie, G. D. (2010). A racing heart, rattling knees, and ruminative thoughts: Defining, explaining, and treating public speaking anxiety. *Communication Education, 59,* 70–105.

Bodon, J., Powell, L., & Hickson, M., III. (1999). Critiques of gatekeeping in scholarly journals: An analysis of perceptions and data. *Journal of the Association for Communication Administration, 28* (May), 60–70.

Bok, S. (1978). *Lying: Moral choice in public and private life.* New York, NY: Pantheon.

Bok, S. (1983). *Secrets.* New York, NY: Vintage.

Bond, C. F., Jr., & Atoum, A. O. (2000). International deception. *Personality & Social Psychology Bulletin, 26* (March), 385–395.

Borden, G. (1991). *Cultural orientation: An approach to understanding intercultural communication.* Englewood Cliffs, NJ: Prentice-Hall.

Bourland, D. D., Jr. (1965–66). A linguistic note: Writing in E-prime. *General Semantics Bulletin, 32–33,* 111–114.

Bourland, D. D., Jr., & Johnston, P. D. (Eds.). (1997). *E-prime III! A third anthology.* Concord, CA: International Society for General Semantics.

Bower, B. (2001). Self-illusions come back to bite students. *Science News, 159,* 148.

Bower, S. A., & Bower, G. A. (2005). *Asserting yourself: A practical guide for positive change.* Cambridge, MA: DaCapo Press.

Brashers, D. E. (2007). A theory of communication and uncertainty management. In B. B. Whaley & W. Samter (Eds.), *Explaining communication: Contemporary theories and exemplars* (pp. 201–218). Mahwah, NJ: Lawrence Erlbaum.

Brauer, M., Judd, C. M., & Gliner, M. D. (1995). The effects of repeated expressions on attitude polarization during group discussions. *Journal of Personality and Social Psychology, 68* (June), 1014–1029.

Bravo, E., & Cassedy, E. (1992). *The 9 to 5 guide to combating sexual harassment.* New York, NY: Wiley.

Brennan, M. (1991). Mismanagement and quality circles: How middle managers influence direct participation. *Employee Relations, 13,* 22–32.

Bridges, C. R. (1996). The characteristics of career achievement perceived by African American college administrators. *Journal of Black Studies, 26* (July), 748–767.

Brilhart, J., & Galanes, G. (1992). *Effective group discussion* (7th ed.). Dubuque, IA: Brown & Benchmark.

Brody, J. E. (1994, March 21). Notions of beauty transcend culture, new study suggests. *New York Times,* p. A14.

Brown, P. (1980). How and why are women more polite: Some evidence from a Mayan community. In S. McConnell-Ginet, R. Borker, & M. Furman (Eds.), *Women and language in literature and society* (pp. 111–136). New York, NY: Praeger.

Brown, P., & Levinson, S. C. (1987). *Politeness: Some universals of language usage.* Cambridge, England: Cambridge University Press.

Brownell, J. (2010). *Listening: Attitudes, principles, and skills* (4th ed.). Boston, MA: Allyn & Bacon.

Bruneau, T. (1985). The time dimension in intercultural communication. In L. A. Samovar & R. E. Porter (Eds.), *Intercultural communication: A reader* (4th ed., pp. 280–289). Belmont, CA: Wadsworth.

Bruneau, T. (2009/2010). Chronemics: Time-binding and the construction of personal time. *General Semantics Bulletin, 76,* 82–94.

Bruneau, T. (1990). Chronemics: The study of time in human interaction. In J. A. DeVito & M. L. Hecht (Eds.), *The nonverbal communication reader* (pp. 301–311). Prospect Heights, IL: Waveland Press.

Buber, M. (1958). *I and thou* (2nd ed.). New York, NY: Scribner's.

Bull, R., & Rumsey, N. (1988). *The social psychology of facial appearance*. New York, NY: Springer-Verlag.

Buller, D. J. (2005). *Adapting minds: Evolutionary psychology and the persistent quest for human nature*. Cambridge, MA: MIT Press.

Buller, D. B., LePoire, B. A., Aune, K., & Eloy, S. (1992). Social perceptions as mediators of the effect of speech rate similarity on compliance. *Human Communication Research, 19* (December), 286–311.

Bullock, C., McCluskey, M., Stamm, K., Tanaka, K., Torres, M. & Scott, C. (2002). Group affiliations, opinion polarization, and global organization: Views of the World Trade Organization before and after Seattle. *Mass Communication & Society, 5*(4), 433–450.

Buss, D. M. (1988). The evolution of human intrasexual competition: Tactics of mate attraction. *Journal of Personality and Social Psychology, 54,* 616–628.

Burgoon, J. K. (2005). Measuring nonverbal indicators of deceit. In V. Manusov (Ed.), *The sourcebook of nonverbal measures: Going beyond words* (pp. 237–250). Mahwah, NJ: Lawrence Erlbaum.

Burgoon, J. K., & Bacue, A. E. (2003). Nonverbal communication skills. In J. O. Greene & B. R. Burleson (Eds.), *Handbook of communication and social interaction skills* (pp. 179–220). Mahwah, NJ: Lawrence Erlbaum.

Burgoon, J. K., & Hoobler, G. D. (2002). Nonverbal signals. In M. L. Knapp & J. A. Daly (Eds.), *Handbook of interpersonal communication* (3rd ed., pp. 240–299). Thousand Oaks, CA: Sage.

Burgoon, J. K., Berger, C. R., & Waldron, V. R. (2000). Mindfulness and interpersonal communication. *Journal of Social Issues, 56,* 105–127.

Burgoon, J. K., Buller, D. B., & Woodall, W. G. (1996). *Nonverbal communication: The unspoken dialogue* (2nd ed.). New York, NY: McGraw-Hill.

Burgoon, J. K., Guerrero, L., & Floyd, K. (2010). *Nonverbal communication*. Boston, MA: Allyn & Bacon.

Burleson, B. R., Kunkel, A. W., & Birch, J. D. (1994). Thoughts about talk in romantic relationships: Similarity makes for attraction (and happiness, too). *Communication Quarterly, 42* (Summer), 259–273.

Burleson, B. R., Samter, W., & Luccetti, A. E. (1992). Similarity in communication values as a predictor of friendship choices: Studies of friends and best friends. *Southern Communication Journal, 57,* 260–276.

Bushman, B. J., & Baumeister, R. F. (1998). Threatened egotism, narcissism, self-esteem, and direct and displaced aggression: Does self-love or self-hate lead to violence? *Journal of Personality and Social Psychology, 75,* 219–229.

Buss, D. M. (2000). *The dangerous passion: Why jealousy is as necessary as love and sex*. New York, NY: Free Press.

Butler, M. M. (2005). Communication apprehension and its impact on individuals in the work place. Howard University. *Dissertation Abstracts International: A. The Humanities and Social Sciences, 65* (9-A), 3215.

Butler, P. E. (1981). *Talking to yourself: Learning the language of self-support*. New York, NY: Harper & Row.

Buunk, B. P., & Dijkastra, P. (2004). Gender differences in rival characteristics that evoke jealousy in response to emotional versus sexual infidelity. *Personal Relationships* 11 (December), 395–408.

C

Cahn, D. D., & Abigail, R. A. (2014). *Managing conflict through communication,* 5th ed. Boston, MA: Allyn & Bacon.

Callan, V. J. (1993). Subordinate-manager communication in different sex dyads: Consequences for job satisfaction. *Journal of Occupational & Organizational Psychology, 66* (March), 1–15.

Canary, D. J., Cupach, W. R., & Messman, S. J. (1995). *Relationship conflict*. Thousand Oaks, CA: Sage.

Canary, D. J., & Hause, K. S. (1993). Is there any reason to research sex differences in communication? *Communication Quarterly, 41* (Spring), 129–144.

Cappella, J. N. (1993). The facial feedback hypothesis in human interaction: Review and speculation. *Journal of Language and Social Psychology, 12,* 13–29.

Carroll, D. W. (1994). Psychology of language (2nd ed.). Pacific Grove, CA: Brooks/Cole.

Castleberry, S. B., & Shepherd, D. D. (1993). Effective interpersonal listening and personal selling. *Journal of Personal Selling and Sales Management, 13,* 35–49.

Cathcart, D., & Cathcart, R. (1985). Japanese social experience and concept of groups. In L. A. Samovar & R. E. Porter (Eds.), *Intercultural communication: A reader* (4th ed., pp. 190–197). Belmont, CA: Wadsworth.

Chadwick-Jones, J. K. (1976). *Social exchange theory: Its structure and influence in social psychology*. New York, NY: Academic Press.

Chang, H.-C., & Holt, G. R. (1996). The changing Chinese interpersonal world: Popular themes in interpersonal communication books in modern Taiwan. *Communication Quarterly, 44* (Winter), 85–106.

Chase, S. (1956). *Guides to straight thinking: With 13 common fallacies*. New York, NY: Harper & Brothers.

Cheney, G., & Tompkins, P. K. (1987). Coming to terms with organizational identification and commitment. *Central States Speech Journal, 38* (Spring), 1–15.

Cho, H. (2000). Asian in America: Cultural shyness can impede Asian Americans' success. *Northwest Asian Weekly, 19* (December 8), 6.

Chung, L. C., & Ting-Toomey, S. (1999). Ethnic identity and relational expectations among Asian Americans. *Communication Research Reports, 16* (Spring), 157–166.

Clance, P. (1985). *The Impostor Phenomenon: Overcoming the fear that haunts your success*. Atlanta, GA: Peachtree Publishers.

Cody, M. J., & Dunn, D. (2007). Accounts. In B. B. Whaley and W. Samter (Eds.), *Explaining communication: Contemporary theories and exemplars* (pp. 237–256). Mahwah, NJ: Lawrence Erlbaum.

Cole, T., & Leets, L. (1999). Attachment styles and intimate television viewing: Insecurely forming relationships in a parasocial way. *Journal of Social and Personal Relationships, 16* (August), 495–511.

Coleman, P. (2002). *How to say it for couples: Communicating with tenderness, openness, and honesty*. Paramus, NJ: Prentice-Hall.

Comadena, M. E. (1984). Brainstorming groups: Ambiguity tolerance, communication apprehension, task attraction, and individual productivity. *Small Group Behavior, 15,* 251–254.

Comer, L. B., & Drollinger, T. (1999). Active emphatic listening and selling success: A conceptual framework. *Journal of Personal Selling and Sales Management, 19,* 15–29.

Congdon, C., & Gall, C. (2013). How culture shapes the office. *Harvard Business Review, 91,* 34–35.

Cornwell, B., & Lundgren, D. C. (2001). Love on the Internet: Involvement and misrepresentation in romantic relationships in cyberspace vs. realspace. *Computers in Human Behavior, 17,* 197–211.

Cooley, C. H. (1922). *Human nature and the social order* (Rev. ed.). New York, NY: Scribners.

Cooper, A., & Sportolari, L. (1997). Romance in cyberspace: Understanding online attraction. *Journal of Sex Education and Therapy, 22,* 7–14.

Coover, G. E., & Murphy, S. T. (2000). The communicated self: Exploring the interaction between self and social context. *Human Communication Research, 26,* 125–147.

Copeland, L., & Griggs, L. (1985). *Going international: How to make friends and deal effectively in the global marketplace*. New York, NY: Random House.

Cragan, J. F., & Wright, D. W. (1990). Small group communication research of the 1980s: A synthesis and critique. *Communication Studies, 41* (Fall), 212–236.

Craig, E., & Wright, K. B. (2012). Computer-mediated relational development and maintenance on Facebook. *Communication Research Reports, 29,* 119–129.

Crampton, S. M., Hodge, J. M., & Mishra, J. M. (1998). The informal communication network: Factors influencing grapevine activity. *Public Personnel Management, 27* (Winter), 569–584.

Cross, E. E., & Madson, L. (1997). Models of the self: Self-construals and gender. *Psychological Bulletin, 122,* 5–37.

Crown, C. L., & Cummins, D. A. (1998). Objective versus perceived vocal interruptions in the dialogues of unacquainted pairs, friends, and couples. Journal of *Language and Social Psychology, 17* (September), 372–389.

Crusco, A. H., & Wetzel, C. G. (1984). The Midas touch: The effects of interpersonal touch on restaurant tipping. *Personality and Social Psychology Bulletin, 10* (December), 512–517.

D

Davis, K. (1980). Management communication and the grapevine. In S. Ferguson & S. D. Ferguson (Eds.), *Intercom: Readings in organizational communication* (pp. 55–66). Rochelle Park, NJ: Hayden Books.

Davis, M. S. (1973). *Intimate relations*. New York, NY: Free Press.

Davison, W. P. (1983). The third-person effects and the differential impact in negative political advertising. *Journalism Quarterly, 68,* 680–688.

Deaux, K., & LaFrance, M. (1998). Gender. In D. Gilbert, S. Fiske & G. Lindzey (Eds.), *The Handbook of Social Psychology*, Vol. 1. (4th ed., pp. 788–828). New York, NY: Freeman.

deBono, E. (1976). *Teaching thinking*. New York, NY: Penguin.

deBono, E. (1987). *The six thinking hats*. New York, NY: Penguin.

DePaulo, B. M., Lindsay, J. J., Malone, B. E., Muhlenbruck, L., Charlton, K., & Cooper, H. (2003). Cues to deception. *Psychological Bulletin, 129,* 74–118.

DePino, D. (2012). Lost to silence. In L. G. Schnoor (Ed.), *Winning orations* (pp. 43–45). Mankato, MN: Interstate Oratorical Association.

Derlega, V. J., Winstead, B. A., Wong, P. T. P., & Greenspan, M. (1987). Self-disclosure and relationship development: An attributional analysis. In M. E. Roloff & G. R. Miller (Eds.), *Interpersonal processes: New directions in communication research* (pp. 172–187). Thousand Oaks, CA: Sage.

Derlega, V. J., Winstead, B. A., Wong, P. T. P., & Hunter, S. (1985). Gender effects in an initial encounter: A case where men exceed women in disclosure. *Journal of Social and Personal Relationships, 2,* 25–44.

DeVito, J. A. (1974). *General semantics: Guide and workbook* (Rev. ed.). DeLand, FL: Everett/Edwards.

DeVito, J. A. (1996). *Brainstorms: How to think more creatively about communication (or about anything else)*. Boston, MA: Allyn & Bacon.

DeVito, J. A. (2014). *The nonverbal communication book*. Dubuque, IA: Kendall-Hunt.

Dewey, J. (1910). *How we think*. Boston: Heath.

Dindia, K., & Canary, D. J. (2006) (Eds.), Sex differences and similarities in communication. Mahwah, NJ: Lawrence Erlbaum.

Dindia, K., & Fitzpatrick, M. A. (1985). Marital communication: Three approaches compared. In S. Duck & D. Perlman (Eds.), *Understanding personal relationships: An interdisciplinary approach* (pp. 137–158). Thousand Oaks, CA: Sage.

Dindia, K., & Timmerman, L. (2003). Accomplishing romantic relationships. In J. O. Greene & B. R. Burleson (Eds.), *Handbook of communication and social interaction skills* (pp. 685–722). Mahwah, NJ: Lawrence Erlbaum.

Dion, K. K., & Dion, K. L. (1996). Cultural perspectives on romantic love. *Personal Relationships, 3,* 5–17.

Dion, K. K., & Dion, K. L. (1993a). Individualistic and collectivist perspectives on gender and the cultural context of love and intimacy. *Journal of Social Issues, 49,* 53–69.

Dion, K. L., & Dion, K. K. (1993b). Gender and ethnocultural comparisons in styles of love. *Psychology of Women Quarterly, 17,* 464–473.

Donaldson, S. (1992). Gender and discourse: The case of interruptions. *Carleton Papers in Applied Language Studies, 9,* 47–66.

Donohue, W. A. (with Kolt, R.). (1992). *Managing interpersonal conflict*. Thousand Oaks, CA: Sage.

Dovidio, J. F., Gaertner, S. E., Kawakami, K., & Hodson, G. (2002). Why can't we just get along? Interpersonal biases and interracial distrust. *Cultural Diversity and Ethnic Minority Psychology, 8,* 88–102.

Drass, K. A. (1986). The effect of gender identity on conversation. Social *Psychology Quarterly, 49,* 294–301.

Dresser, N. (1996). *Multicultural manners: New rules of etiquette for a changing society*. New York, NY: Wiley.

Dresser, N. (2005). *Multicultural manners: Essential rules of etiquette for the 21st century* (Rev. ed.). Hoboken, NJ: Wiley.

Drews, D. R., Allison, C. K., & Probst, J. R. (2000). Behavioral and self-concept differences in tattooed and nontattooed college students. *Psychological Reports, 86,* 475–481.

Dreyfuss, H. (1971). *Symbol sourcebook*. New York, NY: McGraw-Hill.

Dryden, W., & Constantinou, D. (2005). *Assertiveness: Step by step*. London, UK: Sheldon Press.

Drummond, K., & Hopper, R. (1993). Acknowledgment tokens in series. *Communication Reports, 6,* 47–53.

Dunbar, N. E., & Burgoon, J. K. (2005). Measuring nonverbal dominance. In V. Manusov (Ed.). *The sourcebook of nonverbal measures: Going beyond words* (pp. 361–374). Mahwah, NJ: Lawrence Erlbaum.

Dunn, D., & Cody, M. J. (2000). Account credibility and public image: Excuses, justifications, denials, and sexual harassment. *Communication Monographs, 67* (December), 372–391.

Duval, T. S., & Silva, P. J. (2002). Self-awareness, probability of improvement, and the self-serving bias. *Journal of Personality and Social Psychology, 82,* 49–61.

E

Eagly, A. H., & Crowley, M. (1986). Gender and helping behavior: A meta-analytic review of the social psychological literature. *Psychological Bulletin, 100* (November), 283–308.

Eden, D. (1992). Leadership and expectations: Pygmalion effects and other self-fulfilling prophecies in organizations. *Leadership Quarterly, 3* (Winter), 271–305.

Eder, D., & Enke, J. L. (1991). The structure of gossip: Opportunities and constraints on collective expression among adolescents. *American Sociological Review, 56,* 494–508.

Egan, K. G., & Moreno, M. A. (2011). Alcohol references on undergraduate male's Facebook profiles. *American Journal of Men's Health, 5,* 413–420.

Ehrenhaus, P. (1988). Silence and symbolic expression. *Communication Monographs, 55* (March), 41–57.

Einhorn, L. (2006). Using e-prime and English minus absolutisms to provide self-empathy. *Etc.: A Review of General Semantics, 63* (April), 180–186.

Einstein, E. (1995). Success or sabotage: Which self-fulfilling prophecy will the stepfamily create? In D. K. Huntley (Ed.), *Understanding stepfamilies: Implications for assessment and treatment*. Alexandria, VA: American Counseling Association.

Ekman, P. (1985). *Telling lies: Clues to deceit in the marketplace, politics, and marriage*. New York, NY: Norton.

Ekman, P. (2009). *Telling lies: Clues to deceit in the marketplace, politics, and marriage*, 3rd ed. New York: Norton.

Ekman, P., & Friesen, W. V. (1969). The repertoire of nonverbal behavior: Categories, origins, usage, and coding. *Semiotica, 1,* 49–98.

Ekman, P., & Friesen, W. V. (2003). *Unmasking the face: A guide to recognizing emotions from facial expressions*. Cambridge, MA: Malor Book. (Original work published 1975)

Ekman, P., Friesen, W. V., & Ellsworth, P. (1972). *Emotion in the human face: Guidelines for research and an integration of findings*. New York, NY: Pergamon Press.

Elfenbein, H. A., & Ambady, N. (2002). Is there an in-group advantage in emotion recognition? *Psychological Bulletin, 128,* 243–249.

Elmes, M. B., & Gemmill, G. (1990). The psychodynamics of mindlessness and dissent in small groups. *Small Group Research, 21,* 28–44.

Emmert, P. (1994). A definition of listening. *Listening Post, 51,* 6.

Engleberg, I. N., & Wynn, D. R. (2013). *Working in groups* (6th ed.). Boston, MA: Pearson.

Erber, R., & Erber, M. W. (2011). *Intimate relationships: Issues, theories, and research* (2nd ed.). Boston, MA: Allyn and Bacon.

Exline, R. V., Ellyson, S. L., & Long, B. (1975). Visual behavior as an aspect of power role relationships. In P. Pliner, L. Krames, & T. Alloway (Eds.), *Nonverbal communication of aggression*. New York, NY: Plenum Press.

F

Fallows, D. (2005). The Internet and Daily Life, Pew Internet and American Life Project. Retrieved from www.pewinternet.org/PPF/r/131/report_display.asp

Fehr, B., & Broughton, R. (2001). Gender and personality differences in concepts of love: An interpersonal theory analysis. *Personal Relationships, 8,* 115–136.

Feinstein, D. 2006 (October 23), ch 15 Gang violence: An environment of fear www.feinstein.senate,gov/public/index.cfm/speeches?ID=59f0cee8

Felson, R. B. (2002). Violence and gender reexamined. *Law and public policy*. Washington, DC: American Psychological Association.

Fensholt, M. (2003, June). There's nothing wrong with taking written notes to the podium. *Presentations, 17,* 66.

Fernald, C. D. (1995). When in London ... Differences in disability language preferences among English-speaking countries. *Mental Retardation, 33* (April), 99–103.

Festinger, L. (1954). A theory of social comparison processes. *Human Relations, 7,* 117–140.

Fitzpatrick, M. A. (1983). Predicting couples' communication from couples' self-reports. In R. N. Bostrom (Ed.), *Communication Yearbook 7* (pp. 49–82). Thousand Oaks, CA: Sage.

Fitzpatrick, M. A. (1988). *Between husbands and wives: Communication in marriage.* Thousand Oaks, CA: Sage.

Fitzpatrick, M. A. (1991). Sex differences in marital conflict: Social psychophysiological versus cognitive explanations. *Text, 11,* 341–364.

Fitzpatrick, M. A., Jandt, F. E., Myrick, F. L., & Edgar, T. (1994). Gay and lesbian couple relationships. In Ringer, R. J. (Ed.), *Queer words, queer images: Communication and the construction of homosexuality* (pp. 265–285). New York, NY: New York University Press.

Flocker, M. (2006). *Death by Power Point: A modern office survival guide.* Cambridge, MA: DaCapo Press.

Floyd, K., & Mikkelson, A. C. (2005). In *The sourcebook of nonverbal measures: Going beyond words* (pp. 47–56), V. Manusov (Ed.). Mahwah, NJ: Lawrence Erlbaum.

Folger, J. P., Poole, M. S., & Stutman, R. K. (2013). *Working through conflict: A communication perspective* (7th ed.). Boston, MA: Allyn & Bacon.

Folkerts, J., & Lacy, S. (2001). *The media in your life: An introduction to mass communication* (2nd ed.). Boston, MA: Allyn & Bacon.

Forbes, G. B. (2001). College students with tattoos and piercings: Motives, family experiences, personality factors, and perception by others. *Psychological Reports, 89,* 774–786.

Franklin, C. W., & Mizell, C. A. (1995). Some factors influencing success among African-American men: A preliminary study. *Journal of Men's Studies, 3,* 191–204.

Fraser, B. (1990). Perspectives on politeness. *Journal of Pragmatics, 14* (April), 219–236.

French, J. R. P., Jr., & Raven, B. (1968). The bases of social power. In D. Cartwright & A. Zander (Eds.), *Group dynamics: Research and theory* (3rd ed., pp. 259–269). New York, NY: Harper & Row.

Frentz, T. (1976). A general approach to episodic structure. Paper presented at the Western Speech Association Convention, San Francisco, CA. Cited in Reardon (1987).

Friedkin, N. E. (1999). Choice shift and group polarization. *American Sociological Review, 64* (December), 856–875.

Fukushima, S. (2000). *Requests and culture: Politeness in British English and Japanese.* New York, NY: Peter Lang.

Fuller, D. (2004). Electronic manners and netiquette. *Athletic Therapy Today, 9* (March), 40–41.

Furlow, F. B. (1996). The smell of love. *Psychology Today* (March/April), 38–45.

G

Galvin, K., Bylund, C., & Brommel, B. J. (2012). *Family communication: Cohesion and change* (8th ed.). Boston, MA: Allyn & Bacon.

Gamble, T. K., & Gamble, M. W. (2003). *The gender communication connection.* Boston: Houghton Mifflin.

Gao, G., & Gudykunst, W. B. (1995). Attributional confidence, perceived similarity, and network involvement in Chinese and American romantic relationships. *Communication Quarterly, 43,* 431–445.

Geffner, R., Braverman, M., Galasso, J., & Marsh, J. (Eds.). (2004). *Aggression in organizations.* Binghamton, NY: Haworth Maltreatment and Trauma Press.

Georgas, J., et al. (2001). Functional relationships in the nuclear and extended family: A 16-culture study. *International Journal of Psychology, 36,* 289–300.

Gergen, K. J., Greenberg, M. S., & Willis, R. H. (1980). *Social exchange: Advances in theory and research.* New York, NY: Plenum Press.

German, K., Gronbeck, B., Ehninger, D., & Monroe, A. H. (2010). *Principles of public speaking* (17th ed.). Boston, MA: Free Press.

Giles, D. C. (2001). Parasocial interaction: A review of the literature and a model for future research. *Media Psychology, 4,* 279–305.

Giles, H. (2008). Communication accommodation theory. In L. A. Baxter & D. O. Braithwaite (Eds.), *Engaging theories in interpersonal communication: Multiple perspectives* (pp. 161–174). Los Angeles, CA: Sage.

Gladstone, G. L., & Parker, G. B. (2002). When you're smiling, does the whole world smile for you? *Australasian Psychiatry, 10* (June), 44–146.

Glucksberg, S., & Danks, J. H. (1975). *Experimental psycholinguistics: An introduction.* Hillsdale, NJ: Erlbaum.

Goffman, E. (1967). *Interaction ritual: Essays on face-to-face behavior.* New York, NY: Pantheon.

Goffman, E. (1971). *Relations in public: Microstudies of the public order.* New York, NY: HarperCollins.

Goldin-Meadow, S., Nusbaum, H., Kelly, S. D., & Wagner, S. (2001). Gesture—Psychological aspects. *Psychological Science, 12,* 516–522.

Goldsmith, D. J. (2007). Brown and Levinson's politeness theory. In B. B. Whaley, & W. Samter (Eds.), *Explaining communication: Contemporary theories and exemplars* (pp. 219–236). Mahwah, NJ: Lawrence Erlbaum.

Goldsmith, D. J., & Fulfs, P. A. (1999). "You just don't have the evidence": An analysis of claims and evidence. In M. E. Roloff (Ed.), *Communication yearbook, 22* (pp. 1–49). Thousand Oaks, CA: Sage.

Goldstein, N. J., Martin, S. J., & Cialdini, R. B. (2008). *Yes! 50 scientifically proven ways to be persuasive.* New York, NY: Free Press.

Goleman, D. (1995a, February 14). For man and beast, language of love shares many traits. *New York Times,* pp. C1, C9.

Goleman, D. (1995b). *Emotional intelligence.* New York, NY: Bantam.

Gonzaga, G. C., Keltner, D., Lonhahl, E. A., & Smith, M. D. (2001). Love and the commitment problem in romantic relationships and friendships. *Journal of Personality and Social Psychology, 81* (August), 247–262.

Gonzales, A., & Zimbardo, P. G. (1985). Time in perspective. *Psychology Today, 19,* 20–26.

Gonzenbach, W. J., King, C., & Jablonski, P. (1999). Homosexuals and the military: An analysis of the spiral of silence. *Howard Journal of Communication, 10* (October–December), 281–296.

Goodwin, R., & Findlay, C. (1997). "We were just fated together." Chinese love and the concept of yuan in England and Hong Kong. *Personal Relationships, 4,* 85–92.

Goodwin, R., & Gaines, S. O., Jr. (2004). Relationships beliefs and relationship quality across cultures: Country as a moderator of dysfunctional beliefs and relationship quality in three former Communist societies. *Personal Relationships, 11* (September), 267–279.

Goodwin, R., & Lee, I. (1994). Taboo topics among Chinese and English friends: A cross-cultural comparison. *Journal of Cross-Cultural Psychology, 25,* 325–338.

Gordon, T. (1975). *P.E.T.: Parent effectiveness training.* New York, NY: New American Library.

Gosling, S. D., Ko, S. J., Mannarelli, T., & Morris, M. E. (2002). A room with a cue: Personality judgments based on offices and bedrooms. *Journal of Personality and Social Psychology, 82* (March), 379–398.

Gottman, J. (2004). 12-year study of gay & lesbian couples. Retrieved from http://www.gottman.com/research/projects/gaylesbian

Gottman, J. M., & Carrere, S. (1994). Why can't men and women get along? Developmental roots and marital inequities. In D. J. Canary & L. Stafford (Eds.), *Communication and relational maintenance* (pp. 203–229). San Diego, CA: Academic Press.

Gottman, J. M., & Levenson, R. W. (1999). Dysfunctional marital conflict: Women are being unfairly blamed. *Journal of Divorce and Remarriage, 31,* 1–17.

Graham, J. A., & Argyle, M. (1975). The effects of different patterns of gaze, combined with different facial expressions, on impression formation. *Journal of Human Movement Studies, 1* (December), 178–182.

Graham, J. A., Bitti, P. R., & Argyle, M. (1975). A Cross-cultural study of the communication of emotion by facial and gestural cues. *Journal of Human Movement Studies, 1* (June), 68–77.

Greif, E. B. (1980). Sex differences in parent-child conversations. *Women's Studies International Quarterly, 3,* 253–258.

Griffin, E., & Sparks, G. G. (1990). Friends forever: A longitudinal exploration of intimacy in same-sex friends and platonic pairs. *Journal of Social and Personal Relationships, 7,* 29–46.

Grobart, S. (2007, January). Allow me to introduce myself (properly). *Money, 36,* 40–41.

Grossin, W. (1987). Monochronic time, polychronic time and policies for development. *Studi di Sociologia, 25* (January–March), 18–25.

Gu, Y. (1997). Polite phenomena in modern Chinese. *Journal of Pragmatics, 14,* 237–257.

Gudykunst, W. (1993). Toward a theory of effective interpersonal and intergroup communication: An anxiety/uncertainty management (AUM) perspective. In R. L. Wiseman (Ed.), *Intercultural communication competence.* Thousand Oaks, CA: Sage.

Gudykunst, W. B. (1994). *Bridging differences: Effective intergroup communication* (2nd ed.). Thousand Oaks, CA: Sage.

Gudykunst, W. B., & Kim, Y. Y. (1992). *Communicating with strangers: An approach to intercultural communication* (2nd ed.). New York, NY: Random House.

Gudykunst, W. B., Nishida, T., & Chua, E. (1987). Perceptions of social penetration in Japanese-North American dyads. *International Journal of Intercultural Relations, 11,* 171–189.

Gudykunst, W. B., & Ting-Toomey, S., with Chua, E. (1988). *Culture and interpersonal communication.* Thousand Oaks, CA: Sage.

Guéguen, N. (2003). Help on the Web: The effect of the same first name between the sender and the receptor in a request made by e-mail. *Psychological Record, 53* (Summer), 459–466.

Guéguen, N., & Fischer-Lokou, J. (2002). An evaluation of touch on a large request: A field setting. *Psychological Reports, 90,* 267–269.

Guéguen, N., & Fischer-Lokou, J. (2003). Another evaluation of touch and helping behavior. *Psychological Reports, 92,* 62–64.

Guéguen, N., & Vion, M. (2009). The effect of a practitioner's touch on a patient's medication compliance. *Psychology, Health, and Medicine, 14,* 689–694.

Guerin, B. (2003). Combating prejudice and racism: New interventions from a functional analysis of racist language. *Journal of Community and Applied Social Psychology* 13 (January), 29–45.

Guerrero, L. K. (1997). Nonverbal involvement across interactions with same-sex friends, opposite-sex friends, and romantic partners: Consistency or change? *Journal of Social and Personal Relationships, 14,* 31–58.

Guerrero, L. K., & Andersen, P. A. (1991). The waxing and waning of relational intimacy: Touch as a function of relational stage, gender and touch avoidance. *Journal of Social and Personal Relationships, 8,* 147–165.

Guerrero, L. K., & Andersen, P. A. (1994). Patterns of matching and initiation: Touch behavior and touch avoidance across romantic relationship stages. *Journal of Nonverbal Behavior, 18* (Summer), 137–153.

Guerrero, L. K., Andersen, P. A., Jorgensen, P. F., Spitzberg, B. H., & Eloy, S. V. (1995). Coping with the green-eyed monster: Conceptualizing and measuring communicative response to romantic jealousy. *Western Journal of Communication, 59,* 270–304.

Guerrero, L. K., & Hecht, M. L. (2008). *The nonverbal communication reader* (3rd ed.). Long Grove, IL: Waveland Press.

H

Hackman, M. Z., & Johnson, C. E. (1991). *Leadership: A communication perspective.* Prospect Heights, IL: Waveland Press.

Haferkamp, C. J. (1991–92). Orientations to conflict: Gender, attributions, resolution strategies, and self-monitoring. *Current Psychology Research and Reviews, 10* (Winter), 227–240.

Haga, Y. (1988). Traits de langage et caractere Japonais. *Cahiers de Sociologie Economique et Culturelle, 9,* 105–109.

Hall, E. T. (1959). *The silent language.* Garden City, NY: Doubleday.

Hall, E. T. (1963). A system for the notation of proxemic behavior. *American Anthropologist, 65,* 1003–1026.

Hall, E. T. (1976). *Beyond culture.* Garden City, NY: Doubleday.

Hall, E. T., & Hall, M. R. (1987). *Hidden differences: Doing business with the Japanese.* New York, NY: Doubleday.

Hall, J. A. (1998). How big are nonverbal sex differences? The case of smiling and sensitivity to nonverbal cues. In D. J. Canary & K. Dindia (Eds.), *Sex differences and similarities in communication: Critical essays and empirical investigations of sex and gender in interaction* (pp. 155–178). Mahwah, NJ: Lawrence Erlbaum.

Hall, J. K. (1993). Tengo una bomba: The paralinguistic and linguistic conventions of the oral practice Chismeando. *Research on Language and Social Interaction, 26,* 55–83.

Hall, J. A. (2006). Women's and men's nonverbal communication: Similarities, differences, stereotypes, and origins. In V. Manusov & M. L. Patterson (Eds.). *The Sage handbook of nonverbal communication* (pp. 201–218). Thousand Oaks, CA: Sage Publications.

Hampton, K. (2011, June 16). Social networking sites and our lives. Retrieved from www.pewinternet.org/press-release/2011

Haney, W. (1973). *Communication and organizational behavior: Text and cases* (3rd ed.). Homewood, IL: Irwin.

Harris, C. R. (2003). A review of sex differences in sexual jealousy, including self-report data, psychophysiological responses, interpersonal violence, and morbid jealousy. *Personality and Social Psychology Review, 7,* 102–128.

Harris, M., & Johnson, O. (2007). *Cultural anthropology* (7th ed.). Boston, MA: Allyn & Bacon.

Hart, F. (1990). The construction of masculinity in men's friendships: Misogyny, heterosexuality, and homophobia. *Resources for Feminist Research, 19,* 60–67.

Harvard Business School. Working knowledge. Retrieved from http://hbswk.hbs.edu/archive/3481.html

Harvey, J. C., & Katz, C. (1985). *If I'm so successful, why do I feel like a fake: The impostor phenomenon.* New York: St. Martin's Press.

Hatfield, E., & Rapson, R. L. (1996). *Love and sex: Cross-cultural perspectives.* Boston, MA: Allyn & Bacon.

Hayakawa, S. I., & Hayakawa, A. R. (1989). *Language in thought and action* (5th ed.). New York, NY: Harcourt Brace Jovanovich.

Hays, R. B. (1989). The day-to-day functioning of close versus casual friendships. *Journal of Social and Personal Relationships, 6,* 21–37.

Heap, J. L. (1992). Seeing snubs: An introduction to sequential analysis of classroom interaction. *Journal of Classroom Interaction, 27,* 23–28.

Heath, W. P., Stone, J., Darley, J. M., & Grannemann, B. D. (2003). Yes, I did it, but don't blame me: Perceptions of excuse defenses. *Journal of Psychiatry and Law, 31* (Summer), 187–226.

Hecht, M. L., Collier, M. J., & Ribeau, S. (1993). *African American communication: Ethnic identity and cultural interpretation.* Thousand Oaks, CA: Sage.

Hecht, M. L., Jackson, R. L., & Ribeau, S. (2003). *African American communication: Exploring identity and culture* (2nd. ed.). Mahwah, NJ: Erlbaum.

Heenehan, M. (1997). *Networking.* New York, NY: Random House.

Helgeson, V. S. (2009). *Psychology of gende,* (3rd ed.). Upper Saddle River, NJ: Prentice-Hall.

Hellweg, S. A. (1992). Organizational grapevines. In K. L. Hutchinson (Ed.), *Readings in organizational communication* (pp. 159–172). Dubuque, IA: William C. Brown.

Hendrick, C., Hendrick, S., Foote, F. H., & Slapion-Foote, M. J. (1984). Do men and women love differently? *Journal of Social and Personal Relationships, 1,* 177–195.

Herrick, J. A. (2004). *Argumentation: Understanding and shaping arguments* (updated edition). State College, PA: Strata.

Hersey, P., Blanchard, K. H., & Johnson, D. E. (2001). *Management of organizational behavior: Leading human resources* (8th ed.). Upper Saddle River, NJ: Prentice-Hall.

Hertenstein, M. J., Holmes, R., McCullough, M., & Keltner, D. (2009). The communication of emotion via touch. *Emotion, 9,* 566–573.

Hess, U., Kappas, A., McHugo, G. J., Lanzetta, J. T., et al. (1992). The facilitative effect of facial expression on the self-generation of emotion. *International Journal of Psychophysiology, 12* (May), 251–265.

Hewitt, J. P. (1998). *The myth of self-esteem: Finding happiness and solving problems in America.* New York, NY: St. Martin's Press.

Hilton, L. (2000). They heard it through the grapevine. *South Florida Business Journal, 21* (August), 53.

Hirsch, E. D., Jr., Kett, J. F., & Trefil, J. (Eds.). (2002). *The new dictionary of cultural literacy.* Boston, MA: Houghton Mifflin.

Hoffner, C., Plotkin, R. S., Buchanan, M., Anderson, J. D., Kamigaki, S. K., Hubbs, L. A., Kowalczyk, L., Silberg, K., & Pastoret, A. (2001). The third-person effect in perceptions of the influence of television violence. *Journal of Communication, 51* (June), 283–299.

Hofstede, G., Hofstede, G., & Minkov, M. (2010). *Cultures and organizations: Software of the mind* (3rd ed.). New York, NY: McGraw-Hill.

Hofstede, G. (Ed.). (1998). *Masculinity and femininity: The taboo dimension of national cultures.* Thousand Oaks, CA: Sage.

Hofstrand, D. (2006). Retrieved from http://www.extension.iastate.edu

Hoft, N. L. (1995). *International technical communication: How to export information about high technology.* New York, NY: Wiley.

Holmes, J. (1986). Compliments and compliment responses in New Zealand English. *Anthropological Linguistics, 28,* 485–508.

Holmes, J. (1995). *Women, men and politeness.* New York, NY: Longman.

Hopper, R., Knapp, M. L., & Scott, L. (1981). Couples' personal idioms: Exploring intimate talk. *Journal of Communication, 31,* 23–33.

Horenstein, V. D., & Downey, J. L. (2003). A cross-cultural investigation of self-disclosure. *North American Journal of Psychology, 5,* 373–386.

Hunt, M. O. (2000). Status, religion, and the "belief in a just world": Comparing African Americans, Latinos, and whites. *Social Science Quarterly, 81* (March), 325–343.

I

Iizuka, Y. (1993). Regulators in Japanese conversation. *Psychological Reports 72* (February), 203–209.

Imahori, T. T., & Cupach, W. R. (1994). A cross-cultural comparison of the interpretation and management of face: U.S. American and Japanese responses to embarrassing predicaments. *International Journal of Intercultural Relations, 18* (Spring), 193–219.

Infante, D. A. (1988). *Arguing constructively.* Prospect Heights, IL: Waveland Press.

Infante, D. A., & Rancer, A. S. (1982). A conceptualization and measure of argumentativeness. *Journal of Personality Assessment, 46,* 72–80.

Infante, D. A., & Rancer, A. S. (1996). Argumentativeness and verbal aggressiveness: A review of recent theory and research. In B. R. Burleson (Ed.), *Communication Yearbook 19.* Thousand Oaks, CA: Sage.

Infante, D. A., Rancer, A. S., & Avtgis, T. A. (2010). *Contemporary communication theory.* Dubuque, IA: Kendall Hunt.

Infante, D. A., & Wigley, C. J. (1986). Verbal aggressiveness: An interpersonal model and measure. *Communication Monographs, 53,* 61–69.

Iyengar, S. (2010). *The art of choosing.* NY: Twelve.

J

Jablin, F. M. (1981). Cultivating imagination: Factors that enhance and inhibit creativity in brainstorming groups. *Human Communication Research, 7,* 245–258.

Jacobson, D. (1999). Impression formation in cyberspace: Online expectations and offline experiences in text-based virtual communities. *Journal of Computer-Mediated Communication, 5,* n.p.

Jambor, E., & Elliott, M. (2005). Self-esteem and coping strategies among deaf students. *Journal of Deaf Studies and Deaf Education, 10* (Winter), 63–81.

James, D. L. (1995). *The executive guide to Asia-Pacific communications.* New York, NY: Kodansha International.

Jamieson, K. H., & Campbell, K. K. (2006). *The interplay of influence* (6th ed.). Belmont, CA: Wadsworth.

Jandt, F. E. (2004). *Intercultural communication* (4th ed.). Thousand Oaks, CA: Sage.

Janis, I. (1983). *Victims of group thinking: A psychological study of foreign policy decisions and fiascoes* (2nd ed.). Boston, MA: Houghton Mifflin.

Jaworski, A. (1993). *The power of silence: Social and pragmatic perspectives.* Thousand Oaks, CA: Sage.

Jecker, J., & Landy, D. (1969). Liking a person as a function of doing him a favor. *Human Relations, 22,* 371–378.

Jeffres, L. W., Neuendorf, K. A., & Atkin, D. (1999). Spirals of silence: Expressing opinions when the climate of opinion is unambiguous. *Political Communication, 16* (April–June), 115–131.

Joel, B. (1993). *Commencement address Billy Joel.* Retrieved from http://www.berklee.edu/commencement/past/bjoel.html

Johannesen, R. L. (1974). The functions of silence: A plea for communication research. *Western Speech, 38* (Winter), 25–35.

Johannesen, R. L. (2001). *Ethics in human communication* (6th ed.). Prospect Heights, IL: Waveland Press.

Johnson, M. P. (1973). Commitment: A conceptual structure and empirical application. *Sociological Quarterly, 14,* 395–406.

Johnson, M. P. (1982). Social and cognitive features of the dissolution of commitment to relationships. In S. Duck (Ed.), *Personal Relationships: 4. Dissolving personal relationships* (pp. 51–73). New York, NY: Academic Press.

Johnson, M. P. (1991). Commitment to personal relationships. In W. H. Jones & D. Perlman (Eds.), *Advances in personal relationships* (Vol. 3, pp. 117–143). London: Jessica Kingsley.

Johnson, S. D., & Bechler, C. (1998). Examining the relationships between listening effectiveness and leadership emergence: Perceptions, behaviors, and recall. *Small Group Research, 29* (August), 452–471.

Johnson, S. M., & O'Connor, E. (2002). *The gay baby boom: The psychology of gay parenthood.* New York, NY: New York University Press.

Joinson, A. N. (2001). Self-disclosure in computer-mediated communication. The role of self-awareness and visual anonymity. *European Journal of Social Psychology, 31* (March–April), 177–192.

Jones, B. C., DeBruine, L. M., Little, A. C., Burriss, R. P., & Feinberg, D. R. (2007). Social transmission of face preferences among humans. *Proceedings of the Royal Society, 274* (March 22), 899–903.

Jones, S. (2005). The touch log record: A behavioral communication measure. In R. E. Riggio & R. S. Feldman (Eds.), *Applications of nonverbal communication* (pp. 67–82). Mahwah, NJ: Lawrence Erlbaum.

Jones, Q., Ravid, G., & Rafaeli, S. (2004, June). Information overload and the message dynamics of online interaction spaces: A theoretical model and empirical exploration. *Information Systems Research, 15,* 194–210.

Jones, S., & Yarbrough, A. E. (1985). A naturalistic study of the meanings of touch. *Communication Monographs, 52,* 19–56. A version of this paper appears in DeVito and Hecht (1990).

Jourard, S. M. (1968). *Disclosing man to himself.* New York, NY: Van Nostrand Reinhold.

Jourard, S. M. (1971a). *Self-disclosure.* New York, NY: Wiley.

Jourard, S. M. (1971b). *The transparent self* (Rev. ed.). New York, NY: Van Nostrand Reinhold.

Joyner, R. (1993). An auto-interview on the need for E-prime. *Etc.: A Review of General Semantics, 50* (Fall), 317–325.

Judge, T. A., & Cable, D. M. (2004). The effect of physical height on workplace success and income. *Journal of Applied Psychology, 89,* 428–441.

K

Kanner, B. (1989, April 3). Color schemes. *New York Magazine,* pp. 22–23.

Kapoor, S., Hughes, P. C., Baldwin, J. R., & Blue, J. (2003). The relationship of individualism-collectivism and self-construals to communication styles in India and the United States. *International Journal of Intercultural Relations* 27 (November), 683–700.

Katz, S. (2003). *Down to earth sociology: Introductory readings* (12th ed.). Henslin, J. W. (Ed.) pp. 313–320. New York, NY: Free Press.

Kay, A. C., Day., M. V., & Zanna, M. P. (in press). The insidious (and ironic) effects of positive stereotypes. *Journal of Experimental Social Psychology.* Cited in *Psychology Today, 46* (May/June 2013), 16.

Kelly, M. S. (2006). *Communication@work: Ethical, effective, and expressive communication in the workplace.* Boston, MA: Allyn & Bacon.

Kelly, P. K. (1994). *Team decision-making techniques.* Irvine, CA: Richard Chang Associates.

Kennedy, C. W., & Camden, C. T. (1988). A new look at interruptions. *Western Journal of Speech Communication, 47,* 45–58.

Kenrick, D. T., Neuberg, S. L., and Cialdini, R. B. (2010). *Social psychology: Goals in interaction* (4th ed.). Boston: Allyn & Bacon.

Ketcham, H. (1958). *Color planning for business and industry.* New York, NY: Harper.

Keyes, R. (1980). *The height of your life.* New York, NY: Warner Books.

Kim, S. H., & Smith, R. H. (1993). Revenge and conflict escalation. *Negotiation Journal, 9* (January), 37–43.

Kim, Y. Y. (1988). Communication and acculturation. In L. A. Samovar & R. E. Porter (Eds.), *Intercultural communication: A reader* (4th ed., pp. 344–354). Belmont, CA: Wadsworth.

Kindler, H. S. (1996). *Managing disagreement constructively* (Rev. ed.). Menlo Park, CA: Crisp Publications.

Klein, J. (Ed.). (1992). The E-prime controversy: A symposium [Special issue]. *Etc.: A Review of General Semantics, 49*(2).

Kleinke, C. L. (1986). *Meeting and understanding people.* New York, NY: W. H. Freeman.

Kleinke, C. L., & Dean, G. O. (1990). Evaluation of men and women receiving positive and negative responses with various acquaintance strategies. *Journal of Social Behavior and Personality, 5,* 369–377.

Knapp, M. L. (2008). *Lying and deception in human interaction.* Boston, MA: Pearson.

Knapp, M. L., Ellis, D., & Williams, B. A. (1980). Perceptions of communication behavior associated with relationship terms. *Communication Monographs, 47,* 262–278.

Knapp, M. L., & Hall, J. (2010). *Nonverbal behavior in human interaction* (7th ed.). Belmont, CA: Thompson/Wadsworth.

Knapp, M. L., Hart, R. P., Friedrich, G. W., & Shulman, G. M. (1973). The rhetoric of goodbye: Verbal and nonverbal correlates of human leave-taking. *Communication Monographs, 40,* 182–198.

Knapp, M. L., & Taylor, E. H. (1995). Commitment and its communication in romantic relationships. In A. L. Weber & J. H. Harvey (Eds.), *Perspectives on close relationships* (pp. 153–175). Boston, MA: Allyn & Bacon.

Knapp, M. L., & Vangelisti, A. L. (2009). *Interpersonal communication and human relationships* (6th ed.). Boston, MA: Allyn & Bacon.

Knox, D., Daniels, V., Sturdivant, L., & Zusman, M. E. (2001). College student use of the Internet for mate selection. *College Student Journal, 35,* 158–160.

Koerner, A. F., & Fitzpatrick, M. A. (2002). You never leave your family in a fight: The impact of family of origin on conflict behavior in romantic relationships. *Communication Studies, 53* (Fall), 234–252.

Koerner, A. F., & Fitzpatrick, M. A. (1997). Family type and conflict: The impact of conversation orientation and conformity orientation on conflict in family. *Communication Studies, 48,* 59–75.

Kollock, P., & Smith, M. (1996). Managing the virtual commons: Cooperation and conflict in computer communities. In S. Herring (Ed.), *Computer-mediated communication: Linguistic, social, and cross-cultural perspectives* (pp. 109–128). Amsterdam, Netherlands: John Benjamins.

Komarovsky, M. (1964). *Blue collar marriage.* New York, NY: Random House.

Koppelman, K. L., with Goodhart, R. L. (2005). *Understanding human differences: Multicultural education for a diverse America.* Boston, MA: Allyn & Bacon.

Korzybski, A. (1933). *Science and sanity.* Lakeville, CT: International Non-Aristotelian Library.

Kramer, R. (1997). Leading by listening: An empirical test of Carl Rogers's theory of human relationship using interpersonal assessments of leaders by followers. *Dissertation Abstracts International: Section A. Humanities and Social Sciences, 58* (August), 0514.

Krebs, G. L. (1990). *Organizational communication* (2nd ed.). New York, NY: Longman.

Krivonos, P. D., & Knapp, M. L. (1975). Initiating communication: What do you say when you say hello? *Central States Speech Journal, 26,* 115–125.

Kucinich, D. J. (2007, January 8). *Rep. Dennis Kucinich: Out of Iraq and back to the American city.* Retrieved from www.politicalaffairs.net/article/articleview/4666/

Kurdek, L. A. (1994). Areas of conflict for gay, lesbian, and heterosexual couples: What couples argue about influences relationship satisfaction. *Journal of Marriage and the Family, 56* (November), 923–934.

Kurdek, L. A. (1995). Developmental changes in relationship quality in gay and lesbian cohabiting couples. *Developmental Psychology, 31* (January), 86–93.

Kurdek, L. A. (2003). Differences between gay and lesbian cohabiting couples. *Journal of Social and Personal Relationships, 20* (August), 411–436.

Kurdek, L. A. (2004). Are gay and lesbian cohabitating couples really different from heterosexual married couples? *Journal of Marriage and Family, 66* (November), 880–900.

L

Laing, M. (1993). Gossip: Does it play a role in the socialization of nurses? *Journal of Nursing Scholarship, 25* (Spring), 37–43.

Langer, E. J. (1989). *Mindfulness.* Reading, MA: Addison-Wesley.

Larsen, R. J., Kasimatis, M., & Frey, K. (1992). Facilitating the furrowed brow: An unobtrusive test of the facial feedback hypothesis applied to unpleasant affect. *Cognition and Emotion, 6* (September), 321–338.

Latané, B., Williams, K., & Harkins, S. (1979). Many hands make light the work: The causes and consequences of social loafing. *Journal of Personality and Social Psychology, 37,* 822–832.

Lauer, C. S. (2003). Listen to this. *Modern Healthcare, 33* (February 10), 34.

Lea, M., & Spears, R. (1995). Love at first byte? Building personal relationships over computer networks. In J. T. Wood & S. Duck (Eds.), *Under-studied relationships: Off the beaten track* (pp. 197–233). Thousand Oaks, CA: Sage.

Leaper, C., & Holliday, H. (1995). Gossip in same-gender and cross-gender friends' conversations. *Personal Relationships, 2* (September), 237–246.

Leathers, D., & Eaves, M. H. (2008). *Successful nonverbal communication: Principles and applications* (4th ed.). Boston: Allyn & Bacon.

Lederer, W. J. (1984). *Creating a good relationship.* New York, NY: Norton.

Lee, A. M., & Lee, E. B. (1972). *The fine art of propaganda.* San Francisco: International Society for General Semantics.

Lee, A. M., & Lee, E. B. (1995). The iconography of propaganda analysis. *Etc.: A Review of General Semantics, 52* (Spring), 13–17.

Lee, C., & Gudykunst, W. B. (2001). Attraction in initial interethnic interactions. *International Journal of Intercultural Relations, 25* (July), 373–387.

Lee, F. (1993). Being polite and keeping MUM: How bad news is communicated in organizational hierarchies. *Journal of Applied Social Psychology, 23,* 1124–1149.

Lee, H. O., & Boster, F. J. (1992). Collectivism-individualism in perceptions of speech rate: A cross-cultural comparison. *Journal of Cross-Cultural Psychology, 23,* 377–388.

Lee, J. A. (1976). *The colors of love.* New York, NY: Bantam.

Lee, K. (2000, November 1). Information overload threatens employee productivity. *Employee Benefit News* (Securities Data Publishing, Inc.), p. 1.

Lee, R. L. M. (1984). Malaysian queue culture: An ethnography of urban public behavior. *Southeast Asian Journal of Social Science, 12,* 36–50.

Leech, G. (1983). *Principles of pragmatics.* London: Longman.

Lemonick, M. D. (2005). A smile doesn't always mean happy. *Time* (January 17), A29.

Lenhart, A., Madden, M., Smith, A., Purcell, K., Zickuhr, K., & Rainie, L. (2011). Teens, kindness and cruelty on social network sites. Retrieved from http://pewinterest.org/Reports/2011/Teens-and-social-media.aspx

Leon, J. J., Philbrick, J. L., Parra, F., Escobedo, E., et al. (1994). Love styles among university students in Mexico. *Psychological Reports 74,* 307–310.

Leung, K. (1988). Some determinants of conflict avoidance. *Journal of Cross-Cultural Psychology, 19* (March), 125–136.

Leung, S. A. (2001). Editor's introduction. *Asian Journal of Counseling, 8,* 107–109.

Lever, J. (1995, August 22). The 1995 *Advocate* survey of sexuality and relationships: The women, lesbian sex survey. *The Advocate, 687/688,* 22–30.

Levine, D. (2000). Virtual attraction: What rocks your boat. *CyberPsychology & Behavior, 3* (August), 565–573.

Levine, M. (2004, June 1). Tell the doctor all your problems, but keep it to less than a minute. *New York Times,* p. F6.

LeVine, R., & Bartlett, K. (1984). Pace of life, punctuality, and coronary heart disease in six countries. *Journal of Cross-Cultural Psychology, 15,* 233–255.

LeVine, R., Sato, S., Hashimoto, T., & Verma, J. (1994). Love and marriage in eleven cultures. Unpublished manuscript. California State University, Fresno. Cited in Hatfield & Rapson (1996).

Lewin, K. (1947). *Human relations.* New York, NY: Harper & Row.

Lewis, P. H. (1995, November 13). The new Internet gatekeepers. *New York Times,* pp. D1, D6.

Li, C., & Shi, K. (2003). Transformational leadership and its relationship with leadership effectiveness. *Psychological Science, 26* (January), 115–117.

Luft, J. (1984). *Group process: An introduction of group dynamics* (3rd ed.). Palo Alto, CA: Mayfield.

Lustig, M. W., & Koester, J. (2013). *Intercultural competence: Interpersonal communication across cultures* (7th ed.). New York, NY: Pearson.

M

MacLachlan, J. (1979). What people really think of fast talkers. *Psychology Today, 13* (November), 113–117.

Mackey, R. A., Diemer, M. A., & O'Brien, B. A. (2000). Psycho-logical intimacy in the lasting relationships of heterosexual and same-gender couples. *Sex Roles, 43,* 201–227

Madden, M., & Lenhart, A. (2006, March 5). Online dating. Retrieved from www.pewinternet.org/Reports/2006/Online-Dating.aspx

Madon, S., Guyll, M., & Spoth, R. L. (2004). The self-fulfilling prophecy as an intrafamily dynamic. *Journal of Family Psychology, 18,* 459–469.

Mahaffey, A. L., Bryan, A., & Hutchison, K. E. (2005). Using startle eye blink to measure the affective component of antigay bias. *Basic and Applied Social Psychology, 27* (March), 37–45.

Malandro, L. A., Barker, L., & Barker, D. A. (1989). *Nonverbal communication* (2nd ed.). New York, NY: Random House.

Mallen, M. J., Day, S. X., & Green, M. A. (2003). Online versus face-to-face conversation: An examination of relational and discourse variables. *Psychotherapy: Theory, Research, Practice, Training, 40* (Spring–Summer), 155–163.

Manes, J., & Wolfson, N. (1981). The compliment formula. In F. Coulmas (Ed.), *Conversational routines* (pp. 115–132). The Hague: Mouton.

Markman, H. J., Silvern, L., Clements, M., & Kraft-Hanak, S. (1993). Men and women dealing with conflict in heterosexual relationships. *Journal of Social Issues, 49* (Fall), 107–125.

Marsh, P. (1988). *Eye to eye: How people interact.* Topfield, MA: Salem House.

Marshall, A. (2005). *Confronting sexual harassment: The law and policies of everyday life.* Burlington, VT: Ashgate.

Marston, P. J., Hecht, M. L., & Robers, T. (1987). True love ways: The subjective experience and communication of romantic love. *Journal of Personal and Social Relationships, 4,* 387–407.

Martin, G. N. (1998). Human electroencephalographic (EEG) response to olfactory stimulation: Two experiments using the aroma of food. *International Journal of Psychophysiology, 30,* 287–302.

Martin, M. M., & Rubin, R. B. (1998). Affinity-seeking in initial interactions. *Southern Communication Journal, 63,* 131–143.

Martin, S. (2012). Idea watch: 89% of HBR readers love this article. *Harvard Business Review, 90,* 23–25.

Martz, B. (2012). Just do something. In L. G. Schnoor (Ed.), *Winning orations* (pp. 120–122). Mankato, MN: Interstate Oratorical Association.

Maslow, A. (1970). *Motivation and personality.* New York, NY: HarperCollins.

Mastin, T. (1998). Employees' understanding of employer-sponsored retirement plans: A knowledge gap perspective. *Public Relations Review, 24* (Winter), 521–534.

Matsumoto, D. (1991). Cultural influences on facial expressions of emotion. *Southern Communication Journal, 56* (Winter), 128–137.

Matsumoto, D., & Hwang, H. S. (2013). Cultural influences on nonverbal behavior. In D. Matsumoto, M. G. Frank, & H. S. Hwang, H. S. (Eds.), *Nonverbal communication: Science and applications* (pp. 97–120). Los Angeles, CA: Sage.

Matsumoto, D., & Juang, L. (2008). *Culture and psychology,* 4th ed. Boston, MA: Cengage.

Matsumoto, D., & Kudoh, T. (1993). American-Japanese cultural differences in attributions of personality based on smiles. *Journal of Nonverbal Behavior, 17,* 231–243.

McCown, J. A., Fischer, D., Page, R., & Homant, M. (2001). Internet relationships: People who meet people. *CyberPsychology & Behavior, 4* (October), 593–596.

McCroskey, J. C. (1998). *Why we communicate the ways we do: A communibiological perspective.* Boston: Allyn & Bacon.

McCroskey, J. C. (2006). *Introduction to rhetorical communication* (9th ed.). Englewood Cliffs, NJ: Prentice-Hall.

McCroskey, J., & Wheeless, L. (1976). *Introduction to human communication.* Boston, MA: Allyn & Bacon.

McDonald, E. J., McCabe, K., Yeh, M., Lau, A., Garland, A., & Hough, R. L. (2005). Cultural affiliation and self-esteem as predictors of internalizing symptoms among Mexican American adolescents. *Journal of Clinical Child and Adolescent Psychology, 34* (February), 163–171.

McGill, M. E. (1985). *The McGill report on male intimacy.* New York, NY: Harper & Row.

McGinley, S. (2000). Children and lying. Retreived from http://www.ag.arizona.edu/pubs/general/resrpt2000/childrenlying.pdf

McGregor, D. (1980). *The human side of enterprise.* New York, NY: McGraw-Hill.

McGregor, D. (2005). *The human side of enterprise: Annotated edition.* New York, NY: McGraw-Hill.

McNamee, S., & Gergen, K. J. (Eds.). (1999). *Relational responsibility: Resources for sustainable dialogue.* Thousand Oaks, CA: Sage.

McNatt, D. B. (2001). Ancient Pygmalion joins contemporary management: A meta-analysis of the result. *Journal of Applied Psychology, 85,* 314–322.

Media Education Foundation. (2006a). 20 ways to be a media activist. Retrieved from http://www.mediaed.org

Media Education Foundation. (2006b). 10 reasons why media education matters. Retrieved from http://www.mediaed.org

Medora, N. P., Larson, J. H., Hortacsu, N., & Dave, P. (2002). Perceived attitudes towards romanticism: A cross-cultural study of American, Asian-Indian, and Turkish young adults. *Journal of Comparative Family Studies, 33* (Spring), 155–178.

Merton, R. K. (1957). *Social theory and social structure.* New York, NY: Free Press.

Messick, R. M., & Cook, K. S. (Eds.). (1983). *Equity theory: Psychological and sociological perspectives.* New York, NY: Praeger.

Metts, S., & Planalp, S. (2002). Emotional communication. In M. L. Knapp & J. A. Daly (Eds.), *Handbook of interpersonal communication* (3rd ed., pp. 339–373). Thousand Oaks, CA: Sage.

Meyer, J. R. (1994). Effect of situational features on the likelihood of addressing face needs in requests. *Southern Communication Journal, 59* (Spring), 240–254.

Midooka, K. (1990). Characteristics of Japanese style communication. *Media, Culture and Society, 12* (October), 477–489.

Miller, G. R. (1978). The current state of theory and research in interpersonal communication. *Human Communication Research, 4,* 164–178.

Miller, M. J., & Wilcox, C. T. (1986). Measuring perceived hassles and uplifts among the elderly. *Journal of Human Behavior and Learning, 3,* 38–46.

Moghaddam, F. M., Taylor, D. M., & Wright, S. C. (1993). *Social psychology in cross-cultural perspective.* New York, NY: W. H. Freeman.

Molloy, J. (1981). *Molloy's live for success.* New York, NY: Bantam.

Monin, B. (2003). The warm glow heuristic: When liking leads to familiarity. *Journal of Personality and Social Psychology, 85* (December), 1035–1048.

Monk, A., Fellas, E., & Ley, E. (2004). Hearing only one side of normal and mobile phone conversations. *Behaviour & Information Technology, 23* (September/October), 301–306.

Montagu, A. (1971). *Touching: The human significance of the skin.* New York, NY: Harper & Row.

Moore, N., Hickson, M. III, & Stacks, D. W. (2010). Nonverbal communication: Studies and applications. New York, NY: Oxford University Press.

Morreale, S. P., & Pearson, J. C. (2008). Why communication education is important: The centrality of the discipline in the 21st century. *Communication Education, 57* (April), 224–240.

Morrison, T., & Conaway, W. A. (2006). *Kiss, blow, or shake hands: How to do business in sixty countries.* New York, NY: Adams Media.

Morrow, G. D., Clark, E. M., & Brock, K. F. (1995). Individual and partner love styles: Implications for the quality of romantic involvements. *Journal of Social and Personal Relationships, 12,* 363–387.

Mulac, A. (2006). The gender-linked language effect: Do language differences really make a difference? In K. Dindia & D. J. Canary (Eds.), *Sex differences and similarities in communication,* 2nd ed. (pp. 195–215). Mahwah, NJ: Lawrence Erlbaum Associates.

Mullen, B., Salas, E., & Driskell, J. (1989). Salience, motivation, and artifact as contributions to the relation between participation rate and leadership. *Journal of Experimental Social Psychology, 25* (November), 545–559.

Mullen, B., Tara, A., Salas, E., & Driskell, J. E. (1994). Group cohesiveness and quality of decision making: An integration of tests of the groupthink hypothesis. *Small Group Research, 25,* 189–204.

Murstein, B. I., Merighi, J. R., & Vyse, S. A. (1991). Love styles in the United States and France: A cross-cultural comparison. *Journal of Social and Clinical Psychology, 10,* 37–46.

Myers, S. A., & Zhong, M. (2004). Perceived Chinese instructor use of affinity-seeking strategies and Chinese college student motivation. *Journal of Intercultural Communication Research, 33* (September–December), 119–130.

N

Napier, R. W., & Gershenfeld, M. K. (1992). *Groups: Theory and experience* (5th ed.). Boston, MA: Houghton Mifflin.

Neff, K. D., & Harter, S. (2002). The authenticity of conflict resolutions among adult couples: Does women's other-oriented behavior reflect their true selves? *Sex Roles, 47* (November), 403–417.

Neher, W. W., & Sandin, P. (2006). *Communicating ethically.* Boston, MA: Allyn & Bacon.

Neugarten, B. (1979). Time, age, and the life cycle. *American Journal of Psychiatry, 136,* 887–894.

Neuliep, J. W., Chaudoir, M., & McCroskey, J. C. (2001). A cross-cultural comparison of ethnocentrism among Japanese and United States college students. *Communication Research Reports, 18,* 137–146.

Ng, S. H., Loong, C. S. F., He, A. P., Liu, J. H., & Weatherall, A. (2000). Communication correlates of individualism and collectivism: Talk directed at one or more addressees in family conversations. *Journal of Language and Social Psychology, 19* (March), 26–45.

Nice, M. L., & Katzev, R. (1998). Internet romantics: The frequency and nature of romantic on-line relationships. *CyberPsychology and Behavior, 1* (Fall), 217–223.

Nicholas, C. L. (2004). Gaydar: Eye-gaze as identity recognition among gay men and lesbians. *Sexuality and Culture: An Interdisciplinary Quarterly, 8* (Winter), 60–86.

Noble, B. P. (1994, August 14). The gender wars: Talking peace. *New York Times,* p. 21.

Noelle-Neumann, E. (1973). Return to the concept of powerful mass media. In H. Eguchi & K. Sata (Eds.), *Studies in broadcasting: An international annual of broadcasting science* (pp. 67–112). Tokyo, Japan: Nippon Hoso Kyokai.

Noelle-Neumann, E. (1980). Mass media and social change in developed societies. In G. C. Wilhoit & H. de Bock (Eds.), *Mass communication review yearbook* (Vol. 1, pp. 657–678). Thousand Oaks, CA: Sage.

Noelle-Neumann, E. (1991). The theory of public opinion: The concept of the spiral of silence. In J. A. Anderson (Ed.), *Communication yearbook 14* (pp. 256–287). Thousand Oaks, CA: Sage.

Noller, P. (1993). Gender and emotional communication in marriage: Different cultures or differential social power? In *Emotional communication, culture, and power* [Special issue]. *Journal of Language and Social Psychology, 12* (March–June), 132–152.

Noller, P., & Fitzpatrick, M. A. (1993). *Communication in family relationships.* Englewood Cliffs, NJ: Prentice-Hall.

Northouse, P. G. (1997). *Leadership: Theory and practice.* Thousand Oaks, CA: Sage.

O

Obama, B. (2006a). *Dr. Martin Luther King Memorial dedication speech.* Retrieved from http://obama.senate.gov

Obama, B. (2006b). *World Aids Day speech.* Retrieved January 14, 2007, from http://obama.senate.gov

Oggins, J., Veroff, J., & Leber, D. (1993). Perceptions of marital interaction among black and white newlyweds. *Journal of Personality and Social Psychology, 65* (September), 494–511.

O'Hair, D., Cody, M. J., Goss, B., & Krayer, K. J. (1988). The effect of gender, deceit orientation and communicator style on macro-assessments of honesty. *Communication Quarterly, 36,* 77–93.

O'Keefe, D. J. (1999). How to handle opposing arguments in persuasive messages: A meta-analytic review of the effects of one-sided and two-sided messages. In M. E. Roloff (Ed.), *Communication yearbook 22* (pp. 209–249). Thousand Oaks, CA: Sage.

Osborn, A. (1957). *Applied imagination* (Rev. ed.). New York, NY: Scribners.

Ouchi, W. G. (1981). *Theory Z: How American business can meet the Japanese challenge.* Reading, MA: Addison-Wesley.

P

Palmer, M. T. (1989). Controlling conversations: Turns, topics, and interpersonal control. *Communication Monographs, 56,* 1–18.

Parks, M. R. (1995). Webs of influence in interpersonal relationships. In C. R. Berger & M. E. Burgoon (Eds.), *Communication and social influence processes* (pp. 155–178). East Lansing, MI: Michigan State University Press.

Parsons, C. K., Liden, R. C., & Bauer, T. N. (2001). Personal perception in employment interviews. In M. London (Ed.), *How people evaluate others in organizations* (pp. 67–90). Mahwah, NJ: Lawrence Erlbaum.

Paul, A. M. (2001). Self-help: Shattering the myths. *Psychology Today, 34,* 60ff.

Pearson, J. C., & Spitzberg, B. H. (1990). *Interpersonal communication: Concepts, components, and contexts* (2nd ed.). Dubuque, IA: William C. Brown.

Pearson, J. C., West, R., & Turner, L. H. (1995). *Gender and communication* (3rd ed.). Dubuque, IA: William C. Brown.

Penfield, J. (Ed.). (1987). *Women and language in transition.* Albany, NY: State University of New York Press.

Pennebaker, J. W. (1991). *Opening up: The healing power of confiding in others.* New York, NY: Avon.

Perse, E. M., & Rubin, R. B. (1989). Attribution in social and parasocial relationships. *Communication Research, 16* (February), 59–77.

Peter, L. J., & Hull, R. (1969). *The Peter principle.* New York, NY: Bantam.

Peterson, C. C. (1996). The ticking of the social clock: Adults' beliefs about the timing of transition events. *International Journal of Aging and Human Development, 42,* 189–203.

Petrocelli, W., & Repa, B. K. (1992). *Sexual harassment on the job.* Berkeley, CA: Nolo Press.

Petronio, S. (Ed.). (2000). *Balancing the secrets of private disclosures.* Mahwah, NJ: Erlbaum.

Petty, R. E., & Wegener, D. T. (1998). Attitude change: Multiple roles for persuasion variables. In D. T. Gilbert, S. T. Fiske, & G. Lindzey (Eds.), *The handbook of social psychology* (4th ed., Vol. 1, pp. 323–390). New York, NY: McGraw-Hill.

Pilkington, C. J., & Richardson, D. R. (1988). Perceptions of risk in intimacy. *Journal of Social and Personal Relationships, 5,* 503–508.

Pilkington, C., & Woods, S. P. (1999). Risk in intimacy as a chronically accessible schema. *Journal of Social and Personal Relationships, 16,* 249–263.

Pittenger, R. E., Hockett, C. F., & Danehy, J. J. (1960). *The first five minutes.* Ithaca, NY: Paul Martineau.

Place, K. S., & Becker, J. A. (1991). The influence of pragmatic competence on the likeability of grade school children. *Discourse Processes, 14* (April–June), 227–241.

Plaks, J. E., Grant, H., & Dweck, C. S. (2005). Violations of implicit theories and the sense of prediction and control: Implications for motivated person perception. *Journal of Personality and Social Psychology, 88* (February), 245–262.

Pornpitakpan, C. (2003). The effect of personality traits and perceived cultural similarity on attraction. *Journal of International Consumer Marketing, 15,* 5–30.

Postman, N., & Powers, S. (1992). *How to watch TV news.* New York, NY: Penguin.

Pratkanis, A. R., & Aronson, E. (1991). *Age of propaganda: The everyday use and abuse of persuasion.* New York, NY: W. H. Freeman.

Prusank, D. T., Duran, R. L., & DeLillo, D. A. (1993). Interpersonal relationships in women's magazines: Dating and relating in the 1970s and 1980s. *Journal of Social and Personal Relationships, 10* (August), 307–320.

Psychometrics. (2010). *Warring egos, toxic individuals, feeble leadership.* Retrieved July 20, 2013, from http://www.psychometrics.com/docs/conflictstudy_09.pdf

R

Radford, M. L. (1998). Approach or avoidance? The role of nonverbal communication in the academic library user's decision to initiate a reference encounter. *Library Trends, 46* (Spring), 699–717.

Ragins, B. R., & Kram, K. E. (2007). *The handbook of mentoring at work: Research, theory, and practice.* Thousand Oaks, CA: Sage.

Rancer, A. S. (1998). Argumentativeness. In J. C. McCroskey, J. A. Daly, M. M. Martin, & M. J. Beatty (Eds.), *Communication and personality: Trait perspectives* (pp. 149–170). Cresskill, NJ: Hampton Press.

Rancer, A. S., & Avtgis, T. A. (2006). *Argumentative and aggressive communication: Theory, research, and application*. Thousand Oaks, CA: Sage.

Rapsa, R., & Cusack, J. (1990). Psychiatric implications of tattoos. *American Family Physician, 41,* 1481–1486.

The Rand Corporation. Retrieved from http://www.rand.org/pubs

Raven, R., Centers, C., & Rodrigues, A. (1975). The bases of conjugal power. In R. E. Cromwell & D. H. Olson (Eds.), *Power in families* (pp. 217–234). New York, NY: Halsted Press.

Rawlins, W. K. (1989). A dialectical analysis of the tensions, functions, and strategic challenges of communication in young adult friendships. In J. A. Andersen (Ed.), *Communication yearbook 12* (pp. 157–189). Thousand Oaks, CA: Sage.

Rawlins, W. K. (1992). *Friendship matters: Communication, dialectics, and the life course.* Hawthorne, NY: Aldine DeGruyter.

Reardon, K. K. (1987). *Where minds meet: Interpersonal communication.* Belmont, CA: Wadsworth.

Regan, P. C., Kocan, E. R., & Whitlock, T. (1998). Ain't love grand! A prototype analysis of the concept of romantic love. *Journal of Social and Personal Relationships, 15,* 411–420.

Reisman, J. M. (1979). *Anatomy of friendship.* Lexington, MA: Lewis.

Reisman, J. M. (1981). Adult friendships. In S. Duck & R. Gilmour (Eds.), *Personal relationships. 2: Developing personal relationships* (pp. 205–230). New York, NY: Academic Press.

Reynolds, C. L., & Schnoor, L. G. (Eds.). (1991). *1989 championship debates and speeches.* Normal, IL: American Forensic Association.

Rhee, K. Y. & Kim, W-B. (2004). The adoption and use of the Internet in South Korea, *Journal of Computer Mediated Communication, 9*(4).

Rice, M. (2007). Domestic violence. National Center for PTSD fact sheet. Retrieved from http://www.ncptsd.va.gov/ncmain/ncdocs/_fact_shts/fs_domestic_violence.html

Rich, A. L. (1974). *Interracial communication.* New York, NY: Harper & Row.

Richards, I. A. (1968). The secret of "feedforward." *Saturday Review, 51* (February 3), 14–17.

Richmond, V. P., & McCroskey, J. C. (1998). *Communication: Apprehension, avoidance, and effectiveness* (5th ed.). Boston, MA: Allyn & Bacon.

Richmond, V. P., McCroskey, J. C., & Hickson, M. L. (2008). *Nonverbal behavior in interpersonal relations,* 6th ed. Boston: Allyn & Bacon.

Richmond, V. P., McCroskey, J. C., & McCroskey, L. L. (2005). *Organizational communication for survival: Making work, work.* Boston, MA: Allyn & Bacon.

Richmond, V. P., Smith, R., Heisel, A., & McCroskey, J. C. (2001). Nonverbal immediacy in the physician/patient relationship. *Communication Research Reports, 18,* 211–216.

Riggio, R. E. (1987). *The charisma quotient.* New York: Dodd, Mead.

Riggio, R. E., & Feldman, R. S., (Eds.) (2005). *Applications of nonverbal communication.* Mahwah, NJ: Lawrence Erlbaum.

Roberts, W. (1987). *Leadership secrets of Attila the Hun.* New York: Warner.

Rodman, G. (2001). *Making sense of media: An introduction to mass communication.* Boston, MA: Allyn & Bacon.

Rogers, C. (1970). *Carl Rogers on encounter groups.* New York, NY: Harrow Books.

Rogers, C., & Farson, R. (1981). Active listening. In J. A. DeVito (Ed.), *Communication: Concepts and processes* (3rd ed., pp. 137–147). Englewood Cliffs, NJ: Prentice-Hall.

Rohlfing, M. E. (1995). "Doesn't anybody stay in one place anymore?" An exploration of the under-studied phenomenon of long-distance relationships. In J. T. Wood & S. Duck (Eds.), *Under-studied relationships: Off the beaten track* (pp. 173–196). Thousand Oaks, CA: Sage.

Rokach, A. (1998). The relation of cultural background to the causes of loneliness. *Journal of Social and Clinical Psychology, 17,* 75–88.

Rokach, A., & Brock, H. (1995). The effects of gender, marital status, and the chronicity and immediacy of loneliness. *Journal of Social Behavior and Personality, 19,* 833–848.

Rollman, J. B., Krug, K., & Parente, F. (2000). The chat room phenomenon: Reciprocal communication in cyberspace. *CyberPsychology and Behavior, 3* (April), 161–166.

Ronfeldt, H. M., Kimerling, R., & Arias, I. (1998). Satisfaction with relationship power and the perpetration of dating violence. *Journal of Marriage & the Family, 60* (February), 70–78.

Rose, A. J., & Asher, S. R. (1999, January). Children's goals and strategies in response to conflicts within a friendship. *Developmental Psychology, 35,* 69–79.

Rosen, E. (1998, October). Think like a shrink. *Psychology Today,* 54–69.

Rosenbloom, S. (2011, November 13). Love, lies and what they learned. *New York Times,* ST1.

Rosengren, A., et al. (1993, October 19). Stressful life events, social support, and mortality in men born in 1933. *British Medical Journal.* Cited in Goleman (1995a).

Rosenthal, R. (2002). Covert communication in classrooms, clinics, courtroom, and cubicles. *American Psychologist, 57,* 839–849.

Rosenthal, R., & DePaulo, B. M. (1979). Sex differences in accommodation in nonverbal communication. In R. Rosenthal (Ed.), *Skill in nonverbal communication: Individual differences* (pp. 68–103). Cambridge, MA: Oelgeschlager, Gunn & Hain.

Rosenthal, R., & Jacobson, L. (1968). *Pygmalion in the classroom.* New York, NY: Holt, Rinehart & Winston.

Rosenthal, R., & Jacobson, L. (1992). *Pygmalion in the classroom: Teacher expectations and pupils' intellectual development* (Rev. ed.). Norwalk, CT: Crown House.

Rosnow, R. L. (1977). Gossip and marketplace psychology. *Journal of Communication, 27* (Winter), 158–163.

Ruben, B. D. (1985). Human communication and cross-cultural effectiveness. In L. A. Samovar & R. E. Porter (Eds.), *Intercultural communication: A reader* (4th ed., pp. 338–356). Belmont, CA: Wadsworth.

Rubenstein, C. (1993, June 10). Fighting sexual harassment in schools. *New York Times,* p. C8.

Rubin, A., Pearse, E., & Powell, R. (1985). Loneliness, parasocial interaction, and local television news viewing. *Human Communication Research, 12,* 155–180.

Rubin, R. B., Fernandez-Collado, C., & Hernandez-Sampieri, R. (1992). A cross-cultural examination of interpersonal communication motives in Mexico and the United States. *International Journal of Intercultural Relations, 16,* 145–157.

Rubin, R. B., & McHugh, M. (1987). Development of parasocial interaction relationships. *Journal of Broadcasting and Electronic Media, 31,* 279–292.

Rubin, Z. (1973). *Liking and loving: An invitation to social psychology.* New York: Holt, Rinehart & Winston.

Rundquist, S. (1992). Indirectness: A gender study of Fluting Grice's maxims. *Journal of Pragmatics, 18* (November), 431–449.

S

Sabatelli, R. M., & Pearce, J. (1986). Exploring marital expectations. *Journal of Social and Personal Relationships, 3,* 307–321.

Satir, V. (1983). *Conjoint family therapy,* 3d ed. Palo Alto, CA: Science and Behavior Books.

Scandura, T. (1992). Mentorship and career mobility: An empirical investigation. *Journal of Organizational Behavior, 13,* 169–174.

Schaap, C., Buunk, B., & Kerkstra, A. (1988). Marital conflict resolution. In P. Noller & M. A. Fitzpatrick (Eds.), *Perspectives on marital interaction* (pp. 203–244). Philadelphia, PA: Multilingual Matters.

Schafer, M., & Crichlow, S. (1996). Antecedents of groupthink. *Journal of Conflict Resolution, 40* (September), 415–435.

Schegloff, E. (1982). Discourses as an interactional achievement: Some uses of "uh huh" and other things that come between sentences. In D. Tannen (Ed.), *Georgetown University roundtable on language and linguistics* (pp. 71–93). Washington, DC: Georgetown University Press.

Scherer, K. R. (1986). Vocal affect expression. *Psychological Bulletin, 99,* 143–165.

Scheufele, D. A., & Moy, P. (2000). Twenty-five years of the spiral of silence: A conceptual review and empirical outlook. *International Journal of Public Opinion Research, 12* (Spring), 3–28.

Schnoor, L. G. (Ed.). (2008). *Winning orations of the Interstate Oratorical Association.* Mankato, MN: Interstate Oratorical Association.

Schott, G., & Selwyn, N. (2000). Examining the "male, antisocial" stereotype of high computer users. *Journal of Educational Computing Research, 23,* 291–303.

Schultz, B. G. (1996). *Communicating in the small group: Theory and practice* (2nd ed.). New York, NY: HarperCollins.

Schwartz, E. (2005). Watch what you say. *InfoWorld, 27,* (February, 28), 8.

Schwartz, M., and the Task Force on Bias-Free Language of the Association of American University Presses. (1995). *Guidelines for bias-free writing.* Bloomington, IN: Indiana University Press.

Schwarzenegger, A. (2007). *Prepared text of Gov. Schwarzenegger's remarks to tackle California's broken health care system.* Retrieved from http://gov.ca.gov/index.php?/print-version/speech/5066/

Scott, M. L., & Lyman, S. M. (1968). Accounts. *American Sociological Review,* (33), 46–62.

Seiter, J. S. (2007). Ingratiation and gratuity: The effect of complimenting customers on tipping behavior in restaurants. *Journal of Applied Social Psychology, 37* (March), 478–485.

Seiter, J. S., & Sandry, A. (2003). Pierced for success?: The effects of ear and nose piercing on perceptions of job candidates' credibility, attractiveness, and hirability. *Communication Research Reports, 20* (Fall), 287–298.

Severin, W. J., with Tankard, J. W., Jr. (1988). *Communication theories* (2nd ed.). New York, NY: Longman.

Seybert, N. (2013). Size does matter (in signatures). *Harvard Business Review, 91,* 32–33.

Shannon, C. E., & Weaver, W. (1949). *The mathematical theory of communication.* Urbana, IL: University of Illinois Press.

Shaw, M. E., & Gouran, D. S. (1990). Group dynamics and communication. In G. Dahnke & G. W. Clatterbuck (Eds.), *Human communication: Theory and research.* Belmont, CA: Wadsworth.

Sheese, B. E., Brown, E. L, & Graziano, W. G. (2004). Emotional expression in cyberspace: Searching for moderators of the Pennebaker disclosure effect via e-mail. *Health Psychology, 23* (September), 457–464.

Shimanoff, S. (1980). *Communication rules: Theory and research.* Thousand Oaks, CA: Sage.

Shockley-Zalabak, P. (2012). *Fundamentals of organizational communication* (8th ed.). Boston, MA: Pearson.

Shockley-Zalabak, P. (2012). *Fundamentals of organizational communication: Knowledge, sensitivity, skills, values* (8th ed.). Boston, MA: Allyn & Bacon.

Siegert, J. R., & Stamp, G. H. (1994). "Our first big fight" as a milestone in the development of close relationships. *Communication Monographs, 61* (December), 345–360.

Singh, N., & Pereira, A. (2005). *The culturally customized Web site.* Oxford, UK: Elsevier Butterworth-Heinemann.

Skenazy, L. (2013). American cheese. *Psychology Today, 46,* 70–77, 87.

Slade, M. (1995, February 19). We forgot to write a headline. But it's not our fault. *New York Times,* p. 5.

Smith, B. (1996). Care and feeding of the office grapevine. *Management Review, 85* (February), 6.

Smith, D. (2003, December 2). Doctors cultivate a skill: Listening. *New York Times,* p. 6.

Smith-Lovin, L., & Brody, C. (1989). Interruptions in group discussions: The effects of gender and group composition. *American Sociological Review, 54* (June), 424–435.

Smith, M. H. (2003). Body adornment: Know the limits. *Nursing Management, 34,* 22–23.

Smith, S. M., & Shaffer, D. R. (1991). Celerity and cajolery: Rapid speech may promote or inhibit persuasion through its impact on message elaboration. *Personality and Social Psychology Bulletin, 17* (December), 663–669.

Smith, S. M., & Shaffer, D. R. (1995). Speed of speech and persuasion: Evidence for multiple effects. *Personality and Social Psychology Bulletin, 21* (October), 1051–1060.

Smith, T. E., & Frymier, A. B. (2006, February). Get "real": Does practicing speeches before an audience improve performance? *Communication Quarterly, 54,* 111–125.

Smoreda, Z., & Licoppe, C. (2000). Gender-specific use of the domestic telephone. *Social Psychology Quarterly, 63,* 238–252.

Snyder, C. R. (1984). Excuses, excuses. *Psychology Today, 18,* 50–55.

Snyder, C. R., Higgins, R. L., & Stucky, R. J. (1983). *Excuses: Masquerades in search of grace.* New York, NY: Wiley.

Snyder, M. (1992). A gender-informed model of couple and family therapy: Relationship enhancement therapy. *Contemporary Family Therapy: An International Journal, 14* (February), 15–31.

Sojourner, R. J., & Wogalter, M. S. (1998). The influence of pictorials on the comprehension and recall of pharmaceutical safety and warning information. *International Journal of Cognitive Ergonomics,* 2, 93–106.

Solomon, G. B., Striegel, D. A., Eliot, J. F., Heon, S. N., et al. (1996). The self-fulfilling prophecy in college basketball: Implications for effective coaching. *Journal of Applied Sport Psychology, 8* (March), 44–59.

Song, I, LaRose, R., Eastin, M. S., & Lin, C. A. (2004). Internet gratifications Internet addiction: On the uses and abuses of new media. *CyberPsychology & Behavior 7* (August), 384–394.

Sorenson, P. S., Hawkins, K., & Sorenson, R. L. (1995). Gender, psychological type and conflict style preferences. *Management Communication Quarterly, 9* (August), 115–126.

Spitzberg, B. H. (1991). Intercultural communication competence. In L. A. Samovar & R. E. Porter (Eds.), *Intercultural communication: A reader* (pp. 353–365). Belmont, CA: Wadsworth.

Spitzberg, B. H., & Cupach, W. R. (1989). *Handbook of interpersonal competence research.* New York, NY: Springer.

Spitzberg, B. H., & Cupach, W. R. (2002). Interpersonal skills. In M. L. Knapp and J. A. Daly (Eds.), *Handbook of interpersonal communication* (3rd ed., pp. 564–611). Thousand Oaks, CA: Sage.

Spitzberg, B. H., & Cupach, W. R. (2011). Interpersonal skills. In Knapp, M. L., & Daly, J. A. (Eds.), *The sage handbook of interpersonal communication* (4th ed., pp. 481–526). Los Angeles, CA: Sage.

Spitzberg, B. H., & Hecht, M. L. (1984). A component model of relational competence. *Human Communication Research, 10,* 575–599.

Sprecher, S. (1987). The effects of self-disclosure given and received on affection for an intimate partner and stability of the relationship. *Journal of Social and Personal Relationships, 4,* 115–127.

Sprecher, S., & Toro-Morn, M. (2002). A study of men and women from different sides of earth to determine if men are from Mars and women are from Venus in their beliefs about love and romantic relationships. *Sex Roles 46* (March), 131–147.

Steil, L. K., Barker, L. L., & Watson, K. W. (1983). *Effective listening: Key to your success.* Reading, MA: Addison-Wesley.

Stein, M. M., & Bowen, M. (2003). Building a customer satisfaction system: Effective listening when the customer speaks. *Journal of Organizational Excellence, 22* (Summer), 23–34.

Steinmetz, K. (2013, July 8–15). The game of happiness. *Time, 182,* 44–45.

Stephan, W. G., & Stephan, C. W. (1985). Intergroup anxiety. *Journal of Social Issues, 41,* 157–175.

Stewart, L. P., Cooper, P. J., Stewart, A. D., with Friedley, S. A. (2003). *Communication and gender* (4th ed.). Boston, MA: Allyn & Bacon.

Stratford, J. (1998). Women and men in conversation: A consideration of therapists' interruptions in therapeutic discourse. *Journal of Family Therapy, 20,* 383–394.

Suler, J. (2004). The online disinhibition effect. *CyberPsychology and Behavior 7* (June), 321–326.

Sunnafrank, M., & Ramirez, A. (2004). At first sight: Persistent relational effects of get-acquainted conversations. *Journal of Social and Personal Relationships, 21* (June), 361–379.

Surowiecki, J. (2005). *The wisdom of crowds.* New York: Doubleday.

T

Tang, S., & Zuo, J. (2000). Dating attitudes and behaviors of American and Chinese college students. *The Social Science Journal, 37* (January), 67–78.

Tannen, D. (1990). *You just don't understand: Women and men in conversation.* New York, NY: Morrow.

Tannen, D. (1994a). *Gender and discourse.* New York, NY: Oxford University Press.

Tannen, D. (1994b). *Talking from 9 to 5: How women's and men's conversational styles affect who gets heard, who gets credit, and what gets done at work.* New York, NY: Morrow.

Tannen, D. (2006). *You're wearing that? Understanding mothers and daughters in conversation.* New York, NY: Random House.

Taraban, C. B., & Hendrick, C. (1995). Personality perceptions associated with six styles of love. *Journal of Social and Personal Relationships, 12,* 453–461.

Tardy, C. H., & Dindia, K. (2006). Self-disclosure: Strategic revelation of information in personal and professional relationships. In O. Hargie (Ed.), *The handbook of communication skills* (3rd ed., pp. 229–266). New York, NY: Routledge.

Tata, J. (2000). Toward a theoretical framework of intercultural account-giving and account evaluation. *International Journal of Organizational Analysis, 8,* 155–178.

Taylor, J. (2013, March 12). Parenting: Is technology creating a family divide? Retrieved from drjimtaylor.com

Tersine, R. J., & Riggs, W. E. (1980). The Delphi technique: A long-range planning tool. In S. Ferguson & S. D. Ferguson (Eds.), *Intercom: Readings in organizational communication* (pp. 366–373). Rochelle Park, NJ: Hayden Books.

Thibaut, J. W., & Kelley, H. H. (1986). *The social psychology of groups.* New Brunswick, NJ: Transaction.

Thompson, C. A., & Klopf, D. W. (1991). An analysis of social style among disparate cultures. *Communication Research Reports, 8,* 65–72.

Thompson, C. A., Klopf, D. W., & Ishii, S. (1991). A comparison of social style between Japanese and Americans. *Communication Research Reports, 8,* 165–172.

Thorne, B., Kramarae, C., & Henley, N. (Eds.). (1983). *Language, gender and society.* Rowley, MA: Newbury House.

Tichenor, P. J., Donohue, G. A., & Olien, C. N. (1970). Mass media flow and differential growth in knowledge. *Public Opinion Quarterly, 34,* 159–170.

Tierney, P., & Farmer, S. M. (2004). The Pygmalion process and employee creativity. *Journal of Management, 30* (June), 413–432.

Timm, P. R., & DeTienne, K. B. (1995). *Managerial communication: A finger on the pulse* (3rd ed.). Upper Saddle River, NJ: Prentice-Hall.

Ting-Toomey, S. (1981). Ethnic identity and close friendship in Chinese-American college students. *International Journal of Intercultural Relations, 5,* 383–406.

Ting-Toomey, S. (1985). Toward a theory of conflict and culture. *International and Intercultural Communication Annual, 9,* 71–86.

Tinsley, C. H., & Brett, J. M. (2001). Managing workplace conflict in the United States and Hong Kong. *Organizational Behavior and Human Decision Processes, 85,* 360–381.

Trager, G. L. (1958). Paralanguage: A first approximation. *Studies in Linguistics, 13,* 1–12.

Trager, G. L. (1961). The typology of paralanguage. *Anthropological Linguistics, 3,* 17–21.

Trower, P. (1981). Social skill disorder. In S. Duck & R. Gilmour (Eds.), *Personal relationships 3* (pp. 97–110). New York, NY: Academic Press.

Tskhay, K. O., & Rule, N. O. (2013). Accuracy in categorizing perceptually ambiguous groups: A review and meta-analysis. *Personality and Social Psychology Review, 17,* 72–86.

Turner, M. M., Mazur, M. A., Wendel, N., & Winslow, R. (2003). Relational ruin or social glue? The joint effect of relationship type and gossip valence on liking, trust, and expertise. *Communication Monographs, 70* (June), 129–141.

24dash.com. (2007). Married couples have 182 arguments a year. http://www.24dash.com/communities/16903.htm

Tyler, J. J., Feldman, R. S., & Reichert, A. (2006). The price of deceitive behavior: Disliking and lying to people who lie to us. *Journal of Expermental Social Psychology, 42,* 69–77.

U

Ubel, P. (2013). Shared decision making in medicine. *Psychology Today, 46,* 45–46.

Ueleke, W., et al. (1983). Inequity resolving behavior as a response to inequity in a hypothetical marital relationship. *A Quarterly Journal of Human Behavior, 20,* 4–8.

Unger, F. L. (2001). Speech directed at able-bodied adults, disabled adults, and disabled adults with speech impairments. (Doctoral dissertation, Hofstra University, 2001). *Dissertation Abstracts International, 62,* 1146B.

Uris, A. (1986). *101 of the greatest ideas in management.* New York, NY: Wiley.

V

Vainiomaki, T. (2004). Silence as a cultural sign. *Semiotica, 150,* 347–361.

Varma, A., Toh, S. M., & Pichler, S. (2006). Ingratiation in job applications: Impact on selection decisions. *Journal of Managerial Psychology, 21,* 200–210.

Velting, D. M. (1999). Personality and negative expectations: Trait structure of the Beck Hopelessness Scale. *Personality and Individual Differences, 26,* 913–921.

Victor, D. (1992). *International business communication.* New York, NY: HarperCollins.

Viswanath, K., & Finnegan, J. R., Jr. (1995). The knowledge-gap hypothesis: Twenty-five years later. In B. R. Burleson (Ed.), *Communication yearbook 19.* Thousand Oaks, CA: Sage.

Vivian, J. (2011). *The media of mass communication,* 10th ed. Boston, MA: Allyn & Bacon.

Vonk, R. (2002). Self-serving interpretations of flattery: Why ingratiation works. *Journal of Personality and Social Psychology, 82* (April), 515–526.

Vrij, A., & Mann, S. (2001). Telling and detecting lies in a high-stake situation: The case of a convicted murderer. *Applied Cognitive Psychology, 15* (March–April), 187–203.

W

Wallace, K. (1955). An ethical basis of communication. *Communication Education, 4* (January), 1–9.

Walster, E., & Walster, G. W. (1978). *A new look at love.* Reading, MA: Addison-Wesley.

Walster, E., Walster, G. W., & Berscheid, E. (1978). *Equity: Theory and research.* Boston, MA: Allyn & Bacon.

Walster, E., Walster, G. W., & Traupman, J. (1978). Equity and premarital sex. *Journal of Personality and Social Psychology, 36,* 82–92.

Walther, J. B. (1992). Interpersonal effects in computer-mediated interaction. A relational perspective. *Communication Research, 19,* 52–90.

Walther, J. B. (2008). Social information processing theory. In L. A. Baxter & D. O. Braithwaite (Eds.), *Engaging theories in interpersonal communication: Multiple perspectives* (pp. 391–404). Los Angeles, CA: Sage.

Walther, J. B., & Parks, M. R. (2002). Cues filtered out, cues filtered in: Computer-mediated communication and relationships. In M. L. Knapp & J. A. Daly (Eds.). *Handbook of interpersonal communication* (3rd ed., pp. 529–563). Thousand Oaks, CA: Sage.

Watkins, K. (2010). How much time do you spend listening? Retrieved from http://articles.webraydian.com/article4793-How_Much_time_Do_You_Spend_Listening.html

Watzlawick, P. (1977). *How real is real? Confusion, disinformation, communication: An anecdotal introduction to communications theory.* New York, NY: Vintage.

Watzlawick, P. (1978). *The language of change: Elements of therapeutic communication.* New York, NY: Basic Books.

Watzlawick, P., Beavin, J. H., & Jackson, D. D. (1967). *Pragmatics of human communication: A study of interactional patterns, pathologies, and paradoxes.* New York, NY: Norton.

Weathers, M. D., Frank, E. M., & Spell, L. A. (2002). Differences in the communication of affect: Members of the same race versus members of a different race. *Journal of Black Psychology, 28,* 66–77.

Weinberg, H. L. (1958). *Levels of knowing and existence.* New York, NY: Harper & Row.

Weitzman, P. F. (2001). Young adult women resolving interpersonal conflicts. *Journal of Adult Development, 8,* 61–67.

Weitzman, P. F., & Weitzman, E. A. (2000). Interpersonal negotiation strategies in a sample of older women. *Journal of Clinical Geropsychology, 6,* 41–51.

Wennerstrom, A., & Siegel, A. F. (2003). Keeping the floor in multiparty conversation: Intonation, syntax, and pause. *Discourse Processes, 36* (September), 77–107.

Westwood, R. I., Tang, F. F., & Kirkbride, P. S. (1992). Chinese conflict behavior: Cultural antecedents and behavioral consequences. *Organizational Development Journal, 10* (Summer), 13–19.

Wetzel, P. J. (1988). Are "powerless" communication strategies the Japanese norm? *Language in Society, 17,* 555–564.

Wheeless, L. R., & Grotz, J. (1977). The measurement of trust and its relationship to self-disclosure. *Human Communication Research, 3,* 250–257.

Whitty, M. (2003). Cyber-flirting. *Theory and Psychology, 13,* 339–355.

Whitty, M., & Gavin, J. (2001). Age/sex/location: Uncovering the social cues in the development of online relationships. *CyberPsychology and Behavior, 4,* 623–630.

Wiederman, M. W., & Hurd, C. (1999). Extradyadic involvement during dating. *Journal of Social and Personal Relationships, 16,* 265–274.

Wigley, C. J., III. (1998). Verbal aggressiveness. In J. C. McCroskey, J. A. Daly, M. M. Martin, & M. J. Beatty (Eds.), *Communication and personality: Trait perspectives* (pp. 191–214). Cresskill, NJ: Hampton Press.

Wilkins, B. M., & Andersen, P. A. (1991). Gender differences and similarities in management communication: A meta-analysis. *Management Communication Quarterly, 5* (August), 6–35.

Willis, J., & Todorov, A. (2006). First impressions: Making up your mind after a 100-Ms Exposure to a Face. *Psychological Science, 17* (July), 592–598.

Wilson, R. A. (1989). Toward understanding E-prime. *Etc.: A Review of General Semantics, 46,* 316–319.

Windahl, S., & Signitzer, B. (with Olson, J. T.). (1992). *Using communication theory: An introduction to planned communication.* Thousand Oaks, CA: Sage.

Witcher, S. K. (1999, August 9–15). Chief executives in Asia find listening difficult. *Asian Wall Street Journal Weekly, 21,* 11.

Withers, L. A., & Vernon, L. L. (2006, January). To err is human: Embarrassment, attachment, and communication apprehension. *Personality and Individual Differences, 40,* 99–110.

Wolak, J., Mitchell, K. J., & Finkelhor, D. (2003). Escaping or connecting? Characteristics of youth who form close online relationships. *Journal of Adolescence, 26* (February), 105–119.

Wolpe, J. (1957). *Psychotherapy by reciprocal inhibition.* Stanford, CA: Stanford University Press.

Won-Doornink, M.-J. (1985). Self-disclosure and reciprocity in conversation: A cross-national study. *Social Psychology Quarterly, 48,* 97–107.

Wood, J. T. (1994). *Gendered lives: Communication, gender, and culture.* Belmont, CA: Wadsworth.

Wood, W. (2000). Attitude change: Persuasion and social influence. *Annual Review of Psychology, 51,* 539–570.

Wood, A. F., & Smith, M. J. (2005). *Online communication: Linking technology, identity, and culture.* Mahwah, NJ: Lawrence Erlbaum.

Worthington, D. L., & Fitch-Hauser, M. E. (2012). *Listening: Processes, functions and competency.* Boston, MA: Pearson.

Wrench, J. S., & McCroskey, J. C. (2003). A communibiological examination of ethnocentrism and homophobia. *Communication Research Reports, 20,* 24–33.

Wrench, J. S., McCroskey, J. C., & Richmond, V. P. (2008). *Human communication in everyday life: Explanations and applications.* Boston, MA: Allyn & Bacon.

Wright, P. H. (1978). Toward a theory of friendship based on a conception of self. *Human Communication Research, 4,* 196–207.

Wright, P. H. (1984). Self-referent motivation and the intrinsic quality of friendship. *Journal of Social and Personal Relationships, 1,* 115–130.

Wright, P. H. (1988). Interpreting research on gender differences in friendship: A case for moderation and a plea for caution. *Journal of Social and Personal Relationships, 5,* 367–373.

Wyer, R. S. (2012). Your commute can improve your relationship. *Harvard Business Review, 90,* 28–29.

Y

Yau-fair Ho, D., Chan, S. F., Peng, S., & Ng, A. K. (2001). The dialogical self: Converging East-West constructions. *Culture and Psychology, 7,* 393–408.

Young, K. S., Griffin-Shelley, E., Cooper, A., O'Mara, J., & Buchanan, J. (2000). Online infidelity: A new dimension in couple relationships with implications for evaluation and treatment. *Sexual Addiction and Compulsivity, 7,* 59–74.

Yun, H. (1976). The Korean personality and treatment considerations. *Social Casework, 57,* 173–178.

Z

Zane, N., & Yeh, M. (2002). The use of culturally-based variables in assessment: Studies on loss of face. In K. S. Kurasaki (Ed.), *Asian American mental health: Assessment theories and methods* (pp. 123–138). New York, NY: Kluwer Academic/Plenum Publishers.

Zornoza, A., Ripoll, P., & Peiró, J. M. (2002). Conflict management in groups that work in two different communication contexts: Face-to-face and computer-mediated communication. *Small Group Research, 33* (October), 481–508.

Zunin, L. M., & Zunin, N. B. (1972). *Contact: The first four minutes.* Los Angeles, CA: Nash.

Index

Page numbers followed by b, f, or t indicate boxes, figures, and tables, respectively.

A

Academic skills, public speaking and, 283t, 284
Accent, 45, 355–356
Acceptance speech, 377
Accountability, in leadership, 240b
Acculturation, 29
Acquaintanceship, friendship and, 194–195
Action step, 326
Active fighting, 273
Active listening, 92, 93, 94, 94t
Active verbs, 344–345
Adaptors
  body communication and, 127, 127t
  listening and, 80t
Addition, errors of, 355
Ad hominem arguments, 390
Adjustment, 12–13, 18t
Advantages-disadvantages pattern, 326t
Advertising, 250b
Advice, 167–168
  conversation and, 167–168
  giving, 167–168
  meta-advice and, 167
  receiving, 168
Advising listener, 86t
Affect displays, 126–127, 127t
Affectional orientation
  audience and, 295, 296
  as cultural identifier, 113–114
Affective effects, 10
Affiliative cues, 176
Affinity-seeking strategies, 70, 73t
Affirmation, 55
  friendship and, 194
  self-esteem and, 55
Agape love, 198, 202b
Age
  of audience, 295
  as cultural identifier, 114
Ageism, 111–112
Agenda, 238, 239
Agenda-setting organizations, 317b
Aggressor, 229
Agreement, maxim of, 157
All-channel network structure, 254, 254f
Alliteration, 345
Allness, 115, 116
Almanacs, 302
Alter-adaptors, 127
Ambiguity communication, 14–15, 18t
Ambiguity relationship, 14b
Ambiguity tolerance, 33, 36–37
  high, 33, 36
  low, 33, 36–37
Analogies, 313
Anecdotal evidence, 384–385
Anonymous messages, 105
Anti-social deception, 107
Antithesis, 345
Antithetical sentences, 350
Anxiety, public speaking and, 286
Apology, 164–166, 166b
  conversation and, 164–166
  don'ts for effective, 165–166
  dos for effective, 164–165
Appeal to tradition, 385
Appointment, interview, 301
Apprehension. *See* Communication apprehension
Approbation, maxim of, 157
Appropriateness, 346–347, 349t
Argumentativeness, 277, 278t
Articulation, 355
Artifactual communication, 133–134
  body adornment and, 133–134
  clothing and, 133–134
  color communication and, 133
  space decoration and, 134
Assertiveness, in verbal messages, 105–106, 109t
Assertiveness training group, 218
Assimilation, 89
Assimilationist perspective, 30
Asynchronous, 4
Attention step, 325
Attila's theory of leadership, 237b
Attitudes, purpose of speech and, 290–291
Attraction, 179
Attraction messages, 139
Attraction theory, 179–180, 185t, 186f
  personality and, 180
  physical attractiveness and, 180
  proximity and, 179
  reinforcements and, 178–179
  similarity and, 179
Attractiveness
  nonverbal communication and, 124t, 127
  physical, attraction theory and, 180
Attribution of control, 66–67
  fundamental attribution error and, 67
  impression formation and, 66–67
  overattribution and, 66–67, 68b
  self-serving bias and, 67
Audience
  affectional orientation and, 295, 296
  age of, 295
  analyzing (*See* Audience analysis)
  attention, gaining, 328, 329b
  change from, asking for, 392, 394
  cultural factors and, 295
  favorable/unfavorable, 296–297, 296f
  focus on, 367, 370, 370b, 391
  gender of, 295
  identify with, 391, 392
  immediate, 282f
  inattention, 357b
  informative speaking and, 367
  knowledgeable, 297
  media stereotypes and, 295b
  as message senders, 297
  motivating, 391, 391t
  of persuasive speech, 391–392, 392t
  positive labeling of, 392
  questions and, 297, 357
  religion/religiousness and, 296
  remote, 282f
  responses, addressing, 297
  selective exposure and, 392
  social proof and, 394
  specific purpose and, 291
  thesis and, 293
  willingness of, 296
  yes response from, 392
Audience analysis, 294–297
  checklist, 359t
  psychological, 296–297
  sociological, 294–296, 294t
  before speech, 296–297
  during speech, 297
Audios, 319t
Auditory imagery, 346
Authoritarian leader, 236b
Authority
  decision by, 221, 222
  definition by, 314
Autonomy, in relationship dialectics theory, 182
Avoidance
  in conflict, 269, 271t, 273, 273b, 276b
  in small group, 232

B

Backchanneling cues, 84, 154
Backhanded compliment, 166
Balanced split, in family, 205
Balance theories, 383b
Bandwagon, 385
Behavior, speech criticism and, 361, 362
Behavioral approach, to organization, 248b
Behavioral jealousy, 186
Beliefs
  about ethics, 21
  about organizational communication, 250, 251
  cultural, 43b, 241, 295
  self-destructive, 54, 54t
Belonging and love needs, 386, 386f
Beltlining, 275
Biases
  deception, 107
  listening and, 84, 87, 89
  self-serving, 67
  talk and, organizational norms for, 39b
  truth, 107
Biographical materials, 302
Black, meaning of, 141
Blame, 274
Blind self, 52f, 53, 53f
Blocker, 229
Blog citations, 307t
Blogging, 159b
Blog presence, self-concept and, 52
Blue, meaning of, 142
Body action, 356–357
  eye contact, 354, 356
  facial expression, 354, 356
  gestures, 354, 356
  movement, 356–357
  nonverbal messages and, 349t, 354, 355, 356
  posture, 356
Body adornment, 133–134
Body appearance, 127
Body communication, 126–127
  body appearance in, 127
  body gestures in, 126–127, 127t
Body gestures, 126–127, 127t
Body of speech, 323
  main points in, 323
  outlining, 333
Book citations, 306t
Bookstores, 299
Boundary marker, 133
Brainstorming
  electronic, 217
  to find topic, 288
  in idea-generation groups, 216, 217
Breadth, 182
Bromides, 348
Bullying, workplace, 257
Business of conversation, 152, 152f
Business stage of small group, 213
Bypassing, 101–102
  different words, same meaning, 101–102
  same words, different meaning, 102

C

Career skills, public speaking and, 284
Casual friendships, 195
Cause-effect pattern, 324–325
Cell phones, politeness and, 93t
Central marker, 133
Chain network structure, 254, 254f
Channels, 9
  all-channel network structure and, 254, 254f
  backchanneling cues and, 84, 154
  in face-to-face communication, 9
  in messages, 9
  of nonverbal communication, 126–140
  in organizational communication, 253, 254
  of self-disclosure, 57
Character, 389
Character attacks, 390
Charisma, 389–390
Chartboards, 319t
Cheat sheet, 301
Chemicals as tension relievers, 286
Cherishing behaviors, 190
Choice-making, 19, 22t
Chronemics, 137
Circle network structure, 254, 254f
Citing research, 306–307t
Civil inattention, 130
Claim-and-proof pattern, 327

Clarity, 344, 349t
Classroom lecture citations, 307t
Clichés, 348
Closedness, in relationship dialectics theory, 182
Close friendships, 195. *See also* Romantic relationships
Closing, of conversation, 152–153, 152f
Closing stage of small group, 213
Closure, 330
Clothing, 133–134
Code, 8
Coercive power, 216
Cognitive effects, 10
Cognitive jealousy, 186
Cohesiveness, 214
Collaborating style of conflict, 270, 270b, 271t
Collectivism, leadership and, 239, 240
Collectivist culture, 33, 34
Color communication, 133, 141–142
Commencement speech, 398
Commitment, relationship, 176b
Communication, 2. *See also* Face-to-face communication
ambiguity of, 14–15, 18t
benefits of, 4, 5–6
competence (*See* Communication competence)
computer-mediated, 3t, 4, 5t, 8
content and relationship dimensions of, 13–14, 18t
context of, 7–8
effect of, 10
elements of, 7–10, 7f
encoding-decoding in, 8
family and, 204–205
forms of, 2–4, 3t
friendships and, 194–195
impression formation in, 64–69, 69t
impression management in, 70–73, 73t
inevitability of, 16, 18t
interpersonal, 2
interviewing, 2
intrapersonal, 2
irreversibility of, 17, 18t
linear view of, 12f
mass, 3t, 4
messages, 8–10
myths of, 6–7
organizational, 3t, 4
as package of signals, 12, 18t
perception in, 61–64
principles of, 10–17, 18t
as process of adjustment, 12–13, 18t
public speaking, 3t, 4
punctuated, 15, 15f, 18t
as purposeful, 10, 18t
romantic relationships and, 199, 200
self in, 51–61
small group communication, 2, 4
source-receiver in, 8
as transactional, 11–12, 12f, 18t
unrepeatability of, 17, 18t
Communication accommodation theory, 13
Communication apprehension, 284–286
anxiety and, 286
benefits of, 285
chemicals as tension relievers and, 286
fear of failure and, 286
newness of public speaking and, 285
perceived differentness and, 286
performance visualization and, 285–286, 285b
presentation aids and, 317
self-examination of, 285
state apprehension, 284
systematic desensitization and, 288b
trait apprehension and, 284
Communication Choice Point boxes, 6b
apologizing, 166b
approaching public speaking, 284b
arousing the audience, 329b
asserting yourself in a group, 233b
behavior, changing, 396b
conflict, avoiding, 273b
confronting a problem, 266b
credibility, introducing, 390b
critical thinking, 222b
cultural beliefs, 43b
culture *vs.* culture, 31b
defining, 374b
definitions, using, 314b
demonstrating, 375b
directions in high- and low-context situations, 35b
empathetic listening, 90b
errors, correcting, 304b
families, 202b
favor, asking for, 302b
feedforward, 153b
first impressions, 72b
friendship functions, 194b
from friendship to love, 200b
hate speech, 95b
homophobia, 114b
impression correction, 65b
impression management, 212b
individual roles, 231b
information isolation, dealing with, 255b
interruptions, 155b
irreversibility, 17b
jealousy, 187b
joy, dealing with, 92b
listening avoidance, 81b
listening cues, 86b
long-distance relationships, 196b
lying, confronting, 109b
negotiating equity, 184b
networking, 246b
nonverbal impressions, 123b
organizational patterns, 331b
overattribution, 68b
persuasive appeals, 385b
polite and unbiased talk, organizational norms for, 39b
politeness, 105b
proxemics, 132b
rejecting directly, 104b
relationship ambiguity, 14b
relationship dissolution, 179b
relationship résumé, 175b
romance in workplace, 258b
sadness, dealing with, 92b
self-esteem, 56b
silence, 9b
situational leadership, 236b
small group conflicts, 239b
speech of description, 371b
stimulating contributions, 219b
thesis, formulating, 397b
topic appropriateness, 287b
touch boundaries, 135b
unexpected events, 368b
unfavorable audience, 296b
verbal aggressiveness, 277b
violating organizational norms, 252b
win-win solutions, 270b
Communication competence, 17, 19–23, 22t
in choice-making, 19, 22t
conversation and, 157
critical thinking in, 19, 22t
cultural sensitivity in, 20, 22t
culture and, 31
effective listening in, 21–22, 22t
ethics in, 20–21, 22t
media literacy in, 22, 22t, 23
mindfulness in, 19–20, 22t
Communication networks, 254–256
information isolation in, 255–256, 255b
information overload in, 254–255
structures of, 254, 254f
Communication research, 16b. *See also* Research
Communication technology, culture and, 30
Communication theories, 11b
Comparison-and-contrast pattern, 326t
Comparison level, 184
Competence, 388
Competing style of conflict, 269, 271t
Complementarity, 179
Complete declarative sentences in speech outlines, 334
Compliment, 166–167
backhanded, 166
giving, 166–167
receiving, 167
unqualified or qualified, 166
Compliments
conversation and, 166–167
Compromiser, 229
Compromising style of conflict, 270, 271t
Computer-assisted presentations, 320
Computer-mediated communication, 3t, 4
vs. face-to-face communication, 4, 5t
messages in, 8
Conclusion
checklist, 359t
outlining, 333
transitions, 359t
Conclusions to speeches, 330, 332
to motivate, 330
pitfalls in, 332
to summarize, 330
Confidentiality, relationship ethics and, 183b
Confirmation, 110–114
ageism and, 111–112
cultural identifiers and, 112–114
heterosexism and, 110–111
racism and, 110
sexism and, 112
Conflict, 263–280
accommodating style of, 269, 271t
avoiding style of, 269, 271t, 273, 273b, 276b
collaborating style of, 270, 270b, 271t
competing style of, 269, 271t
compromising style of, 270, 271t
confronting, 266b
content, 266, 267
context of, 268–269
cultural context of, 269
emotions and, 272
formal group, 265
gender and, 268b
interdependency and, 264, 265f
interpersonal, 264
issues, 267b
management (*See* Conflict management)
myths about, 266
negative aspects of, 267, 268
online, 264–265
people, 265
physical context of, 268
positive aspects of, 268
principles of, 266–270
procedural, 265
relationship, 267
in small group, 230, 232t, 239b
socio-psychological context of, 268
styles, 269–270, 271t
temporal context of, 268
workplace, 265
in workplace, 265
Conflict issues, 267b
Conflict management, 270–278
after conflict, 271
cognitive assessment in, 272
before conflict, 270–271
emotional state and, 272
family history and, 272
goals, 272
personality and communication competence in, 272
stages of, 272
Conflict management strategies, 271–278
active fighting, 273
argumentativeness, 277, 278t
avoidance, 273, 276b
beltlining, 275
blame, 274
choice of, influences on, 271–272
effective, 272–273
empathy, 265, 274
ethical, 276b
face-detracting, 276, 276b
face-enhancing, 276
force, 273–274, 276b
gunnysacking, 274
manipulation, 274
personal rejection, 275
public relations, 275b
spontaneity, 275
talk, 274

verbal aggressiveness, 276b, 277, 277b, 278t
win-lose, 273
win-win, 273
Conformity-orientation, 203
Connection, in relationship dialectics theory, 182
Connotation, 102, 109t
Consciousness-raising group, 218
Consensual families, 203
Consensus, decision by, 222
Consequences, in organizations, 248
Consistency, 66
Construction of meaning by media users, 91b
Constructive criticism, 361
Contact, 175
Content and relationship dimensions, 13–14, 18t
Content conflict, 266, 267
Content message, 13, 18t
Context, 7
of conflict, 268–269
Context of conflict, 268–269
cultural, 269
physical, 268
socio-psychological, 268
temporal, 268
Contrast, 61
Control
attribution of, 66–67
life, 38
touch and, 135
verbal messages and, 122
Conversation, 150–170
advice and, 167–168
apologies and, 164–166
business of, 152, 152f
closing, 152–153, 152f
compliments and, 166–167
dialogue in, 155–156, 158t
everyday, 158–168
excuses and, 163–164
feedback and, 152, 152f
feedforward and, 152, 152f
flexibility in, 156–157, 158t
gossip and, 165b
immediacy in, 156, 158t
interruptions in, 154, 155b
introductions and, 162–166, 162t
language disorders and, 160t
listening cues in, 154–155
maxims in, 102–103, 157–158
nonverbal communication and, 125
opening, 152, 152f, 163b
politeness in, 157–158, 158t
principles of, 152–158, 158t
process of, 152–153, 152f, 158t
small talk, 158–162
social media and, 159b
speaker cues in, 153–154
speech disorders and, 160t
speech presentation and, 353–354
turn-taking in, 153–155, 153f, 158t
Conversational turns, 153–155, 153f, 158t
turn-denying cues, 153f, 154
turn-maintaining cues, 153, 153f
turn-requesting cues, 153f, 154
turn-yielding cues, 153f, 154
Conversation-orientation, 203
Cooperation, principle of, 102–103
Coordinator, 229
Costs, in social exchange theory, 184
Courage, leadership and, 237b
Credibility, 71, 387
culture and, 95
impressions, 388f
introducing, 391b
listening and, 95
presentation aids and, 317
Credibility, leadership and, 237b
Credibility *(ethos)* proof, 282, 387–390
character and, 389, 390
charisma and, 389–390
competence and, 388–389
listening to, 390
Crisis, controlling, 275b
Critical listening, 86t, 89–99
Critical thinking, 19, 22t
in communication competence, 19, 22t
in small groups, 221t, 222b
Criticism. *See* Speech criticism
Cues
affiliative, 176
backchanneling, 84, 154
in conversation, 154–155
leave-taking, 161
listening, 86, 86b, 92, 96, 154–155
lying, 85b
turn-denying, 153f, 154
turn-maintaining, 153, 153f
turn-requesting, 153f, 154
turn-yielding, 153f, 154
Cultivation theory, 63
Cultural context, 8
of conflict, 269
principle of cooperation and, 102–103
principle of face-saving and, 103
principle of peaceful relations and, 103
principle of self-denigration and, 103
Cultural identifiers, 112–114
affectional orientation, 113–114
age, 114
nationality, 112–113
race, 112–113
sex, 114
Cultural sensitivity
of competent communicator, 20, 22t
importance of, 30
impression formation and, 69
improving, 49
Cultural theories, 29b
Culture, 20, 27–49. *See also* Intercultural communication
audience and, 295
beliefs and, 43b, 241, 295
collectivism and, 239, 240
collectivist, 33, 34
colors and, 141–142
communication competence and, 31
communication technology and, 30
in conflict management, diversity of, 265
credibility and, 95
criticism and, 358, 360
defined, 28–32
demographic changes and, 30
differences in, 33–38
economic interdependency and, 30
ethics and, 44b
exclusionist, 34
face-saving and, 35
facial expression and, 141
family and, 205–206
feedback and, 95
feminine, 33, 36
friendships and, 195
gender and, 28–29
gesture and, 140–141
handshakes and, 162–163, 162t
high-ambiguity-tolerant, 33, 36
high-context, 33, 34–35, 215, 325b
high-power-distance, 33, 35–36
importance of, in communication, 30–31
individualist, 33, 34, 239, 240
indulgent orientation in, 34, 37–38
language and, 95
leadership and, 239–241
leadership styles and, 241
listening and, 94–95
long-term orientation in, 34, 37, 37t
low-ambiguity-tolerant, 33, 36–37
low-context, 33, 34–35, 215, 325b
low-power-distance, 33, 35–36
masculine, 33, 36
member roles and, 241
nonverbal communication and, 95, 140–144
norms in, 251
organizational, 248, 248b, 249
paralanguage and, 142
perspective of, aim of, 31–32
politeness and, 30–31
restraint orientation in, 34, 38
romantic relationships and, 200
rules in, 248, 249
self-disclosure and, 57
sensitivity in, 30, 39
sex and, 28–29
short-term orientation in, 33, 37, 37t
silence and, 142
small groups and, 215
speech and, 95
speech organization and, 325b
teachings in, self-concept and, 52
time and, 142–144, 144t
topic of speech and, 287
touch and, 142
transmission of, 29–30
universalist, 34
workplace values and, 37t
Cute-flippant openers, 163b
Cyberspace communication, ethics in, 313b

D

Date, 117
Deception. *See also* Lying
in nonverbal communication, 125–126
in verbal messages, 106–108, 109t
Deception bias, 107
Decision-making methods
decision by authority, 221, 222
decision by consensus, 222
decision by majority rule, 222
Declarative sentences in speech outlines, 334
Decoder, 8
Decoding, 8
facial communication and, 128
skills, 144–145
Deep Web, 305
Definition, 313, 314
by authority, 314
by etymology, 313, 314
by examples, 314
guides in using, 314
by negotiation, 314
speeches of, 373–375
visualization and, 374b
Delegating style, 238, 238t
Delphi method, 223, 224
Democratic leader, 236b
Demographic changes, culture and, 30
Denotation, 102, 109t
Dependability, leadership and, 237b
Depenetration, 182–183
Depth, 182
Depth listening, 90–91
Desensitization, systematic, 288b
Dialect, 45
Dialogue, 155–156, 158t. *See also* Conversation
Differences of opinion, intolerance of, 232
Dilbert Principle, 253b
Direct messages, 104
Direct openers, 163b
Direct sentences, 348, 349
Disabilities, intercultural communication and, 40t
Disconfirmation, 108–109
Disinhibition effect, 57
Dissolution, 174b, 178–179
Distinctions, messages obscured by, 117
Distractions in listening, 80f, 81, 85, 86
Dominator, 229
Door-in-the-face technique, 393, 393b
Downward communication, 251
Dramatic story, to gain audience attention, 328
Dressing, speech presentation and, 353
Duchenne smiles, 176
Duration, 138
Dyadic consciousness, 195
Dyadic effect, 57

E

Earmarker, 133
Economic interdependency, culture and, 30
Educational or learning groups, 219
Effect, 10
Effect-cause pattern, 325
Effective listening, 21–22, 22t
Ego support, friendship and, 194
Elaborator, 229
Electronic brainstorming (EBS), 217
Emblems, 126, 127t

Emergent leader, 234
Emoticons, 127, 128t
Emotional abuse, 188
Emotional appeals, 385–387
  ethics of, 387b
  hierarchy of needs and, 385–386, 386f, 387
  listening to, 387
Emotional communication, touch and, 134–135
Emotional jealousy, 186
Emotional *(pathos)* proof, 282, 385–387. *See also* Emotional appeals
Emotions. *See also* Emotional appeals
  abuse of, 188
  conflict management and, 272
  jealousy and, 186
  listening to, 88, 88t
  nonverbal communication to express, 126
  touch and, 134–135
Empathy, 274
  advice and, 168
  in conflict management, 265, 274
  leadership and, 237b
  listening and, 88–89, 90b, 92, 94t
  relationship ethics and, 183b
Encoder, 8
Encoding, 8
  facial communication and, 128
  skills, 145
Encoding-decoding, 8
Encounter groups, 218
Encourager, 229
Enculturation, 29
Encyclopedia article citations, 307t
Encyclopedias, 302
Energizer, 229
Envy, 187. *See also* Jealousy
E-prime, 115
Equality, in family, 204–205
Equitable relationship, 184–185
Equity theory, 184–185, 184b, 185t, 186f
Eros love, 197, 202b
Et cetera, 116
Ethics, 20
  beliefs about, 21
  in communication competence, 20–21, 22t
  in conflict management strategies, 276b
  in criticism, 360b
  culture and, 44b
  in cyberspace communication, 313b
  of emotional appeals, 387b
  fighting and, 276b
  gossip and, 165, 165b
  of impression management, 72b
  in Internet communication, 313b
  leadership responsibilities in, 240b
  listening and, 96b
  lying and, 108b
  objective view of, 20
  obligation to self-disclose, 198b
  organizational, five Cs of, 259b
  plagiarism and, 300b
  relationship, 183b
  in self-disclosure, 198b
  of silence, 143b
  of speaking, 369b
  subjective view of, 20–21
  telling secrets and, 214b
Ethnic expressions, 347
Ethnic identity, 41
Ethnocentrism, 41, 46t
Ethos. See Credibility *(ethos)* proof
Etymology, definition by, 313, 314
Eulogy, 376
Euphemisms, 90
Evaluation, listening and, 80f, 84, 87–88
Evaluator-critic, 229
Example
  definition by, 314
  using, 312–313
Exclusionism, 34
Excuses, 163–164
  conversation and, 163–164
  good and bad, 164
  types of, 163–164
Expanding Media Literacy boxes
  advertising, 250b
  agenda setting, 317b
  construction of meaning by media users, 91b
  gatekeeping, 372b
  influence of, 32b
  interpersonal relationships, 196b
  knowledge gap, 234b
  media imperialism, 32b
  parasocial relationship, 173b
  product placement, 125b
  public relations, 275b
  reality constructed by media messages, 63b
  reversing media's influence, 347b
  social media, 159b
  spiral of silence theory, 393b
  stereotypes, media messages as, 295b
  theories of media influence, 63b
  third-person effect, 216b
  value-laden media messages, 113b
Expectancy violations theory, 133, 133b
Expert power, 216
Expert witness testimony, 314
Explanatory knowledge of each other, 151b
Expressions
  in facial feedback hypothesis, 129b
  in speech presentation, 354
Extemporaneous speech, 353
Extensionalize, 115
Extensional orientation, 115
Eye avoidance, 129–130
Eye contact
  conversation and, 156
  listening and, 80t, 86t, 92, 96
  in nonverbal communication, 128–130
  in speech presentation, 354, 356
Eyewitness testimony, 315

F

Face-detracting strategies, 276, 276b
Face-enhancing strategies, 276
Face orientation, 276
Face-saving, 35, 103
Face-to-face communication
  channels in, 9
  vs. computer-mediated communication, 4, 5t
  encoding-decoding in, 8
  message signals in, 8
Facial communication, 127–128
  Duchenne smiles, 176
  emoticons and, 127, 128t
  facial management techniques and, 128
Facial expression
  in nonverbal communication, 141
  in speech presentation, 354, 356
Facial feedback hypothesis, 129, 129b
Facial management techniques, 128
FACQS. *See* Internet resources, evaluating
Fact-inference confusion, 116–117
Facts, listening and, 84
Factual statement, 116
Failure, public speaking and, 286
Fallacies
  listening and, 90
  of reasoning, 384–385
Family, 202–206
  balanced split in, 205
  changes in, 202–203
  characteristics of, 204
  communication and, 204–205
  conformity-orientation and, 203
  consensual, 203
  conversation-orientation and, 203
  culture and, 205–206
  equality in, 204–205
  future of, 204
  gender and, 205–206
  history in, 204
  independents, 203
  laissez-faire, 204
  monopoly in, 205
  pluralistic, 203
  primary relationship in, 203
  protective, 203
  responsibilities in, 204
  roles in, 204
  rules, in rules theory, 180, 181
  separates, 203
  shared living spaces in, 204
  technology and, 206
  traditionals, 203
  types of, 203–204
  unbalanced split in, 205
Fear of failure, public speaking and, 286
Feedback, 9
  conversation and, 152, 152f
  culture and, 95
  listening and, 81, 92, 95
  monotonous feedback giver, 86t
  stage of small group, 213
  unexpected, 346b
Feedforward, 9
  conversation and, 152, 152f
  stage of small group, 213
Feeling empathy, 89
Feminine culture, 33, 36
Fiction-fact pattern, 327
Fighting, ethics and, 276b
Figurative analogies, 313
Figures of speech, 345, 346
First impressions, 72b, 249t
5W pattern, 327t, 372
Flexibility, 156–157
Flip charts, 319t
Focus
  on audience, 367, 370, 370b, 391
  listening and, 80, 87
  of small group, 239
Focus group, 219
Follower, 229
Follow-up, interview, 301
Foot-in-the-door technique, 393, 393b
Force, 273–274, 276b
Forcefulness, 348
Formal communication, 251–252
  downward, 251
  lateral, 251–252
  upward, 251
Formal groups, conflict in, 265
Formal time, 143–144
Formats, small group, 213–214, 213f
Forum, 213
Friendship of association, 193
Friendship of receptivity, 193
Friendship of reciprocity, 193
Friendships, 193–197
  acquaintanceship and, 194–195
  of association, 193
  casual, 195
  close, 195
  communication and, 194–195
  components of, 193
  culture and, 195
  functions of, 194b
  gender and, 196
  initial contact and, 194–195
  as interpersonal relationship, 193
  intimate, 195
  long-distance, 196b
  needs served by, 194
  of receptivity, 193
  of reciprocity, 193
  rules of, in rules theory, 180
  technology and, 197
  types of, 193
Functional approach to leadership, 235
Fundamental attribution error, 67

G

Gatekeeper-expediter, 229
Gatekeeping, 232, 372b
Gender, 29
  audience and, 295
  conflict and, 268b
  context, verbal messages and, 103–104, 109t
  differences, 103b
  family and, 205–206
  friendships and, 196
  intercultural communication and, 39

listening and, 95–96
romantic relationships and, 200–201
self-disclosure and, 57
General purpose, 290–291
General reference works, 302, 303
almanacs, 302
biographical materials, 302
encyclopedias, 302
statistical information, 302, 303
Generosity, maxim of, 157
Gestures
in nonverbal communication, 140–141
in speech presentation, 354, 356
Glittering generality, 390
Gobbledygook, 90
Goodwill speech, 398
Gossip, 165, 165b
Government resources, 304
Grapevine, 252–253
Graphs, 317, 318f
Green, meaning of, 141
Group. *See* Small group
Group building and maintenance roles, 229
Group observer and commentator, 229
Group polarization, 223b
Group power, 217b
Group task roles, 228–229
Groupthink, 232–233, 232t
Gunnysacking, 274

H

Halo effect, 65–66
Handouts, 319t
Haptics, 134. *See also* Touch communication
Harmonizer, 229
Hate speech, 95b
Hearing loss, listening and, 82t
Help
listening and, 79
through communication, 10
Help seeker, 229
Hesitations, 348
Heterosexism, 110–111
Heterosexist language, 110–111
Hidden self, 52f, 53, 53f, 56
Hierarchy of needs, 385–386, 386f, 387
belonging and love needs in, 386, 386f
psychological needs in, 386, 386f
safety needs in, 386, 386f
self-actualization needs in, 386, 386f, 387
self-esteem needs in, 386, 386f
High-ambiguity-tolerant cultures, 33, 36
High-context culture, 33, 34–35, 215, 325b
High-power-distance cultures, 33, 35–36
Home field advantage, 132
Homophobia, 114b
Honesty
in leadership, 240b
relationship ethics and, 183b
Horns effect, 66
Hostile environment harassment, 256
"How?" questions, 289t
Humor, to gain audience attention, 328
Hyperbole, 345

I

Idea-generation groups, 216–217, 224t
Identification, 391, 392
Identification messages, 140
Identity management. *See* Impression management
"I didn't do it" excuses, 163
Idioms, 344
Illustration
to gain audience attention, 328
as presentation aid, 318–319
using, 312–313
Illustrators, 126, 127t
Image-confirming strategies, 73, 73t
Imagery, 346
Images, establishing and repairing, 275b
Immediacy
in conversation, 156, 158t
self-disclosure and, 156
speaking style and, 347, 348
Implicit personality theory, 65
Impolite listening, 91–92
Impostor phenomenon, 55
Impression formation, 64–69, 69t
accuracy in, 68–69
analysis and, 68
attribution of control and, 66–67, 69t
consistency and, 66, 69t
correcting, 65b
cultural sensitivity and, 69
first impressions and, 72b, 249t
perception checking and, 68
personality theory and, 64–66, 69t
primacy-recency and, 66, 69t
processes, 64–68
self-fulfilling prophecy and, 64, 69t
stereotyping and, 64, 69, 69t
Impression management, 70–73, 73t
affinity-seeking strategies in, 70, 73t
credibility strategies in, 71, 73t
ethics of, 72b
image-confirming strategies in, 73, 73t
influencing strategies in, 73, 73t
nonverbal communication and, 123–124, 123b
politeness strategies in, 70–71, 73t
self-deprecating strategies in, 71–72, 73t
self-handicapping strategies in, 71, 73t
self-monitoring strategies in, 72, 73t
in small group, 212b
social networking and, 72b
Impromptu speech, 352
Inactive listening, 92, 93
In A Nutshell tables
communication principles, 18t
competent communicator, 22t
conflict styles, 271t
conversation, 158t
impression formation, 69t
impression management, 73t
informative speaking, 370t
intercultural communication, 46t
leadership functions and skills, 240t
listening style choices, 94t
membership functions and skills, 232t
persuasive speaking, 394t
public speaking checklist, 359t
questions of fact, value, and policy, 400t
relationships and proxemic distances, 131t
relationship theories, 185t
self-disclosure, 60t
small group types, 224t
verbal messages, 109t
wording of speech, 349t
Independents, 203
Index, 117
Indirect messages, 104–105
Indiscrimination, 117
Individualist culture, 33, 34
leadership and, 239, 240
Individual racism, 110
Individual roles, 229
Indulgent orientation, 34, 37–38
Inevitability of communication, 16, 18t
Inferences, listening and, 84
Inferential statement, 116–117
Infinitive phrase, 291
Influence
listening and, 79
media, theories of, 63b
of media imperialism, 32b
of nonverbal communication, 125–126
strategies, 73, 73t
through communication, 10
Informal communication, 252–253
Informal time, 143–144
Information, 367
limiting, 367, 370b
relating new to old, 368, 370b
self-disclosure and, 56
theory, 370b
Information giver, 228
Information isolation, 255–256, 255b
Information overload, 254–255
Information power, 216
Information seeker, 228
Information-sharing groups, 218–219, 224t
educational or learning groups, 219
focus groups, 219
Informative speaking, 366–380
acceptance speech and, 377
audience and, focus on, 367, 370, 370b
complexity in, 367–368
eulogy and, 376
levels of abstraction and, 368, 369, 370b
limiting information in, 367, 370b
memorizing speech and, 369, 370, 370b
presentation speech and, 377
principles of, 367–371, 370b
relating new information to old, 368, 370b
relevance and, 367, 370b
speeches of definition and, 373–375
speeches of demonstration and, 375, 375b, 378
speeches of description and, 371–373
speech of introduction and, 376
toast and, 377
usefulness and, 367, 370b
Informative speech, 290
excellent, 408–410
vs. persuasive speech, 293t
poorly constructed, 406–408
purpose in, 290
Initial contact, friendship and, 194–195
Initiator-contributor, 228
Innocuous openers, 163b
Integrative communication, 187–188
Integrity, in leadership, 240b
Intellectual effects, 10
Intensifiers, 348
Intensional orientation, 115
Interaction
management, relationship ethics and, 183b
process analysis, 230, 230t
rules of, 151b
skills, 5
Interactional contact, 175
Intercultural communication, 13, 38–46
accent and, differences in, 45
adjusting, 45, 46t
among cultures, differences in, 43–44
cultural sensitivity and, 39
dialect and, differences in, 45
disabilities and, people with and without, 40t
ethnocentrism and, 41, 46t
forms of, 38–39
gender and, 39
groups and, recognizing differences in, 44, 46t
improving, 39–46, 46t
interethnic, 39
international, 39
interracial, 39
meaning and, differences in, 44–45
mindfulness and, 43, 46t
model of, 38f
nationality and, 39
nature of, 38–39
overattribution and, 43, 46t
preparing for, 41, 46t
religion and, 39
between smaller cultures existing within larger cultures, 39
stereotypes and, 41–43, 46t
Interdependency, 174, 264, 265f
Interethnic communication, 39
Internal summary transitions, to memorize speech, 369
International communication, 39

Internet
conflict, 264–265
influence of, self-concept and, 51–52
libraries on, 299
news sources on, 304
relationship theories and, 181b
Internet communication, ethics in, 313b
Internet relationships, 197
Internet resources, evaluating, 305–306
accuracy, 305
currency, 305–306
fairness, 305
qualifications, 306
sufficiency, 306
Interpersonal commitment, 176
Interpersonal communication, 2, 3t, 150–170, 151b. *See also* Conversation
Interpersonal conflict, 264. *See also* Conflict
Interpersonal continuum, 151b
Interpersonal relationships, 171–191, 196b
advantages of, 172
bad side of, 186–188
contact and, 174b, 175
deterioration and, 174b, 177
disadvantages of, 172–173
dissolution and, 174b, 178–179
friendship as, 193
interdependency and, 174
intimacy and, 174b, 176, 177
involvement and, 174b, 175
jealousy and, 186–188
media and, 196b
organizational (*See* Organizational relationships)
relationship violence and, 188
repair and, 174b, 178
stages of, 173–179, 174f
theories of, 179–186, 186f
Interpersonal repair, 174b, 178
Interpersonal separation, 178
Interpersonal time, 138
Interpretation-evaluation, 62
Interracial communication, 39
Interruptions, 154, 155b
Intervention group, 218
Interview citations, 307t
Interviewee, selecting, 301
Interviewing, 2, 3t, 301, 302b
Intimacy
jealousy and, 187
as relationship stage, 174b, 176, 177
risk and, 199b
Intimate distance, 131, 131t
Intimate friendships, 195
Intrapersonal communication, 2, 3t
Intrapersonal repair, 178
Introduction
audience attention and, 328, 329b
checklist, 359t
conversation and, 162–166, 162t
excuses and, 163–164
handshakes and, 162–163, 162t
orientation of audience and, 329
outlining, 333
pitfalls in, 332
speaker-audience-topic connection and, 328–329
Introduction, speech of, 376, 404–406
Involvement, 175
Invulnerability, illusion of, 232
Irony, 345
Irreversibility of communication, 17, 18t
"It wasn't so bad" excuses, 164

J
Jargon, 90, 346
Jealousy, 186–188
Johari window, 52–53, 52f, 53f
Journals, 302, 303t
Joy, dealing with, 92b
Judgment
about communication effectiveness, 136
about people, 136
listening and, 87, 89–90, 94t
Just world hypothesis, 67, 67b

K
Key-word presentation, 339, 340
Kinesics, 126
Knowledge gap, 234b

L
Laissez-faire families, 204
Laissez-faire leader, 236b
Language
allness and, 115, 116
culture and, 95
disorders, conversation and, 160t
distinctions obscured by, 117
fact-inference confusion and, 116–117
indiscrimination and, 117
intensional orientation and, 115
listening and, 95
polarization and, 117
reality symbolized by, 115–116
static evaluation and, 117
thought and, 42b
Lateral communication, 251–252
Leadership, 233–239
accountability in, 240b
approaches to, 235–237
Attila's theory of, 237b
authoritarian, 236b
culture and, 239–241
defining, 233–234
democratic, 236b
emergent, 234
ethical responsibilities in, 240b
functional approach to, 235
functions and skills of, 237–239
honesty in, 240b
integrity in, 240b
laissez-faire, 236b
from member to, 233
myths about, 234
responsiveness in, 240b
situational approach to, 235–237, 236b
skills, 6
styles, 236b, 238t
traits approach to, 235
transformational approach to, 235
Learning
listening and, 79
through communication, 10
Leave-taking cues, 161
Legitimate power, 215–216
Leisure, 38
Levels of abstraction, 368, 369, 370b
Liars, behavior of, 107. *See also* Lying
Libraries, 299
Life control, 38
Linear view of communication, 12f
Listener notes, slides with, 320, 321f
Listening, 79–99
active, 92, 93, 94, 94t
adaptors and, 80t
advice and, 167–168
advising listener and, 86t
amount of, 96
assimilation and, 89
avoidance, 81b
barriers, 85–87
biases and, 84, 87, 89
credibility and, 95
critical, 86t, 89–99
cues, 86b, 92, 96, 154–155
culture and, 94–95
depth, 90–91
distractions and, 80f, 81, 85, 86
effective, 21–22, 22t
to emotions, 88, 88t
empathetic, 88–89, 90b, 92, 94t
ethics and, 96b
euphemisms and, 90
evaluation and, 80f, 84, 87–88
eye contact and, 80t, 86t, 92, 96
facts and, 84
fallacies and, 90
feedback and, 81, 92, 95
focus and, 80, 87
gender and, 95–96
gobbledygook and, 90
hearing loss and, 82t
helping and, 79
impolite, 91–92
importance of, 79
inactive, 92, 93
inferences and, 84
influencing and, 79
jargon and, 90
language and, 95
learning and, 79
listeners and (*See* Audience)
lying and, 85b
memory and, 80f, 81, 84
mental distractions and, 86
monotonous feedback giver and, 86t
never-ending listener and, 86t
nonjudgmental, 89–90, 94t
nonverbal behaviors and, 95
note taking and, 80t
objective, 89
offensive, 89
overly expressive listener and, 86t
paraphrasing and, 81, 89, 93, 94
physical distractions and, 85, 86
playing and, 79
polite, 91–92, 93t, 94t
posture and, 80t
power, 80t
prejudices and, 84, 87
premature judgment and, 87
preoccupied listener and, 86t
process of, 79–85
purposes of, 96
questions and, 81, 94
rapport and report talk and, 96
receiving and, 80–81, 80f
relating and, 79
remembering and, 80f, 81, 84
responding and, 80f, 80t, 84, 85, 86t
self-interests and, 84
speech and, 95
static listener and, 86t
styles, 87–94, 94t
surface, 90–91, 94t
thought-completing listener and, 86t
understanding and, 80f, 81, 94
waiting listener and, 86t
weasel words and, 90
Literal analogies, 313
Living spaces, in family, 204
Lobbying, 275b
Logical arguments, 383
Logical (*logos*) proof, 282, 383, 384–385
listening to fallacies of reasoning, 384–385
listening to logical arguments, 384–385
reasoning from causes and effects, 384
reasoning from sign, 384
reasoning from specific instances, 383–384
Logos. See Logical (*logos*) proof
Loneliness-depression cycle, 178
Long-distance friendships, 196b
Long-term orientation, 33, 37, 37t
Looking-glass self, 51
Love. *See* Romantic relationships
Love styles and personality, 202b
Low-ambiguity-tolerant cultures, 33, 36–37
Low-context culture, 33, 34–35, 215, 325b
Low-power-distance cultures, 33, 35–36
Ludus love, 197, 202b
Lying
behavior of liars and, 107
confronting, 109b
cues, 85b
deception bias and, 107
defined, 106–107
ethics and, 108b
listening and, 85b
truth bias and, 107
types of, 107
verbal messages and, 106–108, 109t

M
Magazine article citations, 306t
Main points, 312–327
checklist, 359t
developing, 322–323
goals and, 330
identifying, 330
organizing, 323–327, 326–327t
previewing, 330
for questions of fact, 395

for questions of policy, 400
for questions of value, 396
for speeches of definition, 373
for speeches of demonstration, 378
for speeches of description, 371
supporting materials for, 312–322
Majority rule, decision by, 222
Mania love, 197, 198, 202b
Manipulation, 274
Manner, maxim of, 103
Manuscript speech, 352
Maps, 317, 318
Markers, 133
Masculine culture, 33, 36
Mass communication, 3t, 4
Mate guarding, 187
Maxims in conversation, 102–103, 157–158
Media
gatekeeping and, 372b
imperialism, 32b
influence of, reversing, 347b
influencing, 347b
literacy, 6, 22, 22t, 23 (*See also Expanding Media Literacy boxes*)
of presentation aids, 319t
stereotypes, 295b
Media messages
reality constructed by, 63b
as stereotypes, 295b
value-laden, 113b
Members in small group communication, 228–233. *See also* Roles
asserting yourself and, 233b
culture and, 239–241
emerging as leaders, 233
empowering, 239
functions and skills of, 230–233
interaction process analysis and, 230, 230t
satisfaction of, 237–238
Memorized speech, 352–353, 369, 370, 370b
Memory
focus and, 81
listening and, 80f, 81, 84
messages, 140
organization and, 84
perception and, 63
reconstructing, 83b
repetition and, 84
unity and, 84
Mental distractions, listening and, 86
Mentoring, 258
Message, 8–10. *See also* Nonverbal communication; Verbal messages
channels in, 9
competence, in organizational communication, 256
feedback, 9
feedforward, 9
metamessages, 8–9
noise and, 9–10
nonverbal, 349t, 354, 355, 356 (*See also* Body action)
one-sided *vs.* two-sided, 345b
patterning, to memorize speech, 369, 370
Meta-advice, 167
Metacommunication, 9, 153
Metamessages, 8
Metaphor, 345
Metonymy, 345, 346
Mindfulness
competence and, 19–20, 22t
intercultural communication and, 43, 46t
Models, 317
Modesty, maxim of, 157
Money, raising, 275b
Monochronic time orientation, 144, 144t
Monologue, 155, 162
Monopoly, in family, 205
Monotonous feedback giver, 86t
Monotonous patterns, 353
Morality, assumption of, 232
Motivated sequence, 325–326
action step in, 326
attention step in, 325
need step in, 325
satisfaction step in, 325
visualization step in, 325, 326
Motivation
audience, 391, 391t
conclusion and, 330
Movement, in speech presentation, 356–357
Multiple-definition pattern, 327, 327t

N

Name-calling, 390
Narrative, 312–313
Nationality
as cultural identifier, 112–113
intercultural communication and, 39
Need step, 325
Negative face needs, 70
Negative social proof, 394
Negotiation, definition by, 314
Network convergence, 197
Networking, 159b, 259
Network spread, self-concept and, 51
Never-ending listener, 86t
News items, to find topic, 288
Newspaper article citations, 307t
News sources, 304
Noise, 9–10
Nominal group, 223
Nonjudgmental listening, 89–90, 94t
Nonnegotiation, 273
Nonverbal communication, 121–149. *See also* Body action
accent and, 122
artifactual communication and, 133–134
attractiveness and, 124t
body communication and, 126–127
channels of, 126–140
colors and, 141–142
complement and, 122
contradiction and, 122
control and, 122
conversation structured by, 125
culture and, 95, 140–144
deception of, 125–126
decoding skills and, 144–145
emotions expressed by, 126
encoding skills and, 145
eye communication and, 128–130
facial communication and, 127–128
facial expression and, 141
gesture and, 140–141
impressions and, 123–124
influence of, 125–126
listening and, 95
paralanguage and, 136, 142
principles of, 122–126
relationships formed by, 124
repetition and, 123
silence and, 136–137, 142
skills, 144–145
smell communication and, 139–140
space communication and, 131–133
substitution and, 123
time and, 142–144, 144t
time communication and, 137–139
touch and, 134–136, 142
verbal messages interacting with, 122–124
visual impairments and, 130t
Notes, 298–299
complete, 299
folders for, 298
keying, 298
speech presentation and, 354
taking, listening and, 80t
Novelty, in relationship dialectics theory, 182
Numbers in speeches, 344
Numerical data, 316

O

Object-adaptors, 127
Objective listening, 89
Objective view of ethics, 20
Objectivity, speech criticism and, 361
Offensive listening, 89
Olfactory communication, 139–140
Omission, errors of, 355
One-sided messages *vs.* two-sided messages, 345b
Online conflict, 264–265
Online influence, self-concept and, 51–52
Online libraries, 299
Online news sources, 304
Online relationship theories, 181b
Onymous messages, 105
Open-ended questions, 301
Opening
of conversation, 152, 152f, 163b
lines, 163b
stage of small group, 213, 237
Open-mindedness, 231, 232t
Openness, in relationship dialectics theory, 182
Open self, 52f, 53, 53f, 54, 56
Open Web, 305
Opinion giver, 228
Opinion seeker, 228
Oral citation, 306–307t
Oral style, 344
Organization, 246–249. *See also* Workplace
advertising in, 250b
agenda-setting in, 317b
approaches to, 248b
behavioral approach to, 248b
characteristics of, 247–249
communication networks in, 254–256
consequences in, 248
culture in, 248, 248b, 249
Dilbert Principle and, 253b
division of labor in, 248
ethics in, five Cs of, 259b
first impressions and, 249t
goals in, 254–256
hierarchy of, 246, 247f
importance of, 246
jobs in, 247
messages in (*See* Organizational communication)
nature of, 246–247
people in, 247
perception and, 61–62
Peter Principle and, 253b
of questions of fact, 396
of questions of policy, 401
of questions of value, 397
relationships in (*See* Organizational relationships)
rewards in, 248
by rules, 61–62
rules and regulations in, 247–248
by schemata, 62
scientific approach to, 248b
by scripts, 62
of speeches of definition, 374, 375
of speeches of demonstration, 378
of speeches of description, 372, 373
systems approach to, 248b
Organizational communication, 3t, 4, 249–262
attitudes and beliefs towards, 250, 251
communication channels in, 253, 254
formal, 251–252
grapevine and, 252–253
informal, 252–253
message competence in, 256
Organizational ethics, five Cs of, 259b
Organizational relationships, 256–260
bullying, 257
competence in, 259–260
mentoring, 258
networking, 259
romantic, 258, 258b
sexual harassment and, 256–257
Organized, defined, 246–247
Orientation, 329
affectional, 113–114
audience and, 295, 296
conformity-orientation, 203
conversation-orientation, 203
as cultural identifier, 113–114
extensional, 115
face, 276
family, 203
indulgent, 34, 37–38
intensional, 115
long-term, 33, 37, 37t
monochronic time, 144, 144t
polychronic time, 144, 144t
restraint, 34, 38
short-term, 33, 37, 37t

Orienter, 229
Outlines for speeches, 333–340
complete declarative sentences in, 334
constructing, 333–334
key-word presentation, 339, 340
phrase presentation, 339, 340
preparation, 334, 337
presentation, 340
public speaking sample assistant, 335–336
references listed in, 333–334
samples of, 334–340
symbols in, 334
template, 334, 338, 340
visual aspects in, 334
Overattribution, 67
attribution of control and, 66–67, 68b
intercultural communication and, 43, 46t
Overly expressive listener, 86t
Oxymoron, 346

P

Panel, 213, 213f
Paralanguage, 136, 142
Parallel sentences, 349, 350
Paraphrasing, listening and, 81, 89, 93, 94
Parasocial relationships, 173, 173b
Participating style, 238, 238t
Pathos. See Emotional *(pathos)* proof
Pauses, 356
Peaceful relations, principle of, 103
Peer pressure, 232–233
People, as presentation aid, 318
People conflict, 265
Perceived differentness, public speaking and, 286
Perception, 61–64, 61f
checking, 68
interpretation-evaluation and, 62
memory and, 63
organization and, 61–62
recall and, 63–64
stimulation and, 61
Perceptual contact, 175
Performance visualization, 274b, 285–286, 285b
Periodic sentences, 350
Personal distance, 131, 131t
Personal growth groups, 217, 218, 224t
assertiveness training groups, 218
consciousness-raising groups, 218
encounter groups, 218
intervention groups, 218
Personal interest, 390
Personality
attraction theory and, 180
love styles and, 202b
self-disclosure and, 56–57
Personality theory
halo effect and, 65–66
implicit, 65
impression formation and, 64–66
Personal pronouns, 347
Personal rejection, 275
Personal style, 347, 348, 349t
Personification, 346
Person perception, 64. *See also* Impression formation
Persuasion, 382
Persuasion continuum, 382f
Persuasive proofs, 282, 383, 384–390
credibility *(ethos)*, 282, 387–390
emotional *(pathos)*, 282, 385–387
logical *(logos)*, 282, 383, 384–385
in public speaking, 282
Persuasive speech, 290, 381–403
audience of, 391–394, 392t
change from audience, asking for, 392, 394
excellent, 412–416
focus on audience and, 391
goals of, 382
identify with audience and, 391, 392
vs. informative speech, 293t
motivating audience and, 391, 391t
persuasive proofs in, 383, 384–390
poorly constructed, 411–412
positive labeling and, 392
principles of, 391–394
purpose in, 290–291
on questions of fact, 394–396
on questions of policy, 397, 400–401
on questions of value, 396–397
selective exposure and, 392
social proof and, 394
yes response from audience and, 392
Peter Principle, 253b
Photographs, 318–319
Phrase presentation, 339, 340
Physical abuse, 188
Physical attractiveness, attraction theory and, 180
Physical context, 8
of conflict, 268
Physical distractions, listening and, 85, 86
Physical intimacy, jealousy and, 187
Physical noise, 9–10
Physiological noise, 10
Pie graph, 317, 318f
Pitch, 136
Plagiarism, 300b
Play
listening and, 79
through communication, 10
touch and, 135
Playboy/playgirl, 229
Pluralistic families, 203
Polarization, 117
Politeness, 30, 104
cell phones and, 93t
in conversation, 157–158, 158t
culture and, 30–31
in listening, 91–92, 93t, 94t
strategies, 70–71, 73t
in talk, organizational norms for, 39b
verbal messages and, 104–105, 105b, 109t
Polychronic time orientation, 144, 144t
Popular journals, 302, 303t
Positive face needs, 70
Positive labeling, 392
Positive sentences, 349
Positive social proof, 394
Positivity, speech criticism and, 361
Posture
listening and, 80t
in speech presentation, 356
Power
coercive, 216
in communication networks, 254
expert, 216
information, 216
legitimate, 215–216
listening, 80t
in message competence, 256
personal level of, 215
referent, 216
reward, 216
in small groups, 215–216, 217b
wording of speech and, 348, 349t
Power distances, 33, 35–36
high, 35–36
low, 35–36
Pragma love, 197, 202b
Predictability
in patterns, 353
in relationship dialectics theory, 182
Predictions, 151b
Prejudices, listening and, 84, 87
Premature judgment, listening and, 87
Preoccupied listener, 86t
Preparation outline, 334
Presentation aids, 316–322
benefits of using, 316–317
computer-assisted, 320
to gain audience attention, 328
graphs, 317, 318f
illustrations, 318–319
maps, 317, 318
media of, 319t
models, 317
object itself, 317
people, 318
photographs, 318–319
in speeches of demonstration, 378
types of, 317, 318–319
using, 319
word charts, 317
Presentation outline, 340
Presentation skills, 6
Presentation software, 320–322
rehearsing with, 322
slides and, 319t, 320–322
Presentation speech, 377
Preview transitions, 332
Primacy, 315b
Primacy effect, 66
Primacy-recency, 66
Primary relationship, 203
Primary sources, 301
Primary territories, 132
Principle of cooperation, 102–103
Principle of face-saving, 103
Principle of peaceful relations, 103
Principle of self-denigration, 103
Pro-and-con pattern, 326t
Problem-solution pattern, 324
Problem-solving groups, 219–224, 220b, 224t
critical thinking in, 221t, 222b
decision-making methods in, 221–222
Delphi method in, 223, 224
nominal group technique in, 223
problem-solving sequence in, 220–222, 220f
quality circle in, 224
at work, 222–223
Problem-solving sequence, 220–222, 220f
Procedural conflict, 265
Procedural technician, 229
Process of conversation, 152–153, 152f, 158t
Product placement, 125b
Profit, in social exchange theory, 184
Pronunciation, 355–356
Pro-social deception, 107
Protective families, 203
Proxemic distances, 131–132, 131t
Proxemics, 131
Proximity, 61, 179
Psychological analysis of audience, 296–297
favorable/unfavorable audience and, 296–297, 296f
knowledgeable audience and, 297
willingness of audience and, 296
Psychological needs, 386, 386f
Psychological noise, 10
Psychological time, 137–138
Psychomotor effects, 10
Public distance, 131–132, 131t
Public opinion, influencing, 275b
Public relations, 275b
Public separation, 178
Public speaking, 3t, 4, 282–310
abilities, improving, 283
academic skills and, 283t, 284
audience and, 282f, 294–297
benefits of, 283–284
career skills and, 284
checklist, 359t
communication and (*See* Communication apprehension)
contributions to, 283t
errors in, 304b
growth and development of, 283t
history of, 282–283
performance visualization and, 285–286, 285b
personal competencies in, 283, 284
persuasive appeals and, 282
plagiarism and, 300b
preparation and delivery, steps in, 286f
process and elements of, 282f
purpose of, 290–292, 293t
sample assistant, 335–336
social competencies in, 283, 284
thesis, 292–293, 293t
topic, 287–290, 293t, 298–307

Public territories, 132
Punctuality, 138
Punctuation
 of communication, 15, 15f, 18t
 from speaker's point of view, 89
Purple, meaning of, 142
Purposeful communication, 10, 18t
Purpose of public speaking, 290–292, 293t
 general, 290–291
 in informative speech *vs.* persuasive speech, 293t
 specific, 291–292
Purr words, 102
Pygmalion effect, 65, 65b

Q

Qualified compliment, 166
Quality, maxim of, 103
Quality circle, 224
Quantity, maxim of, 103
Questions
 to gain audience attention, 328
 listening and, 81, 94
 open-ended, 301
 rhetorical, 346
 slides and, 321
 in small group, 239
 small talk and, 161–162
 speaking style and, 347
 "what?," 289t
 "what if?," 297
 "what if," 297
 "when?," 289t
 "where?," 289t
 "who?," 289t
 "why?," 289t
Questions of fact, 394–396
 main points for, 395
 organization of, 396
 summary of, 400t
 support for, 395
 thesis for, 395, 397b
Questions of policy, 397, 400–401
 main points for, 400
 organization of, 401
 summary of, 400t
 support for, 400–401
 thesis for, 397b, 400
Questions of value, 396–397
 main points for, 396
 organization of, 397
 summary of, 400t
 support for, 397
 thesis for, 396, 397b
Quid pro quo harassment, 256
Quotations, to gain audience attention, 328

R

Race, as cultural identifier, 112–113
Racism, 110
Racist language, 110
Rapport, listening and, 96
Rate, 136, 355
Raw numbers, 316
Reality constructed by media messages, 63b
Reasoned choices, 19, 22t
Reasoning from causes and effects, 384
Reasoning from sign, 384
Reasoning from specific instances, 383–384
Recall, perception and, 63–64
Receiver, 8
Receiving, listening and, 80–81, 80f
Recency, 315b
Recency effect, 66
Recognition seeker, 229
Reconstructing memory, 83b
Recorder, 229
Red, meaning of, 141
References
 in speech outline, 333–334
 to written works, self-concept and, 52
Referent power, 216
Regulators, 127, 127t
Rehearsal of speech, 350–351, 359t
Reinforcements, 178–179
Rejection, 109
 direct, 104b
 vs. disconfirmation, 109
Relating
 listening and, 79
 through communication, 10
Relation, maxim of, 103
Relationship commitment, 176b
Relationship competence, 259–260
Relationship conflict, 267
Relationship deterioration, 176b, 177, 177t
Relationship dialectics theory, 182, 185t, 186f
Relationship message, 13–14, 18t
 ignoring, 13
 recognizing, 13–14
Relationship repair, 178
Relationship résumé, 175
Relationship rules theory. *See* Rules theory
Relationships
 commitment and, 176b
 ethics and, 183b
 long-distance, 196b
 nonverbal communication to form, 124
 parasocial, 173b
 proxemic distances and, 131–132, 131t
 skills for, 6
 violence in, 188
Relationship theories, 179–186, 185t, 186f
 attraction theory, 179–180, 185t, 186f
 equity theory, 184–185, 184b, 185t, 186f
 relationship dialectics theory, 182, 185t, 186f
 rules theory, 180, 181–182, 185t, 186f
 social exchange theory, 183, 184, 185t, 186f
 social information processing (SIP) theory, 181b
 social penetration theory, 182–183, 183f, 185t, 186f
 social presence theory, 181b
Relationship time, 138
Relevance, informative speaking and, 367, 370b
Religion/religiousness
 audience and, 296
 intercultural communication and, 39
Remembering. *See* Memory
Report talk, listening and, 96
Research
 bookstores and, 299
 checklist, 359t
 citing, 306–307t
 communication, 16b
 for discovery, 298
 general reference works and, 302, 303
 government and, 304
 integrating, 306
 Internet and, 305–306
 interviewing and, 301, 302b
 journals and, 302, 303t
 libraries and, 299
 news sources and, 304
 notes, 298–299
 sources, 301
 for specifics, 298
 to support a position, 298
 time management and, 298, 299t
 on topic, 298–307
 Web and, 304–305
Responding
 listening and, 80f, 80t, 84, 85, 86t
 to self-disclosure, 59–60, 60t
Responses, 8
Response time, 138–139
Responsiveness, in leadership, 240b
Restraint orientation, 34, 38
Reverse halo effect, 66
Reversing media's influence, 347b
Review transitions, 332
Reward power, 216
Rewards
 of self-disclosure, 58
 in social exchange theory, 184
 systems of, in organizations, 248
Rhetorical questions, 346
Risk
 intimacy and, 199b
 relationship repair and, 178
Ritual touching, 135
Roles, 228
 culture and, 241
 expectations of, 214
 group building and maintenance roles, 229
 group task roles, 228–229
 individual roles, 229, 231b
Romantic relationships, 197–202
 agape love and, 198, 202b
 communication and, 199, 200
 culture and, 200
 eros love and, 197, 202b
 gender and, 200–201
 love styles and, 202b
 love types in, 197–198
 ludus love and, 197, 202b
 mania love and, 197, 198, 202b
 pragma love and, 197, 202b
 risk and, 199b
 self-disclosure in, 198b
 storge love and, 197, 202b
 technology and, 201, 202
 in workplace, 258, 258b
Romantic rules, in rules theory, 180
Round table format, 213, 213f
Rules theory, 180, 181–182, 185t, 186f
 family rules and, 180, 181
 friendship rules and, 180
 romantic rules and, 180
 workplace rules and, 181–182

S

Sadness, dealing with, 92b
Safety needs, 386, 386f
Satisfaction step, 325
Schemata, 62
Scholarly journals, 302, 303t
Scientific approach, to organization, 248b
Script, 62
Search directory, 290
Search engine, self-concept and, 51
Secondary sources, 301
Secondary territories, 132
Secrets, ethics in telling, 214b
Security, friendship and, 194
Selective attention, 61
Selective exposure, 61, 392
Self-actualization needs, 386, 386f, 387
Self-adaptors, 127
Self-awareness, 52–54
 growing in, 53–54
 Johari window and, 52–53, 52f, 53f
Self-censorship, 232
Self-concept, 51–52, 51f
 blog presence and, 52
 cultural teachings and, 52
 network spread and, 51
 online influence and, 51–52
 references to written works and, 52
 search engine and, 51
 self-evaluations and, 52
 self-interpretations and, 52
 Twitter activities and, 52
Self-confessor, 229
Self-critical statements, 348
Self-denigration, principle of, 103
Self-deprecating strategies, 71–72, 73t
Self-destructive beliefs, 54, 54t
Self-disclosure, 56–61
 channel of, 57
 in close relationships, 198b
 corrective, 58b
 culture and, 57
 dangers of, 58
 disinhibition effect and, 57
 dyadic effect in, 57
 ethics in, 198b
 facilitating, 59–60, 60t
 factors influencing, 56–57
 gender and, 57
 in groups, 57
 guidelines for, 58–60, 60t
 immediacy and, 156
 information and, 56
 personality and, 56–57
 pressure to, 60, 60t
 responding to, 59–60, 60t
 rewards of, 58
 topic of, 57
 in workplace, 59t

Self-enhancement deception, 107
Self-esteem, 54–56, 56b, 386
  affirmation and, 55
  dissolution of relationship and, 179
  of group members, 239
  impostor phenomenon and, 55
  needs, 386, 386f
  nourishing people and, 55
  projects resulting in success and, 55
  self-destructive beliefs and, 54, 54t
  successes and, focusing on, 55
Self-evaluations, 52
Self-fulfilling prophecy, 64
Self-handicapping strategies, 71, 73t
Self-interests, listening and, 84
Self-interpretations, 52
Selfish deception, 107
Self-monitoring strategies, 72, 73t
Self-presentation. *See* Impression management
Self-serving bias, 67
Selling style, 238, 238t
Semantic noise, 10
Sentences
  antithetical, 350
  direct, 348, 349
  parallel, 349, 350
  periodic, 350
  phrasing, 348–350
  positive, 349
  short, 348
  types of, varying, 349, 350
Separates, 203
Sequence of events, 15, 15f
Sex, culture and, 28–29, 114
Sexism, 112
Sexist language, 112
Sexual abuse, 188
Sexual harassment, 256–257
Short sentences, 348
Short-term orientation, 33, 37, 37t
Should statements, 168
Signals, communication as package of, 12, 18t
Signal-to-noise ratio, 375, 375b
Signposts
  to memorize speech, 369
  in speeches, 344
  transitions, 332
Silence, 136–137
  ethics and, 143b
  functions of, 136–137
  in nonverbal communication, 136–137, 142
Similarity, 61, 179
Simile, 346
Situational approach to leadership, 235–237, 236b
Skills
  academic, 283t, 284
  career, 284
  in nonverbal communication, 144–145
  in public speaking, 283t, 284
Slang, 346–347, 348
Slides, 319t, 320–322
  charts and, 321
  colors and, 320, 321
  designing, 320–322
  length of, 321
  with listener notes, 320, 321f
  questions and, 321
  size and, 320, 321
  with speaker notes, 320, 322f
  tables and, 321
  technical problems and, 322
  typeface and, 320, 321
Slide show speech, 417–418
Small group, 2, 3t, 4, 210–226
  agenda of, 238, 239
  building and maintenance roles in, 229
  business stage of, 213
  characteristics of, 211
  closing stage of, 213
  conflict in, 230, 232t, 239b
  contributions to, 219b
  culture and, 215
  feedback stage of, 213
  feedforward stage of, 213
  focus of, 239
  follow-up in, 239
  formats, 213–214, 213f
  groupthink in, 232–233, 232t
  idea-generation groups as, 216–217, 224t
  impression management in, 212b
  individuals in, 211
  information-sharing groups as, 218–219, 224t
  interaction in, 238–239
  intercultural communication and, 44, 46t
  interdependence in, 211
  knowledge gap and, 234b
  norms, 214
  observer and commentator, 229
  opening stage of, 213, 237
  open-mindedness in, 231, 232t
  personal growth groups as, 217, 218, 224t
  polarization, 223b
  power in, 215–216, 217b
  problem-solving groups as, 219–224, 220b, 224t
  purpose of, 211
  questions in, 239
  rules in, 211
  secrets and, 214b
  self-disclosure in, 57
  self-perception of, 211
  social loafing in, 231, 232t
  stages, 212–213
  summarizing in, 239
  task roles, 228–229
  teams in, 211–212
  types, summary of, 224t
  understanding in, 231, 232t
  virtual groups as, 212
Small talk, 158–162
  contexts of, 161
  guidelines for effective, 161–162
  leave-taking cues and, 161
  monologuing and, 162
  questions and, 161–162
  situations, 160–161
  topics of, 161, 162
Smell communication, 139–140
Snarl words, 102
Social bonding, 176
Social clock, 142–143
Social distance, 131, 131t
Social exchange theory, 183, 184, 185t, 186f
Social information processing (SIP) theory, 181b
Social loafing, 231, 232t
Social media, 159b
Social networking, 159b
Social penetration theory, 182–183, 183f, 185t, 186f
Social presence theory, 181b
Social-psychological context, 8
Social separation, 178
Social Web, 305
Sociological analysis of audience, 294–296, 294t
  affectional orientation and, 295, 296
  age and, 295
  cultural factors and, 295
  gender and, 295
  media stereotypes and, 295b
  religion/religiousness and, 296
Socio-psychological context of conflict, 268
"So?" questions, 289t
Sounds, errors of adding, 356
Source, 8
Source-receivers, 8
Space communication, 131–133
  proxemic distances and, 131–132, 131t
  territoriality and, 132–133
Space decoration, 134
Space violations, 133b
Spatial distance. *See* Proxemic distances
Spatial pattern, 324
Speaker-audience-topic connection, 328–329
Speaker cues, in conversation, 153–154
  turn-denying cues, 153f, 154
  turn-maintaining cues, 153, 153f
  turn-requesting cues, 153f, 154
  turn-yielding cues, 153f, 154
Speaker notes, slides with, 320, 322f
Speaking, ethics of, 369b
Special interest pleader, 229
Special occasion speeches, 290
  acceptance speech, 377
  commencement speech, 398
  eulogy, 376
  goodwill speech, 398
  presentation speech, 377
  purpose in, 290
  speech of inspiration, 399
  speech of introduction, 376
  toast, 377
Specificity, speech criticism and, 361
Specific purpose, 291–292
  audience and, 291
  infinitive phrase in, 291
  to one idea, 290f, 291
  in persuasive speech, 291
  reasonable, 291–292
  terms in, 292
  vs. thesis, 292–293
Speech
  advantages-disadvantages pattern in, 326t
  changes in, 350–351
  closure in, 330–331
  conclusions to, 330, 332
  criticism, 358–362, 358b
  culture and, 95
  delivery notes and, 350–351
  disorders, conversation and, 160t
  introductions to, 328–330, 332
  listening and, 95
  long-term delivery improvement program and, 351
  main points in, 312–327
  memorizing, 369, 370, 370b
  organizing (*See* Speech organization)
  outlining, 333–340
  presenting, 351–358
  rate, 355b
  rate of, 355b
  rehearsal, 350–351
  rehearsing, 350–351, 359t
  situation, 350
  timing, 350, 351b
  transitions in, 331–332
  wording of, 344–350
Speech criticism, 358–362, 358b
  as attack, 362t
  behavior and, 361, 362
  constructive, 361
  culture and, 358, 360
  defined, 358
  effective, 360–362
  ethics and, 360b
  ethics of, 360b
  objectivity and, 361
  ownership of, 362
  positivity and, 361
  specificity and, 361
  as support, 362t
Speeches of definition, 373–375
  examples of, 373
  main points for, 373
  organization of, 374, 375
  support for, 374
  thesis for, 373
Speeches of demonstration, 375, 375b, 378
  examples of, 375
  main points for, 378
  organization of, 378
  support for, 378
  thesis for, 378
Speeches of description, 371–373, 371b
  examples of, 371
  main points for, 371
  organization of, 372, 373
  support for, 371–372
  thesis for, 371
Speech of inspiration, 399
Speech of introduction, 376, 404–406
Speech organization, 323–327, 326–327t
  advantages-disadvantages pattern in, 326t
  cause-effect pattern in, 324–325
  claim-and-proof pattern in, 327t
  comparison-and-contrast pattern in, 326t
  culture and, 325b
  fiction-fact pattern in, 327t
  5W pattern in, 327t
  motivated sequence in, 325–326

multiple-definition pattern in, 327t
pro-and-con pattern in, 326t
problem-solution pattern in, 324
spatial pattern in, 324
structure-function pattern in, 326t
temporal pattern in, 324
visual aspects to reflect, 334
Speech presentation, 351–358. *See also* Presentation aids
audience questions and, 357
body action and, 356–357
checklist, 359t
conversation and, 353–354
dressing for, 353
effective, 353–354
expression in, 354
extemporaneous, 353
of manuscript speech, 352
memorized, 352
methods of, 352–353
mistakes in, 354
natural, 353
notes and, 354
rate of speech and, 355b
style, 352, 353
variations in, 353
voice and, 355–356
Speech rate, 355b
Speech rehearsal, 350–351
Spiral of silence theory, 393b
Spontaneity, 275
Stages, small group, 212–213
Standard setter, 229
Star network structure, 254, 254f
State apprehension, 284
Static evaluation, 117
Static listener, 86t
Statistics, 302, 303, 316
citing, 307t, 328
numerical data and, 316
Stereotype/stereotyping, 41–43, 46t
impression formation and, 64, 69, 69t
indiscrimination, 117
media messages and, 295b
sex-role, 114
Stewardship, leadership and, 237b
Stimulation
friendship and, 194
perception and, 61
Stimuli, 15
Storge love, 197, 202b
Straw man, 385
Strong verbs, 345
Structure-function pattern, 326t
Styles
conflict, 269–270, 271t
leadership, 236b, 238t
listening, 87–94, 94t
speech presentation, 352, 353
Subjective view of ethics, 20–21
Substitution, errors of, 355
Summarizing, in small group, 239
Summary, 330
Support
for questions of fact, 395
for questions of policy, 400–401
for questions of value, 397
for speeches of definition, 374
for speeches of demonstration, 378
for speeches of description, 371–372
Supporting materials, 312–322
analogies, 313
checklist, 359t
definitions, 313, 314
examples, 312–313
illustrations, 312–313
narratives, 312–313
numerical data, 316
testimony, 314–315
Supportiveness, relationship ethics and, 183b
Surface listening, 90–91, 94t
Surveys, to find topic, 288
Symbols in speech outline, 334
Sympathy, maxim of, 157–158
Symposium, 213, 213f
Symposium-forum, 213, 213f
Synchronous, 4
Synecdoche, 346
Systematic desensitization, 288b
Systems approach, to organization, 248b

T

Tact, maxim of, 157
Tactile imagery, 346
Tag questions, 348
Talk
in conflict management, 274
relationship ethics and, 183b
Talk time, 138
Task-related touching, 135
Taste messages, 140
Team, 211–212, 230, 232t
Technology
family and, 206
friendship and, 197
romantic relationships and, 201, 202
Television show citations, 307t
Telling style, 238, 238t
Template outline, 334, 338, 340
Temporal communication, 137
Temporal context, 8, 268
Temporal pattern, 324, 378
Tension relievers, chemicals as, 286
Terms in speeches, 344, 346
Territoriality, 132–133
territory markers and, 133
territory types and, 132
Tertiary sources, 301
Testimonial, 385
Testimony, 314–315
Theory, 11. *See also Understanding Theory and Research* boxes
Attila's theory of leadership, 237b
attraction, 179–180, 185t, 186f
balance, 383b
communication, 11b
communication accommodation, 13
cultural, 29b
E-prime, 115b
equity, 184–185, 184b, 185t, 186f
expectancy violations, 133b
implicit personality, 65
information, 370b
of media influence, 63b
online relationship, 181b
personality, 64–66
relationship, 179–186, 185t, 186f
relationship dialectics, 182, 185t, 186f
rules, 180, 181–182, 185t, 186f
social exchange, 183, 184, 185t, 186f
social information processing (SIP), 181b
social penetration, 182–183, 183f, 185t, 186f
social presence, 181b
Thesis, 292–293, 293t
audience and, 293
in informative speech *vs.* persuasive speech, 293t
limiting to one idea, 293
main points in, 322–323
for questions of fact, 395
for questions of policy, 400
for questions of value, 396
vs. specific purpose, 292–293
for speeches of definition, 374
for speeches of demonstration, 378
for speeches of description, 371
stating as complete declarative sentence, 293
using, 292–293
wording, 292–293
Thin entering wedge, 385
Thinking empathy, 89
Thinking skills, 5
Third-person effect, 216b
Thought, language and, 42b
Thought-completing listener, 86t
Time
communication, 137–139
culture and, 142–144
formal, 143–144
informal, 143–144
interpersonal, 138–139
management, 298, 299t
monochronic, 144, 144t
nonverbal communication and, 142–144, 144t
polychronic, 144, 144t
psychological, 137–138
social clock and, 142–143
Toast, 377
To be verb, 115b
Topic, 287–290, 293t, 298–307
appropriate, 287
audience and, 296–297
checklist, 359t
culturally sensitive, 287
finding, 288
importance of, stressing, 328
in informative speech *vs.* persuasive speech, 293t
limiting, 288–290
lists, to find topic, 288
researching, 298–307
search directory and, 290
of self-disclosure, 57
of small talk, 161, 162
substantive, 287
system of (topoi), 289, 289t
tree diagrams and, 289, 290t
Topical pattern, 324
Topoi, 289, 289t
Touch
avoidance, 136
boundaries, 135b
control and, 135
culture and, 142
emotional communication of, 134–135
meanings of, 134–135
playfulness and, 135
ritual, 135
task-related, 135
Touch communication, 134–136. *See also* Touch
Traditionals, 203
Trait apprehension, 284
Traits approach to leadership, 235
Transactional view of communication, 11–12, 12f, 18t
Transformational approach to leadership, 235
Transitions, 331–332
internal summary, to memorize speech, 369
pitfalls in, 332
preview, 332
review, 332
signpost, 332
Transparencies, 319t
Tree diagrams, 289, 290t
Truth bias, 107
Turn-denying cues, 153f, 154
Turn-maintaining cues, 153, 153f
Turn-requesting cues, 153f, 154
Turn-taking in conversation, 153–155, 153f, 158t. *See also* Conversational turns
Turn-yielding cues, 153f, 154
Tweeting, 159b
Twitter activities, self-concept and, 52
Two-sided messages, one-sided messages *vs.*, 345b

U

Unanimity, assumption of, 232
Unbalanced split, in family, 205
Uncertainty reduction strategies, 68–69
Understanding
advice and, 168
listening and, 80f, 81, 94
in small group, 231, 232t
Understanding Theory and Research boxes
Attila's theory of leadership, 237b
balance theories, 383b
communication research, 16b
communication theories, 11b
conflict issues, 267b
cultural theories, 29b
culture and speech organization, 325b
Dilbert Principle, 253b
door-in-the-face technique, 393b
E-prime theory, 115b
expectancy violations theory, 133b
facial feedback hypothesis, 129b
foot-in-the-door technique, 393b
gender and conflict, 268b
gender differences, 103b
group polarization, 223b
group power, 217b

Understanding Theory and Research boxes (*Continued*)
information theory, 370b
interpersonal communication, development of, 151b
intimacy and risk, 199b
just world hypothesis, 67b
language and thought, 42b
leadership styles, 236b
love styles and personality, 202b
lying cues, 85b
one-sided *vs.* two-sided messages, 345b
online relationship theories, 181b
opening lines, 163b
organizations, approaches to, 248b
performance visualization, 285b
Peter Principle, 253b
primacy, 315b
Pygmalion effect, 65b
recency, 315b
reconstructing memory, 83b
relationship commitment, 176b
signal-to-noise ratio, 375b
speech rate, 355b
systematic desensitization, 288b
Unfilled pauses, 356
Universalism, 34
Unknown self, 52f, 53, 53f
Unqualified compliment, 166
Unrepeatability of communication, 17, 18t
Upward communication, 251
Usefulness, informative speaking and, 367, 370b
Utility, friendship and, 194

V

Value congruence, 260
Value-laden media messages, 113b
Values, 295
questions of, 396–397
of workplace, culture and, 37t
Verbal abuse, 188
Verbal aggressiveness, 276b, 277, 277b, 278t
Verbal messages, 100–120
accent and, 122
allness and, 115, 116
anonymous, 105
assertiveness in, 105–106, 109t
bypassing and, 101–102
complement and, 122
confirmation and, 110–114
connotation and, 102, 109t
contradiction and, 122
control and, 122
cultural context and, 102–103, 109t
deceptive, 106–108, 109t
denotation and, 102, 109t
direct, 104
disconfirmation and, 108–109
distinctions obscured by, 117
effective use of, 114–117
fact-inference confusion and, 116–117
gender context and, 103–104, 109t
impressions and, 123–124
indirect, 104–105
indiscrimination and, 117
intensional orientation and, 115
meanings dependent on context and, 102–104, 109t
meanings in people, not in things and, 101–102, 109t
nonverbal communication interacting with, 122–124
onymous, 105
polarization and, 117
politeness and, 104–105, 105b, 109t
principles of, 101–108, 109t
purr words and, 102
repetition and, 123
snarl words and, 102
static evaluation and, 117
substitution and, 123
Verbs
active, 344–345
strong, 345
Videos, 319t
Virtual groups, 212
Visual dominance, 129
Visual imagery, 346
Visual impairments, 130t
Visualization, performance, 285–286, 285b, 374b
Visualization step, 325, 326
Vividness, 344, 349t
Voice, 355–356
articulation and, 355
pauses and, 356
pronunciation and, 355–356
qualities, 136
rate and, 355
volume and, 355
Volume, 136, 355
Vulgar expressions, 348

W

Waiting listener, 86t
Wait time, 138
Weakeners, 348
Weasel words, 90
Web, research and, 304–306
"What if?" questions, 297
"What?" questions, 289t
Wheel network structure, 254, 254f
"When?" questions, 289t
"Where?" questions, 289t
White, meaning of, 141
Whiteboards, 319t
"Who?" questions, 289t
"Why?" questions, 289t
Win-lose solution, 273
Win-win solution, 273
Word charts, 317
Wording of speech, 344–350
appropriateness and, 346–347, 349t
clarity and, 344, 349t
forcefulness and, 348
personal style and, 347, 348, 349t
phrasing sentences and, 348–350
power and, 348, 349t
vividness and, 344–345, 346, 349t
words and phrases to avoid in, 347, 348
Workplace. *See also* Organizational communication; Organizational relationships
conflict in, 265 (*See also* Conflict)
networking, 159b
rules, in rules theory, 181–182
self-disclosure in, 59t
Work time, 138

Y

Yellow, meaning of, 142
"Yes, but" excuses, 164
Yes response from audience, 392
Y network structure, 254, 254f

Credits

Text Credits

Pages 19–20: From *Mindfulness* by Ellen J. Langer, copyright © 1989. Reprinted by permission of Da Capo Press, a member of The Perseus Books Group; **p. 37:** Hofstede, G., Hofstede, G., & Minkov, M. (2010). *Cultures and Organizations: Software of the Mind* (3rd ed.). New York, NY: McGraw-Hill; **p. 48:** Hatfield, E., & Rapson, R. L. (1996). *Love and Sex: Cross-Cultural Perspectives.* Boston, MA: Allyn & Bacon; **p. 54:** Based on Butler, P. E. (1981). *Talking to Yourself: Learning the Language of Self-Support.* New York, NY: Harper & Row; **p. 57:** Derlega, V. J., Winstead, B. A., Wong, P. T. P., and Hunter, S. (1985). Gender Effects in an Initial Encounter: A Case where Men Exceed Women in Disclosure. *Journal of Social and Personal Relationships,* 2, 25–44; **p. 66:** Asch, S. (1946). Forming Impressions of Personality. *Journal of Abnormal and Social Psychology,* 41, 258–290; **p. 90:** William Shakespeare; **p. 101:** Haney, W. (1973). *Communication and Organizational Behavior: Text and Cases* (3rd ed.). Homewood, IL: Irwin; **p. 103:** Holmes, J. (1995). *Women, Men and Politeness.* New York, NY: Longman; **p. 104:** Tannen, D. (1994a). *Gender and Discourse.* New York, NY: Oxford University Press; **p. 107:** McGinley, S. (2000). Children and Lying. Retrieved from www.ag.arizona.edu/pubs/general/resrpt2000/childrenlying.pdf; **p. 110:** Rich, A. L. (1974). *Interracial Communication.* New York, NY: Harper & Row; **p. 126:** Axtell, R. E. (1993). Do's and Taboos around the World (3rd ed.). New York, NY: Wiley; Axtell, R. E. (2007). *Essential Do's and Taboos: The Complete Guide to International Business and Leisure Travel.* Hoboken, NJ: Wiley; **p. 133:** Kanner, B. (1989, April 3). Color Schemes. *New York Magazine*, pp. 22–23; **p. 139:** Furlow, F. B. (1996). The Smell of Love. *Psychology Today* (March/April), 38–45; **p. 144:** Hall, E. T., and Hall, M. R. (1987). *Hidden Differences: Doing Business with the Japanese.* New York, NY: Doubleday; **p. 156:** Richmond, Virginia Peck, McCroskey, James G., and Hickson, Mark L., *Nonverbal Behavior In Interpersonal Relations,* 7th ed. ©2012. Reprinted and electronically reproduced by permission of Pearson Education, Inc., Upper Saddle River, New Jersey; **p. 180:** Baxter, L. A. (1986). Gender Differences in the Heterosexual Relationship Rules Embedded in Break-Up Accounts. *Journal of Social and Personal Relationships*, 3, 289–306; **pp. 180–181:** Satir, V. (1983). *Conjoint Family Therapy*, 3rd ed. Palo Alto, CA: Science and Behavior Books; **pp. 205–206:** Moghaddam, F. M., Taylor, D. M., and Wright, S. C. (1993). *Social Psychology in Cross-Cultural Perspective.* New York, NY: W. H. Freeman; **p. 223:** Kelly, P. K. (1994). *Team Decision-Making Techniques.* Irvine, CA: Richard Chang Associates; **p. 265:** DeVito, Joseph A. *The Essential Elements of Public Speaking,* 4th ed., ©2012. Reprinted and electronically reproduced by permission of Pearson Education, Inc., Upper Saddle River, New Jersey; **p. 285:** James C. McCroskey, *An Introduction to Rhetorical Communication*, Figure 3.2, "Personal Report of Communication Apprehension (PRCA 24)," p. 41, © 1997 by Pearson Education, Inc. Adapted by permission of Pearson Education, Inc.; **p. 312:** Kyle Akerman (2010); **p. 314:** Edward deBono; Ambrose Bierce; Ohio Congressman Dennis Kucinich, Wall Street Project Conference on January 8, 2007; **p. 316:** Meagan Hagensick of Wartburg College (Schnoor, 2008); **p. 328:** U.S. Senator from California Dianne Feinstein (2006); **p. 329:** Billy Joel; President Barack Obama (2006); **p. 330:** Christi Liu (2010); Chelsea Anthony, a student from Louisiana State University, Shreveport (2012). Put an End to Convenience Devocalization. In *Winning Orations* (pp. 63–66). L. G. Schnoor (Ed.): Interstate Oratorical Association; Used by permission of the California State Archives; Martz, B. (2012). Just Do Something. In *Winning Orations* (pp. 120–122). L. G. Schnoor (Ed.): Interstate Oratorical Association; **p. 331:** David DePino (2012). Lost to Silence. In *Winning Orations* (pp. 43–45). L. G. Schnoor (Ed.): Interstate Oratorical Association; **p. 354:** Fensholt, M. (2003, June). There's Nothing Wrong with Taking Written Notes to the Podium. *Presentations*, 17, 66; **p. 361:** Noel Coward; **p. 389:** Kofi Annan.

Photo Credits

Page 1: DAJ/Glow Images; **p. 6:** Cardinal/Corbis; **p. 9:** Westend61/SuperStock; **p. 14:** Robin Beckham/BEEPstock/Alamy; **p. 17:** Pixellover RM 7/Alamy; **p. 20:** Ice Tea Media/Alamy; **p. 23:** Pearson; **p. 27:** paul kline/E+/Getty Images; **p. 31:** UpperCut Images/SuperStock; **p. 35:** Spencer Grant/PhotoEdit, Inc; **p. 39:** Radius Images/Alamy; **p. 43:** Kablonk/SuperStock; **p. 46:** Pearson; **p. 50:** All Canada Photos/Glow Images; **p. 56:** Bob Daemmrich/The Image Works; **p. 58:** Artiga Photo/Corbis; **p. 65:** Peter Beavis/Riser/Getty Images; **p. 68:** Peter Bernik/Shutterstock; **p. 72:** Miroslav Georgijevic/Getty Images; **p. 74:** Pearson; **p. 78:** T.Kaiser/ARCO/Glow Images; **p. 81:** Kenneth Sponsler/Shutterstock; **p. 86:** Jean Gill/E+/Getty Images; **p. 90:** Marka/SuperStock; **p. 92:** Ocean/Corbis; **p. 95:** Francisco Cruz/SuperStock; **p. 97:** Pearson; **p. 100:** Inspirestock/Glow Images; **p. 104:** Aaron Amat/Shutterstock; **p. 105:** Beyond/SuperStock; **p. 110:** Bateman Photo/Shutterstock; **p. 114:** UpperCut Images/SuperStock; **p. 118:** Pearson; **p. 121:** Superstock/Glow Images; **p. 123:** Blend Images/Alamy; **p. 132:** Exactostock/SuperStock; **p. 135:** Lisa S./Shutterstock; **p. 139:** Maksim Shmeljov/Shutterstock; **p. 146:** Pearson; **p. 150:** n55ffc/Flickr/Getty Images; **p. 153:** Felicia Martinez Photography/PhotoEdit, Inc.; **p. 155:** Hola Images/Getty Images;

p. 161: Creatista/Shutterstock; **p. 166:** Rosa & Rosa/Corbis; **p. 168:** Pearson; **p. 171:** Annie Katz/Photographer's Choice/Getty Images; **p. 175:** Jari Hindstoerm/Shutterstock; **p. 179:** Medioimages/Photodisc/Getty Images; **p. 184:** Radius/SuperStock; **p. 187:** Radius Images/Glow Images; **p. 189:** Pearson; **p. 192:** Ann & Steve Toon/Robert Harding/Glow Images; **p. 194:** Monty Brinton/CBS/Landov; **p. 197:** Martin Moxter/imagebroker/AGE Fotostock; **p. 200:** AVAVA/Shutterstock; **p. 203:** Petinov Sergey Mihilovich/Shutterstock; **p. 204:** Kablonk/SuperStock; **p. 206:** Pearson; **p. 210:** Angela Waye/Shutterstock; **p. 212:** Stephen Coburn/Shutterstock; **p. 219:** Spencer Grant/PhotoEdit, Inc; **p. 222:** Helen King/Corbis; **p. 224:** Pearson; **p. 227:** Biosphoto/SuperStock; **p. 231:** Glow Images/SuperStock; **p. 232:** PhotoAlto sas/Alamy; **p. 236:** Monkey Business Images/ShutterStock; **p. 239:** Jordan Siemens/Iconica/Getty Images; **p. 241:** Pearson; **p. 245:** StudioSmart/Shutterstock; **p. 246:** IS170/Alamy; **p. 252:** Digital Vision/Getty Images; **p. 255:** Golden Pixels LLC/Shutterstock; **p. 258:** Blend Images/SuperStock; **p. 260:** Pearson; **p. 263:** Biosphoto/SuperStock; **p. 266:** Mark Richardson/Alamy; **p. 270:** Image Source/SuperStock; **p. 273:** Colorblind/Cardinal/Corbis; **p. 277:** Kablonk Micro/Fotolia; **p. 278:** Pearson; **p. 281:** Elena Larina/Shutterstock; **p. 284:** goodluz/Fotolia; **p. 287:** keith morris/Alamy; **p. 296:** OJO Images Ltd/Alamy; **p. 302:** Age fotostock/SuperStock; **p. 304:** Radius Images/Alamy; **p. 308:** Pearson; **p. 311:** zizar/Shutterstock; **p. 314:** Exactostock/SuperStock; **p. 329:** Russell Gordon/DanitaDelimont.com/Newscom; **p. 331:** Natan Dvir/Newscom; **p. 340:** Pearson; **p. 343:** FloridaStock/Shutterstock; **p. 346:** Hill Street Studios/Blend Images/Alamy; **p. 351:** Jeff Greenberg/Alamy; **p. 357:** Cardinal/Corbis; **p. 359:** Angel Simon/Shutterstock; **p. 362:** Pearson; **p. 366:** Pilar Azaña Talán/Flickr Open/Getty Images; **p. 368:** iStock/Thinkstock; **p. 371:** Chris Fitzgerald/Newscom; **p. 374:** Lisette Le Bon/SuperStock; **p. 375:** CJG–Technology/Alamy; **p. 379:** Pearson; **p. 381:** Randy Wells/Corbis; **p. 385:** Marilyn Humphries/The Image Works; **p. 390:** Stockbyte/Getty Images; **p. 396:** Monty Rakusen/Cultura/Getty Images; **p. 397:** Joseph A. DeVito; **p. 401:** Pearson.